Manufacturing Planning and Control Systems

Manufacturing Planning and Control Systems

Thomas E. Vollmann
Boston University

William L. Berry
University of Iowa

D. Clay Whybark
Indiana University

Second Edition

DOW JONES-IRWIN
Homewood, Illinois 60430

Dow Jones-Irwin is a trademark of Dow Jones & Company, Inc.

© Richard D. Irwin, Inc., 1984 and 1988

This publication is designed to provide accurate and
authoritative information in regard to the subject matter
covered. It is sold with the understanding that the
publisher is not engaged in rendering legal, accounting, or
other professional service. If legal advice or other expert
assistance is required, the services of a competent
professional person should be sought.

*From a Declaration of Principles jointly adopted by a Committee
of the American Bar Association and a Committee of Publishers.*

Project editor: Joan A. Hopkins
Production manager: Carma W. Fazio
Compositor: Compset Inc.
Typeface: 10/12 Caledonia
Printer: Arcata Graphics/Kingsport

ISBN 1-55623-015-X

Library of Congress Catalog Card No. 87–72843

Printed in the United States of America

4 5 6 7 8 9 0 K 5 4 3 2 1 0 9 8

In memory of Joseph Orlicky and Oliver Wight:
Pioneers in manufacturing planning and control.

Preface

The world of manufacturing has changed since publication of the first edition of *Manufacturing Planning and Control Systems*. Global competition is a reality, and world class manufacturing companies have been created to engage in sales, manufacturing, and purchasing activities in every corner of the world.

There have been many important changes in manufacturing planning and control (MPC) systems as well. Newer more powerful computer systems have been introduced. Real time and micro-computer systems are in common use. MPC systems are increasingly being integrated with systems for sales, business planning, engineering, and quality control. The just-in-time philosophy has been increasingly adopted and applied to ever more complex product and process environments. New computer-based systems have been developed for dealing with detailed scheduling and other aspects of manufacturing planning and control.

There has been a steady evolution in manufacturing planning and control. Companies will continue changing their practices in MPC. MPC systems have always been an important area for improving the effectiveness of manufacturing. Firms that have implemented a weekly generated MRP system will move into a daily or real time–based system. MRP execution will increasingly be done with just-in-time methods achieving the well-known reductions in lead times, inventories, and waste: also achieved are significant reductions in the overhead costs associated with detailed MRP planning. Effective MRP-based firms will get better at master production scheduling and thereafter see how production planning can help plan and control the entire company. Still other firms are extending their MPC systems outward through their distribution channels using distribution requirements planning (DRP). And other companies are using advanced methods for better coordination with supplier firms.

Although there have been many changes, it is important to draw attention to the things that have remained constant. Our original model of the manufacturing planning and control system has stood the test of time. It is sufficiently broad to include just-in-time, Optimized Production Technology (OPT), and other ideas. It is not limited to Material Requirements Planning (MRP) nor to Manufacturing Resource Planning (MRPII) systems. Newer approaches can be included and the overall MPC system still must perform all of the functions that we have described, or must be consigned to a subsystem role; that is, to enhancing one portion of manufacturing planning and control. Different circumstances require different emphases on different aspects of the system, but we have not encountered a company that did not have to contend with all of the functions described in our model.

Several reviewers have suggested that we change the sequence of the chapters in this book. What has been interesting is that there have been so many different suggestions concerning how to reorder the materials. This means to us that there are many ways to teach a course in manufacturing planning and control. It is important to keep the book organized in such a way as to provide as few roadblocks as possible. We believe that the book design is such that many different paths can be accommodated, not just the one indicated by our chapter sequence.

We have largely stayed with our original design. We personally have found starting with MRP record processing to be pedagogically useful. We believe that understanding the use of time phased records early on allows one to more quickly understand the entire MPC system. The first half of the book is devoted to the basics, believing that there is a need to see the whole MPC system before delving into advanced materials. The second half (chapters 12–20) provides advanced concepts that support the basics. Included are advanced chapters on material requirements planning, scheduling, master production scheduling, production planning, and distribution inventory planning.

Each of the chapters has been revised to include newer materials, and new chapters have been added as well. Major additions to the second addition include a detailed treatment of just-in-time, new materials on production planning and master production scheduling, the scheduling of flexible manufacturing systems (FMS), a much more complete treatment of distribution requirements planning, a description of Optimized Production Technology (OPT) techniques and philosophy, and some new mathematical models for aggregate planning that have appeared in the literature. We have also increased the number of chapter-end problems.

APICS CERTIFICATION EXAMINATION PROGRAM

The American Production and Inventory Control Society (APICS) has an ongoing program of certification based on the successful completion of a set of examinations. At this time, there are six examinations:

- Master Planning
- Material Requirements Planning
- Inventory Management
- Capacity Management
- Production Activity Control
- Just-In-Time

The specific content of the examinations is constantly being updated, and it is very important to secure copies of the study guides and sample examination questions from APICS as part of any plan of study. Each study guide has a list of references, as do the chapters in this book. Additionally, APICS provides training aids and books of reprinted articles that show the concepts in practice.

The combination of using this textbook and the materials provided by APICS is an excellent way to prepare for the certification examinations. The APICS publications tend to focus on case examples rather than on basic methods. The latter type of material is better provided in a text. A similar difference applies to the problems furnished from both sources. The sample tests provided by APICS use the short answer format that are found in the examinations. In fact, all of the questions (50 for each examination) are test items that were at one time on examinations. In this book, we ask more open-ended kinds of chapter-end problems that require calculation and discussion. In some cases there are not single right answers; discussion of the alternatives leads to a deeper understanding of manufacturing planning and control systems.

In the balance of this section, we detail the primary and linkage chapters that address the subject matter of each examination. We also provide information on what is not in our book, sources where the gaps can best be filled, and at least one more reference that complements the materials presented here. We do, however, feel the need to add a few words of caution. Manufacturing planning and control can not be easily partitioned into five or six parts. This is a dynamic ever-changing field that needs to be understood in its entirety. Moreover, the changes will continue and professionals in this area need a framework for understanding change and seeing the opportunities for their companies. We feel that the framework will come from reading all of this book, or at least the first 11 chapters. This set of chapters is recommended reading before going into the more detailed study of each area that follows.

Master Planning

The primary chapters dealing with the materials in the master planning examination are 8, 9, 10, 14, 15, 16 and 19. Chapters 1, 2, 4, 6, and 7 describe linkages to other MPC systems. Chapter 11 deals with issues of implementation. The primary chapters provide coverage of most of the subject matter in this examination. There are two notable exceptions, however. The examination requires some knowledge of basic statistics including the standard deviation and areas under the normal distribution curve. Additionally, there is a need to understand some fundamentals of extrinsic forecasting, such as regression. An article by Chambers, Mullick, and Smith in the July, 1971 *Harvard Business Review* provides a good overview of these ideas. For readers interested in more depth on forecasting, we recommend the book, *Forecasting Methods for Management*, by Wheelright and Makridakis, (Wiley 1980).

Material Requirements Planning

The primary chapters addressing the material requirements planning examination are 1, 2, 3, 11, 12 and 19. Chapters 4, 5, 6, 7, 8, 9, and 10 deal with linkages to other MPC systems. In addition, chapter 17 provides background information on basic inventory models. The primary chapters provide coverage of all of the topical areas of the examination, except for the interfaces with other MPC systems. These are covered in the other set of chapters. For readers desiring another source of reading, we recommend the book, *MRPII: Making It Happen*, by Tom Wallace (Oliver Wight Limited Publications, 1985).

Inventory Management

The primary chapters that delineate the material for the inventory management examination are 2, 7, 12, 16, 17, 18 and 19. Chapters 3, 4, 5, 6, 8, 9, and 10 provide the linkages to other MPC systems and concepts. Chapter 11 deals with implementation issues. This examination also requires knowledge of some basic concepts in statistics and accounting. Included are areas under the normal distribution curve and inventory valuation methods such as LIFO versus FIFO. We recommend the book, *Production and Inventory Management*, by Fogarty and Hoffmann (South-Western, 1983) as an additional reference.

Capacity Management

The primary chapters that deal with the materials found on the capacity management examination are found in chapters 1, 4, 7, 9, 10, and 15. The chapters that provide direct linkages to other MPC systems are 2, 6, 7, and 8. Chapter 11 treats questions of implementation. The capacity management examination requires understanding of the difference between capacity and load, and the difference between nominal, standing, or rated capacity and actual or demonstrated capacity. Also required is awareness of efficiency and utilization. These are explained in the APICS study guide. We also recommend that *Capacity Management Reprints* (APICS) be studied for this examination.

Production Activity Control

The primary set of chapters for preparation for the production activity control examination are 1, 3, 4, 5, 7, and 13. Chapters providing linkages to production activity control are 2, 4, 9, and 10. Chapter 11 is concerned with implementation issues. These two sets of chapters deal with essentially all of the materials as delineated in the study guide, with the possible exception of some basics in cost accounting such as the costing of work in process inventory, shrinkage, and scrap, as well as standard costing techniques and variances. A good additional reading is the book, *Production Activity Control*, by Carter and Melnick (Dow-Jones Irwin, 1987).

Just-in-Time

The primary set of chapters for the just-in-time (JIT) examination module are 5, 6, 7, 13, and 20. Chapters 4, 11, 17, and 18 all provide linkages or supportive theory. This module has just recently been developed, and it will evolve more rapidly than the other examinations. It is, therefore, very important to obtain an up-to-date study guide. We note in our chapter that most directly focuses on JIT (7), that JIT is much more than MPC systems. The examination reflects this wider scope and includes topics such as total quality control, process analysis and layout, JIT philosophy, and implementation issues. Good additional sources for this examination are *World Class Manufacturing*, by R. J. Schonberger (Free Press, 1986) and *Attaining Manufacturing Excellence: Just-in-Time Manufacturing, Total Quality, Total People Involvement* by R.W. Hall (Dow Jones-Irwin, 1987).

We have benefited from a number of manuscript reviews of *Manufacturing Planning and Control Systems*. Notable in the first edition were: Richard Penlesky, *Marquette University*; Robert Millen, *Northeastern University*;

Gene Groff, *Georgia State University.* In the second edition we were fortunate to have manuscript reviewed by: William Sherrard, San Diego State University; Urban Wemmerlov, University of Wisconsin. Jeff Miller at Boston University has also been a major help; each of us has a special relationship with Jeff that goes back many years. And, we gladly extend our recognition and gratitude to Larry Dolinsky of Bentley College for his analytical contribution to Chapter 15. We have also been encouraged by the efforts of Professor Bob Fetter as our series editor through both editions. Bob has been both a champion of the project and a critical reviewer. We have worn out a number of editors at Richard D. Irwin, but Dick Hercher has hung on. Thanks, Dick, for gently guiding and lining up resources when needed.

We appreciate the contributions to our understanding of MPC system practice provided by Oliver Wight, Joe Orlicky, Walt Goddard, Tom Wallace, and Andre Martin. A number of deans have put up with us. Most notable in this edition are George McGurn of Boston University, George Daly of the University of Iowa, and Derek Abell of IMEDE. We also are indebted to the students who so diligently find the mistakes that each of us blames on his coauthors.

Finally, we want to express our appreciation to our families, for the support during all those days when we were working on this book:

Tani	**Jane**	**Neva**
Bill, Ann, and Sarah	Ann, Mike, and Lynn	Mike and Susie

Contents

The DOW JONES-IRWIN / APICS Series in Production Management

*Supported by the American Production
and Inventory Control Society*

1

Manufacturing planning and control

This chapter is devoted to providing a managerial perspective to manufacturing planning and control (MPC) systems. MPC systems deal with all of the activities from acquisition of raw materials to delivery of completed products. MPC systems are also designed to support key management interfaces and activities in various functions of the firm. Included are cost accounting, order entry and customer service, logistics, budgeting, capital budgeting, and strategic planning. Successful management of an MPC system requires planning the correct timing and quantities of purchased and manufactured parts. It also requires specifying the appropriate levels of resources (capacity) to meet the firm's output objectives. MPC system management means more than planning, however. Detailed execution of the plans to a high degree of conformance is critical to the overall MPC process. Successful MPC management also needs to be viewed in an evolutionary context. A firm should never be satisfied with existing achievement levels of its MPC systems. Improvement is always possible and should be sought. Increasingly, the improvements will yield benefits that are critical at the overall company level, such as better responsiveness to customer requests, reduced times for new product introductions, improved quality levels, and better strategic focus.

In this chapter, we address the key role played by MPC systems in maintaining a competitive posture. We also describe the physical systems that are planned and controlled by MPC, that provide a framework for the design of MPC systems, and that show how emphasis on certain aspects of MPC is dictated by company characteristics. Finally, we describe the organization of the text and indicate some different reading sequences. The chapter is organized around the following five topics:

- MPC system payoffs: Why is it important to create effective MPC systems, and what are the returns from doing so?
- Managing the manufacturing process: What are the manufacturing process stages and management concerns with each?
- The manufacturing planning and control system: What does management need from the MPC system, and how is it configured to respond to these needs?
- Matching the MPC system with the needs of the firm: How do manufacturing processes differ, and how can the MPC activities be tailored to an individual firm's situation?
- Organization of the book: How is the book organized, and how can it be used by different readers?

MPC SYSTEM PAYOFFS

We live in an increasingly shrinking world. This has many ramifications, not the least of which is increased availability of raw materials and products from all over the globe. More and more companies find themselves in a global competition, engaging in worldwide sourcing and marketing of their products. The result is a set of key challenges that good MPC systems help to meet. Many successful firms can testify to this claim.

Customer expectations

Global competition carries with it an ever increasing set of demands by the customers. Better quality, more features, better delivery performance, and reduced cost all become part of the expectations for our customers. Mize and Seifert speculate on the kinds of demands that will be placed on manufacturing in the next decade. They start with the manufacturer of a complex engineered product, which presently sells for $35,000 per unit. It presently takes several months to manufacture the item, more time to purchase custom materials, and special features have to be designed to satisfy customer requirements. Figure 1.1 provides a summary of the projected changes in customer expectations that Mize and Seifert identify.

Although we could argue with the specifics of Figure 1.1, it is clear that the directions are correct, and the firms that survive will be those able to

FIGURE 1.1   Trends in customer expectations

	Expectations	
Category	Now	10 years hence
Product quality (rejects)	5%	0.5%
Mean time between failures	15,000 hrs.	50,000 hrs.
Customer lead time	18 months	2 months
Delivery time estimate accuracy	1 month	1 day
Delivery delay tolerance	30 days	0 days
Percent customized	5%	30%
Cost in constant dollars	$35,000	$15,000

Source: J.H. Mize and D.J. Seifert, "CIM—A Global View of the Factory," presented at the Fall Conference of IEE, 1985.

respond to these challenges. The level of customer knowledge is increasing, and some firms can now meet these kinds of expectations. To do so, MPC systems have to be second to none.

Manufacturing improvement plans

If Figure 1.1 lays out the directions for the customers, it is also useful to see how some manufacturing firms are responding, and what specific actions are being taken. The Boston University Manufacturing Futures Survey has been collecting data on the concerns, priorities, and action programs of North American manufacturing firms for five years. There is also a collaborative effort with INSEAD (a business school in France) for European firms and with Waseda University in Tokyo for Japanese manufacturers. MPC systems has been one of the top 10 action programs in every year for all three areas of the world. In the 1986 North American report, three of the top 10 action programs are directly related to MPC in the broad sense: production control systems, manufacturing systems integration, and lead time reduction. Four others are related to quality objectives and two additional top 10 action programs are new product driven. Taken in total, it is clear that MPC systems are playing a key role in the actions being taken by firms to improve manufacturing effectiveness.

A related issue is the current interest in programs that integrate manufacturing activities, both internally within manufacturing and across functional boundaries. These efforts increasingly are called computer integrated manufacturing (CIM). Figure 1.2 is based on analysis from the Boston University Manufacturing Futures Survey data. A question dealing with integration of systems was treated with factor analysis to determine the patterns of systems integration being attempted by North American manufacturers.

FIGURE 1.2 MPC as a central focus for computer integrated manufacturing (CIM)

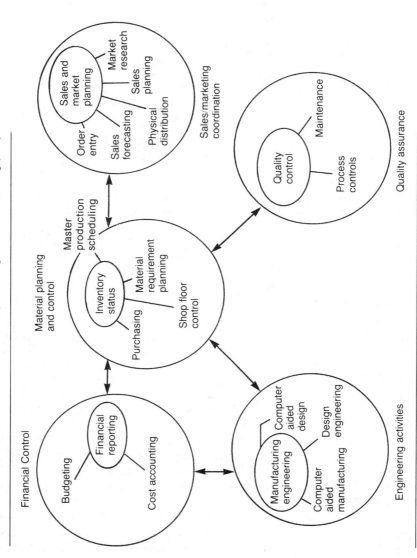

Source: J.G. Miller and T.E. Vollmann, 1985 Manufacturing Futures Survey, Boston University.

There are five distinct "islands" of integration that result. The key point in Figure 1.2 is seen by the critical role played by the center island. It includes the topics we will see as central to manufacturing planning and control. Included are systems to maintain data on accurate inventory balances, master production scheduling (MPS), purchasing, material requirements planning (MRP), and shop-floor control (SFC). Another interesting dimension of Figure 1.2 is that the linkages between islands (the bridges) are almost exclusively to the MPC island. This shows the key role that MPC is playing in computer integrated manufacturing programs.

Actual company performance improvements

MPC system performance is often viewed in terms of specific measures, such as inventory turnover rate, lead time reductions, and so on. A broader view of the goal is in the reduction of what we call "organizational slack." Organizational slack is manifested in excess inventories, excess capacity, excess labor costs, overtime costs, long manufacturing lead times, poor delivery promise performance, fewer new products with longer development cycles, and a lack of responsiveness to changes in the business environment. Hence, a primary payoff from MPC systems is in reducing organizational slack. This payoff can be measured in terms of improved output per man-hour, reduced overtime, reduced inventory investment, reduced obsolescence, improved inventory turnover, lower purchasing costs, reduced distribution costs, improved customer service levels, and the internal generation of capital investment funds. Specific examples of such gains include:

1. The Tennant Company, in a two-year period with its MPC system in place, witnessed the following changes in performances:
   a. Purchased material inventory reduced by 42 percent ($3,129,000).
   b. Production rate increased by 66 percent.
   c. Assembly efficiency increased from 45 percent to 85 percent.
   d. Delivery promises met increased from 60 percent to 90 percent.
2. Steelcase, Inc., put in a new MPC system to better integrate purchasing with manufacturing and found:
   a. The percentage of past due purchase orders dropped from 35.0 to 3.2 percent.
   b. In a two-year period, sales rose 58 percent, while purchased part inventories rose by 12 percent.
   c. During the same period, purchasing cost reduction program savings increased from $500,000 per year to $5 million per year.
   d. During a period of severe nationwide shortages, Steelcase had no vendor lead times over five weeks.

     e. In a sharp economic downturn, Steelcase was able to control inventories and maintain profits.

     f. The purchasing manager stated, "Vendor lead times are virtually irrelevant to Steelcase."

3. Kumera OY implemented an MPC system in six months during a period of heavy competitive pressure and:

     a. Tripled its gross margin.

     b. Increased inventory turnover from 2.5 to 10 times per year.

     c. Eliminated late delivery penalties.

     d. With the funds generated, installed numerically controlled equipment that gave them a distinct competitive advantage.

4. Black & Decker cut work in process in half and cut the average shop lead time from 6 to 2.9 weeks during a period of sales growth. This improvement was accomplished by the use of an approach to MPC called materials requirements planning (MRP). A few years later, building on this foundation with other (just-in-time) methods, the firm was able to increase inventory turns in several of its plants and to achieve other important objectives.

5. Elliott Company, Division of United Technology, improved its performance against customer promise dates by 50 percent while reducing inventory by 23 percent and increasing sales by 32 percent.

6. Toyota Motor Company attributes much of its success to their MPC system which is tailored to the Japanese industrial environment. The firm has the highest labor productivity of any automobile company. Moreover, its turnover of working assets is 10 times that of U.S. and Western European producers.

7. When Jack Waller took over as vice president of manufacturing at Stanley Hardware, the first capital appropriation he received was to purchase more shop boxes for the work-in-process inventory. His response was to deny the request, saying that he intended to put in systems to *empty* the existing shop boxes. Figure 1.3 is a picture of Jack, several years later, with some of the excess shop boxes. He also sold a large quantity of shop boxes to another division. Every year, the volume goes up and the work-in-process goes down.

8. Better MPC systems also are paying dividends in lesser developed countries. For example, the Optical Equipment Corporation in China reduced work-in-process inventories 20 percent, improved equipment utilization, increased the profit rate by 5.4 percent, and decreased late deliveries *during the weeks when their microcomputer MPC system was run in parallel to the manual system.* The No. 5 Shanghai Scarf Factory increased output from one year to the next, profitability by almost 20 percent, and reduced work in process to about a five day supply, using a manual MPC system.

FIGURE 1.3   Inventory reduction at Stanley Hardware

MANAGING THE MANUFACTURING PROCESS

Manufacturing management is tied to the flow of materials and the set of process activities that transforms the products. A flow of materials occurs in any production or logistics process that procures raw materials, produces components, creates products for selling, and moves them to consumers. An entire spectrum of interrelated management problems arises in this overall flow, and systems must be created to deal with these problems on a routine basis. Furthermore, an accurate data base is required to use the system for routine decision making.

The production/logistics process

Figure 1.4 relates several manufacturing process issues to the flow of materials that is typical for many firms. In the bottom portion, we see a physical flow beginning with purchased raw materials and component parts coming from vendors into inventories. Raw materials are transformed into component parts through machining and other fabrication steps. Component parts

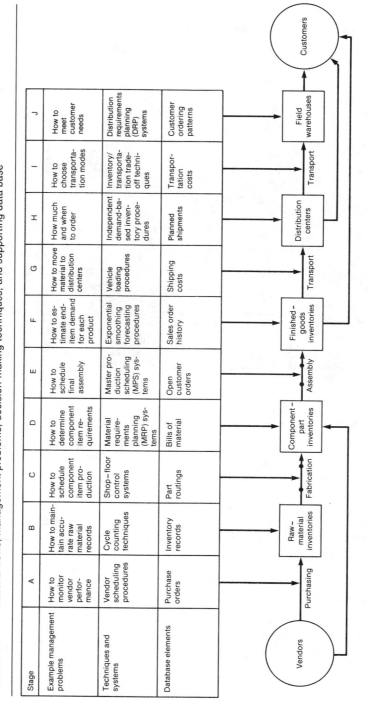

Stage	A	B	C	D	E	F	G	H	I	J
Example management problems	How to monitor vendor performance	How to maintain accurate raw material records	How to schedule component item production	How to determine component item requirements	How to schedule final assembly	How to estimate end-item demand for each product	How to move material to distribution centers	How much and when to order	How to choose transportation modes	How to meet customer needs
Techniques and systems	Vendor scheduling procedures	Cycle counting techniques	Shop-floor control systems	Material requirements planning (MRP) systems	Master production scheduling (MPS) systems	Exponential smoothing forecasting procedures	Vehicle loading procedures	Independent demand-based inventory procedures	Inventory/transportation trade-off techniques	Distribution requirements planning (DRP) systems
Database elements	Purchase orders	Inventory records	Part routings	Bills of material	Open customer orders	Sales order history	Shipping costs	Planned shipments	Transportation costs	Customer ordering patterns

Vendors → Purchasing → Raw-material inventories → Fabrication → Component-part inventories → Assembly → Finished-goods inventories → Transport → Distribution centers → Transport → Field warehouses → Customers are removed from inventory and assembled into finished goods. Finished goods inventories are shipped directly to consumers or by movement through distribution centers and field warehouses. This flow is quite universal, but the specific differences between firms must be taken into account in the detailed design of MPC systems.

One key difference between firms is often seen in the fabrication stage. Some companies have a *job shop* approach, where parts are routed to work centers depending on the production steps required. Other firms have a *flow shop* approach, where one or a few products travel through a set of fabrication activities specially arranged for the particular products. In the latter extreme, we have repetitive manufacturing (e.g., automobiles) and process industries (e.g., chemical plants) in which no significant stoppage in the flow of materials is evidenced, and flow rate becomes the critical decision. The job shop is more flexible in terms of the products that can be produced, while the flow shop offers efficiencies from specially designed equipment and fast through-put times. But both have flows of material that require scheduling. Thus, even though there may be different emphases, criteria, and problem complexity, the fundamental management questions are still there.

Manufacturing companies can also be distinguished by those that manufacture each customer order on a unique basis (make to order), those that assemble a wide variety of finished goods from a smaller set of standardized options (assemble to order), and those that produce goods for inventory (make to stock). In the latter case, finished goods inventories are used to separate the assembly process from customer orders. The assemble-to-order firm, on the other hand, needs to carefully integrate actual customer orders with option planning and final assembly.

Still another distinction between manufacturing firms has to do with the complexity of component part fabrication and assembly. Some firms do little internal fabrication, purchasing most of their component parts prior to assembly. Others, with extensive machining and other conversion processes, have significantly more complex component part fabrication activities. Similarly, vast differences exist in the complexity of finished goods assembly. Some firms make relatively few products with dozens of component parts; others assemble hundreds of end items made from thousands of component parts. These differences, in turn, lead to differences in the details of the MPC systems required by the firms.

Combinations of all sorts can exist in the complexity of fabrication and assembly. Consider, for example, the differences between a make-to-stock furniture manufacturer and a make-to-order transmission/drive train manufacturer. The furniture manufacturer purchases logs, boards, other raw materials, and component parts, such as hinges, drawer pulls, and the like. Wood parts are cut from boards and transformed into component parts by a few fairly standard machining steps. Component parts, such as tops, sides, legs, and so on, are assembled into a large variety of finished goods and thereafter stained and packed. Trucks deliver furniture to warehouses and furniture dealers who sell to final customers. Component fabrication is relatively straightforward, but the assembly scheduling is quite complex in this company.

A somewhat different situation is faced by the company that makes a wide range of heavy-duty transmissions and other drive train equipment for vehicles such as tractors and farm machinery. In this case, final assembly tends to be straightforward, but the number of component fabrication steps can be very large, the machinery utilized is quite expensive (and, therefore, important to utilize effectively), and the company does not build to stock. The furniture manufacturer has many people committed to the assembly stage—this means that an even flow of material becomes important. The drive train manufacturer does not have the same relative need to smooth the assembly work flow, but is more concerned with a flow of material that provides high utilization of the machine tools for component part fabrication. The systems these companies employ cover the same general material flow problems, but specific design features support their different needs.

Management problems

The top row of Figure 1.4 depicts sample managerial problems that relate to the various stages of production/logistics. For each of these stages (coded A through J in Figure 1.4) several critical questions exist. (We have provided one example for each stage.) Figure 1.4 also shows examples of decision-making techniques and systems that have been designed to solve these problems, and the data base elements that must be maintained to provide the correct input for the techniques and systems. We next discuss the questions that face management at each of these stages.

The first stage, A, depicted in Figure 1.4, relates to the purchase of needed raw material and component parts. Some key management problems to be resolved at this stage include how to select vendors, what approaches should be taken to coordinate vendor activities with production needs, and how to monitor and control vendor performance.

Stage B is concerned with raw material inventories. Included are the managerial questions of how to determine desired inventory levels, proper procedures for physical control over raw materials, and the appropriate record-keeping systems for a particular firm.

Stage C is the conversion of raw materials into fabricated component parts. In many firms, this is the most critical step in production. Key managerial problems include the approach to scheduling each fabrication step for each component part, determining the overall level of fabrication activities, and utilizing work center capacities effectively.

Stage D, component part inventories, is directly linked to stage C. This

is because the replenishment of component part inventories places requirements on component part fabrication (or upon vendors for vendor requirements). Some key managerial issues concerning component part inventories
are: how to plan and release replenishment orders, how large a batch to
produce (lot size) for replenishment, and how to maintain physical control
of the inventories.

Stage E is the assembly of component parts into finished goods. Managerial problems at this stage include setting the overall output rate for the
manufacturing facility, determining the build schedule for individual end
items or options, firming up the final assembly schedule, and monitoring
actual performance.

Stage F, finished goods inventories, is linked to assembly in that any difference between desired and actual finished goods inventory levels is a potential source of demand for replenishment orders on assembly. Critical
management problems include how to forecast end item demand, ways of
accomplishing the customer contact functions of order entry and order
promising, setting of safety stocks, and how to establish desired finished
goods inventory levels.

Stage G is the outbound transportation of finished goods inventories to
the physical distribution system. Managerial issues here include determining the frequency of distribution center replenishment, the approach to be
taken in preparing actual truck and freight schedules, and the integration of
product distribution with finished goods inventory level determination.

Stage H, distribution centers, might not be used for all products or even
exist in a particular firm. Key managerial questions include whether to have
distribution centers, the desired distribution center inventory levels, and
the approach used for inventory replenishment.

Stage I is the transportation of goods from distribution centers to field
warehouses. Managerial questions include the choice of transportation
mode, scheduling of replenishment shipments, whether to ship directly to
customers, and whether transhipping between field warehouses is to be
utilized.

The last stage, J, shown in Figure 1.4 is field warehouses. Managerial
questions include whether to utilize this form of physical distribution, which
items to hold and not to hold in these facilities, the approach used for replenishment, and the desired inventory levels.

It should be clear that all of the stages in Figure 1.4 are related, and that
the managerial issues are similarly related. Answers to questions at any stage
need to be examined in terms of their influence on preceding and succeeding stages. That is why this book has a systems perspective. Although topical
areas are treated independently, we have made a concerted attempt to tie
them together in an overall systems framework.

Since the importance and complexity of and emphases on the different
stages varies from company to company and industry to industry, the MPC

systems can be expected to vary. There has been an acceleration of systems and techniques to help answer managerial questions at each of the stages. They are not all found in all firms, however, since the needs of the firms vary. The application of these techniques in successful companies has been most sharply focused on those stages which are key to the success of the firm.

Techniques and systems

We turn our attention here to the discussion of the techniques, systems, and procedures that have been developed to help solve each of the managerial problems listed in Figure 1.4. Some of these problems are infrequent, such as determining distribution centers. The majority of the problems faced in production and inventory management, however, recur, and the need is to create a routine approach, system, or "decision rule" for handling these problems. Perhaps the most basic cornerstone to improved management of material flows is "doing the routine things routinely." Examples of routine problems include component part planning, transaction processing, establishing priorities for unfinished work (open orders) in the fabrication shop, starting the assembly process by launching an assembly order, and determining the replenishment order to be shipped to a particular warehouse.

There has been some lively discussion among production and inventory management experts on the extent to which decisions about these routine problems can be automated—that is, put on a computer. The key point is not whether they can be automated but, rather, that the vast majority of these routine decisions should be made in a very predictable way, guided by tightly defined and consistent policies. These policies should lead to specific procedures that could either be manually or computer supported.

This system or decision rule sets the guidelines for detailed execution of the decisions. The managerial issues are how to design the system, provide the data, set the decision rules, implement the system, monitor performance, and make improvements. Improvement usually comes from better techniques, from better integration of the material flow with the organization, and from better (more accurate and more pertinent) data.

Tightly defined systems for guiding routine decision making are very important in providing the linkages among the managerial problems shown in Figure 1.4. This is so because the predictability that arises leads to a phenomenon called *system transparency*. Simply stated, when the decisions that will be made at any stage of the material flow are clearly defined, that area becomes *transparent* to the other stages (subsystems)—that is, the response or decision that will be made based on any set of input conditions is readily apparent. For example, a change in the bills of materials at stage D will result in a change in the part routings at stage C for a specific item on a specific date.

An interesting aspect of the various techniques and systems shown in Figure 1.4 for stages A through J is a similarity of certain problems. For example, certain stages are concerned with *scheduling* (A, C, E, G, and I). The techniques that are useful for scheduling in one of these stages are often of interest in another. Moreover, the scheduling done in one stage creates a set of conditions for previous and subsequent stages. We then see the need for integrated scheduling.

Another common problem is the control of inventory levels. Stages B, D, F, H, and J all are concerned with inventories. Inventory techniques, systems, and procedures have multiple applications. Moreover, there is critical interaction between the inventory levels and the scheduling stages that replenish and deplete these inventories.

This book is largely devoted to the design of techniques and systems to routinely control the material flow process depicted in Figure 1.4. The decision systems necessarily have to be tailored to differing company environments, but in almost every situation there is a basic core of building blocks required.

The data base

Each technique or system relies on certain basic information, examples of which are shown in Figure 1.4. For example, a machine scheduling system for a large job shop needs data for each part to be produced, including some or all of the following: the steps or routing required for fabrication, the expected time for each fabrication step, the due date, the expected time to complete remaining steps, the estimated labor for each step, the quantity to be completed at each step, and each shop order associated with each part.

The data base elements shown in Figure 1.4 are representative of those necessary to support the techniques and systems. Many problems in manufacturing planning and control are not analytically complex; instead, their complexity derives from the enormity of the underlying data base required to properly support routine decision-making systems. It is not unusual, for example, for a firm to require 5 million individual pieces of data to be accurately maintained and accessed to support a component part planning system.

It is not enough to have well-formulated systems. They must be driven with data that are appropriate, consistent, and accurate. The data elements must be the same in all applications. For example, if the record for part 1234 indicates that 120 are on hand, this number should be found to be correct if a physical count were made and should be the same in the customer service information system, the finance system, the manufacturing system, and so on. Accurate data require rigorous procedures for their maintenance and for the transactions which update those data. For many firms, the achievement of this data base integrity will require profound changes in day-to-day operations. The management of data, like any other company resource, might necessitate major changes in thinking, habits, and procedures.

The importance of information integrity, even in this brief overview, suggests that the notion of data base integration should be mentioned. A modern manufacturing planning and control system virtually requires that the data elements be maintained in an integrated data base, with common definitions of terms, procedures for processing detailed transactions, clear assignment of organizational responsibility for each data base subsection, and a companywide commitment to maintain the integrity of each data base element. The payoffs achieved with good MPC systems derive largely from a substitution of information for organizational slacks. For example, rather than relying on high levels of physical inventory to avoid coordination decisions, decisions can be based on data about inventory. These data indicate not only what is in inventory but what are the planned withdrawals, and the replenishment schedules. To substitute information for inventory, it is necessary to have *high-quality information*. Many chapters in this book deal explicitly with the creation of appropriate data bases and their management. Firms that implement state-of-the-art MPC systems typically find that the day-to-day job becomes management *by* the data base and management *of* the data base.

MANUFACTURING PLANNING AND CONTROL SYSTEMS

We noted above that the field of manufacturing planning and control is concerned with management problems and techniques for their solution, as well as with the linkages or interactions among particular problem areas. It is these interactions that are of interest to us in this section.

A framework for the MPC system

In any firm, manufacturing planning and control encompasses three distinct activities or phases. The first activity is establishment of the overall direction for the firm, with the resulting management plan stated in manufacturing terms, such as end items or product options. The manufacturing plan must be consistent with the company's direction and the plans for other departments of the firm. The second MPC activity is the detailed planning of material flows and capacity to support the overall plans. The third and final MPC activity is the execution of these plans in terms of detailed shop scheduling and purchasing actions.

Overall direction is provided by a game plan that links and coordinates the various departments (e.g., marketing, finance, engineering) of the company. The game plan is the responsibility of top management. It should be at all times consistent with strategic plans, departmental budgets, and the manufacturing plans for production output.

The overall direction phase of manufacturing planning and control includes the estimation of demand for the products sold by the firm. It also is necessary to estimate any additional demand for manufacturing capacity that comes from spare part sales, interplant or intercompany transfers, and branch warehouse requirements. In addition to forecasting the total demand, it is also necessary to manage the consumption (transformation) of the forecast by actual customer orders. That is, one must deal with order entry, customer order promising, and order backlog as these actual orders replace forecast information.

End item planning and customer order entry are where detailed trade-offs are made between marketing and manufacturing. On one hand, it is desirable to provide enough stability so that manufacturing can reasonably be held responsible for meeting plans. On the other hand, it is worthwhile to provide sufficient flexibility so the company can respond competitively to actual customer needs.

The planning of detailed component and raw material needs to support the manufacturing plan can be quite complex. For many firms, this involves the creation of detailed plans for tens or even hundreds of thousands of individual parts.

Detailed capacity planning is the establishment of the individual capacity plans for each machine group, based upon the detailed material plan. Included are the capacity needs for the work already in process as well as the capacity requirements of anticipated orders for all parts.

The system and the framework

Figure 1.5 is a simplified schematic of a modern MPC system. This diagram shows the skeletal framework for the systems described in subsequent chapters. The full system includes other data inputs, system modules, and feedback connections. Figure 1.5 is divided into three parts. The top third, or *front end*, is the set of activities and systems for overall direction setting. This phase establishes the company objectives for manufacturing planning and control. Demand planning encompasses forecasting customer/end product demand, order entry, order promising, accommodating interplant and intercompany demand, and spare parts requirements. In essence, all activities of the business that place demands on manufacturing capacity are coordinated in demand planning. Production planning is that activity which provides the production input to the company game plan and determines the manufacturing role in this agreed-upon strategic plan. The master production schedule (MPS) is the disaggregated version of the production plan. That is, the MPS is a statement to manufacturing of which end items or product options they will build in the future. The MPS must sum up to the production plan.

The middle third, or *engine*, in Figure 1.5, is the set of systems for ac-

FIGURE 1.5   Manufacturing planning and control system (simplified)

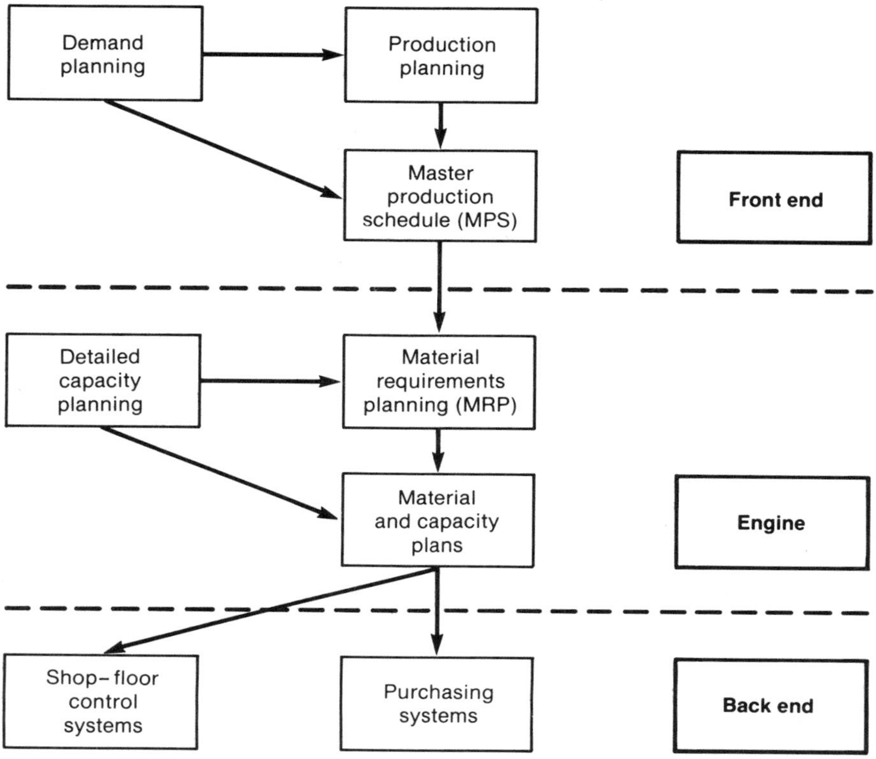

complishing the detailed material and capacity planning. The master production schedule feeds directly into material requirements planning (MRP). MRP determines (explodes) the period-by-period (time-phased) plans for all component parts and raw materials required to produce all the products in the MPS. This material plan can thereafter be utilized in the detailed capacity planning systems to compute labor or machine center capacity required to manufacture all the component parts.

The bottom third, or *back end*, of Figure 1.5 depicts the execution systems. Shop floor control systems establish priorities for all shop orders at each work center so that the orders can be properly scheduled. Purchasing systems provide detailed planning information for vendor scheduling. This information relates to existing purchase orders as well as to planned purchase orders.

For each of the subsystems from master production scheduling down through to the back end systems shown in Figure 1.5, computer hardware and software firms have produced packaged software products that provide information support for the activity. Moreover, the software is integrated to follow the framework. That is, the MPS produces the right input to MRP, which in turn provides the right input to the execution systems.

Execution of the detailed material and capacity plans involves the scheduling of machine and other work centers. In the factory, this scheduling must reflect such routine events as starting and completing orders for parts, and any problem conditions, such as breakdowns or absenteeism. It is usually necessary to update these schedules at least once per day in factories with complex manufacturing processes for producing parts and components.

An analogous detailed schedule is required for purchased parts. In essence, purchasing is the procurement of outside-work-center capacity. It must be planned and scheduled well to minimize the overall cost to the final customers. Good purchasing systems typically separate the procurement activity from routine order release and order follow-up. Procurement is a highly professional job that involves contracting for vendor capacity and establishment of ground rules for order release and order follow-up.

Some firms have used the execution phase to encompass other critical activities. For example, the Elliot Company mentioned above uses a direct analog of shop floor scheduling to plan and control their engineering and drafting activities.

A final activity tied to execution is the measurement of actual results. As products are manufactured, the rate of production and timing of specific completion can be compared to plans. As shipments are made to customers, measures of actual customer service can be obtained. As capacity is used, it too can be compared to plans.

This three-phase framework for material planning and control is supported by a widely applied set of MPC systems and software. The systems are designed to help solve the many problems that arise in managing the flows of material. We now turn to a description of these systems, which in turn provides the information to drive the shop floor control and purchasing systems.

The system and material flows

The system outlined in Figure 1.5 is related to the material flows and problems we discussed earlier. For example, the front end part of Figure 1.5 is addressed to the latter stages shown in Figure 1.4, those concerned with finishing the product and dealing with the market. Note, however, that some of the necessary activities (such as the management of spare parts demand) are not shown explicitly in Figure 1.4.

The engine part of Figure 1.5 is primarily associated with the determination of component item requirements, depicted as stage D in Figure 1.4. Again, Figure 1.4 does not show all of the necessary activities. The issue of capacity planning, for instance, is not shown in Figure 1.4.

The back end part of Figure 1.5 deals with the early stages of material flow, those dealing with component and purchased item scheduling and control (stages A through C in Figure 1.4). Stage C is largely concerned with shop floor control systems, and stage A with purchasing systems, both execution activities of a firm.

Figure 1.4 lists an example of a supporting data base element for each of the systems/techniques that are shown. We noted the need for integration of the data base earlier in our discussion. One of the primary reasons that most professionals today view manufacturing planning and control through the framework of Figure 1.5 is that an integrated data base can be established which is consistent with this framework. The front end data base drives the MRP system. The MRP data base provides the information for the detailed material plans. These plans, in turn, drive the capacity planning system. The data base of detailed material and capacity plans drives the back end systems (shop floor and purchasing), which, in turn, have their own data bases.

We see then, that Figure 1.5 is an overall system that is built upon an integrated data base and an integrated set of systems. The result is an integrated approach to dealing with material flow problems. Moreover, the approach shown in Figure 1.5 is now the way leading authorities *think* about MPC systems, and the way that software packages are conceived and designed. The result forms an important base for professional development in this field.

The system and the individual firm

The activities shown in Figure 1.5 are necessarily performed in *every* manufacturing firm, whether large or small. However, the emphasis given to each of the activities depends strongly on the attributes of the company. The importance of the approach presented in Figure 1.5 is that a consistent set of MPC system modules can ensure that detailed decision making is completely and constantly synchronized with the overall game plan.

It is extremely important *not* to give the impression that all one needs to do is go out and buy the complete set of computer packages depicted in Figure 1.5. That is simply not the case. Purchasing computer hardware and software is the easiest aspect of implementing an MPC system. The complexity and changes required in day-to-day operations to drive the system with accurate data bases are much more profound. Even more significant are the changes in methods, habits, and attitudes of the people involved. New ways of *thinking* about their jobs are required.

The implementation of an advanced MPC system can easily represent the most profound change in operations a firm will ever experience. Moreover, each firm has certain unique features that must be considered in the design of its MPC system. One set of unique characteristics concerns the management policies relating to performance measures and response. For example, how does management measure and evaluate customer service, inventory investment, and productivity? Are there specific goals stated for these? How responsive should the system be to the dynamics of the marketplace?

Certain process/market attributes of each firm influence the way that each of the systems shown in Figure 1.5 is designed and implemented. For some firms, it is necessary to include distribution systems. Others require a multiple factory approach. Some have a much greater need for extensive supplier networks than others. Also, depending upon the products produced, the firm may be more of a job shop than a flow shop, or vice versa. The company may be in the make-to-order business and necessarily need to effectively integrate the engineering and drafting activities with the MPC system. An assemble-to-order firm, on the other hand, needs a very strong linkage of customer order date promising with manufacturing. The make-to-stock firm may have a greater interest in inventory turnover. The nature of the competitive environment is also important. Some firms compete on the basis of price or fast deliveries for stable products, or both. Others are constantly bringing out new products. Products are in different stages of the product life cycle. The MPC system has to be designed to support the market posture of the specific firm in question.

The critical point is that although the basic approach shown in Figure 1.5 applies to any manufacturing firm, it is necessary for the system to be tailored to the specific needs of the firm, which can change over time. We now turn to that topic. In many subsequent chapters, we will show how companies in different kinds of businesses have produced different systems. We also will show that some systems are viewed as more critical in some firms than in others.

MATCHING THE MPC SYSTEM WITH THE NEEDS OF THE FIRM

The requirements placed on the design of an MPC system will vary with the nature of the production process, the customer expectations, and the needs of management. Additionally, MPC requirements are not static. As one gets some aspect of the firm under routine control there is opportunity to tackle new problems. As noted in our discussion of Figure 1.4, the physical sequence of manufacturing activities can be stated in overall terms, but the emphasis varies a great deal from firm to firm. The result is differing emphasis on the various MPC system modules.

We have also noted that the technology of MPC has changed over time.

Material requirements planning, for example, was never a practical approach until random access computers were available. A more recent change is the growing use of on-line systems. There is a fundamental operating difference when on-line systems can be used. Printed paper reports are dramatically reduced, and the planning process can be redone on a daily cycle. This reduces inventories and has other benefits, but it also makes the planning and execution of MPC systems much more dynamic. Changes in the way the users deal with the system and do their routine work are necessary.

Complicating things even more is the fact that even the process itself is not static. In some of the most recent advances in MPC systems, the major breakthroughs have been in changes in the physical process. Job shops have been configured to become lines. Use of small groups of equipment dedicated to production of a group of parts or products (cellular manufacturing) is growing. Fundamental changes are occurring in the relationships between firms and their suppliers.

In this section, we develop a classification schema that shows the relationships between shop complexity, throughput rates, and appropriate MPC approaches. Thereafter we deal with the question of implementation of MPC systems. In the end, this is the real issue: It is not enough to identify MPC opportunities, they need to be realized.

An MPC classification schema

Figure 1.6 shows the relationship between MPC system approaches, the complexity of the manufactured product as expressed in the number of subparts, and the repetitive nature of production, expressed as the time between successive units. Also shown in Figure 1.6 are some example products that fit these time and complexity scales.

Several MPC approaches are presented in Figure 1.6 as appropriate for products that fit in various points in the schema. The intent is to demonstrate that the MPC emphasis changes as the nature of the product or process changes, or both. For example, as a product grows in volume over time, it well might be appropriate for the MPC emphasis to shift from right to left. In any event, it will always be necessary to perform all of activities depicted in Figure 1.5. The way in which these activities are performed, however, changes significantly. The character of the MPC systems and the management requirements are quite different in the left-hand side of Figure 1.6 than they are in the right-hand side.

In the lower left hand corner of Figure 1.6, we show a flow-oriented manufacturing process. This would be typical of many chemical, food, petroleum, and bulk product firms. Since the products are produced in streams instead of discrete batches, there is virtually no time between successive units. The MPC systems are primarily concerned with flow rates that become the master production schedule. Typically, these products have rela-

FIGURE 1.6   MPC classification schema

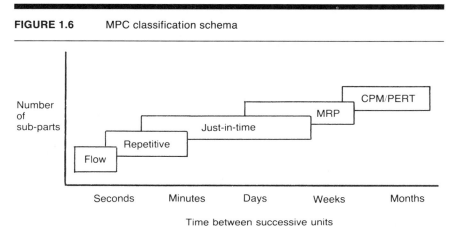

Examples: oil, food, drugs, watches, TV, trucks, planes, houses, ships.

tively few component parts, so management of the "engine" is straightforward. Depending on the ways in which components are purchased, the back end may involve some complexity. Typically, the major cost for these firms is for raw materials, and transportation costs can also be significant.

Repetitive manufacturing activities are found in many plants that assemble similar products. Automobiles, watches, micro computers, pharmaceuticals, and televisions are representative. For such products, component part management is necessary, but everything is coordinated with the flow or assembly rate for the end items.

In the middle of the figure we show a large application area for just-in-time (JIT) systems. We have a chapter devoted to this topic, which continues to grow in importance. For now, we can say that an objective is to move processes from right to left in the figure. That is, the objective is to make processes more repetitive as opposed to unique, and to achieve the MPC operating conditions of repetitive manufacturing (shorter cycles, reduced lead times, lower inventories, and the like). JIT is shown as spanning a wide variety of products and processes. This MPC approach is increasingly being integrated with more traditional MRP based systems. The goal is to achieve better MPC system performance, and to reduce the costs of maintaining the MPC system.

Figure 1.6 also shows material requirements planning as spanning a wide area. MRP is key to any MPC system that involves management of a complicated parts situation. The majority of manufacturing in the United States has this sort of complexity, and MRP based systems continue to be widely applied. For many firms, successful use of MRP is an important step in evolving their approaches to MPC. Once routine MRP operation is achieved, it is possible to select portions of the product and processes that can be executed with JIT methodologies.

The last form of MPC depicted in Figure 1.5 is the project type, which is applied to unique long lead time products, such as ships and highly customized products. The primary concern in these situations is usually management of the time dimension. Related to time is cost, and project management attempts to continually assess the status of partially completed projects in terms of expected completion dates and costs. Some firms have successfully integrated the approaches of MRP with the problems of project management. This is particularly effective in planning and controlling the combined activities of engineering and manufacturing.

The final thoughts we see as important in considering Figure 1.6 are emphasis and evolution. In each of the product/process examples of Figure 1.6 the management concerns are somewhat different, as are the tasks and evaluative criteria for MPC systems. Moreover, once success has been achieved, new opportunities are made available. Processes can be changed and MPC systems similarly can be improved. This leads to the question of *how* to achieve good progress on development and improvement of MPC systems. It is to this topic that we now turn our attention.

For most firms, successful implementation of MPC systems brings about profound changes. People do their day-to-day jobs differently and have new ways of thinking about their jobs and how these relate to other jobs. It is not at all easy. There is no exact formula for success, but there are several critical aspects that we can see as important.

One key to successful implementation is goal setting. It is imperative that performance measures relate to the implementation of MPC systems. Specific targets must be set and evaluated. The manager who implements or enhances one of the MPC system modules should be rewarded. Moreover, after implementation, managerial performance evaluation should not be based on any measure that conflicts with appropriate MPC system performance goals.

A second key to implementation is organizational change. The need is to create an organizational structure consistent with MPC system activities and interfunctional integration. Senior management's attention must be directed toward the MPC system. Organizational changes in some firms consist primarily of changing attitudes and goals. In other firms, formal changes in the organization are required to achieve the desired results. We find that more and more successful firms are implementing a "materials management" form of organization specifically to facilitate MPC system implementation and operation. The objectives of such organizations are to provide an appropriate level of management for each of the goal-setting, detail-planning, and execution activities, and to assign data base responsibility. Finally, organizational design has to be viewed in light of the goal-setting process. As explicit MPC goals are set and modified, it is to be expected that changes in the organization must occur.

A third key to successful implementation is the proper design and use of project teams. A basic feature of good project team design is to have representation from all groups that will later use the system to do their jobs (the "user" groups). Another is to put the *best* people on the project teams—those whom the user groups can least afford to do without. A sure way to undermine the success of the project is to assign implementation responsibility to the newest or least-qualified person or make the assignment *in addition to* the person's other responsibilities. It is critical to find some way to release the project team members from other responsibilities. Leadership of the project team is also important. Overall leadership must *not* be assigned to system design staff groups or technical computer personnel. They should be used only for certain specific aspects, such as computer programming. Finally, proper project team design also requires that the team report to the appropriate management level in the firm. The interdisciplinary nature of MPC systems requires a high level of reporting to implement those key features that cross many functions.

Another key to implementation implicit in every phase of the project is education. It is necessary for people at all levels of the company to know how the system works, who will process certain kinds of transactions, and how their own jobs will be changed as a result of the MPC system.

The final key to success is monitoring the MPC system implementation process itself. It is necessary to periodically audit actual results in relation to plans, look for roadblocks to success, measure costs and benefits, and reestablish directions.

ORGANIZATION OF THE BOOK

In this final section we provide a brief road map of the remainder of the book. The first part of the book is largely devoted to the building blocks of an integrated manufacturing planning and control system (i.e., the basic subsystems). In these chapters we place our primary emphasis on providing a complete understanding of the entire MPC system, rather than developing what are interesting extensions to the basics. The second half of the book provides material of a more technical nature. The emphasis here is on enhancements to the basic MPC systems and on new developments in MPC systems. The organization that is followed in the majority of the chapters is presented next, followed by our logic for the specific topical sequence, and some alternatives to meet the needs of other readers.

Chapter organization

The approach taken in most of the chapters is closely related to the issues summarized in the framework of Figure 1.4. We start with a statement of the managerial objectives of the system module to be discussed. We list the key topics around which the chapter is organized. We then show how the topic area fits within the overall MPC framework shown in Figure 1.5 and provide references to other parts of the book and a description of any special objectives, constraints, or concerns that apply to the area. Thereafter, we present the systems and techniques and data base considerations that are most important to the module. Many of these are illustrated with examples taken from successfully operating systems.

For many of the system modules, we provide an important section on living with the system. In such sections, we provide information on conditions that must be met to ensure successful use of the system, organizational actions required, and ways to use the information provided by the system to improve performance.

We also identify the data base that must be developed and maintained to support the systems and integrate them into the MPC framework. In most chapters, we illustrate the use of the systems for routine decision making with actual company examples. These examples are quite extensive, reflecting our concern for improved practice. The chapters close with a summary of key points in the form of principles appropriate to the topic.

The chapters are relatively independent, although some key vocabulary and concepts appear in the early chapters, and each chapter in the second part of the book depends somewhat on the material from its equivalent fundamental chapter in the first part. Although there is some building to a comprehensive system definition that follows the chapter sequence, it is not essential that the chapters be read in order. We have tried to provide maximum flexibility in this regard. The next section describes the logic of the chapter order and suggests alternatives for different purposes.

Topical sequence

One way that the chapter could have been sequenced is suggested by Figure 1.4. That is, we could present the chapters in a hierarchical order proceeding from overall direction to detailed material planning to shop-floor control and purchasing. In fact, we have not chosen this alternative. Although conceptually appealing, the hierarchical approach is not consistent with our observations on how best to present the material for ease of understanding. It has been our experience that most topics in the front end are easier to understand after studying more simple concepts.

We have found, also, that most firms do not start MPC system implementation with the overall direction phase. Rather, they typically start with detailed material planning, then implement shop floor control, then detailed capacity planning, and only then turn to the tasks of master production scheduling and production planning. We have chosen to follow that basic sequence. It permits us to develop some fundamental concepts in a context where understanding is easier and which parallels implementation practice.

We start with three chapters devoted to the engine. Chapter 2 deals with the detailed planning of component parts. The next chapter deals with two critical MPC system issues: the integrity of the information (data base) and using the system in a dynamic environment. Chapter 4 treats detailed capacity planning.

The next three chapters deal with the back end, or execution, systems. Chapter 5 is devoted to shop floor control and Chapter 6 to purchasing. Chapter 7 describes just-in-time approaches. JIT is most closely associated with the execution portion of MPC systems, but we will see that there are other important dimensions as well. After describing how detailed plans are put into action, we turn to the front end. Chapter 8 deals with master production scheduling. Chapter 9 treats production planning. Chapter 10 is concerned with demand management. Successful implementation of MPC systems necessitates strong managerial leadership, and we devote an entire chapter to this topic. Thus, Chapter 11 is concerned with implementation and organization change as a central focus, rather than as one topic in the study of individual material flow problem areas.

With the set of chapters that comprises the first half of the book, we have presented the overall manufacturing planning and control system. The balance of the book is devoted to supporting technical and theoretical material. These materials amplify many of the ideas presented in Chapters 2 to 11, they make more explicit some of the key trade-offs in manufacturing planning and control, and they present a base of knowledge for the person who wants to be a professional in manufacturing planning and control. The sequence of Chapters 12 to 19 parallels that in the first part of the book, and its topics are presented in the chapter titles.

There are many ways that one can proceed through the book. The choice depends to some extent on the interest of the reader. For someone desiring an understanding of a modern manufacturing planning and control system, we suggest reading Chapter 1 through 11 in sequence, following with the latter chapters that correspond to individual interests. If one is interested in selected aspects of manufacturing planning and control, we suggest reading at least Chapter 2 before moving on to the area(s) of interest. For students in a production planning and control course, the sequence might be both basic and advanced chapters for each topic (e.g., Chapter 2, 3 and 12 followed by Chapters 4, 5, and 13).

Several faculty members have told us that they prefer the hierarchical approach, following Figure 1.4. In that case, a good sequence could be: 1, 9, 10, 19, 15, 8, 14, 2, 3, 12, 4, 5, 6, 7, 13, 11, 20. Chapters 16 through 18 could be positioned in several ways in this sequence.

Another group is those readers interested in becoming certified in a professional society. They will be interested in the certification examination of the American Production and Inventory Control Society (APICS) or the National Association of Purchasing Management (NAPM), for example.

The chapter references for the various modules of the APICS exam are indicated below:

Examination modules	Chapters
Master Planning	8, 9, 10, 14, 15, 16, 19
Material Requirements Planning	1, 2, 3, 11, 12, 19
Capacity Management	1, 4, 7, 9, 10, 15
Inventory Management	2, 3, 7, 12, 16, 17, 18, 19
Production Activity Control	1, 3, 4, 5, 7, 13
Just-in-Time	5, 6, 7, 13, 20

Although each certification examination emphasizes certain areas, the overall interest of professional societies is to foster professionalism. This means that all of the topical materials are relevant. For example, although Chapter 11, Implementation, is not included on any of the APICS examination modules, it should perhaps be on *all* of them. A similar argument holds for Chapter 20.

In closing this first chapter, we would like to make one further point. A great deal of personal experience has gone into this text. We have visited many companies and talked with thousands of people about manufacturing planning and control. We are extremely enthusiastic about the potential for MPC systems, and we hope that our enthusiasm is shared by the readers of the book. Installing an MPC system and seeing the results can be one of the most significant and rewarding activities of one's professional life!

CONCLUDING PRINCIPLES

In this chapter we have laid the groundwork for the rest of the book. It is possible to use the book to achieve many objectives, as we have tried to keep the chapters independent so readers can choose whatever is of most interest. In closing this chapter, we list the following fundamental concepts that underlie MPC systems development and application:

- An effective MPC system can contribute to competitive performance by lowering costs, increasing responsiveness to the customers, and facilitating new product introduction.
- MPC systems should play a central role in the efforts to integrate manufacturing systems for the firm.
- The MPC system needs to reflect the objectives of the company and to use performance measures that are consistent with these objectives.
- Although the manufacturing process and emphasis will vary from firm to firm, all of the elements of MPC must be performed.
- The MPC system is always capable of improvement, and the payoffs to the overall firm are almost always significant.

REFERENCES

Buffa, E. S., and J. G. Miller. *Production-Inventory Systems: Planning and Control.* 3rd ed. Homewood, Ill.: Richard D. Irwin, 1979.

Davis, E. W. "ROA Chart Worksheet," *UVA-OM-300,* and "Return on Assets Problems," *UVA-OM-273R.* Darden School, University of Virginia, Charlottesville, Va, 1981.

Holstein, W. K. "Production Planning and Control Integrated." *Harvard Business Review,* May/June, 1968.

Johnson, G. A. *APICS Bibliography.* Falls Church, Va.: American Production and Inventory Control Society, 1981.

Jacobs, F. R., and V. A. Mabert. *Production Planning, Scheduling, and Inventory Control: Concepts, Techniques, and Systems.* 3rd ed. Atlanta: Institute of Industrial Engineering, Monograph Series, 1986.

Miller, J. G., and T. E. Vollmann. "1985 North American Futures Survey: A Summary of Survey Responses." Boston: Boston University School of Management, 1985.

———, and A. V. Roth. "Report on the 1986 North American Futures Survey." Boston University School of Management, 1986.

Mize, J. H., and D. J. Seifert. "CIM—A Global View of the Factory." IEE Fall Conference, 1985.

Plossl, G. W. *Manufacturing Control—The Last Frontier for Profits.* Reston, Va.: Reston Publishing, 1973.

———. *Production and Inventory Control.* 2nd ed. Englewood Cliffs, N.J.: Prentice-Hall, 1985.

Rosenthal, S. R. "Progress Toward the 'Factory of the Future.'" *Journal of Operations Management* 4, no. 3, 1984.

Schmenner, R. W., and R. L. Cook. "Explaining Productivity Differences in North Carolina Factories." *Journal of Operations Management* 5, no. 3, 1985.

Schultz, T. "MRP to BRP: The Journey of the 80's." *Production and Inventory Management Review and APICS News,* October 1981, pp. 29–32.

Van Dierdonck, R., and J. G. Miller. "Designing Production Planning and Control Systems." *Journal of Operations Management* 1, no. 1, 1980.

Wagner, H. M. "The Design of Production and Inventory Systems for Multi-Facility and Multi-Warehouse Components." *Operations Research* 22, no. 2 (March/April 1974).

Wallace, T. F. *APICS Dictionary.* 5th ed. Falls Church, Va.: American Production and Inventory Control Society, 1984.

———. *MRPII: Making it Happen.* Essex Junction, Vt.: Oliver Wight, Limited Publications, 1985.

Wight, O. W. *Production and Inventory Management in the Computer Age.* Boston: Cahners Books International, 1974.

———. *Manufacturing Resource Planning: MRPII.* Essex Junction, Vt.: Oliver Wight, Limited Publications, 1984.

DISCUSSION QUESTIONS

1. Describe "organizational slack" for some organization with which you are familiar (e.g., the place where you work, the place where you live, an organization that you do business with, or the school where you are studying).

2. The discussion of the framework for manufacturing planning and control seems to imply that the overall direction setting must be done before the detailed material and capacity planning activities can be accomplished. The latter must be done before the execution of the plans is possible. Do you agree? Give an example that supports your position.

3. In Figure 1.4, several stages of material flows are illustrated. For each of these stages, an example management problem is given. Can you list other examples of management problems for each of the stages? How would the importance of each of the stages vary from industry to industry?

4. Examples of data base elements are given in Figure 1.4 but not in Figure 1.5. What are some of the data base elements for the material planning control system of Figure 1.5? What would be the implications of having incorrect or incomplete data along one of the arrows?

5. Implementation is concerned with changing the way people do things, a task that managers face constantly. Provide an example of such a change that you participated in, either as one who did the changing or as one who was changed. As a result of your experience, what things would you do differently if you had the opportunity to make the change again or if you had been responsible for making the change in the first place?

PROBLEMS

1. Assume that the annual sales volume at Ward Manufacturing is $200 million, the cost of goods sold is $.80 per sales dollar, and the inventory turnover is four times per year (in terms of the cost of goods sold).
   a. What is the value of a 12 percent reduction in the firm's inventory investment (due to improved manufacturing planning and control systems)?
   b. If the firm's inventory carrying cost is 10 percent of item value, how many employees (at an annual salary of $25,000) would the savings in inventory carrying cost from a 12 percent reduction in the firm's inventory investment be equivalent to?
   c. Repeat part b, using a 20 percent inventory carrying cost value.

2. The Sumpump Company has been evaluating the benefits of proposed improvements in the firm's manufacturing planning and control system. The materials manager estimates that the direct cost of manufacturing the firm's products ($50/unit) can be reduced by $1/unit through a reduction in organizational slack made possible by the new system. Assume that:
   a. The firm's profit before taxes is 2 percent of sales.
   b. A sales volume of 100,000 units is budgeted for next year.
   c. The product selling price is $100/unit.
   What is the equivalent increase in sales volume provided by the savings resulting from the proposed system?

3. The VP of manufacturing at Vital, Inc., estimates that inventory turnover can be increased from 5 to 10 times per year by installing an improved manufacturing planning and control system. If the current inventory investment is $2 million and the out-of-pocket inventory carrying cost is 20 percent of item value, how many new numerically controlled machines could be purchased each year with the annual savings in inventory carrying cost if the new system is installed? (Each new machine costs $100,000.)

4. A plant manager at Black Manufacturing estimates that fabrication shop lead times can be reduced from six to three weeks by proposed improvements to the firm's manufacturing planning and control system. He also estimates that, at the present sales volume, a reduction of one week in the manufacturing lead time provides a corresponding reduction of $1 million in the work-in-process inventory investment. If the firm's out-of-pocket inventory carrying cost is 15 percent of item value and the average employee earns $25,000, what is the equivalent reduction in employment that the new system provides?

5. The Ace Widebelt Company is contemplating an investment of $500,000 in an improved manufacturing planning and control system. The firm estimates that the new system would improve the final assembly labor efficiency from the current level of 45 percent to a new level of 85 percent. If the firm's annual sales volume is $500 million and the final assembly labor cost is only 1 percent of the total dollar sales volume, would such an investment be worthwhile?

6. The materials manager at Thompson Products has prepared an ROA (return on assets) flow chart (often called a Dupont chart) indicating the relationships between the financial data in the firm's profit and loss (P & L) and balance sheet statements. The top half of Exhibit A contains balance sheet information and the bottom half includes information from the P & L statement. (All data are stated in $1,000 amounts.)

   The firm is evaluating a proposal to update the manufacturing control system by installing a new computer. The estimated benefits of this proposal include:
   a. A 10 percent reduction in raw materials, work-in-process, and finished goods inventories.
   b. A 10 percent reduction in the labor and materials.

   However, the new system will require an additional $100,000/year in overhead, because of the computer rental cost and the need for additional manufacturing staff. Using the ROA flow chart, determine the impact of the proposed system on the firm's ROA.

7. Wilhelm Vandeberg was asked to evaluate several new proposals for material planning and control changes in a small Dutch firm. To make the calculations, he decided to use a simplified ROA worksheet (see Exhibit A, Problem 6). The current assets were made up of 3,487 guilders (G) in cash, and G 46,872 in inventory. The total permanent assets were G 98,760. Sales amounted to G 97,835. Total costs consisted of G 73,376 in cost of goods sold plus other costs of G 13,493. Use a spreadsheet program to determine the change in ROA for each of the following:
   a. A proposal that would reduce inventory 10 percent.
   b. A reduction of lead time that would increase sales by 10 percent (assume that cost of goods sold is 75 percent of sales and inventory turnover remains constant).

EXHIBIT A   ROA work sheet ($000)

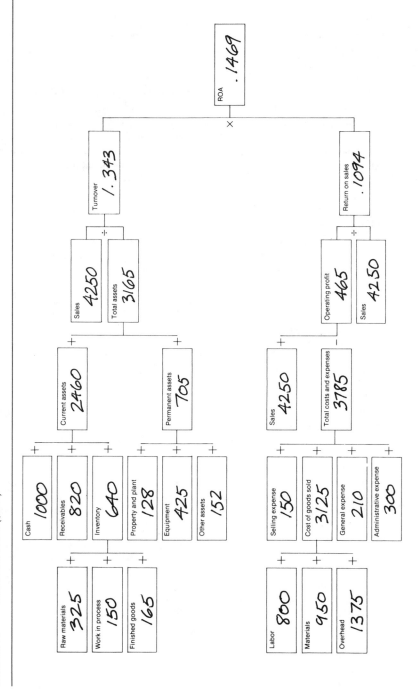

c. A proposal to reduce variable production costs to 74 percent of sales.

d. A combination proposal that would increase the assets by G 12,000, reduce costs of goods sold to 73 percent of sales, increase other costs by G 1,000 per year, increase inventory turnover to four times per year, and increase sales by G 15,000. Would you recommend an investment in the proposal?

8. Construct a simple income statement spreadsheet to evaluate the impact of changes on the profitability of the firm. Use sales of $100, variable costs of 80 percent of sales, fixed costs of $10 plus 20 percent of inventory, inventory of $50 and a tax rate of 50 percent. What is the effect of a 1 percent reduction in the variable costs, a doubling of the inventory turnover, or a 10 percent increase in sales? Which would you prefer, if the effort and cost were the same for each?

9. The following is a simplified income statement for the numerical control division of a Swiss manufacturing firm:

	SFr. (000)*	Percent
Revenue	18,934	100%
Cost of goods sold	7,384	39
Gross profit	11,550	61
Sales expense	2,896	15
Marketing exp.	1,441	8
Inventory Exp.†	1,136	6
Corp. overhead	1,057	5
Product develop.	5,963	31
Profit (loss)	(943)	(5)

*Thousands of Swiss francs.
†Carrying and obsolescence costs combined.

Use a spreadsheet program to determine if you would accept the following project when the firm has a policy of not accepting any project that doesn't have at least a 20 percent return on investment. The project requires an investment of SFr. 24 million. It would increase overhead expenses by SFr. 200,000 and would increase revenues by SFr. 2 million. The project will reduce the cost of goods sold percentage by about 5 percent and will improve the inventory turnover from 3⅓ times per year to 5 times per year.

10. Calculate the time (in hours) between successive units for the following situations:

a. A manufacturer of prefabricated houses that produces a total of 47 houses per year.

b. A breakfast food manufacturer that produces 50,000 cases of 48 boxes of cereal during a 16-hour day.

c. A microcomputer manufacturer that has capacity for 4,000 units per day but only produces an average of 350 per eight-hour shift.

11. Classify the following kinds of companies as to whether they are make-to-stock, make-to-order, or assemble-to-order:

    a. A store that sells ice cream cones.
    b. Fast food hamburgers (e.g., McDonald's).
    c. Student cafeteria.
    d. Exclusive restaurant.
    e. A General Motors assembly line.
    f. A company that makes baseballs.
    g. Hyster fork lift trucks.
    h. Ethan Allen furniture.
    i. Sandoz Laboratories pharmaceuticals.
    j. Black & Decker electric drills.
    k. A company that makes tug boats.

12. The bottom of Figure 1.4 shows material flowing through 5 stages of procurement, manufacture, and distribution, and 5 steps of inventory. Let us assume that each stage takes one week to accomplish. Suppose that just-in-time (JIT) is introduced and the total time for fabrication and assembly is reduced to one week. At the same time, purchasing is done on a JIT basis so that purchased items are delivered as needed directly to fabrication and assembly. What is the overall reduction in material flow time?

13. Continuing with problem **12**, suppose that the customers for the products also are moving to a JIT system. What are the potential lead time savings? What is needed to achieve them?

14. Suppose the company in Figure 1.4 has $5 million in inventory ($1 million in each location)? How much could it afford to spend to eliminate the finished stocks, distribution, and field inventories if capital is worth 20 percent? Are there other "costs" that might be even more important?

15. What kinds of changes will be required in the systems used to plan and control companies with material flows like those in Figure 1.4 in order to achieve the kinds of objectives outlined in Figure 1.1? In what ways do the ideas in Figure 1.2 affect the required changes?

2

Material requirements planning

This chapter deals with material requirements planning (MRP), the central activity in material planning and control (MPC). It is such a key activity that we start the detailed exposition of MPC systems with its description. The managerial objectives of MRP are to provide "the right part at the right time" to meet the schedules for completed products. To do this, MRP provides *formal* plans for each part number, whether raw material, component, or finished good. Accomplishing these plans without excess inventory, overtime, labor, or other resources, is also important. Therefore, the MRP system ensures that the planning is integrated; that is, that the correct number of components is planned for each end item, and raw materials for each component.

Chapter 2 is organized around the following six topics:

- Material requirements planning in manufacturing planning and control: Where does MRP fit in the overall MPC system framework and how is it related to other MPC modules?
- Record processing: What is the basic MRP record and how is it produced?
- Technical issues: What are the additional technical details and supporting systems of which one should be aware?

- Using the MRP system: Who uses the system, how, and how is the exact match between MRP records and physical reality maintained?
- The MRP data base: What are the computer files that support MRP?
- Manual MRP systems: How can the MRP concepts be applied without a computer?

Important related concepts are found in Chapter 3 and 12. Chapter 3 deals with the basic data needs and dynamics of MRP systems. Chapter 12 describes advanced concepts in MRP.

MATERIAL REQUIREMENTS PLANNING IN MANUFACTURING PLANNING AND CONTROL

Figure 2.1 is our general model of a manufacturing planning and control system. Several supporting activities are shown for the front end, engine, and back end of the system. The front end section of the MPC system produces the master production schedule (MPS). The back end, or execution, systems deal with detailed scheduling of the factory and with managing materials coming from vendor plants.

Material requirements planning is the central system in the engine portion of Figure 2.1. It has the primary purpose of taking a period-by-period (time-phased) set of master production schedule requirements and producing a resultant time-phased set of component/raw material requirements.

In addition to master production schedule inputs, MRP has two other basic inputs. A bill of material shows, for each part number, what other part numbers are required as direct components. For example, for an automobile, it could show five wheels required (four plus the spare). For each wheel, the bill of materials could be a hub, tire, valve stem, etc. The second basic input to MRP is inventory status. To know how many wheels to make for a given number of cars, it is necessary to know how many are on hand, how many of those are already allocated to existing needs, and how many have already been ordered.

The MRP data make it possible to construct a time-phased requirement record for any part number. The data can also be used as input to the detailed capacity planning modules.

The MRP system serves a central role in material planning and control. It acts as a translator of the overall plans for production into the detailed individual steps necessary to accomplish those plans. It provides information for developing capacity plans, and it links to the systems that actually get the production accomplished. Because of this key linking role and the central nature of the MRP process and records, we have chosen to describe MRP early in the book. Moreover, the MRP process is where many companies have chosen to start the development of their formal MPC systems.

FIGURE 2.1 Manufacturing planning and control system

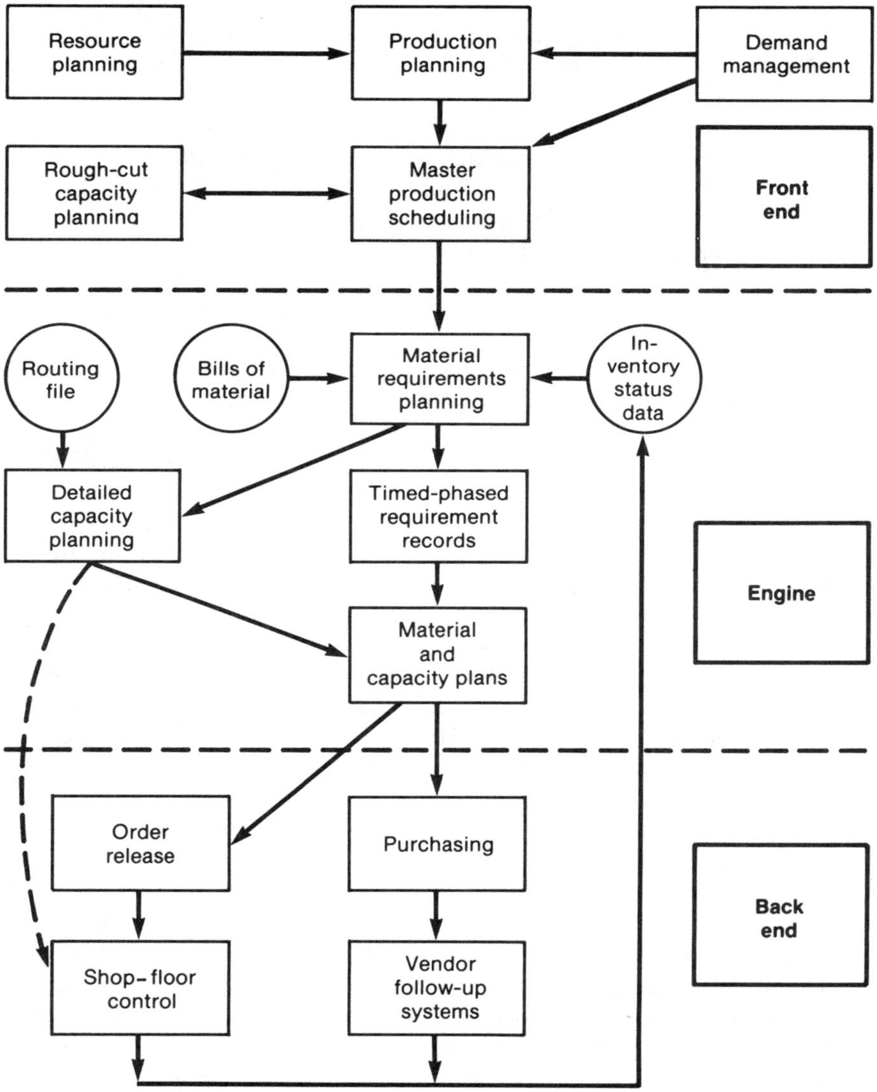

MRP and MRPII

The "engine" section of Figure 2.1 is primarily concerned with the disaggregation of a master production schedule into the resultant set of detailed plans for each manufactured and purchased part number. That is, the MPS is a plan for end items or product options as offered to the customers. MRP is the detailed planning process for components to support the MPS. The box labeled "Material requirements planning" in this section represents the system that does the disaggregation. This was a major breakthrough in MPC made feasible by random access computers. At a later stage of development, it was realized that the due dates for shop orders provided by MRP planning could be updated as needed. This resulted in a rethinking of MRP as more than a disaggregation technique for planning; it was now also seen as a dynamic priority-setting scheme so shop-floor operations could do a better job of execution.

When execution on the shop floor was improved, attention naturally turned to the "front end." The question was how to establish and maintain a viable master production schedule—one that could be executed. When better master production scheduling was incorporated into MRP-based MPC systems, people began to describe them with the term *closed loop MRP systems*.

Additional enhancements included better capacity planning procedures, at the front end, engine, and back end levels. As this occurred, users of these systems began to consider them less as MPC systems and more as company-wide systems. It was now possible to enhance the systems to include financial plans based on the detailed MPC planning process. Because execution was improved, the resultant plans became more and more believable. Simulation possibilities were added, along with various ways to examine "what-if" scenarios. This overall vision of an MRP system for planning and controlling company operations was so fundamentally different from the original concepts of MRP that a new term seemed appropriate. Oliver Wight coined the term *MRPII*. In this case, MRP did not stand for material requirements planning; MRPII means manufacturing resource planning. The old term MRP is now sometimes referred to as mrp or "little MRP." These terms are now widely accepted and most MPC professionals clearly understand the distinction between MRP, mrp, and MRPII.

We will continue in this book to use what we see as the more generic term manufacturing planning and control (MPC) systems. Our reasoning will become clear as we go along, but the fundamental issue is one of evolution. Just as "little MRP" has evolved into MRPII, there have been further improvements, such as just-in-time, optimized production technology (OPT); and more are coming. The question is what to call all of this with a minimum of confusion. Our MPC diagram shown as Figure 1.4 will be expanded in subsequent chapters, but the overall focus will remain the same. We see it as useful to distinguish between the front end or overall direction setting phase of MPC, the detailed disaggregation phase (engine), and the execution aspects associated with detailed shop-floor schedules and procurement. We will see that some of the latest enhancements work in more than one of these areas at the same time.

RECORD PROCESSING

In this section, we present the MRP procedures starting with the basic MRP record, its terminology, timing conventions, and construction. We then turn to an example which illustrates the need to coordinate the planning of component parts with end item planning. We examine several aspects of this coordination and the relationships that must be accounted for. We then look at linking the MRP records to reflect all the required relationships. We intend to show clearly how each MRP record can be managed independently while the *system* keeps them coordinated.

The basic MRP record

At the heart of the MPC system is a universal representation of the status and plans for any single item (part number), whether raw material, component part, or finished good. This universal representation is the MRP time-phased record. Figure 2.2 provides an illustration, displaying the following information:

The anticipated future usage of or demand for the item during the period.

Existing replenishment orders for the item due in at the *beginning* of the period.

FIGURE 2.2   The basic MRP record

Period		1	2	3	4	5
Gross requirements			10		40	10
Scheduled receipts		50				
Projected available balance	4	54	44	44	4	44
Planned order releases					50	
Lead time = 1 period Lot size = 50						

The current and projected inventory status for the item at the *end* of the period.

Planned replenishment orders for the item at the *beginning* of the period.

The top row in Figure 2.2 indicates periods that can vary in length from a day to a quarter or even longer. The period is also called a *time bucket*. The most widely used time bucket or period is one week. A timing convention for developing the MRP record is that the current time is the beginning of the first period. The initial available balance for four units is shown prior to period 1. The number of periods in the record is called the *planning horizon*. In the simplified example shown as Figure 2.2, the planning horizon is five periods. The planning horizon indicates the number of future periods for which plans are made.

The second row, "gross requirements," is a statement of the anticipated future usage of or demand for the item. The gross requirements are *time phased*, which means they are stated on a unique period-by-period basis, rather than aggregated or averaged; that is, the gross requirements are stated as 10 in period 2, 40 in period 4, and 10 in period 5, rather than as a total requirement of 60 or as an average requirement of 12 per period. This method of presentation allows for special orders, seasonality, and periods of no anticipated usage to be explicitly taken into account. A gross requirement in a particular period signifies that a demand is anticipated during that period which will be unsatisfied unless the item is *available* during that period. Availability is achieved by having the item in inventory, or by receiving either an existing replenishment order or a planned replenishment order in time to satisfy the gross requirement.

Another timing convention comes from the question of availability. The convention we use is that the item must be available at the *beginning* of the time bucket in which it is required. This means that plans must be so made that any replenishment order will be in inventory at the beginning of the period in which the gross requirement for that order occurs.

The "scheduled receipt" row describes the status of any open orders (work in process or existing replenishment orders) for the item. This row shows the quantities that have already been ordered and when we expect them to be completed. Scheduled receipts result from previously made ordering decisions and represent a source of the item to meet gross requirements. For example, the gross requirements of 10 in period 2 cannot be satisfied by the 4 units presently available. The scheduled receipts of 50, due in period 1, will be used to satisfy the gross requirement in period 2 if things go according to plan. Scheduled receipts represent a commitment. For an order in the factory, necessary materials have been committed to the order, and capacity at work centers will be required to complete it. For a purchased item, similar commitments have been made to a vendor. The timing convention used for showing scheduled receipts is also at the *beginning* of the period; that is, the order is shown in the period during which the item must be available to satisfy a gross requirement.

The next row in Figure 2.2 is called "projected available balance." The timing convention in this row is the *end* of the period; that is, the row is the projected balance *after* replenishment orders have been received and gross requirements have been satisfied. For this reason, the projected available balance row has an extra time bucket shown at the beginning. This bucket shows the balance *at the present time;* that is, in Figure 2.2, the beginning available balance is four units. The quantity shown in period 1 is the projected balance at the *end* of period 1. This means that the projected available balance shown at the end of a period is available to meet gross requirements in the next (and succeeding) periods. For example, the 54 units shown as the projected available balance at the end of period 1 result from the addition of the 50 units scheduled to be received in period 1 to the beginning balance of 4 units. The gross requirement of 10 units in period 2 reduces the projected balance to 44 units at the end of period 2. The term projected *available* balance is used, instead of projected *on-hand* balance, for a very specific reason. Units of the item might be on hand physically but not available to meet gross requirements because they are already promised or allocated for some other purpose.

The "planned order release" row is determined directly from the projected "available balance" row. Whenever the projected available balance would show a quantity insufficient to satisfy gross requirements (a negative quantity), additional material must be planned for. This is done by creating a *planned order release* in time to keep the projected available balance from becoming negative. For example, in Figure 2.2, the projected available balance at the end of period 4 is four units. This is not sufficient to meet the gross requirement of 10 units in period 5. Since the lead time is one week, the MRP system creates a planned order at the beginning of week 4 providing a *lead time offset* of one week. As we have used a lot size of 50 units, the projected available balance at the end of week 5 is 44 units. Another way that this logic is explained is to note that the balance for the end of period 4 (4 units) is the beginning inventory for period 5, during which there is a gross requirement of 10 units. The difference between the available inventory of 4 and the gross requirement of 10 is a *net requirement* of 6 units in period 5. Thus, an order for at least 6 units must be planned for period 4 to avoid a shortage in period 5.

The MRP system produces the planned order release data in response to the gross requirement, scheduled receipt, and projected available data. When a planned order is created for the most immediate or current period, it is in the *action bucket.* A quantity in the action bucket means that some action is needed now to avoid a future problem. The action is to release the order, which converts it to a scheduled receipt.

The planned order releases are *not* shown in the scheduled receipt row because they have not yet been released for production or purchasing. No material has been committed to their manufacture. The planned order is analogous to an entry on a Christmas list, since the list is comprised of plans. A scheduled receipt is like an order that has been mailed to a catalog firm to send someone on the list a particular gift for Christmas, since a commitment has been made. Like Christmas lists versus mailed orders, planned orders are much easier to change than scheduled receipts. There are many advantages to not converting planned orders into scheduled receipts any earlier than necessary.

The basic MRP record just described provides the correct information on each part in the system. Linking these single part records together is essential in managing the flow of parts needed for a complex product or customer order. Key elements for linking the records are the bill of materials, the explosion process (using inventory and scheduled receipt information), and lead time off-setting. We consider each of these before turning to how the records are linked into a system

An example bill of materials. Figure 2.3 shows a snow shovel, which is end item part number 1605. The complete snow shovel is assembled (using four rivets and two nails) from the top handle assembly, scoop assembly,

---

FIGURE 2.3 The 1605 snow shovel shown with component parts and assemblies

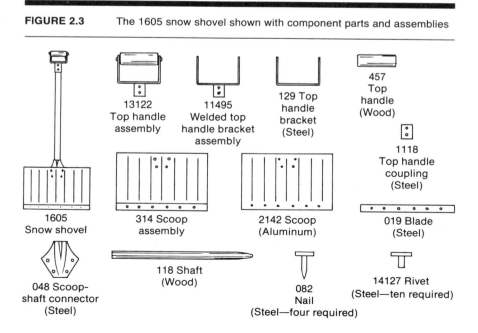

scoop-shaft connector, and shaft. The top handle assembly, in turn, is created by combining the welded top handle bracket assembly with the wooden handle using two nails. The welded top handle bracket assembly is created by welding the top handle coupling to the top handle bracket. In a similar way, the scoop assembly is created by combining the aluminum scoop with the steel blade using six rivets.

Explaining even this simple assembly process is a cumbersome task. Moreover, such diagrams as Figure 2.3 get more complicated as the number of subassemblies, components, and parts used increases, or as they are used in increasingly more places (e.g., rivets and nails). Two techniques that get at this problem nicely are the *product structure diagram* and the *indented bill of materials* (BOM), which are shown in Figure 2.4. Both provide the detailed information of Figure 2.3, but the indented BOM has the added advantage of being easily printed by a computer.

Note that both the product structure diagram and the indented BOM show exactly what goes into what instead of being just a parts list. For example, to make one 13122 top handle assembly, we see by the product structure diagram that one 457 top handle, two 082 nails, and one 11495 bracket assembly are needed. The same information is shown in the indented BOM; the three required parts are indented and shown, one level beneath the 13122. Note also that one does *not* need a top handle bracket (129) or a top handle coupling (1118) to produce a top handle assembly (13122). These are only needed to produce a bracket assembly (11495). In essence, the top handle assembly does not care *how* a bracket assembly is made, only that it is made. The making of the bracket assembly is a separate problem.

Before leaving our brief discussion of bills of material, it is important to stress that the bill of material used to support MRP may be different from other company perceptions of a bill of materials. The BOM to support MRP must be consistent with the way the product is manufactured. For example, if we are making red automobiles, the part numbers should be for red doors. If green automobiles are desired, the part numbers must be for green doors. Also, if we change to a different set of subassemblies, the indentations on the indented BOM should change as well. Engineering and accounting may well not care what color the parts are or what the manufacturing sequence is.

Gross to net explosion. *Explosion* is the process of translating product requirements into component part requirements, taking existing inventories and scheduled receipts into account. Thus, explosion may be viewed as the process of determining, for *any* part number, the quantities of *all* components needed to satisfy its requirements, and continuing this process for *every* part number until all purchased and/or raw material requirements are exactly calculated.

The gross to net explosion process means that, as explosion takes place, only the component part requirements net of any inventory or scheduled

FIGURE 2.4 Parts for snow shovel

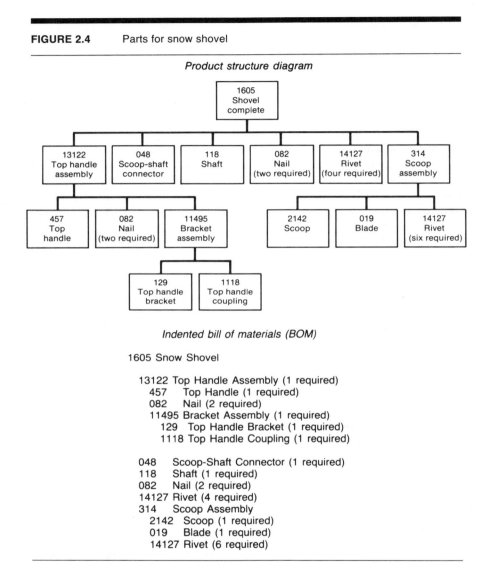

Product structure diagram

Indented bill of materials (BOM)

1605 Snow Shovel

    13122 Top Handle Assembly (1 required)
      457   Top Handle (1 required)
      082   Nail (2 required)
      11495 Bracket Assembly (1 required)
        129 Top Handle Bracket (1 required)
        1118 Top Handle Coupling (1 required)

    048   Scoop-Shaft Connector (1 required)
    118   Shaft (1 required)
    082   Nail (2 required)
    14127 Rivet (4 required)
    314   Scoop Assembly
      2142 Scoop (1 required)
      019   Blade (1 required)
      14127 Rivet (6 required)

receipts are considered. In this way, only the *necessary* requirements are linked through the system. Although this may seem like an obvious goal, the product structure can make determination of net requirements more difficult than it seems. To illustrate, let us return to the snow shovel example.

Suppose the company wanted to produce 100 snow shovels, and we were responsible for making the 13122 top handle assembly. We are given current inventory and scheduled receipt information from which the gross requirements and net requirements for each component of the top handle can be calculated. This is shown in Figure 2.5.

The gross and net requirements shown in Figure 2.5 may not correspond to what one feels they should be. It might at the outset seem that since one top handle coupling (1118) is used per shovel, the gross requirements should be 100 and the net requirement 46, instead of the 48 and zero that are shown. To produce 100 shovels means we need (have a demand for) 100 top handle assemblies (part 13122). Twenty-five of these 100 can come from inventory, resulting in a net requirement of 75. As we need to make only 75 top handle assemblies, we need 75 top handles and bracket assemblies. This 75 is the *gross* requirement for parts 457 and 11495 (as indicated by the circled numbers in Figure 2.5). Since 2 nails (part 082) are used per top handle assembly, the gross requirement for 082 is 150. The 25 units of top handle assembly inventory contain some implicit inventories of handles, brackets, and nails, which the gross to net process takes into account. Looking on down, we see that there are 27 units of the bracket assembly in inventory, so the net requirement is for 48. This becomes the gross requirement for the bracket and coupling. Since there are 39 top handle couplings in inventory and 15 scheduled for receipt, there is *no* net requirement for part 1118.

The gross to net relationship is a key element of MRP systems. It not only provides the basis for the calculation of the appropriate quantities but also serves as the communication link between part numbers. It is the basis for the concept of *dependent demand*; that is, the "demand" (gross requirements) for top handles depends upon the net requirements for top handle assemblies. To correctly do the calculations, the bill of material, inventory, and scheduled receipt data are all necessary. With these data, the dependent demand can be exactly calculated. It need not be forecast. On the other hand, some *independent demand* items, such as the snow shovel, are subject to demand from outside the firm. The need for snow shovels will have to be forecast. The concept of dependent demand is often called the fundamental principle of MRP. It provides the way to remove uncertainty from the requirement calculations.

FIGURE 2.5   Gross and net requirement calculations for the snow shovel

Part description	Part number	Inventory	Scheduled receipts	Gross requirements	Net requirements
Top handle assembly	13122	25	—	100	75
Top handle	457	22	25	75	28
Nail (2 required)	082	4	50	150	96
Bracket assembly	11495	27	—	75	48
Top handle bracket	129	15	—	48	33
Top handle coupling	1118	39	15	48	—

Lead time offsetting. The gross to net explosion tells us how many of each subassembly and component part are needed to support a desired finished product quantity. What it does not do, however, is tell us *when* each of the components and subassemblies is needed. Referring back to Figures 2.3 and 2.4, it is clear that the top handle bracket and top handle coupling need to be welded together before the wooden top handle is attached. These relationships are known as *precedent relationships*. They indicate the order in which things must be done.

In addition to precedent relationships, the determination of when to schedule each component part also depends upon how long it takes to produce the part, that is, the lead time. Perhaps the top handle bracket (129) can be fabricated in one day, while the top handle coupling (1118) takes two weeks. If so, it would be advantageous to start making the coupling before the bracket, since they are both needed at the same time to make a bracket assembly.

Despite the fact that the need to take lead time differences into account may seem obvious, many systems for component part manufacturing ignore them. For example, most furniture manufacturers base production on what is called a *cutting*. In the cutting approach, if a lot of 100 chairs were to be assembled, then 100 of each part (with appropriate multiples) are started at the same time. Figure 2.6 is a Gantt chart (time-oriented bar chart) showing how this cutting approach would be applied to the snow shovel example. (Note that the processing times are shown on the chart.)

Figure 2.6 shows clearly that the cutting approach, which starts all parts as soon as possible, will lead to unnecessary work-in-process inventories. For example, the top handle bracket (129) does not need to be started until the end of day 9, since it must wait for the coupling (1118) before it can be put into its assembly (11495), and part 1118 takes 10 days. In the cutting approach, parts are scheduled earlier than need be. This results from using the *front schedule* logic, that is, scheduling as early as possible.

What should be done is to *back schedule*—start each item as late as possible. Figure 2.7 provides a back schedule for the snow shovel example. The schedules for parts 1118, 11495, 13122, and 1605 do not change, since they in essence form a critical path. All of the other parts, however, are scheduled later in this approach than in the front scheduling approach. A substantial savings in work-in-process inventory is obtained by this shift of dates.

Back scheduling has several obvious advantages. It will reduce work-in-process, postpone the commitment of raw materials to specific products, and minimize storage time of completed components. Implementing the back schedule approach, however, requires a system. The system must have accurate BOM data and lead time estimates, some way to ensure that all component parts are started at the right times, and some means of tracking components and subassemblies to make sure that they are all completed according to plans. The cutting approach is much simpler, since all component parts are started at the same time and left in the pipeline until needed.

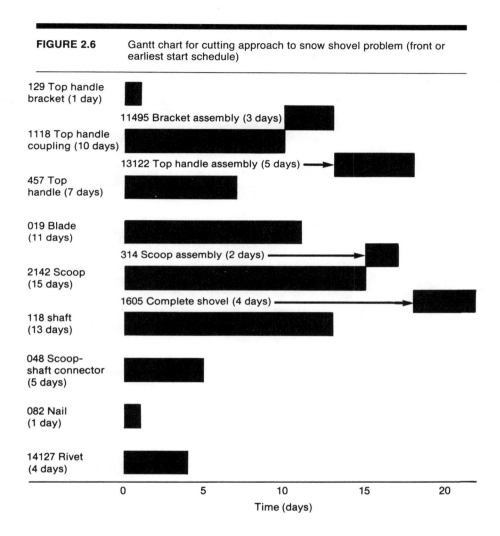

FIGURE 2.6 Gantt chart for cutting approach to snow shovel problem (front or earliest start schedule)

We want to show how MRP achieves the benefits of the back scheduling approach *and* can perform the gross to net explosion. In fact, the combination of back schedules and gross to net explosion is the heart of MRP. We turn now to linking the basic MRP records to see how MRP achieves these goals.

Linking the MRP records

Figure 2.8 shows the linked set of individual time-phased MRP records for the top handle assembly of the snow shovel. We have already used the first five periods of the 082 nail record shown in Figure 2.8 as the basic

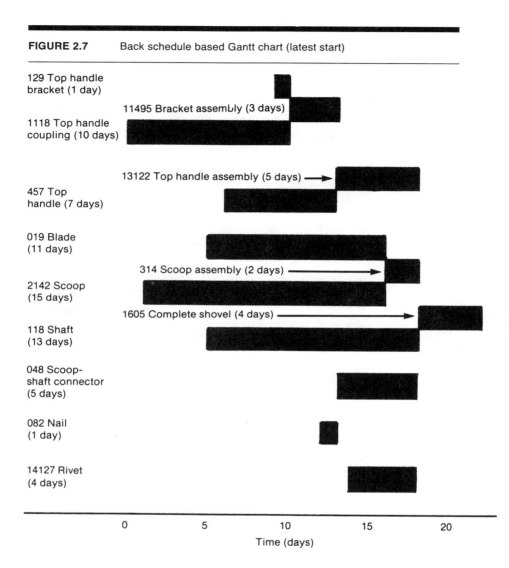

FIGURE 2.7   Back schedule based Gantt chart (latest start)

129 Top handle
bracket (1 day)

11495 Bracket assembly (3 days)

1118 Top handle
coupling (10 days)

13122 Top handle assembly (5 days) ⟶

457 Top
handle (7 days)

019 Blade
(11 days)

314 Scoop assembly (2 days) ⟶

2142 Scoop
(15 days)

1605 Complete shovel (4 days) ⟶

118 Shaft
(13 days)

048 Scoop-
shaft connector
(5 days)

082 Nail
(1 day)

14127 Rivet
(4 days)

0   5   10   15   20

Time (days)

record description in Figure 2.2. To see how that record fits into the whole, we will start with the snow shovels themselves. We said that 100 snow shovels were going to be made, and now we see the timing; that is, the gross requirements row shows the total need of 100 time phased as 20 in week 2, 10 in week 4, 20 in week 6, 5 in week 7, 35 in week 9, and 10 in week 10. Since each snow shovel takes a top handle assembly, the gross requirements row for the top handle shows when shovel assembly is to begin. Note that the total planned orders for the top handle assembly is the net requirement of 75 that we calculated before in the gross to net calculations of Figure 2.5.

The lead time for the top handle assembly is two weeks, calculated as the five days processing time shown in Figure 2.6 plus five days for paperwork. The lead time for each of the other records is similarly calculated; one week (five days) of paperwork time is added to the processing time and the total rounded to the nearest five-day week. The current inventories and scheduled receipts for each part are those shown in Figure 2.5. The scheduled receipts are shown in the appropriate periods. Using the two-week lead time and recognizing a net requirement of five units in week 4 for the top handle assembly, we see the need to plan an order for week 2 of five units.

This planned order release of five units in week 2 becomes a gross requirement in week 2 for the top handles as shown by the circles in Figure 2.8. Note also that the gross requirements for the nails and brackets in period 2 derive from this same planned order release (with two nails per top handle assembly). Thus, the communication between records is the dependent demand that we saw illustrated before in the gross to net calculations of Figure 2.5.

The remaining planned order releases for the top handle assembly exactly meet the net requirements in the remaining periods, offset for the lead time. The ordering policy used for these items is called *lot-for-lot* lot sizing. An exception to the lot-for-lot procedure is the ordering of nails, which is done in lots of 50. In the case of the nails, the total planned orders will not necessarily add up to the net requirements.

Another part for which there is a discrepancy between the planned orders and the net requirements calculated in Figure 2.5 is the top handle coupling. For this part, a safety stock of 20 units is desired. This means the planned order logic will schedule a planned order release to prevent the projected available balance from going below the safety stock level of 20 units. For the top handle couplings, this means a total of 4 units must be planned for period 2 and 10 for period 3 to maintain the 20-unit safety stock.

The one element we have yet to clearly show is the back scheduling effect. We saw before that it would be desirable to delay the start of the top handle bracket (part 129) relative to the top handle coupling (part 1118). The MRP records show that the start of the first planned order for part 129 is not until week 4, two weeks after the first planned order for part 1118. Both of these planned orders are to satisfy a gross requirement of 35 derived from the planned order for the bracket assembly in week 5. We see then that the orders are back scheduled. This relationship can be more complicated than our example, since the planned order release timing depends on the safety stock and inventory levels, as well as the lead times. The MRP system, however, coordinates all of that information and determines the appropriate planned order release dates, based on back scheduling.

At this point, we see fully the linking of the MRP time-phased records.

The planned order release row for the top handle assembly (13122) becomes (with the appropriate multiplier) the gross requirement row for each of its components (part 457, 082, and 11495) and they are linked together. Once all the gross requirement data are available for a particular record, the individual record processing logic is applied and the planned order releases for the part are passed down as gross requirements to its components, following the product structure (BOM) on a level-by-level basis. In some cases, parts will receive their requirements from more than one source (common parts), as is true for the nails and rivets in the snow shovel. In these cases, the gross requirements will reflect needs from more than one planned order release source. Again, the system accounts for this, and incorporates it into the gross to net logic.

We see that the MRP records take proper account of gross to netting. They also incorporate the back scheduling concept, and allow for explicit timings, desired lot sizing procedures, safety stocks, and part commonality. What is of even more importance, however, is independence of the part number planning. With the MRP approach, it is not necessary for the person planning for snow shovels to explicitly coordinate his or her planning with the planning of the component parts. The MRP system accomplishes the coordination. Whatever is done to the MRP record for the snow shovels will result in a set of planned orders that the system will correctly pass down as gross requirements to its components. This means that plans for each part number can be developed independently of the product structures, and the plans at each level will be communicated correctly to the other levels.

So far, we have looked only at the construction of MRP records in the system. It is important to stress that the system is *forward looking*. The records lay out anticipated *future* actions to accomplish product manufacturing objectives. Therefore, it is a proactive system. Problems can be anticipated before they create crises. Since MRP must function in a dynamic world, the system must help managers to be responsive to the problems. Some of the additional technical aspects necessary to make this happen are described next.

TECHNICAL ISSUES

In this section, we briefly introduce some of the technical issues to be considered in the design of MRP systems. The intent is to provide a basic understanding of several additional facets of MRP systems so we can then facilitate the use of the systems.

Processing frequency

Thus far we have looked only at the static construction of the MRP records and how they are linked together. Since conditions change and new information is received, the records must be brought up-to-date so plans can be adjusted to reflect these changes. This means processing the MRP records anew, incorporating the current information. Two issues are involved in the processing decision: how frequently the records should be processed and whether all the records should be processed at the same time.

When all of the records are processed in one computer run, it is called *regeneration*. This signifies that *all* part number records are completely reconstructed each time the records are processed. An alternative is *net change* processing, which means only those records that are affected by the new or changed information are reconstructed. The key issue raised by contrasting regeneration and net change is the frequency of processing. Let us now consider this issue in more detail.

The appropriate frequency for processing the MRP time-phased records is dependent upon the firm, its products, and its operations. The most common current practice is for weekly processing using regeneration. But some firms regenerate every two weeks or even monthly, while others process all the MRP time-phased records twice per week or even more often.

The prime motivation for less frequent processing is the computational cost. This can be especially high with regeneration, since a new record is created for every active part number in the product structure file at each processing. The computational time required, however, varies considerably from company to company, depending upon the computer approach used, the amount of part numbers, the complexity of product structure, and other factors. For companies using regeneration, typically 8 to 24 hours of central processing unit (CPU) time are required. For example, at the Hill-Rom Company in Batesville, Indiana, regeneration for approximately 13,000 active part numbers is done over each weekend and requires approximately 16 hours of computer (CPU) time on an IBM 370-145.

The problem with processing less frequently is that the portrayal of component status and needs expressed in the records becomes increasingly out-of-date and inaccurate. There are both anticipated and unanticipated causes for this decrease in accuracy. As the anticipated scheduled receipts are received and requirements satisfied, the inventory balances change. As unanticipated scrap, requirement changes, stock corrections, or other such transactions occur, they will cause inaccuracies if they are not reflected in all the time-phased records that are influenced by the transactions. The changes in one record are linked to other time-phased records as planned order releases become gross requirements for lower level components. Thus, some change transactions may cascade throughout the product structure. If these transactions are not reflected in the time-phased records early enough, the result could be material shortages.

More frequent processing of the MRP records increases computer costs but results in fewer unpleasant surprises. When the records reflecting the changes are produced, appropriate actions will be indicated to compensate for the changes. Responding to actual events less frequently can increase the magnitude of compensation required. As the inaccuracies increase in number and magnitude, the system's representation of physical reality is less useful. Thus, to manage effectively, there is a need to keep the records synchronized with actuality.

A logical response to the pressure for more frequent processing is to reduce the amount of calculation required by processing only the records affected by the changes. This net change approach only creates a new part number record when a transaction makes the present component plan inaccurate. Although this could be done as the transaction occurs, the typical approach is to accumulate all the transactions in a day and process them overnight.

The argument for the net change approach is that it can reduce computer time enough to make daily or more frequent processing possible. In companies where this can be done, there is the added advantage of smoothing the computational requirements over the week. On the other hand, daily processing of part of the records could lead to even greater overall computational cost than weekly regeneration. Since only part of the records is reviewed at each processing, the need for very accurate computer records and transaction processing procedures is obvious. Some net change users do an occasional regeneration to clean up all of the records.

The question of processing frequency is important, as we have pointed out. The need for frequent processing must be assessed by each company in light of the computational costs, the rapidity of the decline in record accuracy, and the complexity of their products. The benefits of more frequent updating also should be assessed. As computers get faster and faster, firms are increasingly adopting daily processing of the records, either through regeneration or through net change. The state of the art in hardware and software technology now supports on-line systems with a daily updating cycle.

Lot sizing

In the snow shovel example of Figure 2.8, we illustrate a fixed lot size (50 units for the nails) and the lot-for-lot procedure. The lot size of 50 for the nails could have been someone's estimate of a good lot size or the result of calculation. The time-phased information can be used in combination with economic, physical, vendor, and other data to develop lot sizes that conform to organizational needs. One might reach the conclusion, for the top handle (1118) in Figure 2.8, that it is undesirable to set up the equipment for *only* 4 parts in week 2, and again for 10 parts in week 3, and so combine the two orders. The time-phased record permits the development of such *discrete* lot sizes that will exactly satisfy the net requirements for one or more periods.

Several formal procedures have been developed for lot sizing the time-

FIGURE 2.8   MRP records for the snow shovel top handle assembly

			Week									
			1	2	3	4	5	6	7	8	9	10
13122 Top handle assembly Lead time = 2	Gross requirements			20		10		20	5		35	10
	Scheduled receipts											
	Projected available balance	25	25	5	5	0	0	0	0	0	0	0
	Planned order releases			(5)			20	5		35	10	

457 Top handle Lead time = 2	Gross requirements			(5)		20	5		35	10		
	Scheduled receipts				25							
	Projected available balance	22	22	17	42	22	17	17	0	0	0	0
	Planned order releases						18	10				

082 Nail (2 required) Lead time = 1 Lot size = 50	Gross requirements			10		40	10		70	20		
	Scheduled receipts		50									
	Projected available balance	4	54	44	44	4	44	44	24	4	4	4
	Planned order releases					50		50				

11495 Bracket assembly Lead time = 2	Gross requirements			5		20	5		35	10		
	Scheduled receipts											
	Projected available balance	27	27	22	22	2	0	0	0	0	0	0
	Planned order releases				3		35	10				

129 Top handle bracket Lead time = 1	Gross requirements				3		35	10				
	Scheduled receipts											
	Projected available balance	15	15	15	12	12	0	0	0	0	0	0
	Planned order releases					23	10					

1118 Top handle coupling Lead time = 3 Safety stock = 20	Gross requirements				3		35	10				
	Scheduled receipts			15								
	Projected available balance	39	39	54	51	51	20	20	20	20	20	20
	Planned order releases			4	10							

phased requirements. The basic trade-off usually involves elimination of one or more setups at the expense of carrying inventory longer. In many cases, the discrete lot sizes that are possible with MRP are more appealing than the fixed lot sizes that could be used. Compare the residual inventory, in week 10, of the nails with that of the bracket assemblies in Figure 2.8, for example.

The lot-for-lot technique seems at first glance to be somewhat too simple-minded since it does not consider any of the economic trade-offs or physical factors. Recall, however, that batching planned orders at one level will increase the gross requirements at the next level in the product structure. So larger lot sizing near the end item level of the bill of materials cascades down through all levels. Thus, it turns out that lot-for-lot is better than one might expect in actual practice, particularly at the intermediate levels in the bill of materials. This is especially the case when a product structure has many levels, and the cascading effect becomes greatly magnified. This cascading effect can be mitigated to some extent for components and raw materials that are very common. When this is the case, again lot sizing may be appropriate. As a consequence, many firms employ lot sizing primarily at the end item and basic component levels, while intermediate subassemblies are planned on a lot-for-lot basis.

Safety stock and safety lead time

Carrying out detailed component plans is sometimes facilitated by the inclusion of *safety stocks* and/or *safety lead times* in the MRP records. Safety stock is a buffer of stock above and beyond that needed to satisfy the gross requirements. This is illustrated in Figure 2.8 by incorporating safety stock for the top handle coupling. Safety lead time is a procedure whereby shop orders or purchase orders are released and scheduled to arrive one or more periods before necessary to satisfy the gross requirements.

We have seen that safety stocks can be easily incorporated into MRP time-phased records. They are merely included in the analysis so the projected available balance does not fall below the safety stock level instead of zero. To incorporate safety lead time, orders are issued (planned) earlier and are scheduled (planned) to be received into inventory before the time that the MRP logic would indicate it was necessary. Figure 2.9 shows the top handle bracket from Figure 2.8 being planned with a one-week safety lead time. Notice that *both* the planned releases and planned receipt date are changed. Safety lead time is not just inflated lead time.

Both safety stock and safety lead time are used in practice, and there is no structural reason why both cannot be used simultaneously. However, both are hedges that to some extent result in indicating that orders should be released (launched) or that they need to be received when, in fact, this is not strictly true. To use safety stocks and safety lead times effectively, the influence of the techniques on plans must be well understood. If it is not well understood, the wrong orders can be sent to the factory, meaning that workers are trying to get out part A because of safety lead time or safety stock when, in fact, part B will be required to meet a customer order, so it would be better to have them working on that.

Safety stock tends to be used in MRP systems where uncertainty about quantities is the problem, (e.g., where some small amount of scrap, spare

FIGURE 2.9   MRP record with safety lead time

			1	2	3	4	5	6	7	8	9	10
Part 129	Gross requirements				3		35	10				
Top handle bracket lead time = 1	Scheduled receipts											
Lot-for-lot	Projected available balance	15	15	15	12	35	10	0	0	0	0	0
Safety lead time = 1	Planned order releases				23	10						

part demand, or other unplanned usage is a frequent occurrence). Safety lead time, on the other hand, tends to be used when the major uncertainty is in the timing rather than the quantity. For example, if a firm buys from a vendor who often misses delivery dates, safety lead time may provide better results than safety stock. This is particularly true when the planned orders from higher-level parts have been lot sized and safety stock would not cover the requirements. Bringing an order in early, on the other hand, will cover the requirements, since the order size was originally based on the requirement.

Low-level coding

If we refer once again to Figure 2.4, we see that the nails (part 082) and rivets (part 14127) are common parts. The planned order row for completed shovels would be passed down as one part of the gross requirements for both of these parts. But there are additional sources of requirements for the nail (part 082)—from the top handle assembly (13122) and for rivets (14127) from the scoop assembly (314). If we process the time-phased record for either of these common parts before all their gross requirements have been accumulated, the computations will all have to be redone. In Figure 2.8, for example, the record for part 082 only includes the requirements passed down from the top handle assembly and not those from the completed snow shovels.

The way this problem is handled is to assign *low-level code numbers* to each part in the product structure or the indented BOM. By convention, the top final assembly level is denoted as level zero. In our example, the snow shovel would have a low-level code of 0. All immediate component part numbers of this part (13122, 048, 118, 082, 14127, and 314 in Figure 2.4) are given the low-level code number 1. The next level down (part numbers 457, 082, 11495, 2142, 019, and 14127) are low-level coded 2. Note that the two common parts (nails and rivets) have just been recoded as level 2, indicating that they are used lower in the product structure. The higher the level codes, the lower in the product structure the part is used. Consequently, the last level code assigned to a part would indicate the lowest level of usage and is the level code retained for that part. We finish the example when part numbers 129 and 1118 are coded level 3. The level code assigned to any part number is based on the part's usage in all products manufactured by the organization.

Once low-level codes are established, MRP record processing proceeds from one level code to the next, starting at level code 0. This ensures that all gross requirements have been passed down to a part before its MRP record is processed. The result is planning of component parts coordinated with the needs of all higher-level part numbers. Within a level, the MRP record processing is typically done in part number sequence.

Pegging

Pegging relates all the gross requirements for a part to all the planned order releases or other sources of demand that created the requirements. The pegging records contain the specific part number or numbers of the sources of all gross requirements. At level 0, for example, the pegging records might contain the specific customer orders that are to be satisfied by the gross requirements in the end item time-phased records. For lower-level part numbers, the gross requirements are most often pegged to planned orders of higher level items, but might also be pegged to customer orders if the part is sold as a service part.

Pegging information can be used to go up through the MRP records from a raw material gross requirement to some future customer order. In this sense, it is the reverse of the explosion process. Pegging is sometimes compared to where-used data. Where-used data, however, indicate for *each* part number, the part numbers of all items on which the part is used. Pegging, on the other hand, is a *selective* where-used file. Pegging shows only the specific part numbers that produce the specific gross requirements in each time period. Thus, the pegging information can be used to trace the impact of a material problem all the way up to the order it would affect.

Firm planned orders

The logic that was used to illustrate the construction of an MRP record for an individual part number is automatically applied for every processed part number. The result is a series of planned order releases for each part number. If changes have taken place since the last time the record was processed, the planned order releases can be very different from one record-processing cycle to the next. Since the planned orders are passed down as gross requirements to the next level, the differences can cascade throughout the product structure.

One device for preventing this cascading down through the product structure is to create a *firm planned order* (FPO). FPO, as the name implies, is a planned order that the MRP system *does not* automatically change when conditions change. To change either the quantity or timing of a firm planned order, a managerial action is required. This means that the trade-offs in making the change can be evaluated before authorization.

The FPO provides a means for temporarily overriding the system to provide stability or to solve problems. For example, if the changes are coming about because of scrap losses on open orders, the possibility of absorbing those variations with safety stock can be evaluated. If a more rapid delivery of raw material than usual is requested, say by using air freight, to meet a special need, the lead time can be reduced for that one order, and an FPO means the system will not use the normal lead time offset from the net requirement for that order.

Service parts

Service part demand must be included in the MRP record if the material requirements are not to be understated. The service part demand is typically based on a forecast and is added directly into the gross requirements for the part. From the MRP system point of view, the service part demand is simply another source of gross requirements for a part, and the sources of all gross requirements are maintained through pegging records. The low-level code for a part used exclusively for service would be zero. If it is used as a component part as well, the low-level code would be determined the same way as for any other part.

As actual service part needs occur, it is to be expected that demand variations will arise. These can be partially buffered with safety stocks, inventories specifically allocated to service part usage, or by creative use of the MRP system. By careful examination of pegging records, expected shortage conditions for manufacturing part requirements can sometimes be satisfied from available service parts. Conversely, critical service part requirements can perhaps be met with orders destined for higher-level items. Only one safety stock inventory is needed to buffer uncertainties from both sources, however.

Planning horizon

In Figure 2.8, the first planned order for top handle assemblies occurs in week 2 to meet the gross requirement in period 4 of 10 units. This planned order of 5 units in week 2 results in a corresponding gross requirement in that week for the bracket assembly (part 11495). This gross requirement is satisfied from the existing inventory of part 11495. But a different circumstance occurs if we trace the gross requirements for 35 top handle assemblies in week 9.

The net requirement for 35 units in week 9 becomes a planned order release in week 7. This, in turn, becomes a gross requirement for 35 bracket assemblies (part 11495) in week 7 and a planned order release in week 5. This passes down to the top handle coupling (part 1118), which creates a planned order release for 4 units in week 2. This means that the *cumulative lead time* for the top handle assembly is seven weeks (from release of the coupling order in week 2 to receipt of the top handle assemblies in week 9).

The cascading of lead times means that the effective length or visibility of the planning horizon is shortened as one moves down the product structure. This is sometimes referred to as loss of low-level visibility. The 10-week planning horizon for the top handle assembly results in a 6-week planning horizon with only 3 weeks of planned order releases for the coupling. The only way to compensate for this is to extend the planning horizon for the items at the top of the bill of material. It is not uncommon to find one to two years as the planning horizon for MRP systems.

Scheduled receipts versus planned order releases

A true understanding of MRP requires knowledge of certain key differences between a scheduled receipt and a planned order. We noted one such difference before: the scheduled receipt represents a commitment whereas the planned order is only a plan—the former is much more difficult to change than the latter. A scheduled receipt for a purchased item means that a purchase order, which is a formal commitment, has been prepared. Similarly, a scheduled receipt for a manufactured item means there is an open shop order. Raw materials and component parts have *already* been specifically committed to that order and are no longer available for other needs. One major result of this distinction, which can be seen in Figure 2.8, is that planned order releases explode to gross requirements for components, but scheduled receipts (the open orders) do not.

A related issue is seen from the following question: Where would a scheduled receipt for the top handle assembly (13122) in Figure 2.8 of say 20 units in week 2, be reflected in the records for the component parts (457, 082, and 11495)? The answer is nowhere! Scheduled receipts are not reflected in the current records for component parts. For that scheduled receipt to exist, the component parts would have already been assigned to the shop order representing the scheduled receipt for part 13122 and removed from the available balances of the components. As far as MRP is concerned, the 20 part 457s, 40 part 082s, and 20 part 11495s do not exist! They are on their way to becoming 20 part 13122s. It is the 13122 record that controls this process, not the component records.

So far we have examined the basic MRP system and some key technical details. Let us now turn to the *use* of the system: Who does what; how is it done; and what transactions need to be processed?

USING THE MRP SYSTEM

In this section, we discuss the critical aspects of using the MRP system to ensure that the MRP system records are exactly synchronized with the physical flows of material.

The MRP planner

The persons most directly involved with the MRP system outputs are planners. They are typically in the production planning, inventory control, and purchasing departments. The planners have the responsibility for making the detailed decisions that keep the material moving through the plant to achieve the shipment of final products. Their range of discretion is carefully limited (i.e., without higher authorization, they cannot change plans for end items that are destined for customers). It is, however, their actions that are reflected in the MRP records. Well-trained, high-quality MRP planners are essential to effective use of the MRP system.

Computerized MRP systems often encompass tens of thousands of part numbers. The system produces a set of coordinated MRP time-phased records for each part number. As a consequence, planners are generally organized around logical groupings of parts, such as metal parts, wood parts, purchased electronic parts, West Coast distribution center, etc. Even so, it would not be an effective use of the planners' time to review each record every time the records are processed. At any time, many would require no action, so the planner only wants to review and interpret those records which require action.

The primary actions taken by an MRP planner are:

1. Release orders (i.e., launch purchase or shop orders when indicated by the system).
2. Reschedule the due dates of existing open orders when desirable.
3. Analyze and update system planning factors for the part numbers under his or her control. This would involve such things as changing lot sizes, lead times, scrap allowances, or safety stocks.
4. Reconcile errors or inconsistencies and try to eliminate root causes of these errors.
5. Find key problem areas that require action now to prevent future crises.

6. Use the system to solve critical material shortage problems so the actions can be captured in the records for the next processing. This means the planner works *within* the formal MRP rules, *not* by informal methods.

7. Indicate where further system enhancements (outputs, diagnostics, etc.) would make the planner's job easier.

Order launching. Order launching is the process of releasing orders to the shop or to vendors (purchase orders). This process is prompted by MRP when a planned order release is in the current time period, the action bucket. The action converts the planned order into a scheduled receipt in a time period that reflects the lead time offset. Order launching is the opening of shop and purchase orders; closing these orders occurs when the scheduled receipts are received into stockrooms. At that time, a transaction must be processed—to increase the on-hand inventory and eliminate the scheduled receipt. Procedures for opening and closing shop orders have to be carefully defined so that all transactions are properly processed.

The orders indicated by MRP as ready for launching are a function of lot sizing procedures and safety stock, as well as timing. We saw this in our examples where we worked with lot-for-lot approaches and fixed lot sizes. In Figure 2.8, a key responsibility of the planner is to manage with awareness of the implications of these effects. For example, not *all* of a fixed lot may be necessary to cover a requirement, or a planned order that is solely for replenishment of safety stock may be in the action bucket.

When an order is launched, it is sometimes necessary to include a shrinkage allowance for scrap and other process yield situations. The typical approach is to allow some percentage for yield losses that will increase the shop order quantity above the net amount required. To effect good control over open orders, the *total* amount, including the allowance, should be shown on the shop order, and the scheduled receipt should be reduced as actual yield losses occur during production.

Allocation and availability checking. A concept closely related to order launching is that of allocation. An important step prior to order launching involves an availability check for the necessary component or components. From the snow shovel example, if we want to assemble 20 of the top handle assembly (13122) in period 4, the availability check would be whether sufficient components (20 of part 457, 40 of part 082, and 20 of part 11495) are available. If not, the shop order for 20 top handle assemblies (13122) should not be launched, because it cannot be executed without component parts. The planner role is key here, as well. The best course of action might be to release a partial order. The planner should evaluate that possibility.

What most MRP systems do is to first check component availability for any order that a planner desires to launch. If sufficient quantities of each component are available, the shop order can be created. If the order is created, then the system allocates the necessary quantities to the particular shop order. (Shop orders are assigned by the computer, in numerical sequence.) The allocation means that this amount is mortgaged to the particular shop order and is, therefore, not available for any other shop order. Thus, the amounts shown in Figure 2.8 as projected available balances may not be the same as the physical inventory balance. The physical inventory balance could be larger, with the difference representing allocations to specific shop orders that have been released, but for which the component parts have not been removed from inventory.

Creation of the shop order requires more than availability checking and allocation. In addition, *picking tickets* are typically created and sent to the stockroom. The picking ticket calls for a specified amount of some part number to be removed from some inventory location, on some shop order, to be delivered to a particular department or location. When the picking ticket has been satisfied (inventory moved), the allocation is removed and the on-hand balance is reduced accordingly.

Availability checking, allocation, and physical stock picking are a type of double-entry bookkeeping. The result is that the quantity physically on hand should match what the records indicate is available plus what is allocated. If not, corrective action must be taken. The resulting accuracy facilitates inventory counting and other procedures for maintaining data integrity.

Exception codes

Exception codes in MRP systems are used "to separate the vital few from the trivial many." In most systems, if the manufacturing process is under control and the MRP system is functioning correctly, exception coding typically means that only 10 to 20 percent of the part numbers will require planner review at each processing cycle. Exception codes are in two general categories. The first is checking the input data accuracy. Included are checks for dates beyond the planning horizon, quantities larger or smaller than check figures, nonvalid part numbers, or any other desired check for incongruity. The second category of exception codes directly supports the MRP planning activity. Included are the following kinds of exception (action) messages or diagnostics:

1. Part numbers for which a planned order is now in the most immediate time period (the action bucket). It is also possible to report any planned orders two to three periods out to check lead times, on-hand balances, and other factors while there is some time to respond, if necessary.

2. Open order diagnostics when the present timing and/or amount for a scheduled receipt is not satisfactory. Such a message might indi-

cate that an open order exists that is not necessary to cover any of the requirements in the planning horizon. This message might suggest order cancellation. Such a message might be caused by an engineering change that substituted some new part for the one in question. The most common type of open order diagnostic is to show scheduled receipts that are timed to arrive either too late or too early, and should, therefore, have their due dates revised to reflect proper priorities in the factory. An example of this is seen with each of the three scheduled receipts in Figure 2.8. The 457 top handle open order of 25 could be delayed one week. A one-week delay is also indicated for the 082 nail scheduled receipt. For part 1118, the top handle coupling, the scheduled receipt of 15 could be delayed from week 2 until week 5. Another open order exception code is to flag any past-due scheduled receipt (scheduled to have been received in previous periods, but for which no receipt transaction has been processed). MRP systems assume that a past-due scheduled receipt will be received in the immediate time bucket.

3. A third general type of exception message indicates problem areas for production management; in essence, situations where level-zero quantities cannot be satisfied unless the present planning factors used in MRP are changed. One such exception code indicates that a requirement has been offset into the past period and subsequently added to any requirement in the first or most immediate time bucket. This condition means that an order should have been placed in the past. Since it was not, the lead times through the various production item levels need to be compressed to meet the end item schedule. A similar diagnostic indicates that the allocations exceed the on-hand inventory—a condition directly analogous to overdrawing a checking account. Unless more inventory is received soon, the firm will not be able to honor all pick tickets that have been issued, and there may be a material shortage in the factory.

Bottom-up replanning

Bottom-up replanning is the process of using the pegging data to solve material shortage problems. It is best seen through an example. Let us return again to Figure 2.8, concentrating on the top handle assembly and the nails (parts 13122 and 082). Let us suppose that the scheduled receipt of 50 nails arrives on Wednesday of week 1. On Thursday, quality control checks them and finds the vendor sent the wrong size. This means only 4 of the 10 gross requirement in week 2 can be satisfied. By pegging this gross requirement up to its parent planned order (5 units of 13122 in period 2), it can be seen that only 7 of the gross requirement for 10 units in week 4 can be satisfied (the 5 on hand plus 2 made from 4 nails). This, in turn, means that only seven snow shovels can be assembled in week 4.

The pegging analysis shows that 3 of the 10 top handle assemblies cannot be available without taking some special actions. If none are taken, the planned assembly dates for the snow shovels should reflect only seven units in week 4, with the additional three scheduled for week 5. This should be done if some means is not found to overcome the shortfall in nails. The change is necessary because the 10 snow shovels now scheduled for assembly in week 4 also explode to other parts—parts that will not be needed if only 7 snow shovels are to be assembled.

There may, however, be a critical customer requirement for 10 snow shovels to be assembled during week 4. Solving the problem with bottom-up replanning might involve one of the following alternatives (staying *within* the MRP system, as planners must do):

1. Issue an immediate order to the vendor for six nails (the minimum requirement), securing a promised lead time of two days instead of the usual one week. This will create a scheduled receipt for six in week 2.

2. Order more nails for the beginning of week 3, and negotiate a reduction in lead time of one week for the fabrication of this one batch of part 13122, from two weeks to one week. The planned order release for five would be placed in week 3 and be converted to a firm planned order, so it would not change when the record is processed again. The negotiation for a one-week lead time might involve letting the people concerned start work earlier than week 3 on the two part 13122s, for which material already exists, and a reduction in the one-week paperwork time that was included in the lead times.

3. Negotiate a one-week lead time reduction for the assembly of the snow shovels, place a firm planned order for 10 in week 5, which will result in a gross requirement for 10 top handle assemblies in period 5 instead of period 4.

Thus, we see the solution to a material shortage problem might be made by compressing lead times throughout the product structure using the system and bottom-up replanning. The planners work within the system using firm planned orders and net requirements to develop workable (but not standard) production schedules. The creativity they use in solving problems will be reflected in the part records at the next MRP processing cycle. All the implications of planner actions will be correctly coordinated throughout the product structure.

It is important to note that the resolution of problems cannot *always* involve reduced lead time and/or partial lots. Further, none of these actions come for free. In some cases, customer needs will have to be delayed or partial shipments made. Pegging and bottom-up replanning will provide advance warning of these problems so that customers can take appropriate actions.

An MRP system output

Figure 2.10 is an MRP time-phased record for one part number out of a total of 13,000 in one manufacturing company. The header information includes the date the report was run, part number and description, planner code number, buyer code number (for purchased parts), the unit of measure for this part number (pieces, pounds, etc.), rejected parts that have yet to receive disposition by quality control, safety stocks, shrinkage allowance for anticipated scrap loss, lead time, family data (what other parts are very similar to this one), the year-to-date scrap, usage last year, year-to-date usage, and order policy/lot size data. The policy code of 3 for this part means that the order policy is a *period order quantity* (POQ). In this case, the "periods to comb." = 4 means that each order should combine four periods of net requirements.

The first time bucket is "past due." After that, weekly time buckets are presented for the first 28 weeks of data; thereafter, 24 weeks of data are lumped into 4-week buckets. In the computer itself, all data are kept in exact days, with the printouts prepared in summary format for one- and four-week buckets. The company maintains a manufacturing calendar; in this example, the first week is 563 (also shown as 1/22), and the last week is 612.

In this report, safety stock is subtracted from the on-hand balance (except in the past-due bucket). Thus, the exception message indicating that a planned order for 491 should have been issued three periods ago creates no major problem, since the planner noted that this amount is less than the safety stock. This report also shows the use of safety lead time. *Planned* receipts are given a specific row in the report and are scheduled one week ahead of the actual need date. For example, the 337-unit planned order of week 565 is a planned receipt in week 573, although it is not needed until week 574.

The final data on the report is the pegging data section that ties specific requirements to the part numbers from which those requirements came. For example, in week 565 (shop order no. 790305), the requirement for 483 derives from part number F17144. MRP records are printed at this company only for those part numbers for which exception messages exist.

THE MRP DATA BASE

To install and derive maximum benefit from a material planning and control system, a large integrated data base is usually required. The computer hardware and software design aspects of common data bases are beyond the

FIGURE 2.10 Example MRP record

MATERIAL STATUS-PRODUCTION SCHEDULE

DATE- 01/21

******PART NUMBER******
NONJEK OPTY SSV LAM PP UPHL

USTRO40

DESCRIPTION	PLNR CODE	BYR COE	U/M
3/16x7/8 MR P & C STL STRAP	01	9	LFT

****USAGE****

YTD SCRAP	LAST YR	YTD

****** ORDER POLICY AND LOT SIZE DATA ******

POLICY CODE	STANDARD QUANTITY	PERIODS TO COMB.	MINIMUM QTY	REJECT QUANTITY	MAXIMUM QTY	SAFETY STOCK	SHRINKG ALLOWNE	MULTIPLE QTY	LEAD TIME	MIN ORD POINT	FAMILY DATA
3		04				497	1		08		

	PAST DUE	563 01/22	564 01/29	565 02/05	566 02/12	567 02/19	568 02/26	569 03/05	570 03/12	571 03/19	572 03/26	573 04/02
REQUIREMENTS	495											
SCHEDULED RECEIPTS				483				516				
PLANNED RECEIPTS												
AVAILABLE ON-HAND	1,500	508	508		25	25	491					
PLANNED ORDERS	491			337				334				

	574 04/09	575 04/16	576 04/23	577 04/30	578 05/07	579 05/14	580 05/21	581 05/28	582 06/04	583 06/11	584 06/18	585 06/25
REQUIREMENTS	337											
SCHEDULED RECEIPTS												
PLANNED RECEIPTS			334	334								
AVAILABLE						25						
PLANNED ORDERS			334					334				

	586 07/16	587 07/23	588 07/30	589-592 08/06	593-596 09/03	597-600 10/01	601-604 10/29	605-608 11/26	609-612 12/24
VACATION									
REQUIREMENTS									
SCHEDULED RECEIPTS									
PLANNED RECEIPTS									
AVAILABLE									
PLANNED ORDERS									

*******EXCEPTION MESSAGES*********

PLANNED ORDER OF 491 FOR M-WK 568 OFFSET INTO A PAST PERIOD BY 03 PERIODS

*******PEGGING DATA (ALLOC)********
790116   455 JN25220

*******PEGGING DATA (REQMT)********
790205   483 F 17144   790305   516 F 19938
790507   334 F 19938   790409   337 F 17144

scope of this book. Their importance in MPC systems compels us to briefly identify the primary files and communication links that are required. In this section, we treat the data files that would usually be required to support the engine of the MPC system in Figure 2.1. We make no claim that the following approach is optimal, or that one might not group the data in different ways. Rather, our objective is to illustrate one way the data might be supplied and to identify the elements needed. The enormity of the overall data base even for small firms is awesome, but the data needs exist *even if there is no formal system,* as long as people are manufacturing products.

The item master file

The data on an individual part are often contained in two files. The information that remains the same (or nearly so) from period to period is found in the *item master file,* while the information on part status is found in the subordinate file. The item master file typically contains all the data needed to completely describe each part number. These data are used for MRP, purchasing, cost accounting, and other company functions. The objective is to hold, in one file, all of the static data that describe the attributes of individual part numbers. Included are part number, name, low-level code, unit of measure, engineering change number, drawing reference, release date, planner code, order policy code, lead time, safety stock, standard costs, and linkages to other data files, such as routing, where used, bill of material, etc.

The subordinate item master file. A subordinate item master file is often used for changing or dynamic data about individual part numbers. Included are current allocations and the shop order number to which each allocation is tied, time-phased scheduled receipts and associated order numbers, time-phased gross requirements, planned orders, firm planned orders, pegging data, and linkages to the item master file.

The bill of material file. The bill of material file is typically established on a *single level* basis, with each part number linked only to the part numbers of the immediate components required to produce it; that is, the linkages are to one level farther down in the product structure only. By successively linking the part numbers, a full bill of material for each part can be developed from the individual single-level linkings. The data elements held in this file usually include the component part numbers required to make each individual part, number of each required, units of measure, engineering change numbers, effectivity dates, active/inactive coding, and where-used information.

The location file. The location file keeps track of the set of exact physical storage locations for each part number. This can be a highly dynamic file, since the data elements usually include departments, rows, bays, tiers, quantities, units of measure, in dates, original quantities, date of last activity, and so on.

The calendar file.   The calendar file is used to convert the shop day calendar used by the firm to a day/date/year calendar. The file also provides for phenomena such as annual vacations and holidays.

Open order files.   An entire set of files is maintained to support the scheduled receipts (open orders) in the MRP system. These involve both purchase orders and shop orders. For the purchase orders, one needs open purchase orders, open quotations, a vendor master file, vendor performance data, alternate sources, and price/quantity information. Another set of records needs to be maintained to support shop orders in the factory. Included are data files describing open orders, routings, work centers, employees, shifts, tooling, and labor/performance reporting.

Other file linkages.   This brief review of data elements shows the enormity of data acquisition, storage, and the subsequent file maintenance required for an effective MRP system. In addition to the data files needed for the engine, many other data files are necessary to flesh out the entire MPC system. Among them are files for forecasting, capacity planning, production scheduling, cost accounting, budgeting, order entry, shop-floor control, distribution, invoicing, payroll, job standards, and engineering.

MANUAL MRP SYSTEMS

After reviewing the list of required data elements, one might reasonably conclude that MRP is only for the large company with sophisticated computer systems. This is often the case, but a few companies have been able to achieve many of the MRP benefits by using MRP approaches in manual systems. Moreover, computers are becoming less and less expensive and MRP software now exists for microcomputers. Here we will review two manual examples. In both cases, after the manual systems were adopted, it became cost effective to computerize the system. The cost of the computer aspects of MRP continues to decrease. In fact, the significant cost is that of converting company operations over to an MRP-based approach, not the cost of the computer. In both of the following companies, manual MRP was a useful intermediate step in the conversion process.

Dataram

The Dataram company is a manufacturer of high-speed computer core memory units and components used to increase the memory size of a computer's central processing unit. The firm's sales grew from $2.7 million to $10.7 million over a four-year period. At that time, Dataram's products were divided into four major categories: cores, stacks, modules, and systems. Cores are small, doughnut-shaped magnetic storage components. Stacks consist of thousands of cores wired together in grids to form the basis for the storage and transfer of electrical impulses. Modules are assemblies of stacks integrated with timing and control circuits, as well as address and data registers. Systems consist of various numbers of memory modules combined in a chassis with optional internal power-supply units.

The manual production planning and inventory control system at Dataram was based on extensive use of ABC analysis. The company had a total of 1,860 purchased items, and any item representing an expected weekly cost-volume of more than $40 was classified as an A item. The 1,600 B and C purchased components were controlled with a bin reserve system. No formal inventory records were kept, but purchase orders were placed when the inventory reached the reserve quantity. The total investment in B and C items was approximately $250,000. The 260 A items were planned and controlled with a manual MRP system. In this system, an end item production schedule was prepared once per quarter, using six-month buckets. This schedule was used for MRP explosion, with net requirements for modules passed down as gross requirements for both stacks and separately purchased A parts, and as net requirements for stacks passed down as gross requirements to A purchased parts.

Neither chassis systems nor cores were formally considered in the MRP system. Chassis systems are made to order and use available modules, stacks, and purchased parts. Sufficient cores are manufactured to provide a five-to-seven-week buffer inventory.

When the sales were in the range of $5 million per year, the manual system at Dataram represented a reasonable trade-off between the costs of a production control system and its benefits. However, as the firm's rapid growth continued, several significant problems arose:

1. The six-month time bucket meant that all requirements were due in at the beginning of the six-month period—unless scheduled on a separate basis.
2. There were only two people who really understood how the system worked, and they were increasingly becoming involved in other manufacturing problem areas.
3. The analysis of when an item should move from A status to B or C (and vice-versa) was very cumbersome.
4. The impact of any changes in end item build schedules was difficult to assess in terms of projected component availabilities.

As a result, Dataram installed an IBM System 34 computer and implemented the IBM MAPICS software for MRP. The implementation process was facilitated by the experience the company had built up with the manual system. It took about one year to install the new MRP system. The key problems in the change related to transaction processing for all systems and the procedural reform necessary to use the formal system.

Ethan Allen Furniture Company

The Ethan Allen manual method for detailed component scheduling is based upon MRP logic, which utilizes product structures to create demand dependency, lead time offsetting, and gross to netting. The Ethan Allen approach is to establish the assembly date and then prepare a back schedule, or Gantt chart of the form shown in Figure 2.7. The parts are scheduled according to their individual lead times to be ready for final assembly. For MRP planning purposes, Ethan Allen incorporates a one-week safety lead time to allow parts to be exactly counted and prepared for final assembly. When the firm changed to a back schedule based approach from a cutting approach, an immediate reduction of 15 to 20 percent in the work-in-process inventory and lead times was achieved in the plants that were converted. (Old ways die hard, however, and though the benefits of back scheduling were clearly demonstrated, one otherwise well-run factory took eight years to convert to the new system.)

The manual MRP-like system is satisfactory for Ethan Allen furniture factories for two basic reasons. First, although a bill of materials for most items would show indentations of several levels, in fact, subassemblies tend to be phantoms; that is, they are not stored. For example, drawers are not stored. They are produced when the end item is produced, being assembled at the same time from basis components. Thus, there is little need for gross to netting on a level-by-level explosion basis. End item needs are multiplied by the number of components per end item, and gross to netting is performed only against component inventories. The second reason that this approach works well for the company is there is very little commonality among parts and no spare parts requirements. Therefore, component parts generally do not receive gross requirements from more than one source.

Manual MRP systems are still in use at many Ethan Allen factories. However, as was true for Dataram, growth makes the management of these manual systems cumbersome. Ethan Allen now has several computerized MRP systems installed and expects to continue the installation of these systems in other factories as their own knowledge increases, as growth dictates, and as the ever-decreasing costs of computers makes these conversions more attractive.

CONCLUDING PRINCIPLES

Chapter 2 provides an understanding of the MRP approach to planning. It includes a description of the basic techniques and some of the technical issues, as well as how MRP systems are used in practice. MRP, with its time-phased approach to planning, is a basic building-block concept for materials planning and control systems. Later, we will see other applications of the time-phased record. The basic ideas of MRP apply in those situations, too. We see the most important concepts or principles of this chapter as follows:

- Effective use of an MRP system allows development of a forward-looking (planning) approach to managing material flows.
- The MRP system provides a coordinated set of linked product relationships, thereby permitting decentralized decision making on individual part numbers.
- All decisions made to solve problems must be done within the system, and the transactions must be processed to reflect the resultant changes.
- Effective use of exception messages allows focusing attention on the "vital few," not on the "trivial many."
- The system records must reflect the physical reality of the factory if they are to be useful.
- The logical concepts upon which MRP is based apply whether the system is manual or computer based.

REFERENCES

Cox, James F., and Richard R. Jesse, Jr. "An Application of MRP to Higher Education." *Decision Sciences* 12, no. 2 (April 1981), pp. 240–60.

Davis, E. W. *Case Studies in Material Requirements Planning.* Falls Church, Va.: American Production and Inventory Control Society, 1978.

Hyer, N. L. "The Potential of Group Technology for U.S. Manufacturing." *Journal of Operations Management* 4, no. 3, 1984.

Material Requirements Planning Reprints. Falls Church, Va.: American Production and Inventory Control Society, 1986.

Miller, J. G. "Fit Production Systems to the Task." *Harvard Business Review*, January/February 1981.

Miller, J. G., and L. G. Sprague. "Behind the Growth in Materials Requirements Planning." *Harvard Business Review*, September/October 1975.

Myers, K. A.; R. J. Schonberger; and A. Amsari. "Requirements Planning for Control of Information Resources." *Decision Sciences* 14, no. 1 (January 1983), pp. 19–33.

New, C. *Requirements Planning.* New York: Halsted Press, 1973.

Orlicky, J. *Material Requirements Planning.* New York: McGraw-Hill, 1975.

Plossl, George W., and Oliver W. Wight, *MRP Planning by Computer.* Falls Church, Va.: American Production and Inventory Control Society, 1971.

Steinberg, E.; W. B. Lee; and B. M. Khumawala. "MRP Applications in the Space Program." *Journal of Operations Management* 1, no. 2 (1981).

Steinberg, E.; B. M. Khumawala; and R. Scarnell. "Requirements Planning Systems in the Health Care Environment." *Journal of Operations Management* 2, no. 4. (August, 1982).

Wight, Oliver. *Manufacturing Resource Planning: MRPII.* Essex Junction, Vt.: Oliver Wight Limited Publications, 1984.

DISCUSSION QUESTIONS

1. Why is the MRP activity in the "engine" part of the MPC system shown in Figure 2.1?

2. What additional information would be helpful to you in using or following the basic MRP record?

3. Compare a bill of material (BOM) and a cookbook recipe.

4. How does the *system* coordinate the individual item records and provide back schedule information?

5. Provide examples of potential differences between the information system and the physical reality for university activities. What are the consequences of some of these mismatches?

6. What are some of the reasons for wanting to process the records in an MRP system frequently? Provide examples and consequences of delaying the processing of the information.

7. The chapter uses a Christmas list and Christmas gift order analogy for planned order releases and scheduled receipts. What are other analogies of these two concepts? Why is it important to keep them separate in the MRP records?

8. What are the implications of *not* allocating material to a shop order after availability checking?

PROBLEMS

1. The Great GNU Furniture Company is introducing a new product—the dead-end table. You have been asked to construct the product structure diagram for the new table so the company's MRP system can be used in production planning for the new product. The product is described below:

   a. Each table consists of one top assembly and one big leg assembly, connected together with super GNU glue.

   b. A top assembly is constructed by hinging each of two leaves, rectangular sheets of wood, to a center rectangle.

Leaf   Center   Leaf

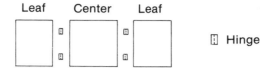

 Hinge

c. Two hinges are used to connect each leaf to the center. (The use of hinges allows the leaves to be raised for a big table or lowered for a small table.)

d. The big leg assembly is made of 2 swing leg subassemblies and one post. Each swing leg subassembly is connected to the post by 1 hinge.

Big leg assembly

Post

e. Each swing leg subassembly consists of 2 L-legs hinged together at the top by one hinge. (The hinges allow the legs to move in for a small table or out to support the leaves for a big table.)

Swing leg subassembly

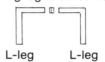

L-leg   L-leg

2. MacRonald's Restaurant sells three kinds of hamburgers—regular, super, and super-duper. The bills of material are:

Regular Burger		*Super Burger*		*Super-Duper Burger*	
⅛ lb. patty	1.0	¼ lb. patty	1.0	⅛ lb. patty	2.0
regular bun	1.0	sesame bun	1.0	sesame bun	1.0
pickle slice	1.0	pickle slices	2.0	pickle slices	4.0
catsup	0.1 oz.	catsup	0.2 oz.	lettuce	0.3 oz.
		onion	0.2 oz.	catsup	0.2 oz.
				cheese	0.5 oz.
				onion	0.2 oz.

a. If the product mix is 20 percent regular, 45 percent supers, and 35 percent super-dupers, and Mac sells 200 burgers a day, how much hamburger meat is used per day?

b. How many pickle slices are needed per day?

c. Suppose that buns are delivered every second day, Mac is ready to order, his on-hand balance of regular buns is 25, and his on-hand balance of sesame buns is 20. How many buns should be ordered?

   d. Reconsider question **c** if Mac has 10 regular hamburgers, 5 supers, and 15 super-dupers all made.

3. How to assemble your P301 computer is shown in the illustration below:

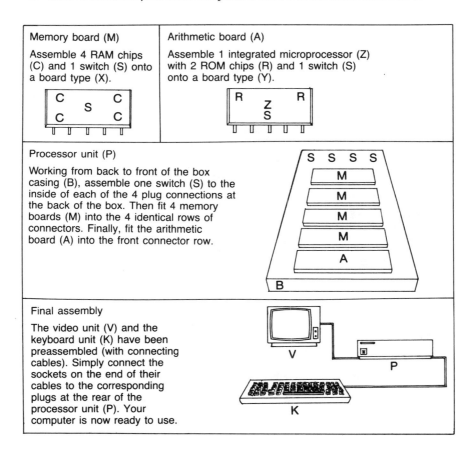

   a. Draw the product structure tree corresponding to the above instructions.

   b. Determine low-level codes for the following items: (1) A—Arithmetic board, (2) B—Box casing, (3) C—RAM chip, (4) K—Keyboard unit, (5) M—Memory board, (6) P—Processor unit, (7) R—ROM chip, (8) S—Switch, (9) V—Video unit, (10) X—Board type X, (11) Y—Board type Y, and (12) Z—Integrated microprocessor.

   c. Assume no inventory of any item. How many of each part should be available to assemble one completed unit?

4. Given the following information related to the Roxy Renolds chair, draw and label the product structure diagram and determine low-level codes for all items.

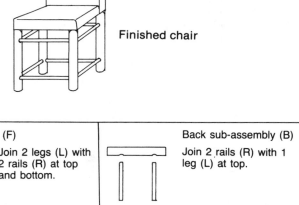

Finished chair

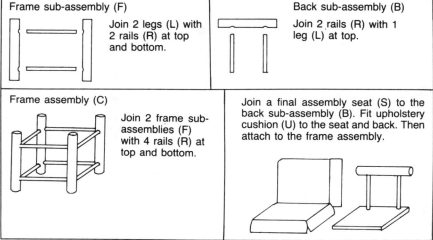

Frame sub-assembly (F)
Join 2 legs (L) with 2 rails (R) at top and bottom.

Back sub-assembly (B)
Join 2 rails (R) with 1 leg (L) at top.

Frame assembly (C)
Join 2 frame sub-assemblies (F) with 4 rails (R) at top and bottom.

Join a final assembly seat (S) to the back sub-assembly (B). Fit upholstery cushion (U) to the seat and back. Then attach to the frame assembly.

5. Weldon Welding, Inc., produces pythagorean triangles as souvenirs for tourists. Its largest product has sides 3, 4, and 5 meters in length. The material for the sides comes from 10-meter lengths of stainless steel bar. The firm uses 5 lengths to cut out 4 sets of parts at a time, with 2 meters of scrap left over. Weldon rolls the bar from 1,000-kilogram ingots, the yield from one ingot being 12 10-meter bars plus 8 meters of scrap.

Weldon has received an order for 100 of its largest triangles. Complete the requirements table:

Item	Lot size	On hand	Gross reqs.	Net reqs.	Order	Ending Inventory
Triangles	1	0	100	——	——	——
Sets of parts	4	12	——	——	——	——
10m bars	12	15	——	——	——	——
Ingots	10	1	——	——	——	——

6. The recipe for 6 drinks of Little Nellie's Triple Polar Bear Comforter calls for 2 dashes of Angostura, 1½ quarts of Southern Comfort, 1 quart of Polish vodka, ½ quart of Cointreau, and 1 bag of ice (for the head?).

   a. Nellie is planning a party for 12 people and wants to make Polar Bear Comforters for openers. How much Polish vodka does she need for 12 drinks if her vodka supply is totally gone?

   b. How many quarts of Southern Comfort must be bought if Nellie already has half a quart of Comfort on hand?

   c. Nellie is planning her party for November 15 and it is currently November 11. The liquor store will deliver quart bottles if they are given one-day notice. Fill in the following MRP record for Cointreau if Nellie has ½-quart on hand and wants the rest delivered. Assume she can mix the drinks on the day of the party.

November		11	12	13	14	15
Gross requirements						
Scheduled receipts						
Projected available balance						
Planned order releases						

7. The Big B Bike and Trike Shop produces two basic bikes, called A and B. Each week, Paul, the owner, plans to assemble 10 A bikes and 5 B bikes. Given this information and the product structure diagrams for A and B presented below, fill out the MRP records (inventory status files) for component parts G and Y for the next seven weeks.

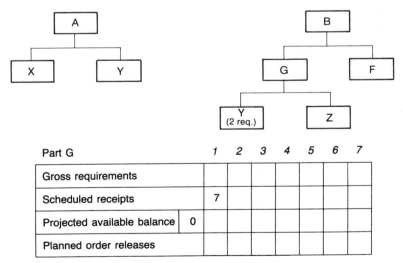

Part G		1	2	3	4	5	6	7
Gross requirements								
Scheduled receipts			7					
Projected available balance	0							
Planned order releases								

Q = lot for lot; LT = 1; SS = 0.

Part Y

		1	2	3	4	5	6	7
Gross requirements								
Scheduled receipts		10						
Projected available balance	28							
Planned order releases								

Q = lot-for-lot; LT = 2; SS = 0.

Suppose 10 units of safety stock are required for part Y. What changes would result in the records? Would the MRP system produce any exception messages?

8. Given the following product structure diagram, complete the MRP records for parts A, B, and C.

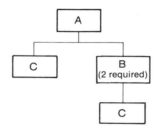

Part A

		1	2	3	4	5	6
Gross requirements		5	15	18	8	12	22
Scheduled receipts							
Projected available balance	21						
Planned order releases							

Q = 20; LT = 1; SS = 0.

Part B

		1	2	3	4	5	6
Gross requirements							
Scheduled receipts		32					
Projected available balance	20						
Planned order releases							

Q = 40; LT = 2; SS = 0.

Part C

	1	2	3	4	5	6
Gross requirements						
Scheduled receipts						
Projected available balance	50						
Planned order releases						

Q = lot-for-lot; LT = 1; SS = 10.

9. Given the following product structure diagrams, complete the MRP records for parts D, E, and F.

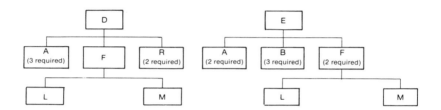

Part D

	1	2	3	4	5	6
Gross requirements	7	11	9	5	8	6
Scheduled receipts						
Projected available balance	10						
Planned order releases						

Q = 30; LT = 1; SS = 0.

Part E

	1	2	3	4	5	6
Gross requirements	10	12	15	11	6	8
Scheduled receipts		11				
Projected available balance	15						
Planned order releases						

Q = lot-for-lot; LT = 2; SS = 3.

Part F

		1	2	3	4	5	6
Gross requirements							
Scheduled receipts		60					
Projected available balance	20						
Planned order releases							

Q = 60; LT = 1; SS = 0.

10. Lucy Davis wants to make 20 picture frames per week with the following product structure (indented bill of materials):

> X Picture frame
>   Y Subassembly (2 required)
>   Z Fastener
>   Z Fastener

Other Data:

	On hand	L.T.	SS	Q
X	41	1	0	25
Y	52	2	0	50
Z	60	1	10	lot-for-lot

Construct the MRP records for week 1–5

11. Foremost Furniture has the following BOM for one of its products:

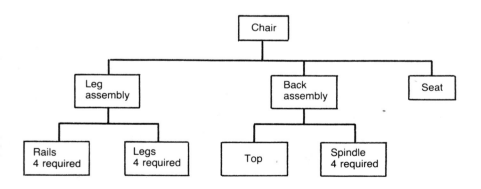

Additional data follow:

	Inventory	Lead time (weeks)
Chairs	100	1
Leg assembly	50	2
Back assembly	25	1
Seats	40	3
Rails	100	1
Legs	150	1
Tops	30	2
Spindles	80	2

The company wants to produce 400 chairs in week 5 and 300 in week 6. Develop a material plan for the parts.

12. Develop an MRP spreadsheet record for six periods using the following parameters for the items:

Requirements	20 units/period
Lead time	1 period
Lot size	40 units
Safety stock	0 units
Inventory	2 units
Scheduled receipt	40 units in period 1

a. In what periods are there planned order releases?
b. What happens to the timing and number of planned order releases if 10 units of safety stock are required?

13. The Ankar High School Supply Company has just perfected the Ardvart (**Part A**) in time for the annual science fair. An Ardvart is composed of 2 backslashes (**Part B**) and a comma (**Part C**). As the demand was running high, Ankar used an MRP system to help manage the material flows. At one point in its attempt to corner the Ardvart market, the company had the status indicated in the records below:

Part A		1	2	3	4	5	6
Gross requirements			25		75	90		50
Scheduled receipts			20					
Projected available balance	15	10	10	5	5	5	5
Planned order releases			70	90		50	

Q = lot-for-lot; LT = 1; SS = 5.

Part B

		1	2	3	4	5	6
Gross requirements			140	180		100	
Scheduled receipts		200					
Projected available balance	10	210	70	90	90	190	190
Planned order releases			200		200		

Q = 200; LT = 1; SS = 0.

Part C

		1	2	3	4	5	6
Gross requirements			70	90		50	
Scheduled receipts							
Projected available balance	56	56	66	56	56	86	86
Planned order releases			80	80		80	

Q = 80; LT = 1; SS = 25.

Ankar heard that the scheduled receipt for 200 backslashes is going to be delayed until period 2. How does this affect the Ardvart schedule? Is there anything to be communicated to the planner for the commas?

14. Actually Ankar got it wrong. The 200 backslashes (in problem 13) are not going to be delayed. Instead there are 100 of them that are rejects. How does this affect the Ardvart schedule? Is there anything that should be said to the planner for the commas because of this new development?

15. The Ward Manufacturing Company has collected 20 periods of data for two of its products, the Snarf and the Barf. Using the two data sets as gross requirements data, construct MRP time-phased records. Using a spread sheet program, create four time-phased records, two for each data set. For one case, use a lot size of 150 units, and for the other use an order quantity equal to the total net requirements for the next three periods. In all four records, start with a beginning inventory of 150 units, and compute the average inventory level held over the 20 periods. What do the results mean?

Snarf		Barf	
Period	Demand	Period	Demand
1	51	1	77
2	46	2	83
3	49	3	90
4	55	4	22
5	52	5	10
6	47	6	80
7	51	7	16
8	48	8	19
9	56	9	27
10	51	10	79
11	45	11	73
12	52	12	88
13	49	13	15
14	48	14	21
15	43	15	85
16	46	16	22
17	55	17	88
18	53	18	75
19	54	19	14
20	49	20	16

═3═════════════════════════════

Maintaining and using the MPC data base

This chapter is concerned with the maintenance of accurate information in the manufacturing planning and control (MPC) data base, given the dynamic changes that occur constantly in the physical flow of materials. The managerial objective is to provide the information necessary to manage the flows of material—to substitute information for inventory and to eliminate other forms of organizational slack. To do so will require high-quality information. This means that the data base elements must reflect the physical reality. Only by keeping the data *in* the system accurate can the outputs *of* the system be truly integrated into day-to-day decision making.

The chapter is organized around the following five topics:

- Integrity of the manufacturing planning and control data base: What are the principles for management *by* a data base and management *of* a data base?
- System dynamics: What is the MRP planner role, how does MRP reflect changing conditions, and why must transactions be processed properly?
- Procedural reform: What are the critical procedures that must be in place to support an effective MRP system?
- Routine auditing: How are transactions audited, errors detected, and corrections made on a routine, timely basis?

- Organizational considerations: How does a firm design, implement, and maintain an integrated data base for MPC systems, and what are the key organizational implications?

The material in Chapter 1 provides an important background for the concepts in this chapter. Chapter 2 covers the basic MRP record, some key technical issues, managerial use of MRP data, and some underlying data base considerations.

INTEGRITY OF THE MPC DATA BASE: MANAGEMENT *BY* AND *OF* A DATA BASE

The users of a truly effective MPC system, including both MRP planners and first-line supervisors, experience changed roles in their day-to-day decision making. It is paramount for them to take the management actions indicated by the formal system and to ensure that all actions necessary to provide the correct data are performed. That is, when the MPC system indicates that some action is required, it is the *sole* signal for taking action—management exclusively *by* the system and its data base with no informal dictates that override the system. If the system is to provide proper signals for action, procedures for entering transactions into the data base and responsibilities for doing so without fail must be developed—management *of* the data base. For this change in managerial perspective to take place, several key principles must be followed. Although we present them couched largely in the terminology and examples of MRP, they clearly apply to all the MPC system modules.

The data base must reflect reality. The objective here is to always have an exact match between what is physically true and the data base representation of the physical entity, viz the data entity. This means that if the inventory balance in a part record indicates that 27 pieces of the part are on hand, then a physical count of that part must yield 27. It also means that if the location file indicates that the 27 pieces are in location N-7, then that is where the 27 pieces must be found, and nowhere else. If a bill of material says three pieces are required for some assembly, there must be three pieces required. If a scheduled receipt indicates that 35 pieces are being worked on in the shop, one can similarly verify that count through physical audit. If someone scraps one or more of these pieces, the system (data base) needs to be informed so the real number of pieces is always reflected. Similarly, the location of the scheduled receipt, work completed, work remaining, due date, etc., all have to be reflected accurately in the system.

A strong principle that comes from experience is that any action, no matter how worthy it may seem, that comes at the expense of data integrity, must be avoided. The costs of ignoring this principle are very high indeed, including complete collapse of the system. It is more important to strive for the goal of an exact match between the data entity and physical reality than to try to determine what is "good enough." Bankers spend dollars to count pennies in order to realize this concept.

Data base transactions must be processed rapidly.   For the system to constantly mirror reality, it is necessary for changes to be processed rapidly as well as accurately. If a scheduled receipt is received and put into stock, the open shop order must be closed out and the on-hand balance increased quickly. Similar speed is required for the processing of customer orders, shipments, orders placed with vendors, receipts from vendors, and any adjustments necessary because of scrap or inventory losses. State-of-the-art systems now process transactions on-line as they occur. Most batch processing systems reflect transactions within 24 hours. The longer the time lag between actual physical change and concomitant change in the data base, the less the data base reflects reality—thereby creating a need for informal systems to find out the truth. For example, in a large service center for distribution of structural steel, this principle has been violated. Inventory transactions are batched and processed by the computer on a time availability basis. As a consequence, the inventory clerks maintain a separate card file to know what is really going on. Their need to know on a daily basis leads them to maintain an informal system — which in turn makes the formal system less useful!

Data base maintenance must be tightly controlled.   There is a critical distinction between *access* to data, which can be available to many users, and authority to *change* a given data element. This distinction must be carefully maintained. If the data base is truly to be managed, then specific individuals must have sole authority to make changes in specific data elements and, similarly, be held responsible for the accuracy of those data. This implies that data accuracy be made a specific part of many job descriptions, and that organizational changes be made to ensure proper data maintenance. A good case in point is the bill of materials file, which traditionally has been managed by the engineering department. The principles of data base accuracy and rapid response to change clearly apply to changes to bills of material. This means that bill of material changes cannot be constrained by antiquated procedures, and that nonengineering uses of the bill of materials must be accommodated. In some companies, these dictates have resulted in maintenance activity for the bill of materials data base being separated from the engineering department and assigned to a materials management group.

All of the data files that are required to support an MPC system have to be tightly controlled. This means organizational assignment of authority to make data base changes. Other areas where reorganization is often dictated by data base maintenance considerations include the functions involving customer order entry, delivery date promising, receipt of purchased parts, quality assurance reporting, and so on.

User actions must be integrated with data base transactions. To achieve data base integrity and to maintain this integrity at high levels, it is desirable to achieve a high degree of congruence between the job actually performed by users and the data which those users provide to the system. If the data collection is simply an added burden to one's job, the chances for mistakes are much greater than if the job performance itself relies upon accurate data. For example, if it can be demonstrated to a first line supervisor that his or her job is actually easier if he or she enters data correctly, higher quality data input should result. To the extent that the transaction reporting on individual orders (scheduled receipts) is integrated with payroll, variance accounting, movements from work in process to finished goods, and the like, there are increased pressures for data accuracy.

The system must tell the truth to the users. This principle is related to the necessity for the data base to reflect reality—but there is an added dimension. It is necessary to so design the system, its parameters, and its data base that unnecessary cushions, personal hedges, and inconsistencies are sorted out. If the formal system is to be used to make day-to-day decisions, the output data must be believable. If it is, the system can substitute information for the physical hedges so often used for buffering in informal systems. A case in point relates to due dates assigned to shop orders launched into the factory. One company had three stamps to be used for its orders: RUSH, CRITICAL, and EMERGENCY! Clearly, here is a case where RUSH stands for *R*outine *U*sual *S*low *H*andling, since it is the lowest order priority. The point to all this is simply that, if everything is marked rush, then nothing is rush. It is essential to establish *relative* priorities for shop orders and purchase orders. This is best done by telling the truth about due dates, lead times, and other system parameters. If everyone has to second guess other people's hedges, the resultant mismatch between the system and reality will be great.

The informal system must die. In many companies, there is a formal system for production planning and inventory control (such as RUSH–CRITICAL–EMERGENCY), and an informal system that gets the products shipped *in spite of* the formal system. These informal systems are usually made up of "hot lists" indicating what is *really* needed to meet shipments, physical staging of the materials to make *sure* that they are available, black books for how to *really* make the products, telephone calls, visits over lunch, etc. As long as there is any vestige of an informal system, the incentive to use the formal system is reduced. The only way to kill off the informal system is to design the formal system so well that users always get better information from it than from the informal system. It is also necessary to continually educate the users so that they understand why the formal system produces better results and why all of their efforts are better devoted to solving problems *with* the system, than in inventing ways of going around it.

SYSTEM DYNAMICS

Murphy's law states that, if anything can go wrong, it will. The corollary to Murphy's law is that Murphy was an optimist! It is also thought that Murphy formulated his famous law by working in manufacturing. Things are constantly going wrong, and it is essential that the MRP system mirror the actual conditions in the shop; that is, both the physical system and the information system have to cope with scrap, incorrect counts, changes in customer needs, incorrect bills of material, engineering design changes, poor vendor performance, and a myriad of other mishaps.

In this section, we look at the need for quick and accurate transaction processing and review the replanning activities of the MRP planner in coping with change. We discuss sources of the problems that will occur as a result of data base changes and actions to be taken to ensure that the system is telling the truth, even if the truth hurts.

Transactions during a period

To illustrate transaction processing issues, we use a simple example for one part. Figure 3.1 shows an MRP record (for part 1234) that has been produced over the weekend preceding week 1. The planner for part 1234 would receive this MRP record on Monday of week 1.

The planner's first action would be to try to launch the planned order for 50 units in period 1; that is, the MPC system would first check availability of the raw materials for this part and then issue an order to the shop to make 50, if sufficient raw material is available. Launching would require allocating the necessary raw materials to the shop order, removing the 50 from the planned order release row for part 1234, and creating a scheduled receipt for 50 in week 3, when they are needed. Thereafter, a pick ticket would be sent to the raw material area and work could begin.

Let us assume that during week 1 the following changes occurred, and the transactions were processed:

- The actual disbursements from stock for item 1234 during week 1 were only 20 instead of the planned 30.
- The scheduled receipt for 50 due in week 1 was received on Tuesday, but 10 units were rejected, so only 40 were actually received into inventory.
- The inventory was counted on Thursday and 20 additional pieces were found.
- The requirement date for the 45 pieces in week 5 was changed to week 4.
- Marketing has requested an additional five pieces for samples in week 2.
- The requirement for week 6 has been set at 25.

FIGURE 3.1 MRP record for part 1234 as of week 1

		1	2	3	4	5
Gross requirements		30	20	20	0	45
Scheduled receipts		50				
Projected available balance	10	30	10	40	40	45
Planned order releases		50		50		

Lead time = 2
Lot size = 50

The resultant MRP record produced over the weekend preceding week 2 is presented as Figure 3.2.

Rescheduling

The MRP record shown in Figure 3.2 illustrates two important activities for MRP planners. These are indicating the sources of problems that will occur as a result of data base changes, and suggesting actions that need to be taken to ensure that the system is telling the truth. Note that the scheduled receipt presently due in week 3 is not needed until week 4. The net result of all the changes to the data base means that it is now scheduled with the wrong due date, and the due date should be changed to week 4. If this

FIGURE 3.2 MRP record for part 1234 as of week 2

		2	3	4	5	6
Gross requirements		25	20	45	0	25
Scheduled receipts			50			
Projected available balance	50	25	55	10	10	35
Planned order release				50		

Lead time = 2
Lot size = 50

change is not made, this job may be worked on ahead of some other job that is really needed earlier, thereby causing problems. The condition shown in Figure 3.2 would be highlighted by an MRP exception message, such as "reschedule the receipt currently due in week 3 to week 4."

For the MRP system to not lie to the users, it is imperative to provide accurate relative priority information to fabrication work centers. The first step in doing this is for the planner to so reschedule the open order that the revised priority can be transmitted to the shop floor. Only in this way will the shop know which job to work on next at each work center. The key to doing this job well is for MRP planners to quickly process due date changes as soon as the MRP records reflect the change transactions. Let us now turn to more complex examples of transaction processing, their impact on MRP records, and the resulting needs for rescheduling.

Complex transaction processing

So far, we have illustrated system dynamics by using a single MRP record. However, an action required on the part of an MRP planner may have been caused by a very complex set of data base transactions involving several levels in the bill of materials. As an example, consider the MRP records shown in Figure 3.3, which includes three levels in the product structure. Part C is used as a component in both parts A and B as well as being sold as a service part. Part C, in turn, is made from parts X and Y. The arrows in Figure 3.3 depict the pegging data.

The part C MRP record is correctly stated at the beginning of week 1. That is, there would be no exception messages produced at this time. In particular, the two scheduled receipts of 95 and 91, respectively, are scheduled correctly, since delaying either by one week would cause a shortage, and neither has to be expedited to cover any projected shortage.

While the two scheduled receipts for part C are currently scheduled correctly, transactions involving parts A and B can have an impact on the proper due dates for these open orders. For example, suppose an inventory count adjustment for part A resulted in a change in the 30 unit planned order release from week 1 to week 3. In this case, the 95 units of part C would not be needed until week 3, necessitating a reschedule. Similarly, any change in timing for the planned order release of 25 units of part A in week 4 would call for a reschedule of the due date for 91 units of part C. Finally, suppose that a transaction requiring 75 additional units of part B in week 5 were processed. This would result in an immediate release of an order for 100 units of part C. This might necessitate rescheduling for parts X and Y. The point here is that actions required on the part of an MRP planner can occur because of a complex set of data base transactions involving many different parts. They may not necessarily directly involve the particular part which is being given attention by the MRP planner.

FIGURE 3.3   MRP record relationships for several parts

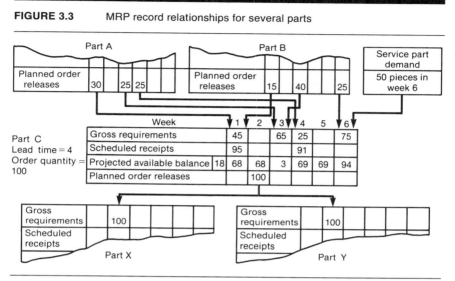

Note: This example is based on one originally developed by Joseph Orlicky, *Material Requirements Planning* (New York: McGraw-Hill, 1975), chap. 3, pp. 44–64.

Procedural inadequacies

MRP replanning and transaction processing activities are two essential aspects of ensuring that the MPC data base remains accurate. However, while these activities are necessary, they are not sufficient to maintain an accurate data base. Some of the procedures used to process transactions simply may be inadequate to the task.

To illustrate inadequate transaction procedures, let us return to the example in Figure 3.3. Note that, if 4 or more pieces are scrapped on the shop order for 95, there will be a shortage in week 3, necessitating rescheduling of the order for 91 one week earlier.

What is even more interesting is to see what would happen if 4 pieces were scrapped on the order for 95, and this scrap transaction were not processed. If the scrap is not reported, the MRP records would appear as shown in Figure 3.3, indicating no required rescheduling—when, in fact, that is not true. *If* the shortage were discovered by the person in charge of the stockroom when he or she puts away this order, then only one week would be lost before the next MRP report will show the problem. If, however, the stockroom person does not count, or the person who made the scrap puts the defective parts at the bottom of the box where they go undetected by quality control, then the problem will only be discovered when the assembly lines are trying to build As and Bs in week 3. Such a discovery comes under the category of unpleasant surprises. An interesting sidelight to this problem is that the cure will be to rush down to the shop to get at least 1 piece from the batch of 91. The very person who failed to report the earlier scrap may well now be screaming, "Why don't those idiots know what they need!"

Still another aspect of the scrap reporting issue can be seen by noting that the 95 and 91 were originally issued as lot sizes of 100. What this probably means is that five and nine pieces of scrap have occurred already, and the appropriate adjustments have been made in the scheduled receipt data. Note that, if these adjustments had *not* been made, the two scheduled receipts would show as 100 each. The resultant 14 (5 + 9) pieces (that do not, in fact, exist) would be reflected in the MRP arithmetic. Thus, the projected available balance at the end of period 5 would be 83 (69 + 14); this is more than enough to cover the gross requirement of 75 in period 6, so the planned order release for 100 in period 2 would not exist and the error would cascade throughout the product structure. Further, even if shop orders are carefully counted as they are put into storage, the five-piece shortage in period 1 is not enough to cause the MRP arithmetic to plan an order. It is only after period 4 (the beginning of period 5) that the additional nine pieces of scrap will be incorporated in the MRP record showing a projected shortage in period 6. This will result in an immediate order, to be completed in one week instead of four! What may be obvious is that, if accurate counting is not done, then the shortage is discovered in week 6, when the assembly line goes down. This means that procedures for issuing scrap tickets when scrap occurs and procedures for ensuring that good parts are accurately counted into inventory must be in place. If not, all of the MPC systems will suffer.

The long and the short of all this is that we are back to the principles calling for data integrity. We have to believe the numbers, and an error of as little as *one* piece can cause severe problems. We have to know the truth. We have to tightly control transactions. Moreover, we have to develop iron-clad procedures for processing MPC data base transactions.

PROCEDURAL REFORM

If one were to apply the ABC inventory control principle (where the A items are most important, B items less important, and C items least important) to MRP implementation, the C items are the computer and computer programs. The B items are the procedures that must be changed, and the A items are the people issues—education, organizational change, etc. With procedural reform, it is quite possible that every single piece of paper going through the factory will need to be changed. Moreover, new procedures and documents will be required to control things that were previously not controlled. Let us now overview some of the key procedures that support MRP.

Cycle counting

We have seen how an error of as little as one unit in an MRP record can lead to the need for managerial actions. If one thinks of an MRP record of 52 weeks in length, and four rows of information, then there are more than 200 numbers that are displayed. Of all these numbers, the one that can be most accurately validated is the on-hand balance. Furthermore, if it is wrong, the result is a tower of gelatin.

It is critical that the on-hand balances reflected in data records exactly match the physical on-hand balances. The only way to be sure of this match is to compare the two numbers by physical counting. This is the purpose of the annual physical inventory. But the annual inventory count is designed for financial purposes and primarily relates to an *overall* imbalance—which can include compensating errors. For MRP purposes, this is not good enough. A shortage of one part and an overage of another are two errors— *both* of which may require managerial actions.

An alternative to taking an annual physical inventory is to continuously monitor on-hand balances using cycle counting. One way to do this is to have personnel whose entire job is to cycle count, checking some item on-hand balances every day. Another way is to have stockroom personnel levels set to readily handle peak loads (ins and outs), with slack times used for cycle counting.

Many firms believe that cycle counting is an extra expense, but this is not necessarily true. If it is done right, cycle counting can and should eliminate the need for taking an annual physical inventory. The records held by the MRP data base and verified by cycle counting should be so good that a total physical inventory would induce more mistakes than it would uncover. The costs of stopping all production for several days can very easily justify having a staff of cycle counters.

Cycle counting represents a critical commitment to the achievement of effective MPC system implementation. We know of *no* first-class system that does not use some form of cycle counting. The concept is to have the numbers in the data base regarded in the same way that they are in a bank. It is no less important to know how many part 1234s are in location N-7 than to know how many $20 bills are in a particular drawer in the bank vault. In fact, it may be much more important, since two $10 bills can be substituted for one $20, whereas other items may not be readily substituted for Part 1234.

The commitment to a cycle counting program conveys a degree of seriousness on the part of management to the factory. Someone should be evaluated on the basis of cycle count accuracy. The stockrooms will have to be physically so arranged that inventory accuracy can be achieved. This implies locked areas, limited entry, containers of known weight, accurate measurement devices, specific item areas, shelving, a system that keeps track of items by individual location, and a set of ironclad procedures that capture every possible transaction as goods move in and out of storage. How is it possible to have accurate records if any of the following conditions can occur? (We have seen them all.)

- The engineers get parts for R&D without proper transactions.
- The president (or anyone else) is free to roam the stockroom—can a bank president roam the vault?
- Parts are stored in old cardboard boxes with holes in them.
- Many parts are piled on top of each other.
- Parts are stored in an open yard where they can be lost in the snow.
- The scale for weighing parts belongs in a museum.
- The containers are of uneven, unknown weights, or people are allowed to throw trash in them.

Once someone has their personal performance evaluated in terms of the cycle count accuracy, all of these causes will be isolated, and proper actions will be taken to correct them. The percentage of error encountered by cycle counting is a good barometer or leading indicator for any MPC system. If this error rate is increasing, one can expect more stockouts, frantic expediting, and missed shipments to closely follow. In many firms, the cycle count error rate is periodically reviewed by senior executives of the company.

Cycle counting systems.   The major message on cycle counting is—do it! However, having said that, let us now turn to the design of a cycle counting system and some successful cycle counting techniques.

One immediate issue in the design of cycle counting systems is how to select the items to be counted. The first need is to determine how many items can be counted in some time period (e.g., a day). With a given work force and some estimates of counts per time period per person, the frequency with which each part is counted can be ascertained. Some companies have found it useful to set the frequency of counting using ABC analysis. A items are counted more frequently than B items, etc. Another selection device is to use the planned order information in the MRP record to advantage. If items are counted just prior to when a new order should be released, any errors can be compensated for by changes in timing and/or amounts. If items are counted just prior to receipt of an order, the on-hand balance should be low. Extending this idea, some firms count when a new batch is put away, since at this time the inventory level should be at a minimum point. Moreover, if the new batch is physically combined with the old, a stockroom person would be handling the parts anyway.

Another selection criterion for cycle counting involves checking any part number that shows a negative on-hand balance, since theoretically this is not possible. Other selection rules include keeping track of the time since the last cycle count, counting items within groups (ABC) in order of last count; keeping track of the item activity (transactions), since those items that have had the most ins and outs may be subject to larger potential error, and applying the opposite logic if transactions are used to verify counts; or allowing users to select parts for counting directly (which can happen for many reasons, including a pending engineering change).

Some companies find it more advantageous to count by location than by part number; that is, the cycle counters are asked to determine the part number and quantity in a specified location. One advantage of this approach is that it is more efficient for cycle counting, since parts in a set of adjacent locations can be counted. It also has the advantage of "finding" parts that are "lost." This scheme is particularly compatible with the use of random storage locations (as opposed to specific locations for each part). In addition to better utilization of space, the random location approach has the advantage that *only* the system knows where a part number is located, so the system *must* be used.

The random location system can also provide for rotating stock, since the pick tickets can be devised to pull stock on a first-in, first-out basis. Alternatively, some companies always pull the smallest quantity first, which tends to consolidate inventories into larger batches. Obviously, this kind of system can also issue commands to consolidate if locations become scarce.

Another nice feature of storage by location is the ability to get "free" cycle counting by picking. A pick ticket can indicate that 24 pieces of part 1234 are to be taken from N-7, and that there should thereafter be 3 left. The stock picker is instructed to identify any discrepancies as the stock is picked. Another free cycle counting device is the use of preprinted zero balance cards. Whenever someone takes the last unit from any location, the item and location are written on the card.

In the design of a cycle counting system it is necessary to specify the tolerance for error that will be acceptable. If 10,000 pieces of a very inexpensive item are to be weigh counted, it seems a bit silly to say that an error has occurred if the scale indicates 9,999. A typical set of tolerances is:

Class	Hand counted	Weigh counted
A	+0% to −0%	+3% to −3%
B	+2% to −2%	+4% to −4%
C	+4% to −4%	+5% to −5%

We have seen some companies approach cycle counting by only verifying the location and eyeballing to see whether the count is way off. This is simply not a satisfactory procedure, and its use will lead to poor MPC system performance.

A final technique we have seen used to great advantage is the establish-ment of a control group of parts, based on a cross section of items, which is counted on a very frequent basis. Initially, this might be only 20 or 30 parts of high activity, which are counted every day. Its purpose is to be able to discover the *causes* of error, because the transactions since the last count are easy to audit. After the cycle counting program is in full operation, the control group might be expanded to about 100 parts, with detailed audit trails of the transactions maintained for each of the parts.

The control group concept leads to a very important point. As important as cycle counting is, in the last analysis its primary purpose is to uncover the causes of errors. The key to achieving cycle count accuracy is to so im-plement ironclad procedures for all transactions that errors are minimized. Let us now turn to two sets of critical procedures that affect the on-hand balance, the maintenance of shop order data integrity, and similar proce-dural issues in purchase order closeout. Thereafter, we deal with some or-ganizational issues in stockroom operations.

Shop order integrity

Internally fabricated parts are typically controlled by a shop order num-ber, which is the authorization for the job. These numbers are usually as-signed sequentially so all shop orders can be opened, monitored, and closed. The opening of a shop order from an MRP point of view is creating a sched-uled receipt, normally as the result of a planned order being launched. This process involves availability checking and allocation.

The shop order typically has a set of shop paper that travels with the material. Included are operation sheets, routings, blueprints, and some means, such as prepunched cards or bar coded data, for reporting work completed.

The open shop order usually produces a pick ticket(s) for the materials to be issued from some storeroom to the shop order. The status of the open order is monitored by the shop-floor control systems. From a data integrity point of view, we have seen that it is also necessary to have procedures for scrap reporting so scheduled receipts are shown with accurate counts in the MRP records. Also required are rework procedures to correct materials that can be salvaged.

The closing of a shop order occurs when the order is put into a stockroom. At that time, the data base needs to be updated. For example, the record now must reflect that the stockroom has put away 147 pieces of part 1234, on shop order 456, in location N-7. When accepted, the scheduled receipt is eliminated and the on-hand balance appropriately adjusted. For the trans-action to be accepted, system checks are performed to determine the agree-ment between the part number and the accompanying shop order, the quan-tity received versus the quantity reported at the last operation in the routing file, whether that last operation has been completed, and whether location N-7 is available.

A key step in this process is the actual counting of the material by stockroom personnel. They should no more accept the count indicated by the last operation than a bank teller would accept your word for the amount of cash in a paper sack you wish to deposit. The operative principle is that the receiver counts. This is the only way that the receiver can be held responsible for the accuracy of the data in his or her area.

Purchase order closeout

Similar procedures are necessary to close out scheduled receipts from vendors. Each "in" transaction is tested against an existing purchase order, the quantity of that order, the previous processing of receiving documentation, etc. We have seen many companies that simply accept the counts on invoices provided by their vendors. The payback from hiring someone to count all receipts (or at least to sample count and keep track of vendor performance) can be very short.

The receiving department is typically the place where a batch of purchased material is first recognized as being on the company premises. An arriving shipment has bills of lading, which are checked against expected deliveries (scheduled receipts for purchased items). This may be done with a file of outstanding purchase orders, preprinted papers, or an on-line computer system that checks the status of the order. In most companies, a detailed count of the parts is not made at this point. Rather, a check for the number of cartons, the stated volume per carton, the total shipment quantity, and for a match against the purchase order is done. The result is a *receiver* transaction, which tells the system that the material has arrived but has not been put into controlled storage on a basis that will allow it to be picked.

Incoming materials are usually routed through receiving inspection before going to the assigned storeroom. At some companies, computerized warehousing (high bay stackers) allows work to be immediately put away— but in a status that is unavailable for picking until inspection has released the batch and inventory control verified the count.

There are, of course, many variations of these procedures, but all accomplish the same basic objectives. For example, we know of one firm that tracks each of the trucks in its large fleet, as well as tracking each unowned truck that enters the area of the factory. This firm has an on-line system to print traveling documentation for each pallet or container as it is unloaded. Again, the objectives are the same: capture the arrival information as soon as possible, track the material flow through the necessary stages prior to storage, count carefully, resolve discrepancies, and perform this quickly. Even if signing bills of lading legally commits the company to some quantity, a speedy verification can usually result in adjustments with vendors.

The stockroom

The stockroom is the place where shop orders and purchase orders are finally closed, as well as where materials for shop orders are issued. As such, the stockroom becomes the nerve center for the entire organization. The most immediate impact of this central role played by the stockroom is in personnel requirements. This is not the place to put tired janitors! The need for absolute integrity in stockroom records and the close monitoring of transactions dictate that the person in charge be an aggressive professional (preferably mean).

Locking the stockroom in many firms is accomplished by building a wire cage around the stock. Thereafter, the night shift goes over with a ladder, so the top is wired. Then someone gets a cutting torch to cut off the lock. The next logical step is to build an impregnable stockroom. We know of one company that did that, followed by an interesting result: no shipments. In fact, the impregnable stockroom was the ultimate frustration to the workers who were getting out the products in spite of the MPC system. The problem? Mainly that the actual components used to build end items were different from those specified by the bills of material, so the assembly department did not have the parts necessary to build end items. Exacerbating this problem was an unrealistic master production schedule At the end of the month, the company would steal production from next month to make the shipment budget. The parts for these orders were still in the stockroom.

One further dimension of stockroom integrity is worthy of mention. It is not a free good—it will take money to hire a mean professional, and the compensation is fully justified in terms of the responsibility assigned. Moreover, it is also necessary to keep tight control over the stockroom at all hours. How can the mean professional be held responsible if the stockroom is open on the second shift—or even if it is locked but the night foremen are allowed to get things out if they need them? Does anyone on the night shift in a bank have access to the vault?

It is often necessary to extend the definition of stockrooms and to hire more personnel to monitor the larger stockroom areas. For example, many firms do not exercise tight control over raw materials, with machine operators getting more as needed. In the MRP world, a bar of one-inch diameter steel, 16 feet long, is just another part number, and the on-hand balance needs to be correct. All transactions to and from raw materials must be recorded accurately, and both cycle counting and limited access may be required. It may also be necessary to establish procedures for a raw materials salvage operation to cope with problems, such as those with parts that are flame cut from large sheets.

The point of all this is simply that tight stockroom control is a necessary but not a sufficient condition for effective MPC implementation. It is necessary to have all data integrity procedures in place and to execute the MPC plans, viz, hit the schedule!

ROUTINE AUDITING

Even the best laid procedural plans will go amuck. Errors will occur, and hopefully the cross checks built into the system will find them. However, when errors do occur, the need still exists to resolve the resulting problems. For example, if an in transaction indicates that 100 pieces of a particular shop order have been put away, and the last fabrication operation before going to stock reported 120 pieces, then there is a discrepancy. Who is right? Where did the other 20 parts go? Is there a need to issue a scrap ticket? Is there an adjustment required in labor reporting? In this section, we review procedures and techniques for routinely auditing data base transactions and for resolving accuracy questions.

Cross checking and "garbage collecting"

An aid to routine auditing of data base transactions is for the systems to provide the maximum amount of cross checking and garbage collecting possible. This includes procedures for using check digits and the like, and, more importantly, any kind of computerized validation checking possible. For example, supposing that employee 123 wants to report the completion of 100 pieces of part 456, on shop order 789, operation 3, included in the cross checking would be the following:

- Is employee 123 a legal employee number?
- Is he or she at work today (checked in)?
- Has this employee already checked in on shop order 789?
- Does this employee work in the department associated with operation 3 for part 456?
- Is this employee assigned to the labor grade consistent with this operation?
- Is part 456 a valid part number?
- Is there an open order (scheduled receipt) for part 456 on shop order 789?
- Is this shop order for 100 pieces?
- Has operation 2 been completed?
- Did operation 2 report 100 pieces?

Any of these cross checks could include tolerances for errors. The objective is to use the computer as much as possible to screen out transaction errors and to focus attention on required remedial actions, such as new counts, scrap not reported, and so on.

Daily reconciliation: an application of principles

The result of any cross check that fails is an exception condition. It will be necessary to have a group of people whose entire job is to audit and reconcile exception conditions. For example, is the in transaction correct or is the purchase order correct? How can we be out of stock in location N-7 when the records indicate that 100 pieces are there? An operator reported work on shop order 1234 which is not valid for the department—was it really shop order 1234? Operation 3 reports 50 pieces and operation 4 reports 48 pieces—is a scrap ticket for 2 pieces needed? Operation 3 reports 50 pieces and operation 4 reports 55 pieces—who is wrong? The assembly department reports none of part 678, yet we show that they have enough to last for three weeks—why?

In an on-line system, many of these discrepancies can be monitored as the transaction is being made. For systems based on batch processing, the minimum goal should be to process all transactions in a 24-hour period or during each night, reconciling all exceptions by about 10 A.M. the following day. It is simply not possible to reconcile errors when the trail gets cold. Going to a machine operator and saying, "Do you remember that job 1234 that you ran three weeks ago?" will usually yield, "No." Moreover, if someone can put in his or her telephone number instead of the part number and get away with it, the system is a joke. Someone will try this, and the objective is to catch the person quickly.

Figure 3.4 is part of an actual daily exception report. This report is the principal auditing tool used by the firm. The document shows 17 parts that generated exception conditions, so they were included on the H/R IN TICKET EXCEPTION REPORT FOR H45. H45 is one of the main stockrooms in this company. The first item, part F16774, shows in the last two columns that 8,375 were reported as finished at the last production operation but only 7,506 have been located or put into stock.

The 4th through 10th items show invalid part numbers. As indicated by the handwriting, the resolution of this problem is that all seven parts were incorrectly given an F prefix (fabricated part), when, in fact, they should have an A prefix (assembly). Note, also, that this exception report shows the location of these seven parts, so they can be checked, if necessary (Department H45, Bay H41, Row WA, Tier LL).

The just-in-time approach

We have now discussed the need for accuracy in the data base, the importance of transactions, the need for auditing, and a new level of discipline in the system. It is important to remember that the need is data base accuracy; transactions, auditing, and discipline are *one* means to that end.

Many firms are beginning to use another approach in their factories. It is called *just-in-time* manufacturing. The relationship to information integrity is most interesting. There is so little inventory in these systems that detailed monitoring of transactions is unnecessary. At the Toyota automobile factory, for example, deliveries of parts from vendors are going out of the door as

FIGURE 3.4 Daily exception report (H/R in ticket exception report for H45)

********PART NUMBER*********

C D E	TRANS. DATE	NUMBER	OPTN SSW LAM	PL/PNT	UPHL	ORDER NUMBER	FROM DEPT	QTY PROD	PROD. BY	U/M	QTY LO LOCTD DEPT BAY RW TR ******SPECIAL INFORMATION	LOCTD BY	TOTAL PROD	TOTAL LOCTD
	04/18	F 16774		PL		JN31318		008375		PCS	0 PARTS PRODUCED ARE NOT LOCATED		008375	007506
	04/19	F 16774		PL		JN35882		006923		PCS	0 PARTS PRODUCED ARE NOT LOCATED		006923	002893
	04/05	F 1677?				JN33270		004785		PCS	0 PARTS PRODUCED ARE NOT LOCATED		004785	004122
IT	04/27	F 17127				JN31782	H41	000322	6149	PCS	000322 H45 H41 WA LL INVALID PART NUMBER. NOT ON PART MASTER	941	0	0
IT	04/27	F 17127				JN31782	H41	000228	6845	PCS	000228 H45 H41 WA LL INVALID PART NUMBER. NOT ON PART MASTER	941	0	0
IT	04/27	F 17127				JN31782	H41	000225	6912	PCS	000225 H45 H41 WA LL INVALID PART NUMBER. NOT ON PART MASTER	941	0	0
IT	04/27	F 17127				JN31782	H41	000221	6912	PCS	000221 H45 H41 WA LL INVALID PART NUMBER. NOT ON PART MASTER	941	0	0
IT	04/27	F 17127				JN31782	H41	000282		PCS	000282 H45 H41 WA LL INVALID PART NUMBER. NOT ON PART MASTER	941	0	0
IT	04/27	F 17127				JN31782	H41	000284	6149	PCS	000284 H45 H41 WA LL INVALID PART NUMBER. NOT ON PART MASTER	941	0	0
IT	04/27	F 17132				JN31074	H41	000269	3254	PCS	000269 H45 H41 WA LL INVALID PART NUMBER. NOT ON PART MASTER	941	0	0
	04/27	F 17133				JN29631		008066		PCS	0 PARTS PRODUCED ARE NOT LOCATED		008066	006450
	04/11	F 18124				M981		000518		PCS	0 PARTS PRODUCED ARE NOT LOCATED		000518	000000
	03/12	F 18855		PL		JN32242		004581		PCS	0 PARTS PRODUCED ARE NOT LOCATED		004581	000000
	04/06	F 18855		PL		JN35424		050000		PCS	0 PARTS PRODUCED ARE NOT LOCATED		050000	004581
	03/23	F 18871				HR79272		008005		PCS	0 PARTS PRODUCED ARE NOT LOCATED		008065	007855
	04/18	F 19219		PL		JN35873		040000		PCS	0 PARTS PRODUCED ARE NOT LOCATED		004000	003600
	03/29	F 19237				JN30112		002430		PCS	0 PARTS PRODUCED ARE NOT LOCATED		002430	000000

[handwritten note pointing to the F 17127 / F 17132 part numbers:] wrong prefix— should be "A"

finished autos within hours. The parts *had* to arrive or the line would stop! Moreover, every worker is also a quality controller, so the parts had to be of the correct quality. In essence the data integrity check for material receipt is product completion.

ORGANIZATIONAL CONSIDERATIONS

Proper maintenance of the MPC data base requires three distinct sets of integrated efforts by the organization. First, there is a set of technical efforts that needs to be supported by the computer specialist—to ensure proper backup of data files, integration among files, consistent system uses of the files, and so on. The second set of efforts is on the part of the system users. In essence, the data base needs to become an integral part of their daily working lives. Finally, some efforts need to be mounted on a companywide basis. These efforts are to encourage a companywide commitment to an integrated data base, and whatever organizational changes are necessary to achieve this goal. This also includes a deliberate effort to base functional planning and decision making on the one integrated data base—for the entire company to sing from the same sheet of music.

The computer side

There is a technical dimension to the design, implementation, and control of an integrated data base, that is largely beyond our present scope. Included are choices of data base languages, computer conversions, architecture of the data base, backup files and backup processing, timing for transaction processing, communication among computer devices, security, and the overall levels of professionalism exhibited by the computer personnel in terms of understanding and ability to deal with integrated data bases. We strongly advise all companies implementing integrated data bases to periodically obtain an independent professional audit of this technical dimension. There is far too much at stake to be subject to unnecessary uncertainties.

At the operational level, it is critical that users and data processing personnel alike understand the nature of linked systems and the transactions in these systems. A revealing analysis in many companies is to ask several different functional areas for some piece of data that should not be subject to uncertainty, such as the shipments two months ago for some particular end item. Many times, the answer to this question is quite different from production to marketing to finance. For instance, at one firm, this question produced three different answers. The differences between production and finance were due to definitions of when the month closed in terms of shipments. Production considered an item shipped when it left the stockroom and entered a truck, whereas finance worked with bills of lading prepared when the trucks left the dock. Thus, reconciliation was possible between production and finance, based on the difference in cutoff dates. However, neither production nor finance could reconcile their version of shipments with that produced by marketing. Marketing used an entirely different system, based on different transactions, linkages, and so forth. It was not surprising that mistakes were made, since there were different views of what was in inventory and available to ship to customers.

The point of this tale is to show how a single definition of shipments (or any other data element) is required, and how all systems and transactions that use and update this data element need to be integrated and controlled. That is, one needs to achieve "procedural" integration. This is more fundamental than the "technical integration" associated with proper bills of material, inventory counts, and so on. An even more fundamental level of integration is "goal integration," which means that different functional areas are working to common overarching objectives.

The user side

In the last analysis, an MPC system will work only if the required actions, procedures, and transactions are consistent with the ways in which MRP planners and first-line supervisors do their jobs. Detailed execution by departmental foremen and MRP planners must be in synchronization with the system. There is an often told joke about the difference between involvement and commitment being well illustrated by ham and eggs—the pig is committed, whereas the chicken is only involved. It is critical for the users of the system to be *committed* to its continued success.

This commitment does not come by executive fiat. It is necessary to educate the users on how the actual system works, their part in the overall system, how errors made in transactions affect everyone, how their particular transactions and procedures are to be done, and how informal "fixes" are to be avoided like the plague. Moreover, it is necessary to review the measures of effectiveness employed to evaluate user performance. If users are rewarded for any actions which come at the expense of data integrity, there are serious problems. The job, as well as the job performance, needs to be synchronized with the system. Users are to be rewarded for using the system to solve problems, and for maintaining the accuracy in the data base at high levels.

It is often necessary to change the communication networks for successful MPC system implementation and maintenance. The elimination of buffer inventories increases the need for better coordination between manufacturing, inventory control, purchasing, and all of the other areas that are linked by material flows. It may be necessary to provide new communication chains for users to solve problems—above and beyond those provided by the MRP system itself. In particular, it is usually necessary to provide fast feedback between users and computer personnel to solve problems of data errors, discrepancies, and so on.

Another dimension of user commitment to the system and its maintenance is the need to understand the changes in social networks that are brought about by the implementation of MPC. The technical system is concerned with the processes, tasks, and technology needed to transform inputs to outputs. The social network in which this technical system operates is concerned with the attitudes of people, the relationships among people, reward systems, and authority structures. In the design and implementation of an MPC system, it is very easy to underestimate the changes required in the social network to adapt to the new technical system, and to underestimate the time and cost necessary for these changes to occur.

When users are indeed committed to the system and its continued maintenance, no immediate problem is important enough to warrant solution at the expense of data base integrity. There are too many other people depending upon the data base for the inputs into their own decision making.

Companywide linkages

A companywide commitment to data base maintenance largely entails an integration of functions and transactions around the one integrated data base. This means, of course, that such problems as how to transact shipments data will be solved. There will be exact divisions of labor and responsibility over specific transactions, and there will be uniform transaction definitions.

More important, other company systems can and should be designed to take advantage of the integrated data base. With this redesign, the company also achieves a new level of data maintenance, because a new group of people with new interests is providing one more audit to the data. Of perhaps even more importance, this interfunctional commitment to an integrated data base provides new avenues for cooperation in strategic planning, budgeting, and control. That is, goal integration is fostered.

A fundamental company linkage is with the cost accounting system. One critical portion of MPC systems is accurately reporting every detailed transaction as materials move in and out of stockrooms and through various production conversion steps. This set of transactions provides the basis for a very detailed cost accounting system. Detailed variance analysis can be done for every shop order, if desired. Labor reporting and material usage reporting can be done by shop order, with variances for usage, productivity, and other deviations from standards noted. Detailed cost implosions (sometimes called cost roll-ups) for each product can be made as needed, or as variations from cost standards dictate. In short, the MPC data base provides the grounds for a most exact cost accounting system.

The other benefit of using the MPC data base for costing derives from the cost accounting need to identify movement from raw materials into work in process into finished goods. The inventory reporting of these financial movements provides another cross check of data base reliability, and the detailed auditing of the transactions which make up these periodic sums is one more audit trail—now based on the same transaction records. Other examples of cost accounting benefits include the detailed resolution of inventory adjustments, the treatment of obsolete inventories, accounting for scrap, reconciliation of accounts payable to in tickets and purchasing, product costing incorporating engineering and tooling changes, and accounting for new product introductions, as well as product phase outs.

With the cost accounting system based on MRP data base transactions, the next logical step is to determine budgets and other financial goals on a consistent basis. In this way, plans are established on the same basis that results are measured. Thus, the establishment of financial budgets and strategic plans becomes integrated with the data base, its operations, its maintenance, and its accounting performance measurement. Still another key linkage for consistency is provided. Moreover, the ability to forecast cash requirements, receivables turnover, and other financial data is substantially increased, because most of these measures are related to material flow decisions.

There can be a negative side to integrating the cost accounting and budgeting procedures as well. If workers are paid based on another system, if cost accounting is only performed in a cursory way, if budgeting is an annual exercise in futility, if forecasting is a game between marketing and production, if a large percentage of the monthly shipments are pushed out in the last few working days with informal methods, or if the performance of first-line supervisors is based on measures that can be contrary to execution of routine tasks, then data base integrity is sure to suffer. The point is that job specification, job performance, and job design need to be tailored to management by and of a data base. Organizational changes may be required.

Finally, it is important to indicate the key organizational linkages to marketing. MPC systems are critically linked to order entry and order promising (setting due dates for customer orders). In essence, the master production schedule (MPS) is the interface between marketing and production. It is here that trade-offs are made and the detailed set of marching orders is provided for manufacturing. Achieving that set of orders is manufacturing's job under MPC system constraints. Marketing, in turn, can depend on manufacturing to achieve the planned results. Moreover, marketing's responsibilities are specified in terms of utilizing these outputs to best achieve the goals of the company from a marketing point of view. The result is a new level of communication and cooperation between marketing and manufacturing—and still further pressure to ensure the integrity of the data base that supports this companywide plan of action.

Jet Spray—An integrated on-line example

Jet Spray Corporation manufactures and sells dispensers for noncarbonated cold beverages (e.g., lemonade) and hot beverages (e.g., coffee). Jet Spray uses a software package called Data 3 for manufacturing planning and control. The package is an integrated on-line system encompassing MRP, capacity planning, shop-floor control, master production scheduling, inventory management, and other functions.

One of the parts at Jet Spray, 3273, is a beverage bowl used for the TJ3 model cold drink dispenser. It is also sold as a replacement or service part, as part number S3273. Figure 3.5 is a portion of the inquiry record for the S3273, where the time-phased record is in vertical format. There are 11 on hand, and a series of customers orders marked C/O. The record begins with the oldest date for a past-due order (8/4); all past-due orders are on credit hold. The projected balance goes negative at 9/25. A work order (W/O 78430) is due on 9/29, but it has a reschedule-in (RSI) message to expedite it to 9/26. Other exception messages are given to help the planner manage the item.

Figure 3.6 is a portion of the report that extracts the exception code information from the individual MRP records like Figure 3.5 into one overall report for the items made in the plastic finishing department. This is where

FIGURE 3.5   Jet Spray MRP system inquiry (part S3273)

```
   9/29/    8:17:23      MRP INQUIRY FOR PART: S3273              C/N   1   RNMRP001
   DESCRIPTION: BOWL  PINCH TYPE
   QTY ON HAND:           11                         LEADTIME DAYS :   3
   SAFETY-STCK:           0                  0   BUYER/PLANNER : 030
```

TYP	ORDER #	REQUIRED QUANTITY	RECEIVABLE QUANTITY	MESSAGE	PROJECTED BALANCE	DUE DATE OPT
C/O	9007987	1			10	8/04/
C/O	9009239	1			9	9/08/
C/O	9009314	1			8	9/10/
C/O	9009344	1			7	9/11/
C/O	0201039	3			4	9/19/
C/O	9009811	1			3	9/24/
C/O	9009830	1			2	9/24/
C/O	9009875	2				9/25/
C/O	9009879	5			5-	9/25/
C/O	9009917	1			6-	9/25/
C/O	9009944	2			8-	9/26/
W/O	0078430		96	RSI 09/26/	88	9/29/
F/C		10			78	9/29/
W/O	0078450		96		174	10/03/
C/O	0201118	50			124	10/03/
C/O	0201129	5			119	10/03/
PLO				96 OPEN SCH REC	215	10/06/
F/C		65			150	10/06/
F/C		65			85	10/13/
PLO				96 OPEN SCH REC	181	10/20/
F/C		65			116	10/20/

FIGURE 3.6   Jet Spray MRP system exception messages (part S3273)

```
001  9/26/  20.56.49          JET SPRAY CORPORATION                      MC SUPVSR          RNMRPP02    PAGE  17
                           MRP EXCEPTION MESSAGE REPORT                              SEQUENCED BY MAKE/BUY
                    FOR BUYER/PLANNER: 030 - J.CAPPADONA--PLASTIC FINISHING
                                                                                                    MAKE/BUY
PART NUMBER --RI DESCRIPTION ----------------*  ACTION MESSAGES----------------------------------------*  CODE


S3170      BOWL GASKET           OPEN A SCHEDULED RECEIPT DUE  9/26/    FOR QTY OF         1.000             IF
                                 OPEN A SCHEDULED RECEIPT DUE 10/03/    FOR QTY OF         1.000
                                 OPEN A SCHEDULED RECEIPT DUE 10/13/    FOR QTY OF         1.000
                                 OPEN A SCHEDULED RECEIPT DUE 10/27/    FOR QTY OF         1.000


S3273      BOWL PINCH TYPE       RESCHEDULE IN  W/O NO. 0078430 TO  9/26/   FROM  9/29/  . QTY IS   96        IF
                                 OPEN A SCHEDULED RECEIPT DUE 10/06/    FOR QTY OF                  96
                                 OPEN A SCHEDULED RECEIPT DUE 10/20/    FOR QTY OF                  96
                                 OPEN A SCHEDULED RECEIPT DUE 10/27/    FOR QTY OF                  96


S3338      BOWL COVER            RESCHEDULE IN  W/O NO. 0079380 TO  9/26/   FROM 10/03/  . QTY IS   50        IF
                                 OPEN A SCHEDULED RECEIPT DUE 10/06/    FOR QTY OF                 100
                                 OPEN A SCHEDULED RECEIPT DUE 10/27/    FOR QTY OF                 100
```

plastic parts sold as service parts are packaged. Item S3273 is shown with the information from Figure 3.5. By looking at the overall report shown as Figure 3.6, work can be efficiently released to the plastic finishing department on a daily basis.

Figure 3.7 presents the inquiry record for part 3273 (not the service part S3273). It contains information derived from the service part record (e.g., the 96 units of WOA 78450 that have not yet been picked) and from records for the end item on which this part is used.

Figure 3.8 shows the daily exception message report for the plastic molding department. It is used to help schedule the extensive changeovers of the molding machines. The exception message for 3273 indicated on Figure 3.7 can be seen in Figure 3.8.

Figures 3.5 through 3.8 show an integrated set of real-time MRP records. They are used on a daily basis at Jet Spray. Many "standard" MRP reports are rarely if ever printed. They are replaced with a "paperless" system. Each day the planners, using video screens, take the actions required for that day. The MRP planning is on a daily cycle. This results in lead time and inventory reductions, but it comes at the cost of all procedures and support activities, such as stockrooms executing instructions in a more timely mode. Again we see pressures for high levels of data integrity and performance. One goal of Jet Spray is to pick orders from stock on the same day they are created by MRP planners.

FIGURE 3.7   Jet Spray MRP system inquiry (part 3273)

9/29/	MRP INQUIRY FOR PART: 3273			
DESCRIPTION: BOWL TJ3				
QTY ON HAND:	1,034		LEADTIME DAYS :	6
SAFETY-STCK:	0		BUYER/PLANNER : 020	
MISC. SHORT:	0			
	REQUIRED		PROJECTED	
TYP ORDER # QUANTITY		MESSAGE	BALANCE	DUE DATE
WOA 0078450	23		1011	9/23/
WOA 0078450	73		938	9/23/
DEP	96		842	9/24/
DEP	20		822	9/26/
DEP	126		696	10/01/
DEP	113		583	10/06/
DEP	96		487	10/07/
DEP	96		391	10/15/
DEP	145		246	10/22/
DEP	150		96	10/24/
PLO		500 OPEN SCH REC	596	10/29/
DEP	120		476	10/29/
DEP	96		380	10/29/
DEP	150		230	10/30/
DEP	96		134	11/04/

FIGURE 3.8 Jet Spray MRP system exception messages (part 3273)

```
001  9/26/

                          JET SPRAY CORPORATION
                       MRP EXCEPTION MESSAGE REPORT
                FOR BUYER/PLANNER: 020      PLASTIC MOLDING

PART NUMBER --RT DESCRIPTION ----------+ ACTION MESSAGES----------------------------+ CODE

3223      SPACER/JT JS EVAP          OPEN A SCHEDULED RECEIPT DUE 10/24/   FOR QTY OF      5,000      IF

3273      BOWL TJ3                   OPEN A SCHEDULED RECEIPT DUE 10/29/   FOR QTY OF       500       IF

3715      FUNNEL COVER HC2 HCL       RESCHEDULE IN W/O NO. 007A990 TO   9/26/   FROM 10/02/86. QTY IS    2,000     IF
```

CONCLUDING PRINCIPLES

In the last analysis, the company with a fully operational MPC system is as different from its prior state as an automobile from a horse. The basic day-to-day operations are different, and the entire approach to problem solving becomes integrated around a single companywide data base. The role of general management in planning and controlling the process of organizational change is critical to success. A superb technical design for an MPC system will never be able to compensate for poor procedures and a lack of control over transaction accuracy. To achieve management by a data base and management of a data base, all of the system dynamics must be understood, and ironclad procedures must be designed to keep the information synchronized with the physical flow of material. We offer the following as a set of principles which summarize these concepts:

- MPC systems substitute information for inventory and other forms of organizational slack; the quality of the information directly influences the ability to make this substitution.
- There must be a constant one-for-one match between the physical system and the information in the data base.
- There must be a match between actions and transactions.
- The organization and the reward systems must change to support data base accuracy.
- The costs and training needed to achieve data base accuracy are substantial but yield quick returns.

REFERENCES

Backes, Robert W. "Cycle Counting—A Better Method for Achieving Accurate Inventory Records." *Production and Inventory Management*, 2nd Quarter 1980, pp. 36–44.

Carlson, J. G. H. "Interactive Systems for the Physical Control of Material." *1975 Conference Proceedings*, American Production and Inventory Control Society, pp. 184–89.

Fenton, T.J., and P.J. Rosa, Jr. "How to Live with Your Net Change System." *1975 Conference Proceedings*, American Production and Inventory Control Society, pp. 24–36.

Hall, R. W. "Data Accuracy in Material Flow Control." *1980 Conference Proceedings*, American Production and Inventory Control Society, pp. 128–30.

Herrick, Terry L. "End Item Pegging Made Easier." *Production and Inventory Management*, 3rd Quarter 1976.

Jackson, J. S. "To Peg or Not to Peg." *1973 Conference Proceedings*, American Production and Inventory Control Society, pp. 84–95.

Jordan, H. H. "How to Start a Cycle Counting Program." *1975 Conference Proceedings*, American Production and Inventory Control Society, pp. 190-98.

―――. "Cycle Counting for Record Accuracy." *1980 Conference Proceedings*, American Production and Inventory Control Society, pp. 385–86.

Kneppelt, L. R. "Real-Time, On-Line, Distribution in the Manufacturing Environment." *1980 Conference Proceedings*, American Production and Inventory Control Society, pp. 58–60.

Kraemer, R. P. "Record Accuracy through CRT and Bar Coded Data Collection Systems." *1980 Conference Proceedings*, American Production and Inventory Control Society, pp. 90–93.

Rose, Harvey N. "Auditing of P&IC Systems—The Necessary Ingredient!" *APICS Annual Conference Proceedings*, 1978, pp. 436–54.

Vollmann, T. E., and W. L. Berry. "The Manufacturing Control System Audit: A Key to Productivity and Profit Improvement." Iowa City: University of Iowa, Business School, Discussion Paper Series no. 83–4.

Wallace, Thomas F. *MRPII: Making It Happen.* Essex Junction, Vt.: Oliver Wight Limited Publications, 1985.

Webber, Michael. "Cycle Counting and Other Physical Controls—What and Why?" *APICS Annual Conference Proceedings*, 1978, pp. 837–45.

DISCUSSION QUESTIONS

1. This chapter refers to the substitution of information for organizational slack. Provide some examples of this concept from your own experience. For instance, when would you have been able to make better use of your time had you had better information?

2. Discuss some of the "informal systems" that exist at a university.

3. Instead of devoting a great deal of effort to the development of transaction processing and error reporting activities in an MPC system, why not devote that effort to eliminating the errors?

4. Someone has just told you that their inventory records are 95 percent accurate. What additional questions would you ask to make sure you understood exactly what was meant? How would you verify the claim?

5. What are examples of transaction processing for individual students at a university? What happens if they are not done well?

6. What are some of the needs for routine auditing at a university? What things might you be interested in trying to "catch" if you had the job?

7. Many firms are now creating positions like "data base manager," "data integrity officer," and "information manager." Discuss the wisdom of the creation of such a role for the MPC data base described in this chapter.

PROBLEMS

1. The following information pertains to the current status of the major product for Acme Manufacturing Company:

Period (week)	Gross requirements	Scheduled receipts
1	25	30
2	10	0
3	5	0
4	30	0
5	15	0
6	20	0

On-hand inventory = 15 units
Lead time = 2 weeks
Order quantity = 30 units
Safety stock = 0

a. Complete the MRP record as it would appear at the beginning of week 1:

Week		1	2	3	4	5	6
Gross requirements							
Scheduled receipts							
Projected available balance							
Planned order releases							

b. Suppose the following transactions occurred *during* week 1:
   1. 20 units were disbursed from inventory.
   2. 25 units were received on the 30-unit scheduled receipt due in week 1 (5 units on this order were scrapped).
   3. An inventory count of the actual stock in week 1 produced a cycle count adjustment of +10.
   4. The new requirement for week 7 is 5 units.
   5. 15 of the 30 requirements in week 4 have been moved to week 5 because of a change in the customer order due dates.

   Update the MRP record, completed in part **a**, as it would appear at the beginning of week 2:

Week		2	3	4	5	6	7
Gross requirements							
Scheduled receipts							
Projected available balance							
Planned order releases							

c. What significant changes have occurred in the MRP record as of week 2 as a result of week 1 transactions? What exception messages would be generated as a result of these changes?

2. The MPC system at the Duckworth Manufacturing Company is run weekly to update the master production schedule (MPS) and MRP records. At the start of week 1, the MPS for end products A and B is:

Master production schedule						
Week number	1	2	3	4	5	6
Product A	10	—	25	5	10	—
Product B	5	20	—	20	—	20

In order to manufacture one unit of either end product A or B, one unit of component C is required. The purchasing lead time for component C is two weeks, an order quantity of 40 units is used, and no (zero) safety stock is maintained for this item. The inventory balance for component C is 5 units at the start of week 1, and there is an open order (scheduled receipt) for 40 units due to be delivered at the beginning of week 1.

a. Complete the MRP record for component C as it would appear at the beginning of week 1:

Week	1	2	3	4	5	6
Gross requirements						
Scheduled receipts						
Projected available balance						
Planned order releases						

b. During week 1, the following transactions occurred for component C:
   1. The open order for 40 units due to be received at the start of week 1 was received on Monday of week 1 with a quantity of 30. (Ten units of component C were scrapped on this order.)
   2. An inventory cycle count during week 1 revealed that five units of component C were missing. An inventory adjustment of −5 was, therefore, processed.
   3. Ten units of component C were actually disbursed (instead of the 15 units that were planned for disbursement to produce endproducts A and B). (The MPS quantity of five in week 1 for product B was canceled due to a customer order cancellation.)
   4. The MPS quantities for week 7 include 15 units for product A and zero units for product B.
   5. Due to a change in customer order requirements, marketing has requested that the MPS quantity of 25 units for product A scheduled in week 3 be moved to week 2.
   6. An order for 40 units was released.

Given this information, complete the MRP record for component C as it would appear at the beginning of week 2:

Week		2	3	4	5	6	7
Gross requirements							
Scheduled receipts							
Projected available balance							
Planned order releases							

What action(s) are required by the inventory planner at the start of week 2 as a result of the transactions which occurred during week 1? What actions should the master scheduler take in order to minimize such problems?

3. Consider the following MRP record for Cactus Cups:

Week		1	2	3	4	5	6
Gross requirements		25	30	5	15	5	10
Scheduled receipts			40		0	15	
Projected available balance	35		20	15		10	
Planned order releases							

Q = lot-for-lot; LT = 5; SS = 0.

Suppose that 5 units of the scheduled receipt for 40 units that is due on Monday of week 2 are scrapped during week 1, and that no scrap ticket is issued. Furthermore, assume that this lot is not counted before it is put away in the stockroom on Monday of week 2, but recorded as a receipt of 40 units. What impact will these actions have on factory operations?

4. Given the following time-phased record, should any open orders be rescheduled, and if so who makes these changes?

		1	2	3	4	5	6	7	8
Gross requirements			25		10		20		30	
Scheduled receipts			20	20						
Projected available balance	30		25	45	35	35	15	15	5	5
Planned order releases							20			

Q = 20; LT = 2; SS = 0.

5. Regenerate the time-phased record for problem 4 at the end of period 1 to include periods 9 and 10, given the following period 1 transactions:
   a. The on-hand balance was cycle counted after the 25 had been withdrawn; 8 parts were found—before the scheduled receipt for period 1 arrived.
   b. The order for 20 pieces in period 1 arrived with an actual quantity of 22.
   c. The scheduled receipt for period 2 was moved out to period 5.
   d. The gross requirement of 10 in period 3 was moved to period 4.
   e. The gross requirements for periods 9 and 10 are 20 and 15 respectively.

	2	3	4	5	6	7	8	9	10
Gross requirements									
Scheduled receipts									
Projected available balance									
Planned order releases									

Is there any action indicated for the MRP planner?

6. Consider the information contained in the planned order row of the MRP record below:

Period		1	2	3	4	5
Gross requirements		5	30	20	20	0
Scheduled receipts			40			
Projected available balance	10	5	15	35	15	15
Planned order releases			40			

   Q = 40; LT = 1; SS = 2.

What transactions would lead to shifting the planned order to period 1 or period 3?

7. The production manager at the Wireless Wizard Company is interested in learning how time-phased MRP records could be used in a manufacturing planning system to better coordinate the final assembly and component manufacturing operations of the firm. He would like you to prepare an example indicating how these operations would be planned and scheduled under MRP. He has supplied the following information concerning one of the firm's end products—the model 101X CB radio:

   Sales forecast = 100 units/week.
   Current on-hand inventory = 150 units.
   Final assembly lead time = 1 week.
   Final assembly standard lot size = 200 units.
   Model 101X safety stock = 0 units.

One of the components required in the final assembly of the model 101X CB radio is the #2100 circuit. Each model 101X requires two of the #2100 circuits and there are currently 300 of these circuits on hand in inventory. Also, the component manufacturing department requires a two-week lead time to make the circuits and there is currently an open order in this department for a standard production lot quantity of 400 due to be delivered in week 2.

    a.   Prepare the MRP records for the next four weeks to illustrate how this type of planning system would function between assembly and the component manufacturing department.

    b.   Indicate what factors are most critical for the effective operation of this type of planning system.

8.   Ajax sells a widget that has a forecasted demand of 25 per week. One of the components of the widget is a framus. The lead time to make widgets is one week and two weeks for framuses. Ajax presently has 35 widgets on hand and 40 framuses. The lot size for widgets is 50 and framuses are made lot-for-lot. There is an open order for 25 framuses due in week 2. Use a spreadsheet to prepare MRP records for widgets and framuses for the next five weeks. Is there any action indicated for the MRP planners?

9.   Consider the following product structure and inventory information:

Item	Inventory
A	10
B	40
C	60
D	60

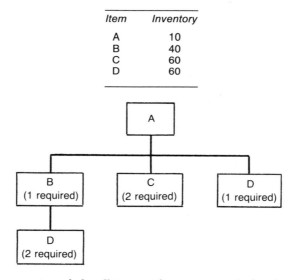

Lead time = 1 week for all items. There are no scheduled receipts for any item.

How many units of product A can be delivered to customers at the start of next week under each of the following circumstances? (Treat each independently; that is, only **a**, only **b**, or only **c**.)

    a.   The bill of materials for B is wrong, it actually takes 2 units of B to make an A.

    b.   The inventory for D is only 40 units.

    c.   There was need to scrap 10 units of the inventory for item C.

10. Are the following cycle counts within tolerance?

Item	Class	Count basis	Record invt.	Actual invt.
1	B	Hand	100	106
2	C	Weigh	10207	10400
3	A	Hand	43	42

11. What kinds of problems arise from the following cycle counting observations? What might be the causes for each of these errors?

Item	Class	Count basis	Record invt.	Actual invt.
1	C	Hand	0	47
2	B	Weigh	1000	1041
3	A	Hand	200	1700

12. Use a spreadsheet program to develop the MRP records for parts A and B from the product structure shown below. Use the data from the table below.

Part	A	B
Requirements	50/period	—
Initial inventory balance	68	8
Lead time	1	1
Lot size	lot-for-lot	250
Safety stock	10	—
Scheduled receipt	—	250 in period 1

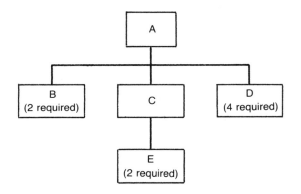

    a. What are the planned orders for item B?

    b. On an unlucky day (it must have been the 13th), the planner for part A found that the inventory was wrong by 13 units. Instead of 68 there were only 55 on hand. What happens to the planned orders for part B?

13. Use the spreadsheet model developed for problem **12,** part **a,** to generate a 10-period material plan for parts A and B. Suppose that in period 1 the actual demand for part A was 60 units instead of 50. Regenerate the spreadsheet for periods 2 through 11. What changes occur in the material plans for parts A and B?

14. Continuing with problem **13,** what is the impact if the 60 unit actual demand for period 1 is repeated for five periods, in each case with a planned demand of 50 units?

15. Using the spreadsheet model generated for problem **12,** part **a,** what is the impact of part B being produced on a machine that only has a 25 percent defect-free yield that is not discovered until part B's are taken from inventory to make part A's (i.e., it takes 4 units of part B inventory to get one good unit of part B)?

4

Capacity planning

In this chapter we discuss the problem of providing sufficient capacity to meet the manufacturing needs of the firm. We focus primarily on techniques for determining the capacity requirements implied in the plans developed by the material planning systems. The managerial objective in planning capacity is to ensure that sufficient capacity is available to accomplish the planned production. The capacity must be available in the right time periods so the production can be completed at the right time, as well. If sufficient capacity cannot be made available either inside or outside the firm, then the only managerial alternative is to change the material plan to conform to the available capacity.

The chapter is organized around the following five topics:

- The role of the capacity planning system in manufacturing planning and control systems: How does it fit? What role does it play?
- Capacity planning and control techniques: How can the capacity implications of a material plan be estimated? How can detailed capacity needs be determined? How can capacity usage be controlled?
- Management and capacity planning: How can managers decide which technique(s) to use? How should they use them?
- Data base requirements: How should the data base be designed for a capacity planning system?

- Example applications: How are capacity planning techniques applied? What outputs are useful for managing capacity?

Some of the techniques in this chapter are closely related to the analogous work in advanced production planning presented in Chapter 15. The description of finite loading is presented in Chapter 5, rather than here, because of its use as a scheduling model. The production planning discussion in Chapter 9 contains managerial considerations useful for the resource-planning activity. The master production schedule, described in Chapter 8, is the primary source of data for capacity planning.

THE ROLE OF CAPACITY PLANNING IN MPC SYSTEMS

A critical activity that parallels the development of the material plans is the development of capacity plans. Without the provision of adequate capacity or recognition of the existence of excess capacity, the benefits of an otherwise effective MPC system cannot be fully realized. On the one hand, insufficient capacity will quickly lead to deteriorating delivery performance, escalating work-in-process inventories, and frustrated manufacturing personnel who will quickly turn back to the informal system to solve problems. On the other hand, excess capacity may be a needless expense that can be reduced. Even firms with advanced material planning capability have found that their inability to provide the appropriate work center capacities is a major stumbling block to achieving maximum benefits. This underscores the importance of developing the capacity planning system in concert with the material planning system—and the need for discussing this topic here.

Hierarchy of capacity planning decisions

The relationship of capacity planning decisions to the other modules of an integrated MPC system is shown in Figure 4.1. Also shown is the scope of capacity planning, starting from an overall plan of resources, proceeding to a rough-cut evaluation of the capacity implications of a particular master production schedule, thereafter moving to the detailed evaluation of capacity requirements based upon detailed MRP records, continuing to finite loading procedures, and ending with input/output techniques to help monitor the plans.

These five levels of capacity planning activities range from large aggregations of capacity for long time periods to very detailed machine scheduling, for an hour or shorter time interval. The primary focus of this chapter will be on rough-cut capacity planning procedures and on the technique called capacity requirements planning. These are central to establishing a correspondence between the capacity plans and the material plans. Since the control of capacity plans is as important as control of material plans, input/output analysis is presented as a method for achieving this control.

FIGURE 4.1   Capacity planning in the MPC system

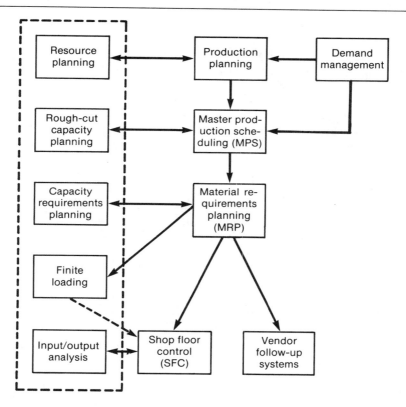

Some authorities distinguish between long-, medium-, and short-range capacity planning and control horizons. This chapter is largely devoted to short- to medium-range capacity planning, involving a planning horizon ranging from next week to a year or more in the future. We consider the following questions: what are the techniques, how do they compare, and what benefits are being obtained in actual practice? Short-range capacity requirements can be determined for individual work centers using the capacity requirements planning technique, and for the medium-range using the rough-cut procedures.

Links to other systems modules

The system linkages for the capacity planning modules follow the basic hierarchy just described and illustrated in Figure 4.1. The capacity planning techniques described in this chapter, rough-cut capacity planning and capacity requirements planning, link with the master production schedule and MRP systems, respectively. The linkages are shown as double-headed arrows for a very specific reason. There must be a correspondence between the capacity *required* to execute a given material plan and that made *available* to execute the plan. If this correspondence does not exist, the plan will either be impossible to execute or inefficiently executed. We do not take the position that capacity must always be changed to meet material plans. In fact, whether this is worthwhile or whether the plans should be changed to meet the capacity is a managerial judgment. The capacity planning systems provide the basic information to make that a reasoned judgment.

The resource planning activity is directly linked to the production planning module. It is the most highly aggregated and longest-range capacity planning decision. Resource planning typically involves converting monthly, quarterly, or even annual data from the production plan into aggregate resources such as gross labor-hours, floor space, machine-hours, and the like. This level of planning involves new capital expansion (brick and mortar, machine tools, warehouse space, and so on), which requires a time horizon of months or years.

The master production schedule is the primary information source for rough-cut capacity planning. The capacity requirements of a particular master schedule can be estimated by any of the following techniques: capacity planning using overall planning factors (CPOF), capacity bills, or resource profiles. These techniques provide information with which to modify the resource levels or material plan in the medium range to ensure efficient execution of the master production schedule.

Substantially more detailed capacity planning is possible using the capacity requirements planning (CRP) technique. To provide this detail, the material plans produced by the MRP system serve as the basis for calculating time-phased capacity requirements. The data files used by the CRP technique include work in process, routing, scheduled receipts, and planned orders. The information provided by the CRP technique can be used to determine the short-term capacity needs for both key machine centers and labor skills.

The finite loading technique also relates to the MRP detail plans, but it can be better viewed as a shop-floor scheduling technique. It, more than any of the other capacity planning techniques, makes clear the relationship between scheduling and capacity availability. Finite loading starts with a specified capacity level for each work center or resource grouping; this capacity is then allocated to work orders. Hence, finite loading is a method for scheduling work orders. The procedures described in this chapter do not deal with scheduling questions. They estimate capacity requirements only, with the schedules of orders considered to be a separate problem. The finite loading process requires linkages to the same files as the CRP technique, as well as to files which specify work center capacities.

Input/output analysis provides a method for monitoring the actual consumption of capacity during the execution of material plans. It is necessarily linked to the execution systems and data base for shop-floor control. Input/output analysis can indicate the need to update capacity plans as actual shop performance deviates from current plans, as well as the need to modify the planning factors used in other capacity-planning techniques.

This overview of the scope of capacity planning sets the stage for the techniques discussed in the chapter. The primary interaction among these techniques is hierarchical; resource planning sets constraints on short- to medium-range capacity planning, which, in turn, constrains detailed scheduling and execution on the shop floor.

CAPACITY PLANNING AND CONTROL TECHNIQUES

In this section, we describe four procedures for capacity planning. The first technique is called capacity planning using overall factors. CPOF is the simplest of the four techniques and is based only on accounting data. The second, capacity bills, requires more detailed product information. The third, resource profiles, adds a further dimension—the specific timing of capacity requirements. The fourth, capacity requirements planning, utilizes the entire MRP data base to calculate the capacity required to produce both the detailed open shop orders (scheduled receipts) and the planned orders. We will also discuss the input/output analysis technique for monitoring and controlling the capacity plans.

To describe the four planning techniques, we use a simple example. The example allows us to clearly see the differences in approach, complexity, level of aggregation, data requirements, timing, and accuracy between the techniques. We will then illustrate the input/output analysis procedure, which could be utilized with any of the four planning procedures. Although the appropriate unit of measure for capacity will vary, depending on the key resources in a particular firm, we will use labor hours for our examples.

Capacity planning using overall factors (CPOF)

CPOF is a relatively simple approach to rough-cut capacity planning, which is typically done on a manual basis. The data inputs come from the master production schedule (MPS), rather than from MRP detailed time-phased record data. This procedure is usually based upon planning factors derived from standards or historical data for end products. When these planning factors are applied to the MPS data, overall labor or machine-hour capacity requirements can be estimated. This overall estimate is thereafter allocated to individual work centers on the basis of historical data on shop workloads. CPOF plans are usually stated in terms of weekly or monthly time periods, and are revised as the firm makes changes to the MPS.

The top portion of Figure 4.2 shows the MPS that will serve as the basis for our example. This schedule specifies the quantity of each of two end products to be assembled during each time period. The first step of the CPOF procedure involves calculating the capacity requirements of this schedule for the overall plant. Direct labor standards, indicating the total direct labor-hours required for each end product, are shown in the lower portion of Figure 4.2. Assuming labor productivity of 100 percent of standard, the total direct labor-hour requirement for the first period is 62.80 hours, as shown in Figure 4.3.

The second step in this procedure involves using historical ratios to allocate the total capacity required each period to individual work centers. The historical percentage of the total direct labor-hours worked in each of the three work centers during the prior year were used to determine allocation ratios. These data could be derived from the company's accounting records. In the example, 60.3 percent, 30.4 percent, and 9.3 percent of the total direct labor-hours were worked in work centers 100, 200, and 300, respectively. These percentages are used to estimate the anticipated direct labor requirements for each work center. The resulting work center capacity requirements are shown in Figure 4.3, for each period in the MPS.

The CPOF procedure, or variants of it, are found in a number of manufacturing firms. The data requirements are minimal, primarily accounting system data, and the calculations straightforward. As a consequence, the CPOF approximations of the capacity requirements at individual work centers are only valid to the extent that product mixes or historical divisions of work between work centers remain constant. The primary advantages of this procedure are its ease of calculation and minimal data requirements. In many firms, the data are readily available and the computations can be done manually.

Capacity bills

The capacity bill procedure provides a much more direct link between individual end products in the MPS and the capacity required for individual work centers. It takes into account any shifts in product mix. Consequently, it requires more data than the CPOF procedure. Bill of material and routing data are required, and direct labor- or machine-hour data must be available for each operation.

To develop a bill of capacity for the example problem, we use the product structure data for A and B shown in Figure 4.4. Additionally, we need the routing and operation time standard data shown in the top portion of Figure 4.5 for the assembly of products A and B, as well as for the manufacture of

FIGURE 4.2 Example problem data

Master production schedule (in units):

End product		Time period												
	1	*2*	*3*	*4*	*5*	*6*	*7*	*8*	*9*	*10*	*11*	*12*	*13*	*Total*
A	33	33	33	40	40	40	30	30	30	37	37	37	37	457
B	17	17	17	13	13	13	25	25	25	27	27	27	27	273

Direct labor time per end product unit:

End product	Total direct labor in standard hours/unit
A	.95 hours
B	1.85 hours

Source: W. L. Berry, T. G. Schmitt, and T. E. Vollmann, "Capacity Planning Techniques for Manufacturing Control Systems: Information Requirements and Operating Features." Reprinted with permission, November 1982 *Journal of Operations Management*, Journal of the American Production and Inventory Control Society, Inc.

FIGURE 4.3 Estimated capacity requirements using overall factors (CPOF) (in standard direct labor-hours)

Work center	Historical percentage	Period													Total hours
		1	2	3	4	5	6	7	8	9	10	11	12	13	
100	60.3	37.87	37.87	37.87	37.41	37.41	37.41	45.07	45.07	45.07	51.32	51.32	51.32	51.32	566.33
200	30.4	19.09	19.09	19.09	18.86	18.86	18.86	22.72	22.72	22.72	25.87	25.87	25.87	25.87	285.49
300	9.3	5.84	5.84	5.84	5.78	5.78	5.78	6.96	6.96	6.96	7.91	7.91	7.91	7.91	87.38
Total required capacity		62.80*	62.80	62.80	62.05	62.05	62.05	74.75	74.75	74.75	85.10	85.10	85.10	85.10	939.20

*62.80 = (.95 × 33) + (1.85 × 17) using the standards from Figure 4.2.

Source: W. L. Berry, T. G. Schmitt, and T. E. Vollmann, "Capacity Planning Techniques for Manufacturing Control Systems: Information Requirements and Operating Features." Reprinted with permission, November 1982 Journal of Operations Management, Journal of the American Production and Inventory Control Society, Inc.

FIGURE 4.4   Product structure data

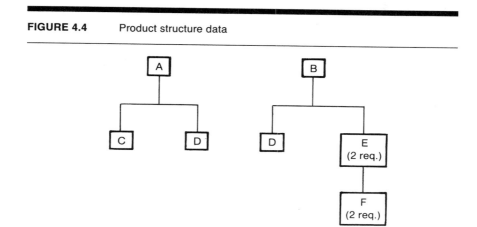

Source: W. L. Berry, T. G. Schmitt, and T. E. Vollmann, "Capacity Planning Techniques for Manufacturing Control Systems: Information Requirements and Operating Features." Reprinted with permission, November 1982 *Journal of Operations Management,* Journal of the American Production and Inventory Control Society, Inc.

component items C, D, E, and F. The bill of capacity indicates the total standard time required to produce one end product in each work center required in its manufacture. The calculations involve multiplying the total time per unit values by the usages indicated in the bill of materials. Summarizing the usage adjusted unit time data by work center produces the bill of capacity for each of the two products shown in the lower portion of Figure 4.5. The bill of capacity can be constructed from engineering data, as we have done here, or similar data might be available in a standard cost system. An alternative approach used by some firms is to prepare the bill of capacity only for those work centers regarded as critical.

Once the bill of capacity for each end product has been prepared, the master production schedule can be used to estimate the capacity requirements at individual work centers. The determination of capacity requirements for our example is shown in Figure 4.6. The resultant work center estimates differ substantially from the CPOF estimates shown in Figure 4.3. The differences reflect the period-to-period changes in product mix between the projected MPS and historical average figures. The estimates obtained from CPOF are based upon an overall historical ratio of work between machine centers, whereas the capacity bill estimates reflect the actual product mix planned for each period.

It is important to note that the total hours shown for the MPS (939.20) are the same in both Figure 4.3 and Figure 4.6; the differences are in work center estimates for each time period. These differences are far more important in firms which experience significant period-to-period product mix variations than in those that have a relatively constant pattern of work.

FIGURE 4.5 Routing and standard time data

End products	Lot sizes	Operation	Work center	Standard setup hours	Standard setup hours per unit	Standard run time hours per unit	Total hours per unit
A	40	1 of 1	100	1.0	.025*	.025	.05†
B	20	1 of 1	100	1.0	.050	1.250	1.30
Components							
C	40	1 of 2	200	1.0	.025	.575	.60
		2 of 2	300	1.0	.025	.175	.20
D	60	1 of 1	200	2.0	.033	.067	.10
E	100	1 of 1	200	2.0	.020	.080	.10
F	100	1 of 1	200	2.0	.020	.0425	.0625

Bill of capacity

	End product	
	A	B
Work center	Total time/unit	Total time/unit
100	.05	1.30
200	.70‡	.55§
300	.20	0.00
Total time/unit	.95	1.85

*.025 = setup time ÷ lot size = 1.0/40.
†.05 = setup time per unit + standard run time per unit = .025 + .025.
‡.70 = .60 + .10 for one C and one D from Figure 4.4.
§.55 = .10 + 2(.10) + 4(.0625) for one D, two Es, and four Fs.

Source: W. L. Berry, T. G. Schmitt, and T. E. Vollmann, "Capacity Planning Techniques for Manufacturing Control Systems: Information Requirements and Operating Features." Reprinted with permission, November 1982 *Journal of Operations Management*, Journal of the American Production and Inventory Control Society, Inc.

FIGURE 4.6   Capacity requirements using capacity bills

Work center	Period													Total hours	Projected work center percentage
	1	2	3	4	5	6	7	8	9	10	11	12	13		
100	23.75*	23.75	23.75	18.90	18.90	18.90	34.00	34.00	34.00	36.95	36.95	36.95	36.95	377.75	40%
200	32.45	32.45	32.45	35.15	35.15	35.15	34.75	34.75	34.75	40.75	40.75	40.75	40.75	470.05	50
300	6.60	6.60	6.60	8.00	8.00	8.00	6.00	6.00	6.00	7.40	7.40	7.40	7.40	91.40	10
Total	62.80	62.80	62.80	62.05	62.05	62.05	74.75	74.75	74.75	85.10	85.10	85.10	85.10	939.20	100%

*23.75 = (33 × .05) + (17 × 1.30) from Figures 4.2 and 4.5.
Source: W. L. Berry, T. G. Schmitt, and T. E. Vollmann, "Capacity Planning Techniques for Manufacturing Control Systems: Information Requirements and Operating Features." Reprinted with permission, November 1982 *Journal of Operations Management, Journal of the American Production and Inventory Control Society, Inc.

Resource profiles

Neither the CPOF nor the capacity bill procedure takes into account the specific timing of the projected workloads at individual work centers. In developing resource profiles, the production lead time data are taken into account to provide time-phased projections of the capacity requirements for individual production facilities.

In the use of any capacity planning technique, the time periods for the capacity plan can be varied (e.g., weeks, months, quarters). Note, however, that when the time periods are long relative to lead times much of the value of the time-phased information may be lost in the aggregation of the data. In many firms, this means that time periods of greater than one week will mask important changes in capacity requirements.

To apply the resource profile procedure to our example, the bills of material, routing, and time standard information in Figures 4.4 and 4.5 are used. We also need to add the production lead time for each end product and component part to our data base. In this simplified example, we use a lead time of one period for the assembly of each end product and one period for each operation required in the production of component parts. Since only one operation is required for producing components D, E, and F, the lead time for producing these components is one time period each. For component C, however, the lead time is two time periods, one for the operation in work center 200 and another for work center 300.

To use the resource profile procedure, a time-phased profile of the capacity requirements for each end item must be prepared. The operation setback charts in Figure 4.7 show this time phasing for end products A and B. The chart for end product A indicates that the final assembly operation is to be completed during period 5. The production of component D must be completed in period 4, prior to the start of final assembly, as must the production of component C. Since component C requires two time periods (one for each operation), it must be started one time period before component D, (i.e., at the start of period 3). There are other conventions that are used to define time phasing, but in this example we assume that the master production schedule specifies the number of units of each end product that must be completed by *the end* of the time period indicated. This implies that *all* components must be completed by the end of the preceding period.

For convenience, we have shown the standard hours required for each operation for each product in Figure 4.7. This information is summarized by work center and time period in Figure 4.8, which also shows the capacity requirements generated by the MPS quantities in time period 5 from Figure 4.2 (40 of end product A and 13 of end product B). The capacity requirements shown in Figure 4.8 are only for the MPS quantities in period 5. The MPS quantities for other periods can increase the capacity needed in each period. For example, Figure 4.8 shows that 7.9 hours of capacity are needed in period 4 at work center 200 to support the MPS for period 5. The MPS

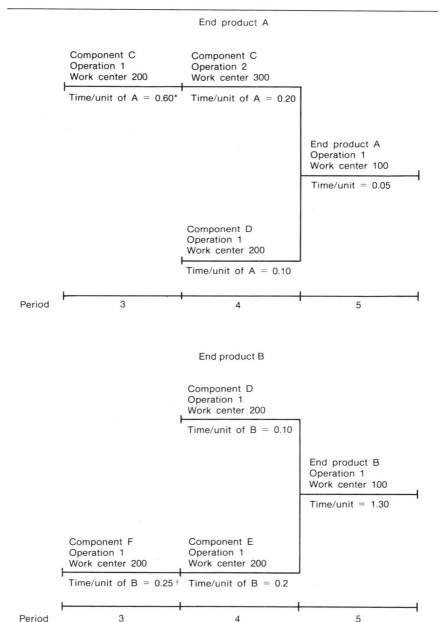

*.60 = Standard time per unit of C × Number of Cs per unit of A = .60 × 1 = .60.
†.25 = Standard time per unit of component F × Number of Fs per unit of B = .0625 × 4 = .25.
Source: W. L. Berry, T. G. Schmitt, and T. E. Vollmann, "Capacity Planning Techniques for Manufacturing Control Systems: Information Requirements and Operating Features." Reprinted with permission, November 1982 *Journal of Operations Management,* Journal of the American Production and Inventory Control Society, Inc.

FIGURE 4.8   Resource profiles by work center

Time required during preceding periods for one end product assembled in period 5:

	Time period		
	3	4	5
End product A			
Work center 100	0	0	.05
Work center 200	.60	.10	0
Work center 300	0	.20	0
End product B			
Work center 100	0	0	1.30
Work center 200	.25	.30	0

Time-phased capacity requirements generated from MPS for 40 As and 13 Bs in time period 5

	Time period		
	3	4	5
40 As			
Work center 100	0	0	2
Work center 200	24	4	0
Work center 300	0	8	0
13 Bs			
Work center 100	0	0	16.9
Work center 200	3.25	3.9	0
Work center 300	0	0	0
Total from period 5 MPS			
Work center 100	0	0	18.9
Work center 200	27.25	7.9	0
Work center 300	0	8.0	0

Source: W. L. Berry, T. G. Schmitt, and T. E. Vollmann, "Capacity Planning Techniques for Manufacturing Control Systems: Information Requirements and Operating Features." Reprinted with permission, November 1982 *Journal of Operations Management*, Journal of the American Production and Inventory Control Society, Inc.

requirements for period 6 will require another 27.25 hours from work center 200. This results in the total of 35.15 hours shown in Figure 4.9, which provides the overall capacity plan for the current MPS using the resource profile procedure.

A comparison of the capacity plans produced by the capacity bills and the resource profile procedures (Figures 4.6 and 4.9) illustrates the impact of the time-phased capacity information. The total workload created by the master production schedule (939.2 hours) remains the same, as do the work center percentage allocations. The period requirements for work centers 200 and 300 projected by the two techniques vary somewhat, however. A capacity requirement of 8 hours was projected for work center 300 in time period 6 using capacity bills versus 6 hours using resource profiles, a difference of

FIGURE 4.9   Capacity requirements using resource profiles

Work center	Past due*														Total hours	Work center percentage
		Period														
		1	2	3	4	5	6	7	8	9	10	11	12	13		
100	0.00	23.75	23.75	23.75	18.90	18.90	18.90	34.00	34.00	34.00	36.95	36.95	36.95	36.95	377.75	40%
200	56.50	32.45	35.65	35.15	35.15	32.15	34.75	34.75	39.45	40.75	40.75	40.75	11.80	0	470.05	50
300	6.60	6.60	6.60	8.00	8.00	8.00	6.00	6.00	6.00	7.40	7.40	7.40	7.40	0	91.40	10
Total	63.10	62.80	66.00	66.90	62.05	59.05	59.65	74.75	79.45	82.15	85.10	85.10	56.15	36.95	939.20	100%

*This work should be completed already for products to meet the master production schedule in periods 1 and 2. (If not, it is past due and will add to the capacity required in the upcoming periods.)

Source: W. L. Berry, T. G. Schmitt, and T. E. Vollmann, "Capacity Planning Techniques for Manufacturing Control Systems: Information Requirements and Operating Features." Reprinted with permission, November 1982 *Journal of Operations Management*, Journal of the American Production and Inventory Control Society, Inc.

more than 30 percent. This change reflects the difference in the timing of resources required to produce the component parts, which is taken into account by the resource bill procedure.

Capacity requirements planning (CRP)

Capacity requirements planning (CRP) differs from the resource profile procedure in four respects. First, CRP utilizes the information produced by the MRP explosion process, which includes consideration of all actual lot sizes, as well as the lead times for both open shop orders (scheduled receipts) and orders that are planned for future release (planned orders). Second, the gross to net feature of the MRP system takes into account the production capacity already stored in the form of inventories of both components and assembled products. Third, the shop-floor control system accounts for the current status of all work in process in the shop, so only the capacity needed to *complete the remaining work* on open shop orders is considered in calculating the required work center capacities. Fourth, CRP takes into account the demand for service parts, other demands that may not be accounted for in the MPS, and any additional capacity that might be required by MRP planners reacting to scrap, item record errors, and so on. To accomplish this, the CRP procedure requires the same input information as the resource profile procedure (bills of material, routing, time standards, lead times) plus information on MRP planned orders and the current status of open shop orders (MRP scheduled receipts) at individual work centers.

The CRP procedure exploits the MRP information so as to calculate only the capacity required to complete the MPS. By calculating the capacity requirements for actual open shop orders and planned orders in the MRP data base, CRP accounts for the capacity already stored in the form of finished and work-in-process inventories. Since the MRP data include the timing of both these open and planned orders, the potential for improved accuracy in the timing of capacity requirements is realized. This accuracy will be of most importance in the most immediate time periods. Rough-cut techniques can overstate the required capacity by the amount of capacity represented in inventories. In Figure 4.9, for example, the past due or already completed portion of the capacity requirements is 63.1 hours, or about a full time period's capacity. This work should already have been completed if we expect to meet the MPS in periods 1 and 2. The potential benefits of CRP are not without cost. A larger data base is required, as well as a much larger computational effort.

The process of preparing a CRP projection is quite similar to that used for resource profiles. The major difference is that the detailed MRP data establish the exact order quantities and timings for use in calculating the capacity required. The resultant capacity needs are summarized by time period and work center in a format similar to that of Figure 4.9. The CRP results would differ from those of the other techniques, primarily in the early periods, but would be a more accurate projection of work center capacity needs. Since the calculations are based on all component parts and end products from the present time period through all periods included in the MRP records (the planning horizon), one can see the enormity of the CRP calculation requirements. This cost is mitigated in some firms by collecting the data as the MRP explosion process is performed.

Figure 4.10 presents one of the MRP records that drive the CRP procedure for our example. To simplify the presentation, we only show the MPS for end product A and the MRP record for one of its components, component

FIGURE 4.10   CRP example: Detailed calculations

Product A MPS

Period	1	2	3	4	5	6	7	8	9	10	11	12	13
	33	33	33	40	40	40	30	30	30	37	37	37	37

Component C
Lot size = 40
Lead time = 2

		Period 1	2	3	4	5	6	7	8	9	10	11	12	13
Gross requirements		33	33	33	40	40	40	30	30	30	37	37	37	37
Scheduled receipts			40											
Projected available balance	37	4	11	18	18	18	18	28	38	8	11	14	17	20
Planned order releases		40	40	40	40	40	40		40	40	40	40		

Work Center 300 Capacity Requirements Using CRP

Hours of capacity*

Period	1	2	3	4	5	6	7	8	9	10	11	12	13
	8	8	8	8	8	8	8	0	8	8	8	8	

Total = 88

*The 8 hours of capacity required is derived from the scheduled receipt and planned order quantities of 40 units multiplied by the time to fabricate a unit of component C in machine center 300, 0.20 hours (see Fig. 4.7).

Source: W. L. Berry, T. G. Schmitt, and T. E. Vollmann, "Capacity Planning Techniques for Manufacturing Control Systems: Information Requirements and Operating Features." Reprinted with permission, November 1982 *Journal of Operations Management,* Journal of the American Production and Inventory Control Society, Inc.

C. We have used these data to calculate the capacity requirements for work center 300. These capacity requirements incorporate the influence of lot sizes, inventories, and scheduled receipts for component C. Since item C is processed at work center 300 during the second period of the two-period lead time, the planned order for 40 units due to be released in period 1 requires capacity in period 2 at work center 300. The capacity required is calculated using the setup and run time data from Figure 4.5 for component C.

For a lot size of 40 units, the total setup and run time in work center 300 is 8 hours (1.0 + [40 × .175]). Each of the planned orders for component C in Figure 4.10 will require eight hours of capacity at work center 300, one period later. Similarly, the scheduled receipt of 40 units due in period 2 will require eight hours of capacity in week 1. Note that the eight hours of capacity required for the scheduled receipt may not, in fact, be required if this job has already been processed at work center 300 before the beginning of period 1. The actual status of the shop order is required to make the analysis.

In comparing CRP to the other capacity planning procedures, one should not expect that the total capacity requirements for the 13 periods or the period-by-period requirements would be the same. A comparison of the capacity requirements for work center 300 developed by the resource profile procedure (Figure 4.9) and CRP (Figure 4.10) indicates that the estimated total capacity requirements for the 13 periods are less using CRP than resource profiles (88 versus 91.4 hours), and vary considerably on a period-by-period basis. The differences are explained by the initial inventory and the use of lot sizing. Any work-in-process that is partially completed would reduce the capacity requirements further.

Input/output control

The basic intent in each of the capacity planning techniques is to provide projections of the capacity needs implied by the current material plan, so timely actions can be taken to balance the capacity needs with capacity available. Once decisions have been made concerning additions to and deletions of capacity, or adjustments to the material plan, a workable capacity plan is the result. The next action is to monitor this plan to determine whether the actions were correct and sufficient. The monitoring also provides the basis for an ongoing correction of capacity planning data.

The basis for monitoring the capacity plan is input/output control. By this we mean that the planned input and planned output of work at a work center will be compared to the actual work input and output. The capacity planning technique used delineates the planned input. The planned output is the result of managerial decision making to specify the capacity level; that is, the planned output is based on manning levels, hours of work, and so forth. In capacity constrained work centers, the planned output is based on the rate of capacity established by management. In noncapacity constrained work centers, the planned output is equal to the planned input (allowing for some lead time offset).

The capacity data in input/output control are usually expressed in hours. The input data are based on the expected arrivals of jobs at a work center. For example, a CRP procedure would examine the status of all open shop orders (scheduled receipts), estimate how long they will take (setup, run, wait, and move) at particular work centers, and thereby derive when they will arrive at subsequent work centers. This would be repeated for all planned orders from the MRP data base. The resultant set of expected arrivals of exact quantities would be multiplied by run time per unit from the routing file. This product would be added to setup time, also from the routing file. The sum is a planned input, expressed in standard hours.

Actual input would use the same routing data, but for the *actual* arrivals of jobs in each time period as reported by the shop floor control system. Actual output would again use the shop floor control data for exact quantities completed in each time period, converted to standard hours with routing time data.

The only time data not based on the routing file are those for planned output. In this case, management has to plan the labor-hours to be expended in the work center. For example, if two people work 9 hours per day for five days, the result is 90 labor-hours per week. This value has to be reduced or inflated by an estimate of the relation of actual hours to standard hours. In our example, if the workers in this work center typically worked at 80 percent efficiency, then the planned output is 72 hours.

The actual output at a work center will deviate from the planned output. Often these deviations can be attributed to conditions at the work center itself, such as lower than expected productivity, breakdowns, absences, random variations, or poor product quality. But less than expected output can occur for reasons outside the control of the work center, such as insufficient output from a preceding work center or improper releasing of planned orders. Either of these problems can lead to insufficient input or a "starved" work center. Another reason for a variation between actual input and planned input was shown by our capacity planning model comparisons; that is, some models do not produce very realistic plans!

Input/output analysis also monitors backlog. Backlog represents the cushion between input and output. Arithmetically, it is equal to prior backlog plus or minus the difference between input and output. The planned backlog calculation is based on planned input and planned output. Actual backlog uses actual input and output. The difference between planned backlog and actual backlog represents one measure of the total, or net, input/output deviations. The monitoring of input, output, and backlog typically involves keeping track of the cumulative deviations and comparing them with preset limits.

The input/output report shown in Figure 4.11 is based on work center 200 for our example problem, now shown in weekly time buckets measured in standard labor-hours. The report was prepared at the end of period 5, so the actual values are current week-by-week variations in planned input. These could be the result of actual planned orders and scheduled receipts; that is, for example, if the input were planned by CRP, the planned inputs would be based upon the timings for planned orders, the status of scheduled receipts, and routing data. The *actual* input that arrives at work center 200 can vary for any of the causes discussed above.

The planned output for work center 200 has been smoothed; that is, management decided to staff this work center so as to achieve a constant output of 11 hours per week. The result should be to absorb the variations in input with changes in the backlog level. The cumulative planned output for the five weeks (55 hours) is 5 hours more than the cumulative planned input. This reflects a management decision to reduce the backlog from the original level of 20 hours. The process of increasing capacity to reduce backlog recognizes explicitly that the flows must be controlled to change backlog; the backlog cannot be changed in and of itself.

The data in Figure 4.11 summarizes the results after five weeks of actual operation. At the end of week 5, the situation requires managerial attention.

FIGURE 4.11   Sample input/output for work center 200* (as of the end of period 5)

		Week				
		1	2	3	4	5
Planned input		15	15	0	10	10
Actual input		14	13	5	9	17
Cumulative deviation		−1	−3	+2	+1	+8
Planned output		11	11	11	11	11
Actual output		8	10	9	11	9
Cumulative deviation		−3	−4	−6	−6	−8
Actual backlog	20	26	29	25	23	31

Desired backlog: 10 hours

*In standard labor-hours.

The cumulative input deviation ($+8$ hours), the cumulative output deviation (-8 hours), the current backlog (31 hours), or all three could have exceeded the desired limits of control. In this example, the increased backlog is a combination of more than expected input and less than expected output.

One other aspect of monitoring the backlog is important. In general, there is little point in releasing orders to a work center that already has an excessive backlog, except when the order to be released is of higher priority than any in the backlog. In general, the idea is to not release work that cannot be done, but to wait and release what is really needed. Oliver Wight sums this up as one of the principles of input/output control: "Never put into a manufacturing facility or to a vendor's facility more than you believe that he can produce. Hold backlogs in production and inventory control."

MANAGEMENT AND CAPACITY PLANNING

In the design and use of the capacity planning system, several management considerations must be taken into account. In this section, we will discuss the design of the systems from the perspective of the MPC framework, consider the capacity measure, look at the choices that must be made in tailoring the capacity-planning system to a particular firm, and consider how to use the capacity planning data. The key elements of management's commitment in the design and use of the system are emphasized.

Capacity planning in the MPC system

In Figure 4.1, we show the relationship between the MPC framework and the various capacity planning modules. The five modules range from long-range resource planning to day-to-day control of capacity utilization. In this chapter, we have concentrated on medium- to short-range planning techniques, rough-cut capacity planning and capacity requirements planning, and the input/output control technique for capacity monitoring. Nevertheless, there is a vertical relationship among the capacity planning modules, as well as the horizontal relationship with the material planning modules of the MPC system. These relationships can affect the managerial choices for the design and use of the capacity planning systems in a specific firm.

An illustration of the importance of the interrelationships in designing and using the capacity planning system comes from considering the impact of production planning and resource planning decisions on shorter-term capacity planning decisions. To the extent that production planning and resource planning are done well, the problems faced in capacity planning can be reduced, since adequate resources have been provided. If, for example, the production plan specifies a very stable rate of output, then changes in the master production schedule (MPS) that require capacity changes are minimal. If the material planning module is functioning effectively, then the MPS will be converted into detailed component production plans with relatively few unexpected capacity requirements.

A good case in point is the use of the *kanban system* by the Toyota Motor Company and other Japanese firms. For these firms, the production plan calls for a stable rate of output (cars per day). Product mix variations are substantially less than for other automobile companies, because Toyota carefully manages the number and timing of option combinations. Order backlogs and finished-goods-inventories also are used to separate the factories from actual customer orders. The result is a shop-floor/vendor control system that is simple, effective, and easy to operate. The careful resource and production planning, and resultant stability, means there is little need for these firms to use either rough-cut capacity planning procedures or CRP.

A quite different but equally important linkage that can affect capacity-planning system design is the linkage with the shop-floor control systems at execution time. A key relationship exists in scheduling the effective use of capacity. If sufficient capacity has been provided, and efficient use of that capacity is ensured by good shop-floor procedures, then few unpleasant surprises will arise that require capacity analysis and change. Effective shop-floor procedures will utilize the available capacity to process orders according to MRP system priorities, provide insight into potential capacity problems in the short range (a few hours to days), and be responsive to changes in the material plans. Thus, an effective shop-floor control system can reduce the necessary degree of detail and intensity of use of the capacity planning system.

In providing effective control of the capacity plans, the shop-floor control system, again, is key. Good shop-floor control leads to plans that are more likely to be met. The net result is a better match between actual input/output and planned input/output. Again we see attention to the material planning side of the MPC system, in this case the shop-floor control module, having an effect on the capacity planning side.

Choosing the measure of capacity

There are several arguments surrounding the choice of capacity measure. They include issues of theory versus practice, calculated versus realized, and labor versus machine time, among others. Several of these are worthy of discussion. Our perspective will be managerial; we are interested in effective use of available resources to meet production plans.

There are three current trends in manufacturing that have a significant bearing on the choice and future choices of capacity measures. One is in direct labor, the second is in make versus buy (i.e., the amount of purchasing or fabrication in a firm), and the last concerns the nature of the manufacturing technology itself. Each of these can have a major impact upon what is important to measure in capacity.

We are seeing a considerable change in the concept of direct labor. There has been a shrinkage of direct labor as a portion of overall manufacturing employment, and the distinctions between direct and indirect labor are shrinking. The ability to change labor capacity by hiring and firing (or even using overtime) has been reduced; notions of "lifetime employment" have further reduced this form of capacity adjustment. In its place is increased emphasis on flexibility of the people. The net result is that the traditional concept of direct labor is changing, and its use as a capacity measure is less meaningful in many firms.

In many companies there has been a decrease in the amount of internal fabrication and increased emphasis on outside purchasing. This trend can alter the conception of what capacity requirements are important. Activities such as procurement analysis, incoming inspection, or engineering liaison may become the critical resources.

For many firms engaged in fabrication, the technology of some of the machines is changing very quickly. Flexible automation has greatly increased the range of parts that can be processed in a machine center. The product mix in the future is likely to be much more variable than in the past, and this can have a marked effect on the kinds of equipment capacity required. Moreover, as equipment becomes more expensive it may be necessary to plan and control the capacity of key pieces of equipment at a detailed level.

All these changes mean that the traditional use of direct labor hours and rough-cut capacity planning methods may not be sufficient for managing capacity in the future. In choosing methods for capacity planning and control, two conclusions emerge: the measure should be related to the key capacity constraints, and the appropriate measure well may change in the future.

The first task in choosing a capacity measure is to creatively identify the resources that are key and in short supply. As has been demonstrated, capacity control is far too complicated to apply to all resources. The next step is to define the unit of measure. If the key resource is people, then labor hours may be appropriate. In other instances, such measures as tons, gallons, number of molds, number of ovens, hours of machine time, square yards, linear feet, and so on have all been used. In some cases, these are converted to some "equivalent" measure to accommodate a wider variety of products or resources.

After the resources and unit of measure have been determined, the next concern is to estimate the capacity available. The primary issue here is theory versus practice. The engineer can provide theoretical capacity from the design specifications for a machine or from time studies of people. A subissue is one of whether "full" capacity or some fraction thereof (often 75 percent to 85 percent) should be used . A further issue is "plasticity" in capacity. For almost *any* resource, if it is *really* important, more output can be achieved. We have seen actual performances that fall short of and that exceed capacity calculations.

The choice of capacity measure follows directly from the objective of providing capacity to meet production plans. The appropriate measure of capacity is what most directly impacts meeting these plans.

The measure, therefore, should be appropriate to the key limited resources, be based on what is achievable, with allowances for maintenance and other necessary activities. It must be possible to convert the mix of products into capacity measurement terms. The results must be understood by the people responsible, and they should be monitored.

Choice of a specific technique

The capacity planning techniques discussed in this chapter convert a material plan into capacity requirements. They vary in accuracy, aggregation level, and ease of preparation. Roughly, as the amount of data and computation time increases, the quality and detail of the capacity requirements improve. The issue is whether the additional costs of supporting more complex procedures are justified by improved decision making and subsequent plant operations. It should also be seen that the quality of the material planning system has an important influence on this trade-off.

Considerations other than that of the quality/cost trade-off can influence the choice of the appropriate capacity planning techniques as well. For example, the length of time it takes to change capacity in particular work centers may necessitate a long-range, aggregate approach. If overtime is not easily used or outside contractors are not readily available, there may be no possible short-term capacity changes. Similarly, if the training period for new employees is quite long or alternate routings are not possible, the effect is the same. In these instances, the need for detailed short-range capacity plans is reduced; the problem often becomes one of utilizing existing capacity more effectively.

If the time frame of the decisions is quarterly or longer, then the accuracy differences between CRP and the rough-cut procedures tend not to be significant. If the inventories are kept low by the MPC systems, the bills of material are shallow (do not have many steps from raw material to finished product), and lead times are short, the differences in the results of the techniques tend to be even less significant.

Another factor that should be taken into account is the need for accuracy in stating the capacity requirements and the magnitude of capacity changes that can be made. If the unit of capacity addition is 1,000 tons per week and requirements vary by only 100 tons, it may be that simpler approximations of the capacity requirements for a particular plan will be sufficient for decision purposes.

One important need in managing the capacity of the company is the ability to perform *what-if analysis*. This implies the ability to look at the capacity implications of alternative material plans. This can be done in detail with CRP, but at a substantial computation cost. Alternatively, what-if analysis can be accomplished using rough-cut methods directly from the MPS at a lower cost. This means that the MPS can be changed and the capacity implications reviewed for several alternatives with the rough-cut procedures in the time it would take CRP to evaluate a single alternative. Some firms have chosen rough-cut procedures for precisely this reason.

It would be easy to conclude from our presentation of the four capacity planning techniques that CRP, with its ability to account for actual shop conditions and plans, is the preferred technique. It does provide the greatest accuracy, but at a substantial cost. We have argued that specific conditions in a company, such as the rapidity with which capacity can be changed, will influence the choice. We also pointed to use of what if analysis as a factor in the choice. Thus, the choice is not a strict cost/accuracy trade-off. The important point is to determine which technique allows the manager to make the best capacity-related decisions.

Using the capacity plan

All the techniques we have described provide data on which a manager can base a decision. The broad choices are clear—if there is a mismatch between available capacity and required capacity, either the capacity or the material plan should be changed. If capacity is to be changed, the choices include: overtime/undertime authorization, hiring/layoff, increasing/decreasing the number of machine tools or times in use, and so on. The capacity requirements can be changed by alternate routings, make or buy decisions, subcontracting, raw material changes, inventory changes, or changing customer promise dates.

In short, the management task is to change the capacity to meet the requirements, the requirements to meet the capacity, or some combination of the two. The factors that enter into this task are costs, market position, flexibility, institutional restrictions, and the like. In Europe, Japan, and South America, the task is oriented more toward changing requirements to meet capacity levels than it is in the United States. This is because it is easier to change capacity levels in the United States than in Europe, Japan, or South America.

The choice of capacity planning units can lead to more effective use of the system. Capacity units need not be work centers as defined for manufacturing, engineering, or routing purposes. They can be groupings of the key resources (human or capital) that are important in defining the levels of output of the factory. Many firms plan the capacity solely for key machines (work centers) and gateway operations. These key areas can be managed in detail, while other areas fall under resource planning and the shop-floor control system.

Capacity planning choices dictate the diameter of the manufacturing pipeline. Only as much material can be produced as there is capacity for its production, *regardless of the material plan*. Not understanding the critical nature of the management of capacity has led more than one firm into production chaos and serious customer service problems. In the same vein, the relationship between flexibility and capacity must be discussed. One cannot have perfectly balanced material and capacity plans *and* be able to easily produce emergency orders! We know one general manager who depicts his capacity as a pie. He has one slice for recurring business, one for spare parts production, one slice for downtime and maintenance, and a final specific slice for opportunity business. He manages to pay for this excess capacity by winning some very lucrative contracts that require rapid responses. He *does not add* that opportunity business to a capacity plan fully committed to the other aspects of his business.

One final note on capacity planning: Many managers have complained that they cannot manage capacity, because they do not know what their capacity is. Therefore, they cannot get started until they have completed some engineering studies, and the engineers are busy right now. In many cases, this is a weak excuse for inaction. Someone has some idea of what capacity is! Use this to get started and then use input/output analysis to improve estimates and knowledge of what can be done. The key is to begin; the major ingredient is courage!

DATA BASE REQUIREMENTS

We have seen that each of the capacity planning techniques requires different systems linkages. These linkages imply different data elements and data base considerations. The managerial use of the different capacity planning techniques and enhancements to improve utility can have data base implications as well.

Data base design consideration

The CPOF, capacity bills, resource profiles, and CRP procedures all use MPS data to develop capacity requirements. The CPOF procedure calculates the overall direct labor requirements for the MPS and allocates this capacity to the work centers on the basis of historically observed workload patterns. By contrast, the capacity bill procedure uses bill of material and routing information to calculate the capacity at work centers and, thus, more accurately reflects the particular mix of end items shown in the MPS. The resource profile procedure time phases the capacity requirements by the lead times for component parts and assemblies used in the manufacture of the end items. The CRP procedure uses additional information from MRP and shop-floor control systems to account for the exact timing, quantities, and status of component part and end-item production orders.

We see that there is an increasing requirement for data starting with relatively simple accounting system data required by CPOF. The capacity bills, resource profiles, and CRP techniques each require increased amounts of production/inventory control, industrial engineering, and shop-floor control data. These latter procedures incur successively increasing computational cost, as well. The specific data linkages with the material planning modules are shown in Figure 4.1.

Although the size of the data base for capacity bills is much smaller than for CRP, the CRP data base already largely exists if the firm has a working MRP system. For this reason, many firms use CRP systems to answer questions that could be analyzed at far lower computational cost with rough-cut techniques. They do so because there are no additional data base requirements. All that is needed is the additional computer run time, which can be expensive but is usually available. However, what they do not usually do is what-if analysis. This would be exceedingly expensive. The result is only *one* capacity plan—the one that is associated with the current MRP-based material plan.

Several other factors influence the design and maintenance of the data base. The level of detail appropriate for capacity management implies a corresponding level of detail in the data base and in data base maintenance. If the capacity assessments are made in terms of sales dollars or average labor-hours, the data may be extracted from the financial accounting data base. This reduces the complexity of the MPC data base but requires some coordinating data base maintenance.

The use of input/output analysis requires a communication link with the shop-floor control system to gather the data for analysis. A closely related issue that affects data base complexity is labor productivity. Many firms have standard time data which differ widely from actual practice. What is more, this difference can vary between work centers. This fact can greatly complicate the data base design and maintenance problem, since it is critical to keep track of actual production rates to make an accurate conversion of material plans into capacity needs.

Extended capabilities and data base design. We have discussed the desirability of incorporating a what-if capability into the capacity planning system. This capability creates demands on the data base design that can be severe. The consideration of computer time has already been raised. The need to evaluate a number of alternative material plans means that the ability to easily change the MPS must be designed in. What is more, the changes must be isolated from the current actual MPS and MRP records, both for the sake of recovery and to not create false signals on the shop floor before appropriate analysis and approval have been accomplished.

Along with the capability of what-if testing runs a parallel set of questions on detailed implementation decisions. The choice of the level of aggregation for capacity planning, the size of the time period for analysis, the number of future periods to be analyzed, and the number and composition of machine centers all influence the size, complexity, and maintenance of the data base. If capacity plans are based on one set of numbers and time periods, and another used for making implementation decisions, mismatches and other problems can occur. On the other hand, designing the system to support any kind of question and any kind of decision may be prohibitively expensive.

We are not arguing here that the manager should be happy with what the computer gives him. Not in the least! The computer can and *should* give the manager what is needed! It is just that the choices of data base design, linkages to other modules, and level of detail required are all closely related. Wise choices in the design stage can lead to more productive systems.

Perhaps the ultimate design objective for the data base and its use is to be able to identify and plan for the key work centers as they change over time. This would require careful attention to the design of the input/output module and the tolerance limits used to trigger attention. It would also require flexibility in the data base to permit analysis of different possible groupings over time and groupings that might not correspond to current work centers or labor categories.

EXAMPLE APPLICATIONS

In this section, we provide examples of the capacity planning techniques in practice. Specifically, we look at the use of CRP by the Black & Decker Company and the use of capacity bills by the Twin Disc Company.

Capacity planning at Black & Decker

The Black & Decker Company produces a broad line of consumer workshop, garden, and household products. The production is mostly to stock. Capacity planning at Black & Decker is largely based upon CRP. Figure 4.12 shows the weekly CRP report for one key machine group (KMG073) in department 8–01 of the Hampstead, Maryland, plant. It is called the BH "group," but is comprised of a single critical machine. The time periods are weeks (from 741 through 775). For each week, the projection is based on the combined open shop orders (MRP scheduled receipts) and MRP planned orders. The times include setup hours (S/U HRS.) and run-time hours (OP HRS.).

The weekly capacity of this machine center is 106 hours. Since there is only one machine, 18 hours per day, five days per week, plus 8 hours each

FIGURE 4.12 Black & Decker CRP report

KMG WEEKLY LOADS, HAMPSTEAD

SEQ 1033 KMG 073 DEPT 8-01 CST/CN 063 KMG NAME BH GROUP MACH QTY 1 WEEKLY CAP 106.0

MFG. WEEK	WIP	741	742	743	744	745	746	747	748	749	750	751	752	753	754	755
S/U HRS.	38	5	4	2	5	2	3	6	4	5	2	4	5	3	4	1
OP HRS.	314	104	102	105	95	94	107	111	84	92	41	101	128	100	72	87
TOTAL	352	109	106	107	100	96	110	117	88	97	43	105	133	103	76	88
% OF CAP		103	100	100	94	90	104	110	83	91	40	100	125	97	72	83

MFG. WEEK	756	757	758	759	760	761	762	763	764	765	766	767	768	769	770	771
S/U HRS.	8	1	3	4	3	3	4	5	3	4	9	1	5	5	2	3
OP HRS.	91	92	107	151	65	96	140	86	68	97	117	62	93	98	83	132
TOTAL	99	93	110	155	68	99	144	91	71	101	126	63	98	103	85	135
% OF CAP	93	88	104	146	64	93	136	86	67	96	119	59	92	97	80	125

MFG. WEEK	772	773	774	775
S/U HRS.	3	6	8	2
OP HRS.	91	121	134	104
TOTAL	94	127	142	106
% OF CAP	89	120	134	100

AVERAGE FOR
1st 10 Wks 92%
2d 13 Wks 99%
3d 12 Wks 98%
Tot 35 Wks 97%

NUMBER WKS OVER 80%
30

Source: R. W. Hall and T. E. Vollmann, "Black & Decker: Pioneers with MRP," *Case Studies in Materials Requirements Planning*, ed. by E. W. Davis (Falls Church, Va.: American Production and Inventory Control Society, 1978), p. 38.

on Saturday and Sunday account for all the capacity. The report shows the percent of capacity (% OF CAP) required by the projected arrival of work in each week (planned input). This is shown on Figure 4.12, where 30 out of the 35 weeks shown are loaded to over 80 percent. Black & Decker keeps track of the number of weeks for which the projected needs are in excess of 80 percent of capacity. This is an indicator of potential serious capacity problems. Moreover, the average level for the total 35-week period is shown to be 97 percent.

The capacity problem may be significantly greater than the percent of capacity indicates. The report shows that the current WIP (work in process) or backlog is 352 standard hours. This work is presently at the machine, with 109 standard hours scheduled to arrive in the upcoming week. The work center is already more than three weeks behind schedule. Given the projected load and present capacity, the backlog will not decrease for the foreseeable future.

To complete the capacity planning picture, Black & Decker uses the MRP data base to analyze capacity loads on a quarterly basis and to prepare a four-week, detailed day-by-day capacity report for each work center. The four-week report is the basis for daily capacity planning decisions. Figure 4.13 shows this daily load report for the next four weeks for the KMG 073 key machine group.

The total values for the weeks show the same capacity problem as does Figure 4.12. Also shown on Figure 4.13 is the actual performance for last week as a part of the input/output control information.

As useful as these capacity planning reports have been to Black & Decker over the years, they do not allow for the level of what-if analysis that is desirable. Recently, Black & Decker designed two new systems to support capacity planning. One is a capacity bill approach to rough-cut capacity planning. It produces total dollar output levels by divisions and product groups, work center loadings, and critical machine group capacity requirements directly from the MPS.

The other aid to capacity planning is called *alternations planning*. This approach to what-if analysis allows use of the MRP data base to determine the effect of changing the timing or quantities of selected MPS values. These changes can be evaluated in terms of the time-phased capacity requirements on particular machine centers without disturbing the operative data base. The output of the report shows both the current plan and revised plan in a format similar to that of Figure 4.12. This report permits a quick assessment of the effect of MPS changes.

Capacity planning at Twin Disc

The Twin Disc Company manufactures gears, transmissions, and other heavy components for the farm implement and heavy-equipment industries.

FIGURE 4.13   Black & Decker daily machine load report

```
09/15/   Week 741-1              HAMPSTEAD MACHINE LOAD REPORT              DEPT. 8-01
COST CTR 002   KMG 073       BHG ROUTING MACH      1 MACH @ 18 HRS/DAY   18 HRS/DAY AVAIL
```

741

SCHED OP HRS	-1	-2	-3	-4	-5	-6	-7*	TOT SCH	TOT AVAIL	PCT LOAD	CUM AVAIL HRS
	18	18	19	19	19	8	8	109	106	103	-3

742

SCHED OP HRS	-1	-2	-3	-4	-5	-6	-7	TOT SCH	TOT AVAIL	PCT LOAD	CUM AVAIL HRS
	18	18	18	18	16	8	10	106	106	100	-3

743

SCHED OP HRS	-1	-2	-3	-4	-5	-6	-7	TOT SCH	TOT AVAIL	PCT LOAD	CUM AVAIL HRS
	19	19	18	18	17	7	8	107	106	100	-4

744

SCHED OP HRS	-1	-2	-3	-4	-5	-6	-7	TOT SCH	TOT AVAIL	PCT LOAD	CUM AVAIL HRS
	20	16	18	19	17	7	4	100	106	94	2

HRS PRODUCED LAST WEEK

	AHEAD	CURR	BHND	TOTAL	BACKLOG
		15	93	108	352

*Days of the week.
Source: R. W. Hall and T. E. Vollmann, "Black & Decker: Pioneers with MRP," *Case Studies in Materials Requirements Planning*, ed. by E. W. Davis (Falls Church, Va.: American Production and Inventory Control Society, 1978), p. 37.

It is primarily a make-to-order firm. One part of the capacity-planning system at Twin Disc involves the use of capacity bills for rough-cut capacity planning. An example output from this system is shown in Figure 4.14.

For each machine or work center, the percentage of available capacity required by each of the nine product lines that Twin Disc uses for master production scheduling purposes is shown. For example, the MPS for product line A requires 22 percent of the 1,561 hours of weekly capacity at the 2AC Chucker. The total capacity requirements for all nine product lines indicate a total load of 95 percent of the 2AC Chucker capacity.

Perhaps the most important aspect of this report is the last column. Illustrated here are the managerial actions taken to overcome capacity problems. For example, the Maag gear grinder is loaded to 113 percent of rated capacity by the present MPS. One Reishauer gear grinder, however, is only loaded to 69 percent of its capacity. A decision has been made to use an alternative gear grinder, taking account of the differences in the capacity of the two grinders, roughly a 3 to 1 ratio in the machine-hours required. Other managerial actions shown on the report include moving an additional machine in from another factory and adding more shifts of capacity. The point is that this document is a working document that is used to make effective capacity decisions.

CONCLUDING PRINCIPLES

Several clear principles for the design and use of the capacity planning system emerge from this chapter. Some of the more important are:

- The capacity plans must be developed concurrently with the material plans if the material plans are to be realized.
- The particular capacity planning technique(s) chosen must match the level of detail and actual company circumstances to permit making effective management decisions.
- The better the resource and production planning process, the less difficult the capacity planning process.
- The better the shop-floor control system, the less short-term capacity planning is required.
- The more detail in the capacity planning system, the more data and data base maintenance required.
- It is not always capacity that should change when capacity availability does not equal need.
- Capacity not only must be planned, but the use of that capacity must also be monitored and controlled.
- Capacity-planning techniques can be applied to selected key resources (which need not correspond to production work centers).
- The capacity measure should reflect realizable output from the key resources.

FIGURE 4.14 Twin Disc capacity bill report

Center '03-05	Type	Qty.	No. of shifts	Cap. (hrs/wks)	A	B	C	D	E	F	G	H	I	TOTAL	Remarks
BD	2AC chucker	4	3	1561	22	22	16	3	8	11	11	2		95	
BR	3AC Warner & Swasey	8	3	2966	3	16	46	1	13	2	1	2		84	
CA	Reishauer gear grinder	2	3	900		38			22		12		—	72	Off load to CAB
CAB	Reishauer gear grinder	2	3	950		10	43		13	2			1	69	
CD	P. & W. gear grinder	1	3	544			59		4					63	3:1 ratio
CEA	Maag gear grinder	4	3	3044		10	76		14	5		8		113	Off load to CA, CD
CG	P. & W. gear grinder	4	3	1190			120		8					128	
CI	Pfauter hobber	5	3	2374	6	22	41		9	2	4		2	86	Off load to CI, CW
CJ	Barber colman hobber	1	3	620	27	39	50	1	29	25		8	1	180	
CN	Gear shaver	3	2.5	700	14	37	15		8	9	4			87	
CQ	Gear pointer	1	1	22	13	56	—		12	3				84	
CS	Fellows shaper	1	3	549		37			8	—				45	
CW	Barber colman hobber	3	3	1530	7	12	26	2	8	9	6			70	Off load to CS
CX	Barber colman shaper	1	3	546	—	38	25	7	6	2	24			102	Off load to CS
CY	Fellows shaper	1	3	514	15	77	17		10	12			2	133	Off load to CS
FD	Internal grinder	1	3	285	8	8	10	5	8	4	6			49	Relieve FI and
FI	Internal grinder	1	3	275	25	59	32	11	25	10	9			171	move machine from PLI2
FJ	Surface grinder	1	1	328	6	41	20	1	11	14				93	
FM	Vertical internal grinder	1	2	368		38	57	1	16	1			3	116	Add ½ shift
FY	Gear hone	2	2	528	19	28	11	12	9	5				84	
H	Engine lathe	1	3	427	26	42	29	—	15	8	6		—	126	Off load to HES
HES	W. & S. Lathe—Special	2	2	234	5	43	18	2	11	12				89	Add 1 shift
JA	Horizontal broach	1	1	90	14	3	53		12	3				87	
NH	Gear chamfer	1	3	307	18	42	10		12	11	5			98	
PC	Magnaflux	1	1	240	3	35	48		12	2	2		—	102	Add ½ shift

Work center description · Percent utilization of capacity by product line

Source: E. S. Buffa and J. G. Miller, *Production-Inventory Systems: Planning and Control*, 3rd ed. (Homewood, Ill.: Richard D. Irwin, 1979), p. 598.

REFERENCES

Aherns, Roger. "Basics of Capacity Planning and Control." *APICS 24th Annual Conference Proceedings*, 1981, pp. 232–35.

Belt, Bill. "Integrating Capacity Planning and Capacity Control." *Production and Inventory Management*, 1st Quarter 1976.

Berry, W. L.; T. Schmitt; and T. E. Vollmann. "Capacity Planning Techniques for Manufacturing Control Systems: Information Requirements and Operational Features." *Journal of Operations Management* 3, no. 1 (November 1982).

————. "An Analysis of Capacity Planning Procedures for a Material Requirements Planning System." *Decision Sciences* 15, no. 4, Fall 1984.

Bolander, Steven F. "Capacity Planning Through Forward Scheduling." *APICS*, Master Planning Seminar Proceedings, Las Vegas, April 1981, pp. 73–80.

Burlingame, L. J. "Extended Capacity Planning." *APICS Annual Conference Proceedings*, 1974, pp. 83–91.

Capacity Planning Reprints. Falls Church, Va.: American Production and Inventory Control Society, 1986.

Hall, R. W., and T. E. Vollmann. "Black & Decker: Pioneers with MRP." *Case Studies in Materials Requirements Planning*. Falls Church, Va.: American Production and Inventory Control Society, 1978, p. 38.

Lankford, Ray. "Short-Term Planning of Manufacturing Capacity." *APICS 21st Annual Conference Proceedings*, 1978, pp. 37–68.

Solberg, James J. "Capacity Planning with a Stochastic Flow Model." *AIIE Transactions* 13, no. 2 (June 1981), pp. 116–22.

Wemmerlov, Urban. "A Note on Capacity Planning." *Production and Inventory Management*, 3rd Quarter, 1980, pp. 85–89.

————. *Capacity Management Techniques for Manufacturing Companies with MRP Systems*. Falls Church, Va.: American Production and Inventory Control Society, 1984.

Wight, O. W. "Input-Output Control, A Real Handle on Lead Time." *Production and Inventory Management*, 3rd Quarter 1970, pp. 9–31.

DISCUSSION QUESTIONS

1. The hierarchy of capacity planning activities shown in Figure 4.1 does not show any direct relationships between them, yet there are constraints imposed by the higher-level activities on the lower-level activities. What are those constraints?

2. There are a variety of resources that must be provided in sufficient quantity to meet the material plans. What are some of the resources that may be planned in a capacity planning system?

3. Provide some examples of the capacity planning activities of a university. What would happen if they were not accomplished well?

4. How might one go about measuring planning factors to use the CPOF procedure?

5. What does the expression, "hold backlogs in production and inventory control," mean?

6. The CRP technique requires a substantially greater amount of computation than the other techniques. Can you cite examples where it might be important to have this level of detail for capacity planning, even for the longer run?

7. Contrast what-if analysis and input-output control.

PROBLEMS

1. Finster Farmware has gathered data on the labor and machine hour requirements for producing their Farmhelper models A and B:

	Year 1	Year 2	Year 3
Production A (units)	1,000	1,200	1,500
Production B (units)	500	580	700
Labor hours A	330	360	420
Labor hours B	60	65	70
Machine hours A	100	120	150
Machine hours B	110	116	125

a. What planning factors should they use for year 4?

b. What capacity requirements for labor and machine hours would you project for year 4 if 50 percent of the labor and machine hours each were worked in departments 101 and 102? Use the quarterly summaries of the master schedule shown below to do the projections:

Year 4 quarter	1	2	3	4	Total
Product A	500	800	200	500	2,000
Product B	200	100	300	200	800

2. Tom Swift, the master scheduler at the Grove Manufacturing Company, has prepared the following master production schedule for one of the firm's major end products—the 101 Spray Gun:

Week #	1	2	3	4	5	6
MPS	100	200	—	120	80	240

Tom is concerned about the impact of this schedule on the Final Test Department. The manager of the Final Test Department has indicated that each 101 spray gun requires one-10th hour of skilled labor capacity to test each unit.

a. Prepare a rough-cut capacity analysis for the Final Test Department using the bill of capacity technique.

b. What are the major advantages and disadvantages of the bill of capacity technique?

3. Sarah Reed, the master scheduler at Walnut Hill, has developed a master production schedule for the XYZ boom box:

Month	MPS
1	250
2	400
3	575
4	980

The XYZ is fabricated in several departments, but the circuit board department and assembly areas are the potential bottlenecks. Capacity is 65 hours per week in circuit board and 80 hours in assembly. Each boom box takes 0.1 hours in circuit board and 0.2 hours in assembly. Prepare a rough-cut analysis of capacity for the MPS above.

4. Bray Manufacturing makes a gizmo, which takes one-half hour to assemble and also takes a total of one hour of welding time for the parts. Bray also makes thingamajigs, which require one hour of assembly and two hours of welding. What are the capacity requirements in assembly and welding for the following MPS?

Quarter	1	2	3	4
Gizmos	250	400	300	700
Thingamajigs	180	150	150	700

5. The management at the Green Valley Furniture Company has just approved the following master production schedule for their make-to-stock products:

End product	Week 1	Week 2	Week 3	Week 4
A	30	0	0	10
B	0	40	36	0
C	10*	0	0	30

*The remaining 10 units from a batch of 30 started last week.

The production control manager is concerned about the capacity requirements for one of the automatic machines in the firm's wood shop—the #10 molder. The #10 molder has a fixed capacity of 40 hours per week. The manager has prepared a rough-cut capacity plan for the #10 molder using a resource profile. His calculations are shown below:

Hours per unit of end product produced		
Product	#10 Molder	Lead time offset
A	0.1	1 week
B	1.5	1 week
C	0.1	1 week

Weekly forecast of final product sales	
Product	Forecast (units/week)
A	10
B	25
C	15

Estimated capacity requirements per week (#10 molder)

Product	Forecast	Resources/unit	Capacity requirements
A	10	0.1 hour	1.0 hours/week
B	25	1.5 hour	37.5 hours/week
C	15	0.1 hour	1.5 hours/week
			40.0 hours/week

Evaluate the rough-cut capacity planning procedure used by the production control manager.

6. The Ticky Tacky Knickknack Company produces a knickknack shelf from two end panels, three shelves, fasteners, and hangers. The end panels and shelves have the following data:

End panel			
Operation	Machine	Run time	Setup time
1	Saw	5 min.	.8 hr.
2	Planer	2 min.	.1 hr.
3	Router	3 min.	.8 hr.

Shelf			
Operation	Machine	Run time	Setup time
1	Saw	2 min.	.3 hr.
2	Molder	3 min.	1.2 hrs.
3	Router	4 min.	.7 hr.
4	Sander	1 min.	.1 hr.

The Knickknack cabinet master schedule for the next three weeks is 25, 40, and 10 units, respectively. There is a setup for each MPS quantity.

a. What is the total number of hours required on each of the five machine centers by knickknack cabinets for this three-week master schedule?

b. If each of the two parts is started into production one week (five days) before needed in assembly, and it takes one day per operation, generate the week-by-week load on the routing machine.

c. If, in question b, the two parts were to arrive at the router on the same day, which would you process first? Why?

7. The machine shop at the Northern Steel Company consists of the following equipment:

Plate shear (PS)	One shear for cutting steel plate up to ⅝" thick.
Burnout table (BO)	One burnout table for cutting shaped parts out of steel plate using a template.
Deburring (DB)	One machine for removing sharp corners and rough edges from metal parts.
Milling (ML)	One machine for producing finished surfaces on metal parts.
Grinding (GR)	One grinding machine for producing precision surfaces on flat metal parts.
Welding (WD)	One arc welding machine for producing fabricated sub-assemblies from metal parts.

Orders received by this shop are processed through these work centers in different sequences, depending on the specifications of the part to be manufactured. All of the orders involve taking material, such as bar or plate, from the warehouse inventory and processing this material to meet the customer's specifications. Some of the orders involve cutting metal parts out of steel plate on the burnout table, removing the sharp corners and rough edges, and grinding a precision finish on the top and bottom surfaces of the part. Still other orders involve cutting steel plate into individual pieces on the plate shear, removing the sharp corners, and machining a finished edge on the part, using the milling machine. Finally, some of the orders involve producing metal parts at the shear, milling, and grinding machines and then welding these parts into fabricated subassemblies.

a. The sample of orders shown in Exhibit A can be divided into two types: orders that are first processed at the plate shear (PS) and orders that begin processing at the burnout table (BO). Using this sample of orders, prepare a capacity bill for each type of order, indicating the work centers required for processing and the processing time (in hours per order) for a typical customer order in each order type.

b. Currently, the machine shop anticipates the incoming order rate to be at a level of 50 orders per week over the next six weeks. Sixty percent of these orders are forecast to be plate shear orders and the remainder burnout orders. Using the capacity bill prepared in part a, prepare an estimate of the weekly capacity requirements for each work center in the shop. Enter your results in the capacity planning worksheet in Exhibit B. What are your conclusions?

EXHIBIT A   Sample orders

JOB: 1	Due date: Monday	
Operation	Machine	Hours
1	PS	1

JOB: 11	Due date: Tuesday	
Operation	Machine	Hours
1	BO	2

JOB: 2	Due date: Monday	
Operation	Machine	Hours
1	BO	1

JOB: 12	Due date: Tuesday	
Operation	Machine	Hours
1	PS	2

JOB: 3	Due date: Monday	
Operation	Machine	Hours
1	PS	2

JOB: 13	Due date: Tuesday	
Operation	Machine	Hours
1	BO	2

JOB: 4	Due date: Monday	
Operation	Machine	Hours
1	BO	2

JOB: 14	Due date: Tuesday	
Operation	Machine	Hours
1	PS	3

JOB: 5	Due date: Monday	
Operation	Machine	Hours
1	PS	1

JOB: 15	Due date: Wednesday	
Operation	Machine	Hours
1	BO	2
2	DB	2
3	ML	2

JOB: 6	Due date: Tuesday	
Operation	Machine	Hours
1	PS	1
2	WD	6

JOB: 16	Due date: Wednesday	
Operation	Machine	Hours
1	PS	3
2	DB	2
3	GR	4

JOB: 7	Due date: Tuesday	
Operation	Machine	Hours
1	BO	2
2	DB	3
3	ML	7

JOB: 17	Due date: Wednesday	
Operation	Machine	Hours
1	PS	3
2	DB	2
3	GR	5
4	WD	5

JOB: 8	Due date: Tuesday	
Operation	Machine	Hours
1	PS	2
2	GR	9
3	WD	5

JOB: 18	Due date: Wednesday	
Operation	Machine	Hours
1	PS	2

JOB: 9	Due date: Tuesday	
Operation	Machine	Hours
1	BO	3
2	DB	1
3	ML	4
4	GR	5

JOB: 19	Due date: Wednesday	
Operation	Machine	Hours
1	BO	2

JOB: 10	Due date: Tuesday	
Operation	Machine	Hours
1	PS	3

JOB: 20	Due date: Wednesday	
Operation	Machine	Hours
1	PS	2

EXHIBIT A (concluded)

JOB: 21	Due date: Wednesday	
Operation	Machine	Hours
1	BO	2

JOB: 22	Due date: Wednesday	
Operation	Machine	Hours
1	PS	1

JOB: 23	Due date: Wednesday	
Operation	Machine	Hours
1	BO	2
2	DB	1
3	ML	3

JOB: 24	Due date: Thursday	
Operation	Machine	Hours
1	BO	2
2	DB	1
3	WD	3

JOB: 25	Due date: Thursday	
Operation	Machine	Hours
1	BO	3
2	DB	1
3	ML	3

JOB: 26	Due date: Thursday	
Operation	Machine	Hours
1	PS	3
2	GR	4

JOB: 27	Due date: Wednesday	
Operation	Machine	Hours
1	BO	1

EXHIBIT B   Capacity planning worksheet

	Projection
Orders	
Shear orders (60%)	
Burnout orders (40%)	
Capacity	
Plate shear (80 hrs/wk)*	
Burnout table (40 hrs/wk)	
Deburring (40 hrs/wk)	
Grinding (40 hrs/wk)	
Welding (40 hrs/wk)	
Milling (40 hrs/wk)	

*Capacity available on the plate shear is 80 hrs/wk.

c. At the start of the current week, the machine shop scheduler received a request from marketing to schedule a special rush order of 180 welded assemblies for the Ajax Company. These welded assemblies are to be delivered in three lots of 60 units each during the next three weeks and are in addition to the regular orders forecast in part **b** above. The Ajax order would require processing at the plate shear, milling, and welding work centers. The processing time per unit for this order at each operation is: plate shear, .2 hour/unit; milling, .2 hour/unit; and welding, .6 hour/unit. Where is there insufficient capacity to schedule the production of the Ajax order and to meet the forecast requirements? What should be done to provide the additional capacity?

8. The partial input/output report below was prepared at the end of week 6 for work center 101 at the Benton Plastics Company:

Week	1	2	3	4	5	6

Planned input*	40	40	40	40	40	40
Actual input*	48	49	42	40	38	32
Cum. deviation						

Planned output*	40	40	40	40	40	40
Actual output*	45	44	43	42	41	40
Cum. deviation						

Actual backlog						

*In standard hours.

Beginning backlog = 10 hours

The company would like to maintain the backlog between 10 and 20 hours at this work center.

a. Complete the input/output report for this work center.

b. What recommendations would you make to the manufacturing manager regarding this work center? Why?

9. Roy Harris is evaluating the palm line at the end of week 5 with input/output analysis. Complete the input/output analysis and describe any problems you see.

	1	2	3	4	5
Planned input	65	70	75	80	80
Actual input	63	63	66	67	67
Cumulative deviation					

	1	2	3	4	5
Planned output	75	75	75	75	75
Actual output	70	69	65	68	70
Cumulative deviation					

Actual backlog	20					

10. In jolly England, a specialized company grew pure germanium crystals for use in some of its medical and atomic research instruments. It took about 24 hours for the crystal puller (the firm had only one) to grow one usable centimeter of product for the fabrication departments. Consequently, the firm used a two-week lead time to produce a "batch" of 10 usable centimeters of crystal. The current MRP record for the crystals is shown below.

		Week					
		1	2	3	4	5	6
Gross requirements		2	8	5	8	6	5
Scheduled receipts			10				
Projected available balance	2	0	2	7	9	3	8
Planned order releases		10	10		10		

Q = 10; LT = 2; SS = 2.

a. There was real concern whether the capacity of the puller had been managed correctly, especially since the firm was having difficulty meeting customer delivery date promises. The puller machine engineers had said the machine was capable of pulling two usable centimeters a day (24 hrs.) while operating. The company engineers had said that it was not correct to count on the "theoretical" capacity, but to use 75 percent as the expected output. On the other hand, only over the last few months had the company been able to consistently get one usable centimeter per 24-hour period. Which capacity value do you think should be used? Why?

b. Given the record above, what are the capacity requirements over the next five weeks? (You can assume that the open order has been in progress for almost a week and is about 5 usable centimeters.) How do they compare to the three possible capacity measures? What advice do you have for the management of the firm?

11. The Single Square Company summarizes the capacity requirements for three of its key resources from each of the three product lines it produces. A typical report (before any action is taken) is shown below.

Key resource type			Percent capacity by line				Remarks
Machine	Number	Shifts	A	B	C	Tot.	
Drill 1	1	3	22	13	24	59	
Drill 2	2	3	36	48	36	120	
Drill 3	1	1	52	24	21	97	
Filer 1	2	3	2	0	14	16	
Filer 2	3	3	12	20	8	40	
Dryer 1	2	2	28	36	52	116	
Dryer 2	2	2	72	51	43	166	
Dryer 3	2	1	84	27	24	135	

a. What actions would you recommend (you can assume each machine type is equivalent in terms of capacity)?

b. What other observations would you have for management, based on the report above?

12. The finishing department of the Ragged Edges Company has just upgraded the finishing machine. The firm hoped the capacity would now be 20 units a day. The machine has been tested one full day and the output fell two units short of what was planned, while the input was exactly as planned. To evaluate the performance of the machine, Ragged Edges decided to use a spreadsheet program to create an input/output control report for the next five days, starting with the deviations and backlog (5 units) from the end of the first day. The firm hoped to maintain a 4-unit backlog.

a. What would the input/output control report look like if the firm planned inputs of 23, 14, 17, 20, and 22 units for each of the five days, and actually did input 22, 15, 21, 23, and 19 units, while output was 22, 20, 20, 18, and 21 units? What observations do you have?

b. Suppose the actual input had been 25 units on the last day. What would the report look like (assume no other changes)? Would your comments change? What if the department reported backlog (instead of output) and they told you that the actual backlog was zero for each of the last four days?

c.   What would the input/output control report be if the input had actually been 14, 18, and 20 in the last three days? What observations can you make?

13. Instant Antiques produces a series of antique knickknacks carefully mounted on a knickknack shelf. One of the components of the knickknack shelf is an ornate mounting bracket, which the firm manufactures. The bracket requires forming, cleaning and inspection, welding, another cleaning, and inspection. Two weeks of lead time is allowed, and the first two operations (forming and the first cleaning and inspection) are normally done in the first week and the remainder in the second. The company is anxious to try capacity requirements planning to help them manage the shop.

The MRP record for the mounting bracket for the next few weeks is shown below, along with the capacities and operations times (in hours) for each of the operations on the mounting bracket. In addition, the loads on each of the three manufacturing areas from other items in the shop are given for the next four weeks. A report from the shop floor says that the open order (to be finished this week for use the next) is a little behind. It has gone through forming but is waiting to be cleaned and inspected.

Mounting bracket		Week					
		1	2	3	4	5	6
Gross requirements		2	17	15	12	6	15
Scheduled receipts			20				
Proj. avail. balance	5	3	6	11	19	13	18
Planned order releases		20	20		20		

Q = 20; LT = 2; SS = 2:

Operations times and capacities (in hours):

	Setup	Hours/unit	Capacity
Forming	1.00	1.00	35
Clean and inspect	0.50	0.25	40
Welding	0.50	0.60	35
Clean and inspect	0.20	0.50	40

Hours of work from other jobs in shop:

		Week			
	Past due	1	2	3	4
Forming	10.00	15.00	5.50	24.00	6.00
Welding	0.00	20.00	24.00	14.50	22.00
Clean and inspect	10.50	31.00	27.00	14.00	16.50

    a. What is the total capacity required in Forming, Cleaning and Inspection, and Welding during the next four weeks? What percentage of the capacity available does it represent?

    b. Management has gotten the agreement of some customers to delay the receipt of their goods. The efforts resulted in a shift of 7 units of gross requirements from week two (from 17 to 10) to week 5 (from 6 to 13) of the mounting bracket. What does this do to the capacity utilization in each shop?

    c. Still not satisfied, management decided also to increase the lot size from 20 to 40, since the managers understood this would save on capacity requirements. What is the effect of this change?

14. Instant Antiques, the company in problem **13**, is interested in evaluating its capacity under different scenarios of demand. Use a spreadsheet program to evaluate the capacity implications for forming, cleaning and inspection, and welding if the gross requirements are 10 percent greater in each week (round up to the next integer value in all cases). Repeat the analysis for 20 percent, 30 percent, and 50 percent.

15. Redo problem **14**, but add to the analysis similar increases in capacity requirements for the work coming from other jobs in the shop; that is, now assume that the capacity increases are general across all products made by Instant Antiques.

5

Shop-floor control

This chapter is concerned with the detailed execution of material plans. It describes the treatment required for individual jobs at work centers on the shop floor in order to satisfy the overall production plans. An effective shop-floor control system can lead to due date performance that ensures meeting the company's customer service goals. Management of the system can lead to reductions in work-in-process inventories and in production lead times. Development of a suitable system means paying close attention to the match between company needs and system design choices. A key dimension involves feedback from the system on the performance of the shop against plans. This loop-closing aspect provides signals for revising the plans, if necessary.

The chapter is organized around the following five topics:

- A framework for shop-floor control: How does shop-floor control relate to other aspects of material planning and control? What concepts are important for individual firm decisions?
- Shop-floor control techniques: What are the basic concepts and models used for shop-floor control?
- Shop-floor control examples: How have shop-floor control systems

been designed and implemented in several different kinds of companies?

- The shop-floor control data base: What are the necessary data elements to support a shop-floor control system, and how are they managed in practice?
- Using the shop-floor control system: What are the critical issues to ensure that shop-floor control plays its proper role in a material planning and control system?

Chapter 5 is linked to Chapter 2 in that MRP provides the material plans that shop-floor control executes. Chapter 3 is also of interest because it is there that we discuss the procedural reforms necessary to ensure accuracy in the shop-floor control data base and priorities. Chapter 13 deals with advanced concepts in scheduling that go beyond the basic scheduling techniques presented in this chapter. Chapter 7 deals with just-in-time (JIT) approaches, including kanban systems, which have an important impact on management of the shop floor. Chapter 20 describes the optimized production technology (OPT) approach to manufacturing planning and control and its impact on shop-floor operations.

A FRAMEWORK FOR SHOP-FLOOR CONTROL

Shop-floor control is one of the back-end modules in the material planning and control (MPC) system shown in Figure 5.1. It is concerned with managing the detailed flow of materials inside the plant. In this section of the chapter, we describe the key MPC system linkages to the shop-floor control (SFC) system and the unique company features which might influence SFC design choices.

MPC system linkages

The primary connection between SFC and the rest of the MPC systems shown in Figure 5.1 comes from the box marked *Material and capacity plans*. The capacity plan is especially critical to managing the detailed shop-floor flow of materials. In essence, the capacity provided represents the resource availabilities for meeting the material plans.

The importance of capacity for SFC is illustrated by considering two extremes. If insufficient capacity is provided, no SFC system will be able to decrease backlogs, improve delivery performance, or improve output. On the other hand, if more than enough capacity exists to produce the peak loads, almost *any* SFC system will achieve material flow objectives. It is in the cases where there are some bottleneck areas and where effective utilization of capacity is important, that we see the utility of good SFC systems.

FIGURE 5.1 Manufacturing planning and control system

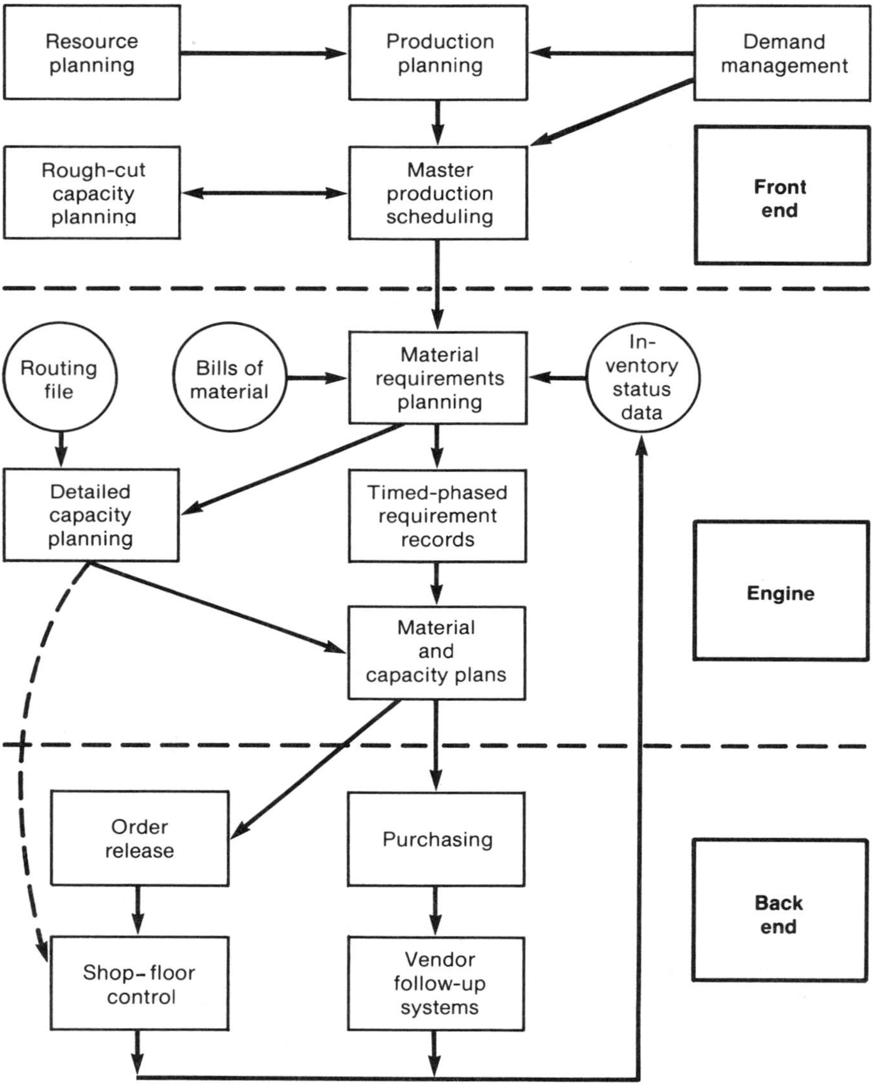

A related issue is the extent to which good capacity planning is done. If the detailed capacity planning activity in Figure 5.1 provides sufficient capacity, with relatively level loading, shop-floor control is straightforward. On the other hand, if peaks and valleys in capacity requirements are passed down to the back end, execution becomes more complex and difficult.

The material plan provides information to the SFC system and sets performance objectives. The essential objective of SFC is to execute the material plan—to build the right part at the right time. This will result in being able to hit the master production schedule and to satisfy customer service objectives.

A critical information service provided by MRP is to keep the SFC system appraised of all changes in material plans. This means revising due dates and quantities for scheduled receipts as needed, so correct priorities can be maintained for SFC. The SFC job begins when a component part planner releases an order. The job thereafter might be likened to a duck hunter following a moving target. The SFC system must keep each shop order lined up with its due date—one that is moving—so overall MPC is supported.

The linkage of shop-floor control with material requirements planning shown in Figure 5.1 clearly implies a due date driven set of priorities for shop-floor control. Also implied is performance measurement of factory operations that is in line with meeting these due dates; that is, shop-floor control is one part of meeting production plans, master production schedules, and detailed MRP-based component plans.

The linkages to SFC are not all one-way. There is an important feedback from the shop floor to the engine. This is the loop-closing aspect of SFC. The feedback is of two types: status information and warning signals. Status information includes where things are, notification of operational completions, count verifications, accounting data, and so on. The warning signals are to help flag inadequacies in material and capacity plans; that is, are we going to be able to do what was planned?

The company environment

We have stated the primary SFC objective as managing the flow of materials to meet MPC plans. In some firms, other objectives relate to efficient use of capacity: labor, machine tools, time, or materials. The role of the particular set of objectives in a firm is critical to the way in which the SFC system is designed. SFC criteria focus on shop orders; capacity criteria focus on the work centers through which the shop orders pass.

The choice of objectives for SFC reflects the position of the firm vis-à-vis its competitors, customers, and vendors. It also reflects the fundamental goals of the company and the constraints under which it operates. In Europe, for example, many firms find changing capacity to be much more difficult than it is in the United States. This viewpoint colors the European view of the SFC system. Similarly, some firms have much more complex products and/or process technologies than others. The result can be a much more difficult shop-floor management problem and a resultant difference in the appropriate SFC system. The net result is that SFC system design must be tailored somewhat to the needs of the particular firm.

SHOP-FLOOR CONTROL TECHNIQUES

This section begins with a description of basic concepts for shop-floor control. Included are priorities, the loading of a particular job onto a machine center, the elements of lead time, and data inputs. We then examine three approaches to shop-floor control. The first, Gantt charts, provides a graphical understanding of the shop-floor control problem; moreover, Gantt chart models can be used in manual shop-floor control systems. The second approach is based on priority rules for sequencing jobs at a work center. The third approach to shop-floor control is finite loading, where an exact schedule of jobs is prepared for each work center.

Basic shop-floor control concepts

Figure 5.2 shows an example product structure for end item A. This example will serve to demonstrate some of the basic concepts that underlie the shop-floor control techniques. One of the essential inputs to the SFC system is the routing and lead time data for each piece. This is presented in Figure 5.3 for part D and part E of the example. The routing specifies each operation to be performed to make the part and which work center will perform the operation.

The production of part D, for example, requires three operations of 4, 5, and 1 days, respectively, for a total of 10 days, or two weeks. Part E requires four operations of 1, 1, 2, and 1 days, respectively, for a total of 5 days, or one week. The remaining lead times shown in Figure 5.2 are all derived the same way. The lead times used for MRP should match those in the routing file. If the MRP time for part E was two weeks instead of one week, the orders would constantly be released one week early.

Lead times are typically made up of four elements:

Run time (operation or machine run time per piece × lot size).
Setup time (time to prepare the work center—independent of lot size).
Move time (from one work center to the next).
Queue time (time spent waiting to be processed at a work center which depends upon workload *and* schedule).

Queue time is the critical element. It frequently accounts for 80 percent or more of the total lead time, and it is the most capable of being managed. Reducing queue time means shorter lead time and, therefore, reduced work-in-process inventory. Achieving the reduction requires better scheduling.

The bottom of Figure 5.3 shows an operation set-back chart based on the lead times for each part. The implications of incorrect MRP lead time can be seen clearly here. If the MRP lead time for part E is not the one week calculated from the routing data, the part will either be released early or late to the shop. Neither of these is a desirable outcome. Note that Figure

FIGURE 5.2   Example product structure diagram

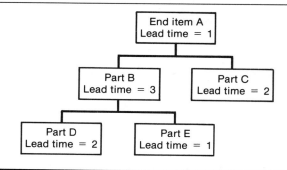

FIGURE 5.3   Routing data and operation setback chart

Part D routing

Operation	Work center	Run time	Setup time	Move time	Queue time	Total time	Rounded time
1	101	1.4	.4	.3	2.0	4.1	4.0
2	109	1.5	.5	.3	2.5	4.8	5.0
3	103	.1	.1	.2	.5	.9	1.0

Total lead time (days) 10.0

Part E routing

Operation	Work center	Run time	Setup time	Move time	Queue time	Total time	Rounded time
1	101	.3	.1	.2	.5	1.1	1.0
2	107	.2	.1	.3	.5	1.1	1.0
3	103	.3	.2	.1	1.5	2.1	2.0
4	109	.1	.1	.1	.5	.9	1.0

Total lead time (days) 5.0

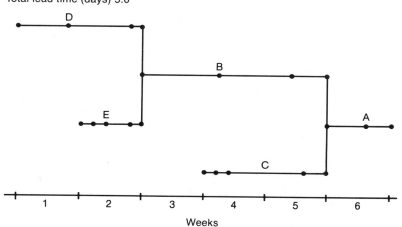

FIGURE 5.4   Work center 101 schedules

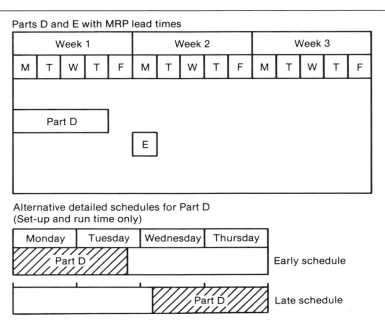

Parts D and E with MRP lead times

Alternative detailed schedules for Part D
(Set-up and run time only)

5.3 shows that both parts D and E go through work center 101 for their first operation. The top half of Figure 5.4 shows the partial schedule for work center 101, with parts D and E scheduled according to the timing given in Figure 5.3.

The bottom half of Figure 5.4 shows two alternative detailed schedules for part D in week 1 at work center 101. The crosshatched portion represents the 1.8 days of lead time required for setup and run time. The first schedule has part D loaded as soon as possible in the four-day schedule shown in the top half of Figure 5.4. The second schedule loads part D into the latest possible time at work center 101.

The key differences between the top and bottom halves of Figure 5.4 are in lead times. The top half includes the queue time. The queue time represents slack that permits the choice of alternative schedules—a form of flexibility. It is also this slack that can be removed by good SFC practice; that is, this schedule allows 4 full days to complete part D, when the actual time on the machine will only be 1.8 days. For the remaining 2.2 days, the part will wait in a queue or be moving between work centers.

The detailed schedules in the bottom half of Figure 5.4 contain no queue time. These schedules represent the loading of a particular job onto a particular work center for a particular time period. The two alternatives shown in the bottom half of Figure 5.4 are different loadings; one typically chooses between alternative loadings so as to utilize the machine center effectively.

Gantt charts

Gantt or bar charts, such as those presented in Figure 5.4, show a schedule. The operation setback chart in Figure 5.3 is very similar. It also represents a schedule for when to make each of the five parts based on lead times that include move and queue times.

One form of shop-floor control is to prepare operation setback charts similar to Figure 5.3 for each job, and use them plus the kind of data presented in Figure 5.3 to prepare Gantt charts, such as those in Figure 5.4; that is, the objective is to prepare a schedule for each machine center. This schedule can be based on the assumptions in either the top or bottom half of Figure 5.4; that is, the schedule may or may not use lead times that include queue and move times.

The more usual practice is to prepare the detailed work center schedule *without* move and queue times. Many firms have systems that do this. The typical approach is a *schedule board* with racks to hold pieces of paper. Each paper is a job and its length represents the time required.

The primary problem with this kind of system is in updating. Actual data must be captured and integrated into an ongoing cycle of replanning. Moreover, a means of communication with the shop floor is usually required, since the schedule boards typically reside in planning offices. However, with personal computers residing on the shop floor, some firms have created what is in essence a fairly dynamic version of the "schedule board."

Priority sequencing rules

Priority sequencing rules are concerned with which job to run next at a work center. To some extent, these rules can be thought of as producing a loading of jobs onto individual machines, but usually only one job is committed at a time; that is, the job to run *next* is only determined near to the time when the prior job has been completed. The priority sequencing rule is just what the name suggests: a *rule* for what job to process next.

Many different priority sequencing rules have been established. A fairly common one is to base priorities on the type of data contained in Figure 5.3. The lower half of that figure contains scheduled due dates for parts and operations. These due dates can be used as priorities. For example, a priority rule could be: the job to process next is the job with the earliest operation due date. An alternative is to next process the job with the earliest *part* due date. Four other commonly used sequencing rules are:

- Order slack: Sum the setup times and run times for all remaining operations, subtract this from the time remaining (now until the part due date), and call the remainder slack. The rule is to work on that job with the least slack. This rule addresses the problem of work remaining.

- Slack per operation: A variant of order slack is to divide the slack by the number of remaining operations, again taking next the job with the smallest value. The reasoning behind slack per operation is that it will be more difficult to complete jobs with more operations because they will have to be scheduled through more work centers.
- Critical ratio: a rule based on the following ratio:

$$\frac{\text{Time remaining}}{\text{Work remaining}}$$

For calculation, the rule is expressed as:

$$\frac{\text{Due date—Now}}{\text{Lead time remaining (including setup,}}$$
$$\text{run, move, and queue)}$$

If the ratio is 1.0, the job is on time. A ratio less than 1.0 indicates a behind-schedule job, while greater than 1.0 indicates an ahead-of-schedule condition. The rule is to always process that job with the smallest critical ratio next.

- Shortest operation next: This rule ignores all due date information as well as all information about work remaining. It simply says, take as the next job the one that can be completed in the shortest time at the work center. This rule maximizes the number of shop orders that go through a work center—and minimizes the number waiting in queue.

In a computerized MRP system, each shop order would be a scheduled receipt for the part. As such, the scheduled receipt has a due date. From this due date, operational due dates could be established by backing off expected operation times, if these data are needed to establish priority sequence. The great advantage of this computer based system is that, whenever the due date for a scheduled receipt changes, the operation due dates can be changed accordingly. These changes, in turn, lead to priority changes for shop-floor control; the result is an execution system that works on the most-needed shop orders first. The objective is for high-priority jobs to move through the shop very quickly, while low-priority jobs are set aside. In this way, the shop-floor control system can indeed execute the dictates of MRP.

In recent times, many companies have developed a preference for sequencing rules that are easy to understand. One straightforward approach to this is to develop operation start and operation due dates, and use them for determining priority sequence decisions.

In a computer based shop-floor control system, due dates would not be printed on any shop paper that travels with the work-in-process inventory. The shop paper would show the routing or sequence of operations (static data), but not any due dates. The changing (dynamic) due date information would be printed daily in the form of a work center schedule or dispatch list for each work center. It is the dispatch list, not the traveling paper, that shows the priority sequence. The dispatch list can be updated as rapidly as transactions are processed to the MRP data base. The daily dispatch list is, in fact, only one option. It is also possible to keep the data even more current, using on-line inquiry for which jobs to run next.

Finite loading

Finite loading systems simulate actual job order starting and stopping to produce a detailed schedule for each shop order and each work center; that is, finite loading does, in fact, *load* all jobs in all necessary work centers for the length of the planning horizon. The result is a set of start and finish dates for each operation at each work center. This schedule is based on the finite capacity limits at each work center. In essence, it is the equivalent of one of the alternative schedules shown in the bottom half of Figure 5.4, but includes *all* of the jobs scheduled for that work center.

Finite loading explicitly establishes a detailed schedule for each job through each work center based on work center capacities and the other jobs that are scheduled. Priority sequencing rules do not consider the work center capacities or the other jobs to be scheduled. For this reason, the priority rules are employed with capacity planning techniques that are based on infinite loading, techniques like resource profiles, or capacity requirements planning.

The difference between finite loading and infinite loading is illustrated by Figure 5.5. The top half shows an infinite loading for work center 101 as it might be produced by capacity requirements planning (CRP). The lower half of Figure 5.5 shows the capacity profile that would result from finite loading. This result (i.e., the capacity profile) is *not* the objective of finite loading; it is the result of scheduling each job through work centers, but never scheduling more work in a center than the center's capacity.

The finite loading approach will only schedule work in a work center up to its capacity. Thus, the 75 hours of work shown as past due in the top half of Figure 5.5 would be scheduled in week 1 under finite loading techniques. Finite loading does not solve the undercapacity problem illustrated in the top half of Figure 5.5. If the capacity is not increased, only 80 hours of work will come out of this work center each week, regardless of the scheduling procedure. Finite loading will determine *which* jobs will come out, based upon priorities.

One output of finite loading is a simulation of how each machine center will operate on a minute-by-minute basis for whatever time horizon is planned. In one approach to finite loading, the simulated running of work

FIGURE 5.5   Infinite versus finite loading (CRP profile for work center 101)

CRP Profile for work center 101

Finite load capacity profile

Open shop orders

Planned orders

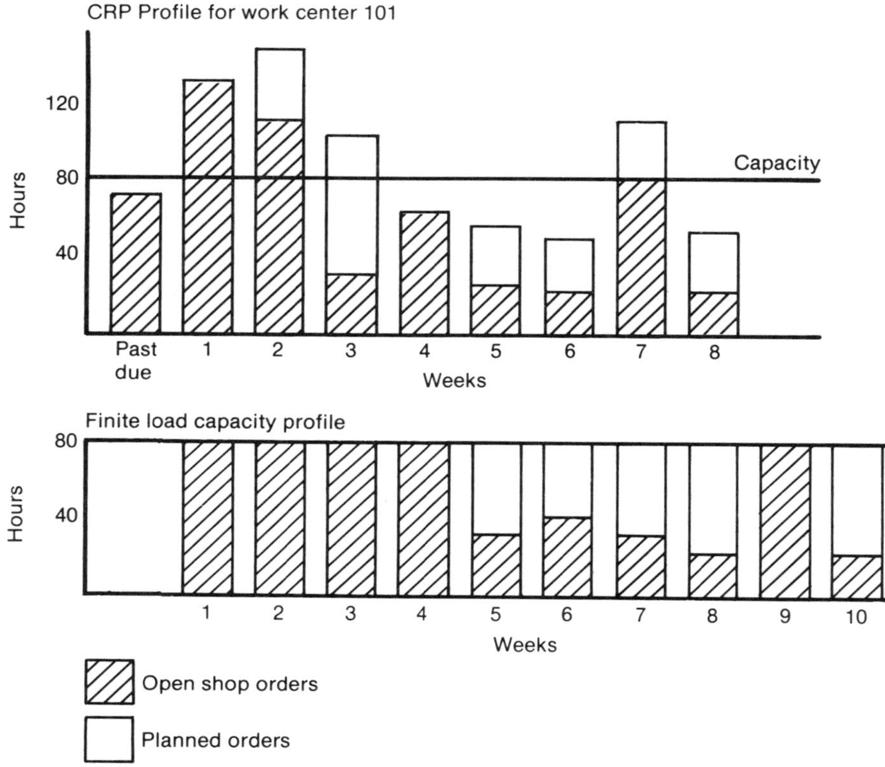

center 101 would proceed as follows, beginning on Monday morning. Assume there is a job already in process, and there are 150 pieces left with a standard time of one minute per piece. Thus, this order would consume the first 150 minutes of capacity; if work started at 8:00 A.M., the machine is loaded until 10:30 A.M. The finite loading system would then select the next order to schedule on the machine, taking account of setup time and run time. This process would be repeated, to simulate the entire working day, then the next day, and so on.

The selection of the next job to schedule is not just based on those jobs that are physically waiting at the work center. Most finite loading systems look at the jobs coming to the work center, when they will be completed at the prior centers, and what priorities these jobs have to decide whether to leave the work center idle and immediately available for the arrival of a particular job. Also, some systems would overlap the operations, so a job might start at a work center before the completion of all work at the prior center.

The approach of filling a work center job by job is called *vertical loading*. It is consistent with the way most job shop scheduling research is conducted, as well as with the priority scheduling viewpoint; that is, one looks at a work center, such as our example center 101, and decides which of a set of jobs (both those at the work center and those scheduled to have had their prior operations processed by the time of the loading) to load next. Another approach is often used for finite loading. It is called *horizontal loading*. In this case, one entire shop order or job (that job with the highest priority) is loaded for all of its operations, then the next highest priority job, and so on. This horizontal approach may well be at odds with a criterion of using a machine center to its maximum capacity. By creating detailed schedules with horizontal loading, the net result can be "holes" in the capacity for a work center. What this implies is that at times a machine is to sit idle, even if a job is available, because a more important job is coming.

Returning to part D in Figure 5.3, we can illustrate the horizontal loading approach. Part D would first be loaded onto work center 101 whenever the previously loaded job is scheduled to be completed. Part D will be scheduled for completion 1.8 days later. At that time, it will be loaded onto work center 109, again as soon as this work center is available. If the prior job at work center 109 has already been completed, this work center will remain idle until part D is completed at work center 101. Finally, part D would be similarly loaded onto work center 103.

Suppose that the next job to be loaded after part D was for part Q, and that the work on part Q commenced in work center 109. Let us also say that, in scheduling part D, the result was idle time at work center 109. *If* (and only if) it were possible to schedule part Q into that idle time *without* disturbing the part D schedule, this would be done.

In addition to the horizontal-vertical distinction, there is also the issue of front scheduling versus back scheduling. The back-scheduling approach would take the job backward from its due date. If the resultant schedule indicates that the *start* date has already passed, one has an infeasible schedule for that job. The front-scheduling approach would load the order in as soon as capacity was available in each work center, and thereby determine the expected *completion* date. If the date is beyond the due date, infeasibility is again indicated. The net result is the need for corrective action.

In either horizontal or vertical loading, there is always the choice of which job to schedule next at a work center. The computer uses priority information somewhat like that used in priority scheduling. The same data (due dates, lead times, and the like) are available, but most finite loading systems can also use managerial weighting factors to augment the other data. These factors are typically used to reflect the urgency of particular orders, the importance of the customer, the nature of the work centers through which the job will travel, and so on.

If the finite loading system were run on a Sunday night, the schedules set for a particular work center for Monday should be reasonably accurate. Part of a particular machine center's capacity may already be allocated to a job in process, and perhaps the other jobs to be scheduled are already waiting in queue at the machine center. However, the schedules for Tuesday must deal with Tuesday's expected starting conditions. Moreover, the jobs scheduled for Tuesday are more likely to come from another work center, rather than already being at the work center. Differences between the simulated operations and actual operations in those centers will be reflected in the actual job arrivals at the work center. These uncertainties on the shop floor mean that there will be a decay in information validity that grows as the time horizon for the schedule is lengthened.

One way to overcome this decay is to redo the planning (finite loading) more often. If it is done each night, the next day's plan will be more accurate. The problem with doing finite loading every night is the cost. Finite loading can easily take 10 times as much computer run time as shop-floor control by priority scheduling.

Because finite loading only schedules a work center up to its capacity (and tries to schedule it up to the limit), it will often be true that matching parts have inconsistent due dates. In our example, assembly A is made up of parts B and C. The due dates for both B and C would be identical under MRP. If part B is delayed for two weeks at some work center, there is no reason to rush completion of part C. Finite loading cannot take explicit account of these product structure relationships in the scheduling process. The use of priority information, other than MRP due dates, can compound this problem.

Proponents of finite loading point to its ability (over CRP) to yield a better forecast of the actual load on each machine center in the near term, say the next few weeks. Although there will be inaccuracies, by simulating the exact flow of orders, the result should be far superior to that based on average queue times. Moreover, the finite loading system will be better than priority scheduling systems for looking out a week or two, because finite systems schedule orders that are one or more work centers away, as well as those at the work center.

The problem of competition between MRP priorities and finite loading, as well as the potential for abusing managerially set priorities, have led many authorities to believe that finite loading is an improper technique that should not be used. The counterargument is that a few companies have, in fact, made it work. It is *not* an easy job. Some critical organizational issues have to be addressed, and the need for accurate standard time estimates, capacities, and other kinds of data integrity is severe.

A partial solution to the problem of MRP priorities versus finite loading is provided by the optimized production technology approach. All jobs are sorted on whether they do or do not use "bottleneck" work centers (a bottleneck work center is one that is loaded to a high level of its capacity). Small subsets of jobs that cross bottlenecks are finite loaded, while the majority of the orders are scheduled using standard MRP approaches. The inconsistency between MRP due dates and those of finite loading is much less severe. Moreover, because OPT only finite loads a small subset of jobs, the computational burden is reduced.

SHOP-FLOOR CONTROL EXAMPLES

In this section we show how the shop-floor control techniques have been applied in three quite different examples. Ethan Allen has a relatively simple product line, with a small number of levels in the bill of materials, a modest number of component parts, and minimal part commonality. Moreover, one portion of their production process is a line flow. The net result is a fairly straightforward shop-floor control environment. They have implemented a manual system based on Gantt chart methods in most of their factories.

The second example is for the Twin Disc Company. Twin Disc has a large number of component parts, complex product structures, long lead times, complex part commonality, and expensive work centers that the firm wishes to heavily utilize. They have implemented a critical ratio based priority sequencing system.

The final example we consider is Swissair. In the Swissair engine maintenance shop the company has a finite loading system for shop-floor control. Each engine to be overhauled is brought in, disassembled, and inspected. It is only at this time that the required work can be determined. Swissair creates a unique routing file for each piece part, based on the inspection decisions. The result is a wide variation in the resulting capacity requirements at each work center. The firm employs a large, highly paid work force that is not easily expanded or contracted. Moreover, overtime is more difficult to schedule than is true for most firms in the United States.

The Ethan Allen shop-floor control system

The Ethan Allen Company manufactures and sells home furniture. Production of wood furniture comes from 14 factories, which are geographically dispersed. The product line comprises about 1,400 items, which can be further condensed into 980 consolidated item numbers (different finishes for the same item). With 980 end items, each made to stock, the average number of products per factory is only about 70. In fact, some plants make as few as 17 end items, while others manufacture as many as 150. The plants with longer product lines tend to have larger numbers of slow-moving items. The result is that, for most factories, the number of items in production at any one time is small, say 5 to 30 items. The average number of component parts per end item is only about 40, with a large percentage purchased, so the number of open shop orders for component parts at any one time is in the low hundreds for most factories. Furthermore, the number of operations per order is not large; a standard series of production line steps results in boards of uniform thickness, length, and width. These typically go through only two or three more operations before becoming completed parts. The sum total of all this is a shop scheduling environment that is not overly complex in terms of the number of orders and operations to be scheduled.

Figure 5.6 is a hypothetical item, in this case a shelf, produced at one of the Ethan Allen factories. Figure 5.6 also shows the necessary component parts for this shelf, and Figure 5.7 shows the Gantt-chart-based schedule for the item. Ethan Allen calls this operation setback chart a "back schedule," because each part is scheduled backwards in time from the desired date for the part to go into the ready-to-assemble inventory (RTA). The RTA stage plays a key role in the Ethan Allen system. This step is designed to achieve proper order closeout for component parts. It also provides a one-week safety lead time.

We now take as an example one part of the shelf, the side (B). Figure 5.8 shows routing information for side B, with the lead time for each operation and the total lead time. As seen in Figure 5.8, there are six operations required to fabricate a side. Figure 5.9 shows the set of shop tickets that correspond to these six operations. In practice, a blank copy of Figure 5.9 is kept in the files, with a copy made for each lot manufactured. Whenever a batch of shelves is to be built, the appropriate due date for each of its component parts, including the side, is taken from the back schedule (Figure 5.7), with the desired assembly date. The due dates for each operation are calculated and handwritten on the shop tickets. There would be one set of

FIGURE 5.6   Ethan Allen product example: shelves

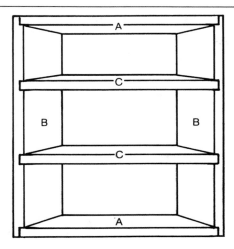

FIGURE 5.7   The Ethan Allen back schedule

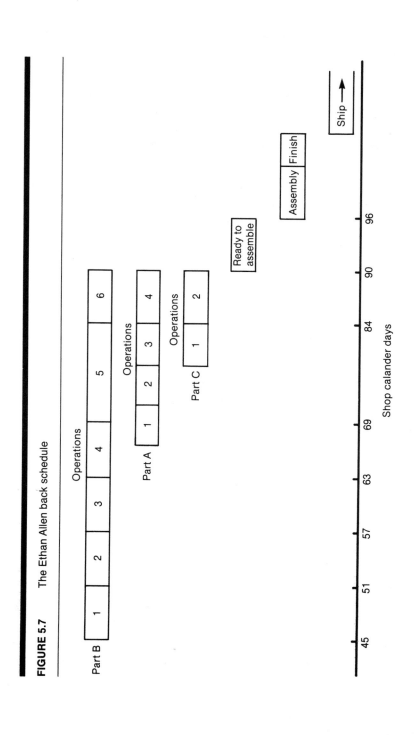

FIGURE 5.8   Routing—side B

Operation	Lead time*
1 Cut to length	1 Week
2 Surface	1 Week
3 Rip	1 Week
4 Surface	1 Week
5 Dado—4 places	2½ Weeks
6 Sand	1 Week

*Consisting of setup time, run time, move time, and queue time.

FIGURE 5.9   Shop paper for side B

Side B	Side B
1 Cut to length	2 Surface
Quantity ———————	Quantity ———————
Due date ———————	Due date ———————
Side B	**Side B**
3 Rip	4 Surface
Quantity ———————	Quantity ———————
Due date ———————	Due date ———————
Side B	**Side B**
5 Dado	6 Sand
Quantity ———————	Quantity ———————
Due date ———————	Due date ———————

shop tickets, such as those shown in Figure 5.9, which would travel with each batch of each component part.

To show how the operational due dates are calculated for the shop tickets, let us assume that the factory wished to assemble 100 shelves in shop week

---

Operation	Due date
1	51
2	57
3	63
4	69
5	84
6	90

272, that the beginning of that week is shop calendar day 96, and that the shop calendar is based upon six-day work weeks. Use of a shop calendar allows ease of calculation of due dates. Signs in the shop remind all workers of what the current shop day is. The resultant operational due dates for side B are shown at the bottom of p. 176.

Sets of shop tickets are created for each batch of component parts, and the resultant orders are issued to the shop according to when they are needed. For example, the side has a due date of 51 for its first operation, cut to length. Since the operation is expected to take six days, this job should ideally be released to the first operation on day 45.

An upside down T-shaped block of wood, called a tilt-up, is placed on top of each batch of component parts. It has clips on both sides of the vertical portion. One clip holds all of the shop tickets in operation sequence. The other is used when an operation has been completed. At that time, the ticket corresponding to the completed operation is removed from the front clip, put on the back clip, and the tilt-up is tipped over. On the bottom it says "move me." A materials handler roams the plant, looking for tilt-ups that indicate movement. When delivered to the department or work center indicated by the next ticket, the back ticket is removed from the load and given to the production control person.

At each work center, the priority sequence rule is to always work on the load with the earliest due date showing on a tilt-up, unless the plant superintendent gives permission to do otherwise. This allows for some deviations to minimize setup or change-over times. These decisions are not left to the workers and first-line supervisors. Their priorities for which job to work on next come from the operational due dates of the back schedule.

In a small office, a copy of each current back schedule is taped to a wall. As each operation is completed, the corresponding portion of the Gantt chart is colored in with a felt-tipped pen. A string is put on the bar chart to indicate the present shop day. Any open space to the left of the string indicates a behind-schedule condition. Any area colored in to the right of the line indicates an ahead-of-schedule condition. By visually reviewing the schedule wall, any scheduling problem can be readily identified.

The exact system described here was implemented in one of Ethan Allen's supplier plants in approximately one month at a critical point in their history. The cash flow situation was critical, with no ready alternative for additional funding. The system was implemented and the result was a reduction in work-in-process inventory of approximately $300,000. A further reduction was obtained after the system had been in operation for about two years, by decreasing the lead time allowed for each operation. Each job went through production faster, spending less time waiting between operations. The result was reduced work in process, reduced lead time, and better responsiveness to actual customer orders. The system was fully maintained by two people, who prepared all back schedules, routing, and shop tickets. They also monitored shop order progress and updated the schedule wall. This firm had annual sales of approximately $5 million and employed about 200 people.

The key limitation of this shop-floor control system is that the operational due dates are static; that is, all back-schedule due dates are based on the date at which each assembly order is to be started, which is fixed. If, for any reason, one wanted to change this date, all shop papers would have to be physically changed in terms of operational due dates. By freezing the master production schedule for eight weeks out, this problem has been minimized at Ethan Allen.

Critical ratio scheduling at Twin Disc

Twin Disc, Inc., is a manufacturer of small-lot, heavy-duty transmission equipment. The products are designed to customer specifications, produced in small lots, and range in unit price from several hundred dollars to over $10,000. Annual sales were approximately $200 million at the time of this writing, with more than one half being to four large customers.

The size of the data base for shop-floor scheduling at Twin Disc is considerably larger than that at Ethan Allen. The number of open shop orders is usually about 3,500. Each order typically passes through 10 to 15 operations, and there are more than 300 different machine centers. The average product is made up of approximately 200 parts, and the total part master data base includes about 60,000 separate part numbers.

Twin Disc installed the critical ratio scheduling system six years after implementing MRP. The MRP system was well understood at that time, and it provided the proper basis for updating the priorities for individual shop orders. Let us now see how this shop-floor scheduling system works.

Figure 5.10 is the daily work center schedule. This report is printed during each night, so it is available to the foremen at the beginning of every working day. The sample report shown as Figure 5.10 was printed for February 6, which was Wednesday of manufacturing week 446. (The manufacturing calendar is based on a five-day week.) It is for the BH machine center which is in plant 3, department 5. This machine center works two shifts and has a weekly rated capacity of 110.9 hours.

The report is divided into two parts. The top portion shows six orders that are presently at the BH work center, and the lower portion shows those orders which are one work center away from BH; that is, the shop orders at the bottom of the page are not now physically at BH, but their routings indicate that, when they are completed at their present work center location, they will be moved to BH for the next operation.

The first two columns on the report are the number and part name. The third column is the shop order number. The fourth and fifth columns are the operation number (i.e., its routing sequence) and a description of the operation. The priority numbers shown in columns 6 and 7 are more easily explained after we discuss the other data. Column 8 shows the quantity that is

FIGURE 5.10 Twin Disc shop-floor control report

```
           DATE 02/06/              DAILY WORK CENTER JOB SCHEDULE        WEEK 446     DAY WEDNESDAY
PLANT 03      DEPT 05            MACH. CTR. BH          SHIFTS WORKED 2.0           CAPACITY 110.9
```

PART # (1)	PART NAME (2)	ORDER # (3)	OP # (4)	OPER DESC (5)	PO (6)	PI (7)	QTY OF OP (8)	QTY AT OP (9)	HOURS (10)	NEXT LOCATION (11)	WORK REM. (12)	TIME REM. (13)
209335H	IMP WHL	@ 438C34	020	FIN	.436		142	142	11.1	0316NB	18.3	8.0
216140A	SPINNER	445C22	010	TURN	1.236		88	88	6.4	0305BQ	18.6	23.0
209308C	IMP WHL	445C67	020	FACE		.430	212	212	16.7	0316NB	18.5	8.0
A 4639A	CARRIER	445B45	010	TURN		2.675	54	54	5.4	**SAME**	8.5	23.0
A 4639A	CARRIER	445B45	020	FACE		2.675	54	54	5.4	0305YE	6.3	23.0
B 1640A	RETAINER	441B22	010	FACE		4.106	108	108	7.3	0305EG	10.4	43.0

TOTAL HOURS IN THIS MACHINE CENTER   52.3

PARTS IN PREVIOUS WORK CENTER

PART #	PART NAME	ORDER #	OP #	OPER DESC	PO	PI	QTY OF OP	QTY AT OP	HOURS	PREVIOUS	WORK REM.	TIME REM.
208346	IMP WHL	443C31	010	TURN	.437		27	27	4.7	0316NBR	18.2	8.0
203587E	FW PILOT	@ 444C98	010	SEMI-TURN	.462		28	28	4.3	0316NBR	17.3	8.0
208346G	IMP WHL	446A09	010	TURN	.742		250	250	15.4	0316NBR	24.2	18.0
208346A	IMP WHL	446A07	010	TURN	.907		1234	1234	62.2	0316NBR	36.3	33.0
B 209335H	IMP WHL	@ 446A10	010	TURN	1.388		141	141	11.1	0316NBR	20.1	28.0
B 5164	RETAINER	445C90	020	TURN		2.006	98	98	6.1	0305BQ	11.4	23.0
A 4639B	CARRIER	446B17	010	TURN		2.215	255	255	12.6	0316NBR	10.3	23.0
208457B	IMPELLER	444A44	010	TURN		3.632	10	10	4.1	0316NBR	10.4	38.0
208346C	IMP WHL	446A08	010	TURN		4.105	50	50	5.8	0316NBR	20.2	83.0

TOTAL HOURS FOR THIS MACHINE CENTER IN PREVIOUS CENTERS   126.3

Source: E. S. Buffa and J. G. Miller, *Production-Inventory Systems: Planning and Control*, 3rd ed. (Homewood, Ill: Richard D. Irwin, 1979), p. 597.

associated with the shop order, while column 9 shows the quantity that is physically at the work center. This distinction facilitates operation overlapping. Column 10 shows the hours that each of the shop orders is expected to take in the BH center. Notice that this column is totaled for both the jobs in the machine center and for the jobs that are one center away. Column 11 shows where each shop order will go when it leaves BH for those jobs at BH, and where each order is for those jobs coming to BH.

Columns 12 and 13 show the work remaining and time remaining for each shop order. In both cases, the figures are stated in days. The time remaining is calculated by subtracting today's date from the due date shown for each of the shop orders as a scheduled receipt in the appropriate MRP record. For example, if one were to go to the time-phased MRP record for part number 209335H, one would find at least two scheduled receipt quantities; one would be for 142 pieces. Although the record might be printed in weekly time buckets, the convention would be to give it a due date of Friday in week 447. The five days of week 447 plus Wednesday, Thursday, and Friday of week 446 yield eight days remaining until this shop order is due to be closed out into inventory. This scheduled receipt for 142 pieces would be pegged to shop order 438C34. A second scheduled receipt for part 209335H would be for 141 pieces, due on Friday of week 451. This order (446A10) is shown as the fifth job in the list of orders one machine center away, with 28 days of time remaining. There could be other open shop orders for part number 209335H as well, but, if so, they are not at BH or at one work center previous to BH.

The work remaining column (12) represents the lead time remaining to complete each order (18.3 days for the first order). This includes setup time, run time, move time, and queue time between operations. We can now define the critical ratio priorities shown as columns 6 and 7:

$$\text{Priority} = \frac{\text{Time remaining}}{\text{Work remaining}}$$

We see there that for the first shop order $(8.0/18.3 = .436)$. This means that this shop order will have to be completed in 43.6 percent of the normal lead time. If this job is not run today, tomorrow's schedule will show a time remaining of 7, and a critical ratio of $7/18.3 = .383$. Any order that has a critical ratio priority greater than 1.0 is ahead of schedule, and any priority less than 1.0 indicates a behind-schedule condition (based on total lead time values).

The distinction between columns 6 and 7, PO versus PI, is that, in the former case, when the shop order is pegged all the way up through product structures, an actual customer order depends upon this particular shop order. It is a priority for *orders*. PI, on the other hand, is a priority for *inventory*. It means that at the present time no customer order promise depends upon the timely completion of this shop order. The order was issued based upon a forecast of customer orders that has not yet materialized.

The work remaining and associated priorities for the orders that are one work center away are based upon completion of the prior operations; that is, the priorities are those that would exist *if* the job were to arrive at BH today. This allows both sets of jobs to be evaluated on a common base.

The jobs are arranged on the daily work center schedule in priority sequence, PO before PI. This is the sequence that the jobs should be run in, all other things being equal; that is, the company believes in running jobs to support customer orders before those to go into stock to support a forecast, and, by running the smallest critical ratio job first, relative priorities are maintained.

In interpreting the shop-floor control report, a foreman knows that a critical ratio of .436 is not a severe problem, providing that *all* of the critical ratios are not less than 1.0. What will happen is that this order will be near the top of the list in each work center schedule as it passes through its routing steps. Since this means that it will be run shortly after arriving at the work center, or perhaps even be started *before* all of the parts are finished at the prior center (i.e., operation overlapping), the queue time will be small and the job should be completed on schedule.

The ability to see jobs that are coming enhances this ability to meet schedules. If the first job in the list of jobs one work center away (part 208346) had a priority of, say, .1, the BH foreman could go to the foreman in 0316NBR (the current location of the job) to see whether the job in BH could be started before all of the parts have been finished in 0316NBR, and perhaps try to overlap the operation following BH, as well.

The report can also be used to sequence jobs to reduce setup times. If the order (446A10) for part number 209335H can be speeded up in 0316NBR, it can be combined on the same setup with order 438C34. Or perhaps running all (or most) of the impeller wheels in sequence makes sense. The report provides relative priority information to the foreman but does not preclude intelligent decision making on his or her part. The extent to which foremen can make decisions at variance with the shop-floor control report should be carefully defined. The key is to provide discretion—but not at the expense of missing due dates.

We have already shown how the priority data change on a daily basis, as the time remaining (numerator) grows smaller, while the lead time remaining (denominator) stays constant. If a job is not completed, its relative priority will increase as it competes against other jobs for the available work center capacity.

The CAPOSS system at Swissair

Swissair operates approximately 50 aircraft on a worldwide basis. Major maintenance is centralized in Zürich, Switzerland, in the Engineering and Maintenance Department (E & M). Approximately 2,600 people are employed in E & M. Swissair also does considerable maintenance work for other airlines.

CAPOSS is an IBM finite scheduling program. The acronym stands for capacity planning and operations sequencing system. The CAPOSS system is used at Swissair for scheduling the engine shop. This shop is responsible for the overhaul of all engines and for the repair of other parts that require operations on engine shop machine tools. The engine shop employs approximately 400 people.

The primary problem in scheduling the engine shop is that more than 60 percent of the repair work on an engine is not definitively known until the engine has been disassembled and inspected. CAPOSS is one of the systems that helps to respond to this inherent level of uncertainty.

Before examining the CAPOSS system itself, it is necessary to briefly overview some other systems and activities that precede it. When an engine is brought in for overhaul, it is disassembled, cleaned, and inspected—all in the minimum time possible. The inspection of a subassembly involves physical measurement and other activities as dictated by detailed maintenance procedures. These procedures originate with the equipment manufacturers. They are translated into German and modified to match Swissair equipment standards. The entire process is done with computerized text editing and is integrated with the overall maintenance control system (MCS) data base.

An inspector uses a video terminal to review the necessary maintenance procedures. Based on tests and measurements, the inspector determines the necessary repair steps for the subassembly and components. This process is, in essence, the determination of a unique routing file for each part and assembly. These data are essential for CAPOSS. The use of interactive computing allows the routing files to be established quickly. A set of shop papers is immediately printed and attached to the work piece. MCS also keeps track of which parts belong to which engine.

A production control group working for the engine shop decides whether a particular part is to be reworked to go back into the same engine or a replacement is to be used. This decision is based upon rework requirements, time availability, capacity loads, replacement part availability, and dictates of the manufacturer.

An engine is defined as being made up of 10 modules. Based upon the completion date for the overall engine, due dates are established for when all the parts of any module are required. These are the due dates by which all parts in that module are to be reworked and are one key input to CAPOSS.

Another key input to CAPOSS is the *external priority*. This is a number from 0 to 9, indicating a production control person's priority to be assigned to this order. It represents a subjective input as to how critical this shop order is relative to other orders.

The CAPOSS system first loads each order with infinite capacity loading assumptions, based on operation times plus standard interoperation times (representing move and queue times). If the resultant completion time is greater than the due date for the reworked parts, a delay factor is computed to augment the external priority. Another step is to reduce the move and queue times. This is based on how late the parts are and can result in inter-operation times being shortened by as much as 50 percent. After this, the external priorities are combined with move and queue time reductions to produce a new priority number. This priority number is used to pick the job sequence for horizontal finite loading for all the jobs through their required work centers.

The system is run daily on a large IBM computer. One output is a schedule of all jobs in each worker center. This serves the same function as a daily dispatch report for shop-floor control. Since the outputs are in German, they are not reproduced here. This listing goes to a production control person assigned to each work center grouping. It is this person's job to actually schedule the work. He or she attempts to combine similar jobs (note that a shop order is issued for each part), attempts to assign jobs to workers best able to do the work, etc. The schedule shows which jobs are in the center as well as those not there. The work center production control person also makes sure that all transactions are accurately entered into the data collection system.

The CAPOSS data base is also sorted by engine. An engine shop production control group gets these data. The result is an ability to foresee part shortages. When this occurs, one typical action is to increase the external priority assigned to the particular shop order. This will result in that order being scheduled earlier on each of the next day's work center schedules.

An engine is always scheduled for overhaul in 21 working days. This time is guaranteed to the customer. The CAPOSS schedule is prepared for 15 days into the future, which is more than the time allowed for machine shop operations. For the work center scheduler, only the first few days in the schedule are of importance. For the engine scheduler, all of the time frame is important; relative priority changes are being made constantly.

At the end of the 15-day schedule, any jobs that have not been scheduled are listed in a separate report, along with their capacity requirements. These data indicate potential work center capacity problems. They are studied closely by the production control supervisor. Remedial actions include overtime, alternate routing, and the increased use of replacement parts instead of reworking parts. The production control supervisor discusses these actions with the manager of the engine shop.

THE SHOP-FLOOR CONTROL DATA BASE

Here we consider the detailed data bases and interactions of the shop-floor scheduling system with other data files and systems. We also raise some managerial issues. As we have seen, the data base for shop-floor scheduling typically includes the open shop orders (scheduled receipts from MRP) and their due dates, routing files, engineering standards or other time estimates for operation times, move and queue time data, and the work centers.

The size and complexity of each of these files varies a great deal from company to company. Some firms, such as Ethan Allen factories, deal with an open order file of less than a few hundred shop orders, whereas Twin Disc typically has 3,500 open shop orders. Similarly, the average number of operations per shop order can also vary widely. The same thing is true for the number of work centers to be scheduled. The net result is that the inherent size of the data base and the number of transactions to be processed each day can vary significantly from firm to firm; the resultant systems and supporting data bases have to reflect these complexities.

Still one other aspect of systems and data base design relates to the kind of questions that will be posed to the system. Some firms like to use their shop-floor control system to answer what-if questions, such as the implications of acceptance of a particular customer order. Others use their systems to track specific orders and want to determine exact order status on a timely basis. These needs must be considered in the design of the shop-floor control system and its underlying data base. Let us now turn to a concrete example of an operating company, where the focus is on the data base and its interactions, rather than on the shop scheduling techniques. Thereafter, we consider new technology being applied to the collection of shop-floor data and management of shop-floor operations.

The Black & Decker Company

Black & Decker manufactures power tools and accessories, such as hand drills, circular saws, impact wrenches, and saw blades for both the consumer and industrial markets. The company's main factory is in Hampstead, Maryland. This factory has approximately 1 million square feet of floor space, annual production in excess of $200 million, and employs about 2,500 people.

The Hampstead plant has about 1,200 machines to be scheduled. The typical number of open shop orders exceeds 3,000. The end items are produced for stock, but almost 15 percent of all parts produced are for service part requirements, and the plant also produces parts for other Black & Decker plants.

The Black & Decker MRP (and related) systems were developed and implemented, starting in 1970. Within five years, the valuation of work-in-process inventory had dropped by 21 percent, while production increased at 10 to 20 percent each year. Job completions on schedule improved by 35 percent, and lead times for components dropped by 30 percent. By 1977, the average shop lead times had been reduced from 6 weeks to 2.9 weeks.

FIGURE 5.11   Black & Decker manufacturing control systems

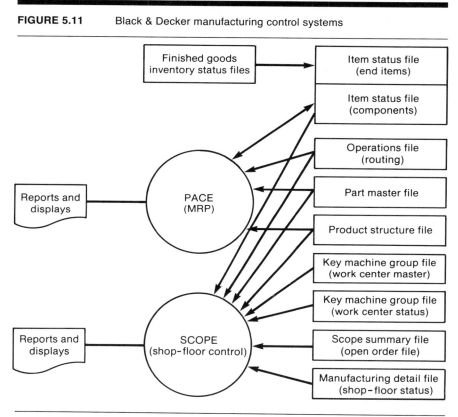

Source: R. W. Hall and T. E. Vollmann, "Black & Decker: Pioneer with MRP," in *Case Studies in Materials Requirements Planning,* ed. E. W. Davis (Falls Church, Va.: American Production and Inventory Control Society, 1978), p. 35.

SCOPE and PACE.   Figure 5.11 shows the primary data base for the Black & Decker manufacturing control systems and the two main programs that interact with the data base, SCOPE and PACE. SCOPE is an acronym meaning: scheduling and control of orders for production economy. PACE stands for planned action and constant evaluation. PACE is the MRP system and SCOPE is the shop-floor system. Parenthetically, Figure 5.11 can be easily compared to Figure 5.1. The finished goods inventory status files are part of the front end, PACE is the engine, and SCOPE is the back end.

SCOPE is the set of computer programs for shop-floor scheduling to execute the plans developed by PACE. SCOPE also has the job of maintaining certain portions of the overall data base. The functions of SCOPE are to:

Schedule orders and plan work center loads.

Coordinate and stage the material for each order.

Release orders to work centers with correct priorities for released orders.

Monitor and control the flow of orders and maintain order priorities.

Maintain order status data.

The SCOPE system is based on the files shown in Figure 5.11. Those that directly interact with SCOPE are:

ITEM STATUS FILES (COMPONENTS). This file is essentially all of the data necessary to prepare MRP time-phased records.

OPERATIONS FILE (ROUTING). This file keeps all the routing data for each fabricated component part.

PART MASTER FILE. This file keeps all of the data for defining each part number. Included are part number, where used, description, low-level code, unit of measure, engineering change status, order policy, lead time, safety stock, planner code, etc.

PRODUCT STRUCTURE FILE. This file is the bill of materials and related data.

KEY MACHINE GROUP FILE (WORK CENTER MASTER). This file contains all of the work centers, as well as related data, such as hours worked per day and hourly capacity per week.

KEY MACHINE GROUP FILE (WORK CENTER STATUS). This file keeps the dynamic data for each work center (called a key machine group), such as which jobs are there, expected jobs, loads, hours ahead, actual results, and backlog.

SCOPE SUMMARY FILE (OPEN ORDER FILE). This file contains all of the scheduled receipts (shop orders) and their present status.

MANUFACTURING DETAIL FILE (SHOP-FLOOR STATUS). This file retains all of the daily transactions for dispatching and labor reporting (e.g., which jobs were worked on, quantities completed, etc.).

The SCOPE system in operation consists of the following 10 programs:

INPUT—Checks all incoming data for consistency and validity.

SCHEDULING—Establishes a detailed schedule file for each shop order.

MACHINE LOAD—Generates a projected four-week detailed load for each work center.

CAPACITY PLANNING—Develops a projected 12-month load for each work center.

MATERIAL AVAILABILITY—Checks material availability two weeks ahead before issuance of shop orders.

PRIORITY DISPATCH—Prints a daily work center schedule similar to that used at Twin Disc, but not using critical ratios.

SHOP PAPER—Generates all the necessary paperwork that travels with the shop order.

STATUS UPDATE—Updates all files from daily transactions.

JOB CLOSEOUT—Closes shop orders, prepares summary data, monitors actual counts and actual times.

WORK IN PROCESS—Collects actual costs of closed orders and prepares various data.

Operation/execution of the SCOPE system is similar to that discussed in the Twin Disc example. As at Twin Disc, the priorities are maintained through interaction between the shop-floor scheduling and MRP programs. We have focused on the Black & Decker example as an effective system for maintaining (in great detail) the data on the shop floor. In fact, Black & Decker regards the job of managing the material flows as "management *by* the data base and management *of* the data base."

Data acquisition and feedback

One of the key requirements of a shop-floor control system is collecting status information on work in process. Included are processing transactions on the completion of a batch at a work center, movement of a batch to another work center, scrap losses, and processing by nonstandard methods.

The need for data integrity is clear, as is the need for promptness of reporting. The ability to update priorities, inform customers, perform CRP calculations, and otherwise adjust plans all depends on data collection being performed effectively. Fortunately, technology is increasingly available. Distributed processing and automatic character recognition help in data acquisition, as well as in changing the balance of effort between a centralized MPC function and one where the shop floor has greater autonomy and responsibility.

Bar coding has made it possible to automate a great deal of data acquisition. Hand-held bar code readers or wands, including those based on laser technology, can quickly and accurately read such information as part numbers and routing steps. While the UPC codes that we see on products in grocery stores generally contain only a limited amount of information, such as the product number, an increasing variety of data is being put in bar code format. Not only is the bar code data base changing, the reader technology is improving, as well. In some cases, local processing can be performed by the wand itself, enabling some of the data editing and processing to take place right at the point of input.

A somewhat different phenomenon is the growth of computational power on the shop floor itself. An evolution from paper systems to "dumb" terminals to "smart" terminals has taken place. The growing power and the shrinking cost of small computers are part of this evolution. It is now practical to have much of the data storage and computational power of mainframe computers on the shop floor.

The combination of improved bar coding, data acquisition, and decentralized computer power means that the character of shop-floor transactions has changed, and that direction for shop-floor management is less in the hands of centralized production control personnel. Some firms with a complex shop environment now have dedicated minicomputers that keep track of the shop data base on a real-time basis. Paper is minimized, and only summary data are transmitted to the mainframe computer.

Shop scheduling based on actual transactions as they occur is a viable approach. In one real-time minicomputer system we have seen, first-line supervisors wand bar coded information from a job card when the job is completed and enter the quantity completed. The computer system does the usual cross checking of data for integrity, and then presents a prioritized list of jobs to work on next, based on up-to-the-minute conditions. The expectation is that the job at the top of the list is chosen, but this choice can be overridden (perhaps another job is more within the capabilities of the particular operator or machine). If the job at the top of the list is not chosen on three consecutive occasions, then the supervisor is blocked from choosing an alternative without higher approval. Jobs passed over, late jobs, and other problem conditions are highlighted for the plant manager. The system uses finite loading for each machine center for a one-week horizon. Beyond that time period, an approach similar to capacity requirements planning (CRP) is used. Alternative routing is readily accommodated, based on local decision making.

A further phase of development in shop-floor control systems is to expand their use beyond traditional MPC system definitions. Quality reporting and equipment maintenance are two problem areas where data can be collected in combination with shop-floor control. Another direction is to integrate shop-floor control systems with computer aided design (CAD) and computer aided manufacturing (CAM). Computer based analysis can be used to develop the routing data base. By integrating these systems, the time frame from product conception to part production can be reduced substantially. Having a good shop-floor control system that routinely plans and controls day-to-day operations is a critical building block for achieving these further levels of system integration.

The managerial tasks of defining the information that should be acquired, and of dealing with the information once gathered, do not go away. The basic conversion of status information into revised plans and determination of early warning data remain as important management tasks. Equally important are a view toward simplification, use of available technology, and integration with other functional systems.

USING THE SHOP-FLOOR CONTROL SYSTEM

The managerial challenge in shop-floor control is to design, implement, and maintain the right system and data base for the company. The design must take account of the inherent complexity of shop scheduling at that firm, as well as of any indirect barriers to implementation, such as an incentive wage system that fosters incorrect reporting. Implementation must also consider the necessary organizational changes, educational requirements, and necessary procedural reforms to achieve data base accuracy.

We have presented several examples that show the necessary match between company conditions and SFC system design. In this section, we consider this issue explicitly. Performance measurement is considered next: Is the SFC system doing what it was designed to do? We then turn to management of lead time—one of the least understood elements of SFC operations. Finally, we discuss some key organizational and management issues facing SFC system users.

Matching the SFC system to the company

We see three critical factors in the design of a specific SFC system. The first relates to the firm's strategic posture in the market. The second factor is the amount and kind of capacity provided for executing the material plans. The third key factor is the nature and complexity of the product, and the process by which the product is produced.

The strategic posture of the company should define the operational objectives of the SFC system. In most of the chapter examples, there is a high implicit customer service objective, which focuses SFC system design on timely production. If a company chooses to compete on the basis of price, however, the primary objective of the SFC system might be to provide high resource utilization. These two objectives, high customer service and high resource utilization, may not be mutually attainable.

There is a close relationship between strategic posture and the amount of capacity provided. In turn, the capacity issue affects the design of the SFC system. One of the costs of providing high levels of customer service may be excess, or highly flexible capacity. An alternative may be a better SFC system. In some market situations, there may be little choice but to provide high service levels. The goal for SFC design in this type of environment is often high flexibility: how to respond to customer needs as quickly as possible. An SFC system that is inherently oriented toward high utilization should not be used. There is no conflict between carrying excess capacity and using it effectively (as opposed to completely).

In some cases, when capacity levels are high relative to demand, the need for a sophisticated SFC system is reduced. When capacity is in short supply, the SFC alternatives have little impact on *average* output rates, but the output of *particular* high-priority jobs can be increased. The key need is to define objectives before finalizing the SFC system design. If capacity is deemed inflexible, the use of finite loading may be indicated, as was the case with Swissair, but finite loading makes less sense if there is surplus capacity.

A concept closely related to the capacity issue is the appropriate unit for shop-floor scheduling. For many firms, it is a group of laborers who get assigned, as needed, to several machines or work centers. In other cases, it may be a unique aggregation of machines that does not match any other work center definition.

The last critical factor in matching the SFC system to the company is the basic product and process design. We saw that Ethan Allen's shallow product structures and short flow times enabled the company to use a manual system with static due dates. With more complicated product structures, there is simply too much data for a manual static system to keep synchronized.

The manufacturing process has several attributes that are important in considering SFC alternatives. One is flexibility; a second is speed of manufacture; and still another is the degree to which all products go through the same sequences (flow shop). If the shop is highly flexible, then alternative routing, operation overlapping, and other techniques can be used, but keeping track of things is more difficult. This may call for greater SFC system sophistication. If the products essentially go through a fixed sequence of steps or through the shop quickly, simple systems may work. The Twin Disc system is designed for long processing times through a variety of routings. Murphy's law has much more time to operate, and the system must respond to all its foibles.

If the operations are long, say weeks, then frequent system updating with short horizons may not be necessary. *But,* if scrap is a significant issue, more frequent updating may be important. If, on the other hand, operations are very short, frequent updating may not be either possible or desirable. Some firms go from raw materials to end items in hours.

Performance measurement

Once the SFC system is in place, a key management issue becomes: Is it performing as expected? For systems with a due date orientation, the obvious measure is the extent to which due dates are met. This is *not* an average measure. Both earliness and lateness need to be taken into account. The objective is to have as small a variation around the due date as possible.

Another issue is to *which* due date performance should be pegged. Since we have seen that due dates change, most firms should be concerned with hitting revised due dates. Note, however, that this measure is highly influenced by the degree of stability in other MPC system modules.

It may be desirable to measure due date changes. Three aspects are important: the number of changes, the magnitude of the change, and any inherent bias in the change process. The more due date changes, the more shop-floor execution is complicated. It is much more difficult to change a due date by five weeks than by one. Also, jobs can't *all* be speeded up (expedited). The expedited jobs should be offset by de-expedited jobs (those given *later* due dates).

A related concept is exemplified by the average priority number in priority sequencing rule systems. For example, if *all* numbers in a critical ratio system are less than 1.0, some corrective action needs to be taken.

Resource utilization is the important objective in some SFC systems. Critical resource units need to be defined, their capacities specified, and measures found for monitoring actual results. Two other measures are work-in-process (WIP) inventory and lead time. These can be monitored in absolute magnitude as well as in terms of some other measure (e.g., percent of sales).

Lead time management

Many people think of lead time as a constant, such as *pi*. In fact, it is not a value to be measured as much as a parameter to be managed. Of the four elements of lead time (setup, processing, move, and queue), the last two can be compressed with good SFC design and practice.

Lead time and WIP are directly related. Moreover, there are critical feedback linkages that operate. The longer the lead time is perceived to be, the longer the time between order launching date and due date. The longer this time, the more orders in the shop. The more orders in the shop, the longer the queue time (and WIP); we have a self-fulfilling prophecy.

Some WIP will be needed at work centers for which high utilization is important. However, a basic principle of MPC systems is to *substitute information for inventory*. The firm does not need to have jobs physically in front of machines. Orders can be held in a computer and converted to physical units only as needed. Studies reported by Plossl and Welch have shown that, for many plants, setup and run time only constitute 10 to 20 percent of the total lead time. The rest is slack that can be substantially cut.

One interesting question is how to manage lead time. This means changing data base elements for both SFC and MRP. One alternative is to go through the data base and systematically change all lead times. If they were reduced, the result could be a transient condition of dry gateway work centers. This might be a reasonable price to pay for the resulting WIP reduction.

Changing lead time data elements naturally leads to the question of how they are established in the first place. For most firms, lead time data are usually an input from some functional area, such as production control. An alternative is to *calculate* lead time. When one thinks about changing lead times as part of a management process, and when one remembers that SFC lead time must be in tune with MRP lead time offset data, this approach has increasing appeal. One firm calculated lead times in the following way:

The lead time for each operation was set equal to setup plus run time (time per piece × lot size), plus queue time (which includes move time).

The nonqueue time was converted to days by dividing the total hours by (7 × number of shifts), assuming 7 productive hours per shift.

The queue time was set equal to two days if the next work center in the routing was in another department, one day if it was in the same department but a different work center, and zero days if it was on the same machine.

The lead time for the total order equals the sum of operation lead times. This time was calculated with an average order quantity, rounded up to a weekly lead time, and used for MRP lead time offsetting.

The selection of the queue time is the critical element in this formula. The values were chosen by taking a sample of 50 parts and using different queue time estimates to yield lead times consistent with production control personnel opinions. The initial estimates were padded, but the company was not very concerned. Once the system was in operation, the estimates for queue times were systematically reduced, a bit at a time. The result was a managed approach to shorter lead times and reduced work in process.

Before leaving this discussion, it is useful to look at the results achieved by one firm. David A. Waliszowski says a $25 million division of Hewlett Packard reduced lead time by 70 percent and increased customer-service levels by 80 percent. This amounted to a $1.7 million reduction in work-in-process inventory and was achieved in three months.

The SFC system users

We turn now to our final issue in using a shop-floor control system. The key questions are: Precisely who is to use the SFC outputs? How are they to be used? What are the relationships between front-line supervisors, MRP planners, and other MPC system personnel?

In the discussion of critical ratio schedules at Twin Disc, we saw how the foremen used the SFC output to make detailed daily decisions that influenced their departments: what to make, when to make it, whom to assign to particular jobs, how to work with other foremen to solve material/ capacity problems, and so on. At Ethan Allen, the scheduling discretion of the foreman was much more limited. At Swissair, the approach is different. A production control person is assigned to groups of work centers. This person plays the key role in making the detailed daily scheduling decisions.

There is a fundamental difference between these approaches, and the difference is intimately related to the SFC system itself. A priority scheduling rule system is usually easy for first-line supervisors to understand. If they have some flexibility in how to use the system, they can become quite knowledgeable about important trade-offs. A key disadvantage of most finite loading systems is that they are *not* transparent to the first-line supervisors. It is difficult for them to see why schedules are as they are. Also, there is an implied centralization of authority. The detailed schedules are determined by "the computer"—and the implication is that one is less free to tinker with the results. The use of personal computers and the philosophy of decentralized computation are changing this view of finite loading. With dedicated computer power on the shop floor, the mysteries of finite loading are being reduced. Moreover, detailed knowledge that only resides in the heads of first-line supervisors can be integrated with the results of computer based analysis.

Within any SFC system, there are always issues that are not formally included in the analysis. Perhaps a particular job is better given to a particular worker or a particular machine. Perhaps if the sequence of jobs run on a particular machine were changed, a faster changeover could be achieved. Sometimes analysis of the schedule discloses potential late jobs, missed due dates, or poor work center utilization that could be improved. Moreover, there can always be the occasional order that must be added to the schedule.

The approach to solving these problems is twofold. First, many finite loading systems are designed to incorporate such flexibilities as alternate routings, overtime, subcontracting (a form of alternate routing), order splitting, operation splitting, operation overlapping, and preparing combinations of front and back schedules.

The second approach to resolving problems is through manual (i.e., nonprogrammed) intervention. A person, usually with a cathode ray tube (CRT) display, locates the order for a missing component part, traces its simulated schedule through work centers, and tries to find some way to get the component order completed faster. The way may be to use one of the flexibilities listed above—but one that was not a formal part of the computer logic. What this means is that the use of finite loading clearly recognizes that not all approaches to solving problems can be reasonably put into the computer.

The issues of precisely *who* is going to make the decisions and how much latitude that person will be given are important. A closely related question is who has the better knowledge of how to make this kind of decision? Is it the foremen who know the machines, people, and other constraints, or is it the production control staff person who knows MPC systems? This question naturally leads to several others, including the basic design of the SFC system itself. If foremen are to be the primary users, a transparent system is important. Also important are education and training for these people. In the last analysis, if information is to be traded for inventory and other kinds of slack, first-line supervision increasingly becomes a job of processing information. This may well lead to new job descriptions for first-line supervisors.

The final managerial challenge is to ensure that the formal SFC system is used—and continues to be used. All informal systems must be killed off and not allowed to reappear. No hot lists or other informal scheduling can be allowed, since these come at the cost of degradation in the formal system. Of course, a successful system remains a success only if the users believe in the system and use it for problem solving, because it is better than any alternative way to solve problems.

CONCLUDING PRINCIPLES

We see the following principles emerging from this chapter:

- Shop-floor control system design must be in concert with the needs of the firm.
- The shop-floor control system should support users and first-line supervisors, not supplant them.
- Organizational goals and incentives must be congruent with good SFC practice.
- Discretion and decision-making responsibilities in shop-floor control practice need to be carefully defined.
- SFC performance should be defined and monitored.
- Feedback from SFC should provide early warning and status information to other MPC modules.
- Automated reading systems and distributed computers are changing data acquisition and shop-floor decision making.
- Lead times are to be managed.
- The informal system must not be allowed to supplant formal use of SFC.

REFERENCES

APICS. *Operations Scheduling Seminar Proceedings*, January 1979.

Baker, Eugene F. "Flow Management: The 'Take Charge' Shop Floor Control System." *APICS 22d Annual Conference Proceedings*, 1979, pp. 169–74.

Belt, Bill. "Input-Output Planning Illustrated." *Production and Inventory Management*, 2nd Quarter 1978.

Biggs, Joseph R. "Priority Rules for Shop Floor Control in a Material Requirements Planning System under Various Levels of Capacity." *International Journal of Production Research* 23, no. 1 (1985), pp. 33–46.

Goddard, W. E. "How to Reduce and Control Lead Times." *1970 APICS Conference Proceedings*, pp. 198–205.

Hall, R. W., and T. E. Vollmann. "Black & Decker: Pioneers with MRP." In *Case Studies in Materials Requirements Planning*, ed. E. W. Davis. Falls Church, Va.: American Production and Inventory Control Society, 1978, pp. 22–47.

Hoffmann, T. R., and G. R. Scudder. "Priority Scheduling with Cost Considerations." *International Journal of Production Research* 21, no. 6 (1983), pp. 881–889.

Lankford, R. I. "Input/Output Control: Making It Work." *1980 APICS Conference Proceedings*, pp. 419–20.

―――. "Scheduling the Job Shop." *1973 APICS Conference Proceedings*, pp. 46–65.

Melnyk, S. A.; S. K. Vickery; and P. L. Carter. "Scheduling, Sequencing, and Dispatching: Alternative Perspectives." *Production and Inventory Management*, 2nd Quarter 1986, pp. 58–68.

Melnyk, S. A.; P. L. Carter; D. M. Dilts; and D. M. Lyth. *Shop Floor Control.* Homewood, Ill.: Dow Jones-Irwin, 1985.

―――. *Production Activity Control.* Homewood, Ill.: Dow Jones-Irwin, 1987.

Nellemann, D. O. "Shop Floor Control: Closing the Financial Loop." *1980 APICS Conference Proceedings*, pp. 308–12.

Philbrook, S. D. "Competency in Bar Code Menus and Templates." *P and IM Review and APICS News*, November 1983.

Plossl, G. W., and W. E. Welch. *The Role of Top Management in the Control of Inventory.* Reston, Va.: Reston Publishing, 1979, p. 78.

Production Activity Control Reprints. American Production and Inventory Control Society, 1986.

Raffish, Norm. "Let's Help Shop Floor Control." *Production and Inventory Management Review* 1, no. 7 (July 1981), pp. 17–19.

Schonberger, Richard J. "Clearest-Road-Ahead Priorities for Shop Floor Control: Moderating Infinite Capacity Loading Unevenness." *Production and Inventory Management*, 2nd Quarter 1979, pp. 17–27.

Waliszowski, David A. "Lead Time Reduction in Multi Flow Job Shops." *1979 APICS Annual Conference Proceedings.*

Wassweiler, W. L. "Fundamentals of Shop Floor Control." *1980 APICS Conference Proceedings*, pp. 352–54.

―――. "Material Requirements Planning: The Key to Critical Ratio Effectiveness." *Production and Inventory Management*, 3rd Quarter 1972, pp. 89–91.

―――. "Shop-Floor Control." *Annual APICS Conference Proceedings*, 1977, pp. 386–91.

Williamson, R. F., and S. S. Dolan. "Distributed Intelligence in Factory Data Collection." *P and IM Review and APICS News*, February 1984.

DISCUSSION QUESTIONS

1. Suppose there were an average of 20 students per year in your major and that the number of graduates varied between 15 and 30 each year. One required course, open to both juniors and seniors, is offered once a year and has a capacity of 20 students. What SFC system would you use to assign students to that course? Would it make any difference if the course capacity was 40 students or 10 students per year?

2. What kind of warning signals would you like fed back from the SFC system to the MRP system?

3. Lead times have sometimes been called "rubbery." What accounts for this concept of elasticity in lead times?

4. In the list of priority rules, there is no first-come/first-served (FCFS) rule, yet most banks, cafeterias, movie theater ticket booths, etc., use this rule in waiting on patrons. Why isn't it a suggested rule for the shop floor?

5. Will vertical loading produce a different schedule than horizontal loading in a finite scheduling system?

6. What is your feeling about having separate priorities for customer orders and inventory orders like they do at Twin Disc?

7. The design of the SFC system involves several trade-offs. Provide some examples of such trade-offs and how they might be resolved.

8. How would you determine how much discretion to give the foreman in combining and reprioritizing jobs?

9. What benefits might be gained by having clerks in a retail store use a wand to read tags on items?

PROBLEMS

1. The Bob Row Ski Company uses three machines to manufacture specialty ski boots. The incoming jobs follow different routes through the shop. For example, a job may be required to be processed on machine 1 first, then machine 3, and finally machine 2. The following table contains information regarding the next four jobs to be scheduled at the company (it is currently April 2):

Job	Job arrival date	Required job/machine routing	Machine 1	Machine 2	Machine 3
A	April 2	2-1-3	1	2	2
B	April 2	3-1-2	1	1	4
C	April 4	1-3-2	3	1	2
D	April 6	3-2-1	2	2	2

Assume that the material for all jobs is ready for processing as soon as the jobs arrive and that a first-come/first-served sequencing rule is used. Assume also that all three machines are idle as work begins on April 2.

a. Construct an appropriately labeled Gantt chart depicting the processing and idle times for the three machines for these four jobs.

b. How many days does each job wait in the queue for processing on machine 3?

2. The production manager at the Knox Machine Company is preparing a production schedule for one of the fabrication shop's machines—the P & W grinder.

He has collected the following information regarding the jobs currently waiting to be processed at this machine:

Job	Machine processing time (in days)*	Date job arrived at this machine	Job due date
A	4	6–23	8–15
B	1	6–24	9–10
C	5	7–01	8–01
D	2	6–19	8–17

*Note: this is the final operation for each of these jobs.

a. The production manager has heard about three dispatching rules—the Shortest Operation Next Rule, the First-Come/First-Served Rule, and the Earliest Due Date Rule. In what sequence would these jobs be processed at the P & W grinder if each of these rules were applied?

b. If it is now the morning of July 10 and the Shortest Operation Next Rule is used, when would each of the four jobs start and be completed on the P & W grinder? (Please express your schedule in terms of the calendar dates involved, assuming that there are 7 working days each week and 30 days per month.)

3. Jobs A, B, and C are waiting to be started on machine centers X and then be completed on machine center Y. The following information pertains to the jobs and work centers:

Job	Hours allowed for machine center X	Hours allowed for machine center Y	Day when due
A	55	16	10
B	128	22	16
C	90	20	20

Machine center X has 60 hours of capacity per week (5 days) and machine center Y has 40 hours of weekly capacity. Two days are allowed to move jobs between machine centers. Scheduling these jobs by earliest due date, can they be completed on time?

4. Are the jobs in problem 3 on time using the critical ratio technique?

5. Can the jobs in problem 3 be completed on time (using the earliest due date or critical ratio technique) if 30 hours of overtime are run in work center X each week?

6. Can the jobs in problem 3 be completed on time (using the earliest due date or critical ratio technique) if only one day is required between operations?

7. The customer for job B in problem 3 has agreed to take half of the order on day 16 and the rest on day 25. Use earliest due date to schedule the four jobs

EXHIBIT A

	Inventory information					Shop information				
Order number	On-hand inventory	Reorder point	Safety stock	Average daily usage	Manufac- turing lead time remaining	Shop time accumulated to date	Time remaining until due date	Current operation processing time	Number of operations remaining	Total processing time remaining
1	80	160	10	10	15	1	7	2	3	8
2	120	160	10	10	15	5	11	3	4	8
3	−10	210	10	10	20	14	−2	5	2	8
4	−40	160	10	10	15	5	−5	4	3	8
5	40	160	10	10	15	13	3	1	12	8

Note: The inventory data is measured in units, and time is measured in days.
Shop time accumulated to date (and also manufacturing lead time remaining) includes both the machine processing time and the length of time orders spend moving and waiting to be processed in a machine queue. Current operation processing time (and also total processing time remaining) do not include any move or queue times.

(A, B1, B2, C). Can they be completed on time assuming that no extra setup time is required for splitting job B?

8. Ms. Mona Hull is in charge of a project to build a 50-foot yacht for a wealthy industrialist from Jasper, Indiana. The yacht is named the *Nauti-Lass* and is scheduled to compete in the famous Lake Lemon Cup Race. Assume that there is a 6-week lead time for constructing the yacht. Assume also that each week consists of 5 work days, for a total lead time of 30 days. The work required to complete the yacht is comprised of 10 operations, three days for each.

   a. On Tuesday morning of week 2, 2 of the 10 operations had been completed and the *Nauti-Lass* was waiting for the third operation. What is the critical ratio priority?

   b. What is the critical ratio priority if only 1 of the 10 operations is completed by Tuesday morning of week 2?

9. The Ace Machine Company is considering the use of a priority scheduling rule in their fabrication shop and must decide whether to use: (1) the Critical Ratio Rule, (2) the Order Slack Rule, (3) the Shortest Operation Next Rule, or (4) the Slack Per Operation Rule. The current inventory and shop status of the company are given in Exhibit A.

   a. State the formula for calculating the priority index for each of the four sequencing rules given above.

   b. Compute the scheduling priority for each order in Exhibit A, using each of the four sequencing rules.

10. The production scheduler at the Bedford Machine Shop has just received the following order for a machined part:

Order No. 6243				
Operation number	1	2	3	4
Machine number	1	4	3	2
Estimated time*	6	4	2	8

*In standard hours.

   a. The Bedford Machine Shop allows two days between machine operations for material handling time, etc. The shop works five days per week on a single work shift, and no overtime is planned for the near future. Given the following loads at each machine center, determined by finite scheduling in the machine shop, determine a schedule for each operation on the new job and indicate when this order can be shipped. (None of the currently scheduled jobs can be changed.)

Machine #	Weekly capacity*	Number of machines	Week #						
			1	2	3	4	5	6	7
1	40	1	40	40	30	20	15	10	5
2	80	2	80	50	80	80	70	60	40
3	40	1	20	15	10	5	2	—	—
4	120	3	120	120	120	120	110	102	90

*In standard hours.

    b. Given the information displayed in the shop load table, what capacity recommendations would you make to management?

11. The XYZ Company uses MRP to plan and schedule plant operations. The plant operates five days per week with no overtime, and all orders are due at 8:00 A.M. on Monday morning of the week required. It is now 8:00 A.M. on Monday morning of week 1, all of the machines are currently idle, and the production manager has been given the information in Exhibit B.

    a. Assuming that the Shortest Operation Next Rule is used to schedule orders in the shop, how should the open orders (scheduled receipts) for items A, B, and C be sequenced at their current operations? What are the implications of this schedule?

    b. Assuming that the Critical Ratio Rule is used to schedule orders in the shop, how should the open orders for items A, B, and C be sequenced at their current operations? What are the implications of this schedule?

EXHIBIT B MRP system data

Item A

Week		1	2	3	4	5	6	7	8
Gross requirements		3	16	8	11	5	18	4	2
Scheduled receipts			30						
Projected available balance	10	7	21	13	2	27	9	5	3
Planned order releases			30						

Q = 30; LT = 2; SS = 0.

Item B

Week		1	2	3	4	5	6	7	8
Gross requirements		2	5	12	4	18	2	7	10
Scheduled receipts				30					
Projected available balance	12	10	5	23	19	1	29	22	12
Planned order releases			30						

Q = 30; LT = 4; SS = 0.

Item C

Week		1	2	3	4	5	6	7	8
Gross requirements			14	4	12	7	8	3	17	2
Scheduled receipts			20						
Projected available balance	17	3	19	7	0	12	9	12	10
Planned order releases		20		20					

Q = 20; LT = 4; SS = 0.

EXHIBIT B (concluded)

Shop floor control system data

Item	Routing					Current operation number
A	Operation number	1	2	3	4	3 (Machine 2)
	Machine number	4	6	2	3	
	Processing time*	1	1	1	1	
B	Operation number	1	2	3	4	2 (Machine 2)
	Machine number	4	2	6	1	
	Processing time*	4	2	5	3	
C	Operation number	1	2	3	4	4 (Machine 2)
	Machine numer	6	3	1	2	
	Processing time*	3	4	6	1.5	

*In days. Assume that there are 1.5 days of move and queue time associated with each operation for computing lead times.

    c.   Suppose that 32 additional units of item B have just been found in the stockroom, as a result of a cycle count. What actions are required on the part of the MRP planner?

12.   Using the data for the Ethan Allen shelves given in Figures 5.6 through 5.9, fill in the four shop tickets shown below for part A. The order is for 100 completed shelves to be assembled, starting on shop day 96. The four operations and lead times are also shown below.

Operation	Lead time	Shop tickets	
1. Cut to length	1 week	**Part A** 1. Cut to length Qty._____ Due date_____	**Part A** 2. Rip Qty._____ Due date_____
2. Rip	1 week		
3. Surface	1 week		
4. Sand	1 week	**Part A** 3. Surface Qty._____ Due date_____	**Part A** 4. Sand Qty._____ Due date_____

13.   On Monday morning of the week before the annual shutdown, the Limited Hours Company had orders in the shop for five products (cleverly called A–E),

which had arrived in alphabetical order. Management had decided not to take any more orders until after the shutdown, and the five orders on hand were assigned priorities in the order of arrival (i.e., A–E). Delivery promises had not been made on any of the orders yet. Each order went through the same three machine centers, but not necessarily in the same sequence. Each order had to be finished at a machine center before another could be started. They could not be split.

The Company worked a demanding three-hour day, and so they were concerned whether there was enough total machine time (capacity) to finish the five orders in the five days remaining before the shutdown. Data on each order are given below (you can assume that the time to move between work centers is negligible).

Order	Machine center routing	Hours at machine center		
		1	2	3
A	1–3–2	2	4	4
B	2–1–3	2	6	3
C	3–1–2	5	1	4
D	1–2–3	3	1	2
E	3–2–1	2	3	1

  a. Is there enough machine time to finish the orders?

  b. Using the horizontal loading technique to schedule each order through the machine centers, on what days can the deliveries be promised?

  c. What changes occur if you use the vertical loading method?

14. On a busy day in June, the Framkrantz Factory had five jobs lined up for processing at machine center 1. Each of the five jobs went to machine center 2 after finishing at machine center 1. After that they had different routings through the factory. It is currently shop day 83 and due dates have been established for each job. Machine time includes setup time, but it does take one day to move between centers and two days of queue time at each center (including Finish). The data are summarized below.

Shop day = 83	Machine center sequence for the jobs and days of machine time required						
Job	1	2	3	4	5	Finish	Due date
A	1	4				X	102
B	3	2	8			X	123
C	3	8		2		X	104
D	6	2	1		3	X	98
E	4	1		8	2	X	110

  a. Use a spreadsheet program to calculate the priorities for the jobs shown above using the critical ratio rule.

b. All of the jobs were at machine 2 by the morning of shop day 96. (Job A took 2 days instead of 1 and Job D took 1 day instead of 6 on machine 1.) Unfortunately, there was a long job on machine 2 and none of the five had started yet. What would their priorities be for machine 2?

c. What would they be if Job A's due date was 96?

15. Shown below is the MRP record for Part Number 483. The current shop day is 100 (with 5-day weeks) and it is Monday of week 1. Open orders (scheduled receipts) are due on Mondays (shop days 100, 105, 110, etc.) of the week for which they are scheduled.

The shop floor has just reported that the batch of 40 on shop order number 32 has just finished at machine center A43 and is waiting to be moved to C06. It takes one day for moving between machine centers (or to I02, which is the inventory location) and one day of queue time at the machine centers. (The inventory location does not require the queue time, but one day of "machine time" is shown for clearing the paper work.) The routing and status of Part number 483 are also given below.

Part No. 483

Week		1	2	3	4	5	6
Gross requirements		14	4	10	20	3	10
Scheduled receipts			40*				
Projected available balance	20	6	42	32	12	9	39
Planned order releases					40		

Q = 40; LT = 2; SS = 5
*Shop Order Number 32

Part No. 483

Routing (mach. cent.):	A12	B17	A43	C06	I02
Machine time (days)	4	1	3	1	1
Status shop ord. 32:	Done	Done	Done		

a. Use a spreadsheet to replicate the MRP record and calculate the critical ratio for Part Number 483. Should the planner take any action?

b. What would the priorities be if the inventory was 23 instead of 20? What action should be taken now?

c. What if inventory was 17 instead of 20?

—6————————————————

Purchasing

It is clearly beyond the scope of this chapter to discuss the entire subject of purchasing. Instead, we concentrate on how manufacturing planning and control (MPC) systems can be integrated into the purchasing activity. The demonstrated results of effecting that integration are impressive. Vendor delivery performance improvements, reduced purchased material inventories, lower prices, sharply decreased vendor lead times, and more satisfactory relationships with vendors have all been attained.

The integration of MPC systems must be viewed in the context of the dramatic changes affecting purchasing today. These include increasing outsourcing, worldwide procurement, pruning of the vendor base, closer integration of vendors with engineering and manufacturing, application of just-in-time (JIT) approaches, and electronic data interchange (EDI) networks to link firms with suppliers. In all of these changes, the role of scheduling takes a central position. MPC systems are not the source of *all* the new payoffs in purchasing, but good MPC systems are a necessary condition to the achievement of dramatic results.

This chapter is organized around the following five topics:

- Purchasing in MPC: How is the purchasing function integrated with a well-designed manufacturing planning and control system?

- Vendor relationships: What are the relationships that should be established with vendors and how are they monitored?
- Purchasing systems and data base: What are the purchasing systems and the underlying data base to support them?
- Organizational change: What changes are necessary to use these systems effectively?
- Results: What improvements in purchasing performance have been achieved by leading-edge companies?

The ideas in this chapter closely parallel those in Chapters 5 and 7, on shop-floor control systems and just-in-time approaches. We view the management of vendor capacity as closely analogous to managing the firm's own capacity resources. Additional technical material on determining purchase order quantities, and some techniques for determining safety stock levels, are found in Chapters 12, 17 and 18.

PURCHASING IN MANUFACTURING PLANNING AND CONTROL

Figure 6.1 is again our general model of a manufacturing planning and control (MPC) system. Purchasing is found in the back end. As an execution system, it has the same role as shop-floor control. Within the MPC system, both purchasing and shop-floor control have the objective of executing the detailed planning developed by the material and capacity planning techniques.

In many firms, for each dollar of sales, $.50 or more is spent for purchased items. The potential for improvement is profound. For example, a study team at the Xerox Corporation recently uncovered a whopping 30 to 40 percent disparity between copier manufacturing costs for Xerox and its Japanese competitors. Since Xerox is not vertically integrated, the purchased material costs in copy machine manufacture ran about 80 percent of total manufacturing cost. The message was clear to the members of the materials management team at Xerox. Supplier costs needed to come down and their quality level to come up.

The integration of MPC systems with purchasing and the vendors represents one part of an overall program to improve supplier cost and quality performance. The object of the MPC system is to improve the planning and control of vendor capabilities through procurement; thereafter, vendor capabilities are scheduled in ways analogous to those used in shop-floor control.

Breadth of the purchasing function

The purchasing function encompasses a multitude of activities. Among the most important are:

FIGURE 6.1   Manufacturing planning and control system

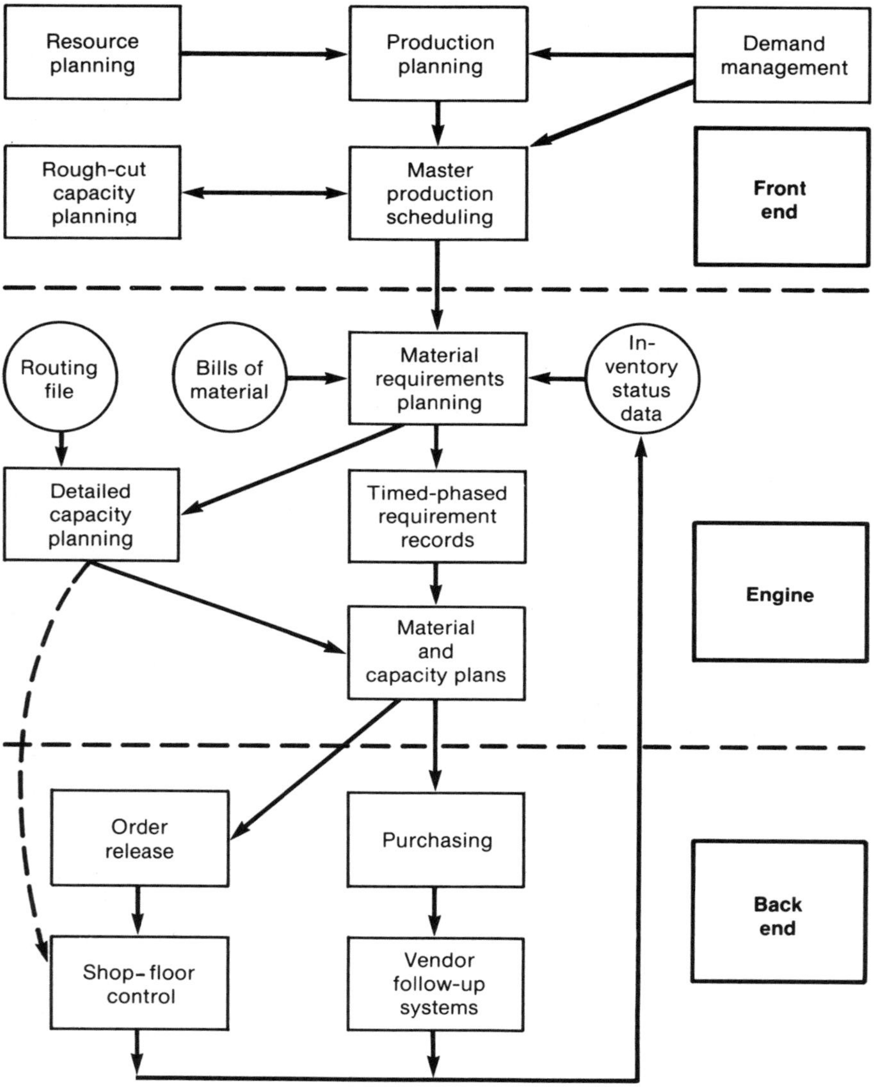

- Sourcing—finding sources of supply, guaranteeing continuity in supply, ensuring alternative sources of supply, gathering knowledge of procurable resources.
- Value analysis—finding less expensive substitutes, helping to isolate

areas where redesign can be particularly appropriate, trying to use more standardized components.

- Contracting—seeking quotations, evaluating quotations, negotiating, establishing relationships with vendors, evaluating vendor performance.
- Budgeting—including price planning, cash-flow forecasting, cost improvement programs, strategic planning.
- Purchasing—committing to specific purchase orders, establishing lot sizes, order releasing.
- Monitoring—controlling the open purchase orders, expediting and deexpediting, order closeout.

The six categories of purchasing activities listed above are arranged from those of strategic importance to the firm to immediate action activities that affect day-to-day operations. Major emphasis is being placed on the purchasing function in many firms as they struggle to compete around the globe. The scope of this activity is being enlarged as purchasing receives increased responsibility for the worldwide sourcing of a greater dollar volume, including parts and even major assemblies. The extent of the changes that such programs require is illustrated by the materials management arm of the Xerox Corporation's reprographic manufacturing group. Highlights of their program are shown in Figure 6.2.

There are many well-known manufacturing firms, such as General Electric, that are adopting a strategy of procuring a much larger portion of their

---

FIGURE 6.2   Purchasing programs at Xerox Corporation

- Drastic pruning of the vendor data base, and the establishment of a centralized commodity management (CCM) organization with worldwide scope.
- Closer relations with design and manufacturing engineers, with buying teams sited right in engineering to support new product development.
- A quantum jump into part-by-part sole sourcing, to take advantage of volume economies and suppliers' know-how.
- Intensive training of suppliers in such techniques as statistical process control (SPC) and just-in-time (JIT), including Xerox-led tours of Japanese firms.
- Longer-term contracts that impel suppliers to become business partners, and build confidence to the point where suppliers share what they've learned—as from trips to Japan—with other firms in their industry.
- Personnel development programs that use functional and geographical shifts of people to build a multinational staff with a broad range of skills.

Source: "Professional Excellence Award: Rank Xerox Our 1985 Winner," *Purchasing*, June 1985.

products. Some of these companies will perform little or no traditional manufacturing and become increasingly service-oriented. In such firms, a variety of profit-making activities are performed, ranging from design to distribution, but without a production base. In contrast to the traditional manufacturing firms, they are "hollow corporations."

MPC functions, such as production planning, master production scheduling, and capacity planning, will be critical in the hollow corporation. However, the MPC back end functions will become almost exclusively concerned with planning and controlling operations of suppliers. As manufacturing, sourcing, and markets take on an increasing global perspective, the MPC systems will require corresponding adaptations.

The MPC focus

There have been many books written on the subject of purchasing, and we have but one chapter. Our focus will be on systems: systems for routinely controlling the flows of materials that are purchased. Although this will touch on some of the purchasing activities delineated above, it will not lead in any direct way to all of them. Our emphasis will be on the systems to support the material and capacity planning decisions for purchased items, and thereafter, on using these systems effectively to implement an organizational climate in which purchasing managers can manage.

At the heart of everything in this chapter is a critical assumption: An MPC system is in place—and it works. There is basic data integrity and a match between planning and execution. The records can be believed and are used for decision making. This assumption is vital, because, in many firms, critical human resources are consumed in expediting and in clerical activities because of not being able to believe what the formal MPC system says.

To free up procurement personnel for the important tasks, it is necessary to develop routine systems for planning the purchase commitments, executing the plans, monitoring actual conditions, replanning as required, and managing the purchasing detail.

VENDOR RELATIONSHIPS

The primary objective in procurement should be to establish reliable sources of supply that effectively augment the firm's internal capabilities. Vendor firms have capabilities that can be utilized. Moreover, if the vendor can improve and better utilize his capabilities, the resultant savings can be passed along to the final consumer. The major savings in purchasing within an integrated manufacturing planning and control system come from a reduction in slack. Slack in purchasing takes the form of larger inventories, extended lead times, extra safety stocks, more obsolete parts, extra capacities, poor vendor performance, expediting, and panic operations. All of these can be reduced if the buyer regards the vendor and his or her capabilities with the same reverence extended to internal capabilities. From the vendor's perspective, his or her master production schedule is made up of purchase orders and planned orders from customers. One objective of purchasing systems is to help the vendors do a better job of master production scheduling. Doing so will help them produce efficiently and on time.

Quantity planning

With a working MPC system as a given, the quantities to be purchased are clearly depicted by the MRP time-phased records. Scheduled receipts are open purchase orders. Planned orders as they mature (move into the most immediate time bucket), represent the need to issue additional purchase orders. This illustrates the close system linkages between purchasing and other MPC modules.

A key factor in slack reduction has to do with the linkage between production control and purchasing. In many companies, the former group issues orders to buy to purchasing (often called traveling requisitions). These documents are an anachronism from the days when production control was the only group close enough to the real world of the shop to estimate actual needs. This practice retards the development of purchasing as a profession. It builds in extra lead times, provides only a very short horizon, takes little account of vendor capacities or discount schedules, and leads to expediting/panic operations as the way of life.

If one can believe in the MPC system, all of the needs are shown by that system as accurately as they can be known. Murphy's law is still in operation, but the effects of all current conditions (good and bad) are reflected in the data base. Purchasing and production control have the same job: To provide material coverage for those part numbers that have been assigned, in the most effective way possible.

Providing purchasing with access to the entire MPC data base for purchased parts has many important potential advantages. The entire set of planned orders can be used to establish relationships with vendors that go well beyond a particular purchase order. The data can be converted to expected vendor capacity needs. The contractual relationship can be for the total volume, say for a year. Release of actual orders is a separate question, as is the vendor's internal decision for lot sizing.

One job of a purchasing professional is to estimate these capacity needs with the vendor, establish a relationship that, in effect, purchases some specified vendor capacity, determine the terms of the agreement, and monitor the agreement and conditions over time. The release of actual purchase orders is constrained by the agreement, and can become a fairly routine interaction between clerical people at the buying firm and clerical people at the vendor.

We have noted how MPC systems substitute information for inventory and other forms of slack. If one considers the vendor's problem of estimating the demands placed by the buying firm, an excellent example of this substitution can be seen. The vendor's forecasting system will tend to average the demand, which well may be lumpy. Safety stocks and other hedges become necessary. The information contained in the planned order rows of the buying firm's MRP records provide a much better estimate of demand. This will enable the vendor to commit short-term capacity to actual orders and to plan longer-term capacity requirements.

The effort to develop this close relationship does not make sense for all vendors. Some represent only trivial or occasional purchases to the buying firm, and others may regard the buying firm as a trivial customer. But for key purchasing relationships, the buyer should recognize that his purchase orders, as well as his planned purchase orders, should be used as a key component of the vendor's master production schedule.

Another approach to joint buyer-vendor quantity planning can be based on capacity-planning models. Many firms now work with their vendors to plan capacity for several years into the future. Old relationships based on fear of being committed to specific firms, single suppliers, or inflexible quantities are now being replaced with an understanding of the need for mutual, ongoing relationships. The benefits of these relationships can often far outweigh the expected costs of commitment, particularly under present world conditions.

The commitment between the buying firm and the vendor can take many forms; for example, the *blanket order* represents a commitment, by which a buying firm specifies some supplier for some specific items for some time period, often a year. In one form, the blanket order does not commit the firm to any specific quantities, but only provides the vendor with an estimate of needs and the commitment to buy solely from him or her, providing the terms of the contract are maintained. A more definitive buyer-vendor relationship provides a *rolling schedule* of requirements for some time period, with a definite commitment for the buying firm to accept those requirements for a given number of weeks. A variation is to commit to buy some specific product for X weeks plus the vendor's raw materials for an additional Y weeks.

In general, the vendor would prefer the more specific set of commitments. With these, capacity can be specifically committed, and reserve capacity to cover customer whims can be minimized. The key to providing these kinds of commitments is through MPC systems.

An example of this approach, providing information and making commitments to vendors, is that used by the Steelcase Company. Figure 6.3 shows a report for one of their vendors; in this case, Cannon Mills. The items purchased are fabrics for upholstered furniture. Note that all of the orders through the week of 8/26 are asterisked, which means that they are firm

FIGURE 6.3 Steelcase requirements for Cannon Mills for the week ending 07/22

ALL TAGGED ORDERS (*) ARE FIRM
OTHER ORDERS ARE EXPECTED DATES AND QUANTITIES

PART NUMBER DIV	FINISH CODE	DESCRIPTION	NO. DATE BUYER	REC'D LAST WEEK	REQUIREMENTS								ON-HAND	ISSUED LAST WEEK
					CURRENT & PAST DUE	7/29	8/05	8/12	8/19	8/26	NEXT 4 WEEKS	FOLLOWING 4 WEEKS		
904550000 4	5350	RED COTTON	9-0553 A 05/08/ 010				400*		400*		400		442	
904550000 4	5351	RED RED ORANGE COTTON	9-0553 A 05/08/ 010		800*	800*	800*	800*	1200*	1200*	1200	1600	359	215
904550000 4	5352	RED ORANGE COTTON	9-0553 A 05/08/ 010	415	785*	800*	800*	400*	800*	800*	400	1200	415	
904550000 4	5353	YELLOW ORANGE COTTON	9-0553 A 05/08/ 010		800* / 400*	400*	400*	1200*	800*	400*	800	1200	50	118
904550000 4	5355	YELLOW COTTON	9-0553 A 05/08/ 010	402	331*		400*	400*		400*	400	400	1804	120
904550000 4	5356	YELLOW YELLOW GREEN COTTON	9-3553 A 05/08/ 010		200*	400*	400*	400*	400*	400*	400	400	237 237H	
904550000 4	5358	GREEN COTTON	9-0553 A 05/08/ 010	416			400*	400*	400*	400*	400	400	384	64
904550000 4	5360	BLUE COTTON	9-0553 A 05/08/ 010	416	384*	400*	400*	400*	400*	400*	400	400	416	
904550000 4	5368	TAN VALUE 1 COTTON	9-0553 A 05/08/ 010	1445	1600* 1600*	800*	400*	800*	800*	800*	1600	1600	1502	234
904550000 4	5369	TAN VALUE 2 COTTON	9-0553 A 05/08/ 010	725	75*				400*	400*	400	400	1305	197

Source: P. L. Carter and R. M. Monczka, "Steelcase, Inc.: MRP in Purchasing," in Case Studies in Materials Requirements Planning, edited by E. W. Davis (Falls Church, Va.: American Production and Inventory Control Society, 1978), p. 215.

commitments on Steelcase's part. Also shown are orders for the next four weeks out. With many of their vendors, Steelcase would commit on these, to the extent of the vendor's investment in raw material.

In this example, the two firms agree on the production of a particular cotton cloth, with a later decision on the specific color it is to be dyed. The job of purchasing is to negotiate the form of the commitment, when and how these "time fences" (cotton versus color) are to be crossed, prices, lot sizes, and so on.

The report shown as Figure 6.3 can be sent directly to the vendor. Steelcase has eliminated the use of formal purchase orders for all but occasional purchases. This not only saves on paperwork but also cuts response time, another form of slack.

At Steelcase there is an informal agreement that is believed in: Help your vendors when they are acting in your interest. An example was that of an important vendor who was in a cash bind. Steelcase loaned this firm $50,000 interest-free to purchase needed raw materials. The purchasing systems are used extensively, but to *support* professional procurement, not to replace it.

An interesting example of a mutually beneficial commitment is that between the Twin Disc Company and one of its vendors, Neenah Foundry, described by Burlingame and Warren.

For Neenah Foundry, the critical measure of capacity is molds per time period for particular molding centers. The Twin Disc data base has all of its Neenah Foundry castings coded as to which mold center at Neenah is required and how many castings are made in one mold. The result is an ability to convert all of the Twin Disc requirements into Neenah capacity units of molds per time period.

The two firms have an agreement on the number of molds per month that are allocated by Neenah to Twin Disc. The length of the agreement is "out as far as Neenah is scheduling into the future." Neenah allowed for changes beyond 90 days and an ability to go 10 percent over or 5 percent under the allotted molds in any one month. The timing for when a commitment to specific end-item castings was required was from 6 to 12 weeks, depending upon the particular casting process.

The benefits from this mold allocation program are significant for both the buyer and the seller. From Twin Disc's point of view, its ability to predict needs is much better in total than for specific items. The firm is able to wait until only 6 to 12 weeks remain to specify end-item castings, when foundries are quoting 50 week delivery times to others. Twin Disc purchases over 80 percent of its castings and forgings in this way.

From Neenah's point of view, they are able to level out their workload. In one year prior to institution of the mold allocation program, they experienced a swing from a 52-week backlog to not enough work to support the labor force. The program also results in reduced clerical costs, because the customers of Neenah on the mold allocation program wait until the last moment to specify end-item castings, avoiding numerous order changes. Neenah has extended the mold allocation program to other customers, and has the goal of devoting at least 50 percent of its capacity to this program.

Price planning

Many authorities believe that price determination is secondary to quantity coordination. If the proper planning for vendors is done, lower prices will be achieved. It is less a matter of bargaining than a matter of cooperating. Moreover, most professionals believe that other considerations, such as continuity of supply, quality, and delivery performance, are at least as important as the price.

The establishment of price is, of course, a matter of negotiation in many cases, and this subject is beyond our present scope. With a good plan for quantities and timing for the quantities, as well as an agreement on the terms of commitment, economies can be achieved by the vendor that can be shared.

A useful model for cost estimation is the learning curve. Again, a thorough discussion of this technique is beyond our present scope. The general concept is that, for each time the cumulative number of units produced doubles, the average cost per unit should be reduced by some constant percentage. For example, if the average unit cost for the first 100 units were $10, and the firm was on an 80 percent learning curve (20 percent improvement), the expected average unit cost for the first 200 units would be $8, for the first 400 units, $6.40, and so on.

The learning model can be built into the price that is negotiated with vendors, either formally or informally. The end result might be a price that is valid for certain quantities with a lower unit price for higher volumes. The quantities expected (and their timing) can be provided by the MPC system.

Another issue in price planning is how the buying firm should respond to a price discount schedule provided by a vendor. The discount may be based on the vendor's perception of learning, or on the allocation of a fixed setup cost over larger volumes. When the demand for an item is lumpy, as it can be with MRP, the determination of the quantity to purchase in each batch is best decided with discrete lot-sizing methods which take into account the price discount schedule.

Vendor scheduling

Vendor scheduling involves release and continuing communication of priorities to released purchase orders. It is the equivalent of shop-floor control, but done for outside work centers. Most of the objectives described for company-owned work centers are applicable to the outside work center, as well. The primary distinction is that, to the vendor, each customer is only one of many sources of demand.

Figure 6.4 is a vendor report that is analogous to a shop-floor control report. Again, it is for the Twin Disc Company; the firm calls it the "Open

FIGURE 6.4   Twin Disc Company, open p.o. buyer fail-safe report

02/05		OPEN P.O. BUYER FAIL-SAFE REPORT.					WEEK-343	
BUYER	VENDOR #	PART #	ORDER #	WEEK #	QTY.	FWEEK	FQTY.
D	52487	# 9670A	791930	345	5	345	1
D3	52487	# 9670B	819371	360	50		
D1	52487	# 9682	789410	344	50	338	19
D1	52487	# 9700B	808601	347	35	347	3
D3	52487	# 9753A	819380	352	100		
D3	52487	# 9791A	789561	345	25	348	25
D3	52487	# 9791A	810201	351	65	351	1
D1	52487	# 9813	810211	354	50		
D3	52487	# 9815B	788760	343	15		
D3	52487	# 9824	819390	350	25		
D3	52487	# 9825	793490	346	50	349	15
D1	52487	# 9841	793730	345	50		
D3	52487	# 9870A	758611	347	50		
D1	52487	# 9957	810220	348	25		
D1	52487	#201522	825880	352	1000		
D3	52487	#203717A	822100	354	250		
D1	52487	#205826	819330	349	100	349	38
D3	52487	#205896	826850	358	25		
D3	52487	#205896L	825890	357	50		
D3	52487	#206207	793770	348	200	346	108
D1	52487	#206331	791841	351	50	350	13

Source: E. S. Buffa and J. G. Miller, *Production-Inventory Systems: Planning and Control,* 3rd ed. (Homewood, Ill.: Richard D. Irwin, 1979), p. 589.

P.O. Buyer Fail-Safe Report." This report lists all of the open purchase orders (scheduled receipts in MRP records), sorted by vendor.

In Figure 6.4, all of the purchase orders listed are for a single vendor. The first column on the report lists the buyer who placed the purchase order. The second column is the vendor number (52487), and the third column is the particular part number on order. The fourth column is the purchase order number for the particular scheduled receipt quantity. Notice, for example, that the sixth and seventh orders are for the same part number, but these are on different purchase orders. The report is printed in part-number sequence within vendor, so *particular* orders can be identified. The fifth column on the report is the due date that was assigned to the purchase order when it was issued. Note that the report was printed at the beginning of week 343. The sixth column is the quantity on the purchase order. Columns seven and eight are of the most interest for vendor scheduling. They are the fail-safe columns. Column seven is the fail week and column eight is the fail quantity. The former is the date at which this order is needed to meet the planned start date of a higher-level assembly. The fail quantity is precisely how many are needed to keep from failing to meet this need.

The first order was issued for five units of part 9670A, with a due date of week 345. As of week 343, this due date is still valid. A failure will occur if it is not met. However, it is not essential that all five pieces be delivered. The company can get by if only one of the five is delivered.

"Getting by" has a definite meaning. The fail week and fail quantity are related to actual customer orders; that is, if one were to peg the scheduled receipt for five pieces under purchase order 791930, for part number 9670A, up through product structures, one would find a customer order depending upon one of the five parts being received in week 345. This concept is the direct analog of separating customer orders from inventory orders for jobs in the shop.

What this means is that, for example, the ninth job on the list (part number 9815B) has a due date of the current week. Since there is no information in the FWEEK—FQTY columns, this order, when pegged up, will not be tied to a customer order. It will only go into Twin Disc's inventory.

Many of Twin Disc's vendors have been so well educated that this report can be mailed directly to them. It provides a means for them to give priorities to all of the orders from Twin Disc, with continuous updating of their priorities. This information can then be integrated with the competing needs of other firms, in their own MPC systems.

For the example shown in Figure 6.4, this report indicates that the third order in the list (part number 9682) is now critical. It is not due until next week, but based on Twin Disc's present conditions, it was needed five weeks ago. *Why* this is true is not important. If one believes the records, this job is now very urgent. Twin Disc will have to shrink five weeks off the combined lead times for all of assemblies above this part in the product structure to meet the customer promise date. Other purchase orders can be delayed if the vendor wishes to do so. However, Twin Disc is ready to accept the parts on the due dates, even though they are not needed until later. This will fulfill its contractual obligations.

Uncertainty protection

Another critical issue in vendor relationships has to do with protection against uncertainty. One approach is the use of safety stocks and safety lead times in MRP systems. A common conclusion is that, when one is interested in protection against the due date for an entire order, safety lead time usually is more effective than safety stock. Since in purchasing it is usually the due date for the entire order that is in question, safety lead time is often used.

Neither safety stocks nor safety lead times are cost-free. In both cases, the end result is added inventory investment and lead time extension. Benefits of working more closely with vendors are available here, as well. If a firm has tools that work, an accurate data base, and proper vendor education, the slacks used for uncertainty protection can be sharply reduced.

A different kind of uncertainty protection has to do with more disastrous circumstances, such as strikes. A European automobile producer keeps an extra two weeks of inventory on parts made in England to protect against strikes in the English facility and in transport. The Swiss government helps to finance the inventory of many strategic materials in Switzerland to protect the economy against any disruptions in supply.

As for genuine disasters, such as a factory burning down, there is really little that can be done to compensate in the way of inventory. In these cases, the only alternative is response: how to build another plant, shift production to sister plants, and the like. In the case of this sort of condition occurring in a supplier plant, one key is to have alternative sourcing plans; another is to help the supplier respond.

Providing protection against these occurrences naturally leads to the concept of multiple sources. Many firms do not want to be totally dependent upon a single source of supply. If they are, it is felt that their bargaining position is weakened. Moreover, some firms want to establish competition among alternative sources for quality, delivery, design improvement, and so on.

The other side of this coin is the learning curve. If one supplier can be given all the volume, perhaps the cost per unit can be driven down significantly. In addition, if uncertainties to the vendor are removed, perhaps the firm will become more integrated (and dependent) upon the buying firm. Also, record-keeping and clerical effort increase with multiple sources. More firms are trying to develop a single supplier relationship, working jointly on vendor scheduling and on other critical aspects of professional procurement, such as value analysis and joint engineering efforts. The MPC system provides the foundation for these relationships.

Quality improvement programs

Another aspect of the evolving relationship with vendors is a major emphasis on quality improvement programs. These programs are closely related to the introduction of just-in-time (JIT) approaches. Both JIT and quality improvement programs have a goal of eliminating uncertainties in vendor performance and support. The goal is perfectly predictable vendor support with no buffer inventories.

Quality improvement programs can have a significant impact on the price and vendor scheduling aspects of purchasing. An improvement in the quality of purchased material can also lead to cost reductions in expediting, production control, inspection, material handling, and indirect labor.

The vendor quality improvement program at Xerox provides an example of the increased emphasis on vendor quality and its impact on MPC systems. A quality assurance (QA) department was created, reporting to the manager of materials management. The QA department includes source surveillance and receiving inspection activities. One of the early programs was to institute statistical process control training for the vendors. This program now includes the European suppliers, and at the time of this writing was being expanded to include all firms in the worldwide centralized commodity management vendor base. As a result of the quality improvement program, 50 percent of all incoming material is now supplier certified, eliminating the need for receiving inspection at Xerox. Instead, the "quality" staff visits suppliers on a weekly to monthly basis, to discuss a variety of improvement and planning topics.

The quality people at Xerox work closely with the procurement managers and buyers located in engineering and with design engineers. They join these groups in attending "supplier concurrence sessions," where topics including materials, processes, and tolerances are discussed. In addition, Xerox has instituted a "forward products procurement program" to involve the suppliers in the early stages of the design of new products. Supplier suggestions on the design of new products have resulted in substantial cost savings through "improved manufacturability." The QA manager explains that eliminating quality problems is a must. "With shorter and shorter product life cycles, we have to hit the market with volume when we enter it. We can't afford slow learning curves. We've got to have good parts coming in from day one."

PURCHASING SYSTEMS AND DATA BASE

We turn now to what is perhaps the most important issue in the chapter. Given the set of vendor relationships defined above, what are the specific tools that successful companies are using? Our discussion is again based on the assumption that there is a working MPC system and data integrity.

The procurement functions

Figure 6.5 shows the detailed interaction of purchasing with the front end, engine, and other parts of the manufacturing planning and control system. The set of activities shown as boxes in the middle column depicts the procurement cycle.

The MRP data base provides time-phased record information to both buying and order release. Buying is the activity that encompasses the establishment of the proper vendor relationships discussed previously. This is an ongoing process of estimating quantities, establishing commitment conditions that are mutually beneficial, and working for continuing improvements.

Order release is primarily a clerical job; it is the determination of detailed quantity and timing decisions as constrained by the conditions of buying. Order release also connotes some form of management by exception; when routine actions cannot be executed, buying personnel need to be so advised.

Order follow-up includes vendor scheduling and an ongoing process of assigning priorities. It also includes some exception coding to highlight any conditions that do not agree with plan.

Receiving and order closeout encompass all of the necessary documentation for the receipt of purchase orders, data integrity check procedures, scrap and quality control, and interfaces with accounts payable. It is critical that appropriate data integrity procedures are in place.

Performance analysis is an ongoing evaluation of vendor performance, commodity performance, buyer performance, and overall procurement performance. We will deal with each of these topics after first identifying the key data base elements.

The data base

Figure 6.5 also shows the key files that comprise the purchasing data base. The MRP data base is used as one important source of information. The right-hand portion of Figure 6.5 depicts some of the critical files in the purchasing data base.

The vendor master file includes all of the information that describes each vendor. Included are name, address, telephone number, vendor code, terms of sale, contact(s) in the firm, and so on. There would also be direct linkages to the quotations, open purchase orders, receipts, and history files, so vendor-order status performance can be assessed.

The buyers file indicates which buyers are responsible for which part numbers, commodities, and vendors. It would also have linkages to the other files. The quotations file would be all open quotations, requests for quotation, "tickler files" for quotation follow-up actions, and any expiration dates of quotation data.

FIGURE 6.5   The purchasing data base and MPC system linkages

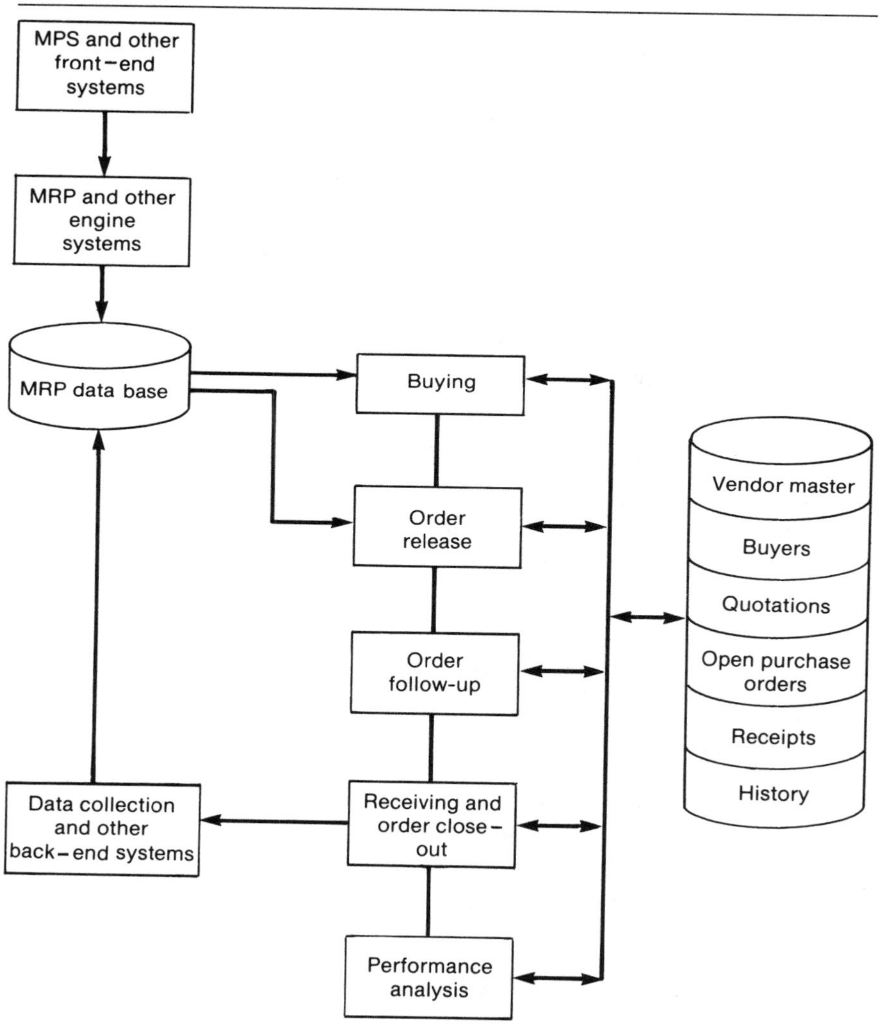

The open purchase orders file is essentially all of the scheduled receipts from MRP records for purchased parts, plus any purchase orders for non-production materials. In addition to quantity and timing data, all of the data held on a purchase order would be maintained, such as destination, shipping means, terms of sale, and so forth.

The receipts file maintains all data on receipts, so order closeout, reconciliation with purchase orders, and accounts payable activities can be supported. The history file contains all of the data on closed purchase orders to support whatever kind of performance analysis is desired by the firm.

Vendor performance

Figure 6.6 is a standard vendor performance report from a software package marketed by Software International Company. This report is for one vendor (ABC Company) for one item (A4792 DPDT SWITCH). This switch is in commodity code DTS, and is bought by ALP.

At the time of the report, there have been two purchase orders closed and one that is still open. The first closed order, issued on 01/15, was due on 02/25, and the last receipt was on 01/25. The order was for 1,000 pieces of which 950 were accepted and 50 were returned. This represents a 5 percent return (RT) rate. The standard cost of those received was $7,125, or $7.125 each. The actual invoice for the 1,000 parts was $7,115.50, or $7.1155 each.

The second closed order shows that the last receipt on 04/05 was later than the due date of 03/30. Also, the returned percentage was 30 percent, and the items were invoiced for $4,000 ($8 each) as against the standard cost of $3,562.50 ($7.125 each). The return percentage as well as the cost overrun were both judged to be significant enough to generate "flag" conditions. These are shown with an asterisk as a quantity (Q) flag (F) and a cost (C) flag (F).

The one open purchase order has had a partial shipment made against it. The cost data are shown for both the total purchase order (bookings) and the portion that has been received (receipts).

The summary data at the bottom of Figure 6.6 allow all of the performance data for closed and open purchase orders to be grouped into one summary set of performance statistics. The result is an ability to compare the performance of any two vendors for the same purchased component.

There are many standardized software packages on the market to support purchasing. This illustration shows how the basic data and definitions of performance can be provided in several forms of analysis. The particular definitions of performance might be different for different applications, but the important concept is the ability to thereafter make comparative analyses. These performance reports perform an important "loop-closing" function in purchasing in a way analogous to that done based on shop-floor and quality performance.

Electronic date interchange (EDI)

Recent advances in computer and information system technology have dramatically changed the way the purchasing function is managed, as well as the linkages between purchasing and the MPC system. Advances in both software and hardware, such as data base management systems and micro-

FIGURE 6.6 Software International, purchasing subsystem report

```
                              VENDOR PERFORMANCE

                          VENDOR PERFORMANCE REPORT
                          *****  DIVISION NAME  *****

AS OF 12/18

VENDOR NO.   VENDOR NAME          TELEPHONE      CONTACT NAME
103927       ABC CO.              301-922-8962   SAM EVANS

                                  COMM.CD        CURRENT BUYER
ITEM NUMBER  ITEM DESCRIPTION     DTS            ALP
A4792        DPDT SWITCH

CLOSED   BUY   ----SCHEDULE----  S  ------------------QUANTITY------------------  SC RT RW Q  ------RECEIPTS------  C
PO NUMBER  ER  ORDERED  DUE   LAST RCPT  F  ORDERED  ACCEPTED  SCRAP  RETURNED  REWORK  Z  Z  Z  F  STANDARD  ACTUAL
10923      MNO  01/15/  02/25/  01/25/   F   1000      950               50              Z  5        7125.00  7115.50
11014      MNO  02/19/  03/30/  04/05/        500      350              150             30  *        3562.50  4000.00 *

OPEN     BUY   ----SCHEDULE----    ------------------QUANTITY------------------   ------BOOKINGS------   ------RECEIPTS------
PO NUMBER  ER  ORDERED  DUE   LAST RCPT  ORDERED  ACCEPTED  SCRAP  RETURNED  REWORK  STANDARD   ACTUAL   STANDARD   ACTUAL
12176      MNO  09/23/  12/07/  11/21/    2000      800               30             13830.00  13790.00  5532.00   5516.00 *

ITEM    PERFORMANCE  LATE ORDER   QUALITY COST        ----------QUANTITY--TOTALS----------   --TOTAL BOOKINGS--    --TOTAL RECEIPTS--
SUMMARY  FLAG  INDEX  PERCENT  RATIO  OVERRUN  ORDERED  ACCEPTED  Z SCRAP  Z RETURN  Z REWORK  STANDARD   ACTUAL   STANDARD   ACTUAL
          *    16.8    56       .87     4.0     3500      2100                 1         1       13830.00  13790.00  16219.00  16631.50 *

TOTALS/VENDOR  PERFORMANCE FLAG=*  INDEX=14  LATE ORD.Z=17  QUA RATIO=.39  COST OR.Z=1.2   TOTALS  41428.50  41009.00  88378.50  89527.40
```

DESCRIPTION: Provides purchasing with a standard method of comparing the relative performance of vendors. Two reports are provided summarizing vendor performance for the last year or for the current calendar year.

SEQUENCE OF DATA: Sequenced by vendor number. Within vendor, by item number and order status (closed and open), respectively.

OPTIONS: Period (last or current year), the reports to be generated (Part I, II, or both), and variable data.

Source: Software International.

computers, have made a major impact on extending the managerial capabilities of the purchasing organization and on improving the communication between purchasing, manufacturing, and the vendors. Likewise, the recent introduction of electronic data interchange networks promises to have an even more profound effect on the management of the purchasing function.

Electronic data interchange permits the computer-to-computer transfer of information and documentation from buying firm to its suppliers. The result is the transfer of information in virtually real time, replacing traditional communication forms, such as mail or telephone. Paperwork costs are significantly reduced. More important, delays for paper processing can be eliminated. EDI thus permits productivity improvements in paperwork and indirect labor, as well as better supplier management.

Caterpillar Tractor Company provides an illustration of the use of EDI in purchasing. Nearly 400 of the firm's domestic and offshore supplier locations are connected, using the standards developed for the automotive industry by the Automotive Industry Action Group (AIAG). Each supplier is assigned an electronic mailbox on the network. Suppliers retrieve information from their mailboxes and can forward information through the mail boxes to Caterpillar. By adopting AIAG, the "mail" is read in a language common to the computers of Caterpillar and its vendors.

Caterpillar's EDI network is called "Speed," for suppliers and purchasers electronically exchanging data. Although Caterpillar has been building the Speed network for several years, it began as an outgrowth of the company's existing MPC systems. The company recognized the need to add effective electronic communications with the outside suppliers to facilitate JIT. The company viewed the advantages of the Speed network to be applicable to both Caterpillar and its vendors. Some of the direct benefits include:

- Reducing transaction time to a few hours, compared with processing through the mail.
- Quicker responses to changes for revised material requirements.
- Reduced paper-handling expenses.
- Reduced errors relative to the transmission of information in a hard-copy environment.

Caterpillar's EDI is focused on the release of purchase orders, advanced shipping notices, invoices, accounts payable transactions, and receiving notices. It supports the firm's JIT program as well as the cost improvement goals for the company. It has also made significant steps toward a paperless environment. Future uses of EDI systems at the company include: transmitting information on engineering specifications, communicating requests for quotations, implementing an on-line status for suppliers to check parts availability, posting quality specifications, and sending engineering drawings to suppliers in conjunction with the firm's CAD/CAM program.

ORGANIZATIONAL CHANGE

We come now to the fourth critical issue in procurement: What are the organizational changes needed to effectively use MPC systems in procurement?

The Steelcase example

With the necessary vendor relationships, data base, and systems in place, the purchasing job undergoes a fundamental change in character. A professional procurement function can be achieved, with more time spent on how to best utilize vendor strengths to the benefit of the ultimate consumer, and less time spent on day-to-day fire fighting.

Let us now examine how the organization of the purchasing group at Steelcase was changed. Figure 6.7 is the purchasing organization prior to the implementation of MPC-based systems. The entire operation used to revolve around one person, who was in charge of purchased item inventory control and order releases. This individual is shown as the inventory control person in Figure 6.7. This employee negotiated blanket orders with vendors, issued monthly releases against the blanket orders using economic lot sizes, controlled all releases to the vendors, based all decisions on a Kardex file system, and carried 1 to 1½ months of safety stock for individual items. Meanwhile, the buyers functioned as expeditors.

This approach to procurement seemed to work as long as the business did

FIGURE 6.7 Steelcase purchasing organization prior to the development of effective MPC systems

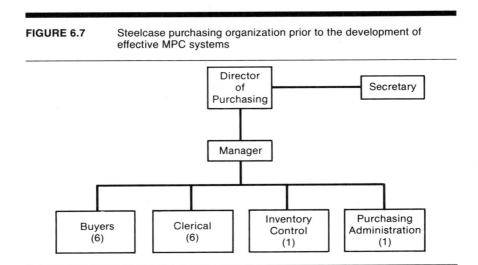

Source: P. L. Carter and R. M. Monczka, "Steelcase, Inc.: MRP in Purchasing," in *Case Studies in Materials Requirements Planning,* ed. by E. W. Davis (Falls Church, Va.: American Production and Inventory Control Society, 1978), p. 123.

not undergo major changes in volume, mix, or design. In fact, when these changes did occur, orders were issued for the wrong parts and wrong quantities, and the resulting expediting activity was sharply intensified. Unfortunately, at one point, Steelcase approached the increasing problems by computerizing the *existing* system and sending the reports to the vendors. The result was a continuing crisis of operation in purchasing.

Figure 6.8 is the purchasing organization after the MPC-oriented systems were installed. Purchasing people now have the responsibility for planning, scheduling, and inventory control on all purchased items. They are totally responsible for any and all shortages on purchased parts, regardless of the cause.

The primary change is that the persons shown on the left-hand side of Figure 6.8 are now concerned with the detailed releasing and scheduling of and assigning priorities of orders to the vendors. Those on the right-hand side are concerned with buying and vendor relationships. The functions have been separated.

The purchasing coordinator is concerned with all capital equipment purchasing, plus the processing of engineering changes. This latter activity is

FIGURE 6.8   Steelcase purchasing organization after implementation of MPC systems

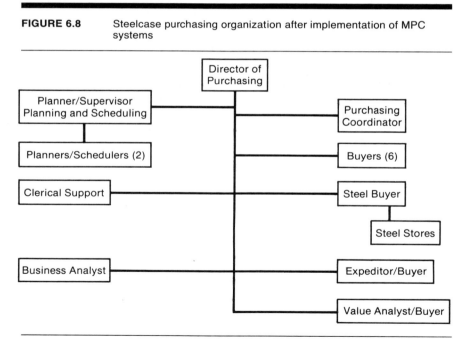

Source: P. L. Carter and R. M. Monczka, "Steelcase, Inc.: MRP in Purchasing," in *Case Studies in Materials Requirements Planning,* ed. by E. W. Davis (Falls Church, Va.: American Production and Inventory Control Society, 1978), p. 123.

absolutely vital to determining the best timing and response to design changes. The six buyers are organized around commodity codes, with one responsible for all maintenance, repair, and nonproduction items. The other five buyers purchase production-oriented items. The steel buyer purchases all steel for the company (the largest single expenditure item), manages the steel inventory, and schedules steel slitting.

There is one expeditor/buyer, who purchases all fasteners for the company. This person also expedites all rejections of purchased parts, including both rework and returns. The expeditor follows a rule that all dispositions must be made within five days; Steelcase recognizes this as a critical problem area. If they are not handled quickly and properly, the result will be a loss in data integrity. The last person shown in the right-hand side of Figure 6.8 is the value analyst/buyer. This person purchases and coordinates all chrome plating and also works as a specialist in value analysis. In fact, all of the buyers are concerned with value analysis as one key aspect of the ongoing improvement in vendor relationships. The goal for all is "to spend their money wisely."

The group that works most closely with the detailed MRP driven data is shown on the left-hand side of Figure 6.8. It is the planner/scheduler group. The two planner/schedulers are in charge of order release, vendor scheduling, and order priority for all purchased parts except fasteners and steel. They manage some 3,800 items, or 1,900 each, on a weekly cycle, since MRP is regenerated over the weekend. On Monday and Tuesday, the planner/schedulers review those 3,800 items, using CRT devices and exception codes. On Tuesday evening, the results are processed to produce the vendor report (Figure 6.3), which is sent to the vendors on Wednesday morning. As we noted before, this report serves as a purchase order; there are no formal purchase orders used for routine purchasing.

The planner/schedulers represent the day-to-day link between Steelcase and its vendors. These people, in effect, interact with detailed order entry personnel in vendor factories. If problems arise that they cannot solve, the problems escalate to their supervisors and from there to buyers at Steelcase, who interact with vendor salespeople.

Use of the vendor report can be illustrated with one of Steelcase's plywood, fiberboard, and fiberglass suppliers. Prior to the installation of the new system, Steelcase would typically telephone specific orders against an open blanket order, on a rush or short lead time basis. This meant that the vendor was constantly reacting to problems and Steelcase was always expediting. With the new report, the activities are very different. The vendor checks the past-due and current columns, and crosses off any orders that have been already shipped but were not reflected on the report because of timing delays. He then puts a high priority on any past-due and current orders not yet shipped, reviews the last two months of demand, and checks the requirements for the next five weeks for any unusual demand to place orders with his vendors. The net result of the new system is that this vendor found his own scheduling much easier because he has better information about future demand.

The benefits that Steelcase achieved from the new system would not have been possible without the organizational changes. The recognition that roles must change and responsibilities shift to use purchasing information as a substitute for inventory, panic operations, and other forms of slack is key. Now, let us generalize from the Steelcase example and take up some related issues.

The procurement job

Figure 6.9 shows the change in a typical buyer's day when MRP-oriented purchasing systems are in use. This figure depicts the changes in procurement that took place at the Tennant Company. As can be seen, prior to the MRP systems, fully one half of the buyer's day was concerned with expediting and very little with de-expediting. After MRP, these two activities are of equal importance and only take up one fourth of the day. (Note, however, that at Steelcase the *buyer* does virtually none of this activity.) The key dif-

FIGURE 6.9   Typical buyer's day

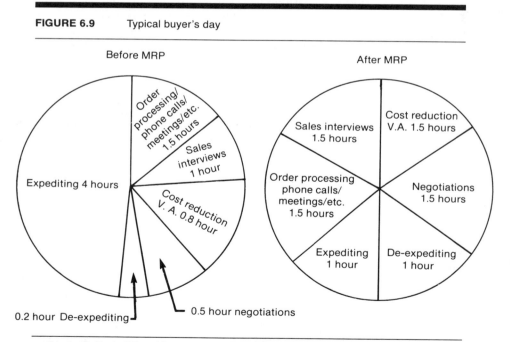

Source: G. Bevis, "Closed-Loop MRP at the Tennant Company." George Bevis Co., P.O. Box 619, Wayzata, Minnesota.

ference reflected in Figure 6.9 is that much more time is spent in the series of activities we have called vendor relationships, and much less in clerical detailed fire fighting.

A similar result was reported by Trill for the Reliance Electric Company. Prior to the installation of the MRP systems, negotiation and vendor selection comprised only 8 percent and 7 percent of the buyers' time, respectively. Moreover, the clerical people in purchasing were spending 30 percent of their time typing purchase orders, change orders, debit memos, and so on, with only 15 percent on expediting. The remaining portion of their time was spent on posting data, filing, and explaining information over the telephone.

With the new system in place, Reliance Electric achieved for buyers a 35 percent savings in time that could now be put to more productive use, a 40 percent savings in overall clerical time, elimination of filing, great reduction of paperwork, savings in equipment and floor space, reductions in lead times, and improved communication between purchasing and other company personnel.

It is important to understand that the substantial changes in the nature of the procurement job that we have identified are not easily achieved. People are used to working with massive paper files. A need for fire fighting breeds a fire fighting organization. Is it possible for these people to change? How about the vendors? Will they believe in the new systems? How will they change their own approaches to scheduling?

All of these are profound issues. The design of the systems to support purchasing from an MPC data base is far easier than the changes that must be made in the way purchasing will operate. Education programs must be an important dimension of the planned changes—both for internal personnel and for the vendors.

Centralization versus decentralization

The final organizational change issue we consider is whether purchasing should be centralized or decentralized in a multiplant environment, and what role the introduction of MPC systems has in this decision. Some of the classical arguments in favor of centralized procurement are increased clout with the vendors, the ability to obtain larger discounts, the potential for better coordinating orders that go to one vendor, the ability to better divide scarce resources among competing company units, economies of scale in the purchasing activity itself, and the ability to develop a more professional staff.

On the other hand, the arguments in favor of decentralized procurement are the coupling of authority for supply with responsibility for a decentralized facility's output, the potential for diminishing returns if the decentralized facility is large in its own right, unique decentralized requirements, extra time lags (lead times), and the public relations aspects of purchasing locally. This latter factor has increasing importance for multinational organizations. In some companies, the development of fairly autonomous procurement units is important insurance against nationalization.

The decentralization-centralization of procurement issue is rarely clear-cut. For many firms, there is one important commodity, such as coffee beans or copper, that is purchased by a central group trying to hedge against price swings. For others, key components may be bought centrally, with local buying of others.

Some people believe that the development of MPC systems forces centralization in purchasing. This is not necessarily true. An MPC data base and related systems in procurement make it possible to achieve better integration in the procurement activities of a multiplant company, regardless of the degree of centralization. Single sourcing and worldwide vendor selection similarly provide opportunities for coordinated procurement. The MPC system provides the basis for the organization to exploit the opportunities for better procurement practice. The use of comparative standard costs, performance by commodity codes, relative vendor performances—all of these are possible in a truly professional multiplant procurement operation supported by modern MPC systems.

RESULTS

The final topic we take up is concerned with the payoffs from integrating effective MPC systems into purchasing. What kind of results have been achieved by the leading-edge companies? The single-word answer is: phenomenal! Many companies have made first-year savings in purchased component costs alone that have more than paid for the entire MPC developmental effort.

Results at Steelcase

We have looked at several examples from the Steelcase Company to illustrate the change in purchasing orientation, as well as to describe some other system reports. Let us now see how these systems have paid off.

One of the most striking results of the system implementation at Steelcase was great improvement in vendor performance against due dates. When the systems were installed, 35 percent of all outstanding purchase orders were past due and many needed to be rescheduled into the future. After one month, only 20 percent were past due, and after 1½ years only 3.2 percent were past due. These were improvements in the *vendor* performance due to effective use of the new systems.

Productivity in the Steelcase plant was improved, as well. After 1½ years, the number of part numbers short in any single week had dropped from an average of 33 to 4. Better service to the production floor resulted in less rescheduling, fewer split lot sizes, and so on.

There was a marked reduction in buyer clerical and follow-up activity. In fact, there was a general reduction in the level of clerical effort throughout purchasing. As noted before, buyers now use their time to spend money wisely, rather than to solve immediate crises.

The purchased-material inventory turnover performance was increased substantially. Historically, the inventory had increased by one half of the rate of increase in sales. Over a two-year period after the systems were installed, sales rose 59 percent while purchased item inventories rose only 12 percent. Moreover, there was a far better ability to control inventory levels during a period of sales decline.

Vendor lead times were also reduced. Steelcase's systems provided the vehicle for a redefinition of the concept of lead time to obtain improved delivery performance. With capacity commitments and the MPC system information, lead times were reduced to an absolute minimum. During a period of severe shortage conditions in the United States, Steelcase had no real lead times in excess of five weeks. Later, the Steelcase purchasing manager stated, "Vendor lead times are virtually irrelevant to Steelcase."

Customer service at Steelcase has also improved. When the Sears Tower was built in Chicago, Steelcase contracted to supply office furniture. The company shipped five truckloads per day, five days per week, for 20 weeks. Every truck arrived within a few minutes of the scheduled time. In an order for 19,000 chairs for the federal government, an unexpected rush order involved delivery of 2,000 within two weeks. Steelcase procured 3,500 yards of special-color fabric that was delivered in 10 days for the order; this fabric has a normal lead time of 10 weeks.

Finally, the procurement function is regarded as truly professional at Steelcase. Buyers are no longer highly paid expeditors. More and more time is spent on value analysis and other vendor relationship efforts. In a two-year period, the targeted cost reductions through better purchasing was increased 10 fold, from approximately $500,000 per year to $5 million per year. These impressive savings were attainable only after the buyers were freed from routine activities to work on those activities that resulted in the large savings.

Results at Xerox

The development of closer relationships with the suppliers has had a measurable impact on operations at Xerox. Since introduction of the program, product costs have been reduced by about 10 percent per year, and inventory has dropped from 3.3 months of supply in 1980 to 1.5 over a four-year period. Also, because of the emphasis on sole sourcing, the vendor base has shrunk from 5,000 suppliers to 300, enabling the cost of operating the materials management department to drop from nine cents per dollar purchased to 3.5 cents. This reduction in the "material overhead" cost has been achieved even with the increased efforts on the quality improvement program with the vendors.

The closer relationships with vendors and improved quality levels have had substantial inputs on the MPC systems. With higher quality assured, transaction reporting and incoming stores activities have been reduced. By moving to JIT deliveries, much shorter response times are being achieved. The "bucket sizes" for planning are also being reduced. In some cases, vendors are put on a "flow basis," with intercompany paperwork reduced to exceptions and changes.

Other results

Steelcase and Xerox are certainly not the only firms that have achieved significant results from improved purchasing based on MPC systems. A similar effort at Signode Corporation, reported by Papesch, resulted in major reductions in shortages, lead time reductions of one fourth to three fourths, faster reaction to increased requirements, and better purging of record error problems.

Although not due to purchasing improvements alone, the Tennant Company has one of the most spectacular MPC success stories. George Bevis, in describing Tennant's results, states that in a 27-month period the purchased material inventory was reduced by 42 percent ($3 million), while the quarterly production rate increased by 66 percent. At the same time, the average daily shortages were reduced from 300 to 5, assembly efficiency increased from 45 to 85 percent, and delivery promises met increased from 50 percent to 90 percent.

Assessing the purchasing function

We are often asked to audit manufacturing planning and control systems. As one portion of this process, it is useful to examine the interactions of MPC systems with purchasing. Here are some of the question we ask:

> How is purchasing organized? Are the buyers and schedulers separated? What is the relationship between buying (vendor relationship) activities and releasing/vendor scheduling activities? How professional is the group? What is the level of formal education and of training in the use of MPC systems? Are there Kardex, tub, or other large noncomputerized files? What are the computer systems? How good are they? Do people use them? Can a purchasing

person (not someone from the computer department) explain their logic to us thoroughly? How are exception conditions handled? With what speed? By whom? Do purchasing people believe in the schedules and MPC systems? Are there any informal systems? How are lead times monitored? Are orders issued as indicated by the MPC systems? What is the frequency of rush orders? How well do the vendors rate this firm as a customer? Is there a formal vendor performance evaluation system? A formal value analysis program? A formal cost improvement program?

What is the state of systems in use relative to the state of the art? Are lead times being reduced? Is there a JIT program? How successful is it? What do the vendors think of the firm's JIT program? What is happening in quality control? Is statistical process control being used? What is the firm doing to reduce paperwork costs, both within the company and with its vendors? Is the firm using electronic data interchange? How?

Answers to these questions can provide a great deal of insight into the potential improvement in purchasing that can be achieved in a particular firm. Furthermore, it is not a one-time effort. There are *always* improvements to be made through a better integration of a firm's needs with the abilities of its vendors.

CONCLUDING PRINCIPLES

This chapter is devoted to showing how MPC-based systems can provide the basis for a new level of professionalism in procurement. By carefully utilizing the information in an operational MPC system, a firm can help their vendors do business better—better for both the buying firm and the vendor. We see the following basic principles as important:

- Vendor capacities should be planned and controlled with as much diligence as are internal capacities.
- A closer, more intimate working relationship between the buying firm and its vendors should be a primary objective.
- The purchasing data base needs to be integrated with other parts of the MPC system data base.
- Clerical work and managerial work should be separated in the purchasing organization.
- Quality improvement programs and single sourcing can have a dramatic impact on purchasing performance and MPC cost.
- High payoffs have been achieved by firms that have purchasing supported by MPC systems. Achieving the payoffs often requires major reorganization and reorientation of jobs.

REFERENCES

Bevis, G. "Closed-Loop MRP at the Tennant Company." George Bevis Co., Wayzata, Minn.

Burlingame, L. J., and R. A. Warren. "Extended Capacity Planning." *1974 APICS Conference Proceedings*, pp. 83–91.

Carlson, J. G. H. "The Effect of Learning on Production Lots." *1974 APICS Conference Proceedings*, pp. 73–82.

Carter, P. L., and R. M. Monczka. "Steelcase, Inc.: MRP in Purchasing." In *Case Studies in Materials Requirements Planning*. Falls Church, Va.: American Production and Inventory Control Society, 1978, p. 125.

Dale, B. G., and R. H. Powley. "Measuring Purchasing Performance." *International Journal of Physical Distribution and Materials Management*, no. 3, 1984, pp. 5–18.

Emmelhorne, Margaret A. *Guide To Purchasing: Electronic Data Interchange*. Oradell, NJ: National Association of Purchasing Management, 1986.

Evans, D. L. "Measuring Purchasing Performance," *1977 APICS Conference Proceedings*, pp. 434–49.

Greenstein, Irwin. "Caterpillar Erects Paperless Network." *Management Information Systems Week*, Jan. 20, 1986.

Hoeffer, E. L. "Production Report." *Purchasing* 90, no. 7 (April 16, 1981), pp. 52–66.

Monczka, R. M., and P. L. Carter. "Productivity and Performance Measurement in Purchasing." *1976 APICS Conference Proceedings*, pp. 6–9.

"Move to MRP System Helped Steelcase Boom." *Purchasing*, January 25, 1977, pp. 60–63.

Papesch, Robert M. "Extending Your MRP System into Your Vendor's Shop." *Production and Inventory Management*, 2nd Quarter 1978, pp. 47–52.

———. "Professional Excellence: Why Xerox is Our '85 Winner." *Purchasing*, June 1985.

Ruhl, J., and J. Schorr. "MRP and Purchasing at Steelcase." Report—Steelcase, Inc., Grand Rapids, Mich.

Schorr, J. E., and T. F. Wallace. *High Performance Purchasing*. Oliver Wight Ltd. Publications, Brattleboro, Vermont: 1986.

Shaughnessy, Thomas E. "Aggregate Inventory Management: Measurement and Control." *Journal of Purchasing and Materials Management*, Fall 1980, pp. 18–24.

Trill, G. P. "Paypor: A Complete CRT, On-Line, Real Time Procurement System." *1977 APICS Conference Proceedings*, pp. 468–80.

Wallace, Tom. *Purchasing and MRP: More Bang for the Buck*. Atlanta: R. D. Garwood, 1983.

Whitmarsh, J. "MRP is the Only Answer." *Purchasing World*, December 1977, pp. 23–28.

Whybark, D. C. "Evaluating Alternative Quantity Discounts." *Journal of Purchasing and Materials Management,* Summer 1971.

DISCUSSION QUESTIONS

1. The MPC system shows purchasing and order releasing as parallel functions in the back end. The elements of material planning and control are much the same for both functions. In what ways, however, is capacity planning different?

2. Describe how buying capacity would work for getting copies of a term paper or a group project. How would buying capacity from a copying service be different for them and for you than the current practice of racing in just before the paper is due to get copies? What would it take to make it work?

3. In what sense does cooperating with vendors lead to lower prices? What aspects of improved MPC would lead a vendor to consider reducing prices?

4. Why would a vendor be interested in shipping just one unit to help Granger Transmission "get by," as is illustrated for Part 9670A in Figure 6.4?

5. Much is made about the switch from an expediting orientation to more planning-oriented activities in the purchasing functions (e.g., Figure 6.9). Why is this important to a firm?

6. Discuss the merits of separating the daily transaction people (schedulers) from the buyers in the purchasing organization.

7. Who should pay for electronic data integration (EDI), the buyer or the supplier?

8. Mike Lawson, owner of Lawson's Axels, said: "I will not increase my quality unless the customers are ready to pay for it." How is this view short sighted?

PROBLEMS

1. Figure 6.3 shows a Steelcase requirements report for Cannon Mills. The quantities are in yards of fabric for the periods shown, for each color or style. Determine the total yards of fabric requested by Steelcase over each of the next 14 weeks (assuming that the 4-week requirements are evenly distributed). What would you think, if you were Cannon?

2. Figure 6.4 is the Twin Disc Open P.O. Buyer Fail-Safe Report. Suppose that vendor 52487 decides to work only on jobs that have entries in the F-week column, and these in order of F week. Generate the list of part numbers in the order in which they will be produced. What are the implications of the sequence to the supplying firm and to Twin Disc?

3. The purchasing manager at Collins Manufacturing was reviewing the performance of the buyers using a software package similar to Exhibit 6.6, which was grouped by buyer. Ivor Morgan, the buyer for integrated circuits, seemed to be performing at a level below that of the other buyers, since he had a higher incidence of cost overruns, quality problems, and late orders. When confronted with this evaluation, Ivor became very angry, saying: "Any bloody fool can buy nuts and bolts." What should the purchasing manager do?

4. Figure 6.9 depicts a large change in the way a typical buyer spends the day after installation of an MRP system. This diagram was shown to Dick Weeks, president of Rhode Island Manufacturing. He said: "This is very nice, but you are asking to spend $200,000 to put in this MRP system in purchasing. How can you convert this chart into a cost justification?"

5. Norman Ware, the parts buyer at the Excello Corporation, received the following three MRP records for purchased parts from the weekly MRP run completed yesterday:
   a. Complete the information in each record. Note: Norman must buy in integer multiples of the order quantity.
   b. What actions should be taken, if any, with regard to the vendor schedule for these items?
   c. Define the computer processing steps required to flag any of the exception notice conditions contained in these records.
   d. Is the activity indicated in question b an appropriate activity for Norman? Why or why not?

Part A

	Week	1	2	3	4	5	6	7	8
Gross requirements		300	100	100	200	200	300	300	200
Scheduled receipts									
Projected available balance	450								
Planned order releases									

Q = 100; LT = 2; SS = 0.

Part B

	Week	1	2	3	4	5	6	7	8
Gross requirements		350	100	250	250	200	300	200	300
Scheduled receipts			500		500				
Projected available balance	50								
Planned order releases									

Q = 500; LT = 4; SS = 0.

Part C

	Week	1	2	3	4	5	6	7	8
Gross requirements		75	75	85	125	175	200	150	125
Scheduled receipts			200						
Projected available balance	100								
Planned order releases									

Q = 200; LT = 4; SS = 0.

6. Hank Rush, the purchasing manager at the Egyptian Papyrus Company, is interested in installing a computer software package for evaluating vendor performance. He has prepared the following information relative to the recent delivery performance of two vendors who supply the Model 1011 integrated circuit. He plans to use this information in choosing a software package for vendor evaluation.

Vendor A		Vendor B	
Order due date	Order receipt date	Order due date	Order receipt date
1–3	1–5	1–10	1–6
1–24	1–17	2–7	2–4
2–14	2–15	2–28	2–28
3–7	3–4	3–14	3–10
3–28	3–21	4–4	4–1
4–25	4–22	4–18	4–13
5–9	5–13	5–16	5–16
5–23	5–21	6–27	6–22
6–13	6–20		

   a. Evaluate the delivery performance of these two vendors.
   b. What particular features would you consider to be desirable in the software package?
   c. What aspects of vendor performance should the software package measure?

7. This morning, Pete Rose, the integrated circuit buyer at Flatbush Products, Inc., received the purchased part MRP record below:

CIRCUIT #101

Week		1	2	3	4	5	6	7	8	9	10	11	12
Gross requirements		50									50	50	50
Scheduled receipts													
Projected available balance	65												
Planned order releases													

Q = 50; LT = 3; SS = 2.

   a. Complete the Circuit #101 MRP record.
   b. Pete noted that the vendor for the Circuit #101 had recently indicated his plant has limited production capacity available. At most, 50 units per four-week period can be provided by this supplier. Pete wondered what action, if any, needs to be taken on this item as a result of this capacity limitation?

8. Each week at Dart, Inc., a vendor report is run using information contained in the MRP records for purchased items. A copy of the June 6 report (Exhibit A) has just been received by the production manager at Jackson Fabrics—a supplier of Dart, Inc. What actions, if any, should the production manager at Jackson take? (Assume that the transportation time between Jackson and Dart is one day.)

9. The materials manager and the vice president of manufacturing at the SCM Transmission Company are currently assessing the capabilities of the firm's suppliers to meet the company's production plan for the next year. The marketing department forecasts the total sales volume to be $70 million, of which 20 percent will be sold in the first quarter, 36 percent in the second quarter, 29 percent in the third quarter, and the remaining 15 percent in the fourth quarter. The average selling price is $1,000/transmission, and the company plans to produce an amount equal to the sales forecast each quarter because of the make-to-order nature of the product and the cost of financing finished goods inventories.

    One of the major purchased items is steel castings, from which machine parts are manufactured. Currently, all of the firm's steel castings are purchased from the Kewanee Foundry. To evaluate the capacity of the Kewanee Foundry to handle SCM's business for the next year, the materials manager has prepared the following capacity bill for steel castings:

    Steel casting capacity bill

    .12 lbs. of steel castings per transmission sales $
    .012 machine molds per transmission sales $
    .024 cast parts per transmission sales $

    The materials manager has indicated that the Kewanee Foundry has an overall capacity to pour 80 tons of metal per day, and it works 90 production days per quarter. *At most*, 15 percent of the daily foundry capacity can be processed through the automated machine molding line. (Equivalently, the automated machine molding line can produce up to 2,400 molds per day, operating 3 shifts per day, 90 days per quarter). The automated machine molding line is the only process at Kewanee that is capable of producing steel castings at a low enough cost to meet SCM's requirements. SCM has used Kewanee as a sole source for its steel casting needs for several years, and the quality and delivery performance of this vendor are excellent. SCM has been able to achieve substantial economies in the purchase of steel castings by consolidating all of its business with Kewanee.

    a. What is your overall evaluation of Kewanee's capability to meet SCM's total requirements for the next year?

    b. The master scheduler at SCM wants to develop the daily production rates for the next four quarters. Express the master schedule in terms of the number of molds required per day. (The Kewanee Foundry manager plans capacity in terms of the number of molds produced per day on the molding machine line.)

EXHIBIT A   Monday June 6, year 5

Vendor report—Jackson Fabrics

Catalog number	Item	ECN* date	ECN* number	Buyer	Received last week	Current and past due	Requirements					Next four weeks	Following four weeks	Dart current on hand	Issued last week
							6/6	6/13	6/20	6/27	7/4				
MX1012	Red cloth	2/10/year 4	22101	60	500	700†	600†	600†	600†	700	700	2800	3600	250	600
MY104	Blue cloth	12/4/year 2	14412	60	100	500†	500†	500	500	500	500	2000	3200	1600	500
MV1010	Yellow cloth	4/6/year 5	25610	60	100	100	100	100	100	100	100	200	—	1800	—
MU469	Green cloth	6/3/year 5	26888	60	150	290†	250†	300†	300†	300†	350†	1600	2500	—	200

*Engineering change notice.
†Firm planned orders.

    c. Can Kewanee meet the master production schedule requirements on a quarterly basis? What alternatives can be discussed with Kewanee?

10. The Strong-Bolt Machine Works, Inc., a manufacturer of machined components for the farm implement industry, purchases eight types of metal alloy from a nearby steel mill. Currently the cost of these alloys is $720/ton for order quantities exceeding 10 tons. Effective February 1, the cost of these alloys will increase by $37/ton to $757/ton. The current status of the eight alloys as of January 25 is given in Exhibit B. Procurement lead time is one week, inventory carrying cost is 23.5 percent of alloy cost per year (52 weeks), and orders are always issued for a minimum quantity of 10 tons. Exhibit B is stated in tons, and no safety stocks are included. Which, if any, of these alloys should be purchased for delivery prior to February 1 at the old cost (of $720/ton)? Why? What decision rules can be developed for this type of situation?

11. Jose Zott is trying to cost justify the introduction of electronic data integration (EDI) at his company. The inventories of purchased items is now $45 million, there are four people in incoming inspection (annual wages are $20,000 each), and the average lead time for purchased items is six weeks. Jose feels that, with good quality control, the inspection staff could be cut in half, but he is not sure that this savings should be attributed to EDI. He does think that overall there should be a clerical savings of several people, both in his company and at the vendor plants. Lead time could be reduced by about two weeks as well. Assuming a two-year payback, how much can Jose spend for EDI?

12. Dynamic Seal sells engine seals to United Aircraft. Dynamic installed statistical process control (at United's request). There is no longer an on-site inspector from United at Dynamic, and seals are not inspected in either plant. Floppy disks with SPC data accompany the shipments of seals and are, thereafter, analyzed at United. What are the benefits of this scheme to United? To Dynamic? Are the benefits worth the cost to Dynamic? Why?

13. The Andrews Manufacturing Company estimates that it costs $5,000 per year for administration of each of its 1,000 vendors. As Andrews moves toward just-in-time production, the company feels that it will spend $1 million per year for vendor education and training. By how many does the vendor base have to be reduced to pay for the education and training?

14. Andrews (problem 13) has reduced the vendor base to 300, but continues to spend $1,000,000 every year on developing better vendor relationships, improved vendor quality, and so on. How much do these efforts have to return per vendor to break even?

15. What influences should reducing the number of vendors and investing in vendor training have on vendor prices? How is the firm (e.g. Andrews of problem 13) going to be sure that it is receiving competitive prices from its vendors?

EXHIBIT B   Status of alloy requirements as of January 25

Alloy	Alloy cost/ton	Estimated annual volume	Current on-hand inventory	Feb 1	Feb 8	Feb 15	Feb 22	Mar 1	Mar 8	Mar 15	Mar 22	Mar 29	Apr 5	Apr 12	Apr 19	Apr 26	May 3
1	$720	200	6				8		20					17			3
2	720	570	43	80					43						75		6
3	720	250	7	20					20			20				20	
4	720	1,200	82					100			150					100	
5	720	600	3	40			25				37						40
6	720	220	10	15							17						13
7	720	660	42	41							33		25	28			
8	720	1,100	20	52							62						83
Total		4,800															

— 7

Just-in-time

This chapter is devoted to the impact of just-in-time (JIT) methods on manufacturing planning and control systems. There has been a great deal of worldwide interest in JIT. The impact of JIT on manufacturing planning and control is very significant, and it continues to grow at a rapid pace. It is, therefore, critical to understand JIT in the context of both existing and potential new MPC systems. JIT is intimately involved in execution, both on the shop floor and in purchasing. Successful JIT systems greatly simplify tracking and transactional requirements in both of these execution areas. In addition, JIT programs provide a broad range of general benefits in efficiency, quality, worker attitudes, and vendor relations. The chapter is organized around the following seven topics:

- JIT in manufacturing planning and control: What are the key features of JIT and how does JIT impact MPC systems?
- A JIT example: How can the basic principles of JIT be illustrated in one simplified example?
- JIT applications: What are some concrete examples of JIT practice?
- Nonrepetitive JIT: How can JIT concepts be applied to the nonrepetitive manufacturing environment?

- JIT in purchasing: What are the changes required and the payoffs to both vendor and vendee?
- JIT software: What are the features of computer packages offered to support JIT?
- Managerial implications: What changes are required to fully pursue the benefits of JIT?

This chapter is closely tied to the MPC execution concepts developed in Chapters 5 and 6. The fit of JIT in a manufacturing firm is illustrated in Chapter 1. Some basic elements of a system based on "pulling" materials are described in Chapter 10. Advanced concepts in scheduling are treated in Chapter 13. In Chapter 20, a Finnish system is described that has level capacity with a variable load and a fixed short cycle time; as such, it is another approach to applying JIT concepts in a nonrepetitive environment.

JIT IN MANUFACTURING PLANNING AND CONTROL

Figure 7.1 shows how just-in-time programs relate to our manufacturing planning and control framework. The cross hatched area indicates the portions of MPC systems that can be affected by implementation of JIT systems. JIT impacts all areas, but the primary application area is in back end execution. However, JIT extends beyond manufacturing planning and control. JIT programs raise fundamental questions about what is really important in manufacturing and how performance should be evaluated. For this reason, we start this section with a discussion of the major elements of an overall JIT program. Thereafter, we turn to the impact of just-in-time on the MPC system and the overhead cost savings from reduced MPC system transaction processing. The section closes with a description of the cornerstones of an overall JIT program and the linkages to MPC systems.

Major elements of just-in-time

Many definitions have been put forward for just-in-time, and they have been evolving as JIT is being more globally adopted. Several of the more popular current definitions focus on JIT as an approach to minimize waste in manufacturing. This focus is so broad as to be of limited use. It helps to subdivide waste into time, energy, material, and errors. A common denominator running through this and other JIT definitions that is useful for our purposes is a broad philosophy of pursuing zero inventories, zero transactions and zero "disturbances;" that is, *zero disturbances* means routine ex-

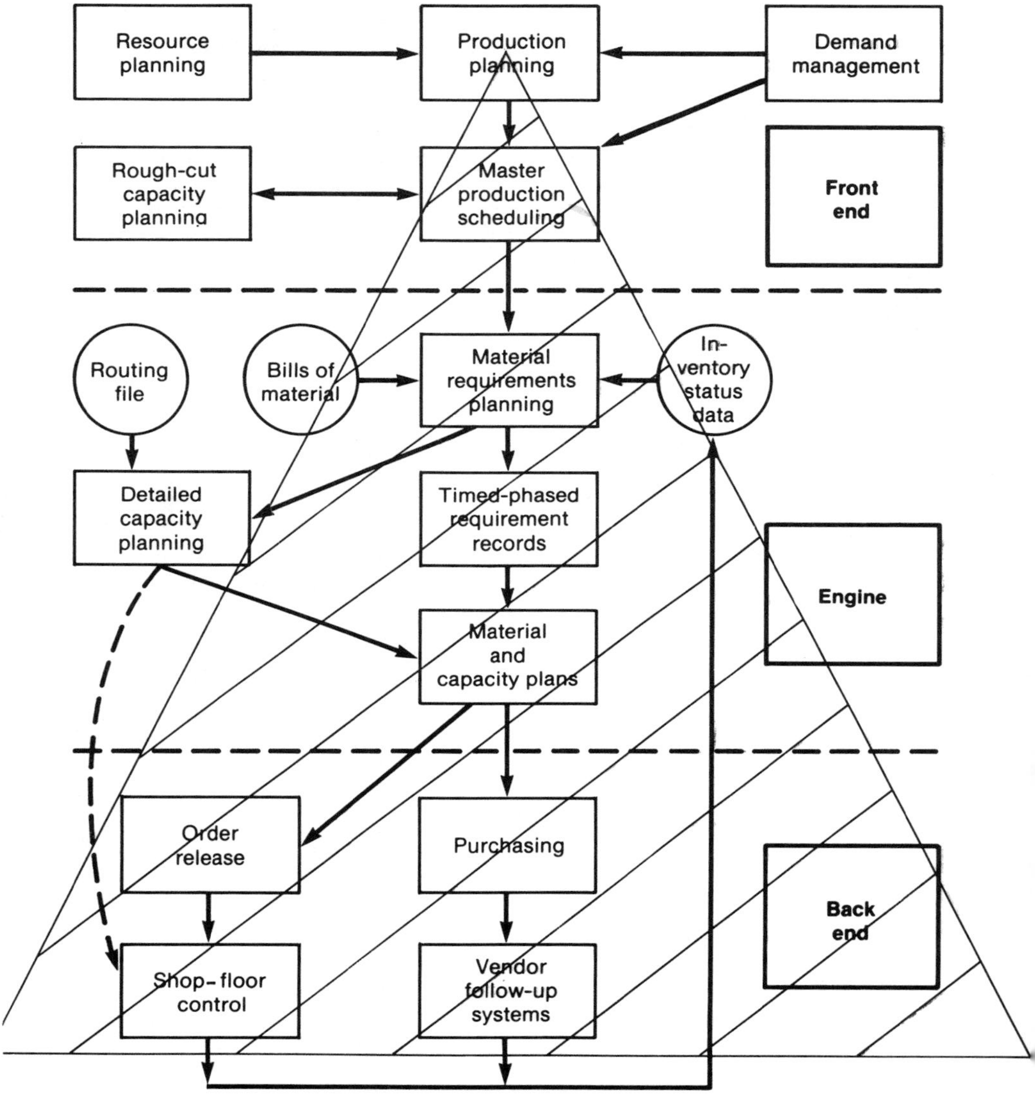

FIGURE 7.1 Manufacturing planning and control system and JIT

ecution of schedule, day in-day out. This sets the conditions for driving what we have termed *organizational slack* to zero.

The literature on JIT is largely one of cases. The best-known JIT examples are from firms with high-volume repetitive manufacturing methods, such as the classic case of Toyota. The most important features of these applications have been the elimination of discrete batches in favor of production rates, the reduction of work-in-process inventories, production schedules that level the capacity loads and keep them level, mixed model plans and master production schedules where all products are made more or less all the time instead of changing over from one model to another, visual control systems where the workers remember how to build the products and execute the schedule without paperwork or complex overhead support, and direct ties to vendors who deliver high quality goods frequently. All of these have MPC implications.

The just-in-time objectives are typically achieved through several physical system changes or projects. One of them is setup time reduction and a drive toward lot sizes that are constantly smaller. This is necessary to make all of the products constantly. It is also consistent with reducing inventory levels. Setup times are typically reduced by the application of fairly common industrial engineering techniques for analyzing the setup process itself, instead of the more usual concentration on operation times. One approach is to turn on a video camera at the beginning of the setup and let the setup workers analyze the results.

Another physical program associated with JIT has been the pursuit of improved quality through process improvement. Most JIT firms have engaged in programs of quality awareness and statistical process control. In a repetitive manufacturing system, any quality problem will result in a stoppage of the entire flow line, unless undesirable buffer inventories are held.

Continual improvement as a goal and as a maxim for day-to-day operations is also a part of what most people now include in a JIT program. The idea is that every day one should get better in some dimension, such as fewer defects, more output, or fewer stoppages. A closely related concept is worker involvement. Most JIT implementations include a strong degree of worker participation. In the words of a union official at the new GM/Toyota (NUMMI) plant in Fremont, California, "This is the way work ought to be. [With JIT] this plant employs our hearts and minds, not just our backs."

JIT firms tend to group their equipment into manufacturing cells; that is, a group of machines is dedicated to the manufacture of some group of parts. The layout of equipment is made to minimize both travel distances and inventories between the machines. Cells are typically U-shaped to increase worker interactions and to reduce material handling. Workers are cross

FIGURE 7.2   Improvement activities—JIT versus non—JIT firms

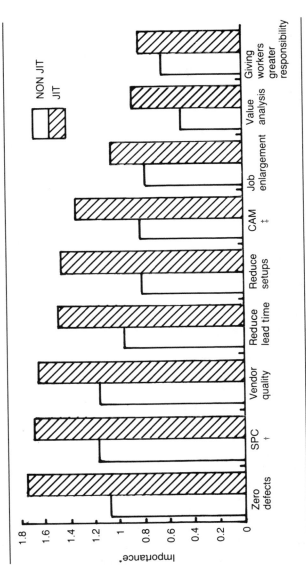

Source: 1986 Manufacturing Futures Survey, Boston University.
*Importance is on a relative scale of 0–2.
†SPC = Statistical process control.
‡CAM = Computer Aided Manufacturing.

FIGURE 7.3   JIT benefit summary

	Improvement	
	Aggregate percent (3–5 years)	Annual percent
Manufacturing cycle time reduction	80–90	30–40
Inventory reductions:		
Raw materials	35–70	10–30
Work-in-process	70–90	30–50
Finished goods	60–90	25–60
Labor cost reductions:		
Direct	10–50	3–20
Indirect	20–60	3–20
Space requirements reduction	40–80	25–50
Quality cost reduction	25–60	10–30
Material cost reduction	5–25	2–10

Source: George W. Plossl, *Just-In-Time: A Special Roundtable.* Atlanta, Ga.: George Plossl Educational Services, Inc., 1985.

trained to be able to run several of the machines. "Capacity" can be made quite flexible in cellular manufacturing, so surges or mix changes can be more readily handled. An extension of the cellular concept is the plant within a plant, where a portion of a factory is focused solely on one group of products.

In summary, a JIT orientation includes several action programs. One is reduction of setup times and lot sizes. A second is a "no defects" goal in manufacturing. A focus on continual improvement is a third. A fourth action program concentrates on involving workers and using their knowledge to a greater extent. Figure 7.2 compares the use of this set of activities (and others) to improve manufacturing between firms employing JIT and those who are not pursuing JIT. A summary of the benefits of undertaking a comprehensive JIT program is provided in Figure 7.3. This summary is the aggregate benefits achieved by a group of JIT companies.

The impact of JIT on manufacturing planning and control

We saw in Figure 7.1 that JIT covers more than MPC activities but does impact all three areas of our MPC framework (front end, engine, and back end). The primary place where JIT makes its contribution is in the back end. JIT provides for greatly streamlined execution on the shop floor and in purchasing. JIT offers the potential for eliminating large portions of standard shop-floor control systems, for sharply reducing the costs of detailed shop scheduling, for significant reductions in work-in-process and lead times, and for better vendor scheduling.

However, although JIT makes its major impact in the back end, it is not without its influence on the front end and engine. In the detailed MRP planning of the engine, JIT plays a strong role in reducing the number of part numbers planned and the number of levels in the bill of materials. Many part numbers formerly planned by MRP analysts can now be treated by different means, such as "phantoms" (i.e., as part numbers that still exist in the bill of materials, but are not expected to be transacted into and out of inventories). The result is often an order of magnitude reduction in the complexity of MRP planning, with a concomitant reduction in the planning personnel required.

In the front end, JIT also gives rise to some important changes. Production plans and master production schedules will be required that provide whatever degree of level capacity loading is necessary for smooth shop operations. In many cases, this also requires a rate-based MPS; that is, so many units per hour or day. This drive toward more stable, level, daily-mix schedules dictates many of the required JIT activities, such as setup time reduction. To the extent that lead times are sufficiently reduced, many make-to-stock firms find themselves becoming more like make-to-order or assemble-to-order companies, as opposed to making inventories in anticipation of customer orders. This, in turn, can impact demand management activities.

Execution under JIT is based on the concept that orders will move through the factory so quickly that it is not necessary to track their progress with a complex shop-floor control system. A similar argument holds for purchased items. If they are converted into finished goods within hours or days of receipt, perhaps it is unnecessary to put them into stockrooms, pick them, and go through all of the details normally associated with receipts from vendors. Instead, the JIT firm can simply pay the vendor for the purchased components in whatever products are completed each time period; there will be so little work-in-process inventory that it is not worth either party keeping track of it for purposes of accrual payments.

The concept of updating component inventory balances when finished items are received into stock is referred to as "backflushing." Instead of creating detailed work-in-process accounting systems based on shop-order transactions, some JIT firms just reduce component part inventory balances by exploding the bills of material for whatever has been delivered into finished goods. It is worth noting, however, that backflushing implies a very high level of data integrity.

The JIT approach in execution is focused on simplicity. The intent is to so design the manufacturing cells, products, and systems that goods flow through very routinely. With problems of quality and disturbances largely eliminated, routine execution becomes just that: routine. Simple systems can be employed by shop people without detailed records or the need for extensive overhead staff support.

The hidden factory

A manufacturing firm can be thought of as comprising two "factories." One makes products and the other (the hidden factory) processes transactions on papers and computer systems. Over time, the former factory has been decreasing in relative cost, compared with the latter. The annual survey of manufacturing firms in North America by the Boston University Manufacturing Round Table has consistently found rising overhead costs to be the number one concern of manufacturing managers. A major driver for these costs is transactions. Logistical transactions include the ordering, execution, and confirmation of materials moving from one location to another. Included are the costs of personnel in receiving, shipping, expediting, data entry, data processing, accounting, and error follow up. Under JIT, the goal is to eliminate the vast majority of this work and the associated costs.

Balancing transactions are those that are largely associated with the planning that generates the logistical transactions. Included are production control, purchasing, master scheduling, forecasting, and customer order processing/maintenance. In most companies, these costs comprise 10 to 20 percent of the total manufacturing overhead costs. JIT again offers a significant opportunity to sharply reduce these costs. MRP planning can be cut by perhaps 75 to 90 percent in complexity. The improvements generated by vendor scheduling can be extended. Vendor firms will no longer have to process *their* sets of transactions that are paid for in hidden factory costs.

Quality transactions extend far beyond what one normally thinks of as quality control. Included are transactions associated with identification and communication of specifications, certification that other transactions have indeed taken place, and recording of required backup data. Many of the costs of quality identified by Crosby and others are largely associated with transactions. JIT, with closer coupling of production and consumption, has faster quality monitoring and response capability.

Still another category is change transactions. Included are engineering changes and all those that update manufacturing planning and control systems, such as routings, bills of material, and material specifications. Engineering change transactions are some of the most expensive of any in the company. A typical engineering change, for example, might require a meeting of people from production control, line management, design engineering, manufacturing engineering, and purchasing. The change has to be approved, scheduled, and monitored for execution.

Japanese firms presently make much heavier use of JIT than manufactur-

FIGURE 7.4   Frequency of engineering changes

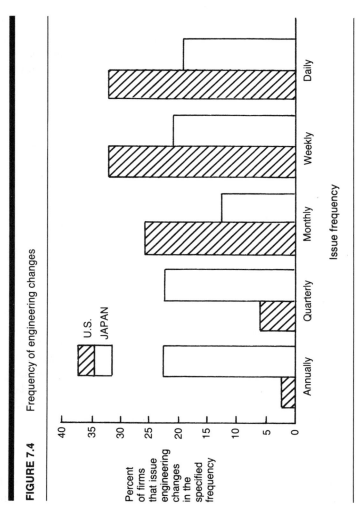

Source: 1986 Manufacturing Futures Survey, Boston University.

ers in other parts of the world. They also make significantly fewer engineering changes. A comparison between Japanese and U.S. firms is provided in Figure 7.4. Just-in-time firms reduce the frequency of engineering changes by batching them. Moreover, JIT greatly reduces the unit cost of these transactions, because there are far less existing inventories that have to be considered, and the monitoring of implementation is more straightforward.

One way in which firms are attacking the hidden factory is by finding ways to significantly reduce the number of transactions. JIT is a major weapon in this attack. Stability is another attack, and again JIT is important. JIT is based on stabilized operations. Still another attack on hidden factory transaction costs is through automation of transactions, such as with bar coding, and the elimination of redundancies in data entry. More integrated systems are also providing payoffs, and so are better data entry methods. But we remain convinced that stability and transaction elimination should be pursued before turning to automation of transactions. JIT is clearly a key in the pursuit of achieving hidden factory cost reductions.

JIT cornerstones and the linkages to MPC

Figure 7.5 provides a holistic view of JIT and the linkages to material planning and control (MPC) systems. This holistic model depicts JIT as having three cornerstones: product design, manufacturing process design, and the whole person concept. These all interact with the MPC system; JIT provides the linkage of these four areas.

Critical activities in product design include quality, designing for manufacture in existing cells, and reducing the number of "real" levels in the bill of materials to as few as possible. Some firms say there should be no more than two or three (phantom levels not controlled separately are not counted). By not having more than three levels in the bill of materials, the products will only have to go into inventory and out again, with MRP-based planning, once or twice as they are produced.

A natural linkage is between the bill of material level reduction and the design of the manufacturing process cells. For the use of fewer levels to be practical, a manufacturing process has to be so put in place that a number of product conversion steps are included in one routing. A related manufacturing process objective has to do with "efficiency." Efficiency in the cells needs to be defined in material terms, not in the more common currencies of labor and capital utilization. The objective is to concentrate on material velocity. Jobs must flow through in short cycle times, so detailed tracking is not required.

"Band width" is another important notion in designing manufacturing processes. A wide band width system is one that has enough surge capacity to take on a fairly mixed set of products, and some variation in demand for the products, as well. The impact on MPC system design is through the focus on inventory and throughput time reduction, which means that inventory is not built to level out capacity requirements. JIT systems are designed to be responsive to as large a set of demands as possible. Superior manufacturing processes support greater band width. The objective is to be able to make any product, right behind any other, with minimal disruption.

The whole person concept is the third cornerstone to JIT. The whole person concept will continually apply training, study, process improvement, and whatever else is needed for the elimination of recurring problems. The objective is continual learning and improvement. The whole person concept recognizes that the workers' range of capabilities and level of knowledge are assets to the firm. Education and cross training are continuing investments in this asset base. As the asset base grows the need for overhead support is reduced, and overhead personnel can be redeployed to address other issues.

The whole person concept has a very significant impact on MPC system design and operation. Band width and not building inventories to utilize direct labor mean that surge capacity must be available. Surge capacity in direct labor personnel means that these people will not be fully utilized in

FIGURE 7.5   Cornerstones of just-in-time

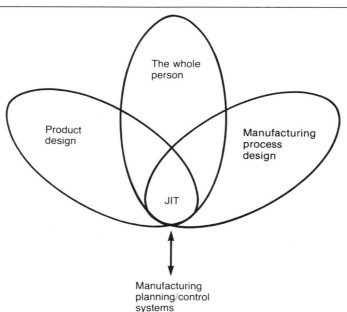

direct production activities. In fact, the whole person concept is based on the premise of hiring *people,* not just their muscles. As a consequence, direct workers are cross trained to take on many tasks not usually associated with "direct labor." Included are maintenance of equipment, education, process improvement, data entry, and scheduling. From an MPC standpoint, the key point is that the whole person concept puts a greater emphasis on scheduling by the workers and less on scheduling by a centralized staff function. The entire process is fostered by the inherent JIT push toward simplification. With no defects, zero inventories, no disturbances, and fast throughput, detailed scheduling is easier; moreover, any problems that arise tend to be local in nature and amenable to solution on a decentralized basis.

Also depicted in Figure 7.5 is the two-way relationship of JIT to manufacturing planning and control. The application of JIT requires most of the critical MPC functions described in this book. It will always be necessary to do master production scheduling, production planning, capacity planning, and material requirements planning based on explosion. If the bill of materials is reduced to two or three levels, the detailed MRP planning and associated transaction costs can be cut significantly. If all detailed tracking is done by direct laborers under the whole person concept, additional savings can be achieved.

We see then that JIT has the potential for changing the character of production control in a company, since it reduces MPC transactions. JIT has the potential for significantly reducing the size of this "hidden factory" that produces papers and computer transactions instead of products. A listing of some building blocks and objectives of JIT is provided in Figure 7.6. Many of these will be described in subsequent sections, after we have detailed some of the basic concepts with the example in the next section.

A JIT EXAMPLE

In this section we develop a detailed but simple example to illustrate the basic concepts of JIT. The product for our example is a 1-quart saucepan produced in four models by the Muth Pots and Pans Company. (See Figure 7.7.) The sales brochure for this product sums up its importance by saying, "If you ain't got a Muth, you ain't got a pot." We will look at elements of a JIT program for the saucepan that range from leveling production to redesigning the product. Some of these elements have a direct MPC relevance and others will affect MPC only indirectly.

Leveling the production

We start the JIT program for the saucepan by considering how to "level and stabilize" production. This means not only planning a level output of 1-quart saucepans but planning to produce the full mix of models each day (or

---

FIGURE 7.6   JIT objectives and building blocks

Ultimate objectives:

- Zero inventory.
- Zero lead time.
- Zero failures.
- Flow process.
- Flexible manufacture.
- Eliminate waste.

Building blocks:

- Product design:
  - —Few bill of material levels.
  - —Manufacturability in production cells.
  - —Achievable quality.
  - —Appropriate quality.
  - —Standard parts.
  - —Modular design.
- Process design:
  - —Setup reduction.
  - —Quality improvement.
  - —Manufacturing cells.
  - —Production band width.
  - —No stockrooms.
  - —Service enhancements.
- Human/organizational elements:
  - —Whole person.
  - —Cross training.
  - —Flexible labor.
  - —Continual improvement.
  - —Limited direct/indirect distinction.
  - —Cost accounting/performance measurement.
  - —Information system changes.
  - —Leadership/project management.
- Manufacturing planning and control:
  - —Pull systems.
  - —Rapid flow times.
  - —Paperless systems.
  - —Visual systems.
  - —Level loading.
  - —MRP interface.
  - —Purchasing/vendor relationships.
  - —JIT software.
  - —Reduced production reporting/inventory transaction processing.
  - —Hidden factory cost reductions.

FIGURE 7.7 The 151 one-quart saucepan line

Basic product:

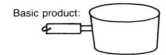

Executive handle option:

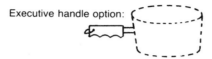

Clad pan option:

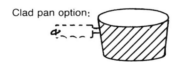

FIGURE 7.8 Annual forecast data

Completed pan model number	Description of model		Annual forecast
	Handle	Metal	
151A	Basic	Sheet	200,000
151B	Basic	Clad	2,500
151C	Executive	Sheet	25,000
151D	Executive	Clad	100,000

week or some other short interval, if volumes are not sufficiently high to warrant daily production). Full-mix production in a short interval provides for less buildup of inventory in each model. Moreover, the schedule can respond to actual custom order conditions more quickly. Level output also implies "freezing" a plan for a time to stabilize the production and related activities on the floor. Before looking at specifically how this might be done, let us consider Muth's current manufacturing situation.

At the present, Muth uses production planning to set the overall production rate. In setting this rate, it is necessary to build inventories in anticipation of the Christmas season peak in demand. The annual forecast for each of the four models is given in Figure 7.8. A product structure and part listing is provided in Figure 7.9. There is a master production schedule, for each of the four models, which is exploded to produce a material requirements planning (MRP) record for each of the part numbers shown on the part listing in Figure 7.9. Safety stock is carried for all components and production is in the lot sizes indicated in Figure 7.9. Figure 7.10 gives lead times and routing data; lead times are computed on the basis of two days per operation, rounded up to the next whole week using five-day weeks. A typical MRP record is shown as Figure 7.11.

To plan for level production, the first step is to convert the forecasts to the daily requirements for each model. Using a 250-day year, this conversion is shown in Figure 7.12. Note the difference between the current lot sizes and the daily requirements. Daily production will put pressure on manufacturing to reduce setup times. Two other possible master production schedules are shown in Figure 7.12, in addition to the one based on daily production batch sizes. The first of these shows the quantities to be produced, if hourly batches are to be made, and the second shows a mixed model MPS. These are the minimum lot sizes to cycle through all models on the final assembly line.

Pull system introduction

A "pull" system of material flow control occurs when a work center is only authorized to produce when it has been signaled there is a need for more parts in a downstream (user) department. In general, a pull system means that no work center is allowed to produce parts just to keep workers or equipment busy. It also means that no work center is allowed to "push" material to a downstream work center. All movements and production are authorized by a pull signal from a downstream work center when it has a need for component parts. Frequently, it is believed that the pull system creates the benefits in JIT. In part, the primary payoffs come from the discipline required to make a pull system work. Included are lot size reductions, limited work-in-process, fast throughput, and line stopping philosophies.

The signals for communicating downstream work center demand vary widely. They include rolling a colored golf ball from a downstream work center to its supplying work center when it wants parts; yelling: "Hey, we need some more"; sending an empty container back to be filled up; and using cards (kanbans) to say that more components are needed. A widely used technique is to paint a space on the floor that holds a specified number of parts. When the space is empty, the producing department is authorized to produce material to fill it. The consuming or using department takes material out of the space as they need it; typically, this only occurs when the space authorizing *their* output is empty. For the Muth example, we will use

FIGURE 7.9   Product structure and parts list

			Finished item number			
Component part	Lot size	Safety stock	151A	151B	151C	151D
Complete pan 151A	8,000	5,000	X			
Complete pan 151B	900	1,000		X		
Complete pan 151C	3,000	3,000			X	
Complete pan 151D	6,000	5,000				X
Regular pan 1936	14,000	10,000	X		X	
Clad pan 1937	8,000	6,000		X		X
Basic han. ass. 137	14,000	8,000	X	X		
Exec. han. ass. 138	8,000	5,000			X	X
Basic han. set 244	9,000	8,000	X	X		
Exec. han. set 245	9,000	8,000			X	X
Bas. han. base 7731	14,000	8,000	X	X		
Ex. han. base 7735	12,000	5,000			X	X
Ring 353	24,000	15,000	X	X	X	X
Rivets 4164	100,000	50,000	X	X	X	X
Sheet metal 621	1 coil	1 coil	X		X	
Clad sheet 624	1 coil	1 coil		X		X
Handle sheet 685	1 coil	1 coil	X	X	X	X
Plastic beads 211	5 tons	1 ton	X	X	X	X

an empty container as the signal for more production; that is, whenever a using department empties a container, it sends the container back to the producing department. An empty container represents authorization to fill it up.

FIGURE 7.10   Routing and lead time data

Department	Item	Routing	Lead time
Final assembly	Complete pan	1. Spot weld	2 days
		2. Inspect	2 days
		3. Package	2 days
		Total = 6 days = 2 weeks	
Punch press	Pan	1. Blank and form	2 days
		2. Roll lip	2 days
		3. Test for flat	2 days
		4. Straighten	2 days
		5. Inspect	2 days
		Total = 10 days = 2 weeks	
Handle base	Handle base	1. Blank and form	2 days
		2. Inspect	2 days
		Total = 4 days = 1 week	
Handle assembly	Handle assembly	1. Rivet	2 days
		2. Inspect	2 days
		Total = 4 days = 1 week	
Injection molding	Plastic handle set	1. Mold	2 days
		2. Deburr	2 days
		3. Inspect	2 days
		Total = 6 days = 2 weeks	

	Purchased items	
Purchasing	Sheet metal	⎧ Purchased
	Clad sheet metal	⎪ Lead time
	Plastic beads	⎨ One week
	Ring	⎪ For all
	Rivets	⎩ Items

FIGURE 7.11   MRP record for basic handle assembly (part 137)

		Week									
		1	2	3	4	5	6	7	8	9	10
Gross requirements			8		8	3	8		8		8
Scheduled receipts											
Proj. avail. bal.	10	10	16	16	8	19	11	11	17	17	9
Planned order rel.		14			14			14			

Q = 14; LT = 1; SS = 8. (All quantities are in thousands.)

FIGURE 7.12   Master production schedule data*

	Model			
Option configurations:	151A	151B	151C	151D
Handle	Basic .	Basic	Executive	Executive
Pan	Sheet	Clad	Sheet	Clad
Annual forecast (units)	200,000	2,500	25,000	100,000
Possible master production schedules:				
Daily batch MPS	800	10	100	400
Hourly batch MPS	100	1.25	12.5	50
Mixed model MPS	80	1	10	40

*Data are based on a 250-day year and an eight-hour work day.

Given that Muth has committed to a level schedule where all models are made every day, the firm is almost ready to move into a pull mode of operation. Two additional issues need to be faced. First, there is the question of stability. For most pull-type systems, it is necessary to keep the schedule firm (frozen) for some reasonable time. This provides stability to the upstream work centers, as well as overall balance of the work flow. For Muth, let us assume that the schedule is frozen for one month, with the daily batch quantities given in Figure 7.12 (1,310 pots per day).

The second issue is determination of the container sizes to transport materials between work centers. For example, let us consider the container used between handle subassembly and final assembly for the basic handle, part 137 (810 are used per day). If the container were to hold 100 parts, this represents just under one eighth of a day's requirements. The determination of the container size is a fairly complicated issue. Involved are material handling considerations, container size commonality, congestion in the shop, proximity of work centers, and, of course, the setup costs. Establishment of container size of 100 for part 137 puts a great deal of pressure on the handle assembly work center to reduce setup times. The center is currently producing in lots of 14,000.

The flow of work in the pull system at Muth is illustrated in Figure 7.13 for handle subassembly to the final assembly line. Only two containers are for part 137; while one is being used at the final assembly line, the other is being filled at handle subassembly. This approach is very simple, and is facilitated by the two departments being in close proximity. Figure 7.14 shows the factory layout. A worker from the final assembly line or a material handler can return empty containers. Any empty container is a signal to

FIGURE 7.13   Pull system for Muth pots and pans

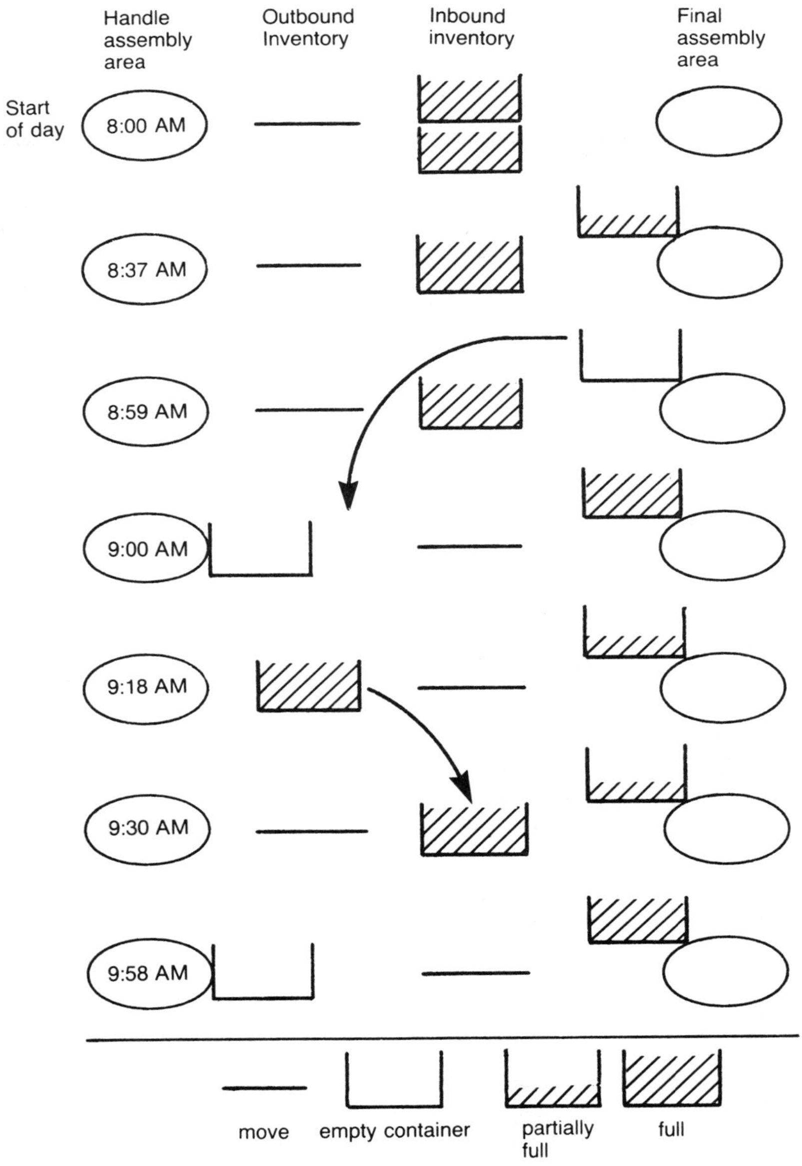

FIGURE 7.14   Factory layout

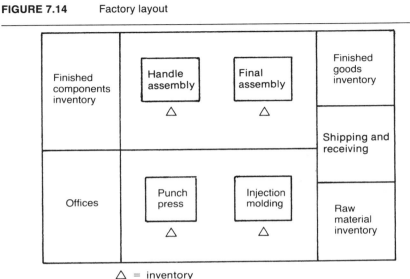

△ = inventory

make a new batch (fill it up). It is interesting to note the difference in average inventory that will be held in this pull system, compared with the former methods based on standard MRP methods and the lot size of 14,000. In the pull system, the average inventory is about 100 units. Compare this to the inventories shown in the MRP record of Figure 7.11.

This pull system example has no buffer at either work center. It would be possible to add another container, which would allow greater flexibility in handle subassembly, at the cost of extra inventory in the system. As it is, the final assembly area would use up a container in just under one hour. This means that the system has to be responsive enough for the empty container to be returned to handle subassembly and a batch made in this time frame. An extra container allows more time for responding to a make signal (an empty container), and it also allows more flexibility in the supplying department. The extra inventory helps resolve problems; for example, when several production requests for different parts (containers) arrive at the same time.

Product design

To illustrate the implications for product design, consider the basic and executive handles for Muth's 1-quart saucepan shown in Figure 7.7. There are two differences between the handles: the grips and the ring placement.

FIGURE 7.15   Redesigned handle base

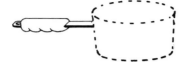

With some redesign of the plastic parts on the executive handle, the handle base and ring could be common between the two handle models, and the methods for handle assembly could also be standardized. The only difference would be the choice of plastic handle parts. Such a redesigned handle base is shown in Figure 7.15.

In addition to the improvements that this design change makes in handle subassembly, there are potential impacts in other areas, as well. For example, there would be one combined lot of production for handle bases, instead of two, with attendant reductions in inventory. Perhaps it might now be possible to run the handle base area on a pull system as well, with containers passing between the handle base area and the handle subassembly area. Another advantage is a simplification in the bill of materials, a reduction in the number of parts that must be planned and controlled with MRP, and a concomitant reduction in the number of transactions that have to be processed.

Process design

The product redesign, in turn, opens opportunities for process improvement. For example, it may now be possible to use the same equipment to attach both kinds of plastic handles to the handle base. Perhaps a cell can be formed, where handle bases are made and assembled as a unit. Figure 7.16 shows a possible way this might be accomplished, including an integration of the handle assembly cell with the final assembly line. Note that, in this example, no significant inventories are anywhere on the line, and both handle base material and plastic handle parts are replenished with a pull system based on containers.

Figure 7.16 also illustrates the "band width" concept. Several open stations along the line would permit adding personnel if volume were increased. Moreover, perhaps Muth would like to establish different production rates for certain times. For example, perhaps this pan might be manufactured in higher volumes near the Christmas season. What is needed is the capacity at the cell to move from one level of output to another. This

FIGURE 7.16   Cellular manufacturing of handle base and handle subassembly

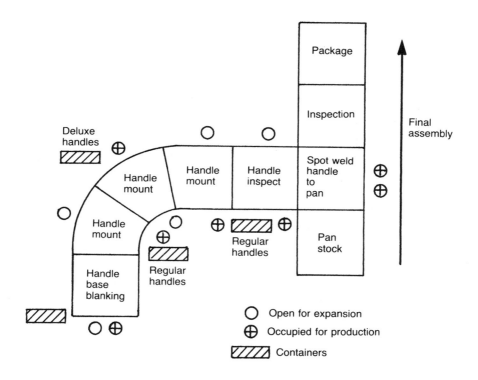

Final assembly line for 1-quart sauce pan

Deluxe handles

Handle mount

Handle mount

Handle mount

Handle inspect

Spot weld handle to pan

Package

Inspection

Pan stock

Regular handles

Regular handles

Handle base blanking

Final assembly

○ Open for expansion

⊕ Occupied for production

▨ Containers

added capacity probably means that the dedicated equipment will not be highly utilized.

The cell is designed to permit variations in manning, to better respond to actual customer demands. If an unexpected surge in demand for executive handle pots comes through, the cellular approach will allow Muth to make the necessary changes faster—and to be able to live with this kind of problem with smaller finished goods inventories. Over time, perhaps this cell can be further expanded in terms of band width to produce handles for other Muth products.

The value of quality can be seen in Figure 7.16. The inspection station takes up valuable space that could be used for production. It adds cost to the product. If bad products are being culled by inspection, buffer stocks will be required to keep the final assembly line going.

FIGURE 7.17   Simplified product structure

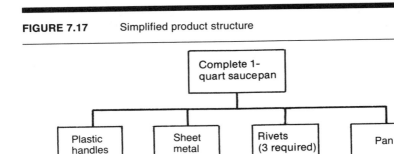

Bill of material implications

The product redesign results in a streamlined bill of materials. The number of options from the customer's point of view has been maintained, but the number of parts required has gone down. With the cellular layout shown in Figure 7.16, the handle base and handle subassembly no longer exist as inventoriable items. They are "phantoms" that will not require direct planning and control with MRP. The product structure given as Figure 7.9 now will look like Figure 7.17.

Several observations can be made about Figure 7.17. One is that handles have ceased to exist as part of the product structure. If one wanted to maintain the handle for engineering and other reasons, it could be treated as a phantom. Figure 7.18 shows what the MRP record would look like in this case. In Figure 7.18, there is some existing inventory to use up; phantom treatment allows this to occur, and will always use this inventory before making more.

Another observation is that pans *do* remain as an inventoriable item. Elimination of this inventory may well be the next goal for product and process redesign. Still another is to understand the magnitude of the reduction in transactions that is represented by the JIT approach illustrated in Figure 7.16. All of the MRP planning for the eliminated part numbers (or phantom treatment) is now gone. This impacts MRP planning as well as stock rooms—and all the other indirect labor associated with MRP control.

Finally, we need to consider the impact on lead times, the resultant ability to better respond to market conditions, the reductions in work-in-process inventories, and the greater velocity with which material moves through the company. If the combined lead times are computed using the data in Figure

FIGURE 7.18   MRP record for phantom part 137

		Week									
		1	2	3	4	5	6	7	8	9	10
Gross requirements		4040	4040	4040	4040	4040	4040	4040	4040	4040	4040
Scheduled receipts											
Projected available balance	15000	10960	6920	2880							
Planned order releases					1160	4040	4040	4040	4040	4040	4040

Q = lot for lot; LT = 0; SS = 0.

7.10, it can be seen that five weeks are required for the flow of sheet metal into pots. With the JIT approach, as illustrated, we have cut that to just over one week, and it could be reduced further.

JIT APPLICATIONS

Toyota is the classic JIT company, in that it has probably gone further than any other firm in terms of truly making the production process into a continuous flow. Much of the Toyota terminology and philosophy is found in other JIT programs. In firms where manufacturing is less repetitive, the application of JIT necessarily has had to be adapted. We start this section with a description of aspects of Toyota's approach. We then describe some variations and close with JIT as it is being implemented at Hewlitt-Packard.

Toyota

The production system at Toyota is in many ways the most advanced JIT system in the world. The results of this system are seen on the highways of the world. By virtually any yardstick, Toyota is truly a great manufacturing company. For example, Toyota turns its inventories at a rate of more than 10 times that of U.S. and European automobile manufacturers. It also turns inventories about 50 percent faster than its Japanese competitors, and it is very competitive in price, quality, and delivery performance.

Figure 7.19 shows the Toyota production system and where JIT fits within the overall approach. To some extent, the role given to JIT in Figure 7.19 is less encompassing than that described above. For example, the "elimination of unnecessaries" is clearly consistent with many definitions of JIT. All of the activities we have described for JIT are in basic agreement with those in Figure 7.19. The box for production methods is basically the same as manufacturing process design in Figure 7.5. Included under this heading is the multifunctional worker, which matches with several aspects of the whole person concept. Also included is "job finishing within cycle time"; this is consistent with the dominance of material flow velocity and the subservient role of direct labor utilization.

Toyota's kanban system

The Toyota view of just-in-time production shown in Figure 7.19 includes "information system," with kanban below it. The information system encompasses the MPC activities necessary to support JIT execution. Kanban is the Toyota technique for controlling material flows. The Japanese word *kanban* means *card*, and Toyota uses a two-card kanban system. The first is a trans-

FIGURE 7.19   Toyota's production system

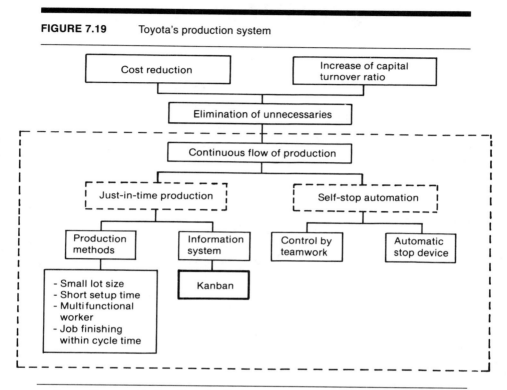

Source: European Working Group for Production Planning and Inventory Control, Lausanne, Switzerland, July 1982.

port, or conveyance, card; and the second is a production card. An example of the two cards, both for the same part number, is shown in Figure 7.20. Figure 7.21 shows the flow of the kanban cards and the resultant "pull" approach to authorizing production.

Starting at the right side of Figure 7.21, work center K123 decides to make one container (50 pieces) of part number 33311-3501 (it did so because a production kanban has just been received in the K123 Box). Someone at work center K123 removed a container of parts awaiting production from stock location A-12. When this container is removed from the location, a conveyance kanban is taken from the container (the top half of Figure 7.20) and placed in the A-12 Box. It authorizes someone to go to stock location A-07 and get a replacement container to put in inventory at stock location A-12 (with the conveyance kanban card). This container, while at stock location A-07, would have a production kanban attached (the lower half of Figure

FIGURE 7.20   Kanban cards

Conveyance Kanban	
Part number: 33311-3501 Container capacity: 50 No. of Kanban released: 7 of 12	Following work center: K123 Stock location no.: A-12
	Stock location no.: A-07 Preceding work center: Y321

Production Kanban

Production Kanban
Work center no.: Y321
Part number to be produced: 33311-3501
Container capacity: 50 units
Stock capacity at which to store: A-07
Materials required:
Material no. 33311-3504   Stock location: A-05
Part no. 33825-2474   Stock location: B-03

Source: R. W. Hall, *Driving the Productivity Machine: Production Planning and Control in Japan* (Falls Church, Va.: American Production and Inventory Control Society, 1981), p. 37. Reprinted with permission, American Production and Inventory Control Society, Inc.

7.20). This production kanban card is removed before the container is moved to stock location A-12, and placed in the A-07 Box. It then flows to the Y321 Box where it becomes the authorization for work center Y321 to remove two containers of components from their input stock locations. These locations are not shown in Figure 7.21, but the production kanban tells us that, to make 50 units of part number 33311-3501, work center Y321 needs material 33311-3504 (location A-05) and part number 33825-2474 (location B-03). In each of these locations, one would find containers with exactly 50 pieces.

The kanban cards replace all work orders and move tickets. To the extent that work-in-process is significantly reduced, the problem of sequencing jobs at work centers is also diminished. The system is completely visual and manual in execution. The chain of dual kanban cards can extend all the way back to the suppliers. Several of Toyota's suppliers receive their authorizations to produce via kanban cards.

FIGURE 7.21 Flow of kanban cards

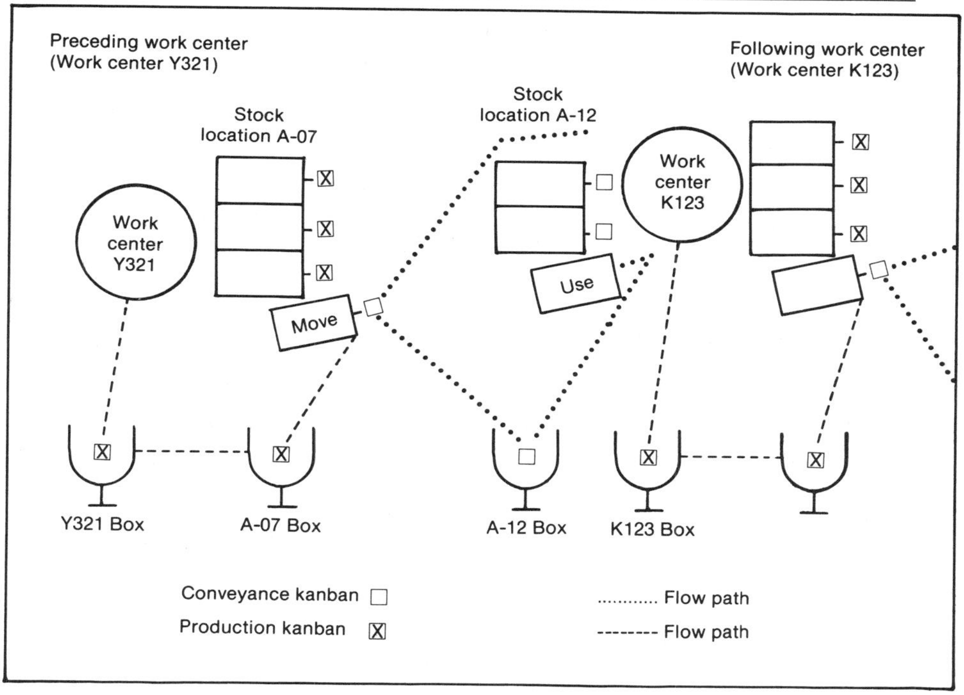

Source: R. W. Hall, *Driving the Productivity Machine: Production Planning and Control in Japan,* (Falls Church, Va.: American Production and Inventory Control Society, 1981), p. 38.

The kanban system is a pull system, because the work centers are only authorized to produce when they have a production kanban. They only get one when a downstream work center pulls a completed container of work from the producing work center's output storage area. No work center is allowed to process input to output merely to keep workers busy. Nor is a work center allowed to transport work (push) to a downstream work center. All movements are pulled, and workers are paced by the flow of kanban cards.

The number of kanban card sets in the system directly determines the level of work-in-process inventory. The more kanban cards, the more containers filled and waiting to be used at a work center. The formula used to calculate the number of kanban cards needed is given in Figure 7.22. In this

---

FIGURE 7.22   Calculating the number of kanbans

$$y = \frac{DL(1 + \alpha)}{a}$$

where:
y = Number of kanban card sets.
D = Demand per unit of time.
L = Lead time.
a = Container capacity.
α = Policy variable (safety stock).

---

formula, there is a factor for including safety stock, which Toyota says should be less than 10 percent. Using the formula, no safety stock, and a container size of 1, we can see the philosophy of the system. If a work center required eight units per day (one per hour) and it took one hour to make one unit, only one set of two kanban cards would be theoretically necessary; that is, just as a unit was finished, it would be needed at the subsequent operation.

The container sizes are kept small and standard. Toyota feels that no container should have more than 10 percent of a day's requirements. Since everything revolves around these containers and the flow of cards, a great deal of discipline is necessary. The following rules are used to keep the system operating:

● Each container of parts must have a kanban card.
● The parts are always pulled. The using department must come to the providing department and not vice versa.
● No parts may be obtained without a conveyance kanban card.
● All containers contain their standard quantities and only the standard container for the part can be used.
● No extra production is permitted. Production can only be started upon receipt of a production kanban card.

These rules keep the shop floor under control. The execution effort is directed toward flawless following of the rules. Execution is also directed toward continual improvement. In kanban terms, this means to reduce the number of kanban cards and, thereby, reduce the level of work-in-process inventory. Reducing the number of cards is consistent with an overall view of inventory as undesirable. It is said at Toyota that inventory is like water that covers up problems that are like rocks. Figure 7.23 depicts this viewpoint. If the inventory is systematically reduced, the problems are exposed—and attention can be directed to their solution. Problems that are obscured by inventory still remain.

FIGURE 7.23   Toyota's view of inventory

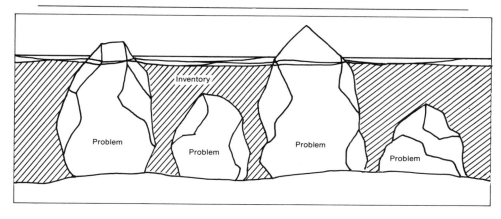

Figure 7.19 shows "continuous flow of production" as hierarchically above just-in-time production. At Toyota, a great deal of care is put into stabilizing production rates. The production plan covers a one-year horizon and is updated monthly. The master production schedule *is* the final assembly schedule. It is frozen for one month. The following two months are specified by model family. All three months are stated in daily buckets. The daily schedule is identical for each day in the month. This degree of stability is critical to use of the kanban system with minimal inventory levels.

The stabilized schedule is also very useful for capacity planning purposes, both within Toyota and for its vendors. The plant is run as much as possible as a continuous flow. Cycle times are easily determined, and problem areas from a capacity point of view can be isolated.

Not everything at Toyota is controlled via kanban cards. Engines, for example, are planned somewhat differently, because there are too many varieties. If done with the standard kanban card approach, it would be necessary to have at least one engine of every variety at both the final assembly station and at the engine assembly output storage area. The number of engine possibilities makes this unwieldy. Instead, the final assembly schedule is transmitted to the engine assembly area for its own scheduling. The schedule is only frozen for several hours, and it can reflect necessary changes due to a body being pulled off the line for rework, and so on. These changes fall within the parameters of the frozen monthly schedule; they are not unchecked reactions to changes in the marketplace.

The same approach, which is often called "broadcasting" of the final assembly schedule, is used to schedule all items that have many options. In some cases, such as for seats, this schedule is electronically transmitted back to vendors, who also can respond to changes within hours. At the Nissan plant in Tennessee, vendor trucks are loaded in the right sequence for final assembly. With about two hours notice, schedules are made, based on approximately four deliveries per hour. The net result is that neither Nissan nor the vendor retains inventories of seats. The raw materials are converted into the exact sequence of required seats for the final assembly line.

Single card kanban

The Toyota system is based on a dual card kanban system, with both a production kanban and a conveyance kanban. There are other approaches involving only one card, its equivalent, or no cards at all. A single card kanban system does not use a production kanban. It is the conveyance kanban that provides the primary control over material movement.

Under one form of a single card kanban system, production is started using a system such as MRP, with daily production rates. Actual delivery to downstream work centers is, however, controlled by the pull of the single kanbans. The primary difference is that a work center is more free to decide what it will work on at a particular time. Each work center has a daily schedule that is to be met, and each is under some obligation to have material finished in its output storage area. For example, returning to Figure 7.21, work center Y321 would know how many of part 33311-3501 it needs to make daily. This information would be provided by a centralized scheduling function. It can decide whether to make these in one container at a time or in more than a one container batch. The output again would be placed in stock location A-07, but the containers would not have production kanbans attached. It is incumbent upon work center Y321 to have at least one container of each part it produces on hand.

Stock location A-12 will generally have less inventory under the single kanban approach. Usually all that is required is that one container be worked on (and perhaps one more) so work center K123 also has the flexibility to work in more than one-container batches. Supporting work center K123 is a delivery system that allows someone to go to stock location A-07 to get more work whenever that is necessary. This could be provided by some periodic delivery system, or by the workers in work center K123 getting the material themselves.

The somewhat greater autonomy provided by the single card kanban approach is not without its costs. To the extent that work centers are allowed schedule flexibility, there necessarily will be greater inventory levels and a concomitant "hiding of the rocks." It is also more cumbersome to reduce inventory levels directly than is the case by removing some of the kanbans from the system. Finally, the dual card approach provides a production schedule with less need for work rates being provided from a central staff activity. Despite these seeming costs of single card kanban system, the single card approach is far more widely used.

Our example with Muth's 1-quart saucepan used a single card variation that captured some of the advantages of the dual card system; that is, when the container was returned to the producing department, this represented the authorization to build more. This approach is simpler, to the extent that the number of parts produced by a work center is relatively small. Simplicity is also aided when the product line is not very complex, so the downstream work center personnel can readily remember what are the parts required and where they are produced. When this is the case, there is less need for the kanban card information, which tells the worker the necessary materials and where they are to be found.

Product complexity and product variety clearly influence the ability of the workers to plan and control materials flow without bill of material and routing information. The ability to use JIT concepts in ever more complex situations is increasing. An example is seen at the Tennant Company. Almost all of the shop lead time for one of the industrial sweepers was accounted for by one complex set of welded subassemblies. A "kanban cart" was constructed that could hold the set of parts required, as well as the completed subassemblies. When a cart was emptied at the final assembly area, it was sent back to the stores area. Parts were picked for the subassemblies, routed through fabrication and painting steps, and delivered back to the final assembly area. All of this was accomplished without any other scheduling or shop-floor control system support. Total flow time for this process was a matter of hours, instead of weeks, and a complete set was delivered in every cart.

Hewlett-Packard

Hewlett-Packard (HP) is one of the more successful users of JIT in the United States. The company started its JIT work in its higher volume product lines, but it has since expanded its efforts into low-volume complex product factories. In Fort Collins, Colorado, HP makes the HP9000 minicomputer, which is an assemble-to-order product sold in almost unlimited end item configurations. JIT has been in use in Fort Collins since 1981. Over the last five years, increasing attention has been devoted to total quality control (TQC) programs, better linkages with suppliers, lead time reductions, relayout of the factory, and continuing improvements in day-to-day operations. Some of the results include an increase in work-in-process turns from 5 to 45 times per year, a decrease in required space of 20 percent while output increased 29 percent, and both scrap and rework decreases of more than 50 percent.

At the Medical Electronics Division in Waltham, Massachusetts, a very

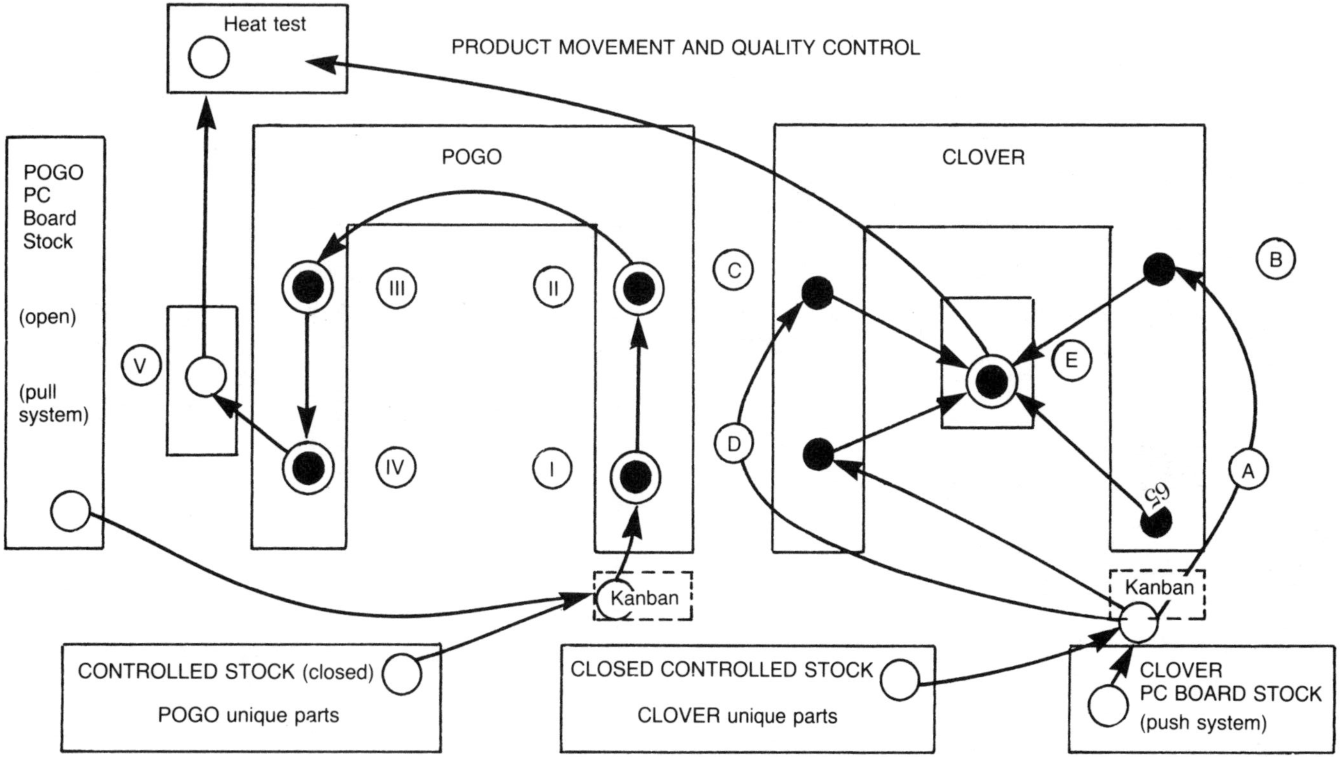

FIGURE 7.24   Hewlett-Packard Waltham Division Pogo/Clover production "U"s

interesting approach to JIT is being implemented. JIT is being used for the assembly of two of the major patient monitoring products called Pogo and Clover. Figure 7.24 shows the layout of the assembly area for these products. Clover is the older, more expensive product, with a larger number of customer specified options. Pogo was designed as a lower-cost alternative. Pogo was also designed with JIT manufacture in mind. The Clover assembly process is made up of four feeder subassemblies (A–D) and a final assembly and test area (E). Pogo is designed to be built in four successive assembly stations in a U shape where a test is performed in each. A final test is performed at station V. Both Clover and Pogo go into a heat test area, shown at the top of Figure 7.24. The series of tests performed on Pogo at each station (I–IV) has allowed HP to more quickly reduce the failure rate in heat testing than was the case for Clover.

Both Clover and Pogo are supported by dedicated component stock areas. Each is also supported with a printed circuit board stock. In the case of Pogo, 12 types of circuit boards are maintained, with a single card kanban approach. They are supplied in lot sizes of four, with coded clothespins acting as the single kanban. The printed circuit boards for Clover are not maintained with a JIT system. As indicated in Figure 7.24, stocks of these boards are maintained with a "push" system. A single card kanban approach is used to pull kits of parts from the controlled stock areas for both Pogo and Clover.

The HP Waltham JIT system is supported by several computer systems, which are MRP-based. These are companywide systems developed for Hewlett-Packard. At Waltham, they are mainly used for component part planning. As time goes by, however, the semimonthly MRP explosion, weekly allocation quantities, and daily release against these allocation quantities are becoming more cumbersome for JIT manufacturing. JIT operates in a very different time frame.

A more profound issue is concerned with the overall philosophy taken by HP Waltham in adopting JIT. The primary emphasis has been on stability. In Pogo, for example, the goal has been to make 10 units per day, each and every day. This goal has been achieved, and it is now possible to get 10 good units between 8:00 A.M. and about 1:30 P.M. on most days. To concentrate on stability, the Pogo assembly area has been buffered on both ends. Extra supplies of component materials have been held, as have extra finished goods inventories.

At the present time, the stability has been achieved. Relatively flawless output can be achieved with regularity. The attention is now shifting to being able to reduce buffers and to increase responsiveness. If the assembly area can produce 15 units on a particular day when necessary, the finished goods can be reduced. With flawless production, lower component inventories can also be attained.

As productivity is increased, new alternatives are presented. For example, perhaps a rebalance of the Pogo line tasks can free up the first worker, so stock picking can be done by that worker instead of using another person. Still another opportunity is for cross training of workers, so an absence or transfer of employee can be better tolerated. The results of JIT at Waltham are impressive. Total plant inventory has been reduced from $56 million to $40 million in 15 months. Work-in-process inventory for the Pogo line has been reduced from 50 units to 4, and the assembly floor space required has been decreased by 65 percent. Quality has been increased substantially by the JIT approach, as well. But all has not been done. There are still new avenues for improvement. Included is further reduction in the printed circuit board inventories and tackling what appear to be bottlenecks in circuit board production.

NONREPETITIVE JIT

Many of the principles of JIT that we have described for high-volume repetitive manufacturing apply in low-volume production environments, as well. However, most low-volume manufacturers have balked at two basic problems presented by the "classical" approaches to JIT: the requirement of setting up high-volume flow lines dedicated to a few products, and level loading. A merging may be taking place, since, even for the classical repetitive manufacturer, it is becoming increasingly important to respond to customer pressures for greater flexibility in volume, product mix, and other service features. High-volume repetitive manufacturers are necessarily learning to cope with greater product variety; the lower-volume job shop manufacturers are in turn learning to adapt JIT to their environments.

A service enhanced view of manufacturing

An examination of service operations can provide insights that are particularly germane to producing products with greater service enhancements. Service operations have limited ability to buffer customer demand with inventories. In service operations, the customer is typically more closely involved in the actual service creation process. Both of these phenomena are present in the environment increasingly faced by manufacturing companies. Rapid response is critical, the number of possible product/service combinations continues to grow so end item forecasting is more difficult, and large buffer inventories are not acceptable. Customers are more actively involved in product/service definition, particularly when one takes into account logistical coupling of firms as vendor and customer.

All of this argues for a JIT mode of manufacture; one whose objective is to be able to accept any customer order and turn it out right behind any other, and one that can have the flexibility to handle surges in volume or mix changes. All of this has to be done on a routine basis. Once again, the service industries provide an example. McDonald's can handle two busloads of Boy Scouts or an unexpected shift from Big Macs to fish sandwiches with little need to resort to some "panic mode" of operation. Manufacturing firms tend to call in the indirect labor "shock troops" and overpower the formal system whenever a significant unexpected event comes along.

Fast-food operations provide still another example. In almost all of the successful fast-food chains, there has been an evolution toward a broader product line (greater band width). McDonald's now serves chicken, for example. The objective in all of this has been to be able to increase market appeal, while maintaining maximum responsiveness, minimal inventories, small lot sizes, short lead times, and so on.

The traditional JIT view of level capacity also changes in adapting to nonrepetitive situations. Responsiveness to fickle demand requires a large band width in terms of surge capacity. No one wants the fire department to be operated at high capacity utilization; immediate response is essential. Surge capacity needs to be in place in both equipment and labor. When carrying these ideas into nonrepetitive manufacturing, a different view of asset management and labor utilization is required. Fixed assets (both capital and people) will be less intensively utilized to increase material velocity and overall system responsiveness.

Labor capacity has to be available to handle surges. To the extent that the whole person concept is achieved, cross training and other investments in personnel development can be focused on better ability to handle surges and more useful application of "excess" time to other enterprise objectives. More and more work now handled by staff personnel can and should be handled by people who have traditionally been considered as direct labor.

Capital utilization also has to be reexamined in light of overall objectives. An example of this is found in a large electronics firm that has two factories making similar products. In one of these factories, automatic insertion equipment was purchased that operates very close to its capacity. The other plant purchased considerably more insertion capacity relative to the expected needs. The first plant initially thought that it had done a better job— it was using capital assets more intensively. After several months, the plant managers changed their minds. They now see the equipment as relatively inexpensive, compared with an ability to respond to surges brought on by changes in requirements. By having "excess" capacity in equipment and people, changes in schedules and design are much easier to handle. The result is routine execution without leveling or the use of complex systems, in a rapidly changing manufacturing environment.

Another example of the kinds of problems brought on by level loading is seen in a manufacturer of small engines sold to OEM manufacturers. The company installed a JIT system, based on standard level loading principles. Unfortunately, the demand for the products is quite seasonal and the number of exact end items sold is high (although there is considerable part commonality). The results of running this JIT system were good efficiencies in manufacturing, but they were achieved at the expense of large seasonal inventories and product mix problems; the wrong end items were frequently in finished goods. Clearly, what is needed in this case is a series of level loaded schedules, where capacity is not utilized at the same rate over the entire year, and where the basics of JIT are maintained.

Flexible systems

The requirements for volume and product flexibility are being understood by leading-edge firms. Some have had experience in repetitive manufacturing applications of JIT and are now moving into nonrepetitive applications. An example is a telecommunications equipment manufacturer, which began JIT in its high-volume telephone handset operations. The firm only made six models; in two years its inventory turns were tripled, work-in-process was reduced by 75 percent, failure rates in manufacturing were cut in half, and setup times were reduced by 50 percent. Thereafter, the firm turned to its low-volume CBX plant, where more than 150 basic circuit boards are manufactured, and every end item is somewhat of a custom order. The company has learned that it must go back to the basics of JIT product engineering, process engineering, and the whole person concept to successfully implement JIT for its nonrepetitive products.

The firm developed cellular designs, cellular manufacturing with great flexibility, and cross trained people with an emphasis on being able to handle volume surges in the CBX plant. MRP is still used for overall planning, but far fewer transactions are processed by the hidden factory of indirect labor. In the first six months, first pass yields on circuit boards improved 27 percent, work-in-process was reduced by 31 percent, the manufacturing cells under JIT hit 100 percent of schedule and then the people helped out other parts of the company that were behind schedule.

Simplified systems and routine execution

A major issue in any JIT firm, repetitive or nonrepetitive, is with flow times. Work must flow through the factory so quickly that detailed tracking is not required. A related idea is in the responsiveness of the systems. In several JIT systems we have seen in nonrepetitive environments, the firm installed what might be called a "weekly wash." In its simplest form, the weekly wash means that week 1's sales orders become week 2's production schedule.

As an example, Stanley Hardware in New Britain, Connecticut, is a make-to-stock firm for most of its items, but some are unique to a particular customer. It has applied JIT with the weekly wash concept to three different production areas. In each case, the weekly sales for a particular week were determined on Friday, and the resultant quantities were manufactured in the next week within some change parameters. In one case, the week-to-week variation in production could be plus or minus 20 percent. For a second product group, the swing was plus or minus 35 percent, and for a third group of products any adjustment could be handled. Because the response times have been shortened, customer service has been enhanced.

The products have to be capable of being manufactured in this time frame, and the manufacturing processes have to have the necessary band width to take on necessary volume and mix changes for this approach to work. For some product lines at Stanley, this was easier than for others. We noted that there were differences among the three production areas in their ability to take week-to-week output variations. This is the band width concept applied to volume. Band width as applied to product diversity was also different across the three lines. In one case, there were less than a dozen end items. For another, the end item possibilities were about two dozen. However, the third product group encompassed several hundred end items. Moreover, the mix among end items varied significantly from week to week, making this the most difficult of the lines to design for mix band width.

Sometimes the required flexibility in volume and mix was provided by product design, and other times it was supported more by the inherent flexibility of the processing unit. Also supporting the weekly wash at Stanley Hardware was creative use of people. For example, when they are not required to make products, the personnel of one department are utilized in packaging other items. There is a large amount of hardware packaging done at Stanley, and the required equipment is not expensive. By having extra equipment available for these workers to use, flexibility is enhanced.

The weekly wash approach to JIT for nonrepetitive manufacturing shifts the emphasis from the scheduling of material to the scheduling of time blocks. The focus is on what is scheduled in the next time frame, rather than on when we will make product X. This focus is driven by the actual requirements, rather than a forecast of needs. It is as though one is scheduling a set of trains or busses. We do not hold the train until it is full, and we can always cram a few more people onto a car, within reason. By scheduling trains on a relatively frequent basis, attempting to keep capacity as flexible as possible, and only assigning "passengers" to a time frame, responsiveness to actual demand can be increased, and detailed scheduling can be made more simple.

JIT IN PURCHASING

JIT has been applied and misapplied in purchasing. Some firms simply ask their suppliers to buffer poor schedules. On the other hand, when done well, the results of a joint JIT approach can be greater bottom line results for both firms and increased competitiveness in the marketplace.

The basics

The first prerequisite to JIT in purchasing is a scheduling system that produces requirements that are reasonably certain. Without predictability, JIT for the vendors is merely a case of their customers exporting the problems. Although this may work in the short run, in the long run it cannot. We have seen a factory where the benefits of JIT were extolled, only to find a new paving project—for vendors' trucks. The inventory had been moved from the warehouse to trailer trucks! Similar war stories abound about warehousing firms in Detroit that are there to buffer suppliers from the demands made on them by the auto companies as they implement JIT.

The features of an integrated MPC system are essential for JIT. As we have noted, JIT has its primary emphasis on execution activities. Good planning precedes excellence in execution. At a more detailed level, we believe that effective internal use of JIT is also a prerequisite for most JIT efforts in purchasing. As a firm becomes used to JIT operations itself, it will produce the right kinds of signals for implementation with vendors. The firm will also pick up the language and understanding of how to solve problems. When people in the firm can truly view inventory as covering up problems, understand the whole person concept, adopt a true zero defects mentality and know what that implies, and adopt a fanatical drive toward continually improved performance, they can be much more effective in extending JIT into vendor firms.

With this understanding, the communications with vendor firms will be fundamentally different than without it. The vendors can learn by observing JIT first hand in their customer's factory. Talking to counterparts at a detailed level is critically important. Instead of exporting problems, with an internally functional JIT program the customer now accepts joint responsibility for solving problems. Vendor and vendee learn together; both are willing to make changes in the ways they do business to achieve the overall improvements that JIT offers.

Another requirement of JIT for purchasing is to achieve, to whatever extent possible, a stable schedule. This is consistent with level schedules for the repetitive manufacturer. To the extent that a firm makes the same products, in the same quantities every day, without defects and without missing the schedule, the schedule for supplier firms is extremely simple. For the nonrepetitive manufacturer, the issue is less one of leveling and more one of no surprises. The level schedule may be violated in nonrepetitive environments, but the cost is a greater need for coordinated information flows and, perhaps, for larger buffer inventories. However, there is a major difference between a *stable* (albeit nonlevel) schedule and one which is simply uncertain. The only cure for the latter case is buffer inventories.

Certainty is a relative commodity. A vendor might be able to live fairly well with a schedule that is unpredictable on a daily basis but very predictable on a weekly basis. A weekly MRP-based total, with some kind of daily call off of exact quantities, could be reasonably effective. The notion of weekly wash as practiced by Stanley Hardware could also be used; that is, an inventory equal to some maximum expected weekly usage could be maintained and replenished on a weekly basis. For high-value products, it might be worth it to go to some kind of biweekly wash, or to obtain better advance information from the customer via MRP and some electronic data interchange.

Other "basics" for JIT in purchasing include all of the action programs discussed earlier in the chapter. These are necessary both inside the customer plant and for the vendors! Setup time reduction, error free production, statistical process control, no work-in-process tracking, worker involvement, cellular manufacturing, cross training of workers, and all the issues associated with product design, manufacturing process design, and the whole person concept need to be actively pursued. Pursuing them on a joint basis and sharing experiences will only improve the speed at which true JIT gets implemented.

A JIT "basic" that is uniquely associated with purchasing relates to pruning the number of vendors. It follows that, if the customer firm is to work closely with supplier firms, it will be important to limit the number of suppliers. Many companies have reduced their vendor base by more than 90 percent to achieve an environment where it is possible to work on a truly cooperative basis with the remaining vendors. Hidden factory issues have to be considered in vendor relations as well. There are those who feel that the secret to JIT is to run MRP in daily or hourly buckets. We are not at all sure that this is the best idea for most firms. The resultant transaction and indirect labor costs associated with such a system could be enormous unless some key changes were made. A better approach might be the use of MRP to provide weekly quantities, agreed upon safety stocks, or amounts by which the sum of daily quantities can exceed weekly totals, and a daily phone call to the supplier for the next day's in-shipment. All of this could be done without intervention of indirect labor personnel.

A computer disk drive manufacturer has such a system where, each day at about 4 P.M., an assembly line worker calls a key vendor and tells it how many of a particular expensive item to deliver the day after tomorrow. The units delivered never go into any stockroom or into any inventory records. They are delivered directly to the line without inspection and are assembled that day. The vendor is paid on the basis of deliveries of finished disk drives into finished goods inventory. Stability is handled by the customer providing the vendor with weekly MRP projections, using time fences that define stability guarantees.

Another issue that relates to frequent deliveries is the cost of transportation. Some firms have approached this by asking vendors to build factories in near proximity. Although this is possible for very large companies, where the output of a plant is largely dedicated to a single customer, this clearly will not be feasible for most vendors.

A different solution is for the customer to pick up the goods from the vendors on some prearranged schedule. This is increasingly being done for several reasons. The most obvious is the savings in transportation costs over having each vendor deliver independently. A second reason relates to stability and predictability. If the customer picks up the material, some of the uncertainty inherent in vendor deliveries can be eliminated. Finally, pickup offers more chances to directly attack hidden factory costs. The customer can, for example, provide containers that hold the desired amounts and that will flow as kanbans through the plant. The savings in packaging materials, as well as the costs of unpacking, are helpful to both parties. Items can also be placed on special racks inside the truck to minimize damage. Defective items can be returned easily for replacement without the usual costly return to vendor procedures and paperwork. Other paperwork can similarly be simplified when third parties are not involved and when the loop is closed between problem and action in a short time frame.

Pickup can also be done in geographic areas beyond the factory. A Hewlett-Packard factory in Boise, Idaho, has outputs from its suppliers in Silicone Valley, California (a distance of about 600 miles), pooled by a trucking firm. Thereafter, the entire shipment is moved to Boise on a daily basis. New United Motor Manufacturing (NUMMI) in Freemont, California, does the same thing with its Midwest suppliers: a Chicago-based trucking company collects trailer loads for daily piggyback shipments to California (a distance of about 2,000 miles). NUMMI started off holding a three-day safety stock of these parts, with plans to reduce it to one day after experience had been gained.

Examples

The Xerox Corporation undertook a JIT program as a response to the stiff competition in the copier business. Over a two-year period, Xerox reduced the number of suppliers from 5000 to 300, who were, thereafter, signed up to long-term supply contracts. The emphasis was both on JIT manufacture and on quality improvements. Unfortunately, the early emphasis was heavily weighted toward making the suppliers hold the inventory, rather than on joint problem identification and solution. This resulted in significant supplier problems, until Xerox stabilized production schedules and became a true partner in JIT with its suppliers. Xerox now runs education classes for supplier firms, helps them become JIT companies, and helps them develop JIT in *their* suppliers.

Harley-Davidson is another well-known U.S. JIT company. The firm originally went into JIT because it found that its Japanese competitors had an operating cost advantage of about 30 percent. The company did not have initial success with its JIT programs in purchasing. The approach had too many legalistic constraints for the suppliers to support, and Harley-Davidson had a reputation with its suppliers for continual expediting and deexpediting. In short, the vendors felt that they were being asked to commit themselves legally to a process that would not have the necessary stability. The JIT approach with vendors was modified. The emphasis shifted to joint problem resolution, including setup time reduction, statistical process control, and joint design efforts. The results have been beneficial for both the vendors and Harley-Davidson.

Purchasing is only one aspect of JIT at Harley-Davidson. In a three-year period, inventory turns for raw materials and work-in-process increased almost 300 percent, setup times were reduced by more than 75 percent on more than 400 machines, productivity per worker was increased by 38 percent, rejected materials were reduced by 66 percent, and other measures of quality were improved substantially.

JIT SOFTWARE

There are several software packages available to support JIT. A well-known one is the Hewlett-Packard system. As will be seen, this package has much in common with the MPC system shown as Figure 7.1. To support the material velocity goal of JIT, the MPS is generated as a rate, and post-deduct logic (backflush) is used for updating component inventory balances.

HP JIT software

Figure 7.25 depicts key blocks of Hewlett-Packard's just-in-time manufacturing software. Rate-based master production scheduling is the approach used for the front end of HP's JIT system. A monthly production plan is converted into the MPS (a daily build schedule) with a spreadsheet program and a personal computer (PC). The resultant schedule is matched against backlogs of customer orders and forecasted orders. Problems highlighted by the program can lead a master scheduler to make changes in the build schedule. The software is designed so that data from the PC can be directly transferred to the HP JIT programs.

Stock areas and deduct lists are used to define the manufacturing process; that is, a stock area is where any part is to be found. A deduct list is the set of parts (and quantities) that are to be decremented from their respective stock areas when a particular stage of product assembly (a deduct point) has been achieved. "Achievement" is transmitted to the system by production reporting. Deduct points in the process are those steps where parts are now to be associated with a higher-level assembly and no longer as individual

FIGURE 7.25   Block diagram of HP's JIT software

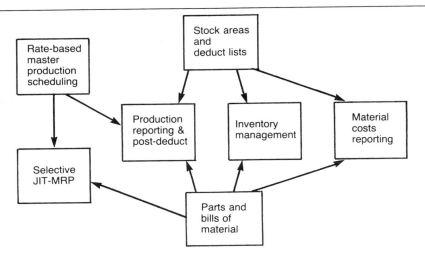

parts. When production at a deduct point has been realized, backflushing of the component inventories (according to the deduct list) is done. In the HP software, this can occur at more than one stage in the assembly process. A deduct list is associated with each assembly for which a deduct point backflush is specified. The list also specifies from which stock areas the deductions are to be made. The sum of all deduct lists has to equal the overall bill of material for the end item.

Production reporting and post-deduct (backflushing) procedures are the subsystem shown in Figure 7.25 to accomplish the deductions from each stock area's inventory balance. Inventory management maintains the current status of inventories in each designated stock location. The numbers, however, are not precisely correct, because of the timing of the post-deduct procedures. Any material already removed from a stock area but not yet having reached a deduct point will incorrectly be treated as on hand in the location by the inventory management subsystem. Material costs reporting summarizes materials consumption during defined accounting periods, subject to the same limitations of post-deduct. These errors are small (and constant) when material velocity is high and the schedules are fairly level.

Selective JIT-MRP means that the HP JIT software can be integrated with an HP traditional MRP package. Shared data bases can be used in both systems, and bills of material can be linked. Parts common to both systems are integrated in the HP MRP package, with the JIT driven requirements treated as independent demand. Some products can be planned with traditional MRP, while others can utilize JIT approaches. This means that adoption of JIT can be a steady evolution from MRP.

An example of how this works can be seen by returning to our earlier HP example, shown in Figure 7.24. Concentrating on the Pogo example, let us suppose that originally this product was built as five separate subassembly and test steps (I–V), going into inventory after each step and was planned and controlled with MRP at each stage of assembly or tests. For each of these discrete steps, the prior assembly would be picked from inventory, along with the unique components associated with the particular subassembly stage. Withdrawals of subassemblies and component parts would be deducted from on-hand inventory balances, as they occurred, in classic MRP tradition.

Under HP JIT, the entire flow might be considered as one step from I to V; that is, the deduct point would be when step V is completed. This is the only step that needs to be reported through production reporting. When this occurs, a deduct list would have all of the components required for steps I–V; all would be deducted at that point in time from the on-hand balance data associated with the Pogo PC board stock and the controlled stock area for unique Pogo parts. We also noted that the printed circuit (PC) boards for Pogo were controlled with a JIT system. This means that receipt of boards into this area would also be a deduct point. When production reporting reports that particular circuit boards have reached the Pogo PC stock area, the deduct lists for the PC board components will be used to decrement the respective parts and locations.

Parts and bills of material in HP JIT are the equivalent of the usual product structure data files in MRP, but they are defined according to deduct points. The JIT based product structures have only a few levels, as was the case in the redesigned 1-quart saucepan of Figure 7.17. Each level corresponds to a deduct point and the components are the deduct list. Standard cost data are associated with the product structures in this JIT format. As products are converted to JIT from MRP, it is necessary to reformat the data according to the deduct points.

The HP JIT system also supports customization by users to match certain individual needs. Some of the customization can be accomplished without additional programming. Included are definitions of system transaction screens and output reports. Advanced customization can also be supported by using predetermined exit points for transactions. This approach to customization allows JIT software to be connected with other operating systems in the company, but the firm is still able to use updated versions of HP JIT software.

JIT using MRP software

Roger Brooks describes a JIT approach used by a firm that had successfully implemented MRP. This company wanted to use JIT for some of its products, while maintaining the MRP systems. The firm schedules these products in daily buckets using firm-planned orders (FPOs). The FPOs will, of course, generate dependent demand for the component parts. The firm does not use a stockroom for the components, the FPOs are never converted into scheduled receipts, and the components are not issued to any shop orders. The FPO data are communicated to the floor for build purposes and are used to sequence the assembly line. As assembled products are completed, they are received into inventory using normal procedures for MRP inventory transactions. These receipts are also netted against the FPO quantities. Consequently, requirements for the corresponding component parts are also reduced.

The result of these steps is a backflush for inventory balances. The firm has high levels of data integrity in the bills of material, it keeps meticulous records of stock balances, and it cycle counts at least once per week. This attention to detail is needed for the back flushing to work properly. The JIT approach of back flushing runs completely counter to standard notions in MPC systems. Back flushing *will* work, but speed in conversion is critical, and so are other methods to ensure data integrity.

MANAGERIAL IMPLICATIONS

The vision of JIT presented in this chapter is much broader than one constrained to only manufacturing planning and control. JIT is best seen as an integrated approach to achieving continued manufacturing excellence. A holistic view of JIT encompasses a set of programs, as well as a process where human resources are continually redeployed in better ways to serve the company objectives in the marketplace. In the balance of this chapter, we feel compelled to speculate a bit on what this implies for manufacturing planning and control and related areas.

Information system implications

Since JIT requires changes in the ways that manufacturing is managed and executed, so are changes required in the ways that computer-based systems are designed to support manufacturing. The changes run counter to many existing approaches to the use of computers in manufacturing.

JIT calls for reducing the number of transactions and the size of the hidden factory. What this means is that large centralized computer systems will tend to be less used than is true for MRP-based execution systems. To the extent that JIT is used for nonrepetitive manufacturing, it well may be that personal computers are used by people on the floor to provide whatever detailed scheduling information is required.

The whole person concept also supports this trend. Shop people can and will learn how to use spreadsheet programs and other user-friendly computer systems. They will use this knowledge to solve execution problems of whatever variety are important. Moreover, if one accepts the notion of constant evolution, the systems will change as needed. For example, at some point a detailed statistical process control program might be needed to solve a quality problem. But, when the problem is clearly solved, the detailed computer system might well be abandoned. The workers no longer need it; moreover, the computer and knowledge resources might be better utilized on a new project.

Current trends in computer technology indicate that powerful computers with ever-increasing user friendliness will become quite inexpensive. Workers will apply this power to problems as perceived at a point in time. To some extent, the result will be an evolutionary approach to CIM (computer integrated manufacturing). Computer power will be applied to problems of an integrative nature, including those that cross company boundaries. The service enhanced view of manufacturing means that firms will increasingly use their computer power in ways that are of value to their customers, and to *their* customers.

Manufacturing planning and control

The implications of JIT for production control and other material planning and control activities are quite profound. JIT offers the potential for eliminating or sharply reducing stockrooms, incoming quality control, receiving, kitting, paper processing associated with deliveries and shipments, the amount of detailed scheduling done by central staff, and all of the detailed tracking associated with a shop-floor control system. It is vital to make estimates of these costs as the MPC system is enhanced to embody JIT. Many of them are "well hidden." There are large benefits that clearly justify the costs associated with a JIT program in manufacturing.

It will not be easy to change the systems in some companies. Organizations have grown around them, cost accounting and other areas seem to require data that are generated by these systems, and many jobs are involved. However, the potential is there, and some of the people presently working in manufacturing planning and control will rise to the challenge and make the company more competitive through implementation of JIT.

Scorekeeping

In the firm that adopts JIT in its fullest context, it will be necessary to think very carefully about reward systems and managerial scorekeeping. Traditional measurement systems tend to focus attention on costs associated with producing the products, using cost accounting systems that have changed little since the Industrial Revolution. These systems are based on an era when direct labor was the major cost source of the products. Now, in many companies, it is materials cost that dominates, with the traditional definition of direct labor cost continually decreasing in relative importance.

Firms are more and more providing a set of "service enhanced" products to their customers. The services include logistical support, fast response, rapid design changes, and hidden factory cost reductions. In most cases, these services are provided with knowledge work, rather than by the usual definitions of direct labor. A chemical firm is now providing a chemical in 3.5-pound bags to a particular customer who uses that amount in each batch of a particular process. The old measurements based on tons produced are not adequate for helping this firm determine the value of manufacturing investments to provide these service enhancements.

JIT is focused on material velocity. This focus is consistent with the objectives of inventory reduction and lead time compression. These programs tend to be cost related. However, under JIT, it is important to be very careful about the way "costs" are measured and the resultant implications for decision making. The values of band width, flexibility, responsiveness, and worker skill enhancement need to be recognized. None of these is incorporated in traditional accounting systems.

The entire approach to capacity utilization will need to be rethought by the JIT firm. Utilization of capital assets may not be as important as responsiveness and material velocity. Being able to take any customer order, even when vastly different from forecast, and doing so with short lead times and no use of "shock troops" is the goal. However, it is the improved responsiveness to the needs of the marketplace that will separate the successful firms from the also-rans.

What all of this means for cost accounting is that many traditional views will need to be scrapped. For example, some Hewlett-Packard factories have given up the cost category of direct labor. They simply have labor. The distinction between direct and indirect is not useful, and basing product costs on multiples of direct labor cost leads to more erroneous implications than some other scheme.

If one follows the idea of lifetime employment or commitment, then labor is a fixed cost. The whole person concept can lead to the conclusion that this labor pool is an asset that can be enhanced. Moreover, it also points to the use of direct labor for activities not normally associated with direct labor. Trying to apportion the labor into various categories may just not be worth the trouble. Even if it were, the continual goal of learning/improvement means that apportionment would be constantly changing. A final scorekeeping issue is the challenge to top management to create the organizational climate where the JIT journey can best take place. We believe that JIT is, in the last analysis, a key means for survival in the years ahead. Leadership will be required to guide manufacturing firms through the necessary changes.

CONCLUDING PRINCIPLES

This chapter is devoted to providing an understanding of JIT and how the concepts of JIT fit into MPC systems. Our view of JIT encompasses more than MPC related activities, but there is a significant overlap between JIT and our approach to MPC systems. In summarizing this chapter, we see the following principles as important:

- Stabilizing, and in some cases leveling, the production schedules is a prerequisite to effective JIT systems.
- Achieving very short lead times supports better customer service and responsiveness.
- Reducing hidden factory costs can be at least as important as reducing costs more usually attributed to factory operations.
- Implementing the whole person concepts reduces distinctions between white- and blue-collar workers and taps the skills of all persons for improving performance.
- Cost accounting and performance measurements need to reflect the shift in emphasis away from direct labor as the primary source of value added.
- To achieve the benefits of JIT in nonrepetitive applications, some of the basic features of repetitive based JIT need to be modified.
- JIT is not incompatible with MRP-based systems. Firms can evolve toward JIT from MRP based systems, adopting JIT as much or as little as they want, with an incremental approach.

REFERENCES

Bitran, G. R., and L. Chang. "A Mathematical Programming Approach to a Deterministic Kanban System." *Management Science* 33, no. 4, April 1987.

Brooks, Roger. "Backflush with Caution." *Oliver Wight Newsletter*, Oliver Wight Companies, 1986.

Crosby, Philip B. *Quality Is Free: The Art of Making Quality Certain*, New York: McGraw-Hill, 1979.

Gelb, Tom. "Harley-Davidson: A Company That's Taking a Different Route." *Target* 9, October 1985.

Goddard, Walter. "Just-In-Time Needs Shop Floor Control." *Modern Materials Handling*, May 7, 1984.

————. *Just-In-Time: Surviving by Breaking Tradition.* Essex Junction, Vermont: Oliver Wight Limited Publications, Inc., 1986.

Hall, R. W. *Driving the Productivity Machine.* Falls Church, Va.: American Production and Inventory Control Society, 1981.

————. *Zero Inventories.* Homewood, Ill.: Dow Jones-Irwin, 1983.

————. *Attaining Manufacturing Excellence.* Homewood, Ill.: Dow Jones-Irwin, 1987.

Huang, P. Y.; L. P. Rees; and B. W. Taylor III. "A Simulation Analysis of the Japanese Just-in-Time Technique (with Kanbans) for a Multiline, Multistage Production System." *Decision Sciences* 14, no. 3, July 1983.

Hutchins, Dexter. "Having a Hard Time with Just-In-Time." *Fortune*, June 9, 1986, pp. 64–66.

Hyer, N. L. "The Potential of Group Technology for U.S. Manufacturing." *Journal of Operations Management* 4, no. 3, 1984.

Krajewski, L. J.; B. E. King; L. P. Ritzman; and D. S. Wong. "Kanban, MRP and Shaping the Manufacturing Environment." *Management Science* 33, no. 1, January 1987.

Miller, J. G., and T. E. Vollmann. "The Hidden Factory." *Harvard Business Review*, September/October 1985, pp. 141–50.

Monden, Yasuhiro. "Adaptable Kanban System Helps Toyota Maintain Just-In-Time Production." *Journal of Industrial Engineering*, May 1981, pp. 29–46.

————. "'A Simulation Analysis of the Japanese Just-in-Time Technique (with Kanbans) for a Multiline, Multistage Production System': A Comment." *Decision Sciences* 15, no. 3, Summer 1984.

Nakane, J., and R. W. Hall. "Management Specs for Stockless Production." *Harvard Business Review*, May/June 1983, pp. 84–91.

Pinto, P. A., and V. A. Mabert. "A Joint Lot-Sizing Rule for Fixed Labor-Cost Situations." *Decision Sciences* 17, no. 2, Spring 1986.

Plossl, George W. (ed.). *Just-In-Time: A Special Roundtable.* Atlanta, Ga.: George Plossl Educational Services, 1985.

Schonberger, Richard J. *Japanese Manufacturing Techniques: Nine Hidden Lessons in Simplicity.* New York: Free Press, 1982.

————. "Some Observations on the Advantages and Implementation Issues of Just-in-Time Production Systems." *Journal of Operations Management* 3, no. 1, 1982.

————. *World Class Manufacturing.* New York: Free Press, 1986.

DISCUSSION QUESTIONS

1. Some people have argued that just-in-time is simply one more inventory control system. How do you think they could arrive at this conclusion?

2. Take one of the common systems at a university—for example, registration. Describe what kinds of "waste" can be found. How might one go about reducing this waste?

3. "Surge" capacity is the ability to take on an extra number of customers or product requests. How do the following three facilities handle surges? A football stadium, a clothing store, and an accounting firm?

4. List several different ways to signal the need for more material in a "pull" type system. Distinguish between situations where the feeder departments are in close proximity and those where they are at some distance.

5. Some companies contend that they can never adopt JIT because their suppliers are located all over the country and the distances are too great. What might you suggest to these firms?

6. "We just can't get anywhere on our JIT program. It is the suppliers' fault. We tell them every week what we want, but they still cannot seem to get it right. I have been over to their shops, and they have mountains of the wrong materials." What do you think is going on here?

7. One manager at a JIT seminar complained that he couldn't see what he would do with his workers if they finished their work before quitting time. How would you respond to this complaint?

8. How do you go about creating the organizational climate for successful JIT? Where do you start?

PROBLEMS

1. Graham Manufacturing has completed the following ABC analysis of the 10 products they make:

Product	Daily sales forecast
1	800
2	500
3	400
4	300
5	200
6	100
7	50
8	25
9	12.5
10	12.5
Total	2400.0

Graham has an assembly line that can produce 300 products per hour and works eight hours per day.

   a. Prepare a daily level schedule for Graham, assuming a batch (container size) of 100 for each product.
   b. Calculate the number of kanban cards required for each product, assuming a 0.5 day lead time and a 20 percent safety stock. What is the total number of kanban cards for all products?
   c. Assuming that storage space is proportional to the number of kanban cards, by what percentage will storage be reduced if the lead time can be reduced to one hour?
   d. What are the benefits, if any, of being able to cut all batch and container sizes to 50 units instead of 100?

2. Larry Dolinski, foreman of the assembly department at Graham Manufacturing, has proposed replacing the two-card kanban system with what he calls "American Kanban." Assembly is fed by two departments, each of which produces parts that are unique to each of the 10 products. This means that the total number of kanban card sets and containers of parts required would be the double of the calculations in problem 1. Based on a safety stock of zero and a container size of 100, Larry has calculated the total number of Kanban card sets for the two supplying departments as 34. Further, Larry has observed that, for products with low sales volumes, such as products 8, 9, and 10, the parts sit in inventory for many days before use.

   American Kanban consists of red, white, and blue containers, a different size for each of the two feeder departments. There are three of each color for each department (a total of 6 containers). Each container holds 100 parts, so a color is one hour's worth of work in final assembly. The rule there is to rotate in the order of red, white, and blue. The feeder departments receive the empty containers as Larry empties them and fill them according to a daily schedule. They can fill them faster than Larry can assemble.

   a. Diagram the flow of parts between one of the departments and assembly.
   b. What are the strengths and weaknesses of Larry's approach? How might it be improved?

3. Mark Davis, the foreman of one of the feeder lines in problems 1 and 2, was discussing the American Kanban with one of his workers, Howie Oden. Howie said that he did not see the benefits of the red, white, and blue system. He would rather have the daily schedule and be free to build it in whatever order he saw fit. He believed that economies could be gained by having some different order to the sequence of products produced in the feeder department. What he really wanted was to be able to be a full day ahead of assembly, which would give Larry greater flexibility as well. Mark agreed with Howie, and suggested that either Howie's one day ahead schedule be used or a fourth color (at the risk of being unpatriotic) be added.

   a. Diagram the new flow of parts for a 1-day-ahead schedule.
   b. What are the strengths and weaknesses of the fourth color suggestion?
   c. How does it compare to the system in problem 2?

4. Larry has been working hard to improve the assembly process described in problem 1. He now believes that assembly rates of 350 per hour can be achieved, instead of 300.

   a. What should the schedule be now?

   b. What, if any, are the benefits of this improvement?

   c. What are the implications?

5. Going back to the data in problem 1, let us suppose that Graham has finished goods inventories of 500 units for products 1 through 5, and 100 units for products 6 through 10. Let us assume a schedule for products 1 through 6 that produces the exact sales forecast each day; products 7 through 10 are produced less frequently than every day.

   a. On day 1, only products 1 through 6 were produced. At the end of the day what are the inventories for products 1 through 6, assuming no forecast errors?

   b. What are the inventories if 900 units of product 1 are sold, but only 300 units of product 2? What does this condition imply for the schedule per day 2?

   c. What happens if less than 2,400 units in total are sold? More than 2,400?

   d. How would improved material velocity and responsiveness help in parts b and c?

6. Fredrick Machine Company prided itself on the ability to keep up with the state of the art in its line of equipment. Although a small firm with only 300 factory workers, it had a fairly extensive line of products. The engineering staff generated an average of ten engineering change orders a week. Over several years, the firm had developed a procedure for processing these changes each week. A group of six people met each Friday morning to make the approvals. About 80 percent of the changes were approved and went on to a scheduling meeting in the afternoon (three people). The company was considering batching the changes for monthly processing (i.e., every four weeks).

   The company was not sure of the savings for doing this, but it gathered the following information:

   It took each person who attended a meeting about ½ hour to prepare for the meeting, regardless of the number of changes.

   It averaged about 10 minutes per engineering change to make either the approval or scheduling decision during the meetings.

   Each Monday, there was a general loss of productivity due to the scheduling changes. It affected about ⅓ of the factory workers and amounted to about ½ hour for each person. Again, this was independent of the number of changes.

   In addition to the general loss, the workers that were affected by the changes (about 10 workers per change) lost about an hour of productive time over three days.

   a. What are the costs over a 12-week period (in terms of labor hours) of the weekly batch system? What would be the change by going to a monthly system? (A spreadsheet might help with this and subsequent analysis.)

   b. Suppose that experience with monthly batching indicated the number of changes dropped (some of the changes that would have been made in the weekly system were superseded in the monthly system). Specifically, the average number of changes per week that were batched for approval dropped to eight and the average number scheduled dropped to seven. What would the quarterly costs be now?

c. The company was considering extending the batching to a quarterly basis. What would the costs be if the number of changes per week to be considered for approval dropped to seven and the number scheduled dropped to six?

7. The Yakima Lash Company produced four models. The forecasts of annual demand for each of the four are shown below.

	Model			
	I	II	III	IV
Forecast of annual demand	500	1,000	2,500	5,000

a. Using a 250-day year and an eight-hour day, determine the level master schedule for a daily batch, hourly batch, and mixed model production with minimum batch sizes.

b. What would the schedule of production look like for an eight-hour day using the mixed model production.

8. The McDougall Manufacturing Company has just finished a product line analysis. The forecasts of the annual demand for their 10 lines is given below (in units of product). Using a 250-day work year and batch sizes of 100 per product, develop a level daily schedule for the assembly line. (The line can produce 300 units of any product per hour.)

Product line	Forecast
1	200,000
2	125,000
3	100,000
4	75,000
5	50,000
6	25,000
7	12,500
8	6,250
9	3,125
10	3,125

9. Produce a "simulation" of the cold water faucet assembly activities on a mixed model refrigerator assembly line. The station where the cold water faucet is installed also installs several other options in refrigerators. Every fourth unit requires the cold water faucet installation. The cycle time is five minutes (i.e., every five minutes a new unit appears at the assembly line station).

Faucets are supplied by a subassembly department in batches of two in a single container. When the assembly line has used both units, the container is immediately returned to the subassembly department, where two more faucet subassemblies are prepared and returned to the assembly line (it takes five minutes to perform the subassembly activities on the faucets, and the subassembly group is told to start immediately on the faucet subassemblies whenever the container appears in the area).

The starting conditions as of 8:00 A.M. are shown below. Refrigerator number 4 is in the options assembly area (they completed units number 1, 2, and 3 the day before). Units number 4, 8, 12, and so on (those marked as Os) require cold water faucets. The container with two subassembly units is at the assembly line.

Refrig. No.	12	11	10	9	8	7	6	5	4	3	2	1
	O	X	X	X	O	X	X	X	O	X	X	X
Subassembly container									Yes			
Subassembly inventory									2			

Using five-minute intervals, record the number of the refrigerator being assembled in the options area, how many water faucet subassemblies are at the station, the location of the container, and whether the subassembly area is working on the faucet subassemblies. Do the "simulation" for more than an hour.

10. Develop the MRP record for the faucet subassemblies (part no. 356) shown in the bill of material below. The faucets are used at the rate of 120/week, the lead time is one week, there is no safety stock, the lot size is 500, and there are 200 units in inventory at the moment.

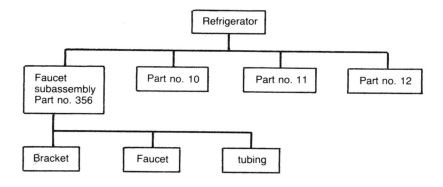

11. Suppose that the faucet subassembly in problem 10 had been "phantomed" (i.e., the faucet would be assembled onto the refrigerator directly from the bracket, faucet, and tubing parts).
   a. What would the bill of material (BOM) look like now?
   b. What would the phantom MRP record look like using the data from problem 10?

12. In one part of its operations, the Wapato Potato Company uses containers that hold 200 units. The usage is an even 25 units per hour in the area.
   a. What is the average inventory (assuming no safety stock) for the area? What if the container size is reduced to 100? 50? 25?
   b. What happens to the average inventory for each container size if the usage is 25 units in the first 15 minutes of each hour and none during the remaining 45 minutes? (You might find it helpful to graph the inventory levels for each container size.)

13. Calculate the number of kanbans required for the following:

	A	B
Usage	120 per week	100 per day
Lead time	1 week	2 weeks
Container size	2 units	50 units
Safety stock	20 percent	0

14. The Elk Sock Company has implemented a JIT program using kanbans to signal the movement and production of product. The average inventory levels have been reduced to where they are roughly proportional to the number of kanbans in use. For one of its products, usage averages 100 units per day, the container size is 20 units, there is no safety stock, and lead time has been one week (five days). The process engineers have been hard at work improving the manufacturing process. They have a proposal to reduce the lead time from five days to three days. What would the percentage change in average inventory be?

15. Merrill's Markers has just installed an expensive machine to produce two of the components for the final assembly line. (It has only been 25 percent depreciated.) The machine produces either component at the rate of 100 units per hour. The setup time is one hour (to go from one product to the other or back again) and the lot size is 500 units. The assembly line requires 40 units per hour of each component.

   The company has just learned of an inexpensive secondhand machine that could produce either of the components at the rate of 50 units per hour. The cost of the machine is $3,500 and no additional people would be required to run it. Would it be worthwhile to purchase the machine and dedicate it to one of the components (the other machine would be dedicated to the production of the other component) if each component was worth $10 at this stage?

16. The Arcane Appliance Company had the following layout for part of the production of its appliances:

Inventory and receiving	Wash room	Subassembly department
Aisle		
Frame shop	Plastic trim	Final assembly

Recently Arcane implemented a JIT delivery system and unit lot size for the frame members for one of its popular appliances. The company instructed the supplier to deliver in lots of 40 frame members every two hours. The lots are delivered to the receiving area, where they are counted and a receipt notice is issued. Next they are issued (with an issue ticket) to the subassembly shop, where they are welded into a subassembly. The subassembly is returned to inventory, where a receipt ticket is issued. Later, an issue transaction will be processed to release two subassemblies to the frame shop, where top and bottom frame units are made and returned to inventory, generating a receipt ticket.

To finish a product, the final assembly shop is issued a top and a bottom unit (now comprising 4 frame members each) for assembly into a completed appliance. The final transaction is receipt back into inventory, which requires another transaction.

a. If each receipt and each issue by the inventory clerk requires a transaction, how many transactions are there for a lot of 40 frame members (i.e., for completing five appliances in total)?

b. If the supplier sticks to the delivery schedule of one lot every two hours, how much time can be spent on an average transaction before the next delivery arrives?

—8—

Master production scheduling

In this chapter, we discuss the basic considerations in constructing and managing a master production schedule. This is a critical module in the manufacturing planning and control system. An effective master production schedule provides the basis for making customer delivery promises, utilizing the capacity of the plant effectively, attaining the strategic objectives of the firm as reflected in the production plan, and resolving trade-offs between manufacturing and marketing. The prerequisites to accomplishing this are to define the master scheduling task in the organization and to provide the master production schedule with the supporting concepts described in this chapter.

The chapter is organized around the following seven topics:

- The master production scheduling activity: What is the role of master production scheduling in manufacturing planning and control and its relation to other business activities?
- Master production scheduling techniques: What are the basic MPS tasks and what techniques are available to aid this process?
- Bill of material structuring for the MPS: How can nonengineering uses of the bill of materials improve master production scheduling?

- The master production scheduler: What does a master production scheduler do and what are the key organizational relationships?
- Examples: How do some actual MPS systems work in practice?
- Master production scheduling stability: How can a stable MPS be developed and maintained?
- Managing the master production schedule: How can MPS performance be monitored and controlled?

Chapter 8 is closely related to Chapter 14, in which advanced concepts in master production scheduling are presented. In particular, detailed examples using complex bill of materials structures are explained in Chapter 14. The production plan, from which the MPS is derived, is discussed in Chapter 9, and Chapter 10 describes the management of the day-to-day demands for plant capacity. Time-phased record concepts, described in Chapters 2 and 3, are building blocks for the material in this chapter.

THE MASTER PRODUCTION SCHEDULING ACTIVITY

We begin with a brief overview of the master production scheduling (MPS) process. What is the MPS activity and how does it relate to other manufacturing planning and control (MPC) systems, and to other company functions? What is the sequence of tasks performed by the master production scheduler?

At an operational level, the most basic decisions relate to how to construct and update the MPS. This involves the processing of MPS transactions, the maintenance of MPS records and reports, a periodic review and update cycle (we call this "rolling through time"), the processing and response to exception conditions, and the measurement of MPS effectiveness on a routine basis.

On a day-to-day basis, marketing and production are coordinated through the MPS in terms of *order promising*. This is the activity by which customer order requests receive shipment dates. The MPS provides the basis for making these decisions extremely effectively, as long as manufacturing executes the MPS according to plan. When customer orders create a backlog and require promise dates that are unacceptable from a marketing viewpoint, trade-off conditions are established for making changes.

The anticipated build schedule

The master production schedule is an anticipated build schedule for manufacturing end products (or product options). As such, it is a statement of production, not a statement of market demand. That is, the MPS is *not* a forecast. The forecast of sales is a critical input into the planning process that is used for the determination of the MPS, but the MPS is different from the forecast in most instances. The MPS takes into account capacity limitations, as well as desires to utilize capacity fully. This means that some items may be built before they are needed for sale, and other items may not be built even though the marketplace could consume them.

The master production schedule forms the basic communication link with manufacturing. It is stated in product specifications; that is, the MPS is stated in part numbers for which bills of material exist. Since it is a build schedule, it must be stated in terms used to determine component-part needs and other requirements. The MPS cannot, therefore, be stated in overall dollars or some other global unit of measure. The specific products in the MPS can be end-item product designations. Alternatively, the specific products may be groups of items such as models instead of end items. For example, a General Motors assembly plant might state the MPS as so many thousand J-body cars per week, with exact product mix (e.g., Chevrolet, four-door, four-cylinder, and so on) determined with a final assembly schedule (FAS), which is not ascertained until the latest possible moment. If the MPS is to be stated in terms of product groups (e.g., J-body cars) then it will be necessary to create special bills of material (planning bills) for these groups (e.g., an average J-body car planning bill).

Linkages to other company activities

Figure 8.1 presents our schematic for an overall manufacturing planning and control system. The detailed plan or schedule produced by the MPS drives all of the engine and back-end systems, as well as the rough-cut capacity planning. Not shown in Figure 8.1 explicitly are the feedback linkages. As execution problems are discovered, there are many mechanisms for their resolution, with feedback both to the MPS and to other MPC modules.

The demand management block shown in Figure 8.1 represents the forecasting, order entry, order promising, and physical distribution activities in a company. This includes all of the activities that place demand (requirements) on manufacturing capacities. These demands may take the form of actual and forecast customer orders, branch warehouse requirements, interplant requirements, international requirements, and service part demands. The resultant capacity needs must be coordinated with the MPS on an ongoing basis.

The production plan represents production's role in the strategic business plan for the company. It reflects the desired aggregate output from manufacturing necessary to support the company game plan. In some firms, the production plan is simply stated in terms of the monthly or quarterly sales dollar output for the company as a whole, or for individual plants or businesses. In other firms, the production plan is stated in terms of the number

FIGURE 8.1 Manufacturing planning and control system

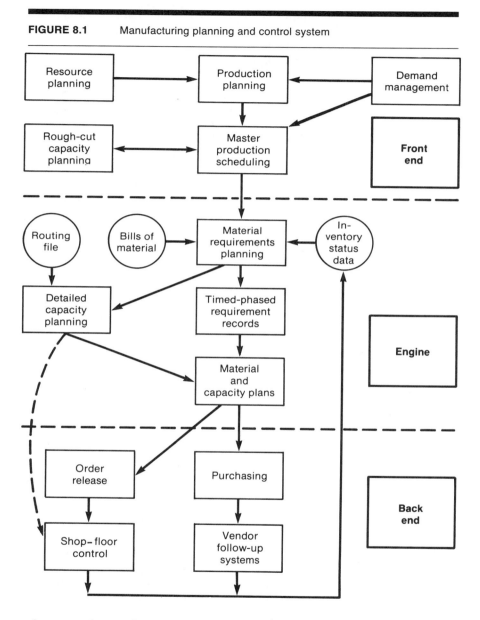

of units to be produced in each major product line monthly for the next year. This aggregate plan constrains the MPS, since the sum of the detailed MPS quantities must always equal the whole dictated by the production plan.

Rough-cut capacity planning involves an analysis of the master production schedule to determine the existence of manufacturing facilities that represent potential bottlenecks in the flow of production; that is, the linkage provides a rough evaluation of potential capacity problems from a particular MPS.

The MPS is the basis for key interfunctional trade-offs. The most profound of these is between production and marketing in terms of exact product definition in the MPS. A request to increase production for any item usually results in the need to reduce production on some other item. If production for no item can be reduced, by definition, the production plan and resultant budget for production must be changed.

Since the MPS becomes the basis for the manufacturing budget, it follows that financial budgets should be integrated with the production planning/MPS activities. When the MPS is extended over a time horizon sufficient to make capital equipment purchases, a better basis is provided for capital budgets. On a day-to-day basis, both cash flow and profits can be better forecast by basing these forecasts on the planned production output specified in the MPS.

The MPS environment

The concept of environment, as it relates to master production scheduling, encompasses the production approach used, the variety of products produced, and the markets served by the company. Three classic types of MPS environments have been identified: make to stock, make to order, and assemble to order. The choice between these alternatives is largely one of the unit used for the MPS; that is, is the MPS to be based on end items, specific customer orders, or some group of end items and product options?

The make-to-stock company produces in batches, carrying finished goods inventories for most, if not all, of its end items. The MPS is the production statement of how much of and when each of those end items is to be produced. Firms that make to stock are often producing consumer products as opposed to industrial goods, but many industrial goods, such as supply items, are also made to stock.

The choice of MPS unit for the make-to-stock company is fairly straightforward. All use end-item catalogue numbers, but many tend to group these end items into model groupings until the latest possible time in the final assembly schedule. Thus, the Ethan Allen Furniture Company uses a *consolidated item number* for items that are identical except for finish color, running a separate system to allocate a lot size in the MPS to specific finishes at the last possible moment. Similarly, the Black & Decker tool manufacturing firm groups models in a series, such as sanders, which are similar, except for horsepower, attachments, and private-brand labels. All of the products so grouped are run together in batches to achieve economical runs for component parts and to exploit the learning curve in the final assembly areas.

The make-to-order company, in general, carries no finished-goods inventory and builds each customer order as needed. This form of production is often necessary when there is a very large number of possible product configurations, and, thus, a small probability of anticipating the exact needs of a customer. In this business environment, customers expect to wait for a large portion of the entire design and manufacturing lead time. Examples include a tugboat manufacturer or a refinery builder.

In the make-to-order company, the MPS unit is typically defined as the particular end item or set of items that comprises a customer order. The definition is difficult since part of the job is to define the product; that is, *design* takes place as the construction takes place. Production often commences before a complete product definition and bill of materials have been determined.

The assemble-to-order firm is typified by an almost limitless number of possible end-item configurations, all of which are made from combinations of basic components and subassemblies. Customer delivery times are often shorter than total lead times, so production must be started in anticipation of customer orders. The large number of end-item possibilities makes forecasting of exact end-item definitions extremely difficult, and stocking of end items very risky. As a result, the assemble-to-order firm attempts to maintain flexibility, starting basic components and subassemblies into production, but, in general, not starting final assembly until a customer order is received.

Examples of assemble-to-order firms include General Motors, with its endless automobile end-option combinations; the Hyster Company, which makes forklift trucks with such options as engine type, lift height, cab design, speed, type of lift mechanism, and safety equipment; and Tennant Company, which makes industrial sweeping machines, with many user-designated options.

The assemble-to-order firm typically does not master production schedule end items. The MPS unit is stated in planning bills of material, such as an average lift truck of some model series. The MPS unit (planning bill) has as its components a set of common parts and options. The option usages are based on percentage estimates, and their planning in the MPS incorporates buffering or hedging techniques to maximize response flexibility to actual customer orders.

The primary difference between make-to-stock, make-to-order, and assemble-to-order firms is in the definition of the MPS unit. However, many of the techniques for master production scheduling are useful for any kind of MPS unit definition. Moreover, the choice of MPS unit is somewhat open to definition by the firm. Thus, some firms may produce end items that they hold in inventory, yet still use assemble-to-order methodologies.

MASTER PRODUCTION SCHEDULING TECHNIQUES

In this section, we present some basic techniques useful for master production scheduling. We start with the time-phased record to show the relationships between the rate of output, the sales forecast, and the expected inventory balance. We then show how revisions to the plans are made as one rolls through time during a review cycle and takes account of actual conditions. Finally, the process of order promising is presented. We show how the entry of actual orders consumes the forecast in this process.

The time-phased record

Using time-phased records as a basis for MPS preparation and maintenance means that they can be produced easily by computer, and they are consistent with MRP record formats. Figure 8.2 shows a highly simplified example of a master production schedule involving an item with a beginning inventory of 20 units, a sales forecast of 10 units per week, and an MPS of 10 units per week as well. The MPS row states the timing for *completion* of units available to meet demand. The data in this record show the expected conditions as of the current week (the first week in the master production schedule). The record covers a 12-week period (planning horizon) for which the total sales forecast is 120 units. The total MPS is also 120 units.

The projected available inventory balance (available) is shown in the second row of the record in Figure 8.2. The "available" row represents the expected inventory position at the end of each week in the 12-week schedule. It results from adding to the starting inventory of 20 units the MPS of 10 units per week, and subtracting the sales forecast of 10 units per week. Any negative values in the projected available inventory row represent expected back orders.

There are several reasons for maintaining a positive projected inventory balance. Forecasts involve some degree of error, and the MPS is a plan for production that may not be exactly achieved. The projected inventory balance provides a tolerance for errors that buffers production from sales variations. For example, in Figure 8.2, if the actual sales in week 1 were 20

FIGURE 8.2   MPS example

	Week number											
	1	*2*	*3*	*4*	*5*	*6*	*7*	*8*	*9*	*10*	*11*	*12*
Forecast	10	10	10	10	10	10	10	10	10	10	10	10
Available	20	20	20	20	20	20	20	20	20	20	20	20
MPS	10	10	10	10	10	10	10	10	10	10	10	10
On hand =	20											

units and the MPS was achieved, there would be no back order. Furthermore, if the marketing department still expected the total sales for the overall 12 weeks to be 120 units (implying that some week's sales would be less than the forecast of 10), production can continue at the rate of 10 units per week and still end up with the same planned inventory at the end of week 12.

The MPS row indicates the quantity and time of completion of production. The details for starting production of the various components and assembly of the product are taken care of by the MRP system. In this sense, the MPS drives the MRP system, as shown in Figure 8.1. There are many alternative MPS plans and we will discuss several. All start from the basic logic that is used to project the expected available inventory balance.

Figure 8.3 presents a different sales forecast from that given in Figure 8.2. In Figure 8.3, the marketing department expects sales of 5 units per week for the first six weeks and 15 units per week for the next six weeks. The overall result is the same: a total sales of 120 units during the 12-week period, but the sales are seasonal. Figures 8.3 and 8.4 show two different master production schedules to meet this sales forecast. The MPS shown in Figure 8.3 represents a level 10 unit per week production rate over the 12-week planning horizon. The MPS in Figure 8.4, however, adjusts for the difference in sales forecasts, calling for 5 units of production per week for the first six weeks, and 15 units per week for the next six weeks.

FIGURE 8.3   A level production MPS approach to seasonal sales

	Week number											
	1	2	3	4	5	6	7	8	9	10	11	12
Forecast	5	5	5	5	5	5	15	15	15	15	15	15
Available	25	30	35	40	45	50	45	40	35	30	25	20
MPS	10	10	10	10	10	10	10	10	10	10	10	10
On hand =	20											

FIGURE 8.4   A chase sales MPS approach to seasonal sales

	Week number											
	1	2	3	4	5	6	7	8	9	10	11	12
Forecast	5	5	5	5	5	5	15	15	15	15	15	15
Available	20	20	20	20	20	20	20	20	20	20	20	20
MPS	5	5	5	5	5	5	15	15	15	15	15	15
On hand =	20											

A comparison of the projected available rows in Figures 8.3 and 8.4 indicates the difference in inventory between the two MPS plans during the 12-week period. They both start and end with the same inventory; but the MPS in Figure 8.3 builds a great deal of inventory during the first six weeks, which is gradually depleted during the last six weeks, while the MPS in Figure 8.4 maintains a constant inventory. These two master production schedules represent two extreme strategies. The MPS in Figure 8.3 is a "leveling" strategy and the MPS in Figure 8.4 is a "chase" strategy. The level MPS calls for no hiring, firing, or capacity adjustments, while the chase MPS, on the other hand, requires production adjustments to chase the demands of the marketplace. There are, obviously, many alternative MPS plans between these two extremes. The goal is to find that plan that best balances the cost and benefits.

Figure 8.5 presents the same sales forecast as Figure 8.3, but it incorporates a lot size of 30 units. In Figure 8.5, a lot of 30 units is scheduled for completion in any week in which the projected available balance would fall below 5 units. This trigger quantity of 5 units reflects a managerial trade-off between carrying inventory and incurring possible back orders.

The projected available balance starts at the beginning inventory position of 20 units and would drop below the 5 unit trigger in the fourth week, so an order is scheduled for the fourth week for 30 units. This order lasts until the eighth week, when the 5 unit level again would be broken. Figure 8.5 shows a total of four batches of 30 units being produced over the 12-week planning horizon. The first batch lasts for six weeks, while subsequent batches last only for two weeks.

Manufacturing in batches of 30 units produces inventories that last between production runs. This inventory is called cycle stock and is part of the projected available inventory row in Figure 8.5. The cycle stock could be reduced by reducing the lot size for the whole schedule or even just during the first six weeks. Similarly, if the company felt that the overall inventory investment was too high for this MPS, the 5 unit trigger could be reduced.

FIGURE 8.5   Lot sizing in the MPS

						Week number						
	1	2	3	4	5	6	7	8	9	10	11	12
Forecast	5	5	5	5	5	5	15	15	15	15	15	15
Available	15	10	5	30	25	20	5	20	5	20	5	20
MPS				30				30		30		30
On hand =	20											

This would provide less protection against forecast errors or manufacturing problems.

Rolling through time

Now let us turn to the inclusion of Murphy's law: If anything can go wrong, it will. Rolling through time requires updating the record to define how actual conditions are reflected in the MPS. It is necessary to not only construct the MPS but also to process actual transactions and make modifications to the MPS.

Figure 8.6 shows the situation at the start of the second week (now for weeks 2 through 13) using the original MPS for the 12-week period as given in Figure 8.5. No material was received during the first week, since none was planned by the MPS. The actual sales, however, were 10 units instead of 5 units, and the actual inventory at the end of the first week (also the start of week 2) is 10 units (instead of 15).

In light of the higher than expected sales during the first week, it is reasonable to ask whether the sales forecast is still valid; that is, does the marketing department still believe that the total sales for weeks 1 through 12 will be 120 units? What is the forecast for week 13? Let us say that the marketing department has decided that the original forecast was incorrect. A new forecast at the end of the first week is for 10 units per week for the next five weeks (2 through 6) and 15 units per week for the following seven weeks (7 through 13). This would total 155 units for the new 12-week planning horizon. Since the new 12-week forecast incorporates 35 more units than the original 12-week forecast, it is greater than the planned production indicated by the MPS of Figure 8.5. Figure 8.6 shows the implications of the new forecast without a revised MPS. Clearly, some adjustment to the MPS is required if anticipated customer needs are to be met. The first potential problem is seen in week 6 of the MPS, where the projected available inventory goes negative. The original master production schedule called for

---

FIGURE 8.6 Using the revised forecast after one week

	2	3	4	5	6	7	8	9	10	11	12	13
						Week number						
Forecast	10	10	10	10	10	10	15	15	15	15	15	15
Available	30	20	10	0	−10	−25	−10	−25	−10	−25	−10	−25
MPS	30						30		30		30	
On hand =	10											

FIGURE 8.7   MPS revision to accommodate revised forecast after one week

	Week number											
	2	3	4	5	6	7	8	9	10	11	12	13
Forecast	10	10	10	10	10	15	15	15	15	15	15	15
Available	30	20	10	30	20	5	20	5	20	5	20	5
MPS	30			30			30		30		30	
On hand =	10											

---

the first batch of 30 units in week 2 and the next batch in week 8. That is not sufficient to meet the revised forecast made at the end of week 2.

The revised MPS shown in Figure 8.7 uses the same 5 unit trigger inventory logic used to establish the lot-sized master schedule in Figure 8.5. Figure 8.7 calls for five batches of 30 units to be produced during the MPS plan, instead of the four batches shown in Figures 8.5 and 8.6. This revision solves the problem of projected negative available inventory but puts in clear focus the question of feasibility. Does the company have the capacity to produce five batches during the next 12 weeks, or to immediately deliver a batch that was planned for next week? The capacity issue must be resolved before the new MPS is put into effect. Furthermore, high costs are typically associated with making production changes. The master production schedule should be buffered from overreaction, with changes made only when essential.

Order promising

For many products, customers do not expect immediate delivery but place orders for delivery in the future. The delivery date (promise date) is negotiated through a cycle of order promising, where the customer either asks when the order can be shipped or specifies a desired shipment date for the order. If the company has a backlog of orders for future shipments, the order promising task is to determine when the shipment can be made. These activities are illustrated in Figures 8.8 and 8.9.

Figure 8.8 builds upon the lot-sized MPS depicted in Figure 8.5. The original sales forecast and MPS as of the beginning of week 1 are shown. In addition, we now consider the sales forecast row to be for shipments. That is, we are forecasting when items will be shipped; and we are closing out the forecast with shipments, not with sales. The distinction separates various forms of sales (e.g., receipt of order or billing) from the manufacturing concern with actual physical movement of the goods.

The row labeled "orders" represents the backlog of orders that the com-

FIGURE 8.8 Order promising example—week 1

					Week number							
	1	2	3	4	5	6	7	8	9	10	11	12
Forecast	5	5	5	5	5	5	15	15	15	15	15	15
Orders	5	3	2									
Available	15	40	35	30	25	20	5	20	5	20	5	20
ATP	15	25						30		30		30
MPS		30						30		30		30
On hand =	20											

FIGURE 8.9 Order promising example—week 2

					Week number							
	2	3	4	5	6	7	8	9	10	11	12	13
Forecast	10	10	10	10	10	15	15	15	15	15	15	15
Orders	5	5	2									
Available	30	20	10	30	20	5	20	5	20	5	20	5
ATP	28			30			30		30		30	
MPS	30			30			30		30		30	
On hand =	10											

pany had at the start of the first week. Five units were promised for shipment in the first week, three more for week 2, and an additional two units were promised for delivery in week 3. Thus, the cumulative order backlog builds to 10 units in week 3. The ATP row will be explained shortly.

As in our previous example, we assume that actual shipments in week 1 were 10 units. This means that five of the units shipped in week 1 were not on the books as sold orders at the start of the week; that is, 50 percent of the orders shipped during week 1 were received during the week. For some companies, this percentage might be significantly higher or lower.

Figure 8.9 shows the status as of week 2. The sales forecast and MPS of Figure 8.8 have been revised in the same way as the revision from Figure 8.5 to Figure 8.7. Furthermore, additional customer orders were received during the first week for shipping in weeks 2 through 4. At the start of week 1, we had three units due to be shipped during week 2. Two additional units have been booked during week 1 for week 2 shipment, so the total backlog at the beginning of week 2 for shipment during that week is five units. An additional three units have been booked for shipment during week 3 and an additional two units for week 4 shipment. We see then that the cumulative order backlog at the beginning of week 2 is 12 units over the 12-week planning horizon. The increase in the cumulative order backlog from 10 to 12 units over a three-week period may well have been one of the key inputs used by the marketing department in the revision of its sales forecasts.

The orders booked for shipment in week 2 in Figure 8.9 are 5 units, while the forecast for the total shipments in this week is 10 units. We expect to receive orders for five additional units during week 2 to be shipped during week 2. Carrying this analysis further, we see the cumulative backlog for weeks 2 and 3 to be 10 units, and the cumulative forecast for the same two weeks to be 20 units. This implies that, between the start of week 2 and the end of week 3, we expect to receive orders for 10 additional units to be shipped during that two-week period.

A more interesting relationship is seen between the order backlog and the MPS. The order backlog for week 2 in Figure 8.9 is 5 units, and the anticipated production plus beginning inventory is 40 units. This means that we still have 35 units to use to meet additional customer requests; that is, we could make total shipments of up to 35 units in addition to what is already promised in week 2.

This is quite true, but we can only accept 28 *additional* units for shipment during week two; that is, we only have 28 units "available to promise" (ATP). The reason is that the next scheduled production for this item does not take place until week 5; therefore, the beginning inventory of 10 units plus the 30 units in the master schedule for week 2 have to cover all existing orders for weeks 2 through 4. Since we already have orders for 12 units on the books for shipment during that period, we can accept only as many as 28 additional units. Thus, Figure 8.9 shows a value of 28 units in ATP for week 2. Those 28 units could be shipped any time during weeks 2, 3, or 4, or any other weeks in the future.

An important convention about the format of the time-phased MPS record shown in Figures 8.8 and 8.9 concerns the available row. The available row is the expected ending inventory. A frequently encountered convention is to use the greater of forecast or booked orders in any period for projecting the available inventory balance, but for the example in Figures 8.8 and 8.9 the actual customer orders never exceed the forecasts for the periods. The general calculation for the available row is: previous available + MPS − (greater of forecast or orders).

The available-to-promise row basically follows the same logic we used before. In Figure 8.9 the on-hand (10) plus the MPS (30) must cover all booked orders (5 + 5 + 2) until the next MPS. The residual ($10 + 30 - 5 - 5 - 2 = 28$) is the amount not presently committed to customer orders and, thus, available to promise.

Some companies may choose to show the available-to-promise (ATP) row as cumulative (58 in week 5). However, keeping the additional increments of ATP separate, makes order promising easier and also has the advantage of not overstating the availability position; that is, there are not really 58

FIGURE 8.10 Order promising example—week 3

	Week number											
	3	4	5	6	7	8	9	10	11	12	13	14
Forecast	10	10	10	10	15	15	15	15	15	15	15	15
Orders	20	2		35		10						
Available	10	0	20	−15	−30	−15	−30	−15	−30	−15	−30	−45
ATP	3		0			20		30		30		
MPS			30			30		30		30		
On hand =	30											

available to promise in week 5 "and" 28 in week 2. Some software packages provide ATP both as indicated in Figures 8.8 through 8.10 *and* in cumulative format.

In many firms, accurate order promising allows the company to operate with reduced inventory levels; that is, the order promising activity allows for the actual shipments to be closer to the MPS. The companies, in effect, buffer uncertainties in demand by their delivery date promises. Rather than carrying safety stocks to absorb uneven customer order patterns, those firms "manage" the delivery dates.

Consuming the forecast

One authority on master production scheduling, Richard Ling, originated the idea that actual customer orders "consume" the forecast; that is, we start out with an estimate (the forecast), and actual orders come in to consume (either partially, fully, or over) the estimate. This can be seen in the data of Figure 8.9. Of the 10 units forecast for week 2, 5 have been consumed. For week 3, 5 of 10 have been consumed, as have 2 of the 10 for week 4.

Let us consider Figure 8.9 and see if, during week 2, we can accept the following hypothetical set of customer orders, assuming they were received in the sequence listed:

Order number	Amount	Desired week
1	5	2
2	15	3
3	35	6
4	10	5

The answer is yes to all but order number 4. Since the total amount re-quested is 65, and the cumulative amount available to promise is only 58 for the next six weeks, only 3 units of order number 4 could be shipped in this period. Let us say that the customer would not accept a partial delivery, so we negotiated for delivery in week 8. Figure 8.10 shows the time-phased record at the beginning of week 3 if no more orders were received in week 2 and the forecast for week 14 is incorporated.

Obviously, the set of orders received during week 2 represents a major deviation from the forecast. However, it does allow us to see clearly how we can use the record to make decisions as we roll through time. Let us first review the arithmetic of the process. To calculate the on-hand inventory at the beginning of week 3, we start with the week 2 beginning inventory of 10. We add the week 2 MPS of 30 and subtract the orders for 5 units shipped in week 2 (shown in Figure 8.9) and we subtract the order for week 2 just promised (5 units). The result is $10 + 30 - 5 - 5 = 30$.

The available row provides the master production scheduler with a projection of the item availability throughout the planning horizon in a manner analogous to projecting an on-hand inventory balance in an MRP record. The convention of subtracting the "greater of forecast or orders" and adding the MPS quantities to calculate the available row has an effect here. For week 3 in Figure 8.10, for example, the available is the 30 units of inventory minus the 20 units on order, for a total of 10. In week 4, the available quantity is 0, the difference between the week 3 available of 10 and the forecast of 10. The use of the greater of forecasts or orders for calculating the available row is consistent with forecast consumption. If actual orders exceed forecast, there has been an "over" consumption that needs to be taken into account. As actual orders are less than forecasts, the result will appear in the on-hand balance (a gross-to-net process); this will also impact the available calculations.

The available position at the end of the planning horizon is an important piece of information for managing the master production schedule, as is the existence of negative available data during the planning horizon. The planning horizon is typically some length of time during which changes are to be made only if absolutely essential, to provide stability for planning and execution. It is at the end of this planning horizon that master production schedulers have maximum flexibility to create additional MPS quantities. If the projected available is positive in the time bucket at the end of the planning horizon, then the scheduling of more production of the item may not be necessary. Note, for example, that at the start of week 2 in Figure 8.9 the week 13 available was five and no MPS quantity was entered for week 13. At the start of week 3 in Figure 8.10, the available for week 14 is $- 45$, due to the consumption of the forecast by the orders booked in week 2. This indicates that in week 3 the master production scheduler should consider scheduling production for completion in week 14. The negative available numbers for weeks 6 through week 14 indicate the desire for more MPS during the planning horizon. Whether this can be achieved is a matter of response time, availability of materials, and competing needs (other items).

The convention of the greater of forecast or orders means that large orders will be immediately reflected in the availability position. This provides signals to the master production scheduler to consider responding to the order by increasing future item availability, which can be used for booking future orders. The available-to-promise row controls the actual order promising. A related question for sales is whether a large order "consumes" forecast for only one period.

To calculate the available-to-promise position, we consider only actual orders and the scheduled production, as indicated by the MPS. We calculate only the incremental available to promise. Note that in Figure 8.10 the 30 units on hand must cover actual orders for weeks 3 and 4, since no additional production is scheduled. In week 5, 30 additional units are scheduled, but none of them is available to promise. The 3 units available to promise in week 3 come from the 30 on hand minus the 20 units ordered for week 2 and the 2 units ordered for week 3. Another 5 units of the on hand are needed for the order of 35 in week 6, since the MPS of 30 units in week 5 is not sufficient. This leaves only three units available to promise for weeks 3 through 7. Of the 30 units that will be produced in week eight, 10 will be used for the order in week 8. This leaves 20 units available to promise in week 8.

Note that the later customer orders are covered by the later MPS quantities. The 10 unit order for week 8 could have been covered by 3 units in week 3 plus 7 units in week 8 instead of all 10 in week 8. This would have left no units for promising from week 3 until week 8, greatly reducing promise flexibility. The convention is to preserve early promise flexibility by reducing the available to promise in as late a period as possible.

The use of both the available row and the available-to-promise (ATP) row is the key to effective master production scheduling. Using the ATP to book orders means that no customer promise will be made that cannot be kept. Note this may mean some orders must be booked at the end of a planning horizon concurrent with the creation of an additional MPS quantity. As actual orders are booked (the order row), or anticipated (the forecast row), or shipped (on-hand inventory), the available row provides a signal for the creation of an MPS quantity. Once created, the MPS quantity provides the items available to promise for future orders.

The final item of interest in Figure 8.10 is to again focus on the negative available quantities from week 6 through 14. These negative quantities indicate potential problems—but only *potential* problems. However, costly MPS changes should not be made to solve "potential" problems. If a condition arises that creates a negative ATP, that represents a "real" problem.

The time-phased records shown in Figures 8.9 and 8.10 are very similar to MRP records. In fact, the same data can be integrated with standard MRP formats. The primary advantage of doing so is to obtain standard record processing. However, it is necessary to keep track of actual customer orders and the timings of MPS quantities to make ATP calculations. The result is that the MRP database will need to be expanded.

BILL OF MATERIAL STRUCTURING FOR THE MPS

The assemble-to-order firm is typified by an almost limitless number of end-item possibilities made from combinations of basic components and sub-assemblies. For example, the number of unique General Motors automobiles runs into billions! Moreover, each new product option offered to the consumer tends to double the number of end-item possibilities. What this means is that the MPS unit in the assemble-to-order environment cannot feasibly be based on end items. Defining other units for master production scheduling means creating special bills of material. In this section, we present a few key definitions to clarify what a bill of material is and is not. Thereafter, we discuss modular bills of materials and planning bills of material that facilitate MPS management. With this background, it is possible to see how master production scheduling takes place in the assemble-to-order environment.

Key definitions

The *bill of material* is narrowly considered to be an engineering document that specifies the ingredients or subordinate components required to physically make each part number or assembly. A *single-level bill of material* is comprised of only those subordinate components that are immediately required, not the components *of* the components. An *indented bill of material* is a listing of the components, from the end item all the way down to the raw materials; it does show the components of the components.

The *bill of material files* are those computer records designed to provide desired output formats. The term *bill of material structure* relates to the architecture or overall design for the arrangement of bill of material files. The bill of material structure must be such that all desired output formats or reports can be provided. A *bill of material processor* is a computer software package that organizes and maintains linkages in the bill of material files as dictated by the overall architecture (bill of material structure). Most bill of material processors operate using the single-level bill of material and maintaining links or chains between single-level files. It is the bill of material processor that is used in MRP to pass the planned orders for a parent part to gross requirements for its components.

The single-level bill and the indented bill are two alternative output formats of the bill of material. Alternative output formats are useful for different purposes. For example, the single-level bill supports order launching by providing the data for component availability checking, allocation, and picking. The fully indented bill is often used by industrial engineers to determine how the product is to be physically put together and by accounting for cost implosions. A fundamental rule is that a company should have one, and only one, set of bills of material or *product structure* records. This set should be maintained as an entity and be so designed that all legitimate company uses can be satisfied.

The concepts presented in the rest of this section present another way of thinking about the bill of material. The traditional approach is from an engineer's point of view; that is, the way the product is *built*. The key change required to achieve superior master production scheduling is to include bill of material structures based on the way the product is *sold*. In this way, the bill of material can support some critical planning and management activities.

Constructing a bill of material structure or architecture based on how the product is sold, rather than how it is built, offers some important advantages. Achieving them, however, is not without cost. The primary cost is that the resultant bills of material may no longer relate to the way the product is built. Activities based on *that* structure (e.g., industrial engineering) will have to be based on some new source of data; that is, if the description of how the parts physically go together is not found in the bill of material, an alternative set of records must be maintained. Providing alternative means to satisfy these needs can be costly in terms of both file creation and maintenance.

The modular bill of material

A key use of bill of material files is in translating the MPS into subordinate component requirements. One bill of material structure or architecture calls for the maintenance of all end-item buildable configurations. This bill of material structure is appropriate for the make-to-stock firm, where the MPS is stated in end items. For each end item, a single-level bill is maintained, which contains those components that physically go into the item. For General Motors, with its billions of possible end items, this bill of material structure is not feasible.

Figure 8.11 shows the dilemma. A solution is to establish the MPS at the option or module level. As indicated, the intent is to state the MPS in units associated with the "waist" of the hourglass. This necessitates that bill of material files be structured accordingly; that is, the option or module will be defined fully in the bill of material files as a single-level bill of material. Thus, the modular bill of material structure has an architecture that links component parts to options, but it does not link either options or components to end-item configurations. If the options are simply buildable subassemblies, then all that is required for the new architecture is to treat the subassemblies as end items; that is, designate them as level zero, instead of

FIGURE 8.11   The MPS hourglass

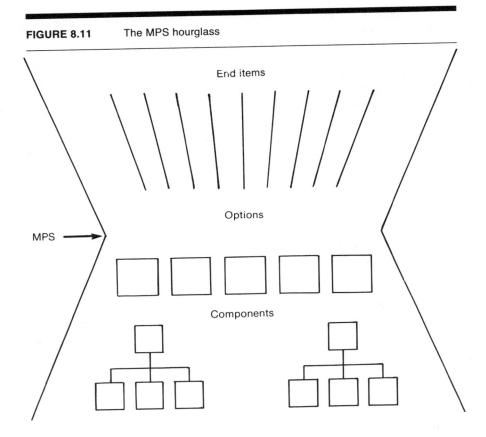

level one. In most cases, however, the options are not stated as buildable subassemblies but as options that provide some services to the customer.

Consider, for example, the air-conditioning option for an automobile. The single-level bill of material would show this option or module as consisting of a particular radiator, fan, hoses, compressor, and interior knobs and levers. These items are not, however, assembled together. They are assembled with still other parts as subassemblies, which eventually are assembled into the automobile.

The use of the air-conditioning option as a bill of material will pass demand from the customer who wants this option down to the necessary parts. It can also be used to forecast demand for air conditioners. However, this bill of material is not useful in the physical building process for air conditioners. For example, the air-conditioning knobs are planned by the bill for the air-conditioning option. They are not planned by the bill of the dashboard assembly where they are installed. Thus, the industrial engineer needs other means to say how the dashboard is to be assembled and from what components.

Using the modular bill of material structure for a firm with a situation similar to that shown in Figure 8.11 permits the MPS to be stated in fewer different units. The MPS is stated in the terms in which it is *sold*, rather than in terms in which it is built; that is, air conditioning, two doors, automatic transmission, fancy trim, and so on. The approach is compatible with marketing perceptions of models, options, and trends in options (e.g., more people buying cars with air conditioning), which tends to improve forecasting. The master scheduling task may be made easier by using modular bills, but order entry tasks are made more complex since each option must be evaluated.

Once the individual customer order (representing a unique collection of options) is entered, it serves the function of a one-time, unique single-level bill of material; that is, it specifies which options or modules are to be included for the particular customer order. It is controlled by a separate final assembly schedule.

The planning bill of material

The restructuring of the bill of material required to better perform MPS activities has led many people to see the techniques and discipline of bill of material approaches as having many applications. An example is the planning bill of material, which is any use of bill of material approaches for planning only, as opposed to use for building the products. The modular bill of material approach just described involves one form of a planning bill, since it is used for developing material plans and modules not all of which are buildable.

The most widely used planning bill of material is the *super bill*. The super bill describes the related options or modules that make up the *average* end item. For example, an average General Motors J-body car might have 0.6 Chevrolet unique parts, 2.6 doors, 4.3 cylinders, 0.4 air conditioners, and the like. This end item is impossible to build; but using bill of material logic, it is very useful for planning and master production scheduling. Bill of material processing dictates that the super bill be established in the product structure files as a legitimate single-level bill of material. This means that the super bill will show all the possible options as components, with their average decimal usage. The logic of bill of material processing permits decimal multiples for single-level component usages. The super bill combines the modules, or options, with the decimal usage rates to describe the average car. The bill of material logic forces arithmetic consistency in the mutually exclusive options; that is, for example, the sum of two possible engine options needs to equal the total number of automobiles.

The super bill is as much a marketing tool as a manufacturing tool. With it, instead of forecasting and controlling individual modules, the forecast is now stated in terms of the total average units, with attention given to percentage breakdowns—to the single-level super bill of material—and to *managing* the inventories of modules using the available-to-promise logic on a day-to-day basis as actual customer orders are booked.

Let us consider an artificially small example. The Garden Till Company makes rototillers in the following options:

> Horsepower: 3HP, 4HP, 5HP.
> Drive train: Chain, Gear.
> Brand name: Taylor, Garden Till, OEM.

The total number of end-item buildable units is 18 (3 × 2 × 3). Management at the end-item level would mean each of these would have to be forecast. A super bill for four-horsepower tillers is given in Figure 8.12. Using this artificial end item, an average four-horsepower tiller, only one forecast is needed from marketing. More important, the MPS unit can be the super bill. The entry of 1,000 four-horsepower super bill units into the MPS would plan the appropriate quantities of each of the options to build

FIGURE 8.12   The four-horsepower super bill

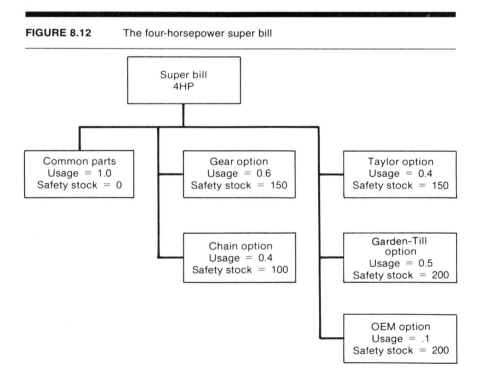

1,000 four-horsepower units in the average option proportions. Actual orders may not reflect the average in the short run, however.

Figure 8.12 shows the use of safety stocks for the options to absorb variations in the mix. No safety stock is shown for the common parts. What this means is that protection is provided for product mix variances but not for variances in the overall MPS quantity of four-horsepower tillers. A commitment made to an MPS quantity for the super bill means that exactly that number of common parts will be needed. In the example of Figure 8.12, if 1,000 four-horsepower super bills were entered, the bill of materials would call for 1,000 common parts modules, 600 gear options, 400 chain options, 400 Taylor options, 500 Garden Till options, and 100 OEM options. The safety stocks allow actual customer orders to differ from the usages specified in the bill of material percentage usage.

Although 600 of the 1,000 four-horsepower tillers are expected to be finished in the gear drive option, as many as 750 can be promised because of the safety stock. Similar flexibility exists for all the other options. The safety stocks are maintained with MRP gross to net logic, so appropriate quantities are maintained as actual conditions become reflected in replenishment orders. Moreover, the safety stock will exist in matched sets because of the modular bill of material structure. Matched sets occur because when one unit of the module is specified for safety stock, *all* parts required for that unit will be planned. Furthermore, the costs of all safety stocks are readily visible; marketing can and should have the responsibility to optimize the mix.

Order entry using planning bill of material concepts tends to be more complex than when the structure is end-item based. To accept a customer order, the available-to-promise logic must be applied to each option in the order, meaning it is necessary to check each of the affected modules. Figure 8.13 shows the flow for a particular customer order, in this case for 25 Taylor four-horsepower in the Gear Option (T4G). The safety stocks are available for promising and will be maintained by the gross to net logic as additional MPS quantities are planned.

THE FINAL ASSEMBLY SCHEDULE

The final assembly schedule (FAS) is a statement of the exact set of end products to be built over some time period. It is the schedule that serves to plan and control final assembly and test operations; included are the launching of final assembly orders, picking of component parts, subassembly, painting or other finishing, scheduling the fabrication or purchase of any component items not under MPS control but needed for final assembly, and packing. In short, the FAS controls that portion of the business from fabricated components to shipable products. It may be stated in terms of cus-

FIGURE 8.13   Available-to-promise logic with modular bill architecture (order for 25T4G)

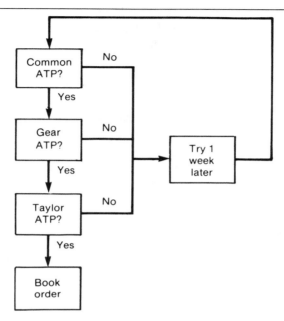

tomer orders, end-product items, serial numbers, or special assembly order numbers.

Relation to the MPS

The master production schedule represents an anticipated build schedule. The FAS is the actual build schedule. The MPS disaggregates the production plan into end items, options, or groups of items, whereas the FAS is the last disaggregation—into exact end-item definitions. The distinction is that the MPS generally incorporates forecasts or estimates of actual customer orders in its preparation, with actual orders thereafter imperfectly consuming these forecasts; the FAS represents the last possible adjustment that can be made to the MPS; therefore, it is advisable to make that adjustment as late as possible. Any unsold items on the FAS will become part of the firm's finished-goods inventory.

The FAS is distinct and separate from the MPS. The distinction is most clearly seen in the assemble-to-order environment. There, the MPS is typically stated in super bills and options, whereas the FAS must be stated in terms of the exact end-item configurations. However, even in make-to-stock firms, such as Ethan Allen or Black & Decker, the MPS is stated in consolidated groups of items, such as all models of a table that differ only in finish, or all models of an electric drill that differ only in speed or gearing. In both cases, flexibility is so maintained that the final commitment to end items can be made as late as possible.

It is important to note that in make-to-stock firms a single-level bill of material is typically maintained for each end item. This means that the conversion from MPS to FAS is simply the substitution of one end-item part number for another. Both are valid, and both explode to components in the same way. For some make-to-stock firms, the MPS is stated in terms of the most common or most complete end item. As actual sales information is received, other end items are substituted. This process continues until a time is reached when all final substitutions are made.

For assemble-to-order and make-to-order firms, end-item bills of material are not maintained. If the FAS is stated in terms of customer orders, it is essential that these orders be translated into the equivalent of a single-level bill of material; that is, these orders must lead to bill of material explosion for order release, picking, and so on. This is easily accommodated if the customer order is stated in the same modules as the planning bill. For the tillers, this would mean that the customer order would be stated in brand name, horsepower, and drive train terms.

Avoidance of firming up the FAS until the last possible moment means that the time horizon for the FAS is only as long as dictated by the final assembly lead time (including document preparation and material release). Techniques that help to delay the FAS commitment include bill structuring, close coupling of order entry/promising systems, partial assembly, the stocking of subassemblies, and process/product designs with this objective.

The Hill-Rom FAS

The Hill-Rom Company, a division of Hillenbrand Industries, manufactures hospital furniture and other health-care equipment. One of the products is an over-bed table, which comes in four different models, 10 alternative color high-pressure laminate tops, and four different options of chrome "boots" (to protect the base) and casters. The result is 160 ($10 \times 4 \times 4$) end-item possibilities. Let us see how a super bill approach to master production scheduling and final assembly scheduling could work in this environment.

Figure 8.14 shows an example super bill of material for this group of products. The cumulative lead time for over-bed tables is 20 weeks, which means that the MPS must extend at least that far into the future. This means that an MPS time-phased record must be maintained over at least this time horizon for each of the 19 common part and option bills of material shown in Figure 8.14.

The final assembly lead time for this product is four weeks. Involved is

FIGURE 8.14   Over-bed table super bill

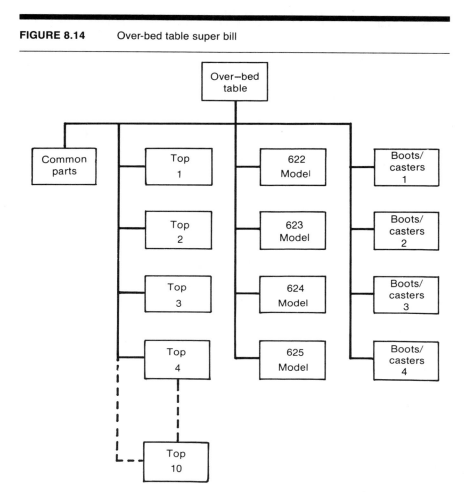

part availability checking, order launching, component part release, welding of subassemblies, snag grinding to smooth welded surfaces, degreasing, painting, subassembly, and final assembly.

Hill-Rom is basically an assemble-to-order company, but some finished-goods inventory is held. This means that, for each of the 160 end-item over-bed tables, an on-hand balance record must be maintained. This is incorporated in a time-phased FAS record. The overall need is for 19 time-phased MPS records for each option and the common parts, maintained for week 5 through at least week 20, plus 160 time-phased FAS records, maintained for each end item for weeks 1 through 4.

The FAS job is to convert MPS records into FAS records as we roll through time. This job is done by the master production scheduler interacting with marketing, since the FAS represents the final culmination of the MPS process.

A related task is order promising, since customer orders may be promised out of the FAS system (on hand or in final assembly) or out of the MPS system (option by option, as done in Figure 8.13). Figures 8.15, 8.16, and 8.17 show this process. In Figure 8.15, we show an FAS record. This record is for one of the 160 end items and is maintained only for the length of the FAS lead time, four weeks. The record is for the 622 model, with "gunstock" colored top, and 01B boots/caster combination; the finished-good item number, which identifies this configuration, is 17123-01B GUN.

Note that there are *only* orders in the record (no forecasts), and they are used to compute the available row. This convention recognizes that the FAS is finishing out products in a specific configuration. The 50 units that will be completed this week are not subject to uncertainty. If no customer order is

FIGURE 8.15   FAS record for 17123-01B GUN table

Part no.		Item	FAS lead time	On hand	
7123-01B GUN		Over-bed Table	4	120	

Week	1	2	3	4	
Orders	10			30	Before
Available	160	160	210	230	booking order
Available to promise	160		50	20	F 5264
FAS	50		50	50	

Week	1	2	3	4	
Orders	10		200	30	After
Available	160	160	10	30	booking order
Available to promise	10			20	F 5264
FAS	50		50	50	

MPS pegging detail				Actual order pegging detail			
Week	Shop Order	Quantities	Action	Week	Quantity	Customer Order	Code
1	011	50		1	10	F 5117	F
3	027	50		3	200	F 5264	F
4	039	50		4	30	F 5193	F

FIGURE 8.16   MPS record for common parts

Part no.	Item	MPS lead time						
1234	Common parts	20						

Week	5	6	7	8	20	21	
Forecast	75	75	75	75	75	75	
Orders	10						Before
Available	−15	210	235	160	125	50	booking
Available to promise	50	300	100				order
MPS	50	300	100	0			

On hand = 10

Week	5	6	7	8	20	21	
Forecast	75	75	75	75	75	75	
Orders	10	200					After
Available	−15	85	110	35	0	−75	booking
Available to promise	50	100	100				order
MPS	50	300	100				

On hand = 10

received for these, they will go into stock; essentially, a "sales order" has been written by the company.

Figure 8.15 also shows an order for 200 units being booked. The customer has requested shipment of the complete order as soon as possible. The available-to-promise (ATP) logic leads to putting the order into week 3, since only 160 units can be promised prior to week 3. This is shown in the "before" and "after" sections of Figure 8.15. The bottom section of the figure shows the supporting pegging data for the orders. The customer orders are pegged with an F code (satisfied from the FAS system).

Next we assume that another customer order is received, requesting shipment in week 6. Since this is outside the FAS, it can be satisfied from the MPS. Figure 8.16 shows the MPS record for the common-parts option. Note that the MPS quantities are for common and option part numbers. Moreover, inventories for these options can exist, even though the physical inventory would be only a collection of parts. (On-hand balance for common parts is 10.) The MPS option quantities can also be committed to final assembly specific end items. When final assembly starts, it takes four weeks to finish out the end item. Figure 8.17 shows the ATP logic required to book any customer order in the Hill-Rom system.

FIGURE 8.17   Available-to-promise logic

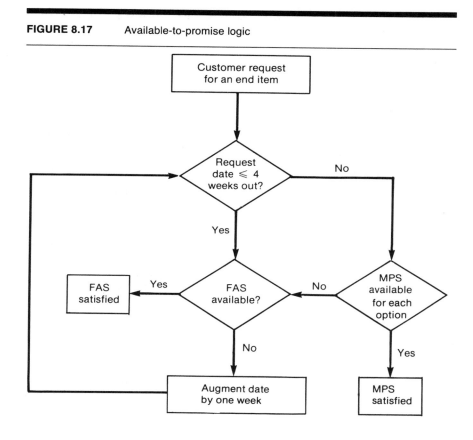

THE MASTER PRODUCTION SCHEDULER

We turn now to the fourth of our seven topics in master production scheduling: Who is the master production scheduler, what does he or she do, and what is the appropriate job description? First, we briefly examine the use of some MRP concepts for the master scheduler.

The MPS as a set of firm planned orders

An interesting advantage of using standard MRP records to manage the master production schedule derives from the firm planned order concept. The firm planned order is similar to any planned order in that it explodes through product structures. However, it is *not* changed in either timing or amount as a result of MRP record processing. It is firm, and it can only be changed as the result of action taken by a responsible person.

It is quite useful to think of the MPS as a set of firm planned orders. Thereafter, the job of the master production scheduler is to convert planned orders to firm planned orders, and to *manage* the timing and amounts of the firm planned orders. The available row in the time-phased record provides the signals for performing this task. Standard MRP exception codes can provide indications of when and to what extent the firm planned orders might not meet the needs.

Managing the timing and amounts of the firm planned orders means that any changes to the MPS have to be carefully evaluated in terms of their resultant impact on material and capacity plans. The key need is to clearly understand the trade-offs between customer needs and other MPC system objectives.

The job

The master production scheduler has the primary responsibility for making any additions or changes to MPS records. He or she also has the primary responsibility for disaggregating the production plan to create the MPS and for ensuring that the sum of the detailed MPS production decisions matches the production plans. This involves analyzing trade-offs, and bringing to the attention of top management any situation in which decisions beyond his or her authority level are required.

As a part of the general feedback process, the master production scheduler should monitor actual performance against the MPS and production plan, and provide a distillation of operating results for higher management. The master production scheduler can also help in the analysis of what-if questions by analyzing the impact on the MPS.

The master production scheduler is often responsible for launching the final assembly schedule. This schedule represents the final commitment, taken as late as physically possible, to exact end items; that is, the final assembly schedule has to be based on specific finished-good items. Other master production scheduler activities include an interface with order entry, and an ongoing relationship with production control to evaluate the feasibility of suggested changes.

Much of this activity is in resolving competing demands for limited capacity. Clearly, if several of the records for the master production schedule show a negative available at the end of the planning horizon, some trade-offs must be made. Not everything can be scheduled at once. The management of the firm planned orders must be done within the capacity constraints. An indication of the priority for making those trade-offs is provided by the available position. The lower the number of periods of supply or the larger the number of periods of backlog the available position shows, the more urgent the need. If too many are urgent, feedback to marketing may be necessary to change budgets.

Figure 8.18 shows the job description for the master production sched-

FIGURE 8.18 Hyster-Portland master production scheduler job description

NAME			JOB TITLE MASTER SCHEDULER	
DEPARTMENT NAME CAPACITY AND MATERIAL PLANNING			DATE ASSIGNED TO PRESENT POSITION	
LOCATION NAME PORTLAND PLANT		LOC. CODE 02	DATE OF LAST EVALUATION	
PREPARED BY: Roger B. Brooks			**JOB DESCRIPTION**	8-23

RATING

INADEQUATE	MARGINAL	SATISFACTORY	GOOD	SUPERIOR

BASIC FUNCTION:

Responsible for planning, organizing, and controlling the activities of the Master Scheduling Section within the Material and Capacity Planning Department.

REPORTS TO: Capacity and Material Planning Manager

SUPERVISES: Order Entry Administrator, Assembly Schedulers, Master Scheduling Planners

RESPONSIBILITIES:

1. Responsible for creating and maintaining a realistic and valid Master Schedule for all Portland Products. The Master Schedule should reflect requirements for Customer Orders, Stock Orders, the Depot, Product Availability Plan and Option Forecast, Interplant and Export Orders with economic and time consideration for Plant Inventory, Manufacturing Efficiencies, Customer Service and Plant Capacity. Proper Master Scheduling will allow the plant to operate at a steady state during periods of oversold order bookings without a build up of past due job orders and inventories, while simultaneously experiencing no idle capacity on bottleneck work centers.

2. Responsible for accurate, timely and organized order entry of Sales Orders, including IMT's and Export Orders, for all Portland manufactured lift trucks, carriers, winches, sold alones and production parts. Responsible for maintaining communications with the Industrial Truck and Tractor Attachment Sales Order desks to provide accurate and timely customer sales order shipping commitments.

3. Responsible for obtaining shipping instructions for all customers orders via communications with the Industrial Truck and Tractor Attachment Sales Order desks to prevent shipping delays.

4. Responsible for scheduling industrial truck, carrier, sold alone and winch assembly to support customer commitments within the constraints of the Master Schedule, Assembly Department and Parts Bank. Responsible for scheduling major weldments and front ends to support the assembly schedule.

5. Responsible for publishing the Daily Production Report and Final Unit Shipment Report in an accurate and timely manner.

6. Select, develop, and evaluate employees so they, as a group, accomplish the foregoing tasks in a businesslike, efficient, and professional manner.

Source: W. L. Berry, T. E. Vollmann, and D. C. Whybark, *Master Production Scheduling: Principles and Practice* (Falls Church, Va.: American Production and Inventory Control Society, 1979), p. 142.

uler at Hyster-Portland. This formal job description makes it clear that the master production scheduler needs to constantly balance conflicting objectives and make trade-offs. The position requires maturity, an understanding of both marketing and finance, and an ability to communicate. Computer software can be a great aid to the master production scheduler, but judgments will always be required.

Managing the MPS data base. For the master production scheduler to operate effectively, it is also critical that there be one single unified data base for the MPS, that it link to the production plan and to MRP, and that clear responsibilities for all transactions be established. This involves not only the usual data integrity issues but also some organizational issues.

In the case of the MPS, many of the transactions occur in different functional areas. For example, the receipts into finished goods may come from completed assemblies (production), the shipments from order closing (marketing), or bills of lading (finance). It is critical that exact responsibilities be established for transaction processing, and that the data linkages to MPS systems and files be rigorously defined and maintained.

Another critical data base requirement for the MPS is proper control over both engineering and nonengineering changes to the bill of material data base. The MPS is often stated in planning bill units that may not be buildable (e.g., an average J-body car). This requires a more complex bill of material or product structure data base. The result is a greater need to procedurally control all changes to the bill of material and to evaluate the impact of changes both from an engineering point of view and in terms of the effect on nonengineering bills of material.

To support the master production scheduler, the time-phased MPS-record-oriented software system must produce the time-phased records to maintain the data base, provide the linkages to other critical systems, provide MPS monitoring and exception messages, and provide for all MPS transactions. Included are entering of order quantities into the MPS, firm planned order treatment, removing MPS order quantities, changing the latter's timing or amount, converting MPS quantities to final assembly schedule (FAS) quantities, launching final assemblies, monitoring FAS scheduled receipts for timing or quantity changes, closing out FAS receipts into finished-goods inventory, and providing for all customer order entry pegging and promising activities.

EXAMPLES

We turn now to two actual MPS examples. We start with an example from Ethan Allen and show its approach to master production scheduling. The approach uses a form of time-phased record, and we will see how standard MRP system approaches can be usefully applied. In presenting this example, aspects of the job of the master production scheduler are highlighted.

The second example illustrates how Jet Spray uses packaged software with an MPS module. The software, Data 3, incorporates available-to-promise logic and other features.

The Ethan Allen master production schedule

The Ethan Allen Furniture Company produces case goods (wood furniture) in 14 geographically dispersed factories. The total product line in these factories is 980 consolidated item numbers (different finishes for the same item make the number of end items about 50 percent larger). Each consolidated item number is uniquely assigned to a particular assembly line or building station in one of the 14 factories. For each assembly line in each factory, there is a capacity established in hours such that, if the hours of capacity are fully utilized on all lines, the overall company objectives as stated in their production plan will be met.

A forecast of demand is made for each consolidated item number, using statistical forecasting methods. A lot size for each item is also determined, based upon economic order quantity concepts. For each assembly lot size, the hours required on the assembly line are estimated. For each product, expected weekly priorities are established by dividing the expected beginning inventory by the forecast. In weeks after the first, expected beginning inventory takes account of production and expected sales. The assembly line is loaded to capacity in priority sequence, smallest to largest. Figure 8.19 provides a simplified example for an assembly line with 35 hours of weekly capacity. The simplified example is based on only four products. Actual lines typically manufacture from 15 to 100 different items.

The top section of Figure 8.19 provides the basic data for each of the four products: the beginning inventory, weekly forecast of sales, lot size, and estimated hours to assemble one lot. Note that for product C there is a beginning backlog or oversold condition.

The middle portion of Figure 8.19 is the set of time-phased priority data. For product A in week 1, the beginning inventory of 20 is divided by the weekly forecast of 5, yielding a priority of 4; that is, at the beginning of week 1 there are four weeks of inventory for product A. Similar priority calculations are made for products B, C, and D in week 1.

The rule for assigning products to the assembly line is to take that product with the smallest priority—the most urgent need. Thus, product C is scheduled for production first. The assignment of product C to the assembly line in week 1 consumes all of the 35 hours of capacity in that week plus 25 hours in week 2. This is so since it takes 60 hours to assemble a batch of 150 of product C.

Moving to week 2, the expected beginning inventory for product A is 15, since the forecast of sales for week 1 is 5. When 15 is divided by the weekly forecast (5) the expected priority for week 2 is 3. Alternatively, if four weeks of sales are in inventory at the beginning of week 1, we would expect to have

FIGURE 8.19 Simplified Ethan Allen MPS example

Basic Data:

Product	Beginning inventory	Weekly forecast	Lot size	Hours per lot size
A	20	5	50	20
B	50	40	250	80
C	−30	35	150	60
D	25	10	100	30

Priorities:

Product	P_1	P_2	P_3	P_4	P_5	P_6	P_7	P_8
A	4	3			0		−2	*
B	1.25	.25			3.5		1.5	.5
C	−.86	*			−.57		*	.71
D	2.5	1.5			−1.5		6.5	5.5

Schedule:

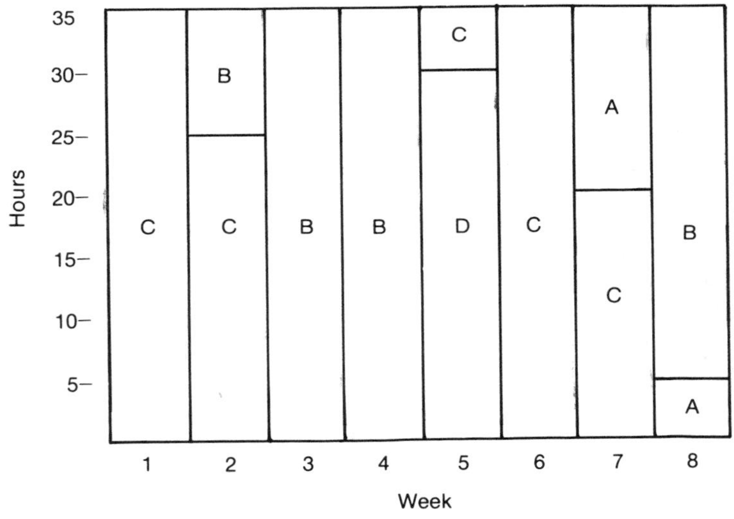

*On the assembly line at the beginning of the week.

three weeks of sales at the beginning of week 2, if no production of product A takes place. This means that, for each product not produced, its priority number in the succeeding week is reduced by 1. The expected priority for product C at the beginning of week 2 can be computed by finding 35/60 of 150, adding this to the beginning inventory −30, subtracting 35 units of forecast demand for week one, and dividing the result by the forecast of 35 to give a value of 0.64. The asterisk, indicating that this product is on the assembly line at the beginning of the week, is used here to simplify the calculations. At Ethan Allen, calculations of all priorities are made.

The lowest priority product for week 2 is B (.25). Since a lot size of the product takes 80 hours, the capacity is fully utilized until the end of week 4. This is why no priority data are given for weeks 3 and 4. A similar situation is true for week 6 when product C, started in week 5, uses the full week's capacity. By loading each line to its weekly capacity, no more and no less, the match between the production plan dictated for each assembly line and detailed MPS decision making is maintained.

Figure 8.20 shows another way to create the Ethan Allen MPS. Here, the same four products are used. For each, a time-phased order point (TPOP) record is developed. The same schedule shown in the bottom portion of Figure 8.19 is achieved when the line is loaded to capacity in the sequence of when planned orders occur in the TPOP records; that is, product C has the first planned order, then B, then D, and so on. Of course, the planned order for D in week 3 is not placed in week 3 because capacity is not available until week 5. There is also a tie shown in week 8. Both products B and C have planned orders in that week. The tie-breaking decision could produce a resultant schedule that differs slightly from that shown in Figure 8.19.

The great advantage to using TPOP approaches to this problem is that specialized MPS software development is reduced. The TPOP records are produced with standard MRP logic, using the forecast quantities as gross requirements. The job of the master production scheduler is to convert these planned orders to firm planned orders, so the capacity is properly utilized. At Ethan Allen, the conversion of TPOP planned orders to firm planned orders is largely an automatic activity, so it has been computerized. Note, however, that the objective is to load the assembly stations to their absolute capacity, in priority sequence. Other firms might use other criteria, such as favoring those jobs with high profitability, favoring certain customers, or allowing flexibility in the definition of capacity. If so, the detailed decisions made by the master production scheduler would be different.

Master production scheduling at Jet Spray

Jet Spray Corporation manufactures and sells dispensers for noncarbonated cold beverages and hot products (coffee and hot chocolate). Jet Spray uses an integrated on-line system encompassing MRP, capacity planning, shop-floor control, master production scheduling, inventory management, and other functions. The software package allows the user to designate part numbers as either being MRP or MPS; that is, MRP part numbers are driven by MPS numbers (but not the opposite). Bills of material need to be designed accordingly (MPS part numbers as parents to MRP part numbers). Any MPS part may also be designed as either make-to-stock or make-to-

FIGURE 8.20   Ethan Allen MPS example using time-phased order point

Week		1	2	3	4	5	6	7	8	
Gross requirements		5	5	5	5	5	5	5	5	
Scheduled receipts										A
On hand	20	15	10	5	0	45	40	35	30	
Planned orders						50				

Week		1	2	3	4	5	6	7	8	
Gross requirements		40	40	40	40	40	40	40	40	
Scheduled receipts										B
On hand	50	10	220	180	140	100	60	20	230	
Planned orders			250						250	

Week		1	2	3	4	5	6	7	8	
Gross requirements		35	35	35	35	35	35	35	35	
Scheduled receipts										C
On hand	−30	85	50	15	130	95	60	25	140	
Planned orders		150			150				150	

Week		1	2	3	4	5	6	7	8	
Gross requirements		10	10	10	10	10	10	10	10	
Scheduled receipts										D
On hand	25	15	5	95	85	75	65	55	45	
Planned orders				100						

order item. The distinction is that, when a shop order is created for a make-to-stock MPS item, the order is closed into finished goods inventory. Subsequent shipment to a customer requires another transaction to remove the items from finished goods into an area awaiting shipment. The inventory in turn is reduced by actual shipment. For a make-to-order item (which includes assemble-to-order) the shop order is driven by an actual customer order and is closed directly into the area awaiting shipment.

One of Jet Spray's best known products is a two product cold beverage dispenser, the Twin Jet 3 (TJ3), which is made to stock. Figure 8.21 is a portion of the basic MPS record for the TJ3.

Figure 8.21 shows the weeks of 11/17 through 1/12, but the system has data to support a one year planning horizon. Notice that the available-to-promise rows are shown in the format described above, as well as in cumulative format. The cumulative data are always the sum of the prior period cumulative plus any ATP in the present period.

The available-to-promise for 11/17 is determined by taking the on-hand quantity (279), subtracting the unavailable (21), and thereafter subtracting the actual demand in the week starting 11/17 (9). The ATP for 11/24 requires looking all the way out to 12/29. In that week, an actual order for 963 completely consumes all MPS quantities for the month of December (286 + 155 + 290 + 225 = 956). Thus, 7 units from the MPS for 11/24 must be promised to the order in the week of 12/29. Additionally, the other actual demand quantities for December (8 + 5 + 4 + 4 = 21) and 11/24 (26) will have to be covered. Thus, the ATP for 11/24 is the MPS (225) − 7 − 21 − 26 = 171. The other ATP figures are relatively straightforward.

The projected balance row (available) for the record is based on a different convention than we have described. The forecast values shown are the *original* forecasts, whereas the software uses the *unconsumed* forecast plus the actual demand in decrementing the projected balance. The unconsumed forecast values are not shown in Figure 8.21.

To get the projected balance for the week of 11/24, one needs to know that the unconsumed forecast for this period is 37 units. Thus, the prior balance of 240 plus the MPS (225) minus the actual demand (26) minus the unconsumed forecast (37) equals 402. The value of 37 is calculated from the original forecast of 63 and the actual customer orders on hand of 26 (63 − 26 = 37). The same calculation logic holds for finding the unconsumed forecast in the weeks of 1/5 and 1/12.

The unconsumed forecast for all weeks in December is zero, since, for the month in total, the actual demand is greater than the forecasts. This leaves us with the unusual forecast for the first week, 11/17. It is 9 units, which cannot be intuitively explained. We would argue for more transparency in the system, but in actual practice the absence of the unconsumed forecast data in Figure 8.21 is not a great problem. The system is on-line, so this number can be obtained whenever it is needed.

The target inventory balance row in Figure 8.21 is worth explaining. The production plan for the TJ3 was not shown here. The actual production plan for the TJ3 is constantly monitored against the MPS. There are tolerances for inventory variations, and, when the projected inventory data exceed the

FIGURE 8.21

JET SPRAY CORPORATION
MASTER PLANNING SCHEDULE -

11/21/

PART NUMBER	DESCRIPTION	QUANTITY ON HAND	SAFETY STOCK	QUANTITY UNAVAIL	LEAD TIME	CUM L/T	FAM GRP	LOT HOR	PLN	TIME FENCE	MASTER SCHEDULE	TYPE*
S3568	TJ3 DOM. TWIN JET	279	0	21	0	92	TJ	5	001	50	MAKE TO STOCK	

BEGIN DATE	11/17/	11/24/	12/01/	12/08/	12/15/	12/22/	12/29/	1/05/	1/12/
DAYS/PERIOD	7	7	7	7	7	7	7	7	7
FORECAST	28	63	147	147	147	146	146	181	181
ACTUAL DEMAND	9	26	8	5	4	4	963	4	1
PROJECTED BAL	240	402	680	830	1,116	1,112	374	493	312
TARGET INV BAL	0	0	0	0	0	0	0	0	0
AVAIL TO PROM	249	171						295	
CUMULATIVE ATP	249	420	420	420	420	420	420	715	715
MPS	0	225	286	155	290	0	225	300	0

limits set by the production plan, this is where those differences are recorded.

This MPS software is an on-line system. Figure 8.21 is only one of several documents available to the master scheduler. Most of the master scheduler's work is supported with a video screen, not paper, and the MPS is reviewed on a daily basis.

MPS STABILITY

A stable master production schedule translates into stable component schedules, which mean improved performance in plant operations. Too many changes in the MPS are costly in terms of reduced productivity. However, too few changes can lead to poor customer service levels and increased inventory. The objective is to strike a balance where stability is monitored and managed. The techniques most used to achieve MPS stability are firm planned order treatment for the MPS quantities, frozen time periods for the MPS, and time fencing to establish clear guidelines for the kinds of changes that can be made in various periods.

Firm planned order treatment at Black & Decker

As noted above, a firm planned order is a planned order with timing and quantity that will not be changed automatically, and the entire MPS can be considered as a set of firm planned orders. That is, once the MPS is established, processing any change in it should be the sole responsibility of the master production scheduler, after careful analysis of the implications of the change. The stability provided by firm planned order treatment of the MPS is particularly important to the rest of the fabrication and purchasing activities in the firm. It ensures that all supporting activities are aiming at the same target.

The firm planned order is particularly useful to ensure that all the changes in physical distribution are not transferred directly back to manufacturing through the MPS. Black & Decker creates the firm planned orders and the MPS in a way that isolates the logistics activities from the shop. First, marketing owns the finished-goods inventories, so they are not considered in the MPS time-phased records by manufacturing. Second, the marketing/ logistics group does use the finished-goods inventories and time-phased order point (TPOP) records to determine when they next need to request an MPS quantity. Third, the times and quantities are negotiated with the master production scheduler. In this way, physical distribution problems are *first* reviewed by marketing/logistics before negotiating for MPS quantities or changes that require expediting in manufacturing.

The Black & Decker approach is illustrated in Figures 8.22 and 8.23. The first shows the MPS time-phased record for a model series of belt sanders.

FIGURE 8.22
Black & Decker time-phased MPS record

WEEK 140 **INVENTORY STATUS** CODE- A FOR 80070581-00 (PART NUMBER OR RAW MATERIAL CODE) CLASS OR FAMILY — I N D I V I D U A L - P A R T (TITLE OF INQUIRY) — REQUESTED BY **VANCE** (NAME) 843 01 (DEPT. NO.)

CATEGORY	PART NUMBER OR RAW MATERIAL CODE	DESCRIPTION	UNIT OF MEASURE	ABC CODE	FAMILY CODE	CLASS CODE	BUYER CODE	STANDARDIZATION CODE	LAST EFFECTIVE ECN NUMBER	PACKAGE ASSEMBLY	UNIT MASTER	UNIT ASSEMBLY	LINE CODE	PHANTOM	SERVICE ONLY	SPECIAL CUTTER	DATE OF LAST C/C	DATE LAST TRANS	ECN PEND	LOC
1	80070681-00	PA BELT SANDERS	50			P07			46812	X			2				000	138	P	8

ORDER CODE	LEAD TIME S/A	LEAD TIME COMP	PRODUCTION LOT SIZE	SCRAP FACTOR	SAFETY STOCK	MINIMUM PURCHASE QUANTITY	PURCHASE CONVERSION QUANTITY	NUMBER ORDERS LAST YEAR	NUMBER ORDERS YEAR TO DATE	USAGE LAST YEAR	EST	USAGE YEAR TO DATE	TOTAL STANDARD COST	SET-UP COST PER LOT	RUN COST (COST EACH LESS SET-UP)	QUANTITY BALANCES ON HAND	QUANTITY BALANCES RECEIVED	QUANTITY BALANCES STAGED	LOCATION PLANT	LOCATION AREA
P				00				0	0	38002		45291	NOT AVAIL						8	

	PAST DUE	CURRENT WEEK	WEEK - 141	WEEK - 142	WEEK - 143	WEEK - 144	WEEK - 145	WEEK - 146	WEEK - 147	WEEK - 148	WEEK - 149	WEEK - 150	WEEK - 151	WEEK - 152
REQUIREMENT	6500	6500			9000				9000				6500	
ALLOCATIONS														
ON ORDER	6500	6500												
AVAILABILITY					9000-	9000-	9000-	9000-	18000-	18000-	18000-	18000-	24500-	24500-
PLANNED ORDERS					9000				9000				6500	

	WEEK - 153	WEEK - 154	WEEK - 155	WEEK - 156	WEEK - 157	WEEK - 158	WEEK - 159	WEEK - 160	WEEK - 161	WEEK - 162	WEEK - 163	WEEK - 164	WEEK - 165	WEEK - 166
REQUIREMENT			8500				8000					9000		
ALLOCATIONS														
ON ORDER														
AVAILABILITY	24500-	24500-	33000-	33000-	33000-	33000-	41000-	41000-	41000-	41000-	41000-	50000-	50000-	50000-
PLANNED ORDERS			8500				8000					9000		

	WEEK - 167	WEEK - 168	WEEK - 169	WEEK - 170	WEEK - 171	WEEK - 172	WEEK - 173	WEEK - 174	WEEK - 175	WEEK - 176	WEEK - 177	WEEK - 178	WEEK - 179	WEEK - 180
REQUIREMENT		9000			9000				9000				9000	
ALLOCATIONS														
ON ORDER														
AVAILABILITY	50000-	59000-	59000-	59000-	68000-	68000-	68000-	68000-	77000-	77000-	77000-	77000-	86000-	86000-
PLANNED ORDERS		9000			9000				9000				9000	

	WEEK - 181	WEEK - 182	WEEK - 183	WEEK - 184	WEEK - 185	WEEK - 186	WEEK - 187	WEEK - 188	WEEK - 189	WEEK - 190	WEEK - 191			TOTALS
REQUIREMENT			9000											101500
ALLOCATIONS														
ON ORDER														6500
AVAILABILITY	86000-	86000-	95000-	95000-	95000-	95000-	95000-	95000-	95000-	95000-	95000-			95000
PLANNED ORDERS			9000											95000

ORDERS OUT OF PHASE — * A - ALLOCATION; B - SERVICE/SUBSIDIARY ALLOCATION; H - PURCHASE ORDER ON HOLD; I - TRANSFER ALLOCATION; J - MFG ORDER - FIRST OPERATION COMPLETE; M - MANUFACTURING ORDER; P - PURCHASE ORDER; R - REQUIREMENT; S - MFG ORDER - SHOP PAPER ISSUED; T - TRANSFER ORDER; U - PLANNED ORDER — † AUTH: P - PART, U - UNIT; CO-ORD: S - SCHEDULE SHEET, C - COORDINATED; CONTROL ECN: A - DROP IN ON USE-UP, B - PKG ASSEM CONTROLS ECN, C - A + B ABOVE

	* CODE	WEEK	REFERENCE NUMBER (LOC, MFG. NO. BUYER / PURCHASE ORDER, LOT, MOD)	QUANTITY	† AUTH	† CO-ORD	† CONTROL ECN	* CODE	WEEK	REFERENCE NUMBER	QUANTITY	† AUTH	† CO-ORD	† CONTROL ECN	* CODE	WEEK	REFERENCE NUMBER	QUANTITY	† AUTH	† CO-ORD	† CONTROL ECN	* CODE	WEEK	REFERENCE NUMBER	QUANTITY	† AUTH	† CO-ORD	† CONTROL ECN
S			REQUIREMENTS					R	139	000706818209	5500	U			R	139	000706818210	1000	U			R	143	000706818309	9000	U		
	R	147	000706818409	9000	U		B	R	151	000706818609	5500	U			R	151	000706818610	1000	U			R	155	000706818801	500	U		B
	R	155	000706818809	7000	U		B	R	155	000706818810	1000	U	B		R	159	000706819009	8000	U		B	R	164	000706819201	500	U		
T	R	164	000706819209	7500	U			R	164	000706819210	1000	U			R	168	000706819401	500				R	168	000706819409	7500			
	R	168	000706819410	1000				R	171	000706819601	1000				R	171	000706819609	6000				R	171	000706819610	2000			
	R	175	000706810209	8000				R	175	000706810210	1000				R	179	000706810409	9000				R	183	000706810601	500			
	R	183	000706810609	7000				R	183	000706810610	1500																	
			OPEN-ORDERS					S	139	000706818209	5500	U	C		S	139	000706818210	1000	U	C								
A			PLND-ORDERS					U	143	000706818309	9000	U			U	147	000706818409	9000	U			U	151	000706818609	5500	U		
	U	151	000706818610	1000	U			U	155	000706818801	500	U			U	155	000706818809	7000	U			U	155	000706818810	1000	U		
	U	159	000706819009	8000	U			U	164	000706819201	500	U			U	164	000706819209	7500	U			U	164	000706819210	1000	U		
	U	168	000706819401	500				U	168	000706819409	7500				U	168	000706819410	1000				U	171	000706819601	1000			
T	U	171	000706819609	6000				U	171	000706819610	2000				U	175	000706810209	8000				U	175	000706810210	1000			
	U	179	000706810409	9000				U	183	000706810601	500				U	183	000706810609	7000				U	183	000706810610	1500			
U	NO WHERE USED							HAS COMPONENTS							HAS OP FILE													
S																												

BLACK & DECKER MFG. CO. FORM NO 30020

Source: W. L. Berry, T. E. Vollmann, and D. C. Whybark, *Master Production Scheduling: Principles and Practice* (Falls Church, Va.: American Production and Inventory Control Society, 1979), p. 67.

FIGURE 8.23 Black & Decker marketing/logistics MPS record

07/01/ MONTHLY TOOL INVENTORY PLANNING REPORT—PLANNING DIVISION 02 PAGE 0167

FAMILY IDENT	PROD CODE	CATALOG NUMBER	DESCRIPTION	MFG-MOD NUMBERS	E C	P-L-A-N-T CUR	LT	FUT	PROD P/GRP	UNIT GSV	UNIT A STD C	LOT SIZE	SAFETY STOCK		END-OF-MONTH BOH	B/O
020560	444	7450-01	BELT SANDER 220V	070681-01		60	00	00	040020	58.20	29.86	25		M	1176	6
	450	7450-06	BELT SNDR 240V	000000-00		60	00	00	020560	59.75	27.14	500		M		
	451	7451	BEST BELT SANDER W/	070681-09		60	00	00	020560	50.15	31.01	5000		M	907	6844
	461	7461	2SPD DUST COLL SNDR	070681-10		60	00	00	020560	61.06	38.23	1000		M	898	

PROD CODE	NET BOH	PAST DUE	JUL 140 ORDERS	JUL 140 SALES	JUL 140 EOM-INV	AUG 143 ORDERS	AUG 143 SALES	AUG 143 EOM-INV	SEP 148 ORDERS	SEP 148 SALES	SEP 148 EOM-INV	OCT 152 ORDERS	OCT 152 SALES	OCT 152 EOM-INV
444	1170	14		95	1089		620	469		25	444		305	139
450														
451	5937-	16	5500	4333	4754-		8278	13032-	19000	5759	901-	5500	5038	329-
461	898	640	1000	443	2095		715	1380		872	508	1000	605	903
TOTALS	3869-	670	6500	4871	1570-		9613	11183-	18000	6656	161	6500	5948	713

Source: W. L. Berry, T. E. Vollmann, and D. C. Whybark, *Master Production Scheduling: Principles and Practice* (Falls Church, Va.: American Production and Inventory Control Society, 1979), p. 68.

Note that it is exactly in MRP format and, in fact, is maintained as any other MRP record. Figure 8.22 does, however, show the creation of the firm planned orders. The gross requirements come down directly as planned orders. This is done by specifying zero lead time, lot-for-lot order sizing, and no on-hand inventories. Any lot can be assembled in the same week it is launched, and the lot sizes put into the gross requirements are those negotiated with logistics. The result is de facto firm planned order status for these planned orders which are the MPS quantities. Just like firm planned orders, the only way they can change is by a manual shift in the gross requirements.

Figure 8.22 is for the model series 80070681–00. Each item in the series is a belt sander but with different accessories, and one is sold under a private brand name. In the pegging data (STATUS) portion of Figure 8.22, the end-item model numbers can be seen as the last two digits of the reference number. This overall model series is comprised of four individual end-item models: 01, 00, 09, and 10. This section is read left to right, requirements first, then open orders, then planned orders. Thus the past-due requirement of 6,500 (also shown as current) is made up of 5,500 model 09 and 1,000 model 10, both due last week, week number 139.

Figure 8.23 shows the same item from the marketing/logistics viewpoint. Marketing/logistics monitor the finished-goods inventory for these make-to-stock-items, and they use data like those in Figure 8.23 in the process. Figure 8.23 is a portion of the TPOP record, which is printed in monthly time buckets. The exact dates, kept inside the computer, are the same as in the manufacturing system except for a lead time offset.

In Figure 8.23, the ORDERS columns show the model 09 order of 5,500 and the model 10 order of 1,000 sanders. The equivalent marketing record uses the product codes of 451 and 461 for 09 and 10, respectively. Each of the remaining orders in Figure 8.23 can be matched with planned orders in Figure 8.22, except that the printout grouping into monthly time buckets combines two manufacturing planned orders for 9,000 each into one marketing order of 18,000 in the month of September.

Note in Figure 8.23 that the inventories (NET BOH) include a −5,937 for model 451, along with positive inventories for two of the other models, and no activity at this time for the 450 model. The negative inventory is for the private-brand product. This product is essentially made to order, not made to stock, and the negative balance is an unfilled order. The key point is that the level and composition of finished-goods inventory is a marketing decision. At Black & Decker, that is where these decisions are made, and the result is a stabilized set of firm planned orders in manufacturing.

Ethan Allen stability

Construction of the Ethan Allen MPS is based upon TPOP records, with assembly lines loaded up to exact capacities, and the sequence of MPS items determined by the date sequence of planned orders. This process might seem to lead to a great deal of repositioning of MPS quantities; that is, as actual sales occur, forecast errors will tend to reorder the MPS. In fact, this does not occur, because the planned orders from TPOP records are "frozen," or firm planned, under certain conditions.

Ethan Allen uses three types of firm planned orders for the MPS. These are illustrated in Figure 8.24. In essence, any firm planned order is frozen in that it will not be automatically repositioned by any computer logic. All MPS quantities for the next eight weeks are considered to be frozen or firm planned at Ethan Allen. In addition, any MPS quantity that has been used to make a customer promise (i.e., a customer order is pegged to that MPS batch) is also a firm planned order. The third type of firm planned order used in the Ethan Allen MPS is for what they call the *manual forecast*. Included are contract sales (e.g., items to a motel chain), market specials (i.e., items to go on special promotion), and new items (MPS is when the product is to be introduced). All of the blank space in Figure 8.24 is filled with the TPOP-based scheduling technique discussed earlier. Computerized MPS logic will fill in the holes up to the capacity limit without disturbing any firm planned order.

Freezing and time fencing

Figure 8.24 shows the first eight weeks in the Ethan Allen MPS as being frozen. This means that *no* changes inside of eight weeks are possible. In reality, "no" may be a bit extreme. If the president dictates a change, it will probably happen, but such occurrences are very rare at Ethan Allen.

Many firms do not like to use the term *frozen*, saying that anything is negotiable—but the negotiations get tougher as we approach the present time. However, the use of a frozen period provides a very stable target for manufacturing to hit. It also removes most alibis for missing the schedule!

Time fencing is an extension of the freeze concept. Many firms set time fences that specify periods in which various types of change can be handled. For example, Black & Decker has three time fences: 26, 13, and 8 weeks. The implication is that beyond 26 weeks the marketing/logistics people can make any change as long as the sum of all MPS records is synchronized with the production plan. From weeks 13 to 25, substitutions of one end item for another are permitted, providing the required component parts will be available and the production plan is not violated. From weeks 8 to 13, the MPS is quite rigid; but minor changes within a model series can be made, if component parts are available. The eight-week time fence at Black & Decker is basically a freeze period similar to that at Ethan Allen, but occasional changes are made within this timing. In fact, assembly lines have been shut down to make changes—but the occurrence is so rare that everyone in the factory remembers when this happens! To achieve the level of productivity necessary to remain competitive, stability in short-range manufacturing plans is essential.

FIGURE 8.24 Ethan Allen firm planned order approach

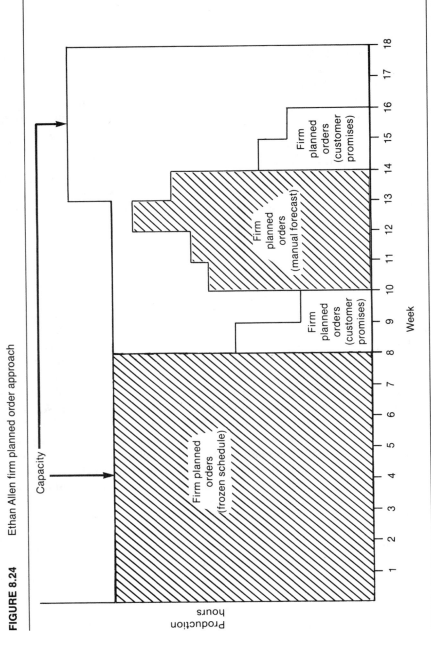

Source: W. L. Berry, T. E. Vollmann, and D. C. Whybark, *Master Production Scheduling: Principles and Practice* (Falls Church, Va.: American Production and Inventory Control Society, 1979), p. 51.

MANAGING THE MPS

We turn now to the management of the MPS: How does one measure, monitor, and control detailed day-to-day performance against the MPS? The first prerequisite for control is to have a realistic MPS. Most basic management textbooks describe how it is critical to only hold people accountable for performance levels that are attainable. This means that the MPS cannot be a wish list, and it should not have any significant portion that is past due. In fact, we claim that significant past due is a major indication of a "sick manufacturing planning and control system."

Stability and proper buffering are also important, because the objective is to remove all alibis and excuses for not attaining the performance for which the proper budget has been provided. Successful companies hit the production plan every month, and they do the best job possible to disaggregate the plan to reflect actual product mix in the MPS.

The overstated MPS

Most authorities have warned that the MPS must not be overstated. To do so destroys the relative priorities developed by MRP and shop-floor control; more importantly, the overstated MPS erodes belief in the formal system, thereby reinstituting the informal system of hot lists and black books. Walter Goddard, a well-known MPS expert, no longer tells companies not to overstate the MPS, because at some point the temptation is overwhelming; he now tells them to learn from the experience so they will not do it again!

A key to not overstating the MPS is to always force the sum of the MPS to equal the production plan. Then, when someone wants to add something, the question is, "Of what do you want less?" The company must give up what is referred to as *the standard manufacturing answer*. The standard manufacturing answer to whether more output of some product is possible is: "We do not know, but we will try like hell!"

The company *must* know. There should be an overall output budget for manufacturing. Capacity should be in place, which matches (is not more or less than) the budget. Manufacturing and marketing should work diligently to respond to product-mix changes, but within the overall budgetary constraint. The correct response to whether more output of some product is possible is, "What else can be reduced?" If nothing, then the answer is either "No," or "The output budget and concomitant resources to increase capacities will have to be changed."

MPS measures

There is an old Vermont story about the fellow who was asked: "How is your wife?" His answer: "Compared to what?" The measurement of the MPS has to be established in concrete terms which reflect the fundamental goals of the firm. This is not as easy as it might seem. At one time, Ethan Allen evaluated each factory on the basis of dollar output per week. At one plant, an assembly line produced both plastic-topped tables and all-wood tables. The plastic-topped tables sold for more and could be assembled in roughly half the time, since the top was purchased as a completed subassembly. Obviously, the factory favored plastic-topped tables, even when the inventories were high on those items and low on wood tables.

It was necessary for Ethan Allen to change the measure for evaluating plant performance. Each line in each plant is now scheduled by the techniques we have described, and performance is based upon hitting the schedule.

Another important measure of MPS and other MPC systems is customer service. In virtually every company, customer service is an area of concern. However, in many firms, a tight definition of precisely how the measure is to be made is lacking. Measurement is a critical step in control, and each firm will need to express the way in which this important aspect of their operation is to be measured.

It is to be expected that whatever measure for customer service is chosen, the firm may have problems similar to those of Ethan Allen when evaluating plants with dollar output. However, the way to find the problems and thereafter eliminate them is, in fact, to start with *some* measure, no matter how crude, and evolve.

Appropriate measures will vary a great deal from firm to firm, reflecting the type of market response typical in the industry and the particular company. Ethan Allen measures customer service in terms of hitting the order acknowledgment or promise dates. Jet Spray measures manufacturing performance against the MPS, as well as monthly performance in "equivalent units" of output versus the budget. The goal is a cumulative performance of at least 95 percent. Black & Decker measures their customer service in distribution, in terms of a 95 percent ability to deliver any customer order from inventory. Some assemble-to-order firms evaluate production against the production plan, which is to deliver a specific number of each model to marketing in the agreed-upon time frame. They also evaluate customer service in terms of how long customers have to wait until they can get a specific end item. This is an indication of how well the production plan is being disaggregated.

Monitoring the MPS at Ethan Allen

The Ethan Allen firm planned order approach to its MPS is depicted in Figure 8.24. We also know that each plant is evaluated on hitting the MPS, so it should be useful to see how the detailed monitoring takes place and how the overall company operations have been affected.

Every Tuesday morning, the Ethan Allen vice president of manufacturing receives a report detailing the performance of each factory in the prior week. Figure 8.25 is an example of this overall performance report, and Figure 8.26 is the detail for one factory, located at Beecher Falls, Vermont.

Figure 8.25 is a short summary of overall performance, showing one plant, Boonville, as having had poor performance. The last two comments about packed production and outside suppliers show the total production achieved in these two categories.

FIGURE 8.25   Ethan Allen summary MPS performance

April 5,

To: Bill Morrissey

From: Marty Stern

Production schedule review
4/1

Summary:

Nine of the 14 factories operating hit their schedules 100 percent.

Performance against schedule was poor this week at one of the factories: Boonville - 75 percent

Packed production was 196 million over total scheduled. 11 of the factories reporting met or exceeded their schedule.

The outside suppliers produced 171 million under their schedule bringing total production to 25 million over scheduled goal.

cc: Marshall Ames
     Barney Kvingedal
     Ray Dinkel
     Walter Blisky
     Andy Boscoe
     Steve Kammerer
     Tom Ericson
     Bob Schneble
     Hank Walker

Source: W. L. Berry, T. E. Vollmann, and D. C. Whybark, *Master Production Scheduling: Principles and Practice* (Falls Church, Va.: American Production and Inventory Control Society, 1979), p. 54.

FIGURE 8.26   Ethan Allen detailed MPS performance (for one factory)

SUMMARY OF SCHEDULE REVIEW

PLANT: BEECHER FALLS   FROM: MARTY STERN

                                                        SCHEDULE DATE 3/27/78
                                                        THRU WEEK OF   8/28/78

STATION	CAPACITY*	PRIORITY	PROD.SCHED. DOLLARS	PRODUCTION GOAL
06-Cases	175.0	1	$ 240.1	232.0
07-C/Hutch	* 10.0	11	10.0	9.0
08-Hutch	* 15.0	14	17.9	19.0
20-Beds	* 60.0	1	85.7	84.0
21-Misc.	3.0	11	3.7	4.0
22-Bookstack	70.0	3	33.0	31.0
24-Desks	* 10.0	8	8.8	10.0
26-Mirrors	25.0	12	23.0	19.0
PLANT TOTAL			$ 422.2	408.0

Station 06 -- Cases: Other than misses caused by reporting date change (Canbury closed Good Friday) no misses. Items such as 10-4017, 4066, 4512P, 4522P, 11-5215, 5223 delayed 1 to 4 weeks. Nine items service position improved. Some jobs outside frozen schedule should have been made "A" jobs and shifting would not have occurred. Priority down to 1 from 2. To schedule through priority 18 requires 10 weeks capacity, slightly higher than last months 9 3/4 weeks.

Station 07 -- C/Hutch: No misses. Delayed 3 of 5 items on this line. Priority down to 11 from 14. 7 weeks capacity will schedule thru priority 18, up from 5 weeks.

Station 08 -- Hutch: No misses, Delayed 2 items, pulled 3 ahead. (Plant comments base the shift on purchase parts). Priority up to 14 from 3. To schedule thru priority 18 requires 3 weeks capacity, down from 6 weeks.

Station 20 -- No misses. Delayed the 11-5632-5. Pulled a number of beds ahead. Priority unchanged at 1. 8 weeks capacity, down from 10 3/4 weeks will schedule thru priority 18.

Station 21 -- Misc.: No misses. Some shifting but orders are O.K, Priority up from 10 to 11. 3 weeks capacity, same as last month, will schedule thru priority 18.

Station 22 -- Bookstack: No misses. Built 1 assembly ahead. Priority up to 3 from 2. To schedule thru priority 18 requires 4 1/2 weeks capacity down from 6 weeks.

Station 24 -- Desks: No misses. Built 1 assembly ahead. Some shifting, no delays. Priority up to 8 from 4. 3 1/2 weeks capacity, down from 5 1/2 weeks, will schedule thru priority 18.

Station 26 -- No misses. Some shifting but ahead only. Priority up to 12 from 1. 2 3/4 weeks capacity, down from 8 weeks will schedule thru priority 18.

Source: W. L. Berry, T. E. Vollmann, and D. C. Whybark, *Master Production Scheduling: Principles and Practice* (Falls Church, Va.: American Production and Inventory Control Society, 1979), p. 55.

The STATIONS in Figure 8.25 are the assembly lines, and their capacities are stated in hours. The PRIORITY data reflect the expected operating conditions 18 weeks in the future. If each of those priority numbers were 18, the expectation is that the plant will be exactly meeting customer needs 18 weeks in the future. This particular factory will be seriously behind in terms of meeting anticipated customer demands. This is a question of capacity that is reflected in the comments about each station. For example, for the 06 station, the detail indicates that 10 extra weeks of capacity are required to catch up. Note, however, that the lack of capacity does not mean that the plant is not meeting its schedule. All eight lines are reported as "no misses." This means that, in the week covered by this report, the plant met its schedule exactly. The jobs in the schedule are being run. The schedule is loaded up to capacity—not in excess of capacity. The lack of adequate capacity will mean longer delivery times to customers, but not missed schedules.

By evaluating the reports illustrated by Figures 8.25 and 8.26, which plants are performing according to expectations is very clear. Life in the factories is much more calm with performance more clearly defined. No longer do salespeople, customers, marketing people, and other executives call the factories. The interface between the functions is reflected in the master production schedule, and the job of each factory is to hit its MPS. In a sense, what the entire master scheduling effort has done for Ethan Allen is to achieve centralized management of decentralized operations. The operations of the factory are geographically dispersed over wide areas, but the evaluation of those operations is very carefully performed in the corporate offices. The execution responsibility and criteria are unambiguously defined for each plant.

One of the most important benefits of the master production scheduling system for Ethan Allen lies in the fact that the system is upward compatible; that is, the system is transparent, and will work with 5 factories or 25 factories, with new ones easily added. Centralized coordination is maintained, and performance is very clear, with the result being an important tool to support orderly growth for the company. The company has roughly tripled in size since the start of the master production scheduling effort.

CONCLUDING PRINCIPLES

The master production schedule (MPS) plays a key role in manufacturing planning and control systems. In this chapter, we have addressed what the MPS is, how it is done, and who does it. We see the following general principles as emerging from this discussion:

- The MPS unit should reflect the company's approach to the business environment in which it operates.
- The MPS is one part of an MPC system—the other parts need to be in place as well.
- Time-phased MPS records should incorporate useful features of standard MRP record processing.
- The order promising activities must be closely coupled to the MPS.
- Available to promise logic provides useful information to the master scheduler and to the sales department.

- The master·production scheduler must keep the sum of the parts (MPS) equal to the whole (production plan).
- The MPS activity must be clearly defined organizationally.
- The MPS can be usefully considered as a set of firm planned orders.
- Stability must be designed into the MPS and managed.
- The MPS should be evaluated with a formal performance measurement system.

REFERENCES

Berry, W. L.; T. E. Vollmann; and D. C. Whybark. *Master Production Scheduling: Principles and Practice.* Falls Church, Va.: American Production and Inventory Control Society, 1979.

Blevins, Preston. "MPS—What It Is and Why You Need It—Without the Jargon and Buzz Words." *APICS Master Planning Seminar Proceedings,* Las Vegas, March 1982, pp. 69–76.

Brongiel, Bob. "A Manual/Mechanical Approach to Master Scheduling and Operations Planning." *Production and Inventory Management,* 1st Quarter 1979, pp. 66–75.

Garwood, R. D. "The Making and Remaking of a Master Schedule—Parts 1, 2, and 3." *Hot List,* January/February and March/June 1978.

Gessnez, R. *Master Production Schedule Planning.* New York: Society of Manufacturing Engineers, 1986.

Hoelscher, D. R. "Executing the Manufacturing Plans." *1975 APICS Conference Proceedings,* pp. 447–57.

Kinsey, John W. "Master Production Planning—The Key to Successful Master Scheduling." *APICS 24th Annual Conference Proceedings,* 1981, pp. 81–85.

Ling, R. C., and K. Widmer. "Master Scheduling in a Make-to-Order Plant." *1974 APICS Conference Proceedings,* pp. 304–19.

Proud, John F. "Controlling the Master Schedule." *APICS 23rd Annual Conference Proceedings,* 1980, pp. 413–16.

———. "Master Scheduling Requires Time Fences." *APICS 24th Annual Conference Proceedings,* 1981, pp. 61–65.

Raffish, Norm. "Stand Alone MPS: Or Why Wait Two Years?" *APICS 24th Annual Conference Proceedings,* 1981, pp. 54–56.

Sulser, Samuel S., "Master Planning Simulation: Playing the 'What-if' Game." *APICS Annual Conference Proceeding,* 1986, pp. 91–93.

Tincher, Michael G. "Master Scheduling—The Bridge Between Marketing and Manufacturing." *APICS Annual Conference Proceedings,* 1981, pp. 57–60.

———. "Master Scheduling and Final Assembly Scheduling: What's the Difference?" *APICS Annual Conference Proceedings,* 1986, pp. 94–96.

Vollmann, Thomas E. *Master Planning Reprints.* Falls Church, Va.: American Production and Inventory Control Society, 1986.

DISCUSSION QUESTIONS

1. Expand on the notion that the master production schedule (MPS) is *not* a forecast.

2. Some companies have tried to increase output simply by increasing the MPS. Discuss this approach.

3. What do you feel would be the key functions of the MPS in each of the following three environments: make to stock, make to order, and assemble to order?

4. What are the similarities and differences in "rolling-through time" for master production scheduling and MRP?

5. Much of the order-promising logic is directed at telling the customers when they can honestly expect delivery. Several firms, on the other hand, simply promise their customers delivery within X weeks (often an unrealistic claim) and then deliver when they can. Contrast these two approaches.

6. One characterization of the available-to-promise record is that the available row is for the master scheduler and the available-to-promise row is for the customers. What is meant by these contentions?

7. Explain how determining the available row with the "greater of forecast or orders" logic can overstate required production.

8. Many companies have come to view their master production schedulers as key people in profitably meeting the strategic goals of the firm. Would you agree? What qualities would you look for in a master production scheduler?

9. The Ethan Allen approach to master production scheduling puts capacity into a primary position instead of a secondary consideration. What is meant by this statement?

10. Discuss the relationship between stability and firm planned orders.

PROBLEMS

1. Excelsior Springs, Ltd., schedules the production of one end product, Hi-Sulphur, in batches of 60 units whenever the projected ending inventory balance in a quarter falls below 10 units. It takes one quarter to make a batch of 60 units. Excelsior currently has 20 units on hand, and the sales forecast for the next four quarters is:

	Quarter			
	1	2	3	4
Forecast	10	50	50	10

   a. Prepare a time-phased MPS record showing the sales forecast and MPS for Hi-Sulphur.
   b. What are the inventory balances at the end of each quarter?

c. During the first quarter, no units were sold. The revised forecast for the rest of the year is:

	Quarter		
	2	3	4
Forecast	20	40	60

How does the MPS change?

2. The production manager at the Neptune Manufacturing Company would like to prepare a master production schedule covering next year's business. The company produces a complete line of fishing boats for both salt and fresh water use and manufactures most of the component parts used in assembling the products. The firm has been using MRP to coordinate the production schedules of the component part manufacturing and assembly operations.

   The production manager has just received the following sales forecast for next year from the marketing division:

Sales forecast (as measured in standard boats)				
Product lines	1st Quarter	2nd Quarter	3rd Quarter	4th Quarter
1000 Series	8,000	9,000	6,000	6,000
2000 Series	4,000	5,000	2,000	2,000
3000 Series	9,000	10,000	6,000	7,000
Total	21,000	24,000	14,000	15,000

The sales forecast is stated in terms of "standard boats," reflecting the total sales volume for each of the firm's three major product lines.

Another item of information supplied by the marketing department is the target ending inventory position for each product line. The marketing department would like for the production manager to plan on having the following number of standard boats on hand at the end of each quarter of next year:

Product line	Quarterly target ending inventory (in standard boats)
1000 Series	3,000 boats
2000 Series	1,000 boats
3000 Series	3,000 boats

Currently, the inventory position for each product is:

Product line	Current inventory level (in standard boats)
1000 Series	15,000 boats
2000 Series	3,000 boats
3000 Series	5,000 boats

The master production schedule is to specify the number of boats (in standard units) to be produced for *each product line in each quarter* of next year on the firm's single assembly line. The assembly line can produce up to 15,000 standard units per quarter (250 boats per day during the 60 days in a quarter).

Two additional factors are taken into account by the production manager in preparing the master production schedule: the assembly line changeover cost and the inventory carrying cost for the finished goods inventory. It costs $5,000 for each assembly line changeover, reflecting material handling costs of changing the stocking of component parts on the line, adjusting the layout, etc. After some discussion with the company comptroller, the production manager concluded that the firm's inventory carrying cost is 10 percent of standard boat cost per year. The item value for each of the product line standard units is:

Product line	Standard boat cost
1000 Series	$100
2000 Series	150
3000 Series	200

The master production scheduler has calculated the EOQ quantities as 5,385; 2,944; and 4,000 units, respectively.

a. Verify the lot size calculations to be used for master scheduling.
b. Develop a master production schedule for next year, by quarter, for each line of fishing boats produced by Neptune. Identify any problems.

3. The Zoro Manufacturing Company has a plant located in Murphysboro, Georgia. Product A is shipped from the firm's plant warehouse in Murphysboro to satisfy East Coast demand. Currently, the sales forecast for Product A at the Murphysboro plant is 30 units per week.

The master production scheduler at the Murphysboro plant considers Product A to be a make-to-stock item for master scheduling purposes. Currently, there are 50 units of Product A on hand in the plant warehouse at Murphysboro, and the desired safety stock level is 10 units for this product. Product A is produced on a lot-for-lot basis. Currently, an order for 30 units is being produced and is due for delivery to the plant warehouse on Monday, one week from today.

The master production scheduler has heard that an MRP record with a lead time of zero and the forecast for gross requirements can be used for master production scheduling. Complete the MRP record below. How can this be used for master production scheduling?

Product A	Week	1	2	3	4	5	6
Gross requirements							
Scheduled receipts							
Projected available balance							
Planned order releases							

Q = lot for lot; LT = 0; SS = 10.

4. The Spencer Optics Company produces an inexpensive line of sunglasses. The manufacturing process consists of assembling two plastic lenses (produced by the firm's Plastic Molding Department) into a finished frame (purchased from an outside supplier). The company is interested in using material requirements planning (MRP) to schedule its operations and has asked you to prepare an example to illustrate the technique.

The firm's sales manager has prepared a 10-week sales forecast for one of the more popular sunglasses (the Classic model) to use in your example. The forecast is 100 orders per week. Spencer has customer orders of 110 units, 80 units, 50 units, and 20 units in weeks 1, 2, 3, and 4, respectively. The sunglasses are assembled in batches of 300. Presently, there are three such batches scheduled, one in week 2, one in week 5, and one in week 8.

a. Complete the MPS time-phased record below.

Classic model MPS record

	Week	1	2	3	4	5	6	7	8	9	10
Forecast											
Orders											
Available	140										
Available to promise											
MPS											

b. Prepare the MRP record for the assembly of the sunglasses using the record below. The final assembly quantity is 300, the lead time is 2 weeks, and there is a scheduled receipt in week 2. Note that there is no inventory shown for the assembled sunglasses in this record, since it is accounted for in the MPS record.

Week	1	2	3	4	5	6	7	8	9	10
Gross requirements										
Scheduled receipts		300								
Projected available balance 0										
Planned order releases										

Q = 300; LT = 2; SS = 0.

5. The MPC system at the Duckworth Manufacturing Company is run weekly to update the MPS and MRP records. At the start of week 1, the MPS for end-products A and B is as follows:

Master Production Schedule				
	Week 1	Week 2	Week 3	Week 4
Product A	10	—	25	5
Product B	5	20	—	20

To manufacture one unit of either end product A or B, one unit of component C is required. The purchasing lead time for component C is two weeks, a fixed order quantity of 40 units is used, and no (zero) safety stock is maintained for this item. The inventory balance for component C is 5 units at the start of week 1, and there is an open order (scheduled receipt) for 40 units due to be delivered at the beginning of week 1.

a. Complete the MRP record for component C as of the beginning of week 1:

Week	1	2	3	4
Gross requirements				
Scheduled receipts				
Projected available balance				
Planned order releases				

Q = 40; LT = 2; SS = 0.

b. During week 1 the following transactions occurred for component C:
1. The open order for 40 units due to be received at the start of week 1 was received on Monday of week 1 for a quantity of 30. (Ten units of component C were scrapped on this order.)
2. An inventory cycle count during week 1 revealed that five units of com-

ponent C were missing. An inventory adjustment of -5 was, therefore, processed.

3. Ten units of component C were actually disbursed (instead of the 15 units that were planned for disbursement to produce end products A and B). (The MPS quantity of 5 in week 1 for product B was canceled due to a customer order cancellation.)

4. The MPS quantities for week 5 include 15 units for product A and zero units for product B.

5. Due to a change in customer order requirements, marketing has requested that the MPS quantity of 25 units for product A scheduled in week 3 be moved to week 2.

6. The MRP planner released an order for 40 units, due in week 3.

Given this information, complete the MRP record for component C as of the start of week 2:

Week	2	3	4	5
Gross requirements				
Scheduled receipts				
Projected available balance				
Planned order releases				

Q = 40; LT = 2; SS = 0.

c. What action(s) are required by the MRP planner at the start of week 2 as a result of the transactions given in question b? What MPS policy issues are raised?

6. Peter Ward has constructed the following (partial) time-phased MPS record:

Weeks	1	2	3	4	5	6
Forecast	20	20	20	20	20	20
Orders	12	6	3			
Available						
Available to promise						
MPS	50		50			50

On hand = 5.

a. Complete the record.
b. Are there any problems?
c. What is the earliest Peter can take an order for 33 units?
d. Assume that an order for 10 is booked for week 4. Assume the order for 33 units in part C is *not* booked, and recompute the record.

7. The Cedar River Manufacturing Company produces a line of furnishings for motels and hotels. Among the items manufactured is an Executive water pitcher whose product structure is shown below:

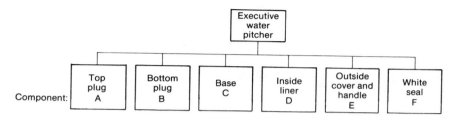

Component items A, B, C, and F are manufactured by the plastic molding shop and components D and E are purchased from a vendor. The Executive water pitcher is completed by the final assembly department.

Currently the following open orders for Executive water pitcher components are waiting to be processed at the #101 injection molding press in the plastic molding shop:

		Plastic molding shop floor control report		
Shop order number	Component item	Order quantity	Order due date	Machine time (weeks)
10–XYZ	F	15	ASAP*	2
10–XXX	B	25	ASAP*	2
10–XZV	A	30	ASAP*	1
10–XXY	C	20	ASAP*	2

*As soon as possible.

All of the orders shown above are made complete in one operation at the #101 injection molding press and are subsequently ready for the final assembly department (final assembly time is negligible).

a. Given the information above, complete the MPS and MRP records for all of the Executive water pitcher items.

MPS record: Executive water pitcher

Week	1	2	3	4	5	6	7
Forecast	10	10	10	10	10	10	10
Orders	12	5	2				
Available							
Available to promise							
MPS							

On hand = 15.
MPS lot size = 20.

MRP records

Component A

Week	1	2	3	4	5	6	7
Gross requirements							
Scheduled receipts	30						
Projected available balance	12						
Planned order releases							

Q = 30; LT = 5; SS = 0.

Component B

Week	1	2	3	4	5	6	7
Gross requirements							
Scheduled receipts	25						
Projected available balance	22						
Planned order releases							

Q = 25; LT = 5; SS = 0.

Component C

Week	1	2	3	4	5	6	7
Gross requirements							
Scheduled receipts	20						
Projected available balance	45						
Planned order releases							

Q = 20; LT = 5; SS = 0.

Component F

Week	1	2	3	4	5	6	7
Gross requirements							
Scheduled receipts	15						
Projected available balance	70						
Planned order releases							

Q = 15; LT = 5; SS = 0.

b. What conclusions can you make with respect to the validity of the current order due dates for the open shop orders at the #101 injection molding press?

8. As a consultant in manufacturing control systems for the R&E accounting firm, you have been invited to do some work for the Green Valley Furniture Com-

pany. It would like you to install a master production scheduling system similar to the one used by the Ethan Allen Furniture Company. Please prepare an illustration of how this system works using the following example data:

End product item	Forecast sales per week	Current on-hand inventory	Final assembly production lot size
A	10	5 units	30 units
B	25	−10*	40
C	15	30	30

*10 units back-ordered.

Currently, there is one final assembly line at the Green Valley plant. This line is run exactly 40 hours per week on a single shift with no overtime. During each week, 40 units of any end product item can be produced in 40 hours on the final assembly line (one hour per unit).

In addition to selling products directly out of finished-goods inventory, the Green Valley Furniture Company also makes a few items on a make-to-order (custom order contract) basis. Currently, there are two such customer orders— one for 20 units of Item D that is scheduled for final assembly in week 2 and another for 15 units of Item E that is scheduled for final assembly in week 4. (Today is Monday of week 1.) The production of these units must be included in the master production schedule.

a. Illustrate the steps in preparing the master production schedule covering the next four weeks using the Ethan Allen procedure. Give the MPS for each end item.

b. Given the master production schedules developed in question a, make a recommendation to the Green Valley Furniture Company regarding changes, if any, that should be made in the final assembly line capacity.

9. Figure 8.19, the Ethan Allen example, is based on the following data:

Product	Beginning inventory	Weekly forecast	Lot size	Hours per lot size
A	20	5	50	20
B	50	40	250	80
C	−30	35	150	60
D	25	10	100	30

Priorities are calculated by dividing expected beginning inventory by forecast. In weeks after the first, expected beginning inventory takes account of production and expected sales.

a. Calculate the weekly priorities and determine the master production schedule for weeks 1 through 8 for these data. Check your answers against Figure 8.19.

b. Assume the actual sales in week 1 were as follows:

Product	Sales
A	10
B	30
C	25
D	25

Given these actual sales data, calculate the weekly priorities and determine the MPS for weeks 2 through 9, assuming the forecasts remain unchanged. What impact do these changes have?

c. Given the actual sales data in question **a**, calculate the weekly priorities and determine the MPS for weeks 7 through 9, assuming the forecasts remain unchanged and weeks 1 through 6 are frozen; that is, the schedule in part a can be revised, but only from week 7 on. What impact would the frozen schedule have on the inventory and customer service levels for products A through D?

d. Assume that the time horizon date is extended to 18 weeks and the following scheduling priorities for week 18 resulted:

Product	Priority
A	2
B	*
C	−1
D	1

Hours	Assembly Load (week 18)
35	
30	
25	C
20	
15	
10	
5	B
0	

What capacity information can be inferred from this schedule?

10. Lou Chin is the master scheduler at Amdur Products. Assembly D is a critical assembly used in products A, B, and C. Assembly D is made in a dedicated work center with a 50 unit per week capacity. Lou has the following demand information and feels that the firm planned order approach to master scheduling will be helpful. Complete the time phased record for Assembly D.

	Product demand		
Period	A(1D)	B(2Ds)	C(1D)
1		10	20
2			
3			
4			
5	50		60
6		40	
7			
8			
9	50	30	40
10			

Week		1	2	3	4	5	6	7	8	9	10
Gross requirements											
Scheduled receipts			30	30							
Projected available balance	20										
Planned orders											
Firm planned orders											

11. The master production scheduler at the XYZ Company is concerned with determining the impact of using different MPS freezing intervals on component part shortages and inventory levels in the firm's fabrication shop. Currently, the firm's end products are produced on a make-to-stock basis. A four-period MPS planning horizon is used. Lot sizing is performed at the start of every period covering all four future periods using a lot-sizing heuristic. Assembly orders are issued at the start of each period. The assembly lead time equals zero periods and the beginning finished product inventory is zero.

The forecast, projected inventory, and MPS are shown in Table A for three consecutive periods for one of the firm's products, using the current freeze policy of one period and assuming perfect forecasts. Similar information is shown in Table B, when a two-period MPS freeze policy is used. Assuming the component part 1234 is only used on this end product, with a usage rate of one unit per unit of end product, prepare the MRP records for this part as of the beginning of each of the three consecutive periods under both MPS freezing policies. Assume that component part 1234 has a planned lead time of two periods, that its lot-size is the net requirement for the next two periods whenever a net requirement is observed and that it has a zero safety stock, a beginning inventory of 450 units in period 1, and there are no scheduled receipts.

   a. What conclusions can be drawn about the effectiveness of the two different freezing policies?

b. What other freezing policies should be considered?
c. What are the appropriate time fences?

TABLE A

Period*	1	2	3	4
Forecast†	177	261	207	309
Available	261	0	309	0
MPS	438	0	516	0

Period	2	3	4	5
Forecast	0	207	309	64
Available	0	373	64	0
MPS	0	580	0	0

Period	3	4	5	6
Forecast	207	309	64	182
Available	0	246	182	0
MPS	207	555	0	0

TABLE B

Period*	1	2	3	4
Forecast†	177	261	207	309
Available	261	0	309	0
MPS	438	0	516	0

Period	2	3	4	5
Forecast	0	207	309	64
Available	0	373	64	0
MPS	0	580	0	0

Period	3	4	5	6
Forecast	207	309	64	182
Available	373	64	0	0
MPS	580	0	0	182

*The forecast is net of beginning inventory.
†The available is the closing inventory balance.

---

12. The Avon Power Tool Company makes a line of snowblowers on a make-to-order basis as well as other types of products. There are eight different end products (catalog numbers) in the snowblower product line, which vary according to the horsepower, drive unit, and starting mechanism. The company expects to sell one third of the snowblowers in 2 horsepower and two thirds in four horsepower. The expected breakdown for drive units is 40 percent and 60 percent, for chain and gear, respectively. Similarly, the breakdown on starters is 50–50.

Catalog number	1000	1100	1200	1300	1400	1500	1600	1700
Horsepower	2	2	2	2	4	4	4	4
Drive unit	Chain	Chain	Gear	Gear	Chain	Chain	Gear	Gear
Starter	Auto	Manual	Auto	Manual	Auto	Manual	Auto	Manual
Component parts	401	401	401	401	801	801	801	801
	200	200	200	200	200	200	200	200
	150	150	160	160	150	150	160	160
	130	135	130	135	130	135	130	135
	115	115	120	120	115	115	120	120
	101	101	101	101	101	101	101	101
	170	175	170	175	170	175	170	175
	600	600	600	600	800	800	800	800

a. Group the component parts. Which are common? Which are associated with horsepower? Drive unit? Starter?

b. Show how super bills can be used to master schedule the snowblower product line, indicating how the requirements for the component items would be exploded. Please prepare sample MRP and MPS records for the 2-HP option and Item #401 to explain and illustrate your two approaches. In preparing these records, assume that the safety stock is zero and the order quantity is 100 for both items. The current on hand quantity for the 2-HP option is 65 units and the on hand for item #401 is 140 units. Booked orders have been accepted for the 2-HP option of: 25 in week 1, 18 in week 2, 6 in week 3, and 4 in week 4. Also, assume that the lead time for Item #401 is two weeks.

c. What are the advantages and disadvantages of this approach?

13. The Ace Electronics Company produces printed circuit boards on a make-to-order basis.

a. Prepare an MPS record for one of its items (catalogue #2400), including the available-to-promise information, using the following data:

Final assembly production lead time = 2 weeks.

Weekly forecast = 100 units.

Current on-hand quantity = 0.

Booked customer orders (already confirmed):
95 units in week 1
105 units in week 2
70 units in week 3
10 units in week 5

Master production schedule:
200 units to be completed at the start of week 1
200 units to be completed at the start of week 3

200 units to be completed at the start of week 5
200 units to be completed at the start of week 7

b. Suppose that the cumulative lead time for the item (catalogue #2400) is 8 weeks. What decision must the master scheduler make this week?

14. Consider the time-phased information relating to the #R907 outboard motor given in Exhibit A. The following transactions occurred during the week of 5/2/83:

1. The MPS for 9/19 was released (360 units).
2. Customer order #6005 requested 3 units in week of 5/9.
3. Customer order #6015 requested 5 units in week of 6/6.
4. Customer order #6028 requested 5 units in week of 6/13.
5. Customer order #6042 requested 15 units in week of 7/4.

a. Can all of the orders received during the week of 5/2 be accepted? Update Exhibit A as it would appear at the beginning of the week of 5/9.

During the week of 5/9, the following additional orders were received:

1. Customer order #6085 requested 20 units in week of 6/6.
2. Customer order #6093 requested 10 units in week of 5/30.
3. Customer order #6142 requested 250 units in week of 8/1/
4. Customer order #6150 requested 100 units in week of 7/25.

b. Discuss the effect of the orders received during the week of 5/9 on the revised Exhibit A.

15. The Parker Corporation is producing and selling a machine for tending golf course greens. The patented device trims the grass, aerates the turf, and injects a metered amount of nitrogen into the soil. The machines are marketed through the Taylor Golf Course Supply Company, under the Parker Company's own original equipment brand and, recently, through a lawn and garden supply house (Brown Thumb), which serves both commercial and consumer accounts. The addition of the lawn and garden outlet and requests to add a 3-HP version have called into question the production planning and control process for the machines.

Of particular difficulty is the forecasting of the products to be produced. At the moment, there are two drive mechanisms, chain and gear, three different body styles (one for each outlet), and two sizes of engine (4 and 5 HP). This gives a total of 12 end items, all of which had some demand (see Exhibit B). The addition of the 3-HP motor would add six more end items, and forecasting the demand for these new items would add to the difficulty of forecasting demand.

The lead times for some of the castings and for 5-HP motors had increased to the extent that it was not possible to wait until firm orders had been received for the end items before the castings and motors had to be ordered. In addition, the firm's business was growing, and it was anticipated that about 120 units would be sold during the next year. Consequently, the production manager arranged to purchase enough material for 10 units per month. There is plenty of capacity for the small amount of parts fabrication that is required, but assembly capacity had to be carefully planned. The current plan called for assembly capacity of 10 units per month.

EXHIBIT A Time-phased requirements

Item #	Description	Assembly lead time	On hand	Lot size	Safety stock	Time fences		Run date
						Demand	Plan	
R907	Outboard motor	1	100	180	0	4	20	5/2

Week	5/2	5/9	5/16	5/23	5/30	6/6	6/13	6/20	6/27	7/4	7/11	7/18	7/25
Forecast	13	14	13	14	13	14	13	14	13	14	13	14	13
Orders	20	5	10	8	10	15	10	8	20	5	10	10	5
Available	80	75	65	57	44	29	196	182	162	148	135	121	288
Available to promise	32						117						175
Master production schedule							180						180

Week	8/1	8/8	8/15	8/22	8/29	9/5	9/12	9/19	9/26	10/3	10/10	10/17	10/24
Forecast	290	290	290	290	290	290	290	290	290	14	13	14	13
Orders	200	200		200		200		200					
Available	178	68	138	28	98	168	58	-232	-522	-536	-549	-563	-576
Available to promise	160		340	180	360	160	180						
Master production schedule	180	180	360	180	360	360	180						

EXHIBIT A   *(concluded)*

MPS pegging detail				Actual demand pegging				Actual demand pegging		
Due date	Shop order	Quantity	Action	Required date	Quantity	Customer order	Required date	Quantity	Customer order	
6/13	M1234	180	Released	5/2	20	5678				
7/25	M1278	180	Released	5/9	5	5789				
8/1	M1347	180	Released	5/16	8	5890				
9/19	—	360	Planned							
9/26	—	180	Planned							

EXHIBIT B   Last year's sales by catalog number

Catalog number			Sales	Key
Body	Horsepower*	Drive	Total = 100	
T	4	C	1	
T	4	G	4	Body:
T	5	C	18	T = Taylor Supply
T	5	G	17	O = "OEM" Parker's own
O	4	C	13	B = Brown Thumb
O	4	G	9	
O	5	C	10	
O	5	G	8	
B	4	C	6	Drive
B	4	G	7	C = Chain
B	5	C	2	G = Gear
B	5	G	5	

*Note: The 3-horsepower machine would be offered in all three body styles and both drives.

With regard to the specific issue of forecasting, the marketing manager summarized the data on the sales of each end item over the past year (see Exhibit B). He felt that a 20 percent growth in the total volume was about right, and that perhaps half of that growth would be accounted for by the 3-HP machines. Of course, once the forecasts had been made, the production manager had to determine which motors and castings (gear or chain) to order. Each machine was made up of many common parts, but the motors, chain or gear drive subassemblies, and bodies were different (though interchangeable).

a. Suggest an improved method of forecasting the demand for the firm's products.

b. As the production manager contemplated the difficulty of forecasting the demand for the firm's products and determining exactly what to schedule into final assembly, two customers called. The first, from Taylor, wanted to know when the company could deliver a model T3G, and the second wanted as early delivery as possible of one of Parker's own machines, an 04C. The Taylor representative said he felt that the 3-horsepower models might "really take off."

Before making any commitment at all, it was necessary to check the material availability and get back to the two customers. It was the firm's practice not to promise immediate delivery, since the units scheduled for

EXHIBIT C   Inventories and on-order

Item	Inventory	On order	Due date	Lot size
Common "kit"	0	5 each	weeks 1,3,5,7,9	5
5-hp motor	10	5	week 5	5
4-hp motor	3	5	weeks 3,8	5
3-hp motor	0	5	week 1	5
Chain drive	14	—	—	10
Gear drive	6	5	week 3	10

EXHIBIT D   Booked orders and delivery dates

Delivery week	1	2	3	4	5	6
Models	2T4G* 105C	1B3G 1T4C 104G	1T5C 1B4C	105G	1T5G	104G
Total	3	3	2	1	1	1

*2 units of T4G

final assembly were usually already promised. The planned assembly schedule called for assembly of three units next week, two units the following week, and alternating three and two thereafter. As a matter of practice, all parts for assembly and delivery in any week would need to be ready at the start of that week.

The current inventory and on-order positions for the common part "kit," the motors, and the drives are shown in Exhibit C. (The production manager did not concern himself with the body styles, since all three styles can be obtained in a week.) In Exhibit D are listed booked orders and promised delivery over the next few weeks. Organize this information to respond to the delivery promise requests (assume that no safety stocks are held). What should the delivery promises be?

—9————————————

Production planning

Production planning is probably the least understood aspect of manufacturing planning and control. However, the payoffs from a well-designed and executed production-planning system are very large. In this chapter, we discuss the process by which the aggregate levels of production are determined. The managerial objective is to develop an integrated game plan for which the manufacturing portion *is* the production plan. The production plan, therefore, links strategic goals to production and is coordinated with sales objectives, resource availabilities, and financial budgets. If the production plan is not integrated, production managers cannot be held responsible for meeting the plan, and informal approaches will develop to overcome inconsistencies.

Our discussion of production planning is organized around the following four topics:

- Production planning in the firm: What is production planning? How does it link with strategic management and other MPC system modules?
- The production-planning process: What are the fundamental activities in production planning and what techniques can be used?

- The new management obligations: What are the key responsibilities for ensuring an effective production-planning system?
- Operating production-planning systems: What is the state of the art in practice?

This chapter is focused on managerial concepts for integrated planning. Advanced concepts in production planning are emphasized in Chapter 15. Useful background for the concepts in this chapter can be found in Chapter 8 on planning bills of material, in Chapter 10 on demand management, and in Chapter 14, which deals with advanced master production scheduling (MPS) concepts.

PRODUCTION PLANNING IN THE FIRM

The production plan provides key communication links from top management to manufacturing. It determines the basis for focusing the detailed production resources to achieve the strategic objectives of the firm. By providing the framework within which the master production schedule is developed, the subsequent MPS systems, material resources, and capacities of the plant are planned and controlled on a basis consistent with these objectives. We now describe the production plan in terms of the role it plays in top management, some of the necessary conditions for effective production planning, the linkages to other MPC system modules, and some of the payoffs from effective production planning.

Production planning and management

The production plan provides a direct and consistent dialogue between manufacturing and top management, as well as between manufacturing and the other functions. As shown in Figure 9.1, many of the key linkages of production planning are *outside* of the manufacturing planning and control (MPC) system. As such, the plan necessarily must be stated in terms that are meaningful to the nonmanufacturing executives of the company. Only in this way can the top-management game plan, shown in Figure 9.1, become consistent for each of the basic functional areas. Moreover, the production plan also has to be stated in terms that can be used by MPC system modules, so detailed manufacturing decisions are kept in concert with the overall strategic objectives reflected in the game plan.

The basis for consistency of the functional plans is the resolution of broad trade-offs at the top-management level. Suppose, for example, there is an opportunity to expand into a new market, and marketing requests additional production to do so. With a specified production plan, this could only be accomplished by decreasing production for some other product group. If this is seen as undesirable (i.e., the new market is to be direct add-on), by definition a new game plan is required—with an updated and consistent set of

FIGURE 9.1   Key linkages of production planning

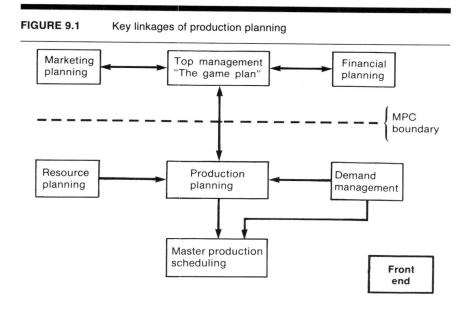

plans in marketing, finance, and production. The feasibility of the added production must be resolved and agreed upon before detailed execution steps are taken.

The production plan states the mission that manufacturing must accomplish if the overall objectives of the firm are to be met. How the production plan is to be accomplished in terms of detailed manufacturing and procurement decisions is a problem for manufacturing management. With an agreed-upon game plan, the job in manufacturing is to "hit the production plan." Similar job definitions should exist in marketing and finance.

An interesting chicken-and-egg question sometimes arises about the production plan and the detailed plans that result from the MPC system. Conceptually, production planning should precede and direct MPC decision making. Production planning provides the basis for making the more detailed set of MPC decisions. In some firms, however, it is only after the other MPC systems are in place that the resultant production-planning decisions are clearly defined. In these cases, the first production plans are no more than a summation of the individual detailed plans. They are the *result* of other detailed decisions, rather than an input to those decisions. Even so, they provide the basis for management review.

The planning performed in other MPC systems is necessarily detailed, and the language is quite different from that required for production planning. The production plan might be in dollars or aggregate units of output per month, while the MPS could be in end products per week. The MPS might be stated in special bills of materials to manage complicated options and not correspond to the units used to communicate with top management.

To perform the necessary communication role, the production plan must be stated in commonly understood, aggregated terms. In some companies, the production plan is stated as the dollar value of total monthly or quarterly output. Other firms break this total output down by individual factories or by major product lines. Still other firms state the production plan in terms of total units for each product line. Measures that relate to capacity, such as direct labor-hours, tons of product, and the like, are also used by some firms. The key requirement is that the production plan be stated in some commonly understood homogeneous unit, that thereafter can be kept in concert with other plans.

The production plan needs to be expressed in meaningful units, but it also needs to be expressed in a manageable number of units. Experience indicates that 5 to 15 family groups seems to be about right for a top-management group to handle. Each has to be considered in terms of expectations on sales, manufacturing, and resultant inventories and backlogs. The overall result, expressed in monetary units, also has to be examined and weighed against overall business plans.

The overall context within which the trade-offs are made and the production plan developed is increasingly called *game planning*. The game plan reflects the strategy (e.g., increased market share) and tactics (e.g., increased inventory for improved service) that are *doable* by the firm. It is not a set of uncoordinated wishes that some people would like to see realized. The manufacturing part of the game plan is the production plan.

The production plan is *not* a forecast of demand! It is the planned production, stated on an aggregate basis, for which manufacturing management is to be held responsible. The production plan is not necessarily equal to a forecast of aggregate demand. For example, it may not be profitable to satisfy all demands, in which case the production would be less than the forecast. Conversely, a strategic objective of improved customer service could result in aggregate production in excess of aggregate demand. These are important management trade-offs.

The production plan for manufacturing is a result of the production planning process. Inputs to the process include sales forecasts; but these need to be stated on the basis of shipments, not bookings. This is necessary so the inventory projections match physical inventories, and so the demands on manufacturing are expressed correctly with respect to time.

Production planning and MPC systems

Up to this point, we have emphasized the linkages of production planning to activities outside of the MPC system boundaries. These linkages are often referred to as top management's handle on the business. To provide execution support for the production plan, it is necessary to have linkages to the MPC systems. The most fundamental linkage is to the master production schedule (MPS), which is a disaggregation of the production plan. The result drives the detailed scheduling through MRP and other MPC systems.

The MPS must be kept in concert with the production plan. As the individual daily scheduling decisions to produce specific mixes of actual end items and/or options are made, the parity between the sum of the MPS quantities and the production plan must be maintained. If the relationship is maintained, then "hitting the schedule" (MPS) means the agreed-upon production plan will be met, as well.

Another critical linkage, shown in Figure 9.1, is the link with demand management. Demand management encompasses order entry, order promising, and physical distribution coordination, as well as forecasting. This module must capture every source of demand against manufacturing capacity, such as interplant transfers, international requirements, and service parts. In some firms, one or more of these sources of demand may be of more consequence than others. For the firm with distribution warehouses, for example, the replenishment of those warehouses may create quite a different set of demands on manufacturing than is true for other firms. The contribution of demand management, insofar as production planning is concerned, is to ensure that the influence of all aspects of demand is included and properly coordinated.

As a tangential activity, the match between actual and forecast demand is monitored in the demand management module. As actual demand conditions depart from forecast, the necessity for revising the production plan increases. Thus, the assessment of the impact of the changes on the production plan and the desirability of making a change is dependent on this linkage. It is critical for top management to change the plans, rather than to let the forecast errors per se change the aggregate production output level.

The other direct MPC linkage to production planning, shown in Figure 9.1, is with resource planning. This activity encompasses the long-range planning of facilities. Involved is the translation of extended production plans into capacity requirements, usually on a gross or aggregate basis. In some firms, the unit of measure might be constant dollar output rates; in others, it might be man-hours, head counts, machine-hours, key-facility-hours, tons of output, or some other output measure. The need is to plan capacity, at least in aggregate terms, for a horizon at least as long as it takes to make major changes.

Resource planning is directly related to production planning, since, in the short term, the resources available provide a set of constraints to production planning. In the longer run, to the extent that production plans call for more resources than available, financial appropriations are indicated. A key goal of the linkage between production planning and resource planning is to answer what-if questions. The maintenance of current resource-planning factors, related to the product groupings used for planning, is the basis for performing this analysis.

Much of the very near-term production plan is constrained by available material supplies. The levels of currently available raw material, parts, and subassemblies limit what can be produced in the short run, even if other resources are available. This is often hard to assess unless the information links from the MRP and shop status data bases are effective.

Links through the MPS system to MRP and other MPC systems provide the basic data to perform the what-if simulations of alternative plans. Having the ability to quickly evaluate alternatives can facilitate the game-planning process. This is *not* an argument to always change the production plan. On the contrary, having the ability to demonstrate the impact of proposed changes may reduce the number of instances in which production "loses" in these negotiations.

The value of the production-planning activity is certainly questionable if there is no monitoring of performance. This requires linkages to the data on shipments/sales, aggregated into the production-planning groupings. The measurement of performance is an important input to the planning process itself. Insofar as deviations in output are occurring, they must be taken into account. If the plan cannot be realized, the entire value of the production-planning process is called into question.

One final performance aspect where effort must be expended is in the reconciliation of the MPS with the production plan. As day-to-day MPS decisions are made, it is possible to move away from the production plan unless constant vigilance is applied. Like other performance monitoring, it requires a frequent evaluation of status and comparison to plan.

Payoffs

Game planning is top-management's handle on the business. It provides important visibility of the critical interactions between marketing, production, and finance. If marketing wants higher inventories, but the top-management decision is that there is not sufficient capital to support the inventories, the production plan will be so designed. Once such critical trade-off decisions are made, the production plan provides the basis for monitoring and controlling manufacturing performance in a way that provides a much more clear division of responsibilities than is true under conventional budgetary controls.

Under such planning, it is manufacturing's job to hit the schedule. This can eliminate the battle over "ownership" of finished-goods inventory. If actual inventory levels do not agree with planned inventory levels, that is basically not a manufacturing problem, *if* they hit the schedule. It is either a marketing problem (they did not sell according to plan) or a problem of product-mix management in the demand management activity (the wrong individual items were made).

The production plan provides the basis for day-to-day, tough-minded trade-off decisions, as well. If marketing wants more of some items, they must be asked "Of what do you want less?" There is no other response, because additional production without a corresponding reduction would violate the agreed-upon production plan. In the absence of a new, expanded production plan, production and marketing must work to allocate the scarce capacity to the competing needs (via the master production schedule).

The reverse situation is also true. If the production plan calls for more than marketing currently needs, detailed decisions should be reached about which items will go into inventory. Manufacturing commits people, capacities, and materials to reach company objectives. The issue is only how best to convert these resources into particular end products.

Better integration between functional areas is one of the major payoffs from production planning. Once a consistent game plan between top levels of the functional areas is developed, it can be translated into detailed plans that are in concert with the top-level agreements. This results in a set of common goals, improved communication, and transparent systems.

Without a production plan, the expectation is that somehow the job will get done—and in fact, it does get done, but at a price. That price is organizational slack: extra inventories, poor customer service, excess capacity, long lead times, panic operations, and poor response to new opportunities. Informal systems will, of necessity, come into being. Detailed decisions will be made by clerical-level personnel with no guiding policy except "get it out the door as best we can." The annual budget cycle will not be tied in with detailed plans and will probably be inconsistent and out of date before it is one month old. Marketing requests for products will not be made so as to keep the sum of the detailed end products in line with the budget. In many cases, the detailed requests for the first month are double the average monthly volume. Only at the end of the year does the reconciliation between requests and budget take place; but in the meantime it has been up to manufacturing to decide what is really needed.

We have seen many companies with these symptoms. Where are these costs reflected? There is no special place in the chart of accounts for them, but they will be paid in the bottom-line profit results. More and more firms are finding that a well-structured monthly production planning meeting allows the various functional areas to operate in a more coordinated fashion and to better respond to the vagaries of the marketplace. The result is a dynamic overall plan for the company, one that changes as needed, and one that fosters the necessary adaptation in each function.

THE PRODUCTION-PLANNING PROCESS

Our interest in this section is on aids to the management of the production-planning process. Specifically, we will be concerned with routinizing the process, the game-planning output, cumulative charting, and the tabular display. We examine these techniques with an example.

Routinizing production and game planning

The game- and production-planning process typically begins with an updated sales forecast covering the next year or more. Any desired increases or decreases to inventory or backlog levels are added or subtracted, and the result is the production plan. The most immediate portion of this plan will not be capable of being changed, since commitments to manpower, equipment, and materials already will have been made. An effective production-planning process will typically have explicit time fences for when the aggregate plan can be increased or decreased; there also well may be tight constraints on the amounts of increase or decrease. An example might be no changes during the most immediate month, up to +10 percent or −20 percent in next month, and so on. Effective production planning also implies periodicity; that is, it is useful to perform the production- and game-planning process on a regular, routine cycle.

Performing the game-planning function on a regular basis has several benefits. It tends to institutionalize the process and force a consideration, which might otherwise be postponed, of changed conditions and trade-offs. The routine also keeps the information channels open for forecast changes, different conditions, and new opportunities. Performing the task routinely helps ensure a separation between the forecasts and the plan.

The frequency of the cycle varies from firm to firm, depending on the stability of the business, the cost of planning, and the ability to monitor performance. The trade-off is a difficult one. There is a high cost to planning involving data gathering, meetings, what-if analysis, and other staff support activities. On the other hand, delaying the planning process increases the chance of significant departures of reality from plan, creating the opportunity for informal systems to take over. Ironically, the more successful firms can use a less frequent cycle because of the ability of their formal systems to keep the firm on plan and warn of impending problems. A common schedule among successful firms is to review the plans monthly and revise the plans quarterly or when necessary. An example of the monthly cycle at Ethan Allen is shown in Figure 9.2.

Ethan Allen is a make-to-stock furniture manufacturer; so much of their demand forecasting is based on routine extrapolation of historical data. The first event shown in Figure 9.2, "determine (manual forecast)," is to forecast the nonroutine items. These include large contract sales (such as to a

FIGURE 9.2 Example monthly cycle for production planning

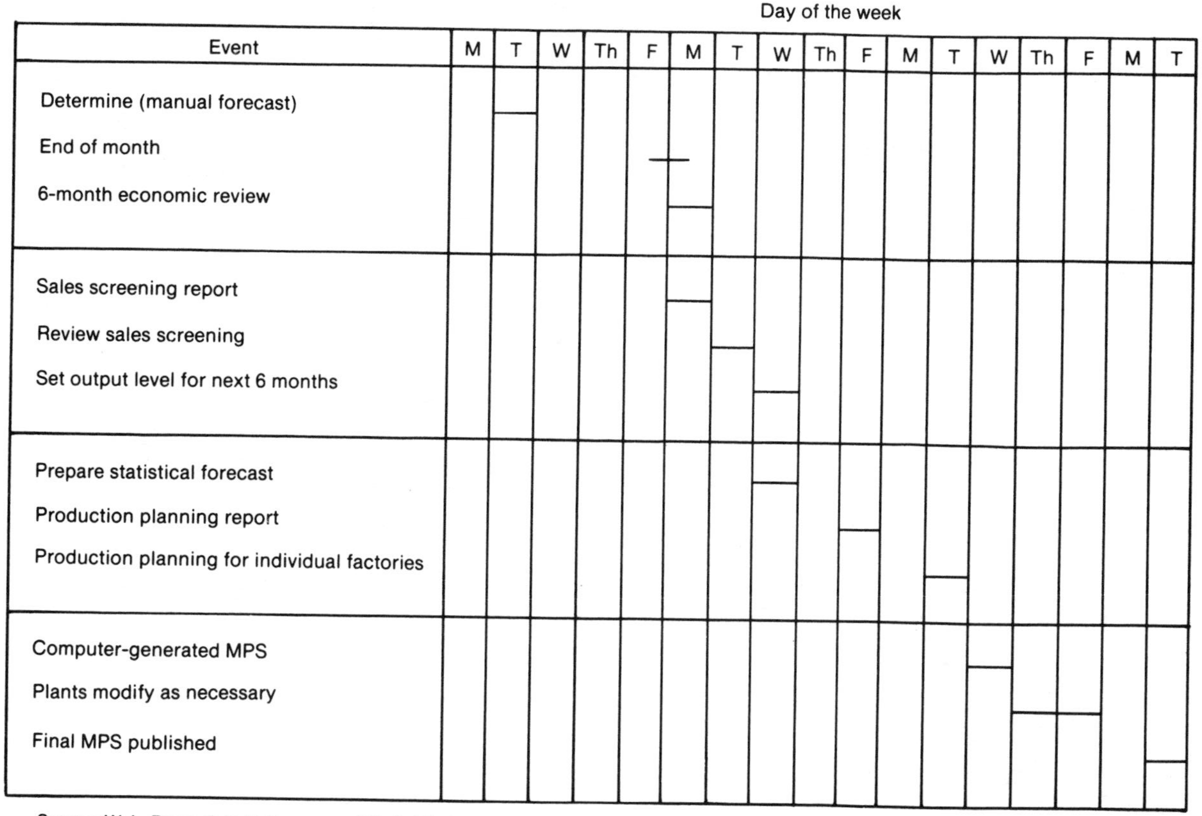

Day of the week

Event	M	T	W	Th	F	M	T	W	Th	F	M	T	W	Th	F	M	T
Determine (manual forecast)																	
End of month																	
6-month economic review																	
Sales screening report																	
Review sales screening																	
Set output level for next 6 months																	
Prepare statistical forecast																	
Production planning report																	
Production planning for individual factories																	
Computer-generated MPS																	
Plants modify as necessary																	
Final MPS published																	

Source: W. L. Berry, T. E. Vollmann, and D. C. Whybark, *Master Production Scheduling: Principles and Practice* (Falls Church, Va.: American Production and Inventory Control Society, 1979), p. 45.

motel chain), new items for which there are no historical data, and market specials.

The second event shown in Figure 9.2 is the end of the month. Following immediately is a six-month economic review. This is a report that attempts to summarize the future economic conditions in the furniture industry. At the same time, the sales screening report is prepared. It is a review of the actual sales in light of the forecast, to make any necessary changes before the preparation of the new routine statistical forecast.

The sixth event shown in Figure 9.2 ("set output level for the next six months"), is the production plan. A group of executives reviews the economic outlook, present inventory levels, statistical forecasts, and other factors. The net result is a rate of output in total dollars for Ethan Allen production. The subsequent events are devoted to preparing reports based on this production plan, allocating the total to individual factories, and preparing the detailed MPS that supports the production plan.

The discipline required in routinizing the production and game-planning process is to replan when conditions indicate it is necessary. If information from the demand management module indicates differences between the forecast and actual have exceeded reasonable error limits, replanning may be necessary. Similarly, if conditions change in manufacturing, or a new market opportunity arises, or the capital market shifts, replanning may be needed. So, though regularizing has its advantages, slavishly following a timetable and ignoring actual conditions is not wise management practice.

Since the purpose of the planning process is to arrive at a coordinated set of plans for each of the functions (a game plan), mechanisms for getting support for the plans are important. Clearly, a minimum step in this is to have the top functional officer involved in the process. This does more than legitimize the plan; it involves the people who can resolve the issues in the trade-off stage. A second step used by some firms is to virtually write contracts between functions on what the agreements are. The contracts serve to underscore the importance of each function performing to plan, rather than returning to informal practices.

To illustrate the nature of production-planning decisions, we now turn to an example based on a firm that has a seasonal sales pattern. We raise the issues in the context of a single facility. In this context, the problem is to find a low-cost combination of inventories, overtime, changes in work force levels, and other capacity variations that meet the production requirements of the company. We first present an example of the cumulative charting approach, and then examine a tabular representation of the alternative strategies.

The basic trade-offs

Figure 9.3 presents the forecast of aggregate sales for our example, the XYZ Company, for the year. The total is aggregated in dollar terms for *all* of

FIGURE 9.3   XYZ Company monthly sales forecast ($000,000)

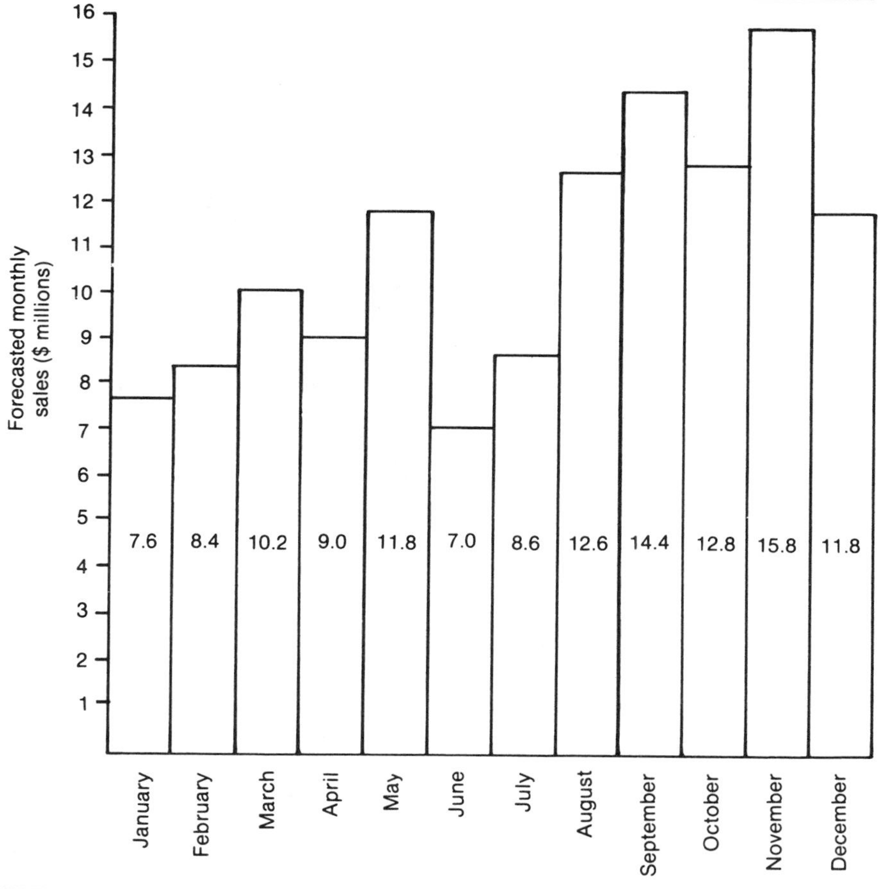

Total sales for the year = $130 million.

the plant's output for the year and is about $130 million. The monthly totals vary from a high of $15.8 million to a low of $7 million. Figure 9.4 shows these monthly sales data in the form of a cumulative chart (solid line). In addition, the dashed straight line in Figure 9.4 represents the cumulative production, at a constant rate of production. The production planning problem is to choose a low-cost cumulative production plan with a line on the cumulative chart that is always on or above the cumulative forecast line.

The cumulative chart shows clearly the implications of alternative plans. For example, the vertical distance between the dashed line and the solid line in our example represents the expected inventory at each point in time.

FIGURE 9.4   XYZ Company cumulative chart

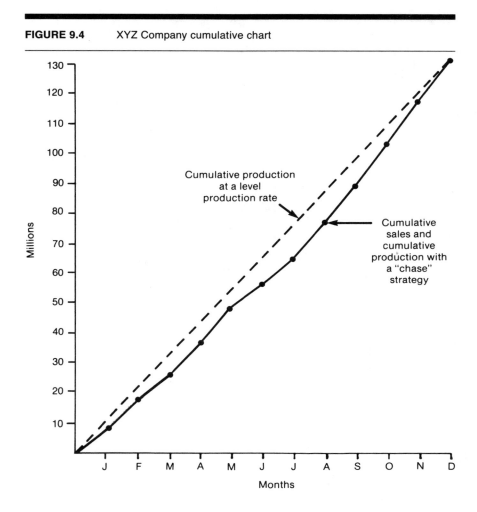

If no inventory is to be held, the cumulative production line would be equal to the cumulative sales line. This policy is a *chase strategy* where production chases sales. The opposite extreme is a *level policy*, where production is at a constant uniform rate of output, with inventory buildups and depletions. Effecting changes in production output requires changes in the work force level, hours worked, and subcontracting.

To convert aggregate output into capacity for planning purposes, a planning factor is used. In our example, the XYZ Company keeps a planning statistic that it uses to convert gross sales dollars into aggregate labor capacity requirements. This statistic, obtained from accounting records, indicates that, on the average, each direct labor-hour produces $30 in sales. This fac-

FIGURE 9.5   XYZ Company labor capacity requirements

Months	Chase strategy (Inventory = 0)				Level production
	Sales in labor-hours (000s)	Working days	Variable work force	Variable workweek	Variable inventory ($000)
January	253	20	1,583	28.4	3,099
February	280	21	1,667	29.6	5,933
March	340	23	1,848	33.1	8,037
April	300	20	1,875	33.7	9,737
May	393	22	2,235	40.2	9,706
June	233	22	1,326	23.9	14,475
July	287	10	3,583	64.4	11,224
August	420	23	2,283	41.0	10,929
September	480	20	3,000	53.8	7,228
October	427	22	2,424	43.5	6,197
November	527	20	3,292	59.1	1,096
December	393	20	2,458	44.2	0‡
Total	4,333	243	2,229*	40.0*	7,305†

*Weighted averages.
†Average inventory.
‡The month-by-month detailed calculations will result in a December ending inventory of approximately −$5,000. This is because a work force of 2,229 workers is slightly less than necessary to create $130 million of sales in 243 working days.

tor is used to convert the sales forecast data in Figure 9.3 into a labor-hour forecast. The first column in Figure 9.5 shows the conversion.

The second column of Figure 9.5 presents the working days in each month for the year. This is an important addition, since the number varies sharply from month to month. The lowest number occurs in July, which only has 10 working days. This is due to the annual two-week shutdown during July for the XYZ Company.

If the total labor-hour requirements for the year's sales (4,333,333 hours) is divided by the number of working days (243), the result (17,832) is the number of labor-hours necessary to work each day if level production is to be employed. Dividing the result by eight working hours per day gives an implied constant labor force of 2,229 workers required to produce the year's forecast.

The third column of Figure 9.5 represents one approach to a pure chase strategy. For this example, the working week is held at 40 hours, and the size of the labor force is varied as needed to only produce the forecast sales. For example, the January forecast sales are $7.6 million. When divided by $30, the resultant labor-hour capacity requirement is 253,333. When this result is divided by 20 working days, we obtain a need for 12,667 labor-hours each day. If each worker puts in an eight-hour day, the implied work force for January is 1,583 workers.

The month-to-month differences between the implied work force levels represent hiring/firing decisions. For example, the decision for February would be to hire an additional 84 workers over the January total (1,667 − 1,583). The impact of the hire/fire decisions is especially severe during the summer months. It would be necessary to fire 909 workers in June, but to hire 2,257 in July.

In most circumstances, it would only be a firm like a summer resort or a farm that harvests an agricultural commodity that could consider such a high level of hiring and firing. In many Western countries, it is very difficult to hire and fire workers. In Western Europe and parts of South America, it is virtually impossible to fire workers—the cost is very high.

The next to last column in Figure 9.5 is another approach to a chase strategy. In this case, the labor force is kept at a constant level of 2,229 workers; but the length of the working week is varied as necessary to provide the labor-hours dictated by the first column. Again, the same kinds of variations are seen, but in the hours worked this time. Clearly the plant shutdown in July causes severe overtime problems, if this strategy is followed. This could be mitigated against by continuing to work at a more normal level of output in June.

The last column in Figure 9.5 shows a "pure" level strategy. This is essentially the dashed line in Figure 9.4, with allowances for the exact numbers of working days in each month. In this example, 2,229 workers would need to be employed for eight hours on each of the 243 working days in the year to meet the forecast sales levels.

In January, the 2,229 workers, working for 20 days of eight hours each, will create $10,699,200 of goods, using the planning factor of $30 of output per labor-hour. Since the sales forecast for January is $7.6 million, the expected inventory at the end of January is $3,099,200. The value shown in Figure 9.5 for February, $5,933,000, includes the January ending inventory plus the net addition to inventory created during February. (Figure 9.5 shows all values rounded to the nearest $1000.) Planned inventory will increase during each month that the implied workweek (next to last column) is less than 40 hours, and decrease if the implied workweek is greater than 40 hours.

The basic trade-offs in production planning are clearly seen in this example. They involve inventory accumulations, hiring and firing, undertime and overtime, and alternative capacity forms, such as outside contracting. The evaluation of these trade-offs is very much firm specific.

Evaluating alternatives

The cumulative chart in Figure 9.4 and the tabular presentation in Figure 9.5 show the implications of the pure chase and level production strategies. So far, in the example, nothing has been said about evaluating the trade-offs involved. The management issue is how to choose between them or how to construct an alternative that is superior to either of the pure strategies. To do this rigorously, it is necessary to establish cost data that relate to the alternative production-planning methods. But in many firms, relevant cost data are not readily available. In such cases, the analysis could be conducted, using executive opinion.

Suppose, for example, that no explicit cost data exist for production planning at the XYZ company. In that case, the executives at XYZ could evaluate such data as those in Figure 9.5 to point out situations they do not like. The implications of revised plans could be quickly calculated, using a programmable calculator or a microcomputer, for subsequent evaluation by the executives. For example, the work force could be allowed to build up as indicated from January through May for the chase strategy and be held at 2,235 for June, instead of dropping to 1,326. The resulting inventory would be included in the analysis performed for July and beyond. If this process of revising and evaluating were continued until the managerial group was satisfied, it could be possible to imply, from the choices made, the relative importance or costs assigned to various conditions.

For illustrating the analysis when cost data are available, we will assume that the cost data in Figure 9.6 were provided for the XYZ company. The cost to hire an employee is estimated to be $200, whereas the cost to fire is $500. The average labor cost at XYZ is $5 per hour, and any overtime work has a 50 percent premium; that is, for overtime work, the average person earns $7.50 for each hour. The cost of "undertime" is more difficult to assess, but clearly there is a heavy morale cost associated with working less than a normal workweek (40 hours). In some firms, the cost may be as much as the regular wage rate, meaning that people are kept on the payroll with no work to do. At the XYZ Company, the people are sent home; but the company estimates the cost is still about $3 per hour, even though no direct payment is made to the work force. The final cost element is the inventory carrying cost. This is estimated to be 2 percent per month, based upon the monthly ending inventory value.

FIGURE 9.6   XYZ Company production-planning data

Hiring cost	$200 per employee
Firing cost	$500 per employee
Regular labor cost	$5 per hour
Overtime premium cost	$2.50 per hour
Undertime premium cost	$3.00 per hour
Inventory carring cost	2 percent per month (applied to the monthly ending inventory)
Beginning inventory	0 units
Beginning labor force	1,583 persons

One question that needs to be addressed before performing the production-planning analysis is the starting conditions; that is, are there any inventories and what is the beginning work force level? From Figure 9.6 we see there is zero beginning inventory and a work force of 1,583 (the desired level for January) at the beginning of the year.

In Figure 9.7, the Hire/Fire column for the first alternative specifically states the necessary additions and deletions to the work force to comply with the levels indicated in Figure 9.5. The Cost column is simply the hire and fire cost for these actions. No regular labor costs are shown in Figure 9.5, since they will be the same for each of the alternative plans considered; that is, the same number of working hours will be used for every plan, although some will be paid an overtime premium. This results in an incremental cost of a pure hire-fire policy, with the given cost values of $2,708,300.

The second alternative in Figure 9.7 is to also maintain a zero inventory level, but to do this with a constant work force of 2,229 persons. The length of the workweek will be adjusted according to the dictates of the next to last column of Figure 9.5, the column that shows the length of the workweek required to produce the sales with 2,229 people. As noted, we again begin with a work force of 1,583, so the first and only hire-fire action is to add 646 workers.

The cost for January ($439,477) is based on the cost of hiring 646 workers (646 × 200 = $129,200) plus the cost of having each worker idle for 11.6 hours (40 − 28.4) per week at $3 per hour. This means that each worker will average undertime work in the amount of 2.32 hours per day (11.6/5). At $3 per hour, 20 working days per month, and 2,229 workers, the undertime premium cost for January is $310,277. When added to the hiring cost of $129,200, the total cost for January is calculated as $439,477.

An illustration of overtime cost can be seen for July. The required workweek is 64.4 hours, or 4.88 hours of overtime per worker each day, on the average. Since there are 10 working days in the month, each overtime hour has a premium cost of $2.50, and there are 2,229 workers, the total overtime premium for the month is $271,938. The total expected cost for the year, with an overtime/undertime strategy, is $2,801,280.

The third alternative shown in Figure 9.7 is the level strategy. In this case, enough people are added to the work force in January to raise it from 1,583 to 2,229 workers. Each worker puts in a constant 40-hour week, and inventories are varied, as indicated in the last column of Figure 9.5. When each of these planned inventory values is multiplied by 2 percent, the costs indicated in Figure 9.7 are obtained (e.g., February = $5,933,000 × .02 = $118,660).

The last alternative evaluated in Figure 9.7 is a mixed strategy. The plan calls for adding employees as necessary from January through May, but thereafter keeps the resultant work force constant (2,235) until September.

FIGURE 9.7 Costs of alternative production plans

Month	Zero inventory hire-fire as required: Hire-fire	Zero inventory hire-fire as required: Cost	Zero inventory/ overtime-undertime/ constant work force = 2,229: Hire-fire	Zero inventory/ overtime-undertime/ constant work force = 2,229: Cost	Level production/ constant work force = 2,229: Hire-fire	Level production/ constant work force = 2,229: Cost	Mixed strategy*: Hire-fire	Mixed strategy*: Work force	Mixed strategy*: Workweek	Mixed strategy*: Inventory ($000)	Mixed strategy*: Cost
January	—	—	+646	$ 439,477	+646	$ 191,180	—	1,583	40.0	$ 0	—
February	+84	$ 16,800	—	292,088	—	118,660	+84	1,667	40.0	0	$ 16,800
March	+181	36,200	—	212,245	—	160,740	+181	1,848	40.0	0	36,200
April	+27	5,400	—	168,512	—	194,740	+27	1,875	40.0	0	5,400
May	+360	72,000	—	4,904	—	194,120	+360	2,235	40.0	0	72,000
June	−909	454,500	—	473,707	—	289,500	—	2,235	40.0	1,081	96,020
July	+2257	451,400	—	271,938	—	224,480	—	2,235	40.0	1,565	31,300
August	−1300	650,000	—	25,633	—	218,580	—	2,235	40.0	1,302	26,040
September	+717	143,400	—	307,602	—	144,560	+494	2,729	40.0	1	98,820
October	−576	288,000	—	85,817	—	123,940	—	2,729	40.0	1,610	33,200
November	+868	173,600	—	425,739	—	21,920	—	2,729	43.3	0	90,875
December	−834	417,000	—	93,618	—	0	−271	2,458	40.0	0	135,000
Total		$2,708,300		$2,801,280		$1,882,420					$641,155

*Hire until May. Constant work force until September (build inventory). Build inventory in October. Overtime in November. Fire in December.

This means that some inventories are held during June, July, and August. In September, the work force is again expanded, this time by 494 workers, to provide the necessary output levels. This is determined by subtracting the August ending inventory of $1,302,000 from the September forecast of $14.4 million to get a net requirement of $13,098,000. At eight hours per day for 20 days and $30 per hour, it takes 2,729 workers to produce this amount.

The plan calls for this work force level to be maintained during October, which results in an addition to inventory of $1,610,000, which is needed in November. To meet the sales forecast of $15 million in November, however, it is necessary to work overtime for 3.3 hours each week. The lower level of forecast in December results in a layoff of 271 workers.

This plan may not be the best plan possible. For example, it is less costly to carry the extra inventory produced by 271 workers in December ($26,016), than to lay off all 271 workers ($135,500). The analysis thus far has not considered the desirable ending conditions in terms of work force levels. The valuation of any particular ending work force level must be made in light of the following year's sales forecast. The determination of mixed strategies that improve costs over those obtained by employing pure strategies can be guided by mathematical models.

Top-management role

The first obligation of top management is to commit to the game-planning process. This means a major change in many firms. The change involves the routine aspects of establishing the framework for game planning: getting the forecasts, setting the meetings, preparing the plans, and so on. The change may also imply modifications of performance measurement and reward structures to align them with the plan. It should be expected at the outset there will be many existing goals and performance measures that are in conflict with the integration provided by a working game-planning system. These should be rooted out and explicitly changed. Enforcing the changes implies a need to abide by and provide an example of the discipline required to manage with the planning system. This implies that even top management must act within the planned flexibility range for individual actions and must evaluate possible changes that lie outside the limits.

As a part of the commitment to the planning process, top management *must force* the resolution of trade-offs between functions prior to approving plans. The production plan provides a transparent basis for resolving these conflicts. It should provide the basic implications of the choices, even if it does not make the decisions any easier. If the trade-offs are not made at this level, they will be forced into the mix of day-to-day activities of operating people who will have to resolve them—perhaps unfavorably. If, for example, manufacturing continues long runs of products in the face of declining demand, the mismatch between production and the market will be in increased inventories.

The game-planning activities must encompass *all* formal plans in an integrated fashion. If budgeting is a separate activity, it will not relate to the game plan and the operating managers will need to make a choice. Similarly, if the profit forecast is based solely on the sales forecast (revenue) and accounting data (standard costs) and does not take into account the implications for production, its value is doubtful. The intention of the game-planning process is to produce plans, budgets, objectives, and goals that are complete and integrated; and all are used by managers to make decisions and provide the basis for evaluating performance. If other planning activities or evaluation documents are in place, the end result will be poor execution. An unfortunate but frequent approach is to invest management time in the production planning activity, but thereafter allow the company to be run by a separate performance measurement system or budget.

Some firms will find the term *game planning* more acceptable than production planning. The latter connotes a functional focus that is not accurate. The production-planning process is interfunctional and needs to be coordinated at the top-management level.

Functional roles

The primary obligation under game planning is to "hit the plan." This is true for all functions involved: manufacturing, sales, engineering, finance, and so on. A secondary obligation is this need to communicate when something will prevent hitting the plan. If there is a problem, the sooner it can be evaluated in terms of other functional plans, the better. The obligation for communication provides the basis for keeping the plans of *all* groups consistent when changes are necessary.

The process of budgeting usually needs to change and to be integrated with game planning and subsequent departmental plans. In many firms, budgeting is done on an annual basis, using data that are not a part of the material planning and control system. The manufacturing budgets are often based upon historical cost relationships and a separation of fixed and variable expenses. These data are not as precise as those that can be obtained by utilizing the material control system data base. By using the data base, tentative master production schedules can be evaluated in terms of component part needs, capacities, and expected costs. The resultant budgets can be analyzed for the effect of product-mix changes as well as for performance against standards.

Another important aspect of relating budgeting to the game-planning activity and underlying MPC systems and data base is that the cycle can be done more frequently. The data will not have to be collected—they always exist in up-to-date form. Moreover, inconsistencies are substantially reduced. The budget should always be in agreement with the production plan, which, in turn, is in concert with the disaggregated end items and components that support the plan. The result should be far fewer occasions when an operating manager has to choose between his budget and satisfying the production plan.

With budgeting and production planning done on the same basis with the same underlying dynamic data base, it is natural to incorporate cost accounting. The result is an ability to perform detailed variance accounting, as well as an important cross check on transaction accuracy.

The most obvious need for integrated planning and control is between marketing and production. Yet it is often the most difficult to accomplish. Firms must ensure product availability for special promotions, match customer orders with specific production lots, coordinate distribution activities with production, and deal with a host of other cross-functional problems.

The job of marketing under integrated game planning is to sell what is in the sales plan. It is necessary to instill the feeling that overselling is just as bad as underselling. In either case, there will be a mismatch with manufacturing output, financial requirements, and inventory/backlog levels. If the opportunity arises to sell more than the plan, it needs to be formally evaluated by means of a change in the game plan. By going through this process, the timing for when this increase can be properly supported by both manufacturing and finance will be ascertained. And once the formal plan has been changed, it is again the job of each function to achieve its specified objectives—no more and no less.

Similarly, it is manufacturing's job to achieve the plan—exactly. Overproduction may well mean that more capacity and resources are being utilized than are required. Underproduction possibly means the reverse (not enough resources) or it means poor performance. In either case, performance against the plan is poor. This can either be the fault of the standard setting process or inadequate performance. Both problems require corrective action.

When manufacturing is hitting the schedule, it is a straightforward job for marketing to be able to provide good customer order promises and other forms of customer service. It is also a straightforward job for finance to plan cash flows and to anticipate financial performance.

If the production-planning results cannot be achieved, it must be the clear responsibility of whoever cannot meet their plan to report this condition promptly. If, for example, a major supplier cannot meet his or her commitments, the impact on the detailed marketing and production plans must be quickly ascertained.

Integrating strategic planning

Strategic planning is an important direction-setting activity that is done in different ways. Some companies approach this problem primarily as an extension of budgeting. Typically, these firms use a bottom-up process, which is largely an extrapolation of the departmental budgets based upon growth assumptions and cost-volume analysis. One key aspect of the strategic plan in these firms is to integrate these bottom-up extrapolations into a coherent whole. Another is to critically evaluate the overall outcome from a corporate point of view.

A more recent approach to strategic planning is to have the plan based more on products and less on organizational units. The company's products are typically grouped into strategic business units (SBUs), with each SBU evaluated in terms of its strengths and weaknesses vis-à-vis similar business units made and marketed by competitors. The budgetary process in this case is done on an SBU basis, rather than on an organizational unit basis. The business units are evaluated in terms of their competitive strength, their relative advantage (sometimes based on learning curve models), life cycles, and cash flow patterns (e.g., when does an SBU need cash and when is it a cash provider?). From a strategic point of view, the objective is to carefully manage a portfolio of SBUs to the overall advantage of the firm.

The role of game planning and the departmental plans to support these strategic planning efforts can be profound. In the case of the production plan, the overall data base and systems must ensure that game plans will be in concert with disaggregated decision making. In other words, the MPS and related systems ensure that the strategic planning decisions are executed!

All the advantages of integrating production planning with budgeting also apply when the SBU focus is taken. It makes sense to state the production plan in the same SBU units; that is, rather than using dollar outputs per time unit, the production plan should be stated in SBU terminology.

Controlling the production plan

A special responsibility involves control of performance against the plan. As a prerequisite to control, the game-planning process should be widely understood in the firm. The seriousness with which it is regarded should also be communicated, as well as the exact planned results that pertain to each of the organization's functional units. In other words, it is necessary that the planning process be transparent, with clear communication of expectations, to control actual results. For the production plan, this means wide dissemination of the plan and its implications for managers.

Another dimension of control is periodic reporting. Performance against the production plan should also be widely disseminated. When actual results differ from plans, analyses of the source of these deviations should be made and communicated.

An example of this communication is seen at the Tennant Company. Some of their more important measures of performance and reporting frequency are:

Measure	Reporting
Conformity of the master production schedule to the production plan	Weekly
Capacity utilization	Weekly
Delivery performance	Daily
Actual production to master production schedule performance	Weekly
Inventory/backlog performance	Weekly

At a recent point in their history, Tennant had not missed a quarterly production plan for the previous 2.5 years. Moreover, the monthly production plan had been met in 10 out of 12 months for each of the previous years. All of these results are well known inside the company, and they are widely disseminated outside, too. The importance of the production plan is well understood at all levels of the firm.

Key issues in production planning are when to make changes to the plan, how often to replan, and how stable to keep the plan from period to period. There is no doubt that a stable production plan results in far fewer execution problems by the detailed master production scheduling, MRP, and other execution systems. Stability also fosters the achievement of some steady state operations, where capacity can be more effectively utilized.

At Tennant, changes to the production plan are batched until the next review, unless they are required to prevent major problems. In other companies, stability in the plan is maintained by providing time fences for changes and permissible ranges of deviation from plan. Flexibility within the plan can be provided by planning adequate inventories or other forms of capacity to absorb deviations within an agreed upon range.

Several companies, such as Toyota, now use just-in-time (JIT) concepts, including a material planning and control system called kanban. There are many aspects of the system that are based on manual controls. One key to making JIT work is a very stable production plan. The output rate is held constant for long time periods, and only modified after extensive analysis. This means that the rate of production at each step of the manufacturing process can be held to very constant levels, providing the benefits of stability and predictability.

The other side of this coin is seen by reviewing the approach of one U.S. automobile manufacturer. In the face of diminishing sales, the company continued to produce in excess of sales. The result was a buildup of finished-goods inventory that exceeded 100 days of sales. The results on the financial statements were very significant. The adjustments in manufacturing were even more severe. Finished-goods inventories and order backlogs can buffer manufacturing from day-to-day shocks, but long-run changes have to be reflected in the basic production plan itself.

OPERATING PRODUCTION-PLANNING SYSTEMS

In this section, we show examples of production-planning practice. In particular, we present some of the organizational aspects of production planning at the Compugraphic Corporation, the entire process for the Mohawk Electric Company, and the way the Hill-Rom Company uses SBU-related bills of material for tying the production plan to their strategic business units.

Production planning at Compugraphic

Compugraphic Corporation is located in the northern suburbs of Boston. The company makes typesetters and related equipment for the printing industry in five separate factory locations. Figure 9.8 shows how production planning fits in the corporation, and Figure 9.9 shows the relationship with master production scheduling in more detail.

The production-planning committee is made up of the top-management group in the company representing all functional areas. The charter of this committee is to develop and monitor the production plan that determines the manufacturing resources to support the business plan and corporate objectives.

The mission of the committee is further delineated as:

- To assure that sales forecasts and production plans are consistent with the annual business plan.
- To establish performance measurements for evaluating the production planning process.
- To communicate sales forecasts for product families on a monthly basis.
- To assure that manufacturing capabilities are consistent with the production plan.
- To monitor actual results against plans and make adjustments as required.
- To manage the finished goods inventory with the targets established in the production and business plans.
- To provide direction to the development and execution of the master production schedule.

At a monthly meeting, each of the 11 product family groups are reviewed. For each family, the forecast and order performance for the current month is reviewed, as well as the outlook for the next 12 months. Next, the manufacturing performance is reviewed. Was the production plan for the last month met? Are there any expected sales or manufacturing deviations in the future? If so, are they to be compensated for in other months? The other major review point is the finished goods inventories in relation to plans,

FIGURE 9.8 Compugraphic production planning

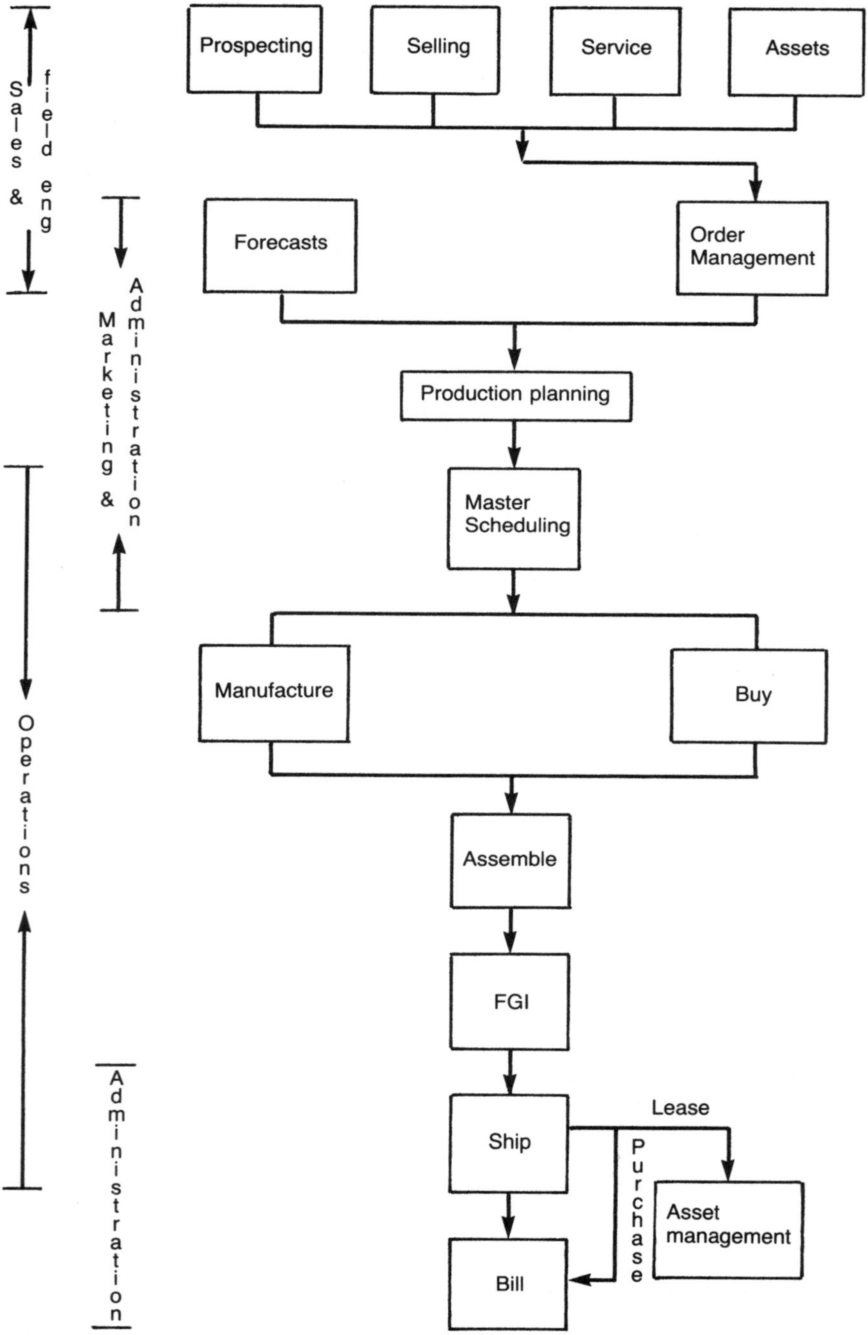

FIGURE 9.9   Compugraphic's production planning and the MPS

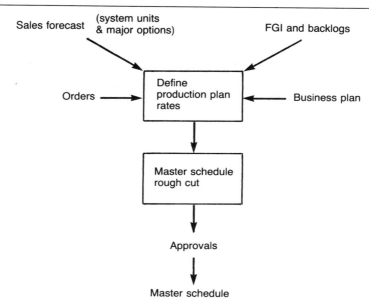

including consideration of established safety stock levels. The projected inventory levels are based on netting the sales and manufacturing data, but they are reviewed independently to see if some revisions in either sales or manufacturing is needed.

Also reviewed at the meeting are several other items that could have an impact on a particular family group's performance. Included are customer backlogs, customer service levels achieved, new marketing plans, such as price changes or sales incentives, and product requirements for demonstration or other nonsales purposes.

Figure 9.10 is an example of the records for one product family. The data were collected during the month of May. The production-planning process is essentially made up of three parts, each corresponding to one of the records. The top third of Figure 9.10 is devoted to the marketing outlook for this product family. At the end of April, the actual shipments and backlog to be shipped were exactly equal to the base line plan (43 units). The original forecast for May was 128 units, but as of the date the data were collected, it appeared that the actual shipments would exceed this plan by 7 units. June was expected to fall short by 54 units (47 cumulative), but marketing expected to catch up during July.

The bottom third of Figure 9.10 gives the production performance. In

FIGURE 9.10   Compugraphic's product planning: Sample family

Product family _Sunline 25_   Month _May_

Shipment performance

		Apr	May	June	July	Aug	Sept	Oct	Nov	Dec	Jan	Feb	Mar
Baseline (plan)		43	128	228	222	311	356	288	288	383	232	232	308
Actual & backlog		43	—	—	—			—			—		—
Shipment outlook		—	135	174	269	311	356	288	288	383	232	232	308
Variance		0	7	<54>	47	0	0	0	0	0	0	0	0
Cum variance		0	7	<47>	0	0	0	0	0	0	0	0	0

Inventory performance

		Apr	May	June	July	Aug	Sept	Oct	Nov	Dec	Jan	Feb	Mar
Baseline (plan)		89	193	22	8	27	1	33	65	2	10	18	10
Actual*	15	103	—										
Outlook		—	86	79	8	27	1	33	65	2	10	18	10
Variance		<147>	7	<47>	0	0	0	0	0	0	0	0	0

Production performance

		Apr	May	June	July	Aug	Sept	Oct	Nov	Dec	Jan	Feb	Mar
Baseline (plan)		117	132	167	199	330	330	320	320	320	240	240	300
Actual	131		—	—	—						—		
Outlook		—	118	167	198	330	330	340	320	320	240	240	300
Variance		14	<147>	0	0	0	0	0	0	0	0	0	0

April Invty

Perpetual   103*
Invty plng 102
Chlc   103

April, manufacturing overbuilt the schedule by 14 units. However, the plan shows them under building in May to get back on the base line schedule for the year.

The middle third of Figure 9.10 nets shipment plans against manufacturing plans to project inventories. This allows top management to examine the overall impact of both forecast errors and manufacturing performance deviations.

The production-planning process at Compugraphic has had an important impact on the company, particularly on the MPC systems. When the firm implemented a new on-line MRP-based system, it became clear that the production plan was critical to provide the necessary direction to master production scheduling and resultant MPC modules. Prior to development of production planning, there was a tendency to not react rapidly to market shifts (particularly downturns). The result was larger than necessary inventories, which, in turn, required more radical adjustments in production. The intent of the production-planning process was to make more frequent smaller adjustments on a regular basis, based on ongoing top-management assessment of where the business was going.

Mohawk's integrated planning process

The Mohawk Electric Company (a disguised name for an actual Midwest firm) manufactures electrical switches, controls, and measurement instruments for industrial applications. Three main product lines—energy management devices, tachographs, and data systems—represent annual sales of $25 to $30 million, with a price range of $15 to $50,000 per unit. About 40,000 units are sold each year, involving some 5,000 unique final-product catalogue numbers. Approximately 70 percent of the sales volume is shipped directly from the finished-goods inventory of the firm.

The production plan and master production schedule are established quarterly as a part of the regular budgetary planning activities of the firm. For most of Mohawk's business, the master production schedule is stated in terms of the number of units to be produced for each end product (catalogue number) during the next four quarters.

The overall production lead time (covering the purchasing, fabrication, and assembly operations) generally exceeds the delivery time quoted to the firm's customers. Thus, the production plan and master production schedule are primarily based on sales forecasts and financial plans—instead of on actual customer orders. The budgetary planning process is outlined in Figure 9.11. Once every quarter, the company's sales, finance, and manufacturing executives prepare an overall business game plan covering the next four quarters that includes: (a) a sales forecast for each of the firm's three product lines (energy management devices, tachographs, and data systems); and (b)

FIGURE 9.11   Mohawk Company's quarterly budgeting cycle activities

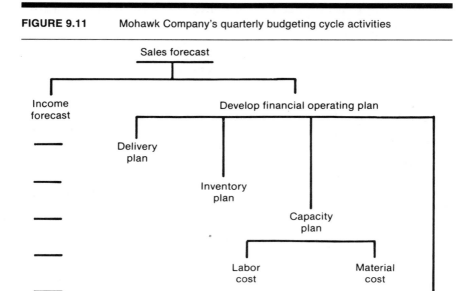

a detailed financial operating plan that specifies a forecast of plant shipments (Mohawk calls this the "delivery plan"; in fact, it is the production plan), inventory level targets (the inventory plan), and a capacity plan (covering both a manpower and a materials budget). Once these plans have been prepared to produce an overall profit forecast for the firm, work can begin on preparing (revising) the master production schedule that also covers the next four quarters.

The budgeting cycle, performed at the midpoint of each quarter, begins with the preparation of a sales forecast for each of the firm's three product lines. Sales forecasting is the responsibility of a general manager, who has the profit responsibility for a particular product line. In preparing the sales forecast, the general manager, the financial staff, and the marketing organization work closely with a separate field sales organization. The initial sales forecast is for one year in the future. This forecast is stated both in terms of dollar sales and unit sales, and it corresponds to the product groupings used by the financial staff to value inventory and measure gross profit levels.

As an example, the energy management product line represents annual sales of $15 to $18 million, in total. This product line includes some 75 individual product categories, each representing annual sales of $25,000 to $2.5 million. While a separate forecast is prepared for all of the 75 different product categories, some of these sales forecasts are combined to reduce the number of product categories considered in the budgeting cycle. In fact, only 21 product groupings are considered in the energy management product line budgeting cycle. They are shown in Figure 9.12, for which the sales forecast was prepared at the midpoint of the second quarter in year 1. In this figure, the sales forecast is expressed in dollars for each product grouping on a monthly basis for the next quarter, and a quarterly basis for the following three quarters. In producing the data in Figure 9.12, the sales for the second quarter of year 1 are treated as actual, even though the quarter is not yet finished. As a result, the monthly forecasts are for the third quarter of year 1, and the quarterly forecasts have been prepared through the second quarter of year 2.

Once the sales forecast has been made, financial and manufacturing representatives become involved in the cycle to prepare a game plan for the product line. One of the first steps is to translate the sales forecast into a delivery plan (production plan) for manufacturing and an income forecast for finance. The company uses a tabular presentation form for preparing these plans.

The delivery plan is a statement of the total planned factory deliveries to customers, to finished-goods inventory, and to other company locations. Representatives from manufacturing, finance, and sales develop the delivery plan. The sales forecast, desired changes to inventory, potential capacity constraints, vendor deliveries, cash requirements, personnel available, and so on, are considered, and adjustments to the sales forecasts (plan), and/or inventory plan are negotiated, if necessary. If, for example, manufacturing cannot produce the volume necessary to satisfy both the sales plan and an increase in inventory, the cycle stops and a new sales and/or inventory plan is agreed upon. This production plan, therefore, is a very important and integral part of the entire process; subsequent planning does *not* proceed until there is complete agreement between the sales, finance, and manufacturing representatives.

The next step in the cycle is the conversion of the delivery plan into a capacity plan for each product line and for the plant in total. Figure 9.13 illustrates the development of the capacity plan for the energy management product line considering the labor content of the sales forecast, the forecast labor content of the two inventories (finished goods and work in process), and the labor content of the forecast interplant transfers both to and from this plant. The bottom line in the energy management section of Figure 9.13 (TOTAL LABOR INPUT) indicates the plant capacity requirements for this product line for the periods indicated where capacity is stated in terms of direct labor dollars. For example, $199,000 of direct labor input is planned for January, year 1. This represents about two thirds of the total direct labor input (capacity) for the Mohawk plant in January ($290,000)—which is shown on the next line of Figure 9.13. Since there are 21 working days in January, this means an average of $13,800 of direct labor input per day. This translates

FIGURE 9.12 Mohawk Company's summary sales forecast, energy management products ($000)*

Product Grouping	History			Year 1						Year 2	
	Year 2	Year 1	Year 0	1st Qtr.	2d Qtr.	July	Aug.	Sept.	4th Qtr.	1 Qtr.	2d Qtr.
Singlephase	886	700	265	51	23	13	14	14	41	41	39
Polyphase	4059	1699	349	46	32	20	20	20	60	60	50
Con-Ed	402	108	—								
Lincoln Billing	1609	1354	1412	451	351	102	161	146	409	527	435
Meter Timeswitch	331	224	188	63	76	20	30	27	77	78	69
Sockets	41	57	84	13	14	2	2	2	6	6	10
	7328	4142	2298	624	496	157	227	209	593	712	603
Lincoln Nonbilling	2301	2721	1837	725	560	149	176	204	529	528	586
Line Controls	615	698	358	97	120	15	21	22	58	83	90
Timeswitch	882	1107	708	186	185	43	55	76	174	262	202
	3798	4526	2903	1008	865	207	252	302	761	873	878
Transformers 600V	2767	3139	2248	666	559	193	254	281	728	756	677
Transformers 15KV	383	528	410	232	110	45	50	60	155	201	175
D.C. Meters	143	200	102	70	59	7	18	18	43	53	56
	3293	3867	2760	968	728	245	322	359	926	1010	908
Survey Recorders	695	826	901	321	355	99	162	132	373	398	367
S.R. Systems				8	95	—	178	45	223	237	141
Digital Pulse Rec.	460	436	225	119	174	43	48	50	141	126	140
C.M.E.	663	448	407	153	168	6	31	57	94	145	145
	1818	1710	1533	601	792	148	419	284	851	906	788
Parts—Winchester & Memphis	1348	1466	1027	405	413	75	135	135	345	395	390
Misc.	407	307	276	224	82	24	32	33	89	120	129
Repairs (Replacement Parts)	37	46	53	16	10	3	3	4	10	10	12
Resale:											
Demand Control	—	2	151								
Sigma-form	482	443	—	64	56	42	52	53	147	172	110
Total	18511	16509	11001	3910	3442	901	1442	1379	3722	4198	3818

*Prepared at the midpoint of the second quarter of year 1.
Source: W. L. Berry, R. A. Mohrman, and T. R. Callarman, "Master Scheduling and Capacity Planning: A Case Study" (Bloomington: Indiana University Graduate School of Business, Discussion Paper No. 73, 1977).

FIGURE 9.13 Mohawk Company's aggregate production and inventory plan ($000)*

Labor forecast	Year 0		Year 1						Year 2	Year 3
	8/31 Actual	12/31 4th Qtr.	1/31 Jan.	2/29 Feb.	3/31 Mar.	6/30 2d Qtr.	9/31 3d Qtr.	12/31 4th Qtr.	12/31 1977	12/31 1978
Energy management:										
Finished Goods inventory	$ 244	$ 240	$ 250	$ 270	$ 275	$ 310	$ 300	$ 300	$ 300	$ 300
Work-in-Process inventory	862	825	825	805	800	800	800	800	800	800
Subtotal	$1,106	$1,065	$1,075	$1,075	$1,075	$1,110	$1,100	$1,100	$1,100	$1,100
Net change		(41)	10	—	—	35	(10)	—	—	—
Labor in sales forecast		599	176	168	210	540	531	542	2,196	2,146
Transfer from Memphis		(54)	(12)	(12)	(12)	(36)	(36)	(36)	(144)	(144)
Transfer to Memphis		72	25	25	15	13	13	13	52	52
Total labor input		$ 576	$ 199	$ 181	$ 213	$ 552	$ 498	$ 519	$2,104	$2,054
Plant total:										
Labor input	$ 210	$ 829	$ 290	$ 273	$ 342	$ 847	$ 745	$ 830	$3,243	$3,706
Days per period	20	61	21	20	25	62	52	57	236	236
Average labor per day	$ 10.5	$ 13.6	$ 13.8	$ 13.6	$ 13.7	$ 13.7	$ 14.3	$ 14.6	$ 13.7	$ 15.7

*Measured in direct labor-dollars.

Source: W. L. Berry, R. A. Mohrman, and T. R. Callarman, "Master Scheduling and Capacity Planning: A Case Study" (Bloomington: Indiana University Graduate School of Business, Discussion Paper No. 73, 1977).

into a total manpower level for the plant, using planning factors for the number of dollars of direct labor per man/day.

Three factors are considered in arriving at the capacity plan. First, the direct labor content of the sales forecast is determined, using standard cost system data. The direct labor content of the sales forecast for the energy management product line is shown in Figure 9.13 (labeled Labor in Sales Forecast). Note that $176,000 of direct labor is required to support the sales forecast for January of year 1. Next, the labor dollars in the sales forecasts are modified to account for any buildup or depletion of inventories that is planned for the coming year. Figure 9.13 indicates the desired levels over the next year, including both finished-goods and work-in-process inventories. The levels (also measured in terms of direct labor dollars) indicate the cash requirements that are needed to finance the inventory during the next year, as well. Note that a reduction in inventory of $41,000 is planned for the fourth quarter of year 0, while an increase of $10,000 is planned for January, year 1. These changes need to be considered in planning the direct labor input for the energy management product line. Thus, the increase of $10,000 in January means that $186,000 of direct labor is needed in this month, instead of $176,000. The third factor needed in determining the plant capacity is interplant sales of equipment. Figure 9.13 shows that $12,000 of labor will be expended in January by the Memphis plant for products sold by this plant. An additional $25,000 in labor will be expended here for products sold by Memphis. Thus, there is a net addition of $13,000 in direct labor required above and beyond the sales by this plant. When added to the $10,000 inventory increase and the $176,000 of labor in the sales forecast, the total labor input for January, year 1, is $199,000.

After all the negotiations are complete, the budgeting cycle has produced an overall game plan for the business that includes an approved sales plan, a delivery plan, an inventory plan, and a capacity plan. Several additional steps are performed in the budgeting cycle, which involve preparing a direct material budget indicating the purchasing dollars required to support the delivery plan, and a cost plan, which specifies a budget of indirect manufacturing and administering expenses. Other operating plans, in addition to the basic production plan, involving engineering and marketing plans, are also included in the budgeting cycle. These plans are then combined by the finance staff to produce a profit forecast for each product line (profit center).

Hill-Rom's use of planning bills of material

The use of planning bill of material concepts can be very useful in the production planning process. For an example, we look at the application developed at Hill-Rom, a manufacturer of hospital beds, related equipment, and accessories for hospitals and nursing homes.

Hill-Rom has expanded the planning bill concept to what it calls the "super-duper" bill. An abbreviated example is shown in Figure 9.14. Using

FIGURE 9.14   Hill-Rom's "super-duper" bill

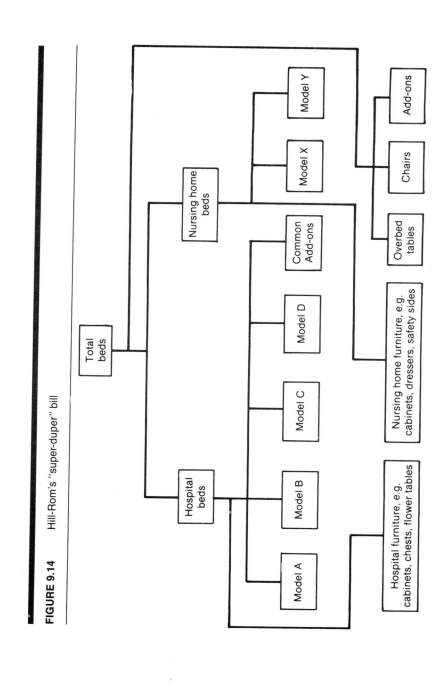

this approach, only one item is forecast, total bed sales. All other forecasts are treated as bill of material relationships. For example, the forecast for the super bill group, over-bed tables, is a percentage of overall bed sales.

One of the marketing-people at Hill-Rom found the super-duper bill concept ideal for implementing an idea he had been thinking about for some time. He believed that the company makes trigger products and trailer products. Beds are trigger products, whereas over-bed tables, chairs, and add-ons, such as trapezes or intravenous fluid rods, are trailer products. The purchase of trailer products is dependent upon the purchase of trigger products in somewhat the same relationship as components to end items. This relationship means that, rather than forecasting the demand for over-bed tables, Hill-Rom tracks and maintains the percentage relationship between the sales of beds and over-bed tables.

This bill of material relationship will probably be a better estimate than a direct forecast of over-bed tables. If one expects bed sales to go up or down, by treating over-bed tables as a trailer product with a bill of material linkage, there is an automatic adjustment made in over-bed table forecasts, as in all the trailer products.

The use of bill of material approaches to forecasting also forces a logical consistency. There was a time when the forecast for 84-inch mattresses at Hill-Rom exceeded the combined forecasts for beds that use 84-inch mattresses. By treating these relationships with bill of material approaches, these inconsistencies, which will always result from independent estimating, are reduced.

The production planning unit for these products at Hill-Rom is total beds. Furthermore, the percentage split into hospital beds and nursing home beds is not only estimated, it is managed. Sales personnel are held to specified tolerance limits on this split because the capacity and net profit implications of the percentage split are important.

Below each of these two super-duper bills are "super" bills for the various model series. Finally, there is another trigger-trailer relationship between the total hospital bed sales and hospital furniture, such as cabinets, flower tables, and the like. The same kind of bill of material relationship is used to forecast nursing home furniture sales. These various bill of material relationships pass the planning information down through the MPC system in a logically consistent way.

Finally, this entire approach is consistent with the way the firm does its strategic planning, which is in terms of strategic business units (SBUs). The SBUs are established as super bills. The result is a very close integration of MPC and strategic planning.

Finally, this entire approach is consistent with the way the firm does its strategic planning, which is in terms of strategic business units (SBUs). The SBUs are to be established as super bills. The result will be a very close integration of MPC and strategic planning.

CONCLUDING PRINCIPLES

Production and game planning are key inputs to MPC systems. They represent management's handle on the business. This chapter emphasizes the key relationships of top management and functional management in the development and maintenance of an effective production plan. We summarize our discussion with the following important principles:

- The production plan is not a forecast; it must be a managerial statement of desired production output.
- The production plan should be a part of the game-planning process, so it will be in complete agreement with the other functional plans (sales plan, budget, and so on) that make up the game plan.
- The trade-offs required to frame the production plan must be made *prior* to final approval of the plan.
- There must be top-management involvement in the game-planning process, which should be directly related to strategic planning.
- The MPC system should be used to perform the routine activities and provide the routine data, so management time can be devoted to the important tasks. The MPC system also should be used to facilitate what-if analyses at the production-planning level.
- Review of performance against plan and forecast performance are both needed to prompt replanning when necessary.
- The production plan should provide the MPS parameters, and flexibility should be specifically defined. The sum of the detailed MPS must always equal the production plan.
- The production plan should tie the strategic activities of the company directly through the MPS to the execution modules of the MPC.

REFERENCES

Berry, W. L.; R. A. Mohrman; and T. Callarman. "Master Scheduling and Capacity Planning: A Case Study. *The Manufacturing Productivity Education Committee,* Purdue University, 1977.

Bitran, Gabriel R.; Elizabeth A. Haas; and Arnoldo C. Hax. "Hierarchical Production Planning: A Single Stage System." *Operations Research* 29, no. 4 (July–August 1981), pp. 717–43.

Dougherty, John R. "Getting Started with Production Planning." *Readings in Production and Inventory Control and Planning,* APICS 27th annual Conference, 1984, pp. 176–79.

Goldratt, Eliyanu. "The Unbalanced Plant." *APICS 24th Annual Conference Proceedings,* 1981, pp. 195–99.

Hall, Robert. "Driving the Productivity Machine: Production Planning and Control in Japan." Falls Church, Va.: APICS, 1981.

Hayes, R. H., and S. C. Wheelright, *Restoring Our Competitive Edge*. New York, John Wiley and Sons, 1984.

Hill, Terry, *Manufacturing Strategy*. London, McMillan Education Ltd., 1985.

Holt, C. C.; F. Modigliani; J. F. Muth; and H. A. Simon. *Planning Production, Inventories, and Workforce*. New York: Prentice-Hall, 1960.

Peterson, Rein, and Edward A. Silver. *Decision Systems for Inventory Management and Production Planning*. 2nd ed. New York: John Wiley & Sons, 1985.

Sari, John F. "Why Don't We Call It Sales and Operations Planning, Not Production Planning?" *APICS 29th Annual Conference Proceedings*, 1986, pp. 22–24.

Skinner, C. W. *Manufacturing in the Corporate Strategy*. New York: John Wiley & Sons, 1978.

Vollmann, T. E. "Capacity Planning: The Missing Link." *Production and Inventory Management*, 1st Quarter, 1973.

DISCUSSION QUESTIONS

1. The production plan is sometimes called "management's handle on manufacturing." Discuss.

2. What would you guess would be the aggregate terms used in managing the university as a whole? The computer center? Buildings and grounds? An individual major?

3. The production plan is stated in aggregate terms; therefore, there will be some error in the resource planning. Wouldn't it be better to use the MPS where the specific product mix is either anticipated or incorporated directly?

4. What are the differences between game planning and budgeting?

5. Some experts argue that the production/game-planning process ought to be done only on exception; that is, only when conditions have changed enough to warrant replanning. Others argue that it should be done on a periodic basis *and* when required by exception. What is your view?

6. Discuss the relative merits of cumulative charts (e.g., Figure 9.4) and tabular plans (e.g., Figure 9.5) for production planning.

7. What are some of the implications of not making the trade-offs explicit in the game-planning process?

8. In incorporating the strategic objectives of the firm into the game planning process, what differences exist between such firms as coal mines or cardboard manufacturers versus fashion or cosmetic manufacturers versus manufacturers of machine tools?

9. What is an analogue to the Hill-Rom "super-duper bill" and their "trigger and trailer" notions in the university setting?

PROBLEMS

1. A production planner for Lavella Chase is developing a production plan that involves the use of backorders. The demand and production rate for the company for the next four periods are shown below:

Period	Demand	Production
1	4,000	3,800
2	7,500	6,000
3	2,200	4,100
4	6,400	6,000

Given that the beginning inventory at the start of period 1 is 200 units, calculate the beginning inventory, ending inventory, average inventory, and the backorder amount, if any, for each of the next four periods.

2. A company that adheres to a policy of level production has a zero beginning inventory and must meet the following demand quantities for its major product:

Period	Demand
1	10
2	2
3	11
4	9
5	8

a. What production rate per period will result in a zero ending inventory for period 5?
b. When, and in what quantities, will backorders occur?
c. What level production rate per period will avoid backorders?
d. Using the production rate computed in question c what will be the ending inventory for period 3?

3. The VP of manufacturing for the N. L. Hyer Company is ready to decide on her aggregate output plan for the next year. The firm's single product (known throughout the adult puzzle trade as "Hyer's Hexagon") is "red hot," according to the VP of marketing, so she has insisted that backorders are not acceptable next year. Since the United Puzzlemakers Union is currently trying to organize the plant, the manufacturing VP has decided that the number of employees must remain constant (i.e., level) throughout all four quarters.

Quarter	Production days	Demand forecast
I	60	10,000
II	58	12,000
III	62	15,000
IV	70	9,000

Beginning inventory = 1,000 units.
Regular time output rate = 10 units/day employee.

    a. What daily production rate and number of employees will be required?

    b. How many units will be in inventory at the end of quarter IV?

4. Below is the plotted cumulative demand for Joan's Joyous Nature Food (in pounds) for the next four months. Beginning inventory is 10 pounds.

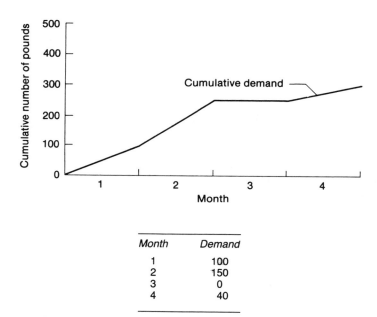

Month	Demand
1	100
2	150
3	0
4	40

    a. How much should Joan produce each month if she wishes to have a level production plan with no backorders or stockouts? Plot your cumulative production on the graph given above.

    b. What is ending inventory for month 4 under this plan?

    c. Joan decides to have a level production, level employment production plan with no ending inventory at the end of the planning horizon. How much should she make each month? What are the monthly backorders?

    d. Given that inventory carrying costs are $2/pound/month (on the average inventory) and backorders are $4/pound/month (based on month-end backorders), calculate the cost of backorders and inventory for the plan in question **c.**

5. The forecast for the first three months of next year for the Oro del Mar Company is as follows: January—100, February—0, March—300 (in 1,000 pounds). The beginning inventory is 100,000 pounds.

    a. Plot the cumulative demand and a level aggregate production plan that meets the demand with no backorders and no ending inventory in March.

    b. What production each month is required to meet the conditions of question a?

6. A portion of the aggregate production plan for the Warmdot Game Company is shown below. Assuming the graph shows cumulative production and demand, is the company expecting an inventory or backorder at the end of August? How many units is this inventory or backorder expected to be?

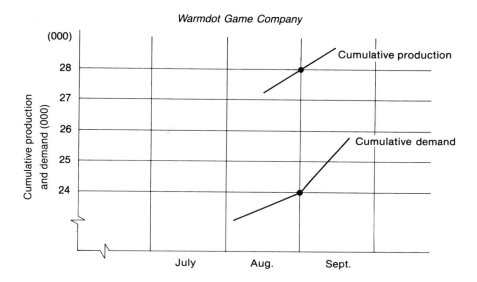

Warmdot Game Company

7. The Crazy Tubb Thumpers use a level plan to produce their snowshoe covers. The beginning inventory for January is zero, and the demand for covers in January, February, and March is given below:

Month	Demand
January	5,000
February	0
March	20,000

a. Graph the cumulative production for a level production plan of 10,000 units per month, the cumulative demand for the months January through March, and indicate the ending inventory for March.

b. Consider the additional data for Crazy Tubb Thumpers below:

Employment = 9 people.
Production = 1,000 units/month/employee (regular time).
Standard hours/month = 166 hours (regular time).
Regular time labor rate = $1,200/month.
Overtime rate = 1½ times regular time rate.

Assuming a production rate of 10,000 units per month, what is the labor cost of one month's production at Crazy Tubb Thumpers?

8. The Bi-Product Company produces two products (A and B) that are quite similar in terms of labor content and skills required. The company's management wishes to "level" the number of employees needed each day, so no hiring or layoffs will be needed during the year. A complication to their problem is that the number of working days each quarter varies.

	Demand		
Quarter	Product A	Product B	Working days
1	9,800	14,500	68
2	12,000	30,000	56
3	14,000	19,500	62
4	31,000	25,000	58

Beginning inventory: 2400 units of Product A
                      900 units of Product B
Inventory holding cost: $10 per unit per quarter (either product)
No backorders allowed
No variations in size of work force allowed
Output rate = 25 units of either product per day per employee

a. What daily production rate will be required to meet the demand forecast and yield zero inventory at end of quarter 4?

b. How many employees will be required each day?

9. Two students who share an apartment decide to use MRP for control over supplies. They shop every day and have the following "master production schedule" for tomorrow: breakfast—6 Bloody Marys, 4 Pop Tarts; lunch—5 peanut butter and jelly sandwiches, 4 cans beer; dinner—3 vodka martinis, 4 hamburgers, 8 oz. potato chips, 4 Hostess Twinkies; snack—18 cans beer, 16 oz. potato chips.

a. Given the following recipes, on-hand inventories, and lot sizes, prepare tomorrow's shopping list:

Recipes	
Bloody Mary	Peanut butter-jelly sandwich
2.5 oz. vodka	2 slices bread
4 oz. tomato juice	1 oz. peanut butter
dash Worcestershire (⅛ oz.)	.5 oz. jelly
dash Tabasco (⅛ oz.)	.5 oz. butter
Vodka martini	Hamburger
4 oz. vodka	4 oz. ground beef
.001 oz. dry vermouth	2 slices bread
ice	1 oz. catsup

Pantry inventory	On-hand	Lot size
Vodka	12 oz.	Quart
Tomato juice	3 oz.	46 oz. can
Worcestershire	6 oz.	8 oz. bottle
Tabasco	0	4 oz. bottle
Pop Tarts	3	8 per package
Peanut butter	6 oz.	12 oz. jar
Jelly	2 oz.	12 oz. jar
Bread	8 slices	20 slice loaf
Butter	4 oz.	1 lb.
Vermouth	5 oz.	16 oz.
Ice	Plenty	—
Hamburger	.8 lb.	1 lb.
Catsup	6 oz.	8 oz. bottle
Potato chips	2 oz.	16 oz. package
Hostess Twinkies	24	1 dozen package
Beer	9 cans	6 pack

b. Student A has just learned that the Bloody Marys must be made in batches of 24. Assuming no change in ingredients or amounts, how does this quantity affect the shopping list?

10. Assume that the two students in problem 9a eat the same set of "meals" each day.

    a. What are their daily "financial" capacity requirements, given the prices below?

Item	Price
Vodka	$.20 per ounce
Tomato juice	.02 per ounce
Worcestershire	.01 per dash
Tabasco	.01 per dash
Pop Tarts	.20 each
Peanut butter	.04 per ounce
Jelly	.03 per ounce
Bread	.03 per slice
Butter	.05 per ounce
Vermouth	.12 per ounce
Ice	no charge
Hamburger	.05 per ounce
Catsup	.02 per ounce
Potato chips	.03 per ounce
Hostess Twinkies	.15 each
Beer	.25 each

    b. What is the out-of-pocket cost of tomorrow's shopping list?

    c. What is the out-of-pocket cost if the Bloody Marys are made in batches of 24 instead of one at a time?

11. Mike Blanford, the master scheduler at General Avionics, has the following demand forecast for one of the lines in his factory:

Quarter	Unit sales
1	5,000
2	10,000
3	8,000
4	2,000

At the beginning of January, there are 1,000 units in inventory. The following data have been prepared by the firm:

Hiring cost per employee = $200
Firing cost per employee = $400
Beginning work force = 60 employees
Inventory carrying cost = $2 per unit per quarter of ending inventory
Stockout cost = $5 per unit
Regular payroll = $1,200 per employee per quarter
Overtime cost = $2 per unit

Each employee can produce 100 units per quarter. Demand not satisfied in any quarter is lost and incurs a stockout penalty. If Mike produces exactly enough to meet demand each quarter, with no inventories at the end of quarters, and no overtime, how much will he produce each quarter, and what is the overall cost (use a spreadsheet model for the calculations)?

12. Use the data in problem 11 to calculate the production amounts and costs for a level rate of output with no ending inventory.

13. The marketing people at General Avionics (problem 11) feel that they are somewhat unsure of their predictions of demand. They want to devise plans that allow for a 10 percent overage in sales in each quarter (i.e., a total sales potential of 27,500 units for the year). Prepare two plans: one a chase strategy and one with level production, and determine the costs.

14. At the end of the first quarter, the actual sales were 4,000 units. Revise both plans for problem 13 to provide for the 10 percent average (i.e., the total sales for the remaining 3 quarters = 22,000).

15. For the data in problem 11, at the end of the first quarter the inventory is 2,000 units. Marketing has revised the forecasts for quarters 2, 3, and 4 with a 20 percent reduction (i.e., total sales = 16,000). Develop a level and chase plan for the revised forecast that provides for an inventory of at least 1,000 units at the end of each quarter.

━━ 10 ━━━━━━━━━━━━━━━━━━━━━━━━

Demand management

This chapter covers the highly integrative activity we call demand management. It is through demand management that all potential demands on manufacturing capacity are collected and coordinated. This activity manages the day-to-day interactions between the customers and the company. A well-developed demand management module within the manufacturing planning and control (MPC) system results in several significant benefits. The proper planning of all externally and internally generated demands means that capacity can be better planned and controlled. Timely and *honest* customer order promises can be made. Physical distribution activities can be improved significantly. This chapter shows how these benefits can be achieved; the focus is less on techniques than on the management underpinnings and concepts necessary to perform this integrative activity.

This chapter is organized around the following four topics:

- Demand management in MPC systems: What role does demand management play in the MPC system?
- Demand management techniques: What techniques have proven useful for demand management in different market environments?
- Managing demand: How to live with demand management on a day-to-day basis.
- Company examples: Effective demand management in practice.

There are several chapters in this book that are closely related to demand management. Chapters 8 and 14 deal with master production scheduling, which is intimately tied to demand management. The production planning process discussed in Chapter 9, addresses overall levels of demand. The details of distribution requirements planning are treated in Chapter 19. Technical material related to forecasting is found in Chapter 16 and to inventory management in Chapters 17 and 18.

DEMAND MANAGEMENT IN MANUFACTURING PLANNING AND CONTROL SYSTEMS

Demand management encompasses forecasting, order entry, order-delivery-date promising, customer order service, physical distribution, and other customer-contact-related activities. Demand management is also concerned with other sources of demand for manufacturing capacity. Included are service-part demands, intracompany requirements, and pipeline inventory stocking. All quantities and timing for demands must be planned and controlled.

For many firms, the planning and control of demand quantities and timings are a day-to-day interactive dialogue with customers. For other firms, particularly in the process industries, the critical coordination is in scheduling large inter- and intracompany requirements. For still others, physical distribution is critical, since the factory must support a warehouse replenishment program, which can differ significantly from the pattern of final customer demand.

Demand management is a gateway module in manufacturing planning and control providing the link to the marketplace. The activities performed here provide the coordination between manufacturing and the marketplace, sister plants, and warehouses. It is through demand management that a channel of communication is maintained between the MPC systems and their "customers." Specific demands initiate actions throughout MPC, which ultimately result in the delivery of products and the consumption of materials and capacities.

The external aspects of the demand management module are depicted in Figure 10.1 as the double-ended arrow connected to the marketplace outside the MPC system. One implication of this connection is the need to forecast demand as a prerequisite to the other MPC activities. An important aspect is providing the forecasts at the appropriate level of detail. It also may imply constraining forecasts to meet certain overall requirements of the company. Both of these considerations are taken into account in the demand management process. Techniques for aggregating and disaggregating demand, such as *pyramid forecasting*, can facilitate this process.

The importance of identifying all sources of demand is obvious, but sometimes overlooked. If the material and capacity resources are to be planned

FIGURE 10.1   Demand management in the MPC system

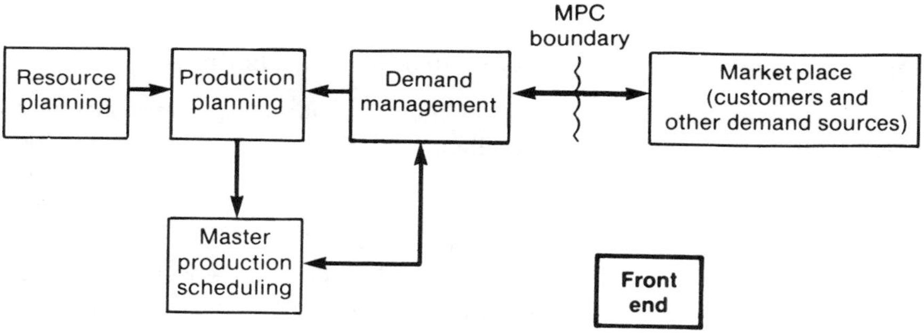

effectively, *all* sources of demand must be identified: spare parts, distribution, inventory changes, new items, promotions, and so on. It is only when all demand sources are accounted for that realistic MPC plans can be developed.

Demand management and production planning

The exact linkage of demand management and production planning depends to some extent on the way in which production planning is done in the firm. If the production plan is a quarterly statement of output in dollars or some other financial measure, then the key requirement for demand planning is for synchronization with this target. If the delivery timings for significant customer orders will affect the production plan, this information needs to be communicated to production planning. Similarly, a major change in distribution inventory policy might influence the production plan.

In addition to the role of synchronization and communication between the market activities and the production plan, a key activity in the demand management module is to assure the completeness of demand information. All sources of demand for manufacturing resources must be identified and incorporated in the production and resource planning processes. Sometimes this is more difficult than it might seem. The difficulty seems to be greatest for companies that have a significant number of interplant transfers. We have often heard plant managers complain that their worst customer was a sister plant or division.

To get a complete picture of the requirements for manufacturing capacity and material means collecting such sources of demand as spare parts demand, intercompany transfers, promotion requirements, pipeline buildups, quality assurance needs, exhibition or pilot project requirements, and even charitable donations. The principle is clear, even though the specifics will differ from firm to firm: All sources of demand must be taken into account. All must be included in the production plan to provide synchronization with other MPC activities.

Demand management and master production scheduling

The interactions of demand management and master production scheduling (MPS) are frequent and detailed. The details vary significantly between make-to-stock, assemble-to-order, and make-to-order environments. In all instances, however, the underlying concept is that of demand being consumed over time by actual customer orders. This is depicted in Figure 10.2. In each case the forecast of future orders lies to the right and above the line, and the actual customer orders are to the left and below the line (these areas are labeled for the make-to-order example).

An important observation from Figure 10.2 is that the position of the three lines is quite different. For make-to-stock environments, there are very few actual customer orders, since demand will be generally satisfied from inventory. Thus, the master production scheduling task is one of providing the inventory to meet forecasted future customer orders.

In the assemble-to-order environment, a key master scheduling task is to provide viable customer promise dates. Usually, there are customer orders already booked for several periods into the future. The master production scheduler uses the *available to promise* concept for each module or customer option to manage the conversion from forecasts to booked orders.

Still different demand management/MPS problems confront the firm with

FIGURE 10.2   MPS time fences—forecasts consumed by orders

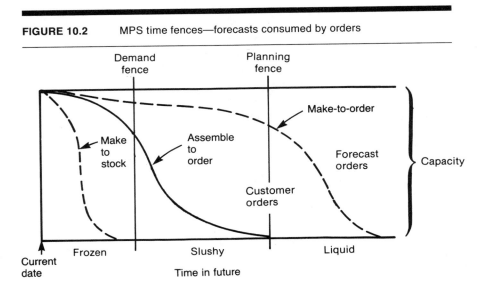

a make-to-order environment, even though there is a relatively larger back-log of customer orders. Some orders can be in progress, even though they are not completely specified and engineered. This means that the master production scheduler is concerned with controlling these custom orders as they progress through all steps in the process. This includes engineering activities, and the impact of those activities on resource requirements, as well as on manufacturing. All of this has to be coordinated with customers as the orders become completely specified.

In each company environment, the objective in the demand management module is to bridge the firm and the customer. This is facilitated by the time fences (the demand and planning fences) shown in Figure 10.2. The two fences result in three areas, which are sometimes termed "frozen," "slushy," and "liquid." The authority for making changes, as well as the way the MPS is stated, is quite different in each of these areas. The fences provide guide-lines to help the master production scheduler as the forecasts become actual orders.

The types of uncertainty also differ from company to company. One aspect of the relationship between master production scheduling and demand management is facilitating the buffering against this uncertainty. In the make-to-stock case, uncertainty is largely in the demand variations around the forecast at each of the inventory locations. In this case, the levels of safety stock (and/or safety lead time) must be set in order to provide the service levels required.

In the assemble-to-order case, the uncertainty involves not only the quantity and timing of customer orders but the product mix, as well. Safety stocks can be used, and the technique of hedging has been proven to be of value. For make-to-order environments, the uncertainty is often not in the timing or quantity of the customer order but, rather, in how much of the company's resources will be required as the engineering is finally completed and the exact requirements are determined.

The demand management task of specifying all sources of demand on the facility impacts master production scheduling in several ways. Some of the sources will be handled directly in the master production schedule, such as pipeline inventory build up, special exhibition requirements, and interplant transfers. Others, such as spare parts, may not be.

The spare-part issue can be quite complex in many firms. The demand for spare parts is typically forecast on an item-by-item basis and added to the gross requirement data in the corresponding MRP records. The actual spare-part demand will, of course, vary around the forecast. The variability can be buffered with safety stocks. The point is, there may not be an explicit treatment of each spare part by a master production schedule. In firms where it would take too long, moreover, the simplified approach will work reasonably well.

A key problem might be raised if spare-part demand is not incorporated at the MPS level; the resulting capacity requirements will not be reflected in rough-cut capacity planning models. The requirements would, however, be seen by the detailed capacity requirements planning models that are driven from MRP records.

To adequately perform rough-cut capacity planning, the service-part demand will have to be included. This could be done on a rough basis by estimating the service-part demand in monetary units and using some base to convert it to the capacity measure. Alternatively, one could prepare a bill of capacity for each service-part and multiply by the forecast service-part demand levels. The principle is clear: The capacity must be provided for *all* sources of demand.

Outbound product flow

Distribution activities are planned on the basis of the information developed in the demand management function. Customer delivery promise dates, inventory resupply shipments, interplant shipments, and so on, are all used to develop short-term transportation schedules. The information used for master production schedules can be integrated with distribution planning, as well. The information can be used to plan and control warehouse resupply. Moreover, transportation capacity, warehouse capacity, and the other resources within which the day-to-day distribution function will operate can also be better planned and controlled with this information.

Integration of distribution with master production scheduling can have very high payoffs for some firms. In essence, the resupply shipping decisions are demand inputs, which must be satisfied by the MPS. Conversely, the MPS provides a set of product availabilities that can be used in the distribution planning system.

It is in demand management that service levels and resultant safety stocks are explicitly defined. The requisite degree of flexibility for responding to mix or engineering design changes is set here as well. This is done through the determination of hedge quantities and timings. The master scheduler is then responsible for maintaining the required level of buffer stocks and timings.

It is through the conversion of the day-to-day customer orders into product shipments that the service levels for the company are realized. Careful management of the actual demands can provide the stability needed for efficient production, and that stability provides the basis for realistic customer promises and service. The booking of actual orders also serves to monitor activity against forecasts. As changes occur in the market place, demand management can and should routinely pick them up, indicating when managerial attention is required.

Data capture

The data capture and monitoring activities of demand management fall into two broad categories: the overall market and the detailed product mix. The activity most appropriate for production planning is basic market trends and patterns. The data should correspond to the units used in production planning. The intent is to determine on an ongoing basis, the general levels of actual business for input to the production planning process.

The second activity is concerned with managing the product mix for purposes of master production scheduling and customer order promising. Since final demand will be in catalog numbers or stockkeeping units, the day-to-day conversion of specific demands to MPC actions requires managing the mix of individual products.

For both the overall market and the detailed product mix, it is important that *demand* data be captured where possible. Many companies use sales instead of demand for purposes of making "demand" projections. Unless all demands have been satisfied, sales can understate the actual demand. In other instances, we know of firms that use shipments as the basis for making demand projections. In one such instance, the company concluded that their demand was increasing since their shipments were increasing. It was not until they had committed to increased raw-material purchases that they realized the increased shipments were replacement orders for two successive overseas shipments lost at sea.

Dealing with day-to-day customer orders

A primary function of the demand management module is converting specific day-to-day customer orders into detailed MPC actions. It is through the demand management function that the actual demands consume the planned materials and capacities. The conversion of actual customer demands into production actions must be performed regardless of whether the firm manufactures make-to-stock, make-to-order, or assemble-to-order products. The details may be somewhat different, depending on the nature of the manufacturing/marketing conditions in the company.

In make-to-order environments, the primary activity is the control of customer orders in order to meet customer delivery dates. This must be related to the master production schedule to determine the impact of any engineering changes on the final customer requirement. While this function is often performed the same way for assemble-to-order products, a communication with the final assembly schedule may also be needed to set promise dates. In both of these environments, there is a communication from the customer (a request) and to the customer (a delivery date) through the demand management module. These aspects of demand management are known by such names as order entry, order booking, and customer order service.

In a make-to-stock environment, demand management does not ordinarily provide customer promise dates. Since the material is in stock, the customer is most often served from inventory. In the event there is insufficient inventory for a specific request, the customer needs to be told when the material will be available or, if there is allocation, told what portion of the request can be satisfied. The conversion of customer orders to MPC actions in the make-to-stock environment triggers resupply of the inventory from which sales are made. This conversion is largely through forecasting, since the resupply decision is in anticipation of customer orders.

In all of the MPS environments, extraordinary demands often must be accommodated. Examples include advance orders in the make-to-stock environment, unexpected interplant needs, large spare-part orders, provision of demonstration units, and increased channel inventories. These all represent "real" demands on the material system.

DEMAND MANAGEMENT TECHNIQUES

This section begins with a general discussion of aggregating and disaggregating forecasts on a consistent basis for demand management at all company levels. Thereafter, three subsections deal with the demand management techniques most useful in the MPS environments of make-to-stock, assemble-to-order, and make-to-order.

Aggregating and disaggregating forecasts

Often forecasts are prepared for a variety of business decisions by many different people in a company. In addition to forecasts for *individual products* (units) used in scheduling operations, top managers utilize forecasts of *overall sales activity* (dollars) to plan and prepare budgets, and product managers frequently prepare forecasts for *groups of products*, (e.g., by horsepower (units), package size (pounds), product brand (dollars), and so on, in developing marketing plans for sales promotions, advertising, and distribution. The fact that sales forecasts are used for so many different decision-making purposes presents a significant coordination problem in many firms. Often these *independent* forecasts are never brought together within the organization to ensure that they are consistent and that the whole equals the sum of the parts.

One means of providing a consistency of forecasts for various purposes is through the bill of material (BOM). Using the BOM to pull together forecasts for different purposes may require special structuring of the bill. The "super bill" is one such example. The bill of materials forces a consistency to the forecasts by explicitly calling out the relationships. The constraint on forecasts for differing "levels" in the bill is a concept that lies behind other techniques for providing forecast consistency.

Another method of "constraining" the forecasts is pyramid forecasting. It provides a means of coordinating, integrating, and forcing consistency between the forecasts prepared in different parts of the organization. These consistent forecasts can then be used to meet the needs in marketing, manufacturing, distribution, and so on. Implementation of techniques to constrain forecasting can be done in a number of ways, but we will focus on a specific example of pyramid forecasting.

The procedure used in implementing the pyramid forecasting approach begins with individual item forecasts at level 3, which are rolled up into forecasts for groupings of individual products shown as level 2 in the example in Figure 10.3. The forecasts for product groupings are then aggregated into a total dollar forecast at level 1 in the product structure. Once the individual item and product grouping forecasts have been rolled up and considered in finalizing the top management forecast (plan), the next step is to force down (constrain) the product grouping and individual item forecasts, so they are consistent with the plan.

In the example, the 11 individual items are divided into two product

FIGURE 10.3   Pyramid forecasting example

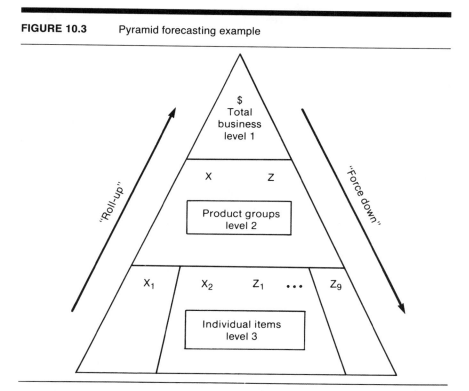

Source: T. L. Newberry and Carl D. Bhame, "How Management Should Use and Interact with Sales Forecasts," *Inventories & Production Magazine,* July–August 1981.

FIGURE 10.4   Initial and roll-up forecasts

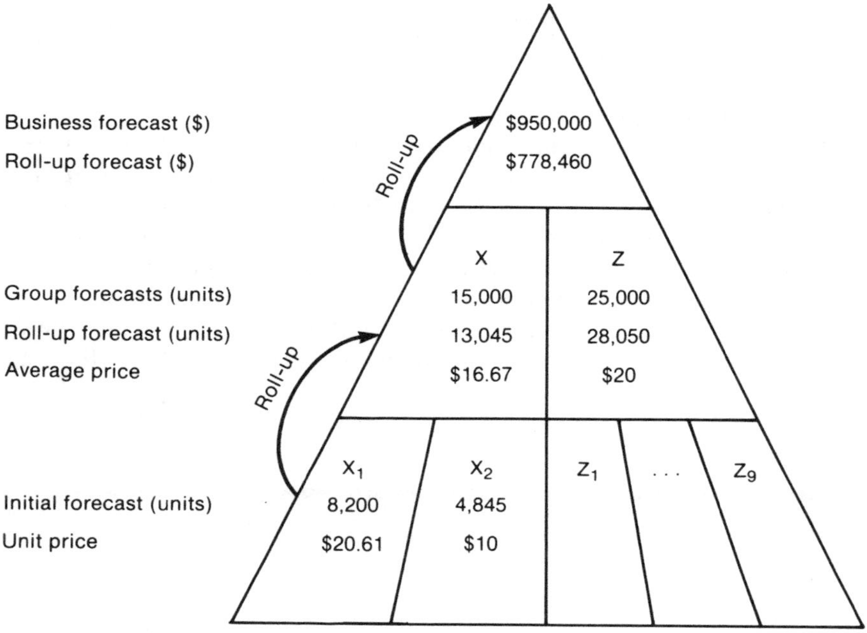

Business forecast ($) — $950,000
Roll-up forecast ($) — $778,460

	X	Z
Group forecasts (units)	15,000	25,000
Roll-up forecast (units)	13,045	28,050
Average price	$16.67	$20

	X_1	X_2	Z_1	...	Z_9
Initial forecast (units)	8,200	4,845			
Unit price	$20.61	$10			

groupings. Two of these items, X_1 and X_2, form product group X (which we will study in detail), while the remaining products, Z_1 through Z_9 are included in product group Z. These two product groups, X and Z, represent the entire line of products sold by the firm. The unit prices and initial forecasts for each level are shown in Figure 10.4.

The roll-up process starts by summing the individual item forecasts (level 3) to provide a total for each group (level 2). For the X group, the roll-up forecast is 13,045 units (8,200 + 4,845). Note that this does not correspond to the independent group forecast of 15,000 units. If there is substantial disagreement at this stage, a reconciliation could take place or an error might be discovered. If there is to be no reconciliation at this level, the independent forecasts for the groups need not be prepared. If dollar forecasts are required at level 2, the prices at level 3 can be used to calculate an average price. For our example, the sum of the individual Z group items gives a forecast of 28,050 units for Z.

To roll up to the level 1 dollar forecasts, the average prices at the group level are combined with the group roll-up forecasts. The total of $778,460 (13,045 × 16.67) + (28,050 × 20.00) is less than the independent business

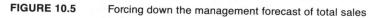

FIGURE 10.5 Forcing down the management forecast of total sales

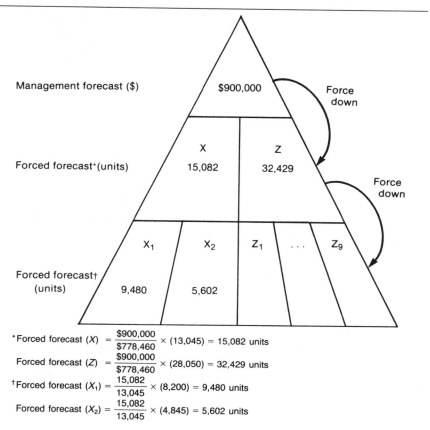

$$\text{*Forced forecast }(X) = \frac{\$900,000}{\$778,460} \times (13,045) = 15,082 \text{ units}$$

$$\text{Forced forecast }(Z) = \frac{\$900,000}{\$778,460} \times (28,050) = 32,429 \text{ units}$$

$$\text{†Forced forecast }(X_1) = \frac{15,082}{13,045} \times (8,200) = 9,480 \text{ units}$$

$$\text{Forced forecast }(X_2) = \frac{15,082}{13,045} \times (4,845) = 5,602 \text{ units}$$

forecast of $950,000. For illustrative purposes, we will assume that management has evaluated the business forecast *and* the roll-up forecast and has decided to use $900,000 as the forecast at level 1. The next task is to make the group and individual forecast consistent with this amount.

The method for bringing about the consistencies is in the forcing-down process. The ratio between the roll-up forecast at level 1 ($778,460) and the management total ($900,000) is used to make the adjustment.

The forecasts at all levels are shown in Figure 10.5. The results are consistent forecasts throughout the organization, and the sum of the parts is forced to be equal to the whole. Note, however, that the process of forcing the consistency needs to be approached with caution. In the example, the forecasts at the lower levels are now higher than they were originally. Even though the sum of the parts equals the whole, there is a possibility that the people responsible for the forecast won't "own" the number. They must not be made to feel they are simply being given an allocation of someone else's wish list.

There are several reasons for aggregating product items in both time and level of detail for forecasting purposes. This must be done with caution, however. The aggregation of individual products into families, geographical areas, or product types, for example, must be done in ways that are compatible with the planning systems. The product groupings must also be developed, so that the forecast unit is sensible to the forecasters. Provided these guidelines are followed, product groupings can be used to facilitate the forecasting task.

It is a well-known phenomenon that *long-term or product-line forecasts are more accurate than detailed forecasts.* This is just a verbalization of a statistical verity. Consider the example shown in Figure 10.6. The monthly sales average 20 units per day, but vary randomly with a standard deviation of 2 units. This means that 95 percent of the monthly demands would lie between 16 and 24 units (assuming a normal distribution). This corresponds to a forecast error of plus or minus 20 percent around the forecast of 20 units per day.

Now suppose that instead of forecasting the demand on a monthly basis, an annual forecast of demand is prepared. In this case, a forecast of 240 units is made for the year. The resulting standard deviation would be 6.9 units (assuming the monthly sales were independent). This corresponds to a 95 percent range of 226 to 254 units or a plus or minus 5.8 percent deviation. The reduction from plus or minus 20 percent to plus or minus 5.8 percent is due to using a much longer time period. The same effect can be seen in forecasting the demand for product families instead of for individual items.

The use of aggregate product forecast data can be illustrated with a survey concerning forecast accuracy, taken by Polysar International of plant, distri-

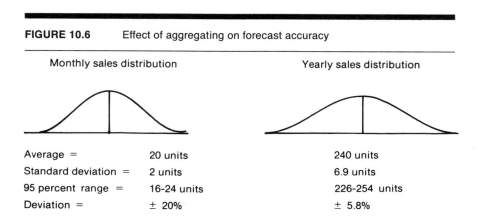

FIGURE 10.6   Effect of aggregating on forecast accuracy

	Monthly sales distribution	Yearly sales distribution
Average =	20 units	240 units
Standard deviation =	2 units	6.9 units
95 percent range =	16-24 units	226-254 units
Deviation =	± 20%	± 5.8%

FIGURE 10.7 Realistic levels of deviation of actual versus forecast (percent)

		1 month	1 quarter	1 year
	Total volume	± 12	8	8
	Family	15	10	8
	Type in family	15		12
	Grade in type	30		
	SKU †	50		

Time →

Item detail

*Average of a Polysar International Survey.
†Stockkeeping unit.

bution, scheduling, sales, and transportation managers. The results of the survey are shown in Figure 10.7. Even though the persons surveyed used detailed information to make labor, inventory, scheduling, traffic, and warehousing decisions, they recognized the magnitude of the forecast error in the detailed product-item forecasts. Their conclusion was to prepare short-term, detailed forecasts routinely and develop methods to live with the forecast errors.

There is one final point about forecast errors: Many efforts to reduce them are wasted—since they will not go away. A better alternative to improved forecasting found by many firms is improved systems for *responding* to forecast errors. The gross to net logic of MRP prevents errors from compounding, since the net requirements are simply changed from period to period as the actual inventory deviates from the projected inventory.

Make-to-stock demand management

Providing adequate inventory to meet the needs of customers throughout the distribution system, and maintaining desired customer service levels, require detailed forecasts. Despite our arguments for the increased accuracy of aggregated forecasts, the need in make-to-stock situations is for item level forecasts by location and by time period. This means we are still confronted with the problem of providing this level of detail.

One means of dealing with the inherent difficulty of forecasting individual items is to forecast ratios or percentages of aggregated forecasts, rather than stockkeeping units (SKUs) directly. Figure 10.8 shows the reduction in detail possible by the technique. For Jag's Coffee Company, there are four grinds, four package sizes, and three brands. This is a maximum total of $4 \times 4 \times 3 = 48$ possible combinations, of which only 20 had sales in the period covered by the example. If the percentages of the total coffee sales

FIGURE 10.8   Sales in tons by brand, size, and grind of Jag's Coffee Company

Brand and size	I	R	D	S	Total
Jingle					
Packet	10				10
Regular	20	40	30		90
Giant		20	10		30
Jangle					
Packet	10				10
Regular	15	10	20		45
Promotion	5	5			10
Giant		5	10		15
Jungle					
Regular		40	40	10	90
Giant		50	50	40	140
Total	60	170	160	50	440

	Total	Percent
Coffee	440	100
Brand		
Jingle	130	30
Jangle	80	18
Jungle	230	52
Size		
Packet	20	4
Regular	225	52
Promotion	10	2
Giant	185	42
Grind		
Grind I	60	14
Grind R	170	39
Grind D	160	36
Grind S	50	11

*I = instant; R = regular; D = drip; S = special.

by each of the brands, sizes, and grinds are computed, there are only 12 separate items (11 mix ratios and total coffee sales) to be concerned with; that is, one could forecast total coffee sales and break them down into brands, sizes, or grinds on a percentage basis.

For many firms, product-mix ratios remain fairly constant over time. In such situations, managerial attention can be directly on forecasting overall sales. Percentage forecasting can be used to routinize the individual item forecasting problem. Moreover, if the master scheduler keeps MPS records for each of the product options, it may not be necessary to forecast individual items. The important job is not *forecasting* individual end items; it is *building* them and providing adequate customer service. Demand management is designed to facilitate the process.

The example of Figure 10.8 also shows the need for applying judgment in forecasting. If the promotion package size was for a single promotion, it should be dropped from the forecast. It also helps if the manufacturing step subject to the greatest forecast error can be postponed as long as possible. For example, if the labeling of the package or the filling of the package can be postponed, a reduction in forecast error might be realized, because some specific customer orders will be on hand before the commitment to any particular item is made.

Once the forecasts have been developed, distribution requirements planning (DRP) can be used to coordinate the replenishment of any distribution

FIGURE 10.9   DRP record for Jag's Jingle brand, regular and drip

Omaha Warehouse

		Period				
		1	*2*	*3*	*4*	*5*
Forecast requirements		10	10	10	10	10
In transit		20				
Projected available balance	6	16	6	16	6	16
Planned shipments			20		20	

LT = 1, Q = 20, SS = 3

inventories. The basic DRP record has the same format and logic as an MRP record but uses the detailed forecasts as the requirements. An example DRP record—for Jag's Jingle brand, regular size, drip grind coffee at the Omaha warehouse—is shown in Figure 10.9. In the DRP record, in-transit is used to indicate material on its way to the warehouse, and planned shipments indicate the plans to send material from central stock to resupply the warehouse. The planned shipments provide a key input to the master production schedule. When summed for all warehouses, they give the demands on the central stock.

In the example of Figure 10.9, we see the use of safety stock in the distribution warehouse as a form of buffer against larger than forecast demands. The use of safety stock in inventories is quite common. Less common is the use of safety lead time. In instances where the finished product is transported to a distant inventory location, such as a warehouse or distribution center, there is often a range of time during which the delivery can take place. The forecast error in this case is in terms of the time of arrival, not the quantity that will arrive. In these circumstances, dispatching shipments earlier than would be necessary on the average provides a safety lead time buffer against late-arriving shipments. In this case, both the shipment date and the scheduled delivery date are advanced by the amount of the safety lead time so the system is driven by the correct data.

Assemble-to-order demand management

In the assemble-to-order environment, we are concerned about making accurate promise dates to customers. This requires MPS stability and predictability. The master scheduler can help to achieve this by using the time

FIGURE 10.10 Application of available-to-promise logic to Jag's instant coffee production

	Period				
	1	2	3	4	5
Forecast	60	60	60	60	60
Booked orders	90	80	50	20	0
Available	80	0	60	0	60
Available to promise	0		50		120
Master schedule production	120		120		120

On hand = 50, Q = 120

fences that were illustrated in Figure 10.2. The "frozen" zone holds schedules firm, and the time fences specify the management level required to formally approve a change request. For assemble-to-order products, stability is also related to the discipline applied in booking customer orders. Key in accomplishing this is the use of the available-to-promise concept. Figure 10.10 provides an example from the Jag's Coffee Company problem, using the 60 tons per period of instant coffee from Figure 10.8 as the basis. We now treat Jag's as an assemble-to-order product for this example.

The example shows that all of the instant coffee available in the first two periods (50 + 120 = 170 tons) is committed to customer orders already booked. No additional promises for delivery in the first two periods are possible without changing the delivery date on one of the orders already booked. There are 120 tons of production planned for period 3, of which 70 tons are already promised. The remaining 50 tons are available for promise as early as period 3. If a customer wanted more than 50 tons to be delivered in one shipment, that customer would have to wait until at least period 5, unless 50 tons of orders presently promised for delivery in periods 1, 2, or 3 could be rescheduled to period 5, or later. The MPS itself might be changed, but the production of 120 tons of instant coffee currently scheduled in period 1 must be nearly completed, and 120 tons for period 3 might be too far along in the process.

If the customers for the instant coffee wanted a unique packaging to meet their specifications, a separate schedule may be needed. Suppose, for example, that the lead time for packaging was one period. A separate packaging schedule (equivalent to a final assembly schedule) could be established for managing this additional level of detail. The packaging schedule need extend only far enough into the future, say two to three periods, to allow for planning the detailed packaging sequences. The booked order entries in the MPS record would have to be offset by one period to allow time for the packaging. The principle of holding the integrity of the customer order promises remains however, and this needs the predictability and discipline of available-to-promise logic.

The focus on stability in the information system and MPS should not be taken as an argument for inflexibility. Indeed, we argued earlier that mechanisms for dealing with the forecast errors were often more important than attempts to reduce forecast errors. This means a form of flexibility is needed, particularly to accommodate short-term variations in the mix of SKUs being sold.

For assemble-to-order products, the use of hedging provides an effective, easily managed buffering technique. An example is given in Figure 10.11 for Jag's regular grind coffee. The figure shows the records for three steps of the production process. Green coffee beans are removed from storage and prepared for roasting. This takes one period. Next, the roasting of the prepared beans is done over three periods. Finally, the roasted beans are ground. The lead time for the final step is one period.

The records trace the planned orders through the process from the master schedule for regular grind coffee to green bean preparation. Since the demand for regular grind coffee is calculated as a percent of the total coffee forecast, and variations can occur in the mix between instant, regular, drip and special grinds, the company wants the flexibility to respond to product-mix changes. However, the firm doesn't want to hold excess regular grind coffee in inventory.

The approach is to establish a hedge of 20 tons five periods from now. This is done by creating a hedge time fence at period 5 and introducing a 20-ton master schedule entry. We presume in this example that this has been done and the system has been operating for some time. Currently, we are at the beginning of period 121 and the hedge of 20 tons has just come over the time fence into period 125. Note that previously placed orders (scheduled receipts) and planned orders balance out the requirements and no inventory is shown except for prepared green coffee beans.

If there is no indication that the mix has changed, the hedge quantity is not required and the 20 hedge tons are pushed back over the fence to period 126 (top arrow in Figure 10.11). This will reduce the gross requirement for regular grind coffee from 360 to 340 tons in period 125 and will change the planned order in period 124. The effect is passed through the roasted bean record to the prepared green beans. At this point, the scheduled receipt of 340 and the inventory of 20 would have been enough to satisfy the gross requirement for 360, but it is not necessary, so the 20 tons will be held in prepared green bean inventory. Pushing out the hedge unit in subsequent periods will leave the 20 tons of prepared green beans in inventory.

If the hedge quantity had been allowed to remain within the time fence,

---

FIGURE 10.11   An example of hedging for regular grind Jag's coffee

---

Regular grind coffee   Hedge time fence = 5 periods

Period		121	122	123	124	125	126
Master schedule		340	0	340	0	340	0
Hedge quantity						20 ⟶ 20	
Gross Requirements		340		340		340 ⟶ 20	
Scheduled receipts		340					
Projected available balance	0	0	0	0	0	0	0
Planned order releases			340		340 ⟶ 20		

Q = lot-for-lot, LT = 1.

Roasted beans

Period		121	122	123	124	125	126
Gross requirements		0	340	0	340 ⟶ 20		0
Scheduled receipts			340				
Projected available balance	0	0	0	0	0	0	0
Planned order releases		340 ⟶ 20					

Q = lot-for-lot, LT = 3.

Prepared green beans

Period		121	122	123	124	125	126
Gross requirements		340 ⟶ 20		0	0	0	0
Scheduled receipts		340	0				
Projected available balance	20	20	0	0	0	0	0
Planned order releases							

Q = lot-for-lot, LT = 1.

---

a planned order for 360 tons of roasted coffee beans would have been issued and the 20 tons of prepared green beans would have started on the way to becoming roasted coffee beans. Should the hedge quantity have been required, it would be ground during period 124 and would be available in period 125. The placement of the hedge fence indicates how quickly a response can be made to product volume changes.

Setting the time fence and managing the hedge units must take into account both economic trade-offs and current conditions. Setting the time fence too early means that the inventory will be carried at higher levels in the product structure, which often decreases alternative uses of basic materials. Also, too short a time fence may not provide enough time to evaluate whether the mix ratio is changing. Similarly, it makes no sense to provide flexibility where it is not needed. Over the period when all the planned available coffee is committed to specific customer orders, there is no need for flexibility since the exact product mix is known (e.g., in the frozen part of Figure 10.2). In this circumstance, the hedge should be pushed out until there is still some forecast usage that has not been consumed by actual orders.

Make-to-order demand management

In the make-to-order environment, we are very much concerned with the control of customer orders after they are entered into the system. In some cases, there will be weeks or months of order backlog at the plant. In many of these orders, a great deal of detailed engineering will take place before the order is completed and sent to the customer. This occurs because the orders are not completely specified when they are booked. Indeed, for products that take many months to manufacture, the technology could even change while the product was in process. Thus, even though the number and timing of customer orders may be known for some time into the future, there can still be a great deal of uncertainty concerning these orders.

In this situation, demand management has to track these orders through all phases of plant activity, including the engineering-related functions. There are three primary reasons for this tracking. First, the master scheduler needs to know what the impact of final specifications will be on parts design, component lead times, and customer promise date for the product as a whole. The second reason is to so manage the overall lead time that satisfactory customer service results. The third reason concerns the impact that the use of engineering resources will have on *other* customer orders in the factory.

Hedging will buffer some of this uncertainty, just as it will for the assemble-to-order product case. This may not be sufficient to cover all changes, however. The use of what-if analysis can help the master production scheduler determine the impact of changes, and the impact as uncertainties in design get resolved. The overall impact can be assessed in terms of the shop load (and load on engineering), and the resultant completion dates for the other products. But other tools are helpful in managing the make-to-order product situation. Some of the newer technologies for manufacturing, especially computer aided design/computer aided manufacture (CAD/CAM), can be helpful in reducing engineering lead times and in improving the pass-off from engineering to manufacturing. Also of value is use of specialized planning bills of material. It is to this topic that we now turn our attention.

Since general parameters for the design of a make-to-order product are known at the time of order entry, a planning bill of materials can be created at that time. It could be patterned after the product made in the past that is believed to be most like the present product, or it could be a generic BOM. The intention is to get something close to what the final product will be into the MPC system as soon as possible, so the management of both the design and manufacturing processes can be all done with one integrated system.

Initial planning must be based on a combination of what is known and what is estimated. The parts of the product that are not completely specified are carried with part number codes indicating that they are "temporary." The planning bill that represents the customer order is carried in the MPS. Modifications to the BOM are entered as the engineering process takes place and the temporary codes are removed from individual part numbers. Overall knowledge of the status of engineering is provided, and the "critical path" for engineering and manufacturing can be determined and managed.

Figure 10.12 illustrates this approach. The initial product structure was developed from a similar product that had been built before. Three of the components are not completely specified, and these are so indicated by the "t" designation in the part numbers. In each case, there is also a range of time given, which is an estimate of the lead time for design and fabrication. Fully specified parts have the standard MPC lead time connotation.

After the engineering has been completed and changes so indicated in the final product structure, there is no longer a need to hedge against initial design uncertainty. Any subsequent engineering changes, however, need to be approved by the customer and managed by the demand management module.

MANAGING DEMAND

In this section we are concerned with managerial issues related to the performance of day-to-day demand management tasks.

Organizing for demand management

Many, if not all, of the activities that we have associated with demand management are already performed in most companies. In many instances, the organizational responsibility for performing these activities is widely scattered throughout the firm. The finance or credit department performs credit-checking and order-screening activities associated with customer orders. The order-entry or booking activities are performed in the sales or customer service departments. The outbound product activities are associated with the distribution, traffic, or logistics departments of firms.

FIGURE 10.12   Planning bill of material before and after specification of the parts

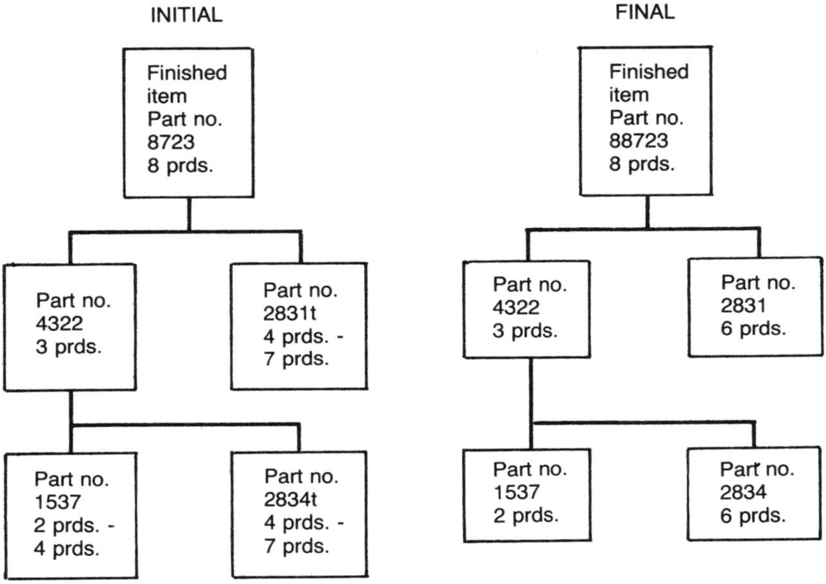

INITIAL

FINAL

Note: All parts require one each of their components.

In some companies, a materials management function has been established that is responsible for coordinating most of the demand management activities. The organizational responsibility for demand management tends to be very much a function of the history and nature of the organization. It is much less important, however, that there be a unified organizational home for all the activities, than that they be appropriately defined and coordinated, with one integrated data base.

In marketing-oriented firms, where close contact with the demand trends and good customer relations are required for success, the demand management function might well be performed by the marketing or sales organization. In those firms for which the development of the product requires close interaction between engineering and customers, the activities might be performed in a technical services department. The materials management organization has grown up in firms that feel it important to manage the flow of materials from purchasing raw materials through the production process to the customer. In such firms, which span both industrial and consumer products, the demand management function can be a part of the materials management activity. In all instances, it is necessary to clearly assign responsibilities to make sure that nothing is left to chance.

If flexibility is a key objective, then the rules for interacting with the system and customers must be carefully designed and enforced by management so the system can provide this flexibility. By this we mean that customer order processing must be established and enforced through the master production scheduling system. It means carefully establishing the rules under which particular special customers will be served. For example, if an extraordinarily large order is received at a field warehouse, procedures need to be established for determining whether that order will be allowed to consume a large portion of the local inventory or be passed back to the factory. Limits within which changes can be made must be defined and enforced. If any of these procedures are violated by a manager who says, "I don't care how you do it but customer X must get his order by time Y," the demand management activity is seriously undercut.

A very useful technique for assisting in defining and managing these areas of responsibility is to tie them to time fences. Abbott Laboratories, Ltd., of Canada has developed a highly formalized set of time fences. Figure 10.13 shows the four levels of change responsibility within the company. As a change request affects the MPS nearer to the current date, the responsibility for authorizing the change moves up in the organization. This procedure does not preclude a change but does force a higher-level of review for schedule changes to be made in the near term.

The underlying concept for approval procedures is to take the informal bargaining out of the system. By establishing and enforcing such procedures for order entry, customer delivery date promising, changes to the material system, and responses to mix changes in the product line, everyone plays by the same rules. In the Abbott example, flexibility is part of the change procedure, but the difficulty of making a change increases as the cost of making that change increases. It is clear that this is more a matter of management discipline than technique. The ability to respond: "What don't you want?" to the "I have to have it right away" for a particular customer request will help immensely in establishing this discipline.

Managing service levels

One way of helping the organization live with a formal system for placing demands on the manufacturing organization is to explicitly set levels of service and to publicize them throughout the organization. Substantial theoretical work has been performed concerning the setting of service levels for finished-goods inventory. This work indicates that inventory investment increases exponentially as service-level objectives are increased. More importantly, there is a need for discipline in the management of service levels. Simply stated, this means understanding that something less than a 100 per-

FIGURE 10.13   Approval fences for master scheduling change at Abbott Laboratories, Ltd.

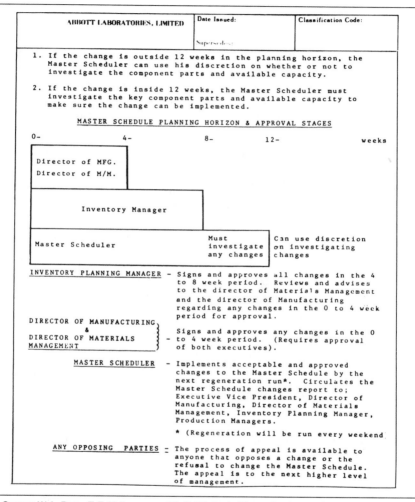

Source: W. L. Berry, T. E. Vollmann, and D. C. Whybark, *Master Production Scheduling: Principles and Practice* (Falls Church, Va.: American Production and Inventory Control Society, 1979), p. 83.

cent service-level target implies that occasionally there *will* be a stock-out. Truly understanding and living with that can be difficult. It is often the case that a stock-out or late delivery focuses so much attention on a given transaction that the people respond to prevent its recurrence. This is frequently the origin of the impossible order given to many inventory clerks: "Keep the inventory low but don't stock-out."

The determination of appropriate service levels requires very careful consideration of the trade-offs. With increasingly high costs of carrying inventory, the levels of service provided to customers from a finished-goods inventory must be reevaluated very honestly. This means assessing the value of maintaining service levels versus the savings from reduced inventory. The statistical methods developed to solve the technical aspects of this trade-off do not solve the difficult managerial problem. Most firms recognize that 100 percent service (i.e., the meeting of every customer demand from inventory or at the time the customer requests it) is simply beyond the realm of financial possibility. For make-to-stock firms, 100 percent service implies huge inventories. For make-to-order firms, immediate delivery implies substantial idle capacity.

Lest one interpret these remarks as a plea for poor customer service, let us state emphatically that such is not the case. We firmly believe that major improvements are possible, but that emotional responses are not the answer. MPC systems are designed to trade information for inventories and other kinds of slack—including poor delivery performances. By using the systems well, one can be close order coupled with customers; that is, demand management can often lead to substantial improvements in customer service *without* massive inventories or idle capacity.

The increasing use of just-in-time is providing significant help as well. A manufacturer of CAD/CAM terminals reduced the lead time from over 15 weeks to four days. At the same time, the company went from make-to-stock to make-to-order. All products are now built to exact customer order.

Using the system

An effective demand management module will gather marketing information, generate forecast information, screen and monitor performance information, and provide detailed action instructions to the material planning and control system. Once implemented, the system can be used to perform routine tasks. A specific example of this is found in the forecasting activity. The system can perform the breakout of item sales within a product family, and management's attention can be focused on the demand for the family itself. Focusing on the broader category both brings attention to bear where it is most needed and prevents squandering human resources on trying to reduce forecast error, which is unlikely. It is only through the support of the system that this redirection of human resources can be accomplished.

The management control function also runs through the formal MPC activities. Gathering intelligence on actual conditions in the marketplace provides the basis for deciding whether or not to change the game plan (production plan, sales plan, budget, and so on) of the organization and for determining the appropriate level of flexibility. Again, the approach is to use the system to gather this information and then apply management talent where it is needed.

Perhaps the most important change that improved management in this area can effect is the ability to be honest with customers. In our experience, customers prefer honest, even if they are unpleasant, answers to inaccurate information. An effective manufacturing planning and control system with discipline in order promising and service-level maintenance provides the basis for honest communication with customers. They can be told when to expect delivery or when inventory will be replenished—and can count on it. Providing the basis for honest communication with the customers can pay handsome dividends in terms of customer loyalty.

COMPANY EXAMPLES

In this section, we present several illustrations of actual demand management practice, as well as records that demonstrate the key concepts we have discussed in this chapter. Material gathered from Abbott Laboratories, the Tennant Company, and the Elliott Company is used in these illustrations.

Abbott Laboratories, Inc.: Forecasting

Abbott Laboratories, Inc., located in North Chicago, Illinois, is a multinational health-care firm. The company's product line includes pharmaceutical products for professional and personal use, medical electronics, cosmetics, and related chemical/pharmaceutical products. The products in this example are produced on a make-to-stock basis; the company has a reputation for maintaining a high level of customer service. Figure 10.14 is an example of the forecasting process used for these products.

The forecasting procedure at Abbott Laboratories uses many of the techniques that were suggested earlier in this chapter. In this example, the first step in the process is to develop the monthly forecasts by product. The initial input is a computer-developed forecast that uses data on customer demand and provides a basis for marketing review and approval. Figure 10.14 shows that marketing left the forecast the same for the months of April and May but changed it for June. Management judgment is used in reviewing the forecast for these monthly totals. Next, the forecast is broken down by distribution center by a computer program using the demand history data base.

The process of dividing up the forecast by distribution center begins with determining the historical percentage of each product sold by each distribution center. This is illustrated in Step III in Figure 10.14. These percentage breakdowns are then applied by the computer to the approved total forecast to develop the monthly forecast by distribution center.

At Step IV in Figure 10.14, the forecast is broken down further by week within the month. Again, this is done by the computer using procedures to take into account split weeks, vacations, and so on. The result is a weekly forecast for each product at each distribution warehouse.

FIGURE 10.14 Developing detailed SKU forecasts at Abbott Laboratories

Illustration of Weekly Forecast
Development for a Product
(by distribution center)

	Month		
	April	*May*	*June*
Week*	1–4	5–8	9–12
Step I: Computer developed forecast by product (preliminary forecast)	520	648	712
Step II: Marketing revision and/or approval (final forecast)	520 (OK)	648 (OK)	620 (Revised by Mkt.)

Step III: Computer proration of
monthly forecast by distribution center (DC)

DC	Forecast[†]	Percent of total FC
#218	155	[‡]31%
#233	310	62%
#244	35	7%
Total	500	100%

April	May	June
[§]160	200	192
320	400	394
40	48	44
520	648	620

Step IV: Development of weekly forecast

DC		Week: 1 2 3 4	5 6 7 8	9
	#218	‖40 40 40 40	50 50 50 50	48
	#233	80 80 80 80	100 100 100 100	96
	#244	10 10 10 10	12 12 12 12	11

*Four weeks per month used to simplify example.
†Each DC Forecast is done independently through the use of an exponential smoothing technique based on past DC sales history.
Sample of calculations (within computer):

‡155 ÷ 500 = 31%
§31% × 520 = 160 (rounded)
‖ 160 ÷ 20 days/mo. × 5 days/wk. = 40/wk.

Source: D. C. Whybark, "Abbott Laboratories, Inc." in *Studies in Material Requirement Planning*, ed. E. W. Davis (Falls Church, Va.: America Production and Inventory Control Society, 1977), p. 17.

These forecasts are then utilized as gross requirements data for the time-phased order point records for each of the warehouses. The result of thereafter applying MRP logic is the planned shipments for replenishing inventory from the factory. Data on actual demand are captured at the warehouses. The gross to net logic and safety stock are used to absorb the fluctuations between sales and forecasts.

An interesting reaction occurred when the weekly projections of product sales at each warehouse were provided to the warehouse supervisors. By having the planned information, in many instances they were able to use their knowledge of the local purchasing patterns to adjust the distribution of the forecast within each month to better plan inventory resupply. Even though the information was quite detailed, they were able to review the weekly patterns and adjust them within the monthly totals provided by the computer breakdown of the marketing approved forecast.

Tennant Company: Order promising and flexibility management

The Tennant Company manufactures industrial floor-maintenance equipment and associated cleaning products. The equipment varies from small walk-behind cleaners to larger operator-driven units. The machines are used for both indoor and outdoor applications. They are divided into families for planning and scheduling purposes. Within each family there are a large number of customer specified options and accessories for each machine.

Customer order promising is done explicitly from the machine availability plan prepared by the material planning and control system. Specifically, this is performed by the order entry function using a report of machine status, an example of which is provided in Figure 10.15. The first line of the document shows the status of machines in E2 family. This report includes machines that have already been assembled and machines in various stages of preparation for customer delivery, as well as machines scheduled for future production. This example shows that all but one of the machines scheduled for production in the next seven weeks are promised to customers. The earliest possible customer delivery date promise is for a machine in week 7 (manufacturing day 211, June 5). Although this report has a different format than the available-to-promise logic illustrated earlier, it contains the same basic information and is used in the same way.

The next two lines indicate two of the options available for the E2 family. They are the gas and LP motor options. This provides a second-level of order entry testing. The only machine that will be available in the week of June 5 is an LP machine. This is seen by the fact that there is no commitment to the LP motor available in the week of June 5. This logic of testing product availability illustrates the process of order entry that matches customer requests to the availability of scheduled machines and options at Tennant.

Figure 10.16 illustrates the production version of the same document in somewhat greater detail. This MPS control report has basic parts, unique gas parts, and unique LP parts, as did the order entry document. It is first important to notice that exactly the same information is available to manufacturing as was available to order entry. Additional information in this report is of interest in illustrating the management of flexibility. First of all, there are specifically identified time fences for the basic parts at manufacturing day 276 and 436 (note the vertical lines of slashes), and different

FIGURE 10.15   Tennant's report of machine status—the customer promising document

DAILY MACHINE RESERVATION REPORT   MFG DATE 182

	FINAL LOGS	1 182 AP26	2 186 MY01	3 191 MY08	4 196 MY15	5 201 MY22	6 206 MY29	7 211 JN05	8 216 JN12	9 221 JN19	10 226 JN26	11 231 JL03	12 236 JL10	13 241 JL17	14 246 JL24	15 251 JL31	LATER CMTMNT

16100 PARTS BASIC E2
PARTS-BASIC   E2LINE #16100
CRTD UNCR TEST RWRK ASSY PULD   SCHEDULED
                                STOCK CMT
                                CUST CMT
3   4   1 DF

17005 FINAL ASSY E2
PARTS-UNIQUE-GAS   E2LINE #16102
CRTD UNCR TEST RWRK ASSY PULD   SCHEDULED
1   1   STOCK CMT
                                CUST CMT
                                1 DF

17006 FINAL ASSY E2 LP
PARTS-UNIQUE-LP   E2LINE #16103
CRTD UNCR TEST RWRK ASSY PULD   SCHEDULED
2   2   STOCK CMT
                                CUST CMT

Source: W. L. Berry, T. E. Vollmann, and D. C. Whybark, *Master Production Scheduling: Principles and Practice* (Falls Church, Va.: American Production and Inventory Control Society, 1979), p. 163.

FIGURE 10.16 Tennant flexibility management document

```
                               M A S T E R   S C H E D U L E   C O N T R O L   R E P O R T
E2 FAMILY                                                          MFG DATE 182
---------

16100   PARTS-BASIC        E2LINE  D.RATIO  SHORT RANGE HEDGE   TIME FENCES    BACKLOG  LONG RANGE HEDGE   LAST REVIEW
                                    100%     10%   15%   20%    00 20 52 00       2        %    %    %         417
SEQ 0560
               -APR/---------MAY--------/--------JUN----/---------JUL---------/---------AUG----/---------SEP----/---------OCT
ADJ.          181  186  191  196  201  206  211  216  221  226  231  236  241  246  251  256  261  266  271  276  281  286  291  296  301  306
PLANNED         1    1    1    2    2    1  (2)    1    1    1    1    1    1    1    1    1    2    1    1   1/    1    1    1    1    1    1
HEDGE W/S       1    1    1    2    2    1    2                                                                1/                   1
COMMITTED       1    1    1    2    2    1    1    1    1    1    1    1    1    1    1    1    2    1    1   2/    1    1    1    2    1    1
                                                                                                                /

               ---------/---------NOV----/---------DEC----/---------JAN---------/---------FEB----/---------MAR----/---------APR
              311  316  321  326  331  336 -341  346  351  356  361  366  371  376  381  386  391  396  401  406  411  416  421  426  431  436
PLANNED         1    1    1    1    1    1    1    1    2    1    1    1    2    1    2    1    1    2    1    1    1    1    1    2    1   1/
HEDGE W/S                 1                   1                   1                   1                   1                                  /
COMMITTED       1    1    2    1    1    1    2    1    2    1    2    1    2    1    3    1    1    2    2    1    1    1    1    2    1   1/
                                                                                                                                            1/

               ---------/---------MAY----/---------JUN----/---------JUL---------/---------AUG----/---------SEP----/---------OCT
              441  446  451  456  461  466  471  476  481  486  491  496  501  506  511  516  521  526  531  536  541  546  551  556  561  566
PLANNED         1    1    1    2    1    2    1    2    1    2    1    2    1    2    1    2    1    2    2    1    2    1    2    1    2    1
HEDGE W/S       1    1    1    2    1    2    1    2    1    2    1    2    1    2    1    2    1    2    2    1    2    1    2    1    2    1

               ---------/---------NOV----/---------DEC---------/---------JAN----/---------FEB----/---------MAR---------/---------
              571  576  581  586  591  596  601  606  611  616  621  626  631  636  641  646  651  656  661  666  671  676  681  686  691  696
PLANNED         2    1    2    1    2    1    2    1    2    1    2    1    2    1    2    1    2    1    2    1    2    1    2    1    2    1
HEDGE W/S       2    1    2    1    2    1    2    1    2    1    2    1    2    1    2    1    2    1    2    1    2    1    2    1    2    1

16102   PARTS-UNIQUE-GAS   E2LINE  D.RATIO  SHORT RANGE HEDGE   TIME FENCES    BACKLOG  LONG RANGE HEDGE   LAST REVIEW
                                     65%     45%   50%   55%    00 03 16 00       2        %    %    %         417
SEQ 0570
               -APR/---------MAY--------/--------JUN----/---------JUL---------/---------AUG----/---------SEP----/---------OCT
ADJ.          181  186  191  196  201  206  211  216  221  226  231  236  241  246  251  256  261  266  271  276  281  286  291  296  301  306
PLANNED         1    1    /    2    2    1    1    1              1    1    1             1/    2    1              1    1    1         1    1
HEDGE                     /                             1    1
W/S             1    1    /    2    2    1    1                                  1         /                   1                   1
COMMITTED       1    1    /    2    2    1    1    1    1    1    1    1    1    1        1/    2    1         1    1    1    1    1    1    1
                                                                                           /

               ---------/---------NOV----/---------DEC----/---------JAN---------/---------FEB----/---------MAR----/---------APR
              311  316  321  326  331  336  341  346  351  356  361  366  371  376  381  386  391  396  401  406  411  416  421  426  431  436
PLANNED         1              1    1         1    1    1    1         1    1    1    1         1    1    1    1         1         1    1
HEDGE W/S                 1                                       1                   1                   1
COMMITTED       1         1    1    1         1    1    1    1    1    1    1    1    2         1    1    2    1         1         1    1
                                                                                                                                             1

               ---------/---------MAY----/---------JUN----/---------JUL---------/---------AUG----/---------SEP----/---------OCT
              441  446  451  456  461  466  471  476  481  486  491  496  501  506  511  516  521  526  531  536  541  546  551  556  561  566
PLANNED              1    1    1    1    1    1    1         1    1    1         1    1    1    1    1    1    1    1         1    1    1    1
HEDGE W/S            1    1    1    1    1    1    1         1    1    1         1    1    1    1    1    1    1    1         1    1    1    1

               ---------/---------NOV----/---------DEC---------/---------JAN----/---------FEB----/---------MAR---------/---------
              571  576  581  586  591  596  601  606  611  616  621  626  631  636  641  646  651  656  661  666  671  676  681  686  691  696
PLANNED         1         1    1    1    1    1    1    1    1    1    1    1         1    1    1    1    1    1    1    1    1    1    1    1
HEDGE W/S       1         1    1    1    1    1    1    1    1    1    1    1         1    1    1    1    1    1    1    1    1    1    1    1
```

FIGURE 10.16 *(concluded)*

```
                              M A S T E R   S C H E D U L E   C O N T R O L   R E P O R T                 TIME 02.45
                                                              MFG DATE 182                                PAGE  21
16103     PARTS-UNIQUE- LP     E2LINE  D.RATIO  SHORT RANGE HEDGE  TIME FENCES  BACKLOG  LONG RANGE HEDGE  LAST REVIEW
                                         35%     45%   50%   55%   00 03 16 00     2       %     %     %       417
SEQ 0580        -APR/--------MAY--------/--------JUN----/--------JUL--------/--------AUG----/--------SEP----/--------OCT
          ADJ. 181 186 191 196 201 206 211 216 221 226 231 236 241 246 251 256 261 266 271 276 281 286 291 296 301 306
PLANNED                1/               1       1   1               1   1   /           1   1               1
HEDGE                   /                   1           1       1           /
M/S                    1/               1   1   1   1   1       1   1   1   /           1   1               1
COMMITTED              1/                                                   /

                --------/--------NOV----/--------DEC----/--------JAN--------/--------FEB----/--------MAR----/--------APR
               311 316 321 326 331 336 341 346 351 356 361 366 371 376 381 386 391 396 401 406 411 416 421 426 431 436
PLANNED              1   1           1           1       1       1       1   1       1           1       1   1       1
HEDGE                                    1
M/S                  1   1           1   1       1       1       1       1   1       1           1       1   1       1
COMMITTED

                --------/--------MAY----/--------JUN----/--------JUL--------/--------AUG----/--------SEP----/--------OCT
               441 446 451 456 461 466 471 476 481 486 491 496 501 506 511 516 521 526 531 536 541 546 551 556 561 566
PLANNED          1           1       1       1   1   1       1   1   1       1       1   1       1   1   1       1
HEDGE
M/S              1           1       1       1   1   1       1   1   1       1       1   1       1   1   1       1

                --------/--------NOV----/--------DEC--------/--------JAN----/--------FEB----/--------MAR--------/-------
               571 576 581 586 591 596 601 606 611 616 621 626 631 636 641 646 651 656 661 666 671 676 681 686 691 696
PLANNED          1   1   1       1       1       1       1       1   1   1       1       1       1       1       1
HEDGE
M/S              1   1   1       1       1       1       1       1   1   1       1       1       1       1       1
```

Source: W. L. Berry, T. E. Vollmann, and D. C. Whybark, *Master Production Scheduling: Principles and Practice* (Falls Church, Va.: American Production and Inventory Control Society, 1979), p. 166–67.

fences identified on the records for the gas and LP parts. These time fences are defined to indicate the time frames in which management wants flexibility. For the basic parts, the fence set at manufacturing day 276 is a *volume hedge* fence. Its purpose is to provide flexibility to accommodate an increase in overall demand for the E2 family. The fence for the gas and LP engines provides the flexibility for adapting to *mix* changes, which occur between these two options.

The hedge concept is applied as illustrated in Figure 10.11. For example, in the basic parts, the hedge unit indicated in period 276 has just crossed the time fence and the master scheduler will move it out unless a management decision is made to increase the volume for the E2 family to include the hedge quantity. The fences for the options indicate the flexibility range for product mix changes. The number of gas and LP options within the time fences exceeds the basic parts that are scheduled. This provides flexibility to adjust to day-to-day swings in the demand for product options without having too large amounts of inventory.

The hedge units are managed explicitly, which means that the amount of flexibility is highly visible and reviewed continually. A great deal of computer information on time fences, hedge percentages, and current status is available to the master production scheduler to assist in the management of the hedges. An important concept is to provide the flexibility in volume and product mix only where necessary. This is noted by the fact that no hedge units are provided prior to manufacturing day 211. There is no need to provide flexibility before that time, since all available machines and options are covered by customer orders.

With all the formality of this system and the support that it provides the planners, there is still a major element of management discipline that makes this system work. On asking Doug Hoelscher, director of manufacturing at the time these reports were gathered, what would happen if a salesperson tried to promise delivery of an E2 prior to week 211, his response was: "We'd fire the person."

The discipline at Tennant runs through to manufacturing, as well. Under the new responsibilities created by formal systems, the manufacturing mandate is to produce the scheduled products. In the event that no customer order is available for an item that is approaching final assembly, management will release a stock commitment for that item. If no customer order is received by the time the item goes to final assembly, it is produced in an easily retrofitted model and goes into inventory. This inventory is owned by *the top-management committee* of Tennant. Top management feels that the commitment to meeting the plans, be they in manufacturing or marketing, is important enough that *they* will own any finished goods that are unsold. They recognize that, if marketing is to meet the sales plan, any currently unsold machines will be sold in the future.

Make-to-order products at Elliott Company, Division of Carrier Corporation

The Jeanette, Pennsylvania, plant of the Elliott Company manufactures large air and gas compressors and steam turbine devices. The products are highly engineered, using state-of-the-art manufacturing techniques and materials. The engineered apparatus products are designed and built to customer specifications, to accomplish a specific function. The products typically weigh 50 tons and take a year or more to produce. More than half of this lead time is made up of order processing, design engineering, and purchasing.

The scheduling of each customer order is based upon the assignment of an imaginary (planning) bill of materials to each major piece of equipment. This bill is established by using elements of previously built products that are similar to the product on the customer order. This imaginary bill of materials is then processed by standard MRP logic. The lead times to produce the components on the imaginary bill of materials include estimated times to perform the engineering design and do the necessary drafting, in addition to the manufacturing lead times. The result is a proper ordering of when each component should be designed, the priorities for all customer orders relative to the due dates, and a capacity requirement profile for each work center. The capacity profiles are produced for engineering and drafting work centers on a routine basis. Figure 10.17 is one of the imaginary bills of material.

Figure 10.18 is part of an exception report showing behind-schedule project activities. For example, the first item on the list is nine weeks behind schedule, has project engineer A in charge, and is presently in engineering department H3P. The report is printed in order of those jobs in the worst status. Elliott uses shop-floor control and other MPC system modules to plan and control each customer order during the several months each is in progress. In two years of using these systems, performance against customer promise dates improved by 50 percent; inventory levels were reduced by 23 percent; and meanwhile, there was a 32 percent increase in sales volume. The advantages were achieved by better planning and control of *all* aspects of the business, from order entry through engineering, to the shop floor. Both hard and soft activities are planned/controlled, with the MPC-based systems for project management.

CONCLUDING PRINCIPLES

This chapter has focused on the integrative nature of demand management. It is necessary to capture all sources of demand, to maintain a proper demand management data base, and to carefully integrate demand management both with production planning and with the detailed MPS decision

FIGURE 10.17 Imaginary bill of materials for Elliott Company

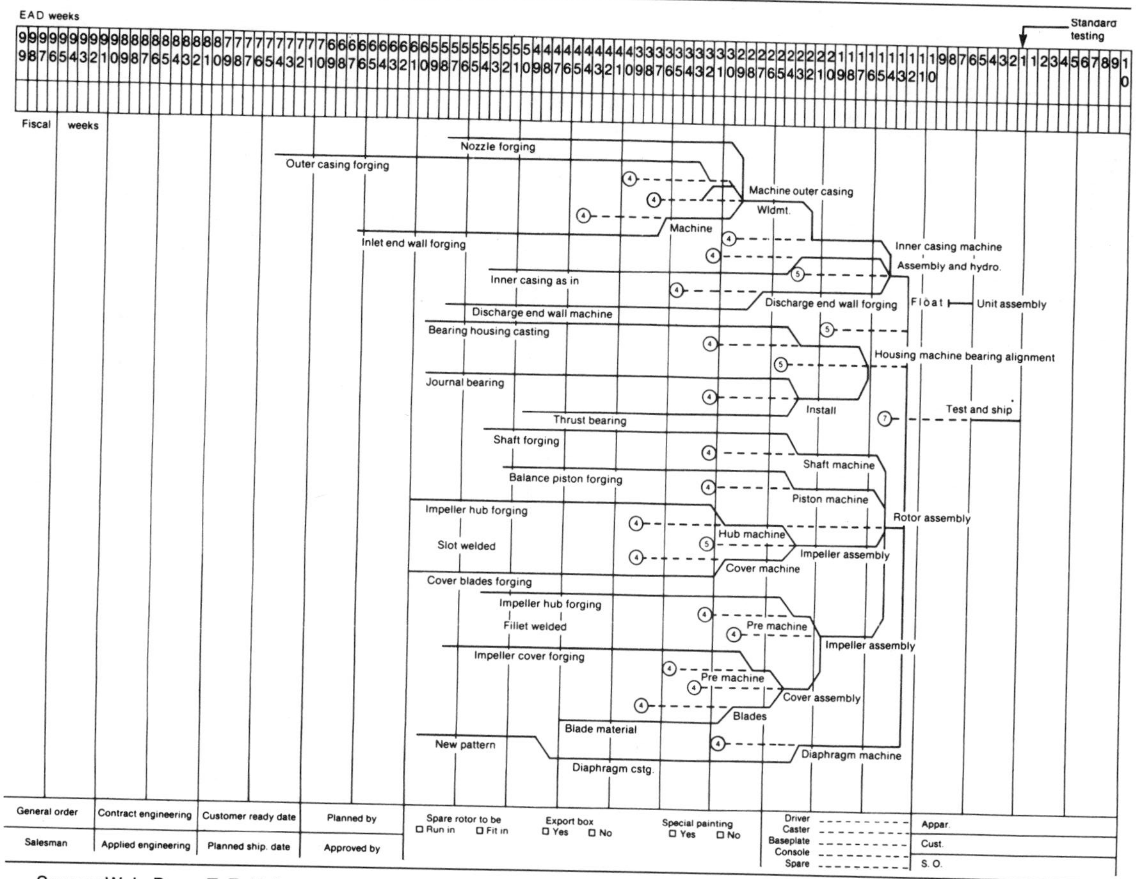

Source: W. L. Berry, T. E. Vollmann, and D. C. Whybark, *Master Production Scheduling: Principles and Practice* (Falls Church, Va.: American Production and Inventory Control Society, 1979), p. 124.

437

FIGURE 10.18   Late project status report for Elliott Company

Report no. ELCH08391

Engineered apparatus project engineering records scheduled for action

Shop order	Description	Quantity	Rel. no.	Project engineer	EAC Project engineering schedule	Project engineer prom.	Status (weeks)
A528156000	Piping Agreement	1.0	H3P	A	356	446	−9
A528157000	Piping Agreement	1.0	H3P	A	376	446	−7
A628502000	Purchase Response	1.0	P3		326	386	−6
A628503000	Purchase Response		P3		326	386	−6
A628505000	Coupling	1.0	S5	V	326	386	−6
A528196000	Major Components	1.0	S5	A	466	516	−5
A628505000	Release of S2	1.0	S3	V	336	386	−5
A528164000	Coupling	1.0	S2T		356	386	−3
	Coupling	1.0	S2T		356	386	−3
A528187000	Oil Schematic	1.0	M1P	A	356	386	−3
	Piping Agreement	1.0	H3P	A	416	446	−3
V025094000	Pipe Agreement	1.0	M3P	O	376	406	−3
A528175000	Piping Agreement	1.0	H3P	A	366	386	−2
A528027000	Place Pr	1.0	S2		376	385	−1
A528043000	Purch Response	1.0	P2P		376	386	−1
	Major Components	1.0	S5	N	376	386	−1
A528131000	Lube Information	1.0	SAP		376	386	−1
	Firm Incomplete	1.0	S1A		376	386	−1
A528142000	Purchase Response	1.0	P3		376	386	−1

Source: W. L. Berry, T. E. Vollmann, and D. C. Whybark, *Master Production Scheduling: Principles and Practice* (Falls Church, Va.: American Production and Inventory Control Society, 1979), p. 125.

making. We see the following key principles as important to accomplishing these objectives:

- MPC systems must take into account *all* sources of demand, properly identified as to time, quantity, location, and source.
- Order promising must be done using available-to-promise concepts.
- Customer-service standards must be developed and maintained.
- The management of outbound product flows must be coordinated through the master production schedule.
- Attaining more accurate forecasts may be an impossible dream. Management attention should be focused on the system to provide appropriate responses to actual conditions and forecast errors.
- The wide variety of demand forecasts prepared by an organization should be so coordinated that top-management business plans and objectives are, in fact, reflected in the detailed forecasts.
- Flexibility must be explicitly planned into the system.
- To provide helpful stability in the factory, demand management and MPS activities need to be closely coordinated.

- Intelligent customer promises should be the rule of the day, rather than wishful thinking.
- Clear definitions of authority and responsibility for demand management activities must be made to obtain the attendant benefits.

REFERENCES

American Production and Inventory Control Society. *Interfaces Seminar Proceedings*, March 1980.

Berry, W. L.; T. E. Vollmann; and D. C. Whybark. *Master Production Scheduling—Principles and Practice.* Falls Church, Va.: *American Production and Inventory Control Society*, 1979.

Borgendale, Mac, "Spare Parts: Deciding What to Stock at Each Location" *APICS Service Parts Seminar Proceedings*, Las Vegas, April 1981, pp. 1–4.

Christopher, Martin. "Creating Effective Policies for Customer Service." *International Journal of Physical Distribution and Materials Management* 13, no. 2 (a special edition of the journal devoted to customer service), 1983.

Haskins, Robert E. "Demand Management by Exception (Not by Exception Report)." *Inventories and Production Magazine*, July–August 1981.

Kuehne, W. A., and P. Leach. "A Sales Forecasting Pyramid for Dow Corning's Planning Endeavors." *Production and Inventory Management Review*, August 1984, pp. 6–11.

Ling, Richard C. "Demand Management: Let's Put More Emphasis on This Term." *26th Annual Conference Proceedings*, American Production and Inventory Control Society, 1983, pp. 11–12.

Martin, Andre. "DRP: Another Resource Planning System." *Production and Inventory Management Review*, December 1982.

———. *DRP: Distribution Resource Planning.* Essex Junction, Vt.: Oliver Wight Limited Publications, 1983.

Perry, W. "The Principles of Distribution Resource Planning (DRP)." *Production and Inventory Management*, December 1982.

Shycon, H. N., and C. R. Sprague. "Put a Price Tag on Your Customer Service." *Harvard Business Review*, July–August 1975.

Tucker, Frances G. "Creative Customer Service Management." *International Journal of Physical Distribution and Materials Management* 13, no. 3, 1983.

DISCUSSION QUESTIONS

1. Discuss the statement, "Demand management is the customer's handle on our business."
2. What is implied by the frozen, slushy, and liquid areas of Figure 10.2?
3. In lower levels of the pyramid forecasting system, how does one prevent abdication of responsibility for forecasting?

4. Can a grocery store capture "demand"data? How would a warehouse capture demand data?

5. Which do you have more confidence in, a forecast of the number of hours that you will have accumulated by the time you graduate or the specific courses that you will have taken? In general, what principle does this illustrate?

6. Describe the relationship between the BOM and the percentage forecasting illustrated in Figure 10.8.

7. How can both stability *and* flexibility be incorporated in the MPS?

8. What part of the organization might have responsibility for demand management in a steel mill, industrial products firm, or children's toy manufacturing firm?

9. How can judgment be incorporated into the demand-management forecasting activity?

PROBLEMS

1. The Tarmack and Pothole Company has capacity to produce 50 potholes per week. The firm currently has booked orders as follows:

Week	Orders
1	43
2	51
3	32
4	21
5	24
6	10
7	7
8	5
9	0
10	2
11+	0

   a. Plot the booked orders against capacity.
   b. Assume the following transactions. In week 1, 45 potholes were shipped. Orders for two potholes were canceled in weeks 2 and 5. Additional orders were booked for 5 in week 2, 20 in week 3, 10 in week 4, 5 in week 6, 4 in week 7, 2 in week 9, and 1 in week 11. What does the plot look like as of week 2?
   c. What problems do you foresee?

2. Five individual products in a product family have identical sales patterns. They each average 100 units per month, with a standard deviation of 10 units. Assuming normal distributions and independent demands:
   a. What is the yearly sales distribution of each product?
   b. What is the monthly sales distribution for all products together?
   c. What is the yearly sales distribution for all products together?

d. Using plus or minus three standard deviations for the values obtained in questions **a, b,** and **c,** compare your results to those of Polysar International in Figure 10.4.

3. Hortense Frobisher has attempted to improve customer delivery performance for the Deluxe Duplicator Company. In her latest effort, she has looked at applying the available-to-promise logic to the most profitable product—the Destructo Deluxe. The sales forecast is for 40 units per week for the next 5 weeks. Hortense will use this time period for her analysis. There are no units on hand, and 87 units are in the master schedule for the upcoming week, and 80 more are in week 3.

    a. If the actual customer orders booked for delivery are 62 for week 1 (past due and week 1 combined), 33 for week 2, and 28 for week 3, can she book an order for 10 units in week 2? Week 3?

    b. What actions should she take?

4. A master production scheduler manages product 1 that has a current inventory of 120 units, a forecast of 50 units per period, a lead time of two periods, no safety stock, and a lot-sizing rule that orders two periods of requirements at a time. Management has said it would like the flexibility to be able to respond to an increase in demand of one unit in six weeks (i.e., in period 7). A second item (part 2) is used to manufacture product 1 at the rate of two units of #2 per single unit of product 1. For product 2, there is no safety stock, no inventory, the lot sizing is lot-for-lot, there is a scheduled receipt of 200 due in the current period, and the lead time is two periods.

    a. Prepare the MRP records for product 1 and product 2 covering the next seven periods. Be sure to indicate how you would respond to management's request for flexibility.

    b. What would the record look like at the start of the second period if demand is exactly 50 in the first period, any planned shipments or orders for period 1 are released, and management wants to increase output by one unit in week 7?

    c. What would the records look like in the second period if management said there was no need to increase output by one unit in week 7 (but did want to maintain the flexibility to increase by one unit in 6 weeks), demand equaled 50, and planned shipments or orders for period 1 are released?

A.

Product 1	1	2	3	4	5	6	7
Forecast							
Scheduled receipts							
Projected available balance							
Planned shipments							

Q = 2 periods supply; LT = 2; SS = 0.

Part 2	1	2	3	4	5	6	7
Gross requirements							
Scheduled receipts							
Projected available balance							
Planned order releases							

Q = lot-for-lot; LT = 2; SS = 0.

B.

Product 1	2	3	4	5	6	7	8
Forecast							
Scheduled receipts							
Projected available balance							
Planned shipments							

Q = 2 periods supply; LT = 2; SS = 0.

Part 2	2	3	4	5	6	7	8
Gross requirements							
Scheduled receipts							
Projected available balance							
Planned order releases							

Q = lot-for-lot; LT = 2; SS = 0.

C.

Product 1	2	3	4	5	6	7	8
Forecast							
Scheduled receipts							
Projected available balance							
Planned shipments							

Q = 2 periods supply; LT = 2; SS = 0.

Part 2

	2	3	4	5	6	7	8
Gross requirements							
Scheduled receipts							
Projected available balance							
Planned order releases							

Q = lot-for-lot; LT = 2; SS = 0.

5. What are the weekly forecasts by distribution center (DC) if the monthly total forecast is 750 units; and the DC percentages of sales are 30, 20, and 50, for DCs A, B, and C, respectively? Assume a four-week month and then recalculate with a five-week month.

6. Suppose the forecast for a particular DC is 20 units per week in one month and 40 per week the next. What recommendations would you make about displaying the forecast in the last week of the first month and the first week of the second month?

7. Frank Stewart operates a series of pharmaceutical warehouses in the state of Arkansas that are served from his central distribution center in Little Rock. Three of the warehouses are located in Pine Bluff, Texarkana, and Fort Smith. Over the last few years, the concentration on service and the increasing number of products that were carried in the line had swelled inventories at the warehouses and distribution center to the point where efficiency and profitability had dropped substantially. It was important for Frank to develop good forecasts of the weekly demand at each of his locations to provide better plans for managing the inventories and staffing the warehouses.

   For the past few weeks, Frank had been keeping detailed records of the demand for two of his products. One of these products is a burn ointment, which had nearly constant demand each week across the state, although there was some variation from warehouse to warehouse, as the nature and number of customers served by the warehouses shifted. The second product is a vitamin tablet that is sold on promotion to many drug stores and has very high seasonal demand peaks during the two times a year when the product is heavily promoted. The information that Frank collected for each of the products at each of the three warehouses is shown in Exhibit A.

   Frank had discussed the forecasting problem with the salesmen and had requested that they develop forecasts by week for each warehouse for each product. After having made an attempt to do this, the salesmen found it difficult, and the forecast errors that resulted were too large for Frank. Even though Frank needed weekly forecasts by item at each warehouse, this involved too great a level of detail for the salesmen. On the other hand, the sales staff had been doing a reasonably good job of forecasting the total demand for each product from all warehouses. They were able to include such influences as the special promotion for the vitamin tablet. These forecasts covered a four-week accounting period (the company's "month") and served as the basis for developing the marketing effort, setting the sales quotas, and submitting the sales budget.

EXHIBIT A   Past demand for two products at all three warehouses for Frank's
Pharmaceuticals

	Burn ointment				Vitamin tablet			
	Warehouse				Warehouse			
Week	FS*	T*	PB*	Total	FS*	T*	PB*	Total
1	20	15	12	47	8	4	2	14
2	18	17	11	46	12	7	0	19
3	22	14	10	46	10	8	5	23
4	23	14	8	45	9	4	1	14
5	19	16	11	46	11	2	3	16

*FS = Fort Smith; T = Texarkana; PB = Pine Bluff.

Frank agreed that the accuracy was much better for the monthly aggregated forecasts than for the attempts at forecasting at the item level.

Frank studied the data on the past five weeks' demand for each of the two products for each of the warehouses (shown in Exhibit A) and considered how he could reconcile his need for detailed forecasts of each product's demand by week at each warehouse, with the forecasts of monthly demand for all of Arkansas provided by the sales staff. The disparity between their projections and his needs is dramatized by the sales staff's forecasts for the next four weeks (weeks 6, 7, 8, and 9). The forecast of demand for the burn ointment is 180 units during the next four weeks, and for the vitamin tablet the demand projection is for 200 units during the next four weeks.

a. Determine how Frank can use the marketing information to make his weekly forecasts at each warehouse, and how he should modify the forecasts as information on actual demand becomes available.

b. The information on the actual demand for week 6 has just been received for the two products at each of the warehouses. This information is summarized in Exhibit B. In addition to this data, marketing has just told Frank that they felt that their projections for the four-week period were still valid for each of the two products. How should this information be incorporated in his forecasts?

EXHIBIT B   Actual demand for week 6 for Frank's Pharmaceuticals

		Burn ointment			Vitamin tablet		
		FS	T	PB	FS	T	PB
	Demand	20	17	9	27	12	4

8. The general sales manager at Knox Products Corporation has just received next year's sales forecast (in units) for two of the firm's major products (Bad and Worse) from the sales managers of the Eastern and Western sales regions:

Eastern region forecast		Western region forecast	
Bad	*Worse*	*Bad*	*Worse*
100	200	200	300

Bad sells for $1 per unit and Worse sells for $2 per unit.

a. The corporate economist has forecast a total corporate-wide sales volume for these two products of $2,000 for next year. What is the disparity between the two forecasts at the *item* level?

b. If top management agrees to a total corporate-wide sales forecast volume of $1,500, what is the sales forecast at the *item* level?

9. Imogene Imaginary has created the following planning bill, based on similar products from the past. Parts A, C, and E have had all engineering completed, and parts B and D have just been estimated.

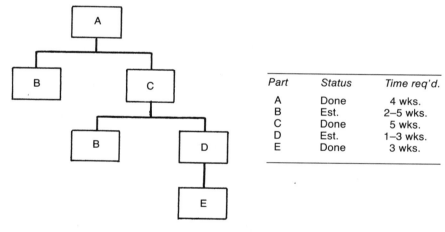

Part	Status	Time req'd.
A	Done	4 wks.
B	Est.	2–5 wks.
C	Done	5 wks.
D	Est.	1–3 wks.
E	Done	3 wks.

a. What would be the delivery time if B could be done in two weeks and D in one week?

b. What would it be if B would take five weeks and D could be done in one week?

c. Which part would you want to watch most closely? Why?

10. Use a spreadsheet to create a DRP warehouse record for a product that has forecast demand of 20 units a period for the first three periods, 25 for period four, and 30 for the next three periods. The shipping quantity is 50 units and the lead time is one period. There are 46 units in inventory. What is the average inventory balance per period if six units of safety stock are used?

11. Using the data in problem **10**, what would it be if one period of safety lead time were used instead of safety stock?

12. The Gonzales Electric Company makes 12 products, which are further grouped into four product families. Products A, B, and C comprise family 1; D, E, and F comprise family 2; G, H, and I comprise family 3; and products J, K, and L make up family 4. Dick Gonzales has the following exponential smoothing forecasts of monthly demand for each product.

Product	Forecast	$/unit
A	10	1,000
B	15	1,200
C	20	900
D	5	5,000
E	3	7,000
F	2	9,000
G	100	250
H	180	100
I	220	100
J	2	10,000
K	4	9,000
L	3	8,000

The salesmen at Gonzales have also come up with the monthly forecasts of sales for each product family.

Family	$ sales
1	50,000
2	50,000
3	75,000
4	75,000

a. Top management has independently set an overall monthly sales goal for the company of $300,000. Roll up the individual product forecasts and compare them with the family data. Use a spreadsheet and the family forecasts to revise the individual item forecasts (in both dollars and units).

b. Roll up the family forecasts to the top level, compare these to the overall forecasts, and roll the forecasts back down to families and to individual unit forecasts (dollars and units).

13. Suppose that in a top-management meeting a decision is reached that the family forecast for product family 3 (products G, H, and I) in problem **12** cannot be increased. At the same meeting, the overall forecast for the company ($300,000) is maintained. Roll the forecasts up and down to determine the dollar and unit forecasts.

14. Suppose that the family forecast data in problem **12** are assumed to be correct, except in any case where the sum of the exponential smoothing forecast data for items exceeds the family forecast. Roll up the resultant overall forecast and roll down the resultant item forecasts.

15. Using the data in problem **12**, suppose that a major customer order has just been received for 10 units of product J. This order was not expected and is in addition to any other forecasts for product J. The company still wants to plan a total monthly sales volume of $300,000. Roll the forecasts up and down to obtain revised individual product forecasts.

11

Implementation of MPC systems

This chapter is devoted to the issue of implementing an effective manufacturing planning and control system. The focus is almost exclusively managerial, since that is where the ultimate responsibility lies. This chapter raises some fundamental issues involving organization, management, procedures, and resources. Addressing these issues is critical to implementing a truly effective MPC system, and doing so on a timely basis with realized results at each step in the process.

The chapter is organized around the following six topics:

- Assessing the situation: How does a firm rigorously determine the magnitude and appropriate direction for the implementation effort?
- Management of and by the data base: Why is management of an integrated data base a critical prerequisite to success?
- Organizational implications: What are the organizational changes needed for implementing a truly effective system?
- Plan of attack: How should the detailed implementation plan be established and managed?
- Education: How should the required educational effort be defined and executed?
- Auditing: Why is periodic auditing of the system essential at

any stage of development? Why is it a general management responsibility?

Elements of implementation issues are raised in virtually every preceding chapter, as the various manufacturing planning and control system modules are discussed. In particular, Chapter 1 discusses differing environments for MPC systems, and Chapter 3 discusses issues of data integrity which are important to successful implementation.

ASSESSING THE SITUATION

In this section, we are interested in developing yardsticks by which the effectiveness of any MPC system can be measured. This is a first step in defining what needs to be done. The second involves developing a sense of the needs of the organization by evaluating the environment in which the system must function and the first areas for improvement. Before turning to some examples, we also want to raise a third issue. This is an evolutionary point of view toward the MPC implementation process.

Establishing the yardstick of performance

Clearly, the model to which we feel a company should be moving is our general MPC schematic, now presented as Figure 11.1. A first step in establishing the current position of the company is to determine how well each of these modules is performed. The first test is one of completeness. Are there any gaps in the current MPC system or is performance so poor in any activity that it might just as well not exist?

A well-known way of assessing MPC system performance was developed by Oliver Wight, who was one of the best known MPC educators. He addressed the implementation issue by defining MRP-based companies as falling into one of the following four categories:

A *Class A* MRP user is one that uses MRP in a closed loop mode. They have material requirements planning, capacity planning and control, shop-floor dispatching, and vendor scheduling systems in place and being used; and management uses the system to run the business. They participate in production planning. They sign off on the production plans. They constantly monitor performance on inventory record accuracy, bill of material accuracy, routing accuracy, attainment of the master schedule, attainment of the capacity plans, etc.

In a Class A company, the MRP system provides the game plan that sales, finance, manufacturing, purchasing, and engineering people all work to. They *use* the formal system. The foremen and the purchasing people work to the schedules. There is no shortage list to override the schedules and answer the

FIGURE 11.1   Manufacturing planning and control system

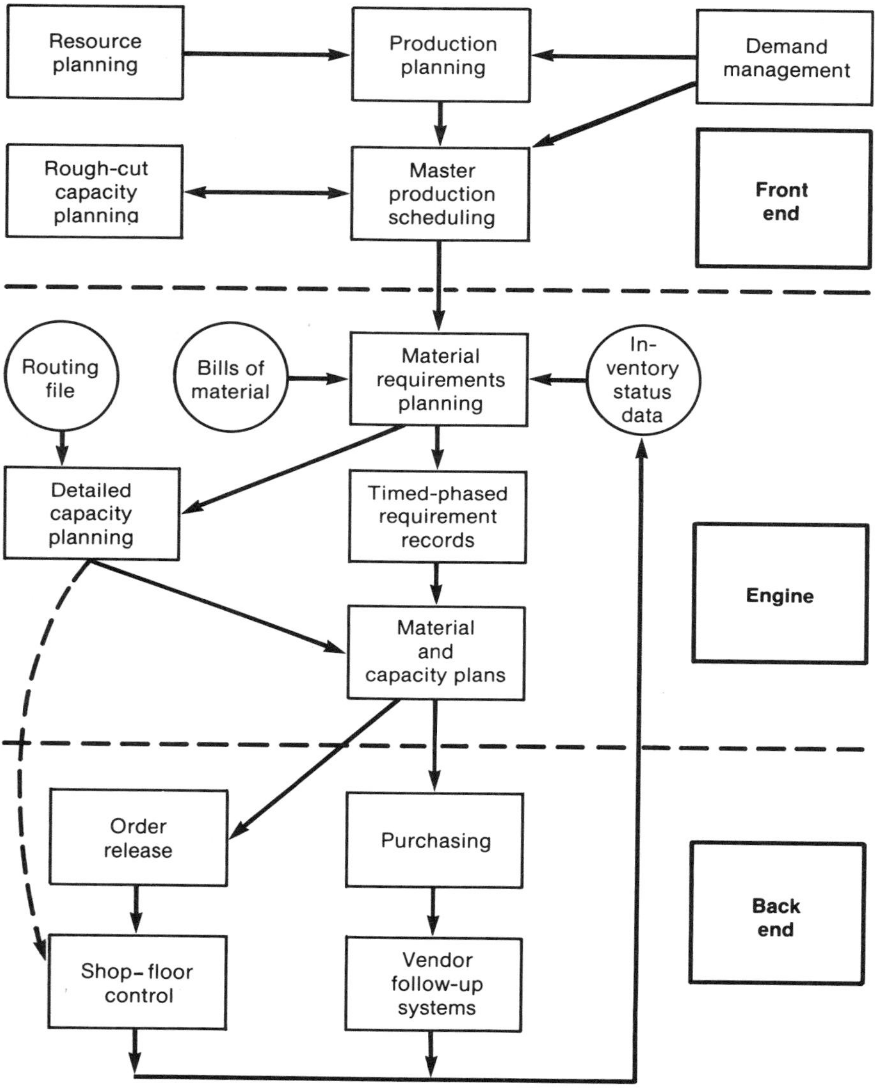

question. What material is really needed when?—that answer comes from the formal MRP system.

Companies using MRP II have gone even a step beyond Class A. They have tied in the financial system and developed simulation capabilities so that the "what-if" questions can be answered using the system. In this type of company, management can work with one set of numbers to run the business, because the operating system and the financial system use the same numbers.

Technically then an MRP II system has the financial and operating systems married together and has a simulation capability. But the important point is that the system is used as a company game plan. This is what really makes a company Class A.

A *Class B* company has material requirements planning and usually capacity requirements planning and shop-floor control systems in place. The Class B user typically hasn't done much with purchasing yet and differs from the Class A user primarily because top management doesn't really use the system to run the business directly. Instead, Class B users see MRP as a production and inventory control system. Because of this, it's easy for a Class B user to become a Class C user very quickly. Another characteristic of the Class B company is that they do *some* scheduling in the shop using MRP, but their shortage list is what really tells them what to make. Class B users typically see most of their benefits from MRP in inventory reduction and improved customer service because they do have more of the right things going through production. Because they haven't succeeded in getting the expediting "monkey" off the backs of the purchasing people and foremen, they haven't seen substantial benefits in reduced purchase costs or improved productivity—and they still have more inventory than they really need.

A *Class C* company uses MRP primarily as an inventory ordering technique, rather than as a scheduling technique. Shop scheduling is still being done from the shortage list, and the master schedule in a Class C company is typically overstated. They have not really closed the loop. They probably will get some benefits in inventory reduction as a result of MRP.

A *Class D* company only has MRP really working in the data processing department. Typically, their inventory records are poor. If they have a defined master schedule, it's usually grossly overstated and mismanaged, and little or no results have come from the installation of the MRP system. Ironically, except for the education costs, a Class D company will have spent almost as much as a Class A company. They will have spent about 80 percent of the total, but not achieved the results.

What is described here as MRP II implies a complete MPC system model, as shown in Figure 11.1, including integration with marketing and financial systems. The MRP in this case means Manufacturing Resource Planning, instead of Material Requirements Planning. The evaluation scheme is interesting, and over the years has been applied to some research efforts. It is also widely referenced by professionals in the field. We will use it in this chapter as one of two yardsticks to judge implementation efforts.

The MPC model in Figure 11.1 is based upon a computer-supported, integrated data base. This model is generally understood by MPC professionals, computer software exists to support this model, and it represents an overall system objective. Furthermore, the MPC model presents a useful way to divide the overall system objective into subsystem projects. The critical implementation question is which projects to take on, and in what order.

The company environment

To some extent, all companies tend to consider themselves as unique—often to the detriment of system implementation. However, there are indeed aspects of each company's situation that make some system modules more appropriate than others for implementation emphasis.

The firm that manufactures many components through complex fabrication steps will want to put in place a shop-floor control system to carefully monitor and manage the progress of the orders. On the other hand, the firm that purchases a large percentage of its components for assembly will be more interested in systems to support purchasing.

A company that has very expensive machine tools in a job-shop environment may be more concerned with capacity planning and control than is the firm that utilizes simple bench-assembly methods. Similarly, a company that has a complex flow of final assembly may be very anxious to establish a level flow of work through these operations.

Many times, the make-to-stock firm will concentrate its original systems effort on distribution and inventories of finished goods. The make-to-order firm that produces complex items in unique designs may require a sophisticated system for the management of customer orders—from quotation through design, to manufacture and shipping. The assemble-to-order firm typically requires a significant effort to create planning bills of material, as well as order-promising logic.

A different sort of environmental consideration is the organization climate and receptiveness to the implementation of various systems. We have seen firms where the achievement of accurate shop-floor reporting is not difficult, and others where such conditions as incentive wage systems virtually preclude the accurate reporting of actual production or shop-floor conditions on a timely basis.

At a more fundamental level, but still a key environmental issue, is the extent of managerial identification with improved systems for materials flow. We list management commitment as a key implementation success variable. Has management recognized the need? Do they have the appropriate *total* level of commitment?

Each of these issues, from the manufacturing process to the management attitudes, are basic elements of the assessment process. They must be honestly addressed if appropriate implementation priorities and resources are to be developed.

An evolutionary point of view

In many instances, the assessment of the company environment will lead to pessimistic conclusions. What can be done in this case? Is the only resort to roll over and play dead? This issue always comes up at the educational seminars we hold. One participant summed up his feelings as: "This is all well and good, and I really see how these systems could do marvelous things for my company. But next week I will return to my job and within hours I will have out my gun and knife, shooting and stabbing as usual."

Our response is that the only way to eat an elephant is one bite at a time, and it doesn't make a great deal of difference if one starts at the tail or the trunk. The key is to critically assess where your company is, and where it would like to be. (Class A in the long run!) Who are you, and what authority and resources do you control? What confederations can you make that will yield results? Where can you take a bite of the elephant that will yield clear-cut results that can be used to widen the commitment? What parts of the elephant should be avoided now because success will be too long in coming?

What all of this means is that, although our general model for MPC systems applies to every firm, and the ultimate goal is Class A status, the emphasis given at any point in time must be assessed on an individual company basis. George Bevis is often quoted for his remark that "MRP is a journey not a destination." There are many ways to drive from New York to California, but the key is always to safely reach some intermediate destination. Let us briefly illustrate these points with two examples.

The Ethan Allen implementation

At a very early stage, the newly appointed assistant vice president of manufacturing at the Ethan Allen Furniture Company saw the clear need to better plan and control production in a widely decentralized set of manufacturing plants. The assessment of where they were at the time versus where they wanted to be revealed a vast need for change. An example of the gap is provided by the product structure data base. Not only did the company not have a computerized bill of materials, it did not even have part drawings! Products were made by launching an end item in terms of rough sizes for wooden pieces, finding a sample piece hanging on a nail somewhere, and making more like it. Tolerances were expressed as: "Machine to fit."

There was no uniformity of building techniques among the factories, and each plant had completely different names for parts as well as ways to make them. It was clear that the company needed to construct a product structure data base, but, when it was considered at the time, management was convinced that this effort could not succeed. The effort was too massive for the very limited resources available, it would be far too long before results would be seen on the bottom line, and the effort would be the first to be set aside for fire fighting or for any cost reduction that was mandated.

The area selected for implementation first was master production scheduling (MPS), and the original effort was confined to only one factory. When this factory could be scheduled in a way that was clearly superior to past practices, word spread throughout the other factories and the plant managers were clamoring to use the new system. Once the MPS system was in use, the need for shop-floor control systems to move parts in sequence with assembly dictates was clear—these systems were put in with minimal effort. Thereafter, the need for data accuracy was keenly felt, so locked storeroom concepts began to be applied. And so it went. Interestingly, this natural evolution eventually came to the product structure data base, the need for standardization of methods and parts, and a consistent cost-accounting system. The journey has taken 15 years and is still not over.

The Black & Decker journey

The Black & Decker systems for controlling material flows have been widely publicized throughout the world. Their MRP system is always included on the list of Class A companies. However, to assume that they have arrived, or that no significant improvement potential exists, or that they cannot make mistakes, is just not correct. In fact, several years ago the company took the actions necessary to free up some of the key people originally responsible for MRP, with the open-ended assignment to look for new improvement potential. They selected engineering as the area, focusing on how to design and group parts for manufacture so as to substantially reduce setup times. They also worked on alterations planning, a technique to assess the capacity impact of proposed changes. Moreover, in a seminar at Indiana University on state-of-the-art MPS systems, it seemed clear that Black & Decker could profit by applying the distribution requirements planning concepts developed by Abbott Laboratories.

Black & Decker has gone on to just-in-time (JIT) systems for many of its factories. In the early 1980s, the firm bought the small appliance businesses from General Electric and integrated them into the overall Black & Decker manufacturing and materials organization. Many of the factories, including the main plant at Hampstead, Maryland, have JIT systems in place. The results have been some inventory turnover rates increasing by 500 percent, significant lead time reductions, faster response to the market place, and reductions in the indirect labor costs (the "hidden factory") to support MPC systems.

Advances in MPC technology

It is important to understand that there is continual advancement in MPC systems, and the results impact both the payoffs that are possible and the implementation approach. In addition to the entire JIT set of systems and approaches, there has been important evolution in the basic MPC computer systems to support the MPC system described in Figure 11.1. The key change has been the development and decreasing cost of on-line systems for

MRP-based operations. On-line systems are important for several reasons. First, the typical MRP system is based on weekly time buckets and a weekly cycle of using the system; for example, run over the weekend, analyze reports on Monday and Tuesday, release orders on Tuesday and Wednesday, update records and data on Thursday and Friday, so the system can be run again over the weekend.

In an on-line environment, many firms in essence achieve a *daily* cycle for using the system. This means that, every day, records are reviewed, orders launched, and data bases updated. One firm tries to issue all orders by 10 A.M. so they can be physically picked from inventory the same day. This approach means that lead times can be significantly reduced. In traditional systems, one week of lead time is usually required for each level in the bill of materials, purely to get the components into inventory, recognize them as available, launch orders for the parent item, pick the components, and move them to the beginning work center. In an on-line environment, this time can be cut to one day. This means, for a product with ten levels in the bill of materials, the total lead time devoted to planning can be cut from ten weeks to two weeks!

An on-line system also helps a great deal in data base integrity. As transactions are input to an on-line system, all of the cross checks for validity of the transaction can be done in real time. This will greatly enhance the data base accuracy and reduce after-the-fact cleanup efforts. This ability has an important impact on implementation, in that the levels of required accuracy *may* be somewhat less. This is *not* meant to be an endorsement of sloppy data base management. However, there is always the implementation issue of when to cut over to the new system and root out the remaining errors with it, rather than root them out prior to conversion. On-line systems favor an earlier cutover, because, for some kinds of problems, they facilitate the data cleanup process.

Another issue with on-line systems is their decreasing cost. A Rhode Island firm found that purchasing a dedicated computer system, with 30 terminals, 15 printers, and state-of-the-art software, would cost about $400,000. The firm was presently paying about twice this much per year for computer costs alone to run an antiquated batch system. The costs for stand alone computer systems continues to fall, and the operation of these systems also gets more and more straightforward. One does not need a staff of computer experts to use the best MPC systems.

MANAGEMENT OF AND BY THE DATA BASE

The achievement of data integrity, the procedural reforms necessary to obtain transaction accuracy, and the necessary changes in job descriptions are critical to success. Virtually every expert states that this aspect of implementation is typically underestimated both in its importance and in the efforts required to attain the required integrity. With poor data integrity, Class D operation is the inevitable best result. In a survey of 326 MRP companies by John Anderson and Roger Schroeder, a strong correlation was found between the degree of record accuracy and the Wight classification scheme. Class A companies have better record accuracy than Class B, which, in turn, have better accuracy performed than Class C, and so on. In this section, we present a checklist of critical data integrity issues.

Data elements

All of the following data elements must be accurate to high levels—more than 90 percent and preferably more than 95 percent —before implementation can be considered successful. The accuracy measure here is an absolute measure, where pluses do not cancel out minuses. A shortage of five part As, each worth $1.00, is not compensated by an overage of ten Bs, each worth $0.50. These are two errors. If the total count was for six parts (A, B, C, D, E, and F), and the last four were accurate, the inventory accuracy measure is $4/6 = 66.7$ percent. Often, in the rush to obtain implementation, a firm may decide to switch over to the new system without achieving desired levels of accuracy in the mistaken view that things will get straightened out. In fact, the result may be just the opposite; the system may become a bad joke, with users scrambling to get information from other sources—a death knell to the implementation project.

- Item Master: Has this critical file been well defined, and have all of the necessary data elements been entered?
- Bill of Materials: Have the product structure records been properly defined for MPC purposes, and have they been checked for accuracy?
- Inventory Records: Does the company have secure storerooms, a cycle counting program, and results that are measured to accuracy levels in excess of 90 percent?
- Routing: Is the set of manufacturing operations for each fabricated part accurate? Has a detailed review been made prior to implementation?
- Open Orders: Does the company have an accurate list of open shop orders, with no tag ends that do not actually exist? Can the quantities be verified by physical count? Can these records be loaded as scheduled receipts in the MRP data base?
- Purchase Orders: Can the tests for open orders be applied to open purchase orders? Is purchase order creation based upon MRP-driven needs? Are purchasing lead times reasonably accurate? Have they been reviewed for MRP lead time offsetting?
- Master Production Schedule: Does the master schedule reflect what is actually being built—on a weekly (or smaller time increment) ba-

sis? Are there any ways that changes to final build schedules can be achieved outside of the formal MPS or FAS (final assembly schedule)?

The above list is not intended to be exhaustive. Clearly, other files, such as locations, rejected materials, vendor master and machine centers, are also required.

Transaction procedures

Hand in hand with accurate initial data is the need to keep the data accurate; that is, data maintenance. It is not enough to get accurate data into the computer once. Tight control over the data elements is required on an ongoing basis. For each data element, some organizational unit or person needs to be assigned the sole responsibility for maintaining the data and making any required changes.

The key to data maintenance is ironclad procedures to control every transaction to the data base. It is imperative that each of the files listed above be maintained so there is no discrepancy between what the file depicts and the actual situation; that is, the system must not lie to the users. To achieve this truth, new procedures are typically required. Some of the most important transaction procedures include:

- Item master maintenance.
- Engineering change (and effectivity dates).
- Cycle counting.
- Inventory adjustments.
- Routing changes (and effectivity dates).
- Order launching—including availability checking and allocation.
- Material and part picking.
- Scrap reporting.
- Rework.
- Receipt tickets and order closeout.
- Receiving, purchase order closeout, returns to vendors, reconciliation, and links to accounts payable.
- Changes, additions, and deletions to the MPS.
- Rejected materials.
- Nonproduction uses of materials.
- Non–bill of material needs for production.
- Order entry, customer due date promising, and changes to open customer orders.

This is a formidable list, and, again, for any particular company there will be other procedures required. The degree of change implied is all too easily underestimated.

Using the system

The final key element in management by a data base and management of a data base is to reemphasize the "by" portion of this dictate. It is absolutely essential that informal systems be supplanted—and kept from reappearing. No handwritten hot lists should be allowed to override the formal system, expediting as a formal job should disappear, and any problem solution which comes at the expense of accurate data is to be avoided at all cost. In short, the system should become the sole basis for decision making, with no other record-keeping systems used. The following dictates are representative of the commitment required:

- Get rid of all kardex or other paper files.
- Don't allow any other set of duplicate records.
- Be sure that only one bill of materials exists.
- Be on constant alert to see whether foremen need black books to run their parts.
- Implement an ongoing audit function.
- Maintain a high level of professional management information system support for the MPC system.
- Expect "the system" to require change and upgrading.
- Insist on an adequate level of system documentation.
- Understand that user education is not a one-time process.

Pitfalls

Figure 11.2 is a list of typical implementation problems that have been observed by James Wagner from the Raytheon Company in his consulting work with many of the decentralized plants in the company. This list is based on implementation of state-of-the-art on-line systems. His observations come from observing the problems that have arisen, and he cautions those implementing new systems to beware of these pitfalls.

The list starts with the purchase of an underpowered computer. Jim's experience is that one almost always needs one more disk drive than the calculations indicate, and that it is intelligent to purchase a computer with more than enough power and disk storage. Related are the next two problems, insufficient terminals and printers. An on-line system will require terminals in many places where they are not currently used, and many of those locations will also need a printer. In some cases, the printer will be largely dedicated to the creation of routine paperwork; in other cases, the printer is used by an analyst so comparisons can be made among different screens of system output.

The next item on Jim Wagner's list is a batch mode mentality. We have

FIGURE 11.2   Typical system implementation problems (Raytheon)

- Computer memory underplanned.
- Disc space underplanned.
- Insufficient number of terminals.
- Insufficient number of slave printers for users.
- Batch mode mentality.
- Modular implementation theory flaws.
- Lack of user involvement:
  —Training.
  —Pilot program with full integration.
- Half staff.
- Different financial, marketing, and manufacturing plans.
- Extended implementation.

seen this problem on many occasions. A frequent example is in purchasing, where the computer system becomes the backup (or nuisance) to the *real* system, which is a set of cards or papers. On-line systems require on-line processing and an on-line mentality. Pencils have no place in this system, and all transactions and documents are updated as they occur, not as someone enters them later into the system.

A modular implementation approach can also lead to problems if it is not done well. The key point is that people can live with dual systems and confusion for a limited length of time. After 60 to 90 days, people just get tired; it is necessary to move completely into the new system environment in that time frame. If it is not possible to do this for the entire firm, then Jim Wagner recommends starting at the shipping dock and implementing systems backwards, moving through the company, but completely phasing into the new systems for each department.

The lack of user involvement and training are often listed as key problems in implementation. Jim Wagner recommends that a pilot program be put together with no more than five or ten parts, and that all people in the firm be trained to do what is needed for these parts. Thereafter, the pilot is to simulate their manufacture, using all the new systems and transactions. It is only after this has been done that the users will clearly see how all parts of the system are linked.

The half-staff concept refers to the often seen situation where only a part of the organization is committed to the implementation plan, with the other part or parts embracing a different plan. This is clearly going to cause confusion in the ranks about which master to serve. Extended implementation is related. It is imperative to get the system in and to get rid of the old ways as quickly as possible.

ORGANIZATIONAL IMPLICATIONS

Implementing a Class A system may well be the largest single change in operations that a company can undertake. The achievement of Class A status requires new levels of discipline, attention to detail, and use of formal systems. With a Class A system, a new level of integration is achieved, so front-end plans and budgets are synchronized with day-to-day detailed decision making. The organizational objective is to make plans that are valid and attainable, and thereafter hold people strictly accountable for achieving these plans.

In company after company we have seen, the first task of the production planning manager is to second guess the sales forecast. Sales personnel resources were consumed in the preparation of the forecast, but no one used it. The budget was produced independently, and production decisions were based on guesses of "real" sales needs. This is a much too common form of management.

In many companies, no one can be held accountable for execution, because the formal plans are simply not used, attainable, or valid. People at the middle-management level ignore the formal plans and execute informal plans, acting in what they think are the best interests of the company. The formal plans call for production of unneeded items, no production of needed items, and sometimes more total production per time period than is possible. In a Class A system, everyone's job is to hit the formally stated schedule. No one is allowed to second guess, and the formal system is always the management plan. No production manager is permitted to say that he or she did not make some item because sales did not need it. The manager's job is always to hit the schedule. This shifts responsibility for preparing a valid schedule squarely to where it belongs.

These suggestions hit people in some organizations very hard. It is assigning new responsibilities and holding people to meet them that raises the greatest number of "we can't do that" responses. The key implementation question is "what is the alternative?" When we ask why a company that is promising all deliveries within two weeks has actual deliveries that vary from four to eight weeks, the answer is often, "We have to promise two weeks because of competition." When confronted with the possibility of *honest* but later than two-week delivery promises, the answer is "We can't do that." The alternative is clear—continued lies to customers.

In one European firm, the organizational cost to implement the MPC system was very high but the alternative was worse. Facing a deteriorating competitive position and profitability, the top management of the firm realized the need for an effective MPC system. The constraints of only making promises to customers from the MPS and not being able to go to the shop floor to get orders for particular customers led the sales manager to resign.

Moreover, the manufacturing manager didn't like the discipline required by the formal system and left, along with the inventory planner.

We are not advocating radical surgery with this example. Organizational change can be costly and requires management commitment. The results for this European firm were tripled gross margins, a fivefold increase in their inventory turns, and a virtual elimination of late delivery penalties. That was certainly preferable to the alternative, and it was worth the high cost in organizational change.

Slack reduction

The firm with poor systems has extra inventories, extra lead times, extra capacity, extra personnel, excessive overtime, long delivery times, and other kinds of slack built into its operations. These elements of slack allow various organizational units to be operated somewhat independently of each other. Under good MPC operations, the objective is, in fact, to reduce these slack conditions. The result is a need for better scheduling and other kinds of improved communication among organizational subunits to compensate for the reduced slack.

The company will have a need for new kinds of dialogue either supported by formal organization changes or by other mechanisms, such as regularly scheduled committee meetings. These committee meetings have to be taken quite seriously, since they usually are a part of a processing cycle that requires a timely decision. If one member doesn't turn up, there will have to be some "default" rule applied, and the no-show will be just as responsible!

One new level of communication that becomes quite important is between first-line management and the computer department. Murphy's law is always at work, and the foremen will occasionally get reports with "mysterious" data. The resolution of these problems on a timely basis is very important for the health of the system.

Job design

Achievement of Class A implementation status means a significant change in the way people do their jobs. It follows, then, that the means of evaluating job effectiveness must change. Jobs must be designed and evaluated on a basis that is consistent with system transactions and system performance measures. Accountability needs to be established on a basis that is congruent with the new job designs. Foremen should be held accountable for meeting the schedules. Stockroom personnel should be evaluated in terms of stockroom accuracy measures. Planners should be evaluated for inventory levels and for shortages of manufactured or purchased materials. Purchasing buyers should be evaluated in terms of material cost reductions, service improvements, and vendor performance.

An interesting implication of job design changes was observed at a large heavy-equipment manufacturer. The continuing addition of systems to be executed on the shop floor resulted in a fundamental change in the job of the foreman. Instead of someone who moved iron and yelled a lot, the foreman became more of an information processor. One result was rethinking the career path that leads to a foreman's job. The MPC-system driven company is fundamentally different from its predecessor.

The organization will have to adapt to the system. Many successful implementers now see that the key is to change the organization to match the system, rather than vice versa. That is not to say that the system is not tailored to meet the needs of a particular environment, but only to say that activities at the operational level after Class A implementation are different. They are as different as the job of a barnstormer is from that of a professional pilot.

The Class A MPC system can be achieved under any form of organization. Many people have asked whether it is necessary to install a materials management organization before implementing MPC systems. The materials management type of formal organization is no guarantee of success and it is not a prerequisite to success. However, because of the interactions among organizational subunits and the reduction of slack that formerly allowed them to operate more independently, many companies have adopted a materials management form of organization to support their systems to control materials flow.

A materials management organization typically integrates production planning, purchasing, traffic, distribution, and all physical inventory control activities within one organizational unit. Also included are formal feedbacks associated with transaction error resolution, shop-floor control, and vendor follow-up systems.

The exact form of a materials management organization can vary from firm to firm over time. However, there is a general evolution toward more complete organizational integration. The reduction of slack requires more close working relationships. The integrated materials management form of organization has been helpful in achieving these relationships in many firms.

An interesting example of introducing the materials management form of organization can be seen in the experience of the Xerox Corporation. The information systems group, the division producing copiers and duplicators, went through a number of changes in their materials management organization as the products went through their life cycle. When the products were new, the designs were in a great state of flux and all emphasis was on design improvements and maximum output. At a later stage, competition was more intense, the designs were stable, and emphasis shifted to productivity and cost reduction.

Top management commitment

The final organizational implication for Class A implementation is the requirement of a deep and lasting commitment from the top management of the company. We have already noted the survey of MRP companies that found a strong correlation between data accuracy and good measures of effectiveness by the Wight classification scheme. An even stronger correlation existed between the level of top-management support and the A, B, C, and D measurement of success. All authorities state that this commitment is critical to success, and empirical evidence backs up this claim.

Another interesting result of this survey was that the authors found a strong correlation between success and the level of support provided by the marketing group. Those companies that have active participation from the marketing department during MPC system design and implementation seem to be more likely to achieve Class A status than those where marketing personnel play a weak or nonexistent role.

Top-management commitment means a great deal more than a chief executive giving his or her blessing to the MPC systems. The key to commitment is not even in providing the necessary funding for the effort. It is first and foremost to recognize that the MPC effort will require the sole use of some of the best people in the organization for a significant period of time. These people have to be identified, they have to be freed from present responsibilities (hire replacements if necessary), they have to be molded into an effective team, and they have to have the authority and responsibility to do the job.

Top-management commitment also relates to understanding how achievement of Class A MPC status will affect the entire company. The top management should provide leadership for the change, rather than playing a passive role. This kind of leadership means that one companywide system is the goal; that this system will be used for budgeting and for strategic planning; that marketing decisions such as customer order promising will be made within the system; that key trade-offs are made in the MPS; that the accounting and finance systems will at some point be integrated with the companywide data base; that engineering will support the effort to whatever degree necessary; that manufacturing's job will be to hit the schedule; and that an ongoing companywide education program, beginning with top management, will be put in place. George Bevis has said that the key to success at the Tennant Company (another Class A system user) was when he clearly understood that he personally had to make an active commitment to the MPC systems. At the time, he was executive vice president for the company. He had to change the way he thought about manufacturing and carry this change through the organization.

In some firms, effective systems have been installed despite lack of top-management support. In one instance we know of, the resources were provided at the vice presidential level and the president never did understand some of the fundamental changes that were taking place in the company. This strategy is risky and is to be avoided if possible. In some cases, however, there is no other way.

PLAN OF ATTACK

We have already discussed how a plan of attack has to be tailored to the company environment and perceptions at a point in time. To some extent, material control systems have been oversold and oversimplified. The result is that many people seriously underestimate the magnitude of the implementation task and have unrealistic expectations of what can be done, how much is reasonable, what subsystems should be started first, and when they should quit.

Defining the scope

The question of where to start is a bit more complex than the analogy of eating an elephant one bite at a time. Some idea of the task and priorities for improvement help define the starting point. For example, many companies only turn to the MPS after the MRP explosion, data integrity, shop-floor control, and purchasing follow-up systems are in place. Without the MPS, the result can often be sophisticated systems to execute insanity. Moreover, with some degree of stability at the front end of the system, the resulting problems in execution are significantly lessened. The other side of the coin is that a sophisticated MPS that cannot be executed will not be widely acclaimed by the organization. But any improvement in the MPS should make management, even with crude execution systems, easier. The resolution of this dilemma hinges on a careful assessment of organizational readiness for change and where change is needed.

One key aspect of defining the project scope is to have in mind a specific group of users for each system that is designed. The system should be designed to support some day-to-day decision problem faced by either an existing group of users or some group of users that is to be put together by a specific organizational change. If the system is designed for some nonexistent group of users or, worse yet, is designed to make decisions automatically, the chances of success are reduced substantially.

Since the first impact of a materials control system will be felt in the factory, it follows that the first group of users should probably be somewhere in the manufacturing organization (including materials management). At least one of the key users should be a member of the design team. In that way, he or she will be continually assessing the system design in terms of what is possible and what key problems are to be solved.

The question of when to quit is partly related to the notion of a journey, rather than a trip. Note that the journey has to be periodically redefined and refunded. A further dimension of this continuing effort is that most companies expect to implement the system and that, thereafter, it will remain relatively static. Experience runs counter to this belief. In most firms, there is an ongoing need for system improvements, reformatting of data, inclusion of different facts on output reports, evolution from paper outputs to cathode ray tubes, new cross checks for data integrity, and so on. These efforts are important and need to be encouraged to some degree, because by so doing the users develop a genuine identity with the systems and they feel that their needs are being met. On the other hand, too much attention to this kind of effort can come at the expense of development in other subsystems. Moreover, sometimes a problem symptom will later be eliminated after other system efforts. The need is for a degree of balance, and an eye to the long term, while not ignoring legitimate short-term user needs. The long-term commitment of the users, obtained by solving their short-term needs, is an important element of this balance.

Project management

Perhaps the most critical dimension to the plan of attack is the proper use of project teams. An MPC system has to be designed and implemented in subsystem units. It is critical to properly define the scope of each subsystem and to manage its design and implementation.

We see the need for three kinds or layers of project management teams, but there are overlaps between them during the evolution of the MPC system. The most important level of project management is what we call the primary project team. This is a group of about five to eight people coming from different functional areas. Their task is to define the detailed set of subsystem projects, order the priorities, make sure that each subsystem project remains congruent with the overall MPC system efforts, and act as a conduit to and from their respective functional areas and user groups.

The primary project team needs to report to a special top-management steering committee. This second group serves as a decision-making group when MPC efforts require coordination that exceeds the authority of the primary project team. An example might be the need to coordinate some aspects of marketing and design engineering. The steering committee is also the source of resources for the project teams. It will be necessary to earmark critical resource persons and allocate funding to the MPC system efforts. The steering committee will be needed to reconcile these needs with competing needs in the company.

The third level of project management is the team assigned to a detailed MPC subsystem, such as stockroom data integrity, bill of material structuring, engineering change control, or master production scheduling. In the early stage of the MPC system effort, it is often true that members of the primary project team serve as members of detailed project teams. This is very useful to broaden their understanding of the MPC system and to develop realistic expectations of how long the subprojects should take, what organizational changes are required, how to define educational needs, and the like.

The primary project team

The group of five to eight persons on the primary project team should definitely include a representative from marketing, one from engineering, one from line manufacturing, and one from the computer department. Beyond this organizational representation, the only need is for bright, hard workers, preferably with some history of getting projects accomplished. Many teams also include a member from finance. This is particularly important when the short-term scope of the project is to incorporate cost-accounting systems or critical interfaces with such systems as labor cost reporting.

The project team should be a core of people who are largely freed from other responsibilities during the course of the project. They should be physically located in some separate area, with minimal contact with their previous jobs and associates. The team should be comprised of people from within the company. There is a tendency to believe that this kind of talent can better be hired. This is not usually the case, for two critical reasons. First, the supply of qualified professionals in this field is severely limited; most of the best ones are happily employed. Second, even if the talent were available, the organization must make the necessary adaptations to use the new systems on its own. It is critical to know what the changes will be, what the major roadblocks are, who will be supportive, and who will need to receive special handling. It is only insiders who have this kind of knowledge.

A further dimension of using insider project teams is the opportunity for individual growth that participation in this kind of project offers. The primary project team is going to evolve into a highly professional group, and materials management based on MPC systems will similarly be more professional than formerly. The result is that there should be some very nice jobs available for productive members of the project teams. There are not many chances for rapid advancement in status and compensation in industrial organizations that outstrip those from achieving demonstrated results on an MPC project team.

The use of insider project teams does not mean that the team should not receive outside counsel. On the contrary, use of a qualified professional consultant can be extremely valuable. This person can help in defining the project scope, in providing education for the project teams, in defining the education program for the company, and in auditing results. Another role that can be well performed by an outsider is that of conscience. It is very useful to have an outsider come around and ask whether the project is on target, whether anyone has been removed from the team or has been diverted, and whether directions are being maintained.

One person on the primary project team has to serve as the project leader. It is tempting to believe that this person needs to be able to perform miracles while serving coffee to the team. People with those qualifications are hard to find. The key attribute of the project leader is that he or she should have a demonstrated track record for management in the company. The person needs to be decisive, to know how to assign task authority and responsibility, and to provide leadership to the team. It is also important to know how to deal with top management.

The primary project team leader must be a user, definitely not someone from the computer department. Ideally, the project leadership will be viewed as a temporary assignment, with the intent to return to a position where he or she uses the system.

A source of leadership in the primary project team is from one key member of the top-management steering committee. This member serves as top management's representative, and should be more knowledgeable about the MPC project than the other members of the steering committee. A good choice might be the vice president of manufacturing. In some firms, this person goes so far as to assume personal responsibility for the success or failure of the MPC project. This level of commitment places MPC system implementation in the same category as any major corporate goal. Building a new factory based on new technology is a useful analog.

The Swissair project team. A good example of how detailed MPC subsystem projects can be defined and managed is provided by Swissair's engineering and maintenance department. Maintenance on Swissair aircraft is performed in Zurich. This facility also provides maintenance service for other airlines. Total employment in the maintenance group is approximately 2,600.

The development of the Swissair integrated maintenance and control system (MCS) is shown as Figure 11.3. It is divided into about 50 subsystems or segments; Figure 11.3 also shows the necessary sequential nature of introducing these segments. Figure 11.4 provides English-language descriptions for those segments that have been implemented and the developmental effort in man-years in the segment. The overall developmental effort for the 15 implemented segments is 260 man-years and costs are estimated at approximately $12.5 million. Annual running costs are approximately $3.5 million.

These costs are more than offset by direct savings, primarily in labor costs, through increased productivity. From a strategic point of view, the Swissair MCS system represents a long-term competitive weapon. Use of

FIGURE 11.3 Swissair's maintenance and control system

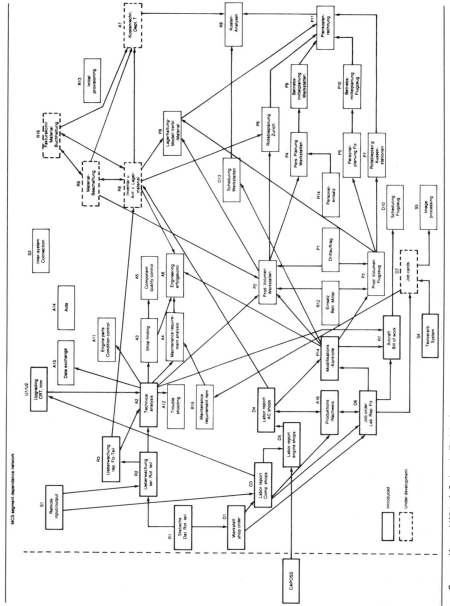

Source: Konrad Wittorf, Swissair, Zurich, Switzerland.

FIGURE 11.4 Swissair implemented system segments

Area	Segment	Function	Development effort (man-years)
Rotable control	R1	Establish a master rotable record, including all static data necessary for rotables control and labor reporting in the rotables workshops.	21.4
	R2	Register location and running times of rotables and control their time limits.	19.7
	R3	Control all rotable and repairable parts during rework time, set workshop priorities, and monitor alert values.	15.3
Time management	D1	Establish a master labor record, including all static data necessary for job planning and control in workshops.	14.4
	D3	Print work papers on request, record and compare man-hours with standards registered in the system for component shops.	24.4
	D4	Same functions as D3 but for aircraft supporting shops.	6.5
	D5	Same function as D3 but for engine workshop. Integration of the CAPOSS package into the MCS.	10.3
	D6	Establish a master labor record and a system for automated printing of work papers and for recording man-hours spent in aircraft maintenance and overhaul.	21.4
	R7	Support the selection of jobs for the next aircraft visit (bill of work).	15.5
Production control	A16	Replace the previous reports about man-hours.	14.1
Technical analysis	A2	Provide statistical data concerning technical occurrences, such as pilot complaints, maintenance complaints, and component changes.	21.8
Modification control	P14	Control origin, implementation, and status of modifications.	15.0
Support segments	S1	Specify and supervise the installation of remote input output facilities.	7.5
	U1/U2	Establish functions for direct access to the central EDP system and introduce CRT terminals. Upgrade some S1 functions to this access mode.	10.0
	S4	Provide a text management system that can be integrated with data processing. First used for overhaul manuals.	3.5

Source: Konrad Wittorf, Swissair, Zurich, Switzerland.

FIGURE 11.5   Swissair's project organization

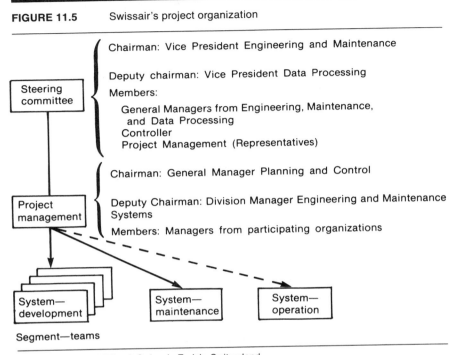

Source: Konrad Wittorf, Swissair, Zurich, Switzerland.

these systems should permit Swissair to obtain an increasing volume of third-party maintenance work. Even though Swiss labor costs are very high, the downtime of aircraft for maintenance can be reduced substantially, resulting in a greater ability to schedule flight hours for each aircraft so maintained.

One key to the Swissair MCS system is the development of each of the segments as a separate project, with its own project team. The segments are constrained to be not longer than approximately 20 man-years of effort and two to three years in elapsed time. The overall organization and management of the MCS project is shown in Figure 11.5. One key aspect of this organization is the general manager—planning and control. This person chairs the project management committee, as well as serving as a member of the steering committee as a project management representative. In essence, he or she is the top-management representative for the detailed MCS project planning and control. This manager spends at least one day per week reviewing the exact status of each segment project.

The management organization for an individual segment project is illustrated in Figure 11.6. Each project encompasses the same set of six phases,

FIGURE 11.6   Swissair's segment teams: Participation in development phases

Skill / Phase	User	System-specialist		Programmer
		System planner (user)	System analyst (EDP)	
Outline	+	⊕	+	
Functional specialist	+	⊕	+	
Program development			⊕	+
User-procedures	+	⊕		
User-tests	+	⊕	+	
Introduction	⊕	+	+	

+   Participation
◯   Responsible

Source: Konrad Wittorf, Swissair, Zurich, Switzerland.

which are clearly defined as the rows in the matrix of Figure 11.6. The columns of this matrix show four key project team members. These entries in the matrix show which of these members participate in each phase, and who is responsible for project leadership during that phase.

The first important observation is that it is a user who will have ultimate responsibility for implementing the system. Since he or she knows this at the outset, there is careful attention given to all of the other phases, so a usable system will result. The second observation is that the EDP (electronic data processing) person is responsible only for computer program development, and it is the only activity that involves the programmers. According to the definition of the project phases, functional specification is not complete until an unambiguous programming job is defined.

The key responsibilities shown in Figure 11.6 are those of the system planner. This is a person who is basically a user, not a computer expert. It is a career assignment for fast-track career persons. They have the major job of defining the exact scope of a segment, including the expected costs, timings, and benefits. They also have the major responsibility of designing the new procedures, testing the system, and making it ready for introduction.

These people have a long-run career interest in becoming managers in a user department. They do not look to careers in data processing. Neither do they have a long-run interest in being project leaders. As one developmental step in their career, they take on one or two of these projects. If the results are favorable, they are eligible for a significant line-management job.

The final aspect of Figure 11.6 of interest is that, in reality, the system planner and the EDP system analyst act as a duo. This is to ensure that, if either of them leaves the company during the duration of the effort, Swissair does not suffer irreparable damage to the project.

Project definition

The precise project definition will be company specific, depending upon their circumstances. However, each plan should have clear timings and milestones, and should perform the tasks in the correct sequences. Some form of project scheduling, such as PERT or CPM, is appropriate, but a bar chart approach can be used. Figure 11.7 is a partial example, which incorporates most of the key elements necessary for a firm starting from informal systems to achieve the basic engine portion of the MPC system in Figure 11.1.

One critical aspect of project definition is to subdivide the overall task into subprojects that each have well-defined milestones. If the project takes too long before concrete benefits are achieved, users will lose interest and chances for success are reduced. We personally feel that a reasonable approach for firms entering into these systems for the first time is to restrict each project to no more than one year in length. If timing slips, and 15 months elapse, the chances for success are probably still fairly good; but if two years elapse before some operating unit sees demonstrable results, the project can be in trouble.

A final comment on project definition is that, once a detailed project plan has been agreed to, try very hard to adhere to the plan, resisting the temptation to go off in other directions. Unless the steering committee has been notified and is in agreement with a revision of the plan, don't permit deviations. Implementation may be a journey instead of a destination, but the journey must not become random.

Project evaluation

The Swissair approach includes means for evaluating the progress of the project on an ongoing basis, but there are some other ideas for evaluation that are also worthy of note. Vincent Piacenti of Compugraphic has developed a "readiness review," which is gone through before any major system module is implemented. The stated purpose of the readiness review is to determine if the particular implementation should proceed or if it should be delayed until improvements are made in certain areas. The readiness review is a formal meeting where the project team for that part of the system makes a presentation to a project review board, including an outside consultant.

The project team needs to present whatever the members think is important to implementation of the particular project, and to identify whatever problems they see. The review board is free to ask any questions not limited

FIGURE 11.7   Sample implementation plan

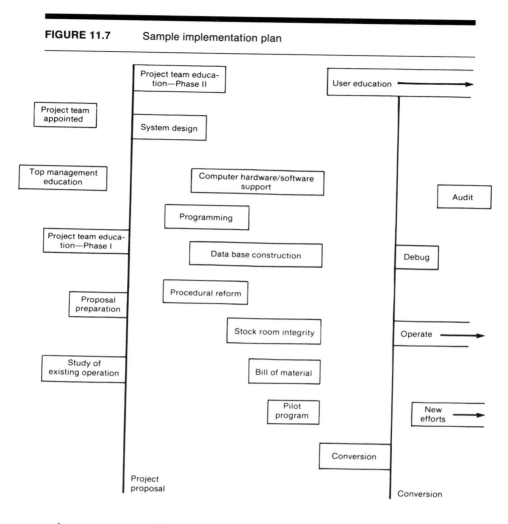

to the presentation. The overall objective is to see if the project team feels comfortable with going on to implementation, or if a delay is required because cutting over to the new system will cause some major confusion for the workers or because some part of the system does not work properly.

The readiness review typically is scheduled for an entire afternoon. The review team takes the next morning to prepare a report on its findings, which is presented to senior management, with the project team in attendance, in the afternoon of the second day. The review team prepares a report based on individual problems it sees.

Figure 11.8 is an example for Compugraphic. The problem involves the ability of the new system to correctly pass requirements down from the Haverhill plant to plant 90, which is a feeder plant making printed circuit boards.

FIGURE 11.8   Compugraphic implementation review

Topic	Haverhill turn-on
Date	4/10
Location	

Critical Area: Haverhill/90 (4.0 - 8.0) Integration

Risk number
1

Risk level _____ Modest _____ High _____ Unacceptable _✓_

Findings - consequences:

Integration process is well defined. However, the initial test yielded many demand mismatches.

Risk is in the validity and timing of subassembly demands to support Master Schedule, as well as component demands.

Supporting evidence:

Eights issues identified for corrective action.

Corrective action underway:

Task list prepared and responsibilities assigned for corrective action. Test run and match-off scheduled.

Recommendations:

If test MRP run is successful (minimal mismatches or none), risk will be eliminated. If mismatches are numerous and cannot be easily reconciled and corrected, turn-on should not occur.

As can be seen, the review board felt that this problem had an unacceptable risk level for implementation. The unacceptable level means that the board felt that if this problem was not solved prior to implementation, it was serious enough to postpone the cutover to the new system.

The readiness review is a great deal of work for the project team, and the teams usually resent the effort required. However, after the fact, the teams typically feel that the effort was worth it. There is a new level of commitment, the problems and potential pitfalls are well known, and the management has an appreciation of the work done and work left to do.

Another useful implementation activity developed by Vince Piacenti is a "control center," which is one central place where any user can call for any problem at any time. The intent is to create a place where anyone in the organization can turn for help, and to eliminate all excuses for not reconciling a problem as soon as it occurs. A related reason for the control center is to demonstrate the commitment to the MPC project in a fundamental way. It will be necessary to provide whatever resources are needed. Included are specialists in communications, specialists in particular techniques and applications, and people who, speaking the language of the shop floor, are able to identify with the frustrations of the users. To the extent that readiness reviews are done well, there should be few surprises in terms of the demands placed on the control center.

EDUCATION

It is almost impossible to overemphasize the role of education in achieving a Class A system implementation. One of the questions asked in the Anderson and Schroeder survey was: "What is the major problem that your firm has faced in implementing MRP?" At the top of the list of replies was: Education of personnel.

Education levels and requirements

We see four distinct foci or levels of education needed for implementation. Figure 11.9 shows these four levels as a pyramid. At the top is the top-management group; this group may be identical to the steering committee. The members need to attend a short course on MPC systems, go to follow-up seminars on a regular basis, read top-management materials dealing with MPC systems, and stay abreast of current company efforts.

The next level of education is for the primary project team and the detailed project teams. The primary project team and the leaders of detailed projects should become true professionals, knowledgeable about the state of the art in this field. This is not an easy job, and it is ongoing. But the size of the MPC investment mandates having this level of knowledge resident within the firm.

This knowledge can be partially purchased through consultants and obtained from hardware/software vendors, but a firm should be especially wary of letting its knowledge base depend too heavily on outsiders, particularly when those outsiders are trying to sell expensive products and services.

The primary project team needs to attend seminars on a regular basis, be active in professional societies, attend conferences and meetings of the societies, read journals in the field, and interact with other professionals in this area of interest. The leaders of detailed projects need to attend educational seminars especially devoted to their particular projects. The American Production and Inventory Control Society (APICS) has a professional certification program based on a series of examinations; achievement of this cer-

FIGURE 11.9   Education requirements

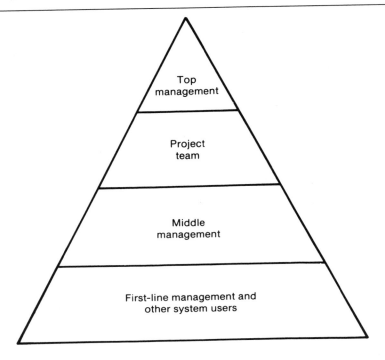

tification status is a reasonable goal for persons who intend to manage through MPC systems.

The third layer of education shown in Figure 11.9 is for the middle managers of the company. It will be necessary for all of these to receive education. This could take the form of attending two or three seminars of three to four days' duration. This group needs to get outside of the company, learn the general approach of these systems, and then see how they have been applied in several other firms. By seeing the before/after conditions through case studies and other means, the general direction of the efforts, as well as the degree of change necessary to make them effective, can be seen. One simply needs to take off the blinders imposed by existing company practices to see what these systems have to offer.

The outside education is followed up by inside education in the systems being designed for the firm. With an outside perspective, the middle managers can now more actively participate in the design of the systems that are going to affect their working lives. This participation goes a long way toward ensuring that the system is *our* system, instead of *the* system.

The final layer of education shown in Figure 11.9 is for first-line supervisors and other system users. In the last analysis, implementation will succeed or fail on the factory floor. It is essential that foremen and others execute the system, process transactions accurately, be rewarded for working within the system, and keep the informal system dead and buried.

There has been a tendency in some companies to consider the education for foremen, stockroom personnel, production planners, buyers, and other users as a narrow job of training. This focus is only on the use of the system as it affects the person's individual area. A much better point of view includes broad-based education about why the system has been adopted, what it does for the firm, and, most important, how decisions made in each area (by specific people) are linked together. When the foreman sees exactly how unreported scrap causes an incorrect scheduled receipt that can result in a rush order back to his or her own department, he or she will be much more interested in data accuracy than if someone simply says, "We want you to always report scrap." The objective is not only to train people in procedures but to provide them with a new framework and understanding. They need to be able to see why certain procedures are necessary and how they should treat some action that has not been previously explained.

Some sort of in-house program for this group is usually most appropriate. Some firms have had success with videotapes; but the best programs we have seen are a mixture of overview concepts and specific company examples. This can often best be achieved by the project team designing an education program, perhaps aided by a consultant. The program can also usefully employ middle managers, who will learn greatly from the process as the teachers.

An education program

The successful firm may find it wise to design the entire education program as part of the project. This can be the best way to address the entire span of educational needs depicted in Figure 11.9. Moreover, it is necessary to include redundancy. We have personal experience with the same users asking questions in a seminar that were clearly covered in an earlier seminar they attended. One simply must take a fairly pessimistic view of how much can be absorbed in one session, and realize that people forget quickly. It will be necessary to give the message several times, hopefully in somewhat different ways.

In addition to the need for redundancy, there is a natural turnover in personnel. People leave or take other assignments, and new personnel must be trained and educated. Since many aspects of executing a Class A system run counter to the work experiences of people, it is important not to expect very much from prior on-the-job training. The new foreman might know how to put some number into a computer terminal, because a prior boss showed him or her how, but the chances are slim that there was a clear explanation of *why*. Often the worst possible training comes from expecting a new person to learn the ropes by watching someone else. The why rarely gets conveyed this way, and professionalism suffers. One further goal of a broad-based education program should be to locate personnel who can get enthusiastic about material control systems and can grow into more responsible positions. There is always a need for these people, particularly those who have firsthand experience.

The final dimension of an educational program we want to mention is the degree of organizational change required to implement Class A systems. This process can be the largest single change in people's working lives. Education can represent a much less direct threat to people than other change approaches. If educational programs and exercises can be set up that clearly show how one way of doing something is better than another, acceptance can be a much easier task and the changes much more easily made.

An example of an overall MPC education effort is seen in Figure 11.10, which provides details for the initial education program at Jet Spray Corporation. It is useful to note that this program includes *every* employee in the company, even the people who wash dishes in the kitchen and who stand guard duty at the doors. The intensity of the education for the senior managers is also worthy of note, as is that for the project team. It is clear that this firm believes strongly in the need for education.

AUDITING

The process of implementing an MPC system deserves some sort of periodic audit. Furthermore, we have closely examined fully implemented systems in many companies, including some of the best in the world. There is not one that could not be improved. Top management should make sure that the best improvement plans are being formulated and that the existing systems are continuing to do the job for which they were designed. In this brief overview of auditing, we present three main ideas. The first is a checklist of system features that should be included in a Class A system. Next, we present a brief view of how we conduct an audit and how one can diagnose poor system health. Finally, we present a section on cost/benefit analysis in the attempt to provide better expectation guidelines for MPC system implementation.

Class A queries

In addition to the brief description of a Class A company presented earlier, the following checklist of system questions should be considered in evaluating any MPC control system.

FIGURE 11.10   Jet Spray's educational program

Initial education—Summarized by hours

Course	Number of people	Hours	Total hours
Teacher/design	14	70	980
Top management	9	41	369
Production & inventory control	3	67	201
Purchasing	3	38	114
Manufacturing managers & supervisors	12	43	516
Manufacturing & industrial engineers	2	40	80
Direct labor employees	135	2	270
Stockroom	20	13	260
Indirect labor employees	12	10	120
Marketing/inside sales	8	32	256
Field sales	13	3	26
Design engineering	6	38	228
Clerical employees	6	13	78
Quality control	3	32	96
Management information systems	4	59	236
Finance & accounting	7	30	210
Vendors	12	7	84
Total			4,124

Initial education — Broken down by number of hours:

Over 60 hours— 17 people
40–59 hours— 27 people
20–39 hours— 27 people
0–19 hours—204 people

Note: In addition to this in-house education, which was largely based on use of video tapes, Jet Spray had 47 attendees at outside courses during the first year of implementation. These courses varied from three to five days covering a range of subjects, including top-management overview, master production scheduling, intensive MPC, purchasing, shop-floor control, bill of material, and computer systems.

- Are the time buckets used for planning no longer than one week?
- Is the planning (regeneration) at least weekly?
- Is performance against schedule evaluated on a weekly or more frequent basis using concrete measurements?
- Is there a defined measure of customer service?
- Is production held responsible for hitting the schedule and not for finished-good inventory levels?
- Is any past-due portion of the master production schedule held to less than one week's capacity?
- Are the capacity implications of the production plan and MPS evaluated on a long-term resource need and a rough-cut basis?

- Are the detailed aspects of capacity planning using capacity require-ments planning a key part of manufacturing planning?
- Is there an input-output or other system in place to compare ma-chine center results with expectations?
- Does the shop-floor control system provide daily dispatch lists for departmental foremen?
- Are the daily dispatch lists the sole source of priority information for the foremen?
- Is an inventory cycle counting procedure in place with periodic mea-surement and evaluation?
- Are all records in the computer (no handwritten documents)?
- Are accuracy levels maintained for bills of material?
- Is there a well-functioning approach to the control of engineering changes?
- Are shop orders closed out religiously (no tag ends, counts recon-ciled, and so on)?
- Are other critical procedures to control transactions adequate, such as rejected materials, rework, and the like?
- Does the system incorporate pegging?
- Does the system have firm planned order capabilities?
- Do planners use bottom-up replanning to solve material availability problems?
- Are state-of-the-art purchasing systems in use, and are vendor ca-pacities planned with the same vigor as internal capacities?
- Is vendor performance routinely measured?
- Is the system integrated with finished-goods planning and control?
- How long has it been since the MPC system was improved?
- How does JIT fit in this firm and is it being pursued?
- Do planners *and* shop floor people use on-line systems?
- What are the approaches being used to reduce lead times?

This is a formidable list of questions, and it is not all-inclusive. Moreover, some negative responses may be more tolerable than others for a given com-pany. Let us now turn to the approach we have found useful in auditing a company's MPC systems.

The routine audit

As one part of a routine audit, we feel that the company's approaches should be evaluated against state-of-the-art system features. The firm that evaluates its approach to material control systems against the set of questions posed above can accomplish this. A somewhat different perspective is to examine the general level of effectiveness of each of the firm's particular systems; that is, whatever the stated system design, do the systems in fact work? Are they in use? What else is needed for users to do their jobs?

Our approach to this issue is a routine audit involving several steps. First, it is necessary to take whatever amount of time is necessary to understand the systems that are in place, how the documents are created, what data files are used to process the records, and so on. This is not to say, however, that one is auditing the computer program or the computerized data base. Effective use of the computer is a separate technical issue. The intent of the MPC audit is to clearly understand the set of output documents, how they are linked, who uses them, and what to do with them.

It is very important to adopt a viewpoint of substantial ignorance at the outset. We ask to be shown actual current output data and examine these documents in considerable detail. We take the position that one needs to understand what all of the data items are on each report or screen, where they come from, and what arithmetical operations are performed to get them. We examine several actual records to see whether we can understand the numbers, and whether the stated logic can be applied to produce the sample results.

One often finds logical inconsistencies in this process, such as negative inventory values, records with all zeros in some field, and the like. These are sure clues that all is not well. It is also of interest to reconcile documents that presumably should have been produced from a common set of data. An example is shipments for some common time period from records in marketing, finance, and manufacturing.

As a side issue of this analysis, one sometimes finds that the in-house experts cannot explain how the documents are created, what they truly contain, who will use them, and how they are used. Inconsistencies in their beliefs must similarly be explained in sufficient detail.

After gaining an understanding of the system, the audit should turn to those who use the output documents. If a foreman who is asked for the daily dispatch list replies: "My daily what?" one begins to wonder whether systems are really being used. On the other hand, if it is in his or her pocket, with pencil lines and fingerprints, one begins to feel that the system outputs are used and the system matches reality. Similar checks should be made in other areas. Is it possible for one of us as an outsider to look important and gain entry into the stockroom? Is the door locked? Who has the keys? What is done on the night shift? Ask a stockroom person to produce the current inventory listing and pick parts at random. Can each of these parts be found in the exact amounts in the exact location? How do the stockroom people feel about data accuracy? Ask them how many times the parts are not there. Ask whether the engineers come in to get parts for R&D without proper paperwork. Check out the receiving area. Are there boxes of goods there? Ask how long they have been there. Find out how the system is notified of arrivals. How are counts verified? Look at the documents that accompany work in process. Do they make sense? Are all fields properly filled out?

Visit the assembly department. Ask whether they are now working on the jobs that the system has indicated they should be working on. Ask whether there is an end-of-the-month bulge in shipments. Ask how many times they run out of parts. Do they use their terminal as indicated?

Talk to the master scheduler. Ask him or her to show you how the MPS is prepared. Ask about the support obtained from marketing. Ask if they get silly forecast data that they have to override.

Audit the level of education being used in the company. Who designed the education program? Who gets it? How often? What is the program? Is an overall level of understanding considered important? Does the foreman know how a shop order is created? Is top management knowledgeable about the MPS system or do they believe that education is important—for my subordinates! Are the members of the design team active professionally? Do they attend seminars, workshops, and conferences?

In sum, the routine audit starts with the posture that one believes nothing unless proven. The objective is to find out what is supposed to be the case and whether actuality matches the system. In the last analysis, a system is only effective when used.

The MPC system audit is not a witch-hunt. Whatever systems are presently in use is simply a matter of fact. It is not the fault of the users that it is not any better. Making it better requires action plans, project teams, and resources. The MPC audit attempts to help the company assess where it truly is, where it might be, and how to get there.

Cost/benefit analysis

We firmly believe that one important aspect of any MPC system implementation should be a well-defined cost/benefit study. There are far too many large system projects that proceed without sufficient analysis of costs and benefits, or that have had the benefits computed on an after-the-fact basis. An MPC system effort represents a substantial investment for the firm; the fact that the data are hard to estimate with precision should not preclude rigorous analysis.

For every project, the costs and benefits will be a bit unique, depending upon the scope of the project and the conditions prevailing at the time. However, to the extent that critical costs and benefits of the effort can be included as a set of time-phased expectations, the steering committee can review the project performance more effectively. Discounted cash flows or payback periods can be calculated, and the monitoring of expenditures and benefits can be made part of a periodic review cycle. Another issue is a tendency in many cases to underestimate the actual expenses. To the extent that major expenditures are specified up front, there will be fewer unpleasant surprises. It may well be easier to sell an entire package with a large price at one time than to be continually "returning to the well."

The kinds of costs that are usually important to plan and budget for are:

- Personnel costs for people assigned to the project on a full-time basis. (Try to identify specific people so that their bosses will be committed to their absence.)
- Personnel costs for people assigned on a part-time basis. (Again, try to obtain a commitment for who and when.)
- Computer hardware costs—any necessary enhancements in hardware should be specified.
- Computer software costs—purchased software and outside personnel to install software.
- Personnel expenses for company systems people who will work on the project (when, who, duration).
- Outside professional services, such as consultants, education, contract programming, and so on.

The indirect costs of managerial time and opportunity costs of placing this system implementation at the highest priority level for the company should perhaps be acknowledged, but not explicitly accounted for.

The benefits can be assessed in a multitude of ways. We feel that the commitment to some concrete statement of benefit measured on an agreed upon basis, rather than precisely how the benefits are measured, is the key. Some possibilities include: Pro forma accounting statements—these can be generally based on certain operating ratios and improvements in those ratios, and thereafter matched with actual results. The problem with the pro forma approach, however, is that bottom-line results are a function of many causes. It may be hard to isolate the exact contribution of the MPC system.

It may be necessary to assess the benefits through improvements in other surrogate measures. Possibilities include:

- Shipping budget performance.
- Labor utilization rates.
- Productivity measures.
- Expediting budget.
- Obsolete inventory write-off.
- Cycle count accuracy.
- Overtime hours.
- Purchased component costs.
- Vendor delivery performance.
- Premium shipment costs.
- Customer delivery promise performance.
- Spare-part service levels.
- Obsolete inventory reduction.

- Raw-material inventory as a percentage of sales.
- Work-in-process inventory as a percentage of sales.
- Finished-goods inventory as a percentage of sales.
- Safety-stock inventory as a percentage of sales.
- Inventory turnover.
- Annual accounting inventory adjustment.
- Hidden factory costs.
- Lead time reduction.

Any of these measures may be appropriate, but the need is to clearly specify how the exact measurement is to be made and when various improvements are to be obtained. Most companies will choose a different set, and perhaps a different way to measure; but this should be part of the upfront effort, so actual progress can be compared to expectations and so project teams can know when they are meeting the agreed-upon expectations.

Many subjective benefits can also be stated, but the problems of concrete measurement are more complex. Among the subjective benefits that firms may wish to achieve are the following:

- Customer relations.
- Competitive position.
- Professionalism.
- Morale and *esprit de corps.*
- Coordination between finance, marketing, and production.
- Accounting control.
- Product quality.

Both the subjective and objective measures should be specified and made a part of each working contract between a particular project team and the steering committee. The original, perhaps tentative, set of objectives should be specified as well as possible and made a part of the formal proposal by the team to the steering committee.

As actual work progresses, any evolution in the anticipated costs and benefits should be directly discussed in progress meetings. A finalized time-phased set of expected costs and benefits should be put forth at the time of major conversion, and continuing audits should be carried out thereafter to measure actual results versus plans.

One final word of caution: These assessments of cost/benefit often look too good! It is probably sensible to focus on a few key measures, ones that have a close relationship to the bottom line, and to be somewhat conservative. A major management responsibility is to truly control the costs. To put a team together with a year to complete the first requirement and then let it drift along will ensure cost overruns. It also will allow enthusiasm to wane, which reduces the possibilities of achieving the long-run benefits. The greatest early leverage is to hold persons responsible to hit the design schedule, and in that way control timings and costs.

The timing issue may be even more critical than the cost issue. The benefits from MPC systems are usually so substantial that cost overruns are easily covered. *But,* if timings are allowed to slip, the result is people resources being used longer than originally planned. This leads to the need for reassigning priorities to project work in the firm. Usually, systems personnel (and others) are being requested to work on many projects. When the actual time durations on these projects slip, one result can be political infighting over resources.

CONCLUDING PRINCIPLES

In this chapter we have tried to focus attention on the major problem in MPC systems—how to get implemented results. The following principles summarize the major points:

- MPC system efforts should start with an assessment of where the firm is and what can be done.
- The total MPC system implementation effort should be divided into manageable subtasks that each yields concrete benefits.
- One should start with a subsystem that can be implemented quickly and that will be of recognized use to some readily identified user group.
- An early goal should be data integrity because of its fundamental importance.
- Management should be prepared to install new organizational forms to facilitate MPC implementation and operation.
- Key users must be on project teams.
- Performance on project teams should be congruent with career planning.
- Education programs should be designed for all levels of the organization.
- The design scope for each particular project should be carefully defined and maintained unless broad agreement on redefinition is reached.
- Project definition and project management techniques should be used to manage the implementation.
- Management should audit, audit, and audit.
- An objective assessment of costs and benefits should be part of any MPC-system implementation program.

REFERENCES

Anderson, J. C., and R. G. Schroeder. "Getting Results from Your MRP System." *Business Horizons*, May/June 1984.

Belt, Bill. "Men, Spindles and Materials Requirements Planning: Enhancing Implementation." *Production and Inventory Management*, 1st Quarter 1979, pp. 54–65.

Benson, P. B.; A. V. Hill; and T. R. Hoffmann. "Manufacturing Systems of the Future—A Delphi Study." *Production and Inventory Management Journal*, 3rd Quarter 1982, pp. 97–98.

Bevis, G. E. "Closed Loop MRP at the Tennant Company." Report—The Tennant Company, Minneapolis, Minn.

Brenezir, Ned W. "The Bottom Line Begins at the Top." *Production and Inventory Management*, 3rd Quarter 1977.

Davis, E. W. "Material Requirements Planning in a Fabrication and Assembly Environment: Ingersoll Rand Case Study." Pennsauken, N.J.: Auerback Publishers, 1982.

Fisher, Kenneth. "How to Implement MRP Successfully." *Production and Inventory Management* 22, no. 4 (4th Quarter 1981), pp. 36–54.

Hall, R. W., and T. E. Vollmann. "Planning Your Material Requirements." *Harvard Business Review*, September/October 1978.

Jordan, H. H. "Developing an Integrated Production and Inventory Control System." *1972 APICS Conference Proceedings*, pp. 28–34.

Lee, S. A., and M. Ebrahimpour. "Just-in-Time Production System: Some Requirements for Implementation." *International Journal of Production Research* 4, no. 4 (1984), pp. 3–15.

Meredith, J. R. "The Implementation of Computer-Based Systems." *Journal of Operations Management* 2, no. 1 (1981).

MRP Re-Implementation: You Too Can Be Successful." *APICS National Conference Proceedings*, Boston, October 1981, pp. 119–20.

Maertz, William E. "MRP's Fourth Requirement." *Production and Inventory Management*, 3rd Quarter 1979, pp. 81–84.

Nicholas, John M. "Developing Effective Teams for Systems Design and Implementation." *Production and Inventory Management*, 3rd Quarter 1980, pp. 37–47.

"Productivity: Out of MRP—A New Game Plan." *Modern Materials Handling*, January 1981, pp. 63–82.

Schroder, R. G. *Material Requirements Planning: A Study of Implementation and Practice*. Falls Church, Va.: American Production and Inventory Control Society, 1981.

Schroder, R. G.; J. C. Anderson; S. E. Tupy; and E. M. White. "A Study of MRP Benefits and Costs." *Journal of Operations Management* 2, no. 1 (October 1981).

Tersine, Richard J. "Production and Operations: A Systems Construct." *Production and Inventory Management*, 4th Quarter 1977.

"The Trick of Materials Requirements Planning." *Business Week,* June 4, 1979, pp. 72D–72J.

Wallace, Thomas F. *MRPII: Making It Happen.* Essex Junction Vt.: Oliver Wight Limited Publications, 1985.

Van Dierdonck, R. J. M., and J. G. Miller. "Designing Production Planning and Control Systems." *Journal of Operations Management* 4, no. 1 (1980), pp. 37–46.

White, E. M.; J. C. Anderson; R. G. Schroeder; and S. E. Tupy. "A Study of the MRP Implementation Process." *Journal of Operations Management* 2, no. 3 (May 1982).

Wight, Oliver W. "MRPII—Manufacturing Resource Planning." *Modern Materials Handling,* September 1979, pp. 78–94.

———. *MRP II: Unlocking America's Productivity Potential.* Williston, Vt.: Oliver Wight Limited Publications, 1981.

DISCUSSION QUESTIONS

1. Are there any differences between the MPC system of Figure 11.1, the "Class A" system, and the notion of "closed-loop MRP"?

2. How would you recognize a "Class D" user or someone in need of improved MPC systems?

3. Where would you put the implementation emphasis for an integrated paper mill, a company that buys cloth and sews fashion garments, or a company manufacturing a new kind of candy bar?

4. How can the implementation process be likened to getting a college degree?

5. Why the emphasis on data accuracy in implementation?

6. What makes coordinated planning in a company (or any enterprise) so difficult? What examples can you think of from your experience?

7. What are some of the difficulties in securing top management support and cooperation for an MPC installation?

8. What is a "user"? Why is it important to have users on the project teams?

9. Who do you think should be the project leader of an implementation? How would you cope with turnover on the project team during a very long implementation period? (Remember, it took Ethan Allen 15 years to get where they are!)

PROBLEMS

1. Critique the following implementation strategies:
   a. A coal mining company that ships unit trains of coal to utility companies started its MPC system implementation with engineering change control.
   b. A toy manufacturer started its effort in finished goods and distribution inventory management.
   c. A custom yacht builder started in the finished-goods area.

2. Would you take the following job?

   We need you. The boss says our inventory is too high, our service is too low, and the shop is a mess. He wants to see some changes in six weeks. He bought a new computer and has hired two computer scientists. They are on the implementation committee, chaired by the chief programmer from our MIS department. Will you be the manufacturing representative on the committee?"

3. What are the accuracy levels for the following counts on items A, B, and C, when the card said 100 in stock each time?

Count	1	2	3
Item A	100	101	99
B	50	107	135
C	20	25	0

4. What are the possible causes of the following problem:

   The assembly manager is 5 parts short on an assembly order that needs only 10 of the parts. The five parts are put on a "hot list" but don't appear on any of the formal records at all (either as open or planned orders).

5. Comment on the following implementation schedule and status:

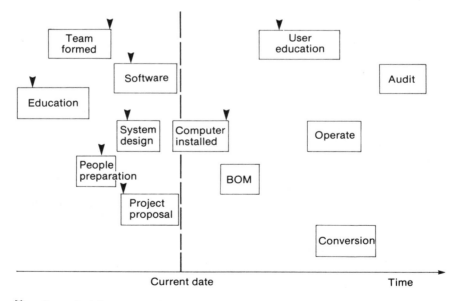

   ▼ = Current status

6. Should the following project be approved if the cost of capital is 25 percent?

Benefits		Costs	
Reduced inventory	$1,000,000	Computer	$500,000
Reduced personnel	100,000/year	System development	750,000
Scrap rework	200,000/year	Ongoing support	400,000/year
Purchase savings	400,000/year	Training	200,000
Improved flow time	—	Forms redesign	50,000
Improved quality	—	New people	200,000/year

7. The Swissair MCS system shown in Figures 11.3 and 11.4 is representative of very large industrial MPC projects requiring long time periods for implementation. If each segment shown on Figure 11.4 had 10 persons assigned to the effort, how long would it take to complete segment R3? How about segment U1/U2? (You may assume that a segment must be completed before a subsequent segment can be started.)

8. Lefty Cardoza heard the yelling from her office. By the time she got to the warehouse, quite a crowd had gathered. The trouble, it seemed, was that nothing was in stock for a particular item, even though the record said there should have been 31 units. The foreman was getting up a lynch party to go after the night shift people, since he felt they had taken the stock. Lefty calmed them down, went back to her office, and retrieved some historical data from the warehouse clerk. It showed the following information:

Count number	1	2	3	4	5
Stock record	37	43	35	32	37
Actual inventory	35	46	43	42	20

   a. What's the inventory record accuracy for this item? Use a spreadsheet program if you've been assigned part c of this problem.)

   b. What observations do you make of the data? Should Lefty join the lynch party?

   c. Would your observations change if the actual inventory for count number 1 and 5 were reversed?

9. The steering committee for an MPC implementation project has identified several measurable costs and benefits of its proposal. The company has requested the committee to perform the financial and what-if analysis using time-phased records for five years. The committee felt that this was useful because not all the costs or benefits were constant for all five years. For example, the inventory savings would be greatest in the second year—building up from $10,000 to $25,000 and then going down to $15,000, $5,000, and 0. On the other hand, the scrap savings would be $15,000 per year. Some costs also varied from year to year. Software costs were high in the first two years ($20,000 and $30,000) and dropped to $5,000, $1,000, and $1,000 in the remaining three years. But wage costs were $10,000 for each of the five years.

The remaining costs were for education ($100,000; $20,000; $10,000; $10,000; and $10,000) and hardware ($5,000; $80,000; $5,000; $2,000; and $2,000). The other benefits were in labor savings ($15,000; $30,000; $75,000; $80,000; and $80,000) and purchase savings, which would end in three years ($35,000; $30,000; and $10,000) because of changes already planned for the product line.

a. In which year would the project break even? (Use a spreadsheet if you are assigned parts **b** and **c** of the problem.)

b. Would this change if the purchase savings had been left at $35,000 per year?

c. What if education costs had been underestimated by 20 percent? (Leave purchasing at $35,000 per year.)

10. What are the accuracy levels for items A, B and C in a transaction reporting system that has the following counts:

	Item		
	A	B	C
Inventory record	1,000	100	10
Actual inventory	990	110	0

11. When Roth Manufacturing converted their monthly regenerated MRP system to a weekly system, the inventory was reduced from $10 million to $6 million. They are considering changing to an on-line system. What inventory savings might they expect? What other benefits can they expect?

12. Ivor Morgan is the materials manager at Rosenthal Inc. One major project line has seven levels in the bill of materials. What is the maximum amount of time that can be saved if Ivor converts the present weekly system to an on-line system?

13. Duncan McDougall, the purchasing manager at Rosenthal Inc., is also interested in converting from a weekly MRP system to an on-line system. At the present time he has about 200 shortages in any one week. Under what conditions will converting from a weekly procurement cycle to an on-line environment provide any help?

14. Suppose the executives at Jet Spray estimated the value of the time of their average employee involved in MPC education at $25 per hour. If the average outside course were four days in duration and cost $2,000 including travel expenses, what is the cost of the initial education program described in Figure 11.10?

15. Anne Shepley was in charge of implementing a new MPC module. There was considerable grumbling about the new system module, and she wondered if this was just the usual process of adapting to a new system or if something was going wrong. At the end of the first two weeks, the following log of calls to resolve problems had been received at the control center.

Day	Calls
1	95
2	125
3	140
4	130
5	140
6	175
7	160
8	180
9	190
10	180

Weekly data for four other MPC modules that have been implemented are:

	Module (number of calls)			
Week	A	B	C	D
1	400	800	25	150
2	300	900	15	95
3	150	400	5	60
4	50	100	0	20
5	5	50	0	10

What should Anne do?

— 12 ——————————————————————

Advanced concepts in material requirements planning

This chapter is concerned with some advanced issues in material requirements planning (MRP). Some of the concepts and conventions discussed can lead to improvement in well-functioning basic systems. Most of the concepts presented are of a "fine tuning" nature and can provide additional benefits to the company.

We take the point of view that the first, most important phase in MRP is to get the system installed, to make it a part of an ongoing managerial process, to get users trained in the use of MRP, to understand the critical linkages with other areas, to achieve high levels of data integrity, and to link MRP with the other modules of the front end, engine, and back end of manufacturing planning and control (MPC) systems. Having achieved this first phase, many firms then turn to the advanced issues discussed in this chapter.

Chapter 12 is organized around the following five topics:

- Determination of manufacturing order quantities: What are the basic trade-offs in lot sizing in the MRP environment, and what techniques are useful?
- Determination of purchase order quantities: How should lot sizes be chosen when purchasing discounts are in effect?

- Buffering concepts: What are the types of uncertainties in MRP, and how can one buffer against these uncertainties?
- Nervousness: Why are MRP systems subject to nervousness, and how do firms deal with system nervousness?
- Other advanced MRP concepts: What conventions have been successfully applied? How are they useful?

Chapter 12 is linked with Chapters 2 and 3 in that this chapter presupposes understanding of MRP systems, record processing, data integrity, and so on. Chapter 12 is also linked to Chapters 17 and 18, where several inventory concepts (lot sizing, buffering, and service levels) are treated. The focus here is on the dependent demand (MRP) environment, whereas Chapters 17 and 18 largely deal with systems for independent demand. Additional buffering concepts are dealt with in Chapters 7 and 14 (master production scheduling) and in Chapter 10 (demand management).

DETERMINATION OF MANUFACTURING ORDER QUANTITIES

The MRP system converts the master production schedule into a time-phased schedule for all intermediate assemblies and component parts. The detailed schedules are comprised of two parts: scheduled receipts (open orders) and planned orders. The scheduled receipts each have had the quantity and timing (due date) determined for release to the shop. The quantities and timings for planned orders are determined by the MRP logic using the inventory position, the gross requirements data, and a specific procedure for determining the quantities—the lot-sizing procedure.

A number of procedures have been developed for MRP systems, ranging from ordering as required (lot-for-lot), to simple decision rules, and finally to extensive optimizing procedures. In this section, we describe five such lot-sizing procedures.

The primary consideration in the development of lot-sizing procedures for MRP is the nature of the requirements data. The demand dependency relationship from the product structures and the time-phased gross requirements mean that the requirements for an item might appear as illustrated in Figure 12.1. First, it is important to notice that the requirements do *not* reflect the key independent demand assumption of a constant uniform demand. Second, the requirements are *discrete*, since they are stated on a period-by-period basis (time phased), rather than as a rate (e.g., an average of so much per month or year). Finally, the requirements can be *lumpy;* that is, they can vary substantially from period to period and even have several periods for which there are no requirements.

MRP lot-sizing procedures are designed specifically for the discrete demand case. One problem in selecting a procedure is that reductions in in-

FIGURE 12.1 Example problem: Weekly requirements schedule

Week number	1	2	3	4	5	6	7	8	9	10	11	12
Requirements	10	10	15	20	70	180	250	270	230	40	0	10

Ordering cost = S = $300 per order
Inventory carrying cost = C_H = $2 per unit per week

Source: W. L. Berry, "Lot-Sizing Procedures for Requirements Planning Systems: A Framework for Analysis," *Production and Inventory Management,* 2nd Quarter 1972, p. 21.

ventory-related costs can generally be achieved only by using increasingly complex procedures. Such procedures require more computations in making lot-sizing determinations. A second problem has to do with local optimization. The lot-sizing procedure used for one part in a MRP system has a direct impact on the gross requirements data passed to its component parts. The use of procedures other than lot-for-lot tends to make the lumpiness of the requirements data grow larger farther down in the product structure.

The manufacturing lot-size problem is basically one of converting the requirements into a series of replenishment orders. If we consider this problem on a local level—that is, only in terms of the one part and not its components—the problem involves determining how to group the time-phased requirements data into a schedule of replenishment orders that minimizes the combined costs of placing manufacturing orders and carrying inventory.

Since MRP systems are normally operated on a daily or weekly basis (i.e., batch-processed), the timing affects the assumptions commonly made in using MRP lot-sizing procedures. These assumptions are as follows. First, since the component requirements are aggregated by time period for planning purposes, we assume that all of the requirements for each period must be available at the beginning of the period. Second, we assume that all of the requirements for a given period must be met and cannot be back ordered. Third, since the system is operated on a periodic basis, the ordering decisions are assumed to occur at regular time intervals (e.g., daily or weekly). Fourth, the requirements are assumed to be properly offset for manufacturing lead time. Finally, we assume that the component requirements are satisfied at a uniform rate during each period. Therefore, the average inventory level will be used in computing the inventory carrying costs.

In the following sections, we shall illustrate the results obtained by applying five different ordering procedures to the example data given in Figure 12.1. Furthermore, this example will be used to illustrate the manner in which these procedures vary in their assumptions and the extent to which they utilize all of the available data in making lot-sizing decisions.

Economic order quantities (EOQ)

Because of its simplicity, the economic order quantity (EOQ) formula is often used as a decision rule for placing orders in a requirements-planning system. As we shall illustrate in the following example, however, the EOQ model frequently must be modified in requirements planning system applications. Since the EOQ is based upon the assumption of constant uniform demand, the resulting total cost expression will not necessarily be valid for requirements planning applications.

The results obtained by ordering material in economic lot sizes for the example data are presented in Figure 12.2. In this example, the average weekly demand of 92.1 units for the entire requirements schedule was used in the EOQ formula to compute the economic lot size. Note, too, that the order quantities are shown when received, and that the average inventory for each period was used in computing the inventory carrying cost.

This example illustrates several problems with using economic lot sizes. When the requirements are not equal from period to period, as is often the case in MRP, fixed EOQ lot sizes result in a mismatch between the order quantities and the requirements values. This can mean excess inventory must be carried forward from week to week. As an example, 41 units are carried over into week 6 when a new order is received.

In addition, the order quantity must be increased in those periods where the requirements exceed the economic lot size plus the amount of inventory carried over into the period. An example of this occurs in week 7. This modification is clearly preferable to the alternative of placing orders earlier to meet the demand in such periods, since this would only increase the inventory carrying costs. Likewise, the alternative of placing multiple orders in a given period would needlessly increase the ordering cost.

FIGURE 12.2   Economic order quantity example

Week number	1	2	3	4	5	6	7	8	9	10	11	12
Requirements	10	10	15	20	70	180	250	270	230	40	0	10
Order quantity	166					166	223	270	230	166		
Beginning inventory	166	156	146	131	111	207	250	270	230	166	126	126
Ending inventory	156	146	131	111	41	27	0	0	0	126	126	116

Ordering cost	$1,800
Inventory carrying cost	3,065
Total cost	$4,865

(Economic lot size = 166)

Source: W. L. Berry, "Lot-Sizing Procedures for Requirements Planning Systems: A Framework for Analysis," *Production and Inventory Management*, 2nd Quarter 1972, p. 22.

Finally, the use of the average weekly requirements figure in computing the economic lot size ignores a considerable amount of other information contained in the requirements schedule. This information has to do with the magnitude of demand. For instance, there appear to be two levels of component demand in this example. The first covers weeks 1 to 4 and 10 to 12; the second covers weeks 5 to 9. By computing an economic lot size for each of these time intervals and placing orders accordingly, the total cost can be reduced by more than $1,000. Yet this proposal would be much more difficult to implement because the determination of different demand levels would require a very complex decision rule.

Periodic order quantities (POQ)

One way of reducing the high inventory carrying cost associated with fixed lot sizes is to use the EOQ formula to compute an economic time interval between replenishment orders. This is done by dividing the EOQ by the mean demand rate. In the example above, the economic time interval would be approximately two weeks (166/92.1 = 1.8). The procedure then calls for ordering *exactly* the requirements for this interval. Applying this procedure to the data in our example (Figure 12.1) produces Figure 12.3. The result is the same number of orders as the EOQ produces, but with lot sizes ranging from 20 to 520 units. Consequently, the inventory carrying cost has been reduced by 30 percent, thereby improving the total cost of the 12-week requirements schedule by 19 percent in comparison with the EOQ result above.

Although the periodic order quantity (POQ) procedure improves the inventory cost performance by allowing the lot sizes to vary, like the EOQ procedure it, too, ignores much of the information contained in the requirements schedule; that is, the replenishment orders are constrained to occur at fixed time intervals, thereby ruling out the possibility of combining orders

---

FIGURE 12.3   Periodic order quantity example

Week number	1	2	3	4	5	6	7	8	9	10	11	12
Requirements	10	10	15	20	70	180	250	270	230	40	0	10
Order quantity	20		35		250		520		270			10
Beginning inventory	20	10	35	20	250	180	520	270	270	40	0	10
Ending inventory	10	0	20	0	180	0	270	0	40	0	0	0

Ordering cost	$1,800
Inventory carrying cost	2,145
Total cost	$3,945

Source: W. L. Berry, "Lot-Sizing Procedures for Requirements Planning Systems: A Framework for Analysis," *Production and Inventory Management,* 2nd Quarter 1972, p. 23.

during periods of light product demand (e.g., during weeks 1 through 4 in the example). If, for example, the orders placed in weeks 1 and 3 were combined and a single order were placed in week 1 for 55 units, the combined costs can be further reduced by $160, or 4 percent.

Part period balancing (PPB)

The part period balancing procedure uses all of the information provided by the requirements schedule. In determining the lot size for an order, this procedure tries to equate the total costs of placing orders and carrying inventory. This point can be illustrated by considering the alternative lot-size choices available at the beginning of week 1. These include placing an order covering the requirements for:

1. Week 1 only.
2. Weeks 1 and 2.
3. Weeks 1, 2, and 3.
4. Weeks 1, 2, 3, and 4.
5. Weeks 1, 2, 3, 4, 5, etc.

The inventory carrying costs for these five alternatives are shown below. These calculations are based on the average inventory per period, hence the 1/2 (average for one week), 3/2 (one week plus the average for the second week), etc.

1. $(\$2) \cdot [(1/2) \cdot (10)] = \$10$.
2. $(\$2) \cdot [(1/2) \cdot (10) + (3/2) \cdot (10)] = \$40$.
3. $(\$2) \cdot [(1/2) \cdot (10) + (3/2) \cdot (10) + (5/2) \cdot (15)] = \$115$.
4. $(\$2) \cdot [(1/2) \cdot (10) + (3/2) \cdot 10 + (5/2) \cdot (15) + (7/2) \cdot (20)] = \$255$.
5. $(\$2) \cdot [(1/2) \cdot (10) + (3/2) \cdot (10) + (5/2) \cdot (15) + (7/2) \cdot (20) + (9/2) \cdot (70)] = \$885$.

In this case, the inventory carrying cost for alternative 4, ordering 55 units to cover the demand for the first four weeks, most nearly approximates the ordering cost of $300; that is, alternative 4 "balances" the cost of carrying inventory when ordering. Therefore, an order should be placed at the beginning of the first week and the next ordering decision need not be made until the beginning of week 5.

When this procedure is applied to the example data, the result is Figure 12.4. As seen, the total inventory cost is reduced by almost $500, or is 13 percent lower than the cost obtained with the periodic order quantity procedure. This procedure permits both the lot size and the time between orders to vary. Thus, for example, in periods of low requirements, it results in smaller lot sizes and longer time intervals between orders than occur for periods of high demand. This results in lower inventory-related costs.

FIGURE 12.4   Part period balancing example

Week number	1	2	3	4	5	6	7	8	9	10	11	12
Requirements	10	10	15	20	70	180	250	270	230	40	0	10
Order quantity	55				70	180	250	270	270			10
Beginning inventory	55	45	35	20	70	180	250	270	270	40	0	10
Ending inventory	45	35	20	0	0	0	0	0	40	0	0	0

Ordering cost	$2,100
Inventory carrying cost	1,385
Total cost	$3,485

Source: W. L. Berry, "Lot-Sizing Procedures for Requirements Planning Systems: A Framework for Analysis," *Production and Inventory Management,* 2nd Quarter 1972, p. 25.

Despite the fact that this procedure utilizes all of the information available, it will not always yield the minimum-cost ordering plan. Although this procedure can produce low-cost ordering plans, it may miss the minimum cost plan, since it does not evaluate all of the possibilities for ordering material to satisfy the demand in each week of the requirements schedule.

McLaren's order moment (MOM)

This procedure is quite similar to the part period balancing procedure. It evaluates the cost of placing orders for an integral number of future periods (e.g., for period 1 only; periods 1 and 2; periods 1, 2, and 3, etc.). However, instead of equating the total costs of placing orders and carrying inventory directly in determining order quantities, as in the case of the part period balancing procedure, the order moment procedure uses a part period accumulation principle.

A part period is one unit of inventory carried for one period. The total number of part periods accumulated across the planning horizon is proportional to the total inventory carrying cost. The McLaren order moment procedure determines the lot size for individual orders by matching the number of accumulated part periods to the number that would be incurred if an order for an EOQ were placed under the conditions of constant demand. This is accomplished by first calculating a target number of part periods, and then accumulating the actual period-by-period part periods until the target is reached. The target value is calculated as follows:

$$OMT = \bar{D} \left[\sum_{t=1}^{T^*-1} t + (TBO - T^*)T^* \right] \qquad (12.1)$$

where:

OMT = Order moment target.
$\bar{D}$ = Average requirements per period.
TBO = EOQ/$\bar{D}$.
T^* = The largest integer less than (or equal to) the TBO.

The order moment procedure accumulates requirements from consecutive periods into a tentative order until the accumulated part periods reach or exceed OMT in period k, using the following equation:

$$\sum_{t=1}^{k} (k - 1)D_k \geqslant OMT \qquad (12.2)$$

In the period when the accumulated part periods first reach or exceed the OMT value, a second test is made before the lot size for the current order quantity is determined.

The second test is made to see whether it is worthwhile to include one more period's requirement in the order. The test involves comparing the carrying cost incurred by including the requirement for period k in the current order with the cost of placing a new order for that period's requirements in period k. This comparison is made using the following equation:

$$C_H(k - 1)D_k \leqslant C_P \qquad (12.3)$$

where:

C_H = The inventory carrying cost per period.
k = The period currently under consideration.
D_k = The requirements for period k.
C_P = The ordering cost.

When the accumulated part periods exceed OMT and $C_H(k - 1) D_k \leqslant C_p$, the order quantity covers the requirements for periods 1 through k. However, when the accumulated part periods exceed OMT and when $C_H (k - 1) D_k > C_p$, the order quantity covers the requirements for periods 1 through $k - 1$.

The example shown in Figure 12.5 applies the MOM procedure to our example data. Note that the accumulated part periods first exceed the OMT target in week 4 when $(1 \cdot 10 + 2 \cdot 15 + 3 \cdot 20) > 73.7$. Since the cost of carrying the 20 units required in week 4 is less than the cost of placing an order in week 4 ($120 < 300$) in this case, the first order is placed in week 1 for 55 units. Then, since the accumulated part periods exceed OMT in weeks 5 through 8, and the cost of carrying the next week's requirement exceeds the ordering cost, weekly orders are placed during that time interval.

The total cost of using the order moment procedure in this example is $3,245, which is 7 percent less than the total cost for the part period balanc-

FIGURE 12.5   McLaren's order moment example

Week number	1	2	3	4	5	6	7	8	9	10	11	12
Requirements	10	10	15	20	70	180	250	270	230	40	0	10
Order quantity	55				70	180	250	270	280			
Beginning inventory	55	45	35	20	70	180	250	270	280	50	10	10
Ending inventory	45	35	20	0	0	0	0	0	50	10	10	0
Part periods	0	10	40	100	180†	250†	270†	230†	0	40	40	70
Exceed target?	No	No	No	Yes	Yes	Yes	Yes	Yes	–	–	–	No, but end of record
$C_H(k-1)D_k$	–	–	–	120	360	500	540	460				60

$\overline{D} = 92.1$

$EOQ = 166.2$

$TBO = 166.2/92.1 = 1.8$

$T^* = 1.0$

$OMT = 92.1[0 + (1.8 - 1)(1)] = 73.7$

Ordering cost	= $1,800
Inventory carrying cost	= 1,445
Total cost	= $3,245

†Measured in the following week.

Source: B. J. McLaren, "A Study of Multiple Level Lot-Sizing Techniques for Material Requirements Planning Systems." (Ph.D. dissertation, Purdue University, 1977).

ing procedure. In fact, the MOM procedure found the optimal solution in this particular example.

Wagner-Whitin algorithm

One optimizing procedure for determining the minimum-cost ordering plan for a time-phased requirements schedule is the Wagner-Whitin algorithm. Basically, this procedure evaluates all of the possible ways of ordering material to meet the demand in each week of the requirements schedule, using dynamic programming. We will not attempt to describe the computational aspects of the Wagner-Whitin algorithm in the space available to us here. Rather, we shall note the difference in performance between this procedure and the part period balancing procedure.

When the Wagner-Whitin algorithm is applied to the example, the results are shown as Figure 12.6. (Note that the order quantities are identical to those in Figure 12.5.) The total inventory cost is reduced by $240, or 7 percent, in comparison with the ordering plan produced by the part period balancing procedure in Figure 12.4. The difference between these two plans occurs in the lot size ordered in week 9. The part period balancing procedure did not consider the combined cost of placing orders in both weeks 9 and 12. By spending an additional $60 to carry 10 units of inventory forward from week 9 to 12, the $300 ordering cost in week 12 is avoided. In this case, a saving of $240 in total cost can be achieved. The increase in the number of ordering alternatives considered, however, clearly increases the computations needed in making ordering decisions.

FIGURE 12.6   Wagner-Whitin example

Week number	1	2	3	4	5	6	7	8	9	10	11	12
Requirements	10	10	15	20	70	180	250	270	230	40	0	10
Order quantity	55				70	180	250	270	280			
Beginning inventory	55	45	35	20	70	180	250	270	280	50	10	10
Ending inventory	45	35	20	0	0	0	0	0	50	10	10	0

Ordering cost	$1,800
Inventory carrying cost	1,445
Total cost	$3,245

Source: W. L. Berry, "Lot-Sizing Procedures for Requirements Planning Systems: A Framework for Analysis," *Production and Inventory Management,* 2nd Quarter 1972, p. 26.

Simulation experiments

The example problem we have used to illustrate the procedures is for only one product item, without regard for *its* components, with no rolling through time, and with only a fixed number of weeks of requirements. To better understand the performance of lot-sizing procedures, they should be compared in circumstances more closely related to the dynamics of an industrial situation. Many simulation experiments have been performed to do exactly that.

Figure 12.7 presents summary experimental results. The first experiment shown in this figure is for a single level (i.e., one MRP record) with no uncertainty. MOM, PPB, POQ, and EOQ are compared to Wagner-Whitin. MOM produces results about 5 percent more costly, PPB about 6 percent, POQ about 11 percent, and EOQ over 30 percent greater than Wagner-Whitin. The size of these differences may be more important than the magnitudes might indicate. Savings of 5 percent in total costs may not be trivial.

Moving down to the third experiment, we see the results for a multilevel situation, again with no uncertainty. In this case, the comparison is not against Wagner-Whitin, but against a dynamic programming procedure that produces close to optimal results in a multilevel environment. The key finding in this experiment is that the results are roughly the same as in the first comparisons, although POQ does a little worse and MOM a little better than in the first experiment.

Perhaps the most interesting result in Figure 12.7 is to compare the first and third experiments to the *second* experiment. The second experiment is for a single-level procedure, but *with* uncertainty expressed in the gross requirements data. The results here are quite mixed. Note that PPB does *better* than Wagner-Whitin, and both MOM and POQ are within 3 percent of Wagner-Whitin.

The conditions modeled in the second experiment replicate conditions

FIGURE 12.7   Summary experimental results

	Procedure				
	Wagner-Whitin	MOM	PPB	POQ	EOQ
Experiment 1: Percent over Wagner-Whitin cost; Single level, no uncertainty*	0	4.93	5.74	10.72	33.87
Experiment 2: Percent over Wagner-Whitin cost; Single level, uncertainty*	0	−0.25	−.67	2.58	.19
Experiment 3: Percent over nearly optimal procedure; Multilevel, no uncertainty†	.77	3.07	6.92	16.91	—
Computing time†	.30	.11	.10	.08	—

*These results are from U. Wemmerlöv and D. C. Whybark, "Lot-Sizing under Uncertainty in a Rolling Schedule Environment," *International Journal of Production Research* 22, no. 3 (1984).
†These results are from B. J. McLaren, "A Study of Multiple Level Lot-Sizing Techniques for Material Requirements Planning Systems" (Ph.D. dissertation, Purdue University, 1977). The multilevel procedure was designed specifically to take into account the relationships of a single part to its components and parents. The computing time is the average CPU time for one sample problem.

likely to be found in actual industrial situations. Moreover, other studies show that as uncertainty grows increasingly larger, it becomes very hard to distinguish between the lot-sizing procedures' performance. What is more, while there were statistically significant differences among procedures in the first experiment, there were none in the second.

The message is clear. Lot-sizing enhancements to an MRP system should only be done *after* major uncertainties have been removed from the system; that is, *after* data integrity is in place, other MPC system modules are working, stability is present at the MPS level, etc. If the MPC is not performing effectively, that is the place to start, *not* with lot-sizing procedures.

DETERMINATION OF PURCHASE ORDER QUANTITIES

So far, we have discussed procedures for determining lot sizes for manufactured items in an MRP environment. In many firms, a high percentage of component items are purchased from external sources. The purchase quantity decision can be very complex when price discounts are available for placing orders in large quantities and/or when transportation savings are available for shipping full carload quantities instead of less than carload lots. We start this section with a brief description of the purchasing discount problem and then turn to three procedures that take into account such discounts: least unit cost, least period cost, and McLaren order moment.

FIGURE 12.8   Example purchase discount problem

Period	1	2	3	4	5	6	7	8	9	10	11	12
Requirements	80	100	124	100	50	50	100	125	125	100	50	100

Ordering cost   = $100
Inventory carrying cost = $2/period/unit
Base price   = $500/unit
Discount price   = $450/unit
Discount quantity   = 350 units

The purchasing discount problem

To illustrate each of these procedures, an example problem will be used based on the first four periods' requirements shown in Figure 12.8. Note that, in addition to the ordering and the inventory carrying costs used in the previous examples, base and discount prices and the discount quantity have been added for this item.

A convention has developed in the purchasing research literature that affects the procedures we will describe. The purchasing procedures use *period-end* inventory balances to calculate the inventory carrying cost. This is not the same convention as that used previously for the manufacturing lot-size calculations. To be consistent with the previous purchasing lot-sizing research, we will use the period-end inventory convention.

The increase of the quantity discount information adds complexity to the solution of this ordering problem. Moreover, the specification of an "all units" discount, such as a $500/unit price for units 1 through 349 and a $450 price for a *total* order quantity exceeding 349 units, presents further computational difficulties. Alternatively, an "additional units" discount is sometimes specified, such as a $500/unit price for units 1 through 349 and a $450/ unit price for any *additional* units ordered in excess of 349. Unlike the additional units discount schedule, the all units discount applies to all units purchased, when at least the discount quantity is purchased. The all units discount is considerably more common in industry than the additional units discount, and it creates a considerably more difficult decision problem.

The ordering procedures we now consider assume the use of an all units discount, as well as the earlier assumptions listed for the manufacturing order quantities under MRP (except average inventory). In addition, several conventions are followed for all of the procedures. One is to consider orders sequentially, which would cover an increasing number of periods. For the example shown in Figure 12.8, this would be orders of 80 (1 period), 180 (2 periods), and so on. In addition, an order for the exact discount quantity (350 units) is considered. Another convention is that calculations are made for at least the number of periods needed to reach the discount quantity (period 4 in the example). An explanation of the details of each procedure is provided in the following paragraphs.

Least unit cost. The least unit cost (LUC) procedure evaluates different order quantities by accumulating requirements, at least through the period in which the discount can be obtained, until the cost/unit starts to increase. The order is placed for the quantity that provides the least unit cost. There are three steps in using this procedure. First, requirements are accumulated through an integral number of periods until the quantity to be ordered is sufficient to qualify for the discount price. The next step is to determine whether the discount should be accepted on the basis of the least unit cost criterion. The final step is to evaluate ordering a quantity exactly equal to the discount quantity. If the least unit cost criterion indicates that neither the integral number of periods nor exactly the discount quantity is the most economical order, the order will be placed for a quantity without the discount.

These steps are illustrated using Figure 12.9 and the example problem shown in Figure 12.8. The setup cost of $100 is incurred once it has been determined that an order will be placed. The inventory carrying cost is accumulated at $2 per unit times the number of periods it will be carried until the period in which it is used. The base price per unit is $500 per unit until a point during period 4, hereafter called "period 3*," the time at which the cumulative requirements exactly equal the discount quantity and where the unit price drops to $450. The additional inventory carrying cost will be (350 − 304) × $2 × 3 periods ($276) as the remaining 46 units would not be used until period 4. The total inventory carrying cost for period 3* is $276 + $696 = $972. Cost per unit is the total cost divided by the cumulative requirements. When the cost per unit increases (as in period 4) and the discount quantity has been surpassed, the LUC heuristic chooses as the lot size the quantity that provides minimum cost per unit (i.e., $453.06, lot size = 350).

FIGURE 12.9   Least unit cost example

Period	Require-ments	Cumulative require-ments	Setup cost	Inventory carrying cost	Unit purchase price	Cumulative total cost	Cost/ unit
1	80	80	$100	$ 0	$500	$ 40,100	$501.25
2	100	180	100	200	500	90,300†	501.67
3	124	304	100	696	500	152,796	502.62
3*	46	350	100	972	450	158,572	453.06
4	100	404	100	1,296	450	183,196	453.46

†(180 × 500) + $100 + $200 = $90,300.

Least period cost. The least period cost (LPC) works in the same manner as the least unit cost procedure, except that the criterion for lot sizing is changed. The calculation of costs in LPC is the same as in the LUC procedure (Figure 12.9). The difference between LPC and LUC is that LPC uses the lowest cost per *period* to determine the lot size, instead of the lowest cost per *unit*. The number of periods of demand considered is the divisor for the cost/period calculation. At period 3* where the exact discount quantity is considered, the period is determined by adding the fraction of the period proportional to the quantity required to qualify for the discount [3 + (350 − 304)/100] = 3.46, where 100 is the requirement in the split period (4). The LPC procedure uses the cost per period as the criterion for lot sizing, and, for this example, the lot size would be 80, as is indicated in Figure 12.10.

McLaren's order moment. The McLaren's order moment (MOM) procedure works somewhat differently. First, the attractiveness of the discount is measured by calculating the number of part periods of inventory that would have to be carried to offset the potential savings from the discount. Part periods are accumulated by summing the number of units to be carried times the number of periods they are carried. Next, the actual number of part periods necessary to qualify for the discount is determined from the requirements and the decision whether to order exactly the discount quantity is made, even if it means splitting requirements to qualify exactly for the discount. If the discount is favorable, the order placed will be for the discount quantity. If it is unfavorable, McLaren's procedure for determining a lot size without discounts is used.

Figure 12.11 presents an application of the McLaren procedure to the example purchase discount problem. The first step is to calculate the number of part periods that would exactly offset the savings available from the discount. This is termed the *target level* and is the dollar savings gained by taking the discount divided by the incremental cost of carrying an additional unit for one period. Equation (12.4) expresses the calculation of the target level. To perform the lot sizing, the actual cumulative part periods until the

FIGURE 12.10   Least period cost example

Period	Cumulative requirements	Cumulative total cost	Cost/period
1	80	$ 40,100	$40,100
2	180	90,300	45,150
3	304	152,796	50,932
3*	350	158,572	45,930
4	404	193,196	45,799

FIGURE 12.11 McLaren's order moment example

Period	Requirements	Cumulative requirements	Part periods	Cumulative part periods
1	80	80	80 × 0 = 0	0
2	100	180	100 × 1 = 100	100
3	124	304	124 × 2 = 248	348
4	100	404	100 × 3 = 300	648

discount quantity is exceeded are computed and tested against the target level, as shown in Figure 12.11.

$$\text{Target level} = \frac{(\text{Base price } - \text{ Discount price}) \times \text{Discount quantity}}{\text{Inventory carrying cost per period}}$$
$$= [(\$500 - \$450) \times 350]/\$2$$
$$= 8,750 \text{ part periods} \qquad (12.4)$$

At period 4, the cumulative requirements exceed the discount quantity, and the cumulative part-periods are less than the target level. This indicates that the discount will more than offset the extra carrying costs associated with the larger quantity. The lot size is set to 350. The requirements in period 4 are then reset to 404 − 350 = 54. Note that, if the number of part periods exceeds the target at four periods, the comparison is made for exactly 350 units to determine whether splitting the period's requirements is worthwhile.

The essence of the MOM procedure is to first answer the question: Is it worthwhile to carry the extra inventory required to qualify for the quantity discount? The target level states how much extra inventory *can* be carried (in part period terms) and still make the discount worthwhile. If the amount that *must* be carried, given the actual requirements, is less, the decision is to order the discount quantity. To decide whether to purchase even more than the discount quantity, the look-ahead feature is employed. It is described next.

Look-ahead feature

Each of the three purchase discount procedures can be used with a *look-ahead* enhancement. After the procedure has determined the initial lot size, the look-ahead feature performs a check to see whether the cost of carrying an additional period's requirements (or the remainder of a period that has had its requirements split), is less than the cost of the setup required to supply that period's requirements in a separate order. If the cost of carrying the additional inventory is less, the requirements are added to the original lot and the look-ahead procedure is repeated on the following period's requirements, and again for the next period until it no longer pays to carry the additional inventory.

An illustration of the look-ahead feature will be developed for the example purchase discount problem. For the least unit cost example in Figure 12.9, a lot size of 350 units has been determined. The remaining requirements in period 4 are 54. Using the look-ahead test, calculate the carrying cost of 54 units to period 4 and compare it to the setup cost:

$$54 \text{ units} \times 3 \text{ periods} \times \$2/\text{unit} = \$324$$
$$\text{Setup cost} = \$100$$

The look-ahead test fails if carrying costs exceed the setup cost; the lot size remains at 350. If the carrying cost had been less than the setup cost, the additional units would be included in the lot size and the look-ahead feature would be applied to the requirements in period 5.

Performance comparisons

Simulation experiments have been conducted to evaluate the performance of these lot-sizing procedures. The results of one set of experiments is presented in Figure 12.12. For this set of results, a mixed integer programming (MIP) procedure was used to provide optimal solutions to the

FIGURE 12.12   Summary of discount procedure comparisons

Procedure	Average % above optimal cost	Max. % above opt. cost	Percent of optimal solutions	Ave. computer time[4]	Max. computer time[4]
MIP[1]	0	0	100	85.76	778.360
WWM[2]	.326	1.35	19	.0121	.014
LUC(LA)[3]	.491	5.406	53	.0017	.004
LPC(LA)[3]	2.136	11.118	6	.0016	.002
MOM(LA)[3]	.486	5.406	50	.0010	.002
LUC	.164	3.355	58	.0015	.003
LPC	2.158	11.118	6	.0017	.003
MOM	.031	.230	53	.0010	.002

[1]Mixed integer program (optimal).
[2]Wagner-Whiten modified.
[3]With look ahead (LA).
[4]CPU seconds on a CDC 6600.
Source: T. E. Callarman and D. C. Whybark, "A Comparison of Procedures for Determining Purchase Quantities for Time-Phased MRP Requirements," *Journal of Purchasing and Materials Management,* Fall 1981.

problems as reference points for the comparisons. The Wagner-Whitin procedure was modified to accommodate the discounts and was used as another approximate procedure.

The other procedures in Figure 12.12 are those described here, both with and without look-ahead. Surprisingly, performance is worse with the look-ahead option for two of the three procedures. The LPC procedure suffers in comparison to the others, on virtually every count. On the other hand, the MOM procedure excels in every category but one: the percent of optimal solutions found. The trade-off between LUC and the Wagner-Whitin modified (WWM) procedure is the dispersion versus the average. WWM is much closer to the optimal solution in the worst case, but has worse overall performance.

Perhaps the biggest practical difference between the MOM and LUC procedures is the ease of understanding. In that category, LUC wins out. Both are superior, on the average, to the other nonoptimal procedures and have very reasonable computer times. Also the cost differences appear small in an absolute sense. Three points must be made about this. First, the comparisons are among reasonable procedures and may understate the saving over practice. Second, even a small unit saving for a company whose purchases represent a large proportion of the cost of goods sold can be a large total that passes right through to the bottom line. Finally, the savings shown are based on *total* cost. If just the controllable costs (setup, inventory, and potential discount) are used, the percentage differences are highly magnified.

These experiments were performed without any uncertainty, using fixed scheduling horizons. In additional experiments performed under conditions of purchase discounts, rolling schedules, and uncertainty, the differences between procedures shrank and absolute costs increased. This is the same result we had pointed out in Figure 12.7 for the single price procedures. The lesson is depicted in the graph in Figure 12.13. It makes little difference about the procedures compared—the results are the same. The overall conclusion is, likewise, the same. Reducing the surprises to a minimum is a worthwhile step in itself and a necessary prelude to reaping the benefits of the differences in the procedures described here.

BUFFERING CONCEPTS

In this section we deal with another advanced concept in MRP, the use of buffering mechanisms to protect against uncertainties. We do, however, want to make the same proviso that was made for lot sizing: Buffering is not the way to make up for a poorly operating MRP system. First things must come first.

FIGURE 12.13   Effect of uncertainty on performance comparisons

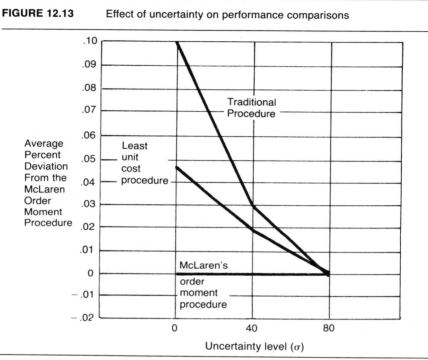

Categories of uncertainty

There are two basic sources of uncertainty that affect an MRP system: demand and supply uncertainty. These are further separated into two types: quantity uncertainty and timing uncertainty. The combination of sources and types provides the four categories of uncertainty that are summarized in Figure 12.14 and illustrated in Figure 12.15.

Demand timing uncertainty is illustrated in Figure 12.15 by timing changes in the requirements from period to period. For example, the projected requirements for 372 units in period 7 have actually occurred in period 4. This shift might have resulted from a change in the promise date to a customer or from a change in a planned order for a higher-level item on which this item is used.

Supply timing uncertainty can arise from variations in vendor lead times

FIGURE 12.14   Categories of uncertainty in MRP systems

	Sources	
Types	Demand	Supply
Timing	Requirements shift from one period to another	Orders not received when due
Quantity	Requirements for more or less than planned	Orders received for more or less than planned

Source: D. C. Whybark and J. G. Williams, "Material Requirements Planning under Uncertainty," *Decision Sciences*, October 1976, p. 598.

FIGURE 12.15   Examples of the four categories of uncertainty

	Periods									
	1	*2*	*3*	*4*	*5*	*6*	*7*	*8*	*9*	*10*
Demand timing:										
Projected requirements	0	0	0	0	0	0	372	130	0	255
Actual requirements	0	0	0	372	130	0	146	255	143	0
Supply timing:										
Planned receipts	0	0	502	0	0	403	0	0	144	0
Actual receipts	502	0	0	0	0	403	0	0	144	0
Demand quantity:										
Projected requirements	85	122	42	190	83	48	41	46	108	207
Actual requirements	103	77	0	101	124	15	0	100	80	226
Supply quantity:										
Planned receipts	0	161	0	271	51	0	81	109	0	327
Actual receipts	0	158	0	277	50	0	77	113	0	321

Source: D. C. Whybark and J. G. Williams, "Material Requirements Planning under Uncertainty," *Decision Sciences*, October 1976, p. 599.

or shop flow times. Thus, once an order is released, the exact timing of its arrival is uncertain. In Figure 12.15, for example, a receipt scheduled for period 3 actually arrived in period 1. Note that in this case the uncertainty is not over the amount of the order but over its timing. The entire order may be late or early.

Demand quantity uncertainty is manifest when the amount of a requirement varies, perhaps randomly, about some mean value. This might occur when the master production schedule is increased or decreased to reflect changes in customer orders or the demand forecast. It can also occur when there are changes on higher level items on which this item is used, or when there are variations in inventory levels. In the example of Figure 12.15, the period 1 projected requirements of 85 actually involved a usage of 103 units.

Supply quantity uncertainty typically arises when there are shortages of lower level material, when production lots incur scrap losses, or when production overruns occur. Figure 12.15 illustrates this category of uncertainty, where the actual quantity received varied around the planned receipts.

Safety stock and safety lead time

There are two basic ways to buffer uncertainty in an MRP system. One of these is to specify a quantity of safety stock in much the same manner as is done with statistical inventory control techniques. The second method, safety lead time, plans order releases earlier than indicated by the requirements plan and schedules their receipt earlier than the required due date. Both approaches produce an increase in inventory levels to provide a buffer against uncertainty, but the techniques operate quite differently. The differences are illustrated in Figure 12.16.

In the first case, shown in Figure 12.16, no buffering is used. A net requirement occurs in period 5, and a planned order is created in period 3 to cover it. In the second case, a safety stock of 20 units is specified. This means that the safety stock level will be broken in period 3 unless an order is received. The MRP logic thus creates a planned order in period 1 to prevent this condition. The final case in Figure 12.16 illustrates use of safety lead time. In this example, a safety lead time of one period is included. The net result is the planned order being created in period 2 with a due date of period 4.

Most MRP software packages can easily accommodate safety stock, since the planned orders can be determined simply by subtracting the safety stock from the initial inventory balance when determining the projected available balance. Safety lead time is a bit more difficult. This cannot be achieved by simply inflating the lead time by the amount of the safety lead time. In our example, this approach would not produce the result shown as the last case in Figure 12.16. The due date for the order would be period 5, instead of period 4. Thus, the planned due date, as well as the planned release date, must be changed.

Both safety stock and safety lead time illustrate the fundamental problem with all MRP buffering techniques: They lie to the system. The *real* need date for the planned order shown in Figure 12.16 is period 5. If the *real* lead time is two periods, the *real* launch date should be period 3. Putting in buffers can lead to behavioral problems in the shop, since the resulting schedules do not tell the truth. An informal system may be created to tell people what is really needed. This, in turn, might lead to larger buffers. There is a critical need to communicate the reasoning behind the use of

FIGURE 12.16   Safety stock and safety lead time buffering

Order quantity = 50 units
Lead time = 2 periods

No buffering used	1	2	3	4	5
Gross requirements		20	40	20	0	30
Scheduled receipts			50			
Projected available balance	40	20	30	10	10	30
Planned order releases				50		

Safety stock = 20 units	1	2	3	4	5
Gross requirements		20	40	20	0	30
Scheduled receipts			50			
Projected available balance	40	20	30	60	60	30
Planned order releases		50				

Safety lead time = 1 period	1	2	3	4	5
Gross requirements		20	40	20	0	30
Scheduled receipts			50			
Projected available balance	40	20	30	10	60	30
Planned order releases			50			

Source: D. C. Whybark and J. G. Williams, "Material Requirements Planning under Uncertainty," *Decision Sciences*, October 1976, p. 601.

safety stock and safety lead times, and to create a working MPC system that minimizes the need for buffers.

Safety stock and safety lead performance comparisons

Simulation experiments have been reported that indicate there is a preference for using either safety stock or safety lead time, depending on the category of uncertainty to be buffered. These results show a distinct preference for using safety lead time in all cases where demand or supply *timing*

FIGURE 12.17 Experimental results: Average inventory versus service level with timing uncertainty

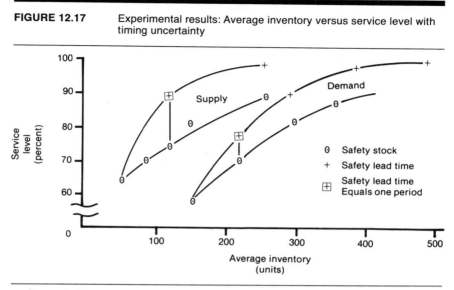

Source: D. C. Whybark and J. G. Williams, "Material Requirements Planning under Uncertainty," *Decision Sciences,* October 1976, p. 602.

uncertainty exists. Likewise, the experiments show a strong preference for using safety stock in all cases where there is uncertainty in either the demand or supply *quantity.*

Typical results from these experiments are shown in Figures 12.17 and 12.18. Figure 12.17 compares safety stock and safety lead time for simulated situations similar to the top two examples shown in Figure 12.15. The horizontal axis shows the average inventory held, and the vertical axis depicts the service level in percentage terms; that is, the horizontal axis is based on the period-by-period actual inventory values in the simulation, the vertical axis is based upon the frequency with which the actual requirements were met from inventory.

For both the supply and the demand timing uncertainty cases, Figure 12.17 shows a strong preference for safety lead time buffering. For any given level of inventory, a higher service level can be achieved with safety lead time than with safety stock. For any given level of service, safety lead time can provide the level with a smaller inventory investment.

Figure 12.18 shows the comparison for uncertainty in quantities. This simulated situation is similar to the bottom two examples shown in Figure 12.15. The results are a bit more difficult to see, since the graphs for supply and demand uncertainty overlap. Nevertheless, the results are again clear. For any given level of inventory investment, higher service levels are

FIGURE 12.18   Experimental results: Average inventory versus service level with quantity uncertainty

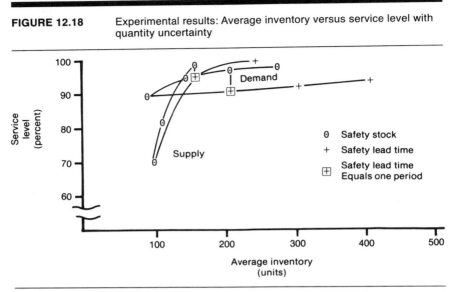

Source: D. C. Whybark and J. G. Williams, "Material Requirements Planning under Uncertainty," *Decision Sciences,* October 1976, p. 603.

achieved by the use of safety stocks than by the use of safety lead times. This result is true for situations involving quantity uncertainty in both demand and supply.

The results of the experiments provide general guidelines for choosing between the two buffering techniques. Under conditions of uncertainty in timing, safety lead time is the preferred technique, while safety stock is preferred under conditions of quantity uncertainty. The experimental conclusions did not change with the source of the uncertainty (demand or supply), lot-sizing technique, lead time, average demand level, uncertainty level, or lumpiness in the gross requirements data. The experiments also indicate that, as the lumpiness and uncertainty levels increase, the importance of making the correct choice between safety stock and safety lead time increases.

There are some important practical implications of these guidelines. Supply timing uncertainty and demand quantity uncertainty are the two categories for which the differences in service levels are largest. An obvious instance of supply timing uncertainty is in vendor lead times. Orders from vendors are subject to timing uncertainty, because of variability in both production and transportation times. These experiments strongly support the use of safety lead time for purchased parts experiencing this type of uncertainty. Demand quantity uncertainty often is found in an MRP system for parts subject to service part demand. Another cause of demand quantity uncertainty is when an end product can be made from very different options or features. The use of safety stock for buffering against these uncertainties is supported by the experimental results.

Other buffering mechanisms

Before leaving the discussion of uncertainty, it is useful to consider some additional alternatives for dealing with uncertainty. One useful way to cope with uncertainty is to reduce it; that is, rather than living with uncertainty, an alternative is to reduce it to an absolute minimum. In fact, that is one of the major objectives of MPC systems.

For example, increasing the accuracy of demand forecasts and the development of effective procedures for translating the demand for products into master schedules reduces the amount of uncertainty that is transmitted to the MRP system. Along these same lines, freezing the master schedule for some time period achieves the same result. Developing an effective priority system for moving parts and components through the shop reduces the uncertainty in lead times. Responsive shop-floor control systems can achieve better due date performance, thereby reducing uncertainty. Procedures that improve the accuracy of the data in the MRP system reduce uncertainty regarding on-hand inventory levels. Increased inspection and more stringent quality control procedures reduce the number of defective units in a production lot. Other activities could be mentioned, but all focus on the reduction of the amount of uncertainty that needs to be accommodated in an MRP system.

Another way to deal with uncertainty in an MRP system is to provide for slack in the production system in one way or another. Production slack is caused by having additional time, manpower, machine capacity, and so on, over what is specifically needed to produce the planned amount of product. This extra production capacity could be used to produce an oversized lot to allow for shrinkage in that lot through the process. It could be used to allow for the production of lots on overtime or for additional machinery to speed their progress through the shop. Thus, providing additional capacity in the shop allows for accommodating greater quantities than are planned in a given time period, or for expediting jobs through the shop. It must be understood, however, that slack costs money. In fact, the objective of a good MPC system should be to *reduce* the slack.

NERVOUSNESS

Several enhancements to MRP systems have been described in this chapter. However, it should be recognized that some of the lot-sizing procedures can contribute to the problem of "nervousness" (i.e., instability) in the MRP plans. In this section, we discuss the problem of nervousness in MRP systems and guidelines for reducing the magnitude of this problem.

Sources of MRP system nervousness

MRP system nervousness is commonly defined as significant changes in MRP plans, which are produced even though there are only minor changes in the higher level MRP records or master production schedule. The changes can involve the quantity or timing of planned orders or scheduled receipts. The example shown as Figure 12.19 illustrates just such a case. Here, a reduction of one unit in the master schedule in week 2 produced a significant change in the planned orders for item A. This change had an even more profound impact on component part B. It is hard to imagine that a *reduction* at the MPS level could create a past-due condition, but that is precisely what is illustrated in Figure 12.19. The example illustrates how the change caused by a relatively minor shift in the master schedule is amplified by the use of the periodic order quantity (POQ) lot-sizing procedure.

There are a number of ways that relatively minor changes in the MRP system can create nervousness and instability in the MRP plans. These include planned orders that are released in an unplanned quantity or which are prematurely released, unplanned demand (as for spare parts or engineering requirements), and shifts in MRP parameter values, such as safety stock, safety lead time, or planned lead-time values. The nervousness created by such changes is most damaging in MRP systems with many levels in the product structure. Furthermore, the use of some lot-sizing techniques, such as POQ, can amplify the system nervousness at lower levels in the product structure, as indicated by the example in Figure 12.19.

Reducing MRP system nervousness

There are several ways of reducing the nervousness in MRP systems. First, it is important to reduce the causes of changes to the MRP plan. It is important to introduce stability into the master schedule through such devices as freezing and time fences. Similarly, it is important to reduce the incidence of unplanned demands by incorporating spare parts forecasts into MRP record gross requirements. Furthermore, it is necessary to follow the MRP plan with regard to the timing and the quantity of planned order releases. Finally, it is important to control the introduction of parameter changes, such as changes in safety stock levels or planned lead times. All of these actions will help dampen the small adjustments that can trigger MRP system nervousness.

A second guideline for reducing MRP system nervousness involves the selective use of lot-sizing procedures; that is, if nervousness still exists after reducing the causes above, different lot-sizing procedures might be used at

FIGURE 12.19   MRP system nervousness example

Before reducing second-week requirements by one unit:
Item A
POQ = 5 weeks
Lead time = 2 weeks

Week		1	2	3	4	5	6	7	8
Gross requirements		2	24	3	5	1	3	4	50
Scheduled receipts									
Projected available balance	28	26	2	13	8	7	4	0	0
Planned order releases		14					50		

Component B
POQ = 5 weeks
Lead time = 4 weeks

Week		1	2	3	4	5	6	7	8
Gross requirements		14					50		
Scheduled receipts		14							
Projected available balance	2	2	2	2	2	2	0	0	0
Planned order releases			48						

After second-week requirement change:
Item A
POQ = 5 weeks
Lead time = 2 weeks

Week		1	2	3	4	5	6	7	8
Gross requirements		2	(23)	3	5	1	3	4	50
Scheduled receipts									
Projected available balance	28	26	3	0	58	57	54	50	0
Planned order releases			63						

Component B
POQ = 5 weeks
Lead time = 4 weeks

Week		1	2	3	4	5	6	7	8
Gross requirements			63						
Scheduled receipts		14							
Projected available balance	2	16	−47						
Planned order releases		(47)							

Past due

different product structure levels. One approach is to use fixed order quantities at the top level, using either fixed order quantities or lot-for-lot at intermediate levels, and using period order quantities at the bottom level. Since the fixed order quantity procedure passes along only order timing changes (and not changes in order quantity), this procedure tends to dampen lot-size-induced nervousness. Clearly, the fixed order quantity values need to be monitored, since changes in the level of requirements may tend to make such quantities uneconomical over time.

A third guideline for reducing nervousness involves the use of the firm planned order in MRP (or in MPS) records. The use of firm planned orders tends to stabilize the requirements for lower-level items. The offsetting cost, however, is the necessary maintenance of firm planned orders by MRP planners.

These guidelines provide methods for reducing nervousness in MRP plans. There is a distinction, however, between nervousness in the MRP *plans* and nervousness in the *execution* of MRP system plans. Nervousness in the execution of the plans can also influence behavior. If the system users see the plans changing, they may make arbitrary or defensive decisions. This can further aggravate changes in plans.

One way to deal with the execution issue is simply to reduce the frequency with which the updated information is passed to system users. This suggestion would argue against the use of net change MRP systems, or at least against publishing every change. An alternative is simply to have more intelligent users. A well-trained user responding to the problem indicated in Figure 12.19 might, through bottom-up replanning, change the lot sizes to eliminate the problem. However, Figure 12.19 does indicate that this is not an easy problem to detect. Many aspects are counter-intuitive. The fact still is, that more intelligent users will make more intelligent execution decisions. User education may be the best investment!

OTHER ADVANCED MRP CONCEPTS

There are several additional MRP concepts or conventions that are used in practice to facilitate use of the system. The applicability of some of these ideas depends upon the company environment. In this section, we briefly deal with timing conventions, bucketless MRP systems, phantom assemblies, scrap allowances, and automatic updating of MRP data base elements.

Timing conventions

The timing convention we have used in the MRP records throughout this book has been that a gross requirement was due at the *beginning* of the period. Other conventions are sometimes used, and, to some extent, any convention will work if it is consistently applied and universally understood.

If shop paper for an order specifies a due date in a particular week, this is interpreted as meaning the *end* of that week; that is, if an order is due in week 3 and is done by Friday of week 3, it is on time. This obviously cannot work if the order is to satisfy a gross requirement for which it was assumed that completion would be at the beginning of week 3.

The problem is only partially solved by making the due date Monday. It still takes time to close out the shop order, recognize the new on-hand balance, create shop orders for the parent item, pick the parts, move them, and begin work. For this reason, some firms make the due dates for a shop order the week prior to the one in which the parent item is to start. This timing convention has the same result as using one week of safety lead time. In fact, the shop may use all of the week except the weekend by not completing the order until Friday.

Bucketless systems

To some extent, the problems of timing conventions are tied to the use of time buckets. When the buckets are small enough, the problems are reduced significantly. However, smaller buckets mean more buckets, which increases the review, storage, and computation costs. A bucketless MRP system specifies the exact release and due dates for each requirement, scheduled receipt, and planned order. The managerial reports are printed out on whatever basis is required, including by exact dates.

Bucketless MRP systems are a better way to use the computer. Above and beyond that, the approach can allow for better maintenance of lead time offsets and provide more precise time-phased information. The approach is consistent with state-of-the-art software, and many firms are now successfully using bucketless systems.

A related concept is real-time systems. Dedicated real-time systems are now the state-of-the-art in MPC. These systems are run on a daily basis (regeneration or net change), utilizing bucketless concepts. The major addition is that the planning cycle itself is bucketless. That is, plans are revised as necessary, not on a periodic schedule, and the entire execution cycle is also shortened.

Phantom assemblies

Another issue related to timing has to do with *phantom assemblies*. In essence, a phantom assembly is any assembly that does not go into and out of inventory; that is, it is an assembly that exists physically but is normally not stored, so inventory transactions are not posted against it. An example would be the assembly of a drawer in a chest that is made as the chest is being assembled. Still another example is the chest itself, which is assembled but thereafter finished (stain, and the rest). We see then that many times there can be phantoms within phantoms.

The need for phantom assemblies can potentially be eliminated by redesigning the bill of materials and engineering drawings. Note that, in the drawer/chest example, this would mean having the drawer parts listed on the single-level bill of materials for the chest, and the drawer itself no longer existing. This will not always work. There are times when the phantom does exist; that is, the drawer does not get assembled into the chest and must be inventoried. This can occur when more subassemblies (drawers) than needed are produced, or when the subassemblies are sold as service parts.

Phantom assembly treatment is widely used as MRP planning evolves into just-in-time (JIT) execution. That is, the number of "real" bill of material levels is reduced so that products go into and out of inventory (requiring MRP planning) fewer times. This by itself can reduce inventory and lead times.

If subassemblies are not treated as phantoms, the bill of material processing logic will necessarily create orders for *both* chests *and* drawers. One reason, therefore, that firms use phantom assemblies is to avoid the work and time associated with closing out shop orders and opening new shop orders; that is, the objective of the phantom assembly treatment of the drawers is to pull drawer parts automatically by only launching orders for chest assemblies and not drawer assemblies.

The phantom condition can also exist in areas that are not truly assemblies. For example, many firms do not typically inventory parts coming off a paint line (even though painted parts have different part numbers than unpainted ones); they simply flow into final assembly and not through inventory, *unless* they are to be used for service parts or extras are produced.

Phantom bill treatment in MRP requires special processing. The net requirements for the phantom bills must be determined (in case there are any inventories), so they can be passed down to the components, but without creating explicit records. The trick to gross to netting the phantom requirements is to explicitly code a phantom bill (to avoid producing the record) and use a zero lead time offset. Whenever a specific need for phantom items occurs, say for service parts, the phantom itself can be treated as any other MRP record item, with usual order-launching treatment.

Scrap allowances

A concept closely tied to buffering is the use of scrap allowances in calculating the lot size to start into production to reach some desired lot size going into the stockroom. It is a fairly straightforward procedure to use any lot-sizing procedure to determine the lot size and then adjust the result to take account of the scrap allowance. One issue that arises is whether the quantity shown on the shop paper (and as a scheduled receipt) should be the *starting* quantity or the *expected finished* quantity. Practice suggests the use of the former. This requires, however, that each actual occurrence of scrap be transacted and reflected in updated plans.

The overall issue of the scrap allowance is similar to the use of safety stocks for quantity uncertainty buffering. In fact, the two issues are clearly related. One or both of these buffers could be used in a particular situation. The point is that, if scrap losses occur, they must be planned for and buffered. It also means that this may be an area where tight control can lead to performance improvements.

An advanced MRP concept related to scrap allowances is how they should be applied in a volatile learning environment, such as is the case in the manufacture of integrated circuits. In such cases, there are typically low initial yields, followed by learning or improvement in yields. Dolinski shows that substantial reductions in mean inventory levels can be realized in low-yield environments if learning is properly included in the order release logic. This finding proves to be robust with respect to modest errors in the estimation of the learning rate.

Automatic updating

The final enhancement issue we consider is the use of the computer to automatically perform a transaction normally done by MRP planners. A good case in point is the updating of scheduled receipt due dates as indicated by exception coding; that is, the computer software tells an MRP planner that the due date for a scheduled receipt needs to be moved from week 7 to week 6. Why not let the computer do it automatically?

We raise this issue here, under advanced concepts, because the operational issue is similar to that of more sophisticated lot sizing: It is OK—*after* one has the basic house in order. When an MRP system is in place, data integrity is good, the other MPC systems are in place, and users are well trained, *then* automatic updating might make sense.

There are two good reasons for doing the updating of scheduled receipt data automatically. First, the new data will be passed more quickly to shop-floor control; the result will be a more responsive shop-floor control system. The second reason is to save time and effort for the MRP planners. Typically, a large percentage of the exception messages involve minor repositioning of scheduled receipt data. If this is done by the computer, time can be freed for more useful pursuits.

A related issue is "back flushing" as done in JIT. There, component inventories are only reduced in quantity after the final products in which they are imbedded are received into finished goods. The benefit is reduced transaction processing; the cost is a slight mismatch between the records and reality. With fast throughput and educated users, the costs can be well worth it.

The key question of whether to do automatic updating or not is behavioral and partly related to system nervousness. Are the users ready for it? Do *they* want it? Will *they* still be accountable for the results? Will *they* have a hand in specifying the logic used to automatically update? Is the system stable enough to not produce too many surprises? Once again, we see this enhancement intimately tied to the development of intelligent system users.

CONCLUDING PRINCIPLES

Chapter 12 describes several advanced concepts and conventions in MRP systems. Many of the ideas are of research interest, but all of them have practical implications, as well. There are, in fact, certain kinds of enhancements that can be made in a well-operating MRP system, if made by knowledgeable professionals, and if implemented with knowledgeable users. We see the following principles as critical:

- MRP enhancement should be done *after* a basic MPC system is in place.
- Discrete lot-sizing procedures for manufacturing can reduce inventory-associated costs. Some procedures work better than others.
- Selecting the appropriate lot-sizing procedure for purchasing can also lead to cost savings.
- Safety stocks are a preferred buffer when the uncertainty is of the quantity category.
- Safety lead times are preferred when uncertainty is of the timing category.
- MRP system nervousness can result from lot-sizing rules, parameter changes, and other causes. The MPC professional must understand this issue and take appropriate precautions.
- MRP system enhancements depend upon the growth of ever more intelligent users.

REFERENCES

Axsater, Sven. "Evaluation of Lot Sizing Techniques." *International Journal of Production Research* 24, no. 1 (1986), pp. 51–57.

Baker, K. R. "Safety Stocks and Component Commonality," *Journal of Operations Management* 6, no. 1 (1986).

Benton, W. C. "Multiple Price Breaks and Alternative Purchase Lot Size Procedures in Material Requirements Planning Systems." *International Journal of Production Research* 23, no. 5 (1985), pp. 1025–1047.

————, and R. Srivastava. "Product Structure Complexity and Multilevel Lot Sizing Using Alternative Costing Policies." *Decision Sciences* 16, no. 4 (Fall 1985).

————, and D. C. Whybark, "Material Requirements Planning (MRP) and Purchase Discounts." *Journal of Operations Management*, February 1982, pp. 137–143.

Berry, W. L. "Lot Sizing Procedures for Requirements Planning Systems: A Framework for Analysis." *Production and Inventory Management* 13, no. 2 (2nd Quarter 1972), pp. 19–33.

Bitran, G. R.; D. M. Marieni; H. Matsuo; and J. W. Noonan. "Multimate MRP." *Journal of Operations Management* 5, no. 2 (1985).

Blackburn, J. D.; D. H. Kropp; and R. A. Millen. "A Comparison of Strategies to Dampen Nervousness in MRP Systems." *Management Science* 32, no. 4 (April 1986).

————, and R. A. Millen. "A Methodology for Predicting Single-Stage Lot-Sizing Performance: Analysis and Experiments." *Journal of Operations Management* 5, no. 4 (1986).

Bobko, P. R., and D. C. Whybark. "The Coefficient of Variation as a Factor in MRP Research." *Decision Sciences* 16, no. 4 (Fall 1985).

Callarman, T. F.; and D. C. Whybark. "Determining Purchase Quantities for MRP Requirements." *Journal of Purchasing and Materials Management* 17, no. 3 (Fall 1981), pp. 25–30.

————, and R. S. Hamrin. "A Comparison of Dynamic Lot Sizing Rules for Use in a Single Stage MRP System with Demand Uncertainty." *International Journal of Operations and Production Management* 4, no. 2, 1984, pp. 39–48.

Carlson, R. C. and C. A. Yano. "Safety Stocks in MRP-Systems with Emergency Setups for Components." *Management Science* 32, no. 4 (April 1986).

Chalmet, L. C.; M. Debodt; and L. Van Wassenhove. "The Effect of Engineering Changes and Demand Uncertainty on MRP Lot Sizing: A Case Study." *International Journal of Production Research* 23, no. 2 (1985), pp. 233–51.

Choi, H. G.; E. M. Malstrom; and R. J. Classen. "Computer Simulation of Lot-Sizing Algorithms in Three-Stage Multi-Echelon Inventory Systems." *Journal of Operations Management* 4, no. 3 (1984).

Collier, D. A. "A Comparison of MRP Lot-Sizing Methods Considering Capacity Change Costs." *Journal of Operations Management* 1, no. 1 (1980).

Dixon, P. S., and E. A. Silver. "A Heuristic Solution Procedure for the Multi-Item, Single Level, Limited Capacity, Lot-Sizing Problem." *Journal of Operations Management* 2, no. 1 (1981).

De Bodt, M. A. and L. N. Van Wassenhove. "Cost Increases Due to Demand Uncertainty in MRP Lot Sizing." *Decision Sciences* 14, no. 3 (July 1983).

Dolinski, Larry R. "Inventory Response to A Material Requirements Planning Environment When Production Yield is Subject to Learning Improvement: A Simulation Study." DBA dissertation, Boston University, 1986.

Elk, Roger D., and James C. Hershauer. "Extended MRP Systems for Evaluating

Master Schedules and Materials Requirements Plans." *Production and Inventory Management*, 2nd Quarter 1980, pp. 53–66.

Gaimon, C. "Optimal Inventory, Backlogging and Machine Loading in a Serial Multistage, Multi-Period Production Environment." *International Journal of Production Research* 24, no. 2 (May–June 1986).

Guerrero, H. H. "The Effect of Various Production Strategies on Product Structures with Commonality." *Journal of Operations Management* 5, no. 4 (1986).

Harl, J. E., and L. P. Ritzman. "A Heuristic Algorithm for Capacity Sensitive Requirements Planning." *Journal of Operations Management* 5, no. 3 (1985).

Hemphill, A. D., and D. C. Whybark. "A Simulation Comparison of MRP Purchase Discount Procedures." Discussion paper no. 96, Indiana University, 1978.

Jesse, Jr., R. R.; and J. H. Blackstone, Jr. "A Note on Using the Lot-Sizing Index for Comparing Discrete Lot-Sizing Techniques." *Journal of Operations Management* 5, no. 4 (1986).

Karmarkar, U. S. "Lot Sizes, Lead Times and In-Process Inventories." *Management Science* 33, no. 3 (1987).

Kerni, R., and Y. Roll. "A Heuristic Algorithm for the Multi-Item, Lot-Sizing Problem with Capacity Constraints." *AIIE Transactions* 14, no. 4 (December 1982).

Kropp, D. H., and R. C. Carlson. "A Lot-Sizing Algorithm for Reducing Nervousness in MRP Systems." *Management Science* 30, no. 2 (February 1984).

————, R. C. Carlson, and J. V. Jucker. "Heuristic Lot-Sizing Approaches for Dealing with MRP System Nervousness." *Decision Sciences* 14, no. 2 (April 1983).

Lambrecht, M. C.; J. A. Muckstadt; and R. Luyten. "Protective Stocks in Multi-Stage Production Systems." *International Journal of Production Research* 22, no. 6 (1984), pp. 1001–25.

McLaren, B. J. "A Study of Multiple Level Lot Sizing Techniques for Material Requirements Planning Systems." Ph.D. dissertation, Purdue University, 1977.

Melnyk, S. A., and C. J. Piper. "Leadtime Errors in MRP: the Lot-sizing Effect." *International Journal of Production Research* 23, no. 2 (1985), pp. 253–64.

Narasimhan, R., and S. A. Melnyk. "Assessing the Transient Impact of Lot Sizing Rules Following MRP Implementation." *International Journal of Production Research* 22, no. 5 (1984), pp. 759–72.

New, C., and J. Mapes. "MRP With High Uncertain Yield Losses." *Journal of Operations Management* 4, no. 4 (1984).

Newson, E. F. P. "Multi-Item Lot Size Scheduling by Heuristic, Part I: With Fixed Resources." *Management Science* 21, no. 10 (1975).

Schmitt, T. G. "Resolving Uncertainty in Manufacturing Systems." *Journal of Operations Management* 4, no. 4 (1984).

St. John, R. "The Cost of Inflated Planned Lead Times in MRP Systems." *Journal of Operations Management* 5, no. 2 (1985).

Silver, E. A., and H. C. Meal. "A Simple Modification of the EOQ for the Case of a

Varying Demand Rate." *Production and Inventory Management,* 4th Quarter 1969.

Smith-Daniels, D. E., and Aquilano, N. J. "Constrained Resource Project Scheduling Subject to Material Constraints." *Journal of Operations Management* 4, no. 4 (1984).

Steele, D. C. "The Nervous MRP System: How to Do Battle." *Production and Inventory Management* 16, no. 4 (April 1973).

Steinberg, E., and A. Napier. "Optimal Multi-level Lot Sizing for Requirements Planning Systems." *Management Science* 26, no. 12 (December 1980), pp. 1258–72.

Vickery, S. K., and R. E. Markland. "Multi-stage Lot Sizing in a Serial Production System." *International Journal of Production Research* 24, no. 3 (1986), pp. 517–34.

Veral, E. A., and R. L. LaForge. "The Performance of a Simple Incremental Lot-Sizing Rule in a Multilevel Inventory Environment." *Decision Sciences* 16, no. 1 (Winter 1985).

Wacker, John G. "A Theory of Material Requirements Planning (MRP): An Empirical Methodology to Reduce Uncertainty in MRP Systems." *International Journal of Production Research* 23, no. 4 (1985), pp. 807–24.

Wagner, H. M., and T. M. Whitin. "Dynamic Version of the Economic Lot Size Model." *Management Science,* October 1958, pp. 89–96.

Wemmerlov, U. "Comments on Cost Increases Due to Demand Uncertainty in MRP Lot Sizing." *Decision Sciences* 16, no. 4 (Fall 1985).

———, and D. C. Whybark. "Lot Sizing under Uncertainty in a Rolling Schedule Environment." *International Journal of Production Research* 22, no. 3 (1984), pp. 467–484.

Whybark, D. C., and J. G. Williams. "Material Requirements Planning under Uncertainty." *Decision Sciences* 7, no. 4 (October 1976).

DISCUSSION QUESTIONS

1. Some practitioners complain that discrete lot-sizing procedures (e.g., POQ, PPB, MOM) aggravate system nervousness because of the changing lot quantities. What do they mean?

2. Reviewing Figure 12.7 and using your own powers of intuition, what would happen to the difference in costs between lot-sizing procedures as uncertainty gets larger and larger? What about the absolute cost values?

3. How do the quantity discount lot-sizing procedures illustrate the contention that advanced concepts are enhancements to sound, basic MPC systems?

4. Why is it necessary that both the release date and the due date be changed for safety lead time?

5. What are some of the difficulties with introducing "organizational slack" as a method of buffering against uncertainty?

6. One suggestion for reducing execution nervousness is to provide the status information to the foreman only at the time of need. Thus, the only time a foreman would need to determine job priorities would be when he or she was choosing the next job to put on a machine. What are the pros and cons of this suggestion?

PROBLEMS

1. Consider the following information about an end product item:

$$\text{Ordering cost} = \$32/\text{order}$$
$$\text{Average usage} = 8 \text{ units/week}$$
$$\text{Inventory carrying cost} = \$2/\text{unit/week}$$

   a. Determine the number of orders that should be placed per year to replenish the inventory of the item based on the average weekly demand.
   b. Given the following time-phased weekly requirements from an MRP record for this item, determine the sequence of planned orders using the economic order quantity and the periodic order quantity procedures. Assume that the lead time equals zero and that the current on-hand inventory equals zero. Calculate the inventory carrying cost on the basis of weekly ending inventory values. Which procedure produces the lowest total cost for the eight-week period?

Week	1	2	3	4	5	6	7	8
Requirements	15	2	10	12	6	0	14	5

2. A final assembly (A) that requires one week to assemble has a component part (B) that requires two weeks to fabricate. There are three units of final assembly A and four units of part B currently on hand. The requirements for assembly A for the next 10 weeks are given below:

Week	1	2	3	4	5	6	7	8	9	10
Requirements	1	4	2	8	1	0	6	2	1	3

   a. What are the planned order releases for part B using lot-for-lot lot sizing for both parts A and B?
   b. What are the planned order releases for part B using POQ = 2 for both parts A and B?

3. A company has estimated the requirements for a particular part as follows:

Month	1	2	3	4	5	6	7	8	9	10	11	12
Requirements	100	10	15	20	70	250	250	250	250	40	0	100

The ordering cost associated with this part is $300. The inventory carrying cost has been estimated as $2 per unit per month. There are currently no parts available in inventory. The company wishes to determine when and how much to order over the next 12 months.

a. Apply the economic order quantity and the part period balancing procedures to solve this problem.

b. What are the important assumptions involved in each of the approaches used in part a?

4. The Chan Hahn Clothing Company is trying to decide which of several lot-sizing procedures to use for its MRP system. The following information pertains to one of the "typical" component parts:

$$\text{Set-up cost} = \$80/\text{order}$$
$$\text{Inventory cost} = \$1/\text{unit/week}$$
$$\text{Current inventory balance} = 0 \text{ units}$$

Demand forecast								
Week	1	2	3	4	5	6	7	8
Demand	60	40	25	5	100	20	60	10

a. Apply the EOQ, POQ, and PPB lot-sizing procedures and show the total cost resulting from each procedure. Calculate the inventory carrying costs on the basis of *average* inventory values. Assume that orders are received into the beginning inventory.

b. Indicate the advantages and disadvantages of using each of the procedures suggested in part a.

5. Apply the McLaren order moment (MOM) lot-sizing procedure to the following 12 periods of requirements data, indicating the size and period of the order receipts. Assume the order costs are $100/order placed and the inventory carrying cost is $1/period. Calculate the inventory carrying costs on the basis of *ending* inventory values.

Period	1	2	3	4	5	6	7	8	9	10	11	12
Requirements	70	30	35	60	60	25	35	70	45	70	80	55

6. Using the requirements data from problem 5, and order costs of $100/order,

inventory carrying cost of $1.00/unit/period, and a unit cost of $50 in lots of less than 100 and $45 for lots of 100 or more. Calculate the inventory carrying costs on the basis of *ending* inventory values.

a. Apply McLaren's order moment (MOM) lot-sizing procedure (with look ahead).

b. Apply the least unit cost (LUC) procedure without look ahead.

7. Ellen Farr is a raw material buyer for the Farr Machine Corporation. She is responsible for purchasing forgings and castings for the firm's raw material stockroom. Ellen's job is to purchase a sufficient number of castings and forgings to meet the weekly demand for these items by the firm's fabrication shop in producing machined parts. She is also interested in low cost and whether to take the discount offered. A forecast of weekly requirements for one item, the Input Shaft Forging, and the cost information for this item are given below:

Week	1	2	3	4	5	6	7	8	9
Forecast	44	2	10	42	46	2	30	10	4

Order cost = $50.
Inventory carrying cost = $5/unit/week.
Item price = $100/unit.*
  *$95/unit if orders are issued for 80 units or more.

Calculate the orders Ellen would place using the least unit cost, the least period cost, and the MOM (with look ahead) procedures. Find the total cost of each solution procedure, assuming that inventory carrying cost is based on the average inventory.

8. The Fisher Products Company produces a line of children's parlor games. The production process for producing games at Fisher includes two departments: fabrication and assembly. The fabrication shop produces game parts, such as plastic men, game markers, special indicators, and so on. The company maintains an inventory of the raw material needed to produce the game parts, as well as an inventory of the finished game parts themselves. The assembly department consists of a single assembly line that is used to collate and package any of the parlor games in Fisher's product line to meet the incoming customer orders. The company maintains no inventory of the finished products (games) but produces only to customer order.

Each week the assembly foreman schedules the assembly line and supervises the withdrawal of game parts from the stockroom that are needed at the stations on the assembly line to meet the production schedule. Sometimes several games are assembled during a single week. Since the company uses MRP to plan and control the production of games and game parts, the assembly foreman prepares a master production schedule for a period covering eight weeks into the future. An example of his master schedule is shown in Exhibit A. Two end products (games A and B) are shown in this master schedule.

a. A component (game part), called the toy cup, is used in producing the two parlor games (A and B). Two units of the toy cup are needed to produce one unit of game A, and one unit of the toy cup is required to produce one unit of game B. Assuming that the toy cup planned lead time is one week, the current on-hand inventory is 44 units, and there are no scheduled receipts, complete the MRP record for the toy cup shown in Exhibit A. Use the period order quantity ordering policy for lot sizing. The ordering cost for the toy cup is $9/order, and the inventory carrying cost is $.10/unit/week.

b. After completing the MRP record for the toy cup in part a, complete the MRP record in Exhibit A for the plastic molding material that is needed to produce the toy cup. Two ounces of the plastic molding material are needed to produce one toy cup, the planned lead time for the plastic material is one week, there are 20 ounces of plastic material currently on hand, there is a scheduled receipt for 90 ounces of plastic material due in week 1 from the supplier, and the periodic ordering policy is used for this

EXHIBIT A   Material requirements planning worksheet

End products	Week number							
	1	2	3	4	5	6	7	8
Game A master schedule	21	0	0	21	20	0	15	0
Game B master schedule	2	2	9	0	6	3	0	9

Toy cup	1	2	3	4	5	6	7	8
Gross requirements								
Scheduled receipts*								
Projected available balance 44								
Planned order releases								

Plastic molding material	1	2	3	4	5	6	7	8
Gross requirements								
Scheduled receipts*	90							
Projected available balance 20								
Planned order releases								

*Received at the beginning of each week.

item. The ordering cost is $5/order and inventory carrying cost is $.04 per ounce per week.

c. The assembly foreman at Fisher has just handed you the MRP records for the toy cup and plastic molding material shown in Exhibit B. These MRP records contain a different master schedule, changed on-hand inventory values, and a new scheduled receipt value. Also, the planned lead time for both items is now two weeks. Complete the new MRP records for both items, assuming that the part period balancing ordering policy is used for the toy cup and for the plastic molding material.

d. What problem(s), if any, are apparent after having completed the MRP records in Exhibit B? What alternative courses of action does the MRP planner have in resolving the problem(s)? What specific course of action should be taken? Why?

EXHIBIT B   Material requirements planning worksheet

End products						Week number				
		1	2	3	4	5	6	7	8	
Game A master schedule			22		21	15				
Game B master schedule		9	1	7	7	3	10	1	2	

Toy cup		1	2	3	4	5	6	7	8
Gross requirements (2 units/game A) (1 unit/game B)									
Scheduled receipts*									
Projected available balance	55								
Planned order releases (Lead time = 2 weeks)									

Plastic molding material		1	2	3	4	5	6	7	8
Gross requirements (2 oz./toy cup)									
Scheduled receipts*			166						
Projected available balance	10								
Planned order releases (Lead time = 2 weeks)									

*Received at the beginning of each week.

9. Using the format of Figure 12.2 and a spreadsheet program, compare the use of EOQ and POQ lot-sizing approaches for ordering to satisfy the requirements sequence given below. The ordering cost is $17 per order, and the carrying cost is $.20 per unit per period (use average inventory).

Week	1	2	3	4	5	6	7	8	9	10
Requirements	48	12	53	91	33	8	60	55	38	22

10. The Silver brothers (Ed, Quick, and Hiho) had their very own factory. Ed was the general manager, and Quick produced the finished product from a part that Hiho made. Selected data are presented below for the finished product and the part. The requirements for the finished product for the next few periods are given as well.

	Quick	Hiho
Order quantity (EOQ)	40	100
Safety stock	5	0
Lead time	1	1
Current inventory	7	12
Scheduled receipt in period 1	40	0

Period	1	2	3	4	5	6	7	8
Requirements	23	13	36	12	21	8	34	23

a. Using a spreadsheet, develop the MRP records for Quick and Hiho. What are the planned order releases for Hiho's part?

b. Devise a different ordering plan for Quick and Hiho that has the same number of orders for both, but reduces the inventory levels *and* has the same amount of closing inventory as the original plan.

11. Develop a spreadsheet to perform the calculations for LUC. Usage of a purchased part averages 20 units per period, the ordering cost is $5.00 per order, the carrying cost is $.20 per unit per period, the purchase price is $1.00. Use these requirements:

Period	1	2	3	4	5	6
Requirements	10	18	30	35	10	16

a. If the price is $1.00 per unit, what is the ordering pattern?

b. If there is a quantity discount of $.05 per unit given for orders of more than 50 units, what happens? (For simplicity, you can assume that you can't split a period's requirements.)

12. Given the following time-phased net requirements from an MRP record, determine *all* of the possible ways that orders can be placed to satisfy the net requirements without incurring a stockout. Assume that the lead time equals zero.

Week	1	2	3
Net requirements	2	6	12

a. If the ordering cost equals $100 per order and the inventory carrying cost equals $10 per unit per week, what is the cost for each ordering alternative?

b. What is the least cost sequence of orders?

13. The production manager at the XYZ Company is investigating the causes of nervousness in the firm's MRP system. His study has produced the following MRP records for product item A. These records show the MRP schedule for this item as of the start of weeks 1, 2, 3, and 4.

LT = 0
SS = 0
Q calculated using the Wagner-Whitin algorithm
Ordering Cost = $400/order
Inventory Carrying Cost = $1.00/unit/week

Item A

Week		1	2	3	4
Gross requirements		177	261	207	309
Scheduled receipts					
Projected available balance	0	261	0	309	0
Planned order releases		438		516	

Item A

Week		2	3	4	5
Gross requirements		261	207	309	64
Scheduled receipts					
Projected available balance	261	0	373	64	0
Planned order releases			580		

Item A

Week		3	4	5	6
Gross requirements		207	309	64	182
Scheduled receipts					
Projected available balance	0	0	246	182	0
Planned order releases		207	555		

Item A

Week		4	5	6	7
Gross requirements		309	64	182	0
Scheduled receipts					
Projected available balance	0	246	182	0	0
Planned order releases		555			

a.   Assume that one unit of raw material item B is required to produce one unit of product item A. Calculate the gross requirements for item B covering a four-week planning horizon as of the start of weeks 1, 2, 3, and 4 (assuming that item B is only used to produce item A). Compare the gross requirements for item B for each week as they are calculated at the start of weeks 1, 2, 3, and 4. What differences do you observe in the gross requirements for item B from week to week?

b.   Given that no changes have been made to either the gross requirements for item A, or the beginning inventory for this item over the four-week interval, how do you explain the changes in the gross requirements for item B observed in part a? How would you explain this situation to the production manager? What impact would such changes in gross requirements for item B have on supplier relations?

14.   The MRP record following is for an item purchased from a supplier requiring a two-week lead time. The percent defective for purchased lots of this item averages 10 percent and has been as large as 20 percent. Defective items are removed and returned to the vendor when found. How would you construct the MRP record to protect against inventory shortages with the degree of defects described? An economic order quantity of 20 units is used for this item.

Week		1	2	3	4	5	6	7	8
Gross requirements		10	0	18	5	23	2	15	20
Scheduled receipts									
Projected available balance	14								
Planned order releases									

15. The MRP record below is for a purchased item having an order quantity of 30 units. The delivery reliability history of the supplier for this item indicates that the average lead time is two weeks. However, a delivery lead time of four weeks has occasionally been experienced. How would you construct the MRP record below so that inventory shortages are not incurred?

Week		1	2	3	4	5	6	7	8	9	10	11	12
Gross requirements		22	8	15	25	17	2	5	21	12	14	0	5
Scheduled receipts		30											
Projected available balance	45												
Planned order releases													

13

Advanced concepts in scheduling

This chapter addresses advanced issues in scheduling, with primary emphasis on the detailed scheduling of individual jobs through work centers in a shop. The intent is to provide direction for the firm that has a working MPC system in place and wishes to enhance the shop-floor control module. This chapter also addresses scheduling issues with some of the newer approaches to manufacturing, including cellular manufacturing and flexible manufacturing systems (FMS).

The approaches in this chapter presume that effective front-end, engine, and back-end systems are in place. Chapter 13 provides an application perspective to some of the research that has been done in scheduling. It is completely beyond our scope to even summarize the vast amount of research done on this topic. Rather, our interest here is to focus on some basic concepts and results, relate them to some of the newer manufacturing approaches, and show how results might be applied in certain operating situations.

Chapter 13 is organized around the following four topical areas:

- A scheduling framework: What are the key definitions, performance criteria, and kinds of scheduling problems studied?
- Basic scheduling research: What are the fundamental scheduling

problem structures? What are the scheduling results that have been consistently verified in the research, and the practical implications?

- Advanced research findings: What findings from advanced research seem to be particularly helpful in assigning jobs or labor to machines?

- Emerging issues: What are the critical scheduling issues in cellular manufacturing and flexible manufacturing systems (FMS), and in what ways do findings from other scheduling research apply?

Chapter 13 is most closely linked to Chapters 5 and 7, which describe basic shop-floor control and just-in-time systems and their place within an overall MPC system framework. There are also indirect links to Chapter 6 concerning the scheduling of vendors, and to Chapters 8 and 14 for master production scheduling. Chapter 20 deals with optimized production technology (OPT), which raises additional scheduling issues.

A SCHEDULING FRAMEWORK

There are many ways to think about scheduling, as well as different kinds of scheduling problems and decisions. Before delving into scheduling research, we think it is useful to first develop a brief framework for scheduling. Included are some key definitions, the criteria for judging scheduling performance, and some important dimensions of scheduling problems.

A schedule may be defined as a plan with reference to the sequence of and time allocated for each item or operation necessary to its completion. This definition allows us to think of a schedule that has a series of sequential steps, or a routing. The entire sequence of operations, the necessary sequential constraints, the time estimates for each activity, and the required resource capacities for each activity are inputs to the development of the detailed plan or schedule.

This definition also allows us to think of component part scheduling based upon product structures, with scheduling of components for subassemblies and, in turn, subassemblies to support end-item assembly. Material requirements planning (MRP) is the system that establishes the necessary disaggregation of end-item scheduling to subassembly and component scheduling. The associated resource capacity requirements are also established by the material plans.

Scheduling can also be thought of as a process; that is, someone prepares a schedule either for when an end item will be completed or for what series of activities or jobs are to be completed during a specified time by the work center of interest. Implied in this definition is repetition of the scheduling task. The schedule is prepared, actual performance is observed, and rescheduling takes place as uncertain events become resolved (e.g., forecasts of customer orders become actual customer orders, planned results become actual results).

Performance criteria

There are three primary objectives or goals that typically apply to scheduling problems. The first goal concerns *due dates:* one typically wants to avoid late job completion. The second goal concerns *flow times:* this objective is to minimize the time that a job spends in the system, from creation or opening of a shop order until it is closed. The final goal concerns *work center utilization:* one wants to fully utilize the capacity of expensive equipment and personnel.

These three objectives are often conflicting. One can do a better job of meeting due dates if more capacity is provided and if the work center capacity is less intensively utilized. Similarly, more capacity will typically reduce flow time, but at reduced capacity utilization. If extra jobs are released to the shop, they will tend to have longer flow times; but capacity can be better utilized and *perhaps* due date performance can be improved.

For each of the three primary scheduling objectives, it is necessary to establish exact performance measures. Moreover, for each objective there are competing measures. Meeting due dates might be simply specified on a yes/no basis. More typically, however, due date performance is based on "lateness." The *average lateness* for jobs is one measure, but this raises the issue of "earliness." Are early jobs allowed to offset late jobs to calculate the average? Is earliness also undesirable? Is maximum lateness an issue? We follow the convention that lateness measures both positive and negative deviations from the due date.

Another alternative is to measure the variability of actual completion dates against due dates with an objective of minimizing the variance of lateness. But this measure raises the question of which due date should be used to measure performance in an MRP environment when due dates are routinely revised by the MRP system.

Similar problems arise with flow times. Is the measure the average flow time, the variance in flow time, or the maximum flow time? Should flow time be weighted by some monetary value to favor shorter flow times for expensive work?

Work-center utilization measures have equal problems. Is one interested in the utilization of all work centers or in selected centers? How does one select? How is utilization to be measured?

The measurement issues are important to the MPC professional, both for understanding what particular research results mean and for establishing the appropriate performance criteria in applying the concepts; that is, an operating scheduling system must have unambiguous definitions of performance, and these measures must be congruent with the basic objectives of the firm. It is imperative to understand the performance criteria utilized in particular research studies and to carefully assess the match between those criteria and what is truly important in an actual company.

Shop structure

Another facet of a scheduling framework relates to the shop structure that is being studied. One important structure is that of the flow-shop variety found in repetitive manufacturing and cellular production systems; that is, all the jobs tend to go through a fixed sequence of the same routing steps. Other structures are more of a job shop nature involving custom-made products. Each particular job tends to have a unique routing, jobs go from one work center to another in a somewhat random pattern, and the time required at a particular work center is also highly variable. The scheduling complexity and constraints in a flow shop can be quite different from those in a job shop. The appropriateness of particular performance criteria and scheduling systems should reflect those differences.

One dimension of shop structure has been clarified in scheduling research. It is tempting to think that what works well in a shop with 10 work centers will not work well in a shop with 100 work centers. This, in fact, is not so. If they both have other attributes that are the same (e.g., shop structure or percentage capacity utilization), the conclusions drawn from a relatively small shop will be very similar to those appropriate for a large shop.

Product structure

Product structure is another facet of the scheduling environment that needs to be defined for a particular situation. One question is the existence of either single part or assembly routings. The issue is whether the scheduling problem is dealing only with individual jobs or if one necessarily must worry about matched sets of parts (jobs); that is, does one have to schedule each of the components of an assembly to ensure that all are done at the same time? Some companies have a large percentage of their jobs that are essentially one piece part per customer order. Others necessarily must produce parts and assemblies.

Assembly scheduling is partially addressed by MRP in that the due dates for components are coordinated by the MRP planning process. It is in this context that MRP is best seen as a scheduling technique. The detailed execution/scheduling of MRP plans is sometimes a separate issue. To the extent that the scheduling procedure attempts to deal with maintaining matched set due dates, the scheduling task becomes very complex. Note that in finite loading approaches due dates are typically adjusted to reflect finite capacity constraints (which implies the performance criterion is work center utilization).

The type of processing time distribution is another product structure issue. Most of the analytical research studies have been based upon processing times which are represented by the negative exponential distribution. Some simulation studies have used empirical distributions. The practical issue is again the extent to which the research results are robust enough to apply to the wide variety of applied scheduling situations.

Another issue in both research and practice is the use of alternative routings. The design and maintenance of alternative routing files can be an enormous job. Moreover, the decision rules for when to use alternative routings can be quite complex. On the other hand, alternative routings can improve operating performance. If one work center is overloaded and another work center is underloaded, improvements in due date performance, flow times, and work center utilization can be achieved by the use of alternative routings.

A related issue is the use of operation overlapping. If a job can be started at a work center *before* it is completely finished on the previous work center, improvements in scheduling performance can be achieved. Overlapping is a form of scheduling that increases flexibility, but it does not come without cost. It is necessary to have good information on time requirements and to start successive operations only when they will not run out of work (i.e., when operation two requires less time per unit than operation one, it can only be started when a sufficient queue at the second operation exists).

Still another issue concerning product structure is the extent to which setup times remain the same, regardless of the sequence in which jobs are processed. Thus, in some firms, there is a potential setup time saving to be made by better sequencing of jobs through a work center. However, it is only after an investment is made in developing a data base and an appropriate scheduling system that these savings can be realized.

A final issue concerning product structure is whether lot sizes are fixed or variable. For most scheduling research, lot sizes are fixed and do not vary as the sequence of operations are performed. In some recent research and practice, lot sizes have been larger for processing through some work centers than for others. Better schedule performance has been achieved.

Work center capacities

A final facet of a framework for scheduling relates to work center capacities. One issue is the extent to which the capacities are fixed or variable. This is analogous to the alternate routing issue. The extent to which the capacity for a particular work center can be increased or decreased and the time delay to achieve the change in capacity both affect scheduling performance.

A related issue is the degree to which the capacity of a particular work center is limited by the capacity of machines or the capacity of labor. The benefit of a labor-limited system versus a machine-limited system is the possibility of increased flexibility, since the same labor capacity can be assigned to several different machines. The extent to which a work force has multiple skills, and the degree of flexibility specified by union contracts on these matters, clearly influence this issue. Most cellular manufacturing and just-in-time (JIT) approaches are based on increasing the scope of jobs and worker crosstraining.

An additional issue in work center capacity is to focus attention on a subset of work centers: the bottlenecks. If the capacity of bottleneck work centers can be more intensely utilized, overall schedule performance can be improved in several ways. Conversely, utilization of nonbottlenecks is *not* a high-priority issue. Attempts to increase nonbottleneck utilization usually increase work-in-process inventories and increase average flow times.

BASIC SCHEDULING RESEARCH

There have been two fundamental kinds of scheduling problems studied in classic scheduling research—static scheduling problems and dynamic scheduling problems. Some, but not all, of the results that apply to one of these situations also apply to the other. The static problem consists of a fixed set of jobs to be scheduled until they are all completed. The dynamic scheduling problem deals with an ongoing situation. New jobs are continually being added to the system, and the emphasis is on the long-term performance of scheduling approaches.

In this section, we describe static and dynamic scheduling problem formulations, and we then present some of the basic research findings detailing appropriate consequences for scheduling practice.

Static scheduling approaches

The static scheduling problem consists of a fixed set of jobs to be run. The typical assumptions are that the entire set of jobs arrive simultaneously and that all work centers are available at that time. Most of the static scheduling research has been conducted using a criterion called minimum "make-span"; that is, the minimum total time to process all of the jobs. This is a flow time criterion, not a due date or work center utilization criterion. Furthermore, the minimum make-span criterion is not the same as the average flow time criterion.

Static scheduling research has been performed using deterministic processing times (known and nonvarying) and stochastic processing times (subject to random variations). Methods for dealing with deterministic times can be divided into those that produce optimum results and those utilizing heuristic scheduling procedures. In general, optimization methods are only applicable to relatively small problems. The computational difficulty tends to increase exponentially with problem size.

Large-scale problems are usually treated with heuristic procedures called dispatching, or sequencing, rules. These are logical rules for choosing which available job to select for processing at a particular machine center. In using dispatching rules, the scheduling decisions are made sequentially, rather than all at once.

Dynamic scheduling approaches

Dynamic scheduling problems are those in which new jobs are continually being added over time. The processing times for these jobs can be either deterministic or stochastic, but most research has focused on the latter case. Analytic approaches have been based on queuing models that provide expected steady state conditions for certain kinds of situations and time distributions. The criteria applied in the queuing studies typically involve the average flow time, the average work-in-process or number of jobs in the system, and the machine center utilization.

One approach in the dynamic scheduling studies is to use different scheduling (dispatching) rules at the work centers. The use of some rules gives better results for certain criteria. The original work in queuing studies was devoted to single-machine systems; later work extended the results to multiple machines. However, as the size of the system increases, simulation is the most frequently used research methodology. Moreover, simulation allows one to forgo the time limiting assumptions that are inherent in most analytical queuing approaches.

Simulation studies of large-scale scheduling problems are again mainly based on dispatching rules. There are a substantial number of these studies, and an understanding of certain basic conclusions is essential for the MPC professional. Some of the results are quite counterintuitive. Furthermore, an understanding of some basic simulation issues, such as sample size requirements and run lengths as a function of problem complexity, are useful for the person contemplating a simulation study for a particular firm.

The one-machine case

Research on single-machine scheduling has been largely based on the static problem of how to best schedule a fixed set of jobs through a single machine, when all jobs are available at the start of the scheduling period. It is further assumed that setup times are independent of the sequence.

If the objective is to *minimize the total time* to run the entire set of jobs (i.e., the minimum make span), it does not make any difference in which order the jobs are run. In this case, the make span will equal the sum of all setup and run times under any sequence of jobs. However, if the objective is to *minimize the average time* that each job spends at the machine (setup plus run plus waiting times), then it can be shown that this will be accomplished by sequencing the jobs in ascending order according to their total processing time (setup plus run time). As an example, if three jobs with individual processing times of one, five, and eight hours, respectively, are scheduled, the *total time* required to run the *entire* batch under any sequence is 14 hours. If the jobs are processed in ascending order, the average time that each job spends in the system is $(1 + 6 + 14) \div 3 = 7$ hours. However, if the jobs are processed in the reverse order, the average time in the system is $(8 + 13 + 14) \div 3 = 11.67$ hours.

This result has an important consequence. The average time in the system will always be minimized by selecting the next job for processing that has the shortest processing time at the current operation. This rule for sequencing jobs at a work center (called shortest processing time, or SPT) provides excellent results when using the average time in system criterion.

SPT also performs well on the criterion of *minimizing the average number of jobs in the system.* We have noted previously that work-in-process inventory levels and average flow time are directly related measures. If one is increased or reduced, the other will change in the same direction. It can be shown analytically that the SPT rule will again provide superior performance when the work-in-process criterion is applied in the single-machine case.

When the criterion is to *minimize the average job lateness,* it can again be demonstrated that SPT is the best rule for sequencing jobs for the single-machine case. To introduce the criterion of lateness, it is first necessary to establish due dates for the jobs. However, an interesting aspect of the research is that, no matter what procedure is used to establish the due dates, the minimization of the *average job lateness* will be achieved by SPT.

Another criterion is to *minimize the maximum job lateness.* In this case, the best sequencing rule is to run the jobs in due date order, from earliest due date to latest due date. This result can also be proven analytically. Still another measure of scheduling performance that is often of interest is that of *minimizing the order lateness variance.* This criterion is also best served by running the jobs in due date sequence, earliest to latest, since doing so minimizes the deviations from due dates of the individual jobs.

Since there are relatively few applied examples of the one-machine scheduling problem, this research tends to be more useful for gaining insights into the behavior of scheduling rules under particular criteria than for direct scheduling applications. The issue from both a pragmatic and research point of view is the extent to which the conclusions from this work are applicable to more complex problem environments.

The most important conclusion to be drawn from the single-machine research is that the SPT rule represents the best way to pick the next job to run, if the objective is to minimize the average time per job, to minimize the average number of jobs in the system, or to minimize the average job lateness. However, if the objective is to minimize either the maximum lateness of any job or the lateness variance, then the jobs should run in due date sequence.

The two-machine case

The development of scheduling procedures for the two-machine case is somewhat more complex than for single-machine systems. In the two-machine case, both machines have to be scheduled to best satisfy whatever criterion is selected. Moreover, job routings need to be considered. In general, any job could be routed to either of the machines for the first operation. In a "flow shop" model (as opposed to a job shop) the assumption is that each of the jobs always goes first to one machine and then to the second. For analytically based research, additional assumptions, such as those for the one-machine case, are made. For example, all jobs are available at the start of the schedule, and setup times are independent.

A set of rules has been developed to minimize the make span in the two-machine case. Note that, while the minimum make span does not depend on the sequencing of jobs in the one-machine case, this is not true in the two-machine case. Additionally, if the total time to run the entire batch of jobs is to be minimized, this does not ensure that either the average time each job spends in the system or the average number of jobs in the system will also be minimized.

The following scheduling rules to minimize make span in a flow shop were developed by Johnson:

> Select the job with the minimum processing time on either machine 1 or machine 2. If this time is associated with machine 1, schedule this job first. If it is for machine 2, schedule this job last in the series of jobs to be run. Remove this job from further consideration.
> Select the job with the next smallest processing time and proceed as above (if machine 1, schedule it second; if machine 2, next to last). Any ties can be broken randomly.
> Continue this process until all of the jobs have been scheduled.

The intuitive logic behind this rule is that the minimum time to complete the set of jobs has to be the larger of the sum of all the run times at the first machine plus the smallest run time at the second machine, or the sum of all the run times at the second machine plus the smallest run time at the first machine.

These rules can also be applied to larger flow shop scheduling problems. For example, an efficient heuristic has been developed by Campbell, Dudek, and Smith (CDS). This procedure uses the Johnson algorithm to solve a series of two-machine approximations to the actual problem having M machine, using the following rules:

Solve the first problem considering only machines 1 and M, ignoring the intervening M-2 machines.

Solve the second problem by pooling the first two machines (1 and 2) and the last two machines (M-1 and M) to form two dummy machines. The processing time at the first dummy machine is the sum of the processing time on machines 1 and 2 for each order, and the processing time at the second dummy machine is the sum of the processing time at machines M-1 and M for each order.

Continue in this manner until M-1 problems have been solved. In the final problem, the first dummy machine contains machines 1 through M-1, and the second dummy machine contains machines 2 through M.

Compute the makespan for each problem solved and select the best sequence.

Additional research using branch and bound algorithms and integer-programming methods has been developed to solve static flow shop three-machine scheduling problems using the minimum makespan criterion. However, the solutions are generally feasible only for very small problems. Currently, heuristic methods such as the Campbell, Dudek, and Smith algorithm are the only means of solving larger-scale flow shop scheduling problems.

There are several important observations to be made from these research efforts. First, the size of problems that can be treated with analytical methods is small and of limited applicability for the "real world." Second, the computer time required to solve scheduling problems with analytical methods grows exponentially with the number of jobs and/or machines to be scheduled. Third, the performance measure, minimizing the make span, is not the same as minimizing the average time in the system or average number of jobs in the system. Moreover, any of these criteria are not necessarily related to the job lateness criterion. Fourth, the static scheduling assumptions (beginning with all machines idle, all jobs available, and ending with all jobs processed and all machines idle) clearly influence the results. Fifth, there is no randomness reflected in any of the machine processing times, which could reduce the applicability of the techniques. Finally, on the positive side, it is important to note that the two-machine scheduling rules utilize the shortest processing time logic. The application of the SPT in the two-machine case is not exactly the same as it was in the single-machine case, but it is clearly an essential element in producing the desired scheduling performance in both problem situations.

Queuing model approaches

The application of queuing models to scheduling problems allows for a relaxation of some of the limiting constraints mentioned above. In particular, the queuing approaches deal with the dynamic problem, rather than the static problem. Randomness in the interarrival and service times are considered, and steady state results are provided for average flow time, average work-in-process, expected work center utilization, and average waiting time.

The queuing research first examined the single-machine case and then was expanded to the multiple-machine case. The single-machine research has shown that, again, the SPT rule for sequencing jobs yields the best performance for the average completion time, average work-in-process level, and average waiting time criteria. Applying the queuing theory to the multiple-machine case requires the use of such limiting assumptions that the results are only interesting from a research point of view. To examine realistic, multiple-machine, dynamic scheduling situations, simulation models are most often used. With simulation, one can examine the performance of various rules against several criteria. The size of the problems studied (work centers and jobs) can be expanded, the effects of startup and ending conditions can be considered, and any kind of product structure, interarrival time patterns, or shop capacity can be accommodated. The primary research questions addressed in simulation studies include the following. Which dispatching rules for sequencing jobs at work centers perform best? For which criteria? Are some "classes" of rules better than others for some classes of criteria or "classes" of problems?

Sequencing rules

Figure 13.1 illustrates a typical scheduling environment for a complex job shop. At any time, if a set of n jobs is to be scheduled on m machines, there are $(n!)^m$ possible ways to schedule the jobs, and the schedule could change with the addition of new jobs. For any problem that involves more than a few machines or a few jobs, the computational complexity of finding the best schedule is beyond the capacity of modern computers.

Complex routings are shown in Figure 13.1. For example, after processing at machine center A, jobs may be sent for further processing to machine centers B, D, or F. Similarly, some jobs are completed after being processed at machine center A and go directly to finished component inventories. Also note that a job might flow from machine center A to machine center D, then back to A.

A sequencing or dispatch rule is depicted in Figure 13.1 between each queue and its associated work center. This indicates that a dispatching rule exists for choosing the next job in the queue for processing. The question of

FIGURE 13.1 The scheduling environment

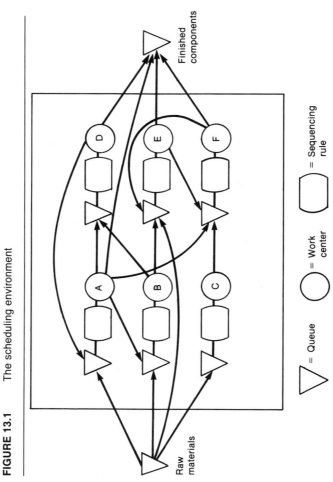

Raw materials

Finished components

▷ = Queue

◯ = Work center

⬡ = Sequencing rule

interest is which sequencing rule will achieve good performance against some scheduling criterion.

There are a large number of sequencing rules that have appeared in research and in practice. Each could be used in scheduling jobs. The following are some well-known rules with their desirable properties:

R (random). Pick any job in the queue with equal probability. This rule is often used as a benchmark for other rules.

FCFS (first come/first serve). This rule is sometimes deemed to be "fair," in that jobs are processed in the order in which they arrived at the work center.

SPT (shortest processing time). As noted, this rule tends to reduce both work-in-process inventory, the average job completion (flow) time, and average job lateness.

EDD (earliest due date). This rule seems to work well for criteria associated with job lateness.

CR (critical ratio). This rule is widely used in practice. The priority index is calculated using (due date—now)/(lead time remaining).

LWR (least work remaining). This rule is an extension of SPT in that it considers *all* of the processing time remaining until the job is completed.

FOR (fewest operations remaining). Another SPT variant that considers the number of successive operations.

ST (slack time). A variant of EDD which subtracts the sum of setup and processing times from the time remaining until the due date. The resulting value is called "slack." Jobs are run in order of the smallest amount of slack.

ST/O (slack time per operation). A variant of ST that divides the slack time by the number of remaining operations, again sequencing jobs in order of the smallest value first.

NQ (next queue). A different kind of rule, which is based on machine utilization. The idea is to consider the queues at each of the succeeding work centers to which the jobs will go and to select the job for processing that is going to the smallest queue (measured either in hours or perhaps in jobs).

LSU (least setup). Still another rule is to pick the job that minimizes the changeover time on the machine. In this way, capacity utilization is maximized. Note this rule explicitly recognizes dependencies between setup times and job sequence.

This list is not meant to be exhaustive. There are many other rules, variants of these rules, and combinations of these rules that have been studied. In some cases, the use of one rule under certain conditions and the use of another under other conditions has been studied.

One issue highlighted in Figure 13.1 is whether the same rule should be used at each work center. One might, for example, build a case for using SPT at the "gateway" work centers and using some due date-oriented rules for downstream centers. Or perhaps the selection of a rule should depend on the size of the queue or the amount of work that is ahead of or behind schedule.

Another issue in selecting sequencing rules is their cost of usage. Some of the rules, such as random, first come/first serve, shortest processing time, earliest due date, and fewest operations remaining, are easily implemented, since they do not require other information than that related to the job itself. Other rules, such as the critical ratio, least work remaining, slack time, and slack time per operation rules, require more complex information, as well as time-dependent calculations. The next queue and least setup rules require even more information, involving the congestion existing at other work centers, or a changeover cost matrix for all jobs currently at a work center.

Sequencing research results

There has been extensive research on the performance of different sequencing rules. We will highlight some of these efforts and draw conclusions for practice. One of the early comprehensive simulation studies on sequencing rules was performed by Conway. He examined 39 different sequencing rules, each tested using the same set of 10,000 jobs. Results from the first 400 and last 900 were not included in the results to eliminate startup and ending conditions. Figure 13.2 reports some results from this study. They are reported for two criteria: the average time in system and the variance of the time in the system. As we have noted, the average time in the system measure is directly related to work-in-process inventory and the average number of jobs in the system. This measure is also directly related to the average job lateness. The results reported in Figure 13.2 clearly show that the SPT rule performs quite well for this set of criteria.

FIGURE 13.2   Simulation results for various sequencing rules

Sequencing rule	Average time in system	Variance of time in system
SPT	34.0	2,318
EDD	63.7	6,780
ST/O	66.1	5,460
FCFS	74.4	5,739
R	74.7	10,822

Source: R. W. Conway, W. L. Maxwell, and L. W. Miller, *Theory of Scheduling* © 1967, Addison-Wesley Publishing Co., Inc., Reading, Ma. Page 287, Table C-3.

There is, however, a concern in using SPT. In many studies, SPT has been found to have a higher variance of time in system than other rules. In addition, it can allow some jobs with long processing times to wait in queue for a substantial time, thereby causing severe due-date problems for a few jobs. However, since the SPT rule can complete the average job in a relatively short time, compared with other rules, it produces a much smaller average job lateness. Therefore, the overall lateness performance might be much less severe than one might think. Figure 13.3 shows simulation results using various lateness criteria.

Figure 13.3 shows that the slack time per operation (ST/O) rule is best in terms of the percentage of jobs late. However, the SPT rule is a close second, and SPT is considerably better than the earliest due date (EDD) rule. The earliest due date rule has a much lower variance of job lateness than SPT, but the *average* lateness measure of SPT might be more than enough to compensate for the high job lateness variance associated with SPT.

Additional studies have been done where job due dates were established using a variety of procedures. The performance of SPT has been shown to be better than other rules, even under those conditions where due dates are assigned a bit less "rationally"; that is, where the due dates are set without regard to the work content involved in processing the job. In studies where the shop utilization was varied, SPT has been found to be less sensitive to changes in the capacity utilization of the work centers than other sequencing rules.

Several rules were tested in a simulation study by Nanot, using very large sample sizes (number of orders scheduled) and several combinations of shop load and routing (job shop versus flow shop) conditions. The general results support SPT as a superior rule in terms of average time in system and the related measures. Again, Nanot found the time in system variance is higher than for some of the other rules. Nanot also concluded that the results did not seem to be sensitive to changes in the shop load and routing conditions.

Other research efforts have attempted to combine SPT with other sched-

---

FIGURE 13.3   Simulation results for other criteria

Sequence rule	Average job lateness*	Variance of job lateness	Percentage of jobs late
ST/O	−12.8	226	3.7
SPT	−44.9	2,878	5.0
EDD	−15.5	432	17.8
FCFS	−4.5	1,686	44.8

*Minus sign means that jobs are early on average.
Source: R. W. Conway, W. L. Maxwell, and L. W. Miller, *Theory of Scheduling* © 1967, Addison-Wesley Publishing Co., Inc., Reading, Ma. Page 287, Table C-3.

uling rules to obtain most of the benefits of SPT without the large time in system variance. One approach has been to alternate SPT with FCFS (first come/first serve) to "clean out the work centers" at periodic intervals. Other combinations of SPT with ST/O or with critical ratio produce similar results.

One of the most consistent results of the simulation experiments has been to demonstrate that SPT is a very good dispatching rule for many criteria. This conclusion is robust and is supported by a variety of simulation studies. This result runs counter to what many practitioners believe: To ignore due dates for sequencing jobs seems irresponsible. But since the use of SPT results in reduced lead times and work-in-process inventories, the benefits might argue for its implementation. Conway sums it up well in one of his conclusions:

> The priority rule under which the job with the shortest processing time is selected (SPT) clearly dominates all the other rules tested. Its performance under every measure was very good, it was an important factor in each of the rules that exhibit a "best" performance under some measure, and is simpler and easier to implement than the rules that surpass it in performance. It surely should be considered the "standard" in scheduling research, against which candidate procedures must demonstrate their virtue.

ADVANCED RESEARCH FINDINGS

In this section, we discuss several additional research studies that we see as being of particular relevance to MPC practice. These studies focus on the determination of lead times (management of due dates) for manufactured items and the determination of labor assignments in manufacturing operations. In most cases, this research has not yet provided definitive conclusions for the practicing professional. However, in each case we think that important practical issues are raised and that the practicing professional can make use of the available, though perhaps tentative, conclusions.

Due date setting procedures

The scheduling procedures presented so far in this chapter have assumed that the order release and due dates for individual jobs are *givens*. In many firms, the setting of such dates is often assigned to manufacturing and is frequently the subject of intense negotiations between manufacturing and marketing personnel. Many times due dates must be set at the time of order receipt or when bidding for an order. An effective MPC system can help by providing appropriate information regarding the availability of material and capacity, as well as information concerning the resource requirements for individual jobs. As an example, the assignment of due dates for make-to-order products is normally made on the basis of raw material and equipment capacity availabilities. Likewise, order release and due dates for manufactured components in MRP systems are set by determining the length of the planned lead time for such items. Therefore, the establishment of lead time offsets and due dates is a vital and ongoing function in a manufacturing system. The achievement of these due dates is fostered by a well-functioning shop-floor control system based on good dispatching rules.

Although very little research has been reported on the management of lead times (due dates), some useful insights have been provided by Baker and Bertrand. They analyzed the effectiveness of three different procedures for estimating lead times and setting due dates for a job shop. Specifically, they set due dates for orders by adding an estimate of the manufacturing time to the date the order is received. The three methods used for establishing the value of manufacturing time are:

CON: A *constant* time allowance for manufacturing *all* jobs; i.e., the same lead time is added to all jobs at receipt date to calculate the due date.

SLK: A time allowance that provides an equal (constant) waiting time or slack for *all* jobs, i.e., the due date is set equal to the receipt date plus the sum of all processing times, plus a fixed additional time for waiting.

TWK: A time allowance that is proportional to the total processing time for a job; that is, the lead time to be added to the receipt date is a multiple of the sum of all processing times.

Each of the procedures has a single parameter (the constant time, the waiting time, or the multiple) to be determined. Other informational needs are similar to those of usual shop-floor control problems. The first procedure is easily implemented in many firms, since the shop-floor control system data base requirements are minimal. The other two procedures, however, require an estimate of the processing time for a job to set the due date.

Research in due date setting is concerned with the degree of improvement in manufacturing performance to be obtained by implementing the more complex due date procedures, SLK and TWK.

The evaluative criterion was "due date tightness." It is presumed that tight due dates (or short lead times) are strategically more desirable than loose due dates. Tight due dates provide a competitive advantage by permitting the firm to offer an improved level of customer service, as well as achieve lower costs through reductions in work-in-process inventory. The approach of the experiments was to so set each of the three parameters that *no* late deliveries occurred; that is, the parameters are so chosen that the longest lead time is just sufficient. Thereafter, the actual lead times are observed in the simulation. The preferred procedure is the one that achieves the smallest mean lead time.

The experiments involved a single-machine system using the shortest processing time (SPT) dispatching rule for all three due date setting rules.

However, they were conducted under a wide variety of operating conditions: 80 percent to 99 percent machine utilization, a variety of jobs, 20 replications, and use of both exponentially and normally distributed processing times. The exponentially distributed processing times gave a much greater degree of variability in achieved lead times (coefficient of variation, $c_v = 1.0$) than the normally distributed processing time $c_v = .25$). Two releasing rules were used, as well. The random release rule meant that orders were issued to the shop as soon as received. The "controlled" release rule meant that jobs were released when work-in-process inventory levels fell below a "trigger point." The trigger point was so chosen to provide a specified average number of jobs in the shop.

The results indicate that the SLK and TWK procedures set tighter due dates than the CON procedure. As shown in Figure 13.4, these two procedures provided as much as a 50 percent reduction in the lead time required for manufacturing (in comparison with the CON procedure) under exponentially distributed processing times. Much smaller differences were noted when normally distributed processing times were used. Furthermore, there was a clear preference for the TWK procedure (as opposed to the SLK procedure) when random work releasing was used. In using controlled work releasing, preference shifts to the TWK procedure at higher levels of machine utilization.

While considerably more research is required (especially for multiple machines) and significant modifications of the procedures may be discovered, we believe there are some important messages that this research suggests. In particular, the results indicate the important potential for reductions in lead time and work-in-process inventory when due dates are set in relation to job processing times. An important step in implementing these procedures is that of determining how much variability exists in the processing times in a shop. An indication of high variability (e.g., coefficient of variation of 1.0 or more) would suggest the potential for major improvements in manufacturing due date setting.

We see these results as particularly important as firms systematically reduce work-in-process inventories. As long as lead times are about 90 percent waiting, the influence of processing times and processing time variability is masked. When lead times are reduced, processing time will become a larger element of the total lead time and, thus, more important to take into account.

Dynamic due dates

A key limitation of all of the research discussed so far is that the assignment of due dates is done once and they are not revised over time. This differs from shop-floor control systems operating as part of an effective MPC system: due dates are continually revised as one portion of the MRP plan-

FIGURE 13.4 Simulation results for manufacturing lead time estimating procedures

Treatment	Mean number of jobs	Utilization	Mean manufacturing lead time			Frequency best*		
			TWK	SLK	CON	TWK	SLK	CON
Exponential times, random release	4.00	0.80	4.43	9.04	10.14	20	0	0
	5.67	0.85	5.63	10.37	11.39	20	0	0
	9.00	0.90	6.20	11.79	12.76	20	0	0
Exponential times, controlled release,	4.00		5.26	4.53	8.79	3	17	0
	5.67		6.51	6.23	10.09	7	13	0
	9.00		8.28	9.51	13.49	17	3	0
Normal times, random release	4.28	0.90	7.20	7.70	7.72	16	2	2
	9.59	0.95	10.06	10.70	10.75	16	2	2
	52.09	0.99	10.44	10.99	11.07	20	0	0
Normal times, controlled release	4.28		6.65	5.31	5.90	0	20	0
	9.59		12.35	10.61	11.18	0	20	0
	52.09		48.53	53.10	53.64	20	0	0

*Number of times in the 20 replications that each procedure performed the best (i.e., produced the lowest mean manufacturing lead time).

Source: K. R. Baker and J. W. M. Bertrand, "A Comparison of Due Date Selection Rules." *AIIE Transactions* 13, no. 2, June 1981, pp. 128–129.

ner's job. The determination of due dates for orders in a job shop is, therefore, only one aspect of the management of due dates in scheduling. A second aspect has to do with maintaining *valid* due dates as orders progress through the manufacturing process. The need for due date maintenance arises from the dynamic nature of the manufacturing environment. Management actions, such as master production schedule changes, planned lead time adjustments, bill of material modifications, and so on, can create the need to reschedule manufacturing orders and to revise the priorities given to the shop. Likewise, variations in shop conditions, such as unexpected scrap, unplanned transactions, and the like, can also create the need to revise job due dates.

Many firms have systems and procedures that result in changes in open order due dates. This practice is referred to as *dynamic due date maintenance*. The primary argument for this practice is that the shop should be using accurate and timely information in dispatching jobs to machines to provide a high level of customer service. In spite of its widespread use, there is some controversy over the advisability of implementing dynamic due date maintenance systems. Some suggest that the use of dynamic due dates can have an adverse impact on scheduling performance because of system "nervousness." Steele, for example, argues that a job shop can function effectively only if open order priorities are stable enough to generate some coherent action on the shop floor. He defines a scheduling system with *unstable* open order priorities as a nervous scheduling system, which can lead to shop floor distrust and overriding of formal priorities. A second behavioral argument against dynamic due date maintenance is that the volume of rescheduling messages might so inundate the production planner that he or she is unable to process the necessary changes in a timely fashion.

In such cases, the production planner may simply stop trying to perform an impossible task; the shop could lose faith in the priority system and revert to using an "informal" system; or ill-chosen or misleading rescheduling messages may be communicated to the shop. Any or all of these responses may cause the shop and inventory system performance to deteriorate.

While much of the scheduling research has been directed at determining the "best" heuristics for scheduling a shop to meet fixed or open order due dates, very little experimental research has addressed the problem of whether and how to respond to these issues when the actual need date for an open order changes while the order is being processed by the shop.

In one study conducted to determine the impact of using *dynamically* updated due dates on manufacturing performance, Berry and Rao evaluated the use of dynamic due dates with the critical ratio scheduling rule in a make-to-stock environment. They studied the scheduling of products produced by a job shop for a finished goods inventory which was controlled using an economic lot size/reorder point system. The *dynamic* due dates used in critical ratio scheduling were produced using the following formula:

$$\text{Due date} = \text{Current date} + \frac{\text{On-hand inventory balance} - \text{Buffer stock}}{\text{Average daily usage}}$$

The result is that larger than expected demand for a product will move the due date for an open order for that item closer to the current date, thereby increasing the critical ratio scheduling priority.

The results of this study were counterintuitive. They showed that the use of dynamic due dates produced a significant increase in the combined costs of setup, carrying work-in-process and finished product inventory, and inventory shortages. Nervousness in the dispatching rule priorities caused both the mean and variance of the job flow times to increase, thereby increasing the work-in-process inventory level and reducing the customer service level.

In a related study by Hausman and Scudder, the use of dynamic inventory information in priority scheduling rules was evaluated for a jet engine repair facility. This facility performed the disassembly, manufacture of component parts, and reassembly of jet engines. Quick turnaround times were of importance to the customer, so the study used the time-weighted final product (engine) back orders as the measure of performance. The inventory management policy was a continuous review, one-for-one (S-1, S) inventory policy, and the product had a multilevel product structure.

The repair facility had 10 machines. The study compared the back order performance of a wide range of priority sequencing rules. These included: static rules (earliest due date, FCFS, etc.), dynamic rules (minimum slack time per operation, critical-ratio, etc.) and rules that consider additional information. Two of the latter rules and their variations proved to be the most effective priority scheduling rules tested. These two rules were:

Inventory based: Select the job with the smallest value of net inventory. (Net inventory equals current on-hand inventory minus back orders for the component type.)

Multiple use: Select the job that is required by the largest number of modules (subassemblies) awaiting parts for assembly.

Both of these rules incorporate dynamic information regarding the expected component work-in-process inventory. In effect, the development of the priority index information used in these rules is similar to the gross-to-netting procedures used in an MRP system.

The use of dynamic work-in-process, finished component, and subassembly requirement information provided significant improvements in operating performance. For example, the inventory based rule resulted in 3.67 mean delay days as opposed to 6.03 for critical ratio and 7.28 for the shortest processing time rule. For the repair facility, a two-day improvement in the mean delay time represents a savings of one engine from the spares inventory, $2 million.

The seemingly contradictory results observed in the previous studies are partially explained in work by Penlesky. He evaluates the use of several dynamic due date procedures. He also examines the use of simple procedures for selectively implementing a few of the many due date changes that would normally be implemented (filtering procedures). In particular, the study is concerned with determining what types of job-related information are important to consider in formulating open order rescheduling procedures and evaluating the impact of the rescheduling on manufacturing performance in MRP systems.

Three different filters for making rescheduling decisions are considered: the ability, the magnitude, and the horizon filters. The purpose of the ability filter is to assure that only attainable due date adjustments are passed along to the shop. In using this procedure:

1. All *rescheduling out* actions (when the new due date is later than the previous due date) are implemented.
2. The implementation of *reschedule-in* actions depends on one of three conditions:
   a. If the machine setup and processing time remaining is less than the time until the new due date, the new due date is implemented.
   b. If the machine setup and processing time remaining is less than the time until the old due date but greater than the time until the new date, the due date is set to the present time plus the machine setup and processing time to complete the order.
   c. If the machine setup and processing time remaining exceeds the time allowed until the old due date, no change is made to the old due date.

Different information is considered by the magnitude and the horizon filters. These procedures are designed to filter out trivial due date adjustments by means of a *threshold* value. In the magnitude procedure, if the absolute value of the difference between the new and the old due dates exceeds a threshold value (T_m), the change in the due date is implemented. Similarly, the horizon procedure is designed to filter out those due date changes that are too far out in the planning horizon to be of any immediate concern to the production planner. Only if the old due date falls within the period of interest (T_H) is the new due date implemented. By setting parameter values for T_m and T_H, the number of rescheduling changes to be filtered out can be adjusted. The procedures will implement all changes when $T_m = 0$ and $T_H = \infty$, providing full dynamic procedures. Static dates are obtained when $T_m = \infty$ and $T_H = 0$.

Simulation experiments were used to investigate the effect of incorporating dynamic due date information in the sequencing rules and the use of the filtering procedures. These experiments were conducted using a make-to-stock job shop simulator, with both component manufacturing and assembly operations, controlled by an MRP system. The procedures were tested under differing values of machine utilization, uncertainty in the master production schedule, length of the planned lead times, and size of production order quantities. The three measures of effectiveness used were the end product customer service level, the combined work-in-process and finished item inventory level, and the number of rescheduling changes implemented.

The results shown in Figure 13.5 indicate that the gains in performance to be obtained by using dynamic due dates depend on the shop operating conditions. These results indicate that, under certain operating conditions, dynamic due date information can provide improvements in customer service and total inventory level. The results help explain the apparently contradictory results reported by Berry/Rao and Hausman/Scudder. While both studies were conducted under high machine utilization conditions, small lot sizes (a single unit) were used in the Hausman and Scudder experiments (these correspond to experiments 6 and 8 in Figure 13.5, where performance gains were obtained), and much larger order quantities (economic order quantities involving several periods of demand) were used in the study reported by Berry and Rao (these correspond to experiments 14 and 16 in Figure 13.5, where no improvements in performance were observed).

Another important conclusion can be drawn from the results in Figure 13.5. The dynamic due dates can provide a reduction in the total inventory level while *simultaneously* providing an improvement in customer service, (e.g., in experiments 3, 6, 8, and 11). Even though the magnitude varies, the attainment of simultaneous improvements in customer service and inventory levels is possible using dynamic due dates.

The performance comparison of the filtering procedures is shown in Figure 13.6 for experiment number 8 of Figure 13.5. Two observations can be made regarding these results. First, there is no significant difference in performance between the filtering procedures and the dynamic due date procedure without filtering. All rescheduling procedures produced a significant improvement in performance over the static procedures. Second, the magnitude and horizon filters provide comparable performance to the dynamic rescheduling procedure—but with far fewer rescheduling actions implemented. Therefore, it would seem that the benefits of dynamic rescheduling can be achieved by *selectively* implementing the rescheduling actions. By filtering the rescheduling messages, the information processing costs and the adverse behavioral effects of system nervousness can be reduced without an adverse effect on operating performance.

FIGURE 13.5 Percentage improvements in service and inventory levels using dynamic due dates*

Periodic order quantity	Planned lead time	Performance measure	Low master schedule uncertainty		High master schedule uncertainty	
			Low machine utilization	High machine utilization	Low machine utilization	High machine utilization
Small	Low	Experiment number	1	2	3	4
		Customer service level	3.4	—	15.2	—
		Total inventory level	—	—	10.5	—
	High	Experiment number	5	6	7	8
		Customer service level	.5	9.3	4.8	31.8
		Total inventory level	—	5.1	—	8.3
Large	Low	Experiment number	9	10	11	12
		Customer service level	4.3	—	14.3	—
		Total inventory level	—	—	8.0	—
	High	Experiment number	13	14	15	16
		Customer service level	2.5	—	6.2	—
		Total inventory level	—	—	—	—

*(Static − Dynamic) ÷ Static) × 100; calculated only in those cases where there was a statistically significant difference in the performance measure between the two procedures.

Source: R. J. Penlesky, "Open Order Rescheduling Heuristics for MRP Systems in Manufacturing Firms," doctoral dissertation, Indiana University, 1982.

FIGURE 13.6   Results of applying the filtering procedures

Procedure	Filter level*	Customer service level		Total inventory level	
		Mean	Standard deviation	Mean	Standard deviation
Static due dates	0	.651	.084	14,357	895
Ability filter	100	.871	.048	12,990	412
Magnitude filter	53	.873	.041	12,873	919
Horizon filter	45	.831	.055	13,190	958
Dynamic due dates without filtering	100	.858	.049	13,161	999

Note: Data from experiment 8 of Figure 13.5.
*Percent of indicated reschedules that were implemented.
Source: R. J. Penlesky, "Open Order Rescheduling Heuristics for MRP Systems in Manufacturing Firms," doctoral dissertation, Indiana University, 1982, p. 148.

Labor limited systems

The scheduling research results presented so far are useful when dispatching (sequencing) rules represent the principal means of controlling the flow of work in a plant. In many firms, in addition to assigning jobs to work centers, there is a need to make labor assignment decisions, as well. Labor assignment decisions are an important factor in controlling work flow when labor capacity is a critical resource in completing work. This can occur even when only one particular labor skill is the bottleneck resource. In such instances, the system is said to be labor limited.

Labor limitations provide an additional dimension to shop-floor scheduling that is particularly important in the present economic climate. In many firms, excess capacity exists in many machine centers. For many JIT and cellular manufacturing situations, labor limited scheduling is also the case. The controllable cost is labor, and the primary scheduling job is how to assign labor to machine centers. Good labor scheduling practice provides the possibility of varying the labor capacity at work centers to better match the day-to-day fluctuations in work loads. To the extent that flexibility in assigning people to work centers exists, improvements in manufacturing performance can be gained (e.g., reduced flow times, better customer service, and decreased work-in-process inventory). However, the degree to which flexibility in making labor assignments exists depends on such factors as the amount of cross training in the work force, the existence of favorable employee work rules, the costs of shifting people between work centers, and so on.

A comprehensive framework for the control of work flow in labor-limited systems has been provided by Nelson. The framework lists three major elements for controlling of work flow in scheduling:

1. Determining which job to do next at a work center (dispatching).
2. Determining when a person is available for transfer to another work center (degree of central control).
3. Determining the work center to which an available person is to be assigned (work center selection).

Various decision rules, using information similar to that used in making dispatching decisions, have been suggested for making the latter two decisions. The decision rules suggested by Nelson for determining the availability of a person for transfer utilize a central control parameter, d, that varies between 0 and 1. When $d = 1$, the person is always available for reassignment to another work center. When $d = 0$, the person cannot be reassigned as long as there are jobs waiting in the queue at the person's current work center assignment. The proportion of scheduling decisions in which a person is available for transfer can be controlled by adjusting the value of d between 0 and 1.

Two different approaches to transfer availability are suggested by Fryer. One considers time, and the other considers the queue. The approach suggests that the person must be idle for t or more minutes before a transfer can be made. The queue-oriented approach suggests making a transfer only when the person's work center queue has less than q jobs waiting for processing. Labor flexibility is increased by decreasing the value of t or increasing the value of q.

The third decision in the framework, deciding to which work center a person should be assigned, can be made using decision rules that are quite similar to dispatching rules. Priorities for assigning labor to unattended work centers can be determined on the basis of which work center has as its next job to process:

1. The shortest job (SPT).
2. The job that has been in the shop the longest (FISFS).
3. The job that has been waiting at the current work center the longest (FCFS).
4. The most jobs in the queue.
5. Random assignment (as a base line for comparison).

These decision rules are combined with the decision rules for making dispatching and labor availability decisions to control the work flow.

Simulation experiments have been conducted to evaluate the performance of the different work flow control rules suggested for labor-limited systems. These studies generally measure the improvement in the job flow time performance. An interesting general finding is that, while changes in dispatching rules involve a trade-off between the mean and variance in job

FIGURE 13.7   Time and number of jobs in system

Size of labor force	Statistic: Queue discipline		Mean time and mean number in system*			Variance of time in system			Variance of number in system		
			FCFS	FISFS	SPT	FCFS	FISFS	SPT	FCFS	FISFS	SPT
4			17.7	17.7	.9.4	488	295	612	201	205	24
3	Labor assignment rule	0	11.0	11.0	7.0	200	125	295	76	80	17
		1	10.2			173			54		
		2		10.5			102			63	
		3			6.6			343			15
		4	10.1	10.1	6.4	169	97	281	50	53	11
2	Labor assignment rule	0	8.7	8.7	6.2	158	147	186	65	67	23
		1	8.7			153			49		
		2		8.7			147			67	
		3			5.0			285			10
		4	8.7	8.8	5.1	154	89	293	46	48	9
1	Labor assignment rule	0	8.3	8.3	5.5	157	174	176	74	69	24
		1	8.3			149			48		
		2		8.3			174			69	
		3			4.2			296			9
		4	8.3	8.3	4.4	150	174	298	45	69	8

Note: Labor assignment rules:
   0 = Random labor assignment to a work center.
   1 = FCFS labor assignment to a work center.
   2 = FISFS labor assignment to a work center.
   3 = SPT labor assignment to a work center.
   4 = Most jobs in queue labor assignment to a work center.
*Parameters so chosen that the mean time and the mean number in the system were equal.
Source: R. T. Nelson, "Labor and Machine Limited Production Systems," *Management Science* 13, no. 9 (May 1967), p. 660.

flow times, changes in labor assignment rules often can reduce both measures simultaneously. These results can be seen in Figure 13.7.

The importance of labor flexibility in a shop is also demonstrated by experiments involving the labor flexibility factor, d. A change between no labor flexibility $(d = 1)$ and complete labor flexibility $(d = 0)$ resulted in a 12 percent and 39 percent reduction in the mean and variance of job flow times, respectively.

The research on labor assignment rules demonstrates the importance of cross-training and labor assignment flexibility. Moreover, it provides a view that both labor and job dispatching can have a major impact in controlling work flow through a shop. With an operating shop-floor control system in place, it well might be that further performance improvements will come from better design of labor assignments and from operational changes that permit greater flexibility in labor assignments.

Lessons for practice

In this section we have overviewed basic scheduling research. This research offers some important insights to the professional who has an operating MPC system and is interested in further enhancements. One important practical result of the research on sequencing methods has been to clearly understand the effectiveness of the shortest processing time (SPT) rule. This suggests the value of a combined rule, such as a critical ratio/SPT, or some other hybrid based on a combined due date-oriented rule and SPT. For example, at Twin Disc, where critical ratio is used, jobs are segregated into PO jobs (pegged to actual customers orders) and PI jobs (pegged to forecasted usage). A hybrid rule is to first run all PO jobs with a critical ratio less than 1.0 in critical ratio sequences, then sequence all other jobs by SPT.

Black & Decker uses a similar hybrid approach in its plant operations where dispatching is used. Most jobs are processed on the basis of SPT. But the importance of lateness grows exponentially until lateness becomes important enough to override SPT. Thus, no jobs can get "lost" because of a long processing time at some operation. This and other practical experiments lead us to believe that hybrid rules will be developed and implemented in other firms with complex job shop processes.

The research on due date setting suggests that important reductions in manufacturing flow times and work-in-process inventory can be achieved by adopting lead time setting procedures that are based on job-processing times. Using this information to set the lead time offset data for MRP and shop-floor control will be particularly important as lead times (and work-in-process inventory levels) are systematically reduced.

The research on managing open order due dates suggests that performance benefits can be gained by implementing dynamic due date procedures under certain operating conditions. The improvements, however, are influenced by shop structure considerations, such as order quantity sizes and lead times. The research on filtering procedures suggests that gains in manufacturing performance can be achieved by implementing a relatively small proportion of the suggested due date changes.

The research on labor-limited scheduling shows the potential that an increase in labor flexibility can have on manufacturing performance. In many firms today, the combined capacity of its work centers far exceeds its labor capacity. Labor limited scheduling is also important in cellular manufacturing, which is an important aspect of JIT.

EMERGING ISSUES IN SCHEDULING

A major shift in direction has occurred in recent research on scheduling methods. It is closely related to the major changes that are occurring today in the design of the production process at many firms. These changes are motivated by the availability of new process technology, such as computer integrated manufacturing (CIM), the introduction of just-in-time (JIT) methods, and the intensity of the worldwide competition in manufacturing. While the scheduling methods described so far in this chapter have been developed for job shop production processes, many of the new processes being installed in firms today are designed to capture the benefits of repetitive manufacturing and continuous flows of material. As a result, much new scheduling research is concerned with the development of new concepts and techniques to schedule repetitive manufacturing operations. The remaining sections of this chapter are concerned with two scheduling approaches. These are concerned with two different process technologies for repetitive manufacturing: cellular manufacturing systems with manned cells and systems with limited manning, like flexible manufacturing systems (FMS).

Cellular manufacturing systems

Cellular manufacturing systems are designed to process part families in dedicated production areas, referred to as manufacturing cells. The benefits associated with the use of manufacturing cells include: reduced order flow time, less work-in-process inventory, smaller setup times, lower material handling costs, improved quality and productivity, improved job satisfaction and status, and simplified planning and control procedures. Wemmerlov describes three types of material that can be processed in cells: piece parts, subassemblies, and assemblies. Cells can also be of a hybrid type, where both machining and assembly can take place in the small cell. As a result, cells can be referred to as machining, fabrication, assembly, and hybrid cells.

Another distinction important for scheduling purposes is whether a cell is manned or has limited manning. A manned cell is staffed by one or more operators who are responsible for both processing and material handling activities. Often there are fewer operators than machines, and the operators move around the cell to process those orders having the highest priority. In many cases, the scheduling of these cells is complicated by the limited availability of labor. This means that the concepts of labor limited scheduling are applicable in some cases.

Other cells involve the application of computer based technology to the processing and material handling activities. Examples of such cells include flexible manufacturing systems (FMS), surface mount technology for the assembly of integrated circuits in the electronics industry, and other applications of computer integrated manufacturing. In these cells, operators perform tool loading, monitoring, and inspection tasks.

The flow pattern within a cell also has an important impact on the selection of a scheduling method in cellular manufacturing. Manufacturing cells can range from being pure flow shops to job shops. In a pure flow shop cell, the job routing is the same for all jobs. Here, the job sequence established for the first machine in the cell is maintained for all of the subsequent machines. Therefore, a sequencing decision is made only once—at the point of entry into the manufacturing cell. For all other flow patterns (e.g., in job shop cells), orders may skip machines, backtrack, or enter the cell at multiple points. In such cases, a sequencing decision must be made at each machine. The next section is concerned with the development of scheduling methods for manned cells, while the following section is concerned with the scheduling of flexible manufacturing systems.

Scheduling manned cellular manufacturing systems

Both static and dynamic scheduling approaches have been applied to the scheduling of flow shop cells. Some of this work uses the analytical methods for solving static scheduling problems developed by Johnson and Campbell, Dudek, and Smith, which were described earlier in this chapter. These methods assume that all of the jobs to be scheduled are available at the first machine in the cell at the beginning of the scheduling period. Recently, work has been reported on the development of dynamic scheduling approaches for flow shop cells. Here, orders arrive at random time intervals for processing in a manufacturing cell. A survey of this research is provided by Wemmerlov. An important part of this effort has been directed toward the development and testing of job shop sequencing heuristics, similar to those described for application to dynamic flow shop scheduling problems earlier in this chapter. In this section we describe two studies that report the development and testing of dynamic scheduling heuristics for dynamic manned manufacturing flow shop cells that are dedicated to the production of certain part families.

Wemmerlov and Vakharia report dynamic scheduling heuristics for a five-stage flow shop cell, with a queue of orders in front of each stage. Each stage in this cell has one machine, and all orders have the same routing through the cell. As many as six part families are processed in this cell, with individual part orders arriving at random time intervals according to a Poisson process. Upon arrival at the cell, each part order is assigned a due date based on the total work content (TWK) to be performed in the cell on the order. The total work content includes the combined values of the part family setup time and the processing time at each stage in the cell.

Simulation studies were conducted to evaluate different scheduling rules, using a computer model of the manufacturing cell. A scheduling rule is used to sequence the orders at the first stage in the cell, and this same sequence is maintained at all of the remaining stages in the cell. The four scheduling rules evaluated were:

FCFS: First come/first served.
SLACK: Slack time.
CDS: Campbell, Dudek, and Smith's procedure.
NEH: Nawaz, Enscore, and Ham's procedure.

The first two rules are job shop sequencing rules and are used to maintain a priority sequence of the orders in the queue at the first stage in the line. However, the second two rules are static scheduling rules. These rules were applied periodically in these experiments to develop a priority sequence of the orders in the queue at the first stage of the line.

While the CDS rule was used as described earlier in this chapter, the NEH rule uses a different sequencing procedure. This heuristic starts with a partial sequence (it could be just one job) of the jobs in queue at the first stage. The makespan is computed for a new job inserted in all positions without disturbing the order of the previous, partial sequence. It is kept in the position that gives the lowest makespan, and another job is evaluated until all available jobs have been considered.

In an effort to minimize the setup time at each stage in the cell, a variation of each of the four rules was developed. The variation simply partitions the queue of orders at the first stage in the line according to a part family. The sequence in which the orders within each part family grouping are processed and the sequence in which the part families are processed are both established. For example, the first come–first served rule processes that family having the oldest order first. After all of the orders in that family are processed, the part family having the next oldest order is processed next.

The family versions for the SLACK, CDS, and the NEH rules are more complex. In the case of the SLACK rule, the orders in the queue at the first stage are partitioned into those orders having negative and positive slack. For those orders having negative slack, the family having the order with the most negative slack is processed first. After all of the orders in this family are processed in the order of their slack time priority, the rule is then applied to determine the next part family to process. For those orders having a positive slack priority, the next part family to be processed is that family having the largest sum of the combined setup and processing time for all of the stages in the cell. Once the next part family to be processed has been selected, the orders within that family are processed in order according to the smallest sum of the combined setup and processing time for all of the stages in the line.

The family versions of the CDS and the NEH rules also develop a sequence for the families represented in the order set, and then a sequence for the jobs in each family. These procedures proceed by first collapsing the five-stage scheduling problem into a series of two-stage scheduling problems, and then use a procedure similar to the Johnson algorithm to solve each two-stage problem. The solution having the minimum makespan is used to sequence both the part family to be processed next and to establish the sequence of the orders within each part family.

Wemmerlov and Vakharia report simulation experiments that evaluate the performance of these rules, considering the following measures of performance: average order flow time and lateness, the total number of early/ total number of late orders, and the total number of family setups/the total number of operations processed. Several factors were varied in these experiments, including: the number of part families, the ratio of family setup time to order processing time, and the cell utilization level.

The simulation results indicate that the family-oriented versions of the sequencing rules consistently outperform the other rules, and that the difference in performance increases as the ratio of the setup to processing time increases. However, these results are quite sensitive to number of part families processed by a cell. When a small number of part families was processed (e.g., 3), the family versions of the FCFS and the SLACK rules outperformed the other rules. However, when the cell processed a larger number of part families (e.g., 6), the FCFS(Family) rule produced the best due date performance while the CDS(Family) rule produced a smaller average flow time. In analyzing the simulation results it appears that the differences between the FCFS(Family) and the CDS(Family) rules are quite small. Therefore when the administrative costs of using the CDS (Family) rule are considered, it may be advantageous to use the simpler FCFS(Family) rule.

In selecting a scheduling rule for a manufacturing cell, these results indicate the value of using a sequencing rule that works toward reducing the setup time in the cell. The resulting increase in effective capacity in the cell provides an important improvement in scheduling performance. Also it is clear that the FCFS(Family) is very effective, especially when the costs of administering the shop-floor control system are considered. However, if a cell is designed to produce a larger number of part families than the number considered in these experiments, the CDS(Family) rule should be considered.

A second study of scheduling heuristics for manufacturing cells is reported by Mosier, Elvers, and Kelly. They examine the performance of sequencing heuristics for the cell shown in Figure 13.8. It contains four machines, each having three queues of orders, with a separate queue for each part family. An order may require processing on one or more of the first three machines, and all orders are processed by the fourth machine. There-

FIGURE 13.8 Schematic of the manufacturing cell used by Mosier, Elvers, and Kelly

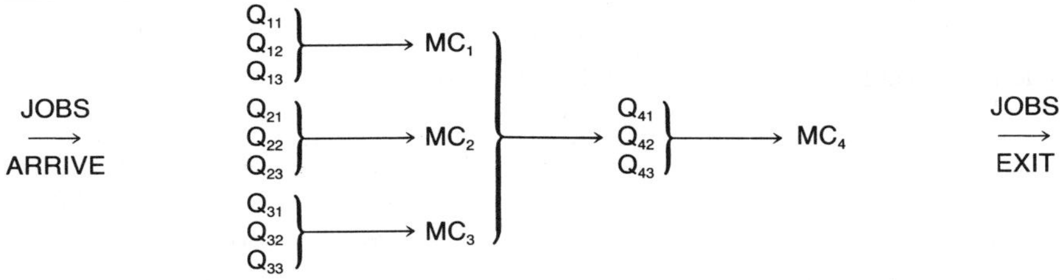

where:
Q_{ij} = Queue at machine i for part family j
MC_i = Machine type i

Source: C. T. Mosier, D. A. Elvers, and D. Kelly, "Analysis of Group Technology Scheduling Heuristics," *International Journal of Production Research* 22, no. 5, 1984.

fore, the part routings are not the same for all orders. The orders arrive at the cell at random time intervals, according to the Poisson process, and the due dates for the cell are assigned on the basis of total work content, using the TWK procedure.

Since this cell is organized as a job shop and orders are not routed to all machines in the same sequence, sequencing decisions must be made at all four machines in the cell. Three decisions are made at each machine:

When to select orders from a different queue (part family).
Which of the two remaining queues (part families) to select orders from.
What order to select from the chosen queue.

Three different rules were used to make the first two decisions:

AVE: Select the part family queue having the highest average order priority and process all of the orders in the queue at the time of the queue selection.

WORK: Select the part family queue having the largest sum of the processing times for this machine; that is, the queue having the largest work content, and process all of the orders in the queue.

ECON: After each order is processed at a machine, calculate the combined expected setup time for all orders in each queue. Switch to the queue having the largest total expected setup time, if that value exceeds the total expected setup time for the queue currently being serviced.

Five different order sequencing rules were used to establish the dispatching priority for the orders in each queue:

1. Slack Time.
2. Modified Critical Ratio 1 (time remaining until the due date divided by the total processing time remaining).
3. Shortest Processing Time.
4. Modified Critical Ratio 2 (time remaining until the due date divided by the remaining number of operations).
5. First In the Shop, First Out.

Simulation experiments were conducted to evaluate these rules using the following criteria: the mean and variance of the order lateness and tardiness, the mean and variance of the order flow times, the proportion of the orders failing to meet the due date, and the total machine setup and idle times. These experiments were conducted using two different levels for the machine setup time and the machine utilization.

The simulation experiments indicate very little difference between the WORK and ECON rules with regard to mean order flow time, mean lateness, and order tardiness. The performance of the AVE rule is inferior to both of the other rules on these measures of performance. However, the AVE rule provides better performance than the WORK and ECON rules when the percentage of late orders is considered. With regard to setup time savings, the WORK and ECON rules provided much greater savings in setup time than the AVE rule.

These studies indicate that important differences exist between different sequencing rules applied to manufacturing cells. In particular, it is important to note that the flow pattern in a cell has an impact on the nature of the scheduling decisions that control the flow of work in the cell. One clear principle emerges: There are important setup savings to be gained by taking family groupings into consideration in the scheduling of work in manufacturing cells, as well as in the basic design of such cells.

In the next section, dealing with flexible manufacturing cells, the nature of the scheduling decision varies from the two cells described in this section. As research continues on the scheduling of manufacturing cells, a better understanding will no doubt emerge of the impact of the characteristics of a cell on the scheduling decisions.

Scheduling FMS systems

The process technology for the low- to medium-volume production of metal parts in job shops has changed dramatically in recent years with the development of flexible manufacturing systems (FMS). Such systems typically have from 2 to 16 machine tools, and they use a computer to control the various steps in the machining process, the material handling activities of moving parts between machines, and the scheduling of the flow of orders through the system. In effect, FMS systems permit many of the efficiencies and utilization levels of mass-production systems while retaining the flexibility of manually operated job shops; that is, very general (random) part flow patterns and machines that are capable of processing a wide variety of different part types. These systems provide important benefits in reducing machine setup times, shortening the overall manufacturing cycle (sometimes from weeks to days) with corresponding reductions in work-in-process inventory, and reduced tooling costs.

Although the development of shop-floor control systems for the scheduling of day-to-day operations in a flexible manufacturing system is still an emerging area of research, the scheduling of such systems can be viewed using many of the job shop scheduling concepts discussed in this chapter. For example, one view could be a static scheduling problem, where a fixed set of orders are to be scheduled, using either optimization or priority scheduling heuristics. Alternatively, the problem could be viewed as a dynamic scheduling problem, where orders arrive periodically for scheduling (e.g., as daily order releases from an MRP system or as individual customer orders). As a static scheduling problem, such performance criteria as minimizing the makespan or the mean order flow time may be of interest, while additional criteria, such as the mean and variance of the order lateness and tardiness, may be of concern in the dynamic version of the problem.

Under either view of the scheduling problem, three different scheduling and control decisions occur in the management of day-to-day operations at the shop floor level of an FMS:

1. Part loading timing: When to load a part into the FMS?
2. Part loading: Which part type to load into the FMS?
3. Dispatching: To which machine should a part be dispatched after it has completed its current operation?

The part loading timing decision is concerned with when to enter a new part into the system at the loading station of an FMS, considering such factors as system congestion, part fixture availability, and the like. The part loading decision concerns the choice of the part type to enter the FMS at the loading station when it is time for a new part to enter the system, considering such factors as the part characteristics and machine workload conditions. The dispatching decision is concerned with the routing of parts through the FMS at the time of actual production, such as the sequencing of parts at the individual machines in an FMS.

These procedures assume that production planning decisions at an aggregate level concerning the types and mix of parts to be run on the FMS have been previously resolved in the development of part routings and in the preparation of the overall material and capacity plans for the company. Stecke has identified five such interrelated production planning problems that need to be solved prior to actual production: FMS part type selection, machine grouping, production ratio determination, resource allocation, and cell loading.

In this chapter, we are concerned with the day-to-day scheduling of FMS operations, and with how FMS performance can be influenced by the choice of the scheduling method used to make these decisions at the shop-floor level. We assume, therefore, that these higher level decisions have been made. Furthermore, other parameters that control the level of work-in-process, such as the number of material handling fixtures for parts and the use of special or general purpose part holding fixtures, can have an important impact on FMS performance, and are also assumed to have been addressed and determined. On this basis, we review some of the results of FMS scheduling studies.

Stecke and Solberg report a study involving the scheduling of a 10 machine FMS built by Sunstrand in the Caterpillar Tractor Company plant in Peoria, Illinois. A diagram of this FMS is shown in Figure 13.9. It includes four large 5-axis machining centers called Omnimills (OM), three 4-axis machining centers Omnidrills (OD), two vertical turret lathes (VTL), and an inspection station. Each machine has a limited capacity tool magazine to hold the tools needed by each operation assigned to the machine. Two transporters run on a straight track and carry parts from machine to machine. A 16-station load/unload area provides a centralized queuing area for work-in-process inventory. This FMS is dedicated to the manufacture of four parts, representing two sizes of transmission housings, with each housing including two matched parts—a transmission case and a cover. The system includes 18 holding fixtures (one fixture holds two parts) to convey the parts through the system. The fixtures are dedicated to individual parts in proportion to the parts demanded.

Simulation experiments were run to evaluate different scheduling and control procedures, using a simulation model of the Caterpillar FMS. These procedures included the following part loading timing, part loading, and dispatching rules:

1. Whenever two parts are completed (one fixture emptied), new parts are loaded into the empty holding fixture at the loading station.
2. The new parts to be loaded have to be of the same type as the completed parts.
3. Sixteen different dispatching rules were tested for deciding which parts to route to an empty machine. These rules are listed in Figure 13.9.

Each simulation experiment consisted of solving a static scheduling problem, in which approximately 172 parts (including an equal number of the four part types) were scheduled during six eight-hour days of simulated time. In all, 80 simulation experiments were run, using 16 different "dis-

FIGURE 13.9   Caterpillar flexible manufacturing system (FMS)

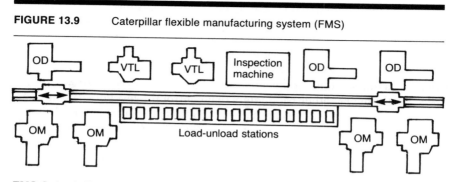

FMS Scheduling Procedures

Part loading timing rule: Load next empty fixture.
Part loading rule: Load same part type as completed part type.
Dispatching rules:

1. Original—for each machine, the assigned operations (obtained at the production planning stage during all loads) are ordered according to the largest workload of the next operation's machine. This was the control strategy originally applied by the FMS and the most complicated, computationally, to apply among all those tested.
2. SPT—the operations are ordered according to the shortest operation time first.
3. LPT—longest operation time first.
4. FOPR—fewest operations remaining for each part.
5. MOPR—most operations remaining.
6. SRPT—shortest remaining processing time of each part.
7. LRPT—longest remaining processing time.
8. SPT·TOT—smallest value of operation time multiplied by the total processing time for the part.
9. SPT/TOT—shortest processing time for the operation divided by the total processing time for the part.
10. LPT/TOT—longest processing time for the operation divided by the total processing time for the part.
11. LPT·TOT—longest processing time for the operation times the total processing time for the part.
12. Part type priority—case, assembly, cover (MOPR).
13. Part type priority—cover, assembly, case (MOPR).
14. Part type priority—assembly, case, cover (MOPR).
15. Part type priority—case, assembly, cover (FOPR).
16. Part type priority—assembly, case, cover (FOPR).

Source: K. E. Stecke and J. J. Solberg, "Loading and Control Procedures for a Flexible Manufacturing System," *International Journal of Production Research* 19, no. 5, 1981.

patching" rules, with five different levels of alternate routing flexibility; that is, moving from the use of fixed routings to an increased number of routing alternatives for each operation. The FMS performance was measured in terms of the number of parts completed during the six-day period.

The SPT/TOT dispatching rule performed the best over all levels of the different alternate routing flexibility, providing an 8 percent to 24 percent improvement over the method originally used to assign orders to machines. Since the objective was to maximize the output of the machine during a given time interval, the performance of the SPT/TOT dispatching rule is consistent with previous research findings. In addition to giving a high priority to short operations, orders requiring a large amount of FMS time and operations that are early in a routing also receive a high scheduling priority.

A different FMS scheduling approach was reported by Denzler and Boe in a study of a 16-machine Kearney and Trecker FMS at the John Deere plant in Waterloo, Iowa. Instead of focusing on the dispatching of parts to machines, this study analyzed different part loading procedures, as well as determining the best number of in-process parts (fixtures) and taking into account congestion on the material handling system. Taken together, the two studies provide an overall view of the performance impact of using different scheduling procedures and criteria for the three different decisions in an FMS shop-floor control system.

A diagram of the Deere FMS is shown in Figure 13.10. This system is dedicated to the manufacture of eight prismatic automatic transmission housings for agricultural tractors. It includes five head indexers, 11 moduline machining stations, two load stations, and two unload stations. A computer controlled material handling system, with 37 carts and 51 dedicated part fixtures, is used to move the eight parts through the system. Because the orientation of several parts differs between operations, the routing for such parts is broken into two or three segments, with each segment requiring a pass through the FMS—resulting in a total of 14 part-items to be processed by the FMS. Instead of a centralized buffer storage queue, this FMS has room for two incoming and two outgoing part fixtures at each machine, and room on the material handling system track for additional part fixtures awaiting assignment to a machine for the next operation on the routing.

A simulation model of the John Deere FMS was used to evaluate the part loading methods shown in Figure 13.10, using the minimum makespan and machine utilization as the performance criteria. In each simulation experiment, a 10-week static scheduling problem was solved, in which 7,590 units of the eight parts were scheduled with five eight-hour days per week. Several experimental factors were varied, including the part loading rule, the number of part fixtures in the system at any given time, and the alternate routing flexibility for the parts. The part loading timing rule used in these experiments was the Next Empty Fixture rule, indicating that a new part was loaded whenever a completed part left the FMS. Also, the dispatching

FIGURE 13.10   Deere & Company flexible manufacturing system (FMS)

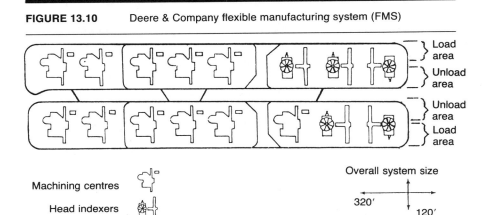

Machining centres

Head indexers

Overall system size

320'

120'

FMS Scheduling Procedures

Part loading timing rule: Next empty fixture (NEF).
Part loading rules:

1. SPJL—Load that part which has the smallest proportion of job launched; that is, the smallest proportion of its batch requirement started.
2. SPT—Load that part with the shortest total processing time.
3. S&S—Load that part with the smallest ratio of loading station time divided by total processing time (Stecke and Solberg's rule).
4. NEF—As each fixture is unloaded, reload it with a like product, if possible.
5. FEM—Find the first empty machine that can do that part on it.
6. HPEM—Find the highest priority empty machine and load that part which can be processed by that machine.

Dispatching rule: Least work in next queue (LWNQ).

Source: D. R. Denzler and W. J. Boe, "Experimental Investigation of Flexible Manufacturing System Scheduling Rules," *International Journal of Production Research,* forthcoming.

of parts to machines was accomplished using the Least Work In Next Queue rule, since small work queues normally exist at each machine in the Deere FMS.

The simulation results indicate that the smallest proportion of jobs launched (SPJL) and the next empty fixture (NEF) part loading rules performed significantly better than the other procedures, producing a shorter schedule length (minimum makespan) with a higher machine utilization. The results also indicated an interesting interaction between two of the experimental factors: alternate routing flexibility and the number of part fixtures in the system. A 12 percent gain in machine utilization was obtained when a high alternate routing flexibility and a large number of in-process part fixtures were used in contrast with the opposite case. Yet, the results also indicate a decreasing marginal improvement in the machine utilization, because the number of in-process part fixtures is increased. Since there is an upper limit on the number of part fixtures available to the system, increasing the number released into the FMS also results in decreasing the choice of part types to be considered by the part loading rule at the loading station.

These studies illustrate the use of scheduling methods in a shop-floor control system for managing the day-to-day operations for an FMS that is dedicated to the production of a relatively small family of similar parts. Very little work has been reported on the scheduling of "random" FMSs—FMS systems designed to process a much larger variety of parts that arrive continuously at random time intervals. The installation of such FMSs represents an important new trend and presents additional customer service criteria to be considered in the scheduling of an FMS.

A recent study by Shanker and Tzen reports early work on methods for planning the workloads on a random FMS, and rules for dispatching orders to individual machines at the time of actual production. Their work considers the planning of balanced workloads at the different machines in an FMS, the arrival pattern of jobs, and the setting of due dates for the jobs processed on an FMS. They evaluate five methods for the planning of FMS workloads in conjunction with four different rules for dispatching jobs to machines: first in/first out, shortest processing time, longest processing time, and most operations remaining first. The simulation experiment results reported by Shanker and Tzen indicate that two dispatching rules (shortest processing time and most operations remaining first) perform effectively using machine utilization as the performance criterion. Furthermore, the FMS performance is improved substantially with the use of a workload planning procedure that achieves a balanced workload between machines.

The work of Shanker and Tzen confirms the effectiveness of the shortest processing time rule observed by Stecke and Solberg in dispatching orders to FMS machines, and indicates the robust nature of this rule under a wide variety of production process configurations. It may well be that, as further research is performed on the scheduling of random FMSs, other parallels will be drawn between the scheduling of job shop and FMS production systems.

A different issue in day-to-day operations of FMS systems is seen in the work by Jaikumar. Figure 13.11 provides a comparison of FMS use by American and Japanese manufacturers. The key differences are in the number of different parts processed by the FMSs, and the utilization of the equipment. There are many lessons in Figure 13.11; but the key, from a scheduling point of view, is that it seems increasingly necessary to utilize FMSs at higher

---

FIGURE 13.11   Jaikumar's comparison of U.S. and Japanese FMS use

	United States	Japan
System development time, years	2.5 to 3	1.25 to 1.75
Number of machines per system	7	6
Types of parts produced per system	10	93
Annual volume per part	1,727	258
Number of parts produced per day	88	120
Number of new parts introduced per year	1	22
Number of systems with untended operations	0	18
Utilization rate, two shifts	52%*	84%*
Average metal-cutting time per day-hours	8.3	20.2

*Ratio of actual metal-cutting time to time available for metal cutting.
Source: R. Jaikumar, "Post Industrial Manufacturing," *Harvard Business Review*, November–December 1986, p. 71.

---

rates, to schedule smaller more frequent lots, and to continually produce new parts on them.

CONCLUDING PRINCIPLES

The advanced scheduling concepts described in this chapter lead to the following concluding principles:

- The objective(s) to be achieved in scheduling must be determined before a sequencing rule can be selected, since different rules provide different results.
- The shortest processing time rule, contrary to one's intuition, can produce effective performance and should be considered as a standard in designing shop-floor control systems.
- Important improvements in manufacturing performance can be gained by introducing flexibility in scheduling (e.g., through the use of alternate routings, adjustments in labor assignments, overlap scheduling, and the like).
- Manufacturing lead time setting is an important consideration in scheduling. Processing times should be a basic data input.
- Proper maintenance of due dates can provide major improvements in manufacturing performance.
- Shop-floor nervousness can be diminished by using due date filtering procedures.
- Increased use of cellular manufacturing systems and FMS are creating new opportunities and challenges for routine scheduling; many job shop scheduling principles are applicable to these situations.

REFERENCES

Bagchi, U.; J. C. Hayya; and J. K. Ord. "Modeling Demand During Lead Time." *Decision Sciences* 15, no. 2 (Spring 1984).

Baker, K. R., *Introduction to Sequencing and Scheduling*. New York: John Wiley & Sons, 1974.

―――. "The Effects of Input Control In a Simple Scheduling Problem and Some Thoughts On 'Managerial Robots.'" *Journal of Operations Management* 4, no. 2 (1984).

―――. "Sequencing Rules and Due-Date Assignments in a Job Shop." *Management Science*, vol. 30, no. 9, September 1984.

Baker, K. R., and J. W. M. Bertrand. "A Comparison of Due-Date Selection Rules." *AIIE Transactions*, June 1981.

Baker, K. R., and J. J. Kanet. "Job Shop Scheduling With Modified Due Dates." *Journal of Operations Management* 4, no. 1 (1983).

Barker, J. R. and G. B. McMahon. "Scheduling the General Job-Shop." *Management Science* 31, no. 5 (May 1985).

Berry, W. L. "Priority Scheduling and Inventory Control in Job Lot Manufacturing Systems." *AIIE Transactions* 4, no. 4 (December 1972).

―――, and V. Rao. "Critical Ratio Scheduling: An Experimental Analysis." *Management Science* 22, no. 2 (October 1975).

Buzacott, J. A., and D. D. Yao. "Flexible Manufacturing Systems: A Review of Analytical Models." *Management Science* 32, no. 7 (July 1986).

Campbell, H. G., R. A. Dudek, and M. L. Smith. "A Heuristic Algorithm for the n Job m Machine Sequencing Problem." *Management Science* 16, no. 10, June 1970.

Carroll, D. C. "Heuristic Sequencing of Single and Multiple Component Jobs." Ph.D. dissertation, Alfred P. Sloan School of Management, Massachusetts Institute of Technology, 1965.

Conway, R. W.; W. L. Maxwell; and L. W. Miller. *Theory of Scheduling*. Reading, Mass.: Addison-Wesley, 1967.

Cruickshanks, A. B.; R. D. Drescher; and S. C. Graves. "A Study of Production Smoothing in a Job Shop Environment." *Management Science* 30, no. 3 (March 1984).

Day, J. E., and M. P. Hottenstein. "Review of Sequencing Research." *Naval Research Logistics Quarterly* 17 (March 1970).

Denzler, D. R., and W. J. Boe. "Experimental Investigation of Flexible Manufacturing System Scheduling Rules." *International Journal of Production Research* (forthcoming).

Eilon, S., and I. G. Chowdbury. "Due Dates in Job Shop Scheduling." *International Journal of Production Research* 14, no. 2 (1976).

Elvers, D. A. "Job Shop Dispatching Using Various Due-Date Setting Criteria." *Production and Inventory Management* 14, no. 4 (December 1973).

Elvers, F. A., and M. D. Treleven. "Job-Shop vs. Hybrid Flow–Shop Routing in a Dual Resource Constrained System." *Decision Sciences* 16, no. 2 (Spring 1985).

Erhorn, Craig R. "Handling Less Than Lead Time Schedule Changes." *Production and Inventory Management* 22, no. 3 (3rd Quarter 1981), pp. 27–32.

Fryer, J. S. "Labor Flexibility in Multiechelon Dual-Constraint Job Shops." *Management Science* 20, no. 7 (March 1974).

————. "Operating Policies in Multiechelon Dual Constraint Job Shops." *Management Science* 19, no. 9 (May 1973).

Graves, S. "A Review of Production Scheduling." *Operations Research* 29, no. 4 (July/August 1981).

Graves, S. C.; H. C. Meal; D. Stefek; and A. H. Zeghmi. "Scheduling of Re-Entrant Flow Shops." *Journal of Operations Management* 3, no. 4 (1983).

Hausman, W. H., and G. D. Scudder. "Priority Scheduling Rules for Repairable Inventory Systems." *Management Science* 28, no. 11 (November 1982).

Hoffmann, T. R., and G. D. Scudder. "Priority Scheduling with Cost Considerations." *International Journal of Production Research* 21, no. 6 (1983).

Holstein, W. K., and W. L. Berry. "The Labor Assignment Decision: An Application of Work Flow Structure Information." *Management Science* 18, no. 7 (March 1972).

Jaikumar, Ramchandran. "Postindustrial Manufacturing." *Harvard Business Review*, November–December 1986, pp. 69–76.

Johnson, S. M. "Optimal Two and Three-Stage Production Schedules with Setup Time Included." *Naval Research Logistics Quarterly* 1 (1954), pp. 61–68.

Karmarkar, U. S. "NOTE: Lot-Sizing and Sequencing Delays." *Management Science* 33, no. 3 (March 1987).

Luthi, H. J. and A. Polymeris. "Scheduling to Minimize Maximum Workload." *Management Science* 31, no. 11 (November 1985).

Mosier, C. T.; D. A. Elvers; and D. Kelly. "Analysis of Group Technology Scheduling Heuristics." *International Journal of Production Research* 22, no. 5 (1984), pp. 857–75.

Nanot, Y. R. "An Experimental Investigation and Comparative Evaluation of Priority Discipline in Job Shop Queueing Networks." Management Sciences Research Project, Research Report no. 87, University of California, Los Angeles, December 1963.

Nawoz, M. A.; M. Enscoci; and E. E. Ham. "A Heuristic Algorithm For the M Machine—N Job Flow Shop Sequencing Problem. *Omega* 41, no. 1, 1983.

Nelson, R. T. "Labor and Machine Limited Production Systems." *Management Science* 13, no. 9 (May 1967).

————. "Dual-Resource Constrained Series Service Systems." *Operations Research* 16, no. 2 (March/April 1968).

————. "A Simulation of Labor Efficiency and Centralized Assignment in a Production Model." *Management Science* 17, no. 2 (Oct–Nov 1970).

Penlesky, R. J. "Open Order Rescheduling Heuristics for MRP Systems in Manufacturing Firms." Ph.D. dissertation, Indiana University, 1982.

Posner, M. E. "A Sequencing Problem with Release Dates and Clustered Jobs." *Management Science* 32, no. 6 (June 1986).

Putnam, A. O.; R. Everdell; G. H. Dorman; R. R. Cronan; and L. H. Lundgren. "Updating Critical Ratio and Slack Time Priority Scheduling Rules." *Production and Inventory Management* 12, no. 4 (1971).

Ragatz, G. L., and V. A. Mabert. "A Simulation Analysis of Due Date Assignment Rules." *Journal of Operations Management* 5, no. 1 (1985).

Russell, R. S. and B. W. Taylor III. "An Evaluation of Sequencing Rules for an Assembly Shop." *Decision Sciences* 16, no. 2 (Spring 1985).

Scudder, G. D. "Scheduling and Labor-Assignment Policies for a Dual-Constrained Repair Shop." *International Journal of Production Research* 24, no. 3 (May–June 1986).

Shanker, K., and Y. S. Tzen. "A Loading and Dispatching Problem in a Random Flexible Manufacturing System." *International Journal of Production Research* 23, no. 3 (1985), pp. 579–95.

Stecke, K. E., and J. J. Solberg. "Loading and Control Procedures for a Flexible Manufacturing System." *International Journal of Production Research* 19, no. 5 (1981), pp. 481–90.

Steele, D. C. "The Nervous MRP System: How to Do Battle." *Production and Inventory Management* 16 (4th Quarter 1975).

Treleven, M. D., and D. A. Elvers. "An Investigation of Labor Assignment Rules in a Dual-Constrained Job Shop." *Journal of Operations Management* 6, no. 1 (1986).

Weeks, J. K. "A Simulation Study of Predictable Due-Dates." *Management Science* 25, no. 4 (April 1973).

Wemmerlov, U. "Design Factors in MRP Systems: A Limited Survey." *Production and Inventory Management* 20, December 1979.

———. *Production Planning and Control Procedures for Cellular Manufacturing Systems: Concepts and Practice.* Falls Church, Va.: American Production and Inventory Control Society, 1987.

Wemmerlov, U., and A. J. Vakharia. "Dynamic and Intermittent Job and Family Structure of a Flow Line Manufacturing Cell." Working paper, University of Wisconsin, 1986.

Whitaker, John H. "Managing—To Get Better Results in Less Time." *Production and Inventory Management,* (4th Quarter 1975).

Woolsey, R. E. D. "A Survey of Quick and Dirty Methods for Production Scheduling." *1972 APICS Conference Proceedings,* pp. 309–30.

Yano, C. A. "Setting Planned Leadtimes in Serial Production Systems with Tardiness Costs." *Management Science* 33, no. 1 (January 1987).

DISCUSSION QUESTIONS

1. Why is the notion of "rescheduling" such an important one in production planning and control?
2. What kinds of performance measures would apply to the "scheduling" at a college or university?
3. Are there college or university equivalents of the following concepts: flow shop structure, matched sets (common due dates), operation overlapping, and alternate routings?
4. Provide some examples of static and dynamic scheduling problems.
5. What sequencing rule do you use to do your homework?
6. If you were asked to audit the lead times for a firm's MRP system, what would you look for?

PROBLEMS

1. The Pohl Pool Company has seven jobs waiting to be processed through its liner department. Each job, estimated processing times, and due dates are listed below:

Job	Processing time (days)	Due date (days from now)
A	4	8
B	13	37
C	6	8
D	3	7
E	11	39
F	9	21
G	8	16

    a. Using the shortest processing time scheduling rule, in what order would the jobs be completed? Processing can start immediately.
    b. What is the average completion time (in days) of the sequence calculated in question a?
    c. What is the average job lateness (in days) of the sequence calculated in question a?

2. The Franklin Furniture Company has the following information on five jobs waiting to be processed in a work center. Processing can start immediately.

Job	Remaining processing time (days)	Due date (days from now)	Remaining number of operations
A	8	15	3
B	4	3	3
C	10	20	5
D	6	6	5
E	7	3	2

    a. Using the slack per operation scheduling rule, in what order would the jobs be completed?

    b. What is the average job lateness (in days) of the sequence calculated in question **a**?

    c. What is the average number of jobs in the system using the sequence in question **a**?

3. The Hyer-Than-Ever Kite Manufacturing Emporium must schedule the latest set of work orders through its frame-making department. Kites begin at frame-making and then proceed through one, two, or three other departments, depending upon the ordered kite's sophistication. It is 8:00 A.M. on Monday morning. Processing can start immediately. Shop scheduler Joan Weber is faced with the following set of orders (listed in order of arrival):

Kite order	Frame-making time (days)	Total processing time (days)	Total number of operations	Frame due date (days from now)
A	10	20	4	25
B	12	18	2	15
C	7	12	2	16
D	5	12	3	17
E	8	10	2	12

    a. Using the order data, evaluate the first come/first served sequencing rule:

        1. In what sequence should the jobs be processed in the frame-making department?

        2. What will the average completion time be in frame-making?

        3. What will be the average number of jobs in the frame-making department?

    b. Using the order data, evaluate the earliest due date sequencing rule:

        1. In what sequence should the jobs be processed in the frame-making department?

        2. Which specific jobs, if any, will be late in leaving frame-making?

        3. What will the average job lateness be in the frame-making department?

    c. Using the order data, evaluate the shortest processing time sequencing rule:

        1. In what sequence should the jobs be processed in the frame-making department?

        2. On what days will order E be in process in frame-making?

        3. What will the average job lateness be in the frame-making department?

    d. While Joan was debating which rule to use, the following memo was delivered to her from Diane Britenbach, the president:

        I have decided that, effective this morning, all departmental job sequencing should be performed using the slack time per operation rule. This should improve scheduling performance throughout the plant.

1. In what sequence should the jobs be processed in the frame-making department, if the slack time per operation rule were used and the due dates are considered to be final due dates?
2. On what day will order D be completed in frame-making?
3. What is the average completion time for this sequence?

4. Prepare a two-machine schedule, using the Johnson procedure for the following four jobs:

	Machine	
Job	I	II
A	4	3
B	1	7
C	8	2
D	8	5

a. In what sequence should the jobs be processed?
b. Construct a Gantt chart of the schedule for both machines.
c. Construct a Gantt chart, assuming there is no buffer storage between the machines (e.g., machine I cannot start a new job until machine II has started the old job).

5. Telly's Deli and Catering Company has five orders. Each order is for a particular type of salad. Making each salad consists of two tasks: prepping and assembling. Assembling cannot be started until prepping for that particular order is complete. The salads must be complete in 24 hours.

Orders	Prepping (hours)	Assembling (hours)
Antipasto	6	4
Indonesian rice	3	4
Mixed vegetables	5	2
Marinated vegetables	8	6
German potato salad	2	1

a. What is the schedule that produces the shortest time span in which these orders can be completed?
b. Is it possible for all orders to be completed in 24 hours? How many hours does it take to complete the five orders?
c. For the schedule in question a, how many hours is the assembling task idle?
d. When will the order for the mixed vegetable salad be completed?
e. What is the average order completion time?

6. Flash Fasttrack is the associate dean of janitorial services at Wombat University. Flash must schedule the regular maintenance performed by his janitorial engineers. There are two crews: the sweeping crew and the waxing crew. Union rules prohibit sweepers from waxing and waxers from sweeping. A building's

floors must first be swept before they can be waxed. Flash must schedule the order in which the maintenance crews will visit each of Wombat U's six buildings. He wishes to minimize the total completion time of the sequence. The times required to sweep and wax each building are as follows:

Building	Sweeping time (hours)	Waxing time (hours)
Astronomy	18	10
Biology	8	9
Chemistry	26	13
Drama	15	16
English	17	20
Foreign language	12	17

   a. Schedule the crews through the buildings.
   b. When will the waxing crew start and stop work in the chemistry building?
   c. During the time of the schedule, how much time is available from sweepers and waxers for other activities?

7. Currently, the marketing manager at Precision Parts, Inc., a manufacturer of custom-made machined parts, promises a six-week delivery time for all customer orders. The production manager is under pressure from top management to improve the firm's performance against quoted delivery dates. In his review of alternative procedures for making customer delivery date promises, he has provided the following data on representative orders:

Order	Total processing time (in weeks)
1	2
2	4
3	6

   a. Determine the delivery time to be quoted on these orders, if the TWK (total work content) procedure is used. (Assume that the average time from order receipt to customer delivery is six weeks.)
   b. Determine the delivery time to be quoted on these orders if the SLK (slack) procedure is used. (Assume that the average time from order receipt to customer delivery is six weeks.)
   c. Suppose that the production manager knows the overall flow time for order #3 has averaged nine weeks in the past, and that the flow time standard deviation for this order is one week. How would this information influence your recommendation of a delivery date setting procedure in this situation?

8. The SCM Corporation has three testing machines in its quality control laboratory, which are manned by a single test operator. Only one machine is run at a time. The SCM Corporation uses two scheduling rules, one for dispatching jobs

at individual machines and another for assigning labor to machines. As of 8:00 this morning (on day 10), the jobs waiting to be processed at each of the three machines are as follows:

Test Machine A			
Job	Due date*	Processing time†	Arrival date*
1	12	1	9
5	18	6	8

Test Machine B			
Job	Due date*	Processing time†	Arrival date*
2	14	3	6
3	16	4	7
6	14	6	6

Test Machine C			
Job	Due date*	Processing time**	Arrival date*
4	13	4	5

* = Day number.
† = In days.

a. Assuming that the shortest processing time rule is used to sequence the orders at each testing machine, determine to which machine the test operator should be assigned and which job will be processed when each of the following labor assignment decision rules are used (assume the operator has just completed his or her last job):
  1. The shortest job.
  2. The job that has been in the laboratory the longest.
  3. The most jobs in the queue.

b. Suppose that the slack time dispatching rule is used to sequence jobs at each testing machine. To which machine should the test operator be assigned and which job will be processed when each of the following labor assignment decision rules are used? (Again it is 8 A.M. and the test operator is available for assignment.)
  1. The shortest job.
  2. The job that has been in the laboratory the longest.
  3. The most jobs in the queue.

c. Would you recommend any other labor assignment decision rule under the conditions indicated in question b above?

9. The materials manager at the Excello Grinding Wheel Company is concerned about the high volume of rescheduling exception messages that his firm's MRP planners have to cope with each week. He is considering implementing one of several possible rescheduling filters (e.g., the Ability, Magnitude, and the Horizon heuristics) and has provided the following example MRP record to illustrate the use of such procedures:

Item A

Week number		1	2	3	4	5	6	7	8	9	10
Gross requirements		16	20	15	20	2	27	1	15	8	10
Scheduled receipts			30		30		30				
Projected available balance	12	-4	6	-9	1	-1	2	1	16	8	28
Planned order releases		30		30							

Q = 30; LT = 7; SS = 0

a. Assume that the total setup, plus run times remaining on the three scheduled receipts in weeks 2, 4, and 6, are 2 weeks, 3.4 weeks (three weeks plus two days), and 4 weeks, respectively. What rescheduling exception messages would be made by the Ability heuristic?

b. Assume that the total setup plus run times remaining on the three scheduled receipts in weeks 2, 4, and 6, are 0.4 weeks (two days), 1 week, and 2 weeks, respectively. What rescheduling exception messages would be made by the Ability heuristic?

c. Assume that $T_m = 1$. What rescheduling exception messages would be made by the Magnitude heuristic?

d. Assume that $T_H = 2$. What rescheduling exception messages would be made by the Horizon heuristic?

e. Assume that $T_m = 0$. What rescheduling exception messages would be made by the Magnitude heuristic?

f. Assume that $T_m = \infty$. What rescheduling exception messages would be made by the Magnitude heuristic?

g. Suppose that a rescheduling exception message calls for moving the 30 units in week 6 to week 8. Would this message be produced if $T_m = 1$?

10. The Medwitz Company has the following processing time data for machines 1, 2, and 3. The routing for each job begins at machine 1 and ends at machine 3:

	Processing time (in hours) Machine		
Job	1	2	3
A	1	5	3
B	6	2	9
C	5	7	2
D	12	1	4

a. Prepare a schedule for a three machine manufacturing cell using the Campbell, Dudek, and Smith (CDS) heuristic.

b. In what sequence should the jobs be processed to minimize the makespan? The same processing sequence is to be followed at each machine in the cell.

c. Construct a Gantt Chart of the best sequence schedule for all three machines.

11. The Philip Company has the following processing time data for machines 1, 2, 3, and 4. The routing for each job begins at machine 1 and ends at machine 4:

| | Processing time (in hours) Machine | | | |
Job	1	2	3	4
A	6	2	4	2
B	1	8	7	5
C	5	7	2	3
D	4	4	1	6

a. Prepare a schedule for a four machine manufacturing cell using the Campbell, Dudek, and Smith (CDS) heuristic.

b. In what sequence should the jobs be processed to minimize the makespan? The same processing sequence is to be followed at each machine in the cell.

c. Construct a Gantt Chart of the best sequence schedule for all four machines.

12. The Arnold Company has the following processing time data for the three-machine manufacturing cell. The routing for each job begins at machine 1 and ends at machine 3:

| | Processing time (in hours) Machine | | |
Job	1	2	3
A	1	7	3
B	4	2	8
C	2	9	2

a. Prepare a schedule for a three-machine manufacturing cell using the Nawaz, Enscore, and Ham (NEH) procedure.

b. A partial schedule, sequencing job A first and job B second, has already been prepared below. Use the NEH procedure that minimizes the makespan to determine the sequence through all three machines in the cell for jobs A, B, and C.

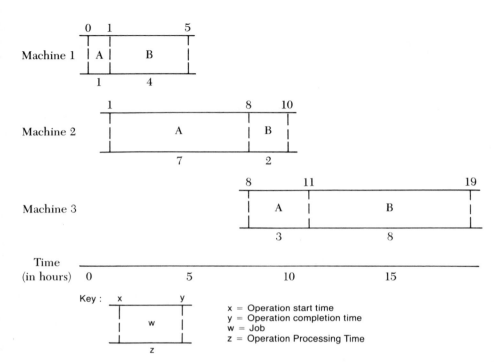

Key :
x = Operation start time
y = Operation completion time
w = Job
z = Operation Processing Time

c. A partial schedule, sequencing job B first and job A second has already been prepared below. Use the NEH procedure to determine the sequence through all three machines in the cell for jobs A, B, and C that minimizes the makespan. How does this schedule compare with that in part b?

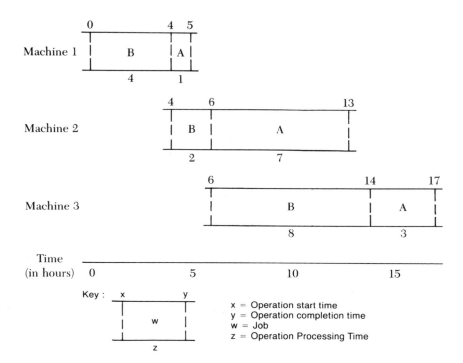

Key :

x = Operation start time
y = Operation completion time
w = Job
z = Operation Processing Time

13. Prepare a schedule for a four-machine manufacturing cell using the Slack Time procedure and the following processing time data for the cell. The routing for each job begins at machine 1 and ends at machine 4.

		Processing time (in hours) Machine				
Job	Family	1	2	3	4	Hours until due date
1	A	2	3	9	2	30
2	B	5	4	2	7	31
3	A	1	6	4	1	24
4	B	4	7	9	8	48

The due date for each order is set using the TKW rule; in this case the TWK is equal to the total processing plus setup time plus an allowance for queuing. The setup time is one hour when a change from one family to another is made and zero if parts of the same family are processed.

a. Using the conventional version of the Slack Time procedure determine the sequence for processing jobs one through four at machine 1 (and through the remaining machines).

b. Using the Family version of the Slack Time procedure determine the sequence for processing jobs one through four at machine 1 (and through the remaining machines).

14. A manufacturing cell containing five machines has been installed to process cylindrical parts in three different part families: A, B, and C. Although the parts within each part family are similar in design, work can be routed through this cell in a variety of ways. Orders typically begin processing at either machine 1 or machine 2, and can be further processed at any or all of the remaining three machines. Therefore, a queue of orders exists at each of the five machines, and sequencing decisions are made at each machine in the cell.

Two decisions are made in sequencing orders at each machine. At the time an order is completed at a machine a decision is made as to which part family to process next. Once the part family to process next has been selected, the slack time dispatching rule is used to decide which order within the part family to process next. A dispatching report for machine 2 in this cell is shown in Exhibit A below. This machine has just completed an order in Part Family A.

   a. Which order should be processed next at machine 2 if the ECON procedure is used to select the part family to process next?

   b. Which order should be processed next at machine 2 if the WORK procedure is used to select the part family to process next?

   c. Which order should be processed next at machine 2 if the AVE procedure is used to select the part family to process next?

EXHIBIT A   Machine 2 dispatching report

Shop order number	Item part number	Operation setup time*	Processing time†	Part family	Order due date‡	Total processing time remaining§
10-1234	5678	1	6.2	A	12	2
10-1240	1082	1	4.3	A	10	4
10-1241	1141	1	5.1	A	7	8
10-1231	1271	1	1.8	B	14	15
10-1229	4252	1	2.3	B	8	6
10-1215	8110	1	0.9	B	10	14
10-1251	1354	1	1.7	B	3	6
10-1249	1278	1	13.2	C	4	1
10-1225	7910	1	3.4	C	9	3
10-1242	6250	1	4.1	C	4	1
10-1260	5140	1	2.8	C	12	4
10-1261	6280	1	3.1	C	15	10
10-1042	1011	1	8.1	C	13	3

*In hours assuming that a change in part family is required; otherwise the setup time is zero
†In hours.
‡Number of manufacturing days until the order due date
§In manufacturing days

15. An FMS with 10 machines has been installed to process a variety of machined parts. These parts are automatically transferred from a 16 location loading station to each machine for processing. Upon completion at a machine the part is either complete and therefore transferred from the FMS, or waits for further processing in the FMS. In the latter case the part is stored in the loading station waiting to be dispatched to the next machine operation.

The FMS dispatching report (Exhibit B) shown below reflects the status of the orders waiting to be processed at the FMS at 8:00 on Monday morning. If the SPT/TOT dispatching rule is to be used in selecting the next order to be processed at each machine, what is the next order to be processed at each machine in the FMS?

EXHIBIT B   FMS dispatching report

Loading station number	Shop order number	Item part number	Operation number	Machine number	Operation processing time*	Total processing time* remaining	Order due date†
1	121-2	1234	10	2	0.5	4.4	2
2	100-10	4213	5	1	0.2	2.6	1
3	60-15	8819	10	2	0.4	8.1	1
4	151-41	1617	5	2	0.8	5.0	2
5	82-92	1002	5	6	0.3	3.4	8
6	130-14	4154	10	5	0.7	2.7	4
7	42-116	8213	10	10	0.6	9.8	4
8	44-210	1234	20	3	0.8	1.7	5
9	61-820	1617	10	3	0.2	4.2	2
10	81-419	1002	10	7	0.4	3.1	1
11	42-161	6150	15	6	0.9	5.6	1
12	45-1	1617	15	4	0.5	10.1	7
13	75-25	1234	30	6	0.8	0.9	1
14	18-191	8819	5	4	1.0	9.1	4
15	46-18	8213	20	2	0.2	6.1	2
16	53-114	1002	20	8	0.6	5.3	1

*In hours.
†Number of manufacturing days until the order due date.

— 14

Advanced concepts in master production scheduling

This chapter addresses advanced concepts in master production scheduling. The techniques described are primarily oriented to the assemble-to-order (ATO) manufacturing environment. This environment is particularly challenging, because companies increasingly find themselves less able to predict the exact end-item configurations that the customers will order. Moreover, the number of these end items is proliferating in many firms. Use of the advanced concepts described in this chapter leads to a reduced number of items to be master-scheduled, a closer relationship between production and sales, and increased flexibility in the MPS. Implementation requires detailed design efforts and added complexities in maintenance of bills of material—but the payoffs are significant.

The chapter is organized around the following four topical areas:

- Two-level master production scheduling: What is the structure of a two-level MPS and how does it work?
- The Hyster lift truck example: How does two-level master production scheduling work in a complex product environment?
- Additional techniques: What are some alternative methods for coping with the assemble-to-order manufacturing environment and how do they work?

- Methods for constructing planning bills of material: How does one construct the planning bills of material to support assemble-to-order manufacturing?

This chapter is most closely related to Chapters 8, 9, and 10. Chapter 8 deals with the basics in master production scheduling, including the time-phased record formats for master scheduling, available to promise logic, and planning bills of material. Chapter 9 describes the linkages between the master production schedule and the production plan. Chapter 10 treats demand management and shows how some forms of planning bills lead to better ways to hedge against uncertainties in demand.

TWO-LEVEL MASTER SCHEDULING

In this section, we start with a simplified example of two-level master production scheduling. The intent is to show how the two-level MPS works, how records are processed as one books actual orders and updates the record from period to period, and how actual orders consume forecasts of demand. The section ends with a description of some benefits of the approach; the net result is a much closer relationship between sales and manufacturing, where each function is better equipped to respond to customer needs.

Two-level MPS example

For our example product, we will use an over-bed table manufactured by the Hill-Rom Company. A simplified version of the super bill of material for this product is presented as Figure 14.1. Customers have the option of ordering any one of four models, in 10 different high-pressure laminate tops, with four different combinations of boots and casters. This results in 160 (4 × 10 × 4 = 160) end-item alternatives.

To illustrate two-level master production scheduling, we will focus attention on two of the four model types: the 622, which represents approximately 50 percent of sales; and the 623 model, which accounts for another 30 percent. Each of the "models" is only a collection number or "bag of parts." It represents the unique parts that, along with the common parts, a top and a boot-caster option, make a unique end item.

Figure 14.2 depicts the MPS records for the over-bed table and the two model options, 622 and 623. The over-bed table is level zero in the bill of materials, and the two model types are at level one. The level-one models, and the level-one common parts record, explode directly into the MRP records, which provide the detailed plans for manufacturing the parts. The collection of parts that are required to make a model 622, for example, are controlled by the level-one MPS, which, in turn, is controlled by the MPS

FIGURE 14.1   Hill-Rom over-bed table super bill

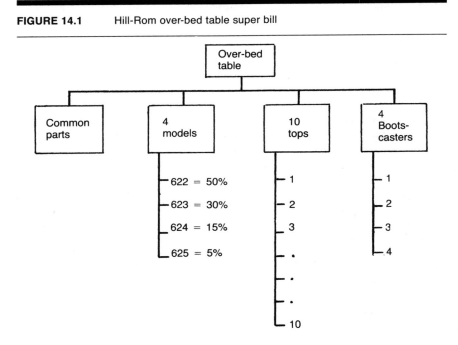

for the over-bed table line. The logic and records are consistent with traditional MRP/MPS logic.

At the top of Figure 14.2, the over-bed table record is driven by the production plan. It shows a constant MPS rate of 100 units per week over the five weeks in our example. The actual orders row shows that the first two weeks of the production plan and the MPS are completely sold. The available-to-promise (ATP) row indicates that no new customer orders can be promised earlier than week 3. There are ATP quantities of 100 units in weeks 3, 4, and 5.

For the second record, the 622 model, the "production forecast" row is exploded from the ATP row of the over-bed table at level zero. The production forecasts of 50 units in weeks 3, 4, and 5 are what we expect to sell of the yet unbooked orders (i.e., 50 percent of the ATP amounts for over-bed tables). Similarly, the 30s in the third record come from the expectation that 30 percent of the over-bed table orders will be for the 623 model.

Explosion of the ATP quantities, rather than the MPS quantities, is because only the unsold items have uncertainty. There is no "production forecast" for the 622 and 623 models in weeks 1 and 2, because all of the 100 units to be built in those periods have been sold (consumed) and their *exact*

FIGURE 14.2 Over-bed table two-level MPS records

			Week		
	1	2	3	4	5
Over-bed table:					
Production plan	100	100	100	100	100
Orders	100	100			
Available					
Available to promise			100	100	100
MPS	100	100	100	100	100
On hand = 0; SS = 0.					
622 model:					
Production forecast			50	50	50
Orders	50	50			
Available	10	10	10	10	10
Available to promise	10		50	50	50
MPS	50	50	50	50	50
On hand = 10; SS = 10.					
623 model:					
Production forecast			30	30	30
Orders	30	30			
Available	15	15	15	15	15
Available to promise	15		30	30	30
MPS	30	30	30	30	30
On hand = 15; SS = 15.					

component requirements have been allocated. For this reason, the production forecast is also called the "unconsumed forecast" in some systems.

The 622 model shows 10 units on hand and available to promise in week 1. This is a safety stock that protects against variability in the 50 percent usage rate estimate for this model. The master scheduler determines when additional quantities should be scheduled to replenish the 622 model parts. Similar conventions apply to the 623 model.

Booking customer orders

Let us now say that a customer requests an order for 40 units of the 623 model to be delivered as soon as possible (we will ignore the top and boot/caster options for this example). The first check is: When are the over-bed units available to promise? Referring to Figure 14.2, we see that week 3 is the first week in which sufficient ATP exists. The next question is whether a week 3 delivery of the 623 model is possible. Again, from Figure 14.2, the answer is yes: 30 units are available to promise (ATP) in week 3, and an additional 15 units are ATP in week 1 (the safety stock).

FIGURE 14.3 Over-bed table two-level MPS records, after booking order for 40 of the 623 Model in week 3

	Week				
	1	2	3	4	5
Over-bed table:					
Production plan	100	100	100	100	100
Orders	100	100	40		
Available					
Available to promise			60	100	100
MPS	100	100	100	100	100
On hand = 0; SS = 0.					
622 model:					
Production forecast			30	50	50
Orders	50	50			
Available	10	10	30	30	30
Available to promise	10		50	50	50
MPS	50	50	50	50	50
On hand = 10; SS = 10.					
623 model:					
Production forecast			18	30	30
Orders	30	30	40		
Available	15	15	-13	-13	-13
Available to promise	5		0	30	30
MPS	30	30	30	30	30
On hand = 15; SS = 15.					

Assuming that the top and boot/caster options are also available to promise in week 3, the three records from Figure 14.2 would look like Figure 14.3 after the order has been booked. The ATP of 100 in week 3 for the over-bed table is now reduced to 60. The former 30 units of ATP in week 3 for the 623 model has been reduced to zero, and the 15 units of ATP in week 1 have been reduced to 5.

The production forecasts are now also recalculated for model 622 and model 623. Since there are only 60 over-bed tables ATP in the level 0 record in week 3, the expected sales volume for the 622 model would be 30 units (50 percent) and 18 units are expected for the 623 model. The records for these two models reflect this new set of expectations. One result is that the 622 now seems to be over-planned (too much expected inventory), whereas the 623 is under-planned (an expected shortfall).

One immediate question is whether to revise the two MPS quantities for period 3 to compensate. If the MPS quantity for the 622 were revised to 30, the projected available balance would return to the safety stock level of 10. Similarly, the MPS for the 623 model in week 3 might be revised to 58 units to return its projected available balance to 15 units. These changes will *not* be made automatically. The MPS quantities are firm planned orders; changing them requires consideration of the overall impact of the changes. Moreover, there is the question of nervousness. Perhaps the next orders will naturally compensate for the order for 40 units of the 623 model. Note that, even if no changes are made, there are still five units of 623 available to promise during the three periods.

Managing with a two-level MPS

Two-level master production scheduling allows the company to focus attention separately on the overall rate of production, as determined by the production plan, and the ways in which various options are selling in the marketplace. When sales orders outstrip production, the ATP dates for the zero-level item will stretch out. The opposite condition results in more near-term ATP and perhaps a decision about making certain items for inventory.

When the zero-level item has near-term ATP, but some level-one items do not, it indicates that the product mix is not meeting expectations—or perhaps that the safety stocks are too small or in the wrong items. Combined marketing and MPS decision making is required.

Overall, the two-level MPS approach helps to align the MPC process closely to the forces of the market. The products are planned and controlled in the way they are *sold*, as opposed to the way they are designed or manufactured. Flexibilities are defined and understood in both the sales and manufacturing organizations.

THE HYSTER LIFT TRUCK EXAMPLE

We now turn to a detailed example of the two-level MPS approach. Actual company records are presented, which show how the MPS is designed and maintained. We will also see how customer order promising is done in a very complex product environment.

The Portland plant

The Portland, Oregon, plant of Hyster, Inc., produces forklift trucks, straddle carriers, and towing winches (for mounting on the rear of crawler tractors). The straddle carriers are made to order, but both towing winches and lift trucks are assemble-to-order products, with virtually unlimited end-item possibilities. The lift trucks are divided into three model series, with a super bill of materials for each; there are six super bills to cover the towing-winch models. Each of these super bills is made up of various options, with percentage usage factors.

Figure 14.4 gives an indication of the end-item definition complexity. This figure represents the option choices for one model series of forklift

FIGURE 14.4 Product option matrix—Model series A lift truck order entry

ORDER ENTRY

LIFT TRK 'A'			GAS O/C	GAS P/S	LPG O/C	LPG P/S	PERKINS O/C	PERKINS P/S	DETROIT O/C	DETROIT P/S
COMMON PARTS			001, 022, 100, 125, 133, 144, 001F, 144F, 125F, 133F, 103F	001, 023, 100, 125, 133, 144, 001F, 144F, 125F, 133F, 108F	001, 024, 100, 125, 133, 144, 001F, 144F, 125F, 133F, 108F	001, 025, 100, 125, 133, 144, 001F, 144F, 125F, 133F, 108F	001, 026, 100, 125, 133, 144, 001F, 144F, 125F, 133F, 108F	001, 027, 100, 125, 133, 144, 001F, 144F, 125F, 133F, 108F	001, 028, 100, 125, 133, 144, 001F, 144F, 125F, 133F, 108F	001, 029, 100, 125, 133, 144, 001F, 144F, 125F, 133F, 108F
ENGINE	GAS		002, 005, 006, 019, 030, 032, 035	001, 005, 006, 020, 031, 032, 036						
	LPG				003, 005, 019, 030, 032	003, 005, 020, 031, 033				
	PERKINS						008, 004, 006, 019, 032, 035	008, 004, 006, 020, 033, 036		
	DETROIT								007, 004, 006, 019, 035	007, 004, 006, 020, 036
AXLE	HYPOID	SOLID	012, 056, 134, 130	021, 037, 056, 134, 130	012, 056, 134, 130	021, 037, 056, 130, 130	012, 056, 134, 130	021, 037, 056, 134, 130	012, 056, 134, 130	021, 038, 056, 134, 130
		PNEUMATIC	012, 056, 134, 060, 130	021, 037, 056, 134, 060, 130	012, 056, 134, 060, 130	021, 037, 056, 134, 060, 130	012, 056, 134, 060, 130	021, 037, 056, 134, 060, 130	012, 056, 134, 060, 130	021, 056, 134, 060, 130
	PLANETARY	SOLID	014, 057, 106, 116, 120	013, 057, 106, 116, 121	014, 057, 106, 116, 120	013, 057, 106, 116, 121	014, 057, 106, 116, 120	013, 057, 106, 116, 121	014, 057, 106, 116, 120	013, 057, 106, 116, 114
		PNEUMATIC	014, 057, 106, 116, 120, 061	013, 057, 106, 116, 121, 061	014, 057, 106, 116, 120, 061	013, 057, 106, 116, 121, 061	014, 057, 106, 116, 120, 061	013, 057, 106, 116, 121, 061	014, 057, 106, 116, 120, 061	013, 057, 106, 116, 114, 061
CAB			181, 619, 620, 626	181, 619, 621, 626	009, 181, 619, 620, 626	009, 181, 619, 621, 626	181, 619, 620, 626	181, 619, 621, 626	181, 619, 620, 626	181, 619, 621, 626
W/O CAB			182	182	010, 182	010, 182	182	182	182	182
HEATER & DEFROSTER			661	661	661	661	662	663	664	665
STANDARD VALVE			017, 080	018, 080	017, 080	018, 080	017, 080	018, 080	017, 080	018, 080
3-WAY VALVE	DIRECT		081, 015, 079, 086, 087	081, 016, 079, 086, 087	081, 015, 079, 086, 087	081, 016, 079, 086, 087	081, 015, 079, 086, 087	081, 016, 079, 086, 087	081, 015, 079, 086, 087	081, 016, 079, 086, 087
	PUSH		082, 015, 079, 086, 087	082, 016, 079, 086, 087	082, 015, 079, 086, 087	082, 016, 079, 086, 087	082, 015, 079, 086, 087	082, 016, 079, 086, 087	082, 015, 079, 086, 087	082, 016, 079, 086, 087
4-WAY VALVE			015, 079, 083, 085, 087	016, 079, 083, 085, 087	015, 079, 083, 085, 087	016, 079, 083, 085, 087	015, 079, 083, 085, 087	016, 079, 083, 085, 087	016, 079, 083, 085, 087	016, 079, 083, 085, 067
5-WAY VALVE			015, 079, 084, 085, 087	016, 079, 084, 085, 087	015, 079, 084, 085, 087	016, 079, 084, 085, 087	015, 079, 084, 085, 087	016, 079, 084, 085, 087	015, 079, 084, 085, 087	016, 079, 084, 085, 087
ATT PARTS – 3			680	680	680	680	680	680	680	680
4			681	681	681	681	681	681	681	681
5			682	682	682	682	682	682	682	682
STD A/C			044, 047, 050	044, 047, 050	044	044	044, 050	044, 050	044, 050	
H.D. A/C			054	054			054	054	STD	STD

Note: Each box represents MPS option groups specified by salable option features for this model.
Source: W. L. Berry, T. E. Vollmann, and D. C. Whybark, *Master Production Scheduling: Principles and Practice* (Falls Church, Va.: American Production and Inventory Control Society, 1979), p. 140.

truck. The option groups used in the super bill are closely related to their sales options; but they are not identical, since some options preclude others and dictate still other options. For example, the gasoline engine option dictates a particular frame and air cleaner. The powershift transmission *with* a gasoline engine dictates still another set of options, such as radiator, flywheel, and hydraulic hoses.

A 12-month production plan is established at corporate headquarters, stated in super bill terms. Each month, this plan is revised (new month added). It is stated in the number of units of each model series to have available to ship in each month. If no customer order exists at the time when commitment must be made to an exact end item (demand time fence), marketing issues a stock order for the model unit, which will become part of marketing's finished-goods inventory.

Order promising is based on available-to-promise logic. The first ATP checked is for the model common parts, then for each optional feature desired. The process is straightforward, but each order is so complex in terms of optional choices that, even with a cathode ray tube (CRT) unit, it takes an average of one hour to promise an order and peg each option to the customer order.

The MPS system at Hyster Portland was installed along with MRP. The MRP and MPS are run daily, using net change, and the MPS produces time-phased records for each of approximately 1,400 MPS super bills and options. The Portland factory had to make major changes in its approach to production planning/inventory control to adapt to the system, but the results have been dramatic. Performance against factory schedules has improved, delivery performance is much better, inventory levels are reduced, and marketing is kept fully informed as each order progresses through the various stages of manufacturing.

Marketing is also extremely happy with the reduction in the lead time at which it has to issue a firm end-item stock order to the plant. Before the system was implemented, marketing had to specify the exact end-item configuration 45 working days before the items were completed. This has been reduced to 14 days, resulting in much greater flexibility in responding to actual customer orders. Manufacturing is also happy, because the amount of lift truck retrofitting has been greatly reduced.

The two-level MPS

The detailed records at Hyster help in illustrating consumption of the forecast by actual customer orders, time fencing, planning bills, and buffering. Before turning to these, we first consider a simplified version of the records to help in understanding.

Figure 14.5 provides an overview of the Hyster two-level approach. The level-zero MPS decisions plan and control the model series (what we have been calling product family), and those at level one deal with the common parts and options. The level-zero MPS record is for the super bill. The quantities are derived directly from the monthly production plan, reflecting the exact working days in each week. The sum of the parts in the level-one options, therefore, is closely coordinated with the dictates of the production plan by the system.

FIGURE 14.5   Hyster two-level MPS

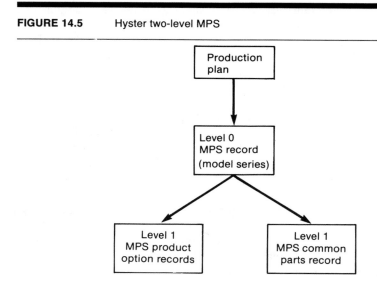

Figure 14.6 extracts data from the actual MPS records to illustrate the two-level MPS approach. The information depicts the first nine weeks of the one-year planning horizon at Hyster. The first MPS record in Figure 14.6 is a portion of the level-zero MPS record for the model series A (one of three lift truck families built at the Portland plant).

The Hyster records are not exactly the same as those we have shown as MPS records. The Hyster records do not have an explicitly named available-to-promise row. They also combine some elements of an MRP record, including a lead-time offset, which results in an MPS start date. The convention we have followed throughout this text is to always show MPS quantities as of the date they will be available for satisfying demand. Finally, the zero-level record does not contain the production plan at the forecast row, but it is netted against sold orders in the MPS start row. Nonetheless, the basic concepts are the same, and the Hyster two-level MPS accomplishes the same results. There are several alternative software packages which accomplish the same results but with slightly different record formats.

The MPS quantities are derived from the production plan for this model series and are translated into weekly requirements that reflect the working days in each week. They are treated as firm planned orders. These production plan quantities are originally shown in the row labeled MPS START, but are decremented by actual orders. The net result is that these MPS START quantities represent the unsold forecasts, and they are the available-to-promise amounts. The time buckets are printed in weekly increments for the weeks 8/21 to 10/16. The production plan for this model series calls for

FIGURE 14.6 Hyster simplified example—Model A series lift truck

Level 0 MPS record

Week Start day	8-21 178	8-28 183	9-5 188	9-11 192	9-18 197	9-25 202	10-2 207	10-9 212	10-16 217
Prod forecast									
Sold									
Sched. rec.									
proj. oh									
MPS start	0	0	2	6	12	13	15	15	15

Level 1 common parts MPS record

Week start day	8-21 178	8-28 183	9-5 188	9-11 192	9-18 197	9-25 202	10-2 207	10-9 212	10-16 217
Prod forecast	0	0	2	6	12	13	15	15	15
Sold		13	10	8	2	2			
Sched. rec.		13							
proj. oh	0	0	0	0	0	0	0	0	0
MPS start	12	14	14	15	15	15	15	15	15

Lead time = 2 weeks
Super bill percentage = 100%

Level 1 oil clutch option parts MPS record

Week Start day	8-21 178	8-28 183	9-5 188	9-11 192	9-18 197	9-25 202	10-2 207	10-9 212	10-16 217
Prod forecast	0	0	2	3	8	8	9	10	9
Sold		8	6	5	2	1			
Sched. rec.		9							
Proj. oh	0	1	0	1	−1	0	0	−1	0
MPS start	7	9	8	10	9	9	10	9	9

Lead time = 2 weeks
Super bill percentage = 62%

the production of 15 lift trucks per five-day week (some weeks have fewer than five working days and their production requirements are adjusted accordingly).

The second record in Figure 14.6 is the level-one record for the common parts. The row titled PROD FORECAST is the same as the MPS START row from the level-zero record; that is, in the same way as in our earlier example, the level-zero record ATP is exploding to production forecasts for the level-one records. For each model series A lift truck to be built, one set of common parts is required. The production forecast row shows this explosion.

The common parts record shown in Figure 14.6 contains other useful information. For example, the customer orders that have been booked for the model series A trucks are displayed in the SOLD row. As an example,

13 model series A units have been booked for the week of 8/28. When customer orders are booked by Hyster, both the PROD FORECAST in the common parts MPS record at level one and the MPS START in the model series A MPS record at level zero are decreased by the amount of the sales order. The resultant data are used to make available-to-promise calculations. For example, in booking an order for one unit for delivery in week 9/5, the value for that week in both the level zero MPS START row and the common parts level-one PROD FORECAST row would decrease from 2 to 1. Likewise, the value of 10 in the level-one common parts SOLD row would increase to 11.

The firm planned orders for the level-one common parts record are shown in the MPS START row. These orders are offset by a planned lead time of two weeks. As an example, the 12 units scheduled to be started in the week beginning 8/21 are completed at the start of week 9/5. This 12-unit firm planned order covers the requirements for 2 units of PROD FORECAST in week 9/5 (exploded from the level-zero MPS record) and 10 units of sold orders in the same week.

The third record in Figure 14.6 is the level-one MPS record for one of the model series A options, an oil clutch. For this record, the row labeled PROD FORECAST is also derived from the MPS START row in the level-zero MPS record for model series A. The super bill percentage for this option is 62 percent. This indicates that Hyster expects 62 percent of the model series A lift trucks to have on oil clutch specification. Thus, the MPS START row data in the level-zero MPS Model series A record are multiplied by .62 to obtain the PROD FORECAST data in the level-one oil clutch MPS option record.

An exact multiplication of the MPS START data in the level-zero model series A MPS record by .62 will not yield the data in the PROD FORECAST row of the level-one oil clutch MPS option record. The system will always round up, but it keeps track of the cumulative round-up to an amount always less than one unit. For example, the MPS START row in the level-zero MPS record for 9/5 is 2. When multiplied by .62, the result is 1.24. The PROD FORECAST row in the level-one oil clutch MPS option record is rounded up to 2. In the following week, the level-zero record MPS START row is 6; when multiplied by .62, the result is 3.72. But since the earlier rounding was .76 (2 − 1.24), the PROD FORECAST row value in the oil clutch MPS option record for week 9/11 is 3. There remains a cumulative round up of .04 (.76 − .72).

Buffering

The safety stock aspects of the common and option parts MPS records shown in Figure 14.6 are contained in the projected on-hand balance (PROJ OH) row. The PROJ OH row for these records equals the expected MPS firm planned order receipts, minus the PROD FORECAST, minus the SOLD (orders), plus any PROJ OH from the previous period. This projected on-hand balance row can be used to determine whether the MPS record contains any safety stock; that is, when the supply of parts exceeds the actual, plus expected usage for the option. Since the PROJ OH row for the common parts in Figure 14.6 contains all zeros, there is no safety stock or overplanning for the common parts.

There is no overplanning for the common parts, since they are used one-for-one on each model series A truck. However, since some safety stock is often planned for product options, the MPS records for these items often deliberately include a projected on-hand balance. Exception messages are generated to indicate those situations; that is, a positive balance in the projected on-hand row indicates that the current material plan (supply) exceeds the projected usage (booked orders, plus production forecast), reflecting the existence of time-phased safety stock. Such an example can be seen for the oil clutch product option in Figure 14.6. Similarly, when the PROJ OH row contains negative figures, the current material plan is inadequate to meet the projected usage for the item, and the exception message signals the need for the master scheduler to review such an item. The negative balance probably does not indicate an inability to meet final assembly needs. It likely indicates a more limited ability to respond to customer orders than is indicated by the percentage usage of that option.

For example, in the oil clutch option parts MPS record in Figure 14.6, the PROJ OH is -1 in the week of 9/18. This comes about because eight units are in the MPS START for 9/5; two units are SOLD for 9/18, and eight units are forecast to be sold that week. There is a PROJ OH of one from the prior week (9/11). This one unit plus the eight-unit MPS is short of the expected total requirements $(8 + 2)$ by one unit. But what this really means is that, if the PROD FORECAST is perfect up to the week of 9/18, only seven more units can be provided for delivery in that week. In the following week, the expected deficiency is recovered.

The Hyster example also illustrates the timing of the safety stock, as well as its quantity. For example, the oil clutch option parts MPS record in Figure 14.6 shows the projected on hand to be zero for the week of 8/21 and to be $+1$ in the week of 8/28; that is, there is no safety stock in 8/21 and one unit in 8/28. But for the week of 8/28, there is also no uncertainty! That is, the PROD FORECAST is zero. The only requirement is eight actual customer orders. Thus, any safety stock would be redundant.

As actual customer orders come in, they will specify the oil clutch option or they will not. The forecast for the oil clutch option will be consumed—albeit somewhat erratically. The 1 unit of projected on hand in week 9/11 means that, although 62 percent of the 6 units of model A left to be sold in week 9/11 are anticipated to be with an oil clutch $(.62 \times 6 = 3$ with cumulative rounding), in fact, actual consumer orders with an oil clutch can be promised for $3 + 1 = 4$ units. The master production scheduler will take this into account when launching the next order for oil clutch options and in any necessary replanning of open shop orders.

What this means is that safety stocks are only used to buffer uncertainty in actual customer orders. As order entry takes place, the uncertainties are resolved. As soon as actual orders are known, there is no need to forecast them. Therefore, all safety stocks can be de-expedited in timing until a period where there is forecast demand. At this point, uncertainty exists about the option mix of customer orders.

The MPS records

The records shown in Figure 14.6 to illustrate the operation of a two-level MPS system were drawn from the actual MPS records from Hyster shown in Figures 14.7, 14.8, and 14.9. These records are printed in weekly time buckets for the weeks 8/21 to 1/15. For the remainder of the one-year MPS planning horizon, they are printed in four-week time buckets. The data in the MPS START row of the level-zero MPS record in Figure 14.6 were taken from the first nine weeks of the MPS START row in Figure 14.7.

The actual MPS records in Figures 14.7, 14.8, and 14.9 contain other useful information. In Figure 14.7, the level-zero MPS record for model series A is shown. The MPS START row quantities in this record are supported by the detail provided in the lower right-hand portion of Figure 14.7. For example, the monthly bucket quantity for 1/15 beginning on day 273 is 49. This is the sum of the quantities shown in the weeks starting on days 273 (13), 278 (12), 283 (12), and 288 (12).

Similar pegging information is shown in the level-one common parts MPS record in Figure 14.8. For example, the customer orders that have been booked for the model series A trucks are displayed in the SOLD row and are listed along with the sales order number in the pegging data section shown in the lower left-hand corner of this record. Note: for the 13 model series A units that have been booked for the week of 8/28, each of the individual orders supporting these sales are shown in the sales order pegging data beginning on day 183. Likewise, the firm planned orders shown in the MPS START row of this record are also listed (pegged) in the lower right-hand corner of Figure 14.8. These data show the due dates for the firm planned orders, instead of the order release dates (e.g., 12 units are due in the week beginning with day 188).

The header information in the level-one oil clutch MPS option record shown in Figure 14.9 includes the super bill forecast percentage for this option. This value is shown under the USER CODE 1 label as 62 percent. The information in these records (Figures 14.7 through 14.9) represents the

FIGURE 14.7 Model series A—Level-zero MPS record

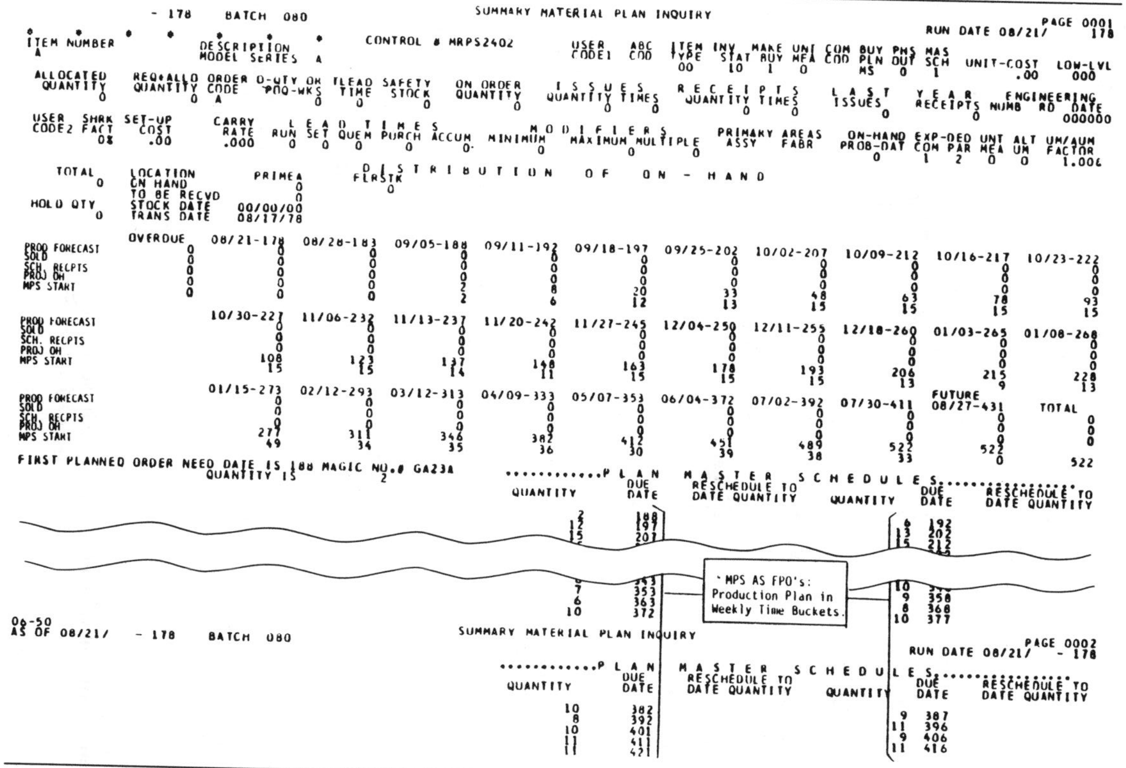

Source: W. L. Berry, T. E. Vollmann, and D. C. Whybark, *Master Production Scheduling: Principles and Practice* (Falls Church, Va.: American Production and Inventory Control Society, 1979), p. 150.

FIGURE 14.8 Model series A common parts level-one MPS record

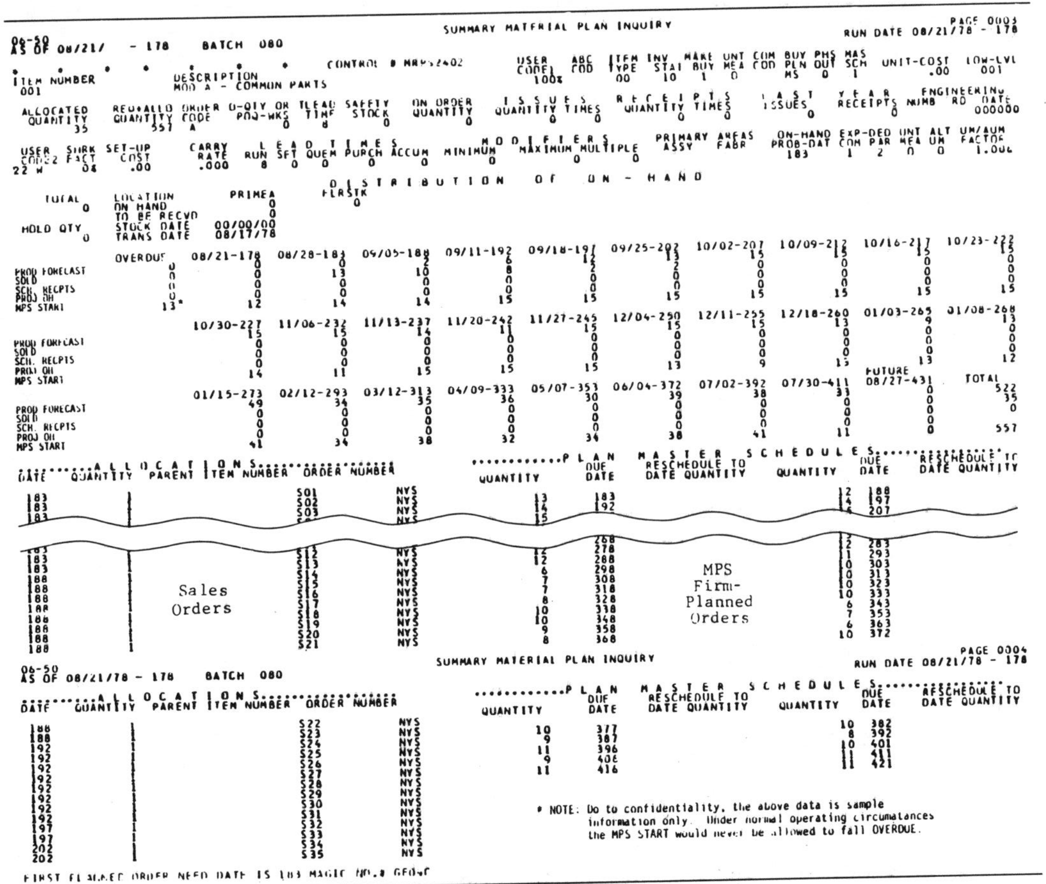

Source: W. L. Berry, T. E. Vollmann, and D. C. Whybark, *Master Production Scheduling: Principles and Practice* (Falls Church, Va.: American Production and Inventory Control Society, 1979), p. 150.

FIGURE 14.9 Model series A—Level-one oil clutch MPS record

```
06-50                                        SUMMARY MATERIAL PLAN INQUIRY                          PAGE 0005
AS OF 08/21/   - 178   BATCH  080                                                     RUN DATE 08/21/   - 178

 •  •  •  •  •  •  •        CONTROL # MRPS2402   USER  ABC  ITEM INV  MAKE UNT COM BUY PHS MAS
ITEM NUMBER     DESCRIPTION                      CODE1 COD  TYPE STAT BUY MFA COD PLN OUT SCH  UNIT-COST  LOW-LVL
 005            MOD A - O/C XMSN                   62%      00   10   1   0       MS  0   1       .00      002

ALLOCATED  REQ+ALLO ORDER O-QTY OR LEAD SAFETY  ON ORDER   I S S U E S    R E C E I P T S   L A S T   Y E A R   ENGINEERING
 QUANTITY  QUANTITY CODE  POQ-WKS  TIME STOCK   QUANTITY  QUANTITY TIMES  QUANTITY TIMES    ISSUES    RECEIPTS  NUMB RD DATE
       22       347 A           0     8     0          0         0     0         0     0         0          0       000000

USER  SHRK SET-UP  CARRY   L E A D   T I M E S       M O D I F I E R S        PRIMARY AREAS  ON-HAND  EXP-DFD UNT ALT UM/AUM
CODE2 FACT  COST    RATE  RUN SFT QUEM PURCH ACCUM  MINIMUM MAXIMUM MULTIPLE   ASSY   FABR   PROB-DAT COM PAR MFA UM  FACTOR
24 W   0%    .00    .000    8   0    0     0     0        0       0        0                    183    1   2   0   0   1.006

                                     D I S T R I B U T I O N   O F   O N - H A N D
   TOTAL    LOCATION       PRIMEA    FLRSTK
       0    ON HAND             0         0
            TO BE RECVD         0
 HOLD QTY   STOCK DATE   00/00/00
       0    TRANS DATE   08/17/
```

	OVERDUE	08/21-178	08/28-183	09/05-188	09/11-192	09/18-197	09/25-202	10/02-207	10/09-212	10/16-217	10/23-222
PROD FORECAST	0	0	0	2	3	8	8	9	10	9	9
SOLD	0	0	8	6	5	2	1	0	0	0	0
SCH. RECPTS	0	0	0	0	0	0	0	0	0	0	0
PROJ OH	0	0	1	0	1	1-	0	0	1-	0	0
MPS START	9 •	7	9	8	10	9	9	10	9	9	10

	10/30-227	11/06-232	11/13-237	11/20-242	11/27-245	12/04-250	12/11-255	12/18-260	01/03-265	01/08-268
PROD FORECAST	10	9	9	6	10	9	9	8	6	8
SOLD	0	0	0	0	0	0	0	0	0	0
SCH. RECPTS	0	0	0	0	0	0	0	0	0	0
PROJ OH	1-	0	1-	0	1-	0	0	0	0	0
MPS START	8	7	9	10	9	8	6	8	8	7

	01/15-273	02/12-293	03/12-313	04/09-333	05/07-353	06/04-372	07/02-392	07/30-411	FUTURE 08/27-431	TOTAL
PROD FORECAST	31	21	21	23	18	25	23	21	0	325
SOLD	0	0	0	0	0	0	0	0	0	22
SCH. RECPTS	0	0	0	0	0	0	0	0	0	0
PROJ OH	1-	1-	0	0	0	1-	0	1-	1-	
MPS START	26	21	24	19	22	23	26	6	0	346

ALLOCATIONS DATE	QUANTITY	PARENT ITEM NUMBER	ORDER NUMBER	PLAN MASTER SCHEDULES QUANTITY	DUE DATE	RESCHEDULE TO DATE QUANTITY	QUANTITY	DUE DATE	RESCHEDULE TO DATE QUANTITY
183	1	S01	NYS						
183	1	S02	NYS	9	183		7	188	
183	1	S03	NYS	9	192		8	197	
192	1	S26	NYS	5	328		6	333	
192	1	S27	NYS	7	338		3	343	
192	1	S28	NYS	7	348		4	353	
197	1	S32	NYS	5	358		4	363	
197	1	S33	NYS	5	368		6	372	

```
06-50                                        SUMMARY MATERIAL PLAN INQUIRY                          PAGE 0006
AS OF 08/21/   - 178   BATCH  080                                                     RUN DATE 08/21/   - 178
```

ALLOCATIONS DATE	QUANTITY	PARENT ITEM NUMBER	ORDER NUMBER	PLAN MASTER SCHEDULES QUANTITY	DUE DATE	RESCHEDULE TO DATE QUANTITY	QUANTITY	DUE DATE	RESCHEDULE TO DATE QUANTITY
202	1	S34	NYS						
				7	377		6	382	
				5	387		5	392	
				7	396		6	401	
				6	406		7	411	
				7	416		6	421	

FIRST PLANNED ORDER NEED DATE IS 183 MAGIC NO.# RK237
QUANTITY IS 9

Note: Due to confidentiality, the above data is sample information only. Under normal operating circumstances, the MPS START would never be allowed to fall OVERDUE.

Source: W. L. Berry, T. E. Vollmann, and D. C. Whybark, *Master Production Scheduling: Principles and Practice* (Falls Church, Va.: American Production and Inventory Control Society, 1979), p. 152.

type of information used on a daily basis by the master scheduler. While such information can be displayed in slightly different formats, the Hyster example provides an illustration of the operation of a two-level master production scheduling system where the MPS and sales order promising are coordinated. The resultant impact on overall company operations has been impressive.

ADDITIONAL TECHNIQUES

In this section, we discuss some additional approaches to the techniques described for two-level master production scheduling. The first involves alternate ways to make available-to-promise calculations and the resultant implications. Thereafter, we treat the topics of consuming forecasts with actual demand, and the enhancing of the MPS with capacity planning that is linked to capacity consumption (based on actual orders).

Alternative ATP explosion conventions

In Figures 14.2 and 14.3, the production forecast (or unconsumed forecast) for level-one items is derived from the ATP quantities at level zero; that is, for example, in Figure 14.3 after the customer order for 40 model 623s had been booked for week 3 delivery, the remaining ATP for the over-bed table (level zero) was 60 units. This quantity was exploded by the appropriate percentages to obtain new forecasts of 30 and 18 units, respectively, for the 622 and 623 models in week 3. This raises the question of whether the original forecasts of 50 percent and 30 percent, respectively, should be revised in light of one actual order. If the long-run percentages are indeed 50 and 30, then the actions taken by the master scheduler based on the information in Figure 14.3 could induce undesirable nervousness into the MPC system. This could occur because the MPS data drive the MRP system. Even though they are firm planned orders, the master scheduler can and should react to some changes. But the system itself may be indicating the need for MPS changes when, in fact, the changes are unwarranted. This issue is illustrated by the question of how to deal with the potential problems indicated in Figure 14.3.

The problem seen as an apparent shortage and surplus in Figure 14.3 will be particularly severe in a firm where demand is lumpy, such as when one customer infrequently buys relatively large amounts of one model. In some instances, the demand coming from a distribution system can create the same effect. We once worked with a firm that sent a ship to South Africa once every four months. That shipment (of just a few models) induced a severe apparent "shortage."

One approach to dealing with this problem has been suggested by John Sari. In essence, he suggests that a longer horizon might be used for allocating the unsold forecast at level zero to the level-one items. His approach starts with the sum of the expected sales for the two models from the data given in Figure 14.2. The 100 units of actual orders and 150 units of forecast for the 622 model over the five weeks add up to 250 units. A similar calculation for the 623 model yields 150 units (60 + 90). After the order for 40 units is booked and the records have been updated in Figure 14.3, the resultant sum for the 622 model is 230 units (100 + 130); the sum for the 623 model is 178 (100 + 78).

Using our example in Figure 14.3, instead of exploding the remaining 60 units of ATP in week 3 by 50 percent and 30 percent, respectively, one might look on a cumulative basis further out into the unsold horizon. In our example at level zero for weeks 3 through 5 inclusive, there are 260 units unsold out of an original forecast of 300 units. The original expectation was that 150 of these 300 units would be sold in the 622 model and 90 in the 623. One sales transaction has been recorded. It consumed 40 of the expected 90 units of model 623 and none of the 622. This infers that the cumulative production forecast for weeks 3 through 5 for the 622 model should remain at 150 units (instead of the 130 in Figure 14.3), and that the cumulative production forecast for 623 should be 50 units (instead of 78).

Achieving this result would require modifications to most MPS software. Even though this could provide more stability to the MPS records, there is a serious question regarding the desirability of doing so. The real issue is whether the firm really believes that the long-run percentages are right; if so, a less responsive (more stable) approach to changing the MPS is indicated. Alternatively, the firm well may believe that each sale is an indication of fundamental changes. If this is so, then the actions indicated on the record in Figure 14.3 should be taken to best deal with the uncertainties inherent in the business. In each case, the master scheduler must manage the situation. To help in that process, the related issue of how best to buffer lumpy demand uncertainty must be addressed. Hedging techniques in demand management appear to be the best approach.

Consumption by actual orders

A problem similar to the issue of adjusting to the long-run or short-run product mix is the question of long-run or short-run consumption of the forecast by actual orders. To illustrate the problem, let us turn to Figure 14.10, which is an extension of the over-bed table record originally depicted in Figures 14.2 and 14.3. We show only the level-zero over-bed table status, assuming that we are just finishing week 3. Weeks 4 to 7 are also shown and have a planned production of 100 units per week.

The issue that is raised in Figure 14.10 is what to do with the unconsumed forecast of 25 units if week 3 finishes with no new orders. Put another way, what should the record look like at the beginning of week 4, and what are the actions required to create this condition? Figure 14.11 depicts the most obvious week 4 record, but we shall see that it has problems.

Figure 14.11 assumes that, since the consumption of forecast by actual orders in week 3 is now complete, we should discard the unconsumed forecast from this week. However, doing so changes, in essence, the production plan. That plan dictated an output rate of 100 units per week; and if we discard 25 units of production plan or forecast in week 3, we will also change the plans for component manufacturing and procurement. The timings for the reductions of different items in the bill of materials will vary, but the impact will be the same: some de-expedite messages, and reductions in planned orders will occur.

FIGURE 14.10   Over-bed table two-level MPS status at the end of week 3

	Week				
	3	4	5	6	7
Over-bed table:					
Production plan	100	100	100	100	100
Orders	75				
Available					
Available to promise	25	100	100	100	100
MPS	100	100	100	100	100

On hand = 0; SS = 0.

FIGURE 14.11   Over-bed table two-level MPS record at the beginning of week 4 (discarding uncomsumed forecast)

	Week				
	4	5	6	7	8
Over-bed table:					
Production plan	100	100	100	100	100
Orders					
Available					
Available to promise	100	100	100	100	100
MPS	100	100	100	100	100

On hand = 0; SS = 0.

An alternative formulation of the records as of the beginning of week 4 is presented as Figure 14.12. In this case, the 25 units of unconsumed forecast is rolled over into the next week (4), thereby maintaining the overall dictates of the production plan and sending the resultant set of signals down to the rest of the items in the bill of materials.

The treatment of the record as shown in Figure 14.12 allows for a quite uneven pattern of consumption of demand over time. The approach in Figure 14.11, on the other hand, may be based on the assumption that a monthly forecast of 400 units is to be nearly evenly divided into 100 units each week. For many firms, this is an unreasonable assumption. There may be considerable week-to-week fluctuations due to random causes. In other cases, a pattern of demand exists where sales are higher near the end of the month or the end of the quarter. Clearly, if this is true, using the approach of Figure 14.11 could cause shortages at the end of the period and undermine the intent of the production plan made for the period.

The same problem exists if actual orders overconsume forecasts and the master scheduler changes the MPS. The net result will be to send signals down the explosion chain to replenish the overconsumption, without reducing any future forecasts to compensate. Richard Ling suggests that one approach to this problem would be to carry another time bucket at the beginning of the planning horizon, which keeps track of the forecast under (or over) consumption. This "demand" could be monitored against some prespecified limits, and it also could be reviewed as one aspect of the production planning meeting.

A variant of this problem is described by Proud, where he points out there will be two separate forecasts to be consumed for many items: production forecasts and service part forecasts. He suggests incorporating two forecast rows in the MPS record, as well as two actual demand rows, and

---

FIGURE 14.12   Over-bed table two-level MPS record alternative formulation at the beginning of week 4 (recognizing unconsumed forecast)

	Week				
	4	5	6	7	8
Over-bed table:					
Production plan	125	100	100	100	100
Orders					
Available	25				
Available to promise	125	100	100	100	100
MPS	100	100	100	100	100

On hand = 25; SS = 0.

two ATP rows. One also needs to keep track of how the available row is apportioned between the two sources of demand. The advantage of Proud's suggestion is that, when the actual demands are lumpy, "borrowing" between supply sources would be much more transparent. Moreover, over- and under-consumption issues might also be examined in terms of the resultant impacts on service part availability.

Capacity planning

The final set of additional techniques for enhancing master production schedule practice deals with capacity planning and capacity consumption. The basic idea is that MPS record formats can be used to monitor capacity as the actual orders consume the available capacity. Suppose, for example, that every over-bed table took 2.5 hours of capacity in the welding department, and every bed model XYZ took 15 hours. If the over-bed table MPS was for 100 units per week and the XYZ bed was for 10, the resultant "production forecast" row in an MPS record for the welding department might look like Figure 14.13. The quantity of 400 hours required in week 1 would actually be for over-bed tables and beds to be sold in subsequent weeks, however, since the lead time for parts manufacture and subassembly must be taken into account.

Figure 14.13 shows an expected capacity requirement of 400 hours per week. This would be determined by the bill of labor or resource profile method of capacity planning. For simplicity here, we will use a constant lead time offset of two weeks for both beds and over-bed tables; that is, let us assume the capacity requirements in week 1 for welding are to support an MPS in week 3. Let us say that the actual orders for over-bed tables are 100, 0, and 4 units for weeks 3, 4, and 5, respectively, and that the orders for the XYZ bed are 10, 5, and 2 for the same weeks. The resultant "orders" for welding are 400, 75, and 40, respectively. Figure 14.13 shows these values, as well as a "master production schedule" of 450 hours per week. This

FIGURE 14.13   Welding department capacity planning*

	Week				
	1	2	3	4	5
Production forecast	400	400	400	400	400
Orders	400	75	40		
Available	50	100	150	200	250
Available to promise	50	375	410	450	450
MPS	450	450	450	450	450

*In welding hours.

450 hours is, in fact, the capacity of the work center. Treating it as a master production schedule allows us to generate ATP data for capacity and to monitor the consumption of capacity in key work centers by actual orders.

This kind of capacity planning will be particularly important in the cases where many products consume capacity in a particular work center. It will also be most useful where potential bottlenecks exist. The approach allows one to examine the consequences of breakdowns or other problems. All that is required is to reduce the "MPS" or available capacity and to examine the impact on customer orders.

The approach can be extended to treatment of key vendors, and it lends itself to "scenario" generation. Most modern MPC systems allow one to create another "company" (in terms of the MPC data base), which is a complete copy of the present firm. This copy company can be used to examine a series of what-if questions without disturbing the data base that is actually being used to plan and control company operations.

METHODS FOR CONSTRUCTION PLANNING BILLS OF MATERIAL

The creation of special planning bills of material to establish the master production schedule at an option level can provide major benefits in terms of reducing the number of items to be master-scheduled, reducing resultant inventories, and increasing responsiveness to customer demands. However, the size and complexity of product structures for assemble-to-order products frequently make it difficult to construct the necessary super bills of material. The major problem is separating the common parts from those that are unique to particular options specified by the customer.

The management and impact of the two-level approach is facilitated by the common parts planning number. For a part to be truly included in the common parts category, it has to remain uncommitted to an exact end item until the final assembly process. Devoting engineering talent to maximize the common parts category has significant payoffs in inventory, since no safety stocks are carried for common parts. Payoffs are also achieved in responsiveness to customer requests, since parts are not committed to the wrong items.

In firms that have product structures with thousands of individual components and vast numbers of optional product features, isolating common parts can be difficult. In this section, we describe two techniques that are useful for developing the super bills of material and for separating the common parts from the unique. The first technique is the matrix bill of material, which is useful for problems of relatively small product complexity. The second approach, the component commonality analysis system, uses commercial software to deal with more complex problems.

The matrix bill of material approach

The matrix bill of material approach is described by Kneppelt. It involves constructing a table with columns for each end item and rows for each sub-assembly, component, and raw material part number. The entries in the table indicate the usage of each component item in the row for each end item in the column. The matrix can be prepared manually or by a computer program. A partial example from Kneppelt is presented as Figure 14.14, based on bicycle components.

The matrix bill of material can be used to identify the common and unique parts in a particular product family and to create "families" based on com-monality. Thereafter, it might be possible to group all of the common parts for planning purposes. The common parts are those that are the same for all end items in the product family; they are also the same in usage quantity for each member of the family. By looking across the rows in Figure 14.14, one can determine which parts have constant usage in all end items in the prod-uct family. For example, the seat post is common to all four models listed in Figure 14.14, but the saddle depends on the particular model. To construct a super bill, the common parts would be removed from the matrix and grouped under one part number; the remaining parts would be grouped by option.

There can be, however, excessive complexity with this approach when a column is defined for each end item. To see this, consider the over-bed table example. We would need 160 columns, since there are 160 unique end-item over-bed table possibilities. A simpler approach is to head the columns with the model or option choices available to the customer. In the case of the over-bed table, the result is 4 models + 10 top options + 4 boot/caster options = 18 columns. Each column would comprise the set of parts asso-ciated with the particular model or option specified by the customer. Those parts common to all columns within a model or option choice (such as the four basic models) would be removed and put into the part number that designates the common parts. The remaining parts in each column are the unique part numbers associated with a particular model or option choice. This approach bases the columns not on how the product is made but on how it is sold in the marketplace.

Commonality and bill of material depth

Because the super bill is based on how it is sold, some potential conflicts with the way the products are manufactured need to be clearly understood. One such conflict is associated with determining the common parts. For example, we see in Figure 14.14 there are four different saddles for the bicycles. It well may be, however, that some saddle part, such as a spring, is common to all four saddles. The first question is how to "disentangle" the

FIGURE 14.14 Matrix bill of material structuring

Number	Component description	Unit	Model number used on			
			SS-53-RM-C-Y	SS-53-TM-C-Y	SS-53-RM-T	SS-53-TM-T
FR-53-S	Silver Frame (53CM)	EA	1		1	
FR-57-S	Silver Frame (57CM)	EA				
FR-60-S	Silver Frame (60CM)	EA		1		1
SA-T-M	Saddle Touring, Men	EA		1		1
SA-T-W	Saddle Touring, Women	EA				
SA-R-M	Saddle Racing, Men	EA			1	
SA-R-W	Saddle Racing, Women	EA	1			
SE-01	Seat Post (25.8MM)	EA	1	1	1	1
WH-C	Wheel Kit, Clincher	EA	1	1		
WH-T	Wheel Kit, Tubular	EA			1	1
CR-01	Crankset Kit	EA	1	1	1	1
PD-01	Pedals Kit	EA	1	1	1	1
De-01	Derailleur Kit	EA	1	1	1	1
BK-01	Brakes Kit	EA	1	1	1	1
HD-01	Handlebar Kit	EA	1	1	1	1
TC-01	Toe Clips/Straps	EA	1	1	1	1

Source: Leland R. Kneppelt, "Product Structuring Considerations for Master Production Scheduling," *Production and Inventory Management*, 1st Quarter 1984.

product structures and, next, how far to go down the structures to find common parts. A more fundamental question is whether to include the parts thus found in the list of common parts. The answer varies with circumstances.

For the over-bed table, the chipboard core for all 10 laminated tops is common. However, because of the lead time to make tops, the core has to be committed to a particular color-laminated top before the final assembly begins. In this case, the core cannot be a common part. Any part that is to be considered common for the purposes of master production scheduling with super bills has to remain uncommitted to a particular end item until the final assembly process.

In the case of the springs in the bicycle saddles, the question is whether the saddles can be assembled as part of the final assembly process. If they are to be built ahead of final assembly, there will have to be overplanning in all of the saddle parts, including the common springs, not just those unique to each particular saddle.

A different way to focus on this issue revolves around customer-response time requirements. Kneppelt points out that all end items in his bicycle example will have to be forecasted and carried in stock *if* competition forces the firm to ship immediately. If a one-week delay is possible, a final assembly process can be used where parts and assemblies are stocked and only be committed to exact end-item specifications after receipt of customer orders. If a two-week delay is possible, frames can be painted to order; if less than two weeks is permissible, the frames have to be held in specific colors.

We see, then, there can be important benefits of very small lead times for final assembly—and for a final assembly process that goes deeply into product structures. The deeper this becomes, the less the planning bills will resemble the physical way the products are built and the way the products are considered from an engineering point of view. Product structures become increasingly "bags of parts," and other MPC techniques are required to dictate the actual assembly of the products. These techniques include phantom bills, routings with operational entry (delivery) data, and just-in-time techniques.

A final concept relating to part commonality and product structures is the design of the super bills so both marketing and manufacturing needs are met. Consider, for example, the Ford Taurus and Mercury Sable; each of these would be independently structured for sales purposes. On the other hand, from a manufacturing point of view, both cars would be built from a single MPS, based on a great deal of part commonality. The same situation exists when part commonality *across* product families is used to define a new "family." The determination of what is in fact a "family" is based on how the product is to be master-scheduled and on how to maximize the dollar content of the common parts (which are not overplanned). In some instances, larger product families can lead to fewer MPS items, but they may lead to a smaller set of common parts.

Component commonality analysis system

Another method for separating common parts from those unique to particular models and options uses relational data base software, which can be installed on many computer systems. This method is called Component Commonality Analysis System (CCAS) by Tallon. CCAS provides a way to analyze computer-based bills of material using the sorting and summarizing features of relational data base software. It does the same work that is done manually in the matrix bill of material approach, but CCAS can analyze complex multiple product structures with high speed and accuracy. It is only limited by the storage capacity of the computer hardware on which it is run.

The CCAS approach includes four steps. First, data and record format descriptions must be checked to ensure that the bill of material data is consistent with the CCAS design. Second, a CCAS data base is established for each product family, using bill of material records to identify the part numbers that make up the product options in the particular product family. Third, the CCAS data base for each family is processed, using the logic shown in Figure 14.15 to determine the common and unique parts. Finally, reports are generated and inquiries can be made to the CCAS data base, using various CCAS features.

Material handling equipment manufacturer example

An analysis of the bill of material records at a material handling equipment manufacturer provides an example of the application of CCAS. Common and unique parts are determined for the purpose of constructing super bills of material for master production scheduling. This analysis was performed for a company that produces material handling vehicles for a variety of specialized applications, including narrow isle units for high-rise, high-density storage warehouses; order picking and selector equipment; and high-speed, low-lift transporters for truck and rail docks. The equipment is custom designed, with many optional features to fit particular customer needs. Business volume has grown over the years, and the manufacturing facilities have retained a job shop orientation involving fabrication and assembly operations.

The CCAS analysis was performed using computer tapes supplied by the company for seven product families. In all, there were 70,651 bill of material records. For each item record, the data include the bill of material level, usage quantity, source (manufactured or purchased), unit cost, and descrip-

FIGURE 14.15 CCAS processing logic

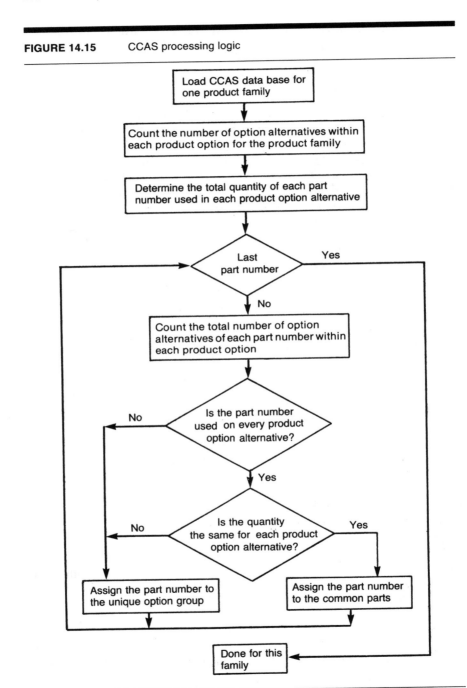

Source: William J. Tallon, "The Design and Performance of Master Production Scheduling Techniques for Assemble-to-Order Products," Ph.D. dissertation, University of Iowa, 1986.

tion. The data cover approximately 20,000 different units sold, out of roughly 240,000 possible end items. The CCAS analysis was used to determine the common parts for each of the seven product families.

An overall summary of the analysis is presented in Figure 14.16, and more detailed results for product family A are presented in Figure 14.17. Turning first to the overall results, we see in section **A** that the sales volumes vary considerably between product lines. Given the product diversity, it is extremely difficult to forecast end-item demand in this kind of firm. Section **B** reinforces this idea; the number of end-item possibilities is huge.

Section **C** develops statistics for an average vehicle across all seven families. The most interesting result of this section is the high percentage of common parts in an average product. Of the material in the average vehicle, 76 percent is made up of common parts. Section **D**, on the other hand, shows that, to cover *all* of the options, it is necessary to carry a higher inventory of unique parts. However, the company should be able to achieve a high inventory turnover on the common parts.

Section **E** breaks out the information in terms of purchased and manufactured parts. An obvious extension of this analysis is to price out the parts and to determine the monetary cost of various safety stock levels. Finally, section **F** shows the number of MPS super bill records required to plan and control each product family using super bills. The entire seven product families can be master scheduled with only 124 MPS records. These records in turn control the 4,243 unique parts and 4,319 common parts.

Figure 14.17 provides the resultant super bill for product family A. As can be seen, product family A has five optional features: options F through J. The 17 MPS option records would be based on this super bill, along with the common parts record for this product family. The CCAS methodology was quite useful to the material handling equipment manufacturer in structuring its approach to master scheduling. After the analysis, the company was surprised at the extent of part commonality and how few MPS records were needed to manage the seven product families.

CONCLUDING PRINCIPLES

This chapter described some advanced concepts in master production scheduling, primarily techniques useful in the assemble-to-order manufacturing environment. Firms that implement these techniques will be able to better respond to customer requests—and to do so at lower costs of operation. We see the following principles as important:

- Managing product mix can be greatly enhanced by appropriate use of super bills and bill structuring techniques.
- The two-level master production schedule allows the firm to closely couple the production plan, the MPS, and order entry.

FIGURE 14.16   Material handling equipment manufacturer: summary statistics

Section	A	B	C	D	E	F	G	Family
					Product family average			
A. Unit sales data:								
Percent sales volume	30%	15%	10%	30%	5%	5%	5%	
B. End-item configurations:								
As engineered	24192	99	129024	24	168	15552	69984	239043
As sold	1200	63	14080	24	54	768	3456	19645
C. Parts for an average vehicle:								
Common parts	1034	813	919	462	486	357	248	4319
Unique parts	287	93	288	49	106	173	283	1279
Total parts	1321	906	1207	511	592	530	531	5598
Percent common	78%	90%	76%	90%	82%	67%	47%	76%
D. Parts for the full family:								
Common parts	1034	813	919	462	486	357	248	4319
Unique parts	786	577	895	121	293	523	1048	4243
Total parts	1820	1390	1814	583	779	880	1296	8562
BOM records	9345	5968	11002	239	4591	16666	21840	70651
E. Purchased vs. manufactured parts:								
Common purchased	651	499	598	280	292	237	158	2715
Common manufactured	383	314	321	182	194	120	90	1604
Unique purchased	455	329	453	57	194	284	663	2435
Unique manufactured	331	248	442	64	99	239	385	1808
F. Super bill MPS records:								
MPS records	18	11	27	10	10	22	26	124
Average vehicle unique purchased vs. manufactured parts:								
Unique purchased	182	55	179	26	72	88	161	753
Unique manufactured	105	38	109	23	34	85	122	516

Source: William J. Tallon, "The Design and Performance of Master Production Scheduling Techniques for Assemble-to-Order Products," Ph.D. dissertation, University of Iowa, 1986.

FIGURE 14.17   Material handling equipment manufacturer: super bill of material

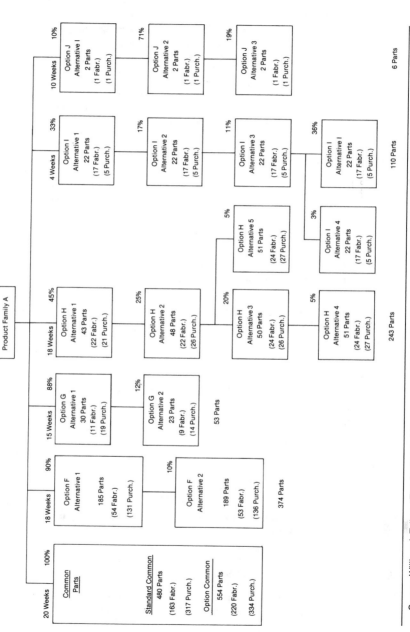

Source: William J. Tallon, "The Design and Performance of Master Production Scheduling Techniques for Assemble-to-Order Products," Ph.D. dissertation, University of Iowa, 1986.

- Very complex product environments can be master-scheduled with relatively few MPS records, with the right product structuring.
- The high costs of developing and maintaining planning bills for the MPS can be offset by the benefits of closer coupling to the market where competition requires rapid response.
- Available-to-promise logic can provide a mechanism for managing the consumption of capacity, as well as materials.
- Structuring the bills of material to determine the common and unique parts must accommodate both the ways the products are sold and the ways in which they are manufactured.

REFERENCES

Berry, W. L.; T. E. Vollmann; and D. C. Whybark. *Master Production Scheduling: Principles and Practice.* Falls Church, Va.: American Production and Inventory Control Society, 1979.

Gessner, Robert A. *Master Production Schedule Planning.* New York: John Wiley & Sons, 1986.

Kneppelt, Leland R. "Product Structuring Considerations for Master Production Scheduling." *Production and Inventory Management* 25, no. 1 (1984), pp. 83–99.

Ling, Richard C. "Demand Management: Let's Put More Emphasis on This Term." *APICS 26th Annual Conference Proceedings,* 1983, pp. 11–12.

Proud, John F. "Consuming the Master Production Schedule with Customer Orders." *APICS 26th Annual Conference Proceedings,* 1983, pp. 21–25.

Sari, John F. "The Planning Bill of Material—All It's Cracked Up to Be?" *APICS 25th Annual Conference Proceedings,* 1982, pp. 324–27.

Sulser, Samuel S. "Advanced Concepts in Master Planning—A Matter of Systems Design." *APICS 27th Annual Conference Proceedings,* 1984.

Tallon, William J. "The Design and Performance of Master Production Scheduling Techniques for Assemble-to-Order Products." Ph.D. dissertation, University of Iowa, 1986.

Vollmann, Thomas E. *Master Planning Reprints.* Falls Church, Va.: American Production and Inventory Control Society, 1986.

Wemmerlov, Urban, "Assemble-to-Order Manufacturing: Implications for Materials Management." *Journal of Operations Management* 4, no. 4 (1984), pp. 347–68.

DISCUSSION QUESTIONS

1. Why does two-level master production scheduling offer increasing benefits as the number of product options available to the customers goes up?

2. Why is the level-one production forecast an explosion of the level-zero available to promise in a two level MPS?

3. Why is safety stock not held in common parts?

4. Upstate University has majors in business administration, nursing, and nuclear physics. How might the university apply the super bill concept to the institution, considering each of the majors as a product family?

5. Upstate has just hired a new dean who believes in a liberal education. At his urging, the curriculum has been revised so that every student takes a liberal arts core of courses during the first two years. How does this change the approach to question 4?

6. Upstate University was using a two-level master production schedule for managing enrollments in the business school. Someone discovered that accounting students apply two months later than the other students. How might this fact influence the way Upstate consumes its forecasts of demand for classes?

7. Why is maximizing the monetary value of the common parts an important goal?

8. Jeff Miller, the master scheduler for Ajax Widgets, has noticed that one of the parts in the circular widget family is used on every end item, but in one case two units are required. As a result, the usage is not the same and the part was not included in common. Jeff asks why he cannot include one unit of the part in common and one more in the unique parts list for the circular widget that requires two units. Will this work?

9. Why is the lead time for the final assembly an important issue?

PROBLEMS

1. Lefty Cardozo has gone to work at Wilbur's Wonderful Widgets as an order entry and master scheduling expert. Flaky Old Lefty (FOL) has come up with the following scheme:

   The company has four distinct products—A, B, C, and D—which come from two basic options. We start with a basic widget, but it can be equipped with either pink or red lining, as well as automatic contour or no automatic contour. The breakdown is:

A = Pink automatic
B = Pink no automatic
C = Red automatic
D = Red no automatic

   FOL is having a hard time with the marketing group in trying to get specific forecast data for A, B, C, and D. However, the FOL thinks a good guess is 3 to 1 for red to pink and 2 to 1 for automatic contours to no automatic contours. Design a super bill of materials for FOL.

2. FOL went to a seminar so he could change back to Smart Old Lefty (SOL). He learned another trick, which eliminates the need for super bills. To get the right number of parts started for his master schedule of 100 per week, he plans the master schedule for 25 Bs (thereby accounting for all needed "pink" plus 25 of the 33 needed "no automatic"); 8 Ds (thereby finishing the "no automatic" and getting 8 of the 75 "red"); and 67 "Cs" (finishing the "red" and "automatic"). At the end of one week, SOL had the following data for a particular master schedule week:

```
15  A
25  C
30  D
```

What is the implied product mix for the remaining 30 widgets?

3. A company makes products on a make-to-order basis instead of stocking finished-goods inventory. Concentrating on one item, product C, we find it with a present inventory of zero and a total of 30 units sold. Assume that the 30-unit present backlog position is made up of 20 units promised in week 1 and 10 in week 2. Also assume an existing master schedule, which includes product C. The resultant master schedule quantities are shown in the weeks in which they are to be made. The following document has been produced.

Item #	Description	Assembly lead time		On hand		Lot size		Time fences	
								Demand	Planning
C		1		0		L–F–L		1	7
Week	1	2	3	4	5	6	7	8	9
Forecast	35	35	35	35	35	35	35	35	35
Orders	20	10							
Available									
Available to promise									
Master production schedule	87	63			12	88	50		

Calculate the "available" and "available-to-promise" rows of the above document.

4. Brent Gibson, the master scheduler at the Vincent Electric Company, explained the firm's approach to scheduling production: "Basically, it is fairly straightforward. We get an annual forecast from marketing, break it up into weeks, and set the lot size at two weeks' worth. Then, depending on the lead time, we can figure out when to order. In the case of the model 47 rotary arm, the forecast works out to 50 per week, which means the lot size is 100. Since there is a four-week lead time, we place an order every other week for delivery four weeks later. Right now, we ordered last week, so there are orders due in weeks 2 and 4. Next week we will order the 100 units for week 6." When asked what happened when the actual sales differed from the constant rate of 50 per week, Brent replied, "Well, first of all, you really have to learn how to handle

those turkeys from marketing. What a bunch of cry babies. I usually just tell them I would like to help them out, then ask where did they come in? By and large, we just hang in there, and the averages work out. If the overall forecast for the year is wrong, then we sometimes have to make an adjustment."

a.   Given the information above and considering the MPS techniques described in this chapter, prepare an analysis based on the *current situation*, stating *all* of the specific problems facing Brent. (Use an 11-week planning horizon in preparing your analysis. Assume assembly time is negligible.)

b.   Suppose that the assembly of a #47 rotary arm requires a critical component, called the #687 link, which is purchased from a supplier. Re-do your analysis in question a, considering the following information about the #687 link:

One #47 rotary arm assembly requires three #687 links. The purchasing lead time for the #687 link equals 3 weeks. There is an open purchase order (scheduled receipt) for 400 units scheduled to be received on Monday morning of week 2 in the future. (The supplier has just advised you that 44 pieces of this order have been scrapped.)

Currently (i.e., at the start of week 1) there are 123 #687 links on hand in inventory. (600 #687 links have already been removed from inventory for use on the two MPS orders for the #47 rotary arm due to be completed in weeks 2 and 4.)

The current order quantity for the #687 link is 400 pieces, and the supplier has made a commitment to ship a maximum of 100 pieces per week or 400 pieces in any four-week time interval.

Mode #47 rotary arm (on-hand inventory = 20)

Booked Orders		
Order number	Promise week	Quantity
1	1	10
2	1	5
3	1	2
4	2	60
5	3	60
6	4	50
7	4	60
8	6	20
9	7	10
New orders to be promised		
10	ASAP*	1
11	ASAP*	10
12	ASAP*	25

*As soon as possible.

c. Now, suppose that there is a $110 ordering cost and a $0.55 inventory carrying cost per piece per week for the #47 rotary arm. Recommend the best ordering policy and the time at which this ordering policy can be implemented. Indicate all of the factors that you considered in this analysis.

d. Considering the problems currently facing Brent (as indicated in question a and supplemented in questions b and c above), identify all of the alternative courses of action that can be taken in the short run to solve these problems. Also, indicate the consequences of and the pros and cons of each alternative solution. Recommend one of the solutions to the current problems and justify your choice.

5. Tani produces several lines of specialty tanning equipment. The most popular line is the Tawny Tanis line. There are several options within the line, but the most popular by far is the "Golden" option, being requested in 80 percent of the orders for any Tawny Tanis product, on the average. Tani uses a planning fence at period 5 for the product line and period 4 for the options. Structure the two-level MPS record for the Tawny Tanis line, the common parts, and the Golden option given the following information:

Production plan for Tawny Tanis:	500/period (1–6)
Master schedule for Tawny Tanis:	500/period (1–5)
Master schedule for common parts:	500/period (1–4)
Master schedule for Goldens:	400/period (1–4)

Actual orders for	Tawny Tanis	Goldens
Period 1	500	423
2	450	354
3	300	250
4	150	112

	Common parts	Tawny Tanis	Goldens
Inventory	0	0	45
Lot sizing	LFL	LFL	LFL
Safety stock	0	0	50

6. Underground Deli produces three sandwiches (jelly, peanut butter, and tunafish) on a roll, a bun, white bread, or dark bread. Each sandwich is carefully wrapped in yesterday's newspaper. It has been a rough job to manage the business, and the owners are thinking about installing an MPC system with a two-level MPS. They wonder about structuring the bill of materials to aid this process. Help them by constructing the matrix for structuring the bill of materials for their twelve products. Use both the option and the end item approach. The bill of materials for white bread sandwiches appears below.

7. Neva's boutique manufactures and sells a number of special nightgowns. One model, the Nevita, is available in several styles, of which the most popular is the "Flimsy," accounting for about 60 percent of sales. Given the record below, update the two-level MPS as of period 2, scheduling the appropriate MPS quantities. At the very end of period 1, a new customer was granted a request

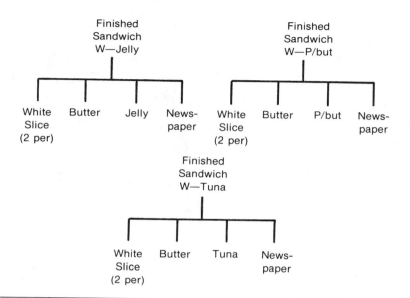

Planning fence at period 5

Nevitas	Period					
	1	2	3	4	5	6
Prod. plan	100	100	100	100	100	100
Act. ords.	90	100	80	20		
Sch. rts.						
Avail.	0	0	0	0	0	−100
ATP	10		20	80	100	
MPS	100	100	100	100	100	

On hand = 0; lot-for-lot; SS = 0.

Planning fence at period 4

Flimsy	Period				
	1	2	3	4	5
Prod. frcst.	6	0	12	48	60
Act. ords.	55	58	43	8	
Sch. rts.					
Avail.	4	6	11	15	−45
ATP	10	2	17	52	
MPS	60	60	60	60	

On hand = 5; lot-for-lot; SS = 5.

for an order of five Nevitas in period 1, all in the Flimsy style, and five for period 5, of which three were Flimsys.

8. Jolly Janes are the latest fad among kids in the third and fourth grades. They come in three models, with the quick Model A accounting for about 50 percent

of the sales. The records below show the two-level MPS for this popular option. What would the records look like after booking an order for six Jolly Janes, of which three were for Model A?

Planning fence at period 5

Jolly Janes			Period			
	1	2	3	4	5	6
Prod. plan	50	50	50	50	60	60
Act. ords.	50	50	40	20		
Sch. rts.						
Avail.	0	0	0	0	0	−60
ATP	0		10	30	60	
MPS	50	50	50	50	60	

On hand = 0; lot-for-lot; SS = 0.

Planning fence at period 4

Model A			Period		
	1	2	3	4	5
Prod. frcst.	0	0	5	15	30
Act. ords.	22	29	22	8	
Sch. rts.					
Avail.	8	4	2	4	−26
ATP	4		3	17	
MPS	25	25	25	25	

On hand = 5; lot-for-lot; SS = 5.

9. Develop a spreadsheet model of the two-level MPS records for Family A and Model I in the following situation. Family A consists of several models, of which Model I represents 50 percent of the demand. The company uses a planning fence at period 5 for the family and period 4 for the models. What happens if the production plan is changed to 8/period for periods 3 through 6 (with no other changes)?

	Production plan for Family A:	10/period (1–6)	
	Master schedule for Family A:	10/period (1–5)	
	Actual Orders for		MPS for
	Family A	Model I	Model I
Period 1	10	6	0
2	8	4	5
3	6	5	6
4	2	1	5
	Family A		**Model I**
Sched. recpt.	0		5 (period 1)
Inventory	0		2
Lot sizing	LFL		LFL
Safety stock	0		3

10. Given the following information in the MPS record, please update the record after entering the four new customer orders. What actions, if any, should the master scheduler take?

	Week						
	1	2	3	4	5	6	7
Forecast	100	100	100	100	100	100	110
Orders	89	22	95	11	5	2	1
Available	12	112	12	112	12	112	12
ATP	23	83		184		197	
MPS		200		200		200	

On Hand = 112   Assembly Lead Time = 3 weeks
Lot Size = 200
Demand Time Fence = 3 weeks
Planning Time Fence = 6 weeks

New Customer Orders:
  15 units customer order number 6042 due in week 1
  19 units customer order number 6044 due in week 1
  14 units customer order number 6051 due in week 5
  25 units customer order number 6056 due in week 3

11. The master production schedule for product family X at the Carlson Company is prepared using a two-level MPS approach. This product family has two options (option 101 and 102). The product structure is shown below.

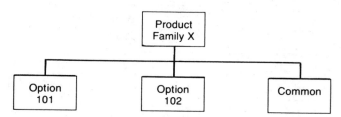

a. Given the following transactions, update the MPS; roll the records ahead to the start of week 2.

Transactions
The MPS quantity of 360 units of item 101 was completed.
A customer order for 15 units of item 101 in week 1 was cancelled.
Ten units of scrap were reported on the MPS of 40 102's due in week 2.
An inventory adjustment of +32 units was reported on item 101.
An inventory adjustment of −12 units was reported on item 102.
No sales order were booked for week 7.

b. On the basis of updated records from question 11a, what actions should the master scheduler take at the start of week 2?

	Week					
Product Family X	1	2	3	4	5	6
Production Plan	200	200	200	200	200	200
Orders	200	200	140	190	50	10
Net	0	0	60	10	150	190

	Week					
Option #101	1	2	3	4	5	6
Forecast	0	0	54	9	135	171
Orders	155	140	91	117	30	6
Available	380	240	455	329	524	347
ATP	380	0	152	0	324	0
MPS (Finish)	360	0	360	0	360	0
MPS (Start)	360		360			

Forecast = 90%   Lead time = 2
Safety stock = 20   weeks
On hand = 175   Lot size = 360

	Week					
Option #102	1	2	3	4	5	6
Forecast	0	0	6	1	15	19
Orders	45	60	49	73	20	4
Available	20	0	−55	−89	−124	−107
ATP	20	−69	0	−53	0	36
MPS (Finish)	0	40	0	40	0	40
MPS (Start)	40		40			

Forecast = 10%   Lead time = 3
Safety stock = 50   weeks
On hand = 65   Lot size = 40

Common Parts	Week					
	1	2	3	4	5	6
Forecast	0	0	60	10	150	190
Orders	200	200	140	190	50	10
Available	200	0	200	0	200	0
ATP	0	0	70	0	340	0
MPS (Finish)	400	0	400	0	400	0
MPS (Start)		400		400		

Forecast = 100%   Lead time = 1 week
Safety stock = 0   Lot size = 400
On hand = 0

12. The Carlson Company in problem 11 has the following product structure for including parts:

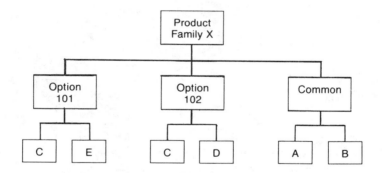

a. Prepare the MRP records for items A, B, C, D, and E, using the data from problem 11, the records below, and the associated lot size, safety stock, and lead time values given for each item. Assume that one unit of each component is used in producing the parent items.

Item A	Week					
	1	2	3	4	5	6
Gross requirements						
Scheduled receipts						
Projected available balance						
Planned order release						

Q = LFL; SS = 10; LT = 1 week; On hand = 12

	Week					
Item B	1	2	3	4	5	6
Gross requirements						
Scheduled receipts						
Projected available balance						
Planned order release						

Q = LFL; SS = 10; LT = 1 week; On hand = 2

	Week					
Item C	1	2	3	4	5	6
Gross requirements						
Scheduled receipts						
Projected available balance						
Planned order release						

Q = LFL; SS = 10; LT = 1 week; On hand = 415

	Week					
Item D	1	2	3	4	5	6
Gross requirements						
Scheduled receipts						
Projected available balance						
Planned order release						

Q = LFL; SS = 50; LT = 1 week; On hand = 95

	Week					
Item E	1	2	3	4	5	6
Gross requirements						
Scheduled receipts						
Projected available balance						
Planned order release						

Q = LFL; SS = 15; LT = 1 week; On hand = 400

b. How would the requirements for item C differ if item C was considered to be a common part? Why might it not be so considered?

13. A revision of the two-level MPS for product family X at the Carlson Company at the start of week 1 is shown below. This product family has two options (see problem 12 for a complete product structure).

a. The firm has just completed substantial work on a set-up time reduction project as well as revisions for product family percentages. Therefore, the lead times and lot sizes for options 101 and 102 have been reduced substantially. Given the revised MPS for product family X, prepare the MRP records for component items A, B, C, D, and E, using the records below and the associated lot size, safety stock, and lead time value given for each item. Also, assume that one unit of each component is used in producing the parent items.

	Week					
Product Family X	1	2	3	4	5	6
Production plan	200	200	200	200	200	200
Orders	200	200	140	190	50	10
Net	0	0	60	10	150	190

	Week					
Option #101	1	2	3	4	5	6
Forecast	0	0	36	6	90	114
Orders	155	140	91	117	30	6
Available	140	120	113	110	110	110
ATP	120	0	29	3	90	114
MPS (Finish)	120	120	120	120	120	120
MPS (Start)	120	120	120	120	120	

Forecast = 60%   Lead time = 1 week
Safety stock = 20   Lot size = 120
On hand = 175

	Week					
Option #102	1	2	3	4	5	6
Forecast	0	0	24	4	60	76
Orders	45	60	49	73	20	4
Available	100	120	127	130	130	130
ATP	100	20	31	7	60	76
MPS (Finish)	80	80	80	80	80	80
MPS (Start)	80	80	80	80	80	

Forecast = 40%   Lead time = 1 week
Safety stock = 50   Lot size = 80
On hand = 65

	Week					
Common Parts	1	2	3	4	5	6
Forecast	0	0	60	10	150	190
Orders	200	200	140	190	50	10
Available	0	0	0	0	0	0
ATP	0	0	60	10	150	190
MPS (Finish)	200	200	200	200	200	200
MPS (Start)	200	200	200	200	200	

Forecast = 100%   Lead time = 1 week
Safety stock = 0   Lot size = 200
On hand = 0

	Week					
Item A	1	2	3	4	5	6
Gross requirements						
Scheduled receipts						
Projected available balance						
Planned order releases						

Q = LFL; SS = 10; LT = 1 week; On hand = 212

Item B

	| Week					
	1	2	3	4	5	6
Gross requirements						
Scheduled receipts						
Projected available balance						
Planned order releases						

Q = LFL; SS = 10; LT = 1 week; On hand = 220

Item C

	| Week					
	1	2	3	4	5	6
Gross requirements						
Scheduled receipts						
Projected available balance						
Planned order releases						

Q = LFL; SS = 50; LT = 1 week; On hand = 415

Item D

	| Week					
	1	2	3	4	5	6
Gross requirements						
Scheduled receipts						
Projected available balance						
Planned order releases						

Q = LFL; SS = 50; LT = 1 week; On hand = 195

Item E

	| Week					
	1	2	3	4	5	6
Gross requirements						
Scheduled receipts						
Projected available balance						
Planned order releases						

Q = LFL; SS = 50; LT = 1 week; On hand = 400

b. How would the requirements for item C differ if item C was considered to be a common part? How (and why) is this answer different from that in problem 12?

c. What would be necessary to use a kanban system be used to control Items A, B, and C?

14. The manager of Master Production Scheduling at Hyster would like to adjust the MPS for the Level 1 oil clutch option shown in Figure 14.9 so that a safety stock of 2 units is maintained in each period in the MPS. Please make the adjustments to the MPS to accomplish this in the record below.

Week		8–21	8–28	9–5	9–11	9–18	9–25	10–2	10–9	10–16
Start Day		178	183	188	192	197	202	207	212	217
Production forecast		0	0	2	3	8	8	9	10	9
Sold			8	6	5	2	1			
Scheduled receipts			9							
Projected on hand										
MPS start										

Lead Time = 2 weeks
Super Bill Percentage = 62%
Beginning On Hand Inventory = 0 units
Safety Stock = 2 units

a. Why might safety stock be desirable on this item?

15. The Fitzsimmons Pump Company produces industrial equipment on a make-to-order basis using general-purpose equipment in job shop facilities. The master production schedule is stated in terms of customer orders for each product family. The master production schedule for the gear reducer product family is shown below. The standard manufacturing lead time quoted for component part production and final assembly is three weeks for this product family.

Gear reducer product family

	Week								
	1	2	3	4	5	6	7	8	9
Forecast	20	20	20	20	20	20	20	20	20
Orders	20	20	20	18	15	12	8	5	2
Available	0	0	0	0	0	0	0	0	0
ATP	0	0	0	2	5	8	12	15	18
MPS (complete)	20	20	20	20	20	20	20	20	20

Lead Time = 3 weeks   Lot Size = LFL
Safety Stock = 0   On Hand = 0

a. The shop is able to complete 20 units per week of this product family. Two work centers currently limit the output: the K & T machining center and the Essex gear hobber. The "typical" gear reducer requires an average of 4 standard hours per end item unit on the K & T machining center and 2 standard hours per unit of end product on the Essex gear hobber. The K & T machining center is operated on a two-shift 80-hour-per-week basis and the Essex gear hobber is run on a single shift 40-hour-per-week basis. Please convert the MPS record for the gear reducer product family into standard hour-capacity equivalents.

b. Suppose that the master production scheduler has just received a new order from sales for 2 gear reducers requiring 3 hours per unit on the K & T machining center and 5 hours per unit on the Essex gear hobber. When can this order be scheduled for delivery, assuming that sufficient capacity exists at the other required work centers?

c. What assumptions are required in using this approach for monitoring shop capacity?

══ 15 ════════════════════════════════

Advanced concepts in production planning

This chapter deals with modeling procedures for the establishment of an overall or aggregate production plan, and the disaggregation of the plan. The basic issue, given a set of product demands stated in some common denominator, is what levels of resources should be provided in each period? There has been a long history of academic research on aggregate production planning models. Theory has outstripped application by a wide margin. However, as firms implement MPC systems, there is a natural evolution toward questions of overall planning which provide direction to the other MPC system modules. We are cautiously optimistic that theory and practice are converging. This chapter provides a basic understanding of how that convergence might occur. It is organized around the following five topics:

- Mathematical programming approaches to the aggregate production planning problem: How can the aggregate production planning problem be formulated as a mathematical programming model?
- Other modeling approaches to aggregate production planning: What are some of the other models that have been developed and how do they compare?
- Disaggregation: What is the framework for disaggregating production plans into the master production schedule?

- Company examples: What are the components of an actual advanced production planning and scheduling system, and what does it provide for the company?
- Applications potential: What are the roadblocks to implementation of advanced production planning methods, and what is the prognosis for the future?

Chapter 15 has a close linkage with Chapter 9, in which basic production planning approaches are described. There are also linkages to Chapters 8 and 14 on master production scheduling, and Chapter 4 on capacity planning. It is the aggregate production plan that constrains the master production schedule in a hierarchical view of manufacturing planning and control. Capacity planning procedures are used to determine the feasibility of an MPS.

MATHEMATICAL PROGRAMMING APPROACHES

In this section, we present an overview of some math programming models which have been suggested for the aggregate production planning problem. The academic literature has long been concerned with the aggregate production planning problem, using formal decision models. We start by formulating the problem as a linear programming model. This approach is relatively straightforward, but is necessarily limited to cases where there are linear relationships in the input data. Thereafter, we describe a mixed integer programming approach for preparing aggregate production plans on a product line basis.

These approaches are already substantially more sophisticated than the practice found in most firms. More common are spreadsheet programs used to explore alternative production plans. Using forecasts of demand and factors relating to employment, productivity, overtime, and inventory levels, a series of what-if analyses helps formulate production plans and evaluate alternative scenarios. "Level" and "chase" strategies are developed to bracket the options, and alternatives can be evaluated against the resultant bench marks. Although the spreadsheet programs do not provide the optimal solutions reached by the models discussed in this chapter, they do help firms understand the inherent trade-offs better, and provide a focal point for important dialog among functional areas of the firm.

Linear programming

There have been many linear programming formulations for the aggregate production planning problem. The objective is typically to find the lowest-cost plan, considering when to hire and fire, how much inventory to hold, when to use overtime and undertime, and so on, while always meeting the sales forecast. One formulation, based on measuring aggregate sales and inventories in terms of direct labor hours, follows:

Minimize:

$$\sum_{t=1}^{m} (C_H H_t + C_F F_t + C_R X_t + C_o O_t + C_I I_t + C_u U_t)$$

Subject to:

1. Inventory constraint:

$$I_{t-1} + X_t + O_t - I_t = D_t$$
$$I_t \geq B_t$$

2. Regular time production constraint:

$$X_t - A_{1t} W_t + U_t = 0$$

3. Overtime production constraint:

$$O_t - A_{2t} W_t + S_t = 0$$

4. Work force level change constraint:

$$W_t - W_{t-1} - H_t + F_t = 0$$

5. Initializing constraints:

$$W_0 = A_3$$
$$I_0 = A_4$$
$$W_m = A_5$$

Where:

C_H = The cost of hiring an employee.
C_F = The cost of firing an employee.
C_R = The cost per labor-hour of regular time production.
C_o = The cost per labor-hour of overtime production.
C_I = The cost per month of carrying one labor-hour of work.
C_u = The cost per labor-hour of idle regular time production.
H_t = The number of employees hired in month t.
F_t = The number of employees fired in month t.
X_t = The regular time production hours scheduled in month t.
O_t = The overtime production hours scheduled in month t.
I_t = The hours stored in inventory at the end of month t.
U_t = The number of idle time regular production hours in month t.
D_t = The hours of production to be sold in month t.

B_t = The minimum number of hours to be stored in inventory in month t.

A_{1t} = The maximum number of regular time hours to be worked per employee per month.

W_t = The number of people employed in month t.

A_{2t} = The maximum number of overtime hours to be worked per employee per month.

S_t = The number of unused overtime hours per month per employee.

A_3 = The initial employment level.

A_4 = The initial inventory level.

A_5 = The desired number of employees in month m (the last month in the planning horizon).

m = The number of months in the planning horizon.

Similar models have been successfully formulated for several variations of the production planning problem. In general, however, few real-world aggregate production planning problems appear to be compatible with the linear assumptions. For some plans, discrete steps, such as adding a second shift, are required. For many companies, the unit cost of hiring or firing large numbers of employees is much larger than that associated with small labor force changes. Moreover, economies of scale are not taken into account by linear programming formulations. Let us now turn to another approach, which partially overcomes the linear assumption limitations.

Mixed integer programming

The linear programming model provides a means of preparing low-cost aggregate plans for overall work force, production, and inventory levels. However, in some firms, aggregate plans are prepared on a product family basis. Product families are defined as groupings of products that share common manufacturing facilities and setup times. In this case, overall production, workforce, and inventory plans for the company are essentially the summation of the plans for individual product lines. Mixed integer programming provides one method for determining the number of units to be produced in each product family. Chung and Krajewski describe a model for accomplishing this.

Minimize:

$$\sum_{i=1}^{n} \sum_{t=1}^{m} [C_{si} \, \sigma(X_{it}) + C_{mi}X_{it} + C_{Ii}I_{it}]$$

$$+ \sum_{t=1}^{m} [C_H H_t + C_F \, F_t + C_o O_t + A_{1t}C_R W_t]$$

Subject to:

1. Inventory constraint:

$$I_{i,t-1} - I_{it} + X_{lt} = D_{it} \qquad \text{(for } i = 1, \ldots, n \text{ and}$$
$$t = 1, \ldots, m)$$

2. Production and setup time constraint:

$$A_{1t}W_t + O_t - \sum_{i=1}^{n} X_{it} - \sum_{i=1}^{n} \beta_i \sigma(X_{it}) \geq 0 \qquad \text{(for } t = 1, \ldots, m)$$

3. Work force level change constraint:

$$W_t - W_{t-1} - H_t + F_t = 0 \qquad \text{(for } t = 1, \ldots, m)$$

4. Overtime constraint:

$$O_t - A_{2t}W_t \leq 0 \qquad \text{(for } t = 1, \ldots, m)$$

5. Setup constraint:

$$- Q_i \, \sigma(X_{it}) + X_{it} \leq 0 \qquad \text{(for } t = 1, \ldots, m \text{ and}$$
$$i = 1, \ldots, n)$$

6. Binary constraint for setups:

$$\sigma(X_{it}) = \begin{cases} 1 \text{ if } X_{it} > 0 \\ 0 \text{ if } X_{it} = 0 \end{cases}$$

7. Non-negativity constraints:

$$X_{it}, I_{it}, H_t, F_t, O_t, W_t \geq 0$$

Where:

X_{it} = Production in hours of product family i scheduled in month t.
I_{it} = The hours of product family i stored in inventory in month t.
D_{it} = The hours of product family i demanded in month t.
H_t = The number of employees hired in month t.
F_t = The number of employees fired in month t.
O_t = Overtime production hours in month t.
W_t = Number of people employed on regular time in month t.
$\sigma(X_{it})$ = Binary setup variable for product family i in month t.
C_{si} = Setup cost of product family i.
C_{Ii} = Inventory carrying cost per month of one labor hour of work for product family i.
C_{mi} = Materials cost per hour of production of family i.
C_H = Hiring cost per employee.
C_F = Firing cost per employee.
C_O = Overtime cost per employee hour.

C_R = Regular-time work force cost per employee hour.

A_{1t} = The maximum number of regular-time hours to be worked per employee in month t.

β_i = Setup time for product family i.

A_{2t} = Maximum number of overtime hours per employee in month t.

Q_i = A large number used to insure the effects of binary variables; that is,

$$Q_i \geq \sum_{t=1}^{m} D_{it}$$

n = Number of product families.

m = Number of months in the planning horizon.

The objective function and constraints in this model are similar to those in the linear programming model. The main difference is in the addition of product family setups in constraints 5 and 6. This model assumes that all of the set-ups for a product family occur in the month in which the end product is to be completed. Constraint 5 is a surrogate constraint for the binary variables used in constraint 6. This constraint forces $\sigma(X_{it})$ to be nonzero when $X_{it} > 0$ since Q_i is defined as the total demand for a product family over the planning horizon.

Additional constraints should be added to the model to specify the initial conditions at the start of the planning horizon; that is, constraints specifying the beginning inventory for the product family, I_{io}, and the work force level in the previous month, W_o, are required. Likewise, constraints specifying the work force level at the end of the planning horizon, and the minimum required closing inventory balance at the end of each month in the planning horizon, may be added.

OTHER APPROACHES

Several other models have been formulated for solving the aggregate production planning problem. In this section, we briefly describe three of them. The first is a classic academic work based on linear and quadratic cost assumptions. The other two approaches are enhancements of this model. The first, management coefficients, is based on managerial behavior as the way to develop the general cost estimates. The second utilizes search approaches that allow for more general cost expressions.

The linear decision rule

The linear decision rule model (LDR) for aggregate production planning was developed by Holt, Modigliani, Muth, and Simon in the 1950s. The primary application was in a paint producing company.

The major difference between the LDR model and linear programming models is the approach taken to cost input data. The four cost elements considered in LDR are regular payroll cost, hire/fire cost, overtime/undertime cost, and inventory/backlog cost.

The regular payroll cost is simply a linear function of the number of workers employed. For the other three cost elements, however, a quadratic cost function is used. For example, the hire/fire cost is defined as:

$$64.3(W_t - W_{t-1})^2$$

Where:

W_t = The work force to be established for the tth month.

W_{t-1} = The prior month's work force.

64.3 = Analytically derived coefficient for best fitting the squared differences in work force levels to actual operating cost results.

Figure 15.1 is an example quadratic hire/fire cost function, along with the presumed actual cost data. The presumed actual cost data only approximate the quadratic function. However, in some ways, the implication that each hire or fire decision results in ever-increasing unit costs is consistent with many managerial opinions.

The total cost function for the paint company was made up of the four cost elements. The problem is to minimize the total cost function. Since the cost data are linear and quadratic, the solution to the problem can be derived by calculus. The result is a set of two decision rules specifying the production output rate and the work force level in each month.

FIGURE 15.1   LDR quadratic cost function for work force changes

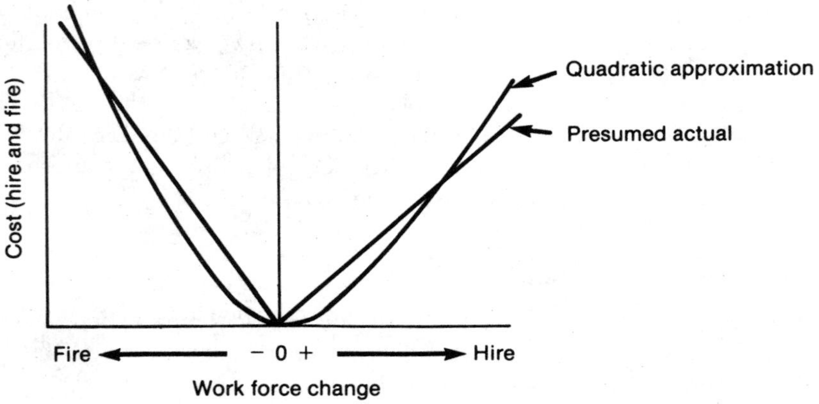

LDR was implemented at the paint company. However, several years later, John Gordon visited the company to assess current results. He describes some of the findings:

> After considerable study and investigation it became apparent that although top management thought the rules were being used to determine aggregate production and work force, a more intuitive and long-standing system was in fact being used. The production control clerk whose responsibility it was to calculate the production and work force sizes, as well as convert these into item orders, was doing just that and posting the results in the form of job tickets on the production control board. When the foremen came into the production control office for a job ticket, they surveyed the available tickets for one that agreed with their intuitive feeling or judgment. If they found one they took it but if they did not they simply wrote out a ticket which corresponded with their feeling. Over the history of the use of the rules it turned out that about 50 percent of the tickets were used and the others ignored. Management, however, had the feeling that the rules were being used except in the odd case when judgment indicated that they should be overruled. At a later date the calculations associated with the rules were centralized with the installation of a data-processing center. The personnel in the center became concerned when their reports indicated that many of the production orders that they had issued were ignored. Consequently, and with the compliance of higher management, they instituted a reporting system, which fed back to the plant management, and the foremen, a cumulative listing of outstanding production orders. After a short delay the length of this cumulative list began to diminish until it all but vanished. But in the meantime the inventory of finished goods associated with this plant rose steadily to alarming proportions, especially in some obsolete items. Further investigation revealed that although the rules were indicating the size of the work force, no action was ever taken to reduce the work force because it was against the policy of the company. This meant that the work force rule was indicating a reduction in the work force; the production rule, attempting to minimize costs given the present work force level but anticipating layoff, called for some production for the excess work force. The rules are interactive, but in this case the interaction had been eliminated.

The moral to the story seems clear: One must never assume that the real world matches the model without auditing. In fact, any system that is not readily understood by the users is more subject to overrides than one where the logic is transparent.

The management coefficients model

A rather unique approach to aggregate production planning has been formulated by Bowman. He suggests that the production rate for any period would be set by the following very general decision rule:

$$P_t = aW_{t-1} - bI_{t-1} + cF_{t+1} + K$$

Where:

P_t = The production rate set for period t.
W_{t-1} = The work force in the previous period.
I_{t-1} = The ending inventory for the previous period.
F_{t+1} = The forecast of demand for the next period.
$a, b, c,$ and K = Constants.

Bowman's approach is to first gather historical data for P, W, I, and F. Thereafter, through regression analysis, the values of a, b, c, and K are estimated. The result is a decision rule based upon past managerial behavior without any explicit cost functions. The assumption is that managers know what is important, even if they cannot readily state explicit costs. However, managers may either overreact to specific circumstances or delay in making adjustments. In both cases, a bias comes into their decision making. The regression analysis of the management coefficients model will average out this bias for future decisions.

Bowman compared the performance of the management coefficient model with LDR and actual company practice in four firms. In three out of four cases, the management coefficient model produced results superior to those made by the company; and in two cases, the results were also superior to LDR. Later research has tended to confirm the efficiency of Bowman's approach, lending credence to approaches that supplement the application of experienced judgment.

Search decision rules

We have noted that linear programming models are limited by the linear cost assumptions. Similarly, LDR is restricted to linear and quadratic costs. The search decision rule (SDR) methodology helps overcome these restrictions. SDR approaches allow one to state the cost data inputs in very general terms. The only requirement is that a computer program be constructed that will unambiguously evaluate the cost of any production plan. The procedure then searches among alternative plans (in a guided fashion) for the plan of minimum cost. Unlike linear programming and LDR, there is no guarantee of mathematical optimality with SDR. However, the increased realism in input data provides the potential for solving a problem more in line with managerial perceptions.

Several researchers have worked with search procedures for the aggregate production planning problem. Taubert compared SDR with LDR for the paint company problem. He found that SDR results were very close to those obtained by LDR. The technique has been applied in a number of companies. The versatility of the underlying approach provided makes it especially attractive for real-world applications.

DISAGGREGATION

Thus far, we have considered only the establishment of a global plan of production. This plan will necessarily have to be broken down or disaggregated into specific products and detailed production actions. Moreover, the aggregate production planning problem, as formulated up to now, has been based on a single facility (although it is conceivable that a facility subscript could be used in the linear programming model). For many firms, the problem of determining which facility will produce which products, in which quantities, is an important prerequisite to planning at each facility. In this section, we first consider an approach to disaggregation that closely parallels the managerial organization for making these decisions. We then turn to a mathematical programming model for determining the MPS within each product family (the product family planning having been done earlier with mixed integer programming).

The disaggregation problem

One of the issues that is receiving increased attention is the conversion of overall aggregate production plans into detailed MPS plans; that is, managers must make day-to-day decisions on a product and unit basis, rather than on the overall output level. The concept of disaggregation facilitates this process and ameliorates mismatches between plan and execution. In essence, disaggregation is concerned with overall production planning, as well as with consistent lower-level capacity decisions. It recognizes that aggregate decisions constrain the disaggregated actions. It is therefore concerned with the issue of how to break the total or aggregate plan into plans for subunits of product.

Disaggregation is an important field of study. There has been some growth in both theory and practice, but the number of applications to date is limited. The disaggregation frame of reference is to maintain a match between the production plan and the master production schedule. The aggregate production plan must be the sum of the production called for by the detailed master production schedule (MPS). At issue is how to keep the two in concert. Some of the new research efforts offer potential help, but there is much to be done.

Hierarchical production planning

One approach to aggregate capacity analysis that is based upon disaggregation concepts and can accommodate multiple facilities is hierarchical production planning. The approach incorporates a philosophy of matching product aggregations to decision-making levels in the organization. Thus, the

FIGURE 15.2   Hierarchical planning schema

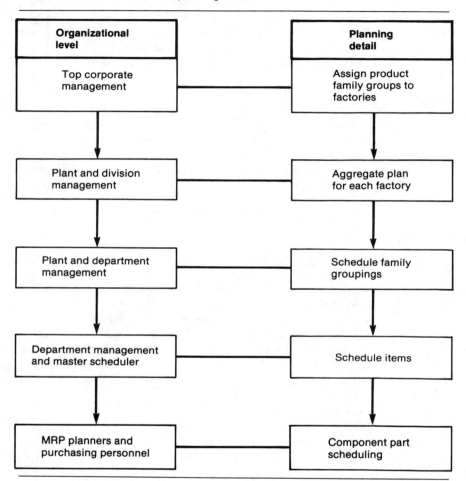

Organizational level	Planning detail
Top corporate management	Assign product family groups to factories
Plant and division management	Aggregate plan for each factory
Plant and department management	Schedule family groupings
Department management and master scheduler	Schedule items
MRP planners and purchasing personnel	Component part scheduling

Source: G. D. Bitran, R. A. Haas, and A. C. Hax, "Hierarchical Production Planning: A Two-Stage System," *Operations Research,* March–April 1982, pp. 232–51.

approach is not a single mathematical model but utilizes a series of models, where they can be formulated. Since the disaggregation follows organization lines, managerial input is possible at each stage. A schema of the approach is shown in Figure 15.2.

The development of hierarchical production planning (HPP) has been the effort of a group of researchers (Bitran, Haas, Hax, Meal, and others) over several years. Some of the work has involved mathematical contributions, while others increase the depth or breadth of application (incorporating distribution centers or levels of detail in a factory). All, however, are based on some fundamental principles.

One principle has been mentioned already: the disaggregation should follow organizational lines. Another principle is that it is only necessary to provide information at the aggregation level appropriate to the decision. Thus, it is not necessary to use detailed part information for the plant assignment decisions. Finally, it is necessary to schedule only for the lead time needed to change decisions. That means that detailed plans can be made for periods as short as the manufacturing lead times.

The process of planning follows the schema of Figure 15.2. It first involves the specification of which products to produce in which factories. The products are combined in logical family groupings to facilitate the aggregation, assignment to factories, and modeling processes. The assignment to factories is based on the minimization of capital investment cost, manufacturing cost, and transportation cost.

Once the assignment to factories has been done and managerial inputs incorporated, an aggregate production plan is made for each plant. The procedure for the determination of the aggregate production plan could be any of those discussed previously. The aggregate plan specifies production levels, inventory levels, overtime, and so on, for the plant. This plan is constrained by the specific products and volumes assigned to the plant.

The next step in the disaggregation calls for scheduling the family groupings within the factory. The schedule is constrained by the aggregate production plan and takes into account any inventories that may exist for the group. The intention at this stage is to realize the economies of producing a family grouping together. The production lots (or share of the aggregate capacity) for the groups are determined and sequenced. If no major economies are achieved by scheduling the group as a unit, the procedure can move directly to the scheduling of individual items, the next stage shown in Figure 15.2.

The determination of the individual item schedule is analogous to making a master production schedule (MPS). In the HPP schema, the MPS is constrained by the previously scheduled family groupings and may cover a shorter planning horizon. In some instances, mathematical models can be used to establish the schedules. In all cases, the items are scheduled within the capacity allocated for the family group to which it belongs. The detailed part and component scheduling can be done with MRP logic, order launching and inventory systems, or even mathematical modeling.

A recent extension to the basic HPP model is to use variable planning periods rather than the fixed planning period of 20 days used in the Bitran, Hass, and Hax approach. Oden develops a recursive algorithm to predict the length of the planning period which minimizes the annual sum of setup and inventory holding costs. Oden's model produces consistently lower production costs (overtime, setup, inventory holding) than those of the fixed period approach.

Disaggregation through mathematical programming

A disaggregation model by Chung and Krajewski illustrates how the aggregate production plan for each family, determined by their mixed integer programming model, can be disaggregated into a detailed master production schedule that specifies the lot size and timing for the individual end products. Since the family production and inventory levels have been established by the aggregate plan, the master production schedule must adhere to the targets set by the aggregate plan. To do this the formulation includes the resource requirements and limitations from the aggregate plan as constraints. The model uses information from the aggregate plan for each family, including: the setup time (β_i), the setup status $(\sigma(X_{it}))$, the production level (X_{it}), and the inventory level (I_{it}). Also used are the overtime (O_t), the work force level (W_t), and the regular time availability (A_{1t}) for each month. The formulation of the disaggregation model follows:

Minimize:

$$\sum_{i=1}^{n} \sum_{k \in K_i} \sum_{t' \in N_t} b_i^k B_{it'}^k + \sum_{t=1}^{m} (w^{3-} d_t^{3-} + w^{3+} d_t^{3+})$$

$$+ \sum_{i=1}^{n} \sum_{t=1}^{m} (w_i^{1-} d_{it}^{1-} + w_i^{1+} d_{it}^{1+} + w_i^{2-} d_{it}^{2-} + w_i^{2+} d_{it}^{2+})$$

Subject to:

1. Inventory Constraint:

$$I_{i,t'-1}^k - I_{it'}^k + X_{it'}^k + B_{it'}^k - B_{i,t'-1}^k = D_{it'}^k$$
$$(\text{for } i = 1, \ldots, n; \; k \in K_i; \; t' \in N_i; \text{ and } t = 1, \ldots, m)$$

2. Regular Time and Overtime Production Constraint:

$$\sum_{i=1}^{n} \sum_{k \in K_i} \sum_{m'=1}^{Li} \sum_{j=1}^{J} (r_{im'j}^k X_{i,t'+Li-m'}^k) + d_{t'}^{o-} - d_{t'}^{o+}$$

$$= \left(\frac{1}{4}\right) \left[A_{1t} W_t - \sum_{i=1}^{n} \beta_i \sigma(X_{it}) \right] (\text{for } t' \in N_t \text{ and } t = 1, \ldots, m)$$

3. Overtime Deviation Constraint:

$$\sum_{t' \in N_t} d_{t'}^{o+} + d_t^{3-} - d_t^{3+} = O_t \qquad (\text{for } t = 1, \ldots, m)$$

4. Regular Time Deviation Constraint:

$$\sum_{k \in K_i} \sum_{t' \in N_t} X_{it'}^k + d_{it}^{1-} - d_{it}^{1+}$$

$$= X_{it} (\text{for } i = 1, \ldots, n \text{ and } t = 1, \ldots, m)$$

5. Inventory Deviation Constraint:

$$\sum_{k \in K_i} \sum_{t' \in N_t} I_{it'}^k + d_{it}^{2-} - d_{it}^{2+} = I_{it}$$

(for $i = 1, \ldots, n$; $t = 1, \ldots, m$; and
$t' = 4(t-1) + 1, \ldots, 4(t-1) + 4$)

6. Non-Negativity Constraints:

$$X_{it'}^k, I_{it'}^k, B_{it'}^k, d_{t'}^{0-}, d_{t'}^{0+}, d_{it}^{2-}, d_{it}^{2+}, d_{it}^{3-}, d_{it}^{3+}, d_{it}^{1-}, d_{it}^{1+} \geq 0$$

Where:

$X_{it'}^k$ = The production hours of end-item k of product family i in week t'.

$I_{it'}^k$ = The hours of end-item k of product family i in inventory at the end of week t'.

b_i^k = Cost to back order one hour of production of end-item k of product family i.

$B_{it'}^k$ = Back order hours of end-item k of product family i in week t'.

$D_{it'}^k$ = The hours of end-item k of product family i demanded in week t'.

$d_{t'}^{0}$ = Undertime in week t'; that is, the number of planned regular time hours not used in week t'.

$d_{t'}^{0+}$ = Overtime hours used in week t'.

d_t^{3-} = Negative deviation from the planned overtime level in month t.

d_t^{3+} = Positive deviation from the planned overtime level in month t.

d_{it}^{1-} = Negative deviation from the planned aggregate production level of product family i in month t.

d_{it}^{1+} = Positive deviation from the planned aggregate production level of product family i in month t.

d_{it}^{2-} = Negative deviation from the planned inventory of product family i at the end of month t.

d_{it}^{2+} = Positive deviation from the planned inventory of product family i at the end of month t.

$w_i^{1-}, w_i^{1+}, w_i^{2-}, w_i^{2+}, w^{3-}, w^{3+}$ = Weights (costs) assigned to the deviation variables.

$r_{im'j}^k$ = Proportion of total production labor hours required for processing item k of product family i at operation or work center j in week m' (the week since production started on k) assuming that at most one operation for each item at each work center j.

L_i = Production lead time for items in product family i.

n = Number of product families.

m = Master production schedule planning horizon length.

J = Number of work centers.

K_i = Set of end items within product family i.

N_t = Set of time-phased weeks, (t')'s, in month t. For this example monthly time buckets are used for the aggregate plans and weekly time buckets are used for the time-phased master production schedule. It is assumed that there are 4 weeks in each month; that is, month 1 $(t = 1)$ has $t' = 1, 2, 3, 4$; and month 2 $(t = 2)$ has $t' = 5, 6, 7, 8$; and so on.

The first constraint represents the production and inventory relationships from week to week with the back order position for the individual product lines included. The second constraint defines the labor hour requirements. The right-hand side value in this constraint is obtained from the aggregate plan solution, and it equals the regular labor hours planned for the month, excluding the hours consumed for setups for product families. The value of ¼ is used to translate the monthly (t) figures into weekly (time-phased t') values, assuming there are four weeks in every month. Therefore, this constraint specifies that the total employee hours at all work centers that produce the items in the product families, including the under and overtime adjustments, should equal the overall employee capacity planned to be available in each week (t').

The third, fourth, and fifth constraints use deviations to force the overtime, family production quantities, and closing inventory values to correspond to the monthly goals set by the aggregate production plan; that is, O_t, X_{it}, and I_{it} respectively. Weights placed on the deviations in the objective function control both the magnitude and the frequency of these deviations.

The initial end-item inventories and work force conditions must be included in the master production scheduling model. The beginning inventories of the end items within a product family must sum to the beginning inventory for the product family used in the aggregate planning model; that is,

$$\sum_{k \in K_i} I_{i,o}^k = I_{i,o}.$$

Also, the lead time (L_i) for each product family must be considered in solving the master production scheduling model. For example, if a four-week production lead time is used for a product family, including one week for the end item and three weeks for the components, then only the master schedule for week 4 and beyond can be changed. The components for weeks 1 to 3 must have been produced in the previous month. Therefore, the resource requirements for these items must be netted from resource capacities given for the first month in the second constraint. Likewise, the demands for weeks 1 to 4 in the master production schedule must also be netted from the planned production in weeks 1 to 3.

A schematic that shows the relationship of the aggregate planning and the

FIGURE 15.3   A schematic diagram of a sequential production planning process

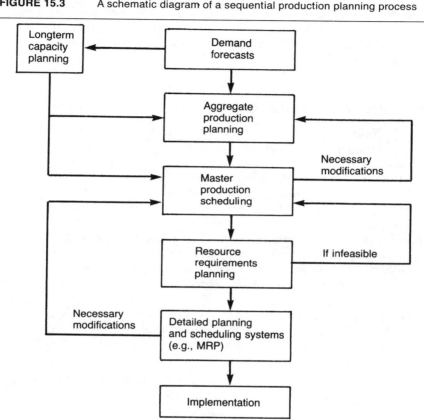

Source: C. Chung and Lee J. Krajewsky, "Planning Horizons for Master Production Scheduling," *Journal of Operations Management*, August 1984.

master production scheduling models to other MPC activities is presented in Figure 15.3. This diagram indicates the sequential nature of the solution process. It begins with aggregate planning for each family. Factor values for X_{it}, I_{it}, $\sigma(X_{it})$, W_t, and O_t are then passed to the master scheduling model. The outputs of the master scheduling model are then passed to the detailed planning and scheduling systems of the company; that is, the material requirements planning (MRP) and to capacity plans driven from the MPS. This cycle is repeated each month.

This approach represents one method for disaggregating overall production plans into detailed master production schedules.

COMPANY EXAMPLE

In this section, we present an application of advanced production planning models. We start with an overview of the problem, then present the aggregate production planning model, and end with a section detailing the disaggregation procedure.

Owens-Corning Fiberglas: Anderson, South Carolina plant

In 1982, Owens-Corning Fiberglas implemented a hierarchical approach for production planning and scheduling decisions at its Anderson, South Carolina, plant—one of the largest plants in the company. The problem structure and results are described by Oliff and Burch; the model details are explained in a subsequent paper by Oliff. The Anderson plant produces a fiberglass mat used in the marine industry for constructing boat hulls, as reinforcement in pipeline construction, and in bathtubs and showers. This mat is sold in a variety of widths and lengths, is treated with one of three process binders, and is frequently trimmed on one or both edges. Over 200 end products are produced, of which 28 represent 80 percent of the sales volume, with the remainder being low-volume special-order products.

The production process for fiberglass mat consists of two high-volume batch production lines for which the demand exceeds the capacity approximately six months of the year. An overview of the hierarchical planning system is shown in Figure 15.4. This system determines:

- An aggregate plan that reflects the relevant costs for inventory, production, and work force.
- Production lot sizes, line assignments, and inventory levels for each standard product.
- Specific production sequences and changeover costs for standard and special-order items.

While this system is an excellent example of the application of advanced techniques for the preparation of aggregate plans, it also illustrates the disaggregation of these plans into the master production schedule for individual end products.

Aggregate production planning. The model used to prepare aggregate inventory level, work force, and production rate plans is a production switching heuristic (PSH). The objective function involves minimizing the direct payroll, overtime, hiring and firing, and relevant inventory costs over a planning horizon that ranges from 3 to 12 months, as shown in the total cost equation below:

FIGURE 15.4   Owens-Corning Fiberglas hierarchical planning system

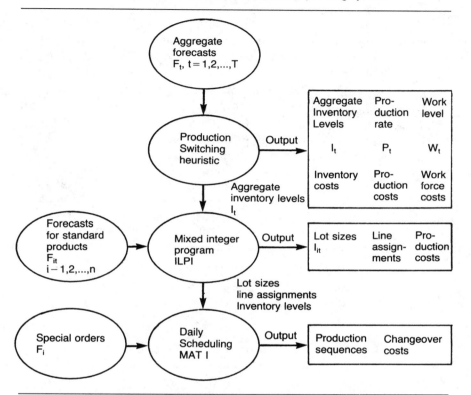

Source: M. D. Oliff and E. E. Burch, "Multiproduct Production Scheduling at Owens-Corning Fiberglas," *Interfaces*, September–October 1985, pp. 25–34.

Minimize:

$$\sum_i \sum_t C_{Ri} S_{it} + \sum_i \sum_t C_{Oi} O_{it}$$
$$+ \sum_i \sum_t C_{Hi} H_{it} + \sum_i \sum_t C_{Fi} F_{it} + \sum_t C(I_t)$$

$$(\text{for } i = 1, \ldots, k \text{ and } t = 1, \ldots, m)$$

Where:

$k =$ number of production lines.

$m =$ number of production months.

$C_{Ri} =$ cost of varible wages per shift on production line i.

$C_{Oi} =$ cost of overtime per shift on production on line i.

$C_{Hi} =$ cost of increasing by 1 shift on production line i.

C_{Fi} = cost of decreasing by 1 shift on production line i.
$C(I_t)$ = cost of holding I_t pounds of inventory, per month.
I_t = pounds of inventory in month t.
S_{it} = number of shifts on line i in month t.
O_{it} = overtime shifts required on line i in month t.
H_{it} = number of shifts added on line i from month $t-1$ to month t.
F_{it} = number of shifts reduced on line i from month $t-1$ to month t.

The decision variables in the aggregate planning model are the monthly plant production rates $P(t)$ over the planning horizon (of m months), which can be adjusted by operating each of the two mat lines at the Anderson plant in one of several shift setups. Full production on line 1 involves using four 6-hour shifts per day with the plant running seven days per week on a 24-hour per day basis, while full production on line 2 is obtained by operating three 8-hour shifts per day on a five-day week, 24-hour per day schedule. A particular shift setting is denoted by (i,j) where i represents the number of shifts on line 1 and j is the number of shifts on line 2. The different shift settings (and monthly production rates) that are feasible because of process and organizational constraints at the Anderson plant are:

Decision variable	Shift setting (i,j)	Production in pounds per month
R_1	(4,2)	1,679,000
R_2	(4,1)	1,571,000
R_3	(3,3)	1,405,000
R_4	(3,2)	1,288,000
R_5	(3,1)	1,180,000

A production switching heuristic is used to fix the production rate for each month in the production plan. The particular heuristic used at the Anderson plant is shown in the equation below:

$$P(t) = \begin{bmatrix} R_1 \text{ if} & D(t) - I(t-1) + A > R_1 \\ R_5 \text{ if} & D(t) - I(t-1) + C < R_5 \\ R_2 \text{ if } R_1 > & D(t) - I(t-1) + A > R_2 \\ R_4 \text{ if } R_5 < & D(t) - I(t-1) + C < R_4 \\ R_3 \text{ otherwise} \end{bmatrix}$$

Where: $R_1 > R_2 > R_3 > R_4 > R_5$.

$D(t)$ = monthly forecast in pounds.
$I(t)$ = inventory level in pounds.
$P(t)$ = production level in pounds (determined by R_i).
S_{it} = number of shifts on line i in month t (determined by R_i)
A = minimum ending inventory target.
C = Maximum ending inventory target. $(A \leqslant C)$

The switching heuristic works by setting the production rate for month t at $R1$ if the demand for month t, $D(t)$ exceeds $R1$, after deducting the starting inventory, $I(t-1)$, and adding the minimum closing inventory target, A. Similarly, the production rate for month t is set at the minimum production rate R_5 if the demand for month t, $D(t)$, net of the starting inventory, $I(t-1)$, and after adding the maximum closing inventory target, C, is less than the minimum production rate $R5$. The monthly production rate can also be set at one of the intermediate production rates, $R2$, $R3$, or $R4$ using the equations above.

An example of a production plan developed using the production switching heuristic is shown in Figure 15.5. This plan was developed using actual sales, an initial inventory of 1,306,000 lbs., and a previous month production rate of $R2$ (4,1). The minimum and maximum inventory targets (A and C) were both set to 1,100,000 in developing this plan.

The production switching heuristic is adaptable to a wide range of operating conditions. It is particularly applicable in production situations where capacity adjustments are made in large increments, such as the addition of extra work shifts. Moreover, a variety of both regular and overtime production settings, inventory targets, and forecasts can be used in this model. In using the model, the production planner can restrict the selection of decision variables and factors to be considered in examining the performance implications of a particular production plan.

This flexibility in the production planning model means that the control

FIGURE 15.5 Example aggregate production plan using last year's sales as forecast data (no overtime)

Month	Forecast (lbs.)	Production (lbs.)	Inventory (lbs.)	Shift schedule (shifts)
0	0	0	1,306,000	41
1	1,190,000	1,180,000	1,296,000	31
2	1,280,000	1,180,000	1,196,000	31
3	1,408,000	1,288,000	1,076,000	32
4	1,714,000	1,679,000	1,041,000	42
5	1,184,000	1,280,000	1,145,000	32
6	1,546,000	1,405,000	1,004,000	33
7	1,216,000	1,288,000	1,076,000	32
8	1,167,000	1,288,000	1,197,000	32
9	1,404,000	1,288,000	1,081,000	32
10	1,204,000	1,288,000	1,165,000	32
11	1,154,000	1,180,000	1,191,000	31
12	1,114,000	1,180,000	1,231,000	31

Inventory cost	Payroll cost	Hire&fire cost	Overtime cost	Total cost
$87,673	$956,026	$65,806	0	$1,109,505

parameters; that is, the production rate factors $(R_1 - R_5)$, the inventory targets (A and C), and the planning horizon length (m), are context dependent. At Owens-Corning Fiberglas, the least cost values for these parameters were determined using a simulation model, which reflected the production planning situation at the company, and direct search methods. At the Anderson plant, production rate increments of 100,000 pounds (less than two days' production) were used in evaluating approximately 100,000 sets of parameter values. Starting conditions were provided to the simulation, and a total cost equation similar to the objective function above was used to determine the least cost set of control parameters. The control parameter values are reviewed periodically at the plant and the model parameters are updated by using the same procedures.

Disaggregating the production plan. The linkage between the production plan and the master production schedule can be seen in Figure 15.4. The aggregate closing inventory position for each month from the production switching heuristic, $I(t)$, is passed to a mixed integer programming formulation that determines the lot sizes, line assignments, and the inventory levels for the 28 standard products (the MPS). The aggregate inventory balance is included as one of the constraints in the mixed integer program. These constraints include:

- Production balance equations to insure that the individual product demand forecasts are satisfied while forcing inventory conservation.
- Inventory equations to adhere to the aggregate inventory constraints, as well as to the safety stock requirements.
- Noninterference equations to insure feasible assignments of individual products to processing lines.
- Changeover equations to incorporate the changeover costs from one product to another.

The mixed integer programming formulation is designed to minimize the combined costs of processing line changeovers and production in determining the assignment of the 28 standard products to the two processing lines. There are three decision variables in the model:

$X_{i,l,t,p}$ = 1 if line l's production capacity during month t and subperiod p is devoted to product i, the wire.

$\sigma_{i,j,l,t,p}$ = 1 if a changeover occurs from product i to product j on line l during month t and at the beginning of subperiod p, and 0 otherwise.

$I_{i,t}$ = the total pounds of product i in inventory at the end of the month t.

While the model determines the production lot sizes, it is not primarily concerned with the sequencing of production lots at this level of decision making in the Owens-Corning Fiberglas manufacturing control system. The production lot sizes for the standard products can be determined from the mixed integer programming solution by simply multiplying the solution value for a particular $X(i,l,t,p)$ by the production rate for line l in month t and subperiod p. The objective function and constraints for this model are as follows:

Minimize:

$$\sum_i \sum_l \sum_t \sum_p (C_{p,i,l} X_{i,l,t,p}) + \sum_i \sum_j \sum_l \sum_t \sum_p C_{s,i,j} \sigma_{i,j,l,t,p}$$

Subject to:

Production balance

$$I_{i,t-1} - I_{i,t} + \sum_l \sum_p r_{p,i,l} \cdot X_{i,l,t,p} = D_{i,t} \text{ (for all } i \text{ and } t)$$

Inventory capacity

$$\sum_i I_{i,t} = I_t \text{ (for all } t)$$

$$I_{i,t} \geq B_{i,t} \text{ (for all } i \text{ and } t)$$

Noninterference

$$\sum_i X_{i,l,t,p} = 1 \text{ (for all } l, t, \text{ and } p)$$

Changeover (one per subperiod, p)

$$X_{i,l,t,p-1} - X_{i,l,t,p} = \sum_j \sigma_{i,j,l,t,p} - \sum_i \sigma_{i,j,l,t,p} \text{ (for all } l, t, p)$$

$$\sum_i \sum_j \sigma_{i,j,l,t,p} = 1 \text{ (for all } l, t, p)$$

Where:

$C_{p,i,l}$ = the production cost of product i on line l, in subperiod p.
$C_{s,i,j}$ = the changeover cost from product i to j.
$D_{i,t}$ = the demand for product i in month t.
$r_{p,i,l}$ = the production in subperiod p for product i on line l.
I_t = the desired aggregate inventory for month t.
$B_{i,t}$ = the desired safety stock for product i in month t.

This mixed integer programming model results in a 10,000 row by 10,000 column matrix. Once a month a linear programming approximation generates feasible, near-optimal solutions to the mixed integer programming problem. The results provide Owen-Corning Fiberglas with monthly, quarterly, or yearly master production schedules. It yields inventory level information, lot sizes, and line assignments for the coming months.

The disaggregation process is carried one step further by the daily scheduling part of the manufacturing control system shown in Figure 15.4. This phase produces a daily production schedule, using both the customer orders for the 170 special ordered products and the lot sizes and processing line assignments for the standard products. A sequencing heuristic is used that considers sequence dependent setups, minimizing the cost of changing from one product to another. This heuristic produces a 7-day to 30-day schedule that includes sequences, complete product descriptions, expected run times, and expected changeover costs. Real-time responses to potential schedule changes, as well as to new schedule requirements, are obtained daily.

The integrated planning and scheduling system has provided Owens-Corning Fiberglas a number of major benefits. The average number of monthly changeovers decreased from 70 in 1981 to less than 40 in 1982 and 1983, providing annual savings of $100,000 or more. Operating savings have improved dramatically, and the system provides real-time cost estimates of actual and potential schedule changes. The system provides an excellent example of the use of advanced techniques for planning and scheduling, as well as the use of a hierarchical process for disaggregating the production plan.

APPLICATIONS POTENTIAL

In this section, we consider the current situation regarding advanced production planning. We start by evaluating a rather disappointing history of the application of formal models. One of the limitations to applying modeling techniques is the data required, a topic we address as well. The section concludes with a prognosis for the future of advanced production planning concepts.

Application of modeling techniques

The application of quantitative models has been disappointing at best. The linear decision rule model (LDR) is more than 25 years old, but has seen very limited application. Linear programming models have been used extensively, but generally for firms that have relatively homogenous output measures and simple product structures, such as oil refineries and feed mixing plants. Hierarchical production planning, which is relatively new and parallels the managerial organization, has had few applications.

Most of the interest in modeling techniques has been academic. In firms where the aggregate production planning problem is treated, the approaches are often combined with the long-range planning and budgeting cycles using simplified tabular or graphical methods. We see three key reasons for the lack of demonstrated applications of the theory.

The first reason is that few firms actually make aggregate decisions in the way implied by the models. For most firms, the aggregate is merely the sum of several lower-level decisions. Among these decisions are output rates for particular factories, product lines, or even work centers. Management guidance on some overall or aggregate basis tends to be of a general nature, rather than one of providing a fixed set of constraints within which a process of disaggregation can unambiguously proceed. A related issue is the assumption of homogeneity. The existence of some uniform measure of output makes more sense in a paint factory than in a multiproduct, multiplant firm. Also, there are great differences among workers. The analytical models treat them as equivalent.

A second reason for the lack of application may be managerial understanding. It is difficult for many managers to understand the analytic underpinnings of the quantitative model forms. Our experience has shown that the logic must be transparent to gain wide acceptance. This seems to be particularly true for aggregate planning models.

A final element inhibiting expanded application of the formal approaches is the data requirements. Often real-world data do not correspond to the model assumptions. In other cases, the data required do not exist. This is an area where data bases like those developed for the manufacturing planning and control (MPC) system can help. The issues are important enough that we devote the next section to them.

Data issues

The existence of high-quality data base for manufacturing, especially if it is linked to the cost accounting and financial analysis system, can help greatly in gathering data for aggregate capacity analysis. Even so, there remain many problems. Looking just at the data requirements for the models raises several issues.

Although of limited applicability in some countries (or companies), one of the most difficult issues is the question of how one would estimate hiring and firing costs. Clearly, the most important aspects of these costs are not part of the accounting records. For determining the hiring costs, the more easily estimated components are those for recruiting, interviewing, and training. More difficult estimations are the length of time to become fully effective, the time to reach the quality levels required, and the ability to become assimilated into the social environment of the firm. Firing costs can be extremely difficult to assess, particularly in terms of the influence on morale.

In most of the methods presented, we treated both hiring and firing costs as linear, with no constraints on the number of persons who could be hired or fired in a time period. In some examples, the resulting labor force changes simply might not be possible. Moreover, the costs of small adjustments are almost surely different from those of large adjustments.

A somewhat similar problem relates to overtime/undertime costs. Overtime in modest amounts does represent a useful means for dealing with short-term capacity problems. However, to go from a 40-hour workweek to a 60-hour workweek is quite severe. Experience indicates that there is a reduction in hourly productivity when people work that many hours. The situation is aggravated when the number of weeks worked on overtime increases. Moreover, the ability to vary the workweek at will is clearly very limited. The costs of undertime are very difficult to measure, especially in terms of the long-term influence on worker morale, turnover, and loss of skill.

The inventory carrying costs might be linear over fairly wide ranges, but could change as capital resources are strained or new opportunities are developed. The percentage rate used to represent inventory carrying costs is presumed to include more than the interest charges from bank loans and direct storage costs. The risks of obsolescence, physical deterioration, and having the wrong items in finished goods also have to be considered.

Again we raise the issue of finding a single aggregate output measure. Many firms rather cavalierly convert sales dollars to labor-hours to get such a measure. The assumptions are that all sales dollars are equal, that any labor-hour can be used to make any sales dollar, and that any inventory is, in fact, useful to meet any marketplace demand. In fact, the existence of an overall single homogenous capacity measure is often not a meaningful concept in many firms. For example, the company with several different product lines, particularly if one product is highly labor intensive and another is capital intensive, will have difficulty finding a uniform capacity measure.

The future

We have some guarded optimism about the use of advanced production planning methods. As more and more firms implement MPC systems and continue to improve them, the applicability of more formal production planning becomes clear. This is typically first manifested in basic production planning, where a monthly production plan is determined by a top-management group. As this process is refined, there is a natural tendency to consider formal models to support the effort. The trade-offs are better understood, as well as the costs to the firm.

Another reason for growing use of advanced production planning models comes from better managerial understanding of the underlying methodologies. Linear programming and other mathematical models are now routinely learned by most business school students.

Finally MPC systems in the years ahead will necessarily be focused on fast response and significantly reduced overhead costs. The high clerical costs of a detailed MPC system with many levels of planning will be reduced as more firms migrate toward just-in-time (JIT) systems. However, the front end planning for these JIT systems becomes critically important.

In summary, we feel that many firms will find the use of advanced production planning methods to be of increasing interest. However, implementing these systems will remain difficult. The lessons learned from application to application indicate that we have a long way to go before well-established guidelines emerge.

CONCLUDING PRINCIPLES

This chapter has reviewed formal approaches to aggregate production planning. We see the following principles as important:

- Making the match between the real world and the model as close as possible makes it easier to build the credibility necessary for the model to be used.
- The match between model and reality is easier to obtain for relatively homogeneous product lines or portions of lines.
- Applying the hierarchical approaches permits management to match the production planning and disaggregation process to the appropriate organizational entity.
- Investments in training, data enhancement, improved basic MPC practices, and determining clear objectives all enhance the potential for using advanced techniques.
- Significant efforts in model formulation, understanding, testing, and explanation all are important to successful applications.
- Advanced techniques must be built on a foundation of good basic practice. Modeling a mess does not make it better.

REFERENCES

Bowman, E. H. "Consistency and Optimality in Managerial Decision Making." *Management Science*, January 1963.

Bitran, G. D.; E. A. Haas; and A. C. Hax. "Hierarchical Production Planning: A Two-Stage System." *Operations Research*, March–April 1982, pp. 232–51.

Chung, C., and L. J. Krajewski. "Planning Horizons for Master Production Scheduling." *Journal of Operations Management*, August 1984, pp. 389–406.

Connell, B. C.; E. E. Adam, Jr.; and A. N. Moore. "Aggregate Planning in Health Care Foodservice Systems with Varying Technologies." *Journal of Operations Management* 5, no. 1, 1985.

Gelders, L. F., and L. N. Van Wassenhover. "Hierarchical Integration in Production Planning: Theory and Practice." *Journal of Operations Management* 3, no. 1, 1982.

Gordon, J. R. M. "A Multi-Model Analysis of an Aggregate Scheduling Decision." Ph.D. dissertation, Sloan School of Management, M.I.T., 1966 (published in Elwood S. Buffa, *Production-Inventory Systems: Planning and Control*. Homewood, Ill.: Richard D. Irwin, 1968, pp. 168–69).

Hansman, W. H., and S. W. Hess. "A Linear Programming Approach to Production and Employment Scheduling." *Management Technology*, January 1960, pp. 46–52.

Holt, C. C.; F. Modigliani; J. F. Muth; and H. A. Simon. *Planning Production, Inventories, and Workforce*. New York: Prentice-Hall, 1960, p. 16.

Holt, J. A. "A Heuristic Method for Aggregate Planning: Production Decision Framework," *Journal of Operations Management* 2, no. 1 (October 1981), pp. 43–51.

Lee, W. B.; E. Steinberg; and B. M. Khumawala. "Aggregate Versus Disaggregate Production Planning: A Simulated Experiment Using LDR and MRP." *International Journal of Production Research* 21, no. 6, pp. 797–811.

Mackulak, G. T.; C. L. Moodie; and T. J. Williams. "Computerized Hierarchical Production Planning in Steel Manufacturing." *International Journal of Production Research* 18, no. 4, pp. 455–65.

Meal, H. L., and D. C. Whybark. "Material Requirements Planning in Hierarchical Planning Systems." *International Journal of Production and Operations Management* 25, no. 7, pp. 947–956, 1987.

Nellemann, David O. "Production Planning and Master Scheduling: Management's Game Plan." *APICS 22d Annual Conference Proceedings*, 1979, pp. 166–68.

Oden, Howard W. "Hierarchical Production Planning with Variable Planning Periods," DBA dissertation, Boston University, 1986.

Oliff, Michael D. "A Discrete Production Switching Rule for Aggregate Planning." *Decision Sciences* 18, no. 4, Fall 1987, pp. 582–597.

Oliff, M. D., and E. E. Burch. "Multiproduct Production Scheduling at Owens-Corning Fiberglas." *Interfaces*, September–October 1985, pp. 25–34.

Sule, Dileep R. "Simple Methods for Uncapacitated Facility Location/Allocation Problems." *Journal of Operations Management* 1, no. 4 (May 1981), pp. 215–24.

Taubert, W. H. "A Search Decision Rule for the Aggregate Scheduling Problem." *Management Science* 14, no. 6 (February 1968).

Tersine, R. J.; W. W. Fisher; and J. S. Morris. "Varying Lot Sizes as an Alternative to Undertime and Days Off in Aggregate Scheduling." *International Journal of Production Research* 24, 1, pp. 97–106.

Vickery, S. K., and R. E. Markland. "Integer Goal Programming for Multistage Lot Sizing: Experimentation and Implementation." *Journal of Operations Management* 5, no. 2, 1985.

Vollmann, T. E. "Capacity Planning: The Missing Link." *Production and Inventory Management Journal*, 1st Quarter 1973.

DISCUSSION QUESTIONS

1. What is the least certain of the data inputs to aggregate production planning models? What can be done about this uncertainty?
2. What does a mixed integer programming formulation add over a linear programming approach?
3. What concerns should managers have about using aggregate production planning models?
4. How does the hierarchical approach match actual managerial practice?
5. How would you explain the Owens-Corning Fiberglas model to the workers?
6. There have been limited documented successes. What are the reasons for this?
7. In the disaggregation process, errors in the product mixes can occur. How do these creep in?
8. Why must we have effective MPC systems in place before we can anticipate adoption of advanced production planning concepts?

PROBLEMS

1. The Seymore Bikini Manufacturing Company of Boise, Idaho, has developed the following demand forecast for next year:

Quarter	Bikini sales
1	5,000
2	10,000
3	8,000
4	2,000

At the beginning of January 1, there are 1,000 units in inventory. The following data have been prepared by the firm:

Hiring cost per employee = $200.
Firing cost per employee = $400.
Beginning work force = 60 employees.
Inventory carrying cost = $2 per unit per quarter of ending inventory.
Stockout cost = $5 per unit.
Regular payroll = $1,200 per employee per quarter.
Overtime cost = $2 per unit.
Each employee can produce 100 units per quarter. Demand not satisfied in any quarter is lost.

Using linear programming:

a. How much will Seymore produce during each quarter?
b. What will be the total budget required by Seymore's plan for the next year?

2. Zebra Enterprises has collected the following information relating to one of its major products. (Use as a spreadsheet to model a and b below.)

Regular production = 1,400 units per period.
Production variation costs = $10 per unit of change (from 1,400 units/period).
Inventory costs = $3 per unit per period (on closing inventory balance).
Shortage costs = $7 per unit per period.
Beginning inventory = 200 units.

Period	Demand (units)
I	2,000
II	1,500
III	1,300
IV	1,800

a. Based on the above demand schedule, calculate a level production schedule which yields zero inventory at the end of period IV.
b. Calculate the total costs associated with the production schedule in part a.

3. The production manager at the Kew Toy Company is trying to decide whether to produce at a level production rate or a chase-sales production rate. In his analysis of the company operations, he has collected the following information:

Beginning employment level = 10 employees.
Beginning inventory = 0.
Hiring cost = $10 per employee.
Firing cost = $5 per employee.
Production per employee = 10 units per quarter.
Inventory carrying costs = $1 per unit per quarter (on ending inventory).
Target inventory at the end of the fourth quarter = 0.
Target employment level at the end of the fourth quarter equals the planned employment level specified by the plan under consideration.

Quarter	Sales forecast
1	50 units
2	80 units
3	120 units
4	150 units

a. Formulate this problem so it can be solved using linear programming.
b. Which of the two policies would result in the lowest annual cost?
c. What is the total annual cost of the policy adopted in part b?
d. What production rate should he use each quarter?

4. The Happy Halter Company had been experimenting with aggregate production plans for several years. As the firm started to lay out the plans for next year the management decided to use a two-month planning horizon to reduce the cost of computation. The basic data the firm had were:
   a. Employment level for this December = 10 people.
   b. Demand forecast for January of next year = 100.
   c. Demand forecast for February of next year = 120.
   d. Inventory level planned for the end of this December = 0.
   e. Backorders are not allowed.
   f. Desired February ending inventory = 0.
   g. Regular time per month = $1,000 per worker-month.
   h. Production = 10 units/person/month.
   i. Overtime premium = 50 percent of regular time.
   j. Overtime limit = 25 percent of regular time per person per month.
   k. Inventory carrying cost = $100/month/unit (on the average month).
   l. Hiring (or firing) cost = $1,000 per person.

   Compare the cost of a fixed employment production plan (i.e., 10 people) that uses overtime to meet demand to a level production plan that uses *no* overtime to meet production. (Use a spreadsheet model.)

5. Consider the following information:

   Production variation cost: $15/unit of change (from a base of 1,300 units).
   Regular production: 1,300 units per period.
   Maximum amount of production capacity: 1,500 units per period.
   Inventory costs: $2/unit per period on the ending inventory.
   Shortage costs: $10/unit per period.
   Subcontracting costs: $12/unit (maximum of 300 units per period).
   Beginning inventory: 400 units.

Period	Demand (units)
1	2,000
2	1,500
3	2,000
4	1,700

   a. As production manager of Big Red Express, you are in charge of meeting the above demand schedule for periods 1 through 4. President Corso specifies that you keep your production plan level for all four months. In addition to this, Corso limits the total amount of production per month to 1,500 units produced. Also, since the market Big Red Express competes in is very competitive, planned stockouts are NOT allowed. Therefore, you must decide if and when to subcontract. Maximum amount of subcontracting available in any one period is 300 units. Ending inventory at the end of period 4 should be zero. Use a spreadsheet to determine the cost of your plan.

b. Assuming the same facts in part **a**, except that NO subcontracting is allowed, could a pure chase strategy be followed and still meet demand? Why or why not?

6. On December 31, the ABC Company forecast its next year's sales to be:

Period	Sales (in units)
1st quarter	9,000
2nd quarter	12,000
3rd quarter	16,000
4th quarter	12,000
	49,000

Currently, the firm has 12 employees, each producing 1,000 units per quarter and earns $2,000 per quarter. The firm estimates its inventory carrying cost to be $2 per unit of ending inventory per quarter and its hiring or layoff costs to be $1,600 per employee. The firm could increase production by working overtime, but overtime work is limited to 25 percent of the regular production rate (or 250 units per employee per quarter). Overtime work is paid at the rate of 1.5 times the regular pay rate of the employees. Idle time costs the firm $4.16 per hour (assume that there are 60 eight-hour days per quarter). The company currently has an inventory of 1,000 units and wishes to have an ending inventory of 1,000 units at the end of the year. The company does not plan to incur inventory shortages.

a. Develop the total incremental cost expression for this problem.
b. Formulate this problem for solution, using linear programming.
c. What is the total incremental cost of a production plan which assumes a constant production rate (include both regular and overtime production) and work force level (assume 12 workers) each quarter.
d. Which production plan would result in the lowest total cost for the firm's operations.
  1. A level production plan (assuming a constant production rate each quarter)?
  2. A plan that sets production equal to sales each quarter?
  3. Some other plan?

7. The production manager at the Bloomington Paint Company is preparing the production and inventory plans for next year. He has supplied the following data concerning his firm:

Quarter	Sales forecast (in units)
1st quarter	3,000
2nd quarter	1,800
3rd quarter	2,400
4th quarter	3,500

Current inventory level = 300 units.
Current employee level = 600 people.

Production rate last quarter = 2,400 units (4 units/employee/quarter).
Inventory carrying cost = $20/unit/quarter (on ending inventory).
Hiring cost = $200/employee hired.
Layoff cost = $200/employee laid off.
Regular time production cost per unit = $320/unit.
Cost of overtime = $60/unit.
Desired closing inventory level = 100 units (minimum).

Furthermore, the production manager sees no equipment capacity limitations during the next two years. (Employees are hired or laid off only at the beginning of each quarter).

a. Specify a linear programming production planning model for use in this company. Formulate the model in sufficient detail so the production manager can solve it to determine his production plan.

b. After considering your recommendations, suppose that the production manager has revised his estimate of: (1) the hiring and layoff cost and (2) the overtime and idle time costs. The new costs are:

Cost of changing the employment level (y_1):

$$y_1 = \$200 \, (Y_n - Y_{n-1})^2$$

Cost of producing on overtime or permitting idle time (y_2):

$$y_2 = \$60(S_n - Ax_n)^2$$

Where:

x_n = The number of people employed in quarter n.
S_n = The planned production rate in quarter n.
A = The number of units produced per employee per quarter.

Given this new information, how would your recommendations to the production manager regarding the formation of a production planning model change?

8. The Old-n-Corny company produced great shower mats. The demand was very seasonal, however (apparently people only get dirty at certain times of the year). The company has a three shift production capability and can change to 1, 2, or 3 shifts at the beginning of each quarter. For each shift in operation, the company can produce 10,000 mats a quarter. At the moment, there are 2,000 mats in inventory and O-n-C would like to keep 2,000 as a hedge against uncertainty. The company is planning production for the next year and has compiled a demand forecast (shown below). Determine production switching heuristics for the number of shifts to schedule each quarter.

	Quarter			
	1	2	3	4
Forecast	10,000	20,000	30,000	10,000

9. Apply the following production switching rules to the forecast below (you might want to use a spreadsheet). What inventory do you end up with each quarter?

Current inventory = 1,250
Max. inventory target = 1,000
Min. inventory target = 1,000
Rules: Production (i) = 1,000 if (Forecast(i) − Inventory$(i-1)$ + Min. inventory target) $\geqslant$ 850
Production(i) = 500 if (Forecast(i) − Inventory$(i-1)$ + Max. inventory target) < 850

	Quarter			
	1	2	3	4
Forecast	750	800	1100	700

10. The Slick Switchers had developed a set of production switching rules for scheduling monthly production. They were quite anxious to try them out in a spreadsheet model. They had three shifts available, each of which could produce 20 switches a month. They had a minimum target inventory of 20 units and a maximum of 40. Current inventory was 35 units. What is the effect of the rules applied to the forecast below? What is the impact of reducing the maximum target inventory to 20 units?

Rules: Production(i) = 60 if (Forecast(i) − Inventory$(i-1)$ + Min. inventory target) > 60
Production(i) = 20 if (Forecast(i) − Inventory$(i-1)$ + Max. inventory target) < 20
Production(i) = 40 otherwise

	Month											
	1	2	3	4	5	6	7	8	9	10	11	12
Forecast	25	30	45	55	40	30	40	50	65	60	30	20

11. The production director and the marketing director at the Pickwick Company are currently negotiating the production and sales plans for the next year. The marketing director confidently forecasts a major sales increase; the forecast is shown in the figures below.

Sales forecast

	Quarter			
	1	2	3	4
Sales forecast (in units)	950	1200	1420	1630

a. Assume that the beginning inventory is 200 units and the target ending inventory for the 4th quarter is 200 units. What production each quarter will provide a level production plan?

b. If the average variable cost per unit for items produced by Pickwick is $500, what will the monetary value of the finished goods inventory at the end of the second quarter be if they use a level production plan?

c. If the average variable labor cost per unit for the items produced by Pickwick is $200 and the average wage rate is $5 per hour, what is the quarterly labor budget in hours and in dollars for a level production plan?

12. The sales manager at the Columbia Manufacturing Company has prepared the following sales forecast for next year:

Sales forecast (in units)

Product Family	Quarter			
	1	2	3	4
A	250	350	500	125
B	150	225	360	75

The production manager has supplied the following data:

Product Family A:
Two direct labor-hours per unit of product.
Setup cost equals $700 per changeover from B.
Setup time equals eight direct labor-hours per changeover.
Inventory carrying cost per quarter equals $1.50 per one direct labor-hour of work left in inventory at the end of the quarter.
Materials cost equals $70 per direct labor-hour of production.
The beginning inventory equals zero.

Product Family B:
One direct labor-hour per unit of product.
Setup cost equals $600 per changeover from A.
Setup time equals 10 direct labor-hours per changeover.
Inventory carrying cost per quarter equals $1 per one direct labor-hour of work in inventory at the end of the quarter.
Materials cost equals $50 per direct labor-hour of production.
The beginning inventory equals zero.

In addition, these factors apply:
Hiring cost per employee equals $1500.
Firing cost per employee equals $500.
Overtime cost per direct labor-hour equals $15.
Regular time cost per direct labor-hour equals $10.
The maximum number of regular time hours to be worked per employee per quarter equals 520.
Employees may not work more than 25 percent of the regular time hours on overtime each quarter.

a. Formulate this problem for solution using mixed integer programming.
b. Why is linear programming not appropriate for solving this production planning problem?

13. The production planning manager at the Columbia Manufacturing Company (in problem 12) has completed work on the firm's production plan for the coming year. He is now concerned with the preparation of the master production schedule for the next two weeks indicating the lot size and timing for the firm's individual products. Selected data concerning the production plan for the next two weeks for Product Family A is shown below.

Product Family A Item	Plan for Next Two Weeks
Production level	38 direct labor-hours during the 2 weeks
Closing inventory	5 direct labor-hours
Overtime hours	0
Family setup made	yes

Additional information:

There are two end-products in Product Family A (75 percent of the demand is for product 1 and the remainder is for product 2)

The plant consists of a single machining center and each end-product is processed in one operation on the machining center.

The cost to backorder one hour of production of either end-product is $100.

The production lead time for each end-product is zero.

a. Formulate this problem for solution using linear programming. Assume that a weight of 1.0 is assigned to each of the deviation variables.
b. What are the advantages and limitations of solving the master production scheduling problem separately from the production planning problem?

14. The sales manager at the Universal Manufacturing Company has prepared the following sales forecast for next year:

Sales forecast (in units)	Quarter			
Product family	1	2	3	4
A	3,500	6,000	4,000	1,300
B	1,200	2,000	2,800	3,600

The production manager has supplied the following data:

Product Family A:

Three direct labor-hours per unit of product.
Setup cost equals $3,000 per changeover from product family B.

Setup time equals 16 direct labor-hours per changeover.
Inventory carrying cost per quarter equals $.50 per one direct labor-hour of
work in inventory at the end of the quarter.
Materials cost equals $130 per direct labor-hour of production.
The beginning inventory equals zero.

Product Family B:

Two direct labor hours per unit of product.
Setup cost equals $1800 per changeover from A.
Setup time equals 24 direct labor hours per changeover.
Inventory carrying cost per quarter equals $.33 per one direct labor hour of
work left in inventory at the end of the quarter.
Materials cost equals $105 per direct labor hour of production.
The beginning inventory equals zero.

Additional information:

Hiring cost per employee equals $2000.
Firing cost per employee equals $1500.
Overtime cost per direct labor-hour equals $18.
Regular time cost per direct labor-hour equals $12.
The maximum number of regular time hours to be worked per employee per
quarter equals 600.
Employees may not work more than 20 percent of the regular time hours on
overtime each quarter.

   a. Formulate this problem for solution using mixed integer programming.
   b. Why is linear programming not appropriate for solving this production
planning problem?

15. The production planning manager at the Universal Manufacturing Company (in
problem 14) has completed work on the firm's production plan for the coming
year. He is now concerned with the preparation of the master production
schedule for the next two weeks indicating the lot size and timing for the firm's
individual products. Selected data concerning the production plan for next two
weeks for Product Family B is shown below.

Product Family B	
Item	*Plan for next two weeks*
Production level	370 direct labor hours during the 2 weeks
Closing inventory	25 direct labor hours
Overtime hours	0
Family setup made	yes

Additional information:

There are two end-products in Product Family B (60 percent of the demand
is for product 1 and the remainder is for product 2).

The plant consists of a single machining center and each end product is processed in one operation on the machining center.

The cost to backorder one hour of production of either end-product is $50. The production lead time for each end-product is zero.

a. Prepare a master production schedule for the next two weeks that conforms to the production plan.

b. What is the cost of labor, material and inventory for this master production schedule?

16

Short-term forecasting systems

Forecasts of demand are one important input to manufacturing planning and control (MPC) systems. In this chapter, we treat short-term forecasting for individual items. Applying effective forecasting systems will result in low-cost routine forecasts and a set of monitors to indicate when forecasting problems are incurred. These forecasts of end items, spare parts, and other independent demand should be a part of the front end modules of the MPC system. A key objective is to provide one, and only one, source for forecast data; this source is to be unbiased and usable by all areas in the firm.

Forecasts used for production and resource planning can be of many types, including subjective estimates, econometric models, Delphi techniques, and so on. A detailed exposition of all these is a book in itself. Although there are many techniques that could be applied to forecasting the demand for individual end items, we focus here on short-term forecasts based on observations of actual demand in the past. The chapter is organized around the following seven topics:

- The forecasting problem: How is the forecasting problem defined for manufacturing planning and control purposes?
- Basic forecasting techniques: What are the basic techniques for forecasting short-term demand?

- Enhancing the basic exponential smoothing model: How can trend, seasonality, and other kinds of information be incorporated?
- Focus forecasting: What is the focus forecasting methodology and how does it produce forecasts?
- Comparisons of methods: Which forecasting techniques work best under which conditions? What are the lessons for managers?
- Using the forecasting system: How does one select initial forecasting parameter values and monitor forecast results?
- Forecasting in industry: How have these techniques been put into practice?

This chapter has very close linkages to Chapter 10 on demand management. The forecasting activities are accomplished in the demand management module of the MPC system. In addition, Chapters 17 and 18, covering independent demand inventory management, presume the existence of effective, routine forecasting procedures.

THE FORECASTING PROBLEM

In this chapter, we deal primarily with short-term forecasting techniques of the type most useful to routine decision making in manufacturing planning and control. However, there are other decision problems both within manufacturing and in other functional areas of the firm that require different approaches to forecasting. We turn first to a brief discussion of these situations before delving more deeply into the development of short-term forecasting techniques for manufacturing. We also treat a vital forecasting question: how to evaluate the performance of a forecasting technique.

Forecasting perspectives

Managers need forecasts for a variety of decisions. Among these are long-run decisions involving such things as constructing a new plant, determining the type and size of aircraft for an airline fleet, extending the guest facilities of a hotel, or changing the curriculum requirements in a university. Generally, these longer-run decisions require forecasts of aggregate levels of demand, utilizing such measures as annual sales volume, expected passenger volume, number of guest nights, or total number of students enrolled. In a sense, this is fortunate, since aggregate levels of an activity can usually be forecast more accurately than individual activities. As an example, a university administration probably has a pretty good estimate of how many students will be enrolled next term, even though the forecast of enrollment for an elective course may be off by a considerable amount.

For aggregate forecasts, we may be able to use causal relationships and the statistical tools of regression and correlation to help us do the job. For example, sales of household fixtures are closely related to housing starts. The number of vacationers at resorts is related to the net disposable income level in the economy. In such instances, the relationship may be statistically modeled, thereby providing the basis for a forecasting procedure. Managerial insight and judgment are also used extensively in developing aggregate forecasts of future activities for long-run decisions. Both statistical and qualitative forecasting methods can also be applied for medium-run decisions, such as the annual budgeting process. It is tempting to classify forecasting techniques as long-run or short-run, but this misses the point of developing and using techniques appropriate to the decision and situation.

Throughout this chapter we will look at fairly mechanical procedures for making forecasts. Specifically, we will look at models for "casting forward" historical information to make the "fore cast." Implicit in this process is a belief that the conditions of the past that produced the historical data will not change. Although the procedures that will be developed are mechanical, one should not draw from this the impression that managers always rely exclusively on past information to make estimates of future activity. In the first place, in certain instances, we simply have no past data. This occurs, for example, when a new product is introduced. Several other examples may come to mind, but we certainly should not ignore plans for a future sales promotion, the appearance of a new competitor, or changes in legislation that will affect our business. These circumstances all illustrate the need for managerial review and modification of the forecast where there is special knowledge to take into account. This should not be lost sight of as we move into the technical aspects of the chapter.

We will largely focus our attention on techniques for converting past information into forecasts. These are often statistical techniques, and we will also use statistical methods for evaluating the quality of the forecasts. The procedures are often called statistical forecasting procedures.

Forecast evaluation

Ultimately, of course, the quality of any forecast is reflected in the quality of the decisions that are based on the forecast. This leads to the suggestion that the ideal comparison of forecasting procedures would be based on the costs of producing the forecast and the value of the forecast for the decision. From these data, the appropriate trade-off between the cost of developing and the cost of making decisions with forecasts of varying quality could be made. Unfortunately, neither of these costs is very easily measured. In addition, such a scheme suggests that a different forecasting procedure might be required for each decision, an undesirably complex possibility. As a result of these complications, we rely on some direct measures of forecast quality.

One important criterion for any forecast procedure would be a low cost per forecast. For many manufacturing planning and control problems, one needs to make forecasts for many thousands of items on a weekly or monthly basis; the result is the need for a procedure that is simple, effective, and low cost. Unlike the rare occasions when the decision is to add more factory capacity, routine short-term decisions are made frequently for many items, and cannot require an expensive, time-consuming forecasting procedure. Moreover, since the resultant decisions are made frequently, any error made in one forecast can be compensated for in the decision made next time. However, the expenditure that an aggregate long-term forecast might require may well be justified in making the factory capacity decision.

Of more general and increasing importance for computer-oriented decision systems are the storage requirements and computer time for producing forecasts. Since the forecasts may be needed for several thousands or tens of thousands of items on a relatively frequent basis, computer time and storage become an increasingly important aspect of forecast procedure evaluation. The procedures that we will focus on in this chapter all have the attribute of simplicity, are easy to use, and have low computer time/storage requirements.

For any forecasting procedure that one develops, an important characteristic is honesty, or lack of bias; that is, the procedure should produce forecasts that are neither consistently high nor consistently low. The forecasts cannot be overly optimistic or pessimistic, but, rather, should tell it like it is. Since we are dealing with projecting past data, lack of bias means smoothing out the randomness of the past data so overforecasts are offset by underforecasts. To measure bias, we will use the mean error as defined by Equation (16.1). In this equation, the forecast error in each period is the actual demand in each period minus the forecast of demand for that period. Figure 16.1 shows an example calculation of bias.

$$\text{Mean error (bias)} = \frac{\sum_{i=1}^{n} (\text{Actual demand}_i - \text{Forecast demand}_i)}{n} \qquad (16.1)$$

where:

i = Period number.
n = Number of periods of data.

$$\text{Bias} = \sum_{i=1}^{4} \text{error}_i/4 = (-100 - 200 + 300 - 100)/4$$
$$= -100/4 = -25$$

As can be seen from Figure 16.1, when the forecast errors tend to cancel one another out, the measure of bias tends to be low. The positive errors in some periods are offset by negative errors in others, which tends to produce an average error or bias near zero. In the example of Figure 16.1, there is a

FIGURE 16.1   Example bias calculation

		Period (i)			
		1	2	3	4
(1)	Actual demand	1,500	1,400	1,700	1,200
(2)	Forecast demand	1,600	1,600	1,400	1,300
	Error (1) − (2)	−100	−200	300	−100

bias and the demand was overforecast by an average of 25 units per period for the four periods.

Having unbiased forecasts is important in manufacturing planning and control, since the estimates, on the average, are about right. But that is not enough. We still need to be concerned with the magnitude of the errors. Note that, for the example in Figure 16.1, we would obtain the identical measure of bias if the actual demand for the four periods had been 100, 100, 5,500, and 100, respectively (see Figure 16.2). However, the individual errors are much larger, and this difference would have to be reflected in buffer inventories if one were to maintain a consistent level of customer service.

Let us now turn to a widely used measure of forecast error, the mean absolute deviation (MAD). The formula is given as Equation (16.2), and example calculations are shown in Figure 16.2.

$$\text{Mean absolute deviation (MAD)} = \frac{\sum\limits_{i=1}^{n}|\text{Actual demand}_i - \text{Forecast demand}_i|}{n} \quad (16.2)$$

where:

i = Period number.
n = Number of periods of data.
$|x|$ = Absolute value of x.

The mean absolute deviation expresses the size of the average error irrespective of whether it is positive or negative. It is the combination of bias and MAD that allows one to evaluate forecasting results. Bias is perhaps the most critical, since forecast errors can be compensated for through safety stocks, expediting, faster delivery means, and other kinds of responses. MAD gives an indication of the size of the expected compensation (e.g., required safety stock). However, if a forecast is consistently lower than demand, the entire material-flow pipeline will run dry; it will be necessary to start over again with raw materials. Similar issues exist for a consistently high forecast. The great advantage of the techniques described in this chapter is that they tend to be unbiased. Moreover, routine monitoring tech-

FIGURE 16.2   Sample MAD calculations

	Period (i)			
	1	2	3	4
(1) Actual demand	1,500	1,400	1,700	1,200
(2) Forecast demand	1,600	1,600	1,400	1,300
Error (1) − (2)	−100	−200	300	−100

$$\text{MAD} = \sum_{i=1} |error_i|/4 = (|-100| + |-200| + |300| + |-100|)/4 = 175$$

$$(16.2)$$

	Period (i)			
	1	2	3	4
(1) Actual demand	100	100	5,500	100
(2) Forecast demand	1,600	1,600	1,400	1,300
Error (1) − (2)	−1,500	−1,500	4,100	−1,200

$$\text{Bias} = \sum_{i=1}^{4} error_i/4 = (-1500 - 1500 + 4100 - 1200)/4$$
$$= -100/4 = -25 \qquad (16.1)$$

$$\text{MAD} = \sum_{i=1}^{4} |error_i|/4$$
$$= (|-1,500| + |-1,500| + |4,100| + |-1,200|)/4$$
$$= 8,300/4 = 2,075 \qquad (16.2)$$

niques identify bias when it is present. Judgmental forecasts, such as those made by marketing groups, are often biased because the forecasting incorporates other goals (e.g., stimulate the sales force). The key is to clearly separate the *process* of forecasting from the *use* of forecasting. The goals for the process are no bias and minimum MAD. What is *done* with the forecast is another issue.

Before turning to the techniques, there is one other relationship that needs to be made. MAD is a measure of error or deviation from an expected result (the forecast). The best-known measure of deviation or dispersion from statistics is the standard deviation. When the errors are distributed normally, the standard deviation of the forecast errors is arithmetically related to MAD by Equation (16.3).

$$\text{Standard deviation of forecast errors} = 1.25 \text{ MAD} \qquad (16.3)$$

BASIC FORECASTING TECHNIQUES

Now that we have identified the objectives of forecasting procedures, let us turn to some procedures that meet the objectives. In this section, we will introduce some of the basic concepts that lie behind two very common short-term forecasting techniques: moving averages and exponential smoothing. Before we discuss these techniques, however, we present an example problem that allows us to continually relate the concepts and formulas to a real-world context.

Example forecasting situation

Enrique Martinez is manager of one of the restaurants located in a large hotel near the Loop in Chicago. The restaurant, Panchos, caters both to guests of the hotel and to local street traffic. Pancho's reputation has been growing, and, a few months ago, the restaurant's capacity was expanded. Enrique was studying ways to improve and routinize his decisions for managing the restaurant operations, and he chose three situations to study in some detail: a new contract offer from his linen service, the trend in tequila-based drinks, and his twice weekly orders to the local wholesale grocery distributor. All of these decisions depended upon his ability to forecast demand. Although the decision in each situation involves placing orders, each presents quite a different forecasting problem. With the variety he had chosen, Enrique felt that he had a good basis for studying forecasting methods for Panchos.

The first situation involved a new contract proposal for tablecloths and napkins from the linen supply service with which the restaurant did business. The owner of the linen supply firm offered an attractive discount if Enrique would prespecify the quantity he wanted each week, rather than continuing the current practice whereby the linen supply firm had to bring enough clean linen to replace whatever quantity of dirty linen there might be each week. Enrique collected data on the number of tables served during the last few weeks as the basis for determining how to forecast his needs. These data are summarized in Figure 16.3.

Before going on to the forecasting techniques, it is worth reiterating a point: We are *not* presently dealing with the decision of how to order table-

---

FIGURE 16.3   Number of tables served during the last nine weeks

	Week number								
	24	25	26	27	28	29	30	31	32
Tables served	1,600	1,500	1,700	900	1,100	1,500	1,400	1,700	1,200

FIGURE 16.4   Number of tequila-based drinks served during the last nine weeks

	Week number								
	24	25	26	27	28	29	30	31	32
Number of drinks	16	71	40	85	196	351	254	261	364

cloths, how many to hold as safety stock, or any other decision. We are simply trying to forecast demand. The premise is that a *good* forecast will allow for better decisions, but we are not combining the act of forecasting with any decision.

The orders for tequila-based drinks in the lounge had been growing rapidly, creating a problem in determining how much tequila to order from the supplier for delivery each week. The number of tequila-based drinks served in each of the last several weeks was collected by Enrique and is presented in Figure 16.4.

The final activity that Enrique chose to review was that of deciding how much to order for the twice weekly delivery from the local wholesale grocery distributor. The distributor delivered on Tuesday (Panchos was closed on Mondays) and Friday mornings. The deliveries consisted of canned goods, staples, condiments, and so on for use during the next three days. There was a substantially smaller volume of business during the first three days of the business week than during the last three. To get an idea of what the pattern might be, Enrique kept track of the usage of number 10 cans of vegetables for each of six three-day periods. The data are shown in Figure 16.5.

Figure 16.6 is a plot of the number of tables served from the data given in Figure 16.3. The number appears relatively stable (for the last nine weeks for which we have data) and seems to fluctuate randomly about some central value. If we were interested in using these past data to forecast the number of tables that would be served in future weeks, a tempting procedure would be to simply draw a line through the data points and use that line as our estimate for week 33 and subsequent weeks. This would produce an estimate of the average or expected demand in future weeks, and the process of draw-

FIGURE 16.5   Number 10 cans of vegetables used during the last six three-day periods

	F–S–Sun	T–W–Th	F–S–Sun	T–W–Th	F–S–Sun	T–W–Th
Week number	29	30	30	31	31	32
Number of cans	48	35	47	30	51	37

FIGURE 16.6   Plot of number of tables served at Panchos during last nine weeks

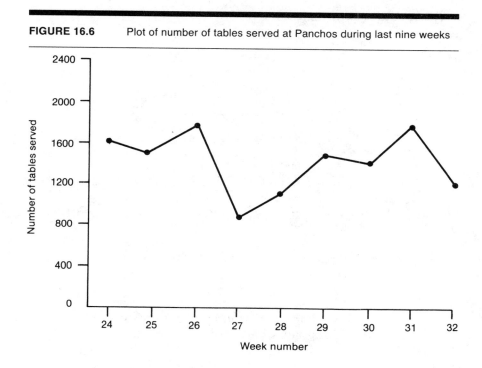

ing that line is an averaging or smoothing process. The process removes fluctuations around the line and focuses on the underlying average. It is this smoothing process that provides the basis for the techniques to which we now turn our attention.

Moving averages

Rather than draw a line through the points in Figure 16.6 to find the average, we could simply calculate the arithmetic average of the nine historical observations. Since we are interested in averaged past data to project into the future, we could use an average of all the past demand data that were available for forecasting purposes. There are several reasons, however, why this may not be a desirable way of smoothing. In the first place, there may be so many periods of past data that storing them all is an issue. Second, it is often true that the most recent history is of most relevance in forecasting the short-term demand in the near future. Recent data may reveal current conditions better than do data that are several months or years old. For these reasons, many firms use the concept of a moving average for forecasting demand.

The moving average model for smoothing historical demand proceeds, as

FIGURE 16.7 Example moving average calculations

			Period			
	27	28	29	30	31	32
Actual demand	900	1,100	1,500	1,400	1,700	1,200

$$\text{6-period MAF made at the end of period 32} = \sum_{27}^{32} \text{Actual demand}/6$$

$$= (900 + 1,100 + 1,500 + 1,400 + 1,700 + 1,200)/6 = 1,300 \qquad (16.4)$$

$$\text{3-period MAF made at the end of period 32} = \sum_{30}^{32} \text{Actual demand}/3$$

$$= (1,400 + 1,700 + 1,200)/3 = 1,433 \qquad (16.4)$$

the name implies, by averaging a selected number of past periods of data. The average moves because a new average can be calculated whenever a period's demand is determined. Whenever a forecast is needed, the most recent past history of demand will be used to do the averaging. The model for finding the moving average is shown in Equation (16.4). The equation shows that the moving average forecast always uses the most recent n periods of historical information available for developing the forecast. Notice that the moving average is the forecast of demand for the next and subsequent periods. This timing convention needs to be clearly understood. One is standing at the end of period t; forecasts are made for periods $t + 1$, or $t + X$ periods into the future. Forecasts are *not* made for period T—the demand for that period is known. Figure 16.7 shows sample calculations for the number of tables served.

$$\text{Moving average forecast (MAF) at the end of period } t\text{: } MAF_t = \sum_{i=t-n+1}^{t} \text{Actual demand}_i/n \qquad (16.4)$$

where:

- i = Period number.
- t = Current period (the period for which the most recent actual demand is known).
- n = Number of periods of moving average.

The basic exponential smoothing model

You will note that the moving average model does smooth the historical data, but it does so with an equal weight on each piece of historical information. Thus, if one were at the end of period 29 with that demand (1,500) known, and the demands for periods 30 and beyond unknown, the three-period moving average forecast for period 30 would be (900 + 1,100 + 1,500)/3 = 1,167. At the end of period 30, the forecast for period 31 would be (1,100 + 1,500 + 1,400)/3 = 1,333. If one looks at a single period's demand, such as the 1,500 in period 29, it is used *only* for forecasts made at the end of periods 29, 30, and 31. In each case, the 1,500 has a weight in the forecast of one third. For forecasts made before the end of period 29 or after the end of period 32, this piece of demand data has no weight.

The exponential smoothing model for forecasting does not eliminate *any* past datum, but so adjusts the weights given to past data that older data get increasingly less weight (hence the name exponential smoothing). The basic idea is a fairly simple one and has a great deal of intuitive appeal. Each forecast is based on an average which is corrected each time there is a forecast error. For example, if we forecast 90 units of demand for an item in a particular period and the actual demand for that item turns out to be 100 units, an appealing idea would be to increase our forecast by some portion of the 10-unit error in making the next period's forecast. In this way, if the error indicated that demand was changing, we would begin to change the forecast. We may not want to incorporate the entire error (i.e., add 10 units), since the error may have just been due to the random variations around the mean. The proportion of the error that will be incorporated into the forecast is called the exponential smoothing constant, and is identified as α. The model for computing the new average is shown in Equation (16.5) as we have just described it. The most common computational form of the exponentially smoothed average is given in Equation (16.6). The new exponentially smoothed average is again the forecast for the next and subsequent periods. The same timing convention is used; that is, the forecast is made at the end of period t for period $t + X$ in the future. Figure 16.8 shows example calculations for the number of tables served.

Exponential smoothing forecast (ESF) at the end of period t:

$$ESF_t = ESF_{t-1} + \alpha \, (\text{Actual demand}_t - ESF_{t-1}) \qquad (16.5)$$
$$= \alpha \, (\text{Actual demand}_t) + (1 - \alpha)ESF_{t-1} \qquad (16.6)$$

where:

α = The smoothing constant ($0 \leqslant \alpha \leqslant 1$).

t = Current period (the period for which the most recent actual demand is known).

ESF_{t-1} = Exponential smoothing forecast made one period previously (at the end of period $t - 1$).

A comparison of exponential smoothing and moving average forecasting procedures can be seen in an example. A five-period MAF is compared to

---

FIGURE 16.8   Example exponential smoothing calculations

	Period	
	27	*28*
Actual demand	900	1,100

Assume:

ESF_{26} = Exponential smoothing forecast made at the end of period 26 = 1,000, α = .1

ESF_{27} (made at the end of period 27 when the actual demand for period 27 is known but the actual demand in period 28 is not known) =

$1,000 + .1(900 - 1,000) = 990$	(16.5)
$.1(900) + (1 - .1)1,000 = 990$	(16.6)

$ESF_{28} = .1(1,100) + (1 - .1)990 = 1001$	(16.6)

FIGURE 16.9   Relative weights given to past demand by a moving average and exponential smoothing model

	Period								
	20	*21*	*22*	*23*	*24*	*25*	*26*	*27**	*28*
5-period MAF weights	0%	0%	0%	20%	20%	20%	20%	20%	—
ESF weights (α = .3)	2%	4%	5%	7%	10%	15%	21%	30%	—

*Forecast made at the end of period 27.

---

an ESF with α = .3 in Figure 16.9. In the preparation of the forecast for period 28, the five-period MAF would apply a 20 percent weight to each of the five most recent actual demands. The ESF model (with α = .3) would apply a 30 percent weight to the actual demand of period 27 as seen here:

$$ESF_{27} = \text{Period 28 forecast} = .3 \text{ (period 27 actual demand)} + .7 \text{ } (ESF_{26})$$

By looking at the ESF made for period 27, at the end of period 26 (i.e., ESF_{26}), we see that it was determined as:

$$ESF_{26} = .3 \text{ (period 26 actual demand)} + .7 \text{ } (ESF_{25})$$

By substitution, ESF_{27} can be shown to be:

$$ESF_{27} = .3 \text{ (period 27 actual demand)}$$
$$+ .7 [.3 \text{ (period 26 actual demand)} + .7 \text{ } (ESF_{25})]$$

This results in a weight of .21 (.7 × .3) being applied to the actual demand in period 26 when the forecast for periods 28 and beyond is made at the end of period 27. By similar substitution, the entire line for the exponential smoothing weights in Figure 16.9 can be derived.

Figure 16.9 shows that, for the forecast made at the end of period 27, 30 percent of the weight is attached to the actual demand in period 27, 21 percent for period 26, and 15 percent for period 25. The sum of these weights, 66 percent, is the weight placed on the last three periods of demand. The sum of all of the weights given for the ESF model in Figure 16.9 is 94 percent. If one continued to find the weights for periods 19, 18, and so on, the sum for all weights is 1.0, which is what intuition would tell us. If the smoothing constant were .1 instead of .3, a table like Figure 16.9 would have values of .1, .09, and .081 for the weights of periods 27, 26, and 25, respectively. The sum of these three (27 percent) is the weight placed on the last three periods. Moreover, $(1 - 27\% = 73\%)$ is the weight given to all actual data *more than* three periods old.

This result shows that larger values of α give more weight to recent demands and utilize older demand data less than is the case for smaller values of α; that is, larger values of α provide more responsive forecasts and smaller values produce more stable forecasts. The same argument can be made for the number of periods in an MAF model. More periods provide more stable but less responsive forecasts. This points out the basic trade-off in determining what smoothing constant (or length of moving average) to use in a forecasting procedure. The higher the smoothing constant or the shorter the moving average, the more responsive the forecasts are to the changes in the underlying demand, but the more "nervous" they are in the presence of randomness. Similarly, smaller smoothing constants or longer moving averages provide stability in the face of randomness but slow reactions to changes in the underlying demand.

ENHANCING THE BASIC EXPONENTIAL SMOOTHING MODEL

Thus far, the exponential smoothing model we have described assumes demand is essentially constant, with only random variations around an average. However, if we have any indication of a pattern underlying the randomness of demand, it is important that it be taken into account to improve our forecast accuracy. Two broad categories of factors might explain nonrandom patterns. The first category of factors includes characteristics of the marketplace, such as cycles and seasonal or trend patterns in demand. Note these need not be natural but could be induced by events like new model introductions or special shows. The second broad category of nonrandom patterns are results of plans we may have for future events that will influence demand. These events could consist of special product promotions, timing of a major customer's orders, special ordering requirements for customers, or new product announcements by either ourselves or our competitors. In this section, we will first look at the changes that can be made to an exponential smoothing model to incorporate market factors, and we will close with methods for taking into account plans or knowledge of events that will affect future demand.

Trend enhancement

The first market characteristic we will take into account is a trend in the demand for the product. This is represented by the increase in tequila-based drinks that Enrique Martinez faces. A cursory glance at the demand for tequila-based drinks (see Figure 16.4) indicates a substantial growth (trend) in demand. To take the trend into account explicitly, we need a method for making an estimate of the trend (i.e., the amount of change in basic demand from period to period). Thinking again of drawing a line through the data to make a smoothed estimate of the trend leads us to consider using smoothing procedures to make the estimate. As a first step in the process of developing the estimate of the trend, we use exponential smoothing to smooth the random fluctuations and create a new base value. As was true with the basic model, we perform the calculations as soon as we find out what actual demand was during the period; that is, at the end of the period. The method for computing the new base value is shown in Equation (16.7).

$$\text{Base value}_t = \alpha\,(\text{Actual demand}_t) +$$
$$(1 - \alpha)(\text{Base value}_{t-1} + \text{Trend}_{t-1}) \quad (16.7)$$

where:

α = Base smoothing constant $(0 \le \alpha \le 1)$.
t = Current period (the period for which the most recent actual demand is known).
Base value_{t-1} = Base value computed one period previously (at the end of period $t - 1$).
Trend_{t-1} = Trend value computed one period previously (at the end of period $t - 1$).

Once the new base value for this period is determined, we apply exponential smoothing to develop the most current estimate of the trend value. A second smoothing constant is introduced to do this, β, and is applied as shown in Equation (16.8).

$$\text{Trend}_t = \beta\,(\text{Base value}_t - \text{Base value}_{t-1}) + (1 - \beta)(\text{Trend}_{t-1}) \quad (16.8)$$

where:

β = Trend smoothing constant $(0 \le \beta \le 1)$.
Base value_t = Base value computed at the end of period t.

Base value$_{t-1}$ = Base value computed one period previously (at the end of period $t - 1$).

Trend$_{t-1}$ = Trend value computed one period previously (at the end of period $t - 1$).

Once the most current trend value and the new base value have been determined, trend-enhanced forecasts of future demand can be made. The method for doing this is given as Equation (16.9). Notice that this equation can be used to forecast for more than one period in the future by multiplying the trend value by the number of periods in the future. Figure 16.10 provides sample calculations.

Trend-enhanced forecast (TEF) for X periods in the future at the end of period t:

$$TEF_{t+x} = \text{Base value}_t + X\,(\text{Trend}_t) \tag{16.9}$$

where:

X = Number of periods beyond period t for which the forecast is desired.

t = Current period for which actual demand is known.

Base value$_t$ = Exponentially smoothed base value computed at the end of period t.

Trend$_t$ = Exponentially smoothed estimate of trend per period computed at the end of period t.

An alternative to the TEF model might be to use the ESF with a high smoothing constant, since we noted how high values of the smoothing constant were responsive to changes in demand. In fact, this alternative will not

---

FIGURE 16.10   Example trend-enhanced forecast calculations

Data: $\alpha = .2$, $\beta = .1$, Trend$_{t-1}$ = 5, Base value$_{t-1}$ = 100

TEF$_t$ (that is, the trend-enhanced forecast made at the end of period $t - 1$ before actual demand for period t was known) =

TEF$_t$ = Base value$_{t-1}$ + Trend$_{t-1}$ = 100 + 5 = 105

At the end of period t, the demand for period t becomes known:
Actual demand$_t$ = 107

We now produce forecasts using equations (16.7), (16.8), and (16.9).

$$\text{Base value}_t = .2(107) + (1 - .2)(100 + 5) = 105.4 \tag{16.7}$$

$$\text{Trend}_t = .1(105.4 - 100) + (1 - .1)(5) = 5.04 \tag{16.8}$$

$$\text{Forecast for next period (i.e., TEF}_{t+1}) = 105.4 + (1)5.04 = 110.44 \tag{16.9}$$

$$\text{Forecast for four periods from now (i.e., TEF}_{t+4}) = 105.4 + (4)5.04 = 125.56 \tag{16.9}$$

FIGURE 16.11 Comparison of trend-enhanced and basic exponential smoothing models

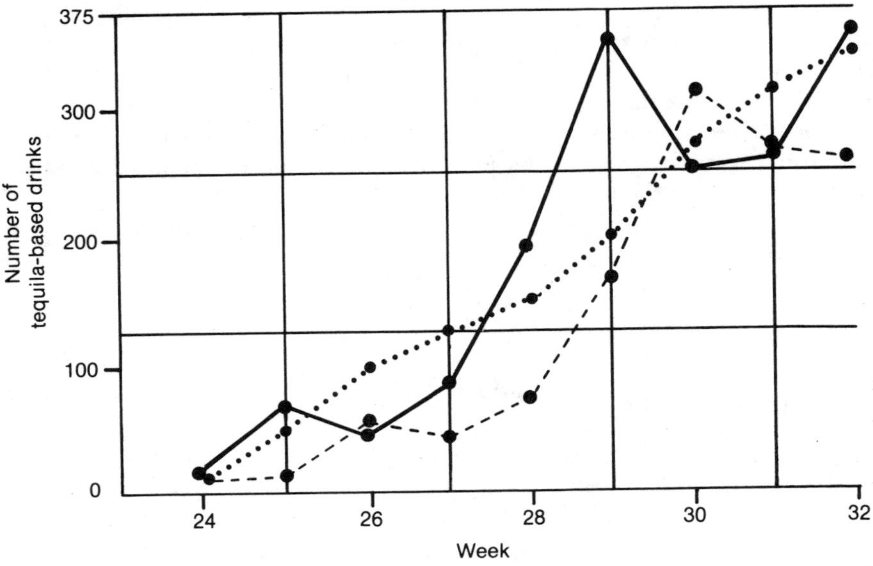

Symbol	Forecast	Bias	MAD
●——————●	Actual demand		
●······●	Trend enhanced $\alpha = .2$, $\beta = .2$	7.26	45.81
●— — —●	Basic model $\alpha = .8$	45.50	65.08

produce results that are as good as the TEF when there is a definitive trend component in the demand. This can be seen in Figure 16.11, which compares an ESF with $\alpha = .8$ and a TEF ($\alpha = .2$, $\beta = .2$) for the tequila-based drink data. As noted, the TEF approach produces better measures of both bias and MAD. By looking at the graph, you will see that the ESF lags the actual demand, which leads to a much higher bias.

Figure 16.11 clearly demonstrates the advantage of explicitly including information about patterns in demand when such patterns do, in fact, exist. However, the opposite statement is also true: If a pattern in demand does not clearly exist, then using a model that assumes such a pattern will lead to poor forecasts. For example, if the TEF model were applied to the data for tables served at Panchos (Figure 16.6), the result could be larger values for both bias and MAD than those obtained with an appropriate ESF.

Seasonal enhancement

Many products have a seasonal demand pattern. We can all think of examples like baseballs, skis, lawn furniture, antifreeze, holiday greeting cards, and so on. Perhaps less obvious are seasons for a product or service during a day, week, or month—like increased bank deposits on paydays—travel on the weekend (or mornings and evenings), mail deposits on Friday afternoons, or long-distance phone calls during the day. A useful indication of the degree of seasonal variation for a product is the seasonal index. This index is an estimate of how much the demand during a season will be above or below the average demand for the product. For example, a bathing-suit line may sell 100 units a month on the average, but 150 suits a month in peak season and 75 in the off-season. The index for peak season sales would be 1.50 and 0.75 for the off-season for bathing suits. The seasonal index is used to adjust forecasts for seasonal patterns.

Much the same kind of logic that was used for adjusting for the trend is applied in adjusting for the seasonality of a product. As before, we will use exponential smoothing to estimate the seasonal indexes of demand for a product. A seasonal pattern during the week is quite clear in the number 10 cans of vegetables used during three-day periods at Panchos (Figure 16.5). Demand is much less in the early part of the week than it is in the latter part of the week. Enrique's forecasting model should take this into account. The seasonally enhanced forecasting procedure (SEF) again involves updating some new base value at the end of some period t. Next, there is an updating of the seasonal index that applies to the period just past. Finally, there is a forecast of demand one or more periods in the future based upon the latest base value and the appropriate seasonal index for the period to be forecast. The formulas for updating the base value and seasonal index are shown as Equations (16.10) and (16.11). The first equation produces the new base by exponentially smoothing the "deseasonalized" demand data (i.e., the actual demand divided by the seasonal index), and the second equation uses another smoothing constant to produce an updated estimate of the seasonal index for the period just past.

$$\text{Base value}_t = \alpha \left(\frac{\text{Actual demand}_t}{\text{Old index}_s} \right) + (1 - \alpha)(\text{Base value}_{t-1}) \quad (16.10)$$

$$\text{New index}_s = \gamma \left(\frac{\text{Actual demand}_t}{\text{Base value}_t} \right) + (1 - \gamma)(\text{Old index}_s) \quad (16.11)$$

where:

α = Smoothing constant for base value.
γ = Smoothing constant for seasonal indexes.
s = Season indicator.

Base value$_{t-1}$ = Base value computed one period previously (at the end of period$_{t-1}$).

Old index$_s$ = Index value for season s, calculated one full cycle ago.

The updating of the base at the end of period t is similar to that done for the TEF model, except the actual demand is first deseasonalized. A seasonal index is maintained and updated for however many periods are included in a cycle of demand. For the number 10 cans of vegetables, there would be two seasonal indexes, one for the three-day period of F–S–Sun, and the other for T–W–Th. For a monthly series in an annual cycle, there would be 12 seasonal indexes, each updated when that month's actual demand became available and used to forecast that month in the future whenever the forecast is desired.

The method for forecasting demand is to multiply the updated base value obtained using Equation (16.10) by the appropriate seasonal index. This is shown as Equation (16.12) and examples are given in Figure 16.12. Seasonal enhanced forecast (SEF) for season s in the future at the end of period t:

$$SEF_s = \text{Base value}_t \, (\text{Index}_s) \qquad (16.12)$$

where:

Base value$_t$ = most recent deseasonalized base value at the end of period t.

Index$_s$ = seasonal index associated with the season s.

If Pancho's wanted to forecast the demand for number 10 cans of vegetables for the next F–S–Sun period now (i.e., at the end of period 5 before the actual demand for period 6 is known); using the data from Figure 16.12:

$$SEF_7 = 40.5(1.23) = 49.8 \qquad (16.12)$$

Trend and seasonal enhancement

A logical extension of either trend enhancement or seasonal enhancement is a model that incorporates both patterns in demand. Without going into a

---

FIGURE 16.12   Example seasonal-enhanced forecast calculations

---

Data: $\alpha = .2$, $\gamma = .3$, old index$_{F-S-Sun}$ = 1.22, old index$_{T-W-Th}$ = .77

Base value$_4$ = 40.2, Actual demand$_5$ = 51 (this was a F–S–Sun)

Base value$_5$ = .2(51/1.22) + (1 − .2)(40.2) = 40.5   (16.10)

New index$_{F-S-Sun}$ = .3(51/40.5) + (1 − .3)1.22 = 1.23   (16.11)

SEF_6 = 40.5(.77) = 31.2 (this was a T–W–Th)   (16.12)

---

detailed explanation, the approach is to first apply an expanded version of Equation (16.10) to update the base value; this is shown as Equation (16.13). Next, the seasonal index is computed with Equation (16.11) as before, and the trend component is updated with Equation (16.8). Finally, the forecast Equation (16.14) incorporates the trend enhancement from Equation (16.9) and the seasonal enhancement from Equation (16.12). The entire sequence would be:

$$\text{Base value}_t = \alpha \left(\frac{\text{Actual demand}_t}{\text{Old index}_s} \right) +$$
$$(1 - \alpha)(\text{Base value}_{t-1} + \text{Trend}_{t-1}) \qquad (16.13)$$

$$\text{New index}_s = \gamma \left(\frac{\text{Actual demand}_t}{\text{Base value}_t} \right) + (1 - \gamma)(\text{Old index}_s) \qquad (16.11)$$

$$\text{Trend}_t = \beta (\text{Base value}_t - \text{Base value}_{t-1})$$
$$+ (1 - \beta)(\text{Trend}_{t-1}) \qquad (16.8)$$

Trend seasonal enhanced forecast (TSEF) for X periods in the future at the end of period t:

$$\text{TSEF}_{t+X} = (\text{Base value}_t + X \text{ trend}_t) \text{ Index}_{t+X-m} \qquad (16.14)$$

where:

Base value_t = Most recent deseasonalized base value at the end of period t.

Index_s = Seasonal index for the season s.

Trend_t = Trend estimate per period calculated at the end of period t.

X = Number of periods beyond period t for which the forecast is desired.

m = Number of periods in the seasonal cycle.

The subscript on the index in Equation (16.14) is worthy of an additional note. The forecast is made at the end of period t, for X periods into the future; hence, $t + X$. The subtraction of m moves the index subscript back to the seasonal value computed at the end of that last season in the cycle. For example, if, at the end of month 5 (May), one wished to forecast for August, the index subscript would be $5 + 3 - 12$, or the seasonal index computed nine months previously at the end of the preceding August.

Other enhancements

We have illustrated the use of multiplicative seasonal factors and additive trend factors. Other approaches have used additive seasonality and/or multiplicative trend. Still other approaches allow for acceleration, which would be applicable to fad products; others utilize the fitting of mathematical functions, such as sine waves to past data. The point is, *if* a genuine pattern in the underlying demand exists, then a model that incorporates this pattern can produce better forecasts. We saw this in Figure 16.11, comparing a trend model and the basic exponential smoothing model for the tequila-based drink data. A similar comparison could be made for the vegetables, using models with and without seasonal enhancement. However, once again we caution against use of these enhanced models if the underlying data do not clearly support their application. We know of a firm that has a definitive seasonal sales pattern with growth—when one is talking about overall sales in dollars. However, the same demand pattern does not exist for many of the individual items in this company.

FOCUS FORECASTING

Two observations lie behind the development of the focus forecasting technique. The first is that the forecasting approach that worked best last time may work best this time. The second observation is that persons experienced in making short-term forecasts tend to use simple models. Bernard Smith developed focus forecasting by putting these two concepts together in a forecasting system.

Focus forecasting uses the *one* forecasting model that would have performed the best in the recent past to make the next forecast. The procedure starts by simulating the forecasts of past periods for a variety of simple forecasting models. Next, the performance that would have been achieved in preceding periods by each of these models is reviewed. Finally, the model that would have had the best performance in the past is used for forecasting the next period.

The focus forecasting procedure works with rolling quarterly data. The mean absolute percentage error (MAPE) is the criterion used to choose the forecasting model for making the next forecast. MAPE is defined as the absolute error (as was used in Equation (16.2) to calculate MAD) divided by the actual demand. The model with the lowest value of MAPE for the last quarter is used to make the forecast for the next quarter.

The models used in the focus forecasting system are ones that have actually been used successfully in practice. They should be understood by the personnel responsible for producing the forecasts. The models are, therefore, quite straightforward approaches to forecasting. Typical of the models used in the system are:

1. The forecast for the next quarter is the actual demand for the same three-month period last year.
2. The forecast for the next quarter is 110 percent of the actual demand for the same three-month period last year.

3. The forecast for the next quarter is half the total actual demand for the last six months (a two-quarter moving average).

4. The forecast for the next quarter is the actual demand for the previous three-month period.

5. The forecast for the next quarter is the actual demand for the same three-month period last year multiplied by the growth or decline since last year as measured by the ratio of the demand for the previous quarter to the demand for the same quarter last year.

6. If the demand in the last six months is less than 40 percent of the demand for the six months preceding that, the forecast for the next quarter is 110 percent of the demand for the same three-month period last year (i.e., we are coming into the upturn of a seasonal swing).

7. If the demand in the last six months is more than 2.5 times the demand for the six months preceding that, the forecast for the next quarter is the same as the demand for the same three-month period last year (i.e., we are starting into the downside of a seasonal swing).

COMPARISONS OF METHODS

At one time we had intended to devote a whole chapter to advanced forecasting techniques. We abandoned that idea after reviewing the work of Spyros Makridakis and his colleagues. Their research and some later work evaluating focus forecasting will be overviewed here. The results contain a key message for practice. Simple models usually outperform more complex procedures, especially for short-term forecasting.

The forecasting competition

A variety of forecasting techniques have been developed and more are being created all the time. They range from very simple to mathematically complex, from aggregate-business oriented to stockkeeping-unit oriented, and from very costly to inexpensive. Among the techniques at the business planning level are those involving expert opinion and consensus, causal or regression approaches that link activities in one sector with those in another sector, and economic or business analysis approaches. For the more operations-oriented forecasts, the techniques range from attempts to characterize past data by using mathematical approaches (e.g., spectral analysis, Box-Jenkins, or trigonometric patterns) to simple projections of past performance using moving averages or exponential smoothing.

Spyros Makridakis organized a forecasting competition in which seven experts evaluated 21 forecasting models. The competition was based on 1,001 different actual time series. Some of these were yearly, some quarterly, and still others monthly. Some of the series were microdata (e.g., for business firms, divisions, or subdivisions), and others were for macrodata (e.g., GNP or its major components). Some series were comprised of seasonal data and others were not. Expert proponents of a variety of forecasting models analyzed the data, determined appropriate model parameters, and made forecasts of the series. The length of the forecasting horizon was varied from 1 to 18 periods into the future. Accuracy of the forecasts was determined with five different measures.

There was no one model that consistently outperformed all the others for all series, all measures, or all forecasting horizons. Some models do better than others on macrodata, while others are better for microdata. Similarly, some models were better for monthly data than for quarterly or yearly data, and still others were good for longer forecasting horizons. Therefore, one conclusion that comes out of this work is that a forecast user can improve forecast accuracy by choosing a model that fits the criterion and the environment in which he or she is interested (e.g., microdata versus macrodata, short versus long horizon, and measure of accuracy).

Since we are concerned here with short-term horizons, the general conclusion that simple methods do better than the more sophisticated models, especially over short horizons for microdata, is an important one. Such techniques as simple exponential smoothing tend to outperform sophisticated methods, such as Box-Jenkins or econometric models.

A summary of the rankings for some of the procedures (for one period forecasting horizons) is given in Figure 16.13. For most of the criteria shown, the exponential smoothing models do quite well. Figure 16.13 is for all the 1,001 data series; the best techniques do even better for just the microdata. One of the surprises of the research is the performance of the combination technique. It indicates that the focused forecasting idea of selecting the *one* forecasting technique with the lowest error to make the forecast was partially right. It might be even better to average the forecasts from the several models that are used each period.

The focus forecasting comparison

To further test the idea that averaging might be better than choosing a single technique, Flores and Whybark performed an experiment involving focus forecasting and an average of all the models' forecasts. Since the focus forecasting approach requires that several forecasting models be in place anyway, averaging the forecasts from all the models was a simple extension of the technique. Averaging could lead to better results—and is also consistent with the desire for simplicity and understandability.

A focus forecasting system comprised of the seven models listed earlier in the chapter was used as the basis for the experiment. The focus forecasting results were compared to the results of averaging all the forecasts, and a

FIGURE 16.13   Performance rank for forecasting techniques among 21 methods for a one-period planning horizon

Criterion*

Method (all adjusted for seasonality)	MAPE (mean average percent error)	MSE (mean squared error)	Average ranking relative to all other techniques	Median APE (median value of percentage error)
Naive (forecast = current actual)	7	17	8	8
Moving average	15	20	10	11
Simple exponential smoothing	3	13	7	7
Exponential smoothing with trend	4	7	2	4
Exponential smoothing with trend and seasonal factors	4	7	2	2
Combination (an average of the forecasts from six methods)	1	10	1	1

*The best performance on the criterion is 1, the worst is 21.
Source: Makridakis et al., "The Accuracy of Extrapolation (Time Series) Methods: Results of a Forecasting Competition," *Journal of Forecasting* 1, no. 2 (1982).

basic exponential smoothing model was used as a point of comparison. Both simulated and actual demand data were used to test the approaches.

MAD and MAPE were used as criteria to evaluate the forecasting performance of the three procedures. The results were the same for both criteria. For the simulated demand data, there were strongly significant differences between all three procedures—going from averaging (best) to exponential smoothing (worst). The rankings were changed and the level of significance reduced when the actual data were used, however. Exponential smoothing performed best, but focus forecasting and averaging were not statistically different.

The pragmatic implications of these experiments are clear. Forecasting actual demand is difficult. Unfortunately, the results do not provide a consistently superior choice of forecasting technique. The results, though, support the use of simple forecasting models.

The important conclusion for practitioners is that more sophisticated and expensive is not necessarily better. It means that those who advocate the use of complex forecasting models need to justify their choice. They need to clearly demonstrate that they can provide better forecasts than the simpler procedures, and that the error measures are consistent with the needs of the forecasts. This "show-me" attitude becomes even more important when one considers the preparation cost for using many of the sophisticated models. In addition to computer and other costs, one should also add the cost to the organization of using a procedure that is difficult for the nonexpert to understand.

USING THE FORECASTING SYSTEM

Using the forecasting system requires a heavy dose of common sense, as well as the application of techniques. In this section, we will look at some methods for incorporating external information into the forecasting system. We will also look at the problem of establishing the forecasting model parameters and of monitoring the forecasting model results. In exponential smoothing, it is not enough to determine the demand patterns and to select the forecasting model that appears to provide minimum bias and MAD. Before we can start making forecasts, it is necessary to choose the smoothing constants and to establish the initial base value, trend value, and seasonal indexes. Once forecasting has started, of course, these initial values are recalculated with each new piece of demand information.

But we are still not done! It is necessary to continue evaluating the quality of the forecasts to make sure the model chosen is still appropriate, to determine whether market conditions have changed, and to learn quickly when something has gone awry. It is to the topics of external information, getting started and monitoring, that we first turn our attention. Thereafter, we briefly raise some strategic issues relating to forecasting.

Incorporating external information

Many kinds of information can and should be used to make good forecasts. For example, in a college town on the day of a football game, traffic around the stadium is a mess. An intelligent forecaster adjusts travel plans on game days to avoid the stadium traffic, if possible. He or she modifies the forecast because of knowledge of the football game's impact on traffic. An exponential smoothing model based upon observations during the week would probably forecast very little traffic around the stadium. We certainly would not use the exponential smoothing forecast without adjusting it for game day. That simple principle is applicable to business forecasting as well, but it is surprising how often people fail to make these adjustments.

Examples of activities that will influence demand and perhaps invalidate the routine forecasting model are special promotions, product changes, competitors' actions, and economic changes. There are two primary ways information about such future activities can be incorporated into the forecast. The first is to change the forecast directly and the second is to change the forecasting model. We might use the first method if we knew, for example, that there was to be a promotion of a product in the future, or that we were going to open more retail outlets, or that we were going to introduce a competing product. In these instances, we could adjust the forecast directly to account for the activities, just as we do for the game day. By recognizing explicitly that future conditions will not reflect past conditions, we can modify the forecast directly to reflect our assessment of the future.

The second method for dealing with future activities would be to change the model itself. This might work best when we are unsure of what the effect of these activities will be. If, for example, we know that one of our competitors is going to introduce a new product, we suspect that the market will change, but we may not be sure just what the direction or magnitude of the change will be. If the product is expensive, we may gain sales; if it is novel, we may lose sales. All we know is that there may be a change. In this instance, we could increase the smoothing constant, making the model more responsive to changes in the marketplace. In this way, we can incorporate changes into our forecasts more quickly. If we know something of what may happen, we could change both the forecast and the smoothing constant. Both of these methods help to incorporate information we have about the future into the forecasts before using the forecasts to make decisions.

Getting started

When historical demand data are available, there is nothing like a plot of those data for getting started. If there is a pattern to the demand, it can be most easily seen from a plot. The plots also help one to set the initial values for doing the forecasting in a way that is consistent with the historical data. If, for example, the plots show that seasonal factors exist, the base value can be estimated by eyeballing the base value line (or by taking the average for at least one seasonal cycle).

The seasonal indexes can be found by averaging the indexes calculated for each of the seasonal peaks and valleys that exist in the data. Similarly, a plot of the values for trend data would enable one to draw in a trend line (or one could average the period-to-period changes) to get an estimate of the trend value. The plot would also help determine the base value to use for starting to make forecasts. In every instance (constant data, trend data, or seasonal data), the plots will help determine whether it is desirable to use the more recent data in setting the starting values.

Once starting values have been determined, one can also use relatively high smoothing constants for the early forecasts to quickly overcome any errors in the starting values. It is also desirable to make simulated forecasts of the last few periods of historical data as test data for the model. By using, say, 75 percent of the historical data to estimate initial values, and then simulating forecasts for the remaining 25 percent of the data, the values for starting the initial forecasts would already have been smoothed by the forecasting model.

The choice of smoothing constants for use in the models for forecasting is a matter of balancing responsiveness with stability. This is not an easy balance, however, and practice has provided some guidance. For smoothing the average or base value, an α of about .1 to .2 has been found useful in practice. The β value is generally held to less than the α value, about .05 to .1. The value for γ depends on how frequently the seasonal index is recalculated. If often, such as every few weeks, a low γ (.1) is acceptable. If less frequently (yearly), $\gamma = .3$ to .4 might be used. In practice, some simulation with past data can be useful. However, our opinion is that this approach is of limited value, since the objective is to forecast well in the *future*. The issue always comes down to the stability-responsiveness trade-off, based on how stable the future environment is judged to be.

Demand filter monitoring

All of the smoothing models presented in this chapter incorporate actual demand data into the forecasts as soon as the information is available. Therefore, it is important that the actual demand data be correct. One way of helping ensure this is through demand filtering (i.e., checking the actual demand against a range of reasonable values). An approach that works well is to screen the actual demand values against some limit before calculating the updated forecasts, and to have some thinking person (not a computer) determine whether exceptions are correct or not. A common screening limit is four MADs in either direction of the forecast of demand for the period. Since 4 MADs correspond to 3.2 standard deviations, this limit provides a probability of less than .001 of the demand value being a random occurrence for normally distributed forecast errors. If an actual demand falls outside this limit, a manual review is applied.

Once the filter catches a value outside the limits, the review might consist of checking to make sure that there wasn't a clerical error in the recording of the demand, that there wasn't some explainable cause for the big change, or that conditions really have changed and demand will be changed significantly. If conditions are changing, the situation may call for using some of the techniques for modifying the forecasts that were discussed earlier.

The limits to use for filtering individual actual demand observations depend upon the costs of a manual review compared to the cost of an error.

The probabilities of exceeding the limits can be determined from a normal table using the relationship between the number of standard deviations and MAD, given in Equation (16.3). This can provide some insight into setting the limits on the observations.

Demand filtering can be very important in actual practice. We have seen many examples where the average demand for some product such as a particular chair at Ethan Allen might be, say, 20 units per month. All of a sudden an order comes along for 300 chairs! Someone opened a restaurant. Demand filtering will pick up this situation, first asking if a data entry error has occurred? The thinking analyst well might not allow this order to influence the average or forecast. At Ethan Allen it would be treated as a "contract sale," which is only forecast in overall dollars. It is too difficult to forecast the exact timings and actual items of contract sales.

Tracking signal monitoring

The approach of exponential smoothing can also be used to compute a useful statistic called a *tracking signal*. The tracking signal helps in monitoring the quality of the forecast. We use the methods of exponential smoothing to make a smoothed average of the bias and MAD. The equations for doing this, (16.15) and (16.16), follow. These equations simply smooth the same error measures that we introduced in Equations (16.1) and (16.2) early in this chapter. By using exponential smoothing, the measures incorporate and weight most heavily the recent demand information. The smoothing constant, δ, is between 0 and 1, and has the same properties as the smoothing constant in the exponential smoothing forecasting model. The larger the δ, the more heavily weighted or responsive to the most recent forecast error. Figure 16.14 shows some sample calculations:

$$\text{Smoothed bias}_t = \delta(\text{Actual demand}_t - \text{Forecast}_t)$$
$$+ (1 - \delta)(\text{Smoothed Bias}_{t-1}) \qquad (16.15)$$
$$\text{Smoothed MAD}_t = \delta|\text{Actual demand}_t - \text{Forecast}_t|$$
$$+ (1 - \delta)(\text{Smoothed MAD}_{t-1}) \qquad (16.16)$$

FIGURE 16.14   Example smoothed bias and MAD calculations

Data: Forecast$_t$ = 100, actual demand$_t$ = 90, δ = .1

Smoothed bias$_{t-1}$ = −1, smoothed MAD$_{t-1}$ = 5

Smoothed bias$_t$ = .1(90 − 100) + (1 − .1)(−1) = −1.9   (16.15)

Smoothed MAD$_t$ = .1|90 − 100| + (1 − .1)(5) = 5.5   (16.16)

Tracking signal = −1.9/5.5 = −.345

where:

$$0 \leq \delta \leq 1.$$

$$|\text{Actual demand}_t - \text{Forecast}_t| = \text{Absolute value of the forecast error observed during period } t.$$

The smoothed bias and smoothed MAD are combined to calculate the tracking signal. The formula for this is given in Equation (16.17). Note that the smoothed MAD provides an estimate of the expected error (i.e., the average error) and the bias shows consistent over- or underforecasting. The tracking signal varies between -1 and $+1$. Either of these extreme values indicates that all of the forecast errors are of the same sign. If the forecast is unbiased, the tracking signal will be near zero, irrespective of the value of MAD. The tracking signal allows one to compute a measure of bias that is independent of MAD; one that will have the same numerical meaning for every item forecast. As the tracking signal deviates from zero in any significant way, manual review of the particular item is called for.

$$\text{Tracking signal}_t = \frac{\text{Smoothed bias}_t}{\text{Smoothed MAD}_t} \qquad (16.17)$$

where:

$$-1 \leq \text{Tracking signal}_t \leq +1.$$

The tracking signal is an indicator of forecast bias that is consistent for all observations. Its use is essentially the same as that described for demand filtering; that is, by isolating those items for which the tracking signal is deviating significantly from the nominal value of zero, one can take corrective actions. For example, if an item were forecast with the basic exponential smoothing model (ESF), and an underlying trend existed in the data, the tracking signal would move away from zero.

The issue of what tracking signal value to use for initiating a review is essentially the same as that for demand filtering. The closer the limit is to zero, the sooner poor forecasts are discovered. On the other hand, with small limits, the number of times that a review will be necessary is increased. Also, the chance for reaching an erroneous conclusion from the review is increased. The appropriate value is also not independent of δ. Small values of the smoothing constant for MAD and bias result in more stability and less responsiveness in these measures. Stability means that it will take longer for the tracking signal to respond to an underlying change in conditions.

Strategic issues

There are a number of strategic and managerial questions about forecasting that we have passed over rather rapidly or have not discussed. Certainly we have not had the space to discuss all the possible forecasting models, and it would not be fair to leave this discussion without indicating there are several more approaches to short-term forecasting than we have mentioned here.

Although it was not indicated for any of the Pancho's restaurant problems, it is often necessary to make longer-term decisions for which the item-level, short-term forecasts simply are not adequate. Among these decisions are capital expansion projects, proposals to develop a new product line, and merger or acquisition opportunities. For these long-term decisions, forecasts based on causal or econometric models, or simply on managerial insight and judgment, can often produce improved results. Causal models are those that relate the business of the firm to indicators that are more easily forecast or are available as general information. Early in this chapter, we used the sales of household fixtures and their relation to housing starts as an indication of a causal relationship. A substantial amount of managerial judgment is required in reviewing the forecasts that form the basis for making long-term decisions. The general principle indicated here is that the nature of the forecast must be matched with the nature of the decision. The level of aggregation, the amount of management review time, the cost, and the quality of the forecast needed really depend upon the nature of the decision being made. Many short-term operating decisions do not warrant the use of expensive forecasting techniques, and that has been one reason for focusing on short-term projection techniques. For strategic decisions with more at risk than two extra bottles of tequila, the investment in more expensive procedures (more management involvement) is called for. A general schema of this is presented as Figure 16.15.

In the ongoing management of forecasts, strategic questions can also come about from a review triggered by forecast monitoring. For example, the forecasting model might be appropriate, but there are insufficient adjustments to account for known actions in the marketplace. The forecasting procedure must be managed to make sure that special knowledge is included in the forecasts.

A review might indicate that the model is no longer appropriate. There may be trend or seasonal effects that should now be included or dropped, or perhaps a compound model that has both trend and seasonal enhancements should be developed. In such cases, the model needs to be adjusted accordingly.

Yet another instance, where the model may not be appropriate, is where the demand is dependent upon other decisions in the firm. For example, the demand for tires in an automobile factory is dependent upon the number of cars being produced. That is quite a different forecasting problem from trying to determine how many cars the public wants to buy. A dependent demand relationship should always be looked for.

It is apparent that forecasting is a pervasive, central activity in the management of operations. To be effective, the forecasting system must be

FIGURE 16.15   Applicability of various forecast attributes to decision attributes*

Decision attributes

Level	Frequency	Money	Time			
Mission	Rare	Much	Long-run			
Strategic	Occasional	Some	Medium-run			
Tactical	Often	Little	Short-run			

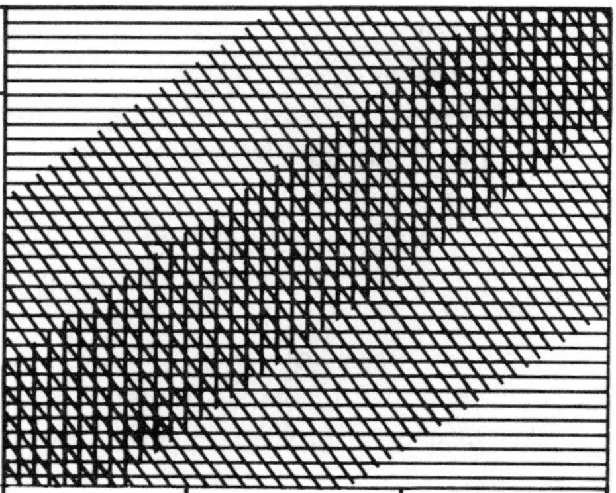

		Increasing aggregation	Item level	Product family	Total sales or output
Forecast attribute		Cost/ forecast	Low	Medium	High
		Degree of management involvement	Low	Medium	High
		Nature of forecast model	Projection technique	Econometric causal	Management judgement

*The darker the area, the greater the applicability.

linked closely to a number of other systems. Certainly, those decisions requiring forecast information must be linked directly to the output of the forecasting system. Since all of the forecasting models presented in this chapter require demand data, there must be close linkage between the order entry system and the forecasting system. Many firms will use sales data or shipment data instead of demand for adjusting their forecasts. In cases where demand information is not available, this may be warranted; but there is a difference between sales, shipments, and demand. Since it is demand that we are interested in forecasting, the link with the order entry system should be capable of picking up demand information. If we do not have the stock available to make the sale or shipment, this will affect our customer service—but not the fact that there was a demand.

FORECASTING IN INDUSTRY

We come now to the last of our seven topical issues in forecasting. In this section, we briefly describe the approach used by one firm, the Ethan Allen Furniture Company. The firm utilizes an exponential-smoothing-based forecasting system to forecast the demand for its products. The forecasting models are part of an overall managerial system that provides for monitoring demand, developing the forecasts, reviewing and modifying forecasts, aggregating the information, producing sales history data, and developing a variety of other management reports. Figure 16.16 provides one example of the type of report that can be produced by the forecasting system. This particular report can be produced by request, for any product that management might wish to scrutinize. The forecasting model used to produce the forecasts shown in Figure 16.16 was a seasonally enhanced model, using a smoothing constant of .2. The monthly seasonal factors are shown on the report, along with the forecasts, actual demand, errors, and percent errors. Note also that manual adjustments can be made and that MAD and the tracking signal can be reported.

The report shown as Figure 16.17 is one of the monitoring reports produced by the system whenever a manual review is indicated by the system. The first product shown in Figure 16.17, a governor's chair, has triggered a review because the error exceeds 50 percent of the forecast. The limit of tolerance is shown at the top of the report. This triggered the inclusion of this particular governor's chair on the sales screening report, which suggests possible manual correction. Information on the last three forecasts, actual demand, MAD, and other review data are also included in the report. Adjustments are made manually, if needed, and will appear in subsequent runs of the report if the actual demand continues to fall outside of the limits for review. The next two items in Figure 16.17 are included in the report, because one individual customer order was larger than the stated percentage of the total forecast. The report shows any information on past changes to the forecast, as well. This keeps the entire process explicit to the reviewer. The sales screening process ensures that the ultimate responsibility for forecasting rests with management.

CONCLUDING PRINCIPLES

Forecasts provide an important input to manufacturing planning and control systems. Although many kinds of forecasts are possible, this chapter has focused on short-term forecasts based on past data. We have shown how exponential smoothing models can be used to make these short-term forecasts and how routine forecast monitoring can be achieved.

We have tried to emphasize that forecasting is too important to leave to

FIGURE 16.16 Ethan Allen, Inc., sales and forecasts

MIRROR   FOR ITEM 11-9008- 225

		JAN	FEB	MAR	APR	MAY	JUN	JUL	AUG	SEP	OCT	NOV	DEC
		.74	1.12	1.39	.63	.72	.85	.79	1.17	1.73	1.01	.79	1.06

AVG SALES 44.5

SEASONAL FACTORS

ADJUSTMENTS TO AMOUNT FOR   ADJUSTMENTS TO AMOUNT FOR   TRACK SGNL   MAD

NUMBER OF UNITS FORECAST AND SOLD

				0...20...40...60...80...100..120..140..160..180..200..220..240
SALES	TOTAL FCST	ERROR	PCT ERROR	DATE
27				FEB
70				MAR
16				APR
20				MAY
28				JUN
29				JUL
66				AUG
53				SEPT
28				OCT
38	26	+12	+46%	NOV
53	37	+16	+43%	DEC
38	25	+13	+52%	JAN
52	38	+14	+36%	FEB
71	48	+23	+47%	MAR
	22			APR
	24			MAY
	29			JUN
	27			JUL
	40			AUG
	59			SEPT
	34			OCT

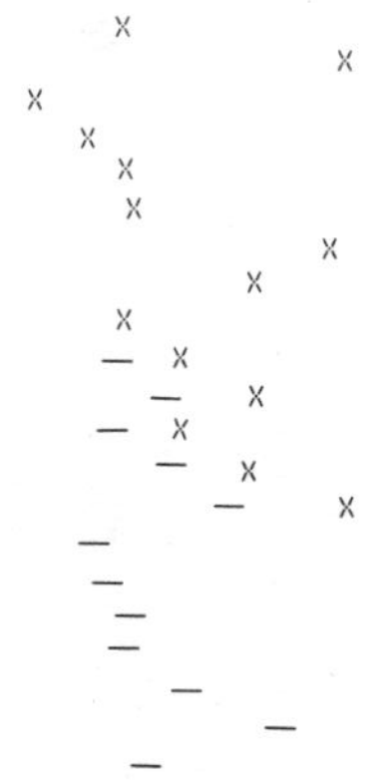

— TOTAL FORECAST
X SALES

FIGURE 16.17 Ethan Allen, Inc., sales screening exception report

FOR MAY

UPPER LIMIT PERCENT = 50%   LOWER LIMIT PERCENT = 50%   NUMBER OF MADS = 2.5

PERCENT/MAD LIMITS EXCEEDED

CHR GOV

ADJUSTED FORECAST	ACTUAL SALES	ERROR	PERCENT ERROR	MAD ERROR	SALES RANGE FROM	TO	AV SLS	SEAS	FORECAST	ADJUSTMENT	REASON	MAD	MAD/AV	MAD LIM	CUMUL ERROR	TRACK SGNL
268	84	-184	-68%	2.2	134	402	372.4	0.72	268			81.7	21%	104%	+225	+5.5
232	282	+50	+21%		TWO MONTHS AGO				232							
534	379	-155	-29%		THREE MONTHS AGO				534							
434	236	-198	-45%		FOUR MONTHS AGO				434							

30-6050-A   218 R   CHR GOV CRVR   CUST ACCT NO 17-4870-0   ORDER DATE 5/21

PERCENTAGE LIMITS EXCEEDED

CONSOLIDATION NO. 30-6050-A   218   FACTORY 018
QUANTITY 12   AVERAGE SALES 97.9   ORDER % OF AV SLS 12%

ADJUSTED FORECAST	ACTUAL SALES	ERROR	PERCENT ERROR	MAD ERROR	SALES RANGE FROM	TO	AV SLS	SEAS	FORECAST	ADJUSTMENT	REASON	MAD	MAD/AV	MAD LIM	CUMUL ERROR	TRACK SGNL
70	34	-36	-51%	0.8	35	105	97.9	0.72	70			40.8	41%			
68	44	-24	-35%		TWO MONTHS AGO				68							
143	171	+28	+19%		THREE MONTHS AGO				143							
123	60	-63	-51%		FOUR MONTHS AGO				123							

30-6052-A   218 R   CHR CPTN   CUST ACCT NO 35-3595-0   ORDER DATE 5/01
                                CUST ACCT NO 13-5448-0   ORDER DATE 5/24

LARGE INDIVIDUAL ORDER
LARGE INDIVIDUAL ORDER

CONSOLIDATION NO. 30-6052-   218   FACTORY 018
QUANTITY 12   AVERAGE SALES 61.3   ORDER % OF AV SLS 19%
QUANTITY 24   AVERAGE SALES 61.3   ORDER % OF AV SLS 39%

ADJUSTED FORECAST	ACTUAL SALES	ERROR	PERCENT ERROR	MAD ERROR	SALES RANGE FROM	TO	AV SLS	SEAS	FORECAST	ADJUSTMENT	REASON	MAD	MAD/AV	MAD LIM	CUMUL ERROR	TRACK SGNL
44	42	-2	-4%	0.0	0	0	61.3	0.72	44			28.4	46%	116%	+22	+0.7
46	12	-34	-73%		TWO MONTHS AGO				46							
95	123	+28	+29%		THREE MONTHS AGO				95							
82	40	-42	-51%		FOUR MONTHS AGO				82							

30-6055-   218 R   DRY SINK

PERCENTAGE LIMITS EXCEEDED

CONSOLIDATION NO. 30-6055-   210   FACTORY 022

ADJUSTED FORECAST	ACTUAL SALES	ERROR	PERCENT ERROR	MAD ERROR	SALES RANGE FROM	TO	AV SLS	SEAS	FORECAST	ADJUSTMENT	REASON	MAD	MAD/AV	MAD LIM	CUMUL ERROR	TRACK SGNL
30	9	-21	-70%	1.3	15	45	42.3	0.72	30			16.0	37%	95%	+109	+6.8
28	23	-5	-17%		TWO MONTHS AGO				28							
58	77	+19	+32%		THREE MONTHS AGO				58							
52	20	-32	-61%		FOUR MONTHS AGO				52							

a forecasting model. Firms that use forecasting models wisely use them to support, not to supplant, managerial judgment. The importance of taking external information into account is one example. Another is the necessary judgment required in a review resulting from forecast monitoring. For example, a tracking signal can indicate a review. It takes a thinking person to decide precisely how to do the review, how (or whether) to change the model, and how to modify the forecasting model data.

The following basic concepts or principles are those we see as particularly important:

- Evaluative criteria must be chosen for the short-term forecasting system. The choices implied in this chapter are minimum bias, minimum MAD, lost cost, and simplicity.
- Controlling bias is the most critical problem. It is easier to live with larger errors (larger MAD) if that is what it takes to reduce bias.
- Use of short-term forecasts must be separated from the act of forecasting.
- Methods for monitoring forecasts over time must be installed.
- Forecasting needs to be embedded in a management structure.
- Forecasting is not a computer program, and the result should not be monitored by the computer department.
- Simple forecasting methods seem to work better than sophisticated procedures for short-term forecasts of microdata.

REFERENCES

Armstrong, J. S. "The Ombudsman: Research on Forecasting: A Quarter Century Review, 1960–1984." *Interfaces*, January–February 1986.

Box, G. E. P., and G. M. Jenkins. *Time Series Analysis: Forecasting and Control.* New York: Holden-Day, 1970.

Brown, R. G. *Smoothing, Forecasting and Prediction of Discrete Time Series.* Englewood Cliffs, N.J.: Prentice-Hall, 1962.

Chambers, J. C.; S. K. Mullick; and D. D. Smith. "How to Choose the Right Forecasting Technique." *Harvard Business Review*, July–August 1971, pp. 45–74.

Flores, B. E., and D. C. Whybark. "A Comparison of Focus Forecasting with Averaging and Exponential Smoothing Strategies." *Production and Inventory Management*, 3rd Quarter 1986.

———. "Forecasting 'Laws' for Management." *Business Horizons*, July/August 1985.

Flowers, A. D. "A Simulation Study of Smoothing Constant Limits for an Adaptive Forecasting System." *Journal of Operations Management* 1, no. 2, 1980.

Forecasting Reprints. Falls Church, Va.: American Production and Inventory Control Society, 1979.

Georgoff, D. M., and R. G. Murdick. "Manager's Guide to Forecasting." *Harvard Business Review*, January–February 1986, pp. 110–20.

Groff, G. R. "Empirical Comparison of Models for Short-Range Forecasting." *Management Science*, September 1973, pp. 22–31.

Gupta, S., and P. C. Wilton. "Combination of Forecasts: An Extension." *Management Science* 33, no. 3, March 1987.

Lawrence, M. J.; R. H. Edmundson; and M. J. O'Connor. "The Accuracy of Combining Judgmental and Statistical Forecasts." *Management Science* 32, no. 12, December 1986.

Lee, T. S., and E. E. Adam, Jr. "Forecasting Error Evaluation in Material Requirements Planning Production-Inventory Systems." *Management Science* 32, no. 9, September 1986.

————, and R. J. Ebert. "An Evaluation of Forecast Error in Master Production Scheduling for Material Requirements Planning Systems." *Decision Sciences* 18, no. 2, Spring 1987.

Mabert, V. A. "An Introduction to Short-Term Forecasting Using the Box Jenkins Methodology." Atlanta: *AIIE Monograph*, 1975.

Makridakis, S.; A. Andersen; R. Carbone; R. Fildes; M. Hibon; R. Lewandowski; J. Newton; E. Parzen; R. Winkler. "The Accuracy of Extrapolation (Time Series) Methods: Results of a Forecasting Competition." *Journal of Forecasting* I (1982), pp. 111–53.

————, and R. L. Winkler, "Averages of Forecasts: Some Empirical Results." *Management Science* 29, no. 9 (September 1983).

Mather, Hal. "Too Much Precision, Not Enough Accuracy." *APICS 22nd Annual Conference Proceedings*, 1979, pp. 116–19.

McLain, F. O. "Restarting a Forecasting System when Demand Suddenly Changes." *Journal of Operations Management*, October 1981, pp. 53–61.

Sickel, Walter F. "Integrating the Forecast into MRP." *APICS 22nd Annual Conference Proceedings*, 1979, pp. 120–22.

Smith, B. T. "A New Level of Accuracy in Product Demand Forecasting." *1979 Conference Proceedings, APICS*.

————. *Focus Forecasting Computer Techniques for Inventory Control*. Boston, Mass.: CBI Publishing Company, 1978.

Trigg, D. W., and A. G. Leach. "Exponential Smoothing with an Adaptive Response Rate." *Operations Research Quarterly*, March 1967, pp. 53–59.

Wheelwright, S. C., and S. Makridakis. *Forecasting Methods for Management*. New York: John Wiley & Sons, 1977.

Winters, P. R. "Forecasting Sales by Exponentially Weighted Moving Averages." *Management Science*, April 1960, pp. 324–42.

DISCUSSION QUESTIONS

1. Provide some examples of both short- and long-term forecast needs. What are some of the "special" types of information that should be taken into account, in addition to the past history, in making these forecasts?

2. Some experts have argued that it is more important to have low bias than to have low forecast error. Why would they argue this way?

3. What concerns would you have with using the data in Figure 16.4 to project the Tequila-based drink demand in the future?

4. Would you use a seasonal-enhanced model for forecasting individual book sales, in the book store?

5. A friend has just installed a focus forecasting system and wants you to add a new model just developed by the statistics department of a major university. What would you advise him?

6. How does the use of a high-smoothing constant for the first few forecasts help in starting a forecasting model?

7. If you had a tracking signal in place and were using it to routinely monitor forecasts, what actions would you take if the tracking signal exceeded your limit and called for a review?

PROBLEMS

1. The master production scheduler at the Acme Machine Company has been analyzing the options on orders received for the firm's industrial valve product line. All customer orders for industrial valves require the use of either option A or option B. During the past six months the following customer order data have been collected. Each customer order is for one valve.

Prior month number	Total number of industrial valve orders received	Number of orders requiring option A	Number of orders requiring option B
February	30	6	24
March	35	10	25
April	40	12	28
May	50	18	32
June	55	25	30
July	65	28	37

a. Develop a basic exponential smoothing model to forecast the percentage of customer orders requiring the use of option A for August. Assume that the initial forecast of orders with option A is 15 percent, and that Acme wants to use a smoothing constant of alpha = .4.

b. What alternative forecasting models might be applied to forecast the percentage of customer orders requiring the use of option A?

2. The manager of shop operations at the Granger Transmission Company is concerned with forecasting the weekly output in terms of standard labor-hours for

the BD Chucker workcenter. He has collected the following data concerning the standard labor-hour output of this workcenter for the past four weeks:

Week Number:	525	526	527	528
Standard Labor Hour Output:	549	579	581	564

a. Using a basic exponential smoothing model, a beginning average of 550 as of the end of week number 524, and a smoothing constant of alpha = .2, prepare a forecast of the standard labor-hour output of this workcenter for week 529 as of the end of week 528.

b. What factors will influence the actual standard labor-hour output of this workcenter? What forecasting model alternatives would you suggest for this situation?

3. The master production scheduler at the Delta Electronics Co. would like to develop a forecasting model for the firm's data entry product line. The following actual sales data have been collected during the past five months for this product line.

Month	Sales (in units)
1	1800
2	1860
3	1920
4	2050
5	2120

a. Using a basic exponential smoothing model, a beginning average at the start of month 1 of 1780 units, and a smoothing constant value of alpha = .2, prepare a forecast for month 6 as of the end of month 5.

b. What alternative forecasting models might be considered for the data entry product line?

4. The master production scheduler at the Delta Electronics Co. would like to develop forecasting models for two of the end-products in the firm's data entry product line. Additional data to those collected in problem 3 have been gathered concerning the sales of two end-products—the J401 and H212 models.

Month	J401 sales (in units)	H212 sales (in units)
July	500	170
August	510	180
September	480	490
October	530	230
November	640	590

a. Develop a basic exponential smoothing model for the J401 model using a beginning average as of the end of June of 480 and a smoothing constant value of alpha = .2. Prepare a forecast of sales for December as of the end of November.

    b. Develop a basic exponential smoothing model for the H212 model using a beginning average as of the end of June of 200 and a smoothing constant value of alpha = .2. Prepare a forecast of sales for December as of the end of November.

    c. What alternative forecasting models might be considered for these products?

5. The production planning manager at the Talbot Publishing Company has provided the following historical sales data for its leading textbook on forecasting:

Year:	4	5	6	7
Sales*:	21	18	20	17

*In 1,000 units

The firm is considering using a basic exponential smoothing model with an α = .2 to forecast the sales of this item.

    a. Assuming that the sales have averaged 20,000 units through year 3, prepare forecasts for years 5 through 7, as of the end of year 4.

    b. Calculate the average MAD value for the forecasts, using the actual sales data provided.

6. Repeat problem 5, updating the forecasts for years 6 and 7 at the end of years 5 and 6, respectively.

7. The ACME Company has recorded the following data for one of its new products over a six month period. (The company assumes no trend or seasonal effects.)

Month	Demand (in units of product)
January	40
February	70
March	60
April	120
May	100
June	90

    a. What would the forecast for February have been if made at the end of January, using exponential smoothing with α = .2 and a forecast for January of 30 units?

    b. What would the forecast for May have been if made at the end of April, using a four-month moving average?

    c. What would be the mean absolute deviation (MAD) of the forecast errors for May and June, given that the forecasts for these two months were 105 and 95 units, respectively?

8. Ms. Sue Sayer is employed as a forecasting analyst for the Barry M. Stiff Casket Corporation. Ms. Sayer has collected the following sales data on Stiff's best-selling casket, Model 12–A:

Period	Sales
1	28
2	32
3	39
4	40
5	38
6	47
7	50
8	59
9	56

a. What is the three-period moving average forecast for period 8 made at the end of period 7?

b. If the forecast for period 5 were 35, what would be the forecast for period 6 made at the end of period 5, using exponential smoothing without trend or seasonality using $\alpha = .2$?

c. If the base at the end of period 7 were 54 and the trend at the end of period 7 were 4 ($\alpha = .2$, $\beta = .4$), what would be the forecast for period 9 made at the end of period 8?

d. Given the model described in c, what would be the forecast for period 10 made at the end of period 9?

e. Given the model described in c and d, what would be the forecast for period 11 made at the end of period 9?

f. What would be the mean absolute deviation (MAD) of forecast errors, given that the forecasts for periods 1, 2, 3, and 4 were 30, 31, 35, and 38, respectively?

9. Edsel Muffler, Inc., showed the following sales figures for its stainless steel muffler, Rusty, over the last six months:

Month	Sales
July	125
August	84
September	60
October	44
November	36
December	44

Assume that the base value at the end of November was 40 units and the trend value was -23 units. What would be the forecast for the following February made at the end of December ($\alpha = .3$, $\beta = .4$)?

10. The sales manager at the Tidy Corporation has given you the following information regarding one of its products—the widget:

Sales history		
Quarter	Year 1	Year 2
1	50	75
2	100	125
3	25	50
4	75	100

a. Plot the quarterly sales data for each year.

b. What seasonal index for each quarter could be used to forecast the sales of this product for year 3?

11. The production manager at the Angel Wing Company is using a trend-enhanced exponential smoothing model to forecast the demand for an end product called Sparkles. At the start of the second quarter, the forecasting model had the following parameter values:

$$\alpha = .5.$$
$$\beta = .5.$$
$$\text{Base}_1 = \text{Base at the end of the first quarter}$$
$$= 50 \text{ units per quarter.}$$
$$\text{Trend} = 5 \text{ units per quarter.}$$
$$\text{Smoothed bias}_1 = -5 \text{ units per quarter.}$$
$$\text{Smoothed MAD}_1 = 10 \text{ units per quarter.}$$

a. What is the forecast for the demand for Sparkles for the third quarter made at the start of the second quarter?

b. If the demand for Sparkles is 60 units during the second quarter, what are the values of the base and trend at the end of the second quarter?

c. Assuming that the demand for Sparkles is 60 units during the second quarter, what is the forecast of demand for Sparkles for the fourth quarter made at the end of the second quarter?

d. What is the value of the tracking signal for Sparkles as of the start of the second quarter?

e. What information does a tracking signal convey to the production manager?

12. The Alpha Corporation has a product with seasonal differences in sales between the halves of the year. The sales in the first part of the year are generally less than for the second part of the year. For this reason they have split the sales from the two previous years 7 and 8 into two parts and would like to use these two parts to predict sales in the coming year (9). They also feel that there is an upward trend in sales. The sales figures from the past two years are:

	Year 7	Year 8
First half (F)	100	105
Second half (S)	110	130

The executives of the company estimated that the trend at the end of year 6 was 5 units per half year (T_{6S} = 5). The base at the end of year 6 (B_{6S}) = 95. The seasonal factors were 1.05 and 0.95 for the first and second half of the year, respectively (note that these factors are set purposely to the opposite of what they should be to demonstrate how they will be corrected).

$$\alpha = .3.$$
$$\beta = .5.$$
$$\gamma = .5.$$

a. Using a trend and seasonally enhanced model, forecast each of the four half years, sequentially updating the model at the end of each half year.
b. At the end of year 8 prepare a forecast for each half year in year 9.
c. Graph the values of the updated seasonal factor for each half year.

13. For the first five months of the year, the demand for Focii has been 14, 23, 12, 17, and 18. Farquart Focus has a focus forecasting system (naturally) using just two forecasting techniques. The first is a two-period moving average and the second is simply that demand this period will equal last period. Farquart uses the MAD for the last three months as the criterion for choosing which model will make the forecast for the next month.
a. What will the forecast be for June and which model will be used?
b. Would it make any difference if the demand for March had been 30 instead of 12?

14. Use a spreadsheet program to compare a three-period moving average forecasting model with a basic (ESF) exponential smoothing model. Five periods of past data exist (27, 26, 32, 41, and 28), and the five future periods to be forecast have demands of 35, 43, 47, 28, and 38. Develop the MAD values for each technique for the five periods.
a. Using the average of the five periods of history to start the exponential smoothing model, what smoothing constant produces the MAD value closest to the moving average approach? Which has the lower MAD?
b. What changes when you use the average of the last three periods to start the exponential model.

15. The following two demand sets are to be used to test two different basic exponential smoothing models. The first model uses α = .1, and the second uses α = .5. In both cases, the model should be initialized with a beginning forecast value of 50; that is, the ESF forecast for period 1 made at the end of period 0 is 50 units. In each of the four cases (two models on two demand sets) compute the average forecast error and MAD. Use a spreadsheet program to do this analysis. What do the results mean?

Demand set I		Demand set II	
Period	Demand	Period	Demand
1	51	1	77
2	46	2	83
3	49	3	90
4	55	4	22
5	52	5	10
6	47	6	80
7	51	7	16
8	48	8	19
9	56	9	27
10	51	10	79
11	45	11	73
12	52	12	88
13	49	13	15
14	48	14	21
15	43	15	85
16	46	16	22
17	55	17	88
18	53	18	75
19	54	19	14
20	49	20	16

— 17 —————————————————

Independent demand inventory management

This chapter is devoted to the management of nonmanufacturing inventories. These include finished goods at the factory or in field warehouses, spare-part inventories, and nonproduction items, such as supplies and maintenance materials. The techniques in this chapter are directed to determining the appropriate order quantities and when to place replenishment orders. If these basic decisions are made well, appropriate levels of customer service will be provided without excess levels of inventory.

This chapter is organized around five topics:

- Basic concepts: What types of inventory are there and why should funds be invested in inventories?
- Measuring inventory performance: What are the costs associated with inventory management?
- Routine inventory decisions: What are the day-to-day decisions for managing independent demand inventories?
- Order timing decisions: How does one buffer uncertainty in demand and how are desired customer-service levels maintained?
- Information systems for inventory control: What systems are in use for managing independent demand inventory items?

This chapter is related to material requirements planning, Chapters 2 and 12. In both of these MRP chapters, lot sizing (order quantity) and order timing decisions are discussed. The principles of independent demand inventory management apply, even though the MRP decisions are based on dependent demand. The issues of Chapter 3 on data base integrity are related to our discussion in this chapter, since data issues exist for any inventory control system. The forecasting material in Chapter 16 covers a topic that is a key input into the inventory management system. More advanced systems for inventory management can be found in Chapter 18.

BASIC CONCEPTS

The investment in inventory typically represents one of the largest single areas of capital in a business, often more than 25 percent of total assets. In this section, we discuss where this investment is made, noting the distinction between independent and dependent demand inventories. We describe the functions of movement inventories and organization inventories (cycle stock, safety stock, and anticipation stock).

Independent versus dependent demand items

This chapter is primarily concerned with the management of independent demand inventories. There are major differences between the methods for managing these inventories and manufacturing inventories. The differences occur mainly because of differences in the sources of demand for the items contained in independent demand inventories and those in manufacturing inventories. The demand for end-product items, such as those stocked in the field warehouses shown in Figure 17.1, is primarily influenced by factors that are independent of the company decisions. These external factors induce a certain amount of random variation in the demand for such items. As a result, forecasts of demand for these items are typically projections of historical demand patterns. These forecasts estimate the average usage rate and the pattern of random variation.

The demand for the items in the manufacturing inventories shown in Figure 17.1 (e.g., the raw material and component items) is directly influenced by internal factors that are well within the control of the firm, such as the assembly and fabrication production schedule; that is, the demand for raw materials and component items is a derived demand, which can be calculated exactly, once the assembly and fabrication production schedules are determined. Therefore, the demand for end-product items is referred to as *independent* demand, while the demand for items contained in manufacturing inventories is referred to as *dependent* demand.

The concepts of independent and dependent demand are important in selecting appropriate inventory management techniques. The inventory

FIGURE 17.1   Materials flow system

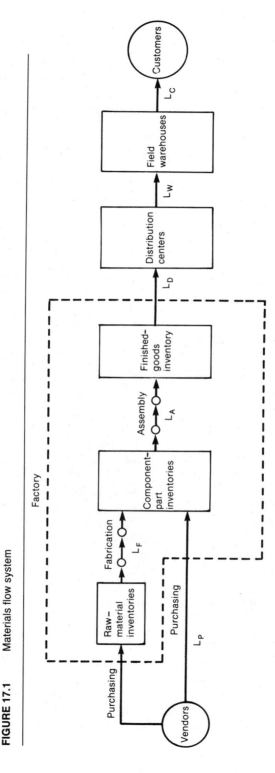

management techniques described in this chapter are best suited for independent demand items, such as those found in distribution inventories, while material requirements planning or just-in-time techniques are best suited for the dependent demand items found in manufacturing inventories.

Functions of inventory

The questions "Why invest funds in inventory?" and "What benefits are derived by investing in inventories?" are frequently raised by industrial executives. An investment in inventory is made for one of two purposes. First, inventory makes it possible to produce goods at some distance from the actual consumer. Second, the existence of inventory provides management with the flexibility to decouple successive production and distribution operations. Therefore, two types of inventory can be found in production and distribution systems: *movement* and *organization* inventories. These two types of inventory are illustrated by the materials flow diagram shown in Figure 17.1. The arrows denote movement inventories, and the boxes indicate organization inventories. Since time is required to accomplish the production and transportation operations in Figure 17.1, a lead time (L) is associated with each of these steps (e.g., L_F represents the time required to fabricate a component item in the factory).

Movement inventories. Movement inventories exist because time is required to manufacture products or to transport goods from one location to another. Movement inventories for transportation purposes are also called in-transit or pipeline inventories. Movement inventories during the manufacturing process are called work-in-process (WIP) inventories. As an example, a WIP inventory is shown in Figure 17.1 between raw material and component part inventories. Since it takes fabrication time (L_F) to convert raw materials into component items, work-in-process inventory is incurred. This inventory takes the form of orders waiting to be transported between machines or of orders waiting to be processed on a particular machine. Management can change the level of WIP by changing the manufacturing process, lot sizes, or production schedules.

Management can influence the magnitude of the movement inventories by changing the design of the production/distribution system. For example, the in-transit inventory between the raw material vendor and the factory can be reduced by: (1) changing the method of transportation (e.g., switching from rail to air freight) or (2) switching to a supplier located closer to the factory to reduce the transit time. These choices, however, involve cost and service trade-offs, which need to be considered carefully. For example, shipping raw material by air freight instead of by rail may cut the transit time in half and therefore reduce the average pipeline inventory by 50 percent; but this might well involve an increase in the unit cost of the raw material because of higher transportation costs. Therefore, the consequences of changing suppliers or transport modes needs to be weighed against investing in more (or less) inventory.

Organization inventories. Organization inventories exist to decouple successive stages in the production and distribution systems. For example, in Figure 17.1, the factory operations are decoupled from the distribution system by the finished-goods inventory. This inventory makes it unnecessary to produce directly to meet the demands from the distribution centers; that is, demand from the distribution centers can be satisfied out of inventory, thereby permitting flexibility in scheduling assembly operations and in fabricating components. There are several types of organization inventory, each having a different purpose: cycle stock, safety stock, and anticipation stock.

Cycle stock. Cycle stock exists whenever one produces (or buys) in larger quantities than are needed to satisfy the immediate requirements. For example, a distribution center may order two units of a given end product weekly from the factory. However, because of the costs of setting up an assembly line and the productivity gained with larger production quantities, the plant might choose to produce a batch of eight units once each month. Thus, the investment in cycle stock provides more economical production costs. Similar savings in unit costs (e.g., transportation costs, purchase price reductions, and clerical costs), are gained by establishing cycle stocks at other points in Figure 17.1 (e.g., for raw materials, component items, and in the distribution centers and field warehouses).

Safety stock. Safety stock exists to provide protection against irregularities or uncertainties in the demand or the supply of an item; that is, when the demand exceeds what is forecast or when the resupply time is longer than anticipated. Safety stock provides insurance that customer demand can be satisfied immediately, and that the customers will not have to wait while their orders are backlogged. For example, a portion of the inventory held at the distribution centers may be safety stock. Suppose the average demand for a given end product is 100 units a week with a restocking lead time of one week, and occasionally the weekly demand might be as large as 150 units and the replenishment lead time as long as two weeks; a safety stock of 100 units might be created to ensure meeting the maximum demand requirements.

Similar investments in safety stock can be made at other stocking points in Figure 17.1 (e.g., for raw materials, component items, finished goods, or in the field warehouses). An important management question concerns the amount of safety stock that is actually required; that is, how much protection is desirable? This question represents another inventory-investment trade-off—between protection against demand and supply uncertainties and the costs of investing in safety stock.

Anticipation stock. Anticipation stock is needed for products whose markets exhibit seasonal patterns of demand and whose production (or supply) is more uniform. Air-conditioner manufacturers, children's toy manufacturers, and calendar manufacturers all face peak demand conditions where the production facility is frequently unable to meet the demand on a period-by-period basis. Therefore, anticipation stocks are built up in advance and depleted during the peak demand periods.

Anticipation stock can be created at several points in Figure 17.1. For example, anticipation stocks may be built up in advance of the peak selling season in the factory warehouse. There are, however, trade-offs to be considered in investing in anticipation stocks. For example, an investment in additional factory capacity could be made, thereby reducing the need for anticipation stocks. It may be that operating the factory at a level production rate and allowing the finished-goods inventory level to fluctuate during the year costs less than investing in additional production facilities and varying the production rate.

MEASURING INVENTORY PERFORMANCE

While the benefits derived from inventory may be evident, the costs of inventory need to be clearly identified. These costs are often not reflected directly in a firm's financial statements. Therefore, inventory performance is sometimes measured in relation to sales volume, using inventory turnover as a surrogate measure; that is, annual sales volume divided by the average inventory investment. For example, annual sales volume for an end product of $200,000 and an average inventory investment during the year of $50,000 produces an inventory turnover of 4.

High inventory turnovers suggest a large return on the inventory investment. Yet an analysis of the costs actually affected by inventory management decisions indicates that inventory turnover is not a comprehensive measure of inventory management performance. There are several pertinent inventory costs that are not reflected in the turnover measure. These include order preparation costs, the costs of carrying inventories, shortage costs, and other customer-service costs.

Order preparation costs

Order preparation costs are incurred in placing orders and are directly related to the frequency with which such orders are placed. These costs include clerical costs associated with writing and issuing replenishment orders and one-time costs incurred in setting up production equipment or in transporting goods between plants and warehouses. Work measurement techniques, such as time study methods, can be used to measure the labor content of order preparation activities. The measurement of other types of order preparation costs is sometimes much more subtle. For instance, in process industries a significant material waste is often incurred in changing from one product to another (e.g., an important paper loss is incurred in switching from one order to another on corregator machines in cardboard box manufacturing plants). Likewise, when the demand for a firm's products exceeds the production capacity, an opportunity cost, such as lost profit, is incurred during the production changeover time. In addition, the learning time is often significant in manual assembly operations, and large replenishment orders can have an important impact on the unit cost of production and, therefore, on a firm's labor productivity.

Inventory carrying cost

Inventory commits management to certain costs that are related to the size of inventories, the value of the items carried in the inventory, and the length of time the inventory is carried. By committing capital to inventory, a firm forgoes the use of these funds for other purposes (e.g., to acquire new equipment, to develop new products, or to invest in short-term securities). Therefore, a cost of capital, which is expressed as an annual interest rate, is incurred on the inventory investment.

The cost of capital may be based on the cost of obtaining bank loans to finance the inventory investment (e.g., 15 to 20 percent), the interest rate on short-term securities that could be earned if the funds were not invested in inventory (e.g., 10 to 15 percent), or the rate of return on capital investment projects that cannot be undertaken because the funds must be committed to inventory. For example, the cost of capital for inventory investment might be 25 percent in the case where a new machine would yield a 25 percent return on investment. In any case, the capital cost for inventory might be determined by alternative uses for funds. The cost of capital typically varies from 6 to 35 percent, but it can be substantially higher in some circumstances.

Once the cost of capital is determined, several additional costs need to be considered. These typically include the costs of taxes and insurance on inventories, the costs of inventory obsolescence or product shelf-life limitations, and operating costs involved in storing inventory (e.g., either in the rental of public warehousing space or in the costs of owning and operating the warehouse facilities, such as heat, light, labor, and so on).

As an example, if the capital cost is 10 percent, and the combined costs of renting warehouse space, product obsolescence, taxes, and insurance amounted to an additional 10 percent of the average value of the inventory investment, the total cost of carrying inventory would be 20 percent of the value of an inventory item. Therefore, a purchased item costing $1 per unit would have an inventory carrying cost of $.20/unit/year.

Shortage and customer-service costs

A final set of inventory-related costs are those incurred when the demand for product exceeds the available inventory for an item. This cost is more difficult to measure than the order preparation and inventory carrying costs. It may be negligible in cases where the customer is willing to have the order backlogged until a product becomes available.

In some cases, this cost may equal the contribution margin of the product when the customer can purchase the item from competing firms. Moreover, this cost may be even more substantial in cases where significant customer goodwill is lost. The major emphasis placed on meeting delivery requirements in many firms suggests that, while shortage and customer-service costs are difficult to measure, they are critical in measuring inventory performance.

One frequently used surrogate measure for inventory shortage costs is the level of customer service achieved in meeting product demand (i.e., the percentage of demand that is shipped from inventory directly upon demand). For example, if the annual demand for an item is 1,000 units and 950 units are shipped directly from inventory, a 95 percent customer-service level is achieved.

The level of customer service can be measured in several ways; for example, as the percentage of units (or of customer orders) shipped directly from inventory (as above), the average length of time required to satisfy back orders, or the percentage of replenishment order cycles in which one or more units are back ordered. The level of customer service can also be translated into the level of inventory investment required to achieve a given level of customer service. As an example, a safety stock of 1,000 units (or $1,000 at a $1 per unit cost) may be required to achieve a 95 percent customer-service level, while 2,000 units of safety stock may be required to achieve a 99 percent customer-service level. Translating customer-service-level objectives into inventory investment dollars often is useful in determining customer-service level/inventory trade-offs.

Incremental inventory costs

Two criteria are useful in determining which costs are relevant to a particular inventory management decision: (1) Does the cost represent an actual out-of-pocket expenditure either as a cash payment or as forgone profit? and (2) Does the cost actually vary with the decision being made? The determination of the item value used in calculating the inventory carrying cost is a good illustration of the application of these criteria.

The item value should represent the actual out-of-pocket cost of placing an item in inventory (i.e., the variable material, labor, and overhead cost of an item). An element of the overhead cost, such as a cost allocation for general administrative expenses, is not an actual out-of-pocket expenditure. Neither does this cost vary with the decision being made (i.e., the size of the inventory investments) and, therefore, it should not be included in the determination of the inventory carrying costs.

Another example involves the measurement of clerical costs incurred in preparing replenishment orders. If the size of the clerical staff remains constant throughout the year, regardless of the number of replenishment orders placed, this neither represents an out-of-pocket cost nor does it vary with the decision being made (i.e., the replenishment order quantity). These examples are not meant to be exhaustive, but rather illustrative of the careful analysis required in determining the costs to be considered in evaluating inventory management performance.

ROUTINE INVENTORY DECISIONS

Two types of routine decisions need to be made in managing inventories at any of the stocking points shown in Figure 17.1. These decisions are concerned with *how much should be ordered (size) and when these orders should be placed (timing)*. Decisions regarding the size and timing of replenishment orders primarily affect the size of the cycle and safety stock inventories. These decisions are influenced by four main factors: the forecast of demand for an item, its replenishment lead time, the inventory related costs for the item, and management policies.

Inventory decision rules

Routine decisions on the size and timing of replenishment orders for independent demand items can be made using any one of the four inventory control decision rules shown in Figure 17.2. These decision rules are designed for use with routine item forecasting systems. The decision rules shown in Figure 17.2 involve placing orders for either a fixed or a variable order quantity, with either a fixed or a variable time between successive orders. For example, under the commonly used order point (Q,R) rule, an order for a fixed quantity (Q) is placed whenever the stock level reaches a reorder point (R). Likewise, under the S,T rule, an order is placed once every T periods for an amount equaling the difference between the current on-hand balance and a desired inventory level (S) upon the receipt of the replenishment order.

The effective use of any of these decision rules involves the proper determination of the decision rule parameter values (e.g., Q, R, S, and T). Procedures for determining the order quantity (Q) and reorder point (R)

FIGURE 17.2   Inventory decision rules

| | Order quantity | |
Order frequency	Fixed (Q)*	Variable (S)†
Variable (R)‡	Q,R	S,R
Fixed (T)§	Q,T	S,T

*Q = Order a fixed quantity (Q).
†S = Order up to a fixed expected opening inventory quantity (S).
‡R = Place an order when the inventory balance drops to (R).
§T = Place an order every (T) periods.

parameters for the order point rule are given in this chapter, while references are provided concerning the determination of the parameter values for the other decision rules in Figure 17.2.

Order quantity decisions.   Order quantity decisions primarily affect the amount of inventory held in cycle stocks at the various stocking points in Figure 17.1. Large order quantities enable orders to be placed infrequently and reduce the costs of preparing replenishment orders, but they also increase the cycle stock inventories and the costs of carrying inventory.

The determination of replenishment order quantities focuses on the question of what lot size provides the most economical trade-off between order preparation and inventory carrying costs. An example item stocked in the field warehouses in Figure 17.1 provides an illustration of this decision.

Example.   The Model 100 movie camera is sold to several hundred retail stores in a surrounding three-state sales region. To avoid excessive inventories, these stores place orders for this item frequently and in small quantities. The resulting demand for the movie camera, measured from the historical records of warehouse sales, averages 5 units per weekday (or 1,250 units per year). The movie camera can be obtained within a one-day lead time from the distribution center (DC) serving the field warehouse. This requires the preparation of a DC order and the transmission of this order over the firm's TELEX system. The cost of preparing a replenishment order is estimated to be $6.25. The firm's cost of carrying inventory is estimated at 25 percent of the item value per year, including the costs of capital, insurance, taxes, and obsolescence. Since the unit cost of the camera is $100, the inventory carrying cost is $25/unit/year.

Currently, the field warehouse orders the Model 100 movie camera on a daily basis in lots of five units. A plot showing the inventory level versus

FIGURE 17.3   Inventory level versus time for Model 100 movie camera

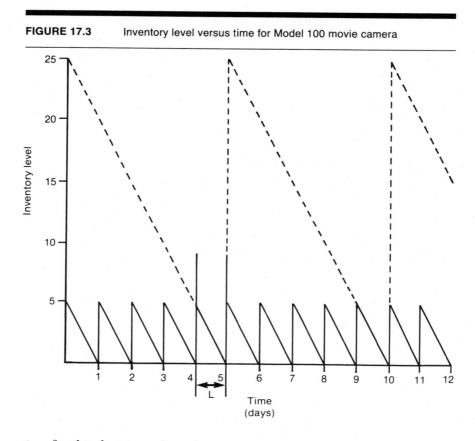

time for this decision rule is shown in Figure 17.3. This plot assumes that the demand rate is a constant 5 units per day, and the resulting average inventory level is 2.5 units. Since orders are placed daily, 250 orders are placed per year, costing a total of $1562.50/year ($6.25 × 250). The average inventory of 2.5 units represents an annual inventory carrying cost of $62.50 a year (2.5 × $25), yielding an overall combined cost of $1,625/year for placing orders and carrying inventory.

The inventory level plot for an alternative order quantity of 25 units, or placing orders weekly, is shown by the dashed line in Figure 17.3. In this case, the average inventory level is 12.5 units and 50 orders are placed annually. The larger order quantity in this case provides important savings in ordering costs ($312.50 versus the previous $1,562.50) with a small increase in the annual inventory costs ($312.50 versus the previous $62.50). Overall, a shift to a larger order quantity would produce a favorable trade-off between the ordering and inventory carrying costs, resulting in a reduction of the total costs to $625 per year.

There are clearly a number of order quantities to be evaluated to determine the best trade-off between ordering and inventory carrying costs. The economic order quantity provides a means of determining the lowest-cost order quantity directly.

Economic order quantity model. The ordering decision is stated in formal terms in the economic order quantity (EOQ) model. This model is an equation that describes the relationship between the costs of placing orders, the costs of carrying inventory, and the order quantity. Several simplifying assumptions are made by this model; these include: the demand rate is constant, costs remain fixed, and production and inventory capacity are unlimited. Despite the fact that these assumptions seem restrictive, the EOQ model provides useful guidelines for ordering decisions—even in operating situations that depart substantially from these assumptions.

The total incremental cost equation for the economic order quantity is shown as:

$$TIC = (A/Q) \, C_p + (Q/2) \, C_H \tag{17.1}$$

This equation contains two terms. The first term, $(A/Q) \, C_p$, represents the annual ordering cost, where A is the annual demand for the item, Q is the order quantity, and C_p is the cost of order preparation. Therefore, the total ordering cost per year is proportional to the number of orders placed annually (A/Q).

The second term, $(Q/2) \, C_H$ represents the annual inventory carrying cost, where the average inventory is assumed to be one half of the order quantity (Q), and C_H is the inventory carrying cost per unit per year; that is, the item value (v) times the annual percentage cost of carrying inventory (C_r).

The combined costs of ordering and carrying inventory are expressed as a function of the order quantity (Q) in Equation (17.1), enabling the total cost of any given order quantity to be evaluated.

Solving the EOQ model. One method of determining the lowest-cost ordering quantity is to plot the total cost equation for various order quantities on a graph. Figure 17.4 shows a plot of the total cost equation for the Model 100 movie camera, based on the following data:

$$A = 1,250.$$
$$C_p = 6.25.$$
$$C_H = 25.$$
$$TC = (1,250/Q)6.25 + (Q/2)25.$$

The total costs for several different order quantities have been plotted in Figure 17.4, and the minimum total cost can be found graphically to equal

FIGURE 17.4   Total inventory related costs versus order quantity for Model 100 movie camera

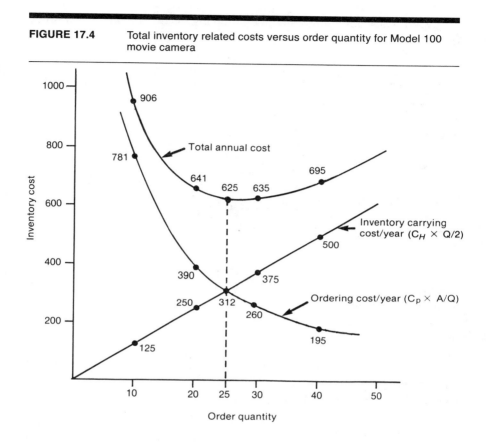

25 (i.e., placing orders weekly). Both terms of the total-cost equation have also been plotted.

Several facts should be noted in these graphs. First, the inventory carrying costs increase in a straight line as the order quantity is increased, while the ordering cost diminishes rapidly at first and then at a slower rate as the ordering cost is allocated over an increasing number of units. Second, in the EOQ model, the minimum cost solution exists where the ordering costs per year equals the annual inventory carrying cost. This observation is used in developing lot-sizing decision rules for dependent demand items. Finally, the total cost is relatively flat around the minimum cost solution (of $Q = 25$ in this case), indicating that inventory management performance is relatively insensitive to small changes in the order quantity around the minimum-cost solution.

A second and more direct method of solving for the minimum cost order quantity is by using the EOQ formula shown in Equation (17.2):

$$EOQ = \sqrt{2C_p\, A/C_H} \qquad (17.2)$$

This formula is derived from the total-cost equation (17.1), using calculus; that is, Equation (17.1) is differentiated with respect to the decision variable Q and solved by setting the resulting equation equal to zero, as is shown in Equations (17.3) through (17.6):

$$dTC/dQ = -C_p(A/Q^2) + C_H/2 \qquad (17.3)$$
$$C_p\, A/Q^2 = C_H/2 \qquad (17.4)$$
$$Q^2 = 2\, C_p\, A/C_H \qquad (17.5)$$
$$Q^* = \sqrt{2C_p\, A/C_H} \qquad (17.6)$$

where:

Q^* = The optimal value of Q = EOQ.

The use of the EOQ formula for the Model 100 movie camera produces a lot size of 25; that is, $\sqrt{[(2)(6.25)(1250)]/25}$. In using this expression, it is important to make sure that both the demand and the inventory carrying cost are measured in the same units (e.g., 1,250 units/year and $25/unit/year, in this case).

In addition to its use in determining order quantities, the EOQ formula can also be used to develop another important measure in the control of inventories—the economic time between orders (*TBO*). The formula to calculate TBO in weeks is shown in Equation (17.7):

$$TBO = Q^*/W \qquad (17.7)$$

where:

W = The average weekly usage rate.

In the case of the Model 100 movie camera, the *TBO* equals one week (25 units/order)/(25 units/week). This measure can be used to determine an economic ordering frequency or time between inventory reviews. As an example, in the case of the movie camera, one might consider using a Q,T decision rule; that is, order an economic lot size weekly.

Quantity discount model.   One of the assumptions underlying the EOQ model is that the unit cost (i.e., the item value) remains fixed over the range of order quantities considered. This frequently is not the case for purchased items where price discounts and transportation rate breaks are quoted when these items are ordered in large quantities. When discounts are possible, the trade-offs reflected in the decision model become more complex, and the solution procedures require more computations. The trade-offs involve a reduction in both the ordering cost and the item cost for an increase in the inventory carrying cost, when the order quantity is increased (and vice versa).

The total cost expression for the quantity discount model includes three terms: the annual purchase cost (vA), the annual ordering cost $(A/Q)C_p$, and the annual inventory carrying cost $(Q/2)C_H$. This expression, shown as Equation (17.8), differs in two respects from the EOQ equation (17.1).

$$TAC = (v)A + (A/Q)C_p + (Q/2)C_H \qquad (17.8)$$

First, the total annual cost of purchasing the item (CA) is a function of the item value (v); second, the inventory carrying cost (C_H) also depends on the item value $(C_H = vC_r$, where C_r is the annual percentage carrying cost). The item value, in turn, depends on the order quantity.

For example, the variable transportation cost for shipping the Model 100 movie camera from the distribution center to the field warehouse is $10 per unit for lot sizes of less than 40 units, and $5 per unit for lot sizes of 40 or more units. If we assume that the $100 unit cost for the movie camera was the delivered cost, based on the daily shipment quantities (5), this means that the item value is $100/unit$(v_1)$ for order quantities of less than 40 units, and $95/unit (v_2) for larger order quantities.

Since the item value is not a continuous function of the order quantity, the quantity discount model cannot be solved for an exact solution using calculus, and the computational procedure involves several steps. Magee and Boodman suggest the following five-step method for the direct calculation of the minimum-cost order quantity:

1. Calculate the economic order quantity, using the minimum unit price; if this quantity falls within the range for which the vendor offers this price, it is a *valid* economic order quantity and will result in the minimum cost for the particular item.
2. If the EOQ calculated in 1 is not valid, find the total annual cost for each price-break quantity.
3. Calculate an EOQ for each unit price.
4. Calculate the total annual cost for each valid EOQ determined in 3.
5. The minimum-cost order quantity is that associated with the lowest cost found in either 2 or 4.

This procedure is illustrated, using the Model 100 movie camera and v_1 = $100, v_2 = $95, and a minimum order quantity (b) of 40 for the $95 price. The calculations at each step are:

1. $EOQ = \sqrt{(2\ (1,250)\ (6.25))/(.25)\ 95} = 26$.
   (This EOQ is *invalid*, since it is less than the minimum order quantity of 40).

2. $TAC_b = (95)\,(1{,}250) + (6.25)(1250/40) + (.25)(95)(40/2) = \$119{,}420.$

3. $EOQ = \sqrt{[(2)\,(1{,}250)\,(6.25)]/(.25)\,(100)} = 25.$

4. $TAC_1 = (100)(1{,}250) + (6.25)\,(1250/25) + (.25)(100)(25/2) = \$125{,}625.$

5. The minimum cost order quantity is therefore the break point $b = 40$.

We see then that the minimum cost order quantity is 40 units. Each step in this process is illustrated in Figure 17.5. Note that the EOQ of 26 on TAC_2 is not a feasible solution, since it lies below the break point b, and that TAC_b is less than TAC_1.

FIGURE 17.5   Purchase discount cost curves

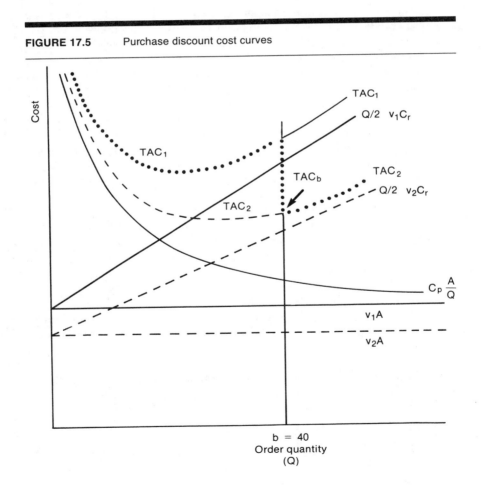

ORDER TIMING DECISIONS

The timing of replenishment orders under the order point rule is determined by the use of a trigger level (i.e., the reorder point). The inventory level is assumed to be under continuous monitoring (review), and, when the stock level reaches the reorder point, a replenishment order for a fixed quantity (Q) is issued. The setting of the reorder point is influenced by four factors: the demand rate, the lead time required to obtain replenishment inventory, the amount of uncertainty in the demand rate and in the replenishment lead time, and the management policy regarding the acceptable level of inventory shortages.

When there is no uncertainty in either the demand rate or the lead time for an item, safety stock is not required, and the determination of the reorder point is straightforward. For example, the demand rate for the Model 100 movie camera is assumed to be exactly five units per day, and the replenishment lead time is exactly one day in Figure 17.3. In this case, a reorder point of five units provides sufficient inventory to cover the demand until the replenishment order is received.

Sources of demand and supply uncertainty

The assumption of a fixed demand rate and a constant replenishment lead time is rarely justified in actual operations. Random fluctuations in the demand for individual products occur because of variations in the timing of the purchase of the product by consumers. Likewise, variations often occur in the length of the replenishment lead time because of machine breakdowns, employee absenteeism, material shortages, or transportation delays in the factory and distribution operations.

The Model 100 movie camera illustrates the amount of uncertainty usually experienced in the demand for end-product items. An analysis of the warehouse sales and inventory records for this item indicates that the replenishment lead time is quite stable, primarily involving a one-day transit time from the distribution center to the field warehouse. However, the daily demand varies considerably for the camera. While the daily demand averages five units, demands of from one to nine units have been experienced, as indicated in Figure 17.6.

If the reorder point is set at five units to cover the average demand during the one-day replenishment lead time, inventory shortages of from one to four units can result when the daily demand exceeds the average of five units; that is, when the demand equals six, seven, eight, or nine units. Therefore, if one is to provide protection against inventory shortages when there is uncertainty in demand, the reorder point must be greater than the average demand during the replenishment lead time, and some level of

FIGURE 17.6   Model 100 movie camera demand

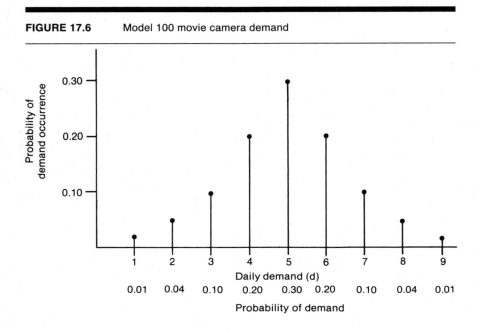

safety stock is required. Increasing the reorder point to nine units would provide a safety stock of four units. It would also prevent any stock-outs from occurring, given the historical pattern of demand for the Model 100 movie camera.

The introduction of safety stock

The introduction of safety stock into the reorder point setting is illustrated in Figure 17.7. The reorder point (R) in this diagram has two components: the safety stock level (S), and the level of inventory $(R - S)$ required to satisfy the average demand (D) during the average replenishment lead time (L). The reorder point is the sum of these two: $R = D + S$. To simplify this explanation, the lead time in Figure 17.7 is assumed to be constant while the demand rate varies.

When a replenishment order is issued (at point a), variations in the demand during the replenishment lead time mean that the inventory level can drop to a point between b and d. In the case of the movie camera, the inventory level may drop by one to nine units (points b and d, respectively) before a replenishment order is received. When the demand equals the average rate of five units, or less, the inventory level reaches a point between b and c, and the safety stock is not needed. However, when the demand rate exceeds the average of five units and the inventory level drops to a point

FIGURE 17.7   Safety stock level

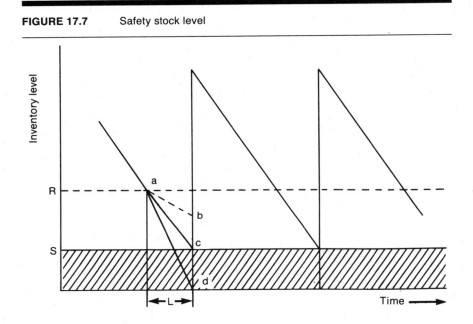

between *c* and *d*, a stock-out will occur unless safety stock is available. (A similar diagram can be constructed when both the demand rate and the lead time vary.)

Determining the safety stock level.   Before the level of safety stock can be decided, a criterion must be established for determining how much protection against inventory shortages is warranted. One of two different criteria is often used: the probability of stocking out in any given replenishment order cycle, or the desired level of customer service in satisfying the product demand immediately out of inventory. Both of these criteria are illustrated using the demand distribution for the Model 100 movie camera shown in Figure 17.6.

Stock-out probability.   One method for determining the required level of safety stock is to specify an acceptable risk of stocking out during any given replenishment lead time (order cycle). The demand distribution data for this analysis for the Model 100 movie camera are shown in Figure 17.6. There is a .05 probability of the demand exceeding seven units (i.e., a demand of either eight or nine units occurring). A safety stock level of two units, which means a reorder point of seven units, would provide a risk of stocking out 5 percent of the time or in 1 out of 20 replenishment order cycles. This safety stock level provides a .95 probability of meeting the demand during any given replenishment order cycle, and a .05 probability of stocking out by either one or two units when the demand exceeds seven units.

The risk of stocking out can be reduced by making a larger investment in safety stock; that is, with a safety stock of three units, the probability of stocking out can be reduced to .01, and with four units of safety stock the risk of stocking out is 0, assuming that the demand distribution does not change. Thus, one method of determining the required level of safety stock is to specify an acceptable trade-off between the probability of stocking out during a replenishment order cycle and the investment of funds in inventory.

Customer-service level. A second method for determining the required level of safety stock is to specify an acceptable level of customer service. For doing this, we define the customer-service level as the percentage of demand, measured in units, that can be supplied directly out of inventory during a stated time period. Data for doing the calculations are provided for the Model 100 movie camera in Figure 17.8. It shows that a safety stock of 1 unit enables 95.8 percent of the annual demand of 1,250 units for this item to be supplied directly out of inventory to the customer. The service level (*SL*) is computed using Equation (17.9):

$$SL = 100 - (100/Q) \sum_{D = R+1}^{D_{MAX}} P(D)(D - R) \qquad (17.9)$$

where:

Q = The order quantity.

D = The average demand during the replenishment lead time (order cycle).

R = The reorder point.

$P(D)$ = The probability of a demand of D units during the replenishment order cycle.

D_{MAX} = The maximum demand during the replenishment order cycle.

For example, when the safety stock is set at one unit in Figure 17.8, the service level is computed as shown in Equation (17.10):

$$SL = 95.8 = 100 - (100/5) [(.01)(3) + (.04)(2) + (.10)(1)] \qquad (17.10)$$

A service level of 95.8 percent means that 4.2 percent of the annual demand, or (.042) (1,250) = 52.5 units, cannot be supplied directly out of inventory. Since the current lot size (*Q*) is 5 units and the item is ordered 250 times per year, the average number of stock-outs per reorder cycle is .21 (i.e., 52.5/250), as is shown in Figure 17.8.

The impact of increasing the safety stock level on both the service level and the average number of shortages per replenishment order cycle are

FIGURE 17.8   Safety stock determination

Reorder point (R)	Safety stock (B)	Demand probability (P(D) = R)	Probability of stocking out (P(D) > R)	Average number of shortages per replenishment order cycle*	Service† level (SL)
5	0	.30	.35	.56	88.8%
6	1	.20	.15	.21	95.8%
7	2	.10	.05	.06	98.8%
8	3	.04	.01	.01	99.8%
9	4	.01	.00	0	100.0%

*This is calculated by:

$$\sum_{D=R+1}^{Dmax} P(D)(D - R)$$

†Assuming the replenishment order quantity is five units.

shown in Figure 17.8. The service level can be raised to 100 percent by increasing safety stock to four units. Again, as in the case of the stock-out probability method described previously, the choice of the required safety stock level depends on determining an acceptable trade-off between the customer service level and the inventory investment.

So far, the determination of the safety stock and the order quantity parameters for an order point system have been considered separately. These two parameters are, however, interdependent in their effect on customer/service-level performance. This interactive effect can be seen in Equation (17.9), since both the safety stock level and the size of the order quantity affect the level of customer service.

As an example, in the case of the Model 100 movie camera, a shift in order quantity from $Q = 5$ to $Q = 25$ raises the customer-service level from 95.8 percent to 99.16 percent when the safety stock equals one unit. This occurs because larger orders are placed less frequently, thereby reducing the number of times this item is exposed to inventory shortages during a year. This reduction in the average ordering frequency and the exposure to inventory shortages, in turn, reduces the average number of inventory shortages per year, effectively raising the level of customer service. Therefore, a change in the order quantity for an item can affect the level of safety stock required to meet a given customer-service-level objective in an order point system.

Continuous distributions

Two different criteria for determining the required level of safety stock and the reorder point have been described (i.e., the use of a stock-out probability and a desired level of customer service). In the discussion of both

FIGURE 17.9   Normal approximation to the empirical demand distribution*

Midpoint X	Discrete distribution probability	Interval	Normal distribution probability	Probability of demand exceeding X − 0.5	Expected number of stock-outs when reorder point = X†
1	.01	.5–1.5	.0085	.9902	4.0068
2	.04	1.5–2.5	.0380	.9522	3.0128
3	.11	2.5–3.5	.1109	.8413	2.0591
4	.20	3.5–4.5	.2108	.6305	1.2303
5	.30	4.5–5.5	.2610	.3695	.5983
6	.20	5.5–6.5	.2108	.1587	.2255
7	.10	6.5–7.5	.1109	.0478	.0641
8	.04	7.5–8.5	.0380	.0098	.0127
9	.01	8.5–9.5	.0085	.0013	.0018

*A χ^2 test indicates that these two distributions are not significantly different. (χ^2 = 8.75 versus 20.09 at the 0.01 level of significance.)

†This is σ_D E(Z) based on the E(Z) values from R. G. Brown, *Decision Rules for Inventory Management* (New York: Holt, Rinehart & Winston, 1967) pp. 95–103.

cases, a discrete distribution is used to describe the uncertainty in demand during the replenishment lead time (order cycle). It is frequently convenient to approximate a discrete distribution with a continuous distribution to simplify safety stock and reorder point calculations. One distribution that often provides a close approximation to empirical data is the normal distribution. In this section, we indicate the changes that are required in the calculations when the normal distribution is used to describe the uncertainty in demand during the replenishment lead time.

The data in Figure 17.9 show a comparison of the empirically derived probability values for the Model 100 movie camera demand shown in Figure 17.6, with similar values derived by using the normal distribution as an approximation for this distribution. The comparison shows that the normal distribution closely approximates the empirical distribution, and can be used to determine the safety stock and reorder point levels.

When the probability of stocking out is used as the safety stock criterion, the required level of safety stock and the reorder point values are easily computed using the normal distribution. First, it is necessary to determine the mean and the standard deviation for the distribution of demand during the replenishment lead time. These values have been calculated using the empirical distribution data for the Model 100 movie camera in Figure 17.6 and are shown in Figure 17.10 along with examples of the area (probability) under the normal distribution.

Next, the safety stock (or reorder point) value can be calculated using a table of normal probability values. For example, suppose sufficient safety stock is desired for the Model 100 movie camera that the probability of stock-

FIGURE 17.10   Daily demand distribution

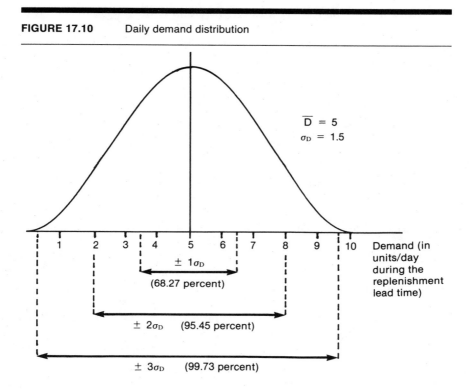

$\overline{D} = 5$
$\sigma_D = 1.5$

1 2 3 4 5 6 7 8 9 10   Demand (in units/day during the replenishment lead time)

$\pm 1\sigma_D$
(68.27 percent)

$\pm 2\sigma_D$ (95.45 percent)

$\pm 3\sigma_D$ (99.73 percent)

ing out in any given replenishment order cycle is .05. The safety stock level and the reorder point are determined, using Equations (17.11) and (17.12), respectively:

$$Safety\ stock = Z\sigma_D \qquad (17.11)$$

$$Reorder\ point = \text{Mean demand during the replenishment}$$
$$\text{lead time} + Z\sigma_D \qquad (17.12)$$

where:

Z = The appropriate value from a table of standard normal distribution probabilities.

σ_D = Demand during the replenishment lead time standard deviation.

The Z value for a .05 probability of stocking out is 1.645. The required level of safety stock, therefore, is 2.5 units—that is, (1.645)(1.5)—and the reorder point is 7.5 units. This can also be seen directly from the data in Figure 17.9, where the probability of demand exceeding 7.5 is shown to be

.0478. In this example, the demand distribution is calculated for one day, the same as the replenishment lead time.

When the time period for the demand distribution is different from the replenishment lead time, an adjustment must be made as shown in Equation (17.13):

$$\text{Safety stock} = Z\,(\sigma_D\,\sqrt{m}) \tag{17.13}$$

where:

m = The lead time expressed as a multiple of the time period used for the demand distribution.

If the lead time for the Model 100 movie camera were three days instead of one day, the required safety stock would be 4.3 units; that is, $(1.645)(1.5)$ $\sqrt{3}$, and the reorder point would be 19.3 units: (3 days)(5 units/day) + 4.3 units. Since the lead time in this example is three times the demand interval of one day, the $\sqrt{3}$ factor has been included in calculating the required safety stock. The resulting safety stock level increases for the three-day lead time to allow for the possible increase in variation in demand over the additional two days.

When the customer-service level is used as the safety stock criterion, the desired level of safety stock can also be determined, using the normal distribution approximation. For this case, we need the average number of stock-outs per replenishment order cycle. To get this, the quantity $\sum_{D=R+1}^{D_{MAX}} P(D)\,(D - R)$ shown in Equations (17.9) and (17.10), is replaced by $\sigma_D E(Z)$. The σ_D still equals the standard deviation of the normal distribution being used to approximate the demand during replenishment lead time. The $E(Z)$ value is the partial expectation of the normal distribution called the service function. It is the expected *number* of stock-outs when Z units of safety stock are held in the standard normal curve. A graph of the service function, $E(Z)$, is plotted in Figure 17.11. Note that when Z is less than -1, the service function, $E(Z)$, is approximately linear.

The safety stock and reorder point calculations are similar to those shown earlier in Equations (17.9) and (17.10). As an illustration, suppose that we want a service level of 95 percent for the Model 100 movie camera, and we go back to the use of an order quantity of five units. The required value for $E(Z)$ is computed, using Equation (17.15), which is derived from Equation (17.14):

$$SL = 100 - (100/Q)\,(\sigma_D E(Z)) \tag{17.14}$$

or

$$E(Z) = [(100 - SL)\,Q]/100\,\sigma_D \tag{17.15}$$

FIGURE 17.11   Service function

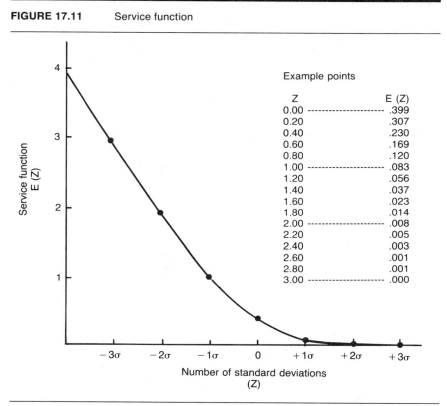

Example points

Z	E (Z)
0.00	.399
0.20	.307
0.40	.230
0.60	.169
0.80	.120
1.00	.083
1.20	.056
1.40	.037
1.60	.023
1.80	.014
2.00	.008
2.20	.005
2.40	.003
2.60	.001
2.80	.001
3.00	.000

Source: R. G. Brown, *Decision Rules for Inventory Management* (New York: Holt, Rinehart & Winston, 1967), pp. 95–103.

In this case, the service function value, $E(Z)$, equals .167; that is:

$$E(Z) = [(100 - 95) (5)]/[(100) (1.5)] = .167$$

and

$$\sigma_D E(Z) = 0.25$$

From the service function table in Figure 17.11, we find that an $E(Z)$ of .167 represents a Z value of approximately $+ .6\, \sigma_D$. The safety stock level therefore is $.9 = (.6) (1.5)$. The reorder point would be 5.9. Alternatively, from Figure 17.9, we find $R = 6$ when $\sigma_D E(Z) = .2255$. Note that this is the same result we got using the empirical discrete distribution earlier.

Forecast error distribution

In many inventory management software packages, the demand values for the economic order quantity and reorder point calculations are forecast, using statistical techniques such as exponential smoothing. When these forecasting techniques are used, the required safety stock level will depend upon the accuracy of the forecasting model—how much variation there is around the forecast. Very little safety stock will be required when the forecast errors are small, and vice versa, for a fixed level of customer service. One commonly used measure of forecasting model accuracy is the mean absolute deviation (MAD) of the forecast errors. This measure can be used directly in determining the required safety stock level.

The methods for determining the safety stock and reorder point levels described earlier in this chapter are also relevant when the product demand is forecast and a MAD value is maintained for the forecasting model. As an illustration, suppose that an exponential smoothing model is used to forecast the demand for the Model 100 movie camera, a .05 probability of stocking out during a reorder cycle is specified, and the forecast errors are normally distributed, as shown in Figure 17.12. The safety stock is calculated using Equation (17.16):

$$\text{Safety stock} = Z\sigma_E = Z\,(1.25\text{ MAD}) \tag{17.16}$$

where:

Z = The appropriate value from a table of standard normal distribution probabilities.

σ_E = Forecast error distribution standard deviation. (The value of σ_E can be approximated by 1.25 MAD when the forecast errors are normally distributed.)

Since the Z value is 1.645 for a .05 probability of stocking out and the MAD value equals 1.2 from Figure 17.12, the required level of safety stock is 2.5 units; that is, $(1.645)\,(1.25)\,(1.2)$. The reorder point would be 7.5 units, as we found before. In this example, the forecast interval is the same as the replenishment lead time—one day. When this is not the case, an adjustment must be made to the MAD value in a manner analogous to equation (17.13). The adjustment is shown in Equation (17.17):

$$\text{Safety stock} = Z\,(1.25\text{ MAD})\,\sqrt{m} \tag{17.17}$$

where:

m = The lead time expressed as a multiple of the forecast interval.

The safety stock can also be determined when customer-service level is used as the safety stock criterion and the product demand is forecast. In this case, Equation (17.15) is modified slightly, as shown in Equation (17.18):

FIGURE 17.12   Model 100 movie camera forecast error distribution

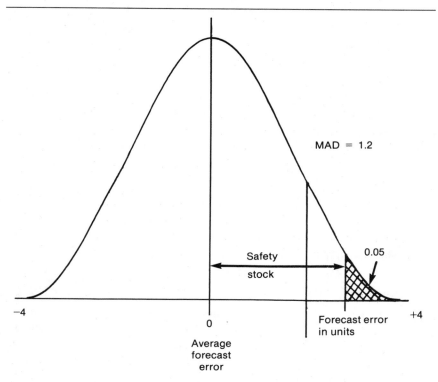

$$E(Z) = [(100 - SL)\, Q] \,/\, [100\,(1.25\ \mathrm{MAD})] \qquad (17.18)$$

After making this change, the safety stock and the reorder point calculations are similar to those involving $E(Z)$, shown earlier in this chapter.

INFORMATION SYSTEMS FOR INVENTORY CONTROL

Attention is focused on the decision-making aspects of the inventory management function for independent items in the previous sections. We discuss the development of routine decision rules for determining the timing and quantity of replenishment orders. The information system aspects of these decisions are, however, also critical in the effective management of inventories. Therefore, attention is now directed toward the information requirements of an effective inventory control system. This information consists of the basic inventory records, the handling of inventory transactions, the reporting of inventory performance, and computer software for managing the inventory system data base. We see these information needs by looking at a series of increasingly complex inventory control systems.

Bin reserve system

The bin reserve system is one of the simplest inventory control systems in terms of its information requirements. In fact, no records are necessary for this system to function. In this system, inventory is carried in two bins. Whenever the first bin is empty, a replenishment order is placed for additional material. The second bin contains sufficient material to last during the replenishment lead time, and it serves as the reorder point quantity.

Although this system is simple to administer, it has several disadvantages. For example, the actual stock balance at any given time is unknown. One knows only whether the stock level is above or below the reorder point. In addition, there is no information available that can be used to estimate the current usage rate for an item. Furthermore, information is also unavailable for management purposes in evaluating inventory performance (e.g., in determining slow-moving and surplus material).

Perpetual inventory systems

Perpetual inventory systems overcome many of the disadvantages inherent in a bin reserve system. A perpetual inventory system maintains a record of the current stock balance for each inventory item, and receipt and disbursement transactions are routinely processed to update the inventory balance, as well as to obtain historical usage data. An example stock status report for such a system is shown in Figure 17.13. This record contains information concerning the present on-hand balance, the quantity currently on order, the date of the last inventory transaction, an estimate of the item usage rate, and so on. It also includes the inventory management parameters for each item (e.g., the order quantity, reorder point, safety stock, and lead time.

The inventory data base provided by a perpetual inventory system enables closer control to be exerted over inventory system performance. For example, the record of stock disbursements enables better estimation of the item usage rates to be prepared, thereby helping avoid excessive inventory levels and inventory shortages. Furthermore, special inventory reports can be prepared to analyze surplus or slow-moving items. Such reports can serve as the basis for inventory parameter changes (i.e., the order quantities or safety stocks) and to initiate special programs to apply surplus inventory to other applications. These improvements in inventory performance are, however, obtained at the expense of the additional administrative effort required

FIGURE 17.13   Perpetual inventory record

```
XYZ COMPANY
REPORT NO. IC-340B                          I N V E N T O R Y   S T O C K   S T A T U S
REQUESTED BY: YOUR NAME                     -------------SELECTION CRITERIA-------------
                                    PART NO   VALUE  TYPE  COMM  NEG    MINUS  DATE
                                    ①         CLASS  CODE  CODE  ON-HAND AVAIL LASTISS  SURPLUS
                              BY REQUEST      XXX    X     XXX   X      X     XXXXX    X
```

PART NO DESCRIPTION	UM	TYP CDE	COM CDE	B A	V C	I	ORD POL	ORDER QTY	SAFTY STOCK	LEAD TIME	STOCK LOC	ON HAND	ON ORDER	ALLOC QTY	AVAIL QTY	GROSS REQMT	YTD USAGE	DATE LASTISS
AA-01 DOUBLE DOOR SET	EA	MFG	END	A	A	R	A/R	0	50	5	A0101	50	100	0	150	650	0	
AA-02 RIGHT DOOR	EA	MFG	ASY	A	A	R	F/T	2	0	5	A0102	250	0	100	150	600	0	
AA-03 LEFT DOOR	EA	MFG	ASY	A	A	R	F/T	2	0	5	A0103	200	0	100	100	600	0	
AA-04 COMMON DOOR	EA	MFG	ASY	A	A	R	F/Q	200	0	VAR	A0104	150	150	0	300	750	0	
AA-05 CENTER MEMBER	EA	PUR	PUR	B	B	R	EOQ	600	100	15	B0102 VENDOR NO VEN075	600	0	450	150	1950	400	12/31

① Stock status reports can be requested by part, value class, type (purchased/manufactured), or commodity to analyze negative-on hand, minus availability, date of last issue for obsolescence, or surplus conditions in any combination selected by user

② Order policies and quantities, safety stock, and leadtime information for order planning

③ Current inventory balances include availability, planned requirements, and year-to-date usage; on hand + on order – allocated = available

Source: *MAC-PAC Manufacturing Planning and Control System General Description Manual* (Chicago: Arthur Andersen & Co., 1980), p. 11.

to maintain a perpetual inventory system. Using a report of the type shown in Figure 17.13, the records for several thousand items can be maintained on a small-scale computer system. Computer software packages for managing a perpetual inventory system data base are widely available from management consulting, computer, and software firms.

ABC analysis

In many firms, an ABC analysis is frequently prepared to determine the most economical method for controlling individual inventory items. Such an analysis can serve, for example, as the basis for determining which items should be controlled, using a perpetual inventory system, and those best controlled by a bin reserve system. An ABC analysis consists of separating the inventory items into three groupings according to their annual cost volume usage (unit cost × annual usage). These groups are then divided into A items having a high dollar volume usage, B items having an intermediate dollar volume usage, and C items having a low dollar volume usage.

The results of a typical ABC analysis are shown in Figure 17.14. For this inventory, 20 percent of the items are A items, which account for 65 percent of the annual cost volume usage. The B category comprises 30 percent of the items and 25 percent of the annual cost usage, while the remaining 50 percent of the items are C items accounting for only 10 percent of the annual cost volume usage. While percentages may vary from firm to firm, it is common to find that a small percentage of the items accounts for a large percentage of the annual cost volume usage.

An ABC analysis provides a tool for identifying those items that will make the largest impact on the firm's inventory performance when improved inventory control procedures are implemented; that is, the use of a perpetual inventory system, improvements in forecasting procedures, and a careful analysis of the order quantity and timing decisions for A items will provide a larger improvement in inventory performance than will similar efforts on the C items. Therefore, conducting an ABC analysis is often a useful first step in designing a program of action to improve inventory performance.

The report shown in Figure 17.15 is included to illustrate the results of conducting an ABC analysis. For this report, several additional criteria have been applied. These include lead time and unit cost, as well as the annual usage value, as is shown in the block labeled Value Class Rules. The A items in each of these categories are clearly candidates for the application of improved inventory control procedures.

Management issues

Several issues have been raised in this chapter, which require action on the part of management for appropriate control of inventories. These in-

FIGURE 17.14   ABC analysis

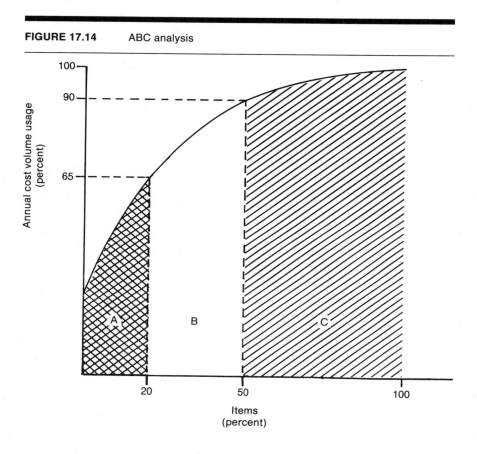

clude: the selection of the appropriate inventory management techniques, the evaluation of inventory management performance, and the proper use of inventories in managing operations. The material presented in this chapter is useful in analyzing these issues.

After all of the analyses have been completed, the critical element in the management of inventories is judgment on when to take action in implementing changes to improve inventory performance. For example, informal procedures for managing inventories may be quite effective for a small-scale warehousing operation. However, as the business experiences growth and there are substantial increases in the number of products stocked and sales volume, more formal inventory control methods are needed to ensure continued business growth. The key to effective inventory management is, therefore, recognizing when to turn to the formal methods for inventory control presented in this chapter, to handle the routine decisions that must be made in managing day-to-day inventory operations.

FIGURE 17.15 ABC analysis

XYZ COMPANY
REPORT NO. IC-480A
REQUESTED BY - YOUR NAME

A B C   I N V E N T O R Y   C L A S S I F I C A T I O N

VALUE CLASS	LEAD TIME	UNIT COST	ANNUAL VALUE	PERCT VALUE	USAGE WEIGHT FACTORS	POST VALUE CLASS
A	20	100.00	100,000	25	YTD 50	N
B	15	50.00	50,000	50	GROSS 50	
C	10	5.00	5,000	80		
D	0	.00	0	100		

PART NO/ DESC	CODES TY AC	PART COUNT	PERCT TOTAL COUNT	ANNUAL USAGE	LEAD TIME DAYS	CURRENT UNIT COST	ANNUAL USAGE VALUE	CUMM USAGE VALUE	PERCT TOTAL VALUE	VALUE CLASS CURR	PREV
AA-05 CENTER MEMBER	1 3	1	14.3	11,000	15 B	10.00 C	110,000 A	110,000	24.5 A	A	A
AA-09 RAW MATERIAL	3 4	2	28.6	-12,500	30 A	7.50 C	93,750 B	203,750	45.4 B	A	A
AA-11 KNOB & LOCK	1 3	3	42.8	20,000	15 B	4.50 D	90,000 B	293,750	65.5 C	B	B
AA-10 GLUE	3 4	4	57.1	15,000	10 C	5.00 C	75,000 B	368,750	82.2 D	B	C
AA-13 HINGE	1 3	5	71.4	240,000	10 C	.25 D	60,000 B	428,750	95.6 D	B	B
AA-12 LOCK CATCH	1 3	6	85.7	30,000	10 C	.50 D	15,000 C	443,750	98.9 D	C	C
AA-14 SCREW	1 3	7	100.0	480,000	5 D	.01 D	4,800 D	448,550	100.0 D	D	D

(1) User specified ABC parameters for leadtime, unit cost, annual dollar value, and per cent total value determine value class rules

(2) Annual usage can be weighted by year-to-date and/or planned usage percentages for more effective ranking

(3) Value class ranking based on highest value in accordance with specified parameters

Source: *MAC-PAC Manufacturing Planning and Control System General Description Manual* (Chicago: Arthur Andersen & Co., 1980). p. 11.

CONCLUDING PRINCIPLES

This chapter presents a considerable amount of theory on independent demand inventory management. Despite the technical nature of the material, several management principles emerge:

- The difference between dependent and independent demand must serve as the first basis for determining the appropriate inventory management procedures.
- Reorder point procedures should be used for independent demand items.
- The organizational criteria must be clearly established before setting safety stock levels.
- The choice of decision rule to use for managing a particular item depends upon where it is in an ABC analysis.
- The performance of the inventory management procedure must be monitored.
- The procedures used to manage inventory should change as the company changes.

REFERENCES

Brown, R. G. *Statistical Forecasting for Inventory Control*. New York: McGraw-Hill, 1959.

————. *Decision Rules for Inventory Management*. New York: Holt, Rinehart & Winston, 1967.

Davis, E. W., and D. C. Whybark. "Inventory Management." *Small Business Bibliography 75*. Washington, D.C.: Small Business Administration, 1980.

Fogarty, D. W., and T. R. Hoffman. *Production and Inventory Control*. Falls Church, Va.: American Production and Inventory Control Society, 1983.

Greene, J. H. *Production and Inventory Control Handbook*. Falls Church, Va.: American Production and Inventory Control Society, 1984.

Inventory Planning Reprints. Falls Church, Va.: American Production and Inventory Control Society, 1978.

MAC-PAC Manufacturing Planning and Control System General Description Manual. Arthur Andersen & Co., Chicago, 1980.

Magee, J. F., and D. M. Boodman. *Production Planning and Inventory Control*. New York: McGraw-Hill, 1967.

Service Parts Management Reprints. Falls Church, Va.: American Production and Inventory Control Society, 1982.

Silver, E. A., and R. Peterson. *Decision Systems for Inventory Management and Production Planning*. 2nd. ed. New York: John Wiley & Sons, 1985.

Vandemark, Robert L. "The Case for the Combination Systems." *APICS 23rd Annual Conference Proceedings*, 1980, pp. 125–27.

DISCUSSION QUESTIONS

1. The concepts of independent and dependent demand are important in inventory management but sometimes not clearly distinguishable. Can you find the elements of dependency and independency in the following situations: selling snacks at a football game, producing bumpers for automobiles, and selling greeting cards at a shopping center.

2. What would you expect to find as the predominant type of inventory in the following businesses: a ski manufacturer, a make-to-order tug boat manufacturer, and a printer?

3. Which of the inventory costs would be most difficult to measure? How would you determine if you needed more precision in the estimate of the cost?

4. Why might the EOQ model not be appropriate for a dependent demand item?

5. How many pairs of socks do you own? How many dress suits? How does this relate to the ABC concept?

PROBLEMS

1. An end product has an average usage of 8 units/period and an ordering cost of $40/order. The inventory carrying cost for the item is $0.10/unit/period. No safety stock is carried for this item.
   a. Calculate the economic order quantity.
   b. Calculate the average cycle stock for this item, using the order quantity in question a.
   c. Assuming that there are 13 periods per year, calculate the total cost per year.

2. Given the following data for a manufactured part, calculate the economic order quantity. State any assumptions made in arriving at a solution.

   Average monthly usage = 32 units.
   Usage standard deviation = 4 units.
   Average production lead time = 1 month.
   Production lead time standard deviation = 0.1 month.
   Production setup time = 3 hours.
   Material cost = $10/unit.
   Direct labor hourly rate = $5/hour.
   Variable shop overhead cost = $1/production hour.
   Fixed shop overhead cost = $1/production hour.
   Cost of capital = 22% per year of part cost.
   Production run time = 1 hour/unit.
   Average overall stockroom inventory investment = $500,000.
   Annual property taxes:
      Stockroom building = $1,000/year.
      Stockroom contents = $5,000/year.

Annual insurance cost:
  Stockroom building = $500/year.
  Stockroom contents = $5,000/year.
  Annual stockroom electric bill = $1,600/year.
  Stockroom clerk = $10,000/year.
  Stockroom fixed overhead = $5,000/year.
  Annual stockroom heating cost = $2,000/year.

3. The Friendly Insurance Company processes an average of 90 checks per day for payment of claims. Each time a check is written, it must be accompanied by a request for payment form (form #RFP–XX). The Friendly clerical staff reproduces the form RFP–XX themselves, using the office photocopy machine. The staff is capable of producing 800 forms in an eight-hour day. The cost of setting up the photocopy machine is $10, which is incurred everytime a batch of forms is started. Holding costs are $0.10 per form per year. Friendly works a total of 250 days per year.

    Bob Collins at Friendly has figured out that the classic EOQ formula needs to be modified when the units are being consumed or used while they are being produced. The revised formula involves multiplying the denominator C_H by $(1 - r/p)$ where r is the usage or demand rate, and p is the production rate (r and p need to be expressed in the same units). Collins is most anxious to see how this model will work at Friendly.

  a. In what size batches should the forms be produced?
  b. How long will it take the clerical staff to produce a batch of form RFP–XX?
  c. How often will a batch of RFP–XXs have to be produced?

4. The Blue Mountain Ice Cream Shoppe sells hand-packed pints of its homemade ice cream. Pints of ice cream are sold at the rate of 10 per day, and the store is open 300 days each year. The ice cream can be made and packed in pints at a rate of 50 pints per day. Storage costs are $0.50 per pint per month, and the cost to prepare the ice cream mixing machine is $15 per batch of ice cream (use the modified EOQ formula given in problem 3).

  a. Calculate the economic run size for a batch of ice cream.
  b. How many batches of ice cream will be produced per year?
  c. What is the maximum inventory level of pints of ice cream?
  d. How long is the cycle time and run time for this operation?

5. The purchasing manager at the Barnes Trucking Company has received the following quote from a supplier on a maintenance item:

Purchase quantity/order	Price
Less than 1,000 units	$100/unit
1,000 units or more	$ 85/unit

If the ordering cost equals $50, the annual volume equals 2,000 units, and the cost of holding inventory is 20 percent of item value per unit per year, what is the total annual cost of the minimum cost order quantity?

6. The Black Forest Company produces a line of hand-carved music boxes with playing units that accept a variety of cassettes. BFC anticipates annual sales of 10,000 music boxes of this type. There is a small reduction in price for the playing units as larger quantities are ordered:

Quantity ordered	Price
Less than 800 units	$10.00/unit
800 through 2,499 units	$ 9.90/unit
2,500 units or more	$ 9.80/unit

If the cost of placing an order is $50 and the carrying cost is 20 percent per year of the unit price, how many playing units should BFC order each time?

7. The inventory control manager at the Denver Auto Parts Supply Center is trying to determine the safety stock and the reorder point for the 1442 mud flap. There is a one week lead time for this item. She has developed the following information for this item:

Sales/week (in units)	Probability
16	.01
17	.02
18	.05
19	.08
20	.10
21	.12
22	.24
23	.12
24	.10
25	.08
26	.05
27	.02
28	.01

a. Determine the required safety stock and the reorder point values that provide a .01, a .08, and a .26 probability of stocking out during a reorder cycle.
b. If the cost per unit of the 1442 mud flap is $10, what is the required inventory investment in safety stock to achieve a .01, a .08, and a .26 probability of stocking out during a reorder cycle?

8. The ICU Optical Clinic has recently introduced a new line of eyeglasses that incorporates a highly fashionable frame and special lenses that darken in sunlight and lighten indoors, thus eliminating the need to purchase a separate pair of sunglasses. The frames for the eyeglasses are purchased from an outside vendor by ICU: however, the lenses are manufactured on site. The clinic has recently been experiencing the following demand distribution for its new eyeglasses:

Demand/month	Probability
12	.10
13	.15
14	.15
15	.20
16	.20
17	.10
18	.05
19	.05

The purchase price of the frames to the ICU Optical Clinic is $30 per unit. The clinic has an ordering cost of $25. The cost of carrying inventory is 25 percent of the item value per unit per year. Order lead time is constant at one month. The work year consists of 12 months.

a. Write the economic order quantity formula for the optimum lot-size quantity using the following notation:

C_u = Unit price of a product.

C_1 = Holding cost per unit per year.

C_2 = Preparation costs per order.

M = Annual demand requirements.

t = Unit time period (i.e., time between orders).

Q = Lot size.

Q* = Optimum lot size.

b. Compute the economic order quantity for the frames purchased by the ICU Clinic.

c. Compute the reorder point and buffer stock level for a 99 percent customer service level. Assume that the order quantity and the reorder point can be computed independently.

d. What is the total annual cost of carrying the buffer stock computed in question c?

9. The corner grocery store orders a two-week supply of flour whenever the on-hand inventory falls below the reorder point. Lead time for the flour is one day. On Tuesday, September 28, the stockboy found 20 bags of flour in stock. Daily sales of the flour are normally distributed with a mean of 18 bags per day and a standard deviation of 10 bags per day. The desired customer service level is 99 percent.

a. How many bags of flour should be ordered on September 28, if the store is open five days per week?

b. What is the safety stock for flour that provides a 99 percent customer service level?

10. A surgical supply item stocked in the pharmacy at the Morningside Hospital is ordered from a supplier having a two-week lead time. Because of the critical nature of this item, a 99 percent service level is desired. The ordering cost is $149 and the inventory carrying cost is $20 per unit per year. The weekly demand for this item is normally distributed with a mean of 42 units and a stan-

dard deviation of 15 units. Determine the economic order quantity, the safety stock, and the reorder point for this item assuming a 52-week year.

11. The spare parts department at the Bath Shipyard stocks an electric component for shipboard sonar systems. This item has a production lead time of one week. The inventory management system record for this item indicates a forecast value of 104 units per week with a MAD value of 40. The ordering cost is $80 and the inventory carrying cost is $5 per unit per year. Assuming that the shipyard would like to maintain a customer service level of 99 percent for this item, determine the economic order quantity, the safety stock level, and the reorder point. (Assume that the forecast error distribution is normally distributed and that there are 52 weeks per year.)

12. The Seldom Seen Ranch in Muckinfut, Texas, is in the process of developing an inventory control system for purchasing hay that will cope with Texas-size uncertainty. The foreman of Seldom Seen, Horace Cints, has prepared the following information on the use of hay at Seldom Seen:

> Average demand during lead time = 1,000 bales.
> Lead time = 1 month.
> Economic order quantity = 2,500 bales.
> Forecast interval = 1 month.
> Mean absolute deviation of forecast error = 40 bales.
> Desired probability of stocking out = 0.10.

   a. How much safety stock will be required?
   b. What is the reorder point?
   c. What is the customer service level for this policy?
   d. What decision rule should Horace Cints use in ordering hay, assuming constant hay usage throughout the year?

13. After the merger, Old Framkranz found himself the only inventory clerk left at Allied Breakwater Company (ABC). The merger had left ABC with only 10 parts in inventory, and he had been told to manage them as effectively as possible. Each part was to be reviewed once a week (ABC worked a very exhausting five-day week). Framkranz knew the inventory carrying cost was 20 percent per dollar of cost per year. He also knew that, to really manage the inventory of a part well, he would have to spend a full day on the review, but he could do a reasonably good job in half a day. Even the most cursory review would require one-quarter day per part, however. The files for the 10 parts contain

Part #	Vendor	Unit cost ($)	Shipping cost/unit	Cost per order ($)	Annual usage	Reorder point	Order quantity
1	A	.20	0	10	1000	50	70
2	B	1.00	.10	20	10	1	45
3	B	.25	.10	15	12	2	95
4	C	3.00	.25	15	100	20	71
5	A	10.00	0	10	300	15	55
6	B	7.00	.10	15	2	1	7
7	C	.50	.25	20	10	2	13
8	A	5.00	0	10	400	20	39
9	C	20.00	.30	20	2	1	4
10	A	2.00	0	10	200	10	100

the information above. How should Framkranz schedule the review of the parts?

14. Develop a general spreadsheet for finding order quantities when there are quantity discounts. Use problem 5 as a test problem. When you have a program that will take different values of the costs and the price/quantity schedules, find the least cost quantity to purchase for the following set of quantity discount data (order cost = $50 and inventory holding cost = 20 percent of item value):

Quantity ordered	Price
Less than 50 units	27.00
50–99 units	26.00
100–199 units	25.50
200–499 units	25.00
More than 499 units	24.75

15. Arthur Hill is evaluating the use of a reorder point system and has asked for your help. Specifically, he would like to examine the use of reorder point models for two items. He has provided you with 20 periods of actual demand data for each item, listed below as demand set I and demand set II. Art has provided the following data (the same for both items) to aid in your analysis:

Item cost = $6.
Carrying cost = 20 percent.
One year = 52 periods.
Setup cost = $15.
Lead time = 1 week (period).
Service level = 95 percent.
Standard deviation = 1.25 MAD

Demand set I		Demand set II	
Period	Demand	Period	Demand
1	51	1	77
2	46	2	83
3	49	3	90
4	55	4	22
5	52	5	10
6	47	6	80
7	51	7	16
8	48	8	19
9	56	9	27
10	51	10	79
11	45	11	73
12	52	12	88
13	49	13	15
14	48	14	21
15	43	15	85
16	46	16	22
17	55	17	88
18	53	18	75
19	54	19	14
20	49	20	16

Calculate the economic order quantity (EOQ) and order point for each item. Using the two sets of data given above estimate average demand and MAD. Thereafter, assume that you are starting period one with an inventory of 150 units of each item. Use a spreadsheet and the results obtained for the order quantity and reorder point to simulate the results of ordering an EOQ each time the inventory drops below the reorder point. Calculate the period by period and the average inventory values, using the two demand sets. Repeat the analysis reversing the reorder point values; that is, use the reorder point calculated for item 1 for item 2 and vice versa. What do the results mean? What are the managerial implications?

— 18

Advanced independent demand systems

In this chapter we present several approaches for improving the management of independent demand items. Most of the improvements derive from increasing the number of problem elements considered and explicitly recognizing interdependencies between problem elements. Applying these concepts to managing independent demand items requires an expanded system perspective but promises important improvements. In addition, a more knowledgeable software selection can be made since many of the ideas are incorporated in commercial software approaches. Applying the ideas presented in this chapter can lead to improved inventory and service performance in independent demand environments. Specifically, we address the following topics:

- A perspective on advanced independent demand systems: How should the advanced concepts be viewed and what is required for their use?
- Order quantity and reorder point interactions: Why is it important to determine the order quantity and reorder point simultaneously, and what form does the analysis take?
- Inventory and transportation mode interactions: How should the im-

pact of alternative transportation choices be incorporated into the analysis?

- Multiple items from a single source: What procedures exist for placing orders for many items from a single vendor?
- Multiple criteria ABC analysis: How can criteria, other than dollar-usage, be incorporated into ABC classifications of inventory items for managerial purposes?
- Living with advanced systems: How can the organization be prepared to use the advanced approaches wisely?

This chapter builds upon the material in Chapter 17 dealing with basic independent demand concepts. The forecasting material in Chapter 16 provides basic inputs to the independent demand management systems. The ideas in Chapter 11 on implementation are germane to installing advanced systems.

A PERSPECTIVE ON ADVANCED SYSTEMS

Throughout this chapter an overriding objective is to present an expanded viewpoint for managing independent demand items. A great deal of the writing on inventory techniques tends to be in watertight compartments; that is, the theoretical materials are based on assumptions that limit the system under study and the evaluative criteria for judging the value of problem solutions. In expanding the system perspective, we necessarily incorporate additional problem elements, break some of the barriers that force problems to be considered in isolation, and consider problems with a more realistic set of objectives or evaluative criteria. Such a viewpoint provides an enhanced understanding of inventory related problems. It also can lead to demonstrable improvements in certain problem environments.

Before turning to the technical issues of particular inventory management systems, a caveat is in order. The ideas presented here depend on having some of the basic system elements in place. These elements include accurate inventory and demand records, clear-cut reporting procedures and transaction controls, timely and effective forecasts of demand, and a managerial willingness to clearly address trade-offs between inventory levels and customer service measures.

In some cases, one needs to take an evolutionary point of view. One first implements a basic system even though it is flawed by the limited system view. With the basic system, the objectives are more straightforward, conformance to procedures can be more easily assessed, and operations of the firm are more easily brought into harmony with the dictates of the system. *Thereafter,* it may be desirable to consider some of the techniques presented here as enhancements.

We begin this chapter by considering advanced reorder point techniques.

These techniques provide performance improvements by combining factors that interact in the determination of the reorder point and order quantity values. These factors include: the inventory required for satisfying customer service level objectives, the interaction between transportation mode and inventory system decisions, and joint ordering of multiple items from a single supplier. We then turn to some of the managerial issues involved in living with these enhanced systems.

In addition to generating important cost savings, the enhancements considered in this chapter often provide major improvements in the productivity of inventory planners. This occurs because many of the clerical tasks performed by the inventory planners can be accomplished routinely using computerized logic. The substitution of routine procedures for manual efforts permits applying the limited personnel resources where they are best utilized in problem-solving activities. When this is done, people can spend more time on decision making and coordinative activities and less time on clerical work.

ORDER QUANTITY AND REORDER POINT INTERACTIONS

In this section, we look at the interaction between the reorder point and order quantity for a small example. We will then present two ways of jointly determining the reorder point and order quantity: a search procedure and an iterative procedure. We consider both service level and total cost criteria.

Service levels and order quantities

Figure 18.1 provides data for a single inventory item that will serve as our example. Note that both the lead time and the weekly demand are prob-

---

FIGURE 18.1   Data for single-item example

Notation

Item value	v	$500 per unit
Average demand	A	35 units per year
Fixed ordering cost	C_p	$45 per order
Shortage cost	C_s	$60 per unit short
Inventory carrying cost rate	C_r	25% of value per year
Economic order quantity	EOQ	5 units
Replenishment lead time	LT	1 week, probability = .8
		2 weeks, probability = .2
		Average lead time = 1.2 weeks
Weekly demand distribution:		0 units, probability = .5
		1 unit, probability = .3
		2 units, probability = .2
		Average demand/week = .7 units

FIGURE 18.2 Tree diagram of possible occurrences of lead time and demand for example problem

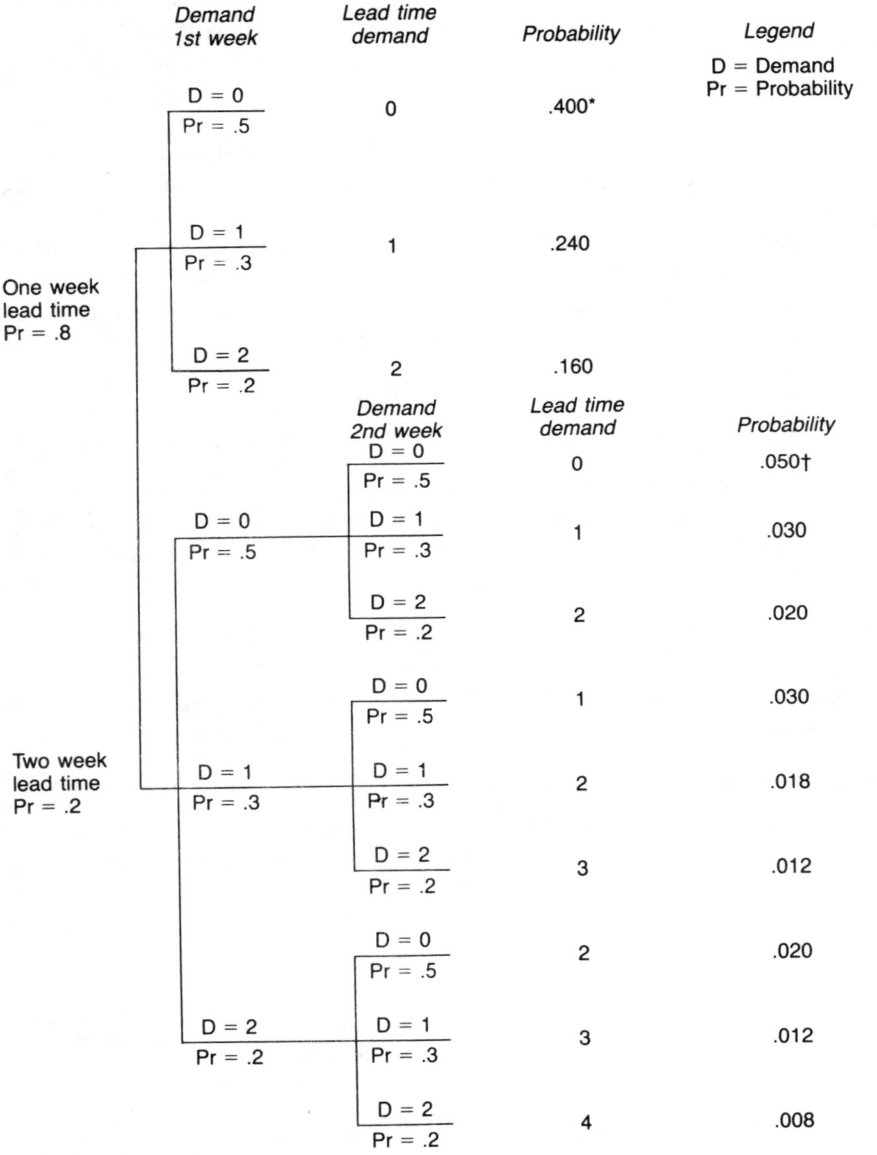

Demand 1st week	Lead time demand	Probability	Legend
			D = Demand
			Pr = Probability
D = 0 Pr = .5	0	.400*	
D = 1 Pr = .3	1	.240	
D = 2 Pr = .2	2	.160	

One week lead time Pr = .8

	Demand 2nd week	Lead time demand	Probability
	D = 0 Pr = .5	0	.050†
D = 0 Pr = .5	D = 1 Pr = .3	1	.030
	D = 2 Pr = .2	2	.020
	D = 0 Pr = .5	1	.030
D = 1 Pr = .3	D = 1 Pr = .3	2	.018
	D = 2 Pr = .2	3	.012
	D = 0 Pr = .5	2	.020
D = 2 Pr = .2	D = 1 Pr = .3	3	.012
	D = 2 Pr = .2	4	.008

Two week lead time Pr = .2

*LT = 1 week (Pr = .8) and D = 0 for that week (Pr = .5). Probability of both occurring is .4 = (.8 × .5).

†LT = 2 weeks (Pr = .2) and D = 0 (Pr = .5) for each week. Probability of all three occurring is .05 = (.2 × .5 × .5).

abilistic (uncertain). This means that the process of determining the distribution of demand during lead time is somewhat complicated. We use a tree diagram to illustrate all possible combinations of demand and lead time that can occur. These are then summarized to give the distribution of demand during lead time.

The lead time and the weekly demand distribution data shown in Figure 18.1 have been used to develop the tree diagram in Figure 18.2. As an example of the calculations, we will use the branch at the bottom of Figure 18.2. The 4-unit demand occurs during the replenishment lead time only when the lead time is 2 weeks and 2 units are demanded each week. The probability of these events occurring is: $(.2)(.2)(.2) = .008$. The remaining combinations of daily demand and lead time values are enumerated in Figure 18.2, and the results are summarized in the demand during lead time distribution, shown in Figure 18.3.

Also shown in Figure 18.3 are the expected number of units short for specified reorder points. A shortage can only occur when the demand exceeds the reorder point. So, for example, when the reorder point is 4, no shortages can occur. If the reorder point is 2, there is a 1-unit shortage if the demand is 3 and a 2-unit-shortage if demand is 4. The probabilities of these demands occurring are .024 and .008, respectively. This means the expected number of stockouts are $(.024 \times 1) + (.008 \times 2) = .040$, when the reorder point is 2.

To show the interaction between reorder point and order quantity, we use the data in Figure 18.3. Suppose the item was currently ordered about five times per year in quantities of 7. If the reorder point was set to 1 unit, the expected number of units short *per reorder cycle* would be .29. This would mean, for the 5 cycles per year, that about 1.5 units would be out of stock in a year. This corresponds to a service level of about 95 percent $[(35 - 1.5)/35]$.

If the order quantity is changed to 35, only 1 reorder cycle per year would occur. There would be an expected .29 units short in the cycle if the reorder point was 1, but that is now the expected number short for the year, as well.

FIGURE 18.3   Demand during lead time distribution

Demand (D)	Probability of demand = D	Probability of demand > D	Reorder point (R)	Expected number of units short (E{s}) when reorder point = R
0	.450	.550	0	.840 units
1	.300	.250	1	.290 units
2	.218	.032	2	.040 units
3	.024	.008	3	.008 units
4	.008	0	4	0 units

Expected demand during lead time = .840

FIGURE 18.4   Inventory costs and service levels

Reorder point	Order quantity					
	4		5		6	
0	$643.75	79%	$627.50	83%	$637.50	86%
1	663.75	93%	647.50	94%	657.50	95%
2	788.75	99%	772.50	99%	782.50	99%

This corresponds to a service level of 99 percent [(35 − .29)/35]. Even a reorder point of 0 would provide a level of service of about 97 percent [(35 − .84)/35] when 35 units are ordered at a time.

The order quantity of 35 provides more cycle stock than the order quantity of 7. For the larger order, the exposure to stockout is only once a year, as opposed to 5 times per year when the order quantity is 7. Thus, the cycle stock protects against demand fluctuations during the year—acting much like safety stock.

In many companies, the determination of shortage costs is very difficult and/or there is a preference to use a service criterion for inventory management. In these firms, the question of the trade-off between service level and inventory cost is still relevant but complicated, because the order quantity and reorder point both affect service levels and inventory costs. One way of providing explicit trade-off data for management consideration is to develop tables like that shown in Figure 18.4. In this table, the inventory holding plus ordering costs and service levels are shown for various order quantities and reorder points using the example data.

To illustrate the calculations for Figure 18.4, consider a reorder point of 2 and an order quantity of 4. The annual ordering cost would be (35/4)(45) = $393.75. The cycle stock carrying cost would be (4/2)(.25)(500) = $250, while the cost of safety stock would be (2 − .84)(.25)(500) = $145. This totals $788.75.

Total cost equation

So far, our example has measured customer service levels as the percentage of the units ordered by the customers met from stock. In some cases, the costs of not having the units in stock (e.g., lost profits, penalty costs, and the loss of customer goodwill) can be quantified. This permits a more global examination of inventory decisions, since the ordering, carrying, and inventory shortage costs can all be considered in determining the inventory parameters.

The equation for total incremental cost per period (18.1) contains terms for the costs of placing orders, carrying inventory, and incurring inventory shortages. This equation requires estimates for all the costs, probably the most difficult of which is the cost of incurring inventory shortages (i.e., the shortage cost). Once the cost estimates are made, the expression can be used to find the lowest total cost set of order quantity (Q) and reorder point (R) parameter values. The equation is:

$$TIC = A/Q \left[C_p + C_s \left(\sum_{D=R+1}^{D_{max}} (D - R) \, P(D) \right) \right] + C_H[Q/2 + (R - \overline{D})] \quad (18.1)$$

where:

$$
\begin{aligned}
A &= \text{Average demand per period.} \\
Q &= \text{Order quantity.} \\
C_p &= \text{Fixed ordering cost.} \\
C_H &= \text{Inventory carrying cost per unit per period} = vc_r. \\
D &= \text{Demand during the replenishment lead time.} \\
\overline{D} &= \text{Average demand during the replenishment lead time.} \\
P(D) &= \text{Probability of demand during lead time equaling } D. \\
R &= \text{Reorder point.} \\
(R - \overline{D}) &= \text{Safety stock level.} \\
C_s &= \text{Shortage } D. \\
R &= \text{Reorder cost.}
\end{aligned}
$$

The first part of Equation (18.1) includes the ordering cost and the stock-out cost. The number of reorder cycles per period is A/Q, and this can be used to convert the costs per cycle to period costs. The expression $(A/Q)C_p$ is the cost per period of placing orders. The expected number of units short $(E\{s\})$, for a reorder point of R is:

$$\left[\sum_{D=R+1}^{D_{max}} (D - R) \, P(D) \right]$$

Multiplying this by $(A/Q)C_s$ gives the cost per period of inventory shortages. The cost per period of carrying cycle stock is $(Q/2)C_H$, and the cost per period of carrying safety stock inventory is $C_H(R - \overline{D})$.

Any particular solution to Equation (18.1) provides the total cost per period for a given setting of the order quantity (Q) and the reorder point (R). If the unit cost of acquiring an item depends on the quantity ordered, additional terms would be required in this model. This can occur when volume or transportation discounts are available.

We shall present two methods for using Equation (18.1) to determine the least cost order point/order quantity values, a grid search approach, and an iterative approach. We will use the example problem to illustrate the approaches.

Grid search procedure

Using the example problem and Equation (18.1) gives an expression for total annual cost as a function of the order quantity Q and reorder point R. The expression is:

$$TC = (35/Q)[45 + 60\ E\{s\}] + 125[(Q/2) + (R - .84)]$$

Evaluating this expression for several values of Q and R provides the results shown in Figure 18.5, which serve as the basis for a grid search.

Our strategy for performing the grid search is to start with Q equal to the economic order quantity (5 units). Next we search on the reorder point (starting at the maximum of $R = 4$) until the costs reach a minimum and start to increase. This occurs at $R = 1$ when $Q = 5$.

The next step is to vary Q around $Q = 5$, when $R = 0$, 1, and 2, to see if costs increase. Since they decrease for $Q = 6$, when $R = 0$ and 1, we continue on to $Q = 7$. At this point only the value at $R = 0$ is still decreasing, so we go on to $Q = 8$, where we finish. (We have underlined the additional values that were provided for completeness.) We have now identified the point of minimum total cost: $R = 1$, $Q = 6$.

Several observations can be made from Figure 18.5. The solution suggested is $Q = 6$, $R = 1$. It trades off some exposure to stockouts by increasing the order quantity over the economic order quantity. In some instances, the solution will reduce the reorder point, as well. That is the reason for checking the costs at $R = 0$ and $Q = 8$. The economic order quantity (EOQ) provides a reasonable starting point for the search, although the solution will be further from the EOQ the larger the stockout cost. We will use some of these observations in the iterative procedure.

The iterative (Q, R) procedure

The iterative procedure is summarized in Figure 18.6. The procedure starts with the EOQ, as we did with the grid search. The value of $P(D > R)$ at step 2 is found by equating the extra annual inventory carrying cost in-

FIGURE 18.5   Total costs for several reorder points and order quantities

Reorder point	Order quantity				
	4	5	6	7	8
0	979.75	875.30	826.50	809.50	812.38
1	816.00	769.30	759.00	769.50	793.00
2	790.85	789.30	796.50	808.70	852.38
3	917.95	899.18	910.30	934.90	967.93
4	1038.75	1022.50	1032.50	1057.50	1091.88

FIGURE 18.6   The iterative procedure for finding Q and R

---

1. Compute the EOQ = $\sqrt{2AC_p/C_H}$

2. Compute $P(D > R) = QC_H/AC_S$ and determine the value of R by comparing the value of $P(D > R)$ with the cumulative demand during lead time distribution values.

3. Determine $E\{s\}$, the expected inventory shortages, using the value of R from step 2.

4. Compute $Q = \sqrt{2A[C_p + C_sE\{s\}_R]/C_H}$

5. Repeat steps 2 through 4 until convergence occurs; i.e., until sequential values for Q at step 4 and R at step 2 are equal.

Source: R. B. Felter and W. C. Dalleck, *Decision Models for Inventory Management* (Homewood, Ill.: Richard D. Irwin, 1961).

---

curred by increasing the reorder point by 1 unit, C_H, to the savings in shortage costs that can be attributed to the additional unit of inventory; that is, $C_H = (A/Q)C_s(E\{s\}_R - E\{s\}_{R+1})$. Since $(E\{s\}_R - E\{s\}_{R-1}) = P(D > R)$; $C_H = (A/Q)C_s \cdot P(D > R)$. The calculation of Q at step 4 is obtained by differentiating Equation (18.1) with respect to Q, setting the resulting expression equal to 0, and solving for Q.

$$Q = \sqrt{\frac{2A[C_p + C_sE\{s\}_R]}{C_H}}$$

To illustrate the procedure, we will use the example problem. Since the procedure iterates from calculating Q to calculating R, it is sometimes called the Q, R procedure.

Step 1: $Q = \sqrt{(2)(35)(45)/(.25)(500)} = 5$.
Step 2: $P(D > R) = (5)(.25)(500)/(35)(60) = .30$
          The closest value in Figure 18.3 is .250 at R = 1.
Step 3: $E\{s\} = .290$ (from Figure 18.3 when R = 1).
Step 4: $Q = \sqrt{2(35)[45 + (.29)(60)]/(.25)(500)} = 5.91 \approx 6$.
Step 5: $P(D > R) = (6)(.25)(500)/(35)(60) = .36$. R = 1.

The five-step procedure converged quickly on the same solution values for Q and R that were indicated in Figure 18.5. Since the procedure considers the expected shortage cost in determining Q in step 4, and since the computation effort is minimal, it is often a very useful approach for determining the order quantity and reorder point values. In cases where the magnitude of the shortage cost, C_s, is large, this procedure will take it into account and adjust the order quantity and reorder point accordingly. This may mean that an increase in the order quantity over the EOQ and a reduction in reorder point is required in order to reduce the total costs. The five-step procedure explicitly accounts for the interaction between inventory shortages and ordering costs in solving for the minimum cost reorder point/order quantity values.

INVENTORY AND TRANSPORTATION MODE INTERACTIONS

In this section we continue to broaden the number of factors which might be included in determining how to order an independent demand inventory item. Specifically, we include the costs of transporting the item from the supplier to the stock-keeping location. In effect, this broadening of the analysis treats the interaction between management of inventories and determination of transportation policy. These considerations interact when alternatives exist for transporting inventory, and each alternative has different inventory management implications. For example, differences in transit time variability could lead to different reorder points, and differences in transportation costs could lead to different order quantities.

Interactions between inventory parameters and transportation alternatives suggest that decisions for these two problem areas should be made simultaneously. This suggestion is rarely carried out in practice, but doing so can lead to important cost savings in some firms. In practice, the determination of a transportation alternative usually starts with the selection of a primary transportation mode (i.e., rail, truck, air, ship) by one group of people. This is often done on the basis of cost or transit time only. Once this decision is made, the selection of a specific transportation company or routing is based on an evaluation of that company's service. This evaluation may not even consider the variability of transportation time. In some instances, the transportation decision is not even made inside the firm (e.g., when a vendor is requested to ship by the "best method"). The resultant transportation decisions are then accepted as givens by another group of people who determine the parameters for managing inventories. Clearly, these organizational boundaries will need to be reduced if an integrated approach is to be applied.

We illustrate the interaction between inventory and transportation decisions by considering one item in a reorder point system. The transportation alternatives involve several different modes, each characterized by three attributes: transportation cost, expected time in transit, and variability of the transit time. In many instances, all alternatives need not be considered since any alternative that is more costly, has a greater time in transit, and has more variability in transit time than another alternative can be eliminated a priori.

The global problem is to determine which transportation alternative and inventory parameters (reorder point and order quantity) lead to the lowest combined inventory and transportation cost. We begin by presenting a total cost expression that combines the transportation attributes and the inventory policy parameters. Next, two procedures are described for solving this cost model: an exact enumeration procedure and a heuristic procedure. Finally, we discuss experiments that evaluate the performance of these procedures and their application in practice.

Total cost equation

The approach taken here is to develop the total cost equation like that previously given as Equation (18.1). To incorporate the transportation considerations, we substitute the expected transit time for the replenishment lead time, incorporate the transit time variance into the demand during lead time, and account for transportation cost. The total cost per period for a specific transportation alternative and set of inventory parameters is comprised of the following cost elements: transportation, in-transit inventory, stored inventory, ordering and shortage.

Equation (18.2) is:

$$TIC = AC_t + C_i vTA + C_H[Q/2 + (R - \overline{D})]$$
$$+ A/Q\left[C_p + C_s\left(\sum_{D=R+1}^{D_{max}} (D - R) P(D)\right)\right] \quad (18.2)$$

where:

A = Average demand per period.
C_t = Transportation cost per unit.
C_i = In-transit inventory cost per dollar of value (can be different for each mode).
v = Item value prior to transport cost.
T = Expected transit time.
C_r = Inventory carrying cost rate per period (percentage).
C_H = $C_r(v + C_t)$.
Q = Order quantity.
R = Reorder point.
$\overline{D}$ = Average demand during lead time (expected transit time).
C_p = Fixed ordering cost.
C_s = Shortage cost.
$P(D)$ = Probability of demand equalling D.

This equation has two inventory parameters, Q and R, as unknowns and incorporates data for a single transportation alternative: C_i, C_t, $\overline{D}$ and $P(D)$. These last two terms are related to the expected time in transit and its variability. The in-transit inventory cost term depends on $\overline{D}$ and the shortage cost term depends on $P(D)$. Faster modes reduce $\overline{D}$, and more reliable modes reduce the variance of demand during lead time. Before illustrating procedures for determining the choice of transport mode and inventory parameters, we will present an example.

Transport mode decision example

An example to illustrate the combined choice of inventory parameters and transport mode is shown in Figure 18.7. Product-related data, including cost and demand information, are provided in the top third of the figure. Three different transportation alternatives for this item are shown in the middle of Figure 18.7. For the modes shown, the unit transportation cost for this product increases as the expected transit time and variability of the transit time decrease.

The demand and the transit time distributions must be combined to develop the demand during lead time distribution for use with Equation (18.2). Since there are two discrete distributions in the example problem, the demand during lead time distribution can be developed using the tree diagramming approach to enumerate the possibilities. For example, since the transport time is either 1 or 3 days for alternative 1 in Figure 18.7, and demand is either 5 or 7 units, the only possibilities are demands of 5, 7, 15, 17, 19, or 21 during the lead time. Each possible demand during lead time and its probability is given for each of the three transport alternatives in the bottom part of Figure 18.7. In addition, the mean and the standard deviation (σ_D) for each demand during lead time distribution has been calculated.

Exact solution methods

The solution of the example problem requires choosing the transportation alternative (1, 2, or 3), order quantity, and reorder point that will minimize the total incremental cost [Equation (18.2)]. In this section we describe exact methods; that is, methods that guarantee minimum cost. One method would be to use the iterative procedure to find the optimal value of Q and R for each transportation alternative. Then Equation (18.2) could be used to calculate the total cost for each transportation alternative using the optimal Q and R. The alternative with the minimum cost is the transportation alternative to use along with the optimal Q and R for that alternative.

Another method is to use partial enumeration to determine the optimal Q and R for each transportation alternative. First, the reorder point, R, is set equal to the maximum demand during lead time for a particular transportation alternative (e.g., 21 units in the case of transport method 1 in Figure 18.6). Next the optimal value of Q and its associated total cost are calculated. Then the value of R is reduced by one, and a new Q value (and its associated total cost) are determined. R is again reduced by 1 and the process repeated until reductions in R begin to increase the total cost. The

FIGURE 18.7   Example: Inventory-transportation mode problem

Product data

Item	Notation	Value
Inventory carrying cost rate	C_r	.000605 per day*
Shortage cost	C_s	$1 per unit short
Order cost	C_p	$10 per order
Item value before transportation cost	V	$2 per unit
Average demand per day	A	6 units
Demand per day standard deviation	σ_A	1 unit
Demand per day distribution		Demand = 5, probability = .5
		Demand = 7, probability = .5.

Transportation alternatives

Item	Notation	Transportation alternative 1	2	3
Transportation cost/unit	C_t	$ .32	$ .38	$ .40
In-transit carrying rate/day	C_i	.001	.001	.001
Expected transit time (days)	T	2.20	1.60	1.40
Transit time standard deviation (days)	σ_T	1.00	.49	.49
Transit time distribution		$\begin{pmatrix} \text{Prob.} = .4 \\ T = 1 \end{pmatrix}$	$\begin{pmatrix} \text{Prob.} = .4 \\ T = 1 \end{pmatrix}$	$\begin{pmatrix} \text{Prob.} = .6 \\ T = 1 \end{pmatrix}$
		$\begin{pmatrix} \text{Prob.} = .6 \\ T = 3 \end{pmatrix}$	$\begin{pmatrix} \text{Prob.} = .6 \\ T = 2 \end{pmatrix}$	$\begin{pmatrix} \text{Prob.} = .4 \\ T = 2 \end{pmatrix}$

Lead time demand distribution

Item	Notation	Transportation alternative 1	2	3
Average demand during lead time (in units)	$\bar{D}$	13.20	9.60	8.40
Standard deviation of demand during lead time	σ_D	6.06	3.20	3.17
Demand during lead time distribution		$\begin{pmatrix} \text{Pr} = .20 \\ D = 5 \text{ or } 7 \end{pmatrix}$	$\begin{pmatrix} \text{Pr} = .20 \\ D = 5 \text{ or } 7 \end{pmatrix}$	$\begin{pmatrix} \text{Pr} = .30 \\ D = 5 \text{ or } 7 \end{pmatrix}$
		$\begin{pmatrix} \text{Pr} = .075 \\ D = 15 \text{ or } 21 \end{pmatrix}$	$\begin{pmatrix} \text{Pr} = .15 \\ D = 10 \text{ or } 14 \end{pmatrix}$	$\begin{pmatrix} \text{Pr} = .10 \\ D = 10 \text{ or } 14 \end{pmatrix}$
		$\begin{pmatrix} \text{Pr} = .225 \\ D = 17 \text{ or } 19 \end{pmatrix}$	$\begin{pmatrix} \text{Pr} = .30 \\ D = 12 \end{pmatrix}$	$\begin{pmatrix} \text{Pr} = .20 \\ D = 12 \end{pmatrix}$

*The period for this example is one day. This is consistent with the period used for describing transit time. The conversion from annual costs assumes a 365-day year.

Q and R that produce the lowest total cost are optimal for the selected transportation alternative.

The results of applying the exact procedures to the example problem are summarized in Figure 18.8. The final choice is to use the first transportation alternative with $R = 19$ and $Q = 277$. The differences in total annual costs

---

FIGURE 18.8   Exact solution to the example problem

Transportation alternative	Reorder point (R)	Order quantity (Q)	Safety stock (R − D̄)	Total cost per year*
1	19	277	5.8	$ 874.34
2	14	271	4.4	1,003.26
3	14	270	5.6	1,047.60

*Assuming 365 days per year.

---

between alternatives are an indication of the potential savings from making the transportation and inventory decisions jointly. When several alternatives exist or the demand and lead time distributions are more complex, the exact procedures require considerable computation time. The heuristic method described next was developed to reduce these computation time requirements.

Heuristic method

The heuristic method uses an estimation process to first choose a transportation alternative. The method does not guarantee that the choice will provide the lowest total cost. However, once the transportation alternative has been selected, all that remains is the calculation of the inventory parameters for that alternative.

The approach involves three phases. First, the exact procedure is used to determine the Q and R (now converted into the number of standard deviations of safety stock) values that provide the minimum expected total cost for any *one* of the transportation alternatives. Second, those Q and safety stock values are used with Equation (18.2) to calculate a total cost for each of the transportation alternatives. The alternative with the lowest total cost at this stage is selected as the transportation alternative for the problem. Finally, the Q and R values that minimize the total cost are determined for the alternative selected in the second phase—if it differs from that used in the first phase.

One additional simplification used in the heuristic method is the use of the normal distribution to approximate the distribution of demand during lead time. This is done even for such "non-normal" distributions as those in the example problem. The steps to making this approximation involve determining the mean and standard deviation of the demand during lead time.

The mean is calculated as:

$$\overline{D} = AT \qquad (18.3)$$

The standard deviation is found, using:

$$\sigma_D = (T\sigma_A{}^2 + A^2 \sigma_T{}^2) \tag{18.4}$$

The example problem, using transportation alternative 2 for the phase one calculation, will illustrate the heuristic method. First the exact procedure is used to find the Q and R values for transportation alternative 2. Using the exact enumeration procedure, we start with a reorder point of 19.2. This is 3 standard deviations of safety stock [i.e., $AT + 3\sigma_D = 9.6 + 3(3.2)$]. The application of the enumeration procedure continues by calculating the expected total cost for successive Q and R values as the value of R is decreased until the expected total cost starts to increase in value. This occurs at $R = 14$ and $Q = 273$ for transportation alternative number 2. The reorder point of 14 implies a safety stock of 4.4 units (14 − 9.6), which is 1.38 standard deviations above the mean demand during lead time.

The value of 1.38 standard deviations is used in phase 2 to estimate the amount of safety stock required for the other two transportation alternatives. This enables us to calculate the reorder point for each alternative. These reorder points and the order quantity (Q), determined for the starting alternative in phase 1, are used to estimate the total costs for the remaining transportation alternatives. The estimates are $875.48 and $1,047.68 for alternatives 1 and 3, respectively. Since the cost of alternative 2 was $1,003.26 (see Figure 18.8), alternative 1 provides the lowest total cost and is selected for use. The appropriate Q and R for alternative 1 are then computed.

In the experiments, performed by Constable and Whybark, the heuristic procedure never failed to choose the same transportation alternative as the exact procedure, and it did so at a considerable savings of computer time. The maximum incremental cost penalty incurred by the heuristic procedure was less than 0.2 percent, even with the normal approximation for the lead time demand distribution. Interestingly, in more than half the cases, the lowest cost transportation mode was optimal. This gives some support to the practice of choosing low-cost transportation when the transport cost represents an important part of the cost of the product.

MULTIPLE ITEMS FROM SINGLE SOURCE

In this section, we consider the economies of jointly ordering several items from a single source. In many independent demand situations, the stocking point may receive different items from the same source. Examples include most wholesale inventories, inventories of spare parts held in a central facility, and indirect supply items being purchased from a single vendor. Placing orders for several of these items at the same time can result in very significant inventory cost savings. Moreover, by so timing the orders to different vendors that receipt of shipments is smoothed out, one can reduce warehouse costs for restocking, shelf space, and demurrage.

We treat joint ordering by successively increasing the amount of inter-dependency among the items considered. The first approaches presented are based on triggering the release of a joint order from individual item reorder points. Several methods for determining how much to order in total and how much of each item to order are presented. The next approaches base the release of the joint order on a group reorder point. We conclude the section with some experimental evidence of the savings possible from applying joint ordering techniques.

The joint ordering circumstance is so common that many companies have developed software packages for managing single supplier items. The approaches differ from package to package. These differences can lead to different service levels and inventory cost performances. The techniques illustrated in this section illustrate the differences. As a specific example, the last technique presented in this section is a modification of the approach used in a commercial software package.

Methods based on individual item reorder points

An example problem is presented in Figure 18.9 for five items from the same source. In the example, the price and weight per unit, the forecasts, and the order quantities and reorder points have been calculated for each item independently. If the inventory were to be managed item by item, the only item to order this period (based on the present problem status) would be item A, since it is the only item below its reorder point. The annual inventory carrying costs and ordering costs for managing these five items independently are about $330 (applying Equation (18.1) and ignoring the stockout and safety stock costs).

One approach to joint ordering is to place a single order whenever any *one* item drops below its reorder point. How much of each item to order could be determined from the individual economic order quantities. These

---

FIGURE 18.9   Example: Five items from same source

Item	Price	Weight (lbs)	Monthly forecast Units	Monthly forecast $	Monthly forecast Lbs	Individual EOQ	Individual ROP	Current on-hand plus on-order
A	$1.10	5	100	110	500	330	79	50
B	.40	1	80	32	80	490	67	200
C	3.80	10	200	760	2,000	250	168	400
D	.25	.5	25	6	13	350	16	75
E	.05	.1	70	4	7	1,300	58	60
			475	912	2,600			

Individual order cost = $10
Joint order cost = $10 + $2/item

Inventory carrying rate = 20%/year
Full truck load quantity = 10,000 lbs.

quantities would then be used to construct one consolidated order. The choice of which items to order could be determined by how close each is to its reorder point. After including any items below reorder point, others could be added using the ratio of the current on-hand plus on-order to the reorder point. This assures ordering those items that are most likely to run out first. Individual items could be added to the joint order until some minimum dollar amount or weight is attained.

Applying this logic to the example problem would mean adding 330 units of item A first, 1,300 units of item E next, item C next, and so on until the joint ordering criterion was met. Note that not all items need to be ordered with this approach although all could be ordered. Using this approach does not necessarily result in a regular timing of orders from the vendor. The next order is placed when the next item reaches the reorder point, and that depends upon how many items are ordered this time, variations in usage rates, etc.

A method that does produce a regular cycle of orders to the vendor is based on developing a joint economic order quantity. This can be done by treating all the items from a vendor as a whole and determining an economic time between orders or an economic dollar value order. In general, the expression for the economic dollar value order is:

$$Q = \sqrt{\frac{2(\sum_i v_i A_i)C_p}{C_r}} \qquad (18.5)$$

where:

$\sum v_i A_i =$ The total dollar volume per period for all items from the vendor (v_i is the value of item i and A_i is the demand per period for item i).

$C_p =$ The cost of placing an order (including any individual item order costs).

$C_r =$ The inventory carrying cost rate per dollar of inventory.

The economic time between orders is:

$$TBO = Q/ \sum_i v_i A_i \qquad (18.6)$$

Applying Equation (18.5) to the data in Figure 18.9 gives the following:

$$Q = \sqrt{2(912 \times 12)20/.2} = \$1,479$$

Note that the dollar forecast has been annualized and that C_p is $20, the joint order cost of $10 plus $2 for each of the five items. Applying Equation (18.6) to this result gives:

FIGURE 18.10 Three joint ordering alternatives for example using individual item reorder points

Item	Economic dollar value order $	Item order quantity*	Simultaneous reorder point — Months supply over reorder point	Item order quantity†	Full truck load — Pounds over reorder point	Pounds to be ordered	Item order quantity‡
A	$ 178	162	−.29	191	−145.0	2,520	504
B	53	130	1.66	—	133.0	247	247
C	1,232	324	1.16	92	2,320.0	7,180	718
D	10	41	2.36	—	29.5	30	60
E	6	113	.03	111	.2	33	330
	$1,479				2,337.7	10,010	

*1.62 months supply (1.62 × monthly forecast).
†For items with less than a 1.62 months supply over reorder point, order = 1.62 months supply − (on-hand + on-order).
‡4.75 months supply − (on-hand + on-order) all values in pounds.

$$TBO = 1,479/912 = 1.62 \text{ months}$$

The individual order quantities now must be established. Using the economic dollar value order basis, we could order each item in 1.62-month supply quantities. The results of applying this logic are shown in the first three columns in Figure 18.10 for each of the five sample items.

Ordering each item in a 1.62-month supply leads to different quantities than using the EOQ for each item but suffers the same limitation. It ignores the present inventory positions. An alternative would be to order individual quantities and bring each item up to a 1.62-month supply above its individual reorder point. This takes into account the current inventory position, and it would mean all items would reach their individual reorder points at the same time if the forecast was perfect.

To illustrate the concept, item A's current inventory position of 50 is 29 units below its reorder point of 79. Thus, the order quantity would be 162 + 29 = 191 units. The middle section of Figure 18.10 shows the present inventory position of each item in terms of the number of months supply in excess of the order point. Items B and D do not need to be ordered, because they have more than a 1.62-month supply over their order points. The order quantities are shown for those items that should be ordered. Note that this procedure will result in a regular pattern of orders to a supplier if the forecasts are generally correct.

A third alternative that uses individual reorder points is to base the combined order on some quantity discount or low-cost transportation alternative. For our example, a full truckload quantity is 10,000 pounds. When an order is made, the question is how to allocate the 10,000 pounds appropriately to the individual items. The analysis starts by noting that a 10,000-pound order represents a 3.85-month supply using the combined demand of 26,000 pounds per month for all items. When the individual item current on-hand plus on-order values are converted to pounds, there is an "excess" of 2,337.7 pounds above the reorder point. This is shown in the last section of Figure 18.10. This represents approximately a 0.9-month supply. Thus, if a 10,000 pound order is to be placed now, it must be so placed to bring the total inventory to 4.75 (3.85 + 0.9) months above the reorder point quantities.

Allocating the 10,000 pound order to the individual items can be illustrated with item A. The present inventory is 29 units, or 145 pounds below the reorder point value for this item. A 4.75-month supply in pounds is 2,375 pounds. To account for the 145 pounds below reorder point, the need is to order 2,520 pounds or 504 units of item A. The pounds and quantities of each item to be ordered are shown in the last section of Figure 18.10. Note the small rounding error in the number of pounds to be ordered.

One weakness of all procedures based on individual reorder points has to do with the service levels attained relative to the service levels expected. In each of these procedures, only *one* item, say item A, needs to be below the reorder point for the combined order to be placed. This means that other items might be above their reorder points, thus providing *higher* service than expected for them. On the next order, it might be another item that is below reorder point, raising the service level for item A as well as for others.

This provision of "over-service" and higher than necessary inventory is difficult to overcome with methods where the joint order is triggered by individual reorder points. One "fix" is to so specify the reorder points for the individual items that they represent the *minimum* service level for each item. Note that only the item below reorder point will be exposed to this low service possibility. In the next section, we look at treating the group as a whole for deciding when to place an order.

Methods based on group reorder points

In using individual reorder points to trigger joint orders, we have argued that individual item and group service levels would be higher than those associated with the independent reorder points. One way to overcome this problem is to create a group reorder point that will provide a service level for the group in total. This can be done by basing the joint reorder point on the individual ones. Several ways of doing this for the example problem of Figure 18.9 are summarized in Figure 18.11. Shown are reorder points that use units, dollars, and months of supply on hand as the basis for reordering.

FIGURE 18.11   Group reorder point alternatives

	Item					Group reorder point
	A	B	C	D	E	
Reorder point units	79	67	168	16	58	388
Reorder point	$86.90	$26.80	$638.40	$4.00	$2.90	$759.00
Average reorder point month's supply	.79	.84	.84	.64	.83	.79
Weighted month's supply		388/475				.82

The first group reorder point in Figure 18.11 is simply the sums of the individual reorder points. A joint order would be triggered whenever the combined inventory positions of items A through E fell below 388 units. This approach can combine "apples and bananas" in summing the reorder points. The second approach converts the item reorder points into dollars and sums these to find a group reorder point based on the dollar value of the joint inventory. The third alternative shown in Figure 18.11 is based on the reorder point for each item expressed in months of supply (dividing the reorder point by the forecast). The group reorder point is the arithmetical average of the individual reorder points. The final approach is similar but weights the group reorder point by the individual reorder points. This is done by dividing the sum of the reorder points by the total item forecast to get a group month's of supply. These same measures can be used to set group service levels directly by using the demand during lead time distribution measured in the same units.

To determine when to place a joint order, the group reorder point values are compared to the inventory position for all items in the group. When the units, dollars, or months of supply *in total* fall below the group reorder point, a group order is placed. In each case, other tests can be added, which prevent a single item from accumulating too many stockouts, falling below some minimum point, or being responsible for creating unjustified orders for everything in the group.

Once a group order is triggered, any of the approaches illustrated in Figure 18.10 can be used to determine the individual order quantities. For the group order point policies, however, only the last two methods shown in Figure 18.10 will provide relative balancing between items.

An alternative approach to joint ordering is to place orders on a single vendor on a periodic basis, where the period is based upon the economic order frequency, Equation (18.6). The quantities ordered could bring the inventory levels for each item up to the level necessary to provide the service desired until the next order. The orders for different vendors could be spread to smooth warehouse labor requirements.

A group service level method

Many commercial software packages contain joint ordering logic. A version of this logic is presented here with an example. The approach uses a group reorder point, based on desired group service levels, to determine when to place an order. The logic used for determining individual order quantities is simultaneous reorder point. The basic flow diagram is presented in Figure 18.12, and the definition of terms is provided in Figure 18.13. After describing the procedure, an example is given.

Periodically, the inventory is reviewed to see if an order should be placed. The decision is based on calculating the expected number of stockouts that would occur for each item if no order was placed. This involves determining the variance of the demand during lead and review time (step 7, Figure 18.12). The variance is used to determine how many standard deviations of each item are currently on hand (step 2). Calculating the expected number of stockouts if no order is placed is done next (step 3).

The total expected number of stockouts is compared to the group level required to meet desired service levels. The allowable level of stockouts is derived from the economic time between orders and the service level in step 8. If the total projected stockouts is greater than the allowed number, an order is initiated.

The order is made at least equal to the economic dollar value order in step 6. It is so allocated that each item has an inventory that will provide its service level and will reach the group reorder point at the same time as the other items given the current forecasts. The allocation is the MRD_j value in steps 9 and 13. Note that not every item needs to be ordered (steps 5 and 14). This cycle is expected to repeat every T periods, so labor smoothing can be done by scheduling other vendors' shipments at other times.

A numerical example of this procedure is presented in Figures 18.14 through 18.16. A two-product example is shown in Figure 18.14. The calculations in Figure 18.15 show that no order is to be placed in period 1, even though there is a 12-unit stockout of item 1 expected. After demands of 2 and 26 units for items 1 and 2, respectively, an order needs to be placed in period 2. The calculations in Figure 18.16 show how the economic dollar value order of $21,689 is allocated to the two products.

Simulation experiments

Kleijnen and Rens performed an extensive set of simulation experiments to evaluate a version of the IMPACT group ordering procedure, modified to incorporate the logic of Figure 18.12. They studied this procedure in a wide variety of operating situations by varying the following factors:

The number of items per group.
The length of the review period (RT).

FIGURE 18.12   Group ordering logic

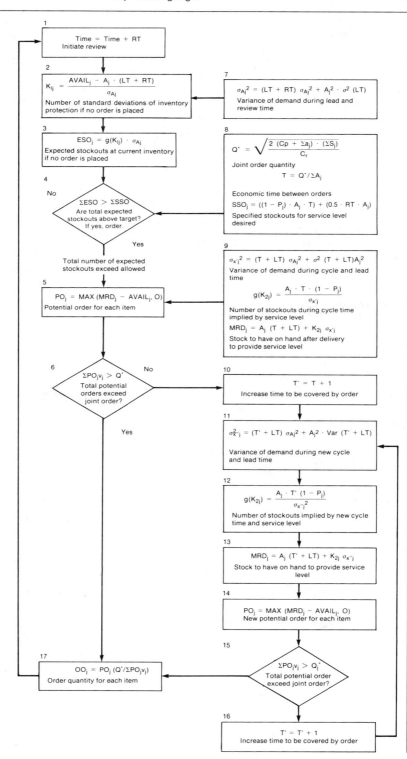

1

Time = Time + RT
Initiate review

2

$$K_{lj} = \frac{AVAIL_j - A_j \cdot (LT + RT)}{\sigma_{Aj}}$$

Number of standard deviations of inventory protection if no order is placed

7

$$\sigma_{Aj}^2 = (LT + RT)\,\sigma_{Aj}^2 + A_j^2 \cdot \sigma^2\,(LT)$$

Variance of demand during lead and review time

3

$$ESO_j = g(K_{lj}) \cdot \sigma_{Aj}$$

Expected stockouts at current inventory if no order is placed

8

$$Q^{\cdot} = \sqrt{\frac{2\,(Cp + \Sigma a_j) \cdot (\Sigma S_j)}{C_r}}$$

Joint order quantity

$$T = Q^{\cdot}/\Sigma A_j$$

Economic time between orders

$$SSO_j = ((1 - P_j) \cdot A_j \cdot T) + (0.5 \cdot RT \cdot A_j)$$

Specified stockouts for service level desired

4

No

$\Sigma ESO > \Sigma SSO$
Are total expected stockouts above target?
If yes, order.

Yes

Total number of expected stockouts exceed allowed

9

$$\sigma_{x'j}^2 = (T + LT)\,\sigma_{Aj}^2 + \sigma^2\,(T + LT)A_j^2$$

Variance of demand during cycle and lead time

$$g(K_{2j}) = \frac{A_j \cdot T \cdot (1 - P_j)}{\sigma_{x'j}}$$

Number of stockouts during cycle time implied by service level

$$MRD_j = A_j\,(T + LT) + K_{2j}\,\sigma_{x'j}$$

Stock to have on hand after delivery to provide service level

5

$$PO_j = MAX\,(MRD_j - AVAIL_j, O)$$

Potential order for each item

6

$\Sigma PO_j v_j > Q^{\cdot}$
Total potential orders exceed joint order?

No

Yes

10

T' = T + 1
Increase time to be covered by order

11

$$\sigma_{\bar{x}''j}^2 = (T' + LT)\,\sigma_{Aj}^2 + A_j^2 \cdot Var\,(T' + LT)$$

Variance of demand during new cycle and lead time

12

$$g(K_{2j}) = \frac{A_j \cdot T' (1 - P_j)}{\sigma_{x''j}^2}$$

Number of stockouts implied by new cycle time and service level

13

$$MRD_j = A_j\,(T' + LT) + K_{2j}\,\sigma_{x''j}$$

Stock to have on hand to provide service level

14

$$PO_j = MAX\,(MRD_j - AVAIL_j, O)$$

New potential order for each item

15

$\Sigma PO_j v_j > Q_j^{\cdot}$
Total potential order exceed joint order?

16

T' = T' + 1
Increase time to be covered by order

17

$$OO_j = PO_j\,(Q^{\cdot}/\Sigma PO_j v_j)$$

Order quantity for each item

Source: J. P. C. Kleignen and P. J. Rens, "Impact Revisited: A Critical Analysis of IBM's Inventory Package—IMPACT," *Production and Inventory Management*, First Quarter 1978.

FIGURE 18.13   Group ordering terminology

RT	= Time between inventory reviews
LT	= Replenishment lead time estimate
T	= Estimated time between two orders
T'	= Estimated time between two orders revised to provide a larger order
$AVAIL_j$	= On hand plus on order inventory (for item j)
A_j	= Mean demand per time period
σ_A	= Demand per time period standard deviation
X_j	= Mean demand during $LT + RT$
X_j'	= Mean demand during $LT + T$
X_j''	= Mean demand during $LT + T'$
K_{1j} and K_{2j}	= Number of standard deviations of inventory
$g(K_{1j})$ and $g(K_{2j})$	= Expected stockouts given K_1 and K_2 standard deviations of inventory [see, for example, R. G. Brown, *Decision Rules for Inventory Management* (New York: Holt, Rinehart and Winston, 1967), p. 179]
ESO_j	= Expected stockout amount during $LT + RT$
SSO_j	= Specified stockout amount during $LT + RT$ at service level P_j
Q^*	= Economic joint order quantity
C_p	= Fixed ordering cost
a_j	= Variable ordering cost (per item)
S_j	= Mean demand per period in dollars
C_r	= Inventory carrying cost rate per period
P_j	= Specified customer service level (percent of annual demand supplied directly from inventory)
MRD_j	= Maximum reasonable demand during $LT + T$ (or during $LT + T'$)
PO_j	= Preliminary order quantity in joint ordering
OO_j	= Final order quantity
v_j	= Value of item j

FIGURE 18.14   Example group ordering situation, period 1

	Product	
Parameter	1	2
Average demand period (A_j)	10	20 units
Demand period standard deviation (σ_j)	2	3 units
Annual demand*	2,600	5,200 units
Lead time (LT)	1	1 period (constant)
Review time (RT)	1	1 period
Desired customer service level (P_j)	.95	.98
Fixed ordering cost (C_p)	$100	$100
Variable (per item) ordering cost (a_j)	$10	$10
Unit cost	$100	$25
Inventory carrying cost per dollar per year (C_r)	.25	.25
Current on-hand plus on-order quantity ($AVAIL_j$)	8	50
Demand during period 1	2	26
Annual demand in dollars (S_j)	$260,000	$130,000
Independent ordering EOQ	151	428
Independent reorder point†	7	21

*260 periods per year.
†$[A_j(LT + .5RT)] + K_j\sigma_j$, with $\sigma_j^2 = (LT + .5RT)\sigma_{A_j}^2 + [(A_j^2\sigma_{LT}^2(LT + .5RT)]$ and $g(K_{jj}) = [EOQ(1 - P_j)/P_j]/\sigma_j$.

FIGURE 18.15   Example reorder calculations

Step	Period 1	Period 2
7	$\sigma_{A1}^2 = (1 + 1)(2)^2 + (10)^2(0)^2 = 8$	—
2	$K_{11} = \dfrac{9 - (10)(1 + 1)}{\sqrt{8}} = -4.24$	$K_{11} = \dfrac{6 - (10)(1 + 1)}{\sqrt{8}} = -4.95$
3	$ESO_1 = (4.24)(2.83) = 12.0$	$ESO_1 = (4.95)(2.83) = 14.0$
7	$\sigma_{A2}^2 = (1 + 1)(3)^2 + (20)^2(0)^2 = 18$	—
2	$K_{12} = \dfrac{50 - (20)(1 + 1)}{\sqrt{18}} = 2.36$	$K_{12} = \dfrac{24 - (20)(1 + 1)}{\sqrt{18}} = -3.77$
3	$ESO_2 = (.003)(4.24) = .013$	$ESO_2 = (3.77)(4.24) = 15.98$
8	$Q^* = \sqrt{\dfrac{2 \cdot 120 \cdot (260{,}000 + 130{,}000)}{.25}}$	—
	$= \$21{,}289$	
8	$T = 434/30 = 14.5$ periods	—
8	$SSO_1 = (1 - .95)(10)(14.5) + (.5)(1)(10)$ $= 12.25$	—
	$SSO_2 = (1 - .98)(20)(14.5) + (.5)(1)(20)$ $= 15.8$	—
4	$ESO_1 + ESO_2 < SSO_1 + SSO_2$ $12.013 < 28.05$	$ESO_1 + ESO_2 > SSO_1 + SSO_2$ $29.98 > 28.05$

The ratio of the order interval to the review period (T/RT).
The ratio of the fixed to the variable ordering cost (C_p/a_j).
The ratio of the optimum to the actual joint order size (Q^*/Q).
The lead-time variance (σ_{LT}^2).
The desired customer service level values (P_j) in a group.

The results of these experiments are summarized for four measures of performance (customer service, inventory carrying cost, ordering cost, and total cost) in Figure 18.17.

The experimental results indicate that the use of the joint ordering procedure can have a major effect on inventory system performance. The use of the joint ordering procedure reduced the total cost by nearly 50 percent in comparison with independent ordering. Much of this improvement came from the reduction in ordering costs, reflecting the objective of the joint ordering procedure. However, this procedure also dominates independent ordering in terms of inventory carrying cost due to the reduction in order quantities.

The modifications incorporated in the procedure provide actual customer service levels close to those obtained by independent ordering. Across all 16 experiments joint ordering averaged within .5 percent of the customer

---

FIGURE 18.16   Period 2 order quantity determination

Step	Calculations
9	$\sigma^2_{x'1} = (14.5 + 1)(2)^2 + (10)^2(0)^2 = 62$
9	$g(K_{21}) = \dfrac{10 \times (14.5)(.05)}{\sqrt{62}} = .92$
9	$MRD_1 = (10)(14.5 + 1) + (-.8)\sqrt{62} = 149$
5	$PO_1 = MAX\,(149 - 6, 0) = 143$
9	$\sigma^2_{x'2} = (14.5 + 1)(3)^2 + (20)^2(0)^2 = 130.5$
9	$g(K_{22}) = \dfrac{(20)(14.5)(.02)}{\sqrt{130.5}} = .51$
9	$MRD_2 = (20)(14.5 + 1) + (-.21)\sqrt{130.5} = 308$
5	$PO_2 = MAX\,(308 - 24, 0) = 284$
6	$\Sigma PO_j v_j > Q^*?$ $143(100) + 284(25) < 21{,}689$ $21{,}400 < 21{,}689$
10	$T' = T + 1 = 14.5 + 1 = 15.5$
11	$\sigma^2_{x'1} = (15.5 + 1)(2)^2 + (10)^2(0)^2 = 66$
12	$g(K_{21}) = \dfrac{(10)(15.5)(.05)}{\sqrt{66}} = .95$
13	$MRD_1 = (10)(15.5 + 1) + (-.84)\sqrt{66} = 158$
14	$PO_1 = MAX\,(158 - 6, 0) = 152$
11	$\sigma^2_{x'2} = (15.5 + 1)(3)^2 + (20)(0)^2 = 148.5$
12	$g(K_{22}) = \dfrac{(20)(15.5)(.02)}{\sqrt{148.5}} = .51$
13	$MRD_2 = (20)(15.5 + 1) + (-.21)\sqrt{148.5} - 327$
14	$PO_2 = MAX\,(327 - 24,0) = 303$
15	$\Sigma PO_j v_j > Q^*?$ $152(100) + 303(25) > 21{,}689$ $22{,}775 > 21{,}689$
17	$00_1 = 152(21{,}689/22{,}775) = 145$
17	$00_2 = 303(21{,}689/22{,}775) = 289$

---

service level for independent ordering. Also, joint ordering is more effective than independent ordering when the actual customer service level is compared with the desired customer service level. The actual customer service level under joint ordering was less than the desired customer service level in half of the experiments, while under independent ordering this occurred in 10 out of the 16 experiments.

In this section, we have evolved an ever expanding view of the "inventory" system and its objectives. First we looked at treating the reorder point

FIGURE 18.17 Experimental results

Experiment number	Customer service level ratio[1]	Inventory carrying cost ratio[2]	Ordering cost ratio[3]	Total cost ratio[4]
1	.999	.489	.664	.555
2	1.041	.787	1.251	.896
3	.989	.452	1.649	.629
4	1.001	.337	.672	.423
5	1.015	.411	.441	.424
6	1.017	.400	.874	.579
7	.988	.599	.614	.605
8	.945	.269	.463	.339
9	.983	.558	.792	.630
10	.981	.361	.528	.430
11	.946	.351	.381	.364
12	.987	.525	.680	.592
13	1.012	.461	1.319	.686
14	1.015	.469	.651	.522
15	1.008	.179	.692	.348
16	1.000	.446	.864	.607
Average	.995	.443	.783	.539

Notes:
1. Average customer service level (group ordering)/average customer service level (independent ordering).
2. Average inventory carrying cost (group ordering)/average inventory carrying cost (independent ordering).
3. Average ordering cost (group ordering)/average ordering cost (independent ordering).
4. Average total cost (group ordering)/average total cost (independent ordering).

Source: J. P. C. Kleijnen and P. J. Rens, "IMPACT Revisited: A Critical Analysis of IBM's Inventory Package—IMPACT," *Production and Inventory Management,* First Quarter 1978.

and order quantity simultaneously. Next, transportation considerations were added to provide a more global view. Finally, we considered combined orders for individual items in a group. By achieving appropriate timing of these group orders, we can improve costs. This again is an expansion of the system view. The potential for improved cost performance that is possible using this expanded view should raise skepticism for single, narrow measures (e.g., 95 percent service level, order full carload only, and the like). The task is to determine what is really important and design the procedures accordingly.

MULTIPLE CRITERIA ABC ANALYSIS

ABC analysis helps focus management attention on what is really important. Managers concentrate on the "significant few" (the A items) and spend less time on the "trivial many" (the C items). Unfortunately, the classification of the items into the A, B, and C categories has generally been based on just one criterion. For inventory management, that criterion is the dollar-usage (value times annual usage) of the items, although it is sometimes just the item cost. In many cases, however, there may be other criteria that are also important.

Multiple criteria ABC distributions

Several noncost criteria have been identified as important in the management of inventories. Among them are lead time, obsolescence, availability, substitutability, and criticality. Flores and Whybark looked into the use of noncost criteria in managing maintenance inventories. Criticality seemed to sum up managers' feelings about most noncost aspects of the maintenance items. It takes into account such factors as the severity of the impact of running out, how quickly the item could be purchased, whether there was an available substitute, and even the political consequences of being out. Some of these criticality notions may even weigh more heavily than dollar-usage in the management of the item—much like the proverbial cobbler's nail.

That is not to say that managers should not still be concerned about cost and dollar-usage implications of maintenance inventory. To have separate ABC categories for dollar usage and criticality, however, could lead to a large number of combinations, each of which could require a different management policy. The potentially large number of different policies violates the principle of simplicity, which is a recurring theme in this book. To keep the number of inventory management policies to a workable few, the number of combinations needs to be kept small. This means combining the criteria somehow (e.g., combining high-cost noncritical items with low-cost critical items).

The procedure for doing this consists of several steps. The first is to produce the dollar-usage distribution and associated ABC categories. This distribution can often come directly from the inventory records of the firm. Typically 10 to 20 percent of the items are designated A and roughly 50 to 60 percent C with this criterion. The second step involves establishing the "ABC" categories of criticality. To keep the confusion level down, we will use I, II, and III to designate the criticality categories. The criteria to establish these categories are more implicit and intuitive. Category I, for example, might include items that would bring the plant to a stop and for which there is no easy substitute, alternative supply, or quick fix. The III items, on the other hand, are the ones for which there would be little if any impact if there were a shortage. The II items are the ones left over. The distributions of dollar usage and criticality for a sample of maintenance inventory items at a consumer durable manufacturing plant are shown in Figure 18.18.

There is substantially less dollar usage in category I than in category A. This should not be surprising, given that the criteria for I included things

FIGURE 18.18 Distributions of dollar-usage and criticality for a sample of maintenance inventory items

	Dollar-usage			Criticality		
Category	No. of items	Percent of items	Percent of dollar-usage	No. of items	Percent of items	Percent of dollar-usage
A-I	15	11%	84%	5	4%	40%
B-II	25	15	15	48	39	56
C-III	88	74	1	75	57	4
Total	128	100	100	128	100	100

Source: B. E. Flores and D. C. Whybark, "Implementing Multiple Criteria ABC Analysis," *Journal of Operations Management* 7, no. 1, Fall 1987.

FIGURE 18.19 Number of items classified by dollar-usage and criticality

		Criticality			
		I	II	III	Total
	A	2	12	1	15
Dollar-usage	B	1	19	5	25
	C	2	17	69	88
	Total	5	48	75	128

Source: B. E. Flores and D. C. Whybark, "Implementing Multiple Criteria ABC Analysis," *Journal of Operations Management* 7, no. 1, Fall 1987.

like impact of outage and ease of replacement. A matrix of the dollar-usage and criticality classifications is shown in Figure 18.19. There is an entry for every combination. That means that both low dollar-usage and high dollar-usage items can have high criticality (or low criticality). It also means that the problem of combining still remains.

Multiple criteria ABC management policies

There are nine possible combinations in Figure 18.19 that could each require a different management policy. The next step is to reduce the number, although R. G. Brown argues this is not necessary when the computer can keep track of any number of policies. We, however, are concerned about having a number with which people can cope. A simple mechanical procedure is used to combine classifications to provide three initial categories of items. These categories, AA, BB, and CC, provide a starting point for management to reassess the classifications of the items. The procedure simply

FIGURE 18.20   Multiple criteria distributions

Combined category	No. of items	Percent of items	Percent of dollar-usage
AA	14	11%	78%
BB	16	13	12
CC	98	76	10
Total	128	100	100

Source: B. E. Flores and D. C. Whybark, "Implementing Multiple Criteria ABC Analysis," *Journal of Operations Management* 7, no. 1, Fall 1987.

assigns every item in A-I (see Figure 18.19), A-II, and B-I to AA; every item in A-III, C-I, and B-II to BB; and every item in B-III, C-II, and C-III to CC. This results in 15 AA items, 22 BB items and 91 CC items.

The next step is to ask management to review the classification of each item. The final step is to define specific policies for managing each category. In fact, it is helpful to develop tentative policies first. These can serve as a guideline to the review of the classification of each item. With the policies in mind, the question to ask when reviewing each item is: Should it be managed with the procedures that apply to its classification? The reclassification of the items by the manager is shown in Figure 18.20. There were changes from the mechanical assignments in each category. The managers even created a fourth category, although we have not shown it. In evaluating the items, they found nearly half should not be carried in inventory at all. This demonstrated our observation that it is hard to enhance a system that does not have sound basics.

Specific inventory management policies are needed for each category to bring meaning to phrases like "closer management" or "more management attention." The policies are developed to cover four areas: inventory record verification, order quantity, safety stock, and the classification of the item itself. The first area, verification, is to prevent the unpleasant surprises that often occur when the computer record does not agree with the physical count. To improve accuracy, more frequent counts should be made. This implies a higher frequency for the AA items than for the BB or CC items. The order quantity and safety stock levels are established for each item depending on both the economics and criticality. Finally, since it is a changing world, a specific period for reconsidering the classification of the item is established.

The specific values chosen for each of these areas are shown in Figure 18.21. The frequency of counting was established using an average counting rate of 40 items per labor hour and taking into account past difficulties with the inventory records and transaction reporting system. The order quan-

FIGURE 18.21   Inventory management policy parameters for multiple criteria ABC items

	Category		
	AA	*BB*	*CC*
Counting frequency	Monthly	Every six months	Yearly
Order quantity	Small for costly items	Medium: EOQ-based	Large quantities
Safety stock	Large for critical items	Large for critical items	Low or none
Reclassify review	Every six months	Every six months	Yearly

Source: B. E. Flores and D. C. Whybark, "Implementing Multiple Criteria ABC Analysis," *Journal of Operations Management* 7, no. 1, Fall 1987.

tities were roughly based on the EOQ values, while safety stock was based on the criticality of the item. For both order quantity and safety stock, each part was considered individually. Finally, in order not to leave the impression that the item's category was "frozen," a specific frequency of review of each item's classification was established.

The multiple criteria ABC categories take into account many factors not normally considered in classifying inventory items for management purposes. When combined with clear, specific policies for each category, they can bring substantial improvements in the use of scarce management talent in managing the inventories.

LIVING WITH ADVANCED SYSTEMS

The installation of many of the advanced concepts discussed in this chapter depends upon having functioning basic systems and minds receptive to organizational change. In addition, several managerial and technical notions are important in keeping the system from taking over once it is installed. In this section, we will discuss some of these concerns.

The importance of organizational preparedness

The first and foremost concern in assessing the value of the advanced concepts for any organization is whether the basic systems are in place. Managers must have a clear understanding of fundamental relationships as well.

If the service level reorder point trade-off is not understood *and* order quantities are not appropriately determined, the interaction between the two can not be well understood. Inventory accuracy, transaction procedures, systems for routine activities, and effective warehouse, traffic, logistics, and inventory groups must all be in place before advanced concepts should be implemented.

The concepts discussed in this chapter all require an expanded view of the system. For example, to incorporate the transportation dimension or to use procedures for group orders requires a nonprovincial view of particular jobs. The implementation of some of these ideas changes the roles of people in the organization. Flexibility and open-mindedness are required. The new coordination tasks may strain the capabilities of otherwise effective persons.

Once the organization is ready, these ideas can lead to improved performance and better response to problems. It depends on whether the right rules and roles can be developed. Expectancies are important as well. A substantial number of small improvements over a large number of items can lead to large totals. But the payoff from any one inventory decision could be small and thus discouraging to the people.

Preparing the organization

Clearly, one of the risks in systematizing the management of independent demand items is that the system will take over; that is, "it's the computer's fault." After one retail organization installed a commercial package, the buyers spent their time changing the suggested group orders because they were triggered by non-key items in the group. Their understanding of the system was insufficient to make it work *for* them. It is clear that one of the key elements in living successfully with advanced systems is training. If there is an insufficient understanding of the purposes, theory, and approach of the system, people will not use it effectively.

Training should be a continuous process. New people come into the organization, and trained ones move on to other tasks. Every now and then a thorough updating of the staff may be warranted. Training is important in monitoring the system outputs and inputs. Even though some of the technical monitoring approaches could be used, the key point is to not let silly things happen because someone doesn't understand.

To do routine things routinely means specifying the routine. This is a management task. With the routine things defined and systematized, the appropriate resources (information, training, authorities, and so on) need to be provided for solving the nonroutine problems. Again, this is the management task. The payoff from these efforts is increasing the productive use of human and system resources.

CONCLUDING PRINCIPLES

In this chapter, we have presented advanced techniques for independent demand systems. Some of these techniques, such as ordering a group of items and multiple criteria ABC analysis, have already been implemented by manufacturing and distribution firms. They are presently enjoying the payoffs from these enhancements to their systems. In many other firms, however, the implementation of these advanced methods awaits the development of a properly functioning basic system; that is, a system built on sound data and the timely handling of transactions. We conclude this chapter by summarizing several principles that we have observed concerning the methods presented in this chapter:

- A well-understood basic independent demand system must be in place before attempting to obtain further benefits from the advanced techniques presented here.
- Savings in inventory related costs can be achieved by a joint determination of the order point and order quantity parameters.
- Savings in firm-wide costs can be obtained by the joint consideration of decision-making activities that are often performed by different groups in an organization.
- Combined ordering of several inventory items obtained from a single source can provide important savings in inventory related costs.
- All criteria should be taken into account in classifying inventory items for management priorities.
- Specific policies for managing each classification of inventory item should be developed and used to guide the classification itself, as well as to the management of the inventories.
- Management must be sure the organization is prepared to take on advanced systems before attempting implementation.

REFERENCES

Baker, K. R.; M. J. Magazine; and H. L. W. Nuttle. "The Effect of Commonality on Safety Stock in a Simple Inventory Model." *Management Science* 32, no. 8, August 1986.

Ballou, Ronald H. "Estimating and Auditing Aggregate Inventory Levels at Multiple Stocking Points." *Journal of Operations Management* 1, no. 3 (February 1981), pp. 143–54.

Billington, P. J. "The Classic Economic Production Quantity Model with Setup Cost as a Function of Capital Expenditure." *Decision Sciences* 18, no. 1, Winter 1987.

Brown, R. G. *Advanced Service Parts Inventory Control.* Materials Management Systems, Inc., 1982, Norwich, Vt.

Bryson, William L. "Profit-Oriented Inventory Management." *APICS 22nd Annual Conference Proceedings*, 1979, pp. 88–91.

Carlson, J. G., and C. S. Gopal. "The Numbering and Taxonomy of Inventoried

Items." *International Journal of Operations and Production Management* 3, no. 1, pp. 10–19.

Chikan, Attila. "Heuristic Modeling of a Multi-Echelon Production-Inventory System." *Production Emerging Trends and Issues,* Netherlands: Elsevier, 1985.

Constable, G. C., and D. C. Whybark. "The Interaction of Transportation and Inventory Decisions." *Decision Sciences* 9, no. 4 (October 1978), pp. 688–99.

Eilon, S., and J. Elmaleh. "An Evaluation of Alternative Inventory Control Policies." *International Journal of Production Research,* July 1968, p. 3–14.

Flores, B. E., and D. C. Whybark. "Multiple Criteria ABC Analysis." *International Journal of Operations & Production Management* 6, no. 3, Fall 1986.

———. "Implementing Multiple Criteria ABC Analysis." *Journal of Operations Management* 7, no. H2, (September 1987).

Hadley, G., and T. M. Whitin. *Analysis of Inventory Systems.* New York: Prentice-Hall, 1963.

Jayaraman, R., and M. T. Tabucanon. "Co-ordinated Versus Independent Replenishment Inventory Control." *International Journal of Operations & Production Management* 4, no. 1, pp. 61–69.

Johnson, L. A., and D. C. Montgomery. *Operations Research in Production Planning, Scheduling and Inventory Control.* New York: John Wiley & Sons, 1979.

Jonsson, H., and E. A. Silver. "Analysis of a Two-Echelon Inventory Control System with Complete Redistribution." *Management Science* 33, no. 2, February 1987.

Kleijnen, J. P. C., and P. J. Rens. "Impact Revisited: A Critical Analysis of IBM's Inventory Package—IMPACT." *Production and Inventory Management,* First Quarter, 1978.

Lewis, C. D., and A. L. Foo. "GIPSI—A General Purpose Inventory Policy Simulation Package." *International Journal of Production Research* 18, no. 1 (January/February 1980), pp. 73–82.

Miltenburg, G. J., and E. A. Silver. "Accounting for Residual Stock in Continuous Review Coordinated Control of a Family of Items." *International Journal of Production Research* 22, no. 4, pp. 607–28.

———. "The Diffusion Process and Residual Stock in Periodic Review, Coordinated Control of Families of Items." *International Journal of Production Research* 22, no. 4, pp. 629–46.

Porteus, E. L. "Investing in Reduced Setups in the EOQ Model." *Management Science* 31, no. 8, August 1985.

Rosenblatt, M. J. "Fixed Cycle, Basic Cycle, and EOQ Approaches to Multi-item Single Supplier Inventory System." *International Journal of Production Research* 22, no. 6, pp. 1131–39.

Silver, E. A. "Operations Research in Inventory Management: A Review and Critique." *Operations Research* 29, no. 4 (July/August 1981).

Wemmerlov, U. "A Time-phased Order Point System in Environments with and without Demand Uncertainty: A Comparative Analysis of Non-monetary Performance Variables." *International Journal of Production Research* 24, no. 2, pp. 343–58.

DISCUSSION QUESTIONS

1. A friend of yours has suggested that she wants to leap-frog the basic independent demand inventory ideas and go directly to implementing some of the more advanced concepts. What arguments would you raise against this strategy? What counter arguments might persuade you that the leap-frog strategy would be OK?

2. Use the analogy of writing home for money to explain the concept of demand during lead time. Be sure to account for the fact that both the lead time and demand are variables.

3. How can Figure 18.4 be used to estimate management's estimated (implied) cost of stockouts?

4. How might you go about convincing a transportation department and inventory control department to join forces in making the transportation-inventory decisions?

5. A manufacturing firm uses a color coding scheme for placing joint orders on a single source of supply. Each vendor is coded with an individual color in the Kardex file. When any one of the items from a vendor reaches reorder point, an economic order quantity is ordered for *all* items from the same vendor, which are easily found by the color coding. Comment on this procedure.

6. How would you classify the three following items using multiple criteria ABC analysis to decide between AA, BB, or CC: a car, a calculator, and writing paper?

PROBLEMS

1. Consider the following demand and lead time data for a company's major product:

Demand per day	Probability	Manufacturing lead time (in days)	Probability
1	.3	2	.4
2	.7	3	.6

a. Determine the distribution for the demand during the lead time and calculate the average demand during the lead time.

b. Assuming that the reorder point is set at 5 units, the item is ordered 10 times per year, and the stockout cost is $10 per unit, what is the expected shortage cost per year?

2. The inventory management of a distribution warehouse for a large chemical firm is experimenting with statistical inventory control policies, which utilize reorder points and economic order quantities. The management has determined that the demand distribution for a specialty product is as follows:

Demand (units/week)	Probability of demand
0	.2
1	.6
2	.2

For the same product, the management has estimated the following costs:

Fixed cost to place an order = $9.
Cost to carry one unit in inventory for one week = $.50.
Stockout cost per unit = $10.

Assuming that the lead time required to order and receive a shipment of replacement inventory is exactly two weeks, what reorder point and order quantity should the warehouse use to minimize cost?

3. A company has an item in stock for which the annual inventory carrying cost is $10 per unit per year, the backorder cost is $4 per unit (stockouts are backordered until replacement stock is available), the ordering cost is $5 per order, and the annual requirement is 100 units. The demand during replenishment lead time has the probability distribution shown below:

Demand during lead time (in units)	Probability
0	.14
1	.27
2	.27
3	.17
4	.09
5	.04
6	.02

What is the minimum cost lot-size and reorder point for this item?

4. Consider the following inventory and distribution data pertaining to the major product of Arnold Manufacturing Company:

Annual sales = 325 units/year.
Ordering cost = $20/order.
Inventory carrying cost = 12.5 percent of item value/year.
Shortage cost = $20/unit.
Item value (before transit) = $6/unit.
Transportation cost:
  Air freight = $10/unit.
  Rail = $8/unit.
In-transit carrying cost: 12.5 percent of the item value/year.

Sales (units/day)	Probability	Air transportation lead time (in days)	Probability	Rail transportation lead time (in days)	Probability
0	0.6	1	.75	2	0.6
1	0.4	2	.25	3	0.4

Assuming that the inventory level is monitored continuously, that lost sales are not backordered, and that there are 250 working days per year, what economic lot-size quantity and reorder point should Arnold use to minimize total costs? Which transportation mode should be used (rail or air freight)?

5. The Regis Book and Stationery store is negotiating with a new vendor that is capable of supplying several grades of paper. Before a final decision can be reached on whether to purchase from this firm, the management desires to know whether to order the various grades of paper separately or to place combined (joint) orders for the items. The following data were collected on a sample of four grades of paper to assist the inventory planner in the analysis:

	Paper grade			
	#1	#2	#3	#4
Daily sales requirements*	2,000 lb.	960 lb.	400 lb.	1,440 lb.
Inventory holding cost (per thousand pounds per day)	$1.00	$.80	$.40	$.60
Purchase cost (per pound)	1.00	.80	.40	.60
Individual order cost	8.00	8.00	8.00	8.00
Joint order cost	$8.00 plus $1.00 per item ordered			
Inventory carrying cost	25% of item cost per year			

*Sales rate based on 250 days per year.

Should Regis Book and Stationery store negotiate for individual orders or not? State any assumptions you made regarding your recommendation.

6. Demand during lead time for Fuzzies is distributed as follows:

Probability =	.1	.1	.3	.2	.1	.1	.1
Demand =	14	15	16	17	18	19	20

a. Use a spreadsheet program to evaluate the expected number of units short per reorder cycle for reorder points of 14–20. What is the expected shortage cost per reorder cycle when the reorder point is 14 and the cost per unit short is $10?

b. What happens to the shortage cost ($R = 14$, $C_s = \$10$) if the demand distribution shifts as follows?

Probability =	.2	.4	.2	.1	.1	0	0
Demand =	14	15	16	17	18	19	20

7. Using the data from Figure 18.1, set up a spreadsheet program to perform the iterative (Q,R) procedure. (Note: you can input the reorder point and expected number of units short by hand if you find it easier.) Once you have been able to duplicate the calculations of the example, determine what happens if the shortage cost drops to $50 per unit.

8. A sample of items from the maintenance inventory of the Soaring Eagle Hang Glider Company is given below. Rank the items in descending dollar-usage order using a spreadsheet. How many items does it take to represent 50 percent of the total? How many does it take to represent the last 10 percent?

					Item					
	a	b	c	d	e	f	g	h	i	j
Cost	83	68	23	45	10	2	94	51	87	24
Usage	14	47	105	24	75	43	56	5	48	81

9. For the items in problem 8, management made A, B, and C as well as I, II, and III assignments for dollar-usage and criticality, respectively, as shown below. Using the mechanical procedure to develop AA, BB, and CC categories, what are the classifications for each item? What is the dollar-usage distribution for AA to CC.

					Item					
	a	b	c	d	e	f	g	h	i	j
A–C	C	B	B	C	C	C	A	C	A	B
I–III	III	II	I	III	I	III	I	II	III	III

10. What observations can you make about the dollar-usage distribution of the following items?

		Item			
	1	2	3	4	5
Cost	1.77	4.78	.89	1.11	.66
Usage	.27	10	54	43	72

11. Solihull Distributors stocks a product having an ordering cost of $216, an inventory carrying cost of $5/unit/year, a stockout cost of $100 per unit short, an annual requirement of 60 units, and a one-month production lead time. The demand during replenishment lead time has the probability distribution shown below:

Demand during lead time (in units)	Probability
0	.01
1	.04
2	.08
3	.12
4	.15
5	.20
6	.15
7	.12
8	.08
9	.04
10	.01

What is the minimum cost lot size and reorder point for this item?

12. The Anderson Company produces a spare part that has an ordering cost of $101, an inventory carrying cost of $20/unit/yr, a stockout cost of $100 per unit short, an annual requirement of 988 units, and a one-week replenishment lead time. The demand during the replenishment lead time has the probability distribution shown below:

Demand during lead time (in units)	Probability
15	.02
16	.05
17	.09
18	.15
19	.38
20	.15
21	.09
22	.05
23	.02

What is the minimum cost lot size and reorder point for this item.

13. Oak Park Furniture Sales Company currently purchases its office furniture line from a supplier located in California. One typical item is characterized by the following data:

Annual Sales = 1000 units/year
Ordering Cost = $250/order
Inventory Carrying Cost = 40% of item value/year
Shortage Cost = $50/unit short
Item Value (before transit) = $300.00

Transportation Cost:
  Rail = $5/unit
  Truck = $10/unit

In-transit carrying cost = 40% of item value/year

Sales (units/week)	Probability
10	.5
20	.5

Rail transportation time	Probability
2 weeks	.2
3 weeks	.8

Truck transportation time	Probability
1 week	.7
2 weeks	.3

Assuming that inventory is monitored continuously and that lost sales are not backordered, what lot size and reorder point should be used to minimize total costs? Which transportation mode should be used (rail or truck)?

14. The Oak Park Furniture Sales Company (in problem 13) has received an air freight transportation quote for the hardware on its office furniture product line, using air freight. Shipping by air freight costs $12/unit and has the following transportation lead time distribution:

Transport Time	Probability
same week	.8
1 week	.2

What is the minimum cost transportation method, lot size, and reorder point, considering all these transportation methods: truck, rail, and air? What solution results if the truck alternative is used as the base case in step 1 of the heuristic method for simultaneously determining mode and inventory policy?

15. The Vickers Automotive Components Company currently purchases two fabricated assemblies from a supplier, items 1234 and 1235. The transportation cost to ship these items from the supplier to Vickers is $250 per order. The trucking firm currently used by Vickers has offered to reduce the transportation cost to $450 per order if Vickers orders the two items jointly. Following is selected data on items 1234 and 1235.

	Item 1234	Item 1235
Annual demand	1000 units	1500 units
Item value	$250/unit	$75/unit
Inventory carrying cost	40% of item value/ year	40% of item value/ year

Determine the minimum cost-independent-order quantity for both items and evaluate whether Vickers should order the two items jointly.

— 19 —————————————————

Distribution requirements planning

This chapter describes a set of techniques for managing distribution inventories. For firms faced with maintaining distribution inventories, the techniques provide an improved ability to bridge between the marketplace and manufacturing. Distribution requirements planning (DRP) provides the basis for tying the physical distribution system to the manufacturing planning and control (MPC) system. It relates the current inventory positions and forecasts of field demand to the master production scheduling and material planning activities of manufacturing. A well-developed DRP system will enable management to better anticipate future requirements in the field, more closely match the material supply to the demand, more effectively deploy inventory to meet customer-service requirements, and more rapidly adjust to the vagaries of the marketplace. In addition, the system can help achieve significant logistics savings through better planning of aggregate transportation capacity needs and dispatching of shipments. This chapter will show how the techniques work, how they are tied into the MPC system, and how they can be used to realize the potential savings.

The chapter is organized around the following four topics:

- Distribution requirements planning in MPC systems: How does DRP fit into the MPC system?

- Distribution requirements planning techniques: How does DRP work and how is it used to manage the demand and supply of field inventories?
- Management issues with DRP: What organizational questions must be addressed to fully realize the potential of the system?
- Company example: How does DRP work in an actual firm?

This chapter of the book is closely related to Chapter 16 on forecasting; to Chapter 10, which treats the topic of demand management; and to Chapters 8 and 14, which cover master production scheduling. The DRP system is driven by forecasts, ties into the demand management activities, and provides a significant input to the master production scheduling process. The record processing in DRP is consistent with that described for material requirements planning (MRP) in Chapters 2 and 3. Some theory on the management of distribution inventories is found in Chapters 17 and 18.

DRP IN MANUFACTURING PLANNING AND CONTROL SYSTEMS

Distribution requirements planning is best conceived of as being one part of demand management. The general relationship of DRP to some of the manufacturing planning and control system modules is shown in Figure 19.1. DRP provides a linkage between the marketplace, demand management, and master production scheduling. The linkage is effected through time-phased information on inventories and through demand and shipping plans that coordinate activities in these modules.

Finished goods inventories are often positioned in a complicated physical

FIGURE 19.1 Distribution requirements planning in the MPC system

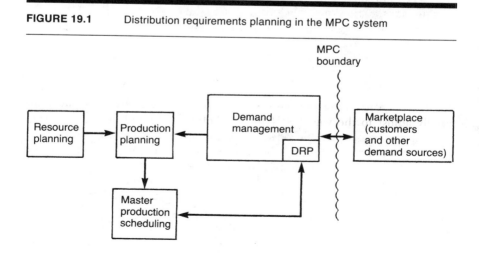

system, consisting of field warehouses, intermediate distribution centers, and a central supply. In such systems, a key task is effectively managing the resultant flow of goods and inventories between the firm and the market. In performing this task, DRP has a central coordinating role, similar to that of material requirements planning in the coordination of materials in manufacturing. The role of DRP is to provide the necessary data for matching customer demand with the supply of products at various stages in the physical distribution system and of those being produced by manufacturing.

Key elements of these data are the planned timings and quantities for replenishing inventories throughout the physical distribution system. These data take into account the currently available field inventories and forecasts. The planners use these data to evaluate the quality of the current match between supply and demand and to make adjustments as required.

Distribution requirements planning provides information to the master production scheduler in a format consistent with that of the MRP records. By using standard MRP software approaches for DRP, the full range of MRP techniques, such as firm planned orders, pegging, and exception messages, are available to manage distribution inventories. This also provides the basis for integrating the data base throughout the material system—from purchasing through distribution. Evaluation of alternative plans, with the integrated data base, provides a complete view of the material planning implications. This is particularly valuable in master production scheduling.

DRP data provide the basis for adjusting the master production schedule (MPS) to reflect changes in demand or in the product mix. If manufacturing and distribution system priorities cannot be adjusted to respond to these requirements, the implications can be evaluated and communicated to customers in a timely fashion. Common records and system integration means there is complete visibility to see how best to use available inventories and to adjust future schedules. DRP provides a solid base of information to make these decisions, instead of relying on political negotiations between the field and the factory.

Distribution requirements planning and the marketplace

DRP starts in the marketplace—or as close to it as possible. In most instances, this means in a warehouse or other distribution facility. In some instances, however, it could actually be at a customer location. We know of some firms that gather information on inventory levels and on product usage directly from some of their key customers. This offers them a major strategic advantage in providing service and advice to these customers.

The DRP records start at the independent demand interface; that is, they are derived from forecasts. Since customers make their own ordering decisions (except in the instance just described, where having knowledge of the customer's inventories and usage may allow the firm to advise the customer on ordering), the demand is "independent" of the company's decisions. From that point on, however, the decisions are under the control of the company. Timing and sizes of replenishment shipments, manufacturing batch sizes, and purchase order policies are all under management control. DRP is the vehicle for integrating the marketing and replenishment information into the overall management control process.

The DRP approach allows one to pick up all of the detailed local information for managing physical distribution and for coordinating with the factory. Since customer demand is independent, detailed forecasts of end-item demand are needed at each warehouse. However, attention to the results may be useful in tailoring the forecasts to local conditions. We know of one instance, for example, where the local warehouse manager was able to identify several products that were purchased late in the month by some large firms. This produced a different demand pattern in the forecast than the constant weekly demand throughout the month resulting from use of a standard forecasting software package. The modified forecasts produced inventory savings by being able to more closely match demand with supply at this location.

Two types of demand data may be available locally that can help in managing the field inventories. Information on future special orders can help in providing service to other customers while satisfying the special orders. Planned inventory adjustments by customers can also be reflected in the system, again providing data for more closely managing the distribution process. In each of these cases, the system allows the company to respond to advance notice of conditions, rather than treating them as "surprises" when they occur.

All management decisions for controlling inventories are reflected in the plans for resupplying warehouses. Planned shipment information provides valuable data for managing the local facility. Personnel required for unloading incoming material and stocking shelves can be planned. If there are problems in satisfying local demands, realistic promises can be made to waiting customers. Also, the amount of capital tied up in local inventory can be more realistically estimated for funds management.

In summary, DRP serves two purposes at the warehouse level. First, DRP provides the means for capturing data, including local demand conditions, for modifying the forecast or for reporting current inventory positions. The second purpose is to provide data for managing the local facility and to provide the data base for consistent communications with the customers and the rest of the company.

Distribution requirements planning and demand management

The demand management module is the gateway between the manufacturing facility and the marketplace. In some systems with field inventories,

FIGURE 19.2   Distribution requirements planning and the logistics system

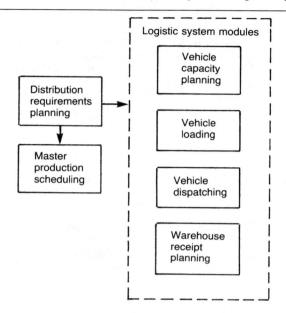

it is where information on demand is taken in and where product for the field warehouses is sent out. This process requires detailed matching of the supply to the demand in every location—and of providing supply to meet all sources of demand. DRP is the method for managing the resultant large volume of dynamic information and for generating the set of plans for manufacturing and replenishment.

The plans that are derived from the DRP information and from the resultant shipping requirements are the basis for managing the logistics process. The relationship between DRP and these activities is shown in Figure 19.2. Vehicle capacity planning is the process of planning the vehicle availability for the set of future shipments as generated by DRP. Shipping requirements also are used to determine vehicle loads, dispatching schedules, and warehouse receipts planning.

By planning future replenishment needs, DRP establishes the basis for more effective vehicle dispatching decisions. These decisions are continually adjusted to reflect current conditions, and long-term plans help to determine the necessary transportation capacity. Near-term needs of the warehouses are used to efficiently load vehicles without compromising customer-service levels. The data on planned resupply of the warehouses can be used for scheduling the labor force in the warehouses.

As actual field demands vary around the forecasts, adjustments to plans are required. DRP continually makes these adjustments, sending the inventories from the central warehouse to those distribution centers where they are most needed. In circumstances where insufficient total inventory exists, DRP provides the basis for making allocation decisions. The planning information facilitates ideas, such as providing stock sufficient to last the same amount of time at each location, or favoring the "best" customers, or even being able to accurately say when availability will be improved and delivery can be expected. DRP, therefore, is a critical component of demand management, of planning, and of updating information while monitoring the outflow of products.

DRP and master production scheduling

Perhaps the greatest payoff of DRP to master production scheduling is from the integration of records and information. Since the formats of DRP and MRP records are compatible and all the MPC modules are linked, DRP provides the means for extending the MPC visibility into the distribution system. This, however, has political implications. One company we know decided not to integrate the records, and it established a committee to resolve issues concerning size and composition of inventories. A sister company installed an integrated system using DRP. When it became evident that the integrated system was superior, the political cost of dismantling the committee was very high. All committee members had "permanent" jobs.

DRP collects detailed information in the field and so summarizes it that MPS decisions can respond to the overall company needs. DRP permits evaluation of current conditions to determine if manufacturing priorities should be revised. It provides insights into how they should be changed and into the implications to the field if they are not. Thus, more reasoned trade-offs can be made in the use of limited capacity or materials.

The shipping plans in DRP provide the master scheduler better information to match manufacturing output with shipping needs. "Demand" based on shipments to the distribution centers can be quite different from "demand" in the field. Manufacturing needs to be closely coordinated with the former. For example, firms matching shipment timings and sizes with manufacturing batches can achieve substantial inventory savings.

In summary, distribution requirements planning serves a central role in coordinating the flow of materials inside the factory with the system modules that place the goods in the hands of the customers. It provides the basis for integrating the MPC system from the firm to the field. We turn next to the technical details of DRP.

DISTRIBUTION REQUIREMENTS PLANNING TECHNIQUES

In this section, we develop the logic of DRP. We start by introducing the basic record and how DRP information is processed. Thereafter, we turn to the "time-phased order point," show how to link several warehouse records, present ways to manage the day-to-day variations from plans, and discuss how safety stocks are used in a DRP-based system.

The basic DRP record

The basic data elements of a DRP system are detailed records for individual products at locations as close to the final customer as possible. The records are maintained centrally as a part of the MPC system data base, but the continually updated information and inventory transaction data are passed between the central location and the field sites either on some periodic basis or on line. For illustrative purposes, we will consider the record for a single stock-keeping unit (SKU) at a field warehouse.

To integrate DRP into the overall MPC system, the bill of materials is expanded beyond its usual context. The zero level in the bill of material is defined as the SKU in a field warehouse. Thus, an item is not seen as completed simply when the raw materials have been transformed into a finished product, but only after it has been delivered to the location from which it will satisfy a customer demand. This extension of the bill of materials into field locations allows us to use standard MRP explosion techniques to link the field with all other MPC systems.

Regardless of the physical location (central inventory at the plant, a distribution center, a field warehouse, or even a customer's shelf), the ultimate demand for the item comes from the customer. The warehouse is where the company's internal world of dependent demand must deal with the independent demand of the customer. The customer, within wide ranges, makes decisions about how much and when to order; these are independent of the company's decisions. Planners in the company, on the other hand, make decisions of when and how much product to make. They also decide when and how much to send to the field locations. To link the company decisions with the customer's we must start with a forecast. This is recorded in the first row of the basic DRP record shown in Figure 19.3.

The record looks like an MRP record, but there are some subtle differences, other than the use of forecast data in the requirements row. For example, since it is for a specific location, it provides not only time-phased data on how much and when but also tells us where. It is not the differences, however, that are important. It is the consistency of format and processing logic that provide many of DRP's benefits. To explain this, we will go through the record in some detail.

In the example shown in Figure 19.3, we show a change in the forecast

FIGURE 19.3   Field warehouse DRP record

		Period						
		1	2	3	4	5	6	7
Forecast requirements		20	20	20	20	30	30	30
In transit			60					
Projected available balance	45	25	65	45	25	55	25	55
Planned shipments				60		60		

Safety stock = 20; shipping quantity = 60; lead time = 2.

in period 5. This could come about because of a revision by someone at the warehouse who has information on local demand, or because of a sales promotion. The fact that these variations can be incorporated into the system at this level provides one of the advantages of using DRP for managing the field inventories.

The second row shows shipments in transit to the warehouse. In Figure 19.3, one shipment is scheduled to arrive in time for use in period 2. Thus, the time for unloading and shelving the products must be accounted for in setting the lead time to show the order available for use in period 2. The equivalent row in a manufacturing MRP record is called "scheduled receipts" (open orders). However, more than the name of the in-transit row is different between manufacturing and distribution. In manufacturing, there is some flexibility in the timing of open orders, in that they can be speeded up or slowed down to a certain extent, by changing priorities in a shop-floor control system. This is more difficult with goods in transit. Once a shipment is on a vehicle bound for a particular location, there is little opportunity to change the arrival time.

The projected inventory balance row contains the current inventory balance (45 for the example provided in Figure 19.3) and the projections of available inventory for each period in the planning horizon (7 periods). A safety stock value of 20 has been determined as sufficient to provide the level of customer service desired for the item. The economics of transportation or packaging indicate that a normal shipment of this product to this location is 60 units. Finally, it takes two periods to load, ship, unload, and store the product.

The projected available balance is generated by using the forecast requirements. The process is identical to that used for processing MRP records. In Figure 19.3, the available balance for the end of period 1 is determined by subtracting the forecast requirement of 20 from the initial inventory of 45. The 25 units at the end of period 1, plus the in-transit quantity of 60 to be received in period 2, minus the forecast of 20 for period 2, give the balance of 65 for period 2.

The planned shipments are indicated for those periods in which a shipment would have to be made to avoid a projected balance having less than the safety stock. The projected balance for period 4, for example, is 25 units. The forecast for period 5 is 30 units. Therefore, a shipment of product that will be available in period 5 is needed. Since the lead time is two periods, a planned shipment of 60 units (the shipping quantity) is shown for period 3. Similarly, the planned shipment of period 5 is needed to cover the forecast of 30 in period 7, since there in only a 25-unit projected available balance at the end of period 6.

The result of these calculations for each product at each location is a plan for future shipments needed to provide the customer-service levels desired by the company. These plans depend on the forecast, but they incorporate management decisions for shipping quantities and safety stocks in planning resupply schedules. It is these plans that provide the visibility needed by the planners to match supply and demand.

Time-phased order point (TPOP)

Many companies use reorder point/economic order or shipping quantity (ROP/EOQ) procedures based on demand forecasts for managing their field inventories. This means the decisions for resupply are made independently at the location, with no integrated forward planning; that is, when the on-hand quantity at a location reaches the reorder point, the shipping quantity is ordered with no thought given to any other items ordered, to the situation at the factory, or to warehouses—or to when the next order might be needed. Time-phased order point can be used as an alternative to ROP/EOQ, even if the forecast is not just a simple constant average usage. Whenever forecast information is used as the requirements and a time-phased MRP approach is used to develop the planned shipments, it is called "time-phased order point." To show the advantages, we use Figure 19.4.

If an ROP/EOQ system were used, the reorder point for the situation depicted in Figure 19.4 would be 25 units, comprised of the safety stock (10) plus the demand during lead time (15), assuming continuous review of inventory balances. If the ROP/EOQ rules were simulated for the data in Figure 19.4, there would be planned shipments in periods 3 and 6, and there would have been an order in transit (placed last period). If DRP logic is used, the planned shipments are in periods 1, 3, and 6. Thus, the timing of the

FIGURE 19.4   Example time-phased order point (TPOP) record

		Period						
		1	*2*	*3*	*4*	*5*	*6*	*7*
Forecast requirements		15	15	15	15	15	15	15
In transit								
Projected available balance	22	7	32	17	42	27	12	37
Planned shipments		40		40			40	

Safety stock = 10; shipping quantity = 40; lead time = 1.

orders in the TPOP record shown in Figure 19.4 does *not* exactly match the expected timing of orders using ROP/EOQ.

The results are, however, very close. The differences would largely disappear if the periods were made small (e.g., days instead of weeks) since they are primarily due to the fact that ROP/EOQ assumes continuous review. The TPOP approach is based on the MRP logic of so triggering (planning) an order that the ending balance in the period when the order arrives will not be below the safety stock level.

One advantage of TPOP over ROP/EOQ is that the TPOP record shows the *planned* shipment data. These are not a part of ROP/EOQ. In addition, TPOP is not limited to the use of constant requirement assumptions. When forecast usages vary, the differences between TPOP and ROP/EOQ can be much larger than those shown in Figure 19.4.

Not only is it important to have planned shipment data it is also critical to capture *all* demand information. Forecast sales requirements are only one source of demand input. DRP can use TPOP, plus actual order data, plus service part requirements, plus interplant demands. *All* of these demand sources can be integrated into the demand data driving DRP.

Linking several warehouse records

Once the records are established for the field warehouses, the information on planned shipments is passed through the distribution centers (if any) to the central facility. This process is sometimes referred to as "implosion." The concept indicates that we are gathering information from a number of

FIGURE 19.5 Field warehouse to central warehouse records for DRP

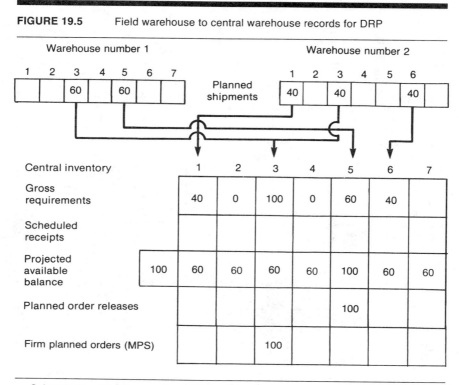

Safety stock = 50; order quantity = 100; lead time = 0.

field locations and aggregating it at the manufacturing facility. This is different from the "explosion" notion in manufacturing, where a finished product is broken into its components, but the process is the same, and in both cases it is based on bills of material.

The record shown in Figure 19.5 is for the central warehouse inventory. The gross requirements correspond to the planned shipments to the two warehouses shown in Figure 19.3 and 19.4. This relationship reflects the logic that, if there were a shipment of 40 units of product to warehouse number 2 in period 1, there would be a "demand" on the central warehouse for 40 units in period 1. The "demand," however, is dependent, having come from the company's shipping department. It is, therefore, a gross requirement and not a forecast requirement. We have crossed over from the independent demand world of the customers to the dependent demand world of the company.

The gross requirement at the central warehouse is shown in the same period as the planned shipment, since the lead time to ship the product has already been accounted for in the field warehouse record. For example, a shipment of 60 units of product planned for period 3 in Figure 19.3 allows for the two-period lead time before it is needed in period 5.

The logic for imploding planned shipment information holds also for much more complicated distribution systems. If there were intermediate distribution centers, they would have gross requirements derived from the warehouses that they served. At distribution centers, gross requirements are established for any period in which replenishment shipments are planned to warehouses.

A primary task at the central facility is to create the master production schedule (MPS). The central inventory record in Figure 19.5 can be used for this purpose. The record shows the projected available balances for the central inventory and the planned order releases, which provide the quantities needed to maintain the safety stock of 50 units. The master production schedule is created by using zero lead time and firm planned orders. Firm planned orders are created by the planners and are not under system control; that is, they are not automatically replanned as conditions change but are maintained in the periods and quantities designated by the planners.

The MPS states when manufacturing is to have the product completed and available for shipment to the field warehouses. In the example shown in Figure 19.5, the MPS quantity (firm planned order) has replaced a planned order, although this need not be the case.

Our example implies creating an MPS for each end item. This may not be desirable in firms that assemble or package a large variety of end items from common modules, subassemblies, or bulk materials. If the MPS is stated in subassemblies or bulk materials, then a final assembly schedule (FAS) needs to be created for managing the conversion to assemblies or

FIGURE 19.6 FAS record for packaging bulk materials

Packaged product		Period						
		1	2	3	4	5	6	7
Gross requirements		40	80	100	0	60	20	100
Scheduled receipts		40						
Projected available balance	10	10	10	10	10	10	10	10
Planned order releases					60	20	100	
Firm planned orders		80	100					

Q = lot for lot; lead time = 1; SS = 10; planning fence: period 3.

FIGURE 19.7   Bulk material record and MPS

200-gram product	Period						
	1	2	3	4	5	6	7
Planned orders					60	40	
Firm planned orders	100		100				

500-gram product	Period						
	1	2	3	4	5	6	7
Planned orders				10	10		20
Firm planned orders		20					

Bulk material—kilograms		Period						
		1	2	3	4	5	6	7
Gross requirements		20	10	20	5	17	8	10
Scheduled receipts								
Projected available balance	5	25	15	35	30	13	5	35
Planned orders								40
Firm planned orders (MPS)		40		40				

Q = 40; SS = 0; lead time = 0; planning fence: period 5.

packed products. The resultant records usually do not need to be frozen or be firm planned over extensive planning horizons, since they only deal with the conversion of, say, bulk material into some specific packaged products.

An example of how this conversion can be managed is provided in Figure 19.6. The gross requirements for this packaged product are exploded from the shipments planned to go to all the field locations. The packaging of this specific product from the bulk material takes one period. Firm planned orders, up to the planning fence at period 3, are used to schedule the packaging operation. The record also shows 10 units of packaged product held at the central facility to provide flexibility in shipping to the field warehouses.

Figure 19.7 shows how the various sizes of packaged products can be combined into a bulk inventory record for creating the MPS for the factory. In the example, two package sizes consume the bulk inventory. The packages are in grams, while the bulk item is in kilograms. The explosion process works from packaged item to bulk, but the grams have been converted to kilograms to get the gross requirements for the bulk material (e.g., for period one: 100 units × 200 grams = 20,000 grams = 20 kilograms). The firm planned orders for the bulk material are the factory MPS, stating when the bulk inventory must be replenished to meet the packaging schedules.

Managing day-to-day variations from plan

On a daily basis, the transactions for actual customer demand, receipts of inventory, and other activities are processed. These transactions are used to periodically update the DRP records. If forecasts and execution of plans were perfect, there would be no need to do anything but add the new period of information at the end of the planning horizon each time the records were processed. Unfortunately, we have not found a company where such conditions hold. An example of a more likely set of circumstances is depicted in Figure 19.8.

In this example, actual sales vary from 16 to 24 around the forecast of 20 units. The actual sales of 18 in period 1 have no impact on the planned shipments, while the actual sales of 24 units in period 2 changes the plan. The additional sales in period 2 have the effect of increasing the net requirements, which leads to planning a shipment in period 3, rather than in period 4. The sales in period 3 were less than expected, so the net requirements are less and the planned shipment in period 5 is changed to period 6. Thus, the gross to net logic results in modifications of the shipping plans to keep them matched to the current market situation.

One negative aspect of the logic is clear from the example of Figure 19.8. The deviations of the actual sales around the forecast were reflected in changed shipping plans. These changes could have a destabilizing impact on the master schedule and shop. Two techniques for stabilizing the information flow are firm planned orders and error addback.

An example of the application of the firm planned order (shipment) concept to the warehouse example is shown in Figure 19.9. By using firm planned shipments, the record shows the what-if results of maintaining the present order pattern. By using DRP records to display this pattern, standard exception messages will be generated; that is, for example, if a present plan violates a stated safety stock objective, this would be highlighted by exception messages.

In the example record for period 3, the firm planned shipment of 40 in period 4 is not rescheduled to period 3, even though the projected available inventory balance for period 4 is less than the safety stock. Thus, the master scheduler can review the implications of *not* changing before deciding

FIGURE 19.8   Records for a single SKU at one warehouse over four periods (lead time = 1 period; shipping quantity = 40; safety stock = 6)

Period		1	2	3	4	5
Forecast requirements		20	20	20	20	20
In transit		40				
Projected available balance	6	26	6	26	6	26
Planned shipments			40		40	

Actual demand for period 1 = 18.

Period		2	3	4	5	6
Forecast requirements		20	20	20	20	20
In transit						
Projected available balance	28	8	28	8	28	8
Planned shipments		40		40		

Actual demand for period 2 = 24.

Period		3	4	5	6	7
Forecast requirements		20	20	20	20	20
In transit		40				
Projected available balance	4	24	44	24	44	24
Planned shipments		40		40		

Actual demand for period 3 = 16.

Period		4	5	6	7	8
Forecast requirements		20	20	20	20	20
In transit		40				
Projected available balance	28	48	28	8	28	8
Planned shipments				40		

FIGURE 19.9   Record for a single SKU at one warehouse with firm planned order (shipments) logic (lead time = 1 period; shipping quantity = 40; safety stock = 6)

Period		1	2	3	4	5
Forecast requirements		20	20	20	20	20
In transit		40				
Projected available balance	6	26	6	26	6	26
Firm planned shipments			40		40	
Actual demand for period 1 = 18.						

Period		2	3	4	5	6
Forecast requirements		20	20	20	20	20
In transit						
Projected available balance	28	8	28	8	28	8
Firm planned shipments		40		40		40
Actual demand for period 2 = 24.						

Period		3	4	5	6	7
Forecast requirements		20	20	20	20	20
In transit		40				
Projected available balance	4	24	4	24	4	24
Firm planned shipments			40		40	
Actual demand for period 3 = 16.						

Period		4	5	6	7	8
Forecast requirements		20	20	20	20	20
In transit						
Projected available balance	28	8	28	8	28	8
Firm planned shipments		40		40		40

FIGURE 19.10   Record for a single SKU at one warehouse with error addback
(lead time = 1; shipping quantity = 40; safety stock = 6)

Period		1	2	3	4	5
Forecast requirements		20	20	20	20	20
In transit		40				
Projected available balance	6	26	6	26	6	26
Planned shipments			40		40	
Period 1 demand = 18; cumulative error = +2.						

Period		2	3	4	5	6
Forecast requirements		22	20	20	20	20
In transit						
Projected available balance	28	6	26	6	26	6
Planned shipments		40		40		
Period 2 demand = 24; cumulative error = −2.						

Period		3	4	5	6	7
Forecast requirements		18	20	20	20	20
In transit		40				
Projected available balance	4	26	6	26	6	26
Planned shipments			40		40	
Period 3 demand = 16; cumulative error = +2.						

Period		4	5	6	7	8
Forecast requirements		22	20	20	20	20
In transit						
Projected available balance	28	6	26	6	26	6
Planned shipments		40		40		
Period 4 demand = 15; cumulative error = +7.						

whether the changes should be made. In this case, the decision might be to opt for consistency in the information, knowing there still is some projected safety stock and that the next order is due to arrive in period 5.

An alternative for stabilizing the information is the error addback method. This approach assumes that the forecasts are unbiased, or accurate on the average. This means that any unsold forecast in one period will be made up for in a subsequent period, or any sales exceeding forecast now will reduce sales in a subsequent period. Using this method, errors are added (or subtracted) from future requirements to reflect the expected impact of actual sales on projected sales. An example is shown in Figure 19.10, which applies this concept to the warehouse example. Note that the planned shipments are under system control; that is, firm planned orders are not used.

The records in this example show the planned orders in exactly the same periods as in the firm planned shipment case. The adjustments to the forecast requirements ensure stability in the information. It is apparent that the effectiveness of this technique diminishes if the forecast is not unbiased. For example, if the reduced demand that occurred in periods 3 and 4 is part of a continuing trend, the procedure will break down. DRP will continue to build inventory as though the reduced demand will be made up in the future. This means that the forecasts must be carefully monitored and changed when necessary so the procedure can be started again. One convenient measure for evaluating forecast accuracy is the cumulative forecast error. If this exceeds a specified quantity, the item forecast should be reviewed. For example, in period 4, the cumulative error has reached a $+7$ (a value exceeding the safety stock); this might be used to indicate the need to review the forecast for this item.

Safety stock in DRP

Distribution requirements planning provides the means for carrying inventories and safety stocks at any location in the system. In the examples of Figures 19.3 through 19.5, we show safety stock in both field locations and at the central facility.

With DRP, it is possible to use safety lead time, as well. In those circumstances where the uncertainty is more likely to be in terms of timing, such as in the delivery of product to the field, it may be better to use safety lead time. In the case of uncertainty in quantity, such as with variable yields in manufacturing, safety stock is more typically used.

Where and how much safety stock (or safety lead time) to carry is still very much an open issue. Research and company experience is just now beginning to provide answers. In terms of the quantity, the theory of relating safety stock to the uncertainty in our demand forecasts is clearly valid. The choice would be made on the basis of trade-offs between customer service levels and inventory required.

On the other hand, in distribution, we are not just concerned about how much uncertainty there is but where it is. Less is known about where to put the safety stocks. One principle is to carry the safety stocks where there is uncertainty. This would imply the location closest to the customer and, perhaps, to intermediate points, where there is some element of independent demand. The argument would imply no safety stock where there is dependent demand.

If the uncertainty from several field locations could be aggregated, it should require less safety stock than having stock at each field location. This argument has led to the concept of a "national level" safety stock popularized by Robert G. Brown in his work on materials management. The idea is to have some central stock that can be sent to field locations as conditions warrant, or to permit transshipments between field warehouses. This added flexibility should provide higher levels of service than maintaining multiple field safety stocks. The issue is clouded, however, by the fact that the stock in the central facility is not where the customers are.

Simulation results for evaluating the question of whether national level safety stocks should be carried or not are provided in Figure 19.11. The

FIGURE 19.11   Service levels as a function of amount and location of safety stock

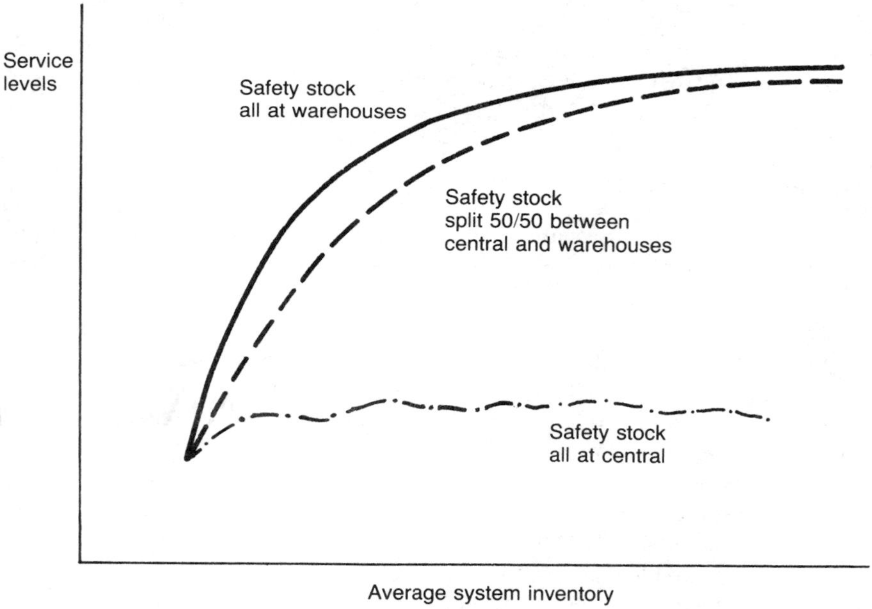

Safety stock
all at warehouses

Safety stock
split 50/50 between
central and warehouses

Safety stock
all at central

Service levels

Average system inventory

Source: W. B. Allen, "A Comparative Simulation of Central Inventory Control Policies for Positioning Safety Stock in a Multi-echelon Distribution System," Ph.D. dissertation, Indiana University, 1983, p. 86.

results of this study indicate it is more efficient to carry the stock in the field than to divide it between field and central. In all of William Allen's runs, the results were the same. Similar conclusions were reached for some of Phillips' TV parts that are distributed throughout Europe. In a study done at Eindhoven University in Holland, K. van Donselaar found that the parts inventory should be sent to the field instead of being split between the field and a central facility.

Still another example of the benefits of pushing safety stocks into the field comes from the experience of a large food company. In one of the divisions, the primary factory has no significant warehouse space and the end items have considerable bulk. The result is a need to ship all production to distribution centers within hours of manufacture. This, in turn, forces the factory to keep in touch with the actual demand and to continually adjust to actual circumstances. The company uses DRP to link the distribution centers to all of its factories; but the products provided by this factory consistently have higher fill rates and fewer stock-outs than other products sold through the same distribution centers. Also, inventory turnover on immediately shipped products is higher than for the other products. The other plants have their own warehouses, where stocks are held. These stocks reduce inventory turns and do not provide immediate service to customers.

MANAGEMENT ISSUES

With an operational DRP system integrated with other MPC systems, management has the ability to rationalize material flows from purchasing through distribution. Achieving this desired state, however, raises several critical management questions. We have already discussed some of the DRP issues, such as planning parameters, safety stock, stability, and the form of the master scheduling interface. More fundamental issues relate to assurances that the system has appropriate data entry procedures, some organizational changes facilitating an integrated MPC approach, and using DRP to solve specific distribution problems. We now turn to each of these managerial topics.

Data integrity and completeness

Let us start by considering the record for an item at a location as close to the customer as possible. We have called this location the field warehouse; but it could be at a distribution center, at the customer location itself, or even at the central facility. The issue concerns *where* the forecast is to be input. Since this is the source of demand data for planning throughout the system, it must be correctly determined and maintained. For this record, there are two key data items on which all plans are based: the forecast requirements and the inventory balance (including any in transit). The axiom of garbage-in, garbage-out holds in DRP as elsewhere. To have confidence in the forecast data, it is necessary to assign responsibility for both forecast preparation and adjustments.

A key issue in forecasting data integrity for DRP systems is the use of aggregate forecasts, which are thereafter broken down into detailed forecasts. An example would be a pharmaceutical firm that forecasts annual U.S. insulin sales in total ounces, based on the number of diabetics in the country. This total is multiplied by the company market share, which is in turn broken down into package sizes, weeks, and locations as the basis for field forecasts. As the total is broken down, the relative errors increase, but the MPS is based on the totals as brought through the DRP system. This is the summation of the detailed forecasts, after field modifications, so the errors should tend to cancel out.

It is imperative, however, that adjustments of the detailed forecasts do not result in a systematic bias that does not balance out. DRP systems are designed to respond to forecast *errors*, but forecast bias is a problem that must be avoided.

Once the basic forecast has been generated, the people in the field can be given some authority to modify it according to local information and needs. This should be constrained by some rule, like "plus or minus 20 percent adjustment," or like "only the timing can be changed but the monthly totals must remain the same." Some mechanism must be put in place for picking up this kind of local intelligence for adjusting the forecasts, but it is important to define the limits for proper control.

Also, management programs should be established to monitor this process. Monitoring is more complex when the records for items are at customer locations (e.g., a large hospital). In all cases, standard forecast monitoring techniques need to be applied, particularly to discover bias introduced through the adjustment process.

Inventory accuracy is dependent on transaction processing routines and discipline. Procedures for quick and accurate reporting of shipments to customers, allocations to customers, returns, adjustments, receipts, and the like must all be in place. Another source of errors is incorrect balances of material in transit; these will affect all calculations in the subsequent record processing. Computer auditing can help find outliers in the data for all of these cases, but tight procedural controls are clearly a necessity.

Organizational support

Figure 19.12 shows conflicting functional objectives and their impact on inventory, customer service, and total costs. This figure illustrates some of the inherent conflicts that need resolution in an integrated MPC system. These conflicts are particularly real when DRP is made a part of the overall MPC system. In many firms, minimization of transportation costs, for ex-

FIGURE 19.12 Conflicting functional objectives

Functional objectives	Impact of objectives on...		
	Inventory	Customer service	Total costs
• High customer service	⬆ (open)	⬆ (filled)	⬆ (open)
• Low transportion costs	⬆ (open)	⬇ (open)	⬇ (filled)
• Low warehousing costs	⬇ (filled)	⬇ (open)	⬇ (filled)
• Reduce inventories	⬇ (filled)	⬇ (open)	⬇ (filled)
• Fast deliveries	⬆ (open)	⬆ (filled)	⬆ (open)
• Reduced labour costs	⬆ (open)	⬇ (open)	⬇ (filled)
• Desired results	⬇ (filled)	⬆ (filled)	⬇ (filled)

Source: T. C. Jones and D. W. Riley, "Using Inventory for Competitive Advantage through Supply Chain Management," *International Journal of Physical Distribution and Materials Management,* 1985, p. 16.

ample, is the objective of a transportation department. The resultant impact on other parts of the organization is often not clearly understood.

In a comprehensive MPC system with DRP, linkages across functional boundaries are encouraged; but organizational support and evaluation measures need to be established that will minimize suboptimization of overall enterprise goals. Many firms have implemented a materials management form of organization to help align responsibilities to the material flow needs. Materials management organizations are responsible for all aspects of materials, from purchasing to final distribution to the customers. Their responsibilities include determining what to make and when, when to take delivery of raw materials, how much to allocate to field locations, and what to do to relieve short-term materials problems.

As firms improve MPC systems either through more comprehensive approaches (e.g., DRP) or through such enhancements as JIT, emphasis shifts from material control to material velocity. Basic discipline and data integrity are not abandoned—they are assumed. Time and responsiveness become the most important objectives. Implied is a need to reduce the organizational fragmentation that has built-in time delays. Organizational structures will increasingly be required, ones that have overarching authority to dictate actions that provide rapid response to customer needs.

Integration of DRP into a comprehensive MPC system in many cases

FIGURE 19.13 Supply chain management

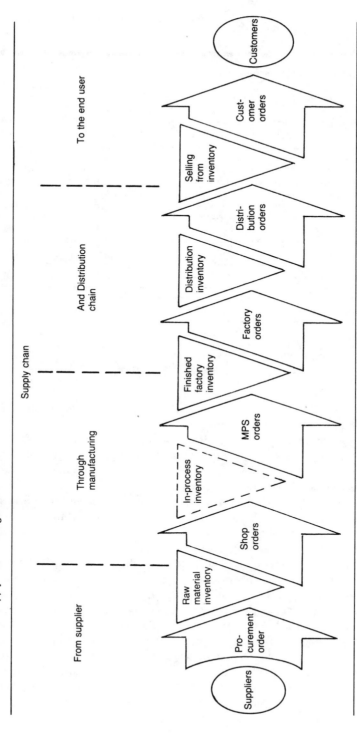

Source: T. C. Jones and D. W. Riley, "Using Inventory for Competitive Advantage through Supply Chain Management," *International Journal of Physical Distribution and Materials Management*, 1985, p. 17.

provides the integrative framework for such an organization. Eli Lilly has recognized this in its materials management organization. Robert Dille, director of purchasing, is quoted by Tom Feare, managing editor of *CPI Purchasing*, as saying, "Our buyers are really requirements analysts. In working with the system, they have seen the advantages of moving to smaller and smaller buckets. Having gone from monthly to weekly, they are now talking about daily buckets."

A concept that has been gaining attention in Europe is called "supply chain management." Figure 19.13 illustrates the concept, showing the many organizational entities that need to be coordinated. The ideas parallel those of materials management, but they focus on the process of building the products. Coordinating the chain shown in Figure 19.13 requires integrated information in the DRP form and an organizational form, such as materials management.

Key to implementing an MPC system with DRP, regardless of the organizational form, is development of the planners. The titles can vary in different organizations. Planners establish firm planned orders, evaluate alternative means to solve short-term problems, coordinate problems that cross functional boundaries, and help evaluate trends. They are also responsible for checking feasibility of changes, monitoring data integrity, and assessing the impact of new situations.

Problem solving

We have already discussed changing conditions due to uncertainty in demand and the techniques that help to deal with them. Other problems come from changing market conditions, product lines, or marketing plans. Examples are product substitutions, promotions, changes in warehouse locations or customer assignments, and controlling the age of stock. DRP records greatly facilitate solution of these problems. We will describe three of these as illustrative: a sales promotion, closing a warehouse, and monitoring stock aging.

Figure 19.14 presents an example of a sales promotion served by a warehouse. For simplicity, we consider only one product at a single warehouse and the packaging line for the product. The process starts with modification of the demand forecast at the warehouse. In the example, the promotion is planned for weeks 5 through 8. The impact is estimated to double sales (from 20 to 40) during the first two weeks and to have a reduced impact during the next two weeks. Note that the promotion "steals" from demand in weeks 9 and 10.

The safety stock has been left at five units for the promotion period, although it might have been increased. The stock for the sales promotion is planned for delivery in the weeks in which needed, although it also might have been planned for earlier delivery if there were a need to set up some

FIGURE 19.14   A sales promotion

Warehouse		1	2	3	4	5	6	7	8	9	10
							Period				
Forecast requirements		20	20	20	20	40	40	30	30	10	10
In transit		20									
Projected available balance	27	27	7	7	7	7	7	17	7	17	7
Planned shipments			20	20	40	40	40	20	20		

$Q = 20$; lead time $= 1$; $SS = 5$.

Packaging		1	2	3	4	5	6	7	8	9	10
							Period				
Gross requirements		0	20	20	40	40	40	20	20		
Scheduled receipts											
Projected available balance	0	0	12	24	16	8	0	0	0		
Planned order releases							20	20			
Firm planned orders		32	32	32	32	32					

$Q = $ lot for lot; lead time $= 1$; $SS = 0$; planning fence: 3.
Note: Packaging capacity $= 35$ units/period.

special display area. The shipping quantity is in multiples of 20, representing a shipping carton or pallet load. The planned shipments are exploded to the packaging record. Using the firm planned orders, the planner has scheduled product packaging at a constant rate of output for the first five weeks (just under the capacity of the packaging line), building inventory in anticipation of the promotion.

The anticipation inventories are shown as remaining at the packaging facility, but they might be sent to the field if there is space available or if a truck were on its way with available cargo space. The pattern of inventory buildup could be different, depending on the trade-off between level production and varying the production levels. The DRP records facilitate both the planning of the buildup and analysis of alternative ways of meeting the need (or even arguing for a postponement if capacity is a problem).

Our second example deals with a warehouse closure. Firms often change their distribution systems, so closing warehouses and changing shipping patterns is an ongoing activity. In the example of Figure 19.15, warehouse No. 1 is scheduled to close at the end of four weeks, and warehouse No. 2 is to start supplying the customers. Again, the process of managing the cutover starts with the forecasts. The requirements at warehouse No. 1 stop at the end of week 4 and are picked up by warehouse No. 2, reflecting the timing and quantities of the closedown and transfer.

In the example, warehouse No. 1 would normally have had a planned shipment for 60 units in week 3. The planner has overridden the planned order with a firm planned order for the exact need, reducing the safety stock to zero. Note that the system plans an order to restore the safety stock and, eventually, the planner will need to change the safety stock parameter to zero in order not to send the wrong signal to the master production scheduler.

As time goes on, the actual quantity needed for warehouse No. 1 may well be different, but there are two weeks before the exact determination must be made. The planner may decide to send even less to warehouse No. 1, because it might be easier to pick up some unsatisfied demand from warehouse No. 2 than to deal with the remnant inventories at warehouse No. 1. The point is that DRP systems provide the visibility for solving these problems. Even though the exact quantity to be sent to warehouse No. 1 will not be determined until week 3, the amount produced and made available to send to either warehouse will be correct, since the planned shipments from both are exploded to the requirements at the central facility. The main questions are how to divide the available stock between the two facilities and how to manage the transient.

Our final example deals with controlling inventory of products for which shelf life is a concern. Certainly one aspect of this problem is to use strict first-in, first-out physical movement, and to make this a part of the training for warehouse personnel. The second way to deal effectively with shelf-life

FIGURE 19.15   Warehouse closure

		Period						
Warehouse 1		*1*	*2*	*3*	*4*	*5*	*6*	*7*
Forecast requirements		30	30	30	30	0	0	0
In transit		60						
Projected available balance	43	73	43	13	60	60	60	60
Planned shipments				60				
Firm planned shipments				17				

Q = 60; lead time = 1; SS = 10.

		Period						
Warehouse 2		*1*	*2*	*3*	*4*	*5*	*6*	*7*
Forecast requirements		100	100	100	100	130	130	130
In transit								
Projected available balance	207	107	207	107	207	77	147	217
Planned shipments							200	200
Firm planned shipments		200		200				

Q = 200; lead time = 1; SS = 20.

problems is to identify those products that may be headed for a problem before it is too late. One way to do this is to use the DRP records and build in exception messages to flag potential shelf-life problems.

If, for example, the demand for a product at some location is dropping for some reason, the forecast should be reduced. This means that any available inventory or in transit stock will cover a longer time period; the result will be that the first planned shipment will be several periods in the future. This condition can be detected, calling for a review of the shelf life of the particular products at this warehouse. Perhaps some of them should be immediately transshipped to another warehouse. This feature is incorporated in the actual system, to which we now turn our attention.

COMPANY EXAMPLE

Abbott Laboratories, Ltd., of Canada produces health-care products. Three lines—pharmaceuticals, hospital products, and infant nutrition products—are produced in three plants. About 750 end items are distributed through DCs (distribution centers) to customers throughout Canada.

Abbott Laboratories uses DRP to manage field inventories. Detailed forecast data are input to warehouse DRP records. These records are represented as the zero level of the bill of materials (BOM). Figure 19.16 illustrates these records for two locations, Vancouver and Montreal. The forecast data are entered as the requirements rows. The first 20 weeks are displayed in weekly time periods (buckets). Thereafter, monthly buckets are used for a total planning horizon of two years.

In the Montreal record, there is an entry of 120 in the week of 8/7, in a row labeled Customer Orders. This row allows the inclusion of specific advance order information. The information is not added to the gross requirements, however. It is there for the detailed planning of shipments and to recognize advanced special orders.

The lead time shown in the Vancouver record is 35 days, or five weeks. This includes safety lead time. The DRP time-phased records are produced using these parameters. For example, the projected on-hand balance at the end of week 9/4 for Vancouver is insufficient to meet the gross requirements of 9/11. The result is a planned order for a quantity of 24, five weeks earlier in the week of 8/7.

Figure 19.17 shows the DRP records for the central warehouse and for the bulk item used to make the end-item product B. The gross requirements for central are based on the planned orders from all the DCs. For example, in the week of 8/7, the gross requirement of 1,908 is comprised of 24 from Vancouver, 1,872 from Montreal, and 12 from some other DC.

The batch size shown for central warehouse in Figure 19.17 is 7,619. In fact, this is the number of product B units yielded from a batch of 4,000 in the unit of measure for the bulk product; that is, the 7,619 shown as a firm planned order in 9/11 becomes a gross requirement of 4,000 for bulk in that week.

The master production scheduler works with the DRP record for central. This person's job is to convert planned orders into firm planned orders, and to manage the timing of the firm planned orders. For example, all of the orders at central are firm planned in Figure 19.17 until 12/31 in the last row. The last three orders (12/31, 2/25, and 4/21) are only planned orders. DRP logic can replan these as needed. Only the master production scheduler can move the firm planned orders that appear early in the record. The result is a stable MPS for the bulk production.

Figure 19.18 illustrates the information available for actual shipment planning. The requirements due to be shipped this week or in the next two weeks (also any past-due shipments) are summarized by distribution center

FIGURE 19.16   Abbot DRP records for Vancouver and Montreal

Description	Size	um	Std bactr	FC	BY	PL	IT	C	Scrap	Total landed costs	OP	Life	O-LT	P-LT	O-LT	QA-LT	T-LT	On hand	OA inventory	Allocated	Safety stock
Product-B	200		24			08	F	C	1.00	0.000		1095	35			0	0	35	36.0	0.0	0.0	0.0

03-VANCOUVER

	PAST DUE	7/24	7/31	08/07	08/14	08/21	08/28	09/04	09/11	09/18	09/25	10/02	10/09	10/16
CUSTOMER ORDERS														
GROSS REQUIREMENTS		5	5	5	5	5	5	5	5	5	5	5	5	5
SCHEDULED RECEIPTS														
ON HAND	36	31	26	21	16	11	6	1	20	15	10	5	24	19
FIRM PLANNED ORDERS														
PLANNED ORDERS				24				24				24		

MONTHLY

	10/23	10/30	11/06	11/13	11/20	11/27	12/04	01/01	01/29	02/26	03/26	04/23	05/21	06/18
CUSTOMER ORDERS														
GROSS REQUIREMENTS	7	7	7	7	5	4	17	21	23	20	20	20	20	20
SCHEDULED RECEIPTS														
ON HAND	12	5	22	15	10	6	13	16	17	21	1	5	9	13
FIRM PLANNED ORDERS														
PLANNED ORDERS			24	24			24	24	24	24	24	24	24	24

	07/16	08/13	09/10	10/08	11/05	12/03	12/31	01/28	02/25	03/24	04/21	05/19	06/16	TOTAL
CUSTOMER ORDERS														
GROSS REQUIREMENTS	20	20	20	24	23	17	20	20	20	20	20	20	26	533
SCHEDULED RECEIPTS														
ON HAND	17	21	1	1	2	9	13	17	21	1	1	9	7	
FIRM PLANNED ORDERS														
PLANNED ORDERS			24	24		24	24	24	24	24	24	24	24	504

NOTES & COMMENTS

Comm list no.
List xyz

Description	Size	um	Std bactr	FC	BY	PL	IT	C	Scrap	Total landed costs	OP	Life	O-LT	P-LT	O-LT	QA-LT	T-LT	On hand	OA inventory	Allocated	Safety stock
Product-B	200	BL	1872	A2		08		C	1.0			1095	14		0	0	14	2520.0	0.0	0.0	0.0

21-MONTREAL

	PAST DUE	7/24	7/31	08/07	08/14	08/21	08/28	09/04	09/11	09/18	09/25	10/02	10/09	10/16
CUSTOMER ORDERS				120										
GROSS REQUIREMENTS		601	601	601	601	576	556	556	556	578	633	633	633	633
SCHEDULED RECEIPTS														
ON HAND	2520.0	1919	1318	717	116	1412	856	300	1616	1038	405	1644	1011	378
FIRM PLANNED ORDERS				1872			1872	3744	1872	1872	3744		1872	
PLANNED ORDERS														

MONTHLY

	10/23	10/30	11/06	11/13	11/20	11/27	12/04	01/01	01/29	02/26	03/26	04/23	05/21	06/18
CUSTOMER ORDERS														
GROSS REQUIREMENTS	777	801	801	801	633	507	2100	2386	2744	2167	2356	2404	2479	2212
SCHEDULED RECEIPTS														
ON HAND	1473	672	1743	942	309	1674	1446	932	60	1637	1153	621	14	1546
FIRM PLANNED ORDERS	1872	1872	1872	1872			1872	3744	1872	1872	3744	1872	1872	1872
PLANNED ORDERS														

	07/16	08/13	09/10	10/08	11/05	12/03	12/31	01/28	02/25	03/24	04/21	05/19	06/16	TOTAL
CUSTOMER ORDERS														
GROSS REQUIREMENTS	2418	2289	2400	2844	2742	2100	2323	2480	2285	2356	2280	2348	2944	62735
SCHEDULED RECEIPTS														
ON HAND	1000	583	55	955	85	1729	1278	670	257	1645	1237	761	1561	
FIRM PLANNED ORDERS	3744	1872	1872	3744	1872	1872	1872	3744	1872	1872	1872	3744	1872	61776
PLANNED ORDERS														

NOTES & COMMENTS

Comm list no.

List xyz

Source: W. L. Berry, T. E. Vollmann, and D. C. Whybark, *Master Production Scheduling: Principles and Practice* (Falls Church, Va.: American Production and Inventory Control Society, 1979), p. 87.

FIGURE 19.17 Abbott DRP records for central and bulk

Description	Size	um	Std bactr	FC	BY	PL	IT	C	Scrap	Total landed costs	OP	Life	O-LT	P-LT	O-LT	QA-LT	T-LT	On hand	OA inventory	Allocated	Safety stock
Product-B	200	BL	7619	A2	00	03	C	0	1.07			1095	0	12	0	11	23	5220.0	0.0	144.0	1000.0

01-CENTRAL

	PAST DUE	7/24	7/31	08/07	08/14	08/21	08/28	09/04	09/11	09/18	09/25	10/02	10/09	10/16
CUSTOMER ORDERS	0	0	0	0	0	0	0	0	0	0	0	0	0	0
GROSS REQUIREMENTS	204	12	12	1908	12	12	2916	156	36	1884	12	1104	1980	12
SCHEDULED RECEIPTS	0	0	0	7619	0	0	0	0	0	0	0	0	0	0
ON HAND	4872	4860	4848	10078	10066	10054	7138	6982	6946	5062	5050	3946	9104	9092
FIRM PLANNED ORDERS	0	0	0	0	0	0	0	0	0	0	0	0	0	0
PLANNED ORDERS	0	0	0	0	0	0	0	0	0	0	0	0	0	0

MONTHLY

	10/23	10/30	11/06	11/13	11/20	11/27	12/04	01/01	01/29	02/26	03/26	04/23	05/21	06/18
CUSTOMER ORDERS	0	0	0	0	0	0	0	0	0	0	0	0	0	0
GROSS REQUIREMENTS	2952	12	36	1884	96	1092	1944	4968	3108	3012	4968	3108	2076	3108
SCHEDULED RECEIPTS	0	0	0	0	0	0	0	0	0	0	0	0	0	0
ON HAND	6140	6128	6092	4208	4112	3020	8214	10384	7276	4264	6434	3326	8388	5280
FIRM PLANNED ORDERS	0	0	0	0	7619	0	7619	0	0	7619	0	7619	0	7619
PLANNED ORDERS	0	0	0	0	0	0	0	0	0	0	0	0	0	0

	07/16	08/13	09/10	10/08	11/05	12/03	12/31	01/28	02/25	03/24	04/21	05/19	06/16	TOTAL
CUSTOMER ORDERS	0	0	0	0	0	0	0	0	0	0	0	0	0	0
GROSS REQUIREMENTS	4740	3120	3108	4980	2052	3108	3012	3108	4980	2964	2052	4956	2808	87612
SCHEDULED RECEIPTS	0	0	0	0	0	0	0	0	0	0	0	0	0	7619
ON HAND	7678	4558	8588	10746	8694	5586	2574	6854	4732	1768	6854	3746	5928	0
FIRM PLANNED ORDERS	0	7619	7619	0	0	0	0	7619	0	0	0	0	0	60952
PLANNED ORDERS	0	0	0	0	0	0	0	0	0	0	7619	7619	7619	22857

NOTES & COMMENTS

Comm list no.

List xyz

Description	Size	um	Std bactr	FC	BY	PL	IT	C	Scrap	Total landed costs	OP	Life	O-LT	P-LT	O-LT	QA-LT	T-LT	On hand	OA inventory	Allocated	Safety stock
Product-B	200	L	4000			00	B	C	1.00		N						0	0	0	0	0

84-Bulk

	PAST DUE	7/24	7/31	08/07	08/14	08/21	08/28	09/04	09/11	09/18	09/25	10/02	10/09	10/16
CUSTOMER ORDERS														
GROSS REQUIREMENTS									4000					
SCHEDULED RECEIPTS														
ON HAND														
FIRM PLANNED ORDERS														
PLANNED ORDERS									4000					

MONTHLY

	10/23	10/30	11/06	11/13	11/20	11/27	12/04	01/01	01/29	02/26	03/26	04/23	05/21	06/18
CUSTOMER ORDERS														
GROSS REQUIREMENTS					4000		4000		4000	4000	4000	4000	4000	4000
SCHEDULED RECEIPTS														
ON HAND														
FIRM PLANNED ORDERS														
PLANNED ORDERS					4000		4000		4000	4000	4000	4000	4000	4000

	07/16	08/13	09/10	10/08	11/05	12/03	12/31	01/28	02/25	03/24	04/21	05/19	06/16	TOTAL
CUSTOMER ORDERS														
GROSS REQUIREMENTS		4000	4000		4000		4000		4000	4000	4000	4000	4000	44000
SCHEDULED RECEIPTS														
ON HAND														
FIRM PLANNED ORDERS														
PLANNED ORDERS		4000	4000		4000		4000		4000	4000	4000	4000	4000	44000

NOTES & COMMENTS

Comm list no.
List xyz

Source: W. L. Berry, T. E. Vollmann, and D. C. Whybark, *Master Production Scheduling: Principles and Practice* (Falls Church, Va.: American Production and Inventory Control Society, 1979), p. 88.

FIGURE 19.18 Abbott short-term shipping information

MPDR0030 DISTRIBUTION REQUIREMENTS PLAN PAGE 206

DC 21 - MONTREAL

DIVISION 2

LIST/SIZE	QUANTITY	PALLET	WEIGHT	CUBE	QUANTITY	PALLET	WEIGHT	CUBE
	PAST DUE				WEEK 1			
XYZ-200 PRODUCT B	0	0.0	0.0	0.0	0	0.0	0.0	0.0
	WEEK 2				WEEK 3			
	0	0.0	0.0	0.0	1872	2.0	3744.0	112.3

PRIORITY 96: 5076 AVAILABLE IN CENTRAL

DC 03 VANCOUVER

LIST/SIZE	QUANTITY	PALLET	WEIGHT	CUBE	QUANTITY	PALLET	WEIGHT	CUBE
	PAST DUE				WEEK 1			
XYZ - 3 PRODUCT B	0	0.0	0.0	0.0	0	0.0	0.0	0.0
	WEEK 2				WEEK 3			
	0	0.0	0.0	0.0	24	0.0	48.0	1.4

PRIORITY 96: 5076 AVAILABLE IN CENTRAL

Source: W. L. Berry, T. E. Vollmann, and D. C. Whybark, *Master Production Scheduling: Principles and Practice* (Falls Church, Va.: American Production and Inventory Control Society, 1979), p. 90.

and product type. This enables the planner to look at the current requirements or future planned shipments in making up carloads destined for a distribution center. Since the information is available in terms of cube, weight, and pallet load, the planner can use the resource that is most limited in making a shipment decision. This flexibility enables planners to efficiently use transportation resources to meet product needs.

CONCLUDING PRINCIPLES

This chapter has presented a technique for integrating field inventories, distribution centers, and warehouses into the manufacturing planning and control system of the firm. The technique, distribution requirements planning (DRP), utilizes record formats and processing logic consistent with MRP. To effectively use DRP, we see the following general principles:

- The top-level records for a DRP system should cover items in a location as close to the customer as possible (or even at the customer, if feasible).
- Local information on demand patterns should be incorporated into the DRP record.
- Matching the supply to the demand requires close control of supply, as well as data on the demand.
- Projections of future requirements should be used to make inventory allocation decisions in periods of short supply.
- Transparent records and consistent processing logic should be used to integrate the system.
- What-if analysis should be based on the integrated records of the system.
- Uncertainty filters, like firm planned orders or error addback, should be available to the master production scheduler.
- Data and performance measurement systems should be put in place to monitor forecast adjustments in the field.
- The organization form should be consistent with the supply chain being managed.

REFERENCES

Allen, W. B. "A Comparative Simulation of Central Inventory Control Policies in Positioning Safety Stock in a Multi-Echelon Distribution System." DBA dissertation, Indiana University, 1984.

Ballou, R. H. "Estimating and Auditing Aggregate Inventory Levels at Multiple Stocking Points." *Journal of Operations Management* 1, no. 3, 1981.

Berry, W. L.; T. E. Vollmann; and D. C. Whybark. *Master Production and Sched-*

uling—Principles and Practice. Falls Church, Va.: American Production and Inventory Control Society, 1979.

Brown, R. G. *Materials Management Systems.* New York: Wiley Interscience, 1977.

Dube, W. R., "Closed Loop Planning for Manufacturing and Distribution." *International Journal of Physical Distribution and Materials Management* 16, no. 1 (1986), pp. 5–13.

Feare, T. "Lilly—How They Buy." *CPI Purchasing,* February 1985, pp. 26–34.

Friedman, W. F. "Physical Distribution: The Concept of Shared Services." *Harvard Business Review,* March—April 1983.

Glover, F.; G. Jones; D. Karney; and J. Mote. "An Integrated Production Distribution and Inventory Planning System." *Interfaces,* November 1979, pp. 21–35.

Heskett, J. L. "Sweeping Changes in Distribution." *Harvard Business Review,* March–April 1973.

Jones, T. C., and D. W. Riley. "Using Inventory for Competitive Advantage through Supply Chain Management." *International Journal of Physical Distribution and Materials Management* 15, no. 1, 1985, pp. 16–26.

Magee, J. F. *Industrial Logistics.* New York: McGraw-Hill, 1968.

Martin, A. "Distribution Resource Planning (DRP II)." *1980 APICS Conference Proceedings,* pp. 161–165.

———. "DRP: Another Resource Planning System." *Production and Inventory Management Review,* December 1982.

———. *Distribution Resource Planning.* Essex Junction, Vt.: Oliver Wight Publications, 1983.

Perry, W. "The Principles of Distribution Resource Planning (DRP)." *Production and Inventory Management,* December 1982.

Schwarz, L. B. "Physical Distribution: The Analysis of Inventory and Location." *AIIE Transactions* 13, no. 2 (June, 1981).

Smith, B. "DRP Improves Productivity, Profit, and Service Levels." *Modern Materials Handling,* July 1985, pp. 63–65.

Stenger, A. J., and J. L. Cavinato. "Adapting MRP to the Outbound Side—Distribution Requirements Planning." *Production and Inventory Management,* 4th Quarter 1979, pp. 1–14.

van Donselaar, K. "Commonality and Safety Stocks." *Pre-Prints of the 4th International Working Seminar on Production Economics,* 1986, pp. 446–80.

DISCUSSION QUESTIONS

1. What is meant by the statement, "The real task of managing materials is matching supply to demand"?

2. Describe how DRP helps bridge the gap between the market and the factory.

3. What are some of the benefits to a warehouse manager in having improved resupply information?

4. Discuss some of the risks and benefits to having local personnel make modifications in the forecast data for the field warehouses.

5. A manufacturer of consumer goods uses a periodic review system for managing the field inventories. This means that, once a period, the field inventory clerks check to see if the inventory is below reorder point; if so they order an amount equal to the EOQ. The materials manager argues this is the same as using TPOP records. What is your opinion?

6. How can you monitor forecast data modifications by field personnel to insure that the changes result in improvements over original computer forecasts?

7. What are the differences between the planned shipments, indicated in Figure 19.3, and planned orders from MRP records?

8. In what ways are the supply chain management concept and materials management similar? How do they differ?

9. The Abbott records on Figure 19.16 show a customer order for Montreal on 8/07. Why do you think this customer order is not added to the forecast requirements (gross requirements in their terminology) in the record?

PROBLEMS

1. For the warehouse of Figure 19.8, suppose the actual demands were 24, 16, and 18, in periods 1, 2, and 3, respectively. The initial DRP record is shown below:

		Period				
		1	2	3	4	5
Forecast requirements		20	20	20	20	20
Scheduled receipts		40				
Projected available balance	6	26	6	26	6	26
Planned shipments			40		40	

Q = 40; lead time = 1; SS = 6.

a. Create the other three DRP records as done in Figure 19.8. What problem is created in period 2? What can be done?

b. Does error addback work for this set of circumstances?

2. The Hazy Company maintains a West Coast distribution center (DC), which is supplied from the plant warehouse in the Midwest. It takes exactly one week to ship to the distribution center from the Midwest. One of its products has an ordering cost of $10 per order, an inventory carrying cost of $1 per unit per week, and an average weekly demand at the DC of 5 units (although it has varied uniformly between 0 and 10 units per week in actuality). Over the years, the safety stock level has varied for this product. There are currently (early

Monday morning) nine units in inventory at the DC. The company is willing to risk a probability of stocking out of 0.10 in any order cycle.

    a. If the company uses a traditional, statistical economic order quantity reorder point system, what should the order quantity and reorder point be?

    b. If the company adapted DRP logic to this DC supply situation and decided to ship only on Mondays (to consolidate shipments), what would you suggest for the planned shipping pattern over the next 10 weeks? (Use a safety stock level of two units.)

    c. If actual demand for the upcoming week were six units, what would the new shipping pattern be? (Assume any planned shipments in the current week are released.)

3. The distribution manager at the Hercules Mining Company has supplied the following information pertaining to one of its products, the H208 oscillator, which is stocked at the firm's field warehouse:

    Average weekly demand = 25 units.
    Current on-hand balance = 15 units.
    Open order (due next week) = 60 units.
    Economic order quantity = 60 units.
    Shipping time = 1 week.
    Safety stock = 0 units.

Complete the record indicating the replenishment stocking schedule for the next eight weeks:

	Week							
	1	2	3	4	5	6	7	8
Forecast requirements								
In transit								
Projected available balance								
Planned shipments								

4. The finance manager at the XYZ Company is currently studying the projected inventory investment for Product 101 at the central (plant) warehouse. Quantities of Product 101 are shipped from the central warehouse to warehouses A and B, based on individual warehouse requirements. This product costs $100 per unit.

    Using the time-phased order point and inventory information for Product 101 in Exhibit A, determine the planned order releases at the central warehouse. Construct a graph indicating the projected inventory investment at warehouse A for this product at the beginning and at the end of each week over the next six-week period. Assume that the demand for this product is equally divided among the days of each week.

EXHIBIT A

| | Week | | | | | |
Product 101 Warehouse A	1	2	3	4	5	6
Forecast requirements	20	20	20	20	20	20
In transit	15					
Projected available balance 10						
Planned shipments						

Q = 40; LT = 1; SS = 0.

| | Week | | | | | |
Product 101 Warehouse B	1	2	3	4	5	6
Forecast requirements	10	10	10	10	10	10
In transit						
Projected available balance 15						
Planned shipments						

Q = 20; LT = 1; SS = 0.

| | Week | | | | | |
Product 101 Warehouse C	1	2	3	4	5	6
Gross requirements						
Scheduled receipts						
Projected available balance 60						
Planned order releases						

Q = lot-for-lot; LT = 1; SS = 0.

5. The distribution of Dyna-Pep is from the plant in Dunham to two warehouses and then to the customers. The distribution pattern is as follows:

For the purpose of analysis, assume that each warehouse will sell *exactly* 20 cases of Dyna Pep per week. Inventory carried either at the plant or at the warehouse locations costs $.10 per week per case (based on Friday night inventory). The ordering cost is $9 per order at each facility, and it takes exactly one week to transport the product from the plant to either of the two warehouses or to produce the product.

    a. Determine the inventory carrying cost plus setup cost per week at Dunham and both warehouses managing the system with EOQ at all locations.

    b. Determine the inventory carrying cost and setup cost per week using DRP to manage the system.

6. The MVA Pet Food Company distributes one of its products, Gro-Pup, through two warehouses located in Seattle and in Portland. A central warehouse located at the St. Louis plant distributes Gro-Pup to these two warehouses in serving the Northwest regional market.

    a. Develop a distribution schedule for the two warehouses and a production schedule for the plant for the next eight-week period, using the DRP worksheet in Exhibit B. (Note that the sales forecast for this product is 20 units per week at the Seattle warehouse and that there are currently 43 units of the product on hand. The shipment order quantity is 60 units, the planned shipment lead time is one week, and there is no safety stock requirement. Similar information is included in the table for the other two facilities.) The product is packed in lots of 50 units at St. Louis. The packaging process takes two weeks.

    b. Each package of Gro-Pup requires one unit of packaging material. Develop a purchasing schedule for the packaging material assuming that:

      1. There are currently 25 units on hand.

      2. An open order for 100 units is due to be received from the vendor next week.

      3. The purchase order quantity equals 100 units.

      4. The purchasing lead time is four weeks.

    c. Update the distribution and production schedules as of the start of week 2, assuming that the following transactions occurred during week 1:

	Receipts	Order releases	Sales/ disbursements	Inventory adjustment	Open order scrap
Gro-Pup/Seattle	0	0	19	−3	0
Gro-Pup/Portland	15	15	20	+3	0
Gro-Pup/Plant	0	50	15	0	0
Gro-Pup/Packaging	90	100	50	+4	10

7. The Drip Producers are planning a promotion of one of its products, the Dead Drop. Dead Drops are distributed through only one of the warehouses. The promotion is to begin in period 4 and run through period 6. The sales forecast is normally 30 per period, but during the promotion the company expects sales to be 60 per period. This is shown below with other data.

		Week							
Gro-Pup Seattle Warehouse		1	2	3	4	5	6	7	8
Forecast requirements		20	20	20	20	20	20	20	20
In transit									
Projected available balance	43								
Planned shipments									

Q = 60; LT = 1; SS = 0.

		Week							
Gro-Pup Portland Warehouse		1	2	3	4	5	6	7	8
Forecast requirements		10	10	10	10	10	10	10	10
In transit		15							
Projected available balance	2								
Planned shipments									

Q = 15; LT = 1; SS = 0.

		Week							
Gro-Pup Plant Warehouse		1	2	3	4	5	6	7	8
Gross requirements									
Scheduled receipts			50						
Projected available balance	30								
Planned order releases									

Q = 50; LT = 2; SS = 0.

		Week							
Gro-Pup Packaging Material		1	2	3	4	5	6	7	8
Gross requirements									
Scheduled receipts		100							
Projected available balance	25								
Planned order releases									

Q = 100; LT = 4; SS = 0.

			Period			
	1	2	3	4	5	6
Sales forecast	30	30	30	60	60	60

	Warehouse	Central
Ship/ord. quantity	40 units	Lot-for-lot
Current inventory	12 units	0 units
Lead time	1 period	1 period
Safety stock	10 units	0 units
Sched. rec./ship.	40 units	40 units
	in period 1	in period 1

    a. Use a spreadsheet to develop the records for the warehouse and central facility.

    b. Suppose the capacity of the central facility was limited to 50 units per period. How would you provide the material for the promotion in the field?

8. Develop a spreadsheet for the Cranstable Company's two warehouses and one central facility system using the data given below. What happens if the central order quantity changes to 200?

	Warehouse 1	Warehouse 2	Central
Forecast requirements	20/period	30/period	
Ship/ord. quantity	48 units	60 units	100 units
Current inventory	23 units	12 units	0 units
Lead time	1 period	1 period	1 period
Safety stock	10 units	10 units	0 units
Sched. rec./ship.	48 units	60 units	none
	in period 1	in period 1	

9. The Cranstable Company was just getting into the swing of DRP when old Barnstable moved away from the region of warehouse 1. Now this would not normally cause problems, but for Cranstable it meant that sales were halved at warehouse 1. Using the data from problem **8**, what is the impact of Barnstable's departure?

10. The demand for Drips averages five per week at a particular warehouse. The Water Company ships Drips in lots of 10 and maintains a safety stock level of 2 Drips at the warehouse. The company currently uses a periodic review system to replenish the warehouse. Each Monday morning, the warehouse inventory clerk checks the inventory of Drips. If it is less than the reorder point of 12 Drips (demand of 10 during lead and review time, plus safety stock of 2 Drips) an order for 10 is placed on the Water Company. It takes one week for the order to arrive at the warehouse. If the demand is not met, the sales are lost (i.e., there are no back orders).

a. Use a spreadsheet to set up the DRP record for the warehouse for the next ten periods and generate the planned shipments. Use an opening inventory of eight units and no in-transit shipments.

b. Develop a spreadsheet that can "simulate" the current practice. Show the Monday morning balance, test for an order, show demand for the week, the Friday balance, and the following Monday balance. The format below may be helpful:

	Week			
	1	*2*	*3*	—
Monday balance				
Demand				
Friday balance				
Order				

c. Compare the orders from the simulation with the planned orders under DRP when the demand is exactly five units per week for all 10 weeks. What happens, in the simulation, when the demand is 7, 3, 5, 1, 4, 6, 5, 9, 6, and 4 for the ten weeks? Is the order pattern different from the DRP plan?

11. Sales forecasting is performed on a national basis at the XYZ Chemical Company. Each month a sales forecast of the monthly sales for the coming year is prepared for each of the firm's end products. Time-phased order point records are maintained at each of the firm's three distribution warehouses for the individual products. The national sales forecast for product A is 2,500 units per four-week period. The sales of this product at each of the three warehouses is split as follows: 50 percent from warehouse A, 30 percent from warehouse B, and 20 percent from warehouse C. An analysis of the sales history of product A at warehouse C indicates that the weekly sales of this product are distributed as follows: 10 percent in week 1, 30 percent in week 2, 50 percent in week 3, and 10 percent in week 4 in a four-week period. Complete the following time-phased order point Record for Product A:

Product A / Warehouse C

		Week							
		1	2	3	4	5	6	7	8
Forecast requirements									
In transit			160	278					
Projected available balance	65								
Planned shipments									

Q = LFL; SS = 0; LT = 3 weeks

12. The distribution planner at the Excello Corporation is concerned about the variability of transit times between the plant in Madison, Indiana, and the firm's distribution center in Atlanta. A decision has been made to incorporate a one-week safety lead time into the time-phased order point records for the items stocked in the Atlanta distribution center. Please complete the record for Product X in the Atlanta distribution center.

Forecast: 200 units per week
In transit: 410 units scheduled for receipt in week 1
On hand inventory: 15 units
Order quantity: 600 units
Lead time: 1 week
Safety stock = 0
Safety lead time = 1 week

Product X		Week							
		1	2	3	4	5	6	7	8
Forecast requirements									
In transit									
Projected available balance									
Planned shipments									

13. The sales director at Allied Products Company has decided to close the firm's warehouse in San Diego and open a new warehouse in Los Angeles. The San Diego warehouse is scheduled to be closed as of the end of week 4 and the new warehouse in Los Angeles is scheduled to be open for business at the start of week 5. Product B is currently stocked in the San Diego warehouse and will be stocked in the new warehouse in Los Angeles. The sales forecast for Product B is 100 units per week. Please complete the time-phased order point records below for product B, reflecting the change in the company's warehousing plans for the item, and the implications for the plant.

Product B / San Diego Warehouse		Week							
		1	2	3	4	5	6	7	8
Forecast requirements									
In transit									
Projected available balance	205								
Planned shipments									

Q = LFL; SS = 10 units; LT = 2 weeks

Product B / Los Angeles Warehouse

	Week							
	1	2	3	4	5	6	7	8
Forecast requirements								
In transit								
Projected available balance								
Planned shipments								

Q = LFL; SS = 10 units; LT = 1 week

Product B / Plant

	Week							
	1	2	3	4	5	6	7	8
Gross requirements								
Scheduled receipts								
Projected available balance	300							
Planned order releases								

Q = 200 units; SS = 15 units; LT = 3 weeks

14. The distribution planning manager at the Stasik Pharmaceutical Company is concerned about the rising cost of out-dated inventory in the firm's distribution warehouses. The shelf life for the company's products should not exceed 4 weeks. Products that have been in stock longer than four weeks must be scrapped according to government regulations. Please devise an exception notice test that can be applied to the time-phased order point records in the firm's distribution warehouses to direct the inventory planner's attention to those items where excess inventory may exist. Apply this procedure to the time-phased order point record for product W below to determine whether out of date inventory is likely to occur on this item.

Product W

		Week							
		1	2	3	4	5	6	7	8
Forecast requirements		300	300	300	300	300	300	300	300
In transit			900						
Projected available balance	350	50	650	350	950	650	1250	950	1550
Firm planned orders			900		900		900		
Planned shipment									

Q = 900; SS = 50 units; LT = 2 weeks

15. Product D is stocked only at the AMC Chemical Company's Dallas warehouse and at the company's plant warehouse in Akron. The sales director has forecast the sales for this product from the Dallas warehouse to be 40 units per week. Product D is manufactured at the firm's plant in Akron using 2 units of Ingredient X per unit of Product D.

   a. Please complete the time-phased order point records for product D at the Dallas warehouse and the Plant warehouse as well as the MRP record for ingredient X using the information supplied below. (Assume that Ingredient X is only used in Product D.)

Product D / Dallas Warehouse		Week							
		1	2	3	4	5	6	7	8
Forecast requirements									
In transit									
Projected available balance	85								
Planned shipments									

Q = LFL; SS = 5 units; LT = 2 weeks

Product D / Plant Warehouse		Week							
		1	2	3	4	5	6	7	8
Gross requirements									
Scheduled receipts									
Projected available balance	42								
Planned order releases									

Q = LFL; SS = 2 units; LT = 2 weeks

Ingredient X		Week							
		1	2	3	4	5	6	7	8
Gross requirements									
Scheduled receipts		320							
Projected available balance	4								
Planned order releases									

Q = 320 units; SS = 2 units; LT = 4 weeks

b. The actual sales for Product D at the Dallas Warehouse in week 1 was 48 units. Prepare the time-phased order point and MRP records as of the beginning of week 2. What actions should the master production scheduler take on the basis of this information?

Product D / Dallas Warehouse	Week							
	2	3	4	5	6	7	8	9
Forecast requirements								
In transit								
Projected available balance								
Planned shipments								

Q = LFL; SS = 5 units; LT = 2 weeks

Product D / Plant Warehouse	Week							
	2	3	4	5	6	7	8	9
Gross requirements								
Scheduled receipts								
Projected available balance								
Planned order releases								

Q = LFL; SS = 2 units; LT = 2 weeks

Ingredient X	Week							
	2	3	4	5	6	7	8	9
Gross requirements								
Scheduled receipts								
Projected available balance								
Planned order releases								

Q = 320 units; SS = 2 units; LT = 4 weeks

c. Suppose the actual sales for Product D at the Dallas warehouse in week 2 were 31 units. What action would the master scheduler take on the basis of this information? In order to avoid this situation, what modifications to the master production schedule might be taken?

	Week							
Product D / Dallas Warehouse	3	4	5	6	7	8	9	10
Forecast requirements								
In transit								
Projected available balance — 85								
Planned shipments								

Q = LFL; SS = 5 units; LT = 2 weeks

	Week							
Product D / Plant Warehouse	3	4	5	6	7	8	9	10
Gross requirements								
Scheduled receipts								
Projected available balance — 42								
Planned order releases								

Q = LFL; SS = 2 units; LT = 2 weeks

	Week							
Ingredient X	3	4	5	6	7	8	9	10
Gross requirements								
Scheduled receipts								
Projected available balance — 4								
Planned order releases								

Q = 320 units; SS = 2 units; LT = 4 weeks

——20————————————————————

MPC frontiers

In this final chapter of the book, we identify some future directions for manufacturing planning and control (MPC) systems. Manufacturing planning and control is a dynamic field that will continue to evolve. MRP was only possible with random access computing. Today's computers are 100 to 1,000 times faster than those available in the early days of MRP, and these computers will be replaced by new ones with the same orders of magnitude in improvements. User-friendly languages and dedicated computers make feasible the use of on-line systems for detailed shop scheduling based on finite loading. Artificial intelligence languages are increasingly being applied to MPC problems. Other uses of computers are focused on integration across functional areas, such as marketing and manufacturing. Computer integrated manufacturing (CIM) carries this integration concept even further.

Not all of the MPC frontiers are being pushed by computer technology. The just-in-time (JIT) approaches and resultant drive for simplicity in many cases results in *less* computerization. The emphasis on hidden factory costs, simplicity, and fast response to customer needs is having a profound impact on MPC design and operation.

This chapter starts with an assessment of MPC systems and where they are headed. We then deal with three related new and different approaches to manufacturing planning and control, followed by discussion of some resultant challenges for evolution in MPC practice.

The chapter is organized around the following five topics:

- The MPC system schematic: How can our general model of a manufacturing planning and control system be used to assess new systems?
- The optimized production technology (OPT) system: What is this approach? How does it work? What have been the results?
- The periodic control system at Kumera Oy: How did a European firm quickly improve manufacturing performance?
- The integrated manufacturing planning system (IMPS): How does this system fit with existing MPC system concepts? How can expert systems be used effectively?
- Observations on the systems and MPC evolution: What generalizations and conclusions can be drawn for future MPC practice?

Chapter 20 is related to many other chapters. The comparison and evaluation of new MPC approaches utilizes some of the ideas in Chapter 1. The OPT system uses finite loading concepts described in Chapter 5. Related scheduling issues are described in Chapter 13. The philosophical ideas of just-in-time are discussed in Chapter 7. Finally, the issues encountered in implementation of MPC systems are discussed in Chapter 11.

THE MANUFACTURING PLANNING AND CONTROL (MPC) SYSTEM SCHEMATIC

In this section, we relate our general model for manufacturing planning and control systems to other systems and approaches. The MPC system schematic is presented as Figure 20.1. We first discuss the concept of a standard for MPC systems and then turn to the question of using the schematic.

The "standard" for MPC systems

It is tempting to say that the MPC system shown in Figure 20.1 is the standard for evaluating and comparing alternative systems. This is accurate in a limited but important sense. The schematic presents a set of functions that must be performed, coordinated, and managed. It does not dictate *how* the functions are to be performed. The standard is that each of these functions must be accomplished in any firm; that is, there must be front-end, engine, and back end activities.

What is not captured in Figure 20.1 is the emphasis or importance that each module will have in a particular company. For example, firms that have only a limited number of suppliers would have a very different emphasis on

FIGURE 20.1   Manufacturing planning and control system

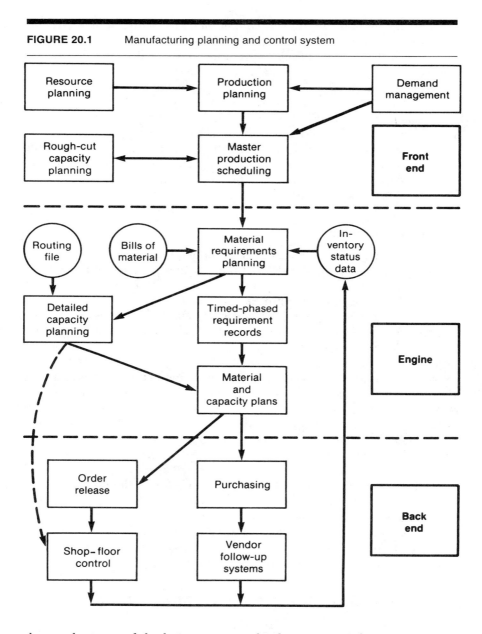

the purchasing module than a company that has many vendors. Figure 20.1 also does not detail the *costs* associated with maintaining satisfactory performance in each of the three areas. Many firms are reducing the transaction costs associated with detailed tracking in the back end.

The differences between firms are not only manifested in different emphases; different systems or techniques will be used, as well. Moreover, all of this needs to be viewed from an evolutionary point of view. *No* system is incapable of improvement. Once a fairly complete integrated (and transparent) system is in place, it is easier to evaluate new items and to implement them.

In summary, we see the MPC system schematic as the standard for the general functions to be performed. The specific procedures that are applied to accomplish these functions must be evaluated on an ongoing basis, both in terms of alternatives and in terms of what is currently viewed as important. In some instances, activities can be combined, performed less frequently, or reduced in importance.

Beyond the schematic

Figure 20.1 can be used as a checklist for auditing an MPC system. The crucial questions are whether each of the activities is performed, how well they are integrated, and how well each of the subsystems works. As noted above, there can always be improvements made in the subsystems.

An example involving no real change in fundamental theory is the increasing use of on-line systems. There are many firms with well-functioning MPC systems based on a weekly cycle for MRP planning. Going to an on-line system allows the company to move to a daily cycle, with resultant reductions in inventory and response times. In many cases, the operating costs of the new system are also reduced. One firm we know had computer charges of $800,000 per year for its weekly regenerated MRP system on a remote computer. It was able to purchase a dedicated computer, 30 terminals, slave printers, and state-of-the-art software for $400,000. The investment provided reduced operating costs *and* better performance!

For many of the newer approaches to MPC, an upgrade of existing methodologies is not enough. It is also necessary to consider the broad management and sociotechnical environments in which MPC systems are embedded. Sometimes it is necessary to make major changes in managerial practice and in the evaluation systems for manufacturing performance to realize improvement. This is particularly true for the firms considering the kinds of approaches to which we now turn our attention.

THE OPTIMIZED PRODUCTION TECHNOLOGY (OPT)

A great deal of attention has recently been focused on a proprietary system called OPT. (This acronym originally stood for optimized production timetable, but now stands for optimized production technology.) OPT is trademarked in two ways. The first trademark is "The OPT Concepts" (the philosophy) and the second is "OPT," which refers to the software package

(OPT/SERVE). There have been many questions about OPT: What does it do? What has been the experience of OPT users? Layered on top of the professionals' questions are broad questions raised by the creators of OPT themselves: What is important in scheduling a factory? What are the impacts of modern-day cost accounting systems on MPC? In addition, those who created and sell OPT have evolved their own thinking and beliefs, so their views today have changed somewhat from those of the past.

We believe that the best way to understand OPT is to view it as an enhancement to basic MPC systems. This view allows those who understand MPC systems to see where OPT fits. We also believe that, when viewed from this vantage point, OPT (at least when OPT is seen as a software product—rather than as a philosophy) can be added to most state-of-the-art MPC software packages as an enhancement. Viewing OPT in terms of software *and* in philosophical terms will permit us to see some important objectives for future enhancements to manufacturing planning and control.

Basic concepts of OPT

When we first studied OPT, the conclusion was that OPT fits into the "back end" section of Figure 20.1; that is, it was a sophisticated shop-floor control system based on finite loading procedures that concentrates on a subset of work centers (the bottlenecks). It uses an algorithm developed by Eliyahu Goldratt (published details of which are still unavailable) to do the finite loading (scheduling) very quickly.

This view does not recognize all OPT's contributions. OPT begins its process by combining the data in the bill of material file with those in the routing file. The result is a network, or extended tree diagram, where each part in the product structure also has its operational data attached directly. These data are then combined with the MPS to form the "Product Network." Figure 20.2 is a symbolic representation of an OPT product network. In the files, starting with the raw material, each operation to be performed is defined in terms of the resources used, setup, and processing times. Additional data typically included in the OPT files are: capacities, maximum inventories, minimum batch quantities, order quantities, due dates, alternate machine routings, manpower constraints, and other data typically used in finite loading models. In Figure 20.3, these data would be part of the "Resource Description." Product network and resource descriptions are then fed into a set of routines called BUILDNET and SERVE that identify the bottleneck resources. The BUILDNET routine combines the product network and resource information to form an engineering network. The SERVE routine uses the information to backward schedule from the order due dates, using logic similar to that of MRP and assuming infinite capacity for the resources. The initial analysis provides reports that indicate the bottleneck resources.

The system incorporates a rough-cut capacity planning routine that pro-

FIGURE 20.2   Sample product network

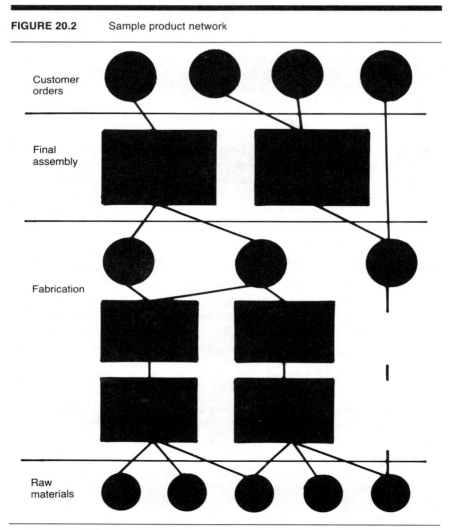

Source: F. Robert Jacobs, "OPT Uncovered: Many Production Planning and Scheduling Concepts Can Be Applied with or without the Software," *Industrial Engineering,* October 1984.

vides much of the information of other capacity planning procedures. Since the OPT product network includes both the parts and their routings, a pass through this network can result in an estimate of the capacity required at each work center. Moreover, a gross-to-net calculation can be made at each step to improve the capacity requirement estimates. Lot sizes at this rough-cut stage are based on lot-for-lot rules. The resultant capacity needs, when divided by the number of weeks in the planning horizon, are the average

FIGURE 20.3 OPT/SERVE information flow

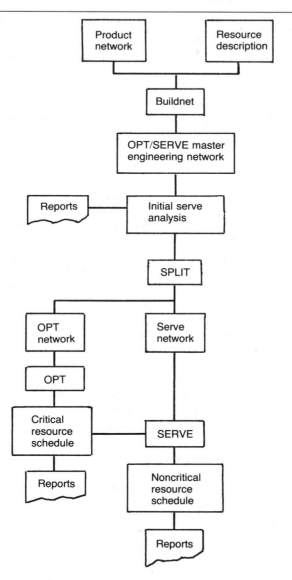

Source: F. Robert Jacobs, "OPT Uncovered: Many Production Planning and Scheduling Concepts Can Be Applied with or without the Software," *Industrial Engineering,* October 1984.

capacity requirements for each resource. When divided by the resource capacities, the result is average expected loads.

The average loads on machine centers are sorted in descending order, and the most heavily loaded are studied. Typical questions include: Are the data correct? Are the time standards accurate? Can we easily increase capacity? Can we use alternate routing for some items? Any changes based on these questions result in another run to see if the bottleneck resources change.

At this point, the OPT product network is split into two portions, using a routine called SPLIT. A symbolic example of the results produced by SPLIT is shown in Figure 20.4. The lower section (the "serve" network) includes all operations that precede the bottleneck resources. The upper portion (the "OPT Network") incorporates all of the bottleneck resources and all succeeding operations, including the market demand for end products that have parts which have processing on the bottleneck resources. The OPT network is forward finite loaded, using Goldratt's algorithm.

The "SERVE Network" (see Figure 20.3) encompasses all the nonbottleneck part operations (the noncritical resource schedule), which are back scheduled using MRP logic. In the initial scheduling pass using SERVE, the due dates are offset from customer order due dates for all part operations. In the second pass, however, the due dates for any part operations that feed bottlenecks are based on those established by the OPT finite loading of bottlenecks. The schedules for those part operations are so set that material will be available in time for the first operation in the OPT network.

One of the advantages of the OPT-MRP split is that from this split we can see where attention should be focused. Not only is bottleneck capacity utilized more intensively by finite loading of this small subset of work centers but identifying the bottlenecks allows one to target efforts in quality and in production improvements on these resources. A significant contribution of OPT logic is that it will vary lot sizes to increase production of limited resources and reduce work in process (WIP) at nonlimiting resources.

It is now that we can identify clearly the primary contribution of the OPT approach. When the finite loading through bottleneck resources has been completed, the result is a doable master production schedule. For this reason, OPT is sometimes considered to be a "front end" system (i.e., a master production scheduling technique). We see it less as an MPS technique than as an enhancement to the MPS. OPT conceivably can take any MPS as input and determine the extent to which it is doable.

What this means is that OPT makes an explicit computer-based analysis of the feedback from the engine (and back end) to the front end. This is an important contribution. It means that a valid MPS is generated, one that the firm has a very good chance of achieving—based on the capacity parameters that were used in the scheduling.

FIGURE 20.4   Product-network: Critical, noncritical SPLIT

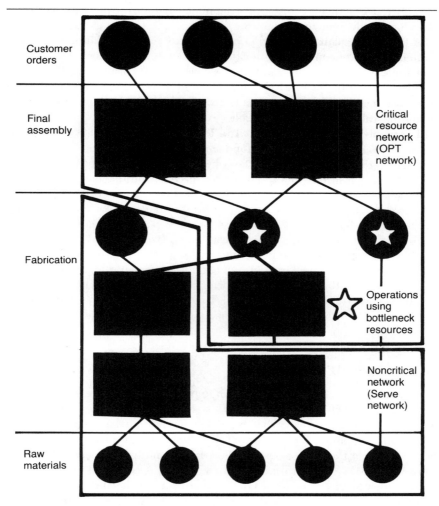

Source: F. Robert Jacobs, "OPT Uncovered: Many Production Planning and Scheduling Concepts Can Be Applied with or without the Software," *Industrial Engineering*, October 1984.

A secondary contribution at this stage comes from the way OPT schedules the nonbottleneck resources. The easiest way to see this is to assume (as is often the case in practice) that there are *no* bottlenecks. In that case, OPT schedules are based on MRP logic. The difference is that OPT in this case will change batch sizes (reducing them) to the point where some resources almost become bottlenecks. The result is less WIP, reduced lead time, greater material velocity, and a move toward "zero inventory" manufacturing. OPT does much of this by overlapping schedules using unequal batch sizes for transferring and processing.

A third important contribution of OPT is to virtually eliminate the fundamental issue of conflicting priorities between MRP and finite loading. By only finite loading a small fraction of the work centers, priority conflict issues should largely disappear. Moreover, the computational time required to do finite loading should be dramatically reduced by only dealing with a subset of orders and work centers/resources.

In operation as a shop-floor control technique, OPT has a few other differences from usual practice. A fundamental tenet in OPT is that an hour lost in a bottleneck resource is an hour lost to the output of the entire factory, while an hour lost in a nonbottleneck resource has no real cost. This means that capacity utilization of bottleneck resources is everything. This is achieved through using WIP buffers in front of bottlenecks, and where the output from a bottleneck joins with some other parts. Utilization of bottlenecks is also achieved by running large batch sizes, thereby reducing the relative time spent in setup downtime.

In practice, the small/large lot size issue has two major implications. The first is that lead times should be shorter: smaller batches will move faster through nonbottleneck work centers. The second implication is less felicitous: procedures have to be developed to split/join batches as they go through production.

OPT and the MPC framework

When OPT was first introduced, some people saw it as a replacement for an integrated MPC system. In fact, this is not correct. OPT is better seen as encompassing much of what is in the engine and back end of Figure 20.1—but combining them in a way that allows one to plan both materials and capacity at the same time; that is, OPT accomplishes many of the functions in the MPC framework, but not all.

A fundamental principle of OPT is that only the bottleneck operations (resources) are of critical scheduling concern. The argument is that production output is limited by the bottleneck operations, and that increased throughput can only come via better capacity utilization of the bottleneck facilities.

To maximize output from bottleneck operations, larger lot sizes are run. The result is to reduce the percentage of nonproductive time devoted to setups in these work centers. For nonbottleneck work centers, the opposite lot-sizing approach is taken. Smaller batches can be made at these work centers, since the only result is to reduce the time these work centers would stand idle. Calculation of the batch sizes is a part of the OPT procedure.

We then see that OPT produces different batch sizes throughout the plant, depending upon whether a work center is or is not a bottleneck. This has several MPC implications. In Figure 20.1, the lot sizes are produced as a part of the MRP explosion process. In typical finite loading procedures, the batch size is fixed. Such is not the case with OPT. It also follows that a batch size for one operation on a part could be different from other operations on the same part. This implies that special treatment will be required for any paperwork that travels with shop orders. In fact, OPT is designed to do order splitting. In usual practice, order splitting is done on backlogged (bottleneck) machines; it is precisely in this situation that OPT would do the opposite.

The key to lot sizing in OPT is distinguishing between a *transfer* batch (that lot size which moves from operation to operation) and a *process* batch (the total lot size released to the shop). Any differences are held in work-in-process inventories in the shop. In essence, no operation can start until at least a transfer batch is built up behind it. Also, whatever the buildup behind the work center, it *only* produces a transfer batch unless the finite scheduling routine calls for multiple batches.

It has been argued that OPT does not have the same needs for data accuracy that are required for MRP scheduling. This statement is partially correct, if one feels that less accuracy is required for nonbottleneck parts and work centers. But going into the process of using OPT, one may not realize very well what these bottleneck operations are. Both OPT and MRP require detailed knowledge of product structures and processes. Data bases, accurate transaction processing, and the right managerial commitment are required for both as well.

Returning to Figure 20.1, we see that OPT cannot uniquely be put in the front end, the engine, or the back end. It works in all three areas, and does some things quite differently than is the case when the scheduling is done exclusively by MRP. However, OPT uses most of the same data as MPC systems. One still needs a front end, engine, and back end (both shop-floor control and purchasing-vendor followup systems). For the firm with an operating MPC system, the basic data base and closed loop understanding exist. Implementing OPT as an enhancement seems to be a logical extension. OPT is another example of separating the vital few from the trivial many, and thereafter providing a mechanism to exploit this knowledge for better manufacturing planning/control. It allows a firm to simultaneously plan materials and capacities and to combine some of the best of MRP with some important concepts in finite loading.

Philosophical underpinnings

There are several philosophical points to OPT. These are summarized in Figure 20.5. Two fundamental principles were identified above: first, the

---

FIGURE 20.5   OPT principles

---

1. Balance flow, not capacity.
2. The level of utilization of a nonbottleneck is determined not by its own potential but by some other constraint in the system.
3. Utilization and activation of a resource are not synonymous.
4. An hour lost at a bottleneck is an hour lost forever.
5. An hour saved at a nonbottleneck is just a mirage.
6. Bottlenecks govern both throughput and inventory in the system.
7. The transfer batch may not, and many times should not, be equal to the process batch.
8. The process batch should be variable, not fixed.
9. Schedules should be established by looking at all of the constraints simultaneously. Lead times are the result of a schedule and cannot be predetermined.

---

utilization of a bottleneck is critical and, second, reduced utilization of non-bottleneck resources costs nothing. On the other hand, in the traditional cost accounting view, people should always be working. But if these people are at nonbottleneck resources, the net result of their work will increase WIP and cause confusion for scheduling at other work centers. Under OPT, it is quite all right to not work if there is not work to do. In fact, working (by the usual definition) in this situation will *cause* problems.

The primary OPT objective is stated as making money. This is achieved by maximizing throughput. Throughput is limited by the bottleneck resources, so all efforts are devoted to maximization of capacity utilization in these work centers. It is *flow* (that can be sold), not overall capacity utilization that is important. Capacity can never be totally balanced. The best way to utilize manpower effectively is to so work on cross training that unique skills are less of a constraint.

This concept is consistent with much of just-in-time manufacturing and the "whole person" concept. Workers who are not at bottleneck operations should not be paced by a 100 percent work load. They should utilize extra time in other activities, such as quality improvement, industrial engineering, and skill enhancement.

The philosophical underpinnings of OPT are important—in their own right. To some extent, many of the basic arguments have been made before, but OPT carries these arguments to a more operational level. The link is clearly made between the OPT position on cost accounting and the resultant scheduling and shop practices. The result is a set of manufacturing practices that are sometimes counter-intuitive—and difficult to implement without a belief at the top in the OPT philosophy.

These philosophical underpinnings are important to achieve OPT benefits and to many manufacturing improvement programs. The net result is a need for education throughout the company, a change in mores for many firms, and a top-management commitment to the basic concept, the philosophy, and the resultant actions required (e.g., let nonbottleneck people do some nondirect production work or even be idle). One OPT firm now says that in the next recession it will not reduce the work force. The firm intends to reduce batch sizes!

Implementation issues

OPT presents several difficulties in implementation. To those who have been through a major MPC system implementation, such as JIT or MRP, there are some similarities and some important differences. In general, OPT is not for the novice. One needs to understand basic finite scheduling concepts. Also needed are sound basic systems, education, top-management support, and a willingness to unlearn some ingrained habits.

Some of these relate directly to the philosophy. The procedures go hand in hand with the philosophical arguments. We know of one firm that has been working for several years to implement OPT, without great success, because it has strong pressures to fully utilize all direct labor hours. The cost accounting tenets of OPT have just not been accepted.

A related issue is the unpublished algorithm used for scheduling the plant. Many of us were brought up on a belief in "system transparency." OPT is anything *but* transparent. It truly is difficult to understand, and it is even more difficult to understand why some schedules have been produced. Many of the OPT results are quite counter-intuitive; it is often difficult to see why they are as they are.

There is always a difficulty of implementation if the basis for the schedule is not clear to the shop-floor people who are responsible for its execution. This is aggravated when the performance evaluation of the shop-floor people is not directly related to schedule execution. Some evidence of these problems was expressed by members of the OPT users group who talked about the time required to get schedule adherence among foremen on the floor.

Another problem of OPT is the certainty assumptions used in processing. To the extent that data are incorrect on capacities, batch time requirements, and so on, the system will produce imperfect results. Use of control techniques, such as input/output, could help in this regard.

OPT buffers the schedules for critical operations at bottleneck operations by using both safety stocks and safety lead time. In scheduling a sequence of jobs on the same machine, safety timing can be introduced between subsequent batches. This provides a cushion against variations adversely affecting the flow of jobs through this same operation.

To protect against having these variations affect subsequent operations on the same job, safety time is again employed. In this case, the start of the next operation on the same job is not scheduled immediately after completion of the current operation. A delay is introduced to perform the buffering here. Note that there can be another job in process during the delay; its completion will affect the actual start date for the arriving job. Each of these allowances means that actual conditions will vary from the OPT schedule. The question for the foremen at some point could easily be *which* job to run next.

To ensure that there is always work at the bottleneck operation (to provide maximum output) there are safety stocks in front of these work centers. Thus, whenever one job is completed, there is another ready to go on the bottleneck machine.

To protect the assembly schedule against shortages that could severely cut output, a safety stock of completed parts from the bottleneck operations are held before assembly. The idea is that disruptions of the bottleneck operation to produce a part that is short will cause reduced output. Part shortages that can be made up by going through operations that are not bottlenecks will not cut capacity.

Additionally, management factors enter into the OPT scheduling system. These help make realistic schedules that meet management criteria. Factors involving the levels of work-in-process inventory, the capacity utilization that is attainable, degree of schedule protection, and batch size controls can all be applied to the procedure. These help take into account the company culture as the procedure is implemented.

The repetitive lot concept

The OPT use of different batch sizes, depending on whether a work center is or is not a bottleneck, has led to related research efforts on the scheduling frontiers of MPC systems. Jacobs and Bragg combine shop scheduling decisions with lot sizes in their work on the "repetitive lot concept." They present simulation results indicating major improvements in the average flow time for manufactured lots and work-in-process inventory using conventional priority scheduling procedures and transfer batches for job shop production.

Jacobs and Bragg permit the original order quantities released to the shop for manufacturing ("operation batches") to be split into smaller batches that can flow immediately to the next operation prior to the completion of the operation at its current work center. The "transfer batches" are, in effect, small predetermined subbatches, which are integral fractions of the original order quantity that provide a work center with the flexibility to begin the production of an order earlier than its completion time at the previous work center. Such flexibility, frequently referred to as "lot-splitting" and "overlap or line scheduling," results in reduced order flow times, improved machine utilization, reduced setup times, and the smoothing of work flow in the shop to yield better use of capacity.

Figure 20.6 shows an example illustrating the use of the repetitive lot concept and its effect on order flow time. Using fixed operation batch sizes of 1,000 in Part A, the order is completed at hour 2250. In Part B, while the original operation batch size is used at operation 1, a transfer batch size of 100 is used to permit processing the order simultaneously at operations 2 and 3 for completion by hour 1125. This example also illustrates that the "operation batch size" (i.e., the number of units produced during a given work center setup) can vary between the original order batch size and the transfer batch size. Although Figure 20.6 does not consider the fact that other jobs may be competing for the resources used for each operation, the simulation took this into account when assessing the potential benefit of lot-splitting and overlap scheduling.

The repetitive lot concept can be applied by using any of the standard priority scheduling methods (e.g., shortest processing time, critical ratio, and the like). When an order is completed under traditional priority scheduling rules, the highest priority order in the queue is selected for processing next. Under the repetitive lot concept, a work center may contain transfer batches coming from many released orders. In this case, the queue is searched for transfer batches of the same type of item that has just been completed at the work center. If such an item is available, it is processed by using the same setup at the work center; otherwise the highest priority transfer batch in the queue is selected and a new setup is made at the work center. In the event that the queue contains no transfer batches, the next batch to arrive at the work center is processed.

Jacobs and Bragg report experimental results in which the repetitive lot size concept is tested, using a simulation model of a shop with 10 work centers. The fixed order quantity for released orders was varied from 120 to 400 in these experiments, and two different transfer batch sizes were used, 50 and 10. A 38 percent average improvement in the mean order flow time was observed when a transfer batch size of 50 was used, and a 44 percent average improvement was obtained with a transfer batch size of 10. A reduction in the total setup time at the work centers of 23 to 27 percent occurred when transfer batches were used in conjunction with small fixed order quantities for the released orders (120 to 200). However, an increase in the total setup time of 13 to 16 percent occurred when larger fixed order release quantities were used (250 to 400).

This study indicates that joint scheduling and batch sizing procedures developed by using "repetitive lot" concepts can provide the benefits of small lot production without requiring capacity increases or an investment in reducing setup times. While the use of the "repetitive lot" concept may result in increased material handling costs and more complexity in tracking

FIGURE 20.6 A comparison of fixed versus variable operation and transfer batch sizes for a single job

	Operation	Time per part (minutes)
Requirements are for 1,000 units of the part. Three	1	1.00
operations are required to produce the part. Processing	2	0.50
time per part is given. There is no setup time required.	3	0.75

A. Fixed operation batch size = 1000
    Transfer batch size = 1000

Operation	Schedule	Completion last batch
1		1000
2		1500
3		2250

0   500   1000   1500   2000
Time

B. Variable operation batch size
    Transfer batch size = 100

Operation	Schedule	Operation batch size	Completion last batch
1		1000	1000
2		200	1050
3		500	1125

0   500   1000   1500   2000
Time

Source: F. Robert Jacobs and Daniel J. Bragg, "The Repetitive Lots Concept: An Evaluation of Job Flow Considerations in Production Dispatching, Sequencing and Batch Sizing," IRMIS working paper no. 505, Indiana University, 1986.

orders in a shop, this concept appears to be a promising new integrative approach for improving manufacturing performance. High-volume manufacturers with limited product lines having numerous operations would appear to benefit most from the reduced order flow times, lower levels of work-in-process inventory, and potential gains in customer service provided by the use of the repetitive lot concept.

THE PERIODIC CONTROL SYSTEM AT KUMERA OY

Kumera Oy is headquartered about 40 miles north of Helsinki in Riihi-mäki, Finland. The company produces a broad range of gear-driven, speed-reducing power transmissions. It engages in all phases of manufacturing, from engineering to parts fabrication and assembly. Kumera employs about 450 people in four manufacturing plants and two sales affiliates located in four countries. The periodic control system has been installed in all plants except one.

A typical product would consist of a housing, mounting devices, shafts, gears, assembly hardware, and perhaps a motor. Some 50 different part numbers would be usual, with 100 or more individual pieces. Of the 50 part numbers, one third to one half would be manufactured (generally the large items, such as gears, shafts, housings, and so on), and the rest purchased. Under usual conditions, the lead times for some of the items would exceed two months, though most are within five weeks. The large number of potential end items possible means virtually no finished-goods inventory can be carried, but competitive pressures require short delivery times to customers. The periodic control system has helped resolve this basic conflict between sales and production.

The system

To describe the periodic control system, we use the manufacturing planning and control system shown in Figure 20.1. The description of the system will start with the front end activities, pass to the engine, and will conclude with the back end. The production planning part of the front end is an intimate part of the company game planning. The resultant commitment to an integrated plan provides direction to the specific production planning and control activities.

The first step in the installation of the periodic control system was the designation of production product groups. The planning and scheduling activities could not be based on specific end items, since the number is too large, and the company must quote delivery times less than total product lead times. Five product groups have been formed on the basis of production process similarities. Within each group, divisions exist for product options. The groupings do not exactly conform to the catalogue product families, but it is easy to translate from customer orders to the groups for order entry purposes.

The groupings facilitate front end activities. Forecasts are made at the main option level and are aggregated by product group as the basis for demand management, budgeting, profit and cash planning, and production planning. Production and resource planning specify the overall production rate and any capacity expansion that the company will undertake. The resulting plan (which reflects sales, finance, and engineering objectives, as well) has a one-year horizon, by week, in units, for each of the five product groups.

The product groups provide the basis for master production scheduling.

FIGURE 20.7   Group forecasts, capacity allocation, and periodic quantities

Product group	Annual forecast	Share of available labor (percent)	Capacity of key machine (percent)	Period quantities
A	500	15	25	50
B	100	20	5	10
C	1,000	10	30	100
D	2,000	25	20	200
E	1,500	30	10	150

Volumes   Labor allocations   Key machine allocations

Source: D. C. Whybark, "Production Planning and Control at Kumera Oy," *Production and Inventory Management*, First Quarter 1984.

The basic process will be illustrated using an example with the five groups, shown in Figure 20.7. To start, rough-cut capacity planning ensures that capacity at key machines will be available to produce the forecast product group mix before going forward with master production scheduling.

The master production schedule is based on the period length of the periodic control system. It is determined by dividing the year into equal increments. Each of the groups of products will be scheduled *once* during a period. Kumera calls the specific products to be produced a *production set*. Actual customer orders are assigned to the production set in a period, using available-to-promise concepts; that is, actual orders replace the period quantities used for planning. The shop orders for production of all of the components necessary to produce the actual customer orders in particular production sets are released at one time. In general, the components are *only* for those specific items in the production set. The sequence of specific products within a production set is based on manufacturing efficiencies in changing from one group to another.

The choice of a repetitive cycle of production helps production control and coordinates the release dates of production orders. The length of period determines how many units of each group will be made in a production set.

FIGURE 20.8   Sequence for releasing production orders for groups

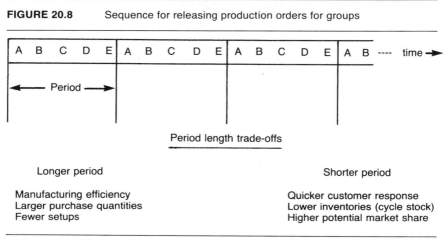

Period length trade-offs

Longer period	Shorter period
Manufacturing efficiency	Quicker customer response
Larger purchase quantities	Lower inventories (cycle stock)
Fewer setups	Higher potential market share

Source: D. C. Whybark, "Production Planning and Control at Kumera Oy," *Production and Inventory Management*, First Quarter 1984.

The quantity effects the manufacturing costs. The length of period also affects how much of the production can be made strictly to order and how much to forecast. These and other factors which influence the length of the period are indicated in Figure 20.8. The final decision requires managerial assessment of the trade-offs between all these factors.

For the example in Figure 20.7, a period of five weeks was chosen. This means each group will be scheduled 10 times per year (using a 50-week year). Once the period length is chosen, forecasts are used to calculate the number of products to be produced in each production set each period. Figure 20.9 shows the master production schedule for the example. The manufacturing objective is to have completed, by the fifth week of the period, all materials required for assembly of the actual products in each production set. This means that, as the next group A is launched, the previous group A is being scheduled into assembly (see the top of the schedule). Kumera thinks in terms of the launch date for each production set (see the bottom of the schedule). They provide wide dissemination of the timing table data to customers and vendors, and within the company.

To specify material requirements, the exact customer orders to be produced in a production set must be determined. This is the job of order entry in demand management. An attempt is made to assign each order to the production schedule that will meet the delivery date requested by the customer. For example, a request for an item from the B product group for delivery in week 14 would be assigned to B_8 if possible (see Figure 20.9).

The order promising is done in accordance with the commitment be-

FIGURE 20.9 Master production schedule (the timing table)

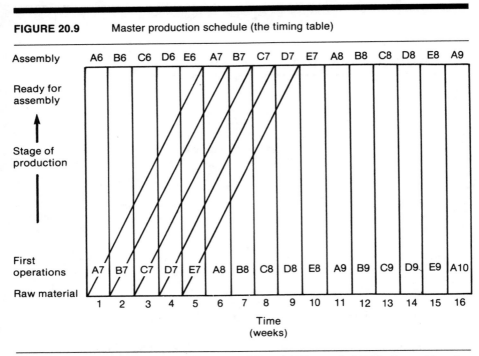

Source: D. C. Whybark, "Production Planning and Control at Kumera Oy," *Production and Inventory Management,* First Quarter 1984.

tween marketing and manufacturing. No more orders may be entered into a production set than the period quantity (e.g., 10 units for B in each production set). Once the period quantity is reached, the next customer order must be delayed until a later production set, or the order must be exchanged for one that is in an earlier set. Kumera looks at the timing table as a train schedule. When the launch date arrives, the production orders for the set are released (the train leaves). The sales department can make any allocation of schedule dates among customers until the train leaves for the factory. After that no more changes, they have to wait for the next train. No release is made for any order that does not have the engineering completed, thereby avoiding potential mix-ups in manufacturing. If the launch date arrives and the "train is not full," sales can decide to make some orders in anticipation (i.e., against a forecast), but this is very dangerous to this firm, since almost all orders are custom-made. The alternative is to pull up an order from a production set scheduled for a later release. At the date of launch, the train *leaves*—sometimes with empty seats! That is, if the production set is not up to the period quantity, the company only makes to order. In the words of one Kumera manager, "If there are empty beds in the hospital, you don't go out and make people sick just to fill the beds."

When the release date has arrived, a composite bill of material is prepared for the actual set of customer orders in the production set. The composite bill is built up from the separate bills for each of the products in the set. Actual inventories and allocations are checked against the computer records (Kumera runs well over 95 percent accuracy) before calculation of the net requirements and release to the shop.

Lot sizing is performed for selected items. The bill of material processor can look ahead to the actual orders in the next and subsequent production sets for end items that use the same parts. Subject to parameters on how far ahead to look, some aggregation of order demands can be used to justify the production of more than the net requirements.

Once the quantities have been determined, items are released to the factory floor and the shop-floor control system carries them through to completion. The purchased items are scheduled to be received as needed on the week before the staging week. (This provides one week of safety lead time.) They are collected into an assembly storage area where they are joined by the manufactured parts.

Purchase and shop orders are released at the same time. Shop orders have an implicit due date at assembly staging time (five weeks hence in the example). Purchased raw materials are due as needed during the five weeks, and purchased assembly components are due prior to the assembly staging week. Kumera numbers the production sets in release date sequence. The sequence numbers are displayed conspicuously on all shop papers associated with the production set. They provide a very simple shop-floor priority rule: "Always work next on the item with lowest-numbered production set."

The production set sequence numbers are also used for other circumstances. For example, emergency production of pieces not required in assembly (e.g., a part needed because a customer's machine is down) can be accomplished by assigning a low number. The scheme can also be used for producing low-priority items as capacity is available (e.g., service parts not immediately required). The assembly foreman schedules the assembly sequence to make an efficient progression through the products in the production set. If any products are still awaiting parts, their assembly can be delayed until the latter part of the week. The late parts will have the lowest number (highest priority) on the shop floor, and so will go through as quickly as possible.

Not all purchase orders can be delayed until the release date for the production set because of long lead times. In these cases, the purchase quantities are calculated to provide just enough inventory to produce the period quantities scheduled for future production. Kumera works at keeping the parts and raw materials that are ordered this way highly common. The commonality and gross to net logic used in calculating the production quantities help keep the residual inventories low. To help key vendors plan their production, Kumera provides them with the timing table data. Vendor follow-up is done from this information or the staged inventories for assembly.

Using the system

The simplicity of the periodic control system enabled Kumera Oy to do the implementation in about six months. The initial system was totally manual. It was converted to the computer two years later. The system required certain disciplines and induced others. Some were necessary to use the system effectively, while others provided the opportunity for later improvements.

Inventory accuracy is essential at the time of net requirement calculation. The physical check at the time the bill of material is processed ensures correct counts. At Kumera, the required accuracy is maintained even though not all inventory is locked up. The short period helps maintain accuracy, since there is less time for shrinkage; short periods also result in smaller production lots and lower inventory quantities.

The marketing disciplines were the most difficult—no more maximization of sales or arbitrary delivery promises. There were to be no more orders in a given production set than the period quantities. The customers were to be told honestly when delivery could be expected and, if it was not good enough, exchanges with previously scheduled customers would have to be worked out or the order lost. There would be no more "we'll try" answers.

At the management level, the adherence to the game plan and a willingness to back the order entry function when difficult decisions were being made was required. Management integrated the budget and profit-planning activities with the periodic control concept. That way, all the management activities were keyed to the same basic information and control reports.

In production, the required disciplines were not as difficult, but some major changes were required. The new priorities had to be followed and reliance on "hot" or shortage lists had to stop. The quantities indicated on the shop orders would be the quantities produced. (No more running a "few extra" since the machine is set up.) The short period meant more setups and lower inventories.

One of the reactions to Kumera's improved delivery capacity was a shift in customer behavior. As they recognized that the promised delivery dates were honest, customers began to rely on them. The distribution of the timing table data to customers shifted their ordering patterns to correspond more closely with Kumera's schedules.

Much the same thing happened with vendors. As vendors realized that the timing table really was used for purchasing, they found they could make better plans. The distribution of the data to key vendors reinforced this. As

Kumera reduced the amount of "panic" buying, the utility of the schedule for the vendors was further reinforced.

Internal changes evolved, as well. Engineering was added to the order entry checks. No customer order is released to the shop without complete engineering. This means that order entry must check before promising a delivery date (assignment to a production set) for any product on which there is a substantial amount of engineering. The same is true for orders needing long lead-time items that are not part of the common items purchased prior to release. Purchasing is consulted before a promise date is given.

Payoffs

There have been many tangible benefits from the installation of the periodic control system and some intangible ones, as well. Principal among the tangible benefits have been the reduction in inventories, improvement in margins and customer service, and reduction in the number of expeditors. These are summarized in Figure 20.10.

The development of the production groupings has greatly facilitated the forecasting task and helped focus marketing on meeting their sales objectives for the groups. The scheduling and priority systems have routinized management of the production and assembly activities. The problems are very visible. This focuses management attention on them quickly, very much as the just-in-time approach does.

The simplicity of the system makes it easy to work with. The system is transparent to everyone in the company, so they can make well-informed decisions. No one guesses at priorities, changes instructions on work in process, or shifts the schedule around. This has improved all working relationships and further enhances the attitude of working together to solve problems as they appear.

Engineering changes are much easier to implement and manage. They are always tied to a particular set, in a way similar to that done by some

---

FIGURE 20.10   Some payoffs from periodic control

	Before periodic control	After implementation	Currently
Inventory turns	2.5	9.2	10.1
Late deliveries	50%	10%	0%
Gross margin (percent)	10	27	30
People: Production control	4	1	1
People: Expediting	2	1	0

Source: D. C. Whybark, "Production Planning and Control at Kumera Oy," *Production and Inventory Management,* First Quarter 1984.

advanced JIT users. With very low inventories in the shop and actual customer orders in every production set, the effectivity dates for engineering changes are much easier to determine and control.

One strong test of the system and its benefits was the recession in Finland. Kumera managed to expand business during the period, largely due to its customer-service capability. At the same time, the firm has vertically integrated. The periodic control system has been installed in its new acquisitions (except the foundry) as a first step in improving the operations.

The periodic control system at Kumera is more than a technique for planning and controlling production. It is a management tool and state of mind. The application of sound management principles at the front end of the system is key to the successful application of the engine and back end techniques. A great deal of attention is focused on the timing table at Kumera. But the timing table is just one aspect of the entire process.

THE IMPS SYSTEM

In this section, we describe an integrated manufacturing planning system (IMPS), developed by Ebner and others at Boston University. IMPS provides an improved linkage between strategic planning and operational execution in manufacturing. A preliminary version of the software is presently being tested with an actual company data base.

IMPS is a "supervisory manufacturing software" system; that is, IMPS is not intended to be a system that replaces existing MPC systems, such as MRP or JIT. IMPS can work well with any and all of these; however, IMPS fosters evolution in MPC systems, such as from MRP to JIT. The IMPS system is best seen as an overlay to detailed manufacturing planning/control systems. It "supervises" these systems, and it continually measures key differences between strategic/tactical objectives of the firm and detailed manufacturing plans. As actual conditions change (e.g., customer orders or Murphy in the factory), IMPS updates the differences that are expressed first in strategic terms (e.g., overall revenue forecasts or gross capacity), and second, in tactical terms (e.g., detailed implications for deliveries, materials, and capacities). When problems occur, IMPS, using expert systems, allows the company to better schedule actual customer orders, so strategic objectives are met more closely, and to better coordinate the detailed planning of each manufacturing unit. The emphasis in IMPS is on coordination, rather than intervention or direct control; that is, IMPS continually simulates factory conditions at a high level of aggregation, intervening only as necessary (if it isn't broken, don't fix it).

IMPS is consistent with a growing trend in manufacturing to provide "service enhanced" products; that is, to survive in manufacturing, high-quality and reasonably priced goods must be produced. But success in manufacturing requires providing a whole new set of additional services to the customers: rapid response, logistics support, more rapid design change, living with poor forecasts, and offering "solutions," rather than products. All of these need to be provided, and systems need to be in place so routine execution can take place on a routine basis; that is, without massive infusions of indirect labor. Manufacturing planning and control is the single largest source of overhead cost in most manufacturing companies. IMPS is designed to reduce these costs by supporting systems that are based on routine execution, with minimal intervention by staff personnel. The desire is to achieve routine MPC system execution, with reduced use of staff personnel, so that these people can increasingly focus their skills on providing service enhancements.

This section describes the IMPS system, its philosophy, the architecture, what we mean by strategic/tactical planning, the resultant implications for both capacity planning and material planning, and the use of expert systems. We start with an overview of the IMPS system architecture. Next we turn to the planning/control systems. The third subsection deals with the way in which IMPS plans and controls both capacity and materials, and the resultant strategic implications. Finally, we show how expert systems are employed to solve the inevitable problems that come up in complex manufacturing environments.

System architecture

There are three ways to view the architecture of IMPS. The first concerns basic functionality, the underlying IMPS data base, and how the data elements are to be controlled. The second view of the IMPS architecture is in terms of the structure of IMPS, focusing on the strategic/tactical hierarchy used for planning and control. The final view is concerned with use of the system and the ways IMPS intervenes in factory operations. The IMPS view of the manufacturing process is presented in Figure 20.11. The factory is considered to be a material conversion process, supported with whatever systems are necessary. A data control unit has the purpose of maintaining integrity in the systems that drive manufacturing; any simulated conditions in IMPS are to remain simulations until intervention is signaled. It is only then that the detailed factory data base is to be updated. Four expert systems are shown in Figure 20.11: strategic planning, vendor management, master scheduling, and reservation management. These are used to evaluate factory conditions and plans.

Activities associated with customer orders, both actual and forecasted, are detailed at the top of Figure 20.12. A strategic plan for the company is translated into manufacturing terms; this is a basic input to order management. The actual customer orders and possible (forecasted) orders have to add up

FIGURE 20.11 The IMPS view of the manufacturing process

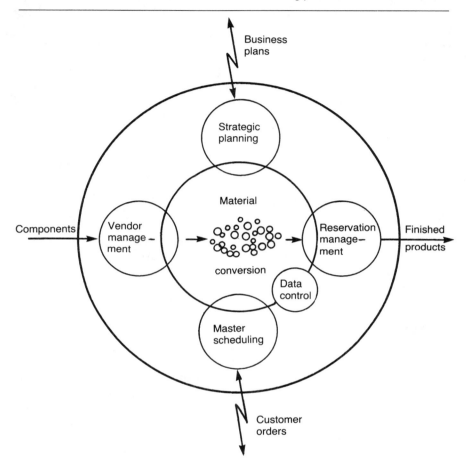

to and support the agreed-upon strategic plan for manufacturing (i.e., the production plan). Order entry consumes the forecast. Actual orders replace forecasted orders in order management. Order scheduling provides promise dates to customer orders and keeps track of them (including changes in configuration). One result of all this is a continually updated set of customer delivery date promises that are based on tests of what is possible in the factories. These tests are guided by several expert systems (three are shown as examples in Figure 20.12) that only pass along bad news to customers as a last resort.

Order scheduling broadcasts the resultant information back, through the

FIGURE 20.12   Organization of the IMPS system at the functional level

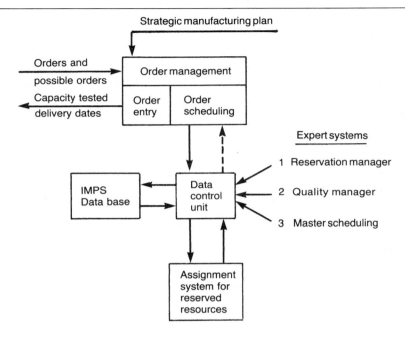

data control unit, to the factories and key vendors so they can bring their scheduling systems to bear on meeting the coordinated delivery dates. Order scheduling also is involved with final assembly scheduling, which is an ongoing process right up until the actual date of shipment for some kinds of products.

The most critical element of Figure 20.12 is seen in what is called "the IMPS data base." This is the *only* set of IMPS-based instructions seen by the factories; that is, the intent is to have only one plan, and not to allow analysis using the expert systems to distort this plan until there is agreement on a new plan. The data control unit provides this data base security. It has a copy of the current IMPS plan, and it also has "hoses" running into other data base elements as needed; that is, for example, if analysis of an existing problem meant that one of the expert systems needed to forward finite load a critical resource, the connection to the necessary data elements would be made. This concept is important to the IMPS architecture, since the intent is to have only the elements in the IMPS data base required to define the current plan and alternative plans, with the highest level of aggregation possible.

The three expert systems shown to the right of the data control unit are only illustrative. The reservation manager would provide continually updated estimates of subassembly completions and match these units with customer orders in ways that best meet revenue and other strategic goals. The quality manager monitors key testing results—looking for situations where scrap and rework problems are significant enough to necessitate replanning; when this is the case, the expert systems aid in resolving the problems.

The box labeled "assignment system for reserved resources," included in Figure 20.12, is the result of the use of expert systems. As each expert system goes through its paces, it works at solving particular problems in light of particular criteria. As this transpires, resources are dedicated or assigned. These assignments need to be "frozen," so they are not reassigned in the next use of the expert systems. Moreover, the assignments need to be kept track of, so subsequent analyses can be aware of prior assignments; perhaps they should be modified, which will call for prior problems being solved again. The key point is that we do not want to undo solutions without careful investigation, but we also do not want to allow "first pig at the trough" to constrain responsiveness.

IMPS is constructed to support scenario generation and evaluation; that is, IMPS is intimately concerned with simulating alternative situations. The scenarios are typically stated in terms of a set of business conditions, which are translated into a set of "customer" orders. These scenarios are then used to evaluate the resultant set of implications for capacities, materials, and strategic/tactical plans. All of this is done without disturbing the existing overall plan. It is only after a plan is adopted that any changes are made to the IMPS data base.

We turn now to the second viewpoint of IMPS architecture, the strategic/ tactical hierarchy. Figure 20.13 shows that IMPS operates at two distinct levels of aggregation. The top box shown in Figure 20.13 depicts the strategic focus and the bottom box the tactical focus.

The strategic focus of IMPS deals with long-term issues facing manufacturing in aggregate dimensions. The primary inputs are the overall business plan for the company, the marketing forecast in gross terms, and the plans for new products and other major inputs from engineering. The outputs are first and foremost a set of plans for the tactical systems to execute. A secondary set of outputs are the necessary modification signals to the overall business plan, the marketing plan, or the engineering plan. These signals can result either from the necessary interaction of plans at the strategic level or from a feedback at the tactical level that says it cannot execute the strategic plan.

The tactical planning system in Figure 20.13 is, in essence, the same as the top box shown in Figure 20.12. It has as inputs the strategic plan and sets of actual/forecasted orders. The output is customer-order delivery dates that are highly realistic.

FIGURE 20.13   The two-level control structure of IMPS for developing a single operating plan

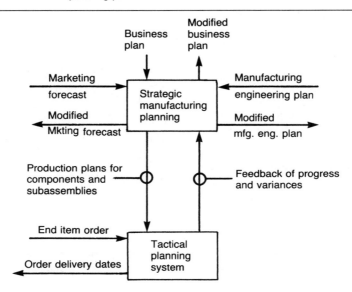

Both the strategic and the tactical planning systems operate in the fashion described for Figure 20.12; that is, in both cases a secure IMPS data base is maintained by a data control unit, expert systems are used to analyze different scenarios, and it is only on careful reflection that changes are made to the actual IMPS data base. The expert systems used in each case are unique to the problems faced and the alternative trade-offs.

Both levels operate in the "currencies" of revenue, capacity, and materials. However, at the strategic level, the level of aggregation is in terms of product families, factories or assembly lines, head counts, square footage, and gross material terms (e.g., integrated circuits). The objective is to plan the necessary number of factories, lines, vendors, and so on with sufficient lead times. Scenario generation and evaluation is a key part of the analysis. What-if questions include new product introductions, the impact on existing product lines, major marketing campaigns, offshore manufacturing, and the impact of new technologies (e.g., more powerful integrated circuits).

An important attribute of Figure 20.13 is that the strategic planning system is directly connected to the tactical planning system; that is, these two levels of planning need to be carried on in parallel, and they overlap. In too many companies, strategic planning is done by different people than those doing the tactical planning; they have different mind-sets, and the connections are weak. IMPS is based on a two-level hierarchy of planning that couples strategic planning and tactical planning, with feedback between the two levels. Moreover, the feedback is in terms of several currencies, where overlapping expert systems provide more than one outcome to a set of problems, and the concept of "plasticity" is employed.

IMPS is based on the belief in some "plasticity" in manufacturing capabilities; that is, even though a particular manufacturing unit says it can only produce X units of a particular product in some time frame, IMPS takes the point of view that this constraint might not be absolute. If a factory knows it is constraining revenue generation for the entire corporation, it well might be able to do a bit more.

The third view of IMPS architecture is in terms of how intervention takes place. Figure 20.14 is divided into two levels. The detailed flow of materials and information as it normally takes place in a firm is shown in the lower level labeled "Action." The upper level, labeled "Control," is IMPS. The top level has a series of data "taps" into the lower level, shown as the dotted arrows in Figure 20.14. As the top level, using the expert systems, decides that a revision in direction is required, an intervention is made (the solid arrows in Figure 20.14).

FIGURE 20.14   The relationship between the IMPS control system and the activity in the factory

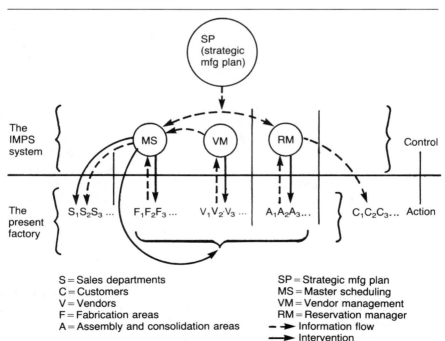

S = Sales departments
C = Customers
V = Vendors
F = Fabrication areas
A = Assembly and consolidation areas

SP = Strategic mfg plan
MS = Master scheduling
VM = Vendor management
RM = Reservation manager
— ▸ Information flow
⟶ Intervention

The action area is shown as composed of sales departments, vendors, shop area, assembly areas, and customers. Data taps are inserted into these areas, and the taps are connected to the hoses described in the data control unit of Figure 20.12. When the top-level planning requires data, in whatever level of detail dictated by the particular problem and expert system, the hoses extract the data through the taps—but do not make any changes to the data elements in the lower level.

When agreed-upon courses of action are determined, a new set of plans is created (the IMPS data base of Figure 20.12). The results are interventions, where resources are newly assigned to best achieve the overall strategic objectives, while taking into account the relevant constraints. The interventions are designed to be as limited as possible, in keeping with a basic IMPS philosophy of minimal intervention.

From the point of view of factory operations, the interventions can be categorized in terms of the degree of invasiveness. At one extreme is a reassignment of a due date to a customer. Although important for customer-service criteria, this kind of intervention should have limited impact on the factory. A notch up is a reschedule, which has an impact on material planning at the factory. Still higher is a necessary capacity adjustment. Going up another level is the need for factory plasticity to meet some overall objective. Finally, in a severe problem, IMPS can be quite invasive—dictating a forward finite loading of some resource that is preventing the company from reaching its objectives.

The intent in IMPS is to only be as invasive as necessary. The goal is to so design factory systems and capacities that factory personnel have maximum control, while simultaneously achieving strategic objectives. IMPS is intended to provide suggestions and directions. It is not a closed-loop hardwired system that controls everything at infinite levels of detail. It is not a step toward the "lights out" factory; quite the contrary. IMPS fosters decentralization, with strong local control, based on overall integrated planning.

Relationships to MPC systems

The strategic focus of IMPS is most consistent with the MPC concept of production planning, shown in Figure 20.1. The objective is to create a version of the overall company plan, in manufacturing terms, which is capable of being executed. IMPS, however, is somewhat different in its orientation to production planning than the approach described in this book. IMPS planning is not just done in material currency, but in capacity currency, and in one or more strategic currencies.

The primary driving force for IMPS at the production planning level is "customer" orders. In most situations, these orders are a mixture of actual orders and forecasted orders. This approach is different from the more widely accepted approach of "super bills" of material that specify "average" products with option percentages. In IMPS, a customer order can call for a mixture of end items, spare parts, accessories, or whatever. Forecasted orders can be configured to provide "maximal" protection against mix configurations. Forecasted orders can also be constructed to depict particular customer characteristics or those of particular industrial groupings; that is, for example, a computer manufacturer could have forecasted orders that represent the educational market, scientific market, communications market, and so on.

Another key difference between IMPS and the production planning of Figure 20.1 is that IMPS works both in a top down manner and in a selected bottom up manner. The selection is based on problems; as IMPS finds a condition not consistent with overall plans, situation dependent bottom up replanning is done, using the expert systems; that is, IMPS starts with the equivalent of a production plan, but that plan is continually updated in light of actual events. In particular, as actual customer orders come in and replace forecasted orders, the resultant set of material and capacity requirements for production units changes. Also impacted by the changes will be revenue forecasts and other financial measures. A bottom up interaction will occur when execution of the plans dictated by IMPS is not possible. For example, if a machine breakdown occurs in some work center, it may not be possible to achieve the desired goals. A forward finite load of what is possible will be made by IMPS, and the resultant set of "best" orders will be replanned on a coordinated basis.

IMPS is continually measuring the remaining flexibility in manufacturing to respond to new conditions. This is accomplished by keeping track of what are called "the deltas." The deltas are simply the differences between what IMPS is asking for in terms of capacity and materials and the available capacity in each manufacturing unit, as well as the existing material plan at each manufacturing unit (the MPS). These deltas are continually changing as actual customer orders are booked, and as material and capacity constraints change. Moreover, there are whole sets of deltas, each associated with a different what-if scenario. IMPS is designed to help manage these deltas. In many cases, the objective will be to have a reasonably large delta in capacity, while reducing the deltas in materials; that is, the objective will be to have highly responsive systems.

This feature of IMPS is very consistent with implementation of just-in-time systems. In JIT systems, the emphasis is on material velocity; materials flow through manufacturing at rates fast enough to negate detailed tracking. This means that the overhead structure to support detailed MPC planning changes. For this to happen, it is necessary for the manufacturing capacities to be large enough not to create backlogs. JIT has a strong orientation on timeliness and on problem-free operations. Both are supported by IMPS.

A key philosophical underpinning for IMPS is "minimal intervention," which means the system will provide common direction for integrated efforts, but it will not provide detailed rules for how to achieve this common direction. This concept is critical for two major reasons. First, very large completely integrated systems are difficult to make work. The larger the integration in whatever way it is measured (people, plants, and so on), the greater the chances that it will cost far more than planned and take far longer—and not work. Individual plants and groups need to feel a sense of ownership of systems. The systems need to be *our* systems, not *the* systems. Moreover, systems should support people, not supplant them. One of the goals for manufacturing should be simplicity based on better execution. This implies an evolution for systems; complex systems may be required at some point, but over time it should be possible to reduce their complexity and cost.

The second reason for minimal intervention comes from statistical process control. The idea is that a control system should be provided with only the most important "control knobs," and these should be used in a sparing way to effect control. More frequent intervention only acts to increase the process variance in the system. This phenomenon is often seen in MRP systems with excess nervousness. The objective in IMPS is to provide the right "nudge" on an infrequent basis.

Minimal intervention is also consistent with many of the philosophical underpinnings of OPT. OPT concentrates attention on a subset of work centers—the bottlenecks. IMPS has a similar focus on whatever material or capacity constraint is most critical in achieving strategic objectives. OPT has a feedback between what is doable in the factory and the strategic planning of the firm, the MPS. IMPS has a similar orientation—by planning in at least the three currencies of material, capacity, and revenue. The major focus of integration in IMPS is somewhat different from the MPC systems as depicted in Figure 20.1, which is from material planning to execution. IMPS is more interested in integration with order entry, customer order maintenance, strategic planning, and capacity planning. IMPS has as its focal point of integration only a high level view of material planning. Instead of a closed loop reaching all the way into detailed execution on the shop floor, IMPS is only interested in the execution of particular activities as they become the constraints for meeting strategic manufacturing objectives. Those constraints can be in either materials or capacities. In either event, IMPS will examine the companywide impact (including revenue implications) and create a new integrated plan.

IMPS is as interested in capacity planning/control as it is in material planning/control. However, the interest is at a high level of aggregation and is selective; that is, in keeping with the concept of minimal intervention, IMPS deals with only the most critical dimensions of plant capacity, and it assumes that each plant or manufacturing unit has its own systems in place to operate within the framework or constraints developed by IMPS. Feedback from the factories to IMPS only takes place as unsolvable problems come up and as each factory reconfigures its capabilities.

IMPS is a "broadcast" system, in that it will continually relay all agreed-upon changes in "customer" requirements (both actual orders and forecasted orders) to the various manufacturing units affected by the change. As these changes occur, the resulting impacts on material and capacity availability are assessed; that is, the deltas are recomputed. When problems are encountered in being able to coordinate the execution of a complex customer order, expert systems are employed to rapidly analyze alternative plans.

IMPS does have full MRP functionality and could be run recursively to completely plan and control each factory, if the data were available. IMPS only uses a small subset of the data base for detailed manufacturing planning/control. It is not the intent to take on the overall manufacturing planning/control. As noted above, the history of these kinds of "total systems" is quite bleak. IMPS can look deeply into a particular factory when that factory is having severe problems and it is a bottleneck for the entire company. As the factory gets its problems resolved, the need for planning/control at this level of detail decreases.

Another important issue in the IMPS approach to manufacturing planning/control is "system robustness." This term means the ability of the manufacturing system to be brought back into control after a major disruption or perturbation. Robustness is an essential quality for a manufacturing planning and control system. Factories inevitably experience unexpected "shocks," such as new equipment that does not work, a machine breakdown, or a large order cancellation. Such shocks may be significant enough to disrupt the previously planned flow of work through multiple factories. What is required is prompt generation of a new coordinated operating plan and subsequent evaluation of the plans by the various organizational entities. The issue of system robustness is closely related to minimal intervention and the level of detail chosen for the MPS. The goal is to allow each factory to adapt to shocks on its own; it is only when the shock affects others that a new integrated plan must be constructed.

The IMPS netting logic

A major advantage of IMPS over conventional manufacturing planning/control is in the detailed planning and monitoring of both material availability and capacity availability. Standard approaches to capacity planning at the master schedule level utilize rough-cut capacity planning techniques, such as the bill of labor. IMPS uses a netting worksheet for each critical resource, which is continually updated as actual orders are booked and as actual conditions in the factory change. This result is the set of deltas that depicts the

FIGURE 20.15   The netting worksheet for a single resource illustrating dynamic netting in IMPS

Resource = RA81 disk assembly.
Units = single RA81 disk.

	Week					
	1	2	3	4	5	6
Strategic demand	500	540	600	400	500	450
Local demand	100	125	175	100	125	120
Total demand	600	665	775	500	625	570
Capacity supply (production)	650	650	650	600	600	600
Inventory supply	50	100	85	0	60	35
Total supply	700	750	735	600	660	635
Units shipped	600	665	735	540	625	570
Units short	—	—	40	—	—	—

degrees of freedom between what the customers want and what the factories are planning to make available. Potential problems and imbalances across manufacturing units can be seen in greater detail and, thus, attention can be focused on their solution with more visibility.

Figure 20.15 is an example netting worksheet from IMPS. The worksheet would normally be displayed on a CRT; Figure 20.15 only shows the first 6 of the 12 to 15 future weeks typically covered. Moreover, it is only one of perhaps 50 to 100 resources that would be planned and controlled in an IMPS implementation. In keeping with the two-level hierarchy, netting is done at both the strategic-level and the tactical level.

The purpose of the display is to provide a comparison of the demand on the resource and the supply or capacity of that resource on a week-by-week basis. Units scheduled to be made in each week (capacity supply) and those available from inventory (inventory supply) are available to meet the demand. Demand is made up of two streams. The first is the strategic demand that comes directly from the production plan. Local demand comes from other sources. Included might be any kind of intercompany demand or spare parts.

The inventory supply starts with an opening balance of 50 units in the example. Production (capacity supply) is 650 units for the first three weeks and 600 units for each of the last three weeks. The inventory balance (inventory supply) is augmented when the capacity supply exceeds the units shipped, and vice versa. The inventory supply plus the capacity supply equals the total supply available to meet total demand. In week 3, a shortage of 40 units is anticipated. The shortage is made up in the next week. This expected shortfall could lead to a decision to increase capacity, or it might lead instead to a reduction of the available-to-promise quantity of this item. Note, however, this decision has an impact on the supply of the other items normally sold with this item. What this means is that making the right decision involves an analysis of the loadings on other resources, and perhaps an analysis of customer promise dates that may have to be revised. IMPS has the ability to perform forward finite loading of critical work centers, and to identify which are the bottlenecks or critical work centers in achieving a given scenario (set of actual and forecasted customer orders).

The resolution of problems in IMPS (using the expert systems) creates different worksheets, which can be reviewed. The analysis typically involves possible changes in order management, strategic management, reservation management, shop operations, and consolidation/delivery management. Determining the best alternatives requires a dialog with the particular problem resource areas. The result is workable schedules with wide participation in their development and in achieving their execution.

Expert systems

Expert systems are needed in IMPS because IMPS is devoted to analysis of manufacturing problems that are dynamic and have multiple criteria; that is, manufacturing necessarily needs to be planned and controlled in more than one currency. It is necessary for factories to meet strategic objectives, such as revenues, while also being constrained by capacity and material availability. Moreover, there are trade-offs among these currencies, but it is not possible to specify the "exchange rates" among them. Particular problems occur. They may be in quality, in material shortages, in vendor deliveries, in forecast errors, in the timing for new product rollouts, in new factory completion dates, in ramp up schedules, or in a host of other categories. The questions: What to do? How is the firm to respond? How can it do so in light of strategic objectives, customer-service criteria, those associated with manufacturing performance, and financial measures? Expert systems are an attractive and reasonable way to attack this multiple criterion problem and to provide a set of alternatives for intelligent managerial choice.

One objective of the expert systems is to resolve problems so that a minimal disruption is felt by the entire company and to best match the resources of the firm to what the customers want. For example, when a shortage of some item is encountered, the system needs, through pegging, to find out which customer orders are impacted. Thereafter, if the shortage condition cannot be resolved, the expert systems have to be employed to examine the consequences. The first order of business is to figure out what factory orders are also tied to that order. Next, it is necessary to examine how the shortfall is to be resolved and what rescheduling actions are possible for the other resource areas. It is also necessary to find out which customer orders *can* be built and, perhaps, to reorder the priorities for the resulting set of components so revenue objectives can be met. At the same time, it is important to meet as many shipping deadlines as possible and to use the resources of the factories as wisely as possible.

Alternative problem scenarios include the following:

- What is the maximum number of some product that could be shipped within some time frame?
- What are the plants or resources that constrain the answer to the last question?
- What are the expected revenues associated with this maximum set of shipments?
- How does this revenue projection compare with the business plan? (What is the delta?)
- What are the sets of deltas associated with all of the major nonbottleneck resources (material and capacity)?
- How far is the maximum build rate above the existing plan and what is required to break this constraint?
- What are the implications for an existing product when a replacement product is introduced?
- How do different scenarios impact different plants, vendors, revenues, and other resources?

Ajax Computer Works example

In this section, we present a simplified problem that illustrates some of the problem scenarios with which IMPS is designed to deal.

The Ajax Computer Works makes and sells four models of computers, the 707, 727, 737, and 747. Each computer is equipped with different CPU units, disk drives, tape drives, and operating system software. There is a separate factory for each of these component types. After manufacture, the components are sent to a consolidation warehouse according to the final product configuration specified by the customer. The end-item products are configured according to the schema given in Figure 20.16 (in the case of disk

---

FIGURE 20.16 Ajax end-item products

	Product			
Component	707	727	737	747
CPU	6	6	8	9
Disk drive	100(1)	200(1–3)	300(1–3)	300(1–5)
Tape drive	70(1)	70(0–4)	70(0–10)	80(0–10)
Operating system	X	X	Y	Y

FIGURE 20.17   Ajax capacity requirements

	Capacity requirements (hours)	Inventory
CPU plant:		
6	2.0	2
8	5.0	3
9	7.0	9
Disk plant:		
100	1.0	15
200	1.5	0
300	2.0	25
Tape plant:		
70	0.5	50
80	1.0	10
Operating system plant:		
X	2.0	5
Y	4.0	6

FIGURE 20.18   Material availability—737 model

Component	Part number	Number required per unit	Number on hand	Units that can be built w/parts
CPU*	8	1	3	3
Disk drive	300	3	25	8
Tape drive	70	10	50	5
Operating system	Y	1	6	6

*CPU #8 limits the number of model 737s that can be built to three.

---

drives and tape drives, the appropriate model number is given, then the variable quantity per end item).

Let us assume that each plant has one critical or bottleneck work center. Further, for simplicity, let us assume that in each case the capacity of the limiting work center is 40 hours per week. We will also assume that each factory has no parts shortages or lead time problems; all of these are solved by the material planning/control systems operating in the factories. The capacity requirements of each component are given in Figure 20.17, along with the present inventories of these components.

Ajax had been concerned about its customer-service levels. In particular, a request has come down about how many of each computer system could be shipped immediately from stock, assuming that in each case the customer ordered the maximum number of components in each option. Which plant(s) is(are) the constraint to achieving maximum shipments? Figure 20.18 shows

FIGURE 20.19   Material availability—all models

Model	CPU		Disk		Tape		Operating system		Max.* ship.
	Part (req)	Avail.	Part (req)	Avail.	Part (req)	Avail.	Part (req)	Avail.	
707	6(1)	2	100(1)	15	70(1)	50	X(1)	5	2
727	6(1)	2	200(3)	0	70(4)	50	X(1)	5	0
737	8(1)	3	300(3)	25	70(10)	50	Y(1)	6	3
747	9(1)	9	300(5)	25	80(10)	10	Y(1)	6	1

*707—Maximum available to ship is two. Constraint is CPU.
727—Unable to ship. Constraint is Disk.
737—Maximum available to ship is three. Constraint is CPU.
747—Maximum available to ship is one. Constraint is Tape.

FIGURE 20.20   Capacity requirements—737 model

A. Calculate average number of parts required:

Component	Part no.	No. required per unit	Average no. of parts required
CPU	8	1	1
Disk drive	300	1–3	(1 + 3)/2 = 2
Tape drive	70	0–10	(0 + 10)/2 = 5
Operating system	Y	1	1

B. Calculate hours required per average part:

Component	Part no.	Average no. of parts required	Hours per part	Hours per avg. unit
CPU	8	1	5.0	5.0
Disk drive	300	2	2.0	4.0
Tape drive	70	5	0.5	2.5
Operating system	Y	1	4.0	4.0

C. Calculate hours required for two average units:

Component	Part no.	Hours per unit	Hours for 2 units
CPU	8	5.0	5 × 2 = 10
Disk drive	300	4.0	4 × 2 = 8
Tape drive	70	2.5	2.5 × 2 = 5
Operating system	Y	4.0	4 × 2 = 8

how this question is evaluated for the 737 model, and Figure 20.19 summarizes the data for all four models.

The second set of questions that Ajax is interested in concerns capacity constraints on meeting customer order patterns. In particular, Ajax asks how much capacity is required by each end-item computer system in each factory, assuming that, in the case of optional numbers of components, the customer picks the average? A further question is how much capacity is required in each factory per week if the sales forecast is to sell two of each computer system each week? Figure 20.20 provides the solution for the 737 model, and Figure 20.21 provides the data for all models.

The Ajax example illustrates two possible problem scenarios that involve trade-offs of material and capacity across product lines and factories. In the first, it is clear that the 737 model is limited by inventories at the CPU plant. Providing extra quantities of other 737 parts will only increase inventory levels. When all products are evaluated, it is seen that the operating system plant inventories are not a constraint to production of any model. It would seem that their output levels have been allowed to get out of synchronization with those of other plants. IMPS would have helped to identify this kind of condition—before it happened.

FIGURE 20.21   Capacity (Cap.) requirements—all models

Model	CPU Avg. × hrs. = Cap.	Disk Avg. × hrs. = Cap.	Tape Avg. × hrs. = Cap.	Operating system Avg. × hrs. = Cap.	Total
707	1 × 2 = 2	1 × 1 = 1	1 × 0.5 = 0.5	1 × 2 = 2	5.5
727	1 × 2 = 2	2 × 1.5 = 3	2 × 0.5 = 1	1 × 2 = 2	8.0
737	1 × 5 = 5	2 × 2 = 4	5 × 0.5 = 2.5	1 × 4 = 4	15.5
747	1 × 7 = 7	3 × 2 = 6	5 × 1 = 5	1 × 4 = 4	22.0
Total	16	14	9	12	51.0
	× 2	× 2	× 2	× 2	
	32	28	18	24	

Capacity requirements

Model 707 requires 2 hrs. CPU, 1 hr. Disk, 0.5 hr. Tape, and 2 hrs. Op. Sys.
Model 727 requires 2 hrs. CPU, 3 hrs. Disk, 1.0 hr. Tape, and 2 hrs. Op. Sys.
Model 737 requires 5 hrs. CPU, 4 hrs. Disk, 2.5 hrs. Tape, and 4 hrs. Op. Sys.
Model 747 requires 7 hrs. CPU, 6 hrs. Disk, 5.0 hrs. Tape, and 4 hrs. Op. Sys.
Two of each model: 32 hrs. CPU, 28 hrs. Disk, 18 hrs. Tape, and 24 hrs. Op. Sys.

The second set of two questions carries the scenario generation to capacity requirements, particularly to those associated with a set of customer orders (two of each product in each week). Comparing these requirements with available capacities results in the deltas for each plant. Other scenarios could be generated here for the impact on revenues, the third currency of IMPS.

OBSERVATIONS

In this chapter, we have examined three quite different approaches to manufacturing planning and control. Each of these represents a frontier for MPC systems. OPT is important because it is much more explicit in the consideration of capacity than is true for "standard" MPC systems. It is also interesting because there are feedbacks from the back end to the front end; the MPS is a *doable* MPS. The separation of work into what crosses bottlenecks and what does not allows a critical focus on what is really important. The OPT philosophy also focuses management attention on what is *not* important: utilization of nonbottleneck resources.

The Kumera Oy system pushes the frontiers because it is a time-driven system, rather than a material-driven system; that is, the Kumera Oy system assigns orders to time periods in the same way that passengers get on a train. If the train is missed, one waits for the next train. The objective is to have high-speed trains and frequent schedules. Factory execution of all material flow dictates is based on the time assignments. By slotting a particular customer into a unique time bucket, all parts of the order are coordinated in a relatively simple way. The series of these time buckets makes up a "train schedule." This schedule is broadcast to both customers and suppliers. The result is an integrative force for better interfirm cooperation.

IMPS goes beyond OPT and Kumera Oy in several key respects. IMPS plans in three "currencies": capacity, material, and strategic planning (revenue dollars). IMPS has the ability to foreword finite load bottlenecks as does OPT, but, with the principle of minimal intervention, it will only do so when a particular problem is blocking the achievement of strategic goals. IMPS also has MRP functionality, but the intent is to use this approach only when necessary. The expectation is that MPC systems will migrate toward just-in-time, with execution done locally. All that remains is an overall set of planning activities to send integrated signals to the factories and to key work centers. The signals are to be sent from a small organization with small hidden factory costs. IMPS uses artificial intelligence/expert systems to trade off capacity, materials, and strategic goals in ways that are unique to each firm.

IMPS has a time focus somewhat akin to that of Kumera Oy, in that an underlying goal is to respond to customer orders as quickly as possible. Customer orders (actual and forecasts) are the drivers for IMPS. These orders make up the MPS, and the objective is to provide fast response to mix and volume changes. IMPS fosters interfunctional cooperation, such as that needed for new product introductions.

CONCLUDING PRINCIPLES

As we review these new approaches and learn of others, we are reminded of the continued evolution of MPC systems and philosophies. From these frontiers, however, some principles do emerge:

- There is no "ultimate weapon" in MPC systems. Firms should continually be evaluating improvements.
- Use of the MPC framework is useful in assessing where a particular approach or system fits within the system.
- Improvements can be made more easily, once a working MPC system is in place.
- Concentration on bottleneck resources focuses attention of material planning and capacity planning on the vital few.
- Time-based planning instead of material-based planning can increase material velocity and manufacturing responsiveness.
- Capacity, materials, and strategic objectives can be simultaneously planned with some of the emerging MPC systems concepts.

REFERENCES

Billington, P. J.; J. O. McClain; and L. J. Thomas. "Heuristics for Multilevel Lot-Sizing with a Bottleneck." *Management Science* 32, no. 8, August 1986.

Bolander, S. F.; R. C. Heard; S. M. Seward; and S. G. Taylor. *Manufacturing Planning and Control in the Process Industries*. Falls Church, Va.: American Production and Inventory Control Society, 1981.

Carlson, J. G. "Microcomputers for Demonstrating G/T, JIT, Kanban and MRP." *Production Emerging Trends and Issues*, Netherlands: Elsevier, 1985.

Ebner, M. L.; L. H. Lindgren; and T. E. Vollmann. "The IMPS System: Its Scope and Applications." Working paper, Manufacturing Engineering Department, Boston University, 1986.

——— and T. E. Vollmann. "Manufacturing Systems for the 1990's." In *Intelligent Manufacturing: Proceedings from the First International Conference on Expert Systems and the Leading Edge in Production Planning and Control*, ed. M. Oliff. Menlo Park, California: Benjamin/Cummings 1987.

Everdell, Romeyn. "MRPII, JIT, and OPT; Not a Choice but a Synergy," *1984 APICS Conference Proceedings*.

Fox, Robert E. "MRP, Kanban or OPT, What's Best?" *Inventories and Production*, January–February 1982.

———. "OPT: An Answer for America, Part II." *Inventories and Production*, November–December 1982.

————. "OPT: An Answer for America, Part III." *Inventories and Production*, January–February 1983.

————. "OPT: An Answer for America, Part IV." *Inventories and Production*, March–April 1983.

————. "OPT vs. MRP: Thoughtware Versus Software, Part I." *Inventories and Production*, November–December 1983.

————. "OPT vs. MRP: Thoughtware Versus Software, Part II." *Inventories and Production*, January–February 1984.

Goldratt, Eliyahu, "The Unbalanced Plant." APICS, 1981 International Conference Proceedings, pp. 195–99.

————. "Optimized Production Timetable (OPT): A Revolutionary Program for Industry." *APICS Annual Conference Proceedings*, 1980, pp. 172–76.

————, and J. Cox, *The Goal*, North River Press, 1984.

Jacobs, F. Robert. "The OPT Scheduling System: A Review of a New Production Scheduling System." *Production and Inventory Management*, 3rd Quarter 1983.

————. "OPT Uncovered: Many Production Planning and Scheduling Concepts Can Be Applied with or without the Software." *Industrial Engineering*, October 1984, pp. 89–95.

———— and D. J. Bragg. "The Repetitive Lot Concept: An Evaluation of Job Flow Considerations in Production Dispatching, Sequencing, and Batch Scheduling." IRMIS Working Paper no. 505, Indiana University, 1986.

Kumpulainen, Vesa. *Periodic Production Control*, 11100 Riihimaki 10, Finland, Kumera Oy. 1983.

Lundrigan, R. "What Is This Thing Called OPT?" *Production and Inventory Management*, Second Quarter, 1986, pp. 2–12.

Mattila, Veli-Pekka. *Periodic Control System*. 11000 Riihimaki 10, Finland, Kumera Oy, 1983.

Meleton, M. P., Jr. "OPT—Fantasy or Breakthrough?" *Production and Inventory Management*, 2nd Quarter 1986, pp. 13–21.

Moily, J. P. "Optimal and Heuristic Procedures for Component Lot-Splitting in Multi-Stage Manufacturing Systems." *Management Science* 32, no. 1, January 1986.

Nakane, J., and R. W. Hall. "Management Specs for Stockless Production." *Harvard Business Review*, May/June 1983, pp. 84–91.

Plenert, G., and T. D. Best. "MRP, JIT, and OPT: What's Best?" *Production and Inventory Management*, 2nd Quarter 1986, pp. 22–29.

Schmenner, R. W. "Comparative Factory Productivity." U.S. Department of Commerce, July 1986.

Steinberg, E.; B. Khumawala; and R. Scamell. "Requirements Planning Systems in the Health Care Environment." *Journal of Operations Management* 2, no. 4, 1982.

Suresh, N. C., and J. R. Meredith. "Achieving Factory Automation through Group Technology Principles." *Journal of Operations Management* 5, no. 2, 1985.

Swann, D. "Using MRP for Optimized Schedules (Emulating OPT)." *Production and Inventory Management*, 2nd Quarter 1986, pp. 30–37.

Vollmann, Thomas E. "OPT as An Enhancement to MRPII." *Production and Inventory Management*, 2nd Quarter 1986, pp. 38–47.

DISCUSSION QUESTIONS

1. How would you respond to the question, "Which is better, MPC or MRP?"

2. How can the MPC system of Figure 20.1 be used to evaluate newly developed software?

3. A recent promotion implied a progression from EOQ to MRP, to JIT, and finally to OPT. How would you react to this claim?

4. What do you feel about the transparency of a system? Is it necessary for people to understand what is going on inside the "black box" to be able to use it?

5. The priority rule used at Kumera is "always work on the items from the lowest-numbered production set next." What shop-floor dispatching rule is that equivalent to? Could it be improved upon?

6. It is tempting to conclude that it is unimportant what the technical choice of the system is, given the importance of management. Can you provide examples of where the technical choice *is* important?

7. In what ways is the scenario given as Figure 20.18 for the Ajax Computer works different from a sales forecast?

8. How could Figure 20.18 incorporate both actual customer orders and expected shipments? Are there any advantages in doing so?

9. How might a spreadsheet model be useful for evaluating Ajax scenarios?

PROBLEMS

1. The Optima Shop has two work centers, Big Mess and No Problem. The Monday list of orders to be filled this week shows the following requirements for capacity at the two centers (in hours):

	Big Mess	No Problem
Customer order 1	Part A, set up 5, run 10	Part C, set up 1, run 2
	Part B, set up 2, run 5	
Customer order 2	Part A, set up 5, run 3	Part D, set up 2, run 2
Customer order 3	Part B, set up 2, run 5	Part C, set up 1, run 3

Joe Biggs, the scheduler at Optima, said that he wants to minimize setups, minimize inventories, and prioritize the customer orders in numerical order.

a. How would you schedule the part production in the two centers? (Please illustrate, using a Gantt chart.)

    b. Can customer delivery promises be met without overtime? Assume capacity is 40 hours in each work center.

    c. How does your answer to question **b** change if only one person is assigned to *both* work centers?

    d. How does your schedule compare with the OPT philosophy?

2. Consider a work center that has a 40-hour per week capacity. The MRP planned orders for that work center show the following requirements for the next several weeks:

Job	A	B	C	D	E	F	G	H
Hours required	5	20	15	30	45	15	20	10
Week release planned	1	1	2	2	3	4	4	4

    a. Plot the weekly load against capacity.

    b. How would you adjust the schedule to meet capacity?

    c. What decision rule could be developed to do the adjustment in a dynamic situation?

3. "What-if" you could get another five hours of capacity for the work center in problem 2? How would your schedule change?

4. A firm considering the use of the periodic control system has divided its product line into four groups, with the following annual forecast in units (assuming a 50-week year):

Group	Forecast
I	400
II	200
III	500
IV	100

    a. The company has decided on an eight-week period. Calculate the period quantities.

    b. If Group I takes 40 direct labor hours per unit, Group II takes 20, Group III takes 5, and Group IV takes 50, what is the allocation of labor capacity to the groups?

    c. Plot the "timing table" for the items.

5. After several months of operation, the order board (promised deliveries) for a company with periodic control and five product groups looked like this:

Product group	Period quantity	Promised delivery date							
		1	2	3	4	5	6	7	8
A	100	50	20	0	0	10	0	0	0
B	50	50	50	50	50	50	50	40	30
C	200	200	200	120	100	50	0	20	0
D	10	10	10	8	5	2	0	1	0
E	40	20	2	0	0	0	0	0	0

a. What do you make of the current situation?

b. What actions would you recommend?

6. What is the composite bill of material for a periodic control group that has 10 items (3 of part 2, 2 of part 7, and 5 of part 10) with the following individual bills?

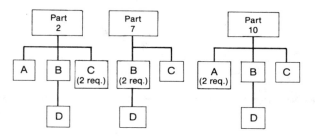

What quantities should be ordered if the inventories are:

Part	Amount
2	0
7	0
10	0
A	10
B	0
C	20
D	100

7. Returning to the Ajax example discussed in the IMPS section, last week each of the Ajax factories was to ship the requirements for customer order #1234 to the consolidation warehouse. This order was for three model 727s, each with two disk drives and two tape drives. A vendor problem with a critical component for the model 200 disk drive kept the disk drive plant from fulfilling its commitment. It will be five weeks before this vendor problem will be resolved. What should Ajax do, assuming the following set of orders need to be filled?

Order #	Quantity	Model #	Disks	Tapes
1235	2	707	1	1
1236	3	727	2	4
1240	2	707	1	1
1245	1	737	3	10
1246	3	747	5	3

8. Table A provides a set of customer delivery data for Ajax in the form of a "scenario"; that is, this table represents one reasonable set of customer orders that Ajax might ship in the future. Table A also provides expected revenues for an average unit of each of these end items. Using the data in Table A, construct a table of expected billings for each week in Table B.

TABLE A

Items	Week								Revenue per average unit
	1	2	3	4	5	6	7	8	
707	2	2	4	3	2	1	2	3	200
727	1	3	4	5	5	6	6	7	300
737	1	1	2	2	2	3	2	2	700
747	3	3	3	4	3	3	3	3	1200

TABLE B

Items	Weekly billings							
	1	2	3	4	5	6	7	8
707								
727								
737								
747								
Total								

9. Use a spreadsheet model, and the data in Table A of problem 8, and the data from Figures 20.16 through 20.21 for this problem. Assume the Table A scenario is for average units and that capacity requirements at each plant occur in the same week as shipments. All plants work a 40-hour week. Complete the weekly capacity analysis (Table C) for each plant. What are the implications?

10. Given your analysis of capacity in problem 9, what is the impact of an expected vacation shutdown in the tape plant during weeks 5 and 6?

11. Assume that a critical component part for the model 200 disk drive (only used on end item Model 727) will be delivered at the rate of four units each over the next eight weeks. One unit is required for each Model 200 disk drive. How should Ajax analyze this issue, and how will it impact the results of Tables A, B, and C?

12. Assume the component in problem 11 can be delivered in unlimited quantities after six weeks. What should Ajax do now?

13. A small Norwegian firm produced several decorative wooden dolls. There were three general types of dolls: Trolls, Gnomes, and Elves. Three manufacturing steps were used to produce the dolls: roughing out the shape, finishing the shaping, and painting. All dolls went through all three departments in the same order, from rough through finish to paint. The total labor-hours required per doll type in each department are shown on the next page.

For several months the company has been trying the periodic control system.

TABLE C

	Weekly capacity analysis							
Plant	*1*	*2*	*3*	*4*	*5*	*6*	*7*	*8*
CPU plant:								
Hours								
Capacity								
Percent utilization								
Disk plant:								
Hours								
Capacity								
Percent utilization								
Tape plant:								
Hours								
Capacity								
Percent utilization								
Operating system plant:								
Hours								
Capacity								
Percent utilization								

It has worked out that a production set of each type can be released each week on a rotating basis. Thus, each three weeks, one doll type will be started into production and it will be completed in three weeks. This means that each department has one week to finish its work on each set. The company has been able to do quite well with the system by using period quantities of 15 for Trolls, 20 for Gnomes and 10 for Elves. The company works a 40 hour week and a little overtime has been required in the finishing department in order to stick to the schedule. The employment by department is given below.

Labor-Hours Required	Work Departments			*Period Quantities*
	Rough	*Finish*	*Paint*	
Trolls	5	3	7	15
Gnomes	3	2	6	20
Elves	8	5	11	10
Employment	2	1	3	

a. Use a spreadsheet to calculate the labor-hour load by department by week. How well is it balanced?

b. After a few more months it became clear that the product mix was changing. The popularity of the Elves was increasing at the expense of the Gnomes. Sales felt that the overall demand for dolls was still about the same, so they suggested a simple change in the period quantities. They reasoned that a switch to 10 for the Gnomes and 20 for the elves would allow them to get back to a reasonable delivery-promise time. They also felt this would make no difference to the factory since the quantities would remain the same. What will be the impact of this suggestion?

c. Using the data from part **b**, what suggestions would you make about employment and staffing for the three departments?

14. The Ace Tool Company is considering implementing the repetitive lot concept in scheduling the firm's fabrication shop. The production manager has selected an example order to use in evaluating the benefits and potential costs of using this scheduling approach. A transfer batch size of 100 units has been suggested for this item. The example order is for a quantity if 1000 units and has the following routing data:

Operation	Work center	Setup time	Run time/ unit
1	1	40 minutes	2.4 minutes/ unit
2	2	20 minutes	1.44 minutes/ unit

a. Assuming a single-shift, eight-hour day, five-day week for work centers 1 and 2, prepare a gantt chart showing the earliest start- and finish-time schedule for this order when the repetitive lot concept is used, and under a conventional scheduling approach when all of the items in the order are processed at one time. What are the earliest start and finish times for each transfer batch at work center 2, assuming that none of the transfer batches are processed together to save setup time?

b. What is the difference in the order-completion times under the two scheduling approaches in part **a** above?

c. What are the benefits and potential costs of this scheduling approach?

15. Recently, the Universal Machine Tool Company introduced the use of the repetitive lot concept in scheduling the firm's fabrication shop. The dispatching report shown on the next page lists the orders ready for processing at the K & T machining center at 8 A.M. on Tuesday. This work center has just completed an order for 20 units of part number 6633 on shop order number WE 433. If the earliest due date dispatching rule is used to schedule orders at this work center, determine the sequence in which the orders should be processed (assuming that no new orders enter the work center).

Shop order number	Part number	Order quantity	Operation quantity	Setup time	Run time	Order due date
XX 234	8965	80	10	0.5	3.0	951
RT 435	6123	50	50	0.1	6.5	918
GI 209	6754	160	16	0.4	5.8	941
TV 244	9087	54	54	0.9	8.2	925
WE 433	6633	100	20	0.8	4.4	944
US 899	7831	210	210	0.7	5.0	923
XX 234	8965	80	10	0.5	3.0	951
WE 433	6633	100	20	0.8	4.4	944
GI 209	6754	160	16	0.4	5.8	941
WE 433	6633	100	20	0.8	4.4	944

Index